RANDOM HOUSE
WEBSTER'S
easy english
dictionary

BEGINNER

RANDOM HOUSE
REFERENCE

NEW YORK TORONTO LONDON SYDNEY AUCKLAND

Random House Webster's Easy English Dictionary Beginner

Copyright © 2001 by Random House, Inc.

Trademarks

Please address inquiries about electronic licensing of reference products, for use on a network or in software or on CD-ROM, to the Subsidiary Rights Department, Random House Reference, fax 212-572-6003.

This book is available for special discounts for bulk purchases for sales promotions or premiums. Special editions, including personalized covers, excerpts of existing books, and corporate imprints, can be created in large quantities for special needs. For more information, write to .Random House, Inc., Special Markets/Premium Sales, 1745 Broadway, MD 6-2, New York, NY, 10019 or e-mail specialmarkets@randomhouse.com.

Library of Congress Cataloging-in-Publication Data is available.

Visit the Random House Reference Web site at www.randomwords.com

Printed in the United States of America

First Edition

0 9 8 7 6 5 4 3 2 1

ISBN: 978-0-375-72211-0

New York   Toronto   London   Sydney   Auckland

CONTENTS

INTRODUCTION

CLEARLY AND SIMPLY, RANDOM HOUSE WEBSTER'S DELIVERS CONFIDENCE.

Random House Webster's Easy English Dictionary Beginner is the first Webster's dictionary truly written for new learners of English. High beginning and low intermediate students will find more usage, grammar, and synonym help than in any other dictionary of its kind.

Students who are ready to begin using an English-only dictionary will find everything they need to understand over 13,000 words and phrases in English. Each definition is clear and simple, written using a strictly controlled vocabulary. Plus, the Dictionary has helpful features not offered by other dictionaries at this level:

- Every derivative form—such as *grammatically* from *grammatical*—has its own full entry, rather than simply being listed at the end of an entry without explanation.
- Warning notes focus on typical errors made by learners of English.
- More examples, usage notes, and illustrations than in any other similar dictionary.

Over 17,000 examples show typical usage and grammatical patterns. Over 150 usage, synonym, and pronunciation notes cover helpful usage topics, such as pronouncing *the* when it's stressed, or how to talk about time. Over 400 illustrations focus on the things that are most difficult to describe, such as easily confused synonyms; prepositions and verbs; and animals and plants.

Finally, at the back of the book, students will find a special Smart Study Section—a complete resource for information on numbers, verbs, adjective word order, countries of the world, and more.

More than just a look-it-up dictionary for beginners, *Random House Webster's Easy English Dictionary Beginner* can actively help students take their confidence in using English to the next level.

══ GUIDE to the DICTIONARY ══

WHAT IS AN ENTRY?

The word or phrase that you look up in a dictionary is called the **main entry**. An entry can be one word: **hearing** . Or it can be more than one word: **hearing aid** . This guide will help you learn about entries. It will teach you where to look for the entry you want. The guide also tells you what an entry shows.

ALPHABETICAL ORDER

In English, letters of the alphabet are put together to make words. The English alphabet has 26 letters, in this order:

Capital letters:　　A B C D E F G H I J K L M N O P Q R S T U V W X Y Z
Lowercase letters:　a b c d e f g h i j k l m n o p q r s t u v w x y z

This order is called **alphabetical order**. The entries in this dictionary are in alphabetical order. So if a word starts with the letter *a* it will be in the first part of the dictionary. If it starts with the letter *z* it will be at the end of the dictionary.

1　Look at these words. They have been written in alphabetical order below.

chance	**gym**	**action**	**tall**	**pool**	**vegetable**

1. action　　　　3. gym　　　　　5. tall

2. chance　　　　4. pool　　　　　6. vegetable

Now, you try writing these words in alphabetical order.

loaf	**cedar**	**knee**	**rich**	**wage**	**address**

1. address　　　　3. _____　　　　5. _____

2. _____　　　　4. _____　　　　6. _____

If two words have the same first letter, look at the second letter. If the first letter and the second letter are the same, look at the third letter. Move from left to right in the words until you see a letter that is different. Use the first letter that is different to put words in alphabetical order.

2 Look at these words and write them in alphabetical order.

| **game** | **gamble** | **giraffe** | **galaxy** | **girl** | **gate** |

1. galaxy _____ 3. _____ 5. _____

2. gamble _____ 4. _____ 6. _____

GUIDE WORDS

The words at the top of a page are guide words. These words are the first and the last main entry words that are on the page. If the word you are looking for belongs in alphabetical order between the two guide words, it will be on that page. Look at the words and guide words below.

3 Draw an arrow (→) from the word to the page that it would appear on.

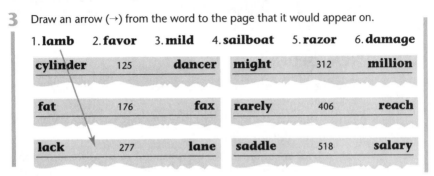

1. **lamb**   2. **favor**   3. **mild**   4. **sailboat**   5. **razor**   6. **damage**

cylinder	125	**dancer**	**might**	312	**million**
fat	176	**fax**	**rarely**	406	**reach**
lack	277	**lane**	**saddle**	518	**salary**

SPELLING

The dictionary entry shows the correct spelling of words. If a word always starts with a capital letter, it will have one in the entry : **Jupiter** . If a word sometimes starts with a capital letter and sometimes starts with a lowercase letter, you will see both: **mom** or **Mom** . You can spell some words two different ways. If a word has two correct spellings, both are in the dictionary: **barbecue** or **barbeque** .

SPECIAL INFORMATION

Many entries in this dictionary have a mark after them. These marks tell you more about the word.

* ***** This mark means that the word is one of the basic words we use to explain meanings in this dictionary. It is an important word for you to learn.

* **T** This mark means that the word is one that you need to know for the TOEFL test (Test of English as a Foreign Language).

Some words, like *active* have more than one mark: ***** **T** . Both of the marks tell you about the word.

4 Look up these words and put the * mark next to basic vocabulary words and a ⊤ next to TOEFL words. If you find more than one mark next to a word, write both marks in the blank.

1. **arrangement** _* ⊤_   5. **fragile** _____   9. **shake** _____
2. **baby** _____   6. **gain** _____   10. **trade** _____
3. **cigarette** _____   7. **habit** _____   11. **valley** _____
4. **dictate** _____   8. **observe** _____   12. **wide** _____

PRONUNCIATIONS

The pronunciations in this dictionary are shown after the main entry. For example, the pronunciation for the word **cat** is shown like this: **cat** /kæt/. The chart on the inside front cover of this dictionary tells you how to read the pronunciation marks. There is also a short guide for pronunciation marks on every right-hand page.

Some pronunciations have high stress marks that look like this ˈ , or low stress marks that look like this ˌ . High stress marks are put in front of the syllable (part of the word) that you say in the strongest voice. Low stress marks are put in front of the syllable that you say in a strong voice, but not as strong as ˈ .

If two or more words that are spelled the same are also pronounced the same, then only the first word has a pronunciation written next to it.

If there are two common ways to say a word, then two pronunciations are shown in the dictionary: **cloths** /klɔðz ; klɔθs/.

If an abbreviation such as **cm.** is only a written abbreviation, then no pronunciation is shown.

5 Look up these words. Draw a line from each word to its pronunciation.

1. **daisy**   /ʌnˈeɪbəl/
2. **dance**   /ˈtrʌbəl/
3. **trouble**   /ˈdeɪzi/
4. **traffic**   /dæns/
5. **unable**   /ˈtræfɪk/

PARTS OF SPEECH

The rules for how words can be used with each other are called **grammar rules**. There are different jobs in a sentence. Grammar rules tell you what kinds of words can do each job. These different kinds of words (like nouns, verbs, and adjectives) are called **parts of speech**.

Words that are spelled the same may be different parts of speech. For example, there is one word *scream* that is a verb. There is another word *scream* that is a noun. Each part of speech has its own

scream[1] /skrim/ [*verb*; **screamed, screaming**] to make a loud cry when you are very afraid or upset: *She screamed when she saw the rat.* | *"Get out of here," he screamed.*

entry. The verb *scream* is the most common, so its entry comes first, and has a ^{1} after it. The noun *scream* is less common, so its entry is second, and has a ^{2} after it.

> **scream**^{2} [*noun*] a loud cry, made when you are very afraid or upset: *No one heard their screams.*

The main parts of speech are: **noun, verb, adjective, adverb, preposition, determiner, pronoun** and **conjunction**. The parts of speech are shown between marks like these: [ ].

noun

A [*noun*] is a word used to name a person, place, thing, idea, or condition.

6   Look up these words. Draw circles around the ones that are nouns.

(tree)	garbled	dog	ramp
blind	shoe	juggle	however
red	letter	lonely	cyclone

If a noun is called [*plural*] or a [*plural noun*] , then it has only a plural form. It cannot be used with *a* or *an*. Plural nouns are always used with plural verbs.

7   Look up these words to see if they are *plural*. (Use the rule: Plural nouns are only used with plural verbs.) Then, mark *correct* if the sentence is right and *incorrect* if the sentence is wrong.

1. Arms is being sent to Washington.   ___correct   ✓ incorrect
2. Bangs are popular in women's haircuts.   ___correct   ___incorrect
3. Politics are not interesting to me   ___correct   ___incorrect
4. The program's graphics aren't very good.   ___correct   ___incorrect
5. Checkers is a fun game.   ___correct   ___incorrect

pronoun

A [*pronoun*] is a word that takes the place of a noun.

8   Look up these words. Draw a circle around the ones that are pronouns.

(mine)	fog	name	you	us	because	she
clear	it	sister	them	they	me	say	theirs
when	her	courage	buy	body	deaf	yours	warn
wife	argue	he	size	hers	shrimp	I	him

determiner/article

A [*determiner*] is a word like *another*, *this*, or *every* that comes before a noun in a sentence. Determiners can tell you many things, like which noun you are talking about (*that* book), whom something belongs to (*his* book), or how many of something there are (*many* books). An [*article*] is a special kind of determiner. The articles in English are *a*, *an*, and *the*. Articles and determiners do the same kinds of jobs in a sentence.

9 Look up these words. Draw a circle around the ones that can be determiners.

**any   sock   (this)   shell   each   by   half   shed   much   rain
often   dozen   sharp   certain   her   circle   bony   either**

adjective

An [*adjective*] is a word like *red*, *happy*, or *boring* that describes a noun.

10 Look up these words. Draw a circle around the ones that can be adjectives.

**swiftly   (funny)   sand   scared   wind   pants   brown   ache   happy
soft   caution   listen   yell   brisk   water   open   silly   bald**

preposition

A [*preposition*] is a word like *at*, *in*, *about*, or *for* that is used before a noun or a pronoun. Prepositions usually give information about direction, time, and position.

11 Look up these words. Draw a circle around the ones that can be prepositions.

**(with)   car   shake   we   dark   to   under   confuse   on
between   in   fast   from   ring   sew   ring   noise   foot**

verb

A [*verb*] is a word like *talk*, *drink*, or *be* that is used to talk about an action or a situation. There are different kinds of verbs. This dictionary will tell you if the verb is a **phrasal verb**, an **auxiliary verb**, a **modal verb**, or a **linking verb**.

phrasal verb

A [*phrasal verb*] is a group of words that acts like a verb, such as *account for* or *grow out of*. Phrasal verbs are shown together after the main meanings, and are in **dark letters**. Phrasal verbs are made with verbs and adverbs, or verbs and prepositions.

12 Look up these phrasal verbs. Write down the meaning for each phrasal verb.

1. **account for** _____ *to be an explanation or reason for something*

2. **chop down** _____

3. **look up** _____

4. **trust in** _____

auxiliary verb

An [*auxiliary verb*] is a verb like *be*, *do*, or *have* that you use before other verbs to make verb tenses and questions.

modal verb

A [*modal verb*] is a verb like *can*, *should* or *would* that you use before another verb or before an auxiliary verb, for example to say that something is possible or should be done.

linking verb

A [*linking verb*] is a verb like *be*, *become*, or *seem* that connects one noun to another noun or adjective. A linking verb tells you that two things are the same.

13 The verbs in this exercise are modal, auxiliary, phrasal or linking. Look up these words and write down what kind of verb they are.

1. **become** _linking verb_   4. **give up** _____

2. **do** _____   5. **will** _____

3. **get** _____   6. **would** _____

adverb

An [*adverb*] is a word like *slowly*, *totally*, or *very* that tells you how, when, or where something is done or happens.

14 Look up these words. Draw a circle around the ones that can be adverbs.

nice   rather   loudly   shiny   slimy   gift   (slowly)
red   quickly   scary   hopefully   neck   really   friendly

conjunction

A [*conjunction*] is a word like *and* or *but* that connects two parts of a sentence.

15 Look up these words. Draw a circle around the ones that are conjunctions.

however   after   but   when   (and)   with   by

name

A [*name*] is what a person or place is called. Names always begin with capital letters.

| Look at page 620 for a list of some common names in English and their pronunciations.

number

A [*number*] is a word that tells you how many, like *one* or *twenty*.

| Look at page 609 for a list of numbers.

SPECIAL FORMS

Some parts of speech have special forms or spellings. If an entry word has an irregular form or is difficult to spell, the special form is shown after the part of speech information.

Regular Forms of Verbs

Most verbs are changed in the same way to show who is speaking and the time they are speaking about. These verbs are called **regular verbs**. Look at page 603 for a guide to regular verb conjugations.

Special Forms of Verbs

All of the verbs in this dictionary show the **past tense, past participle,** and **present participle**. For regular verbs, the past tense and the past participle are the same, so you will see only one word before the present participle, like at the entry
burn[1] * /bɜ·n/ [*verb*; **burned, burning**].
Here *burned* is both the past tense and the past participle.

Sometimes the past participle and the past tense are not the same. If they are different, you will see them both: **break**[1] * /breɪk/ [*verb*; **broke, broken, breaking**]. *Broke* is the past tense and *broken* is the past participle.

The present participle is always the last special form you see, like
talk[1] * /tɔk/ [*verb*; **talked, talking**]   or
drink[1] * /drɪŋk/ [*verb*; **drank, drunk, drinking**].

Some irregular verbs do not change their form for the past tense and the past participle. You will see all of the forms for these verbs, like
cut[1] /kʌt/ [*verb*; **cuts, cut, cut, cutting**].

Many verbs that end with a -y are difficult to spell. When a verb ends with a -y, you will see the third person singular (the form for *he, she,* or *it*) to help you with the right spelling. For example, **carry** /'kɛri/ [*verb*; **carries, carried, carrying**].

Many verbs double the last consonant for the past tense and the past participle. You will see the third person singular (the form for *he, she,* or *it*) for these verbs to tell you that the last consonant is not doubled there. For example,
drip /drɪp/ [*verb*; **drips, dripped, dripping**].

▌ Look at page 592 for more information about irregular verbs. ▐

Special Forms of Nouns

To make a regular noun **plural**, you add an -s. Some nouns do not have a regular plural form. If the plural form of a noun is irregular, or if it could be confusing, the form is shown, like **baby** * /beɪbi/ [noun; plural **babies**] .

16 Look up these words. Draw a circle around the correct plural form.

1. **boss**   boss (bosses) boses
2. **child**   children   childs   childes
3. **life**   lifes   lives   lifs
4. **sister-in-law**   sister-in-law   sister-in-laws   sisters-in-law
5. **sheep**   sheeps   sheep   sheepes

Special Forms of Adjectives

Adjectives have many different forms. To compare two things, you add -er to most adjectives to make the **comparative form**, like *soft → softer*. To make some adjectives comparative, you add *more* before the verb, like *intelligent → more intelligent*.

To say that something is the most, you often add -est to the adjective to make the **superlative form**, like *soft → softest*. To make some adjectives superlative, you add *most* before the verb, like *intelligent → most intelligent*.

If a word has an irregular form for the comparative or superlative, the form is given, like **good**[1] * /ɡʊd/ [adjective; **better, best**] .

Some adjectives cannot be made comparative. If an adjective does not have a comparative form, *no comparative* will be written after the part of speech information, like **global** /ˈɡloʊbəl/ [adjective; *no comparative*] .

For more information about how to use comparative and superlative adjectives, look at the usage note after the entry for **comparative**.

WHERE THE GRAMMAR INFORMATION IS

If the grammar information is true for all of the meanings of an entry word, the information comes at the beginning, before the first definition, like *sing*. If the grammar information is only true for one meaning, it comes before that definition, like *rotten*.

sing * /sɪŋ/ [verb; **sang, sung, singing**]
to make music with your voice: *I could hear someone singing.* I **sing someone something** ▸ *Sing us a song, Grandma!*

rotten /ˈrɑtən/ [adjective]
1 [*no comparative*] having rotted: *She threw the rotten vegetables away.*
2 [**more rotten, most rotten**] very bad or unpleasant: *I had a rotten day.*

DEFINITIONS

A definition tells you what an entry word means. An entry word may have one meaning or more than one meaning. If there is more than one meaning, each definition is shown separately. The most common meaning is shown first.

> **tape**[2] [*verb;* **taped, taping**]
> **1** to record sound or images on a tape: *I'll tape the movie and watch it later*
> **2** to stick a piece of paper or material onto something using tape: *Posters of movies stars were taped on her bedroom walls.*

17 Look up these words. Write down the number of the definition that is shown. Then write down how many total definitions each word has.

ENTRY	DEFINITION	THIS DEFINITION	TOTAL DEFINITIONS
1. **act**[2]	a part of a play	2	3
2. **egg**	an egg of a bird, especially a chicken, used as food	___	___
3. **film**[1]	a very thin layer of a substance on a surface	___	___
4. **heavy**	weighing a lot	___	___
5. **loose**	not close against something or attached firmly	___	___
6. **minority**	the smallest part of a group of people or things	___	___

SYNONYMS AND OPPOSITES

Synonyms are words that mean the same thing, or almost the same thing as each other. An **opposite** is a word that is as far as possible from the meaning of a word.

18 Look at these words. Write down if they are synonyms or opposites.

1. **brag**	**boast**	synonyms
2. **goal**	**aim**[1]	_____
3. **hard**[1]	**difficult**	_____
4. **wide**[1]	**narrow**[1]	_____
5. **import**[1]	**export**[1]	_____
6. **icing**	**frosting**	_____

☛ Be careful. Many words cannot be used in exactly the same way as their synonyms and opposites. Look at the example sentences to be sure that you are using the word correctly.

PHRASES

Phrases are groups of words that have a special meaning when they are used together. In this dictionary, phrases are together in a special group after the other meanings, and are in **dark letters**. Every phrase has its own definition.

Some phrases are parts of sentences, such as **in those days**. Other phrases are whole expressions, such as **I'm afraid so**. Some phrases have a slash **/** in them to show that you can choose which word to use. For example, **the other day/night** means that you can say "the other day" or "the other night." In a phrase like **no matter what/why/how/etc.** the "etc." means that you can use more words like the other words in this phrase, such as **where**, **when**, or **who**.

If part of a phrase can be left out, that part will be inside parentheses ( ). For example, **get acquainted (with someone)** means that you can say "my new neighbor and I got acquainted" or "I got acquainted with my new neighbor."

You will find a phrase at the entry for the main word in that phrase. The main word is usually the first noun. For example, **good afternoon** is at the entry for **afternoon** and **make a face** is at **face**. However, the main word in a phrase can sometimes be another kind of word, such as a verb, an adjective, or pronoun. For example, **call collect** is at the entry for **call**, and **inside out** is at **inside**. If there are choices in the phrase, you will find the phrase at the first main word that is not a choice. For example, **how/what about** is at **about**.

19 Look up these phrases in the dictionary. Write the main entry word where you found the phrase on the line next to the phrase.

1. **for the time being** _____

2. **on account of** _____

3. **out of order** _____

4. **feel at home** _____

5. **on a daily/weekly basis** _____

6. **cut it out!** _____

7. **have high hopes** _____

8. **in return (for)** _____

9. **knock it off** _____

10. **by himself** _____

11. **more or less** _____

12. **break a record** _____

EXAMPLE SENTENCES

In this dictionary, example sentences and phrases show how each meaning is used. For example, *I don't want to* **be a burden to** *you.*

Some parts of the example sentences may be in **dark letters**. The parts in dark letters show other words that are used with the main entry word most often.

20 Look up these words. Choose the phrase that uses the word as you see it in dark letters.

1. **burden**
   he is a burden with you   he is a burden by you   he is a burden to you

2. **crunch**[1]
   he crunched up carrot   he crunched on the carrot   he crunched carrot

3. **heat**[2]
   heat up a cup of tea   heat in a cup of tea   heat on a cup of tea

4. **radar**
   on the radar map   on the image of the radar   on the radar screen

5. **secret**[1]
   I keep the secrets   I can secret   I can keep a secret

If the entry word should be used with other words in a special order, the dark letters show this order before the example sentence. For example, the pattern tells you that you **add something to something** . This means that you can *add milk to coffee*, but you cannot *add milk coffee* or *add to milk coffee*. The only correct pattern is the one in **dark letters**.

21 Look up these words. Draw a circle around the correct pattern.

1. **add**
   add the rice to the water   add rice water   rice add to water

2. **free**[1]
   free go   free to go   go free

3. **keep**
   keep us all night up   keep us up all night   keep up us all night

4. **nominate**
   nominate her president   nominate president by her   nominate her for president

5. **want**
   want to study   want study   want like study

Sometimes a word has parentheses ( ) around it. This means that you can use the word inside the parentheses in this pattern, but it is not always necessary.

Guide to the Dictionary

22 Look up these words. Put parentheses around the word in the pattern that is not always necessary

1. **birth**   give birth (to)
2. **blast**[1]   at full blast
3. **sure**[1]   make sure that
4. **charge**[1]   in charge of

Slashes **/ / /** between words in phrases show a choice of words you can use with the entry word. If the word *etc.* is used, it means you can use other words that are similar to the words between slashes.

23 Look up these words. Draw a circle around the phrase that uses the **wrong** word.

1. **ask**   ask why he left   ask like he left   ask when he left
2. **before**   the week before last   the hour before last   the month before last
3. **follow**   follow instructions   follow orders   follow letters
4. **guess**[2]   bring a guess   take a guess   make a guess
5. **twice**   twice as good   twice as year   twice as wonderful

If a special use of a word in an example sentence needs extra explanation, this information is shown in parentheses following an equals sign (=) . This is called a **gloss**.

24 Look up these words and find the phrases that have a gloss. Then write down their gloss.

1. **butter**   bread and butter   =   _bread with butter on it_
2. **dairy**   dairy products   =   _____
3. **join**   join hands   =   _____
4. **late**   too late to   =   _____
5. **trade**[1]   by trade   =   _____

CROSS REFERENCES

After some definitions, there is an arrow ⇨ that points to another entry word. This means that you can look in another part of the dictionary for more information about the word you have looked up. These directions are called **cross-references**.

See Also **Cross References**

Some cross-references say ⇨ *See also* ___ , like the one at **ashamed** that says ⇨*See also* **shame** . This means that you can look at **shame** because this word is related to the word you have looked up. *See also* can help you find the word or meaning you are looking for if you have looked up a word with a similar meaning.

Compare **Cross References**

Some cross-references say ⇨ *Compare ___* , like ⇨ *Compare* **liftoff** at the entry **takeoff** . This tells you that the difference between the word you are looking up, like **takeoff** , and another word, like **liftoff** , can be confusing. You should look up this other word to see if you are using both words correctly.

Look up **takeoff** and **liftoff** . Do you understand the difference between these two words?

Cross References to Usage and Synonyms

Some cross-references say ⇨ *See the usage note at ___* , like the cross-reference at the main entry **sorry** that says ⇨ *See the usage note at* **apologize** . Others say ⇨ *See the synonym note at ___* , like the cross-reference at **kid** that says ⇨ *See the synonym note at* **child** . This means that there is a note at that entry with more information about the word you have looked up.

Cross References to Pictures

Some cross-references say ⇨ *See the picture at ___* . For example, the entry for **tailgate** says ⇨ *See the picture at* **pickup truck** . This cross-reference means that you will find a picture in another part of the dictionary that will help you understand the word.

Look up the entry for **pickup truck** . Find *tailgate* in the picture.

Some entries have a word in SMALL CAPITAL LETTERS. This means you can find more information or a picture at the entry for that word.

Look up the entry for **lemon**. What word is in small capital letters? Look up that word. What do you find there?

WARNINGS AND NOTES

Warnings have the mark 🖝 in front of them. They tell you about mistakes that students often make with the word you are looking up.

25 Look up these words. Copy the warning for each entry.

1. **baby** _Do not say "baby cat," "baby dog," or "baby cow." Say kitten, puppy, or calf._

2. **beside** _____

3. **friend** _____

4. **rain** _____

5. **unable** _____

Usage notes tell you about special problems you might have when you use the word you have looked up.

> **USAGE** during, for
>
> Use **during** to talk about something that happens within a particular period of time: *She lived in New York during the 1990's.*
>
> Do not use **during** to talk about how long something lasts. Use **for**: *I was in the hospital for six weeks.*

Synonym notes explain the small differences between similar words.

> **SYNONYMS** angry, mad, furious, annoyed
>
> **Angry** is the basic word for what you feel when something happens that you do not like: *He makes me very angry.* **Mad** is a less formal word: *You make me mad!* I *Don't get mad.*
>
> **Furious** means "to be very angry": *She was furious when she realized he was lying.*
>
> **Annoyed** means "a little angry": *He was annoyed at having to wait so long.*

Pronunciation notes tell you about special problems you may have when you pronounce words.

> **PRONUNCIATION** am
>
> When **am** is in the middle of a sentence, pronounce it as /əm/: *What am I going to do?* When **am** is the first or last word in a sentence, pronounce it as /æm/: *Am I tired? Of course I am!*

26 Look up the synonym notes for these words and write down their synonyms. Then, choose the best synonym to use in the sentence and write it on the line.

1. **angry** _____ _____ _____

   She was angrier than she had ever been before. She was _____ with him.

2. **call** _____ _____ _____

   He pressed the buttons on the phone to _____ 555-7537.

3. **mark** _____ _____ _____

   She had a _____ of makeup on her collar.

4. **pay**^{2} _____ _____ _____

   She makes a _____ of $75,000 a year.

Answers for the Guide to the Dictionary

1. 1. address, 2. cedar, 3. knee, 4. loaf, 5. rich, 6. wage

2. 1. galaxy, 2. gamble, 3. game, 4. gate, 5. giraffe, 6. girl

3. 1. page 277, 2. page 176, 3. page 312, 4. page 518, 5. page 406, 6. page 125

4. 1. * T, 2. *, 3. *, 4. T, 5. T, 6. * T, 7. * T, 8. T, 9. *, 10. *, 11. *, 12. *

5. 1. daisy = /ˈdeɪzi/, 2. dance = /dæns/. 3. trouble = /ˈtrʌbəl/, 4. traffic = /ˈtræfɪk/, 5. unable= /ʌnˈeɪbəl/

6. tree, shoe, leather, dog, ramp, cyclone

7. 1. incorrect, 2. correct, 3. incorrect, 4. correct, 5. correct

8. mine, her, them, they, he, you, me, us, hers, because, theirs, yours, she, I, it him

9. any, this, dozen, eacg, certain, her, either

10. soft, funny, scared, brisk, silly, happy, bald

11. with, between, in, from, to, under, on

12. 1. to be an explanation or reason for something, 2. to make a tree fall down by cutting it, 3. to find a particular piece of information in a book or on a computer, 4. to believe that you can depend on someone or something

13. 1. linking verb, 2. auxiliary verb, 3. linking verb, 4. phrasal verb, 5. modal verb, 6. modal verb

14. 1. rather, quickly, loudly, hopefully, slowly, really

15. however, but, and

16. 1. bosses, 2. children, 3. lives, 4. mothers-in-law, 5. sheep

17. 1. 2/3, 2. 2/2, 3. 3/3, 4. 1/4, 5. 1/3, 6. 2/2

18. 1. synonyms, 2. synonyms, 3. synonyms, 4. opposites, 5. opposites, 6. opposites

19. 1. time, 2. account, 3. order, 4. home, 5. basis, 6. cut, 7. hope, 8. return, 9. knock, 10. himself, 11. more, 12. break

20. 1. he is a burden to you, 2. he crunched on the carrot, 3. heat up a cup of tea, 4. on the radar screen, 4. I can keep a secret

21. 1. add rice to water, 2. free to go, 3. keep us up all night, 4. nominate her for president, 5. want to study

22. 1. to, 2. at, 3. that, 4. of

23. 1. ask like he left, 2. the hour before last, 3. follow letters, 4. bring a guess, 5. twice as year

24. 1. bread with butter on it, 2. food such as milk, cheese, etc., 3. hold the hand of the person beside you, 4. there is no time left, 5. I work as __

25. 1. Do not say "baby cat," "baby dog," or "baby cow." Say **kitten**, **puppy** or **calf.**, 2. Do not say "I sat besides her." Say **I sat beside her.**, 3. Do not say "A friend of me." Say **A friend of mine.**, 4. Do not say "big rain." Say **heavy rain.**, 5. Do not use **unable** before a noun.

26. 1. mad, furious, annoyed; furious, 2. phone, telephone, dial; dial, 3. stain, spot, smudge; smudge,, 4. salary, wage, income; salary

A * or **a** /eɪ/ [*noun*]
1 [*plural* **As** or **A's**, **a's**] the first letter of the English alphabet
➪ See the usage note at **ALPHABET**.
2 **A** [*plural* **As** or **A's**] the highest grade in school: *He got an A in English.* | *She always **got straight As** (=received no grade less than A) in college.*

a * /ə; when stressed eɪ/ [*article*]
1 one or any; used before words that begin with consonant sounds: *She wore a blue dress.* | *I need to borrow a pen.*
2 for each one; *synonym* **PER**: *This fabric costs $30 a yard.* | *She visits us about three times a year.*
➪ Compare **AN**.

USAGE   a, an

Use **a** before words, especially countable nouns, that begin with a consonant or a sound like a consonant: *a bowl* | *a house* | *a tiger* | *a useful tool* | *a European country.*
Use **an** before words that begin with a vowel sound: *an egg* | *an idea* | *an honest man* | *an M.A.*

---

abandon /əˈbændən/ [*verb*; **abandoned, abandoning**] to leave someone or something forever: *The house was abandoned many years ago.*

abbreviation * /əˌbriviˈeɪʃən/ [*noun*] a short form of a word, phrase, or name: *"Aug." is an **abbreviation for** "August."*

ABC's /ˈeɪˌbiˈsiz/ [*plural noun*] the English alphabet, as learned by young children: *Has she learned her ABC's yet?*

abdomen /ˈæbdəmən/ [*noun*] the front part of the body of a person or animal between the chest and the legs
➪ Compare **STOMACH** (definition 2).

ability * /əˈbɪliti/ [*noun*; *plural* **abilities**] something you are able to do: *His job really fits his abilities.* | **ability to do something** ▸ *She lost the ability to walk.*

SYNONYMS   ability, skill, talent

Your **ability** to do something is anything you are able to do: *Humans have the ability to talk.* | *Our students have different levels of ability (=some are better at things than others).*

A **skill** is something you are able to do that you need special training in or knowledge about: *We try to develop our students' language skills.* | *The job will need a lot of skill.*
Talent is the ability to do something especially well: *an actor of great talent.*

---

able * /ˈeɪbəl/ [*adjective; no comparative*]
━━ PHRASE ━━
be able to do something to have enough power, skill, time, etc., to do something: *Will you be able to come next week?* | *I wasn't able to hear the speaker.*

aboard[1] /əˈbɔrd/ [*preposition*] if you are aboard a boat, plane, or train, you are on it: *Is everyone aboard the ship now?*

aboard[2] [*adverb*] on or onto a boat, plane, or train: *Come on, let's go aboard.*

abolish /əˈbɑlɪʃ/ [*verb; **abolishes, abolished, abolishing**] to officially end a law or system: *Slavery was finally abolished in the U.S. in 1865.*

abolition /ˌæbəˈlɪʃən/ [*noun*] the ending of a law or system: *the **abolition of** slavery*

about[1] * /əˈbaʊt/ [*preposition*]
1 if a book, movie, conversation, etc., is about something, that is the subject it deals with: *He was reading a book about dinosaurs.* | *We talked about the plan.* | *What was the play about?* | *Did you think about what I said?*
━━ PHRASES ━━
2 **how/what about . . . ?** used to suggest something: *How about some lunch?* | *What about getting a pet?*
3 **what about . . . ?** SPOKEN used to remind someone of something that should be dealt with: *"I'm going away this weekend." "What about your cat?"*

about[2] * [*adverb*]
1 used to show that a number or amount is not exact; *synonyms* **AROUND, APPROXIMATELY**: *I've lived here for about ten years.* | *It weighs about a pound.*
━━ PHRASE ━━
2 **be about to do something** if you are about to do something, you will do it very soon: *I was just about to leave when the phone rang.*

above[1] * /ə'bʌv/ [*preposition*]
1 in a higher POSITION than someone or something; *opposite* BELOW: *There was a clock above the door.* | *The rank above a captain is a major.*
2 more than a particular amount, level, or number; *opposite* BELOW: *The temperature is above normal for this time of year.*
— PHRASE ——
3 above all used at the beginning of a sentence to show that what you are talking about is the most important thing: *Above all, make sure you take the map with you.*

above[2] * [*adverb*] in, into, or toward a higher position, level, amount, etc.; *opposite* BELOW: *Write your name in the space above.* | *You need a grade of C or above to pass the test.*

abroad * ⊤ /ə'brɔd/ [*adverb*] in or to a foreign country: *My aunt spent many years abroad.* | *Have you ever been abroad?*

abrupt ⊤ /ə'brʌpt/ [*adjective*; **more abrupt, most abrupt**] without any warning: *The meeting came to an **abrupt end** (=it stopped suddenly).*

absence * /'æbsəns/ [*noun*]
1 when you are away from a place or not with a person or group: *They made the decision **in my absence** (=when I was not with them).*
2 the fact that something is not present: *The police are worried about the **absence** of proof in the case.*

absent * /'æbsənt/ [*adjective*; *no comparative*] not in a place or not with a particular person or group; *opposite* PRESENT: *Several students are **absent from** school today.*

absolute /'æbsəˌlut/ [*adjective*; *no comparative*] to the greatest degree that is possible, or in every possible way: *I think it's an absolute disgrace!*
☞ Only use **absolute** before a noun.

absolutely ⊤ /ˌæbsə'lutli/ [*adverb*]
1 completely: *The situation is absolutely ridiculous!*
2 used to agree with someone strongly: *"I think they should all be put in jail." "Absolutely!"*

absorb /æb'sɔrb/ [*verb*; **absorbed, absorbing**] to take in liquid, heat, light, etc.: *The drug is quickly **absorbed into** the bloodstream.*

absorbent /æb'sɔrbənt/ [*adjective*; **more absorbent, most absorbent**] an absorbent material is able to take in a lot of liquid: *absorbent paper towels*

absurd ⊤ /æb'sɜrd/ [*adjective*; **more absurd, most absurd**] very silly or wrong: *That's an absurd idea!*

abuse[1] ⊤ /ə'byuz/ [*verb*; **abused, abusing**]
1 to use something in a wrong or harmful way: *Some people abuse alcohol.*
2 to treat a person or animal very badly: *He abused his cat.*

abuse[2] /ə'byus/ [*noun*]
1 the harmful use of drugs, alcohol, etc.: *the problem of drug abuse*
2 unkind language or cruel actions: *verbal abuse* | *physical abuse*

academic /ˌækə'dɛmɪk/ [*adjective*; *no comparative*] relating to schools, colleges, or universities, or the subjects that are studied in them: *an academic institution* | *academic studies*

academy /ə'kædəmi/ [*noun*; *plural* **academies**]
1 a high school, especially a private one: *She goes to Bell's Academy.*
2 a place where people are trained to do something: *a military academy*

accent /'æksɛnt/ [*noun*] the way someone speaks, which shows the country or area he or she is from: *a Russian accent* | *a Spanish accent*

accept * ⊤ /æk'sɛpt/ [*verb*; **accepted, accepting**]
1 to take something that is offered to you, or agree to something that someone has asked for; *opposite* REJECT: *She accepted the money.* | *He asked her to marry him, and she accepted.*
2 to admit someone into a school or organization; *opposite* REJECT: *She was **accepted to** Harvard University.*
3 to agree that something is true: *I **accept that** some changes will have to be made.*

acceptable * ⊤ /æk'sɛptəbəl/ [adjective; more acceptable, most acceptable] of a high enough standard, quality, etc.; synonym SATISFACTORY; opposite UNACCEPTABLE: His homework was not perfect, but it was acceptable.

acceptance /æk'sɛptəns/ [noun]
1 when you take something that is offered, or agree to something that someone has asked for: She made a speech **in acceptance of** the award.
2 when you agree that something is true: This idea is **gaining acceptance**.

access /'æksɛs/ [noun]
1 a way of getting into a place: **Access to** this area is for employees only. | The ramp provides easier access for people in wheelchairs (=makes it easier for them to get into the building).
2 a way of getting information, learning something, talking to someone, etc.: Everyone should have equal **access to** education.

accident * /'æksɪdənt/ [noun]
1 something that happens but is not planned, usually something bad: She was killed **in a car accident**. | He **had an accident** and hurt his arm. | I didn't mean to break it—it was an accident!
═══ PHRASE ═══
2 by accident if you do something by accident, you do not intend to do it; synonym ACCIDENTALLY; opposite DELIBERATELY: By accident, she mailed the letter to the wrong address.

accidental * /ˌæksɪ'dɛntəl/ [adjective; no comparative] not planned; opposites DELIBERATE, INTENTIONAL: The damage was accidental.

accidentally * /ˌæksɪ'dɛntəli/ [adverb] something that happens accidentally is not planned; opposite DELIBERATELY: I accidentally locked myself out of the car.

accommodate /ə'kɑmə,deɪt/ [verb; accommodated, accommodating] to have enough room for people or things; synonym HOLD: The hall doesn't accommodate large crowds.

accommodations /əˌkɑmə'deɪʃənz/ [plural noun] somewhere you can stay, for example in a hotel: The price includes airfare and accommodations.

accompany /ə'kʌmpəni/ [verb; accompanies, accompanied, accompanying]
1 FORMAL to go somewhere with someone: He accompanied me on my walk.
2 to play music that goes with something that someone else is singing or playing on another instrument: She sang, and her brother accompanied her on piano.

accomplish /ə'kɑmplɪʃ/ [verb; accomplishes, accomplished, accomplishing] to succeed in doing something difficult: Think of all the things you've accomplished already!

accomplishment /ə'kɑmplɪʃmənt/ [noun] something you have done well or learn to do well: The article listed her many accomplishments.

accord /ə'kɔrd/ [noun]
═══ PHRASE ═══
of your own accord because you want to: I left of my own accord.

according to * /ə'kɔrdɪŋ ˌtu/ [preposition]
1 used to say who or where your information has come from: According to the weather report, it's going to be hot today.
2 in a way that is decided by something else: You will be paid according to how many hours you work.

account¹ * ⊤ /ə'kaʊnt/ [noun]
1 money that you keep in a bank, that you can take out or add to: I'd like to **open an account**. | I have $150 **in my bank account**. | a savings account
2 a description of an event or series of events: She **gave** us a long **account of** her trip to Europe.
3 accounts [plural] records of the money a company or person receives and spends: Mrs. Brown **keeps the accounts** (=is responsible for organizing them).

/i/ see	/ɪ/ big	/eɪ/ day	/ɛ/ get	/æ/ hat
/ɑ/ father, hot	/ʌ/ up	/ə/ about	/ɔ/ saw	
/oʊ/ hope	/ʊ/ book	/u/ too	/aɪ/ I	/aʊ/ how
/ɔɪ/ boy	/ɝ/ bird	/ɚ/ teacher	/ɪr/ ear	/ɛr/ air
/ɑr/ far	/ɔr/ more	/ʊr/ tour	/aɪr/ fire	
/aʊɚ/ hour	/θ/ nothing	/ð/ mother	/ʃ/ she	
/ʒ/ measure	/tʃ/ church	/dʒ/ jump	/ŋ/ long	

— PHRASES —

4 on account of because of: *She can't play sports on account of her knee.*

5 take something into account to consider something when you are making a decision or judging a situation: *I was late because I didn't take the traffic into account.*

account² T [*verb;* accounted, accounting]

— PHRASAL VERB —

account for [*phrasal verb*]
to be an explanation or reason for something: **account for something** ▸ *How do you account for the missing $80?*

accountant /əˈkaʊntənt/ [*noun*]
someone whose job is to organize and check financial records: *a tax accountant*

accuracy /ˈækyərɔsi/ [*noun*] the fact or quality of being exact or true: *Accuracy is extremely important when you are writing a report.*

accurate T /ˈækyərɪt/ [*adjective;* **more accurate, most accurate**] true and exact; *opposite* INACCURATE: *Do you think her story was accurate?* | *I'll try to work out an accurate figure.*

accurately /ˈækyərɪtli/ [*adverb*]
correctly and exactly: *He accurately predicted who would win the World Series.*

accusation /ˌækyʊˈzeɪʃən/ [*noun*] a statement that someone has done something wrong or illegal: *The accusations against him were false.*

accuse /əˈkyuz/ [*verb;* accused, accusing] to say that someone has done something wrong or illegal: **accuse someone of something** ▸ *She accused him of telling lies about her.* | *He is accused of murder.*

accustomed T /əˈkʌstəmd/ [*adjective;* **more accustomed, most accustomed**]

— PHRASE —

accustomed to familiar with a situation, activity, etc., so that it seems normal and usual to you: *It takes a while to get accustomed to a new school.*
▷ *See also* **be used to** *at* USED².

ache¹ /eɪk/ [*noun*] a continuous pain in a part of your body: *She's always complaining of aches and pains.*

USAGE   ache

Ache is not often used alone, but is usually combined with another word, for example *headache, earache, toothache,* or *stomachache.* For example, do not say "I have an ache in my tooth." Say **I have a toothache.**

ache² [*verb;* ached, aching] if part of your body aches, it hurts with a continuous pain: *My back aches—I've got to get a new chair.*

achieve * /əˈtʃiv/ [*verb;* achieved, achieving] to do something good or difficult: *I feel I've achieved a lot this year.*

achievement * T /əˈtʃivmənt/ [*noun*]
something good or difficult that you do: *Her greatest achievement was winning an Olympic gold medal.*

acid * /ˈæsɪd/ [*noun*] a liquid or substance which contains a chemical that can burn things if it is strong enough: *Vinegar is a fairly weak acid.*

acid rain /ˈæsɪd ˈreɪn/ [*noun*] rain that contains acid, which damages plants, lakes, and rivers

acknowledge T /ækˈnɑlɪdʒ/ [*verb;* acknowledged, acknowledging]
1 to admit that something is true or exists: *He acknowledged that he had made mistakes.*
2 to show that you have seen someone or received something: *I said "hello," but he didn't even acknowledge me!* | *She never acknowledged my letter.*

acorn /ˈeɪkɔrn/ [*noun*]
the nut of the oak tree

acquaintance /əˈkweɪntəns/ [*noun*]
someone you know, but do not know well: *"Is he a friend of yours?" "No, just an acquaintance."*

an acorn

acquainted /əˈkweɪntɪd/ [*adjective;* no comparative]

— PHRASES —

1 get acquainted (with someone) to talk with someone you have just met and learn more about him or her: *Your sister and I have just been getting acquainted.*

2 be acquainted with something/someone to know about something, or to know someone: *I'm not acquainted with that artist's work.*

acquire T /ə'kwaɪr/ [*verb;* **acquired, acquiring**] FORMAL to get or buy something: *The museum acquired this painting in 1956.*

acre /'eɪkɚ/ [*noun*] a unit of land area equal to 43,560 square feet, or about 4,046 square meters: *He owns 20 acres of farm land.*

acrobat /'ækrə,bæt/ [*noun*] someone who performs difficult jumps and other movements to entertain people

across[1] * /ə'krɔs/ [*preposition*]
1 from one side of something to the other: *She ran across the street.* | *They are building a bridge across the river.*
2 in every part of a country or organization: *People across the country will be taking part in the campaign.*

across[2] * [*adverb*]
1 on or to one side of something to the other: *She walked across to the bookcase.*
2 used to talk about how wide something is: *The table measures five feet across.*

acrylic /ə'krɪlɪk/ [*noun*] an artificial substance used to make material, paint, and plastic: *an acrylic sweater*

act[1] * /ækt/ [*verb;* **acted, acting**]
1 to do something or behave in a particular way: *I acted without thinking.* | *Stop acting so silly.*
2 to pretend to be someone else, in a play, movie, television program, etc.: *She has **acted in** only two movies.*

━━ PHRASE ━━
3 act as to do something in a particular situation: *Her husband also acts as her lawyer.*

act[2] * [*noun*]
1 something that is done: *an act of violence*
2 a part of a play, consisting of several scenes: *At the end of Act 2, the heroine's father returns home.*

3 if the way you behave is an act, you are pretending: *He seemed cheerful, but I knew it was just an act.*

─────────────────────
USAGE act, action
Act and **action** can both mean "something you do" when they are used as countable nouns: *a kind act* | *a kind action.* Act is also used in particular phrases: *an act of war* | *an act of kindness.* Do not use **action** in this way.
Action can be uncountable, but **act** cannot: *It was time to take action.* | *It was time for action.*
─────────────────────

acting /'æktɪŋ/ [*noun*] the profession of acting in plays, movies, and television shows: *a successful acting career*

action * /'ækʃən/ [*noun*]
1 something you do, or when you do something: *As a result of his actions, many people were helped.* | *Now is the time for action!*
▷ *See the usage note at* ACT[2].

━━ PHRASES ━━
2 in action working or operating: *When you see him in action, you realize what a great soccer player he is.*
3 out of action not able to work or operate: *His injury means he will be out of action for six weeks.* | *How long will the printer be out of action?*

active * T /'æktɪv/ [*adjective*]
1 [more active, most active] doing a lot of things, or moving around a lot: *She is an active member of the club.* | *It is important to keep active when you get older.*
2 [*no comparative*] GRAMMAR an active verb form or sentence is one whose subject is the person or thing doing something: *"She saw him" is active; "He was seen" is passive.*
▷ *Compare* PASSIVE[2].

activity * /æk'tɪvɪti/ [*noun; plural* **activities**]
1 something you spend time doing,

/i/ **see**	/ɪ/ **big**	/eɪ/ **day**	/ɛ/ **get**	/æ/ **hat**	
/a/ **father, hot**	/ʌ/ **up**	/ə/ **about**	/ɔ/ **saw**		
/oʊ/ **hope**	/ʊ/ **book**	/u/ **too**	/aɪ/ **I**	/aʊ/ **how**	
/ɔɪ/ **boy**	/ɝ/ **bird**	/ɚ/ **teacher**	/ɪr/ **ear**	/ɛr/ **air**	
/ɑr/ **far**	/ɔr/ **more**	/ʊr/ **tour**	/aɪr/ **fire**		
/aʊɚ/ **hour**	/θ/ **nothing**	/ð/ **mother**	/ʃ/ **she**		
/ʒ/ **measure**	/tʃ/ **church**	/dʒ/ **jump**	/ŋ/ **long**		

especially for enjoyment: *My favorite activity is playing computer games.*
2 when someone is doing something or people are doing things: *The office was full of activity.*

actor * /'æktɚ/ [*noun*] someone who acts in plays, movies, and television shows

actress * /'æktrɪs/ [*noun; plural* **actresses**] a woman who acts in plays, movies, and television shows

actual * /'æktʃuəl/ [*adjective; no comparative*]
1 exact or real: *I can't remember the actual time he called.* | *This is the actual room where she was born.*
2 used to talk about the main part of something: *When does the actual ceremony begin?*
☛ Only use **actual** before a noun.

actually * Ⓣ /'æktʃuəli/ [*adverb*]
1 really: *She actually told you she stole the dress?* | *He hasn't actually started his work yet.*
2 used to give your opinion, correct something, or say something new: *Actually, I think it's a pretty good book.* | *"You were born in New York, weren't you?" "Boston, actually."* | *Actually, I wanted to ask you something.*

acupuncture /'ækyʊˌpʌŋktʃɚ/ [*noun*] a form of Chinese medicine which involves sticking long, thin needles into particular parts of the body

acute /ə'kyut/ [*adjective; no comparative*]
1 an acute ANGLE is less than 90 degrees: *Draw an acute angle.*
2 very severe: *acute pain*

A.D. * /'eɪ'di/ an abbreviation used to show that a date is a particular number of years after the year 1: *Claudius became emperor of Rome in 41 A.D.*
↪ Compare B.C.

ad /æd/ [*noun*] INFORMAL a picture, notice, short film, etc., that tries to persuade people to buy something; *synonym* ADVERTISEMENT: *You could put an ad in the paper to sell your piano.*

adapt Ⓣ /ə'dæpt/ [*verb;* **adapted, adapting**]
1 to begin to feel happy or comfortable

in a new situation: *It's hard for some children to **adapt to** a new school.*
2 to change something so it is right for a new purpose: *The book has been **adapted for** television* (=made into a television movie or program).

adaptable /ə'dæptəbəl/ [*adjective;* **more adaptable, most adaptable**] able or willing to change in order to be right for a new situation: *Companies need workers who are adaptable.*

add * /æd/ [*verb;* **added, adding**]
1 to put something with, onto, or in something else: *I think you should add some more salt.* | **add something to something** ▸ *He added the letter to the pile on his desk.*
2 to say something more: *"And it would cost less too," she added.* | *I have nothing to add.*
3 to put two or more numbers together and get a total; *opposite* SUBTRACT: **add something to something** ▸ *Add the tax to the total.*
↪ See also PLUS[1].

— PHRASAL VERB ———

add up [*phrasal verb*]
4 to calculate the total of two or more numbers: **add up something** ▸ *When I added up what I'd spent, it came to $350.* | **add something up** ▸ *She added the figures up.*

addict /'ædɪkt/ [*noun*] someone who keeps taking a harmful drug and feels unable to live without it: *a drug addict*

addicted /ə'dɪktɪd/ [*adjective; no comparative*] feeling unable to be happy without regularly taking a harmful drug: *He's **addicted to** cigarettes.*

addiction /ə'dɪkʃən/ [*noun*] when someone feels unable to live without a harmful drug: *an **addiction to** alcohol*

addition * /ə'dɪʃən/ [*noun*]
1 something that is put with or onto something else, or someone who joins a group: *This vase makes a fine **addition to** my collection.* | *Come and meet the latest **addition to** our family— my baby grandson.*
2 when you put numbers together to get a total; *opposite* SUBTRACTION: *Jim is learning addition and subtraction.*

— PHRASE —

3 in addition (to) used to mention something more that is connected with what you have just said: *In addition to the accident, he lost his job.*

additional * T̄ /ə'dɪʃənəl/ [*adjective; no comparative*] another or more: *We need an additional $2,000.* | *We will be getting some additional help soon.*
☛ Only use **additional** before a noun.

address¹ * /ə'drɛs; 'ædrɛs/ [*noun; plural* **addresses**] the place where someone lives or where an organization, company, etc., is, including the name of the street, the town or city, and the state: *I gave him my address* (=told him where I live).

address² * /ə'drɛs/ [*verb;* **addresses, addressed, addressing**]
1 FORMAL to speak to someone or call someone something: **address somebody by something** ▸ *She addressed me by my first name.*
2 to speak to a group of people formally: *He will address the whole school at 3:00 p.m.*

adequate T̄ /'ædɪkwɪt/ [*adjective;* **more adequate, most adequate**] enough, or good enough; *opposite* INADEQUATE: *They did not allow adequate time to finish the job.*

adhesive /æd'hisɪv/ [*noun*] glue or a similar substance: *Attach the handle with a strong adhesive.*

adj. the written abbreviation of ADJECTIVE

adjective * /'ædʒɪktɪv/ [*noun*] GRAMMAR a word that describes something: *"Big," "angry,"* and *"beautiful"* are all adjectives.

adjust T̄ /ə'dʒʌst/ [*verb;* **adjusted, adjusting**]
1 to begin to feel comfortable in a new situation: *It was easy to adjust to life on the island.*
2 to change or move something slightly: *I adjusted the sound on the TV.*

adjustment T̄ /ə'dʒʌstmənt/ [*noun*]
1 something you do to change or move something slightly: *She made a few adjustments to the flower display.* | *The heating system needs adjustment.*
2 the process of making changes that are right for a new situation: *There's a period of adjustment when a new baby comes home.*

administration /æd,mɪnə'streɪʃən/ [*noun*]
1 the activity of managing an organization or company: *She spends most of her time on administration.*
2 the people who manage or control an organization or government: *He is a member of the school administration.*

administrator /æd'mɪnə,streɪtər/ [*noun*] someone who organizes and manages things in a company or other organization: *a college administrator*

admirable /'ædmərəbəl/ [*adjective;* **more admirable, most admirable**] FORMAL deserving praise: *He showed admirable courage.*

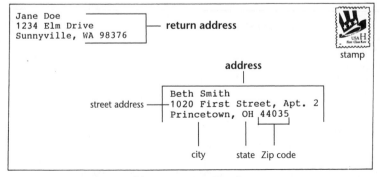

addresses on an envelope

admiral or **Admiral** /'ædmərəl/
[*noun, name*] an officer with the highest
rank in the Navy

admiration * /,ædmə'reɪʃən/ [*noun*]
the feeling of respect you have toward
someone or something that you think is
very good, intelligent, attractive, etc.: *I
have no admiration for him at all.* I *She
gazed at the house in admiration.*

admire * /æd'maɪr/ [*verb; admired,
admiring*]
1 to respect someone or something
because you think that he, she, or it
is very good, intelligent, attractive,
etc.: *I admire her for her courage.* I *I
have always admired your work.*
2 to look at something with pleasure or
approval: *I stopped to admire the view.*

admission /æd'mɪʃən/ [*noun*]
1 a statement that something is true,
especially something bad: *Her
admission that she had lied shocked
everyone.*
2 the money that you must pay to
enter a place: *Admission is $10 for
adults, $5 for students.*
3 permission to enter a place: *They were
refused admission to the movie.*

admit * ⊤ /æd'mɪt/ [*verb; admits,
admitted, admitting*]
1 to say or agree that something is
true, especially something bad: *He
admitted that he did not think he
would win.* I *I admit to feeling a little
nervous.* I **admit doing something** ▶
She admitted stealing the bicycle.
2 to let or accept someone into a
building, an area, or an organization:
*The manager of the café refused to
admit us.* I *He was admitted to the
hospital.*

adolescent /,ædəl'ɛsənt/ [*noun*]
someone who is between a child and an
adult in age and development
↪ *See the synonym note at* TEENAGER.

adopt /ə'dɑpt/ [*verb; adopted, adopting*]
to make someone else's child legally
your own: *They adopted her when she was
a baby.*

adore /ə'dɔr/ [*verb; adored, adoring*] to
like or love someone or something very

much: *Her husband adores her.* I *She
adores singing.*

adult * /ə'dʌlt/ [*noun*] someone who is
grown up: *My parents still don't treat me
like an adult.*

adv. the written abbreviation of ADVERB

advance[1] /æd'væns/ [*noun*]
1 a development or improvement in
something: *There have been great
advances in science in the past century.*
— PHRASE ▬▬▬▬
2 in advance before something
happens, or before you do something:
*She should have told him in advance that
she couldn't come to the meeting.*

advance[2] [*adjective; no comparative*]
happening or done before an event:
*Tours of the building require advance
notice* (=you must say you are coming
before you arrive). I *an advance payment*
☛ Only use **advance** before a noun.

advance[3] [*verb; advanced, advancing*]
to move forward: *Troops are advancing
toward the capital.*

advanced * ⊤ /æd'vænst/ [*adjective;
more advanced, most advanced*] at a
high or difficult level: *She is studying for
an advanced degree in English.*

advantage * ⊤ /æd'væntɪdʒ/ [*noun*]
1 something that is good or that helps
you: *One advantage of this car is that it
doesn't use much gas.* I *His height gives
him an advantage over his opponent.*
— PHRASES ▬▬▬▬
2 to someone's advantage helpful
to someone: *It would be to your
advantage to improve your writing skills.*
3 take advantage of something to
use an opportunity: *We took advantage
of the sunshine and went to the beach.*

adventure * /æd'vɛntʃər/ [*noun*] an
exciting and unusual experience: *She
told us all about her adventures in Africa.*

adventurous /æd'vɛntʃərəs/ [*adjective;
more adventurous, most
adventurous*] liking new or exciting
experiences: *an adventurous child*

adverb * /'ædvɜrb/ [*noun*] GRAMMAR a
word that tells you how, when, or where
something is done or happens: *The
words "slowly," "gently," and "actually"
are all adverbs.*

USAGE Adverbs

Adverbs are often formed by adding -*ly* to an adjective, so *slowly* means "at a slow speed" and *carefully* means "in a careful way." Sometimes, however, adverbs do not end in -*ly*; for example, *most, just, down,* and *back* are used as adverbs in some meanings.

---

advertise * /'ædvɚˌtaɪz/ [*verb;* **advertised, advertising**] to tell the public about something, for example a new product, in a newspaper, on television, etc.: *a billboard advertising a new car* | *The company **is advertising** for a sales manager.*

advertisement * /ˌædvɚ'taɪzmənt/ [*noun*] a picture, notice, short film, etc., that tries to persuade people to buy something; synonym AD: *She appeared in an advertisement for toothpaste.*

advice * T /æd'vaɪs/ [*noun*] information or an opinion about what someone should do: *I need some advice about which college to go to.* | *Let me give you some advice.* | *I wasn't sure what to do, so I asked my dad's advice* (=asked him what to do). | *I took his advice* (=did what he told me to do).

advise * /æd'vaɪz/ [*verb;* **advised, advising**] to tell someone what you think he or she should do: **advise someone to do something** ▸ *The doctor advised me to stop smoking.* | **advise someone on something** ▸ *She advises students on their careers.*

adviser T or **advisor** /æd'vaɪzɚ/ [*noun*] someone who advises people: *the president's advisers*

aerobics /ɛ'roʊbɪks/ [*noun*] a very active kind of exercise to music: *She goes to an aerobics class on Fridays.*
☛ Only use **aerobics** with a singular verb.

aerosol /'ɛrəˌsɔl/ [*noun*] a metal container that sends out liquid in very small drops: *an aerosol hair spray*

affair * /ə'fɛr/ [*noun*]
1 an event, situation, or something you are involved in: *This affair could embarrass the company.*
2 affairs [*plural*] things that a person, organization, or country does or is

involved in: *They did not want to get involved in the affairs of another country.*

affect * T /ə'fɛkt/ [*verb;* **affected, affecting**] to produce an effect or change in someone or something: *Bad weather is still affecting the area.*

USAGE affect, effect

Do not confuse **affect** and **effect**. **Affect** is a verb meaning "to produce an effect or change in someone or something": *How will this affect the situation?* | *This decision affects me too.*

Effect is a noun meaning "a change or difference that happens as a result of something": *What effect will this have on the situation?* | *The effect was gross.*

---

affection /ə'fɛkʃən/ [*noun*] a feeling of liking and caring about someone or something: *His affection for his father is obvious.*

affectionate /ə'fɛkʃənɪt/ [*adjective*] showing that you like and care about someone: *an affectionate kiss*

afford * T /ə'fɔrd/ [*verb*] if you can afford something, you have enough money to buy it or do it: *Do you think we can an we afford a bigger house?* | **afford to do something** ▸ *I can't afford to go on vacation this year.*
☛ Only use **afford** with "can," "could," or "be able to."

afraid * /ə'freɪd/ [*adjective;* **more afraid, most afraid**]
1 worried that something is dangerous or bad; synonyms FRIGHTENED, SCARED: *Is she afraid of dogs?* | **afraid (that)** ▸ *I'm afraid I might get hurt.* | **afraid to do something** ▸ *He was afraid to go into the cave.*
☛ Do not say "I am afraid to make mistakes." Say I **am afraid of making mistakes.**
☛ Do not use **afraid** before a noun.

/i/ **see** /ɪ/ **big** /eɪ/ **day** /ɛ/ **get** /æ/ **hat**
/ɑ/ **father, hot** /ʌ/ **up** /ə/ **about** /ɔ/ **saw**
/oʊ/ **hope** /ʊ/ **book** /u/ **too** /aɪ/ **I** /aʊ/ **how**
/ɔɪ/ **boy** /ɚ/ **bird** /ɚ/ **teacher** /ɪr/ **ear** /ɛr/ **air**
/ɑr/ **far** /ɔr/ **more** /ʊr/ **tour** /aɪr/ **fire**
/aʊɚ/ **hour** /θ/ **nothing** /ð/ **mother** /ʃ/ **she**
/ʒ/ **measure** /tʃ/ **church** /dʒ/ **jump** /ŋ/ **long**

— PHRASE ——

2 I'm afraid so or **I'm afraid not**
used to say yes or no to a question
when you are sorry about the answer:
*"Is he badly hurt?" "I'm afraid so." |
"Did you get the tickets?" "I'm afraid
not."*

Africa * /'æfrɪkə/ [*name*] the large area
of land south of Europe between the
Atlantic Ocean and the Indian Ocean

African[1] * /'æfrɪkən/ [*countable noun*]
someone who comes from Africa

African[2] * [*adjective; no comparative*]
belonging to, from, or relating to
Africa: *The African elephant is larger than
the Indian elephant.*

African American /'æfrɪkən
ə'merɪkən/ [*noun*] an American whose
family originally came from Africa;
synonym **BLACK**

African-American [*adjective; no
comparative*] relating to Americans
whose families originally came from
Africa; *synonym* **BLACK**: *African-American
culture*

after[1] * /'æftɚ/ [*preposition*]
1 later than a particular time or event:
*I'll meet you after lunch. | It's twenty
after five. | I'm leaving the day after
tomorrow. | There was a lot of cleaning
up to do after the party.*
2 behind, or in the next position: *You're
after me in line. | In the word "piece,"
the "e" comes after the "i."*
  ⇨ *See the picture at* LINE[1].
3 later than someone else: *She arrived
after me.*
  ⇨ *Compare* BEFORE[1].

— PHRASES ——

4 be after something to want to get
something: *I think he's after my job.*
5 after all
  a used to say that there is a good
  reason for doing or thinking
  something: *I think you should help
  him. After all, he is your friend.*
  b in spite of what happened or what
  you expected: *We didn't need our
  umbrellas after all—it was sunny all
  day.*

after[2] * [*conjunction*] when something
has or had happened; *opposite* BEFORE:

*I'll call you back after I've asked my
mother. | After I left college I worked as
a nurse.*

after[3] * [*adverb*] later in time, or
following; *opposite* BEFORE: *He left the
company soon after. | I received no reply
that day, or the day after.*
  ☛ The adverb **after** is nearly always
  used after an adverb such as "soon" or
  "shortly," or a noun such as "day" or
  "week."

afternoon * /,æftɚ'nun/ [*noun*]
1 the part of the day between noon and
the evening: *I saw her yesterday
afternoon at the library. | We spent the
afternoon shopping. | The afternoon
session starts at one o'clock.*
  ☛ Do not say "in afternoon." Say **in
  the afternoon.**

— PHRASE ——

2 good afternoon SPOKEN used as a
polite greeting to someone you meet
or talk to in the afternoon: *Good
afternoon. May I speak to Mrs. Gray?*

afterward * Ⓣ /'æftɚwɚd/ or
afterwards /'æftɚwɚdz/ [*adverb*]
after something happened or happens;
opposite BEFOREHAND: *Let's visit the art
gallery, then afterward we can get
something to eat.*

again * /ə'gɛn/ [*adverb*]
1 for a second, third, etc., time: *Try
ringing the bell again. | I thought I
would never see you again.*
2 back into the previous position or
state: *She opened the door, looked
around, and closed it again.*

— PHRASE ——

3 again and again many times: *He
shouted for help again and again.*

against * /ə'gɛnst/ [*preposition*]
1 not agreeing with something: **be
against something** ▸ *I'm against
changing the schedule. | She went to the
party against her parents' wishes
(=even though they did not want her
to go).*
2 touching or leaning on something:
*There was a desk against the wall on one
side of the room. | She leaned her bicycle
against the fence.*
3 trying to defeat, harm, or stop

someone or something: *I would never use violence against anyone.*

4 in order to be protected from something: *Is your car insured against theft?*

age * /eɪdʒ/ [*noun*]
1 the amount of time that someone has lived or that something has existed: *The two boys looked about the same age.* | *I left school at the age of 18* (=when I was 18 years old).
☛ Do not say "What age is he?" Say **How old is he?**
2 a period in someone's life: *I plan to spend my old age living near the ocean.*
3 a period of history: *the Stone Age*
4 the state of being old: *Wisdom comes with age.*
5 ages [*plural*] INFORMAL a long time: *We waited ages for the bus.* | *I haven't seen her for ages.*

aged /'eɪdʒɪd for definition 1; eɪdʒd for definition 2/ [*adjective; no comparative*]
1 FORMAL very old: *He takes care of his aged parents.*
2 used to say how old someone is: *He died last Tuesday, aged 93.*
☛ Always use **aged** before a number in this meaning.
➪ *See also* MIDDLE-AGED.

agency /'eɪdʒənsi/ [*noun; plural* **agencies**] a company or organization that provides a service for other companies or for a government: *a travel agency* | *a federal agency*

agenda /ə'dʒɛndə/ [*noun; plural* **agendas**] a list of things to be discussed at a meeting: *The first item on the agenda is the company picnic.*

agent /'eɪdʒənt/ [*noun*]
1 someone who helps writers and artists sell their work, or helps actors and musicians to find work
2 someone who works in an agency: *a travel agent*

aggression /ə'grɛʃən/ [*noun*] angry, rude, or threatening behavior: *You need to control your aggression.*

aggressive /ə'grɛsɪv/ [*adjective;* **more aggressive, most aggressive**] often attacking people or saying rude or

angry things to them: *His aggressive behavior will get him into trouble.*

ago * /ə'goʊ/ [*adverb*] in the past: *I moved here eight years ago.* | *A long time ago, dinosaurs lived in this area.*
☛ Only use **ago** after a noun. For example, do not say "It happened ago three weeks." Say **It happened three weeks ago.**

USAGE ago, since, for

Use **ago** with a word such as "month," "day," or "time" to talk about something that happened in the past: *A long time ago, this area was a forest.* | *That happened years ago.*

Both **since** and **for** are used to talk about what has been happening between a time in the past and now.

Use **since** with particular times and events: *I've been waiting since three o'clock.* | *She has been happier since she moved here.*

Use **for** with amounts of time, either in the past or the future: *I have been waiting for three hours.* | *The building will last for years.*

Do not say "I have been waiting since three hours." Use **for.**

agony /'ægəni/ [*noun*] very great pain: *I was in agony after the accident.*

agree * /ə'gri/ [*verb;* **agrees, agreed, agreeing**]
1 to have or say you have the same opinion as someone else; *opposite* DISAGREE: *He agreed with me about the need for research.* | *They couldn't agree on a name for the company.* | *I agree (that)* ▸ *I agree that we need a bigger house.*
2 to say yes to something that someone has suggested or asked for: *He agreed to all their demands.* | *agree to do something* ▸ *They agreed to finish the work in two weeks.*

/i/ **see**	/ɪ/ **big**	/eɪ/ **day**	/ɛ/ **get**	/æ/ **hat**
/a/ **father, hot**	/ʌ/ **up**	/ə/ **about**	/ɔ/ **saw**	
/oʊ/ **hope**	/ʊ/ **book**	/u/ **too**	/aɪ/ **I**	/aʊ/ **how**
/ɔɪ/ **boy**	/ɜ/ **bird**	/ɚ/ **teacher**	/ɪr/ **ear**	/ɛr/ **air**
/ar/ **far**	/ɔr/ **more**	/ʊr/ **tour**	/aɪr/ **fire**	
/aʊɚ/ **hour**	/θ/ **nothing**	/ð/ **mother**	/ʃ/ **she**	
/ʒ/ **measure**	/tʃ/ **church**	/dʒ/ **jump**	/ŋ/ **long**	

agreement * /ə'grimənt/ [*noun*]
1 something such as an arrangement that people have agreed on: *The two sides* **have reached an agreement**.
2 when people agree about something; *opposite* DISAGREEMENT: *I think there is general* **agreement on** *that point.* | *Everyone is* **in agreement**.

USAGE Agreement of subjects and verbs

Singular subjects are used with singular verbs, and plural subjects are used with plural verbs. This is called "subject-verb agreement." Sometimes it is hard to know what the subject is. Look at these sentences below:

A **list** *of words* **is** *on the blackboard.*
  ("A list" is the subject.)
Joe, *as well as his friends,* **likes** *soccer.*
  ("Joe" is the subject.)
A number *of people* **were** *laughing.*
  ("A number" means "several" here.)
The number *of students* **is** *the same as last year.*
  ("The number" is just one amount.)
Fifty dollars is *too much to pay.*
  ("Fifty dollars" is just one amount.)

---

agricultural /ˌægrɪ'kʌltʃərəl/ [*adjective; no comparative*] relating to farming: *agricultural methods* | *agricultural laborers*
agriculture /'ægrɪˌkʌltʃɚ/ [*noun*] the business of growing crops and raising animals for food; *synonym* FARMING
ahead * /ə'hɛd/ [*adverb*]
1 in a forward direction: *She was staring straight ahead.*
2 some distance in front of you: *There is a bridge over the river ahead.* | *There was a large truck* **ahead of** *us.*
3 more successful than someone or something else: *She's always been* **ahead of** *the other students.*
  ⇨ Compare BEHIND[1] (definition 2).
4 in the future: *He has a busy day* **ahead of** *him.*
  ⇨ See also **ahead of schedule** at SCHEDULE[1] *and* **ahead of time** *at* TIME[1].
aid /eɪd/ [*noun*] help or money that is given to someone who needs it: *Should we give more aid to other nations?*

aide /eɪd/ [*noun*] someone who helps someone important such as a president or government minister: *The president and his aides flew to Rome.*
AIDS /eɪdz/ [*noun*] a serious condition that makes a person's body unable to fight illness
aim[1] * /eɪm/ [*noun*]
1 what you want to achieve; *synonym* GOAL: *My aim is to get more young people interested in the theater.*
2 how well you point a gun or weapon: *His aim was so bad he didn't hit the target at all.*
— PHRASE ——
3 **take aim** to point a gun or weapon at someone or something you want to hit: *She took aim at the target.*
aim[2] * [*verb; aimed, aiming*]
1 to want to achieve something: *Exams give students something to* **aim for.** | **aim to do something** ▸ *We are aiming to win more games this season.*
2 to point a gun or weapon at someone or something you want to hit: *She was* **aiming at** *a deer, but she missed.* | *Ready! Aim! Fire!*
ain't /eɪnt/ [*verb*] NONSTANDARD a short form of "am not," "are not," "is not," "have not," and "has not": *I ain't talking to you.*
☛ You should learn what **ain't** means, but do not use it.
air * /ɛr/ [*noun*]
1 the gases around Earth, which we breathe: *Could you open a window? I need some* **fresh air.**
2 used to talk about traveling in airplanes: *It is much quicker* **by air** *than by train.*
3 **the air** the space above or around things: *She threw the ball into the air.*
air conditioner /'ɛr kənˌdɪʃənɚ/ [*noun*] a machine that cools the air in a room or building
air conditioning /'ɛr kənˌdɪʃənɪŋ/ [*noun*] a system in a building or car that keeps the air in it cool
aircraft * /'ɛrˌkræft/ [*noun; plural* **aircraft**] a vehicle that can fly: *Military aircraft have gone to the area.*

airfare /'ɛr,fɛr/ [*noun*] the price you pay to fly somewhere on a plane: *The airfare to New York is $520 round trip.*

airfield /'ɛr,fild/ [*noun*] an area where airplanes take off and land, smaller than an airport

air force or **Air Force** /'ɛr ,fɔrs/ [*noun*] the part of a country's military that fights using airplanes: *My daughter is in the Air Force.*

airline /'ɛr,laɪn/ [*noun*] a company that organizes flights to different places: *Have you traveled with this airline before? I an airline pilot*

airmail /'ɛr,meɪl/ [*noun*] the system of carrying letters, packages, etc., on an airplane: *an airmail letter*

airplane * /'ɛr,pleɪn/ [*noun*] a vehicle that flies, that has an engine and wings; *synonym* PLANE

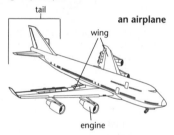

an airplane

tail
wing
engine

airport * /'ɛr,pɔrt/ [*noun*] a place where airplanes take off and land, used by the public: *I was late getting to the airport.*

air raid /'ɛr ,reɪd/ [*noun*] an attack on a place when bombs are dropped from airplanes

airspace /'ɛr,speɪs/ [*noun*] the sky over a country, which is considered to belong to that country: *Canadian airspace*

airtight /'ɛr,taɪt/ [*adjective; no comparative*] an airtight container is one which air cannot get in or out of: *Put the leftovers in an airtight container.*

aisle /aɪl/ [*noun*] a path between rows of seats in a church, theater, plane, etc., or between rows of shelves in a store: *We had seats next to the aisle. I Canned vegetables are in aisle 3.*

ajar /ə'dʒar/ [*adjective; no comparative*] a DOOR that is ajar is slightly open: *The door to his room was ajar.*

☛ Do not use **ajar** before a noun.

alarm /ə'larm/ [*noun*]
1 a bell or other sound that warns you of danger: *I was at lunch when the fire alarm went off. I a burglar alarm*
2 sudden fear: *A dog barked, and she jumped in alarm.*

alarm clock /ə'larm ,klak/ [*noun*] a clock that makes a sound at the time you have planned, usually to wake you up: *He set his alarm clock for 6:30 in the morning.*

alarmed /ə'larmd/ [*adjective;* **more alarmed, most alarmed**] feeling suddenly afraid or worried: *Don't be alarmed—the dog won't bite.*

alarming /ə'larmɪŋ/ [*adjective;* **more alarming, most alarming**] making you feel afraid or worried: *alarming news I an alarming noise*

album /'ælbəm/ [*noun*]
1 a book in which you put things such as photographs and cards that you want to keep: *I looked through the old photo album.*
2 a collection of songs or pieces of music on a CD, tape, or record: *Her last two albums sold very well.*

alcohol * /'ælkə,hɔl/ [*noun*] the substance in beer, wine, etc., that can make people drunk, or drinks like these: *Wine is about 12% alcohol. I I never drink alcohol.*

alcoholic[1] * 🅣 /,ælkə'hɔlɪk/ [*adjective;* **more alcoholic, most alcoholic**] an alcoholic drink contains alcohol: *Wine is more alcoholic than beer.*

alcoholic[2] 🅣 [*noun*] someone who drinks a lot of alcohol and feels unable to live without it

alert /ə'lɜt/ [*adjective;* **more alert, most alert**] ready or able to notice things: *The guards needed to stay alert.*

algae /'ældʒi/ [*plural noun*] simple plants that grow in water: *The sides of the fish tank were covered in algae.*

/i/	see	/ɪ/	big	/eɪ/	day	/ɛ/ get	/æ/ hat
/a/	father, hot	/ʌ/	up	/ə/	about	/ɔ/	saw
/oʊ/	hope	/ʊ/	book	/u/	too	/aɪ/ I	/aʊ/ how
/ɔɪ/	boy	/ɚ/	bird	/ɚ/	teacher	/ɪr/ ear	/ɛr/ air
/ɑr/	far	/ɔr/	more	/ʊr/	tour	/aɪr/ fire
/aʊɚ/	**hour**	/θ/	nothing	/ð/	mother	/ʃ/ she
/ʒ/	measure	/tʃ/	**church**	/dʒ/	jump	/ŋ/ long

algebra /'ældʒəbrə/ [*noun*] a kind of mathematics in which letters are used to represent numbers

alien /'eɪlyən; 'eɪliyən/ [*noun*]
1 someone who is not a legal citizen of the country that he or she is living in: *an illegal alien*
2 a creature from space: *Do you think Earth has been visited by aliens?*

alike * /ə'laɪk/ [*adjective;* **more alike, most alike**] people or things that are alike are similar to each other: *He and his father are very alike.* | *All the houses look alike.*
☛ Do not use **alike** before a noun.

alive * /ə'laɪv/ [*adjective; no comparative*] breathing or growing; *opposite* DEAD: *Is that plant still alive?*
☛ Do not use **alive** before a noun.

all¹ * /ɔl/ [*determiner*]
1 the whole of something, or every one of the things in a group: *She spent all the money I gave her.* | *All her friends were there.*
☛ Do not say "all them" or "all they." Say **all of them.**
▷ *See the usage note at* EACH¹.
═ PHRASE ═
2 **all day/night/week/month/year** for a whole day, week, etc.: *He waited all day long for her to call.*

all² * [*pronoun*]
1 the whole of something, or every one of the things in a group: *He was liked by all of his colleagues.* | *You ate it all!*
☛ You can say **it/us/you/them all,** but do not use **all** after a noun.
═ PHRASES ═
2 **all along** the whole time, from the beginning: *I thought all along that our team would win.*
3 **at all** used with questions and negatives to mean "considering everything" or "even one": *I didn't like her at all.* | *Did he give any reason at all for not going?*
4 **not at all** not in any way: *She said she's not at all tired.*
5 **all in all** considering everything: *All in all, we've had a pretty good day.*
6 **in all** used to talk about a total: *There are 30 students in all.*

all³ * [*adverb*]
1 completely: *I was all alone in the dark.* | *Oh, no! I forgot all about meeting her.*
═ PHRASE ═
2 **all over** affecting or going to every part of something: *She accidentally poured tea all over him.* | *People celebrated all over the country.*

Allah /'ɑlə/ [*name*] the spirit that Muslims believe is the only god

allegiance /ə'lidʒəns/ [*noun*] loyalty to a person, group, country, etc.: *His allegiance to the team is strong.*

allergic /ə'lɜrdʒɪk/ [*adjective; no comparative*] becoming ill when you eat, smell, or touch a particular thing: *I'm allergic to peanuts.*

allergy /'ælərdʒi/ [*noun; plural* **allergies**] when you become ill if you eat, smell, or touch a particular thing: *an allergy to cats*

alley /'æli/ [*noun; plural* **alleys**] a narrow street or path between buildings or walls: *The workers' entrance is in the alley behind the restaurant.*

alliance /ə'laɪəns/ [*noun*] when two or more countries or groups work together or support each other: *an alliance between the political parties*

alligator /'ælɪˌgeɪtər/ [*noun*] a large animal with a long mouth, big teeth, short legs, and a long thick tail

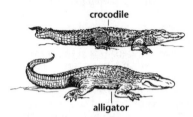

crocodile

alligator

allow * Ⓣ /ə'laʊ/ [*verb;* **allowed, allowing**] to let someone do something, or to give permission for something: *They don't allow smoking on the airplane.* | **allow someone to do something** ▸ *She allowed us to play in her yard.* | *You aren't allowed to touch the sculptures.*

allowance /ə'laʊəns/ [*noun*] a set amount of money given to someone to spend in a particular way: *a food* allowance | *Our parents give each of us a weekly allowance.*

all right¹ /ˌɔl 'raɪt/ [*adjective; no comparative*]
  1 used to say that there are no problems, or that something is satisfactory; synonym **OK**: *"I'm sorry I didn't call you." "That's all right."* | *Everything's all right now.*
  2 well, or not hurt; synonym **OK**: *Are you all right? You look awful.*

all right² [*adverb*]
  1 used to say yes, or when you agree with something; synonym **OK**: *"Can I borrow your bicycle?" "All right."*
  2 used when you start talking; synonym **OK**: *All right, everybody listen now.*
  3 in a way that is satisfactory but not excellent; synonym **OK**: *I did all right on my history test.*

ally /'ælaɪ/ [*noun; plural* **allies**] a country or person that helps or supports another: *political allies* | *military allies*

almond /'amənd/ [*noun*] a long pale **NUT**: *The cake is flavored with almonds.*

almost ∗ /'ɔlmoʊst/ [*adverb*] not quite doing something, not quite in a particular state or place, etc., but close to it; synonym **NEARLY**: *My mother is almost forty.* | *I swim almost every day.*

alone¹ ∗ /ə'loʊn/ [*adjective; no comparative*]
  1 without anyone else present: *When she was alone, she opened the letter.*
  ☛ Do not use **alone** before a noun.
  ━━ **PHRASE** ━━
  2 leave someone/something alone to not talk to or touch someone or something: *I wish you'd all leave me alone.* | *Leave the food alone—it's not time to eat yet.*

alone² ∗ [*adverb*]
  1 without anyone else present or helping you: *He's lived alone since his wife died.* | *She made her decision alone.*
  2 with nothing or no one else: *He alone knows where she went.*

━━━━━━━━━━━━━━━━━━━━
SYNONYMS   alone, on your own, lonely

  Alone means "without any other people": *She sat alone in the cafeteria.*

  On your own means the same as **alone,** but is often used to emphasize that no one else is with you or helping you: *Did you come all this way on your own?*
  Lonely means "unhappy because you are alone": *I felt lonely when I went to college.*
━━━━━━━━━━━━━━━━━━━━

along¹ ∗ /ə'lɔŋ/ [*preposition*] following a path, road, etc.: *I was walking along the street when I saw her.*

along² ∗ [*adverb*]
  1 forward, on a path, road, etc.: *They were driving along, talking cheerfully to each other.*
  2 if you bring someone or something along, you bring that person or thing with you to a place: *Bring your friends along!*

alongside 🔲 /ə'lɔŋ'saɪd/ [*preposition*] next to the side of: *A tractor was parked alongside the barn.*

aloud /ə'laʊd/ [*adverb*] if you say something aloud, you say it so that people can hear: *My father **read aloud** to me every night.*

alphabet ∗ /'ælfə,bɛt/ [*noun*] the group of letters used to write the words of a language, especially when they are said or written in a fixed order: *There are 26 letters in the English alphabet.*

━━━━━━━━━━━━━━━━━━━━
USAGE   The alphabet

  The letters of the alphabet can be countable nouns or uncountable nouns: *There are three g's in "giggle."* | *Not many words begin with X.*
━━━━━━━━━━━━━━━━━━━━

alphabetical /,ælfə'bɛtɪkəl/ [*adjective; no comparative*] arranged according to the normal order of letters in the alphabet: *The names were listed in alphabetical order.*

already ∗ /ɔl'rɛdi/ [*adverb*]
  1 before now, or before a particular time: *"Will you speak to Dad?" "I*

━━━━━━━━━━━━━━━━━━━━
/i/ **see** /ɪ/ **big** /eɪ/ **day** /ɛ/ **get** /æ/ **hat**
/a/ **father, hot** /ʌ/ **up** /ə/ **about** /ɔ/ **saw**
/oʊ/ **hope** /ʊ/ **book** /u/ **too** /aɪ/ **I** /aʊ/ **how**
/ɔɪ/ **boy** /ɝ/ **bird** /ɚ/ **teacher** /ɪr/ **ear** /ɛr/ **air**
/ɑr/ **far** /ɔr/ **more** /aɪr/ **fire**
/aʊɚ/ **hour** /θ/ **nothing** /ð/ **mother** /ʃ/ **she**
/ʒ/ **measure** /tʃ/ **church** /dʒ/ **jump** /ŋ/ **long**

already did." | I called her, but she had
already left.

2 now, or at a particular time: *Can't it
wait? I'm late already.* | *When they got
there, the theater was already full.*

also * /ˈɔlsoʊ/ [*adverb*]
  1 used to mention something more: *We
  visited the museum and also the park.*
  2 used to talk about someone or
  something else that is similar: *You
  study medicine? My best friend also
  wants to be a doctor.*

USAGE   also, as well, as well as, too

All of these words are used when you
add something more to what you have
been talking about. However, they cannot
be used in the same way in sentences.

Also can be used before a noun, or at
the beginning or end of a sentence: *I
want some pie, and also some coffee.* |
I want some coffee also. **Also** can be used
before a verb, or after the verb **be**: *I also
want to come.* | *Also, I want some coffee.* |
I'm also hungry.

As well is used at the end of a sentence:
I want some coffee as well. | *I want to
come as well.*

As well as is used before a noun or a
noun phrase: *I want some pie as well as
some coffee.* | *As well as pie, I want coffee.*

Too is usually used at the end of a
sentence: *I want some pie, and some coffee
too.* | *"I want to come." "Me too."* (=
I want to come too.)

---

altar /ˈɔltɚ/ [*noun*] a special piece of
furniture that is used as a table in
religious ceremonies

alter ⊤ /ˈɔltɚ/ [*verb; altered, altering*]
to change, or to change something: *We
had to alter our plans.* | *The place had
altered since he was last there.*

alteration /ˌɔltəˈreɪʃən/ [*noun*]
a change, especially a small change: *I
made a few alterations in the schedule.*

alternate[1] /ˈɔltɚˌneɪt/ [*verb;
alternated, alternating*] to do one
thing, then another, then the first thing
again, and so on: *He is alternating
between working nights and weekends.*

alternate[2] /ˈɔltɚnɪt/ [*adjective; no
comparative*] every second one: *I work on
alternate days.*
  ☛ Only use **alternate** before a plural
  noun. For example, do not say "on
  alternate day." Say **on alternate days**.

alternative[1] ⊤ /ɔlˈtɚnətɪv/ [*noun*]
something else you can do or use in a
situation: *I don't want to leave, but I
have no alternative.*

alternative[2] ⊤ [*adjective; no
comparative*] other or different: *Do you
have any alternative suggestions?*
  ☛ Only use **alternative** before a noun.

although * ⊤ /ɔlˈðoʊ/ [*conjunction*] in
spite of a fact; *synonym* THOUGH: *You can
come with me, although you might get
bored.*
  ☛ Do not say "Although he is young,
  but he is wise." Say **Although he is
  young, he is wise.**
  ⟳ Compare **even though** at THOUGH[1].

altitude /ˈæltɪˌtud/ [*noun*] height above
the ground or ocean: *It can be hard to
breathe at high altitudes.*

altogether /ˌɔltəˈgɛðɚ/ [*adverb*]
  1 used to talk about a total number or
  amount: *Altogether, the vacation cost
  me $1,400.*
  2 completely: *He had forgotten about
  their argument altogether.*

aluminum /əˈlumənəm/ [*noun*] a
silver-white metal used for making
strong light objects, such as airplane
parts

aluminum foil /əˈlumənəm ˌfɔɪl/
[*noun*] aluminum that is as thin as
paper and is used to wrap things,
especially food: *a roll of aluminum foil*

always * /ˈɔlweɪz/ [*adverb*]
  1 whenever a particular situation
  happens or happened: *I always take a
  hot bath when I get home.* | *My mother
  always read me stories at bedtime.*
  2 all the time, or forever: *It's always hot
  here.* | *I'll always remember this visit.*
  — PHRASE —
  3 can/could always used to suggest
  something: *You could always ask your
  dad what he thinks of your idea.*

am * /æm/ [*verb*] the present form of BE that is used with "I": *I am so tired!* | *"Who's ready for dessert?" "I am."*

PRONUNCIATION   am

When **am** is in the middle of a sentence, pronounce it as /əm/: *What am I going to do?* When **am** is the first or last word in a sentence, pronounce it as /æm/: *Am I tired? Of course I am!*

---

a.m. or **A.M.** /'eɪ'ɛm/ an abbreviation used to show that a time is in the morning, before 12:00 noon: *The meeting will begin at 8:30 a.m.* ⇨ *Compare* P.M.

amateur /'æmə,tʃʊr/ [*adjective; no comparative*] doing something because you enjoy it, not as a job; *opposite* PROFESSIONAL: *an amateur photographer* | *an amateur boxer*

amaze Ⓣ /ə'meɪz/ [*verb; amazed, amazing*] to make someone very surprised: *It amazes me that he finished so quickly.*

amazed /ə'meɪzd/ [*adjective; more amazed, most amazed*] very surprised: *I was amazed at the size of the school.* | *I was amazed how big the school was.* | *She seemed amazed that I had heard of her hometown.*

amazement /ə'meɪzmənt/ [*noun*] very great surprise: *They stared at him in amazement.*

amazing Ⓣ /ə'meɪzɪŋ/ [*adjective; more amazing, most amazing*] very surprising or impressive: *I think it's an amazing achievement.* | *It's amazing that the palace has survived so long.*

ambassador /æm'bæsədɚ/ [*noun*] an important official who represents his or her country's government in a foreign country: *He has just been appointed ambassador to France.* | *the U.S./Russian/Chinese ambassador* (=the ambassador representing the U.S./ Russia/China)

ambition /æm'bɪʃən/ [*noun*]
1 a desire to do something important, difficult, or interesting, or the thing you want to do: *It has always been her ambition to climb Mount Everest.*
2 the desire to be successful or

powerful: *His father was disappointed by his lack of ambition.*

ambitious Ⓣ /æm'bɪʃəs/ [*adjective; more ambitious, most ambitious*] wanting to be powerful or successful: *an ambitious young doctor*

ambulance /'æmbyələns/ [*noun*] a vehicle in which people who are injured or very ill are taken to a hospital

amendment /ə'mɛndmənt/ [*noun*] a change or addition to a law or agreement: *They wanted to make amendments to the contract.*

America * /ə'mɛrɪkə/ [*name*] the United States of America

SYNONYMS   America, the U.S.A., U.S., the States

The **United States of America** is the full name of the country. There are many shorter forms that can be used instead.

America is often used to mean the United States of America: *She comes from America.*

The **U.S.A.** is an abbreviation of "the United States of America": *The U.S.A. is a member of the United Nations.*

U.S. is the abbreviation for "United States": *How long have you been in the U.S.?* It is often used before a noun to talk about something that comes from the United States: *the U.S. Army* | *U.S. exports*

The **States** is a less formal way of talking about the U.S.A., and is used especially in spoken English: *Have you ever been to the States?*

American[1] * /ə'mɛrɪkən/ [*noun*] someone who comes from the United States of America

American[2] * [*adjective; no comparative*] belonging to, from, or relating to America: *the American Embassy* | *an American company*

American Indian /ə'mɛrɪkən 'ɪndiən/ [*noun*] someone from one of the groups

---

/i/ **see** /ɪ/ **big** /eɪ/ **day** /ɛ/ **get** /æ/ **hat**
/ɑ/ **father, hot** /ʌ/ **up** /ə/ **about** /ɔ/ **saw**
/oʊ/ **hope** /ʊ/ **book** /u/ **too** /aɪ/ **I** /aʊ/ **how**
/ɔɪ/ **boy** /ɝ/ **bird** /ɚ/ **teacher** /ɪr/ **ear** /ɛr/ **air**
/ɑr/ **far** /ɔr/ **more** /ʊr/ **tour** /aɪr/ **fire**
/aʊɚ/ **hour** /θ/ **nothing** /ð/ **mother** /ʃ/ **she**
/ʒ/ **measure** /tʃ/ **church** /dʒ/ **jump** /ŋ/ **long**

of people who lived in North America before Europeans arrived; *synonym* NATIVE AMERICAN
➪ Compare INDIAN¹ (definition 1).

ammunition /ˌæmyəˈnɪʃən/ [*noun*] things such as bullets that can be fired from a gun

among * /əˈmʌŋ/ [*preposition*]
1 used to show that something involves or is shared by three or more people: *The toys were shared among the children.*
➪ See the usage note at BETWEEN¹.
2 existing within the things or people in a particular group: *The disease is rare among young people.*
3 used to talk about something that is in the middle of or is surrounded by many other things: *We saw a little house among the trees.*

amount * /əˈmaʊnt/ [*noun*] how much there is of something: *She was carrying a large amount of cash.* | *Vitamins should be taken in small amounts.*

USAGE   amount, number

Use **amount** with uncountable nouns: *a large amount of work* | *an amount of money.* Use **number** with countable nouns: *a large number of people* | *a number of times.*

---

amp /æmp/ [*noun*] a measure of electrical current: *a 15-amp cord*

amphibian /æmˈfɪbiən/ [*noun*] an animal that can live both on land and in water: *Alligators, crocodiles, and frogs are all amphibians.*

ample Ⓣ /ˈæmpəl/ [*adjective; no comparative*] as much of something as you need and more: *There was ample space in the car for all our things.*
➪ See also PLENTY. ➪ Compare ENOUGH¹.

amuse * /əˈmyuz/ [*verb; amused, amusing*]
1 to make someone think something or someone is funny: *She seemed amused by the little boy.*
2 to do something to keep someone interested and stop him or her from being bored: *They played card games to amuse themselves on the trip.*

amusement * Ⓣ /əˈmyuzmənt/ [*noun*]
1 when you enjoy something or think

that it is funny: *His comments caused a lot of amusement.*
2 an activity or game you enjoy doing: *The hotel provides video games, movies, and other amusements.*

amusement park /əˈmyuzmənt ˌpɑrk/ [*noun*] a place with exciting machines to ride on and games to play where people go for entertainment

amusing * /əˈmyuzɪŋ/ [*adjective; more amusing, most amusing*] making you laugh or smile; *synonym* FUNNY: *I didn't think that joke was amusing.*

an * /ən; *when stressed* æn/ [*article*] one or any; used before words that begin with the vowel sounds of a, e, i, o, and u: *an elephant* | *The job will take about an hour.* | *Would you like an orange?*
➪ See the usage note at A.

analysis /əˈnæləsɪs/ [*noun; plural* analyses /əˈnæləˌsiz/] when you study or write about something carefully: *All seniors must do an analysis of their science experiments.*

analyze Ⓣ /ˈænəˌlaɪz/ [*verb; analyzed, analyzing*] to study something carefully so that you understand it better or know more about it: *The test results were analyzed in the lab.* | *They asked an expert to analyze the problem.*

anatomy /əˈnætəmi/ [*noun*]
1 the scientific study of the parts of humans and other living things
2 the way the parts of the body of humans and other living things are formed or work together: *the anatomy of a plant*

ancestor /ˈænsɛstər/ [*noun*] someone in your family who lived a long time before you were born: *My ancestors came from Asia.*
➪ Compare DESCENDANT.

anchor /ˈæŋkər/ [*noun*] a heavy weight that is dropped from a ship to the bottom of the water to stop the ship from moving away: *The ship raised the anchor and sailed away.*

ancient * Ⓣ /ˈeɪnʃənt/ [*adjective; more ancient, most ancient*] very old or from a very long time ago: *an ancient civilization* | *This chair looks ancient.*

and * /ænd/ [*conjunction*] used to join two words, phrases, or parts of a sentence: *Were Tim and Joe at the party?* | *He stood up and walked out of the room.* | *She's good at sports, and she's smart too.* ☛ Do not say "I don't like French and Spanish." Say **I don't like French or Spanish.**

anesthetic /ˌænəs'θɛtɪk/ [*noun*] a drug that is given to someone to stop him or her from feeling pain, especially while he or she is receiving medical treatment

angel /'eɪndʒəl/ [*noun*]
1 a spirit that is believed to live with God and protect people. In pictures, it is often shown as a human with wings
2 a kind or helpful person: *Thanks for helping out—you're an angel.*

anger * /'æŋgɚ/ [*noun*] a strong feeling of wanting to hurt or criticize someone because of something he or she has done that you do not like: *She was full of anger at the way he had treated her.*
⤷ *Compare* FURY, RAGE.

angle * /'æŋgəl/ [*noun*] the space between two lines that meet or cross each other: *an angle of 45 degrees*

angrily * /'æŋgrəli/ [*adverb*] in a way that shows anger: *He angrily tore the letter in two.*

angry * /'æŋgri/ [*adjective; **angrier, angriest**] feeling very strongly that you want to hurt or criticize someone because of something he or she has done that you do not like; *synonym* MAD: *He was **angry that** the coach would not let him play.* | *Don't tell Mom—she'll only **get angry about** it.*
⤷ *See the picture at* EMOTION.

right angle

acute angle

obtuse angle

angles

SYNONYMS angry, mad, furious, annoyed

Angry is the basic word for what you feel when something happens that you do not like: *He makes me very angry.* **Mad** is a less formal word: *You make me mad!* | *Don't get mad.*
Furious means "extremely angry": *She was furious when she realized he was lying.*
Annoyed means "a little angry": *He was annoyed at having to wait so long.*

animal * /'ænəməl/ [*noun*] a living thing that is not a person or a plant: *They keep pigs, cows, and other animals.* | *Bears are **wild animals** (=animals that do not belong to humans).*

ankle * /'æŋkəl/ [*noun*] the bottom part of your leg just above your foot which bends when you walk
⤷ *See the picture at* BODY.

anniversary /ˌænə'vɚsəri/ [*noun; plural* **anniversaries**] a day that is an exact number of years after the day when something important happened: *My parents are celebrating their 25th **wedding anniversary** on Saturday.* | *the 300th **anniversary** of Mozart's birth*
⤷ *Compare* BIRTHDAY.

announce * /ə'naʊns/ [*verb;* **announced, announcing**] to tell people something, especially something important: *The judge will announce the winners of the competition.* | *He announced that he had resigned.*

announcement * /ə'naʊnsmənt/ [*noun*] when someone gives people some important news: *I need to **make an announcement.***

announcer /ə'naʊnsɚ/ [*noun*] someone who introduces programs or gives information on television, the radio, etc.: *The announcer introduced the band.*

annoy * /ə'nɔɪ/ [*verb;* **annoys, annoyed, annoying**] to make someone feel a little angry: *Waiting annoys me.*

annoyance /ə'nɔɪəns/ [*noun*]
1 the feeling you have when you are a little angry: *He looked at his watch **in annoyance**: his son was late again.*

/i/ **see** /ɪ/ **big** /eɪ/ **day** /ɛ/ **get** /æ/ **hat** /ɑ/ **father, hot** /ʌ/ **up** /ə/ **about** /ɔ/ **saw** /oʊ/ **hope** /ʊ/ **book** /u/ **too** /aɪ/ **I** /aʊ/ **how** /ɔɪ/ **boy** /ɝ/ **bird** /ɚ/ **teacher** /ɪr/ **ear** /ɛr/ **air** /ɑr/ **far** /ɔr/ **more** /ʊr/ **tour** /aɪr/ **fire** /aʊɚ/ **hour** /θ/ **nothing** /ð/ **mother** /ʃ/ **she** /ʒ/ **measure** /tʃ/ **church** /dʒ/ **jump** /ŋ/ **long**

2 something that makes you a little angry: *That loud noise is an annoyance.*

annoyed * /ə'nɔɪd/ [*adjective;* **more annoyed, most annoyed**] a little angry: *He's still **annoyed with** me for losing his keys.* | *She was **annoyed that** she had missed the start of the movie.*
▷ *See the synonym note at* ANGRY.

annoying * Ⓣ /ə'nɔɪɪŋ/ [*adjective;* **more annoying, most annoying**] making you feel a little angry: *The way he sings all the time is really annoying.* | *It's **annoying that** I wasn't told about this.*

annual /'ænyuəl/ [*adjective; no comparative*] happening, done, or produced every year; *synonym* YEARLY: *I'm playing in the annual school concert.*
☛ Only use **annual** before a noun.

annually /'ænyuəli/ [*adverb*] every year; *synonym* YEARLY: *I visit my relatives in Mexico annually.*

anonymous /ə'nɑnəməs/ [*adjective; no comparative*] if you get an anonymous letter, telephone call, or gift, you do not know who sent it or is responsible for it: *an anonymous donation*

another[1] * /ə'nʌðɚ/ [*determiner*]
1 one more of the same kind, or several more: *Can I have another cookie?* | *We waited another ten minutes, then left.*
2 a different one: *His parents were in another part of the store.* | *That spoon was dirty so I got **another one**.*

USAGE Using "another" with singular and plural nouns

Use **another** before a singular noun: *We had another day of rain.*

Do not use "another" directly before a plural noun. Instead, use "few" or a number before a plural noun: *another few days* | *another five days*

---

another[2] * [*pronoun*]
1 one more of the same kind: *No, you can't have another.* | *She heard one bell ring, and then another.*
2 a different one: *I took the dress back and exchanged it for another.*
▷ *See also* **one another** *at* ONE[2].

answer[1] * /'ænsɚ/ [*verb;* **answered, answering**]
1 to say or write something back to

someone who has spoken or written to you: *I couldn't answer any of her questions.* | *I asked her if she was all right, but she didn't answer.*
2 to speak into a telephone when it rings: *No one's answering.* | *Her dad answered the phone.*
— PHRASE —
3 answer the door to open the door when someone knocks or rings the bell: *Please answer the door.*

answer[2] * [*noun*]
1 what you say or write after someone asks you a question or writes to you: *His answer was "No."*
2 information that you are asked for in a test or competition: *What's the **answer to** question 4?*
3 something that will stop a problem; *synonym* SOLUTION: *This could be the **answer to** our worries.*

answering machine /'ænsərɪŋ mə,ʃin/ [*noun*] a machine that records telephone messages, for example when you are not there: *When I got back, there were over twenty messages on my answering machine.*

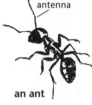
antenna

ant /ænt/ [*noun*] a small red or black insect that lives in large groups in the ground

an ant

Antarctic /ænt'ɑrktɪk/ [*name*]
the Antarctic the area around the South Pole: *Penguins live in the Antarctic.*
▷ *Compare* ARCTIC.

antarctic /ænt'ɑrktɪk/ [*adjective, no comparative*] from or relating to the South Pole: *an antarctic research project*

Antarctica * /ænt'ɑrktɪkə/ [*name*] the large area of land around the South Pole

antelope /'æntə,loʊp/ [*noun; plural* **antelopes** or **antelope**] a large animal like a deer that can run very fast

antenna /æn'tɛnə/ [*noun*]
1 [*plural* **antennas**] a wire or object that receives or sends out radio waves: *a radio antenna* | *a car antenna*

⋄ See the pictures at CELLULAR PHONE and HOUSE.

2 [plural **antennae** /æn'tɛni/] one of the long thin parts on the head of an insect or sea creature, which it uses to feel things: a lobster's antennae

⋄ See the pictures at ANT and LOBSTER.

anthill /'ænt‚hɪl/ [noun] a place in or on the ground where ants live

antibiotic /‚æntɪbaɪ'atɪk/ [noun] a medicine that can cure infections: The doctor **put her on antibiotics** (=gave her this medicine to take).

anticipate ⊤ /æn'tɪsə‚peɪt/ [verb; anticipated, anticipating] FORMAL to expect something: We **are anticipating** that 5,000 people will attend the event.

anticipation /æn‚tɪsə'peɪʃən/ [noun] a feeling of excitement as you wait for something to happen or arrive: We waited **with great anticipation** for the game to begin.

antique¹ /æn'tik/ [noun] a valuable old object or piece of furniture: a room full of beautiful antiques

antique² [adjective; no comparative] an antique object is old and valuable: She collects antique furniture.

☞ Only use **antique** before a noun.

antiseptic /‚æntə'sɛptɪk/ [noun] a substance that makes skin or objects clean so that they do not cause infection: He put some antiseptic on the cut. | a powerful antiseptic

anxiety ✶ /æŋ'zaɪti/ [noun; plural anxieties] a worried feeling, especially about the future: Her **anxiety about** the science test increased. | His anxieties kept him awake at night.

anxious ✶ /'æŋkʃəs/ [adjective; **more anxious, most anxious**]

1 worried about something that might happen: He was **anxious about** his friends because they were late.

⋄ See the usage note at NERVOUS.

2 wanting to do or have something, and a little worried about it: They were **anxious to** hear our news.

☞ Do not use **anxious** before a noun in this meaning.

USAGE   anxious, eager

Both **anxious** and **eager** are used to talk about wanting to do or have something. Use **anxious** when someone is a little worried: He is anxious to please his boss. Use **eager** when someone is a little excited: He is eager to please his girlfriend.

---

anxiously ✶ /'æŋkʃəsli/ [adverb] in a worried or nervous way: She waited anxiously for her son to arrive.

any¹ ✶ /'ɛni/ [determiner, pronoun]

1 used in questions and negative sentences to mean "one," "none," or "some": I don't have any money with me. | Are there any questions? | Do **any** of you want to come for a walk? | "Have some dessert." "No thanks, I don't want any." | He has **hardly any** hair (=very little hair).

2 all, every, or every kind of: Any citizen can become governor. | You can call me at any time. | Look through these books and choose any you want.

any² ✶ [adverb] used with comparatives to make a question or negative stronger: The tree hasn't grown any bigger since it was planted. | Can't you walk any faster?

anybody /'ɛni‚badi/ [pronoun]

1 used in questions and negative sentences to mean "a person"; synonym ANYONE: I didn't see anybody else there.

2 every person, it does not matter which; synonym ANYONE: Anybody can make a mistake.

anyhow /'ɛni‚haʊ/ [adverb] INFORMAL in spite of something; synonym ANYWAY: It was the wrong color but I bought it anyhow.

anymore /‚ɛni'mɔr/ [adverb] if something does not happen anymore, it used to happen but does not happen now: He doesn't love me anymore. | She doesn't play tennis anymore.

☞ Only use **anymore** in negative sentences.

/i/ **see**	/ɪ/ **big**	/eɪ/ **day**	/ɛ/ **get**	/æ/ **hat**
/ɑ/ **father**, **hot**	/ʌ/ **up**	/ə/ **about**	/ɔ/ **saw**	
/oʊ/ **hope**	/ʊ/ **book**	/u/ **too**	/aɪ/ **I**	/aʊ/ **how**
/ɔɪ/ **boy**	/ɚ/ **bird**	/ɚ/ **teacher**	/ɪr/ **ear**	/ɛr/ **air**
/ɑr/ **far**	/ɔr/ **more**	/ʊr/ **tour**	/aɪr/ **fire**	
/aʊɚ/ **hour**	/θ/ **nothing**	/ð/ **mother**	/ʃ/ **she**	
/ʒ/ **measure**	/tʃ/ **church**	/dʒ/ **jump**	/ŋ/ **long**	

anyone * /'ɛni‚wʌn/ [*pronoun*]
  1 used in questions and negative sentences to mean "a person"; <u>synonym</u> ANYBODY: *There wasn't anyone in the building.* | *Has anyone seen my wallet?*
  2 every person, it does not matter which; <u>synonym</u> ANYBODY: *Anyone can enter the competition.*

anyplace¹ /'ɛni‚pleɪs/ [*adverb*] INFORMAL
in or to any place; <u>synonym</u> ANYWHERE: *He could be anyplace.*

anyplace² [*pronoun*] any place; <u>synonym</u> ANYWHERE: *I can't think of anyplace I want to go.*

anything * /'ɛni‚θɪŋ/ [*pronoun*]
  1 used in questions and negative sentences to mean "something": *She didn't say anything.* | *Was there anything interesting in the mail?*
  2 every thing, it does not matter which: *You can do anything you like.*

anyway /'ɛni‚weɪ/ [*adverb*]
  1 in spite of something: *It was raining, but they went out anyway.*
  2 used to add something which makes what has just been said not important: *I don't really want to go to her party, and anyway I haven't been invited.*
  3 used to change the subject you are talking about: *We had a good time. Anyway, how was your weekend?*

anywhere * /'ɛni‚wɛr/ [*adverb, pronoun*]
any place, or in or to any place: *I couldn't find my pen anywhere.* | *Are you going anywhere this weekend?* | *We can't find anywhere else to stay.*
  ⭗ *Compare* SOMEWHERE.

apart * /ə'pɑrt/ [*adverb*]
  1 into pieces or parts: *He took the fan apart to clean it.* | *The explosion blew the building apart.*
  2 not next to someone or something else: *Our houses are only a few streets apart.* | *The boy was standing **apart** from the others.*
  ━━ PHRASE ━━
  3 **apart from** used to say that someone or something is not included in what you say; <u>synonym</u> EXCEPT: *Everyone apart from Mom had left.*

apartment * /ə'pɑrtmənt/ [*noun*] a room or set of rooms where someone lives, which is part of a larger building: *I'm looking for an apartment to rent that is not too expensive.*

ape /eɪp/ [*noun*] an animal like a large monkey, with no tail

chimpanzee

apes

orangutan

gorilla

apiece /ə'pis/ [*adverb*] each: *I gave the children two cookies apiece.*

apologize /ə'pɑlə‚dʒaɪz/ [*verb*; **apologized, apologizing**] to tell someone you are sorry for doing something: *He **apologized for** being late.*

I *She apologized to the teacher.* I *If I was rude, I apologize.*

USAGE Ways of apologizing

You can say that you are sorry for doing something wrong in different ways.

Excuse me is the most informal. If you do something that is not very serious, such as walking into someone by accident or walking in front of people in a theater to get to your seat, say **Excuse me**. You can also say **Pardon me** if the situation is more formal.

I'm sorry is used when something you do by accident causes a bigger problem, such as hurting someone when you walk into him or her, or phoning someone at a bad time. There are several ways to use **I'm sorry**: *I'm sorry that I said that.* I *I'm sorry for what I said.* I *I'm sorry for saying* that. I *I'm very sorry.*

☞ Only use "I'm sorry to" when you are actually doing the thing you are apologizing for I *I'm sorry to call so late, but this is important.*

Apologize is the verb that means "to say you are sorry." You can also use **I apologize** instead of **I'm sorry**, but not in as many ways, and it is more formal: *I apologize for what I said.* I *I apologize for saying* that.

---

apology /ə'pɑlədʒi/ [*noun; plural* **apologies**] when you tell someone you are sorry for doing something: *I want an apology from the company.* I *I think I owe you an apology* (=should tell you that I am sorry). I *She sent him a letter of apology.*

apostrophe /ə'pɑstrəfi/ [*noun*] a mark used in writing. It looks like this: '
⇨ *See* Punctuation *in the Smart Study section.*

apparatus /ˌæpə'rætəs/ [*noun*] equipment or tools used for doing something: *a piece of scientific apparatus in a laboratory*

apparent T /ə'pærənt/ [*adjective;* **more apparent, most apparent**] if a quality or situation is apparent, it is clear: *It soon became apparent that he knew nothing about soccer.*
☞ Do not use **apparent** before a noun.

apparently T /ə'pærəntli/ [*adverb*] used to say that you think something is true, but you are not sure: *Apparently, he asked her to dance and she said no.*

appeal¹ T /ə'pil/ [*verb;* **appealed, appealing**]
1 to ask someone for something in a strong or emotional way: **appeal to someone for something** ▸ *He appealed to his neighbors for help.*
2 to seem nice or attractive to someone: *This movie will probably appeal to young people.*

appeal² T [*noun*] a strong or emotional request: *The mayor made an appeal for calm.*

appear * /ə'pɪr/ [*verb;* **appeared, appearing**]
1 to arrive or move into a position where you can be seen: *He didn't appear until the party was nearly over.* I *A figure appeared at the window.*
2 [*linking*] to seem to be true, or seem to have a particular quality: *It appears that the fire was an accident.* I *She appeared to be calm.*

appearance * /ə'pɪrəns/ [*noun*]
1 the way someone or something looks: *How can I improve my appearance?*
2 when someone or something arrives: *A famous movie star is expected to make an appearance at the event.*

appetite /'æpɪˌtaɪt/ [*noun*] the feeling that you want to eat: *I've lost my appetite* (=I don't feel hungry anymore). I *She has a healthy appetite* (=likes to eat a lot).

applaud /ə'plɔd/ [*verb;* **applauded, applauding**] to hit your hands together many times, to show that you enjoyed something or that you approve of something: *Everyone stood up and applauded.* I *We applauded his speech.*
⇨ *Compare* CLAP.

/i/ **see**	/ɪ/ **big**	/eɪ/ **day**	/ɛ/ **get**	/æ/ **hat**	
/ɑ/ **father, hot**	/ʌ/ **up**	/ə/ **about**	/ɔ/ **saw**		
/oʊ/ **hope**	/ʊ/ **book**	/u/ **too**	/aɪ/ **I**	/aʊ/ **how**	
/ɔɪ/ **boy**	/ɝ/ **bird**	/ɚ/ **teacher**	/ɪr/ **ear**	/ɛr/ **air**	
/ɑr/ **far**	/ɔr/ **more**	/ʊr/ **tour**	/aɪr/ **fire**		
/aʊə/ **hour**	/θ/ **nothing**	/ð/ **mother**	/ʃ/ **she**		
/ʒ/ **measure**	/tʃ/ **church**	/dʒ/ **jump**	/ŋ/ **long**		

applause /ə'plɔz/ [*noun*] when people hit their hands together many times, to show that they enjoyed watching or listening to something: *They gave him **a round of applause**.*

apple * /'æpəl/ [*noun*] a round, hard, sweet FRUIT that is white inside, has green, red, or yellow skin, and grows on trees

appliance /ə'plaɪəns/ [*noun*] a tool or machine that you use in the home to do cooking or cleaning: *The store sells vacuum cleaners and other **household appliances**.*

applicant /'æplɪkənt/ [*noun*] someone who has written to ask for a job, for permission to study at a school, etc.: *We interviewed five **applicants for** the job.*

application Ⓣ /ˌæplɪ'keɪʃən/ [*noun*] a letter or form in which you ask for a job, to study at a school, etc.: *I forgot to sign the **application form**.*

apply Ⓣ /ə'plaɪ/ [*verb;* **applies, applied, applying**]
1 to write asking for a job, to study at a school, etc.: *I **applied for** a job as a salesman.* | *She is intending to **apply to** college next year.*
  ☛ Do not say that someone "applied a job" or "applied a school." Say that he or she **applied for a job** or **applied to a school**.
2 to be suitable or right in a particular situation or for a particular person: *In this case, the rule does not **apply**.* | *My remarks don't **apply to** you.*
3 FORMAL to put a substance on a surface: *She applied her makeup carefully.*
  ⇨ *See also* **put on** *at* PUT (definition 8).

appoint /ə'pɔɪnt/ [*verb;* **appointed, appointing**] to choose someone for a particular job or position: **appoint someone as something** ▸ *They decided to appoint her as principal.* | **appoint**

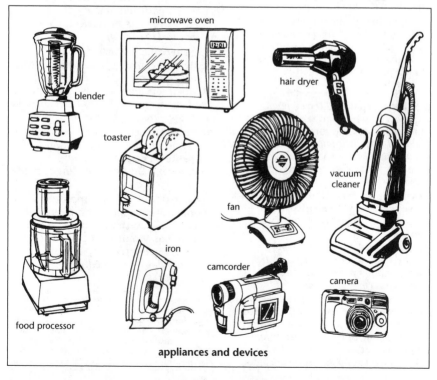

microwave oven

blender

toaster

hair dryer

fan

iron

camcorder

camera

vacuum cleaner

food processor

appliances and devices

someone something ▸ *He was recently appointed ambassador to Italy.*

appointment /ə'pɔɪntmənt/ [*noun*]
1 an arrangement to see someone or do something at a particular time: *I have an appointment at 11.*
2 when someone is chosen to have a particular job or position: *The appointment of such a young man as chairman was surprising.*

appreciate /ə'priʃi,eɪt/ [*verb*; appreciated, appreciating]
1 to be grateful for something: *I'd appreciate your help with these math problems.* | **appreciate someone's doing something** ▸ *I really appreciate your helping me.* | **appreciate that** ▸ *I appreciate that you cleaned your room.*
2 to like something and realize that it is good or important: *I like cooking for people who appreciate good food.*
3 to realize something: *I don't think you appreciate the danger you're in.*

appreciation /ə,priʃi'eɪʃən/ [*noun*] the feeling of being grateful for something: *I'd like to show my appreciation by buying you dinner.*

approach /ə'proʊtʃ/ [*verb*; approaches, approached, approaching]
1 to get nearer: *Winter is approaching.* | *As we approached the house, a dog started barking.*
☛ Do not say "approach to a place." Say **approach a place.**
2 to deal with something in a particular way: *I wasn't sure how to approach the problem.*

appropriate * ⊺ /ə'proʊpriɪt/ [*adjective*; more appropriate, most appropriate] right or suitable for a particular situation or person; *opposite* INAPPROPRIATE: *Would a camera be an appropriate present for a ten-year-old?*

approval * /ə'pruvəl/ [*noun*] when you think that something is good or right; *opposite* DISAPPROVAL: *Does my idea have your approval?*

approve * ⊺ /ə'pruv/ [*verb*; approved, approving] to think that something is good or right; *opposite* DISAPPROVE: *I don't approve of smoking.* | *I'd love to go skating with you if my parents approve.*

approximate /ə'praksəmɪt/ [*adjective*; no comparative*] an approximate number is not exact, but is close to the exact one: *I can only give you an approximate figure.*

approximately ⊺ /ə'praksəmɪtli/ [*adverb*] used to show that a number or amount is not exact, but is close to the exact one; *synonyms* AROUND, ABOUT: *The flight will take approximately four hours.* | *There were approximately ten thousand people there.*

Apr. the written abbreviation of APRIL

apricot /'æprɪ,kat/ [*noun*] a small, pale orange FRUIT with one large seed and skin that feels like short fur

April * /'eɪprəl/ [*noun*] the fourth month of the year: *The meeting is on April 11th.* | *I will be on vacation in April.*
⇨ See the usage note at MONTH.

apron /'eɪprən/ [*noun*] a piece of clothing worn to keep your clothes clean, especially when you are cooking

aptitude /'æptɪ,tud/ [*noun*] a natural ability to do something: *She has an aptitude for playing the violin.*

an apron

aquarium /ə'kwɛriəm/ [*noun*] a large container in which live fish are kept, or a building where sea creatures are shown to the public

Arab[1] /'ærəb/ [*noun*] someone who comes from a country where Arabic is spoken, or whose family originally came from such a country

Arab[2] [*adjective*; no comparative] belonging to or relating to Arabs: *This custom exists all over the Arab world.*

Arabic[1] /'ærəbɪk/ [*noun*] a language spoken in some countries in the Middle East and North Africa

/i/ **see**	/ɪ/ **big**	/eɪ/ **day**	/ɛ/ **get**	/æ/ **hat**
/ɑ/ **father, hot**	/ʌ/ **up**	/ə/ **about**	/ɔ/ **saw**	
/oʊ/ **hope**	/ʊ/ **book**	/u/ **too**	/aɪ/ **I**	/aʊ/ **how**
/ɔɪ/ **boy**	/ɝ/ **bird**	/ɚ/ **teacher**	/ɪr/ **ear**	/ɛr/ **air**
/ɑr/ **far**	/ɔr/ **more**	/ʊr/ **tour**	/aɪr/ **fire**	
/aʊɚ/ **hour**	/θ/ **nothing**	/ð/ **mother**	/ʃ/ **she**	
/ʒ/ **measure**	/tʃ/ **church**	/dʒ/ **jump**	/ŋ/ **long**	

Arabic² [adjective; no comparative] relating to the language, art, history, etc., of the Arabs: Arabic art

arch /artʃ/ [noun; plural **arches**] a curved structure or shape

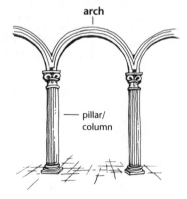

arch

pillar/ column

archaeologist /ˌɑrki'ɑlədʒɪst/ [noun] someone who studies the buildings and objects left by people who lived a long time ago

archaeology /ˌɑrki'ɑlədʒi/ [noun] the study of buildings and objects left by people who lived a long time ago

architect /'ɑrkɪˌtɛkt/ [noun] someone whose job is to design buildings

architecture /'ɑrkɪˌtɛktʃɚ/ [noun] the style and structure of buildings: The city is known for its magnificent architecture.

architectural /ˌɑrkɪ'tɛktʃərəl/ [adjective; no comparative] relating to the style and structure of buildings: an interesting architectural feature

Arctic /'ɑrktɪk/ [name]
the Arctic the area around the North Pole: Polar bears live in the Arctic.
⇨ Compare **ANTARCTIC**.

arctic /'ɑrktɪk/ [adjective; no comparative] from or relating to the North Pole: freezing arctic winds

Arctic Ocean /ˌɑrktɪk 'oʊʃən/ [name]
the Arctic Ocean the ocean near the North Pole

are * /ɑr/ [verb] the present form of BE that is used with "you," "we," and "they": They are sisters. | "Are you ready?" "Yes, we are."

PRONUNCIATION   are
   When **are** is the first or last word in a sentence, pronounce it as /ɑr/: Are you ready? | I'm taller than you are. When **are** is in the middle of a sentence, pronounce it as /ɚ/: When are you leaving?

area * /'ɛriə/ [noun; plural **areas**]
   1 a part of a place or surface: What area of town do you live in? | There is a worn area on the carpet.
   2 the amount of space that something covers: The forest covers **an area of** 60 square miles. | The offices are up to 1,200 square meters **in area**.

arena /ə'rinə/ [noun; plural **arenas**] a large round structure with seats around a central space, where sports games and other public events take place: There were cheers as the athletes entered the arena.

aren't * /'ɑrənt/
   1 the short form of "are not": Your shoes aren't very clean. | Aren't you ready yet?
   2 the short form of "am not," used in questions: Aren't I smart?
   ☛ Do not say "Am not I lucky?" Say **Aren't I lucky?**

argue * /'ɑrgyu/ [verb; **argues, argued, arguing**]
   1 to discuss something that you do not agree about, in a slightly angry way: My parents sometimes **argue about** money. | I **was arguing with** her over which band is best.
   ☛ Do not say that two people "argue each other." Say that they **argue with each other.**
   2 to give your opinion and the reasons for it in order to persuade other people that you are right: He **argued against** buying a car. | I **argued that** it would be unfair to punish the entire class.

SYNONYMS   argue, disagree, fight
   If you **argue** with someone, you disagree in a slightly angry way: They were arguing about the restaurant check. If you **disagree** with someone, it does not mean that you are angry or annoyed with him or her; you just have a different opinion: We disagreed about the quickest way to get there.

Fight is a less formal word that can mean the same as **argue**. However, **fight** is used more often about people who know each other well and who are very angry and loud: *My brothers are always fighting.*

---

argument * /'ɑrgyəmənt/ [*noun*]
1 when people discuss something they do not agree about, in an angry way: *He had an argument with his sister.*
2 the reason someone gives for his or her opinion: *Her argument was that it would be cheaper to buy a new radio than to get the old one repaired.*

arid Ⓣ /'ærɪd/ [*adjective; more arid, most arid*] very dry and without much rain: *Arizona has an arid climate.*

arise /ə'raɪz/ [*verb; arose, arisen* /ə'rɪzən/, **arising**] to happen, or to be mentioned: *If any more problems arise, please let us know.*

arithmetic /ə'rɪθmətɪk/ [*noun*] when you calculate numbers by adding, multiplying, etc.: *You'd better check my arithmetic.*

arm * /ɑrm/ [*noun*]
1 one of the two long parts of your BODY that are attached to your shoulders and end with your hands
2 one of the two parts at the sides of a chair on which you can rest your arms
3 **arms** [*plural*] guns, bombs, and other weapons: *They smuggled arms into the country.*

armband /'ɑrm,bænd/ [*noun*] a piece of cloth that you wear around your arm: *The officials in charge of the event wore special armbands.*

armchair /'ɑrm,tʃɛr/ [*noun*] a large comfortable CHAIR with arms

armed /ɑrmd/ [*adjective; no comparative*] having a gun or other weapon; opposite UNARMED: *The robbers were armed with shotguns.*

armed forces /ɑrmd 'fɔrsɪz/ [*plural noun*] a country's military groups, such as an army, navy, or air force

armful /'ɑrmfʊl/ [*noun; plural armfuls*] as much of something as you can hold in your arms: *several armfuls of dirty laundry* | *an armful of roses*

armor /'ɑrmɚ/ [*noun*] metal clothes worn by soldiers a long time ago to protect their bodies: *a suit of armor*

armored /'ɑrmɚd/ [*adjective; no comparative*] an armored vehicle is made from or covered with a special strong metal to protect it from bullets, bombs, etc.: *an armored car*

armpit /'ɑrm,pɪt/ [*noun*] the part of your BODY underneath where your arm joins your shoulder

army * or **Army** /'ɑrmi/ [*noun; plural armies*] the part of a country's military that fights mainly on land: *Dad is a colonel in the Army.*

aroma /ə'roumə/ [*noun; plural aromas*] a pleasant smell, especially of food or drink: *The aroma of fresh bread came from the kitchen.*
  ⇨ See the synonym note at SMELL[1].

arose /ə'rouz/ [*verb*] the past tense of ARISE

around[1] * /ə'raʊnd/ [*preposition*]
1 to many parts of a place: *The kids were running around the yard.*
2 on all sides of or surrounding something: *She had a gold chain around her neck.* | *a fence around the house*
  ☛ Do not say "around of the house." Say **around the house**.
3 to the other side of something curved, round, or with a corner: *The car had come around the corner too fast and skidded off the road.*

around[2] * [*adverb*]
1 in many directions or to many places: *I spent all day rushing around.*
2 on all sides of something: *There were trees all around.* | *The children gathered around to see what she had brought.*
3 in the opposite direction, and perhaps back again: *She turned around and drove back home.* | *Turn around so I can see how you look.*

/i/ see	/ɪ/ big	/eɪ/ day	/ɛ/ get	/æ/ hat
/ɑ/ father, hot	/ʌ/ up	/ə/ about	/ɔ/ saw	
/ou/ hope	/ʊ/ book	/u/ too	/aɪ/ I	/aʊ/ how
/ɔɪ/ boy	/ɚ/ bird	/ɚ/ teacher	/ɪr/ ear	/ɛr/ air
/ɑr/ far	/ɔr/ more	/ʊr/ tour	/aɪr/ fire	
/aʊɚ/ hour	/θ/ nothing	/ð/ mother	/ʃ/ she	
/ʒ/ measure	/tʃ/ church	/dʒ/ jump	/ŋ/ long	

4 somewhere near: *"Where's Dad?"* *"He's around somewhere."*

5 used to show that a number or amount is not exact; *synonyms* ABOUT, APPROXIMATELY: *It costs around $200.*

arrange * T /ə'reɪndʒ/ [*verb;* **arranged, arranging**]

1 to make plans for something to happen; *synonym* ORGANIZE: *We had arranged a trip to the beach.* I **arrange to do something** ▸ *I arranged to meet her after school.* I **arrange for someone to do something** ▸ *Mom arranged for me to have tennis lessons.* ☛ Do not say "arranged doing something. For example, do not say "I arranged meeting her." Say I **arranged to meet her.**

2 to put things next to each other so that they are neat or look nice: *He arranged the chairs in a line.*

arrangement * T /ə'reɪndʒmənt/ [*noun*]

1 a plan for something to happen: *I'll make arrangements for the food to be delivered.*

2 a group of things put next to each other so that they are neat or look nice: *a flower arrangement*

arrest[1] T /ə'rɛst/ [*verb;* **arrested, arresting**] if the police arrest someone who they think is guilty of a crime, they officially and legally take him or her away to answer questions: **be arrested (for something)** ▸ *He's been arrested for robbery.*

arrest[2] [*noun*]

1 when the police seize someone who they think is guilty of a crime: *The police made an arrest.*

━━━ PHRASE ━━━

2 under arrest if someone is under arrest, he or she is being kept and questioned by the police because they think he or she is guilty of a crime: *The police placed him under arrest.*

arrival * T /ə'raɪvəl/ [*noun*] when someone or something comes to a place; *opposite* DEPARTURE: *She gave them her arrival time.*

arrive * /ə'raɪv/ [*verb;* **arrived, arriving**] to come to a place that you have been traveling toward; *opposite* DEPART: *I should arrive at about 2:30.* I *When does the train arrive?* I *We arrived at the airport in plenty of time.* ☛ Do not say "We arrived the airport." Say We **arrived at the airport.**

arrogant /'ærəgənt/ [*adjective;* **more arrogant, most arrogant**] someone who is arrogant thinks he or she is better than other people and behaves in a rude and proud way; *opposite* MODEST: *He's unpopular because he's so arrogant.*

arrow /'ærou/ [*noun*]

1 a stick with a metal point that is shot from a BOW

2 a sign that points to something, shaped like a V on its side: *We went in the direction indicated by the arrow.*

arson /'arsən/ [*noun*] the crime of burning property: *The police suspect the fire was the result of arson.*

art * /art/ [*noun*]

1 the activity or skill of painting or drawing pictures: *She's great at art— look at this picture.*

2 paintings and other beautiful objects that people have made or designed: *I really like 19th-century French art.* I *We visited the local art gallery.*

3 arts [*plural*] subjects such as literature, languages, and history, rather than science subjects: *I'm more interested in the arts than the sciences.* I *The School of Performing Arts*

artery /'artəri/ [*noun; plural* **arteries**] a tube in your body through which blood flows from the heart to other parts of the body ▷ *Compare* VEIN.

arthritis /ar'θraɪtɪs/ [*noun*] a disease in which your joints are stiff and painful

artichoke /'artɪtʃouk/ [*noun*] a VEGETABLE with many flat hard leaves that grow tightly together, which is eaten cooked

article * /'artɪkəl/ [*noun*]

1 a piece of writing in a newspaper or magazine: *There's an interesting article on education in today's newspaper.* I *a magazine article*

2 GRAMMAR the word "a" or "an" (the indefinite article) or the word "the"

(the definite article): *You have used the wrong article before the noun.*

3 FORMAL an object that is a member of a group of things: *There were **articles of clothing** (=clothes) scattered on the floor.*

artificial * /ˌɑrtəˈfɪʃəl/ [*adjective; no comparative*] made by people rather than being natural; *synonym* MAN-MADE: *artificial coloring | artificial flowers*

artillery /ɑrˈtɪləri/ [*noun*] large guns used by an army

artist * /ˈɑrtɪst/ [*noun*] someone who makes beautiful or interesting things, such as paintings: *That sculpture was done by a local artist.*

artistic /ɑrˈtɪstɪk/ [*adjective;* **more artistic, most artistic**]
1 good at making beautiful or interesting things: *He is very artistic, and decorated his room himself.*
2 relating to art: *I want to improve my artistic skills.*

as¹ * /æz/ [*conjunction*]
1 used to say that one thing happens at the same time as another: *As I worked, I grew more and more tired. | He called as I was finishing my dinner.*
2 used to say that something is done or happens in a particular way, or in the same way as something else: *Do exactly as I say. | As I said earlier, this can cause problems.*
3 used to describe something, such as someone's feelings or an event: *The award came as a surprise to her* (=she did not expect it).
4 used to give the reason for something; *synonym* BECAUSE: *I don't know if my letter has arrived, as I haven't received a reply yet.*

━━ PHRASES ━━
5 **as well (as)** in addition to something or someone: *They have a dog and two cats as well. | She was wearing a coat as well as a sweater.*
⇨ *See the usage note at* ALSO.
6 **as if** or **as though** used to say how someone or something appears or seems: *She looked as if she would faint. | I feel as though I've known him forever.*

as² * [*adverb*] used to compare one thing with another: *The rock was as big as a house. | I came as soon as I could. | There's not as much time as I thought. | This one's twice as expensive.*

as³ * [*preposition*] used to say what someone or something does, for example as a job: *He works as a sales assistant right now. | The parachute acts as a brake. | You'd be great as a teacher.*

ASAP or **a.s.a.p.** /ˈeɪˌsæp; ˈeɪˌɛsˌeɪˈpi/ an abbreviation of "as soon as possible": *I need that report ASAP.*

ascend /əˈsɛnd/ [*verb;* **ascended, ascending**] to go up; *opposite* DESCEND: *Birds use the wind to help them ascend.*

ash * /æʃ/ [*noun; plural* **ashes**] small gray pieces that are left when something has burned: *There was cigarette ash on his jacket. | The letter had been **burned to ashes** (=completely burned).*

ashamed * /əˈʃeɪmd/ [*adjective;* **more ashamed, most ashamed**] feeling bad and sorry about something bad or wrong you have done: *He was **ashamed of** what he had done. | **ashamed to do something** ▸ She was ashamed to admit that she had cheated. | **ashamed of doing something** ▸ Aren't you ashamed of hurting the dog?*
⇨ *See also* SHAME. ⇨ *Compare* GUILTY, EMBARRASSED.

ashore /əˈʃɔr/ [*adverb*] on or onto land, from the sea: *They jumped out of the boat and waded ashore.*

ashtray /ˈæʃˌtreɪ/ [*noun; plural* **ashtrays**] a small bowl to put cigarette ashes in

Asia * /ˈeɪʒə/ [*name*]
1 the large area of land between Europe and the Pacific Ocean, north of the Indian Ocean
2 the area of the world that includes the continent of Asia, Japan,

/i/ **see**	/ɪ/ **big**	/eɪ/ **day**	/ɛ/ **get**	/æ/ **hat**
/ɑ/ **father, hot**	/ʌ/ **up**	/ə/ **about**	/ɔ/ **saw**
/oʊ/ **hope**	/ʊ/ **book**	/u/ **too**	/aɪ/ **I**	/aʊ/ **how**
/ɔɪ/ **boy**	/ɝ/ **bird**	/ɚ/ **teacher**	/ɪr/ **ear**	/ɛr/ **air**
/ɑr/ **far**	/ɔr/ **more**	/ʊr/ **tour**	/aɪr/ **fire**
/aʊɚ/ **hour**	/θ/ **nothing**	/ð/ **mother**	/ʃ/ **she**
/ʒ/ **measure**	/tʃ/ **church**	/dʒ/ **jump**	/ŋ/ **long**

Indonesia, and Malaysia: *We sell many books to Asia.*

Asian[1] * /'eɪʒən/ [*noun*] someone who comes from Asia

Asian[2] * [*adjective; no comparative*] belonging to, from, or relating to Asia: *I'm interested in Asian cultures.*

Asian American /'eɪʒən ə'mɛrɪkən/ [*noun*] an American whose family originally came from Asia

Asian-American [*adjective; no comparative*] relating to Americans whose families originally came from Asia: *an Asian-American arts festival*

aside /ə'saɪd/ [*adverb*] to one side: *A man rushed past, **pushing** her **aside**. | He **took** her **aside** (=talked to her away from other people) and asked her what was wrong. | They **had put** some money **aside** (=saved it) for a new car.*

ask * /æsk/ [*verb;* asked, asking]
1 to say something to get information from someone: *You **ask** too many questions. | ask when/what/how/ etc.* ► *Ask when the next train leaves. |* **ask someone something** ► *She asked me the way to the zoo. |* **ask someone about something** ► *He never asked me about my vacation.*
2 to say that you want someone to give you something: *He **asked for** a glass of water. |* **ask someone for something** ► *She asked her mother for $20.*
☞ Do not say "She asked some money." Say **She asked for some money.**
3 to say that you want someone to do something or come somewhere: **ask someone to do something** ► *The teacher asked me to open the window. |* **ask someone to something** ► *Have you asked her to your party?*
☞ Do not say "ask someone doing something." For example, do not say "I asked him helping me." Say **I asked him to help me.**

asleep * /ə'slip/ [*adjective; no comparative*]
1 if someone is asleep, he or she is sleeping; <u>opposite</u> AWAKE: *He got into bed and was soon **fast asleep** (=very deeply asleep).*

☞ Do not use **asleep** before a noun.
⇨ *Compare* SLEEPY.
— PHRASE —
2 fall asleep to start sleeping: *She finally **fell asleep** at around midnight.*
⇨ *Compare* **wake up** *at* WAKE.

asparagus /ə'spærəgəs/ [*noun*] a VEGETABLE with long, pale green stems

aspect ⊤ /'æspɛkt/ [*noun*] one part of a situation: *There are several aspects to consider.*

aspirin /'æspərɪn/ [*noun; plural* **aspirins** or **aspirin**] a drug you take when you feel pain or have a fever: *I **took** a couple of aspirins.*

assassin /ə'sæsɪn/ [*noun*] someone who kills someone important or powerful, especially a politician

assassinate /ə'sæsə,neɪt/ [*verb;* assassinated, assassinating] to kill someone important or powerful: *He planned to assassinate the governor.*

assault[1] /ə'sɔlt/ [*verb;* assaulted, assaulting] to attack someone: *He said the owner of the store had assaulted him.*

assault[2] [*noun*] when one person attacks another: *a vicious assault*

assemble /ə'sɛmbəl/ [*verb;* assembled, assembling]
1 to gather together in a group or at a place: *We were told to assemble in front of the school.*
⇨ *See the synonym note at* MEET[1].
2 to fit together the parts of something: *He bought the parts separately and assembled his own computer.*

assembly /ə'sɛmbli/ [*noun; plural* **assemblies**]
1 when a group of people gather for a special reason: *We have school assemblies on Fridays.*
2 also **Assembly;** a group of elected government officials: *the state assembly*

assertive /ə'sɝtɪv/ [*adjective;* **more assertive, most assertive**] confident about saying what you really think or want: *Try to be more assertive.*

asset /'æsɛt/ [*noun*]
1 something or someone that is useful:

Your skill at languages is a great asset. I
He is an asset to the school.
2 something that is owned such as
property, part of a company, etc.: *The
company may have to sell some of its
assets to pay its debts.*
☛ This meaning is usually used in the
plural.

assign /əˈsaɪn/ [*verb; assigned,
assigning*]
1 to choose someone to do a job: *I was
assigned to collect tickets at the door.*
2 to give someone a piece of work to
do: *Our teachers assign too much
homework.*

assignment /əˈsaɪnmənt/ [*noun*] a
piece of work that you have been given
to do, especially as part of a course of
study: *I finished my history assignment
last night.*

assist Ⓣ /əˈsɪst/ [*verb; assisted, assisting*]
FORMAL to help someone: *Can I assist in
any way?* I **assist someone with
something** ▸ *Our staff will assist you with
anything you need.*

assistance Ⓣ /əˈsɪstəns/ [*noun*] FORMAL
help with something: *Call if you need
any assistance.* I *Can I **be of assistance?***
(=can I help you)

assistant¹ /əˈsɪstənt/ [*noun*] someone
whose job is to help someone: *He left
most of the work to his assistant.* I *She is a
sales assistant in a hardware store* (=she
serves customers).

assistant² [*adjective; no comparative*]
═ PHRASE ═
**assistant manager/director/
editor/etc.** someone whose job is just
below that of a manager, director,
editor, etc., in rank: *We just hired two
new assistant editors.*

associate Ⓣ /əˈsoʊʃiˌeɪt/ [*verb;
associated, associating*]
1 to connect things in your mind:
**associate something with
something** ▸ *I associate cherry trees
with spring.*
2 to spend time with someone: *I don't
like the people she **is associating with**.*

association * /əˌsoʊsiˈeɪʃən/ [*noun*] an
organization whose members share an
interest, activity, or profession: *The
Association of Nurses will meet next week.*

assume /əˈsum/ [*verb; assumed,
assuming*] to believe something
because it seems very likely to be true:
assume (that) ▸ *I assume that you don't
want to come with us.* I *"Will they be at
the party?" "I assume so."*

assumption /əˈsʌmpʃən/ [*noun*] a belief
that you think is very likely to be true:
*You're **making** too many **assumptions**.*

assurance /əˈʃʊrəns/ [*noun*] when
someone says that something will
definitely happen: *Despite all his
assurances, he never paid us the money.*

assure /əˈʃʊr/ [*verb; assured, assuring*]
to tell someone that something will
definitely happen: **assure someone
(that)** ▸ *I can assure you that the package
will arrive tomorrow.*

asterisk /ˈæstərɪsk/ [*noun*] a mark (∗)
used in writing to show that there is
something special to notice about a
word or sentence: *In this dictionary, an
asterisk is used to show a basic vocabulary
word.*

asthma /ˈæzmə/ [*noun*] a disease that
makes breathing difficult

astonish Ⓣ /əˈstɑnɪʃ/ [*verb; astonishes,
astonished, astonishing*] to make
someone extremely surprised: *His
ignorance astonishes me.*

astonishment /əˈstɑnɪʃmənt/ [*noun*]
very great surprise; <u>synonym</u> AMAZEMENT:
*To my **astonishment**, I won first prize.*

astrology /əˈstrɑlədʒi/ [*noun*] the study
of how the position of planets and stars
are thought to affect people's lives

astronaut /ˈæstrəˌnɔt/ [*noun*] someone
who travels into space: *In 1969,
astronauts landed on the moon.*

astronomer /əˈstrɑnəmɚ/ [*noun*]
someone who studies stars and planets

astronomy /əˈstrɑnəmi/ [*noun*] the
scientific study of stars and planets

at ∗ /æt/ [*preposition*]
1 used to talk about a place or an event

/i/ see	/ɪ/ big	/eɪ/ day /ɛ/ get /æ/ hat
/ɑ/ father, hot	/ʌ/ up	/ə/ about /ɔ/ saw
/oʊ/ hope	/ʊ/ book	/u/ too /aɪ/ I /aʊ/ how
/ɔɪ/ boy	/ɝ/ bird	/ɚ/ teacher /ɪr/ ear /ɛr/ air
/ɑr/ far	/ɔr/ more	/ʊr/ tour /aɪr/ fire
/aʊɚ/ hour	/θ/ nothing	/ð/ mother /ʃ/ she
/ʒ/ measure	/tʃ/ church	/dʒ/ jump /ŋ/ long

in a place: *He was waiting at the station for me.* | *She lives at 23 Oak Street.* | *I met them at a party.*
2 toward someone or something: *She noticed a girl staring at her.* | *I threw a cushion at him.*
3 used to give a time: *I'll call you at eight o'clock.*
4 used to give a speed, age, amount, etc.: *He was driving at 65 m.p.h.* | *I moved here at the age of seven.* | *Roses were priced at $20.00 a dozen.*

atchoo /æ'tʃu/ [*interjection*] used to represent the sound of someone sneezing

ate * /eɪt/ [*verb*] the past tense of EAT

atheist /'eɪθiɪst/ [*noun*] someone who does not believe that God or a god exists

athlete /'æθlit/ [*noun*] someone who regularly plays a sport or sports, especially as a job: *He was a professional athlete for many years.*

athletic /æθ'lɛtɪk/ [*adjective*]
1 [*no comparative*] relating to sports: *An injury finished her athletic career.*
2 [**more athletic, most athletic**] strong and able to move quickly and with energy: *He is an athletic dancer.*

athletics /æθ'lɛtɪks/ [*noun*] sports, especially ones that are taught in schools and colleges: *The university she goes to has a great athletics program.*
☛ Only use **athletics** with a singular verb.

Atlantic * /æt'læntɪk/ [*name*]
the Atlantic (Ocean) the large ocean between North and South America on the west, and Europe and Africa on the east

atlas /'ætləs/ [*noun; plural* **atlases**] a book of maps: *an atlas of the world* | *I need a road atlas.*

ATM /'ɛɪˌti'ɛm/ [*noun; plural* **ATMs** or **ATM's**] a machine that gives you money from your bank account when you put in a plastic card

atmosphere /'ætməsˌfɪr/ [*noun*]
1 the general feeling in a place: *The school has a friendly atmosphere.*
2 the gases around the earth or another planet: *Scientists are worried about changes in the earth's atmosphere.*

atom * /'ætəm/ [*noun*] the smallest unit of a chemical element that can exist: *Two hydrogen atoms and one oxygen atom form one molecule of water.*
↪ Compare MOLECULE.

atomic /ə'tamɪk/ [*adjective; no comparative*] relating to or using atoms: *an atomic bomb* | *atomic energy* (=power that comes from splitting atoms)

attach * /ə'tætʃ/ [*verb;* **attaches, attached, attaching**] to join one thing to another: **attach something with something** ▸ *The bottle labels are attached with glue.* | **attach something to something** ▸ *There was a note attached to the package.*

attached /ə'tætʃt/ [*adjective;* **more attached, most attached**] if someone is attached to another person, he or she likes that person very much: *He is very attached to his mother.*
☛ Do not use **attached** before a noun.

attachment /ə'tætʃmənt/ [*noun*] a computer document that is attached to an electronic mail message so it can be sent: *I couldn't open the attachment you sent.*

attack[1] * /ə'tæk/ [*verb;* **attacked, attacking**]
1 to try to harm someone physically: *He was attacked walking home through the park.* | *Will the dog attack again?*
2 to criticize someone or something strongly: *His ideas were attacked by many people.*

attack[2] * [*noun*]
1 an attempt to harm someone physically: *There were several **attacks on** women near here.* | *The soldiers **came under attack** (=were attacked).*
2 strong criticism: *His **attack on** his former friend surprised everyone.* | *The president's plans **came under attack**.*
3 when you are suddenly affected by an illness or feeling: *a **heart attack***

attacker /ə'tækɚ/ [*noun*] the person who attacks someone: *Her attacker was a tall man with a deep voice.*

attempt[1] * /ə'tɛmpt/ [*verb;* **attempted, attempting**] to try to do something: **attempt to do something** ▸ *He attempted to escape, but he failed.*

attempt² * [noun] when someone tries to do something: *He **made an attempt to** fix the car himself.* | **an attempt at doing something** ▸ *My attempts at scoring a goal were unsuccessful.*

attend * /ə'tɛnd/ [verb; **attended, attending**] to go to a class, meeting, etc.: *There are 800 children attending the school.* | *How many people attended the conference?*

attendance /ə'tɛndəns/ [noun] when someone goes to a class, a meeting, etc.: *Her school attendance record is very bad.* | *Sit down so I can **take attendance** (=check to see who is and is not in a class).*

attendant /ə'tɛndənt/ [noun] someone whose job is to take care of a place or the people who come there: *The attendant at the gallery told us where to go.* | *a gas station attendant*

attention * /ə'tɛnʃən/ [noun]
1 when you are watching someone or something closely or listening to him, her, or it carefully: *May I **have your attention**, please?* | *I **gave** him my full **attention**.*
— PHRASE —
2 pay attention (to) to watch or listen carefully to someone or something: *He wasn't paying attention to the teacher.*

attentive /ə'tɛntɪv/ [adjective; **more attentive, most attentive**]
1 watching or listening to someone or something carefully: *You should be more attentive in class.*
2 making sure that someone is comfortable and that he or she has everything he or she needs: *The waiter was polite and attentive.*

attic /'ætɪk/ [noun] a room at the top of a HOUSE, just below the roof

attitude * Ⓣ /'ætɪˌtud/ [noun] a general opinion about something: *My father and I have different **attitudes toward** life.*

attorney /ə'tɜ˞ni/ [noun; plural **attorneys**] someone whose job involves helping people with legal matters; synonym LAWYER: *He consulted an attorney about the contract.*

attract * Ⓣ /ə'trækt/ [verb; **attracted, attracting**] to make people or animals like something or come nearer to something: *Insects are attracted by lights.* | **attract someone to something** ▸ *What attracted you to this town?*

attraction /ə'trækʃən/ [noun] something that attracts you to someone or something: *The chance to travel was the main attraction of the job.*

attractive * /ə'træktɪv/ [adjective; **more attractive, most attractive**] looking or seeming pleasant or nice in a way that makes you interested; opposite UNATTRACTIVE: *She's an attractive woman.* | *It's a very attractive offer.*
⟳ *See the synonym note at* BEAUTIFUL.

auction /'ɔkʃən/ [noun] a public sale, when each thing is sold to the person who offers the highest price: *My parents bought the table at an auction.*

audience /'ɔdiəns/ [noun] the people who are watching or listening to a play, concert, TV show, etc.: *The audience laughed and clapped.*

audio /'ɔdiˌoʊ/ [adjective; no comparative] relating to the production or recording of sound: *Our audio equipment is new.*
☛ Only use **audio** before a noun.

audiovisual /ˌɔdioʊ'vɪʒuəl/ [adjective; no comparative] relating to the production and recording of both sound and pictures; synonym AV: *Some teachers use VCRs and other audiovisual aids.*
☛ Only use **audiovisual** before a noun.

audition /ɔ'dɪʃən/ [noun] a short performance by a singer, actor, or dancer in order for him or her to prove that he or she is suitable to be in a play, movie, band, etc.: *Her audition went well.*

auditorium /ˌɔdɪ'tɔriəm/ [noun] a large room where concerts, speeches, etc., are given: *Our school auditorium holds more than 1,000 people.*

/i/ **see** /ɪ/ **big** /eɪ/ **day** /ɛ/ **get** /æ/ **hat**
/ɑ/ **father, hot** /ʌ/ **up** /ə/ **about** /ɔ/ **saw**
/oʊ/ **hope** /ʊ/ **book** /u/ **too** /aɪ/ **I** /aʊ/ **how**
/ɔɪ/ **boy** /ɝ/ **bird** /ɚ/ **teacher** /ɪr/ **ear** /ɛr/ **air**
/ɑr/ **far** /ɔr/ **more** /ʊr/ **tour** /aɪr/ **fire**
/aʊɚ/ **hour** /θ/ **nothing** /ð/ **mother** /ʃ/ **she**
/ʒ/ **measure** /tʃ/ **church** /dʒ/ **jump** /ŋ/ **long**

Aug. the written abbreviation of
AUGUST

August ✳ /ˈɔgəst/ [noun] the eighth
month of the year: *He left on August
5th.* | *I will be eighteen in August.*
➪ *See the usage note at* MONTH.

aunt ✳ or **Aunt** [name, name] a sister of
your mother or father, or your uncle's
wife: *We're going to visit Aunt Mary.* |
One of my aunts lives in Philadelphia.
➪ *See the picture at* FAMILY TREE.

Australia ✳ /ɔˈstreɪlyə/ [name] the large
area of land between the Indian Ocean
and the Pacific Ocean, that is one large
country

Australian[1] ✳ /ɔˈstreɪlyən/ [noun]
someone who comes from Australia

Australian[2] ✳ [adjective; no comparative]
belonging to, from, or relating to
Australia: *The kangaroo is an Australian
animal.*

author /ˈɔθɚ/ [noun] someone who
writes books or stories: *a well-known
author*

authority ✳ ⊤ /əˈθɔrɪti/ [noun; plural
authorities]
1 the power to decide and control
things and people: *Do you have the
authority to make that decision?* | *a
person in a position of authority*
2 a person or group that has official
power in a country: **The authorities**
have refused to let him enter the country.
☛ This meaning is usually used in the
plural.

authorize ⊤ /ˈɔθəˌraɪz/ [verb;
authorized, authorizing] to give
official permission for something: *Who
authorized his visit?*

authorized /ˈɔθəˌraɪzd/ [adjective; no
comparative] officially allowed to do
something, or officially allowed to
happen: *You are not **authorized to** enter
this area.*

auto /ˈɔtoʊ/ [adjective; no comparative]
OLD-FASHIONED relating to cars: *He works
in an auto factory.*

autobiography ⊤ /ˌɔtəbaɪˈɑgrəfi/
[noun; plural **autobiographies**] the story
of someone's life, written by that
person: *The 70-year-old actor is planning*

to write his autobiography.
➪ *Compare* BIOGRAPHY.

autograph ⊤ /ˈɔtəˌgræf/ [noun] a
famous person's name, written by him
or her for someone to keep: *Can I have
your autograph?*

automatic ⊤ /ˌɔtəˈmætɪk/ [adjective; no
comparative]
1 an automatic machine works without
much human control or effort: *The
street lights are on an automatic timer.*
2 always happening in a particular
situation unless someone makes it
stop: *There's an automatic charge of $25
if your payment is late.*

automatically ⊤ /ˌɔtəˈmætɪkli/ [adverb]
1 if a machine works automatically, it
works without much human control or
effort: *The doors opened automatically.*
2 if something happens automatically,
it always happens in a particular
situation unless someone makes it
stop: *Your account will be automatically
billed $15 every month.*
3 if you do something automatically,
you do it without thinking, often
because you always do it: *As he left the
room, he automatically turned off the
light.*

automobile /ˈɔtəməˌbil/ [noun] OLD-
FASHIONED a car: *He was driving a bright
yellow automobile.*

autumn ✳ /ˈɔtəm/ [noun] the season
between summer and winter; synonym
FALL
➪ *See the usage note at* SEASON.

auxiliary verb ✳ /ɔgˈzɪlyəri ˈvɝb/
[noun] GRAMMAR a verb such as "be,"
"have," or "do," which is used before
other verbs to form tenses, questions,
etc., as in "She is reading," "They have
gone," and "Do you like it?"

AV /ˈeɪˈvi/ the abbreviation of
AUDIOVISUAL: *We sell video cameras,
projectors, and other AV equipment.*

available ✳ ⊤ /əˈveɪləbəl/ [adjective; no
comparative]
1 not busy or not already being used,
and therefore able to be seen or used:
*Is Dr. Black available? I'd like to talk to
him.* | *There are no seats available on
that flight.*

2 if a job is available, a company or organization needs someone to do it: *We have nothing available at the moment.*

avalanche /'ævə,læntʃ/ [*noun*] a sudden, powerful, and dangerous fall of snow down a mountain: *Three people were almost killed in the avalanche.*

Ave. the written abbreviation of AVENUE: *526 3rd Ave.*

avenue or **Avenue** /'ævə,nyu/ [*noun; plural* **avenues**] a wide street in a town: *He lives on Third Avenue.*

average[1] * T /'ævrɪdʒ/ [*adjective; no comparative*]
1 an average number is one you get when you add a group of numbers and divide the total by the number of numbers you added: *The average temperature here is 78° in the summer.*
2 ordinary or typical: *The average teenager is not interested in gardening.* | **above/below average** ▸ *Her grades are above average.*

average[2] * [*noun*]
1 a number you get by adding numbers and dividing the total by the number of numbers you added: *People spend an average of four hours a day watching TV.*
— PHRASE —
2 **on average** used to say what usually or typically happens: *It takes me a week to read a book, on average.*

avocado /,ævə'kadou/ [*noun; plural* **avocados**] a fruit with a hard, dark skin and a soft, pale green inside, eaten as a VEGETABLE

avoid * T /ə'vɔɪd/ [*verb;* **avoided, avoiding**]
1 to not do something, or not become involved with something: *I try to avoid arguments.* | **avoid doing something** ▸ *He wanted to avoid upsetting her.*
☛ Do not say "avoid to do something." For example, do not say "We avoided to get wet." Say **We avoided getting wet.**
2 to not meet or speak with someone deliberately: *Why are you avoiding me?*

await /ə'weɪt/ [*verb;* **awaited, awaiting**] FORMAL
1 to be waiting for something: *I eagerly await your decision.*

2 if something awaits you, you are about to experience it: *There was a surprise awaiting them.*

awake * /ə'weɪk/ [*adjective; no comparative*] not asleep: *He was already* **wide awake** (=completely awake). | *I lay awake all night hinking about the exam.*
☛ Do not say that someone is "very awake." Say that he or she is **wide awake.**
☛ Do not use **awake** before a noun.
↪ See also WAKE.

award[1] /ə'wɔrd/ [*verb;* **awarded, awarding**] to officially give someone a prize or amount of money: **award something to someone** ▸ *First prize was awarded to Anna Brown.* | **award someone something** ▸ *The judge awarded him $1,000.*

award[2] [*noun*] a prize or amount of money that is officially given to someone: *She was given a special award for her bravery.*

aware T /ə'wɛr/ [*adjective;* **more aware, most aware**] knowing that something exists or is happening; *opposite* UNAWARE: *He was not* **aware of** *the facts.* | *The teacher was* **aware that** *the children were finding the work extremely difficult.*

away * /ə'weɪ/ [*adverb*]
1 from a place or person: *She turned and walked away.* | *He took the knife* **away from** *the child.*
↪ Compare TOWARD (definition 1).
2 into a place where you can keep something: *She put her dress away in the closet.* | *He locked the letter away in his desk.*
3 used to say how far something is from you or from a place: *The nearest gas station was only two blocks away.*
↪ See the synonym note at FAR[1].
4 not at home or at work: *She's away for three weeks.*

awesome /'ɔsəm/ [*adjective;* **more awesome, most awesome**] impressive, powerful, or surprising: *an awesome waterfall*

awful /'ɔfəl/ [*adjective;* **more awful, most awful**]
1 very bad or unpleasant; *synonym* TERRIBLE: *The movie was awful.* | *I've had an awful day.*
2 used to emphasize that something is large in amount or degree: *It must have cost an awful lot of money.*

awfully /'ɔfli/ [*adverb*] INFORMAL very: *It took me an awfully long time to get there.*

awhile /ə'wɪl/ [*adverb*] for a short period of time: *I had to wait awhile before the doctor could see me.*
⇨ Compare **a while** at WHILE².

awkward * /'ɔkwəd/ [*adjective;* **more awkward, most awkward**]
1 an awkward situation is one that has a lot of problems and that can be embarrassing: *I'm in an awkward position.* | *It's awkward to try to explain.*
2 not in a comfortable position: *This desk is at an awkward height.*

3 moving in a way that looks uncomfortable, stiff, or silly; *opposite* GRACEFUL: *Many birds look awkward when they walk.*
4 uncomfortable in social situations: *I was shy and awkward as a child.*

awkwardly /'ɔkwədli/ [*adverb*] in a way that shows you are not comfortable, or in a way that is uncomfortable; *synonym* GRACEFULLY: *He danced a little awkwardly.* | *She sat awkwardly on the stool.*

ax or **axe** /æks/ [*noun; plural* **axes**] a TOOL with a heavy metal blade and a long wooden handle, used for cutting down trees

axis /'æksɪs/ [*noun; plural* **axes** /'æksiz/]
1 a line through the middle of something, around which it turns: *The earth's axis goes through the North and South Poles.*
2 one of the lines that mark the edge of a graph: *The x axis shows the months and the y axis shows the average temperature.*

B

B * or **b** /bi/ [*noun*]
1 [*plural* **Bs** or **B's, b's**] the second letter in the English alphabet
⇨ See the usage note at ALPHABET.
2 **B** [*plural* **Bs** or **B's**] a grade in school that is good but not excellent: *I got a B on my geography test.*

B.A. /'bi'eɪ/ [*noun; plural* **B.A.s** or **B.A.'s**] Bachelor of Arts; a degree given for four years of study in subjects such as history, literature, or a language: *She's studying for a B.A.*
⇨ Compare **B.S., M.A., M.S., PH.D.**

baby * /'beɪbi/ [*noun; plural* **babies**]
1 a very young child, especially one that is less than a year old: **baby boy/girl** ▸ *They have a baby boy.* | *My sister has just had a baby* (=her baby has just been born).
2 a very young animal: *a mother elephant with her baby* | *a baby monkey*
☛ Do not say "a baby cat," "a baby

dog," or "a baby cow." Say **a kitten, a puppy,** or **a calf.**

baby carriage /'beɪbi ˌkærɪdʒ/ [*noun*] a small bed with four wheels and a handle in which a baby can lie or sit and be moved from place to place; *synonym* CARRIAGE

babysit /'beɪbi ˌsɪt/ [*verb;* **babysat, babysitting**] to take care of a child when his or her parents leave the house for a short time: *I'm babysitting for my aunt tonight.* | *They often asked me to babysit their kids.*

babysitter Ⓣ /'beɪbi ˌsɪtə/ [*noun*] someone who takes care of a child while his or her parents are away for a short time

bachelor /'bætʃələ/ [*noun*] a man who is not married: *A bachelor lives next door.*

back¹ * /bæk/ [*adverb*]
1 in the direction opposite the way you are moving or facing: *Take two steps*

forward and three steps back. | *She looked back to see if he was following.*
2 in a movement that returns to a place or person: *We'd better go back to the house.* | *Give me back my pen.* | *I'll be back in an hour.* | *I put the book back on the shelf.*
3 some distance away from someone or something: *Please stand back and give us more room.* | *The crowd was kept back by a line of police.*

━━ PHRASE ━━
4 back and forth in one direction and then in the opposite direction: *She hurried back and forth bringing food from the kitchen.*
⟳ *See also* TO AND FRO.

back² * [*noun*]
1 the part of the body that is behind you, from the neck to below your waist: *She sat with her back straight.* | *He carried a large pack on his back.*
2 the back the part of something that is farthest from the front: *He always sits at the back of the class.* | *Their furniture was in the back of the truck.* | *The book has an index at the back.*
⟳ *Compare* **the front** *at* FRONT¹.
3 the side or surface of something that is not the important side; *opposite* FRONT: *Write your address on the back of the envelope.* | *The backs of the houses face the alley.*

━━ PHRASES ━━
4 in back behind, or in the part of something that is farthest from the front: *There's a big yard in back of the house.* | *The kids rode in back (=in the back of a car).* | *They sat in back of us.*
☛ *Do not say "in the back of us."*
5 with your back to
a facing away from someone or something: *He was standing with his back to us.*
b leaning against something behind you: *We stood with our backs to the wall.*

back³ * [*adjective; no comparative*]
1 at or in the back of something; *opposite* BACK: *They left by the back door.* | *the back room*
☛ *Only use* **back** *before a noun.*

━━ PHRASE ━━
2 back street or **back road** a street

or road that is not wide or important: *I live on a back street near the station.*

back⁴ [*verb;* **backed, backing**]
1 to move backward without turning around: *He began to back away from the doorway.*
2 to move a car backward without turning it around: *Can you back your car a little way?* | *You'll have to back into the garage.*
3 to support a person, idea, or plan, especially with money: *The state is backing our plans for the town.* | *Several leading scientists backed her theory.*

━━ PHRASAL VERB ━━
back up [*phrasal verb*]
4 to support what someone is saying, and say or show that it is true: **back someone/something up** ▸ *Tell them what happened, and we'll back you up.* | **back up someone/something** ▸ *The evidence backs up his statement.*
5 to make a copy of work that you have done on a computer: **back up something** ▸ *Remember to back up your work every day.* | **back something up** ▸ *The file has disappeared and I didn't back it up.*
6 to move backward without turning around, or to move a car in this way: *I backed up to let them go by.* | **back up something** ▸ *Please back up your car. It's blocking the driveway.* | **back something up** ▸ *Back the car up a little.*

backbone /'bæk,boʊn/ [*noun*] the line of bones down the center of your back; *synonym* SPINE
⟳ *See the picture at* SKELETON.

background * ⊤ /'bæk,graʊnd/ [*noun*]
1 the part of a picture, a design, or a scene that is behind the main part: *The flag has seven gold stars on a blue background.* | *The statue stood against a background of flowering trees.* | *Our house is in the background of the photo.*

/i/ **see**	/ɪ/ **big**	/eɪ/ **day**	/ɛ/ **get**	/æ/ **hat**
/ɑ/ **father, hot**	/ʌ/ **up**	/ə/ **about**	/ɔ/ **saw**	
/oʊ/ **hope**	/ʊ/ **book**	/u/ **too**	/aɪ/ **I**	/aʊ/ **how**
/ɔɪ/ **boy**	/ɝ/ **bird**	/ə/ **teacher**	/ɪr/ **ear**	/ɛr/ **air**
/ɑr/ **far**	/ɔr/ **more**	/ʊr/ **tour**	/aɪr/ **fire**	
/aʊə/ **hour**	/θ/ **nothing**	/ð/ **mother**	/ʃ/ **she**	
/ʒ/ **measure**	/tʃ/ **church**	/dʒ/ **jump**	/ŋ/ **long**	

2 the family, social group, and conditions in which someone grew up: *I don't know much about his background.* | *Our students come from many different backgrounds.*

backpack /'bæk,pæk/ [*noun*] a large bag made of cloth that you wear on your back, used for carrying things; *synonym* PACK

backpacking /'bæk,pækɪŋ/ [*noun*] the activity of walking or traveling for pleasure, carrying a backpack: *He quit his job to **go backpacking** across Asia.*

a backpack/a pack

backstage /'bæk'steɪdʒ/ [*adverb*] behind the stage in a theater: *We were invited to **go backstage** and meet the actors.*

backstroke /'bæk,stroʊk/ [*noun*] a kind of swimming that you do on your back: *The women's backstroke race is next.*

backup /'bæk,ʌp/ [*noun*] a copy of a computer program or of work that you have done on a computer: *Remember to **make a backup** of your work.* | *Keep your **backup disks** in a safe place.*

backward[1] * /'bækwəd/ also **backwards** /'bækwədz/ [*adverb*]
1 in the direction opposite the way you are facing; *opposite* FORWARD: *Take three steps backward.* | *He was coming backwards down the stairs.* | *Lean backward and let your partner catch you.*
2 in the order or direction opposite the usual one: *Count backward from ten.*

backward[2] * [*adjective*]
1 [*no comparative*] in the direction opposite the way you are facing: *She left with one last **backward glance** (=a look back).* | *He did a backward somersault into the pool.*
☛ Only use **backward** before a noun in this meaning.
2 [**more backward, most backward**] a backward place or society does not have many modern developments; *opposite* ADVANCED: *They brought new*

farming methods to the more backward areas.

backyard /'bæk'yɑrd/ [*noun*] the area behind a house: *The kids are playing **in the backyard**.* | *a backyard barbecue*

bacon /'beɪkən/ [*noun*] meat from a pig that has been preserved using salt or smoke: *They had bacon and eggs for breakfast.*

bacteria * /bæk'tɪriə/ [*plural noun*] very small living things, some of which cause illness: *There are harmful bacteria in the water of this river.*

bad * /bæd/ [*adjective*; **worse, worst**]
1 not good in quality: *That's the worst movie I've ever seen.* | *I know I've made some bad decisions.*
2 not good or pleasant: *I've had a really bad day.* | *The weather is getting worse.* | *I'm afraid I have some bad news for you.*
3 having a serious or harmful effect: *There was a bad accident on the highway yesterday.* | *He had a bad cold.* | *Pollution is **bad for** (=it is harmful to) the environment.*
4 not morally acceptable or right: *Lying is a bad thing to do.*
5 not helpful or kind, or not behaving well: *I don't think he's really a bad man.* | *You've been a bad girl today.*
6 not skillful at doing or dealing with something: *She's an even worse teacher than Mr. Green.* | *I'm really **bad at** math.*
7 food that is bad cannot be eaten because it is not fresh: *There were a few bad tomatoes in the bowl.* | *The meat has **gone bad**.*
↪ Compare GOOD[1].

━ PHRASES ━
8 not bad SPOKEN fairly good: *"Did you have a good time?" "Not bad."*
9 too bad SPOKEN used to say that you are sorry about a situation: ***It's too bad that** she couldn't finish college.* | *"Brenda can't come." "That's too bad."*
10 feel bad
 a to feel sorry or ashamed: *I **feel really bad about** breaking your vase.*
 b to feel sick: *Don't go to class if you're feeling bad.*

badge /bædʒ/ [*noun*] a small object that you wear to show what organization

you belong to, or the work that you do:
The police officer showed them his badge.

badly * /'bædli/ [*adverb;* **worse, worst**]
1 in a way that is not good,
satisfactory, or skillful; *opposite* WELL:
*Most workers in that factory are **badly
paid**.* | *The shoes were **badly made** and
falling apart.* | *You have treated your
brother very **badly**.*
2 very much: *We **badly need** more books
and writing materials.* | *I **wanted** a
vacation very **badly**.*
3 seriously: *Is he **badly hurt?*** | *The
building was **badly damaged** in the
earthquake.* | *The tension was beginning
to affect us **badly**.*

badminton /'bædmɪntən/ [*noun*] a
sport or activity played by hitting a
small light object over a net with
rackets: *We **play badminton** every
Monday evening.* | *a **badminton court***

bag * /bæg/ [*noun*] a container, made
from a soft material, that opens at the
top for carrying things: *a paper grocery
bag* | *a **bag of** rice* | *a **shoulder bag*** | *My
bags are packed and I'm ready to go.*

bags

handles

paper bag

plastic bag

shopping
bag

bagel /'beɪgəl/ [*noun*] a small, round,
ring-shaped bread: *I had tuna fish salad
on a bagel for lunch.*

baggage /'bægɪdʒ/ [*noun*] cases and
bags that you take with you when you
travel somewhere; *synonym* LUGGAGE:
*Don't take more than two **pieces of
baggage**.*
☞ Do not say "baggages." Say **pieces of
baggage**.

baggage claim /'bægɪdʒ ˌkleɪm/
[*noun*] the place in an airport where
you get your baggage after a flight: *I'll
meet you at the baggage claim.*

baggy /'bægi/ [*adjective;* **baggier,
baggiest**] baggy clothing is big and
loose: *He wore jeans and a baggy shirt.*

bait /beɪt/ [*noun*] food used to attract
and catch animals or fish: *We use
worms as bait when we go fishing.*

bake * /beɪk/ [*verb;* **baked, baking**] to
cook food such as bread or cakes in an
oven, or to be cooked in this way: *Mom
baked a cake for dessert.* | *I baked all
morning.* | *The cookies are still baking.*
↪ *See the synonym note at* COOK[1].

baker /'beɪkɚ/ [*noun*] someone whose
job is to make bread and cakes

bakery /'beɪkəri/ [*noun; plural* **bakeries**]
a store or place where bread and cakes
are made or sold

balance[1] * ⊺ /'bæləns/ [*noun*]
1 the ability to stand or walk without
leaning to one side and falling: *It was
hard to **keep my balance** on the ice.* |
*He **lost his balance** and fell.*
2 when two or more things have equal
importance, or each one has the right
amount of importance: *Try to keep a
good **balance between** your work and
your social life.*

balance[2] * [*verb;* **balanced, balancing**]
1 to keep steady or keep something
steady: *He **balanced on** the back of the
sofa to change the light bulb.* | **balance
something on something** ▸ *She
balanced the basket on her head.*
2 to give equal importance, or the right
amount of importance, to two or more
things: *Try to **balance** classwork **with**
outdoor activities.* | *You'll have to
balance your family's needs **against**
your own.*

balcony /'bælkəni/ [*noun; plural*
balconies]
1 a small structure that sticks out from
the wall of a building, outside a
window or a door that is in a wall
above the main level: *We watched the*

/i/ **see** /ɪ/ **big** /eɪ/ **day** /ɛ/ **get** /æ/ **hat**
/ɑ/ **father, hot** /ʌ/ **up** /ə/ **about** /ɔ/ **saw**
/oʊ/ **hope** /ʊ/ **book** /u/ **too** /aɪ/ **I** /aʊ/ **how**
/ɔɪ/ **boy** /ɝ/ **bird** /ɚ/ **teacher** /ɪr/ **ear** /ɛr/ **air**
/ɑr/ **far** /ɔr/ **more** /ʊr/ **tour** /aɪr/ **fire**
/aʊɚ/ **hour** /θ/ **nothing** /ð/ **mother** /ʃ/ **she**
/ʒ/ **measure** /tʃ/ **church** /dʒ/ **jump** /ŋ/ **long**

parade *from the balcony.* | *They sat on the balcony.*

2 an upstairs area in a theater where people sit: *We had seats in the balcony.*

bald /bɔld/ [*adjective;* **balder, baldest**] with no HAIR or not much hair on your head: *He was completely bald.* | *I started going bald when I was thirty.*

ball * /bɔl/ [*noun*]

1 a round object that is used in sports or as a child's toy: *The kids were playing with a ball.* | *He hit the ball very hard.* | *Throw the ball to me!*

2 a round shape: *Roll the dough into balls.* | *a ball of string*

3 a large formal party with dancing: *a New Year's ball*

— PHRASE

4 be on the ball INFORMAL to know what needs to be done, and be ready to do it: *She's lucky that her secretary is always on the ball.*

football

soccer ball

baseball

basketball

tennis ball

balls

ballerina /ˌbælə'rinə/ [*noun; plural* **ballerinas**] a woman who dances in ballet

ballet /bæ'leɪ/ [*noun*] a kind of dancing that is done in a theater, and often tells a story: *We saw the famous ballet, "Swan Lake."* | *a ballet dancer*

balloon /bə'lun/ [*noun*]

1 an object like a thin rubber bag that is filled with air or gas and used as a toy or for decoration: *Help me to blow up these balloons for the party.*

2 an extremely large cloth bag that is tied to a basket, filled with hot air, and used for carrying people above the ground: *I'd love to go up in a hot-air balloon.*

ballot /'bælət/ [*noun*] a piece of paper on which someone writes a vote: *The ballots aren't all counted yet.*

ballpark /'bɔl,park/ [*noun*] a place where baseball is played and watched

ballpoint pen /'bɔl,pɔɪnt 'pɛn/ also **ballpoint** [*noun*] a PEN with a very small ball at its point, where the ink comes out

ballroom /'bɔl,rum/ [*noun*] a large room used for parties and dancing: *the hotel ballroom* | *ballroom dancing*

bamboo /bæm'bu/ [*noun*] a tall plant with hard, usually hollow, stems: *a bamboo chair*

ban¹ Ⓣ /bæn/ [*verb;* **bans, banned, banning**] to forbid people to have, use, or do something: *Smoking is banned in all public places.* | *a banned book*

ban² Ⓣ [*noun*] an official order that forbids people to have, use, or do something: *a ban on the sale of guns*

banana /bə'nænə/ [*noun; plural* **bananas**] a long, curved, sweet yellow FRUIT that grows on trees in hot places: *a bunch of bananas*

band * /bænd/ [*noun*]

1 a group of people who play music together, especially popular music: *I play the flute in the high school band.*

2 a thin flat piece of material that is placed around something or used to hold things together: *A velvet band held back her long hair.*

⮑ *See also* ARMBAND, RUBBER BAND.

3 an area of color, light, or darkness that is longer than it is wide: *A rainbow has seven bands of color.*

4 a group of people who do something together, especially something dangerous or illegal: *a band of rebels*

bandage¹ /'bændɪdʒ/ [*noun*] a piece of cloth or plastic that you put on or around an injury or wound: *She had an elastic bandage around her ankle.*

bandage² [*verb;* **bandaged, bandaging**] to wrap a bandage around an injury or wound: *His foot was tightly bandaged.*

Band-Aid /'bænd,eɪd/ [*noun*] TRADEMARK a small bandage that sticks to your skin

bandit /'bændɪt/ [*noun*] a member of a group of thieves who attack travelers

bang[1] /bæŋ/ [*verb;* **banged, banging**]
  1 to hit something hard with something else and make a loud noise: *I banged on the door until she let me in.* | *She angrily banged the tray down on the table.* | *The screen door banged against the house.*
  2 to hurt a part of your body by knocking it against something: *She banged her head on the window frame.* | *I banged my elbow against the wall.*

bang[2] [*noun*]
  1 a loud noise made by something knocking against something else or by an explosion: *He put his books down with a bang.* | *We heard a loud bang from upstairs.*
  2 bangs [*plural*] HAIR that is cut so that it hangs in a straight line above the eyes

banister /'bænəstɚ/ [*noun*] a bar along the side of a set of STAIRS, that you can hold while you go up or down

banjo /'bændʒoʊ/ [*noun; plural* **banjos** or **banjoes**] a MUSICAL INSTRUMENT with five strings, a round body, and a long neck, that you play with your fingers: *I'm learning to play the banjo.*

bank[1] * T /bæŋk/ [*noun*]
  1 a business that keeps people's money safe, and lends money: *I need to go to the bank at lunchtime.* | *How much money do we have in the bank?*
  2 the land at the side of a river: *Mike stood on the bank of the river.*

bank[2] [*verb;* **banked, banking**] to put or keep money in a bank: *We bank at City National.* | *I went downtown and banked the money.*

banker /'bæŋkɚ/ [*noun*] someone who works in a bank and has the power to make decisions about people's money: *an investment banker*

banking /'bæŋkɪŋ/ [*noun*] the business that banks do: *a career in banking*

bankrupt /'bæŋkrʌpt/ [*adjective; no comparative*] not having enough money to pay your debts: *He started a business but then went bankrupt.*

banner /'bænɚ/ [*noun*] a long sign made of cloth or paper: *The banner over the door said "Congratulations!"*

banquet /'bæŋkwɪt/ [*noun*] a big impressive formal meal, made for a special occasion: *Every Christmas, the governor gives a banquet.* | *a wedding banquet*

baptism /'bæptɪzəm/ [*noun*] a Christian ceremony at which someone is baptized

baptize /'bæptaɪz/ [*verb;* **baptized, baptizing**] to make someone a member of a Christian church, by a ceremony in which water is used: *Do you wish to be baptized?*

bar[1] * /bɑr/ [*noun*]
  1 a long piece of metal or wood, especially one that is used to keep people or animals in or out of a place: *The apartment had bars on the windows.* | *the bars of a cage*
  2 a small block of something: *a bar of soap* | *a candy bar*
  3 a place where people buy and drink alcohol: *I'll meet you in the hotel bar.*
  4 a long narrow table where alcoholic drinks are sold and served: *We sat at the bar.*

bar[2] * [*verb;* **bars, barred, barring**]
  1 to officially prevent people from going somewhere or doing something: *Reporters were barred from the meeting.*
  2 to put a bar across a door to stop people from getting in: *They went into the house and barred the doors.*

━━ PHRASE ━━━━━━━
  3 bar someone's way to prevent someone from going somewhere by standing in front of him or her: *He stood in the doorway, barring my way.*

barbecue[1] or **barbeque** /'bɑrbɪ,kyu/ [*noun; plural* **barbecues** or **barbeques**]
  1 a meal which is cooked and eaten outdoors: *Let's have a barbecue.*

/i/ **see**	/ɪ/ **big**	/eɪ/ **day**	/ɛ/ **get**	/æ/ **hat**
/ɑ/ **father, hot**	/ʌ/ **up**	/ə/ **about**	/ɔ/ **saw**	
/oʊ/ **hope**	/ʊ/ **book**	/u/ **too**	/aɪ/ **I**	/aʊ/ **how**
/ɔɪ/ **boy**	/ɚ/ **bird**	/ɚ/ **teacher**	/ɪr/ **ear**	/ɛr/ **air**
/ɑr/ **far**	/ɔr/ **more**	/ʊr/ **tour**	/aɪr/ **fire**	
/aʊɚ/ **hour**	/θ/ **nothing**	/ð/ **mother**	/ʃ/ **she**	
/ʒ/ **measure**	/tʃ/ **church**	/dʒ/ **jump**	/ŋ/ **long**	

2 a piece of equipment for cooking food outdoors: *He put the steaks on the barbecue.*

barbecue² or **barbeque** [*verb;* **barbecues, barbecued, barbecuing; barbeques, barbequed, barbequeing**] to cook food on a barbecue: *barbecued chicken legs*

barbed wire /barbd 'waɪr/ [*noun*] wire with sharp points sticking out from it, used to make fences: *There is a barbed wire fence all around the ranch.*

barber /'barbɚ/ [*noun*] someone whose job is to cut men's hair: *I went to the barber's this afternoon.*

bare /bɛr/ [*adjective;* **barer, barest**]
1 not covered or protected by clothes or shoes: *Don't go outside with bare feet.*
2 not containing anything or covered by anything: *I prefer bare walls without pictures.* | *We camped out on the bare rock ledge.* | *The refrigerator is almost bare* (=almost empty).

barefoot¹ /'bɛr,fʊt/ [*adverb*] without wearing shoes or socks: *I like to go barefoot in the summer.*

barefoot² [*adjective; no comparative*] not wearing shoes or socks: *barefoot children*

barely /'bɛrli/ [*adverb*]
1 almost not at all, almost none at all, etc.; synonyms HARDLY, SCARCELY: *We had barely enough money to pay the rent.* | *I could barely hear what he was saying.*
2 only just: *They had barely sat down when the phone rang.*

bargain¹ /'bargən/ [*noun*]
1 something good or useful that you are able to buy at less than its usual price: *You can find some good bargains there.* | *This TV was a real bargain.*
2 an agreement between two people or groups about what they will do for each other: *I'll make a bargain with you—finish your homework, and I'll take you swimming.*

bargain² [*verb;* **bargained, bargaining**] to argue with someone and try to reach an agreement, especially about money: *She enjoys bargaining for antiques.* | *We bargained with the car salesman.*

barge /bardʒ/ [*noun*] a large boat with a flat bottom, used for carrying goods

bark¹ /bark/ [*verb;* **barked, barking**] if a dog barks, it makes a loud, sudden noise: *The dog barked at the cat.*

bark² [*noun*]
1 the substance that covers the outside of a tree: *Oak trees have rough bark.*
2 the loud noise that a dog makes: *Her dog gave a fierce bark.*

barley /'barli/ [*noun*] a kind of grain that is used as food and to make beer and other drinks

barn /barn/ [*noun*] a building on a farm used for storing crops or keeping animals in

barnyard /'barn,yard/ [*noun*] an area of ground next to a barn on a farm

barracks /'bærəks/ [*plural noun*] buildings in which soldiers live: *Officers don't have to live in the barracks.*

barrel /'bærəl/ [*noun*]
1 a large round container in which liquids and some foods are stored, or the amount this container holds: *a barrel of oil*
2 the long hollow part of a gun: *a rifle barrel*

a barrel

barrier /'bæriɚ/ [*noun*]
1 a structure, for example a fence, that is put up to stop people from moving from one place to another: *There was a barrier across the road at the frontier.*
2 something that stops people from doing or achieving something: *Racism is a barrier to success.*

bartender /'bar,tɛndɚ/ [*noun*] someone whose job is to serve drinks in a bar

base¹ * /beɪs/ [*noun*]
1 the bottom of something, or its lowest part: *There was a path at the base of the cliff.* | *The statue stands on a concrete base.* | *a lamp base*
⇨ See the pictures at LAMP and TELEPHONE.
2 the main place from which an activity, business, or military group is organized: *The company's base is in New York.* | *an army base*
3 one of the four places that a player

must touch after hitting the ball in baseball: *He ran toward first base.*

base² * [*verb; based, basing*]

— PHRASE —

1 be based in/on/at to be organized from a particular place: *Our firm is based in Chicago.* I *The Marines were based on the largest island.*

— PHRASAL VERB —

base on/upon [*phrasal verb*]

2 to form or develop something from something else: **base something on/upon something** ▶ *The movie is based on a mystery novel.*

baseball * /'beɪs,bɔl/ [*noun*]

1 a sport or game played by two teams, in which players try to hit a ball with a **BAT** and then run around a field, touching all four bases: *He loves playing baseball.* I *a baseball field*

2 the **BALL** that is used in this game

baseball cap

/'beɪs,bɔl ,kæp/ [*noun*] a cap with a long curved part sticking out at the front

visor

a baseball cap

basement

/'beɪsmənt/ [*noun*] a part of a house or building that is below the level of the ground: *The laundry room is in the basement.*

↪ Compare **CELLAR**.

basic * Ⓣ /'beɪsɪk/ [*adjective; more basic, most basic*] simple and necessary or important: *There are some basic rules to remember.* I *He earns enough for the family's basic needs.*

basically /'beɪsɪkli/ [*adverb*] used when you give the most important fact about something: *Basically, you need to work harder.*

basics /'beɪsɪks/ [*plural noun*]

the basics the simple and most important parts of something: *I'm not an expert, but I can teach you the basics.* I *the basics of a healthy diet*

basin /'beɪsən/ [*noun*] a large bowl for holding liquid: *The nurse brought a basin of warm water.*

basis /'beɪsɪs/ [*noun*]

1 the main facts or ideas that support

an opinion, plan, or decision: *What is the basis of his theory?*

☛ The plural from of **basis** is rare.

— PHRASES —

2 on the basis of something for a particular reason: *The winners were chosen on the basis of talent.*

3 on a daily/weekly/regular/etc. basis every day, every week, regularly, etc.: *The rooms are cleaned on a daily basis.* I *We agreed to meet on a regular basis.*

handles

shopping basket

baskets

basket * /'bæskɪt/ [*noun*]

1 a container made of woven material, used mainly for carrying things: *She was carrying a basket of apples.*

2 a high ring with a net hanging from it, into which players try to throw the ball in a game of basketball: *The boys spent an hour shooting baskets* (=trying to throw a ball into a basket).

basketball * /'bæskɪt,bɔl/ [*noun*]

1 a sport or game played by two teams, in which points are scored by throwing a large ball into a high ring with a net hanging from it: *The girls are at the gym playing basketball.* I *a basketball court*

2 the **BALL** that is used in this game

/i/ see	/ɪ/ big	/eɪ/ day	/ɛ/ get	/æ/ hat
/ɑ/ father, hot	/ʌ/ up	/ə/ about	/ɔ/ saw
/oʊ/ hope	/ʊ/ book	/u/ too	/aɪ/ I	/aʊ/ how
/ɔɪ/ boy	/ɝ/ bird	/ɪr/ ear	/ɛr/ air
/ɑr/ far	/ɔr/ more	/ʊr/ tour	/aɪr/ fire
/aʊɚ/ hour	/θ/ nothing	/ð/ mother	/ʃ/ she
/ʒ/ measure	/tʃ/ church	/dʒ/ jump	/ŋ/ long

bat[1] * /bæt/ [noun]
1 a small animal with wings that hangs upside down and flies at night
2 a long, round, heavy stick used to hit the ball in games such as baseball

a bat

a baseball bat

bat[2] [verb; bats, batted, batting] to hit a ball in a game such as baseball: *It's your turn to bat.*

batch /bætʃ/ [noun; plural **batches**] a group or number of things that are done or made together: *I made three batches of cookies.*

bath * /bæθ/ [noun; plural **baths** /bæðz/] an act of washing your whole body in a bathtub: *I'm going to take a bath.*

bathe /beɪð/ [verb; **bathed, bathing**]
1 to wash yourself or someone else in a bathtub: *I bathed and changed my clothes.* | *He was bathing the children.*
2 to wash part of your body with a liquid, especially a part that is hurt: *Bathe the cut with warm water.*

bathing suit /'beɪðɪŋ ˌsut/ [noun] a piece of CLOTHING that you wear for swimming; <u>synonym</u> SWIMSUIT

bathrobe /'bæθˌroʊb/ [noun] a piece of CLOTHING like a long loose coat, which people wear in their homes, for example before getting dressed; <u>synonym</u> ROBE: *He put on his bathrobe and went downstairs.*

bathroom * /'bæθˌrum/ [noun]
1 a room in a house that contains a toilet and a bathtub or a shower
↪ *Compare* RESTROOM.

═══ PHRASE ═══

2 go to the bathroom to use the toilet: *I need to go to the bathroom.*

bathtub * /'bæθˌtʌb/ [noun] a large container that you fill with water and sit in to wash your body; <u>synonym</u> TUB

batter[1] /'bætɚ/ [noun]
1 a liquid mixture of flour, eggs, and milk, used in cooking: *pancake batter*
2 the person who tries to hit the ball in a game of baseball

batter[2] [verb; **battered, battering**] to

hit someone or something hard a lot of times: *Huge waves battered the ship.*

battery /'bætəri/ [noun; plural **batteries**] an object that stores and produces electricity: *My radio needs new batteries.* | *a car battery* | *The flashlight battery is dead* (=has stopped producing electricity).

battle * /'bætəl/ [noun]
1 a fight between two groups of people, especially in a war: *They had fought in many battles.* | *He was killed in battle* (=while fighting in a war).
2 an angry or difficult argument, competition, or struggle: *the battle for political power*

bay /beɪ/ [noun; plural **bays**] a curved part of an ocean or lake that has land on two or three sides of it: *Korea Bay*

B.C. * /'bi'si/ [adverb] before Christ; an abbreviation used in dates to show a particular number of years before the birth of Jesus Christ: *Confucius died in 479 B.C.* | *in the seventh century B.C.*
↪ *Compare* A.D.

be[1] * /bi/ [linking verb]
1 used to give information about someone or something: *I am a student.*

Forms of *be*		
	present tense	past tense
singular	I **am**, I'**m** he **is**, he'**s** she **is**, she'**s** it **is**, it'**s** you **are**, you'**re**	I **was** he **was** she **was** it **was** you **were**
plural	we **are**, we'**re** they **are**, they'**re** you **are**, you'**re**	we **were** they **were** you **were**
negatives	I'**m not** he **isn't** she **isn't** it **isn't** you **aren't** we **aren't** they **aren't**	I **wasn't** he **wasn't** she **wasn't** it **wasn't** you **weren't** we **weren't** they **weren't**
participles	*being*	*been*

| *The lecture will be on Thursday.* | *He was in love with her.* | *I would have been really sorry to miss the party.*
➪ *See also* BEING².

— **PHRASES** —

2 it is/was/will be/etc. used to describe a situation or give an opinion: *It's a beautiful day.* | *It will be a pity if he fails the exam.* | *It was lucky that Rachel knew how to drive.*

3 there is/are/was/were/will be/ etc. used to say that something exists, is true, or happens: *There's a lot more dessert left.* | *There will be time for questions after the lecture.*

be² * [*auxiliary verb*] GRAMMAR
1 used with a present participle to show the continuous tense of a verb: *What are you doing?* | *They were watching TV when I arrived.* | *Don't come this afternoon—I'll be studying for the test.*
2 used with a past participle to show the passive form of a verb: *I was taught by a famous musician.* | *English is spoken in many parts of the world.*

beach * /bitʃ/ [*noun; plural* **beaches**] a flat area of land, usually covered with sand, along the edge of an ocean: *Let's go to the beach.* | *a picnic **on the beach***
➪ *Compare* SHORE.

bead /bid/ [*noun*] a small object with a hole through it that is put on a thread to make jewelry: *She wore a **string of beads** around her neck.*

beak * /bik/ [*noun*] the hard, pointed, outer part of a BIRD's mouth

beam¹ * /bim/ [*noun*]
1 a line of light coming from a light or the sun

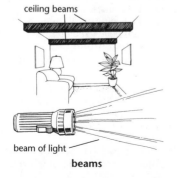

ceiling beams

beam of light

beams

2 a long, thick piece of wood or metal used to support a roof: *wooden ceiling beams*

beam² [*verb;* **beamed, beaming**] to smile in an extremely happy way: *Dad beamed at me from across the room.*

bean * /bin/ [*noun*]
1 a long, thin, green vegetable that has small seeds inside it: *string beans*
2 a small dried seed from some kinds of plants, that is cooked and eaten as a VEGETABLE: *kidney beans* (=dark red curved beans)

bean sprouts /'bin ˌspraʊts/ [*plural noun*] seeds that have just started to grow, that are eaten as a vegetable: *a tuna sandwich with bean sprouts*

bear¹ * /bɛr/ [*verb;* **bore, borne, bearing**]
1 to support the weight of something: *That chair won't bear your weight.*
2 to deal with something without becoming upset or angry: *The pain was more than she could bear.* | *I can't bear sad music* (=I hate it).
➪ *Compare* **can't stand** *at* STAND¹.
3 FORMAL to hold or carry something: *An official entered bearing the documents.* | *All citizens have the right to **bear arms*** (=carry weapons).

cub

bears

bear² * T [*noun*] a large dangerous animal with thick fur

beard * /bɪrd/ [*noun*] HAIR that grows on a man's face, especially on his chin

/i/ **see**	/ɪ/ **big**	/eɪ/ **day**	/ɛ/ **get**	/æ/ **hat**
/ɑ/ **father, hot**	/ʌ/ **up**	/ə/ **about**	/ɔ/ **saw**	
/oʊ/ **hope**	/ʊ/ **book**	/u/ **too**	/aɪ/ **I**	/aʊ/ **how**
/ɔɪ/ **boy**	/ɚ/ **bird**	/ɚ/ **teacher**	/ɪr/ **ear**	/ɛr/ **air**
/ɑr/ **far**	/ɔr/ **more**	/ʊr/ **tour**	/aɪr/ **fire**	
/aʊɚ/ **hour**	/θ/ **nothing**	/ð/ **mother**	/ʃ/ **she**	
/ʒ/ **measure**	/tʃ/ **church**	/dʒ/ **jump**	/ŋ/ **long**	

beast /bist/ [noun] FORMAL a large animal, especially a dangerous one: *He knew all the birds and beasts of the forest.*

beat[1] * /bit/ [verb; **beat, beaten** /'bitən/, **beating**]
1 to defeat someone in a fight, game, or competition: *We were beaten three games to one.* | *My brother usually beats me at chess.*
2 to hit someone or something again and again: *Beating children is a crime.* | *I beat on the door with my fists.* | *The rain beat against the window.*
3 if your heart beats, it makes the regular movements that send blood through your body: *My heart began to beat faster.*

━ PHRASE ━
4 **beat it** SPOKEN used to tell someone to go away: *Stop bothering the animals—go on, beat it!*

━ PHRASAL VERB ━
beat up [phrasal verb]
5 to hit someone again and again and hurt him or her: **beat someone up ▸** *The guards beat him up.* | **beat up someone ▸** *They beat up anyone who disagreed with them.*

beat[2] * [noun]
1 a single hit, movement, or sound that is part of a regular series: *My heart rate is 72 beats per minute.*
2 a regular series of hits, movements, or sounds: *The music had a lively beat.*

beating /'bitɪŋ/ [noun]
1 when a person or group is defeated: *Our team took a beating on Saturday.*
2 when something is used without enough attention to whether it will be damaged or not: *Air travel really gives your luggage a beating.*
3 when someone hits another person again and again: *The prisoners were given frequent beatings.*

beautiful * /'byutəfəl/ [adjective; **more beautiful, most beautiful**]
1 a beautiful woman or child is extremely attractive; *opposite* UGLY: *His wife was very beautiful.* | *What beautiful children you have!*
☛ Do not describe a man as "beautiful." Say that he is **handsome** or **attractive**.

2 very pleasant to see, hear, or experience: *Our room had a beautiful view of the mountains.* | *It's a beautiful sunny day.* | *beautiful music*
☛ Do not say "I had a beautiful time." Say **I had a wonderful time** or **I had a great time.**

SYNONYMS   beautiful, pretty, good-looking, attractive, handsome
All of these words are used to describe someone who looks nice.
    Beautiful is usually used to describe women or children: *She is a talented and beautiful actress.*
    Pretty is used to describe young women or girls who look very attractive, but not in an unusual way: *She's the prettiest girl in my class.*
    You can say that both men and women are **good-looking** or **attractive**: *My son is very good-looking.* | *Your cousin is a very attractive woman.*
    You can describe a man as **handsome**, especially when he is tall and looks strong: *A handsome young man with a beard approached us.*

beautifully * /'byutəfli/ [adverb] in a beautiful way: *She was beautifully dressed.* | *The girls sang beautifully.*

beauty * /'byuti/ [noun; plural **beauties**]
1 the quality of being very attractive: *She was a woman of great beauty.* | *He admired the beauty of the landscape.*
2 a very attractive woman or machine: *She was always considered a beauty.* | *Wow, that car's a real beauty!*

━ PHRASE ━
3 **the beauty of something** the thing that makes something very good: *The beauty of this game is that anyone can play.* | *You don't have to pay, that's the beauty of it.*

became * /bɪ'keɪm/ [verb] the past tense of BECOME

because * /bɪ'kɔz/ [conjunction]
1 used to give the reason for something: *He stayed at home because he was sick.* | *Because they had worked hard, I let them go home early.*
☛ Do not use **because** with **so**. For example, do not say "Because I was

tired, so I didn't go." Say **Because I was tired, I didn't go** or **I didn't go because I was tired.**

— PHRASE —

2 because of someone/something for a particular reason: *We stayed at home because of the rain.* | *Because of the accident, no trains were running.*

☛ Do not use **because of** to connect two full sentences. For example, do not say "I was worried because of he was late." Say **I was worried because he was late.**

become ✳ /bɪˈkʌm/ [*linking verb*; **became, become, becoming**] to reach a new state, position, or stage of development: *After listening for an hour, I became very bored.* | *It was getting dark and the wind was becoming stronger.* | *In a short time, the caterpillar becomes a butterfly.* | *He became a doctor.*

☛ Do not say "He became to be a doctor." Say **He became a doctor.**

SYNONYMS become, get, grow, go

All these words can be used to mean "to change from one state or condition into another." **Become** is more formal than **get** and is used mainly in writing: *He suddenly became angry and violent.* You usually use **get** in conversation: *It's getting cold—let's go home.*

Grow is used when something changes slowly and gradually, and is used mainly in stories and descriptions: *The sound of music grew louder.*

Go is used especially in some fixed phrases: *Everything has gone wrong!*

---

bed ✳ /bɛd/ [*noun*]

1 a piece of furniture that you sleep on: *She sat down on the edge of the bed.* | *Are you still in bed?* (=lying in your bed)

☛ Do not say "Are you in the bed?" Say **Are you in bed?**

2 a piece of ground that is prepared for growing flowers or vegetables: *a bed of roses* | *a flower bed*

3 the land beneath a river, a lake, or the ocean: *The water is so clear that you can see the bed of the river.*

— PHRASES —

4 go to bed to get into your bed at the end of the day: *It's time to go to bed.*

5 make the bed or **make your bed** to make a bed neat after someone has slept in it: *She went to make her bed.*

USAGE go to bed, go to sleep

Do not confuse **go to bed** and **go to sleep**.

When you **go to bed**, you get into your bed at the end of the day, but you may not sleep immediately: *I'm going to go to bed and read for a while.*

When you **go to sleep**, your eyes are closed and you relax completely: *Turn off the light and go to sleep now.*

---

bedding /ˈbɛdɪŋ/ [*noun*] the sheets and other covers on a bed: *The bedding was clean and new.*

bedroom ✳ /ˈbɛdˌrum/ [*noun*] a room where you sleep

bedside /ˈbɛdˌsaɪd/ [*adjective; no comparative*] beside someone's bed: *a bedside lamp*

bedspread /ˈbɛdˌsprɛd/ [*noun*] a large piece of cloth used to cover a bed and everything on it

bedtime /ˈbɛdˌtaɪm/ [*noun*] the time when someone usually goes to bed: *He drinks warm milk at bedtime.* | *The kids stayed up way past their bedtime* (=after they should have been in bed).

bee /bi/ [*noun; plural* **bees**] an insect with yellow and black lines on it, that makes honey: *a swarm of bees*

beef ✳ /bif/ [*noun*] meat from a cow: *I don't eat beef often.* | *beef stew*

beehive /ˈbiˌhaɪv/ [*noun*] a place in which bees live; *synonym* HIVE

been ✳ /bɪn/ [*verb*] the past participle of BE: *Where have you been?* | *I've been working very hard.*

⇨ *See the usage note at* GONE.

/i/ **see**	/ɪ/ **big**	/eɪ/ **day**	/ɛ/ **get**	/æ/ **hat**
/ɑ/ **father, hot**	/ʌ/ **up**	/ə/ **about**	/ɔ/ **saw**	
/oʊ/ **hope**	/ʊ/ **book**	/u/ **too**	/aɪ/ **I**	/aʊ/ **how**
/ɔɪ/ **boy**	/ɝ/ **bird**	/ɚ/ **teacher**	/ɪr/ **ear**	/ɛr/ **air**
/ɑr/ **far**	/ɔr/ **more**	/ʊr/ **tour**	/aɪr/ **fire**	
/aʊɚ/ **hour**	/θ/ **nothing**	/ð/ **mother**	/ʃ/ **she**	
/ʒ/ **measure**	/tʃ/ **church**	/dʒ/ **jump**	/ŋ/ **long**	

beep /bip/ [*verb;* **beeped, beeping**] if an electronic machine beeps, it makes short high sounds: *When the food's done, the microwave will beep until you open the door.*

beeper /'bipɚ/ [*noun*] a small electronic machine that you carry or wear, that beeps when you have a message or need to phone someone; *synonym* PAGER: *Excuse me—my beeper's going off.*

beer * /bɪr/ [*noun*]
1 an alcoholic drink made from grain: *a glass of beer*
2 a glass, can, or bottle of this drink: *Let me buy you a beer.*

beet /bit/ [*noun*] a round, dark red root that is cooked and eaten as a VEGETABLE

beetle /'bitəl/ [*noun*] an insect with a smooth hard back

before[1] * /bɪ'fɔr/ [*preposition*]
1 earlier than a particular time or event: *Come and see me before school.* | *I was ready an hour before the meeting.* | **before doing something** ▸ *Please sign the visitors' book before leaving the hotel.* | *I read the book* **the week before** *the test.*
2 earlier than someone else: *My sister finished her homework before me.*
3 ahead of someone or something: *I was before him in the line.* | *M comes before N in the alphabet.*
4 FORMAL in front of someone or something: *He stood before the judge.* | *A meal was set before us.*
☛ Only use this meaning of **before** in very formal writing. For example, do not say "I put the desk before the window." Say **I put the desk in front of the window.**
↪ *Compare* AFTER[1].

━━ PHRASES ━━
5 before long fairly soon: *She'll probably write to me before long.* | *Before long, I got bored.*
6 the day before yesterday two days ago: *I called her the day before yesterday.*
7 the week/month/year before last two weeks, months, or years ago: *His birthday was the week before last.*

before[2] * [*conjunction*] earlier than the time when something happens; *opposite*

AFTER: *I worked in a store before I got this job.* | *It'll be dark before we get home.* | *Before you go, please answer one question.*
☛ Do not say "before you will go." Say **before you go.**

before[3] * [*adverb*] earlier; *opposite* AFTER: *I've seen this movie before.* | *I had ordered the flowers* **the day before.**

beforehand /bɪ'fɔr,hænd/ [*adverb*] before doing something; *opposite* AFTERWARD: *Never give a speech without practicing it beforehand.*

beg /bɛg/ [*verb;* **begs, begged, begging**]
1 to ask for something in a very serious or anxious way, because you want very much: *I need your help, but I'm not going to beg.* | **beg (someone) for something** ▸ *He begged his mother for money.* | **beg someone to do something** ▸ *I begged him to listen to me.* | **beg to do something** ▸ *The kids begged to go too.*
☛ Do not say "I begged him listening to me" or "I begged him that he would listen to me." Say **I begged him to listen to me.**
2 if a poor person begs, he or she asks other people for money or food: **beg (someone) for something** ▸ *Small children begged us for money.*

━━ PHRASE ━━
3 I beg your pardon
a used to say politely that you are sorry for doing something that is slightly wrong or not polite, or that may annoy someone: *I beg your pardon, I didn't mean to interrupt you.*
↪ *See also* **pardon me** *at* PARDON[1].
b used to ask someone politely to repeat something: *"I beg your pardon?" "I said it's starting to rain."*
↪ *See also* **pardon (me)** *at* PARDON[1].

began * /bɪ'gæn/ [*verb*] the past tense of BEGIN

beggar /'bɛgɚ/ [*noun*] a poor person who asks other people for money or food: *The streets were full of beggars.*

begin * /bɪ'gɪn/ [*verb;* **began, begun, beginning**]
1 to start to do or feel something: *Begin when you're ready.* | *They began their dinner at seven o'clock.* | **begin to do**

something ▸ *I was beginning to feel angry.* | **begin doing something** ▸ *She began sweeping the floor.*
☛ Do not say "I was beginning getting angry." Say **I was beginning to get angry** or **I was getting angry.**
2 to start to happen or exist: *The cold weather will begin next month.*
━━ PHRASE ━━
3 to begin with at the beginning of something: *He was shy to begin with, but then he got more confident.*
↪ See also **to start with** at START[1].

━━━━━━━━━━━━━━━━━━━━
USAGE begin, start
Begin and **start** mean the same, but **begin** is more formal and is used less often in conversation.
━━━━━━━━━━━━━━━━━━━━

beginner /bɪˈɡɪnɚ/ [noun] someone who has just started to do something: *She teaches piano to beginners.*
beginning ✳ Ⓣ /bɪˈɡɪnɪŋ/ [noun] the start of something; *opposite* END: *At the beginning of the class, some students arrived late.* | *Go back to the beginning, and read it through again.*
☛ The plural use of **beginning** is rare.
↪ Compare FINISH[2].
begun ✳ /bɪˈɡʌn/ [verb] the past participle of BEGIN
behalf /bɪˈhæf/ [noun]
━━ PHRASE ━━
on behalf (of) for or instead of someone: **on behalf of someone** ▸ *On behalf of everyone here, I want to thank you for your help.* | **on someone's behalf** ▸ *The mayor has asked me to speak on his behalf.*
behave ✳ /bɪˈheɪv/ [verb; behaved, behaving]
1 to do things in a particular way; *synonym* ACT: *She's been behaving strangely lately.*
2 to do things in a correct, polite way: *If you can't behave, you'll have to leave the room.* | *You can come if you promise to behave yourself.*
━━ PHRASES ━━
3 well-behaved doing things in a correct, polite way: *The students were very well-behaved in class.*
4 badly behaved doing things in a

way that is not correct or polite: *I have never met such badly behaved kids.*
behavior ✳ /bɪˈheɪvjɚ/ [noun] the way in which someone behaves: *Your behavior in class will affect your final grade.*
☛ Do not say "a behavior" or "behaviors." Say **behavior.**
behind[1] ✳ /bɪˈhaɪnd/ [preposition]
1 at the back of someone or something: *There was a big yard behind the house.* | *Look behind you.*
↪ Compare **in front** at FRONT[1].
2 less successful than someone or something else: *He is behind the rest of the class in math.*
↪ Compare AHEAD (definition 3).
↪ See also **behind schedule** at SCHEDULE[1].
behind[2] ✳ [adverb]
1 in or to a position at the back of someone or something: *The other runners were **close behind**.*
↪ Compare **in front** at FRONT[1].
2 in a place that someone has left: *Emily, please **stay behind** after class.* | *I realized I had **left** my books **behind**.*
beige[1] /beɪʒ/ [noun] a very light brown color: *She often wears beige.*
beige[2] [adjective; no comparative] of the color beige: *a beige scarf*
being[1] ✳ /ˈbiɪŋ/ [verb] the present participle of BE[1]
being[2] [noun] a person, or a creature that is like a person: *She believes she has talked to beings from other planets.*
↪ See also HUMAN BEING.
belief ✳ /bɪˈlif/ [noun]
1 a strong feeling that something is true or exists: *Her **belief in** God remained strong.*
2 something that you believe is true or right: *His religious beliefs don't allow him to eat meat.*

━━━━━━━━━━━━━━━━━━━━
/i/ **see** /ɪ/ **big** /eɪ/ **day** /ɛ/ **get** /æ/ **hat**
/ɑ/ **father, hot** /ʌ/ **up** /ə/ **about** /ɔ/ **saw**
/oʊ/ **hope** /ʊ/ **book** /u/ **too** /aɪ/ **I** /aʊ/ **how**
/ɔɪ/ **boy** /ɚ/ **bird** /ɚ/ **teacher** /ɪr/ **ear** /ɛr/ **air**
/ɑr/ **far** /ɔr/ **more** /ʊr/ **tour** /aɪr/ **fire**
/aʊɚ/ **hour** /θ/ **nothing** /ð/ **mother** /ʃ/ **she**
/ʒ/ **measure** /tʃ/ **church** /dʒ/ **jump** /ŋ/ **long**

believe * /bɪ'liv/ [*verb;* **believed, believing**]
  1 to think that what someone says is true: *He says he didn't do it, and I believe him.* | *They believed his story.*
  2 to think that something is probably true: *I believe that he is coming tomorrow.* | *I don't believe she's home* (=I think she is not home).
  ☛ Don't say "I believe she isn't home."
  ═══ PHRASES ═══
  3 I can't believe used to say that you are very surprised or shocked by something: *I can't believe they didn't offer you lunch.* | *I couldn't believe how mean he was.*
  4 believe it or not used to say that something is true although it is surprising: *I'm his aunt, believe it or not.*
  ═══ PHRASAL VERB ═══
  believe in [*phrasal verb*]
  5 to think that someone or something exists: *I believe in God.* | *Do you believe in miracles?*
  6 to think that something is good or right: *My father believes in hard work.*
  7 to think that someone is honest or able to succeed: *His students still believe in him.* | *You must **believe in yourself**.*

bell * /bɛl/ [*noun*]
  1 an electrical or metal object that makes a ringing sound, used as a signal that it is time to do something
  2 a musical instrument that is hollow and made of metal, with a piece of metal hanging inside it that hits the outer part to make a sound: *The church bell was ringing.*

belly /'bɛli/ [*noun; plural* **bellies**] *INFORMAL* someone's stomach: *a big belly*

belong * /bɪ'lɔŋ/ [*verb;* **belonged, belonging**]
  1 to be in the right place or situation: *Your bicycle belongs outside, not in the house.* | *Put those tools back where they belong.* | *Violent programs don't belong on television.*
  ═══ PHRASAL VERB ═══
  belong to [*phrasal verb*]
  2 to be owned by someone: **belong to someone** ▸ *The house belongs to my aunt.* | *Who do these books belong to?*

3 to be part of a group or organization: **belong to something** ▸ *I belonged to several student organizations.*

belongings /bɪ'lɔŋɪŋz/ [*plural noun*] the things you own, especially things that you are carrying or traveling with: *They put all their belongings in the truck.*

below¹ * /bɪ'loʊ/ [*preposition*]
  1 in a lower POSITION than someone or something; *opposite* ABOVE: *They live in the apartment below ours.* | *The files are on that shelf below the window.*
  2 less than a particular amount, level, or number; *opposite* ABOVE: *Keep your speed below fifty miles per hour.* | *Your work is **below average** (=worse than the average).*

below² * [*adverb*] in, into, or toward a lower position, level, amount, etc.; *opposite* ABOVE: *The people on the floor below are noisy.* | *Temperatures may fall to zero or below.*

belt * /bɛlt/ [*noun*] a thin piece of cloth or leather that you tie or fasten around your waist

bench /bɛntʃ/ [*noun; plural* **benches**] a long seat that several people can sit on, usually outdoors: *a park bench*

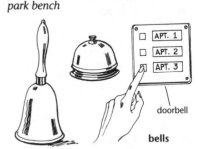

doorbell

bells

bend¹ * /bɛnd/ [*verb;* **bent, bending**]
  1 to lean your body forward and downward: ***Bend over** and touch your toes.* | *She **bent down** to put on her shoes.* | **bend over something** ▸ *He bent over the sink to do the dishes.*
  2 to move a part of your body so that it is not straight: *Stand with your knees slightly bent.* | *Bend your arms and touch your shoulders.*

3 to force something into a curved shape: *He bent the antenna on my car.*
4 to change from a straight line to a curved shape: *The road bends to the left just outside the town.*
  ⇨ *See also* BENT².

The trees are **bending** in the wind.

He's **bending over**.

bend² * [*noun*] a place where something bends, especially a road: *He slowed down at the **bend in** the road.* I *There's a gas station just **around the bend**.*

beneath * /bɪ'niθ/ [*adverb, preposition*] FORMAL below something or covered by something; synonym UNDER: *They rested beneath the trees.* I *A rock fell from the cliff onto the beach beneath.*

benefit¹ /'bɛnəfɪt/ [*noun*] an advantage that is gained from something: *the **benefits of** regular exercise* I *All this was done **for your benefit** (=to help you).*

benefit² [*verb; benefited, benefiting or benefitted, benefitting*] to gain an advantage from something: *If health care is improved, everyone will benefit.*
☛ Do not say that something "will benefit to you." Say that it **will benefit you** or that **you will benefit from it**.

bent¹ * /bɛnt/ [*verb*] the past tense and past participle of BEND¹

bent² [*adjective; more bent, most bent*] curved, especially as a result of being damaged; opposite STRAIGHT: *The knives and forks were old and bent.*

beret /bə'reɪ/ [*noun*] a soft hat that is round and flat: *She wore a blue beret.*

berry * /'bɛri/ [*noun; plural* **berries**] a small, soft, round fruit with seeds, which is usually red or purple

beside * /bɪ'saɪd/ [*preposition*]
1 close to the side of someone or something: *They were selling fruit beside the road.* I *I sat down beside my mother.*
☛ Do not say "I sat besides her." Say **I sat beside her.**
  ⇨ *See also* **next to** *at* NEXT¹. ⇨ *See the picture at* POSITION.
2 when seen with and compared to another person or thing: *He was a tall man, but looked small beside his father.*

besides¹ * /bɪ'saɪdz/ [*preposition*] in addition to someone or something: *I have other people to consider besides you.* I **besides doing something** ▶ *Besides teaching math, he coaches baseball.*

besides² * [*adverb*]
1 used to give an additional reason or point that you think is important: *I wouldn't enjoy the show. Besides, it's too expensive.*
2 in addition to the people or things you have mentioned: *He knows about art, and a lot more besides.*

best¹ * /bɛst/ [*adjective*]
1 better than anyone or anything else; the superlative of GOOD¹: *This is the best meal I have ever tasted.* I *She was wearing her best clothes.* I *The best athletes will receive medals.*
2 most suitable or most likely to be successful: *Are you sure that's **the best thing to do**?*

━━ PHRASES ━━
3 your best friend the friend you like the most and spend the most time with: *Anna was my best friend when we were in school.*
4 best of all used to say what is the best thing about a situation: *There was a tennis court, a baseball field, and best of all, a swimming pool.*

/i/ **see** /ɪ/ **big** /eɪ/ **day** /ɛ/ **get** /æ/ **hat**
/ɑ/ **father, hot** /ʌ/ **up** /ə/ **about** /ɔ/ **saw**
/oʊ/ **hope** /ʊ/ **book** /u/ **too** /aɪ/ **I** /aʊ/ **how**
/ɔɪ/ **boy** /ɝ/ **bird** /ɚ/ **teacher** /ɪr/ **ear** /ɛr/ **air**
/ɑr/ **far** /ɔr/ **more** /ʊr/ **tour** /aɪr/ **fire**
/aʊɚ/ **hour** /θ/ **nothing** /ð/ **mother** /ʃ/ **she**
/ʒ/ **measure** /tʃ/ **church** /dʒ/ **jump** /ŋ/ **long**

5 best wishes used as a greeting at the end of a letter or in a birthday card: *Best wishes from all the family.* | *With our very best wishes for a happy birthday.*

best[2] * [*adverb*]
  1 the superlative of WELL[1]: *I work best early in the morning.*
  2 more than any other thing or person: *Which of the boys do you like best?* | *He likes chocolate best of all.*

best[3] * [*noun*]
  1 the best
    a the best possible thing or things: *Your parents want the best for you.* | *This is the best we can do* (=we cannot do anything better) *right now.*
    b the person or thing that is best or that does something best: *If you're buying a computer, buy the best.* | *He is the best of our new employees.*
  ═══ PHRASE ═══
  2 do your best to try very hard: *I'm sorry you didn't win, but I'm sure you did your best.*

best man /'bɛst 'mæn/ [*noun*] a man who has been specially chosen by a man who is getting married, to take part in the wedding and make some of the arrangements: *My cousin has asked me to be his best man.*

bet[1] /bɛt/ [*verb*; **bets, bet** or **betted, betting**]
  1 to risk money by playing cards, guessing the result of a race, or other action: *What horse did you bet on?* | *He bet $10 on our team.* | *I bet you $5 that she won't dance with you.*
  ═══ PHRASE ═══
  2 I bet SPOKEN used to say what you think happened, is happening, or will happen: *I bet they'll be glad to see us.* | *I bet he was angry when you told him what happened.*

bet[2] [*noun*] the action of risking money, or the money that is risked: *She climbed the tree on a bet* (=because of a bet between her and someone else). | *I placed a $5 bet on Silver Star.*

betray /bɪ'treɪ/ [*verb*; **betrays, betrayed, betraying**] to harm your country, a friend, or a group that you are a member of, by helping an enemy or telling a secret: *I would rather die than betray my country.*

better[1] * /'bɛtɚ/ [*adjective*]
  1 the comparative of GOOD[1]: *Your bicycle is much better than mine.* | *She's a better dancer than her sister.* | *Your English is getting better.*
  2 more suitable or likely to be successful: *It would be better to go by car.* | *A soft pencil is better for drawing.*
  3 well again after an illness: *I hope you feel better soon.* | *He's getting better every day.*
  ⇨ See the synonym note at RECOVER.
  ═══ PHRASE ═══
  4 better off in a better situation or position than you were before, for example by having more money: *He's better off now that he has a new job.*

better[2] * [*adverb*]
  1 the comparative of WELL[1]: *She plays tennis much better than I do.*
  2 more than someone or something else, or more than before: *I like baseball better than football.*
  ═══ PHRASE ═══
  3 had better used to say what someone should do: *I'd better write to him soon.* | *I'd better go or I'll be late.*
  ☛ Do not say that someone "had better not to do something." Say that he or she **had better not do something.**

between[1] * /bɪ'twin/ [*preposition*]
  1 in the space that separates two people, places, or things: *I was sitting between my mother and father.*
  2 in the period that separates two times or events: *Come today between two and four.* | *the years between 1980 and 1995*
  3 within the range that separates two amounts, ages, etc.: *It will cost between $500 and $750.*
  4 used to show the two people or groups involved in a fight, game, argument, etc.: *a game between Florida State and Boston University* | *a war between two countries*
  5 used to show how two people, places, or things are related: *There's a great difference between high school and college.* | *a flight between Denver and Seattle*

6 used to show that something involves or is shared by two people: *His money was divided equally between his two children.*

7 used to show the two things involved when a choice is made: *We had to choose between English and Spanish.*

USAGE   between, among

Use **between** to talk about two people, things, times, etc.: *The students are between 16 and 19 years old.* I *Her umbrella was caught between the elevator doors.* I *I'll arrive between 11:30 and 12:30.*

Use **among** to talk about three or more people, things, etc.: *They shared the candy among the five children.* I *I could see a house among the trees.*

between² [*adverb*]

━ PHRASE ━━

in between in the space, period, or range that separates two things: *My classes end at 2:00 and dinner is at 5:30, so I have time in between for sports.*

beware /bɪ'wɛr/ [*verb*] FORMAL

━ PHRASE ━━

beware (of) used to warn someone about something dangerous: *Travelers should beware of pickpockets.* I *Beware of the dog!*

⊃ *See also* **be careful (of)** *at* CAREFUL.

bewildering /bɪ'wɪldərɪŋ/ [*adjective;* **more bewildering, most bewildering**] making you feel confused: *There was a bewildering choice of desserts.*

beyond¹ * /bi'ɑnd/ [*preposition*]

1 past something, or on the other side of it: *Beyond the river we could see a great forest.* I *She lived beyond the city limits.*

2 past or later than a particular time or event: *I don't have plans beyond next weekend.*

3 outside a particular range or limit: *The work was beyond his abilities.* I *The handle was **beyond my reach** (=too far away for me to reach it).*

━ PHRASE ━━

4 beyond someone too difficult for someone to understand: *Algebra is beyond me.*

beyond² * [*adverb*]

1 past something or on the other side of it: *He looked at the mountains and wondered what lay beyond.*

2 past or later than a particular time or event: *We are planning for the next year and beyond.*

biased ⊤ /'baɪəst/ [*adjective;* **more biased, most biased**] unfairly influenced by ideas about whether a situation, person, or group is good or bad: *The judge's decision was biased.* I *That's a **biased opinion**.*

bib /bɪb/ [*noun*] a piece of cloth or plastic that is tied around a young child's neck to keep his or her clothes clean while eating

Bible or **bible** /'baɪbəl/ [*noun*] the name of the holy book of the Christian and Jewish religions: *He read a passage from the Bible.* I *a young girl holding a bible*

biblical /'bɪblɪkəl/ [*adjective; no comparative*] from the Bible: *a biblical name*

bicycle * /'baɪsɪkəl/ [*noun*] a vehicle with two wheels, a seat, and pedals that you push with your feet to make it move; *synonym* BIKE: *I **ride my bicycle** to work every day.* I *A boy **on a bicycle** came around the corner.* I *She came **by bicycle**.* ☛ Do not say "I went by my bicycle." Say **I went by bicycle** or **I went on my bicycle**.

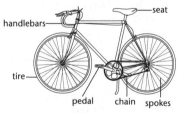

a bicycle

bid¹ /bɪd/ [*verb;* **bids, bid, bid, bidding**]

1 to offer to buy something for a

/i/ **see**	/ɪ/ **big**	/eɪ/ **day**	/ɛ/ **get**	/æ/ **hat**
/ɑ/ **father, hot**	/ʌ/ **up**	/ə/ **about**	/ɔ/ **saw**	
/oʊ/ **hope**	/ʊ/ **book**	/u/ **too**	/aɪ/ **I**	/aʊ/ **how**
/ɔɪ/ **boy**	/ɚ/ **bird**	/ɚ/ **teacher**	/ɪr/ **ear**	/ɛr/ **air**
/ɑr/ **far**	/ɔr/ **more**	/ʊr/ **tour**	/aɪr/ **fire**	
/aʊɚ/ **hour**	/θ/ **nothing**	/ð/ **mother**	/ʃ/ **she**	
/ʒ/ **measure**	/tʃ/ **church**	/dʒ/ **jump**	/ŋ/ **long**	

particular amount of money: *I want to bid on the vase.* | *He bid $500 for the necklace.*
2 to offer to do a job for a particular price: *Several companies are bidding for the contract.*

bid² [*noun*] an offer of an amount of money to buy something: *I made a bid for the painting.*

big * /bɪg/ [*adjective; bigger, biggest*]
1 having a size that uses a lot of space; *opposites* LITTLE, SMALL: *He was a big strong man.* | *I want to live in a big city.* | *We need a bigger house.*
2 important or serious; *opposites* MINOR, SMALL: *You're making a big decision.* | *This is the biggest game of the season.*
3 involving a lot of people or things: *A big crowd came to watch the parade.*
4 successful or popular: *His sister is a big movie star.* | *The band is big in Peru.*
═══ PHRASE ═══
5 **big deal** INFORMAL something important: *Don't worry about being late, it's no big deal* (=it's not important).

bike /baɪk/ [*noun*]
1 a short form of BICYCLE: *Can I borrow your bike?* | *We came by bike.*
2 a short form of MOTORBIKE: *His bike ran out of gas on the highway.*

bikini /bɪˈkini/ [*noun; plural* **bikinis**] a piece of clothing with a separate top and bottom that women wear for swimming: *I don't look good in a bikini.*
↪ *Compare* BATHING SUIT.

bilingual /baɪˈlɪŋgwəl/ [*adjective; no comparative*]
1 able to speak two languages easily: *Most of these children are bilingual in English and Japanese.*
2 using or written in two languages: *I use a bilingual dictionary.*

bill¹ * /bɪl/ [*noun*]
1 a written statement of the money that is owed for goods or services: *He sent me a bill for $75.* | *a phone bill*
2 a piece of paper money: *I had a ten-dollar bill and some change.*
3 a document that will become a law if it is approved by the people who make a country's laws: *The bill was passed by Congress.*

bill² [*verb; billed, billing*] to send someone a bill for goods or services: *We'll bill you at the end of every month.*

billboard /ˈbɪlˌbɔrd/ [*noun*] a large sign on which advertisements are shown: *The road was lined with billboards.*

billion * /ˈbɪlyən/ [*number, noun*] one thousand million: 1,000,000,000: *The full cost will be four billion dollars.* | *billions of dollars*

bin /bɪn/ [*noun*] a large container for storing something: *The grain was stored in bins.*

binary /ˈbaɪnəri/ [*adjective; no comparative*] relating to the system of counting that uses only 1 and 0: *Computers use the binary system.*

bind /baɪnd/ [*verb; bound, binding*] to tie someone or something with string, rope, etc.: *The broom was made of twigs bound together with cords.*

binder /ˈbaɪndɚ/ [*noun*] an object like a book for holding loose pieces of paper together, with a stiff cover and metal rings inside it: *Keep all your English homework in a binder.*
↪ *See the picture at* CLASSROOM.

bingo /ˈbɪŋgoʊ/ [*noun*] a game in which you match numbers on a card with numbers that are called out. The first person to match a set of the numbers in a straight line wins: *We played bingo in English class to help us learn numbers.*

binoculars
/bəˈnɑkyəlɚz/ [*plural noun*] a pair of tubes with curved pieces of glass in them, that you look through to see distant things: *a pair of very powerful binoculars*

binoculars

biography /baɪˈɑgrəfi/ [*noun; plural* **biographies**] the story of someone's life, written by another person: *She has written a biography of President Bush.*
↪ *Compare* AUTOBIOGRAPHY.

biological /ˌbaɪəˈlɑdʒɪkəl/ [*adjective; no comparative*] relating to living things or the study of biology: *Digestion is a biological process.*

biologist /baɪˈɑlədʒɪst/ [noun] a scientist who studies living things, such as animals and plants

biology /baɪˈɑlədʒi/ [noun] the science that deals with living things, such as animals and plants: *a biology class*

bird * /bɜrd/ [noun] a creature with wings and feathers

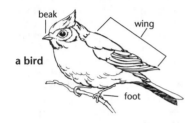

beak
wing
a bird
foot

birth * /bɜrθ/ [noun]
1 when a baby is born: *The baby weighed seven pounds at birth.* | *She had helped with the birth of our son.*
2 the social or family conditions into which someone is born: *She is Russian by birth, but she lives in the U.S.*
— PHRASES —
3 **give birth (to)** to have a baby: *A day later she gave birth to a healthy boy.* | *The vet came to help our cow give birth.*
4 **date of birth** the date when you were born: *Please put your date of birth on the form.*

birthday * /ˈbɜrθˌdeɪ/ [noun; plural birthdays]
1 the day of the year on which someone was born: *It's my birthday tomorrow.* | *They took me out for dinner on my birthday.* | *I'm going to my nephew's birthday party.*
— PHRASE —
2 **happy birthday** used to wish someone happiness on his or her birthday: *Happy birthday, Dad.* | *I just called to say happy birthday.*
⇨ Compare ANNIVERSARY.

birthplace /ˈbɜrθˌpleɪs/ [noun] the place where someone was born: *Many people visit the poet's birthplace.*

biscuit /ˈbɪskɪt/ [noun] a kind of bread baked in small round pieces and eaten hot: *We had biscuits for breakfast.*

bishop or **Bishop** /ˈbɪʃəp/ [noun, name] an important priest in some Christian churches: *the Bishop of London*

bit[1] * /bɪt/ [noun]
1 a small piece or amount of something: *There were bits of paper all over the table.* | *You have a bit of of food on your chin.*
2 the smallest unit of information that a computer stores: *How many bits are there in a byte?*
— PHRASES —
3 **a (little) bit** slightly: *I'm a bit busy right now.* | *She's a little bit upset.*
4 **quite a bit** a lot: *A new car would cost quite a bit.*
5 **bit by bit** slowly and gradually: *Bit by bit his confidence increased.*

bit[2] * [verb] the past tense of BITE[1]

bite[1] * /baɪt/ [verb; bit, bitten, biting]
1 to cut something with your teeth: *I was afraid the dog would bite me.* | *He bit into the sandwich.*
2 if an insect bites, it takes blood from you: *Most spiders don't bite people.*

bite[2] * [noun]
1 an act of biting something: *She took a bite of the cookie.*
2 a mark where an insect has taken blood from you: *We were covered in mosquito bites.*

bitten * /ˈbɪtən/ [verb] the past participle of BITE[1]

bitter * /ˈbɪtər/ [adjective; more bitter, most bitter]
1 having a sour and often unpleasant taste: *The coffee tasted bitter.*
2 angry and disappointed: *She is bitter about the way she has been treated.*
3 extremely cold and unpleasant: *January brought bitter weather.*

bitterly /ˈbɪtərli/ [adverb]
1 in a way that shows that you are disappointed and angry or unhappy: *She complained bitterly about not being invited.*

/i/ **see** /ɪ/ **big** /eɪ/ **day** /ɛ/ **get** /æ/ **hat**
/ɑ/ **father, hot** /ʌ/ **up** /ə/ **about** /ɔ/ **saw**
/oʊ/ **hope** /ʊ/ **book** /u/ **too** /aɪ/ **I** /aʊ/ **how**
/ɔɪ/ **boy** /ɜr/ **bird** /ər/ **teacher** /ɪr/ **ear** /ɛr/ **air**
/ɑr/ **far** /ɔr/ **more** /ʊr/ **tour** /aɪr/ **fire**
/aʊər/ **hour** /θ/ **nothing** /ð/ **mother** /ʃ/ **she**
/ʒ/ **measure** /tʃ/ **church** /dʒ/ **jump** /ŋ/ **long**

— PHRASE —

2 bitterly cold extremely cold: *a bitterly cold December day*

black[1] * /blæk/ [*noun*]

1 the color of the sky at night: *People usually wear black at funerals.*

2 also **Black;** someone with brown skin, whose family originally came from Africa: *There are nine other Blacks in my class.*

⇨ Compare AFRICAN AMERICAN.

— PHRASE —

3 in black and white in black, white, and gray, without any other colors: *Most of the pictures are in black and white.*

black[2] * [*adjective*]

1 [**blacker, blackest**] of the color black: *He rode a black horse.* | *I can't find my black dress.*

2 [*no comparative*] also **Black;** used to describe someone with brown skin, whose family originally came from Africa: *My teacher is Black.* | *a black person*

⇨ Compare AFRICAN-AMERICAN.

3 [*no comparative*] black coffee has no milk in it: *Do you like your coffee black or with cream?*

black-and-blue /ˌblækənˈblu/ [*adjective; no comparative*] with dark marks on the skin from being hurt: *My knees were black-and-blue after I fell.*

black-and-white /ˌblækənˈwaɪt/ [*adjective; no comparative*] with pictures in black, white, and gray, without any other colors: *He has an old black-and-white TV.* | *black-and-white photography*

blackberry /ˈblækˌbɛri/ [*noun; plural* **blackberries**] a small, soft, blue-black fruit that grows on low plants

blackbird /ˈblækˌbɚd/ [*noun*] a bird with black feathers

blackboard /ˈblækˌbɔrd/ [*noun*] a large dark board or surface that you write on with chalk, especially in a CLASSROOM; *synonym* CHALKBOARD

black eye /ˌblæk ˈaɪ/ [*noun; plural* **black eyes**] a dark mark around someone's eye, where it has been hit: *He gave the other boy a black eye.*

blade * /bleɪd/ [*noun*]

1 the sharp thin metal part of a knife or sword: *a pocket knife with six blades*

2 a single piece of grass: *A few blades of grass showed between the cracks in the sidewalk.*

blame[1] * /bleɪm/ [*verb;* **blamed, blaming**]

1 to think that someone or something is responsible for something bad: *Don't blame her—it was my fault.* | **blame someone for something** ▸ *Dad blamed me for the accident.* | **blame something on someone/something** ▸ *He always blames his failures on others.*

☛ Do not say that you "blame someone to do something." Say that you **blame someone for doing something.**

— PHRASE —

2 I don't blame or **you can't blame** used to say that you think that someone is being reasonable: *She's angry with him, and I don't blame her.*

blame[2] * [*noun*] when people say that someone is responsible for something bad that has happened: *I always get the blame when things go wrong.* | *They're trying to put the blame on me* (=say that I was responsible).

bland /blænd/ [*adjective;* **blander, blandest**] food that is bland does not have a strong or interesting taste: *Their diet was very bland.*

blank[1] Ⓣ /blæŋk/ [*adjective; no comparative*]

1 not containing any written information or sounds: *If you don't know the answer, just leave the space blank.* | *I need a blank tape to record the program.*

2 not showing any thought or expression: *I asked him about it, but he just looked blank.* | *He had a blank look on his face.*

blank[2] [*noun*] an empty space where something can be written: *Fill in all the blanks on the form.*

blanket /ˈblæŋkɪt/ [*noun*] a thick warm piece of cloth that you use to cover yourself, especially in bed: *She pulled the blankets up around her neck.*

⇨ See the picture at UNDER[1].

blare /blɛr/ [*verb;* **blared, blaring**] to make a loud unpleasant noise: *Car horns were blaring.* | *A radio* **blared out** *music from a window upstairs.*

blast[1] /blæst/ [*noun*]
1 a strong current of air: *A* **blast** *of hot air came from the furnace.*
2 an explosion: *The blast could be heard from miles away.*
3 a sudden loud noise: *The driver gave a blast on his horn.*

— PHRASE —
4 **(at) full blast** as loudly as possible: *He was playing his radio at full blast.*

blast[2] [*verb;* **blasted, blasting**]
1 to break rock with an explosion: *A tunnel had been blasted through the mountain.*
2 to make a lot of loud noise: *Our neighbors always blast their stereo.*

— PHRASAL VERB —
blast off [*phrasal verb*]
3 if a space vehicle blasts off, it leaves the ground: *The shuttle blasted off at noon.*

blastoff /'blæst‚ɔf/ [*noun*] when a space vehicle leaves the ground: *Three, two, one, blastoff!*

blaze[1] /bleɪz/ [*verb;* **blazed, blazing**] to burn or shine very brightly: *The sun blazed down on the fields.* | *We sat in front of a blazing fire.*

blaze[2] [*noun*]
1 a strong hot fire: *The blaze destroyed three buildings.*
2 a bright light or color: *A* **blaze** *of light came from the store windows.*

blazer /'bleɪzər/ [*noun*] a short coat that is worn with pants or a skirt, but is not part of a suit: *He wore gray pants and a dark blue blazer.*

bleach[1] /blitʃ/ [*noun*] a chemical used to make things white or very clean

bleach[2] [*verb;* **bleaches, bleached, bleaching**] to make something paler or white: *The sails were bleached by the sun.*

bleachers /'blitʃərz/ [*plural noun*] high rows of seats without backs, where people sit to watch sports events: *We were sitting high up in the bleachers.*

bleed * /blid/ [*verb;* **bled** /blɛd/, **bleeding**] to lose blood, especially through a cut in the body: *She was bleeding from a cut above her eye.*
☛ Do not say "His blood was bleeding." Say **He was bleeding.**

blend[1] /blɛnd/ [*verb;* **blended, blending**]
1 to mix two or more substances together until they become one substance: *Blend the yogurt and honey together.*
2 to look or sound pleasant together: *The cello blends beautifully with the violin.*

blend[2] [*noun*] a mixture of things or substances: *His music is a blend of new and traditional styles.*

blender /'blɛndər/ [*noun*] a small electric machine for mixing liquids or turning soft foods to liquid
↪ See the picture at APPLIANCE.

bless /blɛs/ [*verb;* **blesses, blessed, blessing**]
1 to ask God to protect someone or to make good things happen: *The priest blessed the people.*

— PHRASES —
2 **Bless you** said after someone sneezes: *"Atchoo!" "Bless you."*
3 **God bless you** used to say that you hope good things will always happen to someone: *Goodbye and God bless you.* | *God bless you for your kindness.*

blew * /blu/ [*verb*] the past tense of BLOW[1]

blind[1] * ⊤ /blaɪnd/ [*adjective;* **blinder, blindest**] unable to see: *She began to go blind.* | *He is blind in one eye.*

blind[2] ⊤ [*verb;* **blinded, blinding**] to make someone unable to see: *He was blinded in an accident.*

blind[3] [*noun*]
1 **the blind** people who are blind: *She goes to a special school for the blind.*
☛ Only use **the blind** with a plural verb in this meaning.

/i/ see	/ɪ/ big	/eɪ/ day	/ɛ/ get	/æ/ hat
/ɑ/ father, hot	/ʌ/ up	/ə/ about	/ɔ/ saw	
/oʊ/ hope	/ʊ/ book	/u/ too	/aɪ/ I	/aʊ/ how
/ɔɪ/ boy	/ɝ/ bird	/ɚ/ teacher	/ɪr/ ear	/ɛr/ air
/ɑr/ far	/ɔr/ more	/ʊr/ tour	/aɪr/ fire	
/aʊə/ hour	/θ/ nothing	/ð/ mother	/ʃ/ she	
/ʒ/ measure	/tʃ/ church	/dʒ/ jump	/ŋ/ long	

2 a cover for a window made of thin pieces of plastic or wood that are joined together: *Pull down the blinds.*
⇨ Compare SHADE[1] (definition 2).

blind date /'blaɪnd 'deɪt/ [*noun*] a romantic meeting between two people who have not met before, arranged by someone who is friends with both of them: *It was the first time I had been on a blind date.*

blindfold[1] /'blaɪnd,foʊld/ [*noun*] a cloth that covers someone's eyes so that he or she cannot see: *He tried to pull off the blindfold.*

blindfold[2] [*verb;* **blindfolded, blindfolding**] to cover someone's eyes so that he or she cannot see: *The prisoners were blindfolded.*

blindness /'blaɪndnɪs/ [*noun*] when you are not able to see: *That disease sometimes causes blindness.*

blink /blɪŋk/ [*verb;* **blinked, blinking**]
1 to close your eyes and open them again very quickly: *She blinked her eyes in the sunlight.*
2 if a light blinks, it goes on and off quickly several times: *A light on the printer started blinking.*

bliss /blɪs/ [*noun*] when you are extremely happy and comfortable: *It was bliss to sink into the tub of hot water.*

blister /'blɪstɚ/ [*noun*] a small raised sore area on your skin that forms when something rubs against it or burns it: *She had walked so far that she had blisters on her feet.*

blizzard /'blɪzɚd/ [*noun*] a severe snow storm: *We were caught in a blizzard on our way home.*

blob /blab/ [*noun*] a small amount of a thick liquid: *a blob of glue*

block[1] * 🔟 /blak/ [*noun*]
1 a solid piece of something, with straight sides: *The fish were displayed on a block of ice.* | *The kids were building a tower with wooden blocks.*
2 the distance or area between two streets in a town: *The movie theater's just two blocks from here.* | *There were a lot of big old houses on our block.*

block[2] * [*verb;* **blocked, blocking**]
1 to stop movement along a road, pipe,

etc., by being in it or putting something in it: *Police blocked the roads to the airport.* | *Something's blocking up the drains.*
2 to stop something from happening or developing: *They've blocked the progress of our plans.*

blonde[1] or **blond** /bland/ [*adjective;* **blonder, blondest**] having light-colored hair: *She was tall and blonde.* | *He has blond hair.*

blonde[2] [*noun*] a woman with light-colored hair

blood * /blʌd/ [*noun*]
1 the red liquid that flows through the body of a person or animal
2 someone's family and social group: *There is some Turkish blood in the family.*

blood donor /'blʌd ,doʊnɚ/ [*noun*] someone who gives blood to be used to help other people

bloodshot /'blʌd,ʃat/ [*adjective;* **more bloodshot, most bloodshot**] if you have bloodshot eyes, your eyes are red, especially because you are tired or sick: *Your eyes are all bloodshot.*

bloodstream /'blʌd,strim/ [*noun*] the blood flowing around in your body: *It will take a while for the medicine to get into your bloodstream.*

blood type /'blʌd ,taɪp/ [*noun*] one of the groups into which human blood is divided: *Do you know your blood type?*

bloom[1] /blum/ [*verb;* **bloomed, blooming**] if plants bloom, they have open flowers: *The roses bloom in June.*

bloom[2] [*noun*]
1 a flower that is open: *What beautiful blooms!*

═══ PHRASE ═══
2 **be in (full) bloom** to have open flowers: *The roses were in full bloom.*

blossom[1] /'blasəm/ [*noun*] a flower or flowers on a tree or bush: *cherry blossoms* | *The trees were all in blossom* (=their flowers were open).

blossom[2] [*verb;* **blossomed, blossoming**] if a tree blossoms, it has open flowers: *They sat beneath a blossoming apple tree.*

blouse /blaʊs/ [*noun*] a woman's shirt
⇨ *See the picture at* CLOTHING.

blow[1] * /bloʊ/ [*verb;* **blew, blown, blowing**]
1 to breathe out hard, making a current of air, or to move something in this way: *He **blew on** his coffee.* | *She blew her hair away from her face.*
2 if the wind blows, it moves the air: *A strong wind was blowing.*
3 to move by the force of the wind, or to be moved by the wind: *The paper blew across the road.* | *I thought my hat would be **blown away**.*
4 to make a noise by sending air through an object: *The whistle blew at the end of the game.* | *The referee blew his whistle.*

— PHRASES
5 **blow your nose** to clear the inside of your nose by breathing hard through it, into a soft cloth or paper: *Stop sniffing and blow your nose.*
6 **blow it** SPOKEN to fail by making a mistake: *This is your best chance, so **don't blow it!***

— PHRASAL VERBS
blow out [*phrasal verb*]
7 to make a flame go out by blowing on it: **blow something out** ▸ *I'll help you blow the candles out.* | **blow out something** ▸ *He blew out the match.*
blow up [*phrasal verb*]
8 to destroy something or be destroyed in an explosion: *The bridge **blew up** just after we crossed it.* | **blow up something** ▸ *They planned to blow up the factory.* | **blow something up** ▸ *They blew the factory up.*
9 to fill something with a gas or air; synonym INFLATE: **blow up something** ▸ *Help me blow up the balloons for the party.* | **blow something up** ▸ *We stopped at a garage to blow the tires up.*

blow[2] * [*noun*]
1 when someone or something is hit hard: *He received a blow to the head.*
2 something bad that happens and makes someone very sad or disappointed, or less confident: *Her son's death was a terrible blow to her.*

blown * /bloʊn/ [*verb*] the past participle of BLOW[1]

blue[1] * /blu/ [*noun*]
1 the color of the sky when there are no clouds: *His eyes were a clear blue*
2 **blues** [*plural*] a kind of slow, sad music that was developed by black musicians in the U.S.: *He loves to play the blues.* | *a blues singer*

— PHRASE
3 **have the blues** or **get the blues** INFORMAL to feel or become sad: *She was always kind to me when I had the blues.*

blue[2] * [*adjective;* **bluer, bluest**]
1 of the color blue: *a **dark blue** shirt*
2 INFORMAL sad: *You're looking kind of blue—what's the matter?*

blueberry /ˈblu,bɛri/ [*noun; plural* **blueberries**] a small, round, blue fruit that grows on low bushes

blunt /blʌnt/ [*adjective;* **blunter, bluntest**] without a sharp point or edge: *This knife's too blunt.* | *a blunt pencil*
⇨ *Compare* DULL (definition 2).

blurred /blɜrd/ [*adjective;* **more blurred, most blurred**] not clear, and without definite edges: *The photo was a little blurred.* | *blurred images*

blush[1] /blʌʃ/ [*verb;* **blushes, blushed, blushing**] to become pink in the face because you are embarrassed: *The boys were trying to make her blush.*

blush[2] [*noun*] a pink or red substance that women put on their cheeks

board[1] * /bɔrd/ [*noun*]
1 a long flat piece of wood with straight sides: *Some boards were missing from the floor.*
2 a flat piece of wood, cardboard, or plastic that is used for a special purpose: *She put the herbs on the **cutting board**.* | *I looked at the **bulletin board**.* | *a **chess board*** | *I like playing **board games** (=games that are played on a board).*
3 a group of people who make decisions and rules for an organization,

/i/ **see**	/ɪ/ **big**	/eɪ/ **day**	/ɛ/ **get**	/æ/ **hat**
/ɑ/ **father, hot**	/ʌ/ **up**	/ə/ **about**	/ɔ/ **saw**	
/oʊ/ **hope**	/ʊ/ **book**	/u/ **too**	/aɪ/ **I**	/aʊ/ **how**
/ɔɪ/ **boy**	/ɝ/ **bird**	/ɚ/ **teacher**	/ɪr/ **ear**	/ɛr/ **air**
/ɑr/ **far**	/ɔr/ **more**	/ʊr/ **tour**	/aɪr/ **fire**	
/aʊɚ/ **hour**	/θ/ **nothing**	/ð/ **mother**	/ʃ/ **she**	
/ʒ/ **measure**	/tʃ/ **church**	/dʒ/ **jump**	/ŋ/ **long**	

especially a business: *She is **on the
school board**. | the company's **Board of
Directors***

4 the meals that are provided at a
place where you stay, and must be
paid for: *Students pay $500 a month for
room and board.*

☛ Do not say "It's $300 a month for
the board." Say It's $300 a month for
board.

══ PHRASE ══

5 on board on a ship, plane, or train:
*There were 300 passengers on board the
plane.*

board² [*verb*; **boarded, boarding**]

1 to go onto a ship, plane, or train: *We
boarded the ship at noon.*

2 if a ship, plane, or train is boarding,
people are going onto it: *Flight 301 is
now boarding at Gate 10.*

3 to stay in someone's home and pay
for your room and meals: *I **boarded
with** a Greek family on Maple Street.*

══ PHRASAL VERB ══

board up [*phrasal verb*]

4 to put boards over a door, window,
etc.: **board up something** ▸ *We
boarded up the windows to protect the
house during the hurricane.*

boarding school /'bɔrdɪŋ ˌskul/ [*noun*]
a school where the students live as well
as study: *When I was ten, I went away to
boarding school.*

boast /boʊst/ [*verb*; **boasted, boasting**]
to talk too proudly about what you
have, what you can do, or what you
have done; synonym BRAG: *She was
always **boasting about** her grades. | He
boasted that he could run faster than
anyone else.*

boastful /'boʊstfəl/ [*adjective*; **more
boastful, most boastful**] talking too
proudly about what you have, what
you can do, or what you have done: *He
was a great athlete, but he was boastful.*

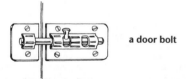

a door bolt

boat ∗ /boʊt/ [*noun*]

1 a thing in which people travel across
water: *We traveled up the coast in a
fishing boat. | If you go **by boat** it will
take five days.*

↪ Compare SHIP¹.

══ PHRASE ══

2 be in the same boat to be in the
same difficult or unpleasant situation
as someone else: *I got some advice from
other people who were in the same boat.*

bob /bab/ [*verb*; **bobs, bobbed, bobbing**]
to move up and down with small quick
movements: *The boats **bobbed up and
down** behind the great ship.*

body ∗ /'badi/ [*noun*; *plural* **bodies**]

1 the whole of a person or animal,
with all its physical parts: *My whole
body felt warm and relaxed. | His **body
temperature** was normal.*

2 a dead person; synonym CORPSE: *His
body was found by a neighbor.*

3 FORMAL all the people who belong to a
group: *The **student body** elects two
representatives.*

bodybuilding /'badiˌbɪldɪŋ/ [*noun*] the
activity of developing your muscles by
lifting heavy weights: *He is the world
bodybuilding champion.*

bodyguard /'badiˌgard/ [*noun*]
someone whose job is to protect an
important person: *The movie star was
surrounded by bodyguards.*

boil ∗ /bɔɪl/ [*verb*; **boiled, boiling**]

1 if water boils or you boil it, it
becomes very hot, has bubbles in it,
and begins to turn into steam: *I'll boil
some water for tea. | Is the water boiling
yet? | The **boiling point** of water is 212°
Fahrenheit, or 100° Celsius.*

2 to cook food in boiling water: *Boil the
rice for twenty minutes. | a boiled egg*

↪ See the synonym note at COOK¹.

bold /boʊld/ [*adjective*; **bolder, boldest**]
brave, confident, and determined:
*Steven was the boldest of the three boys. |
He had made a bold decision.*

bolt¹ /boʊlt/ [*noun*]

1 a bar of metal that you slide across
the edge of a door to hold it shut

2 a screw without a point

↪ See the picture at TOOL.

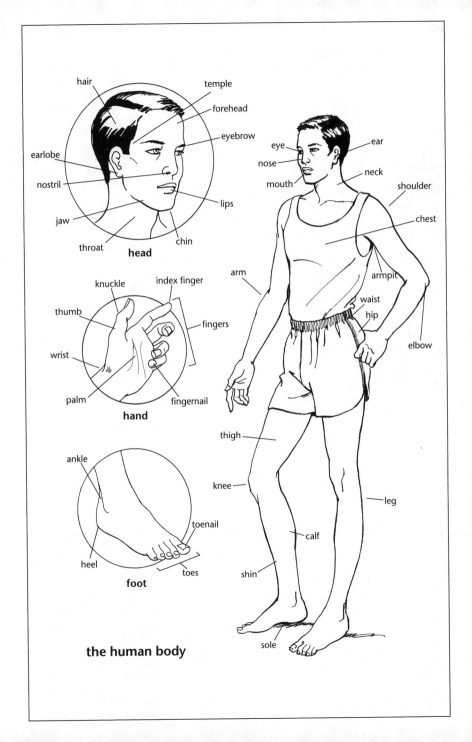

hair

temple

forehead

eyebrow

earlobe

nostril

jaw

throat

head

eye

nose

mouth

ear

neck

shoulder

chest

armpit

arm

waist

hip

elbow

chin

lips

knuckle

index finger

thumb

fingers

wrist

palm

fingernail

hand

ankle

toenail

thigh

knee

leg

heel

toes

calf

foot

shin

sole

the human body

bolt[2] [*verb;* **bolted, bolting**]
1 to fasten a door or window with a special bar of metal: *He shut the door and bolted it.*
2 to fasten things together with bolts: *The chairs were bolted to the floor.*
3 to suddenly run very fast: *The horse bolted when its rider fell off.* | *He bolted from the room.*

bomb[1] * /bɑm/ [*noun*] a weapon that kills or destroys by exploding: *The planes dropped bombs on the town.* | *The bomb went off in a crowded mall.*

bomb[2] * [*verb;* **bombed, bombing**] to attack a place with bombs: *Enemy aircraft bombed the town.*

bomber /'bɑmɚ/ [*noun*]
1 a plane that drops bombs: *He flew a bomber in the war.*
2 someone who explodes a bomb: *The bomber has not been caught.*

bone[1] * /boʊn/ [*noun*] the white, hard parts in a human's or animal's body: *There are many small bones in the foot.* | *ancient tools made of bone*

bone[2] [*verb;* **boned, boning**] to remove the bones from meat or fish: *I'd like four boned chicken breasts, please.*

bonfire /'bɑnˌfaɪr/ [*noun*] a large outdoor fire

bonnet /'bɑnɪt/ [*noun*] a hat that ties under the chin: *a baby bonnet*

bonus /'boʊnəs/ [*noun; plural* **bonuses**] something extra that you get, especially money: *All the workers received a special bonus.*

bony /'boʊni/ [*adjective;* **bonier, boniest**] very thin, so that the shape of your bones can be seen: *He had long bony fingers.*

boo[1] /bu/ [*verb;* **boos, booed, booing**] to say "boo" loudly to show you do not like like a performer, speaker, etc.: *The band was booed by the audience.*

boo[2] [*interjection*]
1 a sound you make to show you do not like a performer, speaker, etc.: *Loud boos came from the audience.*
2 a word used to frighten someone who does not know you are there: *She jumped out from behind the door and shouted "Boo!"*

book[1] * /bʊk/ [*noun*] a piece of writing printed on many pieces of paper that are fastened together inside a cover: *She was reading a book about dinosaurs.* | *Take care of your school books.* | *a new book by Stephen King*

book[2] [*verb;* **booked, booking**] to arrange for a restaurant table, a hotel room, etc., to be kept available for you; *synonym* RESERVE: *I've booked us a room at the Hilton Hotel.* | *All the hotels are fully booked* (=there were no rooms available).

bookcase /'bʊkˌkeɪs/ [*noun*] a piece of furniture in which books are kept
⇨ *See the pictures at* OFFICE *and* CLASSROOM.

booklet /'bʊklɪt/ [*noun*] a small book with a paper cover, containing information: *The doctor's office had booklets on lots of health topics.*

bookmark /'bʊkˌmɑrk/ [*noun*] something that you put inside a book so that it will open at the right page: *He used his train ticket as a bookmark.*

bookshelf /'bʊkˌʃɛlf/ [*noun; plural* **bookshelves** /'bʊkˌʃɛlvz/] a shelf on which books are kept: *My office needs more bookshelves.*
⇨ *See the picture at* OFFICE.

bookstore /'bʊkˌstɔr/ [*noun*] a store that sells books

boom /bum/ [*noun*] a sudden, loud, deep noise: *The tree fell to the ground with a loud boom.*

boot * /but/ [*noun*] a shoe that covers your whole foot and part of your leg: *a pair of hiking boots* | *winter boots*
⇨ *See the picture at* CLOTHING.

booth /buθ/ [*noun; plural* **booths** /buðz/]
1 a small structure: *a phone booth* | *a ticket booth*
2 one of a set of tables along a restaurant wall that have long seats with soft covers built around them: *Let's sit in that booth in the corner.*

border * /'bɔrdɚ/ [*noun*]
1 the place where two countries meet: *the border between the U.S. and Mexico*
2 a line or pattern around the edge of something: *a tablecloth with a red border*

bore[1] /bɔr/ [*verb;* **bored, boring**]
  1 to be dull and make someone feel tired and unhappy: *Classical music bores him.*
  2 to make a hole in something by pushing and turning a special tool: *He bored a hole in the wall.*

bore[2] * [*verb*] the past tense of BEAR[1]

bored * /bɔrd/ [*adjective;* **more bored, most bored**] feeling tired and annoyed because something does not interest you: *The children were bored and hungry.*

USAGE bored, boring

  Bored and **boring** are both adjectives, but only people can be **bored**: *The trip was long, and the kids got bored.* Events, speeches, activities, etc., can be **boring**, but cannot be **bored**: *The trip was long and boring.*
  You can describe another person as **boring** (although this is not polite) if he or she makes you feel **bored**: *He's so boring—all he talks about is cars!*

---

boring * /'bɔrɪŋ/ [*adjective;* **more boring, most boring**] very dull, so that you feel tired and annoyed; *opposite* INTERESTING: *I think museums are boring.*
  ⇨ *See the usage note at* BORED.

born * /bɔrn/ [*adjective; no comparative*]
  ▬ PHRASE ▬
  be born to come from your mother's body and begin life: *I was born in Korea.* | *He was born in 1902 and died in 1985.*

borne * /bɔrn/ [*verb*] the past participle of BEAR[1]

borrow * /'barou/ [*verb;* **borrowed, borrowing**]
  1 to use something that someone else owns for a short time: *Can I borrow your pen?* | **borrow something from someone** ▸ *I borrowed a ladder from my neighbor.*
  2 to receive money from a person or organization and give it back after some time: **borrow something from someone** ▸ *We borrowed $4,000 from the bank.*
  ⇨ *See the usage note at* LEND.

boss[1] /bɔs/ [*noun; plural* **bosses**] an employer or manager who is in charge of other people: *My boss gave me a raise.*

boss[2] [*verb;* **bosses, bossed, bossing**] to tell people what to do, especially in an way that is not reasonable or without having authority: *Stop bossing me around!*

bossy /'bɔsi/ [*adjective;* **bossier, bossiest**] liking to tell other people what to do: *a bossy older brother*

botanist /'batənɪst/ [*noun*] a scientist who studies plants

botany /'batəni/ [*noun*] the scientific study of plants

both[1] * /bouθ/ [*determiner, pronoun*] each of two people or things: *We both like swimming.* | *My parents are both teachers.* | *Both boys went to the zoo.* | *Both of them had brown hair.* | *Write on both sides of the paper.* | *I bought only one book because I couldn't afford both.* | *Both the books are expensive.*
  ☛ Do not say "the both books." Say **both books** or **both the books**.
  ☛ You can say **we/they/us/them both**, but do not use **both** after a noun.
  ⇨ *Compare* EITHER[1], NEITHER[1]. ⇨ *See the usage note at* EACH[1].

both[2] * [*conjunction*]
  ▬ PHRASE ▬
  both . . . and used to emphasize that each of two people or things is involved: *Both Cynthia and her sister are tall.* | *He speaks both French and German.*

bother[1] /'baðɚ/ [*verb;* **bothered, bothering**]
  1 to interrupt, annoy, or worry someone: *Don't bother your mother—she's resting.* | *Is something bothering you?* | **bother someone with something** ▸ *I didn't want to bother him with all the details.*
  2 to make the necessary effort to do something: *"Would you like some coffee?" "Please don't bother—I'm fine."* | *Why bother talking to her? It won't make any difference.* | **bother to**

/i/ s**ee**	/ɪ/ b**i**g	/eɪ/ d**ay**	/ɛ/ g**e**t	/æ/ h**a**t
/a/ f**a**ther, h**o**t	/ʌ/ **u**p	/ə/ **a**bout	/ɔ/ s**aw**
/ou/ h**o**pe	/ʊ/ b**oo**k	/u/ t**oo**	/aɪ/ **I**	/aʊ/ h**ow**
/ɔɪ/ b**oy**	/ɝ/ b**ir**d	/ɚ/ t**ea**cher	/ɪr/ **ear**	/ɛr/ **air**
/ɑr/ f**ar**	/ɔr/ m**ore**	/ʊr/ t**our**	/ɜ/ **fire**
/aʊɚ/ h**our**	/θ/ n**o**thing	/ð/ m**o**ther	/ʃ/ **she**
/ʒ/ mea**s**ure	/tʃ/ **ch**urch	/dʒ/ **j**ump	/ŋ/ lo**ng**

do something ▸ *I didn't bother to make a copy of the letter.*

bother² [*noun*] effort or trouble: *"You don't have to help me." "Don't worry—it's no bother."*

bottle¹ ∗ /ˈbɑtəl/ [*noun*] a glass or plastic container with a lid, used for storing liquid: *a bottle of soda.*

bottles

bottle² [*verb*; **bottled, bottling**] to put liquid into bottles: *We only drank bottled water.* | *a bottling plant*

bottom¹ ∗ /ˈbɑtəm/ [*noun*]
1 the lowest part or surface of something; <u>opposite</u> TOP: *They lived at the bottom of the hill.* | *There's a hole in the bottom of my shoe.* | *There's some tea left in the bottom of the pot.*
2 INFORMAL the part of the body that you sit on: *He fell and landed on his bottom.*
━ PHRASE ━
3 the bottom (of) the lowest or worst position on a list, in an organization, etc.: *Sign your name there, at the bottom.* | *He's near the bottom of the class in English.*

bottom² [*adjective*; *no comparative*] in the lowest position; <u>opposite</u> TOP: *She stood on the bottom step, looking up.* | *The files are in the bottom drawer.*
☛ Only use **bottom** before a noun.

bought ∗ /bɔt/ [*verb*] the past tense and past participle of BUY

boulder /ˈboʊldɚ/ [*noun*] a large rock: *The hill was covered with boulders.*

bounce /baʊns/ [*verb*; **bounced, bouncing**]
1 if a ball bounces or you bounce a ball, it hits a hard surface and comes up or back again: *The ball bounced off the post.* | *She was bouncing a ball against the wall.*
⇨ *See the picture at* PLAY¹.

2 to jump or move quickly up and down: *The kids were bouncing on the trampoline.* | *He bounced around the tennis court.*

bound¹ /baʊnd/ [*verb*] the past tense and past participle of BIND

bound² [*adjective*; *no comparative*]
1 going to a particular place: *We were bound for the West Coast.*
━ PHRASE ━
2 be bound to do something to be very likely or certain to do something: *If we tell her, she's bound to tell her mother.* | *The train is bound to be late.*

bound³ [*verb*; **bounded, bounding**] to move with a lot of energy, so that you are almost jumping: *He came bounding across the lawn.*

bound⁴ [*noun*] a long high jump: *He crossed the stream with one bound.*

boundary /ˈbaʊndəri; ˈbaʊndri/ [*noun*; *plural* **boundaries**] a line that separates two places: *The river forms a boundary between the mountains and the plain.*

bouquet /buˈkeɪ/ [*noun*] a bunch of flowers, often tied together, and usually given to a woman as a gift: *a bouquet of roses*

bow¹ /baʊ/ [*verb*; **bowed, bowing**]
1 to bend your body forward as a sign of respect or thanks: *He bowed to the audience.*
━ PHRASE ━
2 bow your head to bend your head forward: *His head was bowed in thought.*

bow² /baʊ/ [*noun*]
1 when you bend your body forward as a sign of respect: *The young man gave a bow.*
2 the pointed front part of a ship: *We sat in the bow.*

bow³ /boʊ/ [*noun*]
1 a kind of knot with two curved parts, which looks attractive
2 a weapon made from a curved piece of wood with a string attached to the ends, from

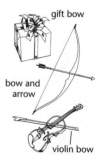

gift bow

bow and arrow

violin bow

bows

which arrows are shot: *He hunted deer with a **bow and arrow**.*

3 a straight piece of wood with threads stretched along it, used for playing an instrument with strings such as a violin

bowl * /boʊl/ [noun] a round container without a lid, used for holding liquids, mixing food, eating from, etc.: *Put the fruit in a bowl.* | *He ate **a bowl of** soup.*

bowling /ˈboʊlɪŋ/ [noun] the sport or activity of rolling a large ball down a narrow track to knock down a set of objects standing at the other end: *We **go bowling** on Monday nights.* | *a **bowling alley** (=where people go bowling)*

bow tie /ˈboʊ ˈtaɪ/ [noun; plural **bow ties**] a thin piece of cloth tied in a bow that is worn around the neck of a shirt
⇨ *See the picture at* TIE².

box¹ * /baks/ [noun; plural **boxes**]
1 a CONTAINER with stiff straight sides and usually a lid or cover, used for storing things: *Please take the books out of those boxes.* | *a cardboard box* | *He gave her **a** heart-shaped **box of** candy.*
2 a place on a printed page with lines around it, that contains information or a space to write something: *Check the box next to your choice.*

box² [verb; **boxes, boxed, boxing**] to fight someone as a sport, using your closed hands with special gloves on: *My uncle used to box when he was younger.*

boxer /ˈbaksɚ/ [noun] someone who takes part in the sport of boxing

boxing /ˈbaksɪŋ/ [noun] the sport of fighting someone using your closed hands with special gloves on: *a **boxing match** (=when boxers fight)* | *the **boxing ring** (=square area where a boxing match takes place)*

box office /ˈbaks ˌɔfɪs/ [noun] a place in a theater where tickets are sold

boy * /bɔɪ/ [noun; plural **boys**] a male child: *The boys played soccer in the yard.* | *We have two children, a boy and a girl.*

boyfriend /ˈbɔɪˌfrɛnd/ [noun] a boy or man with whom someone is having a romantic relationship: *My boyfriend and I went to the movies.*

Boy Scout /ˈbɔɪ ˌskaʊt/ [noun]
1 the Boy Scouts an organization for boys that teaches skills they will need in life: *A lot of boys in my class are in the Boy Scouts.*
☛ Only use **the Boy Scouts** with a singular verb in this meaning.
2 a boy who is a member of the Boy Scouts: *I want to be a Boy Scout.*

bra /bra/ [noun; plural **bras**] a piece of underwear that a woman wears to support her breasts

bracelet /ˈbreɪslɪt/ [noun] a piece of JEWELRY that is worn around the wrist

braces /ˈbreɪsɪz/ [plural noun] a set of wires that is put on a child's teeth to make them grow straight: *I had to wear braces for two years.*

brackets /ˈbrækɪts/ [noun] a pair of marks used in writing. They look like this: [ ]
⇨ *See* Punctuation *in the Smart Study section.*

brag /bræg/ [verb; **brags, bragged, bragging**] to talk too proudly about what you have, what you can do, or what you have done; synonym BOAST: *She **brags about** her son all the time.* | *He **bragged that** he caught the most fish.*

braid¹ /breɪd/ [verb; **braided, braiding**] to weave three long pieces of hair, wool, etc., over and under each other to make one thick piece: *She **braided her hair**.*

braid² [noun] pieces of HAIR that have been put over and under each other to form a thick piece: *She wore her hair **in braids**.*

braille /breɪl/ [noun] a kind of writing for blind people, in which letters are shown by raised marks: *They have many books **in braille**.*

brain * /breɪn/ [noun]
1 the organ inside your head with which you think
2 also **brains**; your intelligence and ability to think: *She has a good brain.* | *Just **use your brains**!*

/i/ see	/ɪ/ big	/eɪ/ day	/ɛ/ get /æ/ hat
/a/ father, hot	/ʌ/ up	/ə/ about	/ɔ/ saw
/oʊ/ hope	/ʊ/ book	/u/ too	/aɪ/ I /aʊ/ how
/ɔɪ/ boy	/ɝ/ bird	/ɚ/ teacher	/ɪr/ ear /ɛr/ air
/ɑr/ far	/ɔr/ more	/ʊr/ tour	/aɪr/ fire
/aʊɚ/ hour	/θ/ nothing	/ð/ mother	/ʃ/ she
/ʒ/ measure	/tʃ/ church	/dʒ/ jump	/ŋ/ long

brake[1] /breɪk/ [noun] a piece of equipment in a car, on a bicycle, etc., that you use to make it stop: *She* **stepped on the brakes.**

brake[2] [verb; braked, braking] to stop a car, bicycle, etc., or make it go more slowly by using its brake: *He braked hard and the car jerked.*

branch * /bræntʃ/ [noun; plural branches]
1 a part of a tree that grows out from the trunk: *Monkeys sat in the branches of the trees.* | *I saw a bird on a high branch.*
2 a local office of a business or organization that has offices in many different places: *You can return the car to our Dallas branch.*
3 one part of something that has many parts: *Which branch of medicine do you study?*

brand /brænd/ [noun] a kind of thing that people buy, that is made by a particular company: *She always drinks the same brand of coffee.*

brand-new /'brænd'nu/ [adjective; no comparative] never used before, or completely new: *We are buying a brand-new computer.*

brass /bræs/ [noun] a hard, shiny, yellow metal that is a mixture of copper and zinc: *a brass trumpet*

brave * /breɪv/ [adjective; braver, bravest] not feeling or showing fear: *You were very brave to go there alone.* | *It was brave of him to say what he thought.*

bravely * /'breɪvli/ [adverb] without showing any fear: *He fought bravely for his country.*

bravery /'breɪvəri/ [noun] the quality of not feeling or showing fear: *Many of their soldiers showed great bravery.*

bread * /brɛd/ [noun] a food made of flour mixed with water and yeast and then baked: *I bought a loaf of bread.* | *She was eating a piece of bread.* | *He cut another slice of bread.*
↪ *See the picture at* THICK.

break[1] * /breɪk/ [verb; broke, broken, breaking]
1 to separate into pieces, for example when hit or damaged, or to make

something separate in this way: *The string broke and the kite blew away.* | *The plate broke into pieces.* | *Who broke the window?* | *He fell off his bike and broke his arm.*
2 to be damaged and stop working, or to damage something so that it does not work: *My alarm clock broke.* | *He broke my camera.*
3 to not do what a rule or law says you should do: *She was in trouble for breaking school rules.* | *You're asking me to break the law!*

— PHRASES —
4 **break a promise/agreement/etc.** to not do what you promised or agreed to do: *He said he would come, but he broke his word.*
5 **break a record** to do something faster, better, etc., than it has ever been done before: *He broke the world record for the 400 meters.*

— PHRASAL VERBS —
break down [phrasal verb]
6 if a vehicle or a large machine breaks down, it stops working: *Our truck broke down three miles out of town.*

break in or **break into** [phrasal verb]
7 to enter a building, room, etc., using force: *Thieves broke in and robbed us.* | *Our house was broken into last night.*
↪ *See also* BREAK-IN.

break off [phrasal verb]
8 to separate from something because of being hit, pulled, etc., or to separate something from another thing in this way: *One of the handles has broken off.* | **break off something** ▸ *He broke off a twig from the tree.* | **break something off** ▸ *I broke a piece off the loaf.*

break out [phrasal verb]
9 if fighting, disease, or a fire breaks out, it starts: *The fire broke out on the third floor of the building.*

break up [phrasal verb]
10 to end a relationship with someone: *He broke up with his girlfriend.*

break[2] [noun]
1 a short rest from your work: *Let's take a break for a few minutes.* | *I'll go to the store during my lunch break.* | *a coffee break* | *You need a break from work.*
2 when something stops and then

starts again: *The line of cars stretched for a mile* **without a break**. | *The sun shone through a* **break** *in the clouds.*

breakable /'breɪkəbəl/ [*adjective; no comparative*] made of something that breaks easily: *Don't put anything breakable in your suitcase.*

breakdown /'breɪkˌdaʊn/ [*noun*] when something such as a car, machine, or system stops working: *We* **had a breakdown** *on the highway.*

breakfast * /'brɛkfəst/ [*noun*] the first meal of the day, eaten in the morning: *What did you have* **for breakfast?** | *We often* **have breakfast** *on the deck.*

break-in /'breɪkˌɪn/ [*noun*] when someone enters a building using force, especially to steal something

breast * /brɛst/ [*noun*]
1 one of the two soft round parts of a woman's chest that can produce milk
2 the front part of a body, above the stomach; synonym CHEST: *a bird with a red breast*

breaststroke /'brɛstˌstroʊk/ [*noun*] a style of swimming in which you push your arms straight forward and then pull them back through the water

breath * /brɛθ/ [*noun*]
1 the air that comes out of your nose and mouth when you breathe: *Her breath smelled of toothpaste.*
2 when you breathe once: *Take a* **deep breath**, *and let it out slowly.*

=== PHRASES ===
3 **hold your breath** to stop yourself from breathing for a short time: *I can hold my breath longer than you can.*
4 **be out of breath** to be breathing hard because you have been using a lot of energy: *He was out of breath when he reached the top of the hill.*
5 **catch your breath** to rest until you stop breathing hard: *I stopped to catch my breath.*

breathe * /brið/ [*verb*; **breathed, breathing**]
1 to take air into your lungs through your nose or mouth and let it out again: *The room was so hot I could hardly breathe.*

=== PHRASAL VERBS ===
breathe in [*phrasal verb*]
2 to take air into your lungs: *Breathe in before you start to sing.*
breathe out [*phrasal verb*]
3 to send air out from your lungs: *Now breathe out slowly.*

breathless /'brɛθlɪs/ [*adjective; no comparative*] breathing hard or with difficulty, for example because you have been using a lot of energy: *I was breathless after an hour of exercise.*

breed[1] * /brid/ [*verb;* **bred** /brɛd/, **breeding**]
1 to keep animals and control the way they produce babies, in order to produce better animals: *I breed dogs.*
2 if animals breed, they produce babies: *Pandas do not breed very often.*

breed[2] * [*noun*] a particular kind of animal, which has been developed in farming or as a pet: *This* **breed of** *cattle produces plenty of milk.*

breeze /briz/ [*noun*] a light wind: *A cool breeze was blowing.* | *The leaves were rustling in the breeze.*

brew /bru/ [*verb;* **brewed, brewing**] to prepare coffee or tea with hot water, or to make beer: *The tea is brewing.* | *freshly brewed coffee*

bribe[1] /braɪb/ [*verb;* **bribed, bribing**] to give someone money or a gift so that he or she will do something: **bribe someone to do something** ▸ *He bribed the janitor to let him into the building.*

bribe[2] [*noun*] money or a gift that is given to persuade someone to do something: *He was fired from his job for* **taking bribes.**

brick * /brɪk/ [*noun*] a block of baked clay used for building: *a brick wall*

bride /braɪd/ [*noun*] the woman who is getting married at a wedding, or has just gotten married
↪ *Compare* GROOM.

/i/ see /ɪ/ big /eɪ/ day /ɛ/ get /æ/ hat
/ɑ/ father, hot /ʌ/ up /ə/ about /ɔ/ saw
/oʊ/ hope /ʊ/ book /u/ too /aɪ/ I /aʊ/ how
/ɔɪ/ boy /ɝ/ bird /ɚ/ teacher /ɪr/ ear /ɛr/ air
/ɑr/ far /ɔr/ more /ʊr/ tour /aɪr/ fire
/aʊɚ/ hour /θ/ nothing /ð/ mother /ʃ/ she
/ʒ/ measure /tʃ/ church /dʒ/ jump /ŋ/ long

bridesmaid /'braɪdzˌmeɪd/ [*noun*] a woman who helps a bride and takes part in the wedding with her

bridge * /brɪdʒ/ [*noun*] a structure that is built over a river, railroad, etc., so that people or vehicles can cross it: *We drove across the bridge.*

brief /brif/ [*adjective;* briefer, briefest]
1 continuing only a short time; <u>opposite</u> LONG: *They came for a brief visit.*
2 not using many words: *Give a brief description of the experiment.* | *Please be brief* (=do not say too much).

briefcase /'brif,keɪs/ [*noun*] a thin case with a handle, used for carrying documents

briefly T /'brifli/ [*adverb*]
1 for a short time: *The general appeared briefly on the balcony.*
2 using few words: *Could you explain briefly why we are here?*

briefs /brifs/ [*plural noun*] men's underwear that fits closely: *a pair of briefs*

bright * T /braɪt/ [*adjective;* brighter, brightest]
1 shining strongly, or full of light; <u>opposite</u> DIM: *The light was so bright it hurt my eyes.* | *The class was held in a bright room.*
2 bright colors are strong and not dark; <u>opposite</u> PALE: *The flags were bright red.*
3 able to learn and understand things quickly; <u>synonyms</u> INTELLIGENT, SMART: *Some of the kids were not very bright.*

brighten /'braɪtən/ [*verb;* brightened, brightening] to become brighter, more colorful, or more cheerful, or to make something or someone do this: *When she opened the letter, her face brightened.* | *We could brighten up the hall with some paint.* | *The flowers brightened the room up.*

brightly * /'braɪtli/ [*adverb*]
1 with a strong light: *The moon shone brightly.*
2 with strong colors that are not dark: *The room was brightly decorated.*

brilliant T /'brɪlyənt/ [*adjective;* more brilliant, most brilliant]
1 extremely intelligent or skillful: *a brilliant student* | *a brilliant idea*

2 very bright, clear, and strong: *a brilliant light* | *I love brilliant colors.*

brilliantly /'brɪlyəntli/ [*adverb*]
1 with a lot of intelligence or skill: *He handled the situation brilliantly.*
2 very brightly: *brilliantly colored birds*

brim /brɪm/ [*noun*]
1 the edge of a hat that sticks out: *She wore a straw hat with a wide brim.*
   ⇨ See the picture at CLOTHING.
2 the edge of a bowl, cup, etc.: *Our glasses were filled to the brim.*

bring * /brɪŋ/ [*verb;* brought, bringing]
1 to have something or someone with you when you come to a place: *Have you all brought your notebooks?* | *Can I bring a friend to the party?* | *Bring Anna with you the next time you come to see us.* | **bring someone something** ▸ *I've brought you a present.*
2 to have an effect or make something happen: *Every year, technology brings new changes.* | **bring someone something** ▸ *Money can't bring you happiness.*

━━ PHRASAL VERBS ━━

bring back [*phrasal verb*]
3 to have someone or something with you when you return to a place: **bring back someone/something** ▸ *Bring back a newspaper, will you?* | **bring someone/something back** ▸ *Find Dan and bring him back.* | **bring someone back something** ▸ *Please bring me back a T-shirt from New York.*

bring up [*phrasal verb*]
4 to take care of a child from a young age until he or she is grown; <u>synonym</u> RAISE: **bring someone up** ▸ *My aunt brought me up.* | **bring up someone** ▸ *They have brought up three children.*

USAGE   bring, take

You use **bring** and **take** to talk about carrying something or going with someone to a place. If you say that someone **brings** something to a place, you are in the place that he or she carries it to: *Can you bring some CDs when you come?*

If you say that someone **takes** something to a place, you are not in the place that he or she carries it to: *Don't forget to take your CDs when you go home.*

brisk /brɪsk/ [adjective; brisker, briskest] quickly and with a lot of energy: We went for **a brisk walk**. | They traveled at **a brisk pace**.

brittle /ˈbrɪtəl/ [adjective; brittler, brittlest] a brittle substance is hard, and breaks easily: People's bones become brittle as they get older.

British * /ˈbrɪtɪʃ/ [adjective; no comparative] belonging to, from, or relating to the island of Great Britain: a British passport

broad * Ⓣ /brɔd/ [adjective; broader, broadest]
1 measuring a lot from one side to the other; synonym WIDE; opposite NARROW: We came to a broad river. | broad streets | He has broad shoulders.
2 including many different things or people: They study a **broad range** of subjects.
3 not including all the details; synonym GENERAL: He gave us a **broad outline** (=a general description) of the course.

broadcast¹ * /ˈbrɔdˌkæst/ [verb; broadcasts, broadcast, broadcast, broadcasting] to send out radio or television programs: The Olympics will be broadcast on Channel 2.

broadcast² [noun] a radio or television program: We interrupt this broadcast to bring you a special announcement.

broccoli /ˈbrakəli/ [noun] a dark green VEGETABLE that looks like a little bush

brochure Ⓣ /broʊˈʃʊr/ [noun] a thin book that gives information, especially about something that you can buy: a travel brochure

broil [verb; broiled, broiling] to cook food on a metal object under direct heat or fire, or to be cooked this way: While the fish broiled, I made the salad. | broiled chicken breasts
▷ See the synonym note at COOK¹.

broke¹ * /broʊk/ [verb] the past tense of BREAK¹

broke² [adjective; more broke, most broke] INFORMAL without any money: I'm completely broke until Friday.

broken¹ * /ˈbroʊkən/ [verb] the past participle of BREAK¹

broken² * [adjective; no comparative]
1 damaged and separated into pieces: a broken window
2 damaged and not working: My watch is broken.
═══ PHRASE ═══
3 **broken English/Spanish/etc.** English, Spanish, etc., that is not correct and is spoken by someone who does not know it well: He questioned me in broken English.

bronze¹ /branz/ [noun]
1 a brown metal made of a mixture of copper and tin: old coins made of bronze
2 a shiny brown-red color: The leaves had turned to bronze and red.

bronze² [adjective; no comparative] made of bronze: a bronze statue | a **bronze medal** (=a medal given as third prize in a competition)

brooch /broʊtʃ; brutʃ/ [noun; plural brooches] a piece of jewelry with a PIN attached to it that you fasten to your clothes: She wore a gold brooch.

broom /brum/ [noun] a brush with a long handle for sweeping floors, paths, etc.: Get a broom and sweep up that mess!

brother * /ˈbrʌðɚ/ [noun] a boy or man who has the same parents as you do: My **older brother** is getting married.
▷ See the picture at FAMILY TREE.

brother-in-law /ˈbrʌðɚ-ɪnˌlɔ/ [noun; plural brothers-in-law] your sister's husband, or the brother of your husband or wife
▷ See the picture at FAMILY TREE.

brought * /brɔt/ [verb] the past tense and past participle of BRING

brown¹ * /braʊn/ [noun] the color of earth or chocolate: I often wear brown.

brown² * [adjective; browner, brownest] of the color brown: She has brown eyes and hair. | The package was wrapped in brown paper.

/i/ see	/ɪ/ big	/eɪ/ day	/ɛ/ get	/æ/ hat
/a/ father, hot	/ʌ/ up	/ə/ about	/ɔ/ saw	
/oʊ/ hope	/ʊ/ book	/u/ too	/aɪ/ I	/aʊ/ how
/ɔɪ/ boy	/ɚ/ bird	/ɚ/ teacher	/ɪr/ ear	/ɛr/ air
/ar/ far	/ɔr/ more	/ʊr/ tour	/aɪr/ fire	
/aʊɚ/ hour	/θ/ nothing	/ð/ mother	/ʃ/ she	
/ʒ/ measure	/tʃ/ church	/dʒ/ jump	/ŋ/ long	

Brownie /'braʊni/ [*noun; plural* Brownies]

1 the Brownies the Girl Scout organization for younger girls: *I have a lot of fun in the Brownies.*
☛ Only use **the Brownies** with a singular verb in this meaning.

2 a girl who is a member of the Brownies: *Now I'm a Brownie, but next year I'll be a Girl Scout.*

bruise[1] /bruz/ [*noun*] a dark mark on the skin caused by falling, being hit, etc.: *He had a bruise on his cheek.*

bruise[2] [*verb; bruised, bruising*] to hurt a part of your body so that a dark mark is formed on the skin: *I fell and bruised my knee.* | *Her arm was badly bruised.*

brunette /bru'nɛt/ [*noun*] a woman with dark hair

brush[1] ✳ /brʌʃ/ [*noun; plural* brushes] a small tool consisting of a lot of hairs or stiff threads fixed to a handle, used for painting or for making things clean or neat: *a comb and brush* | *Get a dustpan and brush.* | *Clean your brushes carefully after painting.*

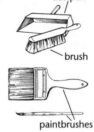

dustpan

brush

paintbrushes

hairbrush

brushes

brush[2] ✳ [*verb; brushes, brushed, brushing*]

1 to make something clean or neat with a brush: *I brush my teeth after I eat.* | *Wait while I brush my hair.*

2 to remove something with a brush or with your hand: **brush something off/from something** ▸ *The waiter brushed the crumbs off the table.* | *She came in, brushing snow from her coat.*

Brussels sprout /'brʌsəlz 'spraʊt/ [*noun*] a green vegetable that looks like a very small cabbage, that is eaten cooked

brutal /'brutəl/ [*adjective; more brutal, most brutal*] cruel and violent: *It was a brutal murder.* | *The murderer was a brutal man.*

B.S. /'bi'ɛs/ [*noun; plural* B.S.s or B.S.'s] Bachelor of Science; a degree given for four years of study in subjects such as mathematics or a science
↪ *Compare* **B.A., M.A., M.S., PH.D.**

bubble[1] ✳ /'bʌbəl/ [*noun*] a ball of air or gas in a liquid: *It's fun to blow bubbles* (=put a plastic ring into liquid soap, then blow through the ring to make bubbles).

bubble[2] [*verb; bubbled, bubbling*] if a liquid bubbles, bubbles form in it: *The stew was bubbling on the stove.*

bubble bath /'bʌbəl ˌbæθ/ [*noun; plural* bubble baths /'bʌbəl ˌbæðz/] liquid soap that you pour into bath water to make bubbles, or a bath you take in this water: *Children love bubble baths.*

bubble gum /'bʌbəl ˌgʌm/ [*noun*] chewing gum that you can blow into to make a bubble come out of your mouth: *fruit-flavored bubble gum*

buck /bʌk/ [*noun*] INFORMAL a dollar: *The ticket cost twenty bucks.*

bucket ✳ /'bʌkɪt/ [*noun*] a round open container with a handle over the top: *a bucket of water*

buckle[1] /'bʌkəl/ [*noun*] a metal or plastic object used for fastening BELTS, shoes, etc.

buckle[2] [*verb; buckled, buckling*] to fasten something with a buckle: *Buckle your seat belts, everybody.*

bud /bʌd/ [*noun*] a new flower or leaf before it opens: *The plants were showing a few buds.*

Buddha /'budə/ [*name*] the man whose life and beliefs the Buddhist religion is based on

Buddhism /'budɪzəm/ [*noun*] a religion of east and central Asia, based on the things taught by the religious teacher called Buddha

Buddhist[1] /'budɪst/ [*noun*] someone whose religion is Buddhism

Buddhist[2] [*adjective; no comparative*] relating to Buddhism: *Buddhist beliefs*

budget[1] /'bʌdʒɪt/ [*noun*] the money you have to spend on something, or a plan of how to spend it: *They have a budget of $25,000.* | *You must try to stay within* *your budget* (=do not spend more than you have).

budget² [*verb;* **budgeted, budgeting**] to plan how you will spend your money: *You will have to **budget for** the trip* (=make sure you will have enough money for it).

buffalo /ˈbʌfəˌloʊ/ [*noun; plural* **buffalo** or **buffaloes** or **buffalos**] a North American animal that is larger than a cow and has a big, hairy head

bug /bʌg/ [*noun*] INFORMAL
1 a small insect: *There are little black bugs all over the window.*
2 an illness that is not serious: *I've been in bed with a bug of some kind.*
3 a fault in a computer program: *There are a few bugs we still have to work on.*

build * /bɪld/ [*verb;* **built, building**]
1 to make something, especially something big, by putting the parts of it together: *This house was built 150 years ago.* | *They're building a new road to the airport.* | *The wall is **built of** stone.*
2 to develop something gradually, or to increase gradually: *They **built up** the business over many years.* | *Pressure began to **build up** inside the engine.*

builder /ˈbɪldɚ/ [*noun*]
1 someone who builds something: *the **builders of** the Great Wall*
2 someone whose job is to make or repair houses and other buildings: *The builders are still working on the house.*

building * /ˈbɪldɪŋ/ [*noun*]
1 a structure with walls and a roof: *a tall office building*
2 the activity or business of building things: *the building industry*

built * /bɪlt/ [*verb*] the past tense and past participle of BUILD

bulb /bʌlb/ [*noun*]
1 the round glass part of an electric light, from which light shines when electricity passes through it: *a 60-watt **light bulb***
2 the fat round root from which some plants grow: *tulip bulbs*

bulge /bʌldʒ/ [*verb;* **bulged, bulging**] to stick out in a round shape, especially because of being full: *The sacks were **bulging with** rice.*

horn

a bull

hoof

bull /bʊl/ [*noun*] a male cow

bulldozer /ˈbʊlˌdoʊzɚ/ [*noun*] a large machine that you drive and use to move dirt, rocks, etc.: *The workmen used a bulldozer to move the pile of sand.*

bullet * /ˈbʊlɪt/ [*noun*] a small piece of metal that is fired from a gun: *He had a **bullet wound** in his leg.*

bulletin /ˈbʊlɪtən/ [*noun*]
1 a short news report on radio or television: *Our next news bulletin will be at ten o'clock.*
2 a regular printed report that an organization sends to its members: *I get the club's bulletin every month.*

bulletin board /ˈbʊlɪtən ˌbɔrd/ [*noun*]
1 a board on a wall for putting up notices
   ➪ *See the picture at* OFFICE.
2 a place in a computer system where you can write things for other people to read: *He runs a bulletin board for students learning English.*

bully¹ /ˈbʊli/ [*noun; plural* **bullies**] someone who hurts or frightens people who are weaker or less powerful: *You're acting like a bully. Stop it right now.*

bully² [*verb;* **bullies, bullied, bullying**] to hurt or frighten people who are weaker or less powerful: *If someone is bullying you, tell your teacher.*

bump¹ /bʌmp/ [*verb;* **bumped, bumping**]
1 to knock against someone or something without intending to: *I*

/i/ **see**	/ɪ/ **big**	/eɪ/ **day**	/ɛ/ **get**	/æ/ **hat**
/ɑ/ **father, hot**	/ʌ/ **up**	/ə/ **about**	/ɔ/ **saw**	
/oʊ/ **hope**	/ʊ/ **book**	/u/ **too**	/aɪ/ **I**	/aʊ/ **how**
/ɔɪ/ **boy**	/ɝ/ **bird**	/ɚ/ **teacher**	/ɪr/ **ear**	/ɛr/ **air**
/ɑr/ **far**	/ɔr/ **more**	/ʊr/ **tour**	/aɪr/ **fire**	
/aʊɚ/ **hour**	/θ/ **nothing**	/ð/ **mother**	/ʃ/ **she**	
/ʒ/ **measure**	/tʃ/ **church**	/dʒ/ **jump**	/ŋ/ **long**	

bumped my head on the door frame. I
He came running downstairs and
bumped into me.

══ PHRASAL VERB ══

bump into [*phrasal verb*]
2 to meet someone without intending
to: **bump into someone** ▸ *I bumped
into an old friend at the mall today.*
 ⟳ *See the synonym note at* MEET¹.

bump² [*noun*]
1 a raised place on your body where you
have knocked it against something:
*How did you get that bump on your
head?*
2 a raised part on a surface such as a
road: *The car rattled over the bumps in
the road.*

bumper /'bʌmpɚ/ [*noun*] a long piece
of metal at the front or back of a CAR
that protects the main part of the car if
it hits something: *We hit the **back
bumper** of the car in front of us.*

bumpy /'bʌmpi/ [*adjective;* **bumpier,
bumpiest**] a bumpy road, path, or
surface has many raised parts; synonym
UNEVEN; *opposite* SMOOTH: *A bumpy road
led to the farm.*

bun /bʌn/ [*noun*]
1 bread that has been baked in a
special small shape to eat with
particular foods: *a **hot dog bun** | a
burger on a bun*
2 long hair arranged in a tight round
shape at the back of the head: *She
wore her hair **in a bun,** and always
carried an umbrella.*

bunch ✳ /bʌntʃ/ [*noun; plural* **bunches**]
1 a group of people or things: *A **bunch
of** kids were playing in the park.* | *a
bunch of keys | a **bunch of flowers**
(=flowers that have been picked and
tied together) | a **bunch of grapes/
bananas** (=an amount of fruit that
grows and is picked together)*
2 INFORMAL a lot of something: *I have **a
whole bunch of** work to do.*

bundle /'bʌndəl/ [*noun*] a group of
things that are tied or wrapped together
so that they are easy to carry: *a **bundle
of** clothes*

bunk /bʌŋk/ [*noun*] a narrow bed that is
attached to a wall or is part of a bunk
bed: *The sailors sleep in bunks.*

bunk bed /'bʌŋk ˌbɛd/ [*noun*] a piece of
furniture with two narrow beds, one
above the other

burden /'bɝdən/ [*noun*]
1 something or someone that worries
you or causes you problems: *a **heavy
burden** of debt | I don't want to **be a
burden to** you.*
2 FORMAL a heavy load that is being
carried: *He lifted his burden again and
walked on.*

burger /'bɝgɚ/ [*noun*] a HAMBURGER: *Do
you want fries with your burger?*

burglar /'bɝglɚ/ [*noun*] a thief who
enters buildings to steal things: *The
burglars had taken the TV.*

burglarize /'bɝgləˌraɪz/ [*verb;*
burglarized, burglarizing] to enter a
building and steal things: *Our house was
burglarized last year.*

burglary /'bɝgləri/ [*noun; plural*
burglaries] the crime of entering a
building to steal things: *There have been
several burglaries in our neighborhood.*

burial /'bɛriəl/ [*noun*] when a dead
body is put into the ground: *They had a
short ceremony at her burial.*

burn¹ ✳ /bɝn/ [*verb;* **burned, burning**]
1 to be destroyed or harmed by fire or
strong heat: *It smells like your dinner is
burning.* | *We **burned up** most of the
wood.* | *Careful—don't **burn yourself** on
that hot stove.*
2 if a fire or a flame burns, it produces
heat and light: *A nice warm fire was
burning in the fireplace.*
3 to feel very hot, for example because
you are ill or embarrassed: *My cheeks
were burning.* | *She was burning with a
fever.*

══ PHRASAL VERBS ══

burn down [*phrasal verb*]
4 if a building burns down or is burned
down, it is destroyed by fire: *His house
had burned down while he was away.*

burn out [*phrasal verb*]
5 to stop burning or producing light
after using up all the fuel there is: *One
of your car's headlights has burned out.*

burn[2] * [noun] an injury caused by fire or heat: *He had a bad burn on his arm.*

burner /'bɝnɚ/ [noun] one of the four parts on the top of a STOVE that get extremely hot, where you put pans to cook things

burnt * /bɝnt/ [adjective; **more burnt, most burnt**] damaged by fire or heat: *I hate burnt toast.*

burp /bɝp/ [verb; **burped, burping**] to let gas come up from your stomach and out of your mouth: *It's not polite to burp out loud.*

burrow /'bɝroʊ/ [noun] a hole in the ground that an animal lives in: *The rabbit ran into its burrow.*

burst[1] * /bɝst/ [verb; **bursts, burst, burst, bursting**]
1 to break because of being very full or containing a lot of pressure, or to break something like this: *The dam burst and water flooded the village.* | *His pants were so tight that he burst a seam.*
2 to enter a place suddenly, especially with a lot of noise or energy: *She burst into his office and demanded a meeting.*
━ PHRASES ━
3 **burst into tears/song/laughter/ etc.** to suddenly start doing something: *The wood burst into flames.*
4 **burst out laughing** or **burst out crying** to suddenly start laughing or crying: *She burst out laughing as soon as she saw me.*
5 **be bursting with**
a to be very full of people or things: *The museum was bursting with visitors.*
b to have a lot of a feeling or quality: *We were bursting with excitement.*

burst[2] [noun] a sudden short period of noise or activity: *a burst of laughter* | *a burst of energy*

bury * /'bɛri/ [verb; **buries, buried, burying**]
1 to put a dead body into the ground: *He is buried in the local cemetery.*
2 to put something into a hole in the ground and cover it with earth: *They say pirates buried treasure near here.*
3 to cover someone or something with a large amount of something: *The photo was buried under a pile of papers.*

bus * /bʌs/ [noun; plural **buses**] a large vehicle that has a motor and carries many passengers: *There were not many people on the bus.* | *Get off the bus at the next stop.* | *We can go by bus.*

bush * /bʊʃ/ [noun; plural **bushes**] a plant like a small short tree: *The gardens were full of trees and bushes.* | *a lilac bush*

busily * /'bɪzəli/ [adverb] with a lot of activity and energy: *They were busily packing the goods into boxes.*
⇨ See also BUSY.

business * /'bɪznɪs/ [noun; plural **businesses**]
1 the activity of earning money by buying and selling things or providing services: *They do a lot of business with Australia.* | *He decided to go into business* (=start a company). | *The company has gone out of business* (=stopped its business activities).
2 an organization that sells things, makes things, or provides a service: *He wants to work in the family business.*
━ PHRASES ━
3 **on business** as part of your job, and not for any other reason: *He travels a lot on company business.*
4 **mind your own business** SPOKEN used to say rudely that someone should not try to ask about or help with things that are private: *"What are you two talking about?" "Mind your own business!"*
5 **it's none of your business** SPOKEN used to tell someone rudely that he or she does not have the right to ask about or get involved in something: *My plans are none of your business.*

businessman /'bɪznɪs,mæn/ [noun; plural **businessmen** /'bɪznɪs,mɛn/] a man who owns a business or has an important position in a company

/i/ **see**	/ɪ/ **big**	/eɪ/ **day**	/ɛ/ **get**	/æ/ **hat**
/ɑ/ **father, hot**	/ʌ/ **up**	/ə/ **about**	/ɔ/ **saw**	
/oʊ/ **hope**	/ʊ/ **book**	/u/ **too**	/aɪ/ **I**	/aʊ/ **how**
/ɔɪ/ **boy**	/ɝ/ **bird**	/ɚ/ **teacher**	/ɪr/ **ear**	/ɛr/ **air**
/ɑr/ **far**	/ɔr/ **more**	/ʊr/ **tour**	/aɪr/ **fire**	
/aʊɚ/ **hour**	/θ/ **nothing**	/ð/ **mother**	/ʃ/ **she**	
/ʒ/ **measure**	/tʃ/ **church**	/dʒ/ **jump**	/ŋ/ **long**	

businesswoman /'bɪznɪs,wʊmən/ [noun; plural **businesswomen** /'bɪznɪs,wɪmən/] a woman who owns a business or has an important position in a company

bus station /'bʌs ,steɪʃən/ [noun] a place where buses start and end their trips

bus stop /'bʌs ,stap/ [noun] a place where buses stop to let people get on or off: *She was waiting at the bus stop.*

busy * /'bɪzi/ [adjective; busier, busiest]
1 having a lot of things to do: *Can I see you this morning, or are you busy?* I be **busy doing something** ▸ *We're busy getting ready for the meeting.*
⇨ *See also* BUSILY.
2 full of activity; *opposite* QUIET: *Spring is a busy time for us.* I *The market is busiest in the morning.* I *a busy street* (=a street with a lot of traffic)
3 a telephone line that is busy is being used: *I tried to call you earlier, but your line was busy.*

but[1] * /bʌt/ [conjunction]
1 used to say that something happened or is true in spite of something else: *She is very quiet but has lots of friends.*
2 used to say that something was done or can be done instead of something else: *I don't have his address, but I can give you his phone number.*
3 used to give the reason something is wrong, cannot be done, etc.: *This dress is nice, but it's too big for me.*

but[2] [preposition] used to say that someone or something is not included in what you are saying; *synonym* EXCEPT: *They invited everyone but me.* I *No one but you knows I'm here.*

butcher /'bʊtʃɚ/ [noun] someone who sells meat

butter * /'bʌtɚ/ [noun] a yellow fat made from milk, that is eaten with bread and used in cooking: *Fry the chicken pieces in butter.* I *a piece of **bread and butter*** (=bread with butter on it)

butterfly /'bʌtɚ,flaɪ/ [noun; plural **butterflies**] an insect with large, attractive, colored wings

a butterfly

buttocks /'bʌtək/ [plural noun] the part of your body that you sit on; *synonym* BOTTOM

button[1] * /'bʌtən/ [noun]
1 a small round object on a piece of CLOTHING that is passed through a hole to fasten the piece of clothing: *He undid the top button of his shirt.*
2 a small round or square part of a machine or piece of electrical equipment that you press to make it do something: *I pressed the wrong button on the keyboard.* I *Push the lower button to turn on the stereo.*
⇨ *See the picture at* TELEPHONE.

button[2] [verb; buttoned, buttoning]
1 to fasten a piece of clothing that has buttons: *Look, you buttoned your shirt the wrong way.* I *Button up your coat. It's cold outside.*
2 used to say where the buttons are that fasten a piece of clothing: *a blouse that buttons in back*

buttonhole /'bʌtən,hoʊl/ [noun] a hole in a shirt, coat, etc., used to fasten something by passing a button through it: *The buttonholes on this dress are too big for the buttons.*

buy * /baɪ/ [verb; buys, bought, buying] to get something in exchange for money: *I bought this shirt two years ago.* I **buy someone something** ▸ *His parents have bought him a bicycle.* I **buy something for someone** ▸ *I am buying the book for my sister.*
⇨ *Compare* SELL.

buzz[1] /bʌz/ [verb; buzzes, buzzed, buzzing] to make a noise like the sound that a bee makes: *A small plane buzzed overhead.*

buzz[2] [noun] a continuous low noise like the sound that a bee makes: *I heard a **buzz of conversation** in the next room.*

by[1] * /baɪ/ [preposition]
1 beside or near someone or something: *She was standing by her mother.* I *Our house is just by the school.* I *We sat by the river.*
2 used with a passive verb to show who or what does something: *He was bitten by a dog.* I *English is spoken by many people.* I *The crops had been damaged by a storm.*

3 used to show the method used to do something: *We communicate by e-mail.* | *I paid by check.* | *We traveled by bus.* | **by doing something** ▸ *She reached the shelf by standing on a chair.*

4 used to say who wrote a book, play, piece of music, etc., or did a piece of art: *"Hamlet" is a play by William Shakespeare.* | *Who is this painting by?*

5 past someone or something: *We drove by the market.*

6 not later than a particular date or time: *Can you send me the information by Friday?* | *I'll be back by five o'clock.*

7 used to mention the amount of an increase, decrease, or difference: *Our team was leading by eight points.*

8 used to say what part of someone or something is held: *He took her by the hand and led her away.* | *Hold the bucket by its handle.*

═══ **PHRASE** ═══

9 by yourself/himself/etc. alone, without company or help: *He was sitting by himself in a corner.* | *Did you paint the room all by yourself?*

by² [*adverb*]
1 past someone or something: *She waved as she drove by.* | *We watched the parade go by.*
2 if time goes by, it passes: *Several days went by without any news from him.*

═══ **PHRASES** ═══

3 stop by or **drop by** to visit someone: *Thanks for stopping by.*
4 by and by after a period of time: *By and by, they came to a small stream.*

bye /baɪ/ also **bye-bye** /ˌbaɪˈbaɪ/ [*interjection*] INFORMAL used to say goodbye: *Bye! See you later.*

byte /baɪt/ [*noun*] a basic unit for measuring how much information a computer or a computer document can hold: *A byte usually has 8 bits.*

═══ **C** ═══

C ✳ or **c** /si/ [*noun*]
1 [*plural* **Cs** or **C's, c's**] the third letter of the English alphabet
➪ *See the usage note at* ALPHABET.
2 **C** [*plural* **Cs** or **C's**] a fairly low grade in school: *I got a C on my history test.*

C. the written abbreviation of CELSIUS or CENTIGRADE: *Water boils at 100°C.*

c or **c.** the written abbreviation of CUP or CUPS: *Add 2 c flour and 1/4 c sugar.*

cab /kæb/ [*noun*]
1 a car with a driver you pay to take you somewhere; *synonym* TAXI: *We took a cab from the airport to the hotel.*
2 the part of a truck or train where the driver sits
➪ *See the picture at* PICKUP TRUCK.

cabbage /ˈkæbɪdʒ/ [*noun*] a large round VEGETABLE with thick green leaves

cabin /ˈkæbɪn/ [*noun*]
1 a small house made of wood
2 a small room where passengers sleep on a ship: *Each cabin has a bathroom and shower.*
3 the part of a plane where the passengers sit: *The cabin holds about 300 people.*

cabinet /ˈkæbənɪt/ [*noun*] a piece of furniture with a door and shelves or drawers, where you keep dishes, knives, medicines, etc.: *a bathroom cabinet*

cable /ˈkeɪbəl/ [*noun*]
1 a thick wire that carries electricity, electronic signals, telephone messages, etc.: *Attach the cable to the back of your computer.* | *a telephone cable*
2 a system of television broadcasting that you pay for, that connects to your home through cables: *Do you have cable TV?*
3 a thick, strong, metal rope: *The bridge is held up with cables.*

cactus /ˈkæktəs/ [*noun; plural* **cactuses** or **cacti** /ˈkæktaɪ/] a plant covered in sharp points with a thick stem, that grows in hot places

café or **cafe** /kæˈfeɪ/ [*noun; plural* **cafés** or **cafes**] a small restaurant

cafeteria [T] /ˌkæfɪˈtɪriə/ [noun; plural **cafeterias**] a restaurant or part of a building where people get their own food and then take it to a table to eat

caffeine /kæˈfin/ [noun] a substance in drinks such as coffee and tea that can keep you awake or make you nervous: *There's a lot of caffeine in cola.*

cage /keɪdʒ/ [noun] a structure with bars or wires in which birds or animals are kept: *A bird was singing in its cage.*

cake * /keɪk/ [noun] a sweet food made from flour, eggs, butter, etc.: *Who wants a slice of cake?*
⇨ See the picture at **SLICE**[1].

calcium /ˈkælsiəm/ [noun] a silver-white chemical substance that is very important for building and keeping strong bones: *Milk provides lots of calcium.*

calculate * /ˈkælkyəˌleɪt/ [verb; **calculated, calculating**] to use numbers to find an exact figure or result: *You'll need to calculate exactly how much the vacation will cost.*

calculation * /ˌkælkyəˈleɪʃən/ [noun] the use of numbers to find out an exact figure or result, or the result that you get: *budget calculations | I got the calculations wrong when I did my taxes.*

calculator /ˈkælkyəˌleɪtɚ/ [noun] a small electronic machine used to add, multiply, divide, etc., numbers

calendar /ˈkæləndɚ/ [noun] a set of pages showing the days, weeks, and months of a year: *Let me look at my calendar to see if I'm free on Friday.*
⇨ See the picture at **OFFICE**.

calf /kæf/ [noun; plural **calves**]
1 a young cow
2 the back part of your leg below your knee: *an exercise to strengthen the calf muscles*
⇨ See the picture at **BODY**.

call[1] * /kɔl/ [verb; **called, calling**]
1 to use a telephone to talk to someone; synonym PHONE: *I'll call you later. | Dad called while you were out.*
2 to say something in a loud voice, especially to get someone's attention: *He called out her name. | "Are you ready yet?" she called.*
⇨ See also **SHOUT**[1] (definition 1).

3 to give someone or something a name: *They called the baby Maria. | What's this flower called in English?* (=what is its English name)
4 to ask someone to come to you: *Call a doctor quickly!*

— PHRASAL VERBS —

call back [phrasal verb]
5 to telephone someone again after he or she has telephoned you: **call someone back** ▸ *Dad's not here right now. I'll get him to call you back.*

call off [phrasal verb]
6 to decide that something you have planned will not happen: **call off something** ▸ *I was sick, so I had to call off the party.*

call on [phrasal verb]
7 to ask someone to speak or answer a question: **call on someone** ▸ *The teacher never calls on me.*

call up [phrasal verb]
8 to telephone someone: **call up someone** ▸ *He called up Susan to chat. |* **call someone up** ▸ *He called her up on Tuesday.*
☛ Use **call up someone** only with a name: **He called up Susan.** Don't say "He called up her."

SYNONYMS call, telephone, phone, dial

These words are all verbs meaning "to use a telephone to talk to someone." **Call** is the most usual word: *I call my grandmother every week. | Call the police!* You can also use **phone**: *Your cousin phoned earlier.*

Telephone is a more formal word, and is not usually used in spoken English: *Customers may telephone our Information Service.*

If you **dial** a number, you press the numbers or turn the dial on a telephone: *He dialed 540–1817.*

call[2] [noun]
1 when you talk to someone using a telephone; synonyms PHONE CALL, TELEPHONE CALL: *You got a call from Michael while you were out* (=he telephoned you). *| I'll give him a call* (=telephone him) *tomorrow.*

2 a shout to get someone's attention: *He could hear the calls of the street vendors outside.*

3 a short visit to someone: *We should pay Donna a call* (=visit Donna) *while we're here.*

— PHRASE

4 **on call** someone who is on call must be ready to work if he or she is needed: *Which doctor is on call this weekend?*

caller /'kɔlɚ/ [*noun*] someone who makes a telephone call: *The caller asked to leave a message.*

calm[1] * T /kam/ [*adjective;* **calmer, calmest**]
1 relaxed and not angry, upset, or afraid: *The captain told the passengers to stay calm.*
 ⇨ *Compare* WILD[1] (definition 2).
2 not moving much; *opposite* ROUGH: *The water was calm and blue.*
 ⇨ *Compare* STILL[2].

calm[2] [*verb;* **calmed, calming**] to stop or to make someone stop being angry, upset or afraid: *We can't talk about this until you calm down.*

calmly * /'kamli/ [*adverb*] in a way that is relaxed and not angry, afraid, or upset: *She listened to them calmly.*

calves /kævz/ [*noun*] the plural of CALF

camcorder /'kæm,kɔrdɚ/ [*noun*] a camera that you carry with you and use to make movies, for example of your family or of your vacation
 ⇨ *See the picture at* APPLIANCE.

came * /keɪm/ [*verb*] the past tense of COME

camel /'kæməl/ [*noun*] a large desert animal with one or two humps, used to carry people and goods

hump

a camel

camera * /'kæmərə/ [*noun; plural* **cameras**] a piece of equipment for taking photographs
 ⇨ *See the picture at* APPLIANCE.

camp[1] * /kæmp/ [*noun*]
1 a place where young people stay for a short time and do sports and other activities: *He's going to summer camp next week.* | *I met her at camp.*
2 a place where a group of people sleep in tents or other temporary shelters: *an army camp*

camp[2] * [*verb;* **camped, camping**] to stay in a tent or camper for a short time: *They camped in the mountains last weekend.*

campaign /kæm'peɪn/ [*noun*] an organized activity that is intended to achieve something: *a political campaign* | *an advertising campaign*

camper /'kæmpɚ/ [*noun*]
1 someone who stays in a camp or a campground, or who attends a camp: *The campers began to put up their tents.*
2 a structure with beds in it that is used instead of a tent for camping: *Our camper fits onto a truck.*

campfire /'kæmp,faɪr/ [*noun*] a small fire outdoors, used for cooking on when you are camping

campground /'kæmp,graʊnd/ [*noun*] a place where people stay in tents for a short time, especially when they are on vacation: *The campground has toilets and showers.*
 ⇨ *Compare* CAMPSITE.

camping /'kæmpɪŋ/ [*noun*] the activity of staying in a tent for a short time, especially when you are on vacation: *I love to go camping.* | *We're taking the kids camping next month.*

campsite /'kæmp,saɪt/ [*noun*] a place in a campground where you can stay in your tent or camper: *We picked a campsite near the river.*

/i/ **see** /ɪ/ **big** /eɪ/ **day** /ɛ/ **get** /æ/ **hat**
/ɑ/ **father, hot** /ʌ/ **up** /ə/ **about** /ɔ/ **saw**
/oʊ/ **hope** /ʊ/ **book** /u/ **too** /aɪ/ **I** /aʊ/ **how**
/ɔɪ/ **boy** /ɝ/ **bird** /ɚ/ **teacher** /ɪr/ **ear** /ɛr/ **air**
/ɑr/ **far** /ɔr/ **more** /ʊr/ **tour** /aɪr/ **fire**
/aʊɚ/ **hour** /θ/ **nothing** /ð/ **mother** /ʃ/ **she**
/ʒ/ **measure** /tʃ/ **church** /dʒ/ **jump** /ŋ/ **long**

campus /'kæmpəs/ [*noun; plural* **campuses**] the buildings of a college or school and the land around them: *He's one of the smartest guys on campus.*

can¹ * /kæn/ [*modal verb; past* **could**]
  1 to be able to do something: *Can you swim?* | *She can play the violin.*
  2 to have permission to do something: *We can leave school early tomorrow.*
  3 used to ask for permission to do something: *Can I talk to you for a minute?*
  ▷ Compare MAY (definition 2).
  4 used to say that something is possible, or to offer to do something: *We can get some pizza before the movie.* | *I can feed your cat while you're gone.*

can² * [*noun*]
  1 a metal CONTAINER for food, drinks, etc.: *a can of tomatoes* | *a soda can*
  2 a large container for waste: *a trash can* | *a garbage can*

canal /kə'næl/ [*noun*] an artificial river that ships and boats travel along: *the Panama Canal*

canary /kə'nɛri/ [*noun; plural* **canaries**] a small yellow bird that sings and is kept as a pet

cancel /'kænsəl/ [*verb;* **canceled, canceling**] to decide that a planned event or activity will now not happen: *We canceled the trip because I was ill.*

cancer /'kænsɚ/ [*noun*] a disease that can spread through someone's body and makes cells grow in a way that is not normal: *Her father died of cancer.*

candidate /'kændɪˌdeɪt/ [*noun*] someone who might be chosen for a job or a political position: *There were three candidates for the sales job.* | *She was a candidate for mayor*

candle * /'kændəl/ [*noun*] a piece of wax with a string in the middle that burns to give light

candlestick /'kændəlˌstɪk/ [*noun*] a tall thin object that holds a candle

candy * /'kændi/ [*noun; plural* **candies**] sweet

a candle

a candlestick

food made from sugar or chocolate: *a bag of mint candies* | *I don't eat candy.*

candy bar /'kændi ˌbar/ [*noun*] soft candy in the shape of a bar, usually made of chocolate or covered in chocolate: *Mom, can I have a candy bar?*

candy cane /'kændi ˌkeɪn/ [*noun*] hard candy in the shape of a stick with a curved end, usually eaten at Christmas

cane /keɪn/ [*noun*] a stick that some people use to support them as they walk: *My grandmother walks with a cane.*

canned /kænd/ [*adjective; no comparative*] canned food is in a closed metal container that keeps it fresh: *canned vegetables*

cannon /'kænən/ [*noun; plural* **cannons** or **cannon**] a big heavy gun used for firing metal balls, used especially in the past: *They defended the fort with guns and cannons.*

cannot * /'kænat; kæ'nat/ [*modal verb*] FORMAL the negative form of CAN: *He cannot swim.*
  ▷ See also CAN'T.

canoe /kə'nu/ [*noun; plural* **canoes**] a small narrow boat for one or two people, that is pointed at both ends
  ▷ See the picture at KAYAK.

can't * /kænt/ the short form of CANNOT: *I can't see very well without my glasses.* | *You can ride a horse, can't you?*

cantaloupe /'kæntəˌloʊp/ [*noun*] a large round fruit that is pale green on the outside and has orange flesh
  ▷ See the picture at MELON.

canvas /'kænvəs/ [*noun*] strong cotton cloth: *My jacket is made of canvas.* | *a canvas bag*

canyon /'kænyən/ [*noun*] a deep valley with steep sides: *There was a river running through the canyon.*

cap * /kæp/ [*noun*]
  1 a soft hat that fits closely to your head: *He was wearing a baseball cap.*
  ▷ See the picture at BASEBALL CAP.
  2 a lid of a CONTAINER or bottle: *Put the cap back on the toothpaste.*

capable ⊤ /'keɪpəbəl/ [*adjective;* **more capable, most capable**]
  1 good at something: *Charles and Beth*

are both extremely capable students.
⇨ Compare **INCAPABLE**.

═══ **PHRASE** ═══

2 be capable of to have the skill or ability to do something: *The car is capable of speeds up to 120 miles per hour.*

capacity /kə'pæsɪti/ [*noun; plural* **capacities**] the amount that something can hold or can make: *containers of different capacities* | *The factory has increased its capacity.*

cape /keɪp/ [*noun*] a piece of clothing that hangs from the shoulders and is worn instead of a coat

capital * /'kæpɪtəl/ [*noun*]
1 the main city in a country or state: *The capital of China is Beijing.*
2 also **capital letter;** a letter of the alphabet with the form "B," "F," "K," etc., rather than "b," "f," "k," etc.; *synonym* **UPPERCASE**; *opposite* **LOWERCASE**: *"China" is spelled capital C, h, i, n, a.* | *Please print your name in capitals.*

SPELLING   Capital letters

Use a capital letter to begin a sentence. You should also always use a capital letter at the beginning of the name of a person, place, day, or month: *Dr. Margaret Rivers* | *Hello, John.* | *Have you ever been to Mexico?* | *I'll see you on Monday.* | *Her birthday is in February.* However, capital letters are not usually used for the names of seasons: *That summer was very hot.*

Use a capital letter for the name of a nationality or language: *He's Chinese.* | *Do you speak English?*

Use a capital letter for words such as Mom and Grandpa when they are used as names: *Dad, can I go outside and play?* | *Hi, Grandma!* However, do not use a capital letter at other times: *My dad said I could go out.* | *She's going to visit her grandma.*

---

capsule /'kæpsul/ [*noun*] a small object containing medicine that you swallow: *Take two capsules every four hours.*
⇨ See the picture at **PILL**.

captain /'kæptən/ [*noun*]
1 the leader of a sports team: *She's the captain of the hockey team.*
2 [*name*] also **Captain;** an officer with a fairly high rank in the Army, Navy, police, fire department, etc.
3 the person who is in charge of a ship: *a ferry captain*

captive /'kæptɪv/ [*noun*] a prisoner: *The kidnapper's captive was treated well.*

captivity /kæp'tɪvɪti/ [*noun*] the condition of being kept as a prisoner: *They were released from captivity.*

capture /'kæptʃɚ/ [*verb;* **captured, capturing**]
1 to catch someone and keep him or her as a prisoner: *He was captured by soldiers in the desert.*
2 to show or describe a situation or feeling very well in a picture or story: *Her photographs really capture the beauty of the area.*

car * /kɑr/ [*noun*]
1 a vehicle that has a motor and four wheels: *He got into the car and started the engine.* | *We went to Ohio by car.*

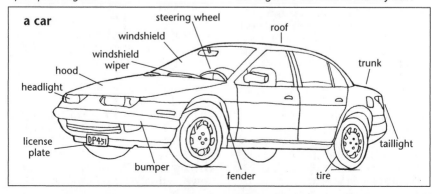

a car — steering wheel, windshield, windshield wiper, hood, headlight, roof, trunk, license plate, bumper, fender, tire, taillight

2 one of the parts of a train that you sit inside: *The train had eight cars.*

carbon /ˈkɑrbən/ [*noun*] a chemical substance that is in all living things and in many other substances: *Coal and diamonds are made of carbon.*

card * /kɑrd/ [*noun*]
1 a piece of stiff paper with a picture on the front and a message inside that you send someone on his or her birthday, wedding day, etc.: *a birthday card* | *an anniversary card*
2 a small piece of plastic that you use to pay for things, take money out of a bank, etc.
⊃ *See also* CREDIT CARD.
3 a small piece of stiff paper that has information on it: *an identification card* (=a card that shows who you are) | *a business card* (=with your name, company, position, and address on it)
4 one of a set of 52 pieces of stiff paper with pictures and numbers on them, that are used for playing various games: *They were playing a card game.*

cards

cardboard * /ˈkɑrdˌbɔrd/ [*noun*] thick stiff paper, used especially for making boxes: *a cardboard box*

cardinal /ˈkɑrdənəl/ or **cardinal number** /ˈkɑrdənəl ˈnʌmbɚ/ [*noun*] a number that is used for counting: *The cardinals are "one," "two," "three," etc.*
⊃ *Compare* ORDINAL.

care[1] * /kɛr/ [*verb*; **cared, caring**]
1 to feel interested in or worried about someone or something: *I really care about you.* | *Do you care what we do today?* | *I don't care if we go or not.*
— PHRASE —
2 not care for something to not like something: *I don't care for grapes.*
— PHRASAL VERB —
care for [*phrasal verb*]
3 to take care of someone who is not able to take care of himself or herself: **care for someone** ▸ *He has to care for his mother and younger sister.*

care[2] * [*noun*]
1 the process or activity of looking after someone or something: *The book gives advice on the care that animals need.* | *Skin care is very important.*
2 when you are careful to avoid damaging something or making a mistake: *You must handle old photographs with care.*
— PHRASES —
3 take care to be careful: *Take care when you go sailing.*
4 take care of to watch someone or something and make sure he, she, or it is safe: *I take care of the kids while my wife works.* | *They took care of our apartment while we were on vacation.*

career /kəˈrɪr/ [*noun*] someone's main job or profession, especially one that he or she does for most of his or her life: *a teaching career* | *a career in politics.*

careful * /ˈkɛrfəl/ [*adjective*; **more careful, most careful**]
1 thinking about what you are doing, to avoid mistakes or accidents: *He's a very careful driver.*
— PHRASE —
2 be careful (of) used to warn someone about something that could be dangerous: *Be careful how you cross the road.*

carefully * /ˈkɛrfəli/ [*adverb*] in a careful way: *She opened the package carefully.*

careless * /ˈkɛrlɪs/ [*adjective*; **more careless, most careless**] not thinking about what you are doing, so that you make mistakes or cause damage: *He makes careless mistakes in his work.*

carelessly * Ⓣ /ˈkɛrlɪsli/ [*adverb*] in a careless way: *The writing had been done quickly and carelessly.*

caretaker /ˈkɛrˌteɪkɚ/ [*noun*] someone whose job is to take care of a building or land

cargo /ˈkɑrgoʊ/ [*noun*; *plural* **cargos** or **cargoes**] the goods that a ship, plane, etc., carries: *a cargo of fresh fruit and vegetables*

caring /ˈkɛrɪŋ/ [*adjective*; **more caring, most caring**] often thinking about what other people need and trying to help them: *Lisa is a very caring person.*

carnation /kar'neɪʃən/ [*noun*] a FLOWER with a nice smell that people often pin to a jacket or dress on special occasions

carnival /'karnəvəl/ [*noun*] a traveling show with games and machines that you can ride on

carol /'kærəl/ [*noun*] a song that people sing at Christmas: *We sang carols around the Christmas tree.*

carousel /'kærə,sɛl/ [*noun*] a large machine that goes around and around, and has model horses that children ride on for fun

carpenter /'karpəntə/ [*noun*] someone whose job is to make things from wood: *A carpenter made us some bookshelves.*

carpet /'karpɪt/ [*noun*] a piece of heavy thick material that covers a floor: *a red carpet* | *a piece of carpet ten feet wide* ⇨ *Compare* RUG.

carriage * /'kærɪdʒ/ [*noun*]
1 a vehicle that is pulled by horses, that was used especially in past times
2 a small bed with four wheels and a handle in which a baby can lie or sit and be moved from place to place; *synonym* BABY CARRIAGE

carrier /'kæriə/ [*noun*]
1 a company whose business is to move goods, people, or information from one place to another: *We didn't like their phone service, so we switched to a different carrier.*
2 someone whose job is to deliver mail and packages: *a mail carrier*

carrot /'kærət/ [*noun*] a long orange root that is eaten as a VEGETABLE

carry * T /'kæri/ [*verb;* **carries, carried, carrying**]
1 to take something somewhere by holding it in your hands, in your arms, on your back, etc.: *He was carrying two bags.* | *She carried the baby into the house.*
2 to take people or goods from one place to another: *The bus can carry 60 passengers.*
3 if a pipe, wire, etc., carries a liquid or electricity somewhere, the liquid or

electricity flows along it: *Underground cables carry electricity to the houses.*

━━ **PHRASAL VERBS** ━━

carry on [*phrasal verb*]
4 to continue to do something that has already been started: **carry on something** ▸ *It was difficult to carry on the conversation after he left.*

carry out [*phrasal verb*]
5 to do something that you have promised to do or something that someone has asked you to do: **carry out something** ▸ *The city is carrying out road repairs.* | **carry something out** ▸ *I expect you to carry my orders out immediately.*

SYNONYMS carry, hold, lift

If you **carry** something, you take it from one place to another, especially in your hands or arms: *She was carrying a heavy grocery bag.*

If you **hold** something, you have it in your hand or hands, though you do not always take it from one place to another: *He was holding a piece of paper.*

If you **lift** something, you use your hands or arms to raise it from a lower place to a higher one: *She lifted the basket onto the table.*

---

cart /kart/ [*noun*]
1 a container or frame on wheels that you use in a food store, airport, etc., to carry things around: *a shopping cart*
2 a vehicle with two wheels that a horse pulls: *a horse and cart*

luggage cart
shopping cart
carts

cartilage /'kartəlɪdʒ/ [*noun*] a strong substance in the body, especially

---

/i/ **see** /ɪ/ **big** /eɪ/ **day** /ɛ/ **get** /æ/ **hat** /a/ **father, hot** /ʌ/ **up** /ə/ **about** /ɔ/ **saw** /oʊ/ **hope** /ʊ/ **book** /u/ **too** /aɪ/ **I** /aʊ/ **how** /ɔɪ/ **boy** /ɝ/ **bird** /ɚ/ **teacher** /ɪr/ **ear** /ɛr/ **air** /ar/ **far** /ɔr/ **more** /ʊr/ **tour** /aɪr/ **fire** /aʊɚ/ **hour** /θ/ **nothing** /ð/ **mother** /ʃ/ **she** /ʒ/ **measure** /tʃ/ **church** /dʒ/ **jump** /ŋ/ **long**

between the bones: *He tore the cartilage in his knee while playing football.*

carton /'kɑrtən/ [*noun*]
1 a small CONTAINER made of plastic or stiff paper for food or drinks: *a carton of milk*
2 a large box: *a carton of books*

cartoon /kɑr'tun/ [*noun*]
1 a funny drawing or series of drawings in a newspaper or magazine
2 a short movie, usually funny, that uses drawings rather than real actors to tell the story: *I like watching cartoons on TV.*

cartridge /'kɑrtrɪdʒ/ [*noun*] a small container or case with something in it, that you put inside something else: *an ink cartridge for a computer printer* | *an electronic game cartridge*

carve /kɑrv/ [*verb*; carved, carving]
1 to cut shapes in wood or stone: **carve something out of something** ▸ *She carved the figure out of marble.*

carving

2 to cut a cooked bird or a large piece of cooked meat into smaller pieces for people to put on their plates: *He carved the turkey and put it onto a plate.*

case * /keɪs/ [*noun*]
1 an example of a situation or a legal or business problem: *In some cases, the illness is caused by lack of sleep.* | *Their case will be decided in court.*
2 a container used to hold or protect something: *Have you seen my sunglasses case?* | *a jewelry case*

━━ PHRASES ━━

3 **in case** because something may happen: *Take the map in case we get lost.*
4 **in that case** because or if a situation is true: *"What if there's rain?" "In that case, we'll stay home."*

cash[1] /kæʃ/ [*noun*] money in the form of coins and paper: *If you don't have any cash, you can pay by check.*

cash[2] [*verb; cashes, cashed, cashing*] to exchange a check for coins or paper money: *Can I cash a check, please?*

cashew /'kæʃu/ [*noun*] a small, curved, yellow-brown NUT

cashier /kæ'ʃɪr/ [*noun*] the person who takes the money when you pay in a store: *The cashier gave me my change.*

cash machine /'kæʃ mə,ʃin/ [*noun*] a machine that you get money from; *synonym* ATM: *She went to get some money from the cash machine.*

cash register /'kæʃ ,rɛdʒɪstɚ/ [*noun*] a machine in a store that holds the money and shows how much each sale is: *There are cash registers on every floor.*

casino /kə'sinoʊ/ [*noun; plural* casinos] a place where people try to win money by playing games: *They were gambling in the casino.*

casserole /'kæsə,roʊl/ [*noun*] a hot dish made of a mixture of foods, or the heavy pan this is baked in: *a tuna casserole* | *a casserole dish*
↪ *See the picture at* POT.

cassette /kə'sɛt/ [*noun*] a flat plastic case with TAPE inside that is used to record sounds or pictures: *a video cassette* | *She bought two cassettes of her favorite singer.*

cast /kæst/ [*noun*]
1 the people who act in a play or movie: *The movie had an excellent cast.*
2 something hard that is put around a broken bone to protect it: *His broken arm was in a cast.*

castle * /'kæsəl/ [*noun*] an old stone building built to protect the people inside it from attack: *In Scotland, we visited an old castle.*

casual ⊤ /'kæʒuəl/ [*adjective;* more casual, most casual]
1 friendly and relaxed, or suitable for times when you are not doing anything special; *synonym* INFORMAL: *casual clothes* | *a casual dinner*
2 not seeming to care or worry about something: *He has a very casual attitude toward schoolwork.*

casually /'kæʒuəli/ [*adverb*] in a casual way: *She was casually dressed in a T-shirt and jeans.* | *He walked casually up to her.*

cat * /kæt/ [*noun*] an animal with four legs and a tail that catches birds and mice, that is kept as a pet

a cat

catalog /'kætə,lɔg/ [*noun*]
1 a set of pictures and descriptions of things you can buy, in a small book or shown on a computer: *She bought a new suit from the store catalog.*
2 a long list, especially of all the books in a library: *He looked in the catalog to see if they had the book.*

catastrophe /kə'tæstrəfi/ [*noun*] an extremely bad event or situation: *The earthquake was a total catastrophe.*

catch[1] * /kætʃ/ [*verb*; catches, caught, catching]
1 to stop something that is moving through the air and hold it: *He threw the ball and his dog caught it.*
   ⇨ *See the picture at* PLAY[1].
2 to get and keep a person or animal after you have been chasing or hunting him, her, or it: *The police are trying to catch the robber.* | *Look, I caught a fish!*
3 to get an illness: **catch something from someone** ▸ *I caught a cold from my brother.*

━━━ PHRASE ━━━
4 **catch a bus/plane/train** to get on a bus, plane, or train: *Hurry, or you won't catch the bus.*

━━━ PHRASAL VERB ━━━
catch up [*phrasal verb*]
5 to reach someone who is moving in front of you: **catch up with someone** ▸ *I ran to catch up with her.*

catch[2] [*noun*; plural **catches**]
1 when you catch a ball that someone has thrown or hit: *That was a great catch.*
2 a game of throwing and catching a ball played by two or more people: *Let's play catch.*

catcher /'kætʃɚ/ [*noun*] the player in baseball who catches the ball if the person who is supposed to hit it does not hit it

category /'kætɪ,gɔri/ [*noun*; plural **categories**] a group of people or things that have the same qualities or features: *He divided the books into three categories.*

caterpillar /'kætə,pɪlɚ/ [*noun*] the young form of some flying insects, that looks like a hairy or colored worm with legs

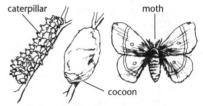

caterpillar   moth

cocoon

The **caterpillar** becomes a moth.

cathedral /kə'θidrəl/ [*noun*] a big important church

cattle * /'kætəl/ [*plural noun*] animals such as cows and bulls: *Cattle were grazing in the field.*
☛ Do not say "a cattle." **Cattle** is plural, and it is used with a plural verb.

caught * /kɔt/ [*verb*] the past tense and past participle of CATCH[1]

cauliflower /'kɔlɪ,flauɚ/ [*noun*] a VEGETABLE with large green leaves and a large, round, hard, white center

cause[1] * /kɔz/ [*verb*; caused, causing] to make something happen: *The accident was caused by driving too fast.*

cause[2] * [*noun*]
1 the thing that makes something happen: *The **cause of** the accident is not known.*
☛ Do not say "the cause for" in this meaning. Say **the cause of**.

/i/ **see** /ɪ/ **big** /eɪ/ **day** /ɛ/ **get** /æ/ **hat** /a/ **father, hot** /ʌ/ **up** /ə/ **about** /ɔ/ **saw** /oʊ/ **hope** /ʊ/ **book** /u/ **too** /aɪ/ **I** /aʊ/ **how** /ɔɪ/ **boy** /ɝ/ **bird** /ɚ/ **teacher** /ɪr/ **ear** /ɛr/ **air** /ar/ **far** /ɔr/ **more** /ʊr/ **tour** /aɪr/ **fire** /aʊɚ/ **hour** /θ/ **nothing** /ð/ **mother** /ʃ/ **she** /ʒ/ **measure** /tʃ/ **church** /dʒ/ **jump** /ŋ/ **long**

2 a reason that makes it right for you to feel or do something: *There's no cause for concern.*

USAGE cause, reason

A **cause** is what makes something happen, and a **reason** is why it happens. Use **of** with **cause**: *What was the cause of the computer failure?* Use **for** with **reason**: *There's no reason for you to be so angry.*

---

caution ⊤ /'kɔʃən/ [*noun*] when someone is very careful: *Open the box with caution.*

cautious ⊤ /'kɔʃəs/ [*adjective;* **more cautious, most cautious**] careful to avoid danger or trouble: *Be cautious walking home in the dark.*

cave /keɪv/ [*noun*] a hollow space under the ground or in the side of a mountain or cliff: *It was cold inside the cave.*

cc[1] /'si'si/ [*plural* **cc's**]
1 an abbreviation of "carbon copy," used in a business letter or electronic mail message to show that you are sending a copy to someone else:
To: John Bell
cc: Mary Harms, Cynthia London
2 an abbreviation of "cubic centimeter": *4 cc's of water*

cc[2] [*verb;* **cc's, cc'ed, cc'ing**] to send a copy of a business letter or electronic mail message to someone else: *She cc'ed the e-mail to the whole department.*

CD /'si'di/ [*noun; plural* **CDs** or **CD's**] a compact disc; a flat, round piece of plastic that sound or computer information can be stored on
⇨ *See the picture at* DISK.

CD player /'si'di ˌpleɪɚ/ [*noun*] a piece of equipment used to listen to CDs

CD-ROM /'si,di 'rɑm/ [*noun; plural* **CD-ROMs** or **CD-ROM's**] a CD containing information that can be read by a computer: *The program comes on CD-ROM.*

cease /sis/ [*verb;* **ceased, ceasing**] FORMAL to stop doing something: *We want the fighting to cease.* | *The newspaper will cease publication.*

cease-fire /'sis 'faɪr/ [*noun*] an agreement to stop fighting a war: *The cease-fire did not last* (=the fighting started again).

ceaseless /'sislɪs/ [*adjective; no comparative*] continuing and not stopping: *the ceaseless movement of ocean waves*

cedar /'sidɚ/ [*noun*] a tree with leaves like thick needles, which do not all fall off in winter, or the wood from this tree

ceiling * /'silɪŋ/ [*noun*] the flat surface at the top of a room

celebrate * ⊤ /'sɛləˌbreɪt/ [*verb;* **celebrated, celebrating**] to show that a day or event is special by having a party, special meal, etc.: *Mom and Dad had a party to celebrate their anniversary.*

celebration * /ˌsɛlə'breɪʃən/ [*noun*] a party or other special event when you celebrate something: *We're having a big New Year's celebration.*

celebrity /sə'lɛbrɪti/ [*noun; plural* **celebrities**] someone who is famous: *a television celebrity*

celery /'sɛləri/ [*noun*] a light green VEGETABLE with long thin parts

cell * /sɛl/ [*noun*]
1 one of the small rooms in a prison: *There were three prisoners in the cell.*
2 one of the smallest parts of all living things: *red blood cells*

cellar /'sɛlɚ/ [*noun*] a room under a building, used especially for storing food: *The wine is kept in the cellar.*
⇨ *Compare* BASEMENT.

cello /'tʃɛloʊ/ [*noun; plural* **cellos**] a MUSICAL INSTRUMENT with four strings that you hold between your legs and play with a BOW: *My sister plays the cello.*

cellular phone /'sɛlyəlɚ 'foʊn/ or **cell phone** /'sɛl ˌfoʊn/ [*noun*] a small phone that you carry around with you

antenna

a cellular phone

Celsius /'sɛlsiəs/ [*adverb*] according to a scale for measuring TEMPERATURE in which water freezes at 0° and boils at 100°; *synonym* CENTIGRADE: *It's 25° Celsius today.*
⇨ *Compare* FAHRENHEIT.

cement /sɪ'mɛnt/ [*noun*] a hard gray substance used in building that is made from powder and water: *a cement sidewalk*

cemetery /'sɛmɪˌtɛri/ [*noun; plural* **cemeteries**] a piece of land where dead people are buried; <u>synonym</u> GRAVEYARD: *She went to the cemetery to visit her grandmother's grave.*

cent ✳ /sɛnt/ [*noun*] the smallest unit of money in the U.S. and Canada: *That candy bar costs 75¢* (=spoken as: *seventy-five cents*). | *There are 100 cents in a dollar.*

center ✳ /'sɛntɚ/ [*noun*]
1 the middle of something: *We live near the center of town.* | *The Japanese flag is white with a red circle in the center.*
2 a place that is used for a particular activity: *a center for scientific research*

USAGE center, middle

Use **center** to talk about the exact center of an area: *Put the flowers in the center of the table.*

Use **middle** to talk more generally about a place in or near the center: *He was in the middle of the street.*

---

centigrade /'sɛntɪˌgreɪd/ [*adverb*] according to a scale for measuring TEMPERATURE in which water freezes at 0° and boils at 100°; <u>synonym</u> CELSIUS: *It's 25° centigrade today.*
➪ *Compare* FAHRENHEIT.

centimeter ✳ /'sɛntəˌmitɚ/ [*noun*] a unit for measuring length: *There are 100 centimeters in a meter.*

central ✳ /'sɛntrəl/ [*adjective;* **more central, most central**]
1 in the middle of an area: *Central Asia*
2 extremely important: *She had a central role in planning the event.*
3 a central system or organization controls what other systems and organizations do: *a central computer network*
☛ Only use **central** before a noun in this meaning.

century ✳ /'sɛntʃəri/ [*noun; plural* **centuries**] a period of 100 years: *The year 2001 marks the start of the 21st century.*

cereal /'sɪriəl/ [*noun*]
1 a food made from grains that people eat with milk, especially for breakfast: *Do you want toast or cereal?*
2 a plant such as wheat or rice: *a cereal crop*

ceremony ✳ /'sɛrəˌmouni/ [*noun; plural* **ceremonies**] a set of actions and words that are used at special social or religious events: *a wedding ceremony*

certain[1] ✳ /'sɝtən/ [*adjective;* **more certain, most certain**]
1 sure about something; <u>opposite</u> UNCERTAIN: *Are you **certain that** he saw you?* | *You must be **certain about** your facts.*
☛ Do not use **certain** before a noun
━━ PHRASE ━━
2 **make certain** to be sure something happens or is done: *Make certain you sign your application form.*

certain[2] ✳ [*determiner*] used to talk about someone or something that you do not name exactly: *Certain animals come out only at night.*

certainly ✳ /'sɝtənli/ [*adverb*]
1 without any doubt; <u>synonym</u> DEFINITELY: *Carlos is certainly taller than I am.*
2 SPOKEN used to say yes: *"May I sit here?" "Certainly."*
3 used to emphasize what you are saying; <u>synonym</u> SURE: *I'm certainly glad that he's safe.*

certificate /sɚ'tɪfɪkɪt/ [*noun*] an important piece of paper that shows that something is true or that you have achieved something: *a **birth certificate*** (=that says when and where you were born)

chain[1] ✳ /tʃeɪn/ [*noun*]
a series of metal rings that are joined together: *There is a chain holding the gate closed.*

link

a chain

chain[2] [*verb;* **chained, chaining**] to fasten something with a chain: *The*

/i/ **see**	/ɪ/ **big**	/eɪ/ **day**	/ɛ/ **get**	/æ/ **hat**
/ɑ/ **father, hot**	/ʌ/ **up**	/ə/ **about**	/ɔ/ **saw**	
/oʊ/ **hope**	/ʊ/ **book**	/u/ **too**	/aɪ/ **I**	/aʊ/ **how**
/ɔɪ/ **boy**	/ɝ/ **bird**	/ɚ/ **teacher**	/ɪr/ **ear**	/ɛr/ **air**
/ɑr/ **far**	/ɔr/ **more**	/ʊr/ **tour**	/aɪr/ **fire**	
/aʊə/ **hour**	/θ/ **nothing**	/ð/ **mother**	/ʃ/ **she**	
/ʒ/ **measure**	/tʃ/ **church**	/dʒ/ **jump**	/ŋ/ **long**	

doors were chained. | Did you **chain up** your bike before you went into the store?

chair * /tʃɛr/ [noun]
1 a piece of furniture for one person to sit on that has a back and four legs: She sat down in the chair by the window.
2 someone who leads a meeting: The chair called for a vote.

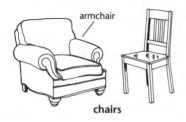

armchair

chairs

chairlift /'tʃɛr,lɪft/ [noun] several chairs that hang from a thick, strong, metal rope and are used to carry people up a mountain

chairman /'tʃɛrmən/ [noun; plural **chairmen** /'tʃɛrmən/]
1 someone, especially a man, who leads a meeting: The chairman ended the meeting by thanking everyone.
2 the leader of a political party: the Democratic Party chairman

USAGE   chairman, chairperson, chairwoman

Chairperson (/'tʃɛr,pɜrsən/) is often used instead of **chairman**, especially for a woman. **Chairwoman** (/'tʃɛr,wʊmən/) can also be used for a woman.

chalk * /tʃɔk/ [noun]
1 soft white or gray rock: The soil contains a lot of chalk.
2 a piece of this used for writing and drawing: a **piece of chalk**

chalkboard /'tʃɔk,bɔrd/ [noun] a large dark board or surface that you write on with chalk, especially in a school; synonym BLACKBOARD
⇨ See the picture at CLASSROOM.

challenge[1] ⊤ /'tʃælɪndʒ/ [noun]
1 something that is interesting and tests your skill and strength: The competition will be a challenge. | the challenge of skiing

2 an invitation to someone to compete against you in a game, fight, etc.: We accepted the challenge to play them at basketball.
3 when you show that you doubt that something is right: His speech was a **challenge to** the president's programs.

challenge[2] ⊤ [verb; challenged, challenging]
1 to say that you do not think something is right: He challenged the umpire's decision.
2 to invite someone to compete against you in a game: **challenge someone to something** ▸ They challenged us to a game of baseball.

challenging /'tʃælɪndʒɪŋ/ [adjective; more challenging, most challenging] difficult but interesting and exciting: My job is very challenging.

chamber /'tʃeɪmbər/ [noun] FORMAL a room, especially one used for important meetings: the Senate chamber

champagne /ʃæm'peɪn/ [noun] a white wine from France that has bubbles in it

champion /'tʃæmpiən/ [noun] someone who has won a competition: She's a tennis champion.

championship /'tʃæmpiən,ʃɪp/ [noun] a competition to see who is the best in a sport: the basketball championship

chance * /tʃæns/ [noun]
1 a possibility that something will happen: There's **a chance that** we will go to Japan. | There's **no chance** that they will win now.
2 an occasion when it is possible for you to do something good, enjoyable, useful, etc.; synonym OPPORTUNITY: **chance to do something** ▸ I haven't had a chance to read the book yet.
━ PHRASES ━
3 **by chance** if something happens by chance, you did not plan it: I met him by chance.
4 **take a chance** to do something although you know it may not be successful: We took a chance that the store would be open.

change[1] * /tʃeɪndʒ/ [verb; changed, changing]
1 to become different, or to make

someone or something different: *The city has changed in the last few years.* | *Becoming famous has changed his life.*

2 to stop doing, using, or having one thing and do, use, or have something else: *She changed the light bulb.* | *Can you change these dollars for yen, please?* | *They changed places in line.*

3 to get off a bus, train, etc., and get onto another one: *We changed at Fir Road.* | *We'll change planes in Reno.*

4 to take off your clothes and put on different ones: *I always change when I get home from school.* | *She changed her dress.* | *You should change into more comfortable clothes.*

change² * [*noun*]

1 the process or fact of becoming different: *There's been a change in the weather.* | *Change can be difficult.*

2 money that you get back when you pay more than something costs: *The cashier gave me the wrong change* (=did not give back the right amount).

3 money in the form of coins: *I don't have any change.*

— PHRASE

4 for a change used to emphasize that something is different from what you would normally do: *Let's go to the movies for a change.*

channel /'tʃænəl/ [*noun*]

1 a television station and the programs that it shows: *There's a great program on channel 5 tonight.*

2 a narrow area of water between two larger ones: *the English Channel*

chaos /'keɪɑs/ [*noun*] when a situation is completely uncontrolled and no one knows what is happening: *The airport was in complete chaos.*

chapel /'tʃæpəl/ [*noun*] a small church or an area in a church or other building for prayer: *the hospital's chapel*

chapter /'tʃæptɚ/ [*noun*] a part into which a book is divided: *Be prepared to discuss chapter two on Monday.*

character * /'kærɪktɚ/ [*noun*]

1 all the qualities that make someone behave the way he or she does: *He has a quiet side to his character.*

2 someone in a book, play, or movie: *The main character is a teacher.*

3 a sign in an Asian language that represents a word, an idea, or a sound: *This character means "person."*

charcoal /'tʃɑr,koʊl/ [*noun*] a black substance that results from burning wood: *a bag of charcoal*

charge¹ * ⊤ /tʃɑrdʒ/ [*noun*]

1 the price you pay for a thing or a service: *There's a charge of $10 to get into the museum.*

↪ See the synonym note at COST².

2 a statement from the police saying that someone is guilty of a crime: *He's in jail on a charge of murder.*

— PHRASE

3 be in charge (of) or **take charge (of)** to be the person who controls something, or begin to do this: *Who's in charge of this department?*

charge² * ⊤ [*verb*; **charged, charging**]

1 to ask a particular amount of money for something: **charge something for something** ▸ *They charge $2.50 for a cup of coffee.*

2 to buy something and pay for it later: *I'll use my credit card and charge our lunch.*

3 if the police charge someone, they officially say that they think he or she is guilty of a particular crime: **charge someone with something** ▸ *She was charged with robbery.*

charity /'tʃærɪti/ [*noun*; *plural* **charities**]

1 an organization that collects money to help people or animals that are poor, sick, or old: *a charity that helps homeless people*

2 money that is given to people or animals that are poor, sick, or old: *All profits from the show will go to charity.*

charm¹ /tʃɑrm/ [*verb*; **charmed, charming**] to be pleasing and attractive to other people: *She charms everyone she meets.*

/i/ **see** /ɪ/ **big** /eɪ/ **day** /ɛ/ **get** /æ/ **hat**
/ɑ/ **father, hot** /ʌ/ **up** /ə/ **about** /ɔ/ **saw**
/oʊ/ **hope** /ʊ/ **book** /u/ **too** /aɪ/ **I** /aʊ/ **how**
/ɔɪ/ **boy** /ɝ/ **bird** /ɚ/ **teacher** /ɪr/ **ear** /ɛr/ **air**
/ɑr/ **far** /ɔr/ **more** /ʊr/ **tour** /aɪr/ **fire**
/aʊɚ/ **hour** /θ/ **nothing** /ð/ **mother** /ʃ/ **she**
/ʒ/ **measure** /tʃ/ **church** /dʒ/ **jump** /ŋ/ **long**

charm^2 [*noun*]
1 a quality someone has that makes him or her pleasing and attractive: *He has a lot of charm.*
2 an object thought to bring good luck: *This penny is my lucky charm.*

charming /'tʃɑrmɪŋ/ [*adjective;* **more charming, most charming**] pleasing and attractive: *a charming young lady*

chart /tʃɑrt/ [*noun*] a picture that shows information, especially information that relates to amounts: *The chart shows how tall each child is.*
➷ Compare GRAPH, TABLE (definition 2).

chase^1 ＊ /tʃeɪs/ [*verb;* **chased, chasing**] to follow someone or something to catch him, her, or it: *The cat was chasing a mouse.*

chase^2 [*noun*] when you follow someone or something to catch him, her, or it: *There's an exciting car chase in the movie.*

chat^1 /tʃæt/ [*noun*] a friendly conversation: *We had a nice chat.*

chat^2 [*verb;* **chats, chatted, chatting**] to talk in a friendly way: *We chatted about our school.*

chatter /'tʃætɚ/ [*verb;* **chattered, chattering**] to talk a lot, especially about things that are not important: *teenagers chattering on the phone*

cheap ＊ /tʃip/ [*adjective;* **cheaper, cheapest**]
1 not costing much money: *The book was very cheap.*
2 not of good quality: *a cheap shirt*

cheat^1 ＊ /tʃit/ [*verb;* **cheated, cheating**] to behave in a dishonest way to try to win a game or do well on a test: *She cheated on her history test.*

cheat^2 [*noun*] someone who behaves in a dishonest way to try to win a game or do well on a test: *You cheat! You looked at my cards.*

check^1 ＊ /tʃɛk/ [*verb;* **checked, checking**]
1 to make sure that something is correct, true, etc.: *"Is the baby asleep?" "I'll go and check."* | *I'd better check that I locked the door.*
2 to make a mark on paper to show that something is correct, finished, etc.: *The teacher checked my work.*

check in [*phrasal verb*]
3 to tell someone at an airport or hotel that you have arrived: *We checked in an hour before the flight.*
check out [*phrasal verb*]
4 to leave a hotel after paying: *Guests must check out by 12:00.*

check^2 ＊ [*noun*]
1 when someone looks at something to see if it is safe, true, etc.: *They are doing safety checks on the machines in the factory.*
2 a piece of paper that you sign and use instead of money to pay for something: *You can pay by check.* | **write someone a check** ▸ *I'll write you a check for the groceries.*
3 a piece of paper that shows how much money you must pay in a restaurant: *We're ready for the check.*
4 a mark on paper (✔) to show that something is right: *The teacher put a check by every correct answer.*

checkbook /'tʃɛk,bʊk/ [*noun*] a book that a bank gives you with pieces of paper that you sign and use to pay for things: *Oh no—I forgot my checkbook.*

checked /tʃɛkt/ [*adjective; no comparative*] having a regular PATTERN of dark and light squares: *a checked tablecloth*

checkers /'tʃɛkɚz/ [*noun*] a game for two people, played by moving round pieces on a board with black and red squares: *Dad and I often play checkers.*
☛ Only use **checkers** with a singular verb.

checking account /'tʃɛkɪŋ ə,kaʊnt/ [*noun*] a bank account in which you keep the money you need to have ready to spend
➷ Compare SAVINGS ACCOUNT.

checkout /'tʃɛk,aʊt/ [*noun*]
1 also **checkout counter** /'tʃɛk,aʊt ,kaʊntɚ/ the place where you pay for things in a large store: *She took all the things to the checkout.*
2 the time when people must leave a hotel: *Checkout is at noon.*

checkup /'tʃɛk,ʌp/ [*noun*] an examination that a doctor gives you to make sure you are healthy: *It's time for my yearly checkup.*

cheek * /tʃik/ [*noun*] one of the two soft parts at the side of your face: *Tears ran down her cheeks.*
  ⇨ *See the picture at* BODY.

cheer[1] /tʃɪr/ [*verb; cheered, cheering*]
  1 to shout loudly because you are happy or want to encourage someone: *We cheered when Dave hit a home run.*
  ━ **PHRASAL VERB** ━━━
cheer up [*phrasal verb*]
  2 to become less sad, or to make someone less sad: *He cheered up when his friends arrived.* | **cheer someone up** ▸ *I tried to cheer her up.*
  ⇨ *Compare* DEPRESS.

cheer[2] [*noun*] a shout you make when you are happy or want to encourage someone: *The crowd gave a cheer.*

cheerful * /'tʃɪrfəl/ [*adjective; more cheerful, most cheerful*] behaving in a happy, friendly way: *She was always cheerful, even when things went wrong.*
  ⇨ *See the synonym note at* HAPPY.

cheerfully * /'tʃɪrfəli/ [*adverb*] in a happy, friendly way: *"Good morning everyone!" he said cheerfully.*

cheerleader /'tʃɪr,lidɚ/ [*noun*] one of an organized group of young people who encourage a team's supporters to cheer and shout during a sports game

cheese * /tʃiz/ [*noun*] a hard or soft food made from milk, or a kind of this food: *a cheese sandwich* | *cream cheese* | *She bought several hard cheeses.*

cheeseburger /'tʃiz,bɚgɚ/ [*noun*] a sandwich made of a round piece of ground beef with melted cheese, between two thick round pieces of bread: *I'll have a cheeseburger with pickles and onions, please.*
  ⇨ *Compare* HAMBURGER.

cheesecake /'tʃiz,keɪk/ [*noun*] a cake made with soft cheese and sugar: *a slice of cherry cheesecake*

chef /ʃɛf/ [*noun*] someone whose job is to cook in a hotel or restaurant

chemical[1] * T /'kɛmɪkəl/ [*noun*] a natural substance that is used in or produced by chemistry: *Chemicals are very important in certain industries.*

chemical[2] * T [*adjective; no comparative*] relating to chemicals or chemistry: *a chemical reaction*

chemist /'kɛmɪst/ [*noun*] a scientist who knows a lot about chemistry

chemistry * /'kɛməstri/ [*noun*] the science that studies what substances are made of and how they change

cherry /'tʃɛri/ [*noun; plural cherries*] a small, soft, round, red FRUIT that grows on trees

chess /tʃɛs/ [*noun*] a game for two people, played by moving different shaped pieces on a board with black and white squares: *Do you play chess?*

chest * /tʃɛst/ [*noun*]
  1 the part of your BODY that is between your neck and your stomach
  2 a big box made from wood that you keep things in: *a toy chest*

chew * /tʃu/ [*verb; chewed, chewing*] to bite food several times before you swallow it: *The candy was hard to chew.*

chewing gum /'tʃuɪŋ ,gʌm/ [*noun*] soft candy that you chew but do not swallow; *synonym* GUM: *He always has some chewing gum in his mouth.*

chick /tʃɪk/ [*noun*] a young chicken or other bird: *There was a chick in the nest.*

chicken * /'tʃɪkən/ [*noun*] a bird that is kept for its meat and eggs, or the meat from this bird: *a chicken sandwich*

hen

rooster

chickens

chief[1] * T /tʃif/ [*adjective; no comparative*] most important: *the hospital's chief surgeon*

chief[2] * [*noun*] the most important person in an organization or a tribe: *the Chief of Police*

chiefly ⊤ /'tʃifli/ [*adverb*] in the main or most important way: *He's chiefly responsible for organizing the concerts.*

child * /tʃaɪld/ [*noun; plural* **children**]
1 someone who is older than a baby but is not yet 13: *There are 40 children in the class.*
2 someone's son or daughter: *Do you have any children?* | *He's an only child* (=without any brothers or sisters).

SYNONYMS   child, kid, toddler

A **child** is a person who is not yet a teenager: *The children were playing in the yard.*

Kid is an informal word for a child or young person: *Hey, you kids! Come over here!* | *a kids' game*

A **toddler** is a very young child who has just learned to walk: *My son is a toddler now.*

---

childhood /'tʃaɪldhʊd/ [*noun*] the time when someone is a child: *She had a happy childhood.*

childish /'tʃaɪldɪʃ/ [*adjective;* **more childish, most childish**] behaving in a silly way: *Stop being so childish!*

children * /'tʃɪldrən/ [*noun*] the plural of CHILD

chili /'tʃɪli/ [*noun; plural* **chilies**]
1 a small thin vegetable with a very strong hot taste: *Mexican food uses a lot of chilies.* | *chili powder*
2 a dish like thick soup made from beans, tomatoes, and meat, that tastes hot: *a bowl of chili*

chilly /'tʃɪli/ [*adjective;* **chillier, chilliest**] cold, but not extremely cold: *It's chilly outside.*

chimney /'tʃɪmni/ [*noun; plural* **chimneys**] a pipe that carries smoke from a fire out through the roof of a HOUSE or other building

chimpanzee /ˌtʃɪmpæn'zi/ [*noun; plural* **chimpanzees**] an animal like a monkey, with no tail
⇨ *See the picture at* APE.

chin * /tʃɪn/ [*noun*] the area on your face that is below your mouth
⇨ *See the picture at* BODY.

china /'tʃaɪnə/ [*noun*]
1 a hard substance that cups and plates are made from: *china cups and saucers*
2 plates, cups, etc., that are made of china: *They had some beautiful china.*

chinos /'tʃinoʊz/ [*plural noun*] pants that are made of a soft cotton cloth: *a pair of chinos*

chips

chip¹ /tʃɪp/ [*noun*]
1 thin pieces of food that have been fried until they are hard: *potato chips* | *tortilla chips* (=made from ground corn)
2 a small hole or mark on a plate, glass, etc., where a piece has broken off: *There's a chip in the cup.*
3 a very small object with electronic connections on it, used to make computers or other electronic equipment work; *synonym* MICROCHIP: *a memory chip*

chip² [*verb;* **chips, chipped, chipping**] if something chips, or if you chip it, a small piece breaks off it: *The dish fell and chipped.* | *She chipped her tooth.*

chipmunk /'tʃɪpmʌŋk/ [*noun*] a small animal with a long tail and black lines on its fur

a chipmunk

chipped /tʃɪpt/ [*adjective; no comparative*] something hard that is chipped has a piece missing from it: *a chipped tooth* | *a chipped cup*
⇨ *See the picture at* CRACKED.

chirp /tʃɜrp/ [*verb;* **chirped, chirping**] if birds or particular insects chirp, they make short high sounds: *The birds began to chirp at five o'clock this morning.*

chisel /'tʃɪzəl/ [*noun*] a metal TOOL used to shape wood or stone

chocolate * /'tʃɔkəlɪt/ [*noun*]
1 a sweet brown food made from cocoa and sugar: *a bar of chocolate* | *a chocolate cake*
2 a piece of candy made from chocolate: *a box of chocolates*

choice * /tʃɔɪs/ [*noun*]
1 a decision that you make about what you want: *I had to **make a choice between** the red shirt and the blue one.*
2 the person or thing that you choose: *Hawaii was a good choice for our trip.*
3 all the things that you can choose from: *There is **a wide choice** of courses* (=a lot you can choose from).
4 the chance to choose between several things: *You **have a choice** of hotels in the area.*

choir /kwaɪr/ [*noun*] a group of people who sing together: *She sings in the school choir.*

choke /tʃoʊk/ [*verb*; **choked, choking**] to be unable to breathe because there is something in your throat: *He was **choking on** a piece of food.*

choose * /tʃuz/ [*verb*; **chose, chosen, choosing**] to decide which of several things, ideas, people, etc., you want: *I don't care what we eat—you choose.* | *She chose a red dress to wear to the party.*

chop[1] /tʃɑp/ [*verb*; **chops, chopped, chopping**]
1 to cut food or wood into smaller pieces: ***Chop up** the vegetables, please.* | *He was chopping wood.*

━━ **PHRASAL VERB** ━━━━━

chop down [*phrasal verb*]
2 to make a tree fall down by cutting it: **chop something down** ▸ *They chopped the old oak tree down.* | **chop down something** ▸ *They chopped down the tree next to the house.*

chop[2] [*noun*] a flat piece of meat with a bone in it: *a pork chop*

chopstick /'tʃɑp,stɪk/ [*noun*] one of the two long thin pieces of wood or plastic that some people use to eat food: *a **pair** of chopsticks*

chore /tʃɔr/ [*noun*] a small job you must do regularly, often one that you do not like: *My brother and I have to do chores every week, like mowing the lawn, taking out the garbage, and cleaning our rooms.*

chorus /'kɔrəs/ [*noun*; *plural* **choruses**]
1 a part of a song that you repeat several times: *We all sang the chorus.*
2 a large group of people who sing together: *an opera's chorus*

chose * /tʃoʊz/ [*verb*] the past tense of CHOOSE

chosen * /'tʃoʊzən/ [*verb*] the past participle of CHOOSE

chowder /'tʃaʊdər/ [*noun*] thick soup made with fish or corn and milk: *a bowl of clam chowder*

Christian[1] /'krɪstʃən/ [*noun*] someone who believes in Jesus Christ and the things he taught

Christian[2] [*adjective*; *no comparative*] based on the things that Jesus Christ taught: *the Christian religion*

Christianity /ˌkrɪstʃi'ænɪti/ [*noun*] the religion that is based on Jesus Christ and the things that he taught

Christmas /'krɪsməs/ [*noun*] December 25th, a holiday when people give each other gifts. It traditionally celebrates the birth of Jesus Christ: *What are you giving your parents **for Christmas**?* | ***Merry Christmas!*** (=I hope you have a happy Christmas)

Christmas Eve /'krɪsməs 'iv/ [*noun*] December 24th, the evening before Christmas: *We decorate the tree on Christmas Eve.*

Christmas tree /'krɪsməs ˌtri/ [*noun*; *plural* **Christmas trees**] a small tree that people decorate and have in their houses at Christmas: *We put lights on the Christmas tree.*

chubby /'tʃʌbi/ [*adjective*; **chubbier, chubbiest**] slightly fat, but in a pleasant way: *a chubby baby*

/i/ **see**	/ɪ/ **big**	/eɪ/ **day**	/ɛ/ **get**	/æ/ **hat**
/ɑ/ **father, hot**	/ʌ/ **up**	/ə/ **about**	/ɔ/ **saw**	
/oʊ/ **hope**	/ʊ/ **book**	/u/ **too**	/aɪ/ **I**	/aʊ/ **how**
/ɔɪ/ **boy**	/ɚ/ **bird**	/ə/ **teacher**	/ɪr/ **ear**	/ɛr/ **air**
/ɑr/ **far**	/ɔr/ **more**	/ʊr/ **tour**	/aɪr/ **fire**	
/aʊə/ **hour**	/θ/ **nothing**	/ð/ **mother**	/ʃ/ **she**	
/ʒ/ **measure**	/tʃ/ **church**	/dʒ/ **jump**	/ŋ/ **long**	

chuckle /'tʃʌkəl/ [verb; chuckled, chuckling] to laugh in a quiet way: *She chuckled as she read the letter.*

chunk /tʃʌŋk/ [noun] a large piece or amount of something: *a chunk of cheese*

church * /tʃɜrtʃ/ [noun; plural **churches**] a building where Christians meet and pray to God: *They go to church* (=go to a meeting there) *every Sunday.*

cider /'saɪdər/ [noun] a drink made from apples: *a glass of cider*

cigar /sɪ'gɑr/ [noun] a thick tube of tobacco that is smoked

cigarette * /ˌsɪgə'rɛt/ [noun] a thin tube of paper with tobacco inside that is smoked: *a pack of cigarettes*

cinema /'sɪnəmə/ [noun; plural **cinemas**] a word used in the names of buildings where you go to see movies; synonym MOVIE THEATER: *We saw a good movie at the Crossroads Cinemas.*

cinnamon /'sɪnəmɪn/ [n.u.] a brown spice that is sold as a powder or in sticks, and is often used in baking

circle * /'sɜrkəl/ [noun] a round shape, or several people or things arranged in a round shape: *She drew a circle on the paper.* | *They stood in a circle.*
⇨ See Shapes in the Smart Study section.

circular * /'sɜrkyələr/ [adjective; no comparative] in the shape of a circle, or moving in a circle: *a circular racetrack*

circulate Ⓣ /'sɜrkyəˌleɪt/ [verb; circulated, circulating] to move around and around: *Blood circulates around your body.*

circumference /sɜr'kʌmfərəns/ [noun] the distance around a circle or a ball: *the circumference of a circle* | *a sphere 12 centimeters in circumference*
⇨ See the picture at DIAMETER.

circumstances /'sɜrkəmˌstænsɪz/ [plural noun] the conditions that affect a situation or event: *What were the circumstances surrounding his death?* | *Under the circumstances* (=because of them), *we can ignore the rules.* | *Under no circumstances* (=never) *will I go!*

circus /'sɜrkəs/ [noun; plural **circuses**] a show with people and animals doing tricks, often in a big tent

citizen * /'sɪtəzən/ [noun] someone who lives in a particular town or country: *Korean citizens* | *a U.S. citizen*

citizenship /'sɪtəzənˌʃɪp/ [noun] the right to live in a particular country: *He is applying for U.S. citizenship.*

city * /'sɪti/ [noun; plural **cities**] a large place with many houses and businesses that has a central government: *Los Angeles is the largest city in California.* | *I like the excitement of the city.*

civilian /sɪ'vɪlyən/ [noun] someone who is not in the army, navy, etc.: *Many civilians and soldiers died in the war.*

civilization /ˌsɪvələ'zeɪʃən/ [noun] a society that has laws, education, art, etc.: *modern civilization* | *the civilizations of the ancient world*

civilized /'sɪvəˌlaɪzd/ [adjective; **more civilized, most civilized**] having laws, education, art, etc.: *a civilized country*

civil war /'sɪvəl 'wɔr/ [noun] a war between groups of people in a country who are trying to get political control: *The civil war lasted for several years.*

claim[1] * /kleɪm/ [verb; **claimed, claiming**]
1 to say that something is true although you cannot prove it: *She claims that she saw a ghost.* | *He claimed he had been robbed.*
2 to ask for something that you have a right to: *She claimed her prize.* | *He claimed compensation for his injury.*

claim[2] [noun] something that you say is true: *I don't believe their advertising claims.*

clam /klæm/ [noun] a sea creature that you can eat, that has two smooth shells that close around it
⇨ See the picture at SHELLFISH.

clamp /klæmp/ [noun] a TOOL with parts that can close tightly to hold things together

clap /klæp/ [verb; **claps, clapped, clapping**] to hit your hands together to show that you enjoyed something or to get people's attention: *The audience clapped and yelled.*
⇨ Compare APPLAUD.

clarinet /ˌklærəˈnɛt/ [*noun*] a MUSICAL INSTRUMENT that is a long wooden tube, with an end you blow into and buttons you press: *I can **play the clarinet**.*

clash[1] /klæʃ/ [*verb*; **clashes, clashed, clashing**]
 1 to disagree or fight with someone: *He often **clashed with** his father.*
 2 if colors clash, they do not look good together: *I think purple and red clash.*

clash[2] [*noun; plural* **clashes**]
 1 when people disagree or fight: *She had a **clash with** her boss.*
 2 a loud sound of metal hitting metal: *the clash of cymbals*

clasp /klæsp/ [*noun*] a small metal object that fastens a belt, a piece of jewelry, etc.: *The clasp on her necklace was broken.*

class * /klæs/ [*noun; plural* **classes**]
 1 a group of people who are being taught: *There are 30 kids in my class.*
 2 a meeting of a group of people to learn something: *a French class* | *We're not allowed to eat **in class**.*
 ➪ Compare LESSON.
 3 a group of students who graduate in the same year: *the class of '98*

4 one of the groups in a society that people are divided into depending on their job, education, etc.: *the middle class*

classic /ˈklæsɪk/ [*adjective; no comparative*] used about the best or most typical example of something: *a classic mystery movie*

classical /ˈklæsɪkəl/ [*adjective; no comparative*] classical music or art is serious and is considered to be more important than popular songs or art: *classical composers like Mozart*

classmate /ˈklæsˌmeɪt/ [*noun*] someone who is in your class at school: *I get along well with my classmates.*

classroom /ˈklæsˌrum/ [*noun*] a room where you are taught in a school or college

classwork /ˈklæsˌwɜk/ [*noun*] the activities that students do in a classroom, such as writing, tests, and group work: *Your classwork will count for 30 percent of your total grade.*
 ➪ Compare HOMEWORK.

clause /klɔz/ [*noun*] GRAMMAR a group of words that has a subject and a verb and forms part of a sentence: *In the sentence*

in a classroom
a clock
a bookcase
a map of the U.S.A.
a chalkboard/a blackboard
an equation
$$x^2 + 10x$$
$$(\tfrac{1}{2} \cdot 10)^2 = (5)^2 = 25$$
$$x^2 - 10x$$
$$[\tfrac{1}{2}(-3)]^2 = (-\tfrac{3}{2})^2 = \tfrac{9}{4}$$
a teacher
a book
a desk
a chair
a binder
a ruler
a notebook
a student/a pupil

"I ate an apple but I didn't like it," "but I didn't like it" is a clause.

claw /klɔ/ [*noun*]
1 a hard sharp part on the foot of an animal or bird: *The cat had sharp claws.* ⇨ *See the picture at* EAGLE.
2 the hard part at the end of the leg of some sea animals, such as LOBSTERS, that they use for holding things

clay * /kleɪ/ [*noun*] a substance that is soft when it is wet, and is used to make bricks and containers: *a clay flowerpot*

clean[1] * /klin/ [*adjective*; **cleaner, cleanest**]
1 not dirty: *He keeps the apartment very clean.*
2 not used: *Write your name on a clean sheet of paper.*

clean[2] * [*verb*; **cleaned, cleaning**]
1 to make something clean: *The house needs cleaning.*
— PHRASAL VERB —
clean up [*phrasal verb*]
2 to make something completely clean: *They were cleaning up after the party.* I **clean something up** ▸ *I have to clean this mess up.* I **clean up something** ▸ *Clean up your room.*

cleaner /ˈklinɚ/ [*noun*]
1 someone whose job is to clean a building or house: *The cleaners come once a week.*
2 a substance or machine used for cleaning things: *a new bathroom cleaner*
3 **the cleaner's** a store where you take clothes to be cleaned with chemicals instead of water; *synonym* DRY CLEANER: *I picked up my suit from the cleaner's.*

clear[1] * /klɪr/ [*adjective*; **clearer, clearest**]
1 easy to understand: *The instructions were very clear.*
2 easy to see, hear, or notice; *synonym* OBVIOUS: *It's clear that she's ill.*
3 a clear object or substance is easy to see through because it is not dirty or colored: *clear water* I *a clear glass vase*
4 empty or easy to pass through: *The roads are clear.*
5 easy to recognize or be certain about; *synonym* OBVIOUS: *It was clear we would be late.*

6 with no clouds, rain, or mist; *opposite* CLOUDY: *It was a clear day.*

SYNONYMS   clear, transparent
    Both of these words are used to describe things you can see through. **Clear** things are usually not colored. For example, a glass window is **clear**, but a **transparent** glass cup could be blue or green. Only **clear** can be used to describe substances such as water, and only **transparent** can be used to describe things such as cloth.

clear[2] * [*verb*; **cleared, clearing**]
1 to take things away so that a place is neater: *Please clear the table.* I *Can you clear your books off the table?*
— PHRASAL VERB —
clear up [*phrasal verb*]
2 to help make something easier to understand or deal with: **clear up something** ▸ *His explanation cleared up her confusion.*
3 if weather clears up, clouds go away or a storm stops: *It's supposed to clear up tomorrow.*

clearly * /ˈklɪrli/ [*adverb*] in a way that is easy to see, hear, or understand: *The teacher explained the problem clearly.* I *He was clearly very angry.*

clerk * /klɚk/ [*noun*]
1 someone who sells things in a store: *a grocery store clerk*
2 someone who does general jobs in an office: *My sister's a clerk in an accounting office.*

clever 🔲 /ˈklɛvɚ/ [*adjective*; **cleverer, cleverest**]
1 intelligent and quick to learn; *synonym* SMART: *a clever child* I *She's very clever.*
2 unusual and effective: *a clever tool for opening bottles*

click[1] /klɪk/ [*verb*; **clicked, clicking**]
1 to make a short, sharp sound, or to make something make this sound: *The gate clicked shut behind her.*
— PHRASAL VERB —
click on [*phrasal verb*]
2 to press a button on a computer mouse in order to do something on a computer: **click on something** ▸ *Click on the bar at the top of the screen.*

click[2] [*noun*] a short sound:
I heard the click of the door lock.

client /'klaɪənt/ [*noun*] someone who pays for work done by a business person: *He's in a meeting with an important client.*

cliff * /klɪf/ [*noun*] a high, steep place where the land or rock suddenly ends: *They stood on the cliffs above the beach.*

climate /'klaɪmɪt/ [*noun*] the kind of weather that an area usually has

climb[1] * /klaɪm/ [*verb*; **climbed, climbing**]
1 to go up, down, or over something, sometimes using your hands as well as your feet: *They climbed a hill to get a better view.* | *I climbed down the ladder.*
2 to go higher: *The airplane climbed higher and higher.*

climb[2] [*noun*] when you go up something such as a mountain: *It was a difficult climb.*

cling /klɪŋ/ [*verb*; **clung, clinging**] to hold onto something or someone very tightly, especially so that you do not fall: *She clung to him as they rode on his motorcycle.*

clinic /'klɪnɪk/ [*noun*] a place where people go for medical care and help: *She brought her baby to the health clinic.*

clip[1] /klɪp/ [*noun*] a small metal or plastic object used to hold things or fasten them together: *a hair clip* | *a paper clip*

clip[2] [*verb*; **clips, clipped, clipping**]
1 to hold or fasten something to another thing, using a clip: *A small microphone was clipped to her collar.*
2 to cut a small piece from something larger: *She clipped the article from the newspaper.*

clock * /klɑk/ [*noun*] an object on a wall, table, etc., that tells you what time it is
⇨ *See also* O'CLOCK. ⇨ *Compare* WATCH.
⇨ *See the pictures at* CLASSROOM *and* OFFICE.

clockwise /'klɑk,waɪz/ [*adverb*] in the same direction as the movement of the hands of a clock; *opposite* COUNTERCLOCKWISE: *Turn the cap clockwise to close it.*

close[1] * /kloʊs/ [*adjective*; **closer, closest**]
1 only a short distance from a place or thing; *synonym* NEAR: *The school is very close.* | *I took a closer look.*
2 very careful: *Pay close attention to your teacher.*
3 if two people are close, they like each other and talk to each other a lot: *Michael is one of my closest friends.*

— PHRASE —
4 close to almost doing something, or almost in a particular state or place: *He's close to graduating.* | *The temperature is close to freezing.*

close[2] * /kloʊs/ [*adverb*; **closer, closest**] only a short distance from a place or thing; *synonym* NEAR: *We live close to the airport.* | *My friends all live close by.*

close[3] * /kloʊz/ [*verb*; **closed, closing**]
1 to move part of something so it is no longer open, or to move and no longer be open; *synonym* SHUT: *Would you close the window, please?* | *She closed her eyes and tried to sleep.* | *There was a gust of wind and the door closed.*
2 to stop doing business for the day; *synonym* SHUT; *opposite* OPEN: *We close the library at six o'clock.* | *The office closes at five o'clock.*
3 to stop using a computer document or program, so that you can not see it any longer: *Close all your programs before you shut down your computer.*

— PHRASAL VERB —
close down [*phrasal verb*]
4 if a business or store closes down or is closed down, it does not do business any longer: *The movie theater closed down last year.* | **close down something** ▸ *They closed down the restaurant.*

closed * /kloʊzd/ [*adjective*; no comparative]
1 if something with parts that can move is closed, its parts are as close together as possible; *synonym* SHUT;

/i/ **see**	/ɪ/ **big**	/eɪ/ **day**	/ɛ/ **get**	/æ/ **hat**
/ɑ/ **father, hot**	/ʌ/ **up**	/ə/ **about**	/ɔ/ **saw**	
/oʊ/ **hope**	/ʊ/ **book**	/u/ **too**	/aɪ/ **I**	/aʊ/ **how**
/ɔɪ/ **boy**	/ɝ/ **bird**	/ɚ/ **teacher**	/ɪr/ **ear**	/ɛr/ **air**
/ɑr/ **far**	/ɔr/ **more**	/ʊr/ **tour**	/aɪr/ **fire**	
/aʊɚ/ **hour**	/θ/ **nothing**	/ð/ **mother**	/ʃ/ **she**	
/ʒ/ **measure**	/tʃ/ **church**	/dʒ/ **jump**	/ŋ/ **long**	

suits

a coat

sweaters

a vest

pocket

sleeve

cuff

a shirt

a blouse

a skirt

pants/trousers

a jumper

a dress

kinds of clothing

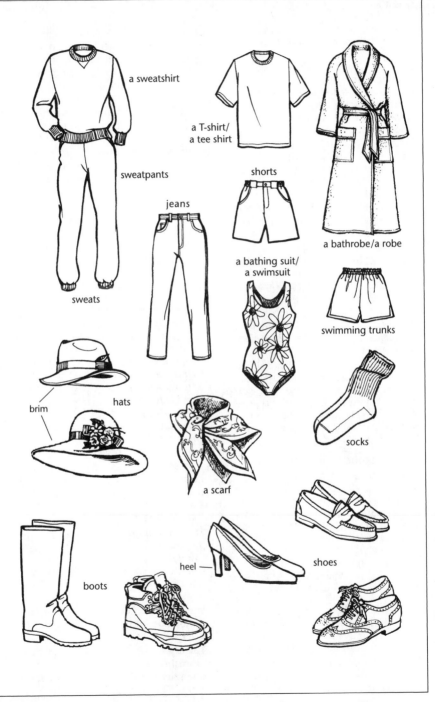

a sweatshirt

a T-shirt/
a tee shirt

sweatpants

shorts

jeans

a bathrobe/a robe

a bathing suit/
a swimsuit

sweats

swimming trunks

hats

brim

socks

a scarf

shoes

heel

boots

opposite OPEN: *Please keep the door closed.* | *Keep your mouth closed when you chew.*
2 not open for business; *synonym* SHUT: *The store was closed.*
3 not available for people to do or take part in; *opposite* OPEN: *The Senior Club is now **closed** to new members* (=no new members can join).

closely * /'kloʊsli/ [*adverb*]
1 in a place that is only a short distance from another place or thing: *The baby ducks followed closely behind their mother.*
2 in a careful way: *He listened closely.*

closet * /'klazɪt/ [*noun*] a tall cupboard or small room that you keep clothes in: *He hung his pants in the closet.*

closeup /'kloʊs,ʌp/ [*noun*] a photograph that is taken from very near to something: *a closeup of the boy's face*

cloth * /klɔθ/ [*noun; plural* **cloths** /klɔðz; klɔθs/] material made from cotton, wool, etc., or a piece of this material: *The table was covered with a blue cloth.*
➡ *See the usage note at* CLOTHES.

clothes * /kloʊz/ [*plural noun*] things that you wear, such as shirts, pants, dresses, and coats: *Don't get your clothes dirty!* | *The store sells clothes and shoes.*
☞ You can say **some clothes** or **a lot of clothes**, but do not say "a clothe" or "three clothes."

USAGE clothes, clothing, cloth

Use **clothes** to talk about the shirts, pants, skirts, etc., that you wear: *He always wears nice clothes.* Use **clothing** to talk about clothes in general or a particular kind of clothes: *All children need food and clothing.* | *Casual clothing is not allowed in the restaurant.*
Do not confuse **clothes** and **cloth**. **Cloth** is the material such as cotton, wool, etc., that **clothes** are made from.

---

clothesline /'kloʊz,laɪn/ [*noun*] a rope that is hung outside, where you hang clothes you have washed until they are dry: *He hung his shirt on the clothesline.*

clothespin /'kloʊz,pɪn/ [*noun*] a small piece of wood or plastic that is used to fasten clothes to a clothesline

clothing * /'kloʊðɪŋ/ [*noun*] clothes in general, or a particular kind of clothes: *Take plenty of warm clothing when you go camping.* | *a **piece of clothing** (=one shirt, one dress, etc.)*
➡ *See the usage note at* CLOTHES.

cloud * 🆃 /klaʊd/ [*noun*] a white or gray mass in the sky made of drops of water: *There were lots of white clouds in the sky.*

cloudy /'klaʊdi/ [*adjective;* **cloudier, cloudiest**] having a lot of clouds in the sky; *opposite* CLEAR: *It was a cloudy day.*

clown /klaʊn/ [*noun*] someone who wears funny clothes and makes people laugh

a clown

club * /klʌb/ [*noun*]
1 an organization whose members share an interest or activity: *I'm a **member of** the school chess **club.***
2 an organization that people join in order to get exercise or play a sport, that has its own building and equipment: *a health club* | *a tennis club*
3 a place where you can go to dance and listen to music: *They go to a club every Saturday night.*
4 a big heavy stick: *Someone hit him with a club.*
➡ *See also* GOLF CLUB.

club soda /'klʌb 'soʊdə/ [*noun; plural* **club sodas**] water that has bubbles in it, or a glass or bottle of this; *synonym* SODA: *Would you like some club soda?* | *Two club sodas, please.*

clue /klu/ [*noun; plural* **clues**]
1 a piece of information that helps you find the answer to a question or mystery: *I can't think of the answer— give me a clue.*
— PHRASE —
2 not have a clue INFORMAL to not know something at all: *I don't have a clue where he is.*

clumsy /'klʌmzi/ [*adjective;* **clumsier, clumsiest**] someone who is clumsy often drops things or knocks them over: *Sorry—I'm so clumsy!*

clung /klʌŋ/ [verb] the past tense and past participle of CLING

clutch /klʌtʃ/ [verb; **clutches, clutched, clutching**] to hold something or someone tightly: *He was clutching a book in his left hand.*

cm the written abbreviation of CENTIMETER or CENTIMETERS: *It measures 10 cm in length.*

Co. 1 the written abbreviation of COMPANY

2 the written abbreviation of COUNTY

coach[1] /koʊtʃ/ [noun; plural **coaches**] someone who teaches people how to play a sport: *He's a basketball coach.*

coach[2] [verb; **coaches, coached, coaching**] to teach someone how to play a sport: *She coaches our softball team.*

coal * /koʊl/ [noun] a black mineral that is burned to produce heat and energy: *a coal mine*

coarse ⊤ /kɔrs/ [adjective; **coarser, coarsest**] having a rough surface or feel: *The sack was made of coarse cloth.*

coast * /koʊst/ [noun]
1 the land next to the ocean: *They have a house on the coast.*

— PHRASE —

2 the East/West Coast the U.S. states that are farthest east or west: *They moved to the West Coast last year.*

coastline /ˈkoʊstˌlaɪn/ [noun] the part of a country that is next to the ocean

coat[1] * /koʊt/ [noun]
1 a piece of CLOTHING with sleeves that you wear over your clothes when you go outside: *a warm wool coat*
2 a thin layer of a substance that you put on something: *a coat of paint*

coat[2] [verb; **coated, coating**] to cover something with a thin layer of a substance: **coat something with something** ▸ *Coat the fish with flour.*

coating /ˈkoʊtɪŋ/ [noun] a layer of something that covers a surface: *A coating of dust covered the shelves.*

coax /koʊks/ [verb; **coaxes, coaxed, coaxing**] to gently persuade someone to do something: *I coaxed her into joining us for dinner.*

cob /kab/ [noun] the hard part of a corn plant that the small yellow seeds are attached to: *corn on the cob*

cobra /ˈkoʊbrə/ [noun; plural **cobras**] a poisonous snake that spreads out the skin on the sides of its head

cobweb /ˈkabˌwɛb/ [noun] a net of threads that a spider makes to catch insects

cockroach /ˈkakˌroʊtʃ/ [noun; plural **cockroaches**] a large insect that is often found where food is kept

cocoa /ˈkoʊkoʊ/ [noun] a mixture of cocoa powder and sugar used to make a hot drink, or the drink itself: *a cup of cocoa*
▷ *See also* HOT CHOCOLATE.

cocoa powder /ˈkoʊkoʊ ˌpaʊdɚ/ [noun] a brown powder made from the seeds of a tree, used to make cocoa and chocolate: *Add two tablespoons of cocoa powder.*

coconut /ˈkoʊkəˌnʌt/ [noun] a large brown seed that contains a liquid like milk and has a white inside that you eat

cocoon /kəˈkun/ [noun] the case that some insects, such as moths, make to protect themselves until they change into their adult form
▷ *See the picture at* CATERPILLAR.

cod /kad/ [noun; plural **cod**] a large sea fish that is eaten

code /koʊd/ [noun]
1 a system used to keep a message secret by using special signs or words instead of the real words: *The message must be in code.*
2 a set of numbers or letters used to represent something: *Each product has its own code.*

coed or **co-ed** /ˈkoʊˈɛd/ [adjective; no comparative] including or for both male and female students: *a coed volleyball team | a coed dorm*

/i/ **see**	/ɪ/ **big**	/eɪ/ **day**	/ɛ/ **get** /æ/ **hat**
/a/ **father, hot**	/ʌ/ **up**	/ə/ **about**	/ɔ/ **saw**
/oʊ/ **hope**	/ʊ/ **book**	/u/ **too**	/aɪ/ **I** /aʊ/ **how**
/ɔɪ/ **boy**	/ɝ/ **bird**	/ɚ/ **teacher**	/ɪr/ **ear** /ɛr/ **air**
/ɑr/ **far**	/ɔr/ **more**	/ʊr/ **tour**	/aɪr/ **fire**
/aʊɚ/ **hour**	/θ/ **nothing**	/ð/ **mother**	/ʃ/ **she**
/ʒ/ **measure**	/tʃ/ **church**	/dʒ/ **jump**	/ŋ/ **long**

coffee * /'kɔfi/ [noun; plural **coffees**]
a hot drink made from beans that have
a strong taste, or a cup of this: *We had a
cup of coffee.* | *I'd like two coffees to go,
please.* | *black coffee* (=coffee without
milk in it)

coffee shop /'kɔfi ˌʃap/ [noun] a small
restaurant where you can buy small,
cheap meals

coffin /'kɔfɪn/ [noun] a box that a dead
person is put in: *The coffin was lowered
into the grave.*

coil /kɔɪl/ [noun] a piece of
wire or rope that curls
around and around to form
a circle or tube shape: *He
tripped over a coil of rope.*

coin * /kɔɪn/ [noun] a piece
of money made from
a coil/
a spring
metal: *Christopher and Sarah have been
collecting foreign coins for several years.*

a fifty-cent piece   a quarter (25¢)

a dime (10¢)   a nickel (5¢)   a penny (1¢)

U.S. coins

coincidence /kou'ɪnsɪdəns/ [noun]
when two things happen at the same
time, in the same place, or to the same
people, without being planned: *What a
coincidence! I was born in Dallas too.*

Coke /kouk/ [noun] TRADEMARK the name
of a kind of cola; often used to mean
any drink of this type: *I'll have a Coke,
please.*

cola /'koulə/ [noun; plural **colas**] a sweet
brown drink that has no alcohol: *Do
you want a can of cola?*

colander /'kɑləndɚ/ [noun] a piece of
kitchen equipment like a bowl with

many small holes in it, used to separate
liquid from solid pieces of food

cold[1] * /kould/ [adjective; **colder,
coldest**]
1 having a low temperature; *opposite*
HOT: *a cold drink* | *It's cold today* (=the
weather is cold). | *I'm cold.*
2 not at all friendly; *opposite* WARM: *a
cold stare*

SYNONYMS   cold, freezing, cool

  Cold means "having a low
temperature": *It's very cold outside.* | *Close
the window—I'm cold!*
  Freezing is a less formal word meaning
cold: *I'm freezing!* | *It's freezing in here!*
  Use **cool** to talk about something that is
cold, but in a pleasant way: *It's nice and
cool here in the shade.*

---

cold[2] * [noun]
1 an illness that affects your nose and
throat: *He has a cold.* | *I hope I don't
catch a cold* (=become ill from a cold).
2 **the cold** cold weather: *Come in out of
the cold.*

cold-blooded /'kould 'blʌdɪd/
[adjective; no comparative] a cold-blooded
animal is one whose body temperature
changes with the temperature of the
place it is in: *Snakes are cold-blooded.*

collapse /kə'læps/ [verb; **collapsed,
collapsing**] to fall down suddenly: *The
building collapsed in the earthquake.* | *He
just collapsed in the movie theater.*

collar * /'kɑlɚ/ [noun]
1 the part of a shirt, JACKET, coat, etc.,
that goes around your neck: *This collar
feels too tight.*
2 a band that a dog or cat wears
around its neck: *a flea collar* (=that
protects an animal from insect bites)

colleague /'kɑlig/ [noun; plural
colleagues] someone who works with
you: *She discussed the problem with one
of her colleagues.*

collect[1] * T /kə'lɛkt/ [verb; **collected,
collecting**]
1 to get things of the same kind from
different places or people, and put
them together: *The teacher collected
everyone's homework.*
2 to get things of the same kind and

save them to look at, because they are interesting or for fun: *I collect stamps.*

3 to get money from people: *We collected nearly $200 for charity.*

4 to come together to form a group or a larger amount: *There's a leak where rain has collected on the roof.*

collect[2] [*adverb*]

— PHRASE

call collect if you call someone collect, he or she pays for the call even though you make it: *Mom said we could call collect.*

collection * /kə'lɛkʃən/ [*noun*]

1 a group of similar things that you have collected because they are interesting: *They have an interesting **collection of** books.* I *a coin collection*

2 when mail, waste, etc., is taken from a place: *The garbage collection is on Thursdays.*

collector /kə'lɛktər/ [*noun*]

1 someone whose job is to collect things: *a ticket collector*

2 someone who collects things because they are interesting: *a stamp collector*

collective noun /kə'lɛktɪv 'naʊn/ [*noun*] GRAMMAR a noun such as "family" or "team" that is used to mention a group of people or things: *Collective nouns are sometimes followed by "of."*

college * /'kɑlɪdʒ/ [*noun*] a place where you can study after high school and get a degree: *My sister **goes to college.** I She's **in college** right now.*

collide /kə'laɪd/ [*verb*; **collided, colliding**] to hit someone or something while moving: *Her car **collided with** a tree.*

collision /kə'lɪʒən/ [*noun*] an accident in which two or more moving vehicles hit each other: *There was a **collision between** two trains.*

colon /'koʊlən/ [*noun*] a mark (:) used in writing

⇨ *See* Punctuation *in the Smart Study section.*

colonel or **Colonel** /'kɜ˞nəl/ [*noun, name*] an officer with a high rank in the Army, Air Force, or Marine Corps

colony /'kɑləni/ [*noun; plural* **colonies**] a country that is governed by another

country: *Hong Kong used to be a British colony.*

color[1] * T /'kʌlər/ [*noun*]

1 red, blue, green, yellow, etc.: *"What's your favorite color?" "Purple."* I *What color is your bedroom?*

2 how dark or light someone's skin is: *People of all colors live here.* I ***people of color*** (=people who are not white)

color[2] * T [*verb*; **colored, coloring**] to use colored pens, pencils, etc., to put color onto a picture: *She was coloring a picture of a horse.*

colored * /'kʌlərd/ [*adjective; no comparative*] having a color such as red, yellow, etc.: *colored paper* I *a dark-colored hat*

colorful * /'kʌlərfəl/ [*adjective*; **more colorful, most colorful**] having many bright colors: *Colorful butterflies flew around them.*

column /'kɑləm/ [*noun*]

1 a large post that supports part of a building; *synonym* PILLAR: *There were two columns at the building's entrance.* ⇨ *See the picture at* ARCH.

2 numbers or words written below each other: *Add up the figures in the left column.*

coma /'koʊmə/ [*noun; plural* **comas**] a long period when someone is not conscious: *He was **in a coma** for a week.*

comb[1] * /koʊm/ [*noun*] a thin piece of plastic that you use to arrange your hair: *a brush and comb*

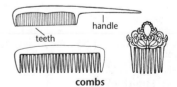

handle

teeth

combs

comb[2] * [*verb*; **combed, combing**] to use a comb to make your hair neat: *Bob combed his hair.*

---

combat /'kɑmbæt/ [noun] fighting in a war: He was wounded in combat.

combination * T /ˌkɑmbə'neɪʃən/ [noun] two or more things that exist together or are put together: She was late for a combination of reasons.

combine * /kəm'baɪn/ [verb; combined, combining] if you combine two or more things or if they combine, you put them together or they exist together: combine something with something ▸ He combined his business trip with a visit to his parents.

come * /kʌm/ [verb; came, come, coming]

1 to move toward the place where you are or the person or place you are talking about: Come and sit next to me. I We came by bus. I Please come in (=enter the room). I Are you coming with us to the zoo?

2 to arrive somewhere: They came to a wide river. I Your package came today.

3 to happen: The news came as a surprise (=was a surprise).

4 to become: The button on my shirt came loose. I Did the knob come off the radio?

— PHRASES —

5 come (in) first/second/last/etc. to be the one who wins in a race or competition, or to be second, last, etc.: She came second in the 200 meters.

6 come on SPOKEN used to tell someone to hurry up: Come on, or we'll miss the train.

7 come to $50/$100/etc. if two or more amounts come to $50, $100, etc., that is their total when they are added together: Lunch for the three of us comes to $45.

— PHRASAL VERBS —

come about [phrasal verb]

8 to happen, especially when it is difficult to believe: How did such a terrible situation come about?

come across [phrasal verb]

9 to meet someone or find something that you did not expect: come across someone/something ▸ I just came across my old school photograph.

come along [phrasal verb]

10 to go somewhere with someone: We're going to the movies. Do you want to come along?

11 to appear or arrive: Another job will come along if he doesn't get this one.

12 if something is coming along, it is developing or improving: Her schoolwork is coming along well.

come back [phrasal verb]

13 to return to a place: He didn't come back for two hours.

come down [phrasal verb]

14 if prices come down, they become lower: The price of milk has come down.

come from [phrasal verb]

15 to have been born in a particular place or to have been obtained from a particular thing: come from something ▸ Gasoline comes from oil. I come from ▸ I come from Boston.
☛ Do not say "I am coming from Boston." Say I come from Boston.

come on [phrasal verb]

16 if a machine, light, etc., comes on, it starts to work: The light comes on automatically.

come out [phrasal verb]

17 to become known by a lot of people: Will the truth ever come out?

18 if the sun or a flower comes out, it starts to appear: The sun came out in the afternoon.

come up [phrasal verb]

19 to be mentioned or suggested: The subject came up at the meeting.

20 if the sun comes up, it starts to appear in the morning: We watched the sun coming up.

21 if an event is coming up, it will happen soon: My birthday is coming up.

comedian /kə'midiən/ [noun] someone whose job is to tell jokes and make people laugh: He is a popular comedian.

comedy /'kɑmɪdi/ [noun; plural comedies] a play, movie, etc., that makes people laugh
⤷ Compare TRAGEDY (definition 2).

comet /'kɑmɪt/ [noun] a bright object in space that has a tail and moves around the sun

comfort[1] * /'kʌmfɚt/ [noun]

1 a state in which you do not have any pain, worry, trouble, etc.: They lived in

comfort (=they had everything they needed).
2 something that makes your life easier or happier, or makes you less sad: *He was glad to be back among the comforts of home.*

comfort[2] * [*verb;* **comforted, comforting**] to say or do something to make someone feel less sad: *She held the baby and tried to comfort him.*

comfortable * /'kʌmftəbəl/ [*adjective;* **more comfortable, most comfortable**]
1 comfortable clothes, furniture, etc., are pleasant to wear or use; *opposite* UNCOMFORTABLE: *The bed was very comfortable.*
2 feeling relaxed and not having any worry or pain; *opposite* UNCOMFORTABLE: *I didn't feel comfortable in her house.*

comic /'kamɪk/ [*adjective;* **more comic, most comic**] funny and making you laugh: *a comic story*

comic book /'kamɪk ˌbʊk/ [*noun*] a magazine that tells stories using drawn pictures: *I love reading comic books.*

comic strip /'kamɪk ˌstrɪp/ [*noun*] a number of drawn pictures that tell a story: *What's your favorite comic strip?*

comma /'kamə/ [*noun; plural* **commas**] a mark used in writing. It looks like this: ,
⇨ *See* Punctuation *in the Smart Study section.*

command[1] * /kə'mænd/ [*noun*]
1 an order that you must do something: *The officer gave the command to retreat.*
2 the control of a group of people or situation: *You don't need to worry. He's in command of the situation.*

command[2] [*verb;* **commanded, commanding**] to order someone to do something: *The officer commanded his men to attack.*

comment[1] /'kamɛnt/ [*noun*] something that you say about someone or something; *synonym* REMARK: *May I make a comment?*

comment[2] [*verb;* **commented, commenting**] to say something about someone or something; *synonym* REMARK: *No one commented on my new haircut.*

commentary /'kamən,tɛri/ [*noun; plural* **commentaries**] a spoken description of an event that is made while the event is happening: *They were listening to the radio commentary on the basketball game.*

commentator /'kamən,teɪtɚ/ [*noun*]
1 someone who talks on television or radio about an event while it is happening: *a baseball commentator*
2 someone who knows a lot about a subject and talks about it on television or radio: *an economic commentator*

commerce /'kamɚs/ [*noun*] FORMAL the business of buying and selling things: *He works in commerce.*

commercial /kə'mɜrʃəl/ [*noun*] an advertisement on television or radio: *a commercial for a new fruit drink*

commit /kə'mɪt/ [*verb;* **commits, committed, committing**] to do something wrong or illegal: *He already has committed several crimes.* | *She committed murder.*

commitment /kə'mɪtmənt/ [*noun*] when you are determined to work hard at something and make it successful: *His commitment to the project is not in doubt.*

committee * /kə'mɪti/ [*noun; plural* **committees**] a group of people who are chosen to make decisions or look at something for a larger group of people: *Who's on the committee?* | *The committee appointed a new secretary.*

common[1] * /'kamən/ [*adjective*]
1 [**commoner** or **more common, commonest** or **most common**] existing in a lot of places or happening often; *opposites* RARE, UNCOMMON: *Colds are common in winter.* | *It's a common problem.*
2 [*no comparative*] shared by two or more people: *They have common interests.*

common[2] [noun]
━━ PHRASE ━━
have something in common (with)
to have the same interests, experiences,
etc., as someone else: *I have a lot in
common with my best friend.*

common sense /ˈkamən ˈsɛns/ [noun]
the ability that people have to think
about things and make good decisions:
*You left the car lights on! Where's your
common sense?*

communicate ∗ T /kəˈmyunɪˌkeɪt/
[verb; communicated, communicating]
to use words or actions to express what
you think or feel: *They communicated
with each other by e-mail.*

communication ∗ T
/kəˌmyunɪˈkeɪʃən/ [noun]
1 when people talk or write to each
other and understand each other: *Poor
communication hurt their relationship.*
2 communications [plural] ways of
sending information such as radio,
telephone, etc.: *electronic
communications systems*

community T /kəˈmyunɪti/ [noun;
plural **communities**] a group of people
who live near each other or have the
same interests, religion, etc.: *The city has
a large Spanish-speaking community.* | *a
community park* (=shared by everyone in
the community)

commute /kəˈmyut/ [verb; commuted,
commuting] to travel a long way to
work every day: *She commutes from her
home in the country to the city.*

commuter /kəˈmyutɚ/ [noun] someone
who travels a long way to work every
day: *The train was full of very tired
commuters.*

compact disc /ˈkampækt ˈdɪsk/ [noun]
a flat round piece of plastic used for
recording music, storing programs on a
computer, etc.; synonyms **CD**, DISC
➪ *See the picture at* DISK.

companion /kəmˈpænyən/ [noun]
FORMAL a person or animal you go
somewhere with or spend a lot of time
with: *A dog can be a good companion.*

company ∗ /ˈkʌmpəni/ [noun; plural
companies]
1 a legal business that is owned by a

person or a group: *She works for a
publishing company.*
2 a person or people that are with you:
We had company over for dinner. | *I
always enjoy his company* (=I like being
with him).
━━ PHRASE ━━
3 keep someone company to be
with someone so that he or she is not
lonely: *I wanted to keep you company.*

comparative ∗ /kəmˈpærətɪv/ [noun]
GRAMMAR the form of an adjective or
adverb used when comparing two
things or people, and saying that one
has more of a quality than the other:
"Smaller" is the comparative of "small." |
a comparative form

USAGE Comparatives and
superlatives
In this dictionary, you can find the
comparative or superlative form of a
word right next to the part of speech.
For example, **funny** shows **funnier** and
funniest; acceptable shows **more
acceptable** and **most acceptable**.
Do not use **more** with an -er form,
or **most** with an -est form. For example,
do not say "more funnier" or "most
funniest."
---

compare ∗ T /kəmˈpɛr/ [verb;
compared, comparing]
1 to look at two things or people and
say how they are the same or how
they are different: *We compared prices
for stoves.* | *He compared the signature
with the one on the card* (=he looked to
see if they were different). | *A family
can be compared to a tree with many
branches* (=they are alike in some
ways).
2 to be different from something else
in some way: *How does life in Korea
compare with life in the U.S.?*
━━ PHRASE ━━
3 compared with or **compared to**
used to say that one thing or person
has more or less of a quality than
another: *Her grades are good compared
to mine* (=her grades are bad, but mine
are worse). | *Profits have decreased by
8% compared with last year.*

USAGE   compare with, compare to

When you **compare** similar things **with** each other, you talk about how they are different: *He compared his camera with mine.* When you **compare** different things **to** each other, you talk about how they are alike: *Books can be compared to friends.*

However, when you use the fixed phrases **compared with** and **compared to** to talk about the qualities of two people or two things of the same type, the meaning is the same: *You're tall compared with/to me.*

---

comparison * ⊤ /kəm'pærəsən/ [*noun*]
1 when two things are compared: *It's hard to make a comparison between the two cases.* I *Here's one of his earlier pictures for comparison.*

══ PHRASE ══

2 in comparison (to/with) used to say that one thing or person has more of a quality than another: *Our car seemed old in comparison to theirs.*

compartment /kəm'partmənt/ [*noun*]
1 a separate part of an object which is used to hold or store things: *a refrigerator's butter compartment* I *a car's* **glove compartment** (=usually used for maps)
2 a small room on a train for people to sit in: *Our compartment was full.*

compass /'kʌmpəs/ [*noun; plural* compasses]
1 a tool that always points north and is used to help you find the correct direction to travel: *Take a map and compass when you go hiking.*
2 a tool with two points that you use for drawing circles

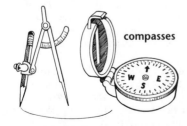

compasses

compensation ⊤ /ˌkampən'seɪʃən/ [*noun*] money that is given to someone

who has been harmed, paid by the person or organization that caused the harm: *He claimed* **compensation for** *his injury.*

compete * /kəm'pit/ [*verb;* competed, competing]
1 to try to be more successful than someone else or another organization: *Dan and Rob* **are** *always* **competing for** *the teacher's attention.* I *Businesses have to* **compete with** *each other.*
2 to take part in a competition or race: *He* **competed in** *the Olympic Games.*

competition * /ˌkampɪ'tɪʃən/ [*noun*]
1 an event in which someone tries to be the best: *a swimming competition*
2 when people, groups, or companies are trying to be more successful than each other: *There was a lot of* **competition between** *the children.*

competitive /kəm'pɛtɪtɪv/ [*adjective;* more competitive, most competitive] wanting very much to be more successful than other people: *Steve is very competitive.*

competitor * /kəm'pɛtɪtɚ/ [*noun*] a person, group, or company that is competing with another for something: *There were 50 competitors in the race.*

complain * ⊤ /kəm'pleɪn/ [*verb;* complained, complaining] to say that you are angry or unhappy about something: *My dad* **complained about** *the food.* I *She* **complained that** *her hotel room was dirty.*

complaint * /kəm'pleɪnt/ [*noun*] something you say or write to show that you are angry or unhappy about something: *During the party we received several* **complaints about** *noise.* I *I'd like to* **make a complaint.**

complete[1] * /kəm'plit/ [*adjective; no comparative*]
1 whole and with nothing missing; <u>opposite</u> **INCOMPLETE**: *We were given a complete set of instructions.*

/i/ **see** /ɪ/ **big** /eɪ/ **day** /ɛ/ **get** /æ/ **hat** /ɑ/ **father**, **hot** /ʌ/ **up** /ə/ **about** /ɔ/ **saw** /oʊ/ **hope** /ʊ/ **book** /u/ **too** /aɪ/ **I** /aʊ/ **how** /ɔɪ/ **boy** /ɝ/ **bird** /ɚ/ **teacher** /ɪr/ **ear** /ɛr/ **air** /ɑr/ **far** /ɔr/ **more** /ʊr/ **tour** /aɪr/ **fire** /aʊɚ/ **hour** /θ/ **nothing** /ð/ **mother** /ʃ/ **she** /ʒ/ **measure** /tʃ/ **church** /dʒ/ **jump** /ŋ/ **long**

2 to the greatest degree that is possible, or in every possible way; _synonym_ TOTAL: _I have complete confidence in him._
☞ Only use **complete** before a noun in this meaning.

complete[2] * [_verb;_ **completed, completing**] to finish doing or making something: _It took a year to complete the building work._

completely * /kəm'plitli/ [_adverb_] as much as is possible, or in every possible way; _synonym_ TOTALLY: _The dress was completely ruined._

complex [T] /kəm'plɛks/ [_adjective;_ **more complex, most complex**] having many different parts: _a complex machine_

complicated * [T] /'kampli,keɪtɪd/ [_adjective;_ **more complicated, most complicated**] difficult to understand or explain because it has many parts; _opposite_ SIMPLE: _It's a very complicated situation._

compliment[1] /'kampləmənt/ [_noun_] something nice that you say about someone: _She gets lots of compliments about her work._

compliment[2] [_verb;_ **complimented, complimenting**] to say something nice about someone: _We complimented her on her wonderful cooking._

compose /kəm'poʊz/ [_verb;_ **composed, composing**] to write a piece of music: _Mozart composed many pieces of music._

composer /kəm'poʊzɚ/ [_noun_] someone who writes music

composition /,kampə'zɪʃən/ [_noun_] something you write, such as a story, description, or piece of music: _The class wrote compositions about the city._

compound * /'kampaʊnd/ [_adjective; no comparative_] GRAMMAR a compound noun, adjective, or verb is formed from two or more other words: _"Comic book" is a compound noun._

computer * /kəm'pyutɚ/ [_noun_] an electronic machine that can store information and organize it very quickly: _She looked up the information on her computer._ | _I like computer games._
➪ See the picture at OFFICE.

computerize /kəm'pyutəraɪz/ [_verb;_ **computerized, computerizing**]

to store and organize information on a computer: _The college has computerized all student information._

computer program /kəm'pyutɚ ,proʊɡræm/ [_noun_] a set of instructions that make a computer do something: _She writes computer programs._

conceal [T] /kən'sil/ [_verb;_ **concealed, concealing**] FORMAL to hide something: _He tried to conceal his fright._

concentrate /'kansən,treɪt/ [_verb;_ **concentrated, concentrating**] to think carefully about what you are doing: _It was so noisy, I couldn't concentrate._ | _He doesn't concentrate on his schoolwork._

concentration /,kansən'treɪʃən/ [_noun_] when you think carefully about what you are doing: _The task requires a lot of concentration._

concern[1] * [_verb;_ **concerned, concerning**]
1 to be about a particular person or thing: _The story concerns a child growing up in Africa._
2 to involve someone: _Don't ask about things that don't concern you._
3 to make someone feel worried: _The pollution level concerns many people._

concern[2] /kən'sɜn/ [_noun_]
1 a feeling of worry, or something that worries you: _There were concerns about the safety of the building._
— PHRASE ——
2 not be your concern to not be something that you have the right or duty to ask about or get involved in: _The details are not our concern._

concerned * /kən'sɜnd/ [_adjective;_ **more concerned, most concerned**] worried about something: _Police were concerned about the little girl's safety._

concerning * /kən'sɜnɪŋ/ [_preposition_] FORMAL about a person or thing: _The leaders will discuss issues concerning both countries._

concert * /'kansɜt/ [_noun_] a public event at which music is performed: _a rock concert_ | _a jazz concert_

conclude /kən'klud/ [_verb;_ **concluded, concluding**] FORMAL
1 to finish something: _He concluded his speech with a joke._

2 to decide that something is true after thinking about the facts you know: *Police concluded that the burglar was a woman.*

conclusion /kən'kluʒən/ [*noun*]
1 something that you decide is true after thinking about the facts you know: *I came to the conclusion that she was lying* (=that is what I decided).
2 the end of a piece of writing: *You need to rewrite your conclusion.*

concrete Ⓣ /'kaŋkrit/ [*noun*] a wet gray mixture of minerals that becomes very hard when it dries, and is used in building: *a concrete wall*

condemn /kən'dɛm/ [*verb;* **condemned, condemning**] to say that an action is bad and wrong: *The mayor condemned the violence.*

condition * /kən'dɪʃən/ [*noun*]
1 the state that something is in: *The old book was in very good condition.*
2 a health problem that affects you for a very long time: *a heart condition*
3 something in an agreement that must be done: *a condition of employment* | *I won't tell Mom, on one condition—that you never do it again.*
4 conditions [*plural*] the situation in which people live or work: *Working conditions at the factory have improved.*

conditioner /kən'dɪʃənɚ/ [*noun*] a liquid that you put on your hair to make it softer after you have washed it

condominium Ⓣ /,kandə'mɪniəm/ [*noun*] an apartment that someone owns in a building with a lot of other apartments, or the building itself

conduct /kən'dʌkt/ [*verb;* **conducted, conducting**]
1 to direct a group of people who are playing musical instruments or singing: *The orchestra was conducted by James Levine.*
2 to use a special process to find something out, especially in science or police work: *Tests are being conducted on a new drug.*

conductor /kən'dʌktɚ/ [*noun*]
1 someone who directs a group of people who are playing musical

instruments or singing: *The choir has a new conductor.*
2 someone who works on a bus or train but does not drive it: *The conductor came to check our tickets.*

cone /koʊn/ [*noun*]
1 a shape that is round at the bottom and has sloping sides and a point at the top
⇨ See **Shapes** in the **Smart Study** section.
2 an object with a shape like this
⇨ See the picture at **ICE-CREAM CONE.**

conference /'kanfərəns/ [*noun*] a large, important meeting where a lot of people discuss something, especially for several days: *He attended a conference on world trade.*

confess /kən'fɛs/ [*verb;* **confesses, confessed, confessing**] to tell someone that you have done something bad: *She confessed to lying to the police.* | *He confessed that he did it.*

confession /kən'fɛʃən/ [*noun*] when you say formally that you did something wrong or illegal: *I have a confession to make.*

confetti /kən'fɛti/ [*noun*] pieces of colored paper that you throw in the air at a celebration

confidence * /'kanfɪdəns/ [*noun*] the feeling that you can do things well and will be successful: *She did not have much confidence in herself.*

confident * /'kanfɪdənt/ [*adjective;* **more confident, most confident**]
1 feeling that you can do things well and will be successful: *He looks very confident and relaxed.*
2 sure that something will happen or is true: *I'm confident that he'll be there.*
☞ Do not use **confident** before a noun in this meaning.

confidential Ⓣ /,kanfɪ'dɛnʃəl/ [*adjective; no comparative*] a confidential document or piece of information is or should be secret: *a confidential report*

/i/ see /ɪ/ big /eɪ/ day /ɛ/ get /æ/ hat /ɑ/ father, hot /ʌ/ up /ə/ about /ɔ/ saw /oʊ/ hope /ʊ/ book /u/ too /aɪ/ I /aʊ/ how /ɔɪ/ boy /ɝ/ bird /ɚ/ teacher /ɪr/ ear /ɛr/ air /ɑr/ far /ɔr/ more /ʊr/ tour /aɪr/ fire /aʊɚ/ hour /θ/ nothing /ð/ mother /ʃ/ she /ʒ/ measure /tʃ/ church /dʒ/ jump /ŋ/ long

confirm T /kən'fɜ·m/ [verb; confirmed, confirming] to say or show that something is definitely true: *Your flight for January 20 has been confirmed.* | *He confirmed that he would be at the meeting.*

confirmation /ˌkɑnfə·'meɪʃən/ [noun] something that shows or says that something is definitely true: *We need confirmation of your order.*

conflict[1] T /'kɑnflɪkt/ [noun] an argument or fight: *The decision caused a lot of conflict between them.*

conflict[2] /kən'flɪkt/ [verb; conflicted, conflicting] to not agree or to be completely different: *That conflicts with what you said last week.*

confuse * /kən'fyuz/ [verb; confused, confusing]
1 to make someone unable to think clearly: *He talked so fast that he completely confused me.*
2 to think that a person or thing is someone or something else: **confuse someone with someone** ▶ *Everyone confuses me with my sister.*

confused * /kən'fyuzd/ [adjective; **more confused, most confused**] unable to understand something or think clearly: *She explained, but I was still confused.*

confusing * /kən'fyuzɪŋ/ [adjective; **more confusing, most confusing**] hard to understand, or making it hard to think what to do: *The instructions were confusing.*

confusion /kən'fyuʒən/ [noun] when people do not know what is happening or do not understand something: *There was some confusion about the time of the concert.*

congratulate /kən'grætʃəˌleɪt/ [verb; congratulated, congratulating] to tell someone that you are happy because something good has happened to him or her: **congratulate someone on something** ▶ *She congratulated me on getting my driver's license.*

congratulations /kənˌgrætʃə'leɪʃənz/ [plural noun] something that you say when something nice has happened to someone: *Congratulations on the birth of your baby.*

Congress /'kɑŋgrɪs/ [noun] the part of the U.S. government that includes the two groups of people who make national laws: *Congress approved the new budget.*
⊃ *See also* **HOUSE OF REPRESENTATIVES, SENATE.**

congressman or **Congressman** /'kɑŋgrɪsmən/ [noun, name; plural **congressmen** /'kɑŋgrɪsmən/] a man who is a member of Congress

congresswoman or **Congresswoman** /'kɑŋgrɪsˌwʊmən/ [noun, name; plural **congresswomen** /'kɑŋgrɪsˌwɪmən/] a woman who is a member of Congress

conjunction * /kən'dʒʌŋkʃən/ [noun] GRAMMAR a word such as "and" or "but" that connects two parts of a sentence: *How is the conjunction "nor" used?*

connect * T /kə'nɛkt/ [verb; connected, connecting] to join two things together; *opposite* DISCONNECT: *Make sure you connect the wires correctly.* | *Connect the hose to the faucet.*

connected /kə'nɛktɪd/ [adjective; no comparative]
1 if two things are connected, they are joined: *The printer is connected to the computer.*
2 if events, situations, etc., are connected, they are related in some way; *opposite* UNCONNECTED: *Is his illness connected with his work?*

connection * /kə'nɛkʃən/ [noun] the fact that two things or people are related; *synonym* LINK: *There is a clear connection between diet and heart disease.* | *This man has no connection with the college.*

conquer T /'kɑŋkə·/ [verb; conquered, conquering] to defeat people in a war and take their land: *They conquered the area in 1342.*

conscience * /'kɑnʃəns/ [noun] the part of your mind that tells you whether something is morally right or wrong: *He had a guilty conscience* (=felt bad because he had done something wrong).

conscious * /'kɑnʃəs/ [adjective; no comparative]
1 awake and knowing what is

happening around you; *opposite*
UNCONSCIOUS: *She hit her head, but was
still conscious.*
2 noticing something a lot; *synonym*
AWARE: *I'm very conscious of my age.*
☛ Do not use **conscious** before a noun
in this meaning.

consecutive /kən'sɛkyətɪv/ [*adjective;
no comparative*] coming or happening
one after the other: *We're taking tests on
two consecutive days.*

consent[1] /kən'sɛnt/ [*noun*] FORMAL
permission for something: *He borrowed
the car **without** his mother's **consent**.*

consent[2] [*verb; consented, consenting*]
FORMAL to give permission for something
to happen: *The owner finally **consented
to** renting me the apartment.*

consequence /'kansɪ,kwɛns/ [*noun*]
something that happens as a result of
something else: *He never thought about
the **consequences of** his actions.*

conservation [T] /,kansə-'veɪʃən/ [*noun*]
the protection of animals, plants, land,
etc., so that they are not destroyed:
*People now realize the importance of
conservation.*

conservative [T] /kən'sɜ-vətɪv/ [*adjective;
more conservative, most conservative*]
not liking new ways of doing things: *My
dad is too conservative.*

consider * /kən'sɪdə-/ [*verb; considered,
considering*] to think about something
for a while: *I'll need to consider the idea
first.* | **consider doing something** ▸
*He's considering studying English next
year.*

considerate /kən'sɪdərɪt/ [*adjective;
more considerate, most considerate*]
caring about how your actions will
affect people, and trying not to upset
them; *opposite* INCONSIDERATE: *Our
neighbors are always considerate.*
↪ Compare THOUGHTFUL. ↪ See the
synonym note at KIND[2].

consideration /kən,sɪdə'reɪʃən/ [*noun*]
1 care and respect for another person:
*He **showed consideration for** her
feelings.*
2 a lot of thought and attention: *We
gave consideration to both proposals.*

consist * [T] /kən'sɪst/ [*verb; consisted,
consisting*]
━━ **PHRASAL VERB** ━━
consist of [*phrasal verb*]
to be made of different things or parts:
consist of something ▸ *Air consists of
nitrogen, oxygen, and a small amount of
other gases.*
☛ Do not say that something "is
consisting of something." Say that it
consists of something.

consonant * /'kansənənt/ [*noun*]
1 a sound that is produced when the
air from your throat is partly stopped
by your lips, tongue, or teeth: *He found
some consonants difficult to pronounce.*
2 a letter used to represent a consonant
sound: *"B" and "m" are consonants.*
↪ Compare VOWEL.

constant [T] /'kanstənt/ [*adjective; no
comparative*]
1 happening or existing all the time:
He was in constant pain.
2 staying the same: *Driving at a
constant speed saves gas.*

constantly [T] /'kanstəntli/ [*adverb*]
all the time: *She is constantly tired.*

constitution /,kanstɪ'tuʃən/ [*noun*]
the laws governing something such as a
country, state, or organization: *the
Constitution of the United States*

constitutional /,kanstɪ'tuʃənəl/
[*adjective; no comparative*] relating to
what is contained in a constitution: *a
constitutional issue*

construct /kən'strʌkt/ [*verb;
constructed, constructing*] to build a
building, road, etc.: *The theater was
constructed in 1970.*

construction [T] /kən'strʌkʃən/ [*noun*]
the building of roads, buildings, etc.:
*The bridge is still **under construction**
(=being built).*

consul /'kansəl/ [*noun*] a representative
of a government who lives in a foreign

/i/ **see** /ɪ/ **big** /eɪ/ **day** /ɛ/ **get** /æ/ **hat**
/a/ **father, hot** /ʌ/ **up** /ə/ **about** /ɔ/ **saw**
/oʊ/ **hope** /ʊ/ **book** /u/ **too** /aɪ/ **I** /aʊ/ **how**
/ɔɪ/ **boy** /ɝ/ **bird** /ə-/ **teacher** /ɪr/ **ear** /ɛr/ **air**
/ar/ **far** /ɔr/ **more** /ʊr/ **tour** /aɪr/ **fire**
/aʊə-/ **hour** /θ/ **nothing** /ð/ **mother** /ʃ/ **she**
/ʒ/ **measure** /tʃ/ **church** /dʒ/ **jump** /ŋ/ **long**

city and helps people there who are from his or her country

consult /kən'sʌlt/ [*verb;* **consulted, consulting**] to talk to someone in order to get information or advice: *I think she should consult a lawyer.*

consume ⊤ /kən'sum/ [*verb;* **consumed, consuming**] to use energy, goods, or food: *Americans consume a lot of gas and electricity.*

consumer /kən'sumɚ/ [*noun*] someone who buys and uses things: *There will be new laws to protect consumers.*

contact[1] /'kantækt/ [*verb;* **contacted, contacting**] to write to someone or speak to someone on the telephone: *I'll contact you when I know what time we're leaving.*

contact[2] [*noun*] communication with someone by letter, telephone, etc.: *She hasn't had any contact with her brother.* I *They stayed in contact after college.*

contact lens /'kantækt ˌlɛnz/ [*noun;* plural **contact lenses**] a small piece of plastic that you wear in your eye to help you see clearly

contagious /kən'teɪdʒəs/ [*adjective;* **more contagious, most contagious**] if an illness or a person with an illness is contagious, other people can easily get the illness: *Colds are highly contagious.* I *The doctor says I'm not contagious.*

SYNONYMS   contagious, infectious

A **contagious** illness such as a cold or the flu is one that people usually get from another person during the first days the other person is ill.

An **infectious** disease is usually more serious, and can be passed to another person at any time.

contain * /kən'teɪn/ [*verb;* **contained, containing**] to have a particular thing inside: *The box contained some old books.*

container * /kən'teɪnɚ/ [*noun*] a box, bottle, etc., that you can keep things in: *Put the leftovers in a plastic container.*

content /kən'tɛnt/ [*adjective;* **more content, most content**] happy and not needing anything more: *He seemed content with his life.* I **content to do something** ▸ *She was content to watch the others play.*

☛ Do not use **content** before a noun.

contented /kən'tɛntɪd/ [*adjective;* **more contented, most contented**] happy and not needing anything more: *You don't seem very contented.*

contents /'kantɛnts/ [*plural noun*] the things that are inside a box, bag, etc: *She dropped the bag and its contents fell out.*

contest /'kantɛst/ [*noun*] a competition: *She won an essay contest.*

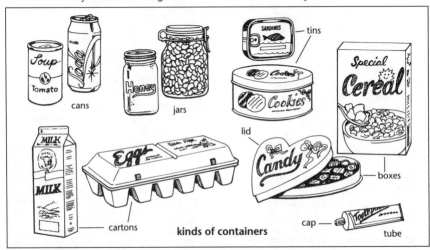

kinds of containers

contestant /kən'tɛstənt/ [*noun*] someone who competes in a contest: *None of the contestants knew the answer.*

continent * /'kɑntənənt/ [*noun*] one of the seven large areas of land on the earth: *Asia and Africa are two of the continents.*

continual /kən'tɪnyuəl/ [*adjective; no comparative*] happening often, or continuing for a long time: *There were continual interruptions.*

continually T /kən'tɪnyuəli/ [*adverb*] often or for a long time: *One student continually asked questions.*

continue * T /kən'tɪnyu/ [*verb; continues, continued, continuing*]
1 to keep doing something or keep happening without stopping: **continue to do something** ▸ *If you continue to feel sick, go and see a doctor.* I **continue doing something** ▸ *He continued reading.*
2 to start again or to start something again: *They continued their game after lunch.*
3 to go farther: *The flight stops in Denver, then continues to Los Angeles.*

continuing education /kən'tɪnyuɪŋ ‚ɛdʒə'keɪʃən/ [*noun*] education for adults after they have left school, but not at a university: *continuing education classes* ⇨ *Compare* HIGHER EDUCATION.

continuous[1] * /kən'tɪnyuəs/ [*adjective; no comparative*]
1 happening without changing or stopping; *opposite* UNINTERRUPTED: *There has been a continuous improvement in her grades.*
2 GRAMMAR the continuous form of a verb shows that something is continuing to happen: *In "She is playing tennis," "is playing" is in the continuous form.*

continuous[2] * [*noun*] GRAMMAR **the continuous** another way to say the PRESENT CONTINUOUS

USAGE　Continuous tenses

A continuous tense is the form of a verb used to show continuing states or actions in the past, present, or future. Continuous verbs are formed with the past, present, or future tense of "be" and a present participle:

the past continuous: *I was watching TV when the phone rang.*
the present continuous: *Be quiet. I'm watching TV.*
the future continuous: *I will be watching TV tonight.*

---

continuously * /kən'tɪnyuəsli/ [*adverb*] all the time, without stopping: *It rained continuously for three days.*

contract * /'kɑntrækt/ [*noun*] a written agreement between two people that says what each of them must do: *We signed a contract for the loan.*

contraction * /kən'trækʃən/ [*noun*] GRAMMAR two words that have been put together into one short form, with some letters removed: *"Don't" is a contraction of "do not."*
⇨ *See "apostrophe" at* Punctuation *in the Smart Study section.*

contradict /‚kɑntrə'dɪkt/ [*verb; contradicted, contradicting*] to say that what someone has just said is not true: *She always contradicts her father.*

contrast /'kɑntræst/ [*noun*] a difference between people or things: *The contrast between the two pictures was amazing.*

contribute T /kən'trɪbyut/ [*verb; contributed, contributing*] to give part of the money, help, or information that is needed: **contribute something to/ toward something** ▸ *We each contributed $10 toward the gift.*

contribution /‚kɑntrə'byuʃən/ [*noun*] money, help, or information given that is part of what is needed: *Thank you for your contribution to our organization.*

control[1] * /kən'troʊl/ [*verb; controls, controlled, controlling*]
1 to make someone or something do what you want: *The pilot controls the plane.* I *She couldn't control her son.*
2 to succeed in behaving calmly

/i/ **see**	/ɪ/ **big**	/eɪ/ **day**	/ɛ/ **get** /æ/ **hat**
/ɑ/ **father, hot**	/ʌ/ **up**	/ə/ **about**	/ɔ/ **saw**
/oʊ/ **hope**	/ʊ/ **book**	/u/ **too**	/aɪ/ **I** /aʊ/ **how**
/ɔɪ/ **boy**	/ɝ/ **bird**	/ɚ/ **teacher**	/ɪr/ **ear** /ɛr/ **air**
/ɑr/ **far**	/ɔr/ **more**	/ʊr/ **tour**	/aɪr/ **fire**
/aʊɚ/ **hour**	/θ/ **nothing**	/ð/ **mother**	/ʃ/ **she**
/ʒ/ **measure**	/tʃ/ **church**	/dʒ/ **jump**	/ŋ/ **long**

although you feel angry, sad, etc.: *Try to control your temper.*

control² * [*noun*]
1 the ability to make someone or something do what you want: *She lost control of the car.* | *The situation is out of control* (=cannot be controlled). | *He wasn't in control of the horse* (=could not control the horse). | *The teacher kept the class under control* (=was able to control the class).
2 the ability to behave calmly even though you feel very angry or excited: *I lost control and shouted at him.*
3 controls [*plural*] the things that you press or turn to make a vehicle or machine work: *He took over the controls of the airplane.*

convenient * [T] /kən'vinyənt/ [*adjective;* **more convenient, most convenient**] good for what you need; *opposite* INCONVENIENT: *It's very convenient living next to a grocery store.* | *Is that time more convenient for you?*

convent /'kɑnvɛnt/ [*noun*] a place where nuns live

convention [T] /kən'vɛnʃən/ [*noun*] a very large meeting of people who are interested in the same thing: *a computer software convention*

conversation * /ˌkɑnvɚ'seɪʃən/ [*noun*] a talk that two or more people have: *I had a conversation with her on the phone.* | *They were deep in conversation.*

conversion /kən'vɝʒən/ [*noun*]
1 when something is changed into something else: *Several conversions to the building have been made.*
2 when someone changes from one religion to another: *His conversion to Judaism happened in 1997.*

convert [T] /kən'vɝt/ [*verb;* **converted, converting**]
1 to change or make something change from one thing to another: *This couch can convert to a bed.* | *I convert something into something* ▶ *They converted the garage into a tiny house.*
2 to change or make someone change from one religion to another: *He converted to Buddhism.*

convict¹ /'kɑnvɪkt/ [*noun*] someone who is in prison for a crime

convict² /kən'vɪkt/ [*verb;* **convicted, convicting**] to prove that someone is guilty of a crime in a court of law: **be convicted of something** ▶ *He was convicted of robbery.*

convince [T] /kən'vɪns/ [*verb;* **convinced, convincing**] to make someone feel sure that something is true: **convince someone that** ▶ *She convinced me that the plan would succeed.*

convinced /kən'vɪnst/ [*adjective;* **more convinced, most convinced**] feeling sure that something is true or that something will happen: *I'm convinced that I've failed the test.*
☛ Do not use **convinced** before a noun.

cook¹ * /kʊk/ [*verb;* **cooked, cooking**]
1 to make food ready to eat by using heat: *I cooked dinner every night last week.* | *I learned to cook when I was a teenager.*
2 if food is cooking, it is being heated: *Turkeys take a long time to cook.*

SYNONYMS   cook, bake, roast, fry, broil, grill, boil, steam

If you **cook** food, you prepare it for eating using heat: *What are you going to cook tonight?* | *I'm cooking dinner.*

If you **bake** something, especially bread, cake, or cookies, you cook it in an oven: *I spent all afternoon baking cookies.* You **roast** things in an oven as well, especially meat or vegetables: *How long will the chicken take to roast?*

To **fry** something means to cook it in hot oil: *Fry the onions until they are soft.* To **broil** something means to cook it directly under heat or fire: *broiled steak.* To **grill** something means to cook it directly over a fire: *grilled pork chops.*

If you **boil** something, you cook it in very hot water: *Boil the rice for about 15 minutes.* If you **steam** something, you cook it over very hot water: *steamed vegetables.*

cook² * [*noun*] someone who cooks food, especially as a job: *He's a cook in a small restaurant.* | *She's a great cook!*

cookbook /'kʊkˌbʊk/ [noun] a book that tells you how to cook food

cookie * /'kʊki/ [noun; plural **cookies**] a small, flat, dry cake: She was eating chocolate chip cookies.

cooking /'kʊkɪŋ/ [noun] the process of making food ready to eat: I love cooking.

cool[1] /kul/ [adjective; **cooler, coolest**]
1 fairly cold, in a pleasant way; _opposite_ WARM: It was a hot day but there was a nice cool breeze.
⇨ See the synonym note at COLD[1].
2 calm and not nervous or excited: How can you be so cool before a test?
3 SPOKEN very good or fashionable: "I rode a motorcycle." "Cool!" | What a cool jacket!

cool[2] [verb; **cooled, cooling**] to become colder or make something become colder; _opposite_ WARM: I left the coffee to **cool down** a little. | The weather has **cooled off**. | He blew on his tea to cool it.

cooperate T /koʊ'apəreɪt/ [verb; **cooperated, cooperating**] to work together with someone in a helpful way: How can we cooperate?

cooperation /koʊˌapə'reɪʃən/ [noun] when people are willing to help and work together with others: We need everyone's cooperation.

cooperative /koʊ'apərətɪv/ [adjective; **more cooperative, most cooperative**] willing to work with others and help them: You're not being very cooperative.

cop /kap/ [noun] INFORMAL a **POLICE OFFICER**: The cops arrested him.

cope /koʊp/ [verb; **coped, coping**] to be able to deal with a difficult situation or problem: He **is coping well** so far. | I'm not sure I could **cope with** the extra work.

copper /'kapɚ/ [noun] a soft red-brown metal which electricity moves through quickly: a copper wire

copy[1] * /'kapi/ [noun; plural **copies**]
1 something that you make to look exactly the same as something else: Please send a **copy of** your birth certificate.
2 a short form of PHOTOCOPY: Please make two copies of the article.

3 one of several books, newspapers, etc., that are exactly the same: Do you have a **copy of** today's paper?

copy[2] * [verb; **copies, copied, copying**]
1 to make or produce something that is exactly like something else: He copied the picture from the book.
2 a short form of PHOTOCOPY: Please copy this article for me.
3 to do what someone else does in exactly the same way; _synonym_ IMITATE: Children often copy their parents without realizing it.

copybook /'kapiˌbʊk/ [noun] a set of pieces of paper fastened together like a book, for writing in; _synonym_ NOTEBOOK: Write these sentences in your copybook.

cord /kɔrd/ [noun]
1 the wire that joins a piece of electrical equipment to the electrical supply: She almost tripped over the TV cord.
⇨ See the picture at OUTLET.
2 a kind of thick string: Pull that cord to open the curtains.

cordless /'kɔrdlɪs/ [adjective; no comparative] a piece of electrical equipment that is cordless does not have an electric cord: I got a cordless phone for my birthday.

core T /kɔr/ [noun]
1 the main part or the middle of something: the **core of** the problem
2 the hard part in the middle of some fruits: an **apple core**

cork /kɔrk/ [noun] the round piece of soft wood that is put in the top of a bottle to close it: We couldn't get the cork out of the bottle.

corkscrew /'kɔrkˌskru/ [noun] a tool that you use to remove a cork from a bottle

corn * /kɔrn/ [noun]
1 the juicy yellow seeds of a tall plant that are eaten as a vegetable, or the

/i/ **see**	/ɪ/ **big**	/eɪ/ **day**	/ɛ/ **get**	/æ/ **hat**
/ɑ/ **father, hot**		/ʌ/ **up**	/ə/ **about**	/ɔ/ **saw**
/oʊ/ **hope**	/ʊ/ **book**	/u/ **too**	/aɪ/ **I**	/aʊ/ **how**
/ɔɪ/ **boy**	/ɝ/ **bird**	/ɚ/ **teacher**	/ɪr/ **ear**	/ɛr/ **air**
/ɑr/ **far**	/ɔr/ **more**	/ʊr/ **tour**	/aɪr/ **fire**	
/aʊɚ/ **hour**	/θ/ **nothing**	/ð/ **mother**	/ʃ/ **she**	
/ʒ/ **measure**	/tʃ/ **church**	/dʒ/ **jump**	/ŋ/ **long**	

plant itself: *I bought six ears of corn* (=pieces with the seeds attached).

━━ **PHRASE** ━━

2 corn on the cob pieces of corn cooked with the seeds attached: *Corn on the cob is my favorite picnic food.*

an ear of **corn**

corn² [*adjective; no comparative*] made from dried ground corn: *corn muffins* | *corn chips*

corner * ⊤ /'kɔrnə/ [*noun*]
  1 the place where two lines, sides, or walls join: *There was a chair in the corner of the room.*
  2 the place where two streets meet: *Our house is on the corner of Main Street and Lincoln Avenue.*

corporal or **Corporal** /'kɔrpərəl/ [*noun, name*] an officer with a low rank in the Army, Air Force, Navy, or Marine Corps

corporation ⊤ /ˌkɔrpə'reɪʃən/ [*noun*] a large company: *Their corporation has factories in several countries.*

corpse /kɔrps/ [*noun*] a dead body: *The corpse was found in the river.*

correct¹ * /kə'rɛkt/ [*adjective; no comparative*] right or true and without a mistake; *opposites* INCORRECT, WRONG: *Does anyone know the correct answer?* | *My guess was correct.*

correct² * [*verb; corrected, correcting*] to make something right, for example by fixing mistakes: *Teachers spend a long time correcting homework.*

correction /kə'rɛkʃən/ [*noun*] a change that makes something right: *There were lots of corrections on my homework.*

correctly * /kə'rɛktli/ [*adverb*] in the right way; *opposite* INCORRECTLY: *Have I spelled your name correctly?*

correspond /ˌkɔrə'spand/ [*verb; corresponded, corresponding*]
  1 if one thing corresponds to another, they are connected or similar: *Each letter in the code corresponds to a number.*
  2 FORMAL to write letters to someone: *I have corresponded with him for a year.*

correspondence /ˌkɔrə'spandəns/ [*noun*] letters that people write to each other: *My correspondence is in that file.*

correspondent /ˌkɔrə'spandənt/ [*noun*] someone whose job is to report news for a newspaper, television company, etc.; *synonym* REPORTER: *Here's a report from our correspondent in Russia.*

corridor /'kɔridə/ [*noun*] a passageway in a building, on a ship, on a train, etc.: *Our classroom is at the end of the corridor.*

cosmetics /kaz'mɛtɪks/ [*plural noun*] colored substances that you put on your face to make yourself look more attractive: *I don't use any cosmetics.*

cost¹ * /kɔst/ [*verb; costs, cost, cost, costing*] to have a particular price: *That coat costs $80.* | *cost someone something* ▸ *It cost me a lot of money.*
  ☛ Do not say "The suit cost $100 to me." Say **The suit cost me $100.**

cost² * [*noun*] the amount of money that you must pay for something: *The cost of living is increasing* (=cost of buying food, clothes, etc.). | *The house was repaired at a cost of $50,000.*

SYNONYMS cost, price, fare, charge, fee

  The **cost** of something is how much money you need to pay for something: *What will the cost of the vacation be?*

  The **price** of something is the exact amount you must pay to buy it in a store, restaurant, etc.: *What's the price of this hat?*

  A **fare** is the price you pay for a trip on a bus, train, plane, etc.: *"How much was the plane fare?" "Four hundred dollars."*

  The word **charge** is used especially about a particular service: *Is there a charge for using the telephone?*

  A **fee** is what you pay for a service from someone such as a doctor or lawyer: *Her fee is $200 an hour.*

---

costly /'kɔstli/ [*adjective; costlier, costliest*] very expensive: *The furniture will be costly to replace.*

costume /'kastum/ [*noun*]
  1 a set of clothes that an actor or performer wears: *The actor playing the king was trying on his costume.*

2 a set of clothes that make you look like a person in stories, an animal, etc.: *Grandma is making my witch costume for Halloween.*

3 clothes that are typical of a particular place or time: *The people at the carnival were wearing their national costume.*

cot /kɑt/ [*noun*] a bed that you can fold up and carry

cottage /'kɑtɪdʒ/ [*noun*] a small house in the country

cotton * /'kɑtən/ [*noun*]

1 cloth or thread made from the cotton plant: *a cotton shirt*

2 a plant with a lot of white hair on its seeds: *We drove past cotton fields.*

cotton ball /'kɑtən ˌbɔl/ [*noun*] a small ball of cotton for cleaning your skin

couch /kaʊtʃ/ [*noun; plural* **couches**] a long soft chair for two or more people to sit on; *synonym* SOFA

cougar /'kugɚ/ [*noun*] a large wild cat that lives in North and South America

cough[1] * /kɔf/ [*verb;* **coughed, coughing**] to push air out through your mouth with a short rough sound: *My chest hurt and I couldn't stop coughing.*

cough[2] * [*noun*]

1 an illness in which you keep coughing: *I have a terrible cough.*

2 the action or sound of coughing: *a loud cough*

could * /kʊd/ [*modal verb*]

1 the past tense of CAN: *He could read when he was three.*

2 used to say that something is or was possible: *He could help if he wanted to.* I *The fire could have been prevented.*

3 used to make a polite request: *Could you give me a ride to school?*

4 used to make a suggestion: *We could go to the beach.*

couldn't * /'kʊdnt/ the short form of "could not": *I couldn't see without my glasses.*

could've /'kʊdəv/ SPOKEN the short form of "could have": *You could've visited me in Boston.*

council * /'kaʊnsəl/ [*noun*] a group of people who are chosen to make rules or to give advice about something: *the Security Council of the United Nations*

counselor /'kaʊnsələ/ [*noun*] someone whose job is to listen to people and help them solve their problems: *a marriage counselor*

count[1] * /kaʊnt/ [*verb;* **counted, counting**]

1 to say numbers in the correct order: *Can you count in English?*

2 to say a number for each one of a group of people or things in order to find out how many there are: *She was counting the stamps in her collection.* I **count up something** ▶ *Count up your pennies and see how many you have.*

3 to be important or worth something: *Honesty counts.*

━━ PHRASAL VERB ━━

count on [*phrasal verb*]

4 to need and expect someone to do something or something to happen: **count on someone/something** ▶ *I'll be there. You can count on it.* I **count on someone to do something** ▶ *I'm counting on you to score some points.*

count[2] [*noun*]

━━ PHRASES ━━

1 keep count (of) to make sure you know what the changing total of something is: *You keep count of how many invitations we send, okay?*

2 lose count (of) to not remember how many times you have done something, or how many times something has happened: *I've lost count of how often I've been to Canada.*

countable noun * /'kaʊntəbəl 'naʊn/ [*noun*] GRAMMAR a noun that can be used with "a" or a plural form: *"Dog" is a countable noun.*

↪ *Compare* UNCOUNTABLE NOUN.

counter /'kaʊntɚ/ [*noun*]

1 the place in a store, bank, etc., where you pay for things or ask for things: *He works behind the counter in a video store.*

2 a flat surface in a kitchen that you

prepare food on: *Bob was at the counter chopping carrots and onions.*

counterclockwise /ˌkaʊntɚˈklɑkˌwaɪz/ [*adverb*] in the opposite direction of the movement of the hands of a clock; *opposite* CLOCKWISE: *Turn the handle counterclockwise.*

countless T /ˈkaʊntlɪs/ [*adjective; no comparative*] so many of something that you cannot count them all: *Twenty people were killed and countless others were injured.*

☛ Only use **countless** before a noun.

country * /ˈkʌntri/ [*noun; plural* countries]
1 an area that is ruled by one government: *China is one of the largest countries in the world.*
2 **the country** an area of land away from towns and cities: *They have a house in the country.*

SYNONYMS country, state, nation

A **country** is an area that is ruled by one government: *France is a country in Europe.* | *What country was he born in?*

A **state** is also a country, especially its government and political organization: *They promised loyalty to the state.* | *a head of state.* However, a **state** can also be a separate political area within a bigger country: *the state of California.*

A **nation** is a country and the people who belong to it: *The whole nation was shocked by the president's death.*

---

country music /ˈkʌntri ˈmyuzɪk/ [*noun*] music in the style that is typical of the south and west of the U.S.

countryside * /ˈkʌntriˌsaɪd/ [*noun*] land that has few or no buildings on it

county /ˈkaʊnti/ [*noun; plural* counties] one of the areas that some states or countries are divided into for government: *I live in the next county.*

couple T /ˈkʌpəl/ [*noun*]
1 two people who are married or having a romantic relationship: *We live next door to a young couple.*
— PHRASE —
2 **a couple** two things or people of the same kind: *We need a couple more cups.* | *She has a couple of dogs.*

USAGE couple, pair

A **couple** of things is any two things of the same kind: *a couple of dollars* | *a couple of apples.* Sometimes **couple** is used to talk about a small number of something: *Wait a couple of minutes.*

A **pair** of things is two things that are used or worn together: *a pair of shoes* | *a pair of socks.* It is also used about a single thing that has two parts that are joined together: *a pair of pants* | *a pair of scissors.*

---

coupon /ˈkupɑn/ [*noun*] a piece of paper that is used to buy a product at a lower price: *I have a half-price coupon for this cereal.*

courage * /ˈkɜrɪdʒ/ [*noun*] the ability to do things although you are afraid, in pain, etc.: *He didn't **have the courage to** leave.* | *It **took courage** (=he needed courage) to admit he was wrong.*

courier /ˈkɜriɚ/ [*noun*] someone whose job is to take packages, important papers, etc., from one place to another

course * /kɔrs/ [*noun*]
1 the planned direction of a ship, plane, etc.: *The plane **changed** its course.* | *The boat was blown **off** course.*
2 a set of classes that you have in a particular subject: *I'm **taking** a computer course.*
3 one of the parts of a meal: *For the first course, we had soup.*
4 the way something happens or develops: *the course of events*
— PHRASE —
5 **of course**
  a used to say that something is clear or not surprising: *Of course he was tired from traveling.* | *She was delighted, of course.*
  b used to say "yes" strongly: *"Can I borrow your pen?" "Of course."*

court * /kɔrt/ [*noun*]
1 a building or room where people decide if someone is guilty of a crime: *He is appearing **in court** next week.* | *a court of law*
2 an area for playing games such as tennis and basketball: *a volleyball court*

courteous /'kɜ·tiəs/ [adjective; **more courteous, most courteous**] FORMAL very polite: *a courteous young man*

courtesy /'kɜ·təsi/ [noun] very polite behavior: *We were treated with courtesy.*

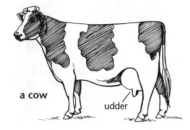

a cow

udder

courthouse /'kɔrt,haʊs/ [noun; plural **courthouses** /'kɔrt,haʊzɪz/] a building with courts of law inside it: *Reporters waited outside the courthouse.*

courtroom /'kɔrt,rum/ [noun] a room where people decide if someone is guilty of a crime

courtyard /'kɔrt,yard/ [noun] a space with buildings on all sides: *The doors opened onto a courtyard.*

cousin * /'kʌzən/ [noun] a son or daughter of your uncle or aunt
⇨ *See the picture at* FAMILY TREE.

cover¹ * T /'kʌvɚ/ [verb; **covered, covering**]
1 to put something over or on top of something else in order to hide it or protect it: **cover something with something** ▸ *She covered her head with a red scarf.*
2 to be on top of something or to be over a whole area: *Snow covered the ground.* | **be covered with/in something** ▸ *All the soccer players were covered with mud.*
3 to include or deal with particular things: *The course covers English grammar and spelling.*

cover² * T [noun]
1 something that is put over something else to protect it: *a pillow cover*
2 the outside of a book or magazine: *There was a picture of a dog on the cover.*
3 protection or shelter: *It began to rain and the boys ran for cover.* | *We took cover from the storm in a doorway.*

coveralls /'kʌvər,ɔlz/ [plural noun] a piece of clothing that you wear over your other clothes to keep them clean when you are working
⇨ *See the picture at* OVERALLS.

cow * /kaʊ/ [noun] a large female animal that is kept on a farm and produces milk

coward /'kaʊɚd/ [noun] someone who is too afraid to do things: *He was too much of a coward to ask her for a date.*

cowardly /'kaʊɚdli/ [adjective; **more cowardly, most cowardly**] too afraid to do things; *opposite* BRAVE: *I'm too cowardly to be a good soldier.*

cowboy /'kaʊ,bɔɪ/ [noun; plural **cowboys**] a man who rides a horse and takes care of cattle

coyote /kaɪ'oʊti/ [noun] a wild dog that lives in North America

cozy /'koʊzi/ [adjective; **cozier, coziest**] warm and comfortable: *a cozy room* | *It was very cozy in bed.*

CPU /'si'pi'yu/ [noun; plural **CPUs**] central processing unit; the part of a computer that does almost all its calculations, and that deals with electronic instructions: *In most PCs, the CPU is just one microchip.*
⇨ *See also* PROCESSOR.

crab /kræb/ [noun] a sea creature that you can eat, that has ten legs and a hard shell on its back

claw

a crab

crack¹ * T /kræk/ [verb; **cracked, cracking**]
1 to break slightly or make something break slightly, so that there is a line on the surface: *I cracked the cup while I was washing it.*
2 to make a short, loud noise: *My knee cracked.*

/i/ **see** /ɪ/ **big** /eɪ/ **day** /ɛ/ **get** /æ/ **hat**
/ɑ/ **father, hot** /ʌ/ **up** /ə/ **about** /ɔ/ **saw**
/oʊ/ **hope** /ʊ/ **book** /u/ **too** /aɪ/ **I** /aʊ/ **how**
/ɔɪ/ **boy** /ɚ/ **bird** /ɚ/ **teacher** /ɪr/ **ear** /ɛr/ **air**
/ɑr/ **far** /ɔr/ **more** /ʊr/ **tour** /aɪr/ **fire**
/aʊɚ/ **hour** /θ/ **nothing** /ð/ **mother** /ʃ/ **she**
/ʒ/ **measure** /tʃ/ **church** /dʒ/ **jump** /ŋ/ **long**

━━ PHRASAL VERB ━━

crack down on [phrasal verb]
3 to become more strict in making sure that rules are obeyed: *Police are cracking down on speeding drivers.*

crack² * T [noun]
1 a line on the surface of something where it has started to break: *There was a crack in the vase.*
2 a very narrow space between two things: *He could see light through a crack in the curtains.*
3 a sudden loud, sharp sound: *a crack of thunder*

cracked /krækt/
[adjective; no comparative]
something that is cracked has a line on the surface where it is starting to break

This cup is **cracked.**

cracker /'krækɚ/
[noun] a thin hard cake, usually not

This cup is **chipped.**

sweet: *He was eating crackers and cheese.*

cradle /'kreɪdəl/ [noun] a very small bed that a baby sleeps in, that can move from side to side

craft /kræft/ [noun]
1 [plural **crafts**] an activity that involves making something with your hands: *The children are taught crafts such as sewing and weaving.*
2 [plural **craft**] a boat, airplane, or space vehicle: *Their little craft hit a rock and sank.*

craftsman /'kræftsmən/ [noun; plural **craftsmen** /'kræftsmən/] someone who is good at making something with his or her hands: *This furniture was made by a skilled craftsman.*

crafty /'kræfti/ [adjective; **craftier, craftiest**] good at getting what you want, especially by deceiving other people: *He's a crafty lawyer.*

cram /kræm/ [verb; **crams, crammed, cramming**] to force more things or people into something than it can easily hold: **cram something into something** ▸ *She crammed her clothes into a bag.*

cramped /kræmpt/ [adjective; **more cramped, most cramped**] a house, room, etc., that is cramped does not have enough space in it: *The kitchen is very cramped.*

cranberry /'kræn,bɛri/ [noun; plural **cranberries**] a small, sour, round, red fruit with smooth skin, that grows in wet places and in used in cooking

crane /kreɪn/ [noun]
1 a machine that is used for lifting very heavy things: *The builders used a crane to move the concrete pipes.*
2 a large bird that has long legs and a long neck and eats fish

cranky /'kræŋki/ [adjective; **crankier, crankiest**] INFORMAL feeling slightly angry, and easily annoyed: *Why are you so cranky today?*

crash¹ * /kræʃ/ [verb; **crashes, crashed, crashing**]
1 to have an accident in a car, train, or plane by hitting something: *My older brother crashed his car.* I *The helicopter **crashed into** a mountain.*
2 if a computer crashes or if you crash it, it suddenly stops working: *The computer crashed and I lost a lot of work.*
3 to hit something while moving and make a lot of noise: *A brick came **crashing through** the window.*

crash² * [noun; plural **crashes**]
1 an accident in which a car, train, or plane hits something: *Fortunately, no one was hurt in the **car crash**.*
2 a loud sound that is made when something hits something else: *There was a loud crash as the tree hit the ground.*
3 when a computer suddenly stops working: *We want to reduce the number of crashes.*

crate /kreɪt/ [noun] a large strong box made of plastic or wood that is used for carrying things: *a **crate of** oranges*

crawl T /krɔl/ [verb; **crawled, crawling**]
1 to move on your hands and knees like a baby: *The baby is just learning to crawl.*
2 if an insect crawls somewhere, it moves on its legs: *A spider was crawling up the wall.*

crayon /ˈkreɪən/ [*noun*] a colored pencil or a stick of colored wax that is used for drawing: *a box of crayons*

crazy * /ˈkreɪzi/ [*adjective;* **crazier, craziest**] INFORMAL
1 not at all sensible, or very strange: *That's a crazy idea! | You'd be crazy to go out in this storm.*
━━ PHRASE ━━
2 **be crazy about** to like or love someone or something very much: *She's crazy about my brother.*

creak /krik/ [*verb;* **creaked, creaking**] if a door, bed, etc., creaks, it makes a high noise when you open it, sit on it, etc.: *The stairs creaked as she climbed them.*

cream * /krim/ [*noun*]
1 the thick part of milk: *coffee with cream*
2 a thick substance that you put on your skin, especially to make it softer: *a jar of face cream*
3 a yellow-white color: *These pants come in cream or brown.*

cream-colored /ˈkrim ˌkʌlɚd/ [*adjective; no comparative*] of the color cream: *The room had cream-colored walls.*

creamy /ˈkrimi/ [*adjective;* **creamier, creamiest**] full of cream, or tasting like cream: *a rich, creamy, chocolate dessert*

crease /kris/ [*noun*] a line in paper or cloth that has been made by folding or pressing it: *His pants had two neat creases down the front.*

create * ⊤ /kriˈeɪt/ [*verb;* **created, creating**] to make something exist that did not exist before: *The new shopping mall has created a lot of traffic.*

creation /kriˈeɪʃən/ [*noun*]
1 something new that is made: *artistic creations*
2 the act of making something new: *job creation*

creative ⊤ /kriˈeɪtɪv/ [*adjective;* **more creative, most creative**] producing or involving interesting new ideas or things: *a creative artist | a creative idea*

creature * /ˈkritʃɚ/ [*noun*] an animal, insect, bird, etc.: *I think giraffes are beautiful creatures.*

credit[1] /ˈkredɪt/ [*noun*]
1 a way of buying something in which you pay for it later: *Furniture can often be bought on credit. | Cash or credit, sir?*
2 praise given to someone because he or she did something good: *She worked very hard but didn't get any credit for it.*
3 a point that a student gets for a class or part of a class, depending on a school's system: *I need 15 more credits to graduate.*

credit[2] [*verb;* **credited, crediting**] to put money into a bank account or other financial account: *Fifty dollars has been credited to your account.*

credit card /ˈkredɪt ˌkard/ [*noun*] a plastic card that you use to buy things and pay for them later: *Put it on my credit card.*

creek /krik/ [*noun*] a narrow stream or river: *They went fishing in the creek.*

creep ⊤ /krip/ [*verb;* **crept, creeping**] to move very quietly because you do not want people to hear you: *She crept downstairs to the kitchen.*

creepy /ˈkripi/ [*adjective;* **creepier, creepiest**] INFORMAL making you feel slightly frightened: *a creepy old building*

cremate /ˈkrimeɪt/ [*verb;* **cremated, cremating**] to completely burn someone's body after he or she dies: *My grandfather was cremated.*

crept /krept/ [*verb*] the past tense and past participle of CREEP

crescent /ˈkresənt/ [*noun*] a curved shape that has a point at each end
⇨ See the picture at MOON.

crest ⊤ /krest/ [*noun*] the top of a hill or wave: *the crest of a ridge*

crew /kru/ [*noun*] the people who work on a boat or aircraft: *The ship has a crew of 25.*

crib /krib/ [*noun*] a small bed with high sides for a baby to sleep in: *He's getting too big for a crib.*

cricket /ˈkrɪkɪt/ [*noun*] an insect that jumps and makes a noise

/i/ **see**	/ɪ/ **big**	/eɪ/ **day**	/ɛ/ **get**	/æ/ **hat**
/ɑ/ **father, hot**	/ʌ/ **up**	/ə/ **about**	/ɔ/ **saw**	
/oʊ/ **hope**	/ʊ/ **book**	/u/ **too**	/aɪ/ **I**	/aʊ/ **how**
/ɔɪ/ **boy**	/ɝ/ **bird**	/ɚ/ **teacher**	/ɪr/ **ear**	/ɛr/ **air**
/ɑr/ **far**	/ɔr/ **more**	/ʊr/ **tour**	/aɪr/ **fire**	
/aʊɚ/ **hour**	/θ/ **nothing**	/ð/ **mother**	/ʃ/ **she**	
/ʒ/ **measure**	/tʃ/ **church**	/dʒ/ **jump**	/ŋ/ **long**	

cried * /kraɪd/ [*verb*] the past tense and past participle of CRY¹

crime * /kraɪm/ [*noun*] an action that is not allowed by the laws of a country: *Murder is a crime.* I *Crime has increased in many cities.* I *He **committed** several **crimes**.*
☛ Do not say "do a crime." Say **commit a crime**.

criminal * /'krɪmənəl/ [*noun*] someone who has committed a crime: *Do you think criminals should go to jail?*

cripple /'krɪpəl/ [*verb*; **crippled, crippling**] to be injured and no longer able to use one or both of your arms or legs: *She was crippled in a car accident.*

crisis /'kraɪsɪs/ [*noun*; plural **crises** /'kraɪsiz/*] a time when something is happening that is dangerous or difficult to deal with: *a time of crisis*

crisp /krɪsp/ [*adjective*; **crisper, crispest**] food that is crisp is pleasantly hard: *a crisp apple* I *crisp bacon*

critic /'krɪtɪk/ [*noun*] someone whose job is to write about movies, plays, works of art, etc., and say whether they are good or bad: *an art critic* I *a restaurant critic*

critical Ⓣ /'krɪtɪkəl/ [*adjective*; **more critical, most critical**]
1 saying that something or someone is bad in some way, especially when this is unfair: *The teacher is always very **critical of** my work.*
2 a critical time or thing is very important: *At this critical point in the game, the home team scored.*

criticism * /'krɪtə,sɪzəm/ [*noun*] when you say that something is bad in some way: *My only **criticism of** the hotel is that the rooms are small.* I *There was a lot of criticism of the mayor's speech.*

criticize * Ⓣ /'krɪtə,saɪz/ [*verb*; **criticized, criticizing**] to say that someone or something is bad in some way: *My father criticizes my clothes.*

crocodile /'krakə,daɪl/ [*noun*] a large, dangerous animal with a long mouth and a lot of teeth that lives in water in some hot countries
⊃ *See the picture at* ALLIGATOR.

crook /krʊk/ [*noun*] INFORMAL someone who is dishonest or steals things: *Don't buy anything from that crook!*

crooked /'krʊkɪd/ [*adjective*; **more crooked, most crooked**]
1 not straight: *His teeth were crooked.*
2 INFORMAL dishonest: *a crooked banker*

crop * /krap/ [*noun*]
1 a plant such as rice or corn that farmers grow for people to eat: *The farmer's main crop was rice.*
2 the amount of rice, corn, etc., that is produced at one time: *We'll have a good crop this year.*

cross¹ * /krɔs/ [*verb*; **crosses, crossed, crossing**]
1 to go from one side of something to the other side: *Look both ways before crossing the street.*
2 if two lines, roads, etc., cross, they meet and continue: *Highway 67 crosses Route 80 right here.*

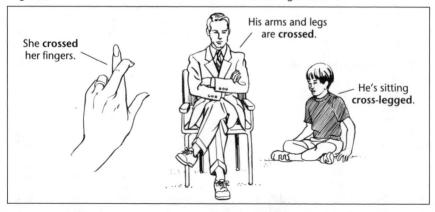

She **crossed** her fingers.

His arms and legs are **crossed**.

He's sitting **cross-legged**.

━ **PHRASE** ━━━

3 cross your arms/legs/fingers to bend one leg, arm, or finger over the other: *She was sitting with her legs crossed.* | *Cross your fingers, everybody!* (=to wish for good luck)

cross² * [*noun; plural* **crosses**]
1 a shape or object with two straight lines or pieces that cross each other: *She put a cross next to all the wrong answers.*
2 something that is a mixture of two other things: *A mule is a cross between a horse and a donkey.*

crossing /'krɔsɪŋ/ [*noun*] a marked place where you can cross a road, railroad, etc.: *We waited at the crossing.*

cross-legged /'krɔs ˌlegɪd/ [*adverb*] if you are sitting cross-legged, you are not on a chair, and your legs are crossing each other: *The boy was sitting cross-legged on the floor.*

crossroads /'krɔsˌroʊdz/ [*noun; plural* **crossroads**] a place where two roads cross each other: *Turn left at the next crossroads.*

crosswalk /'krɔsˌwɔk/ [*noun*] a marked place where cars have to stop to let people walk across the road

crossword puzzle /'krɔsˌwɜ˞d ˌpʌzəl/ [*noun*] a game in which the answers to questions are written into a pattern of squares

crouch /kraʊtʃ/ [*verb;* **crouches, crouched, crouching**] to bend or be bending your knees so that you are close to the ground: *She crouched down to talk to the little boy.*
⇨ *See the picture at* MOVEMENT.

crow¹ /kroʊ/ [*noun*] a big black bird

crow² [*verb;* **crowed, crowing**] to make the long loud sound of a rooster: *I was often awake before the rooster crowed.*

crowd¹ * /kraʊd/ [*noun*] a large group of people: *There was a crowd of people outside the White House.*

crowd² * [*verb;* **crowded, crowding**] if people crowd into a place or crowd around something, they are very close together: *Thousands of soccer fans crowded into the stadium.* | *Everyone crowded around the TV.*

crowded /'kraʊdɪd/ [*adjective;* **more crowded, most crowded**] a place or vehicle that is crowded has a lot of people in it: *The store was very crowded.* | *a crowded train*

crown /kraʊn/ [*noun*] a metal object that a king or queen wears on his or her head: *a gold crown*

crude /krud/ [*adjective;* **cruder, crudest**]
1 in a natural form: *Crude oil is refined for use as fuel.*
2 not polite: *I don't like his crude jokes.*

cruel * /'kruəl/ [*adjective;* **crueler, cruelest**] deliberately hurting people or animals, or making them unhappy: *Someone played a cruel joke on her.* | *He was very cruel to his dog.*

cruelty /'kruəlti/ [*noun*] the quality or activity of being cruel: *cruelty to animals*

cruise¹ /kruz/ [*noun*] a trip for pleasure on a large boat: *My parents went on a Caribbean cruise.*

cruise² [*verb;* **cruised, cruising**] to sail slowly: *They were cruising along the river.*

crumb /krʌm/ [*noun*] a very small piece of dry food, for example from bread or a cake: *He dropped crumbs on the floor.*

crumble /'krʌmbəl/ [*verb;* **crumbled, crumbling**] to break into very small pieces, or to make something do this: *The walls of the building were crumbling.*

crumple /'krʌmpəl/ [*verb;* **crumpled, crumpling**] to press a piece of paper, cloth, etc., together in a rough way so that it has folds in it: *He crumpled up the letter and threw it away.*

crunch¹ /krʌntʃ/ [*verb;* **crunches, crunched, crunching**]
1 to eat hard food in a way that makes noise: *She was crunching a carrot as she read.* | *The dog crunched on a bone.*
2 to make the noise of something being crushed: *The snow crunched as we walked.*

/i/ **see** /ɪ/ **big** /eɪ/ **day** /ɛ/ **get** /æ/ **hat**
/ɑ/ **father, hot** /ʌ/ **up** /ə/ **about** /ɔ/ **saw**
/oʊ/ **hope** /ʊ/ **book** /u/ **too** /aɪ/ **I** /aʊ/ **how**
/ɔɪ/ **boy** /ɝ/ **bird** /ɚ/ **teacher** /ɪr/ **ear** /ɛr/ **air**
/ɑr/ **far** /ɔr/ **more** /ʊr/ **tour** /aɪr/ **fire**
/aʊɚ/ **hour** /θ/ **nothing** /ð/ **mother** /ʃ/ **she**
/ʒ/ **measure** /tʃ/ **church** /dʒ/ **jump** /ŋ/ **long**

crunch[2] [*noun*] the sound of something hard being crushed: *There was a loud crunch as the car hit the tree.*

crush * T /krʌʃ/ [*verb;* **crushes, crushed, crushing**] to press something so that it becomes flatter or breaks into small pieces: *The hat will get crushed in your bag.* | *Crush the berries to make a sauce.*

crust /krʌst/ [*noun*] the hard brown surface of something that is baked, such as bread: *She cut the crusts off the sandwiches.*

crutch /krʌtʃ/ [*noun; plural* **crutches**] a stick that you put under your arm to help you walk if you have hurt your leg

cry[1] * /kraɪ/ [*verb;* **cries, cried, crying**]
1 to produce water from your eyes because you are sad, in pain, etc.: *I cried when my dog died.*
⇨ *See the picture at* EMOTION.
2 to shout something loudly: *"Go away!" he cried.*

cry[2] * [*noun; plural* **cries**] a loud shout: *They heard cries of "Help!"*

crystal /ˈkrɪstəl/ [*noun*]
1 an amount of a hard substance that has formed in a regular shape: *salt crystals*
2 rock or glass that is clear like ice: *a crystal ornament*

cub /kʌb/ [*noun*] a young BEAR, lion, tiger, or fox

cube * /kyub/ [*noun*]
1 a shape with six equal square sides
⇨ *See* Shapes *in the Smart Study section.*
2 an object with a shape like this: *ice cubes*

cubed /kyubd/ [*adjective; no comparative*] used to describe a number that is multiplied by itself two times: *2 cubed is 8.*

cubic /ˈkyubɪk/ [*adjective*]
━━ PHRASE ━━
a cubic centimeter/inch/meter/ etc. a measurement that says how much a cube can hold when its sides are a centimeter, inch, meter, etc., long: *The volume of the box is 150 cubic inches.*

cubicle /ˈkyubɪkəl/ [*noun*] a small area that is separated from the rest of a room so that people cannot see you: *a shower cubicle*

Cub Scout /kʌb ˌskaʊt/ [*noun*]
1 **the Cub Scouts** the Boy Scouts organization for younger boys: *Mom, can I join the Cub Scouts?*
☛ Only use **the Cub Scouts** with a singular verb in this meaning.
2 a boy who is a member of the Cub Scouts: *My youngest son is a Cub Scout.*

cucumber /ˈkyukʌmbɚ/ [*noun*] a long green VEGETABLE that is white inside, which you eat raw

cuddle /ˈkʌdəl/ [*verb;* **cuddled, cuddling**] to gently hold someone or something close to you with both arms: *She cuddled the little dog.*

cuff /kʌf/ [*noun*] the part of a sleeve that is closest to your hand
⇨ *See the picture at* CLOTHING.

cultivate T /ˈkʌltəˌveɪt/ [*verb;* **cultivated, cultivating**] to prepare and use land for growing crops: *The land is rocky and hard to cultivate.*

cultivation /ˌkʌltɪˈveɪʃən/ [*noun*] the growing of crops: *the cultivation of rice*

cultural T /ˈkʌltʃərəl/ [*adjective; no comparative*]
1 connected with a particular society: *I was aware of the cultural differences between our two countries.*
2 related to art, music, etc.: *He enjoys many cultural activities.*

culture T /ˈkʌltʃɚ/ [*noun*]
1 a particular society and its ideas, beliefs, ways of doing things, etc.: *Chinese culture* | *Western culture*
2 art, plays, music, etc.: *The city has plenty of culture.*

cup * /kʌp/ [*noun*]
1 a small container for drinking from, usually with a handle: *a china cup*
⇨ *See the picture at* TEAPOT.
2 a drink in a cup: *a cup of tea*
3 a measurement equal to 8 ounces, used in cooking: *Mix 2 cups of sugar with 1 cup of butter.*
⇨ *See the picture at* Measurements *in the Smart Study section.*
4 a silver container that is given as a prize: *She won a cup in the golf tournament.*

cupboard * /ˈkʌbɚd/ [*noun*] a piece of furniture or a small closet with a door on it, where you keep dishes, food, etc.: *There's no sugar in the cupboard.*

cupcake /'kʌp,keɪk/ [*noun*] a small round cake: *I ate three cupcakes.*

cupful /'kʌpfʊl/ [*noun; plural* **cupfuls**] as much of something as a cup can hold: *She spilled a whole cupful of coffee.*

curb /kɜ·b/ [*noun*] the edge of a sidewalk next to the road
⇨ *See the picture at* HOUSE.

cure[1] * /kyʊr/ [*verb*; **cured, curing**] to make someone who is sick become well: *Will the doctors be able to cure him?*

cure[2] * [*noun*] a medicine or form of treatment that can make an illness disappear: *a **cure for** cancer*

curiosity /,kyʊri'asɪti/ [*noun*] the feeling of wanting to know something: *I'd like to try sailing, just **out of curiosity** (=to see what it is like).*

curious ⊤ /'kyʊriəs/ [*adjective;* **more curious, most curious**]
1 wanting to know something: *I'm **curious about** why they left so early.*
2 strange and unusual: *There was a curious smell in the kitchen.*

curiously /'kyʊriəsli/ [*adverb*] in a strange or unusual way: *The children were curiously quiet.*

curl[1] * /kɜ·l/ [*noun*] a piece of hair that is not straight and curves around: *a little girl with lots of dark curls*

curl[2] * [*verb;* **curled, curling**]
1 to form a curved shape, or to make something do this: *I curl my hair every morning.*

═══ PHRASAL VERB ═══

curl up [*phrasal verb*]
2 to move so that you are sitting or lying with your arms and legs close to your body: *He was curled up in bed, reading a book.*

curly /'kɜ·li/ [*adjective;* **curlier, curliest**] HAIR that is curly has lots of tight curves in it

currant /'kɜrənt/ [*noun*] a very small, black, dried fruit

currency ⊤ /'kɜrənsi/ [*noun; plural* **currencies**] the kind of money that is used in a particular country: *The dollar*

is the currency used in the U.S. | *foreign currency* | *French currency*

current[1] ⊤ /'kɜrənt/ [*adjective*] happening or existing now: *In his current job he deals with sales.*
☛ Only use **current** before a noun.

current[2] * [*noun*] a flow of water or electricity: *The river has **strong currents** here.*

currently /'kɜrəntli/ [*adverb*] now, at this time: *The school currently has 600 students.*

curriculum /kə'rɪkyələm/ [*noun; plural* **curricula** /kə'rɪkyələ/ or **curriculums**] the subjects that a school or college teaches: *The school has a broad curriculum.*

curry /'kɜri/ [*noun*] a food consisting of meat or vegetables in a liquid with a hot taste: *We had chicken curry and rice.*

curse[1] /kɜ·s/ [*verb;* **cursed, cursing**]
1 to use rude and offensive words; synonym SWEAR: *She cursed when she dropped the vase.*
2 to say or think bad things about someone or something that has made you angry: **curse someone for doing something** ▸ *She cursed him for forgetting to phone her.*

curse[2] [*noun*] something you say when you are very angry or that uses rude words: *He screamed curses at them.*

cursor /'kɜ·sə·/ [*noun*] a mark that moves around a computer screen to show where you are working: *Put the cursor at the end of the word and press "Enter."*

curtain * /'kɜ·tən/ [*noun*]
1 a piece of cloth that you pull across a window to cover it: *Sandy **drew the curtains** (=closed the curtains).*
2 a large piece of material in front of the stage in a theater: *The **curtain***

/i/ see	/ɪ/ big	/eɪ/ day	/ɛ/ get	/æ/ hat
/ɑ/ father, hot	/ʌ/ up	/ə/ about	/ɔ/ saw
/oʊ/ hope	/ʊ/ book	/u/ too	/aɪ/ I	/aʊ/ how
/ɔɪ/ boy	/ɚ/ bird	/ə·/ teacher	/ɪr/ ear	/ɛr/ air
/ɑr/ far	/ɔr/ more	/ʊr/ tour	/aɪr/ fire
/aʊə·/ hour	/θ/ nothing	/ð/ mother	/ʃ/ she
/ʒ/ measure	/tʃ/ church	/dʒ/ jump	/ŋ/ long

goes up at 7 o'clock (=that is when the performance starts).

curve¹ * /kɜ˞v/ [*noun*] a line that bends, like part of a circle: *a long curve in a road*

curve² * [*verb;* **curved, curving**] to be in the shape of a line that bends: *Route 17 curves around the mountain.*

curved /kɜvd/ [*adjective; no comparative*] having a shape like part of a circle or ball; _opposite_ STRAIGHT: *a curved knife*

cushion /ˈkʊʃən/ [*noun*] a cloth bag filled with soft material that you put on a chair to make it more comfortable: *She had colorful cushions on the sofa.*

custard /ˈkʌstə˞d/ [*noun*] a soft, sweet food made by cooking eggs, milk, and sugar: *We had custard for dessert.*

custom * ⊤ /ˈkʌstəm/ [*noun*]
1 something that people do in a particular country or area because they have done it for a long time: *the Japanese custom of bowing to greet someone*
  ↪ *See the usage note at* HABIT.
2 customs the place where your bags are checked when you go into a country, in order to make sure you do not have anything you should not have: *There was a long line **at customs**.*
  ☛ Only use a singular verb with **customs** in this meaning.

customer * /ˈkʌstəmə˞/ [*noun*] someone who buys something from a store or business: *We like to please our customers.*

cut¹ * /kʌt/ [*verb;* **cuts, cut, cut, cutting**]
1 to divide something, remove something, or make a hole in something using a knife, scissors, etc.: *Cut the string.* I *She's outside cutting flowers.* I *Did you **cut up** the carrots?* I **cut something in/ into something** ▸ *Cut two holes in the mask.* I **cut something in half/in two** ▸

cutting

Would you cut the sandwich in half, please? I **cut something into pieces/ quarters/** etc. ▸ *He cut the apple into quarters.* I **cut someone a piece/slice** ▸ *Cut me another slice of cake, please?*
2 to make something shorter using scissors or another tool: *I need **to get my hair cut.***
3 to accidentally hurt yourself with something sharp that makes your skin bleed: *He cut his finger on a piece of broken glass.* I *Ouch! I cut myself!*
4 to make something smaller in size, amount, number, etc.: *The price was cut, so I bought the computer.*

━━ PHRASE ━━
5 cut it out! SPOKEN used to tell someone to stop doing something: *Cut it out! That tickles!*

━━ PHRASAL VERBS ━━
cut down [*phrasal verb*]
6 to cut through a tree so that it falls to the ground: **cut down something** ▸ *Trees were cut down to build the road.* I **cut something down** ▸ *They cut my favorite tree down.*

cut off [*phrasal verb*]
7 to separate something from a larger thing by cutting: **cut something off** ▸ *He cut the label off his new shirt.*
8 to stop a supply of water, electricity, etc.: *Their gas **was cut off** because they didn't pay the bill.*

cut out [*phrasal verb*]
9 to remove part of something, usually a piece of paper, by cutting: **cut out something** ▸ *I think I'll cut out this article and keep it.*

cut² * [*noun*]
1 an injury where something sharp cut your skin: *She had a cut on her knee.*
2 a reduction in the amount of something: *a **price cut***

cute /kyut/ [*adjective;* **cuter, cutest**] INFORMAL attractive and pretty: *a cute little girl* I *What a cute outfit!*

cycle * /ˈsaɪkəl/ [*noun*] a number of connected events that keep happening in the same order: *the cycle of the four seasons*

cyclist /ˈsaɪklɪst/ [*noun*] someone who rides a bicycle

cylinder /'sɪlɪndɚ/ [*noun*]
1 a shape like a short straight pipe
➪ *See* Shapes *in the Smart Study section.*
2 a container that has a shape like this: *a gas cylinder*

cyclone /'saɪkloʊn/ [*noun*] a violent storm with very strong spinning winds: *Tornadoes and hurricanes are cyclones.*
➪ *Compare* GALE, HURRICANE, TORNADO.

cymbal /'sɪmbəl/ [*noun*] a MUSICAL INSTRUMENT consisting of a flat round piece of metal that you play by hitting it with a stick: *She **plays the cymbals**.*
☛ This word is usually used in the plural.

D

D * or **d** /di/ [*noun*]
1 [*plural* **Ds** or **D's, d's**] the fourth letter of the English alphabet
➪ *See the usage note at* ALPHABET.
2 **D** [*plural* **Ds** or **D's**] a bad grade in school: *I **got a D** on my math test.*

dab /dæb/ [*verb;* **dabs, dabbed, dabbing**] to press something lightly with a cloth or other material, especially something wet: *She dabbed her eyes with a handkerchief* (=because she was crying).

dad or **Dad** /dæd/ [*noun, name*] *INFORMAL* father: *My dad will drive us home.* | *Come and look at this, Dad!*
➪ *See the usage note at* CAPITAL.

daddy or **Daddy** /'dædi/ [*noun, name; plural* **daddies**] *INFORMAL* a word meaning FATHER, used especially by children: *Daddy, can I have a soda?*
➪ *See the usage note at* CAPITAL.

daffodil /'dæfədɪl/ [*noun*] a tall yellow FLOWER that grows in spring

daily[1] * /'deɪli/ [*adjective; no comparative*] happening, done, or produced every day: *a **daily newspaper*** | *He takes a daily walk.*
☛ Only use **daily** before a noun.

daily[2] * [*adverb*] every day: *The museum is open daily from 9 until 6.*

dairy /'dɛri/ [*noun; plural* **dairies**] a place where milk, butter, cream, etc., is produced: ***dairy products*** (=food such as milk, cheese, etc.)

daisy /'deɪzi/ [*noun; plural* **daisies**] a small white FLOWER with a yellow center, that grows in grass

dam[1] /dæm/ [*noun*] a wall built across a river, especially in order to collect a supply of water behind it: *The dam broke and flooded the surrounding area.*

dam[2] [*verb;* **dams, dammed, damming**] to build a dam across something: *They dammed the river.*

damage[1] * /'dæmɪdʒ/ [*noun*] physical harm done to something: *The floods caused **severe damage**.* | *Did you **do any damage to** your car?*
☛ Do not say "make damage." Say **do damage**.

damage[2] * [*verb;* **damaged, damaging**] to physically harm something: *Smoking can **damage your health**.*

damaged /'dæmɪdʒd/ [*adjective;* **more damaged, most damaged**] harmed by something such as an accident: *The bike is too damaged to fix.* | *a damaged book*

damp /dæmp/ [*adjective;* **damper, dampest**] slightly wet, often in an unpleasant way: *It was a cold, damp morning.* | *a damp cloth*

dance[1] * /dæns/ [*verb;* **danced, dancing**] to move your feet and body as music plays, for enjoyment: *The kids were **dancing to** pop music.*
☛ Do not say that someone "dances music" or "dances with music." Say that he or she **dances to music**.

dance[2] * [*noun*]
1 a party where people dance: *I met my husband at a dance.*
2 when you move your feet and body as music plays, for enjoyment: *Let's have one last dance before we go.*

dancer * /'dænsɚ/ [*noun*] someone who dances, especially as his or her job: *Her younger son's **a ballet dancer**.*

dancing /'dænsɪŋ/ [noun] when people move their feet and bodies as music plays, for enjoyment: *Dancing is fun.*

dandelion /'dændə,laɪən/ [noun] a small, yellow, wild flower that becomes a white ball of seeds

dandruff /'dændrəf/ [noun] small white pieces of dead skin from your head

danger * /'deɪndʒɚ/ [noun]
  1 the possibility that someone or something will be harmed or killed: *The sign read "Danger—Keep Out!"* | *She felt that she was in danger* (=in a dangerous situation).
  2 something that might harm or kill you: *the dangers of smoking*

dangerous * Ⓣ /'deɪndʒərəs/ [adjective; more dangerous, most dangerous] likely to harm or kill you: *It can be dangerous to go out alone at night.* | *That man is a dangerous criminal.*

dangle /'dæŋgəl/ [verb; dangled, dangling] to swing or hang loosely, or to make something do this: *She dangled her legs from the top bunk.*

danish /'deɪnɪʃ/ [noun; plural danishes] a small round food made of sweet bread, often with fruit in the middle

dare Ⓣ /dɛr/ [verb; dared, daring]
  1 to be brave or confident enough to do something: **dare do something** ▸ *He wouldn't dare leave without asking.* | *How dare you speak to your mother like that!* | *Don't you dare do that again!*
  2 to try to persuade someone to do something that is dangerous or embarrassing, to prove that he or she is not afraid: **dare someone to do something** ▸ *He dared me to climb the tree.* | *You go first—I dare you!*

dark¹ * /dɑrk/ [adjective; darker, darkest]
  1 with little or no light: *It's getting dark.* | *I walked down the dark hall.*
  2 a dark color is closer to black than to white; *opposite* LIGHT: *a dark blue suit* | *a boy with dark hair*

dark² * [noun]
  the dark when there is no light: *I'm afraid of the dark.*

darkness * /'dɑrknɪs/ [noun] when there is little or no light: *The room was in total darkness* (=completely dark).
  ☛ Do not say that someone is "afraid of the darkness." Say that he or she is **afraid of the dark.**

darling /'dɑrlɪŋ/ [noun] used as a name for someone you love, especially in a romantic relationship: *Would you like some more tea, darling?*

dash¹ /dæʃ/ [verb; dashes, dashed, dashing] to run somewhere very quickly: *She dashed out the door.*

dash² [noun; plural dashes] a mark used in writing. It looks like this: —
  ↪ See Punctuation *in the Smart Study section.*

data /'deɪtə; 'dætə/ [noun]
  1 [singular] information: *The data is available on the Internet.*
  2 [plural] facts: *The data are hard to discover.*

database /'deɪtə,beɪs; 'dætə,beɪs/ [noun] a collection of information on computer: *We have a database of information about different colleges.*

date¹ * /deɪt/ [noun]
  1 a particular day of the month or of the year: *What's the date of your party?* | *Today's date is January 26th.*
  ☛ Do not say "at the same date." Say **on the same date.**
  ↪ See the usage note at SECOND².
  2 an arrangement to go out with someone you like in a romantic way: *He has a date with my cousin tonight.*
  ↪ See also OUT-OF-DATE, UP-TO-DATE.

date² [verb; dated, dating] to go places together with someone you like in a romantic way: *He's dating my cousin.*

daughter * /'dɔtɚ/ [noun] someone's female child
  ↪ See the picture at FAMILY TREE.

daughter-in-law /'dɔtɚ ɪn ,lɔ/ [noun; plural daughters-in-law] the wife of your son
  ↪ See the picture at FAMILY TREE.

dawn /dɔn/ [noun] the time of day when it first becomes light: *We woke up at dawn.*

day * /deɪ/ [noun; plural days]
  1 a period of 24 hours: *We're spending*

ten days in Bangkok. | *"What day is it?"* *"Tuesday."* | *I had my hair cut the day before yesterday.* | *The wedding's the day after tomorrow.*
2 the time when it is light; *opposite* NIGHT: *It's a beautiful day.* | *I'm home during the day.* | *It rained all day and all night.*

— PHRASES —

3 **one day** at some time in the future; *synonym* SOMEDAY: *One day I'll be rich.*
4 **these days** used to say what the situation is now compared with the past: *I don't go to the movies much these days.*
5 **in those days** during a period of time in the past: *There was no TV in those days.*
6 **day off** a day when you do not have to go to work or to school: *Monday's my day off.*
⋄ *See also* **all day/night/week/month/ year** *at* ALL[1]. *See also* **the other day/ night** *at* OTHER[1].

USAGE　**Talking about days**

Use **on** to talk about what happens, happened, or will happen on a particular day of the week: *She always visits on Tuesdays.* | *I last saw him on Sunday.* | *I start school on Monday.*

Use **last** to talk about a particular day in the week before this one: *Where were you last Monday?* | *Last Friday we went to the beach.*

Use **next** to talk about a day in the week after this one: *Will you be at the party next Saturday?* | *It's her birthday next Thursday.*

day care Ⓣ /'deɪ ˌkɛr/ [*noun*] a place where very young children are cared for during the day while their parents are working

daydream[1] /'deɪˌdrim/ [*verb;* **daydreamed, daydreaming**] to think about something pleasant, so that you forget about what you should be doing: *Stop daydreaming and get to work.*

daydream[2] [*noun*] pleasant thoughts that make you forget about what you should be doing: *She seemed lost in a daydream.*

daylight /'deɪˌlaɪt/ [*noun*] the light produced by the sun

daytime /'deɪˌtaɪm/ [*noun*] the time during the day when it is light: *He sleeps in the daytime and works at night.*

dead ✳ /dɛd/ [*adjective; no comparative*]
1 no longer alive: *His father has been dead for six years.* | *The grass is covered with dead leaves.*
2 no longer operating: *a dead battery*

USAGE　**dead, died**

Dead is an adjective, not a verb: *I think he's dead!* | *a dead body.* Do not say that someone "has dead." Say that someone **dies, died,** or **has died.**
Use the verb **die,** not the adjective **dead,** to say how someone died: *She died in a car crash.*

dead end /'dɛd 'ɛnd/ [*noun*] an end of a street that does not connect to another street, so that you cannot get out: *That street is a dead end.*

deadline /'dɛdˌlaɪn/ [*noun*] the time by which something must be finished: *Friday is the deadline for our essays.*

deadly /'dɛdli/ [*adjective;* **deadlier, deadliest**] likely to kill a person or animal: *Some mushrooms are deadly.*

deaf[1] /dɛf/ [*adjective;* **deafer, deafest**] unable to hear because there is something wrong with your ears: *I think I'm going deaf* (=becoming deaf).
☛ Do not say "His ears are deaf." Say **He is deaf.**

deaf[2] [*noun*]
the deaf people who are deaf: *There are special telephones for the deaf.*
☛ Only use **the deaf** with a plural verb.

deafness /'dɛfnɪs/ [*noun*] when someone is unable to hear because there is something wrong with his or her ears

deal[1] ✳ /dil/ [*noun*]
1 an arrangement or agreement,

/i/ see	/ɪ/ big	/eɪ/ **day**	/ɛ/ get	/æ/ **hat**
/ɑ/ **father, hot**	/ʌ/ **up**	/ə/ **about**	/ɔ/ **saw**
/oʊ/ **hope**	/ʊ/ **book**	/u/ **too**	/aɪ/ **I**	/aʊ/ **how**
/ɔɪ/ **boy**	/ɝ/ **bird**	/ɚ/ **teacher**	/ɪr/ **ear**	/ɛr/ **air**
/ɑr/ **far**	/ɔr/ **more**	/ʊr/ **tour**	/aɪr/ **fire**
/aʊɚ/ **hour**	/θ/ **nothing**	/ð/ **mother**	/ʃ/ **she**
/ʒ/ **measure**	/tʃ/ **church**	/dʒ/ **jump**	/ŋ/ **long**

especially in relationships, business, or politics, that helps both groups involved: *Let's **make a deal**: I'll cook and you clean.* | *You can **get some good deals on** computers right now* (=buy them at a good price).

— PHRASE —

2 a good deal or **a great deal** a lot: *He knows a great deal about African art.* | *I spend a good deal of time on homework.*
☞ Do not say "Her patience is a great deal." Say **She has a great deal of patience.**

deal[2] * [*verb*; **dealt, dealing**]
1 to give cards to the people playing a card game: *It's your turn to deal.*

— PHRASAL VERB —

deal with [*phrasal verb*]
2 to do what is necessary in a situation: **deal with someone/something** ▸ *We're dealing with the problem.*
3 to do business with a person or a company: **deal with someone/something** ▸ *We've dealt with the company for years.*

dealer /'dilə/ [*noun*] someone who buys and sells a particular kind of thing: *My father is a car dealer.*

dealt * /dɛlt/ [*verb*] the past tense and past participle of DEAL[2]

dear[1] /dɪr/ [*adjective*; **dearer, dearest**]
1 used before someone's name at the beginning of a letter: *Dear Jasmine, How have you been?*
2 used to talk about someone you like very much: *He's a dear friend.*

dear[2] [*noun*] used as a name for someone you like or love, for example a family member: *How are you, dear?*

dear[3] [*interjection*] said when you are upset, surprised, or annoyed: *Oh dear! I spilled my soda.*

death * /dɛθ/ [*noun*] the end of a person or animal's life: *He was lonely after the **death** of his wife.* | *The janitor almost **burned to death** (=died by being burned in a fire).*

debate[1] /dɪ'beɪt/ [*noun*] a formal discussion about a subject that people have different opinions about: *They held a **debate about** taxes.*

debate[2] [*verb*; **debated, debating**] to discuss a subject in order to make a decision: *The Senate is debating defense spending.* | **debate how/what/who/which/etc.** ▸ *We're still debating which car to buy.*

debt * /dɛt/ [*noun*]
1 money that you owe someone: *She took a second job **to pay off** her **debts**.*

— PHRASE —

2 be in debt to owe money: *We are **heavily in debt** (=owe a lot of money).*
☞ Do not say "be in the debt." Say **be in debt.**

decade 🆃 /'dɛkeɪd/ [*noun*] a period of ten years: *The hotel has been empty for more than a decade.*

decaf /'di,kæf/ [*noun*] coffee that the caffeine has been removed from

decaffeinated /di'kæfə,neɪtɪd/ [*adjective; no comparative*] decaffeinated drinks such as coffee and tea have had the caffeine removed from them: *decaffeinated soda*

decay[1] * /dɪ'keɪ/ [*noun*] when something is slowly destroyed by natural chemicals: ***Tooth decay** is caused by eating too much sugar.*

decay[2] * [*verb*; **decays, decayed, decaying**] to be slowly destroyed by natural chemicals, or to destroy something in this way; synonym ROT: *The fallen tree had begun to decay.*

deceit * /dɪ'sit/ [*noun*] dishonest behavior: *I'm sick of his lies and deceit.*

deceive * /dɪ'siv/ [*verb*; **deceived, deceiving**] to make someone believe something that is not true; synonym TRICK: *She managed to deceive us all.*

December * /dɪ'sɛmbə/ [*noun*] the twelfth and last month of the year: *Christmas Day is **on** December 25th.* | *It's very cold here **in** December.*
➪ See the usage note at MONTH.

decent /'disənt/ [*adjective*; **more decent, most decent**]
1 good enough for most situations: *Don't you have a decent suit to wear?*
2 honest and treating people fairly: *Her father was a decent, respectable man.*

decide * /dɪ'saɪd/ [*verb*; **decided, deciding**] to make a choice about

something: **decide to do something ▸** *He decided to take the job in Oklahoma.* | **decide who/what/when/etc. ▸** *I can't decide what to wear.* | **decide (that) ▸** *We decided that we wouldn't go on vacation.*
☛ Do not say "'I decided going to the party." Say **I decided to go to the party** or **I decided (that) I would go to the party.**

decimal /'dɛsəməl/ [*noun*] a part of a whole number written as a number following a decimal point: *The decimal 0.3 is the same as 30% and 3/10.*

decimal point /'dɛsəməl ˌpɔɪnt/ [*noun*] a mark [.] used to separate a whole number from the part that follows: *In prices, cents are shown after the decimal point, as in $1.25*

decision * /dɪ'sɪʒən/ [*noun*] a choice or judgment that you make: *Have you made a decision about what to study?*

deck /dɛk/ [*noun*]
1 a flat floor of a ship, especially one that is outside: *Let's go out on deck.*
2 a set of playing cards; *synonym* PACK: *a deck of cards*
3 a wooden floor built onto the outside of a house, where you can relax: *She loved to sit on the deck and read.*

declare ⊤ /dɪ'klɛr/ [*verb*; **declared, declaring**] to state something officially or formally: *The two countries declared war in 1757.*

declaration /ˌdɛklə'reɪʃən/ [*noun*] an official, public statement: *a declaration of war* | *the Declaration of Independence*

decline[1] ⊤ /dɪ'klaɪn/ [*verb*; **declined, declining**] to become lower in amount or quality: *The school's enrollment is declining.*

decline[2] [*noun*] when the amount or quality of something becomes lower: *There has been a decline in the number of applicants.* | *Her health is in decline.*

decorate * /'dɛkəˌreɪt/ [*verb*; **decorated, decorating**] to make something look more attractive by adding things to it: *We decorated the walls with posters.*

decoration * /ˌdɛkə'reɪʃən/ [*noun*] something pretty that you put on something else to make it look more attractive: *We're putting the holiday decorations up tomorrow.*

decorator /'dɛkəˌreɪtɚ/ [*noun*] someone whose job is to choose furniture, curtains, paint, etc., for someone else's house or office

decrease[1] * ⊤ /dɪ'kris/ [*verb*; **decreased, decreasing**] to become less, or to make something less in amount, level, or degree; *synonym* REDUCE; *opposite* INCREASE: *We need to decrease the amount of water we use.* | *Sales have decreased this month.*

decrease[2] * ⊤ /'dikris/ [*noun*] when an amount, level, or degree becomes less; *synonym* REDUCTION; *opposite* INCREASE: *There has been a decrease in deaths from heart attack.*

deed /did/ [*noun*] LITERARY something someone does: *I did a good deed and helped clean the house.*

deep[1] * ⊤ /dip/ [*adjective*; **deeper, deepest**]
1 going down a long way from the top or from the surface; *opposite* SHALLOW: *The deepest water is beyond the rocks.* | *a deep bowl*
☛ Do not say "'What is the deep of the pool?" Say **How deep is the pool?** or **What is the depth of the pool?**
↪ See also DEPTH.
2 a deep sound is very low: *He has a very deep voice.*
3 a deep color is strong and dark: *deep red flowers*
4 very strong in degree: *deep sadness* | *deep joy* | *a deep breath* | *deep sleep*

deep[2] * ⊤ [*adverb*]
1 a long way down from the top or surface of something: *Use a pan that is at least three inches deep.*
2 a long way into something: *The cut went deep into his finger.*

deeply /'dipli/ [*adverb*] very strongly or very much: *She found his behavior deeply upsetting.* | *deeply held beliefs*
☛ Do not use **deeply** to talk about how far down something goes. For example,

/i/ see	/ɪ/ big	/eɪ/ day	/ɛ/ get	/æ/ hat
/ɑ/ father, hot	/ʌ/ up	/ə/ about	/ɔ/ saw
/oʊ/ hope	/ʊ/ book	/u/ too	/aɪ/ I	/aʊ/ how
/ɔɪ/ boy	/ɝ/ bird	/ɚ/ teacher	/ɪr/ ear	/ɛr/ air
/ɑr/ far	/ɔr/ more	/ʊr/ tour	/aɪr/ fire
/aʊɚ/ hour	/θ/ nothing	/ð/ mother	/ʃ/ she
/ʒ/ measure	/tʃ/ church	/dʒ/ jump	/ŋ/ long

do not say "They are digging deeply." Say **They are digging deep.**

deer * /dɪr/ [*noun; plural* **deer**] a brown animal with long thin legs, which can run fast. The male deer has horns like branches

defeat[1] * /dɪ'fit/ [*noun*] when a person, team, or group is beaten; *opposite* VICTORY: *It was the team's third defeat in three weeks.*

defeat[2] * [*verb;* **defeated, defeating**] to beat someone in a war, game, election, etc.: *The army was defeated.*

defend * /dɪ'fɛnd/ [*verb;* **defended, defending**] to do something to protect someone or something from being attacked: *We should all learn how to defend ourselves.*

defense * T /dɪ'fɛns for definition 1; 'difɛns for definition 2/ [*noun*]
1 the activities, weapons, and people connected with protecting a country from attack: *Governments spend millions of dollars on defense.*
2 the part of a team that tries to stop the opposite team from scoring in football, soccer, basketball, etc.; *opposite* OFFENSE: *The Bulls' defense looked very strong.* I *I prefer to play defense.*

define T /dɪ'faɪn/ [*verb;* **defined, defining**] to explain what a word means, in a few words: *How would you define the word "delicious"?*

definite * T /'dɛfənɪt/ [*adjective;* **more definite, most definite**] completely certain; *opposite* INDEFINITE: *Have you made any definite arrangements yet?*

definite article /'dɛfənɪt 'ɑrtɪkəl/ [*noun*] GRAMMAR the word THE: *The definite article is used with singular nouns.*
↪ *Compare* INDEFINITE ARTICLE.

definitely * /'dɛfənɪtli/ [*adverb*] certainly and without any doubt: *I'm definitely not taking French next year.*

definition /ˌdɛfə'nɪʃən/ [*noun*] an explanation of the meaning of a word, especially in a dictionary: *What's the definition of "poor"?*

degree * /dɪ'gri/ [*noun; plural* **degrees**]
1 a unit for measuring temperatures or angles. Its symbol is (°): *It was 95*

degrees in the shade. I *a 180° turn*
2 used to talk about the amount of a quality that exists, or about how true something is: *I want some degree of responsibility in my job.* I *Exercise can improve health to a great degree.*
3 a document given by a college or university to students who complete a course of study: *a degree in history*
☞ Do not say "a degree of history." Say **a degree in history.**

degree

delay[1] * T /dɪ'leɪ/ [*noun; plural* **delays**] when something happens later than it should, or the length of time you have to wait until it happens: *The airlines report delays of up to an hour.* I *See your doctor without delay* (=immediately).

delay[2] * T [*verb;* **delays, delayed, delaying**] to wait until a later time to do something, or to make someone wait: *We had to delay our departure.*

delete T /dɪ'lit/ [*verb;* **deleted, deleting**] to remove a word from a piece of writing, a document from a computer, etc.: *I accidentally deleted two files.*

deli /'dɛli/ [*noun; plural* **delis**] INFORMAL delicatessen; a store that sells cooked meats, cheese, salads, etc.

deliberate * /dɪ'lɪbərɪt/ [*adjective; no comparative*] intended or planned; *synonym* INTENTIONAL; *opposite* ACCIDENTAL: *a deliberate insult*

deliberately * T /dɪ'lɪbərɪtli/ [*adverb*] done in a way that is intended or planned; *opposite* ACCIDENTALLY: *Are you deliberately ignoring me?*

delicate * T /'dɛlɪkɪt/ [*adjective;* **more delicate, most delicate**] easily broken, harmed, or damaged: *a delicate piece of china*

delicatessen /ˌdɛlɪkə'tɛsən/ [*noun*] a DELI

delicious /dɪ'lɪʃəs/ [*adjective;* **more delicious, most delicious**] tasting or smelling extremely good: *That soup smells delicious.*

delight[1] /dɪˈlaɪt/ [noun] a feeling of great happiness and pleasure: *The children squealed with delight.*

delight[2] [verb; delighted, delighting] to give someone a feeling of happiness or pleasure: *The story delighted them.*

delighted ⊤ /dɪˈlaɪtɪd/ [adjective; **more delighted, most delighted**] very happy and pleased about something that has happened: *I was delighted to hear your news.*

delightful /dɪˈlaɪtfəl/ [adjective; **more delightful, most delightful**] very nice or attractive: *What a delightful child!*

deliver * /dɪˈlɪvɚ/ [verb; delivered, delivering]
1 to take a letter, package, or goods to a place: *Your new stove will be delivered on Friday.*
2 to help a baby come out of his or her mother's body: *The doctor delivered her baby at 3:15.*

delivery /dɪˈlɪvəri/ [noun; plural **deliveries**]
1 when a letter, a package, or goods are taken to a place: *Does that store charge extra for delivery?*
2 an amount of something that is to be taken somewhere: *The zoo is waiting for a delivery of hay.*

demand[1] * ⊤ /dɪˈmænd/ [noun]
1 how much of something people want or need to buy or use: *The demand for oil increases in the winter.*
2 when you ask firmly for something that you think you have a right to: *Dad makes a lot of demands on us.*
— PHRASE —
3 be in demand to be wanted by a lot of people: *His paintings are in great demand at the moment.*

demand[2] * ⊤ [verb; demanded, demanding] to ask for something very firmly, because you think you have a right to it: *I demand an apology!* | **demand to do something** ▸ *She demanded to see the manager.* | **demand that someone do something** ▸ *They demanded that he apologize.*
☛ Do not say "She demanded seeing him." Say **She demanded to see him.**
☛ Do not use a pronoun as the object of

demand. For example, do not say "He demanded me to pay." Say **He demanded that I pay.**

democracy /dɪˈmɑkrəsi/ [noun; plural **democracies**] a country or system of government in which the people have the right to choose their own leaders: *The people fought for democracy.* | *India is one of the world's biggest democracies.*

Democrat /ˈdɛməˌkræt/ [noun] someone who belongs to or supports the Democratic Party (=a political party in the U.S.)

democratic /ˌdɛməˈkrætɪk/ [adjective; **more democratic, most democratic**] giving everyone the right to vote, speak, etc.: *a democratic system of government*

demolish /dɪˈmɑlɪʃ/ [verb; demolishes, demolished, demolishing] to destroy a building completely, because it is no longer wanted: *The old school was demolished.*

demolition /ˌdɛməˈlɪʃən/ [noun] when a building is completely destroyed, because it is no longer wanted

demonstrate /ˈdɛmənˌstreɪt/ [verb; demonstrated, demonstrating]
1 to show or prove something clearly: *Someone's coming to demonstrate how to use the new fax machine.*
⋄ Compare ILLUSTRATE (definition 1).
2 if a group of people demonstrate, they meet in a public place to protest about something: *People demonstrated against the war.*

demonstration ⊤ /ˌdɛmənˈstreɪʃən/ [noun]
1 when you show or explain to someone how something is done: *a cooking demonstration*
2 an event at which a group of people meet in a public place to protest something: *There have been street demonstrations against the war.*

/i/ **see**	/ɪ/ **big**	/eɪ/ **day**	/ɛ/ **get**	/æ/ **hat**
/ɑ/ **father, hot**	/ʌ/ **up**	/ə/ **about**	/ɔ/ **saw**	
/oʊ/ **hope**	/ʊ/ **book**	/u/ **too**	/aɪ/ **I**	/aʊ/ **how**
/ɔɪ/ **boy**	/ɝ/ **bird**	/ɚ/ **teacher**	/ɪr/ **ear**	/ɛr/ **air**
/ɑr/ **far**	/ɔr/ **more**	/ʊr/ **tour**	/aɪr/ **fire**	
/aʊɚ/ **hour**	/θ/ **nothing**	/ð/ **mother**	/ʃ/ **she**	
/ʒ/ **measure**	/tʃ/ **church**	/dʒ/ **jump**	/ŋ/ **long**	

den /dɛn/ [noun]
1 a place where some kinds of wild animals live: *a bear's den*
2 a room in a house where you can relax, watch television, listen to music, etc.: *Dad's in the den reading.*

denim /'dɛnəm/ [noun] strong, blue, cotton cloth, of the type used for making jeans: *a denim jacket*

dense T /dɛns/ [adjective; denser, densest] full of things or small parts that are very close together; *synonym* THICK: *an area of dense forest | dense fog*

densely /'dɛnsli/ [adverb] in a way that fills an area with little space in between; *opposite* THINLY: *a densely populated area*

dent¹ /dɛnt/ [verb; dented, denting] to hit the surface of an object and make part of it bend in: *How did your car get dented?*

dent² [noun] an area where the surface of an object has been hit so that it bends in: *If a can of food has a dent in it, don't buy it.*

dental /'dɛntəl/ [adjective; no comparative] relating to your teeth: *dental care | dental surgery*

dentist /'dɛntɪst/ [noun] a doctor who treats people's teeth and diseases of the mouth

dentures /'dɛntʃəz/ [plural noun] a set of artificial teeth: *Grandpa wears dentures.*

deny /dɪ'naɪ/ [verb; denies, denied, denying] to say that something is not true: *deny doing something ▸ He denies stealing the money.*
☞ Do not say that someone "denies to do something." Say that he or she **denies doing something**.

deodorant /di'oʊdərənt/ [noun] a substance that you put on your skin to stop yourself from smelling unpleasant

depart /dɪ'part/ [verb; departed, departing] FORMAL to leave; *opposite* ARRIVE: *The next train will depart at 9:15. | Passengers departing for Miami should go to Gate 12.*
☞ Do not say "depart to a place." Say **depart for a place**. Do not say "depart a place." Say **depart from a place**.

department * T /dɪ'partmənt/ [noun] a group of people that forms part of an organization such as a company, government, or college: *My job was in the sales department.*

department store /dɪ'partmənt ˌstɔr/ [noun] a large store that sells a lot of different products such as clothes, furniture, and kitchen equipment

departure /dɪ'partʃə/ [noun] when someone or something leaves a place; *opposite* ARRIVAL: *What time is your departure?*

depend * T /dɪ'pɛnd/ [verb; depended, depending]
━━ PHRASE ━━
1 **it depends** or **that depends** SPOKEN used when you cannot say what you are going to do because the answer could change according to what happens first: *"Are you coming over later?" "I don't know. It depends."*
━━ PHRASAL VERB ━━
depend on [phrasal verb]
2 to need the help and support of someone very much: **depend on someone** ▸ *I can depend on my friends.*
3 if one thing depends on another, how or whether it happens is influenced by how or whether the first thing happens: **depend on something** ▸ *"Are you going camping this weekend?" "It depends on the weather."*

dependable /dɪ'pɛndəbəl/ [adjective; more dependable, most dependable] always working well or doing things in the way you expect, and therefore easy to trust; *synonym* RELIABLE; *opposite* UNRELIABLE: *a dependable car | a dependable babysitter*

dependent¹ * /dɪ'pɛndənt/ [adjective; more dependent, most dependent]
━━ PHRASE ━━
dependent on needing someone or something to live, be successful, or be healthy: *The young cubs are dependent on their mother.*

dependent² * [noun] a child or other person whose needs are paid for and taken care of by someone such as a parent: *I have three dependents.*

deposit¹ /dɪ'pazɪt/ [noun] part of the cost of something that you pay before you receive it: *We put a deposit down on a new car.*

deposit[2] [*verb; deposited, depositing*] to put money in a bank: *I need to deposit my paycheck.*

depress /dɪ'prɛs/ [*verb; depresses, depressed, depressing*] to make someone feel sad: *That movie really depressed me.*
⇨ Compare **cheer up** at CHEER[1].

depressed T /dɪ'prɛst/ [*adjective; more depressed, most depressed*] upset in a sad, tired way: *He was depressed when his father died.*

depressing /dɪ'prɛsɪŋ/ [*adjective; more depressing, most depressing*] making you feel sad and quiet: *a depressing story*

depression /dɪ'prɛʃən/ [*noun*] when you feel very sad, especially for a long time: *He's been suffering from severe depression for almost a year.*

dept. the written abbreviation of DEPARTMENT: *the English Dept.*

depth * /dɛpθ/ [*noun*] used to talk about how deep something is: *What is the depth of the swimming pool?*
⇨ See the warning at DEEP[1] (definition 1).

deputy /'dɛpyəti/ [*noun; plural deputies*] someone who has the second most important job in some organizations: *the deputy mayor*

descend /dɪ'sɛnd/ [*verb; descended, descending*] to go down; *opposite* ASCEND: *The plane began to descend.*

descendant /dɪ'sɛndənt/ [*noun*] someone who is related through their parents, grandparents, etc., to a particular person who lived a long time ago: *a descendant of George Washington*
⇨ Compare ANCESTOR.

describe * /dɪ'skraɪb/ [*verb; described, describing*] to say what someone or something is like: *Describe the picture to me.* | *I'd describe him as a kind man.*
☛ Do not say "describe someone something." Say **describe something to someone.**

description * T /dɪ'skrɪpʃən/ [*noun*] a piece of writing or speech that says what someone or something is like: *She gave the police a description of her lost dog.*

desert * /'dɛzə˞t/ [*noun*] a large area of land covered with sand or rocks, where it is very hot and dry and very little grows: *The world's biggest desert is the Sahara.* | *a large area of desert*

deserted /dɪ'zɜ˞tɪd/ [*adjective; no comparative*] a deserted place has no people in it: *By ten o'clock the streets were deserted.*

deserve * T /dɪ'zɜ˞v/ [*verb; deserved, deserving*] if you deserve something, you should get it because of the way you have behaved: *You deserve a good rest.* | **deserve to do something** ▸ *He deserves to do well on his exams.*

design[1] * /dɪ'zaɪn/ [*noun*]
1 the way in which something has been planned and made: *They've improved the **design of** their computer.*
2 a pattern: *a rug with a fancy design*
3 a drawing that shows how something will be made or built: *The **designs for** the building are on display.*

design[2] * [*verb; designed, designing*] to make a drawing or plan of how something will be made: *A famous architect designed the new museum.*

designer /dɪ'zaɪnə˞/ [*noun*] someone whose job is to think of ideas for new clothes, cars, etc., and for how they will be made: *a fashion designer*

desirable * /dɪ'zaɪrəbəl/ [*adjective; more desirable, most desirable*] worth being wanted or wished for: *a desirable house*

desire[1] * /dɪ'zaɪr/ [*noun*] a strong wish for something: *I have no desire to meet him* (=I do not want to meet him).

desire[2] * [*verb; desired, desiring*] FORMAL to want something: *He gave her everything she desired.*

desk * /dɛsk/ [*noun*] a table that you can sit at to write or work, which often has drawers under it
⇨ See the pictures at CLASSROOM and OFFICE.

---

despair[1] /dɪ'spɛr/ [noun] a feeling of being very unhappy and having no hope: "What will we do?" she asked in despair.

despair[2] [verb; despaired, despairing] to have no hope left: Don't despair! Things will be fine.

desperate /'dɛspərɪt/ [adjective; more desperate, most desperate] to have a great need for something: I was desperate for a glass of water.

despise /dɪ'spaɪz/ [verb; despised, despising] to hate someone or something very much; synonym DETEST: Why do you despise her so much?

despite /dɪ'spaɪt/ [preposition] used to say that something happens even though something else, which you would expect to prevent it, also happens: Despite our warnings, she walked onto the frozen river.
➪ See also in spite of at SPITE.

dessert /dɪ'zɜt/ [noun] sweet food that you eat at the end of a meal: For dessert there's chocolate pudding.

destination /ˌdɛstə'neɪʃən/ [noun] the place that someone or something is going to: a popular tourist destination

destroy * T /dɪ'strɔɪ/ [verb; destroys, destroyed, destroying] to damage or spoil something completely: Many homes were destroyed in the earthquake.

destruction * /dɪ'strʌkʃən/ [noun] when something is completely destroyed: People are worried about the destruction of the rain forests.

detail * /'diteɪl/ [noun]
1 a single fact about something: I want to hear all the details.
▬▬ PHRASE ▬▬
2 in detail if you describe something in detail, you give many pieces of information about it: Describe in detail how this process works.

detailed /dɪ'teɪld/ [adjective; more detailed, most detailed] including many pieces of information: I want a detailed report on Monday.

detect T /dɪ'tɛkt/ [verb; detected, detecting] to notice or discover something: He detected the odor of gas.

detective /dɪ'tɛktɪv/ [noun] a police officer whose job is to get information about crimes and catch criminals

detergent /dɪ'tɜdʒənt/ [noun] a liquid or powder containing soap, that you use to wash clothes or dishes

deteriorate T /dɪ'tɪriəˌreɪt/ [verb; deteriorated, deteriorating] to become worse: His health was deteriorating.

determination * /dɪˌtɜmə'neɪʃən/ [noun] when someone continues trying to do something even though it is very difficult: determination to do something ▸ I admired her determination to succeed.

determined * T /dɪ'tɜmɪnd/ [adjective; more determined, most determined] wanting to do something very much and not allowing anything to stop you: She's a very determined woman.

determiner * /dɪ'tɜmɪnɚ/ [noun] GRAMMAR a word such as THE, SOME, or A, used before a noun or adjective: You used the wrong determiner.

detest /dɪ'tɛst/ [verb; detested, detesting] to hate something or someone very much; synonym DESPISE: I detest all this new technology.

detour /'ditʊr/ [noun] a way of going somewhere that is not as direct as the one you usually use: We took a detour around the road work.

develop * T /dɪ'vɛləp/ [verb; developed, developing]
1 to grow or change into something bigger or more important, or to make something or someone do this: I've developed my leg muscles by running. I There are plans to develop a new mall.
2 to treat film from a camera with chemicals to make a photograph: I had the pictures developed last week.

developing country /dɪ'vɛləpɪŋ 'kʌntri/ [noun; plural developing countries] a country without much money or industry: the developing countries of Africa

development * /dɪ'vɛləpmənt/ [noun]
1 the process of becoming bigger or more advanced: the development of the computer industry

2 an event that changes a situation: *He reported on the latest developments.*

device /dɪ'vaɪs/ [*noun*] a small tool that you use for a particular job: *a device for opening cans*

devil /'dɛvəl/ [*noun*]
1 the Devil the most powerful evil spirit: *Do you believe in the Devil?* (=do you think that the Devil exists)
2 an evil spirit: *Old stories are full of devils and fairies.*

devise /dɪ'vaɪz/ [*verb*; devised, devising] to plan, invent, or create something: *He tried to devise a new way to develop photographs.*

devote /dɪ'voʊt/ [*verb*; devoted, devoting] to spend a lot of time or effort doing something: *She devoted herself to studying* (=spent all her time studying).

dew /du/ [*noun*] the small drops of water that form on the ground during the night: *There is dew on the grass.*

diagnosis /ˌdaɪəg'noʊsɪs/ [*noun; plural* diagnoses /ˌdaɪəg'noʊsiz/] when a doctor says what illness someone has: *The diagnosis was asthma.*

diagonal /daɪ'ægənəl/ [*adjective; no comparative*] going from one corner to the opposite corner: *Draw a diagonal line between two corners of the square.*

diagram /'daɪəˌgræm/ [*noun*] a picture that explains an idea, or shows how something works or is put together: *a diagram of an air conditioner*

dial[1] /'daɪəl/ [*verb*; dialed, dialing] to press the numbers or turn the dial on a telephone: *Are you sure you dialed the right number?*
➪ *See the synonym note at* CALL[1].

dial[2] [*noun*] a round object on a piece of equipment such as a radio that you turn to choose a station, make it louder or softer, etc.: *Turn the dial to the right.*

dialect /'daɪəˌlɛkt/ [*noun*] a form of a language that is spoken in one area and has different sounds and words than the form spoken in another area
➪ *Compare* ACCENT.

dialogue * or **dialog** /'daɪəˌlɔg/ [*noun*] conversation between characters in a book, play, or movie

diameter /daɪ'æmɪtɚ/ [*noun*] a line or distance from one side of a circle to the other, that passes through the center: *Draw a circle 10 cm in diameter.*

diamond /'daɪmənd/ [*noun*]
1 a very hard, clear, valuable stone that is used to make jewelry: *She wore a diamond ring.*
2 a shape with four sides of equal length and no right angles
➪ *See* Shapes *in the Smart Study section.*

diaper /'daɪpɚ/ [*noun*] a piece of soft material that is put around a baby's bottom to collect waste from its body: *Please change the baby's diaper.*

diarrhea /ˌdaɪə'riə/ [*noun*] an illness in which waste from the body has a lot of water in it and comes out very often

diary /'daɪəri/ [*noun; plural* diaries] a book in which you write what you think and feel, and what happened during the day; synonym JOURNAL: *I used to keep a diary when I was younger.*

dice /daɪs/ [*plural noun*] two small blocks of wood or plastic, each with a different number of spots on each side, that are used in games: *He threw the dice.*

dictate ⊤ /'dɪkteɪt/ [*verb*; dictated, dictating] to say something for someone to write down: *She was dictating a letter to her secretary.*

dictation /dɪk'teɪʃən/ [*noun*] a language test in which you have to write down what a teacher says without making any mistakes: *Spanish dictations are very difficult for me.*

dictator /'dɪkteɪtɚ/ [*noun*] a very strong leader of a country who controls everything with the help of soldiers, and is often not liked by the people: *a military dictator*

dictionary * /'dɪkʃəˌnɛri/ [*noun; plural* dictionaries] a book that contains a list of words and their meanings

did * /dɪd/ [*verb*] the past tense of DO

/i/ **see**	/ɪ/ **big**	/eɪ/ **day**	/ɛ/ **get**	/æ/ **hat**
/ɑ/ **father,**	**hot**	/ʌ/ **up**	/ə/ **about**	/ɔ/ **saw**
/oʊ/ **hope**	/ʊ/ **book**	/u/ **too**	/aɪ/ **I**	/aʊ/ **how**
/ɔɪ/ **boy**	/ɝ/ **bird**	/ɚ/ **teacher**	/ɪr/ **ear**	/ɛr/ **air**
/ɑr/ **far**	/ɔr/ **more**	/ʊr/ **tour**	/aɪr/ **fire**	
/aʊɚ/ **hour**	/θ/ **nothing**	/ð/ **mother**	/ʃ/ **she**	
/ʒ/ **measure**	/tʃ/ **church**	/dʒ/ **jump**	/ŋ/ **long**	

didn't * /'dɪdənt/ the short form of "did not": *I didn't see a thing.*

die * /daɪ/ [*verb;* **dies, died, dying**]
1 to stop living: *The flowers died.* | *Jack died of lung cancer.* | **die from something** ▸ *He won't die from his injuries.*
☛ Do not say that someone "has died for a long time." Say that he or she **has been dead for a long time** or **died a long time ago.**
↪ *See the usage note at* DEAD.
— PHRASE —
2 be dying to do something SPOKEN to want to do something very much: *I'm dying to meet her fiancé.*
☛ Do not say that someone "died to meet" someone else. Say that he or she **was dying to meet** him or her.

diet[1] /'daɪɪt/ [*noun*]
1 the kind of food that you eat each day: *Do you have a **healthy diet**?* | *Some illnesses can be controlled by diet.*
2 when you eat less food than usual for a period of time, in order to become thinner: *I'm **going on a diet.***

diet[2] [*verb;* **dieted, dieting**] to eat less food than usual for a period of time, in order to become thinner: *You don't need to diet!*

difference * /'dɪfərəns/ [*noun*]
1 a way in which two or more things are not the same: *"What's the **difference between** the two computers?" "There are **differences in** price and quality."*
↪ *Compare* SIMILARITY.
— PHRASES —
2 make a difference or **make no difference** to have a good effect or no effect on a situation or person: *It **makes no difference to** me what you think.*
3 tell the difference to be able to recognize that people or things are different: *I can't **tell the difference between** Emily and her twin sister.*

different * Ⓣ /'dɪfərənt/ [*adjective;* **more different, most different**] not the same as someone or something, or not the same as before: *You **look so different***

with that new haircut. | *Life in the country is **different from** life in the city.*
☛ Do not say that two things are "different with" each other. Say that they are **different from** each other.
↪ *Compare* SIMILAR.

differently * /'dɪfərəntli/ [*adverb*] in a different way: *They behaved differently when they were alone.*
↪ *Compare* **the same (as)** *at* SAME[3].

difficult * /'dɪfɪ,kʌlt/ [*adjective;* **more difficult, most difficult**] not easy to do or understand; *synonym* HARD; *opposite* SIMPLE: *My math homework is difficult.*
☛ Do not say "I'm difficult to understand it." Say **It's difficult to understand.**

difficulty * /'dɪfɪ,kʌlti/ [*noun; plural* **difficulties**] a problem: *He's **having difficulties** in school.*

dig * /dɪg/ [*verb;* **dug, digging**] to remove earth from the ground using a shovel: *It took a year to dig the tunnel.*

digest /daɪ'dʒɛst/ [*verb;* **digested, digesting**]
1 to change the food in your stomach into a form that can be used by your body: *Some people can't digest milk.*
2 to completely understand some information: *It took me a long time to digest the news.*

digestion /daɪ'dʒɛstʃən/ [*noun*] the process of digesting food: *Milk is bad for my digestion.*

digestive /daɪ'dʒɛstɪv/ [*adjective; no comparative*] relating to digestion: *the digestive system*

digit /'dɪdʒɪt/ [*noun*] a number from 0 to 9: *a seven-digit phone number*

digital /'dɪdʒɪtəl/ [*adjective; no comparative*] a digital watch or clock shows information as numbers: *I have a digital alarm clock.*

dignified /'dɪgnə,faɪd/ [*adjective;* **more dignified, most dignified**] behaving in a proud and calm way, so that people respect you: *a very dignified woman*

dignity /'dɪgnɪti/ [*noun*] proud and calm behavior that makes people respect you

dim Ⓣ /dɪm/ [*adjective;* **dimmer, dimmest**] not bright: *The light **was growing dim.***

dime /daɪm/ [*noun*] an American or Canadian COIN worth ten cents

diner /'daɪnɚ/ [*noun*] a small restaurant where the food is not expensive

dining room /'daɪnɪŋ ˌrum/ [*noun*] a room in a house that is specially for eating meals in

dinner * /'dɪnɚ/ [*noun*] the main meal of the day, usually eaten in the evening: *My new friends are coming for dinner tonight.* | *Mom cooked a great dinner.*
➪ Compare SUPPER.

dinnertime /'dɪnɚˌtaɪm/ [*noun*] the time during the day when you have your main meal, usually in the evening: *We get together at dinnertime.*

dinosaur /'daɪnəˌsɔr/ [*noun*] a very large animal that existed millions of years ago

dip¹ * /dɪp/ [*verb*; **dips, dipped, dipping**] to put something into a liquid and quickly take it out again: *She dipped her foot into the water.*

dip² [*noun*] a soft food served with raw vegetables or other foods: *a sour cream and onion dip* | *potato chips and dip*

diploma /dɪ'ploumə/ [*noun*; *plural* **diplomas**] an official paper that is given to someone who has finished a course of study or passed an exam: *a high school diploma*

direct¹ * /dɪ'rɛkt/ [*adjective*; **more direct, most direct**]
 1 going the straightest way to a place, without stopping; *opposite* INDIRECT: *We took a direct flight to Washington, D.C.*
 2 saying what you mean, without being careful about offending people: *He was very direct with his answers.*
 3 without anything or anyone coming between: *She has direct access to the president.*

direct² [*verb*; **directed, directing**]
 1 to show or tell someone what to do or how to do it: *A secretary directed them to an office down the hall.*
 2 to give instructions to the actors in a movie or play: *My sister directed the school play.*

direction * /dɪ'rɛkʃən/ [*noun*] the way that someone or something is moving, facing, or pointing: *Bob drove off in the opposite direction.* | *We walked in the direction of the station* (=toward it).
 ☛ Do not say "toward the direction of" or "to the direction of." Say **in the direction of.**

USAGE   Talking about directions
  Words such as **east, west, north,** and **south** are not usually written with capital letters: *They live north of us.* | *My office is in the southeast corner of the building.*
  Use a capital letter with nouns that are the names of areas of the U.S.: *I'm from the South.* | *He grew up in the Northwest.*

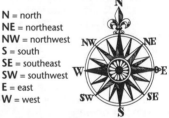

N = north
NE = northeast
NW = northwest
S = south
SE = southeast
SW = southwest
E = east
W = west

directions of the compass

directly * /dɪ'rɛktli/ [*adverb*]
 1 straight to a place without stopping: *She drove directly to the house.*
 2 in a clear way, or without anything or anyone coming between: *He looked directly at her.* | *She spoke directly and honestly.*

direct object * /dɪ'rɛkt 'abdʒɛkt/ [*noun*] GRAMMAR a word or group of words that refers to the person or thing directly affected by the subject of the verb: *In the phrase "I love you," "you" is the direct object of the verb "love."*
 ➪ Compare INDIRECT OBJECT.

director /dɪ'rɛktɚ/ [*noun*]
 1 someone who controls a business or an organization: *a sales director*
 2 someone who gives instructions to the actors in a movie or play

---

/i/ **see** /ɪ/ **big** /eɪ/ **day** /ɛ/ **get** /æ/ **hat**
/ɑ/ **father, hot** /ʌ/ **up** /ə/ **about** /ɔ/ **saw**
/oʊ/ **hope** /ʊ/ **book** /u/ **too** /aɪ/ **I** /aʊ/ **how**
/ɔɪ/ **boy** /ɝ/ **bird** /ɚ/ **teacher** /ɪr/ **ear** /ɛr/ **air**
/ɑr/ **far** /ɔr/ **more** /ʊr/ **tour** /aɪr/ **fire**
/aʊɚ/ **hour** /θ/ **nothing** /ð/ **mother** /ʃ/ **she**
/ʒ/ **measure** /tʃ/ **church** /dʒ/ **jump** /ŋ/ **long**

directory /dɪ'rɛktəri/ [*noun; plural* **directories**] a book or list of names or facts in alphabetical order: *a **telephone directory*** (=telephone book) I *a directory of* Internet sites

dirt * /dɜt/ [*noun*] earth, or anything that makes things dirty: *a **dirt road*** I *There was dirt all over the floor.*

dirty * /'dɜti/ [*adjective;* **dirtier, dirtiest**] not clean: *Don't get your shirt **dirty**!*

disabled /dɪs'eɪbəld/ [*adjective; no comparative*] unable to use a part of your body or mind in the usual way: *A car accident left him disabled.*

disadvantage ⊤ /,dɪsəd'væntɪdʒ/ [*noun*] something that may make it more difficult for you to do something: *What are the **disadvantages of** living in the country?*

disagree * /,dɪsə'gri/ [*verb;* **disagrees, disagreed, disagreeing**] to have or express an opinion that is different from someone else's; *opposite* AGREE: *I'm sorry, but I **disagree with** you.* I *My sister and I **disagree about** everything.*
☛ Do not say "disagree to someone." Say **disagree with someone**.
⊃ *See the synonym note at* ARGUE.

disagreement * /,dɪsə'grimənt/ [*noun*] when people do not agree about something; *opposite* AGREEMENT: *There was **disagreement about** who won.* I *I had a **disagreement with** Mom.*

disappear * ⊤ /,dɪsə'pɪr/ [*verb;* **disappeared, disappearing**] to become impossible to see or find: *The sun disappeared behind a cloud.*

disappearance /,dɪsə'pɪrəns/ [*noun*] when someone or something becomes impossible to see or find: *The plane's disappearance shocked everyone.*

disappoint * /,dɪsə'pɔɪnt/ [*verb;* **disappointed, disappointing**] to make someone unhappy because something that he or she hoped for did not happen or was not done: *She didn't want to disappoint her parents.*

disappointed /,dɪsə'pɔɪntɪd/ [*adjective;* **more disappointed, most disappointed**] unhappy because something good that you hoped for did not happen: *He was very **disappointed** with his grades.* I **disappointed (that)** ▸ *I was disappointed that he couldn't come.*

disappointing * /,dɪsə'pɔɪntɪŋ/ [*adjective;* **more disappointing, most disappointing**] not as good as you hoped: *It was a disappointing meeting.*

disappointment /,dɪsə'pɔɪntmənt/ [*noun*] the sadness you feel when something is not as good as you hoped or does not happen: *You could see his disappointment at losing the race.*

disapproval ⊤ /,dɪsə'pruvəl/ [*noun*] when you think something or someone is bad or wrong; *opposite* APPROVAL: *The principal shook his head in **disapproval**.*

disapprove /,dɪsə'pruv/ [*verb;* **disapproved, disapproving**] to think that something or someone is bad or wrong; *opposite* APPROVE: *His father **disapproves of** his clothes.*

disaster /dɪ'zæstə/ [*noun*] a sudden event such as a storm, flood, or accident that causes a lot of damage or injuries: *a mining disaster*

disastrous /dɪ'zæstrəs/ [*adjective;* **more disastrous, most disastrous**] causing a lot of damage or problems: *It would be disastrous if my computer broke.*

disc /dɪsk/ [*noun*] a short form of COMPACT DISC
⊃ *See the picture at* DISK.

discipline /'dɪsəplɪn/ [*noun*] a way of training people to obey rules and behave well: *The school is known for its strict discipline.*

disc jockey /'dɪsk ,dʒaki/ [*noun; plural* **disc jockeys**] someone whose job is to play music on the radio or at a dance club; *synonym* DJ

disconnect /,dɪskə'nɛkt/ [*verb;* **disconnected, disconnecting**] to separate one thing or part of something from another; *opposite* CONNECT: ***Disconnect** the computer **from** the power source.*

discount ⊤ /'dɪskaʊnt/ [*noun*] a reduction in the price of something: *There is a 10% **discount on** these shoes.*

discourage /dɪ'skɜrɪdʒ/ [*verb;* **discouraged, discouraging**] to persuade someone not to do something by making him or her feel less

confident; _opposite_ ENCOURAGE:
**discourage someone from doing
something** ▶ _I discouraged her from
driving in the storm._

discouraged /dɪˈskɜrɪdʒd/ [_adjective;_
more discouraged, most discouraged]
no longer confident or hopeful; _opposite_
ENCOURAGED: _She's discouraged because
she hasn't got a job._

discouraging /dɪˈskɜrɪdʒɪŋ/ [_adjective;_
**more discouraging, most
discouraging**] making you feel less
confident or hopeful; _opposite_
ENCOURAGING: _I had a discouraging
interview._

discover * /dɪˈskʌvɚ/ [_verb;_ **discovered,
discovering**] to find something that
was hidden or that many people did
not know about: _Galileo discovered that
the earth moves around the sun._
⇨ _See the usage note at_ INVENT.

discovery * /dɪˈskʌvəri/ [_noun; plural_
discoveries] a fact or object that
someone discovers: _scientific discoveries_

discriminate Ⓣ /dɪˈskrɪməˌneɪt/ [_verb;_
discriminated, discriminating] to treat
a person in an unfair way, because he
or she belongs to a different group: _The
company was accused of **discriminating**
against women._

discrimination Ⓣ /dɪˌskrɪməˈneɪʃən/
[_noun_] when someone is treated in an
unfair way, because he or she belongs
to a different group: _We will not tolerate
racial discrimination._

discuss * /dɪˈskʌs/ [_verb;_ **discusses,
discussed, discussing**] to talk about
something with someone: _I need to
discuss your paper **with** you._
☛ Do not say "discuss about something"
or "discuss on something." Say **discuss
something**.

discussion * /dɪˈskʌʃən/ [_noun_] when
you talk about something with
someone: _We **had a long discussion
about** politics._ | _Your proposal is **under
discussion**_ (=being discussed).

disease * /dɪˈziz/ [_noun_] a serious
medical condition caused by something
in a persons's or animal's body: _She is
suffering from an unknown disease._ |
childhood diseases such as mumps

SYNONYMS   disease, illness, sickness
   Use **disease** to talk about the thing that
is making a person or animal sick, or the
part of the body that is affected by the
disease: _Cancer is a terrible disease._ | _heart
disease_
   Use **illness** to talk in general about the
fact or time that someone is sick. An
illness can be caused by something like
being poisoned or getting an infection,
not just by a disease: _He took care of her
during her illness_
   Sickness is used about less serious
illness or in the names of some illnesses:
motion sickness | _sleeping sickness_

disgrace /dɪsˈɡreɪs/ [_noun_]
   1 a bad thing that someone does that
makes people lose respect for him or
her: _You are **a disgrace to** the family._
   2 when someone loses people's respect
because he or she has done something
wrong: _She was sent home **in disgrace**._

disgraceful /dɪsˈɡreɪsfəl/ [_adjective;_
more disgraceful, most disgraceful]
very bad and not acceptable: _Your
grades are disgraceful!_

disguise¹ Ⓣ /dɪsˈɡaɪz/ [_verb;_ **disguised,
disguising**] to change someone's
appearance, clothes, or voice so that
people do not know who he or she is:
He was **disguised as** a guard.

disguise² Ⓣ [_noun_] something that you
wear to change your appearance so
that people do not know who you are:
That's a great disguise. | _He entered the
bank **in disguise**_ (=wearing a disguise).

disgust /dɪsˈɡʌst/ [_noun_] a strong feeling
that you do not like and do not approve
of someone or something: _We waited an
hour, then left the restaurant **in disgust**._

disgusted /dɪsˈɡʌstɪd/ [_adjective;_ **more
disgusted, most disgusted**] feeling that
you do not like and do not approve of
something or someone: _I was disgusted
by his behavior._

/i/ **see**	/ɪ/ **big**	/eɪ/ **day**	/ɛ/ **get**	/æ/ **hat**	
/ɑ/ **father, hot**	/ʌ/ **up**	/ə/ **about**	/ɔ/ **saw**		
/ou/ **hope**	/ʊ/ **book**	/u/ **too**	/aɪ/ **I**	/aʊ/ **how**	
/ɔɪ/ **boy**	/ɚ/ **bird**	/ɚ/ **teacher**	/ɪr/ **ear**	/ɛr/ **air**	
/ɑr/ **far**	/ɔr/ **more**	/ʊr/ **tour**	/aɪr/ **fire**		
/aʊɚ/ **hour**	/θ/ **nothing**	/ð/ **mother**	/ʃ/ **she**		
/ʒ/ **measure**	/tʃ/ **church**	/dʒ/ **jump**	/ŋ/ **long**		

disgusting /dɪs'gʌstɪŋ/ [*adjective;* **more disgusting, most disgusting**] extremely unpleasant: *What a disgusting smell!*

dish * /dɪʃ/ [*noun; plural* **dishes**]
1 a container used for cooking or serving food: *Where do you keep your serving dishes?*
2 food cooked or prepared in a particular way: *My favorite dish is sweet and sour chicken.*
3 dishes [*plural*]
  a plates and bowls: *The dishes are in this cupboard, the glasses are in that one.*
  b dirty plates, knives, glasses, etc., that need to be washed I *Who's going to do the dishes* (=wash them)?

dishonest * /dɪs'anɪst/ [*adjective;* **more dishonest, most dishonest**] someone who is dishonest lies or steals; *opposite* HONEST: *a dishonest salesman*

dishtowel /'dɪʃ,taʊəl/ [*noun*] a cloth for drying dishes: *Get me a clean dishtowel.*

dishwasher T /'dɪʃ,waʃɚ/ [*noun*] a machine that washes dishes: *unload the dishwasher* (=take the clean dishes out of it) I *load the dishwasher* (=put the dirty dishes into it)

disinfectant /,dɪsɪn'fɛktənt/ [*noun*] a chemical that cleans things and kills bacteria

compact disc/
CD

disk/
floppy disk/
diskette

disk /dɪsk/ [*noun*]
1 a piece of square plastic with a round flat piece of plastic inside it, used for storing computer information; *synonyms* DISKETTE, FLOPPY DISK: *Would you like my work on disk?*
2 a flat round object or shape: *The saw has different cutting disks.*

disk drive /'dɪsk ,draɪv/ [*noun*] a piece of equipment in a computer that is used to take information from a disk or put information onto it: *Put the diskette into the disk drive.*

diskette /dɪ'skɛt/ [*noun*] a DISK (definition 1): *a box of diskettes*

disk jockey /'dɪsk ,dʒaki/ [*noun; plural* **disk jockeys**] another spelling of DISC JOCKEY

dislike T /dɪs'laɪk/ [*verb;* **disliked, disliking**] FORMAL to not like someone or something: *dislike doing something* ▸ *I dislike doing homework.*
☛ Do not say that you "dislike to do something." Say that you **dislike doing something**.
⇨ Compare HATE¹.

dislikes /'dɪslaɪks/ [*plural noun*] things that someone does not like: *Tell me about your* **likes and dislikes**.

disloyal /dɪs'lɔɪəl/ [*adjective;* **more disloyal, most disloyal**] not faithful to a friend, employer, member of your family, etc.; *opposite* LOYAL: *He said I had been disloyal to my family.*

dismay /dɪs'meɪ/ [*noun*] the feeling of being disappointed and shocked: *He stared in dismay at the broken statue.*

dismiss * /dɪs'mɪs/ [*verb;* **dismisses, dismissed, dismissing**]
1 to send someone away from a place: *Class is dismissed.*
☛ Do not say "The class dismissed." Say **The class was dismissed**.
2 to think that someone's ideas or opinions are not worth considering: *He dismissed all her suggestions.*

disobedience /,dɪsə'bidiəns/ [*noun*] when someone deliberately does not do what you tell him or her to do; *opposite* OBEDIENCE: *You will be punished for your disobedience.*

disobedient /,dɪsə'bidiənt/ [*adjective;* **more disobedient, most disobedient**] deliberately not doing what someone tells you to do; *opposite* OBEDIENT: *You are a disobedient child!*

disobey /,dɪsə'beɪ/ [*verb;* **disobeys, disobeyed, disobeying**] to refuse to do what someone tells you to do; *opposite* OBEY: *How dare you disobey me?*

disorganized T /dɪs'ɔrgə,naɪzd/ [*adjective;* **more disorganized, most disorganized**]
1 not arranged or planned well;

opposite ORGANIZED: *How can you work in this disorganized office?*
2 not planning or arranging things well; *opposite* ORGANIZED: *I'm so disorganized today.*

display[1] ⊤ /dɪ'spleɪ/ [*noun; plural* **displays**]
1 an arrangement of things for people to look at: *We looked at a **display of** children's books.*

══ PHRASE ══
2 be on display to be in a public place for people to look at: *The CD player I want is on display.*

display[2] ⊤ [*verb;* **displays, displayed, displaying**] to put things where people can see them easily: *The children display their work on the classroom walls.*

disposable /dɪ'spoʊzəbəl/ [*adjective; no comparative*] designed to be thrown away: *I always use disposable razors.*

dispose /dɪ'spoʊz/ [*verb;* **disposed, disposing**]
══ PHRASAL VERB ══
dispose of [*phrasal verb*]
to throw away something you no longer want or need: *You should dispose of old newspapers in this box.*

dispute /dɪ'spyut/ [*noun*] a serious disagreement: *The two countries are **in a dispute over** trade.*

disrupt /dɪs'rʌpt/ [*verb;* **disrupted, disrupting**] to stop something from continuing for a period of time: *Maria, you are disrupting the whole class.*

dissatisfied /dɪs'sætɪs‚faɪd/ [*adjective;* **more dissatisfied, most dissatisfied**] not happy because something is not good enough; *opposite* SATISFIED: *Her parents are **dissatisfied with** the school.*

dissect /daɪ'sɛkt/ [*verb;* **dissected, dissecting**] to cut a plant or part of a dead animal, in order to study what is inside it: *We are dissecting frogs in biology class.*

dissolve /dɪ'zɑlv/ [*verb;* **dissolved, dissolving**] to mix completely with a liquid and become part of it, or to make something do this: *Stir the sauce until the sugar dissolves.* I ***Dissolve** the tablet **in** warm water.*

distance ∗ /'dɪstəns/ [*noun*]
1 the amount of space between two places: *What's the **distance from** Chicago **to** Dallas?*

══ PHRASE ══
2 in the distance or **from a distance** at or from a place that is fairly far away: *We could see a house in the distance.* I *From a distance, the mountains seem smaller.*
☛ Do not say "at the distance" or "in a distance." Say **in the distance** or **from a distance**.

distant ∗ /'dɪstənt/ [*adjective;* **more distant, most distant**] far away from where you are now, or at a very different time: *a distant galaxy* I *It happened in **the distant past**.*

distinct ⊤ /dɪ'stɪŋkt/ [*adjective;* **more distinct, most distinct**] clear and easy to see, hear, taste, or understand: *As we got closer, the mountains became more distinct.* I *a distinct difference*

distinctly /dɪ'stɪŋktli/ [*adverb*] very clearly: *I **distinctly remember** locking the door.*

distinguish ⊤ /dɪ'stɪŋgwɪʃ/ [*verb;* **distinguishes, distinguished, distinguishing**] to recognize or understand the difference between things: *Some people cannot **distinguish between** red and green.*

distinguished /dɪ'stɪŋgwɪʃt/ [*adjective;* **more distinguished, most distinguished**] successful and respected: *a distinguished professor*

distract /dɪ'strækt/ [*verb;* **distracted, distracting**] to stop someone from paying attention to what he or she is doing: **distract someone from something** ▸ *Don't distract your sister from her homework.*

distribute ⊤ /dɪ'strɪbyut/ [*verb;* **distributed, distributing**] to divide something and give it to a number of

---

/i/ **see** /ɪ/ **big** /eɪ/ **day** /ɛ/ **get** /æ/ **hat**
/ɑ/ **father, hot** /ʌ/ **up** /ə/ **about** /ɔ/ **saw**
/oʊ/ **hope** /ʊ/ **book** /u/ **too** /aɪ/ **I** /aʊ/ **how**
/ɔɪ/ **boy** /ɝ/ **bird** /ɚ/ **teacher** /ɪr/ **ear** /ɛr/ **air**
/ɑr/ **far** /ɔr/ **more** /ʊr/ **tour** /aɪr/ **fire**
/aʊɚ/ **hour** /θ/ **nothing** /ð/ **mother** /ʃ/ **she**
/ʒ/ **measure** /tʃ/ **church** /dʒ/ **jump** /ŋ/ **long**

people: **distribute something to someone** ▸ *Volunteers are distributing clothes to the homeless.*

district /'dɪstrɪkt/ [noun] a particular area of a city or country: *The business district is downtown.*

disturb Ⓣ /dɪ'stɜ·b/ [verb; **disturbed, disturbing**] to make someone stop what he or she is doing by asking questions, making noise, etc.: *Don't disturb your mother.*

☛ Don't say "Sorry I disturbed you working." Say **Sorry I disturbed you.**

disturbance /dɪ'stɜ·bəns/ [noun]
1 something that interrupts you so that you cannot continue what you are doing: *I need to work **without** any disturbance.*
2 a situation in which people behave violently in public: *There have been disturbances in several areas of the city.*

ditch /dɪtʃ/ [noun; plural **ditches**] a long narrow hole dug in the ground, that is not very deep and is open at the top

dive /daɪv/ [verb; **dived** or **dove, dived, diving**] to jump into water with your arms and head going in first: *Boys were diving into the lake.*

diver /'daɪvɚ/ [noun] someone who swims under water using special equipment to help him or her breathe: *a **deep-sea diver***

divide * /dɪ'vaɪd/ [verb; **divided, dividing**]
1 to separate something into parts, or to become separated in this way: *When the road divides, stay to the left.* I **divide something into something** ▸ *Divide the children into three groups.*
☛ Do not say "divide something in something." Say **divide something into something.**
2 to calculate how many times one number is contained in a bigger number; *opposite* MULTIPLY: *Twenty-eight divided by seven equals four (28 ÷ 7 = 4).*

divine /dɪ'vaɪn/ [adjective; no comparative] coming from God or gods, or relating to God or gods: *a divine being*

diving /'daɪvɪŋ/ [noun] the sport or activity of diving or being a diver: *a diving competition*

diving board /'daɪvɪŋ ˌbɔrd/ [noun] a board above a swimming pool that bends a little, that you can stand on to dive or jump into the water

division Ⓣ /dɪ'vɪʒən/ [noun]
1 when you calculate how many times one number will go into another; *opposite* MULTIPLICATION: *Children this age are able to do division.*
2 a part of a large company or organization: *I work in the **sales division**.*
3 when something is separated into parts: *Mr. King supervised the **division** of the money.*

divorce[1] Ⓣ /dɪ'vɔrs/ [noun] the legal ending of a marriage: *They **got a divorce**.* I *Many marriages end in divorce.*

divorce[2] Ⓣ [verb; **divorced, divorcing**] to legally end a marriage: *They divorced in 1998.* I *I think she'll divorce him.*

divorced Ⓣ /dɪ'vɔrst/ [adjective; no comparative] no longer married: *Her parents are divorced.* I *They **got divorced** (=ended their marriage).*

dizzy /'dɪzi/ [adjective; **dizzier, dizziest**] feeling as though things are going around and around: *She felt dizzier and dizzier.*

DJ /'diˌdʒeɪ/ [noun; plural **DJs** or **DJ's**] disc jockey; someone whose job is to play music on the radio or at a dance club

Forms of *do*		
	present tense	past tense
singular	*I* **do** *he/she/it* **does** *you* **do**	*I* **did** *he/she/it* **did** *you* **did**
plural	*we* **do** *they* **do** *you* **do**	*we* **did** *they* **did** *you* **did**
negatives	*I* **don't** *he/she/it* **doesn't** *you/we/they* **don't**	*I* **didn't** *he/she/it* **didn't** *you/we/they* **didn't**
participles	**doing**	**done**

do[1] * /du/ [auxiliary verb]
1 used with another verb to form questions and negatives: *Do you like swimming?* I *Cindy doesn't want to go to the movies.* I *Don't run in the house.*

2 used to avoid repeating a verb: *"I love pizza." "So do I."*

do² ⋆ [*verb*]

1 to perform an action or a job: *Have you done your homework? | I need to do some shopping. | What are you doing?*

2 to make progress: *How is your daughter doing in school? | She did well in math. | Grandma's doing very well since her operation.*

3 to be enough for or suitable for a particular purpose: *The recipe says to use cream, but yogurt will do.*

— PHRASES —

4 What do you do? used to ask someone what his or her job is: *"What do you do, Mike?" "I'm a police officer."*

5 How do you do? a polite formal greeting: *"I'm Christopher Black." "How do you do?"*

6 How are you doing? used to ask someone if he or she is well and happy: *"Hi, Kimberly, how are you doing?" "Oh fine, thanks."*

7 have to do with something to be about a particular thing or involved in a particular thing: *I had nothing to do with that decision.*

8 could do with something to need or want something: *I could do with a shower.*

9 What did you do with . . . ? SPOKEN used to ask someone where he or she has put something: *What did you do with my watch?*

dock¹ Ⓣ /dak/ [*noun*] a long flat structure that sticks out into a river, lake, etc.: *Stay away from the edge of the dock.*

dock² [*verb*; **docked, docking**] to bring a boat or ship to a dock: *The ferry docks over there.*

doctor ⋆ /'daktɚ/ [*noun*] someone who treats people who are sick; written as "Dr." before a name: *I've made an appointment to see the doctor. | Dr. Banks can see you at 10:15.*

document ⋆ /'dakyəmənt/ [*noun*]

1 a piece of paper with official information written on it: *Bring all your travel documents.*

2 a piece of writing on a computer: *Remember to save your document.*

documentary /ˌdakyə'mentəri/ [*noun*; *plural* **documentaries**] a movie or television program that gives information about a subject: *Did you see the documentary about whales?*

does ⋆ /dʌz/ [*verb*] the present form of DO that is used with "he," "she," "it," and names: *Does this purse belong to you? | She does beautiful paintings.*

doesn't ⋆ /'dʌzənt/ the short form of "does not": *He doesn't want to go.*

dog ⋆ /dɔg/ [*noun*] an animal with four legs and a tail that is kept as a pet or as a working animal

a dog

doll /dal/ [*noun*] a child's toy that is like a small person

dollar ⋆ /'dalɚ/ [*noun*] the money used in the U.S., Canada, Australia, New Zealand, and some other countries; written as $ before a number: *There are 100 cents in one dollar. | I gave him $50.*
☛ When saying a price such as $3.50, do not say "three dollars fifty." Say **three-fifty** or **three dollars and fifty cents.**

dolphin /'dalfɪn/ [*noun*] a large, intelligent sea animal like a gray fish with a long pointed nose

flipper

a dolphin

/i/ **see**	/ɪ/ **big**	/eɪ/ **day**	/ɛ/ **get**	/æ/ **hat**
/a/ **father, hot**	/ʌ/ **up**	/ə/ **about**	/ɔ/ **saw**	
/oʊ/ **hope**	/ʊ/ **book**	/u/ **too**	/aɪ/ **I**	/aʊ/ **how**
/ɔɪ/ **boy**	/ɚ/ **bird**	/ə/ **teacher**	/ɪr/ **ear**	/ɛr/ **air**
/ɑr/ **far**	/ɔr/ **more**	/ʊr/ **tour**	/aɪr/ **fire**	
/aʊɚ/ **hour**	/θ/ **nothing**	/ð/ **mother**	/ʃ/ **she**	
/ʒ/ **measure**	/tʃ/ **church**	/dʒ/ **jump**	/ŋ/ **long**	

dome /doʊm/ [*noun*] a round curved roof of a building: *They could see the dome of the cathedral.*

domestic /də'mɛstɪk/ [*adjective; no comparative*] FORMAL
1 happening within one country and not concerning any other countries: *You are not allowed to smoke on domestic flights.*
2 relating to your family or your life at home: *He has a happy domestic life.*
☛ Only use **domestic** before a noun.

dominate /'dɑmə,neɪt/ [*verb; dominated, dominating*] to have power or control over someone or something: *Which company dominates the telephone market?*

dominoes /'dɑmɪ,noʊz/ [*noun*] a game played with small blocks that have a different number of spots on each half of one side: *Let's play dominoes.*

donate /'doʊneɪt/ [*verb; donated, donating*] to give money or something useful to a person or organization that needs it: *A local businessman has donated $5000 to the museum.*

donation /doʊ'neɪʃən/ [*noun*] something that you give to help a person or organization: *a donation of $10* | *Would you like to make a donation to the church?*

done[1] * /dʌn/ [*verb*] the past participle of DO

done[2] * [*adjective; no comparative*]
1 finished or completed: *The work on the house is nearly done.*
2 cooked and ready to be eaten: *Is the chicken done?*
☛ Do not use **done** before a noun.

donkey /'dɑŋki/ [*noun; plural* **donkeys**] a gray or brown animal like a small horse with long ears

a donkey

don't * /doʊnt/ the short form of "do not": *I don't like peas.*

donut /'doʊnʌt/ [*noun*] another spelling of DOUGHNUT

The door   The door   The door
is **open**.   is **ajar**.   is **closed**.

door * /dɔr/ [*noun*]
1 the large flat object that you open or close to go into or out of a room, building, vehicle, etc.: *Did you lock the front door?* | *Could someone please open the door for me?* | *Please don't slam the door* (=shut the door hard so that it makes a loud noise).
2 the entrance to a room or building: *Go through that door on the right.*
═══ PHRASES ═══
3 answer the door or **get the door** to open the door when someone knocks or rings the bell: *Someone answer the door! I'm on the phone.*
4 at the door waiting outside the door for it to be opened: *Go see who's at the door.*
5 next door (to) in the building or apartment next to where you are: *The people next door are very friendly.*
↪ See also DOOR-TO-DOOR.

doorbell /'dɔr,bɛl/ [*noun*] a button outside a door that you press to make a sound, so people inside open the door
↪ See the picture at BELL.

doorknob /'dɔr,nɑb/ [*noun*] a round handle that you turn to open a door

doorman /'dɔr,mæn/ [*noun; plural* **doormen** /'dɔr,mɛn/] a man who works in a hotel or apartment building and opens the door for people, finds them taxis, etc.

doormat /'dɔr,mæt/ [*noun*] a thick piece of material just inside or outside a door that you clean the bottom of your shoes on: *Wipe your feet on the doormat.*

doorstep /'dɔr,stɛp/ [*noun*] a step just outside a door to a building

door-to-door /'dɔr tə 'dɔr/ [*adverb, adjective; no comparative*] going to every house in a street, for example to sell things or to collect money: *My brother sells magazines door-to-door.* | *a door-to-door salesperson*

doorway /'dɔr,weɪ/ [*noun; plural* **doorways**] a space that can be covered by a door, or a space just outside a door: *James was standing in the doorway.*

dorm /dɔrm/ [*noun*] dormitory; a building at a school where students live: *A friend in her dorm lent her a dress.*

dormitory /'dɔrmɪ,tɔri/ [*noun; plural* **dormitories**] a DORM

dose /doʊs/ [*noun*] a measured amount of medicine that you should take: *a dose of cough medicine*

dot /dɑt/ [*noun*] a colored spot that is part of a PATTERN

double[1] ＊ T /'dʌbəl/ [*adjective; no comparative*]
1 twice the usual amount or size: *a double scoop ice-cream cone* (=with two balls of ice cream)
2 done two times: *a double count of votes*
3 intended to be used by two people: *a double bed*
  ↪ Compare SINGLE[1] (definition 3).
4 having two parts that are the same: *The kitchen has a double sink.*
☞ Only use **double** before a noun.

double[2] ＊ T [*verb;* **doubled, doubling**] to become twice as big, or to make something twice as big: *His salary has doubled in the last five years.* | *Think of a number and then double it.*

double[3] ＊ T [*adverb*] twice as much: *Why did they charge us double?*

doubt[1] ＊ T /daʊt/ [*verb;* **doubted, doubting**] to think that something is probably not true or is not likely to happen: *"Do you think we'll win?" "I doubt it."* | **doubt (that)** ▸ *I doubt that it will rain.*

doubt[2] ＊ T [*noun*]
1 when you are not sure that something is true, possible, good, etc.: *I have doubts about his plan.*
━ PHRASES ━
2 no doubt used when you think that something is very likely or almost certain: *No doubt it'll rain soon.*
3 without (a) doubt used to emphasize that you think something is definitely true: *Jason is, without doubt, a fine athlete.*

doubtful T /'daʊtfəl/ [*adjective;* **more doubtful, most doubtful**] not likely to happen: *It is doubtful that Tom will play in tomorrow's game.*

dough ＊ /doʊ/ [*noun*] a soft mixture of flour, water, and fat or eggs, that you cook in different ways: *bread dough* | *Carefully place the dough in the pie pan.*

doughnut T /'doʊnʌt/ [*noun*] a small round cake that is cooked in oil and covered in sugar: *a jelly doughnut* (=that is filled with fruit jelly)

dove[1] /dʌv/ [*noun*] a white bird that is often used as a sign of peace

dove[2] /doʊv/ [*verb*] a past tense of DIVE

down[1] ＊ /daʊn/ [*adverb*]
1 to or in a lower place or position: *She put the package down on the table.* | *They stopped on the bridge and watched the water down below.* | *I went down to the basement.* | *The sun was going down* (=leaving the sky in the evening).
2 to a lower rate, amount, level, etc., than before: *Could you turn the radio down, please?* | *The price of milk may come down.*
3 in or into a flat or sitting position: *Please sit down.* | *I think I'll lie down for a while.*
4 written on paper: *He wrote down the address.*
5 toward or in the south: *She lives down in Florida.*
  ↪ Compare UP[1].

/i/ **see**	/ɪ/ **big**	/eɪ/ **day**	/ɛ/ **get**	/æ/ **hat**
/ɑ/ **father, hot**	/ʌ/ **up**	/ə/ **about**	/ɔ/ **saw**	
/oʊ/ **hope**	/ʊ/ **book**	/u/ **too**	/aɪ/ **I**	/aʊ/ **how**
/ɔɪ/ **boy**	/ɝ/ **bird**	/ɚ/ **teacher**	/ɪr/ **ear**	/ɛr/ **air**
/ɑr/ **far**	/ɔr/ **more**	/ʊr/ **tour**	/aɪr/ **fire**	
/aʊɚ/ **hour**	/θ/ **nothing**	/ð/ **mother**	/ʃ/ **she**	
/ʒ/ **measure**	/tʃ/ **church**	/dʒ/ **jump**	/ŋ/ **long**	

6 go down to SPOKEN to go somewhere in order to get something or do something: *We're just going down to the store.*

down² ** [preposition]*

down² * [preposition]

1 toward the ground or a lower level or position; *opposite* UP: *He fell down the stairs.* I *The church is just down the hill.*

2 along something or toward the far end of a place; *synonym* UP: *Her room is down the corridor.*

down³ [adjective; no comparative]

1 INFORMAL sad: *I've been feeling down lately.*

2 if a computer is down, it is not working: *My computer's down again.*

3 if a number or amount is down, it is lower than before; *opposite* UP: *His temperature is down today.*

☛ Do not use **down** before a noun.

downhill¹ /'daʊn'hɪl/ [adjective; no comparative] involving going down a slope; *opposite* UPHILL: *downhill skiing*

downhill² [adverb] down a slope; *opposite* UPHILL: *The path runs downhill to the lake.*

download /'daʊnˌloʊd/ [verb; downloaded, downloading] to move information onto your computer from another computer: *I'm downloading a picture from the Internet.*

downstairs¹ /'daʊn'sterz/ [adverb] on or to a lower floor of a building; *opposite* UPSTAIRS: *There are three large rooms downstairs.* I *She ran downstairs to answer the door.*

☛ Do not say that someone "went to downstairs." Say that he or she **went downstairs.**

downstairs² /'daʊnˌsterz/ [adjective; no comparative] on the main floor of a building; *opposite* UPSTAIRS: *a downstairs bathroom*

☛ Only use **downstairs** before a noun.

downtown¹ ⊤ /'daʊn'taʊn/ [adverb] in or to the business center of a town or city: *I'm going downtown for a meeting.*
⊅ Compare UPTOWN¹.

downtown² ⊤ [adjective; no comparative] used to talk about the business center of a town or city: *They have offices in downtown New York.*

☛ Only use **downtown** before a noun.
⊅ Compare UPTOWN².

downward * /'daʊnwəd/ or **downwards** /'daʊnwədz/ [adverb] toward a lower position or level; *opposite* UPWARD: *The feather floated slowly downward.*

doze /doʊz/ [verb; dozed, dozing]

1 to sleep lightly or for a short time: *Mom is dozing on the couch.*

doze off [phrasal verb]

2 to begin to sleep, especially if you did not intend to: *I dozed off during the concert.*

dozen /'dʌzən/ [determiner]

1 twelve things or people: *There are a dozen eggs in the refrigerator.* I *She bought two dozen eggs.*

☛ Do not say "two dozens eggs" or "two dozens of eggs." Say **two dozen eggs.** However, use "of" before "the," "those," or "these": **I want two dozen of those eggs.**

2 dozens of very many: *I've been to the theater dozens of times.*

Dr. the written abbreviation of DOCTOR: *Dr. Jones*

draft /dræft/ [noun] a cold wind coming into a room: *There's a bad draft near the windows.*

drag /dræg/ [verb; drags, dragged, dragging] to pull something or someone along the ground: *We dragged the box out from under the bed.*

dragon /'drægən/ [noun] an imaginary animal that has wings and a long tail and makes fire come out of its mouth

a dragon

drain[1] /dreɪn/ [*noun*] a pipe that carries liquid away from a sink, bathtub, shower, etc.: *You can pour that water down the drain.*

drain[2] [*verb;* **drained, draining**] to flow away, or to make the liquid in or around something flow away: *The water slowly drained out of the bathtub.* | *Drain the pasta well.*

drama /'drɑmə/ [*noun; plural* **dramas**]
1 a play for the theater, television, or radio, or plays and acting generally: *I'm studying drama.* | *a TV drama*
2 an exciting situation or event: *the drama of a big thunderstorm*

dramatic T /drə'mætɪk/ [*adjective*]
1 [**more dramatic, most dramatic**] exciting and impressive, or very noticeable: *a dramatic rescue* | *a dramatic difference in price*
2 [*no comparative*] relating to plays or the theater: *Shaw's dramatic works*
☛ Only use **dramatic** before a noun in this meaning.

drank * /dræŋk/ [*verb*] the past tense of **DRINK**[1]

draw * /drɔ/ [*verb;* **drew, drawn, drawing**]
1 to make a picture using a pen or pencil: *He draws beautifully.* | *I drew a picture of you, Mommy.*
↪ See also **DRAWING**.
2 to take something out of a place or container: *I'd like to draw $50 out of my savings account.* | *He drew a gun.*
3 to move somewhere: *The train was drawing into the station.*
4 to attract people to a place or to interest people in something: *The museum draws millions of visitors.*

═══ PHRASES ═══
5 **draw a conclusion** to decide what is true: *I heard what happened and drew my own conclusion.*
6 **draw someone's attention to** to make someone notice something: *I drew his attention to the "No smoking" sign.*
7 **draw the curtains** to pull curtains across so that they cover a window: *She drew the curtains and went to bed.*

drawer * /drɔr/ [*noun*] a part of a piece of furniture that can be pulled out and is used for keeping things in: *There are stamps in the top drawer of the desk.*
↪ See the picture at **OFFICE**.

drawing /'drɔɪŋ/ [*noun*]
1 a picture made with a pen or pencil: *He did a drawing of a ship.*
2 the skill of making pictures using a pen or pencil: *He's great at drawing.*

drawn * /drɔn/ [*verb*] the past participle of **DRAW**

dream[1] * /drim/ [*noun*]
1 pictures and thoughts that come into your mind while you are asleep: *I had a strange dream last night.*
2 something that you want very much to happen: *It's always been my dream to go to India.*

dream[2] * [*verb;* **dreamed** or **dreamt** /drɛmt/, **dreaming**]
1 to have a series of pictures and thoughts in your mind while you are asleep: *I dreamed I was on a big boat.* | *I dreamed about you last week.*
2 to think about something that you would like to happen: *As a child she dreamed of becoming a musician.*
☛ Do not say "dream to do something." Say **dream of doing something**.

drench /drɛntʃ/ [*verb;* **drenches, drenched, drenching**] to be or become completely wet: *The rain drenched us.*

dress[1] * /drɛs/ [*noun; plural* **dresses**]
1 a piece of **CLOTHING** worn by a woman or girl that covers her body and part or all of her legs: *She was wearing a short cotton dress.*
2 clothes of a particular kind or for a particular purpose: *a man in evening dress*

dress[2] * [*verb;* **dresses, dressed, dressing**]
1 to put clothes on yourself or on someone else; *opposite* **UNDRESS**: *She*

washed and dressed and went downstairs. | He dressed the children.

☛ Do not say "Dress yourself" or "Dress clothes." Say **Get dressed**.

— PHRASAL VERB —

dress up [phrasal verb]

2 to wear more formal clothes than you usually wear: You don't have to dress up for the party.

3 to wear special clothes for fun, or dress someone in special clothes: She **dressed up as** a witch on Halloween.

SYNONYMS dress, get dressed, be dressed in, put on, wear

When **dress** means "put on clothes," it often means "put on very nice clothes": Are you dressing for dinner? Use **get dressed** as the more general phrase: Get up and get dressed now. Use **dress**, especially **be dressed in**, to talk about what someone is wearing: She was dressed in black.

Use **put on** to talk about when you get dressed in a particular piece of clothing: He put on his hat. | Put a coat on, or you'll get cold.

Wear means "to have clothes on, especially a particular kind of clothes": She was wearing a red suit.

---

dressed /drɛst/ [adjective; no comparative]

— PHRASES —

1 be dressed to be wearing clothes: I'm not dressed yet. | She was **dressed in** jeans and a sweatshirt.

2 get dressed to put on your clothes: Hurry up and get dressed.

⇨ See the synonym note at DRESS[2].

dresser /ˈdrɛsɚ/ [noun] a piece of bedroom furniture with several drawers for keeping clothes in: The handkerchiefs are in my top **dresser drawer**.

dressing /ˈdrɛsɪŋ/ [noun] a liquid that you can pour over salad or other food: oil and vinegar dressing

dressing room /ˈdrɛsɪŋ ˌrum/ [noun] a room where a performer gets ready before a performance

dressmaker /ˈdrɛsˌmeɪkɚ/ [noun] someone whose job is to make women's clothes, especially high-quality women's clothes: I'm going to the dressmaker to pick up my gown.

drew * /dru/ [verb] the past tense of DRAW

dried[1] * /draɪd/ [verb] the past tense and past participle of DRY[2]

dried[2] [adjective; no comparative] dried fruits, flowers, etc., have had most of the water removed from them: Put the dried flowers in a vase.

drift /drɪft/ [verb; drifted, drifting] to be moved somewhere slowly and gently by the air or by water: The smell of cooking drifted through the house. | The boat drifted away.

drill[1] /drɪl/ [noun]

1 a TOOL or machine that you use to make a hole in something hard

2 when you practice doing something many times so that you can do it well: a **fire drill** (=to practice leaving a building if there is a fire)

drill[2] [verb; drilled, drilling] to make a hole in something hard with a special tool or machine: The company is **drilling for** oil in this area.

drink[1] * /drɪŋk/ [verb; drank, drunk, drinking] to take a liquid into your mouth and swallow it: Richard doesn't drink tea or coffee. | Please **don't drink from** the bottle, Adam.

⇨ See also DRUNK[2].

drink[2] * [noun]

1 an amount of a liquid that you drink: Could I have a **drink of** water?

2 liquid that you can drink, usually alcohol: Why don't you come over for drinks on Saturday?

☛ **Would you like a drink?** usually means you are being offered alcohol. **Would you like something to drink?** means any kind of drink.

drinking fountain /ˈdrɪŋkɪŋ ˌfaʊntən/ [noun] an object in a public place that looks like a small sink, that sends out water for people to drink

drip /drɪp/ [verb; drips, dripped, dripping]

1 to fall or let something fall in drops: Rain dripped off the roof. | She dripped mustard on her blouse.

2 to produce drops of liquid: The faucet in the bathroom is dripping.

drive[1] * /draɪv/ [verb; drove, driven, driving]
1 to make a vehicle move, and control where it goes: *Can you drive?* | *He slammed the car door and **drove off*** (=left). | *I'll drive and you give directions.*
2 to travel in a car or take someone somewhere in a car: *Dad drove us home after the movie.*

— PHRASE —

3 **drive someone nuts/crazy/mad** to make someone feel very angry or upset: *He drives me crazy with his constant questions.*

drive[2] * [noun]
1 a trip in a car: *We like to **go for a drive** on Sundays.*
2 used in the names of some city roads: *Sunset Drive*
⮑ *See also* DISK DRIVE.

driven * /'drɪvən/ [verb] the past participle of DRIVE[1]

driver * /'draɪvɚ/ [noun] someone who drives a vehicle: *a truck driver*

driver's license /'draɪvɚz ˌlaɪsɪns/ [noun] an official document that says you are legally allowed to drive

drive-through /'draɪv ˌθru/ [adjective; no comparative] made in a way that people can use a service without parking or leaving their cars: *The bank has a drive-through window.*

driveway /'draɪvˌweɪ/ [noun; plural driveways] the hard area or road between the garage of a HOUSE and the street

droop /drup/ [verb; drooped, drooping] to hang over or bend down in a loose way: *The plants drooped in the hot sun.*

drop[1] * /drap/ [verb; drops, dropped, dropping]
1 to fall or let something fall: *An apple dropped from the tree.* | *Excuse me, but you dropped your wallet.*
2 to fall suddenly in

He **dropped** his books.

amount, level, or degree: *The water level of the lake has dropped.*

— PHRASAL VERBS —

drop by or **drop in** [phrasal verb]
3 to visit someone when he or she is not expecting you: *Michelle dropped by yesterday.* | *Let's **drop in on** Karen.*

drop out [phrasal verb]
4 to stop going to school or college without finishing your courses: *He dropped out of high school.*

drop[2] * [noun]
1 a very small amount of liquid that falls in a round shape: *The rain was falling in big drops.*
2 a small amount of a liquid: *We haven't had a **drop of** rain in months.*
3 a fall in the amount, level, or degree of something: *a drop in temperature*

drought /draʊt/ [noun] a long period of dry weather when there is not enough water: *The drought lasted for months.*

drove * /droʊv/ [verb] the past tense of DRIVE[1]

drown /draʊn/ [verb; drowned, drowning] to die from being under water for too long, or to kill someone in this way: *Hundreds of people drowned in the floods.*

drowsy /'draʊzi/ [adjective; drowsier, drowsiest] feeling that you want to sleep: *Alcohol can make you feel drowsy.*

drug * /drʌg/ [noun]
1 a medicine: *The doctor prescribed this new drug.*
2 an illegal substance that people smoke, swallow, etc., to make themselves feel good: *I'm sure that guy **takes drugs**.*

drugstore /'drʌgˌstɔr/ [noun] a store that sells medicines, soap, and many other things: *Get me some toothpaste when you're **at the drugstore**.*

drum[1] * /drʌm/ [noun] a MUSICAL INSTRUMENT made of a round frame with a skin stretched over the top that you

/i/ **see**	/ɪ/ **big**	/eɪ/ **day**	/ɛ/ **get**	/æ/ **hat**
/ɑ/ **father, hot**	/ʌ/ **up**	/ə/ **about**	/ɔ/ **saw**	
/oʊ/ **hope**	/ʊ/ **book**	/u/ **too**	/aɪ/ **I**	/aʊ/ **how**
/ɔɪ/ **boy**	/ɚ/ **bird**	/ɚ/ **teacher**	/ɪr/ **ear**	/ɛr/ **air**
/ɑr/ **far**	/ɔr/ **more**	/ʊr/ **tour**	/aɪr/ **fire**	
/aʊɚ/ **hour**	/θ/ **nothing**	/ð/ **mother**	/ʃ/ **she**	
/ʒ/ **measure**	/tʃ/ **church**	/dʒ/ **jump**	/ŋ/ **long**	

play by hitting it with your hand or a stick: *I used to play the drums.*

☞ **Drum** is usually used in the plural.

drum² [*verb;* **drums, drummed, drumming**] to hit something again and again, and make sounds: *She drummed her fingers on the table.* | *Rain drummed against the window.*

drunk¹ ✱ /drʌŋk/ [*verb*] the past participle of **DRINK¹**

drunk² [*adjective;* **drunker, drunkest**] unable to behave or speak normally because you have drunk too much alcohol; *opposite* **SOBER**: *I don't like to get drunk.*

dry¹ ✱ T /draɪ/ [*adjective;* **drier, driest**]
1 having no water or other liquid on it or in it; *opposite* **WET**: *dry clothes* | *The ground is dry enough to sit on.*
2 without any rain: *a dry, sunny day*

dry² ✱ T [*verb;* **dries, dried, drying**]
1 to become dry, or to make something dry; *opposite* **WET**: *The laundry is drying.* | *I need to dry my hair.*

══ **PHRASAL VERBS** ══

dry out [*phrasal verb*]
2 to become dry: *My coat needs to dry out.*
3 to make something dry: **dry something out** ▸ *I dried my socks out by the fire.*

dry up [*phrasal verb*]
4 to lose all water: *The river dried up.*

dry cleaner /'draɪ ˌklinər/ [*noun*] a store where you take clothes to be cleaned with chemicals instead of water: *Remind me to get my jacket from the dry cleaner's.*

dryer /'draɪər/ [*noun*] a machine used to dry things, especially wet clothes: *The clothes are in the dryer.*

duck¹ ✱ /dʌk/ [*noun*] a bird that swims on water and is sometimes kept for its eggs and meat

duck² [*verb;* **ducked, ducking**] to bend your head to avoid hitting it on something: *He ducked under the low beam.*
↪ *See the picture at* **MOVEMENT.**

due T /du/ [*adjective*]
1 expected at a particular time: *Her baby is due in early December.* | *My*

library books are due back tomorrow. | **due to do something** ▸ *When is the plane due to arrive?*
2 if a bill is due, it needs to be paid: *The car payment is due on the 24th.*
☞ Do not use **due** before a noun.

══ **PHRASE** ══

3 **due to** because of something: *The delay was due to an accident.*

duet /du'ɛt/ [*noun*] a piece of music or a song for two performers: *She and her sister played a piano duet.*

dug ✱ /dʌg/ [*verb*] the past tense and past participle of **DIG**

dull ✱ /dʌl/ [*adjective;* **duller, dullest**]
1 not interesting or exciting; *synonym* **BORING**: *a dull speech*
2 no longer sharp: *All my kitchen knives are too dull.*
↪ *Compare* **BLUNT.**
3 not bright or shiny: *a dull red color*

dumb /dʌm/ [*adjective;* **dumber, dumbest**] *INFORMAL* stupid; *opposite* **SMART**: *That was a dumb thing to do!*

dump¹ /dʌmp/ [*verb;* **dumped, dumping**] *INFORMAL*
1 to drop something or put something down with a lot of force: *She dumped her books on the table.*
2 to get rid of something or someone you no longer want: *The milk smelled bad, so I dumped it.*

dump² [*noun*] *INFORMAL* a place where waste and things you no longer want are collected and kept: *a garbage dump*

dune /dun/ [*noun*] a hill made of sand near the ocean or in the desert

duo /'duoʊ/ [*noun; plural* **duos**] two musicians or singers who perform together: *The duo had their own weekly television show.*

a goose

a duck

during * /'dʊrɪŋ/ [*preposition*]
  1 all through a period of time or an event: *We go to the beach during the summer.* | *Don't talk during the show.*
  2 at some point in a period of time or while something else is happening: *The soldier died during the night.*

USAGE during, for

  Use **during** to talk about something that happens within a particular period of time: *She lived in New York during the 1990s.*
  Do not use **during** to talk about how long something lasts. Use **for**: *I was in the hospital for six weeks.*

dusk /dʌsk/ [*noun*] the time in the evening when the sky is becoming darker: *The park closes at dusk.*

dust¹ * /dʌst/ [*noun*] very small pieces of dirt like a powder: *a thick layer of dust*

dust² [*verb; dusted, dusting*] to remove the dust from the surface of something: *Are you done dusting the furniture?*

dustpan /'dʌst,pæn/ [*noun*] a flat container with a handle that you use with a BRUSH to remove dust, dirt, etc., from the floor

dusty /'dʌsti/ [*adjective; dustier, dustiest*] covered with dust: *a dusty road* | *The old records were very dusty.*

duty * /'duti/ [*noun; plural duties*]
  1 something that someone must do because it is his or her job or because it is right: *He carried out his duties well.*
  — PHRASES —
  2 on duty doing your job: *I go on duty* (=start work) *at 3:00 p.m.*
  3 off duty not doing your job: *What time do you go off duty?* (=leave work)
  ☞ **On duty** and **off duty** are only used about people such as police officers, soldiers, and doctors, who need to watch very carefully what is happening when they are at work.

dye¹ /daɪ/ [*noun; plural dyes*] a liquid or powder that you use to change the color of something such as your hair or a piece of clothing: *hair dye*

dye² [*verb; dyes, dyed, dyeing*] to use a substance to make something a different color: *I dyed the curtains pink.*

dying /'daɪɪŋ/ [*verb*] the present participle of DIE

dynamite /'daɪnə,maɪt/ [*noun*] a substance used to cause explosions: *a stick of dynamite*

E

E * or **e** /i/ [*noun; plural Es or E's, e's*] the fifth letter of the English alphabet
  ⇨ *See the usage note at* ALPHABET.

E. or **E** a written abbreviation for EAST: *201 E. 50th St.* | *32 E 103 Street*
  ⇨ *Compare* N., S., W.

each¹ * /itʃ/ [*determiner, pronoun*]
  1 every person or thing in a group: *Each document has a number.* | *We each have our own room.* | *Each of the boxes is labeled.*
  ☞ Do not say "on each sides." Say **on each side**.
  — PHRASE —
  2 each other if two or more people do something to or with each other, each person does it to or with the other person or other people: *John and Bill looked at each other and laughed.* | *They danced with each other all evening.*

USAGE each, every, all, both

  Use **each** to talk about two or more things or people considered separately: *Put a candle on each cake.*
  Use **every** to talk about more than two things or people considered together: *Make sure every cake has a candle on it.*
  All is used with the plural forms of countable nouns to talk about more than two things together: *All (of) the cakes had candles on them* (=there are more than two cakes).
  Use **both** to talk about two things considered together: *Both (of) the cakes had candles on them* (=there are only two cakes).

each[2] * [*adverb*] for each one: *The chairs cost $200 each.*

eager * /'igɚ/ [*adjective;* **more eager, most eager**] wanting very much to do or have something: **eager to do something** ▸ *I was eager to meet him.* | *They were eager for news.*
⇨ *See the usage note at* ANXIOUS.

eagerly * /'igɚli/ [*adverb*] in a way that shows that you want very much to do or have something: *"I'll come with you!" John said eagerly.*

eagle /'igəl/ [*noun*] a large, powerful bird that eats small animals

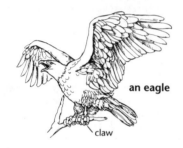

an eagle

claw

ear * /ɪr/ [*noun*]
1 one of the two parts on either side of your head that you hear with: *The man had big ears.*
⇨ *See the picture at* BODY.
2 the part of a CORN plant that contains the seeds: *an ear of corn*

earache /'ɪr,eɪk/ [*noun*] a pain in one or both of your ears: *I have a bad earache.*

earlier[1] /'ɚliɚ/ [*adverb*] at a time before the present time or before a time in the past: *You said something earlier that I didn't understand.* | *The war had ended three weeks earlier.*

earlier[2] [*adjective; no comparative*] happening or coming before now, or before the time you are talking about; synonym PREVIOUS: *She had an earlier meeting with them that went well.*

earliest /'ɚliɪst/ [*adjective; no comparative*] least recent: *Her earliest book was her best.*

earlobe /'ɪr,loʊb/ [*noun*] the soft part at the lower edge of your ear
⇨ *See the picture at* BODY.

early[1] * /'ɚli/ [*adjective;* **earlier, earliest**]
1 before the usual or expected time; opposite LATE: *You're early. We're not ready yet.*
2 near the beginning of a period of time; opposite LATE: *They met in the early afternoon.* | *I'd like an earlier appointment on Friday.*

early[2] * [*adverb;* **earlier, earliest**]
1 before the usual or expected time; opposite LATE: *You should get to bed early tonight.* | *We arrived earlier than the other guests.*
2 near the beginning of a period of time; opposite LATE: *The accident happened early this morning.*

USAGE   **early, soon**

Use **early** to talk about the beginning of a period of time: *We should arrive early to get a good seat.*

Use **soon** to talk about a time that is not long from now: *The train should arrive very soon.*

earn * /ɚn/ [*verb;* **earned, earning**]
1 to get money for the work you do: *She earns $40,000 a year.* | *We all have to* **earn a living** (=earn enough money for food, clothes, and other basic things).
⇨ *See the synonym note at* GAIN.
2 to do something that makes you deserve something: *He has earned our respect.*

earphones /'ɪr,foʊnz/ [*plural noun*] a piece of electrical equipment with parts you wear in each ear, used for listening privately to recorded music, people speaking to you, etc.
⇨ *Compare* HEADPHONES.

earring /'ɪrɪŋ/ [*noun*] a piece of JEWELRY that you wear hanging from or through the bottom part of your ear: *She wore pearl earrings.*

earth * /ɚθ/ [*noun*]
1 also **Earth**; the planet that we live on, that is third from our sun: *Earth is the fifth largest planet.* | *We must protect* **the earth.** | *It is the coldest place on* **Earth.**
2 soil: *Press the earth down firmly around the plant's roots.*

— PHRASE —

3 why/who/what/etc. on Earth
SPOKEN used to make a question sound stronger when you are angry, upset, surprised, etc.: *Why on Earth didn't you tell me?*

earthquake /'ɜ·θ,kweɪk/ [*noun*] when the ground shakes strongly, often causing a lot of damage: *The earthquake killed over 100 people.*

ease[1] /iz/ [*noun*]

— PHRASES —

1 with ease easily: *She caught the ball with ease.*

2 at ease feeling relaxed and not worried or nervous: *He tried to make the new students feel at ease.*

ease[2] [*verb*; **eased, easing**] to make an unpleasant feeling or situation less severe, or to become less painful, difficult, etc.: *The pain has eased a little.*

easel /'izəl/ [*noun*] a frame that supports a picture while someone is painting or drawing: *There was a half-finished painting on the easel.*

easily * /'izəli/ [*adverb*]
1 without difficulty: *We'll beat them easily.*

— PHRASE —

2 might easily or **could easily** used to say that something is very likely: *They might easily change their minds.*

east[1] * /ist/ [*noun*]
1 the east the direction in which the sun rises, or an area in that direction: *There is a desert in the east. | a small town to the east of the capital*
↪ See the usage note at **DIRECTION**.

2 the East countries in the eastern part of the world, especially eastern Asia: *She has studied the religions of the East.*

east[2] * [*adjective; no comparative*] in, toward, or coming from the east: *The east part of the forest is much drier. | They live on the east side of town. | an east wind*
☛ Only use **east** before a noun.

east[3] * [*adverb*] toward or in the east: *The ship sailed east. | Our house is east of the lake.*

Easter /'istɚ/ [*noun*] a Christian holiday in the spring: *It's traditional to decorate eggs at Easter.*

Easter egg /'istɚ ,ɛg/ [*noun*] a boiled egg in its shell, which has been colored and decorated for Easter: *We colored Easter eggs last night.*

eastern * /'istɚn/ [*adjective; no comparative*]
1 in or from the east: *the eastern part of the country | an eastern accent*
2 Eastern from or relating to Asia: *He is very interested in Eastern philosophy.*

Easterner /'istɚnɚ/ [*noun*] someone who comes from the east of a country: *Many Easterners never visit the West Coast.*

eastward /'istwɚd/ or **eastwards** /'istwɚdz/ [*adverb*] toward the east: *We traveled eastward for three days.*

easy * /'izi/ [*adjective*; **easier, easiest**]
1 not needing much effort, experience, or skill to understand or do; *opposites* DIFFICULT, HARD: *That was the easiest test I've ever taken. | easy to do something* ▸ *It's easy to ride a bicycle. | It's easy for her to learn new songs.*

— PHRASE —

2 take it easy or **take things easy** to relax and not do much: *The doctor says I should take it easy for a while.*

easygoing Ⓣ /'izi'goʊɪŋ/ [*adjective*; **more easygoing, most easygoing**] not strict and not easily worried about things: *He's an easygoing kind of guy.*

eat * /it/ [*verb*; **ate, eaten** /'itən/, **eating**]
1 to put food in your mouth and swallow it: *She was eating an apple.*
2 to have a meal: *Where should we eat tonight?*

— PHRASE —

3 something to eat a little food, or a meal: *Let's have something to eat before we go.*

/i/ **see**	/ɪ/ **big**	/eɪ/ **day**	/ɛ/ **get**	/æ/ **hat**

/i/ **see** /ɪ/ **big** /eɪ/ **day** /ɛ/ **get** /æ/ **hat**
/ɑ/ **father, hot** /ʌ/ **up** /ə/ **about** /ɔ/ **saw**
/oʊ/ **hope** /ʊ/ **book** /u/ **too** /aɪ/ **I** /aʊ/ **how**
/ɔɪ/ **boy** /ɚ/ **bird** /ɚ/ **teacher** /ɪr/ **ear** /ɛr/ **air**
/ɑr/ **far** /ɔr/ **more** /ʊr/ **tour** /aɪr/ **fire**
/aʊɚ/ **hour** /θ/ **nothing** /ð/ **mother** /ʃ/ **she**
/ʒ/ **measure** /tʃ/ **church** /dʒ/ **jump** /ŋ/ **long**

═══ PHRASAL VERB ═══

eat out [*phrasal verb*]
  4 to have a meal in a restaurant rather than at home: *Let's eat out tonight.*

eater /'itə/ [*noun*] a word meaning "someone who eats," used to talk about the way he or she eats: *a fast eater*

echo¹ /'ɛkoʊ/ [*noun; plural* echoes] a sound that comes back from a surface so that you hear it again, for example in an empty room, or in the mountains: *We could hear the echo of our voices.*

echo² [*verb;* echoes, echoed, echoing] if a sound echoes, it comes back from a surface so that you hear it again: *Our footsteps echoed in the long corridor.*

eclipse /ɪ'klɪps/ [*noun*] an occasion when the sun has the moon's shadow on it, or the moon has the earth's shadow on it, so that all or part of it is dark: *an eclipse of the sun*

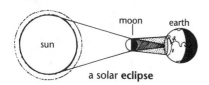

moon   earth

sun

a solar eclipse

economic * 🔲 /,ɛkə'namɪk/ [*adjective; no comparative*] relating to money, trade, and industry: *an economic crisis*

economical 🔲 /,ɛkə'namɪkəl/ [*adjective;* more economical, most economical] not using a lot of something, for example fuel: *an economical car*

economics /,ɛkə'namɪks/ [*noun*] the study of money, trade, and industry: *She's interested in politics and economics.*
  ☛ Only use **economics** with a singular verb.

economy /ɪ'kanəmi/ [*noun; plural* economies] the money, trade, and industry of a country: *a strong economy*

edge * /ɛdʒ/ [*noun*]
  1 the part of an object or area that is farthest from the center, or is where it ends: *a path at the edge of the lake | The edge of the scarf was torn.*
  2 the sharp side of something such as a knife: *He cut his finger on the edge of the blade.*

═══ PHRASE ═══

  3 on edge worried and nervous: *Everyone was feeling on edge.*

edition /ɪ'dɪʃən/ [*noun*] one of the copies of a book, a magazine, etc., that are printed at the same time: *Do you have last week's edition of "Newsweek"?*

editor /'ɛdɪtə/ [*noun*]
  1 someone who is in charge of a newspaper or magazine, or in charge of a part of it: *He is the political editor of a local newspaper.*
  2 someone who prepares books, magazines, movies, etc., to be printed or broadcast by checking for mistakes, removing parts, etc.: *The TV show has three editors.*

educate * /'ɛdʒʊ,keɪt/ [*verb;* educated, educating] to teach someone, especially in a school: *I was educated at Yale University. | Young people should be educated about the dangers of drugs.*

educated * /'ɛdʒʊ,keɪtɪd/ [*adjective;* more educated, most educated] having learned a lot about many subjects; *opposite* UNEDUCATED: *a highly educated man*

education * /,ɛdʒʊ'keɪʃən/ [*noun*] the process of teaching and learning: *Every child deserves a good education.*

educational /,ɛdʒʊ'keɪʃənəl/ [*adjective*]
  1 [*no comparative*] relating to the process of teaching and learning: *the state's educational program | books and other educational materials*
  2 [more educational, most educational] teaching you something: *The guided tour was very educational.*

eel /il/ [*noun*] a long fish that looks like a snake and can be eaten

effect * 🔲 /ɪ'fɛkt/ [*noun*]
  1 a change or difference that happens as a result of something: *The medicine seemed to have no effect. | the effect of pollution on the environment*
  ⇨ *See the usage note at* AFFECT.

═══ PHRASE ═══

  2 take effect to start being used or done or producing a result: *When will the law take effect?*

effective * /ɪ'fɛktɪv/ [*adjective;* more effective, most effective] producing the result that you want: *effective pain medication* | *an effective ad campaign*

efficient /ɪ'fɪʃənt/ [*adjective;* **more efficient, most efficient**] working well, especially without wasting time or energy; *opposite* INEFFICIENT: *She's an efficient manager.*

efficiently /ɪ'fɪʃəntli/ [*adverb*] doing the work that is needed, and not wasting time, energy, or materials: *an efficiently run farm*

effort * T /'ɛfɚt/ [*noun*]
  1 trying hard to do something difficult: *She* **puts** *a lot of* **effort into** *her schoolwork.* | *Repairing this table was* **worth the effort.**
  2 an attempt to do something: *She* **made an effort** *to talk to them.* | **effort to do something** ▶ *The man died in spite of their efforts to save him.*

EFL /'i,ɛf'ɛl/ [*noun*] English as a Foreign Language; the teaching of English to people whose first language is not English and who live in a country where English is not the main language: *She taught EFL in Japan.*

e.g. /'i'dʒi/ an abbreviation meaning "for example": *Bring anything you need to stay overnight, e.g., a towel and a toothbrush.*

egg * /ɛg/ [*noun*]
  1 a round object with a shell that a bird, reptile, or insect produces, in which a baby creature grows: *I saw five eggs in the nest.* | *Hens* **lay eggs.**
  2 an egg of a bird, especially a chicken, used as food: *We ate eggs for breakfast.* | *You have some egg on your tie.*

eggplant /'ɛg,plænt/ [*noun*] a shiny purple VEGETABLE that is white inside, and is eaten cooked

eggshell /'ɛg,ʃɛl/ [*noun*] the hard covering of a bird's egg
  ⇨ See the picture at HATCH.

eight * /eɪt/ [*number, noun*] 8: *You are allowed to borrow eight books from the library.*

eighteen * /'eɪ'tin/ [*number*] 18: *She will be eighteen in January.*

eighteenth * /'eɪ'tinθ/ [*adverb, adjective; no comparative*] coming after 17 other

people, things, or events; sometimes written as "18th": *She works on the 18th floor.* | *I finished eighteenth in the race.*
  ⇨ See the usage note at SECOND[2].

eighth[1] * /eɪθ/ [*adverb, adjective; no comparative*] coming after seven other people, things, or events; sometimes written as "8th": *August is the 8th month of the year.* | *I finished eighth in the race.*

eighth[2] * [*noun*] one of eight equal parts: *Cut the cake* **into eighths.** | *Five is* **an eighth of** *40.*
  ⇨ See the usage note at SECOND[2].

eightieth * /'eɪtiiθ/ [*adjective, adverb; no comparative*] coming after 79 other people, things, or events; sometimes written as "80th": *He enjoyed his eightieth birthday very much.*
  ⇨ See the usage note at SECOND[2].

eighty * /'eɪti/ [*number, noun; plural* **eighties**] 80: *Over eighty people applied for the job.*
  ⇨ See the usage note at TEENS.

either[1] * /'iðɚ; 'aɪðɚ/ [*determiner, pronoun*]
  1 one of two people or things, it does not matter which: *You can spell it either way.* | *Either would be fine.*
  2 not one and not the other of two people or things: *I don't like either of them.* | *I don't trust either brother.*
  ☞ Only use this meaning of **either** in negative sentences.
  ⇨ *Compare* BOTH[1], NEITHER[1].
  3 both of two things: *On either side of the road, there were tall trees.*
  ⇨ See also EACH[1] (definition 1).
  ☞ Use **either** before a singular noun, not a plural noun.

either[2] * [*conjunction*]
  — PHRASE —
  either ... or one of two things, but not both: *Either Emily or I will meet you at the airport.*

/i/ **see** /ɪ/ **big** /eɪ/ **day** /ɛ/ **get** /æ/ **hat** /ɑ/ **father, hot** /ʌ/ **up** /ə/ **about** /ɔ/ **saw** /oʊ/ **hope** /ʊ/ **book** /u/ **too** /aɪ/ **I** /aʊ/ **how** /ɔɪ/ **boy** /ɚ/ **bird** /ɚ/ **teacher** /ɪr/ **ear** /ɛr/ **air** /ɑr/ **far** /ɔr/ **more** /ʊr/ **tour** /aɪr/ **fire** /aʊɚ/ **hour** /θ/ **nothing** /ð/ **mother** /ʃ/ **she** /ʒ/ **measure** /tʃ/ **church** /dʒ/ **jump** /ŋ/ **long**

USAGE either . . . or, neither . . . nor

Use **either . . . or** to say that one of two things could happen, could be done, etc.: *Either you or John should tell her.* | *I'll either take the train or the bus.*

Use **neither . . . nor** with negative statements: *Neither John nor I wanted to tell her.* | *He took neither the train nor the bus.* **Neither . . . nor** is fairly formal, and is used especially in written English.

elaborate Ⓣ /ɪ'læbərɪt/ [*adjective;* **more elaborate, most elaborate**] having a complicated design or having many parts: *an elaborate hairstyle* | *an elaborate plan*

elastic /ɪ'læstɪk/ [*noun*] material that can stretch and return to its original shape, often used in making clothes: *The skirt has elastic around the waist.*

elbow * /'ɛlboʊ/ [*noun*] the joint in your arm where it bends
  ⊳ *See the picture at* BODY.

elder /'ɛldɚ/ [*adjective;* superlative **eldest**] older than another family member or members: *her elder sisters* | *The eldest of her sons is at Harvard.*
  ☛ Do not confuse **elder** and **older**. **Elder** is only used about people. **Older** can be used about people or things.

elderly /'ɛldɚli/ [*adjective;* **more elderly, most elderly**] someone who is elderly is old. "Elderly" is a more polite word than "old": *I live with my elderly aunt.*

elect * /ɪ'lɛkt/ [*verb;* **elected, electing**] to choose a person or group for a particular job or position by voting: *We elect a mayor in November.* | **elect someone something** ▸ *Kennedy was elected president in 1960.*

election * /ɪ'lɛkʃən/ [*noun*] the process of voting for a person or group, especially for a position of political power: *Did you vote in the last election?*

electric * /ɪ'lɛktrɪk/ [*adjective; no comparative*]
  1 using electricity to work: *an electric razor* | *Is your stove electric or gas?*
  2 consisting of or produced by electricity; *synonym* ELECTRICAL: *an electric current*

electrical * /ɪ'lɛktrɪkəl/ [*adjective; no comparative*]
  1 designed to use electricity: *electrical equipment*
  2 consisting of or produced by electricity; *synonym* ELECTRIC: *an electrical storm* | *electrical energy*

electrician /ɪlɛk'trɪʃən/ [*noun*] someone whose job is to put in and repair electrical equipment and systems

electricity * /ɪlɛk'trɪsɪti/ [*noun*] a form of energy that is carried by wires and used to make things such as lights, televisions, and computers work: *Does the cabin have electricity?* | *The electricity had been **cut off** (=electricity was no longer supplied to the building).*

electron /ɪ'lɛktran/ [*noun*] a part of an atom that has a negative charge: *An atom consists of a nucleus surrounded by electrons.* | *an electron microscope* (=a microscope that can see extremely small things)
  ⊳ *Compare* NEUTRON, PROTON.

electronic * /ɪlɛk'tranɪk/ [*adjective; no comparative*] containing or using extremely small electrical parts: *an electronic calculator*

electronics /ɪlɪk'tranɪks/ [*noun*] the use, study of, and production of electronic equipment and systems: *Advances in electronics have made computers faster.*
  ☛ Only use **electronics** with a singular verb.

elegant /'ɛlɪgənt/ [*adjective;* **more elegant, most elegant**] beautiful in a simple but often expensive way: *She was wearing an elegant black dress.*

element Ⓣ /'ɛləmənt/ [*noun*]
  1 a chemical substance, for example oxygen or iron, that is not a mixture of other substances
  2 a part of something: *The salary was a major element in her choice of jobs.*
  3 a small amount: *All sports activities contain **an element of** risk.*

elementary Ⓣ /,ɛlə'mɛntəri/ [*adjective;* **more elementary, most elementary**]
  1 FORMAL simple or basic: *elementary mathematics*
  2 relating to the first stages of a learning process: *elementary education*

elementary school /ˌɛləˈmɛntəri ˌskul/ [noun] a school in the U.S. for children in the first five or six years of education; _synonym_ GRADE SCHOOL

elephant /ˈɛləfənt/ [noun] a very big animal with thick, gray skin, big ears, and a long nose called a trunk

an elephant

tusk

trunk

elevator /ˈɛləˌveɪtɚ/ [noun] a machine that takes people and goods between the levels of a building: _Take the elevator up to the sixth floor._

eleven ✲ /ɪˈlɛvən/ [number] 11: _There were eleven children on the bus._

eleventh ✲ /ɪˈlɛvənθ/ [adverb, adjective; no comparative] coming after ten other people, things, or events; sometimes written as "11th": _November is the 11th month of the year._ | _I finished eleventh in the race._
↪ _See the usage note at_ SECOND[2].

elf /ɛlf/ [noun; plural **elves**] an imaginary creature that looks like a small person with pointed ears: _a story about an elf_

elite /ɪˈlit/ [noun] a small group of people who have a lot of power or have special abilities: _Political power is in the hands of a small elite._

else ✲ 🔲 /ɛls/ [adverb]
   1 a different or other thing, person, or place: _Get someone else to do it._ | _I have nowhere else to go._ | _What else can I do?_
   2 in addition to the other thing, person, or place you have already mentioned: _What else did you do?_ | _There's no one else here._
   ☛ Only use **else** after a pronoun or adverb.
— PHRASE
   3 or else SPOKEN used to say what will happen if something is not done or is not true: _Go now, or else you'll be late._

elsewhere /ˈɛlsˌwɛr/ [adverb] FORMAL in another place or places: _Elsewhere, the storm was less severe._

elves /ɛlvz/ [noun] the plural of ELF

e-mail[1] or **E-mail** /ˈi ˌmeɪl/ [noun]
   1 electronic mail; the system of sending written messages from one computer to another: _They'll send me the documents by e-mail._
   2 a message sent by e-mail: _I got an e-mail from a friend in Mexico today._

e-mail[2] or **E-mail** [verb; e-mailed, e-mailing; E-mailed, E-mailing] to send a written message from your computer to someone else's: **e-mail someone something** ▸ _I'll e-mail you my answer._

embarrass ✲ /ɛmˈbærəs/ [verb; embarrasses, embarrassed, embarrassing] to make you feel ashamed or uncomfortable, as if other people were laughing at you or criticizing you: _All this attention embarrasses her._

embarrassed ✲ /ɛmˈbærəst/ [adjective; more embarrassed, most embarrassed] feeling ashamed or uncomfortable, especially because of what other people might think about you: **embarrassed to do something** ▸ _I was embarrassed to admit I'd forgotten his name._
   ↪ _Compare_ ASHAMED, GUILTY.

embarrassing ✲ /ɛmˈbærəˌsɪŋ/ [adjective; more embarrassing, most embarrassing] making you feel ashamed or uncomfortable: _an embarrassing mistake_

embarrassment /ɛmˈbærəsmənt/ [noun] an uncomfortable feeling of shame: _She covered her face in embarrassment._

embassy /ˈɛmbəsi/ [noun; plural **embassies**] the building where the

---

/i/ see	/ɪ/ big	/eɪ/ day	/ɛ/ get	/æ/ hat
/a/ father, hot	/ʌ/ up	/ə/ about	/ɔ/ saw
/oʊ/ hope	/ʊ/ book	/u/ too	/aɪ/ I	/aʊ/ how
/ɔɪ/ boy	/ɚ/ bird	/ɚ/ teacher	/ɪr/ ear	/ɛr/ air
/ɑr/ far	/ɔr/ more	/ʊr/ tour	/aɪr/ fire
/aʊɚ/ hour	/θ/ nothing	/ð/ mother	/ʃ/ she
/ʒ/ measure	/tʃ/ church	/dʒ/ jump	/ŋ/ long

people who represent a foreign government work: *the Greek embassy*

embrace[1] /ɛmˈbreɪs/ [*verb;* **embraced, embracing**] to put your arms around someone as a greeting or in a loving way: *She embraced her daughter.*

embrace[2] [*noun*] an act of embracing someone: *He held her in a tight embrace.*

embroider /ɛmˈbrɔɪdɚ/ [*verb;* **embroidered, embroidering**] to sew patterns or designs on cloth: *She embroidered flowers on the dress.*

embroidery /ɛmˈbrɔɪdəri/ [*noun*] a pattern or design sewn on cloth: *a tablecloth decorated with embroidery*

emerald /ˈɛmərəld/ [*noun*] a valuable green stone that is used to make jewelry: *an emerald ring*

emerge /ɪˈmɝdʒ/ [*verb;* **emerged, emerging**] to come out from a place where you could not be seen before: *A deer suddenly emerged from the forest.*

emergency /ɪˈmɝdʒənsi/ [*noun;* **emergencies**] a serious situation in which action must be taken quickly: *Only call an ambulance in an emergency.*

emergency room /ɪˈmɝdʒənsi ˌrum/ [*noun*] the part of a hospital where people who need treatment quickly are dealt with; *synonym* **ER**: *He was rushed to the emergency room.*

emigrant /ˈɛmɪgrənt/ [*noun*] someone who goes to live permanently in another country: *The emigrants waited to board the plane.*
⇨ *Compare* **IMMIGRANT**.

emigrate T /ˈɛmɪˌgreɪt/ [*verb;* **emigrated, emigrating**] to leave your own country and go to live permanently in another country: *Her grandparents emigrated from Sweden.*
⇨ *Compare* **IMMIGRATE**.

emigration /ˌɛmɪˈgreɪʃən/ [*noun*] when people go to live permanently in another country: *Emigration was one result of the famine.*
⇨ *Compare* **IMMIGRATION** (definition 1).

emotion * /ɪˈmoʊʃən/ [*noun*] a feeling such as happiness, sadness, or anger: *He was unable to control his emotions.* | *Her voice shook with emotion.*

emotional * T /ɪˈmoʊʃənəl/ [*adjective;* **more emotional, most emotional**] feeling, showing, or involving strong emotions: *She's very emotional.* | *an emotional scene in a movie*

emperor /ˈɛmpərɚ/ [*noun*] a very powerful king who rules one country or a lot of countries: *the emperor of Japan* | *an ancient Roman emperor*

emphasis T /ˈɛmfəsɪs/ [*noun*] special importance that is given to something you do or say: *He put great emphasis on the need for a good education.*

emphasize * T /ˈɛmfəˌsaɪz/ [*verb;* **emphasized, emphasizing**] to give special or additional importance to something, or to make people notice it: *Our teacher emphasizes correct grammar.*

empire /ˈɛmpaɪr/ [*noun*] a group of countries that is ruled by one person or one government: *the British Empire*

employ * /ɛmˈplɔɪ/ [*verb;* **employs, employed, employing**] to pay someone to work for you: *We employ 30 people.*

employee /ɛmˈplɔɪi/ [*noun;* plural **employees**] someone who works for a company or person: *a company with over 1000 employees*

employer * /ɛmˈplɔɪɚ/ [*noun*] a company or person that employs someone: *Our company is the biggest local employer.*

employment * /ɛmˈplɔɪmənt/ [*noun*] paid work: *She looked for employment as a journalist.*

empress /ˈɛmprɪs/ [*noun;* **empresses**] a powerful queen who rules a country or a lot of countries, or the wife of an emperor: *the Empress Josephine*

empty[1] * /ˈɛmpti/ [*adjective; no comparative*] something that is empty

He's happy.   He's angry.   He's sad.
He's smiling. He's frowning. He's crying.

emotions

has nothing or no one in it; *opposite*
FULL: *an empty box* | *The room was empty.*

empty[2] * [*verb;* **empties, emptied,
emptying**] to make something empty
or to become empty: *Please* **empty out**
the wastebasket. | *When the bell rang, the
classroom emptied.*

enable /ɛnˈeɪbəl/ [*verb;* **enabled,
enabling**] to make it possible for
someone to do something: **enable
someone to do something** ▶ *The money
will enable him to buy a truck.*

enclose * /ɛnˈkloʊz/ [*verb;* **enclosed,
enclosing**]
1 to send something with a letter: *I've
enclosed some pictures of our new house.*
2 to surround something: *The yard was
enclosed by a wooden fence.*

encourage * ⊤ /ɛnˈkɜrɪdʒ/ [*verb;*
encouraged, encouraging] to make
someone feel more confident or hopeful
about doing something; *opposite*
DISCOURAGE: **encourage someone to do
something** ▶ *His parents encouraged him
to learn the piano.*

encouraged * /ɛnˈkɜrɪdʒd/ [*adjective;*
more encouraged, most encouraged]
confident or hopeful about something;
opposite DISCOURAGED: *The team felt more
encouraged after winning some games.*

encouragement /ɛnˈkɜrɪdʒmənt/
[*noun*] when someone is made to feel
more confident or hopeful about
something: *My parents* **gave me** *a lot of
encouragement.*

encouraging /ɛnˈkɜrɪdʒɪŋ/ [*adjective;*
more encouraging, most encouraging]
making someone feel more confident or
hopeful; *opposite* DISCOURAGING: *This is
encouraging news.*

encyclopedia ⊤ /ɛnˌsaɪkləˈpidiə/ [*noun;*
plural encyclopedias] a book that
contains facts about many different
subjects or about a particular subject: *I
looked up "airplanes" in an encyclopedia.*
| *an encyclopedia of horses*

end[1] * /ɛnd/ [*noun*]
1 the last part of something; *opposites*
BEGINNING, START: *I left Mexico* **at the
end** *of 1997.* | *The author's name was
given* **at the end** *of the article.* | *The
assignment must be done* **by the end** *of*

the week (=no later than the last day of
the week).
⟳ Compare FINISH[2].
2 the part of something where it stops:
They sat at each **end of** *the bench.*

━ **PHRASE** ━
3 **in the end** finally, or after you have
thought about something carefully: *In
the end I decided to study chemistry.*

end[2] * [*verb;* **ended, ending**] to stop
happening, or to make something stop
happening; *opposite* START: *The
discussion* **ended in** *a fight.* | *A big dance
number ended the show.*

ending /ˈɛndɪŋ/ [*noun*] the last part of a
book, play, or movie: *a happy ending*

endless /ˈɛndlɪs/ [*adjective; no
comparative*] continuing or seeming to
continue for a very long time: *They have
endless discussions.*

enemy * /ˈɛnəmi/ [*noun; plural* **enemies**]
1 the country or group you are fighting
in a war: *Their enemies had gained
control of the city.*
2 someone who does not like you and
tries to harm you: *My enemies are
spreading lies about me.*

energetic ⊤ /ˌɛnərˈdʒɛtɪk/ [*adjective;*
more energetic, most energetic]
having a lot of energy and always very
active: *He's an energetic teacher.*

energy * /ˈɛnərdʒi/ [*noun*]
1 the strength to do physical activities
or hard work: *Grandfather still has a lot
of energy.* | *I feel full of energy.*
2 a form of power, such as heat or
electricity: *solar energy* (=from the sun)

engaged /ɛnˈgeɪdʒd/ [*adjective; no
comparative*] having officially promised
to marry someone: *She's* **engaged to** *my
cousin.*

engagement /ɛnˈgeɪdʒmənt/ [*noun*]
1 an official agreement that you will
marry someone, or the period of time

/i/ **see**	/ɪ/ **big**	/eɪ/ **day**	/ɛ/ **get**	/æ/ **hat**
/ɑ/ **father, hot**	/ʌ/ **up**	/ə/ **about**	/ɔ/ **saw**
/oʊ/ **hope**	/ʊ/ **book**	/u/ **too**	/aɪ/ **I**	/aʊ/ **how**
/ɔɪ/ **boy**	/ɝ/ **bird**	/ɚ/ **teacher**	/ɪr/ **ear**	/ɛr/ **air**
/ɑr/ **far**	/ɔr/ **more**	/ʊr/ **tour**	/aɪr/ **fire**
/aʊɚ/ **hour**	/θ/ **nothing**	/ð/ **mother**	/ʃ/ **she**
/ʒ/ **measure**	/tʃ/ **church**	/dʒ/ **jump**	/ŋ/ **long**

the agreement lasts: *They announced their engagement.*
2 FORMAL an arrangement to see someone or do something: *I have a dinner engagement.*

engine * /'ɛndʒən/ [*noun*] the part of a vehicle or large machine that produces the power to make it move or work: *Something's wrong with my car's engine.*

engineer * T /ˌɛndʒə'nɪr/ [*noun*]
1 someone who designs, builds, or fixes machines, vehicles, or large structures such as bridges: *She's an engineer for a car company.* | *an electrical engineer*
2 someone who drives a train

engineering /ˌɛndʒə'nɪrɪŋ/ [*noun*] the profession or activity of designing and building machines, vehicles, or large structures such as bridges

England /'ɪŋglənd/ [*name*] a country in the south of Great Britain

English[1] * /'ɪŋglɪʃ/ [*noun*] the official language of the United States, Canada, Britain, Australia, and some other countries: *I am studying English.* | *The book is only available in English.*

USAGE   English

The language spoken in the U.S., the U.K., Australia, Canada, and many other countries is **English**. The way English is spoken in the U.S., the U.K., etc., is sometimes different, so it is sometimes called **American English, British English,** etc.

English[2] * [*adjective; no comparative*] relating to the English language: *English spelling can be very difficult.*

enjoy * /ɛn'dʒɔɪ/ [*verb; enjoys, enjoyed, enjoying*]
1 to get pleasure from doing something or experiencing something; synonym LIKE: **enjoy doing something** ▸ *I enjoy playing tennis.* | *She enjoyed the book.*
━━ PHRASE ━━
2 **enjoy yourself** to have a good time: *I hope you are all enjoying yourselves.*

enjoyable * /ɛn'dʒɔɪəbəl/ [*adjective; more enjoyable, most enjoyable*] giving you a lot of pleasure: *We had a very enjoyable day.*

enjoyment * /ɛn'dʒɔɪmənt/ [*noun*] pleasure that you get from doing or experiencing something: *Our enjoyment of the play was spoiled by people talking.*

enlarge /ɛn'lardʒ/ [*verb; enlarged, enlarging*] to make something bigger: *We're planning to enlarge the school.*

enormous T /ɪ'nɔrməs/ [*adjective; more enormous, most enormous*] extremely large or great; synonym HUGE: *The new airport will cost an enormous amount of money.* | *an enormous task*

enough[1] * /ɪ'nʌf/ [*determiner, pronoun*] as much as is needed, or as many as are needed: *We don't have enough chairs for everyone.* | **enough . . . to do something** ▸ *There is enough time to go shopping.* | *Did you get enough to eat?*

SYNONYMS   enough, sufficient, plenty

If you have **enough** of something, you have all of it that you need: *We had enough gas to drive home.* **Sufficient** means the same as **enough**, but is formal: *We did not have sufficient funds to complete the project.* If you have **plenty of** something, you have enough of it and more: *There's plenty of rice left.*

---

enough[2] * [*adverb*] to as great a degree as is needed: *You aren't working hard enough!* | *I don't think those shoes are big enough for you.*
☞ Use the adverb **enough** after an adjective, adverb, or verb, not before it.

enroll /ɛn'roʊl/ [*verb; enrolled, enrolling*] to join or arrange for someone to join a course, school, or group: *I enrolled in an art class.* | *They enrolled their son in a private school.*

enrollment /ɛn'roʊlmənt/ [*noun*] when people can join a course, school, or group: *Enrollment takes place on Monday.*

enter * /'ɛntər/ [*verb; entered, entering*]
1 to go into a place: *Everyone stood up when he entered the room.* | *Please knock before you enter.*
2 FORMAL to become a member of a profession, a school, etc.: *He entered the medical profession in 1984.*
3 to take part in a competition or race, or arrange for someone or something

to be in it: *Three hundred people entered the contest.* | *She entered a poem in the literature competition.*

4 to put information on a list or record, or into a computer: **enter something on/in/into something** ▸ *The data is then entered into our database.*

entertain * /ˌɛntɚ'teɪn/ [verb; entertained, entertaining]
1 to amuse or interest someone by saying or doing something: *He entertained everyone with his stories.*
2 to have guests and give them food and drinks: *We entertain often.*

entertainer /ˌɛntɚ'teɪnɚ/ [noun] someone who sings songs, tells jokes, or performs in some other way

entertaining /ˌɛntɚ'teɪnɪŋ/ [adjective; more entertaining, most entertaining] funny and interesting: *an entertaining story*

entertainment * T /ˌɛntɚ'teɪnmənt/ [noun] performances or other activities intended to amuse or interest people: *Who will organize the entertainment?*

enthusiasm /ɛn'θuzi,æzəm/ [noun] a feeling of really wanting to do something and considering it to be very enjoyable, interesting, important, etc.: *The crowd showed great enthusiasm for the singer.*

enthusiastic /ɛn,θuzi'æstɪk/ [adjective; more enthusiastic, most enthusiastic] showing a lot of interest and excitement about something: *We are looking for enthusiastic volunteers.*

entire /ɛn'taɪr/ [adjective; no comparative] every part of something; synonym WHOLE: *I spent the entire day reading.* | *He ate the entire pie.*

entirely /ɛn'taɪrli/ [adverb] completely: *It was entirely my fault.*

entitle /ɛn'taɪtəl/ [verb; entitled, entitling] to give someone a right to have or do something: **be entitled to something** ▸ *He's entitled to a fair trial.*

entrance * /'ɛntrəns/ [noun]
1 a door or way into a place: *She waited for me at the entrance to the park.*
2 the right or opportunity to enter a place; synonym ENTRY: *He was denied entrance to the club.*

entry /'ɛntri/ [noun; plural entries]
1 the right or opportunity to enter a place; synonym ENTRANCE: *They were refused entry.*
2 what someone writes or produces to take part in a competition: *The winning entry came from someone in Chicago.*

envelope * /'ɛnvə,loʊp/ [noun] a paper cover in which a letter is sent: *He sealed the envelope and put a stamp on it.*

envious /'ɛnviəs/ [adjective; more envious, most envious] unhappy because you do not have something that someone else has; synonym JEALOUS: *He was envious of his friend.*

environment * T /ɛn'vaɪrənmənt/ [noun]
1 the natural world, for example the land, ocean, and living things: *Pollution is bad for the environment.*
2 the situation or conditions that a person or animal is in: *a good working environment*

environmental /ɛn,vaɪrən'mɛntəl/ [adjective; no comparative] relating to the natural world: *environmental laws* (=for protecting the environment)

envy[1] /'ɛnvi/ [noun] the unhappy feeling you have when you wish you had what someone else has; synonym JEALOUSY: *She looked at Carla's new dress with envy.*

envy[2] [verb; envies, envied, envying] to wish you had what someone else has: *It's hard not to envy someone who is so successful.*

enzyme /'ɛnzaɪm/ [noun] a substance produced by animal or plant cells that causes a chemical change: *Digestive juices contain enzymes that break down food.*

epidemic /ˌɛpɪ'dɛmɪk/ [noun] when a disease spreads very quickly to a lot of people: *a flu epidemic*

/i/ **see**	/ɪ/ **big**	/eɪ/ **day**	/ɛ/ **get**	/æ/ **hat**	
/a/ **father, hot**	/ʌ/ **up**	/ə/ **about**	/ɔ/ **saw**		
/oʊ/ **hope**	/ʊ/ **book**	/u/ **too**	/aɪ/ **I**	/aʊ/ **how**	
/ɔɪ/ **boy**	/ɚ/ **bird**	/ə/ **teacher**	/ɪr/ **ear**	/ɛr/ **air**	
/ɑr/ **far**	/ɔr/ **more**	/ʊr/ **tour**	/aɪr/ **fire**		
/aʊɚ/ **hour**	/θ/ **nothing**	/ð/ **mother**	/ʃ/ **she**		
/ʒ/ **measure**	/tʃ/ **church**	/dʒ/ **jump**	/ŋ/ **long**		

equal[1] * [T] /'ikwəl/ [adjective; no comparative] the same size, rank, etc.: Give the dogs equal amounts of food. | One quart is **equal to** 32 ounces.

equal[2] * [T] [noun] if you are someone's equal, you are as good as he or she is: He treats all his workers as equals.

equal[3] * [verb; equaled, equaling]
1 to be the same amount as: Two plus two equals four.
2 to achieve the same thing, or do as well as someone or something else: We are hoping to equal the amount of money we raised last year.

equality /ɪ'kwɑlɪti/ [noun] when everyone in a society is treated the same and has the same rights: All citizens have equality under the law.

equally * /'ikwəli/ [adverb]
1 in amounts of the same size: His wealth was divided equally among his children.
2 used to say that two or more things have the same amount of a quality: The two methods work equally well.
☞ Do not say "equally as well." Say equally well.

equal sign or **equals sign** /'ikwəl ˌsaɪn/ [noun] the sign (=) which shows that two amounts are the same, as in 5 + 6 = 11

equation /ɪ'kweɪʒən/ [noun] a mathematical statement that two amounts are equal: *Solve the equation* $6x + 52 = 64$ (=work out what x represents).
☼ See the picture at CLASSROOM.

equator /ɪ'kweɪtɚ/ [noun] the imaginary line around the middle of the earth, through the hottest parts of the world

equip /ɪ'kwɪp/ [verb; equips, equipped, equipping] to provide tools and other things that someone needs: **be equipped with something** ▸ The lab is equipped with all the latest technology.

equipment * /ɪ'kwɪpmənt/ [noun] tools, machines, or other things that you need in order to do something: camping equipment | electrical equipment

ER /'i'ɑr/ emergency room; the part of a hospital where people who need treatment quickly are dealt with: I went to the ER when I broke my ankle.

era /'ɪrə/ [noun; plural eras] a long period of time in history: the modern era

erase /ɪ'reɪs/ [verb; erased, erasing] to remove something, especially something written or drawn in pencil or chalk: She erased her answer and wrote in the right one.

eraser /ɪ'reɪsɚ/ [noun] something that removes pencil or chalk marks

errand /'ɛrənd/ [noun] a short trip you make in order to do something, for example to take a message to someone or buy something: I **ran some errands** (=did some errands) for my mother.

error /'ɛrɚ/ [noun] a mistake or something that has been done wrong: Your essay is full of spelling errors.

erupt /ɪ'rʌpt/ [verb; erupted, erupting] if a volcano erupts, hot rock and ash come out of it: No one is sure when the volcano will erupt next.

escalator /'ɛskəˌleɪtɚ/ [noun] a set of metal stairs that moves continuously up or down: The escalator isn't working.

escape[1] * /ɪ'skeɪp/ [verb; escaped, escaping] to manage to leave a place where you are being kept or are trapped: Three prisoners escaped. | They escaped from the burning building.

escape[2] * [noun] when you manage to leave a place you do not want to be in: He spent months planning his escape.

escort[1] /ɪ'skɔrt/ [verb; escorted, escorting] FORMAL to go with someone to guard, protect, or help him or her: **escort someone somewhere** ▸ Let me escort you to your car.

escort[2] /'ɛskɔrt/ [noun] a person or group of people going with someone to guard, protect, or help him or her: The president always has a security escort.

ESL /'iˌɛs'ɛl/ [noun] English as a Second Language; the teaching of English to people in the U.S. whose first language is not English: She's an ESL teacher in Chicago. | an ESL dictionary

especially * /ɪ'spɛʃəli/ [adverb] more than other people or things, or more than in other situations: I love animals, *especially horses.* | *I am especially interested in working with children.*

essay /ˈeseɪ/ [*noun; plural* **essays**] a short piece of writing about a particular subject, especially done as school work: *Your essays are due on Friday.*

essential ⊤ /əˈsenʃəl/ [*adjective; more essential, most essential*] completely necessary: *A quiet office is **essential for my work**.*

establish ✶ ⊤ /ɪˈstæblɪʃ/ [*verb; establishes, established, establishing*]
1 to start something such as a school, a company, or a new way of doing things: *The business was established in 1878.*
2 to find out or show something: *We have **established that** the drug is safe.*

estate /ɪˈsteɪt/ [*noun*] a large house with land surrounding it, owned by a rich person: *a country estate*

estimate[1] ⊤ /ˈestəˌmeɪt/ [*verb; estimated, estimating*] to guess what the size or amount of something is: *Try to estimate how tall the building is.*

estimate[2] ⊤ /ˈestəmɪt/ [*noun*] an amount or figure that you guess, but do not know exactly: *You'll need **an estimate of** how much the trip will cost.*

etc. /et ˈsetərə/ an abbreviation meaning "and other things of the same kind": *a shop selling hats, scarves, etc.*

ethnic ⊤ /ˈeθnɪk/ [*adjective; no comparative*] relating to someone's race or home country: *people from different ethnic groups*

Europe ✶ /ˈyʊrəp/ [*name*] the large area of land between the Atlantic Ocean and Asia, north of Africa

European[1] ✶ /ˌyʊrəˈpiən/ [*noun*] someone who comes from Europe: *She had not met many Europeans before.*

European[2] ✶ [*adjective; no comparative*] belonging to, from, or relating to Europe: *a meeting of European leaders*

evacuate /ɪˈvækyuˌeɪt/ [*verb; evacuated, evacuating*] to move people out of a dangerous area: *The town has been evacuated.*

evaporate ⊤ /ɪˈvæpəˌreɪt/ [*verb; evaporated, evaporating*] if a liquid

evaporates, it disappears into the air: *The spilled gasoline quickly evaporated.*

eve /iv/ [*noun*] the day before a special day or event, especially the end of that day: *Everyone was nervous **on the eve of** the election.* | *New Year's Eve*

even[1] ✶ ⊤ /ˈivən/ [*adverb*]
1 used before you mention something surprising that is included: *Even my cat liked him.* | *I liked everything about the town, even the noise.*
2 used to talk about something that is more than something else that is already big, fast, good, etc.: *Even more people now watch the show.* | *This new software works even faster.*
━ PHRASE ━
3 even if used to say that something that may happen will not affect a situation: *Even if we win this game, we can't win the tournament.*

even[2] ✶ ⊤ [*adjective; more even, most even*]
1 at the same level everywhere, or the same level as something else: *The hem of your dress isn't even.* | *Please cut my hair even with my chin.*
2 not changing; *synonym* STEADY: *Store the wine at an even temperature.*
3 an even number is one that can be divided by two; *opposite* ODD: *Six is an even number.*
4 not owing someone money any longer: *I bought dinner, so that makes us even.*
━ PHRASE ━
5 get even with to do something to harm someone who has harmed you: *One day I'll get even with him.*

even[3] [*verb; evened, evening*]
━ PHRASAL VERBS ━
even out [*phrasal verb*]
1 to become or make something the same in all parts: **even something out** ▸ *My bangs need to be evened out.* | *We need one more player to even the*

/i/ **see**	/ɪ/ **big**	/eɪ/ **day**	/ɛ/ **get**	/æ/ **hat**
/ɑ/ **father, hot**	/ʌ/ **up**	/ə/ **about**	/ɔ/ **saw**
/oʊ/ **hope**	/ʊ/ **book**	/u/ **too**	/aɪ/ **I**	/aʊ/ **how**
/ɔɪ/ **boy**	/ɝ/ **bird**	/ɪr/ **teacher**	/ɪr/ **ear**	/ɛr/ **air**
/ɑr/ **far**	/ɔr/ **more**	/ʊr/ **tour**	/aɪr/ **fire**
/aʊɚ/ **hour**	/θ/ **nothing**	/ð/ **mother**	/ʃ/ **she**
/ʒ/ **measure**	/tʃ/ **church**	/dʒ/ **jump**	/ŋ/ **long**

teams out (=so that each has the same number of players).

even up [phrasal verb]
2 to make something equal: *Our team has evened up the score.*

evening * /'ivnɪŋ/ [noun] the part of the day between the afternoon and the night: *Let's see a movie this evening.* | *They go bowling on Friday evenings.*
☛ Do not say "at evening." Say **in the evening**.

evenly /'ivənli/ [adverb] so that each part of a number or amount is the same: *She divided the candy evenly among the children.*

event * ⊤ /ɪ'vɛnt/ [noun]
1 something that happens: *The events of the past week have shocked everyone.*
— PHRASE —
2 in the event of something if something happens: *In the event of a fire, leave your room immediately.*

eventually ⊤ /ɪ'vɛntʃuəli/ [adverb] after a long time: *We got lost, but eventually we found the hotel.*

ever * /'ɛvɚ/ [adverb]
1 at any time: *Have you ever been to Shanghai?* | *I don't think I will ever forget her.*
☛ Only use **ever** in questions, and in sentences with a negative.
— PHRASE —
2 ever since for all the time since a particular time: *I've wanted to be an actor ever since I was a young.*

evergreen /'ɛvɚˌgrin/ [noun] a tree or bush that keeps its leaves all through the year: *Fir trees are evergreens.*

every * /'ɛvri/ [determiner] all the things or people in a group: *She comes to see me every day.* | *Every letter needs to be checked before it is sent out.*
☛ Only use a singular noun after **every**, not a plural noun.
☛ Do not say "every of them." Say **each of them**.
⇨ See the usage note at EACH[1].

everybody /'ɛvriˌbadi/ [pronoun] all the people in a group; synonym EVERYONE: *Everybody in my family is good at music.*
☛ Only use **everybody** with a singular verb.

everyday /'ɛvriˌdeɪ/ [adjective; no comparative] ordinary and usual: *The corner drugstore sells everyday items.*
☛ Only use **everyday** before a noun. Also, do not confuse **everyday** with **every day. Every day** means "each day."

everyone * /'ɛvriˌwʌn/ [pronoun] all the people in a group; synonym EVERYBODY: *Everyone was sorry to see him leave.*
☛ Only use **everyone** with a singular verb.

everything * /'ɛvriˌθɪŋ/ [pronoun] all the things in a group: *Do you have everything you need?*
☛ Only use **everything** with a singular verb.

everywhere * /'ɛvriˌwɛr/ [adverb] in all places: *I've looked everywhere for my pen.* | *Everywhere he went, people stared at him.*
☛ Do not say "to everywhere" or "in everywhere."

evidence ⊤ /'ɛvɪdəns/ [noun] something that shows that something happened or is true: *There's evidence that he cheated.*

evil * /'ivəl/ [adjective; **more evil, most evil**] morally bad; synonym WICKED: *He thought up an evil plan.* | *an evil spirit*

evolution /ˌɛvə'luʃən/ [noun] the way that living things in the present time have developed from living things in the past

exact * /ɪg'zækt/ [adjective; **more exact, most exact**] completely correct in every detail; synonym ACCURATE; opposite APPROXIMATE: *I can't give you an exact figure.*

exactly * /ɪg'zæktli/ [adverb]
1 not more and not less, not later and not earlier, etc.; opposite APPROXIMATELY: *It's five o'clock exactly.*
2 with nothing more or less than all the details; opposite ROUGHLY: *Tell me exactly what happened.*
3 without any difference: *She looks exactly like my cousin.*
4 SPOKEN used to say you completely agree with what someone has said: *"We should have worked out a schedule first." "Exactly."*

exaggerate ⊤ /ɪg'zædʒəˌreɪt/ [verb; **exaggerated, exaggerating**] to say that something is bigger, better, worse, etc., than it really is: *I think he's exaggerating the problem.*

exaggeration /ɪɡˌzædʒəˈreɪʃən/ [*noun*] a statement saying that something is bigger, better, worse, etc., than it really is: *It would be an exaggeration to call it a disaster.*

exam * /ɪɡˈzæm/ [*noun*] an important test to find out how well a student knows a subject; *synonym* EXAMINATION: *I passed my history exam.* | *She's **taking** two exams today.*

examination * /ɪɡˌzæməˈneɪʃən/ [*noun*] **1** a careful and thorough look at something: *The doctor **carried out an examination** of the patient.*
2 FORMAL an important test to find out how well a student knows a subject; *synonym* EXAM: *She passed all her examinations.*

examine * ⊤ /ɪɡˈzæmɪn/ [*verb;* examined, examining] to look at something carefully: *He examined the picture to see if it was genuine.*

example * /ɪɡˈzæmpəl/ [*noun*] **1** one thing of a particular type, that shows what the type is like: *This is a very fine **example of** his work.* | *Can you **give me an example**?*
— PHRASE —
2 for example used to show you are giving an example: *Many animals, for example bats, hunt at night.*
↪ *See also* E.G. *and* **for instance** *at* INSTANCE.

exceed /ɪkˈsid/ [*verb;* exceeded, exceeding] to be bigger, better, or more than something else: *The number of students in the school exceeds 800.*

excellent * /ˈɛksələnt/ [*adjective; no comparative*] extremely good; *synonym* SUPERB: *We had an excellent meal at the hotel.* | *His English is excellent.*

except * ⊤ /ɪkˈsɛpt/ [*preposition, conjunction*] used to say that someone or something is not included in what you are saying; *synonym* BUT: *Everyone except Thomas had gone home.* | *We had nothing to do except read and play cards.* | *The room was empty except for a chair.*

exception /ɪkˈsɛpʃən/ [*noun*] someone or something that is not included in what you say: *I want you all in bed by ten—**no exceptions**!* | *Everyone, **with the exception of** Lisa, was there* (=Lisa was the only person not there).

exceptional /ɪkˈsɛpʃənəl/ [*adjective; more exceptional, most exceptional*] **1** extremely and unusually good: *His work is exceptional.*
2 unusual or extreme: *They were sent home because of the exceptional heat.*

exceptionally /ɪkˈsɛpʃənəli/ [*adverb*] extremely and unusually: *She is exceptionally good at art.*

excess[1] /ˈɛksɛs/ [*adjective; no comparative*] too much: *The airline charges you for excess baggage.*
☛ Only use **excess** before a noun.

excess[2] /ɪkˈsɛs; ˈɛksɛs/ [*noun*]
— PHRASE —
in excess of more than: *There are in excess of a million kinds of beetles.*

excessive ⊤ /ɪkˈsɛsɪv/ [*adjective; no comparative*] too much: *He watches an excessive amount of television.*

exchange[1] * /ɪksˈtʃeɪndʒ/ [*verb;* exchanged, exchanging] to give something to someone and get something similar back: *She **exchanged** the shirt **for** a smaller one.* | *They exchanged addresses.*

exchange[2] * [*noun*] **1** when something is given and a similar thing is given back: *At the end of the war there was an **exchange of** prisoners.*
— PHRASE —
2 in exchange for in return for something you give someone: *I got a sweater in exchange for this blouse.*

exchange rate /ɪksˈtʃeɪndʒ ˌreɪt/ [*noun*] the amount of one country's money that you get for an amount of another

---

/i/ **see** /ɪ/ **big** /eɪ/ **day** /ɛ/ **get** /æ/ **hat** /ɑ/ **father, hot** /ʌ/ **up** /ə/ **about** /ɔ/ **saw** /oʊ/ **hope** /ʊ/ **book** /u/ **too** /aɪ/ **I** /aʊ/ **how** /ɔɪ/ **boy** /ɚ/ **bird** /ɚ/ **teacher** /ɪr/ **ear** /ɛr/ **air** /ɑr/ **far** /ɔr/ **more** /ʊr/ **tour** /aɪr/ **fire** /aʊɚ/ **hour** /θ/ **nothing** /ð/ **mother** /ʃ/ **she** /ʒ/ **measure** /tʃ/ **church** /dʒ/ **jump** /ŋ/ **long**

country's money: *The exchange rate is eight Chinese yuan to the dollar.*

excite * /ɪkˈsaɪt/ [*verb;* **excited, exciting**] to make someone feel eager and happy: *The thought of a trip to the mountains excited him.*

excited * /ɪkˈsaɪtɪd/ [*adjective;* **more excited, most excited**] eager and happy about something: *She seemed very excited about the news.*

excitement * /ɪkˈsaɪtmənt/ [*noun*] an excited feeling: *Her face was glowing with excitement.*

exciting * /ɪkˈsaɪtɪŋ/ [*adjective;* **more exciting, most exciting**] making you feel eager and happy: *an exciting game | an exciting opportunity*

exclaim /ˌɪkˈskleɪm/ [*verb;* **exclaimed, exclaiming**] to suddenly say something when you are excited, surprised, or angry: *"Don't go!" Leo exclaimed.*

exclamation point /ˌɛkskləˈmeɪʃən ˌpɔɪnt/ [*noun*] a mark used in writing. It looks like this: !
▷ *See* Punctuation *in the Smart Study section.*

exclude ⊤ /ɪkˈsklud/ [*verb;* **excluded, excluding**] to not include someone or something, or not allow someone into a place; *opposite* INCLUDE: **exclude someone/something from something** ► | *Don't exclude her from the conversation.*

excluding /ɪkˈskludɪŋ/ [*preposition*] used to say that something is not included in what you say: *It costs $84, excluding tax.*

exclusive ⊤ /ɪkˈsklusɪv/ [*adjective;* **more exclusive, most exclusive**]
1 used only by rich people: *He stayed at an exclusive hotel.*
2 only allowing a limited number of people to join or take part: *an exclusive sports club*

excuse¹ * /ɪkˈskyuz/ [*verb;* **excused, excusing**]
1 to forgive or to give a good reason for something bad that someone has done: *She excused his rudeness.*
2 to allow someone to leave a place or to not do something: **be excused from something** ► *She was excused from classes for two weeks.*

— PHRASE —
3 excuse me SPOKEN
a used to get someone's attention: *Excuse me—is this the way to the park?*
b used to say politely that you are sorry for doing something that is slightly wrong or not polite, or that may annoy someone: *Oh, excuse me, I didn't realize this room was being used.*
▷ *See the usage note at* APOLOGIZE.
c used to ask someone politely to repeat something: *Excuse me, did you say "fifteen" or "fifty"?*

excuse² /ɪkˈskyus/ [*noun*]
1 a reason that you give for doing something wrong or bad, which is often not true or not good enough: *He always makes excuses for being late.*
▷ *See the synonym note at* REASON.
— PHRASE —
2 no excuse not a good reason: *There's no excuse for cheating on a test.*

execute /ˈɛksɪˌkyut/ [*verb;* **executed, executing**] to kill someone as an official punishment for a crime: *The murderer will be executed tomorrow.*

execution /ˌɛksɪˈkyuʃən/ [*noun*] the killing of someone as an official punishment for a crime: *There have been four executions in this state this year.*

exercise¹ * /ˈɛksɚˌsaɪz/ [*noun*]
1 physical activity that makes your body stronger and healthier: *You need to get more exercise. | I do exercises every morning.*
2 something you do as practice or in order to learn something: *a book of English exercises*

exercise² * [*verb;* **exercised, exercising**] to run, walk, swim, dance, etc., in order to make your body stronger and healthier: *We should exercise regularly.*

exhaust¹ ⊤ /ɪgˈzɔst/ [*verb;* **exhausted, exhausting**] to make someone very tired: *The long climb exhausted her.*

exhaust² [*noun*] the gases that come out of the back of a car, or the pipe they come out of

exhausted /ɪgˈzɔstɪd/ [*adjective;* **more exhausted, most exhausted**] extremely tired: *He was so exhausted he fell asleep immediately.*

exhausting /ɪɡ'zɔstɪŋ/ [*adjective;* **more exhausting, most exhausting**] making you very tired: *Getting ready for the wedding was exhausting.*

exhibit[1] T /ɪɡ'zɪbɪt/ [*verb;* **exhibited, exhibiting**] to show things such as paintings to the public: *Her pictures have been exhibited all over the world.*

exhibit[2] T [*noun*] a collection of things such as paintings that are being shown to the public: *Have you been to the Monet exhibit yet?*

exile[1] /'ɛɡzaɪl/ [*verb;* **exiled, exiling**] to force someone to live in a foreign country: *He was **exiled from** his country five years ago.*

exile[2] [*noun*] when someone is forced to live in a foreign country: *She is now **living in exile**.*

exist ✲ /ɪɡ'zɪst/ [*verb;* **existed, existing**]
1 to be real and not just imagined by someone: *Do you think ghosts really exist? | Poverty exists everywhere.*
2 to live: *We couldn't exist without water.*

existence ✲ T /ɪɡ'zɪstəns/ [*noun*] when something is real and present in the world: *It is the oldest building still **in existence** (=still existing).*

existing /ɛɡ'zɪstɪŋ/ [*adjective; no comparative*] being real or present now: *A new library will replace the existing one.*
☛ Only use **existing** before a noun.

exit T /'ɛɡzɪt/ [*noun*] a way out of a building or enclosed area: *Please go to the nearest exit.*

expand T /ɪk'spænd/ [*verb;* **expanded, expanding**] to become bigger or make something bigger: *We want to expand our business.*

expect ✲ /ɪk'spɛkt/ [*verb;* **expected, expecting**]
1 to think that something will happen or will be true: *I'm expecting a phone call. | I **expect that** they'll be tired when they get here. | **be expected to do something** ▸ The movie is expected to be very popular.*
2 to think strongly that someone should do something: **be expected to do something** ▸ *We are expected to arrive early every day. | I **expect better***

of you (=think you should behave better than you did).
═ PHRASE ═
3 be expecting (a baby) to be going to have a baby: *She's expecting in May.*

expedition /ˌɛkspɪ'dɪʃən/ [*noun*] a trip to a place that is unknown or difficult to get to: *He and four other people are **going on an expedition to** the Antarctic.*

expel /ɪk'spɛl/ [*verb;* **expels, expelled, expelling**] to force someone to leave a school, club, country, etc: *He was **expelled from** school for fighting.*

expense T /ɪk'spɛns/ [*noun*] money that you spend on something: *Please keep a record of your expenses.*

expensive ✲ T /ɪk'spɛnsɪv/ [*adjective;* **more expensive, most expensive**] costing a lot of money: *Those shoes are too expensive.*
☛ Do not say "The price of this watch is too expensive." Say **This watch is too expensive.**

experience[1] ✲ /ɪk'spɪriəns/ [*noun*]
1 something that happens to you: *Flying in a helicopter was an amazing experience.*
2 knowledge of something that you get from having done it a lot: *We need someone with experience for this job. | I don't have much **experience in** dealing with children.*

experience[2] ✲ T [*verb;* **experienced, experiencing**] to have something happen to you: *He experienced sudden nausea.*

experienced /ɪk'spɪriənst/ [*adjective;* **more experienced, most experienced**] having done a job or activity a lot, and therefore being good at it; *opposite* INEXPERIENCED: *an experienced pilot*

experiment[1] /ɪk'spɛrəmənt/ [*noun*] a formal test that is done, especially by a scientist, to find out something: *a*

/i/ see	/ɪ/ big	/eɪ/ day	/ɛ/ get	/æ/ hat
/ɑ/ father, hot	/ʌ/ up	/ə/ about	/ɔ/ saw	
/oʊ/ hope	/ʊ/ book	/u/ too	/aɪ/ I	/aʊ/ how
/ɔɪ/ boy	/ɝ/ bird	/ɚ/ teacher	/ɪr/ ear	/ɛr/ air
/ɑr/ far	/ɔr/ more	/ʊr/ tour	/aɪr/ fire	
/aʊɚ/ hour	/θ/ nothing	/ð/ mother	/ʃ/ she	
/ʒ/ measure	/tʃ/ church	/dʒ/ jump	/ŋ/ long	

medical experiment I *They* **conducted an experiment** (=did an experiment).

experiment[2] /ɪk'spɛrəˌmɛnt/ [*verb;* **experimented, experimenting**] to do something in order to discover more about it or to see if something will work: *Scientists often* **experiment on** *animals* (=use animals in their experiments).

expert[1] /'ɛkspɚt/ [*noun*] someone who knows a lot about a particular subject: *We need a computer* **expert** *to fix this problem.* I *an* **expert in** *physics*

expert[2] [*adjective; no comparative*] knowing a lot about something, or coming from someone who knows a lot: *an* **expert** *painter* I **expert** *advice*

expire /ɪk'spaɪr/ [*verb;* **expired, expiring**] to not be able to be used after a particular date: *My visa will* **expire** *in November.*

explain * T /ɪk'spleɪn/ [*verb;* **explained, explaining**] to tell someone about something, or say why something happened: **explain something to someone** ▸ *He* **explained** *his plan* **to** *her.* I *Could you* **explain** *how it works?* I *I tried to* **explain** *why I was late.* I *She* **explained** *that she had lost her keys.*
☛ Do not say that someone "explained me the meaning of this poem." Say that he or she **explained the meaning of the poem to me**.

explanation * /ˌɛksplə'neɪʃən/ [*noun*] when something is explained or can be explained: *Did he give any* **explanation for** *why he left?* I *Thank you for that clear* **explanation**.
↪ *See the synonym note at* **REASON**.

explode * /ɪk'sploʊd/ [*verb;* **exploded, exploding**] to burst with a very strong force, usually causing a lot of damage: *The bomb* **exploded**, *destroying the building.* I *The car* **exploded** *in flames.*
↪ *See also* **blow up** *at* **BLOW**[1] (definition 9).

exploration /ˌɛksplə'reɪʃən/ [*noun*] when you go to a place to learn more about it: *an* **exploration** *of the cave* I *space* **exploration**

explore /ɪk'splɔr/ [*verb;* **explored, exploring**] to go all around a place to

find out what is there: *We* **explored** *the city during the week we were there.*

explorer /ɪk'splɔrɚ/ [*noun*] someone who goes into an unknown area of the world to find out what is there: *Antarctic* **explorers**

explosion * /ɪk'sploʊʒən/ [*noun*] when something bursts apart with a very strong force, usually causing damage: *A huge* **explosion** *destroyed the house.*

explosive[1] * /ɪk'sploʊsɪv/ [*adjective, no comparative*] able to cause an explosion: *an* **explosive** *device*

explosive[2] * [*noun*] a substance that can cause an explosion: **Explosives** *were used to break apart the rock.*

export[1] T /ɪk'spɔrt/ [*verb;* **exported, exporting**] to sell and send goods to a foreign country; *opposite* **IMPORT**: *We* **export** *most of our coffee* **to** *the U.S.*

export[2] T /'ɛkspɔrt/ [*noun*] something that is sold and sent to a foreign country; *opposite* **IMPORT**: *The country's main* **exports** *are cocoa and timber.*
☛ The noun **export** is usually used in the plural.

exporter /ɛk'spɔrtɚ/ [*noun*] a company or country that sells things to foreign countries; *opposite* **IMPORTER**: *an* **exporter** *of grain*

express[1] * /ɪk'sprɛs/ [*verb;* **expresses, expressed, expressing**] to say or show what you are thinking or feeling: *It's hard for him to* **express** *his feelings.*

express[2] [*adjective; no comparative*] an **express** train or bus goes fast and does not stop at many places: *We can get there in 50 minutes on the* **express** *train.*
↪ *Compare* **LOCAL**[1] (definition 2).

express[3] [*noun; plural* **expresses**] a train or bus that goes fast and does not stop at many places: *Take the* **express** *to 125th Street.*
↪ *Compare* **LOCAL**[2] (definition 1).

expression * /ɪk'sprɛʃən/ [*noun*]
1 two or more words that are used together with a special meaning: *The* **expression** *"I'm full" means "I've had enough to eat."*
2 the appearance of your face, which shows how you feel: *She had such a worried* **expression**.

expressway /ɪk'sprɛsˌweɪ/ [*noun; plural* **expressways**] a wide road on which vehicles can travel very fast

extend /ɪk'stɛnd/ [*verb;* **extended, extending**]
1 to make something longer or larger: *We are planning to extend our house.*
2 to cover an area: *The site extends over an area of 30 acres.*

extension /ɪk'stɛnʃən/ [*noun*]
1 something that is added to make something longer or bigger: *They put an extension on their house.*
2 a telephone line to a particular phone in a building: *I'll give you my extension number.*

extensive T /ɪk'stɛnsɪv/ [*adjective;* **more extensive, most extensive**] covering a wide area or a lot of things: *an extensive ranch* I *He has extensive experience.*

extent /ɪk'stɛnt/ [*noun*] how far or how much something is affected: *The extent of the storm damage is not yet known.*

exterior[1] /ɪk'stɪriɚ/ [*noun*] the outside of something; *opposite* INTERIOR: *The exterior of the building is painted white.*

exterior[2] [*adjective; no comparative*] on the outside of something; *opposite* INTERIOR: *an exterior wall*
☛ Only use **exterior** before a noun.

external /ɪk'stɝnəl/ [*adjective; no comparative*] outside, or happening outside; *opposite* INTERNAL: *This medicine is for external use only* (=for use only on the skin).

extinct /ɪk'stɪŋkt/ [*adjective; no comparative*] if an animal or plant is extinct, not even one still lives on the earth: *Dinosaurs became extinct millions of years ago.*

extinction /ɪk'stɪŋkʃən/ [*noun*] when the last animal or plant of a particular type dies: *Tigers are facing extinction* (=in danger of becoming extinct).

extra[1] * /'ɛkstrə/ [*adjective; no comparative*] more than is normally given, used, or done: *I like extra ketchup on my hamburger.* I *You can have an extra day to finish your assignment.*

extra[2] [*adverb*]
1 more than normal: *It costs $15 extra for a room with a view.*

2 more than normally: *I wonder why she's being extra nice to me lately.*

extra[3] [*noun; plural* **extras**] something that is not a basic or usual part of something: *This car has lots of extras, like air conditioning and a CD player.*

extract T /'ɛkstrækt/ [*noun*] a short part of a book or article: *I'll read you an extract from her most recent novel.*

extra large or **extra-large** /'ɛkstrə 'lɑrdʒ/ [*noun*] a size of clothing that is very big: *My son wears an extra large.* I *Do you have this shirt in extra large?*
⟡ *Compare* SMALL[2], MEDIUM[2], LARGE[2].

extraordinary /ɪk'strɔrdənˌɛri/ [*adjective;* **more extraordinary, most extraordinary**] very unusual, surprising, or impressive: *She was an extraordinary woman.*

extreme * T /ɪk'strim/ [*adjective*]
1 [**more extreme, most extreme**] very great in degree: *Not many animals live here, because of the extreme cold.*
2 [*no comparative*] at the farthest point of something: *Our house is at the extreme end of the road.*
☛ Only use **extreme** before a noun in this meaning.

extremely * T /ɪk'strimli/ [*adverb*] used to emphasize that something is very good, big, tall, etc.: *They live in an extremely large house.*

eye * /aɪ/ [*noun; plural* **eyes**]
1 one of the two parts of your face that you see with
⟡ *See the picture at* BODY.
2 the small hole at the end of a needle that the thread goes through: *the eye of a needle*

— PHRASES —
3 keep an eye on something/ someone to watch something or someone to make sure he, she, or it is safe: *Could you keep an eye on my bag?*

/i/ **see** /ɪ/ **big** /eɪ/ **day** /ɛ/ **get** /æ/ **hat** /ɑ/ **father, hot** /ʌ/ **up** /ə/ **about** /ɔ/ **saw** /oʊ/ **hope** /ʊ/ **book** /u/ **too** /aɪ/ **I** /aʊ/ **how** /ɔɪ/ **boy** /ɝ/ **bird** /ɚ/ **teacher** /ɪr/ **ear** /ɛr/ **air** /ɑr/ **far** /ɔr/ **more** /ʊr/ **tour** /aɪr/ **fire** /aʊɚ/ **hour** /θ/ **nothing** /ð/ **mother** /ʃ/ **she** /ʒ/ **measure** /tʃ/ **church** /dʒ/ **jump** /ŋ/ **long**

4 see eye to eye to agree with someone: *We always see eye to eye.*

eyebrow /'aɪˌbraʊ/ [*noun*] the line of hair above each eye
⊳ *See the picture at* BODY.

eyelash /'aɪˌlæʃ/ [*noun; plural* **eyelashes**] one of the hairs at the edge of your

eyelid; *synonym* LASH: *She has very long, beautiful, thick, dark eyelashes.*

eyelid /'aɪˌlɪd/ [*noun*] the skin that covers your eye when you close it

eyesight /'aɪˌsaɪt/ [*noun*] your ability to see; *synonyms* SIGHT, VISION: *He lost his eyesight in an accident.* | *bad eyesight*

F

F * or **f** /ɛf/ [*noun*]
   1 [*plural* **Fs** or **F's, f's**] the sixth letter of the English alphabet
   ⊳ *See the usage note at* ALPHABET.
   2 F [*plural* **Fs** or **F's**] a grade in school that means you have failed: *If you keep getting Fs, you'll never graduate.*

F. the written abbreviation of FAHRENHEIT, a measure of temperature: *Water freezes at 32° F.*

fable /'feɪbəl/ [*noun*] a short story, often about animals, that teaches people how to behave: *Aesop's fables*

fabric /'fæbrɪk/ [*noun*] cloth used to make clothes, covers for furniture, etc.; *synonym* MATERIAL: *The bag was made from dark blue fabric.*

fabulous /'fæbyələs/ [*adjective; no comparative*] extremely good or beautiful; *synonym* WONDERFUL: *Thanks. We had a fabulous time.*

face¹ * Ⓣ /feɪs/ [*noun*]
   1 the front part of your head where your eyes, nose, and mouth are: *He cut his face while he was shaving.* | *You should have seen her face* (=seen the expression on her face) *when we surprised her!*
   ⊳ *See the picture at* BODY.
   2 the front of a clock or watch: *The face of my watch got cracked.*
   ━ PHRASE ━
   3 make a face to change your expression to show that you are angry or disappointed, or to make people laugh: *The children made faces at each other.*

face² * Ⓣ [*verb; faced, facing*]
   1 to accept that a problem exists and try to deal with it: *He couldn't face the*

fact that he would never walk again. | *You must face up to your own faults.*
   2 to look at or toward someone or something: *Could you all turn to face me, please?* | *Our apartment faces south.*
   3 to talk to someone you are frightened of or who you do not want to talk to: *She was scared to face her father after the accident.*

facility Ⓣ /fə'sɪlɪti/ [*noun; plural* **facilities**] equipment, rooms, or a building that you use for an activity: *The school has excellent facilities.*

fact * /fækt/ [*noun*]
   1 something that is definitely true or has definitely happened: *It's a fact that he sold his business.* | *We don't have all the facts yet* (=we do not know everything that happened).
   ━ PHRASES ━
   2 in fact used to emphasize something that you are saying, especially when this seems surprising: *She's a good player. In fact, she won three tournaments.*
   3 as a matter of fact used to emphasize something that you are saying, especially when you are annoyed with someone or do not agree with him or her: *"Do you mind if I come too?" "As a matter of fact, I do."*

factory * Ⓣ /'fæktəri/ [*noun; plural* **factories**] a place where large quantities of things are made using machinery: *a car factory*

faculty /'fækəlti/ [*noun; plural* **faculties**]
   1 a department within a school, college, or university: *the modern languages faculty*
   2 the faculty the teachers at a school

or college: *The faculty met at 10 a.m. yesterday.*

☛ Only use **the faculty** with a singular verb.

fade /feɪd/ [*verb;* **faded, fading**]
1 to become less colorful and bright: *My T-shirt faded after several washes.* | *The sun faded the curtains.*
2 to gradually disappear: *They drove home as the light was fading.*

Fahrenheit /ˈfærən,haɪt/ [*adverb*] according to a scale for measuring TEMPERATURE in which water freezes at 32° and boils at 212°: *Put on a warm jacket! It's only 40° Fahrenheit today.*
➪ *Compare* CELSIUS, CENTIGRADE.

fail * /feɪl/ [*verb;* **failed, failing**]
1 to not pass a test or course: *I failed my French test.*
2 to not work correctly: *The brakes failed on my car.*
3 to not do or achieve what is expected or needed; *opposite* SUCCEED: **fail to do something** ▸ *They failed to finish the work on time.*

failure * /ˈfeɪlyɚ/ [*noun*] someone or something that does not succeed; *opposite* SUCCESS: *The project was a complete failure.*

faint[1] * ⊤ /feɪnt/ [*adjective;* **fainter, faintest**] difficult to see, hear, etc.: *He drew a faint line on the map.* | *She thought she heard a faint knock.*

faint[2] * ⊤ [*verb;* **fainted, fainting**] to suddenly not be conscious, usually for a short time: *He fainted in the heat.*
➪ *See also* **pass out** *at* PASS[1].

fair[1] * /fɛr/ [*adjective;* **fairer, fairest**]
1 someone or something that is fair treats people in an equal way, giving them what they deserve; *opposite* UNFAIR: *Teachers must be fair to all their students.* | *This is the fairest way to divide the chores.* | *Why can't I go too? It's not fair!*
2 done according to the rules: *It was a fair contest.*
3 acceptable, but not very good: *His math skills are only fair.*
4 fair hair or skin is light in color; *opposite* DARK: *a tall girl with fair skin*

fair[2] [*noun*] an outdoor event where people can ride on special machines, play games for prizes, and where farm animals are sometimes judged and sold: *Every year, we go to the county fair.*

fairground /ˈfɛr,graʊnd/ [*noun*] an area of land where fairs and other events take place

fairly * /ˈfɛrli/ [*adverb*]
1 a little, but not very or not completely; *synonym* RATHER: *We played fairly well.* | *I was up fairly late last night.*
☛ Do not use **fairly** with comparatives. For example, do not say "It's fairly warmer." Say **It's a little warmer.**
☛ Put **fairly** after **a**, not before it. Say **It's a fairly nice day.**
2 in a way that is reasonable and equal; *opposite* UNFAIRLY: *It's important to treat all the children fairly.*

USAGE   **fairly**

Fairly is used to make adjectives and adverbs weaker. For example, if you say "Her grades are fairly good," her grades are not bad, but they are not as good as they could be.

---

fairy /ˈfɛri/ [*noun; plural* **fairies**] a small, imaginary creature in stories that has wings and the power to do magic: *The good fairy granted his wishes.*

fairy tale /ˈfɛri ,teɪl/ [*noun*] a children's story about strange creatures and events, in which magic things happen

faith * /feɪθ/ [*noun*]
1 belief and trust in someone or something: *I have great faith in him.*
2 belief and trust in God or a religion: *Her faith is very strong.*

faithful * /ˈfeɪθfəl/ [*adjective;* **more faithful, most faithful**] continuing to support someone; *synonym* LOYAL: *a faithful friend*

/i/ **see**	/ɪ/ **big**	/eɪ/ **day**	/ɛ/ **get**	/æ/ **hat**
/ɑ/ **father, hot**	/ʌ/ **up**	/ə/ **about**	/ɔ/ **saw**
/oʊ/ **hope**	/ʊ/ **book**	/u/ **too**	/aɪ/ **I**	/aʊ/ **how**
/ɔɪ/ **boy**	/ɝ/ **bird**	/ɚ/ **teacher**	/ɪr/ **ear**	/ɛr/ **air**
/ɑr/ **far**	/ɔr/ **more**	/ʊr/ **tour**	/aɪr/ **fire**
/aʊə/ **hour**	/θ/ **nothing**	/ð/ **mother**	/ʃ/ **she**
/ʒ/ **measure**	/tʃ/ **church**	/dʒ/ **jump**	/ŋ/ **long**

fake /feɪk/ [adjective; no comparative] not true or real; _synonym_ PHONY: a fake diamond

fall[1] * /fɔl/ [verb; fell, fallen, falling]
1 to move directly toward the ground from a higher place; _opposite_ RISE: Leaves **fell from** the trees. | Several books had **fallen off** the shelf. | The cup fell to the floor.
2 to go down onto the ground by accident when you are standing, walking, etc.: She slipped and fell on the ice. | I **fell off** my bike. | He **fell down** and hurt his knee.
3 to go down to a lower amount, level, or degree; _opposite_ RISE: The price of cars has fallen recently. | Temperatures will fall during the night.
— PHRASES
4 **fall asleep** to start to sleep: I fell asleep watching television.
5 **fall in love** to start to love someone in a romantic way: They fell in love in April and got married in December.
— PHRASAL VERBS
fall apart [phrasal verb]
6 to break into pieces or parts: That chair will fall apart if anyone sits on it.
fall behind [phrasal verb]
7 to not do as much of something as you should: I **fell behind in** my math.
fall for [phrasal verb]
8 to be deceived or tricked into believing something: **fall for something** ▸ I think he fell for it.
fall out [phrasal verb]
9 if someone's hair or teeth fall out, they come out of the place where they grow: Two of his front teeth fell out.

fall[2] * [noun]
1 the season between summer and winter; _synonym_ AUTUMN
↪ See the usage note at SEASON.
2 when an amount, level, or degree goes down suddenly; _opposite_ RISE: There's been a sharp **fall in** car sales.
— PHRASE
3 **have a (bad) fall** to fall and hurt yourself: He had a bad fall and broke his ankle.

fallen * /'fɔlən/ [verb] the past participle of FALL[1]

false * T /fɔls/ [adjective; no comparative]
1 not true: Are the following statements true or false?
2 not real, but made to look real: false teeth

fame /feɪm/ [noun] the attention and admiration from a lot of people that famous people get: He first **achieved fame** in the movie "Behind the Walls."

familiar * T /fə'mɪlyɚ/ [adjective; more familiar, most familiar]
1 well known and easy to recognize; _opposite_ UNFAMILIAR: I was glad to be home, in my old familiar room.
— PHRASE
2 **be familiar with** to have knowledge of something: I'm not familiar with this particular program.

family * /'fæməli/ [noun; plural families] a group of people who are related to each other, especially a mother, father, and their children

family tree /'fæməli 'tri/ [noun; plural family trees] a drawing that shows all the members of a family and how they are related to each other

famine /'fæmɪn/ [noun] when a lot of people in an area or country do not have enough food to eat: Thousands of people died as a result of the famine.

famous * /'feɪməs/ [adjective; more famous, most famous] known about by a lot of people in different places: Las Vegas is **famous for** its casinos. | a famous scientist

SYNONYMS famous, well-known, notorious

Use **famous** only about people and places: a famous singer | a famous landmark. **Well-known** can be used about facts as well as people and places: a well-known cause of cancer. **Notorious** also means well-known, but for something bad: a notorious criminal.

fan[1] /fæn/ [noun]
1 someone who likes an activity or admires a famous person very much: baseball fans | I'm a great **fan of** his.
2 someone who is interested in a particular team and always wants it to win: We're Chicago Cubs fans.

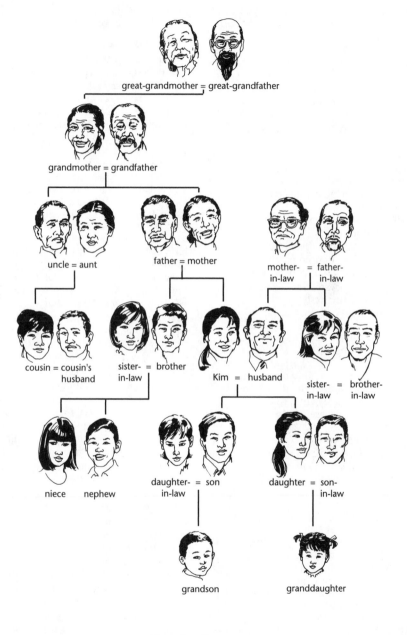

great-grandmother = great-grandfather

grandmother = grandfather

uncle = aunt   father = mother   mother- = father-
                                   in-law   in-law

cousin = cousin's   sister- = brother   Kim = husband   sister- = brother-
         husband   in-law   in-law   in-law

niece   nephew   daughter- = son   daughter = son-
                   in-law   in-law

grandson   granddaughter

Kim's family tree

3 a machine, or a thing that you wave with your hand, that moves the air and makes you cooler: *Turn on the fan.*
⇨ *See the picture at* APPLIANCE.

fan² [*verb;* **fans, fanned, fanning**] to wave something, especially near your face, in order to move the air: *He fanned himself with the magazine.*

fancy /ˈfænsi/ [*adjective;* **fancier, fanciest**] having a lot of decoration and not plain or ordinary; *opposite* SIMPLE: *a fancy restaurant*

fantastic /fænˈtæstɪk/ [*adjective;* **more fantastic, most fantastic**] SPOKEN very good or enjoyable: *I had a fantastic weekend!*
☛ Do not use the comparative forms of **fantastic** in writing.

fantasy /ˈfæntəsi/ [*noun; plural* **fantasies**] an imaginary situation or event: *I have fantasies of being rich.*

far¹ * /fɑr/ [*adverb;* **farther** or **further**, **farthest** or **furthest**]
1 used to talk about a distance, especially a long distance: *How far is it to Wilmington?* | *The hotel's not far from the airport.* | *The sign was too far away to read.* | *My birthday isn't very far off* (=is not a long time from now). | *The store was farther than I thought.*
⇨ *See the usage note at* FURTHER¹.
2 to a great degree: *He works far too hard.*
━ PHRASES ━
3 as far as to a particular place: *Drive as far as the next light and turn left.*
☛ Do not use "so far as" for distances.
4 as/so far as I know used to give all the information you have now: *As far as I know, he's planning to be here.*
5 as/so far as I'm concerned used when you give a strong opinion: *As far as I'm concerned, he's nasty.*
6 by far used to say that someone or something is much better, worse, bigger, etc., than someone or something else: *Michael is by far the best student in the class.*
7 so far until now: *The team has been playing well so far.*
8 so far, so good used to say that something is happening the way you

want, although this may change: *"How's school going?" "So far, so good."*

SYNONYMS far, away, a long way
   When talking about distances, only use **far** in questions or negative sentences: *Is it far to the motel?* | *It's not far to the motel.* | *There's not far to go now.*
   Use **away** with a word or phrase for a particular distance: *The airport is ten miles away.* | *She lives two blocks away.* Do not say "The airport is away ten miles" or "She lives away two blocks."
   If you want to talk about something that is a long distance from you, say it is **a long way (away)**: *It's a long way to the motel.* | *The motel is a long way away.*

far² * [*adjective; no comparative*] being a long distance away or the most distant of two ends, sides, etc.: *These plants only grow in the far south of the country.* | *the far side of the river*
☛ Only use **far** before a noun.

fare /fɛr/ [*noun*] the price you pay for a trip on a bus, train, plane, etc.: *How much is the plane fare to Toronto?*
⇨ *See the synonym note at* COST².

farm¹ * /fɑrm/ [*noun*] an area of land where people raise animals and grow crops for food

farm² * [*verb;* **farmed, farming**] to use land for growing crops and raising animals: *People have farmed the land here for hundreds of years.*

farmer * /ˈfɑrmɚ/ [*noun*] someone who owns and works on a farm

farmhouse /ˈfɑrmˌhaʊs/ [*noun; plural* **farmhouses** /ˈfɑrmˌhaʊzɪz/] the house on a farm where the farmer lives

farming /ˈfɑrmɪŋ/ [*noun*] the business of raising animals and growing crops for food; *synonym* AGRICULTURE: *Modern equipment has made farming easier.*

farmyard /ˈfɑrmˌyɑrd/ [*noun*] an area surrounded by farm buildings

farsighted /ˈfɑrˈsaɪtɪd/ [*adjective; no comparative*] unable to see things clearly if they are very close to you; *opposite* NEARSIGHTED: *My mother's farsighted and needs glasses to read.*

farther * /'fɑrðɚ/ [adverb] the comparative of FAR[1]: *I can't walk any farther.*
↪ *See the warning at* FURTHER[1].

USAGE   farther, further
Do not confuse the adverbs **farther** and **further**. **Farther** is usually only used to talk about distance. **Further** can be used to talk about distance or time, and is also used to mean "more" or "additional."

farthest * /'fɑrðɪst/ [adverb] the superlative of FAR[1]: *The farthest I've run is eight miles.*

fascinate 〒 /'fæsə,neɪt/ [verb; fascinated, fascinating] to strongly interest someone: *They were **fascinated** by the magician.*

fascinating /'fæsə,neɪtɪŋ/ [adjective; more fascinating, most fascinating] extremely interesting: *Visiting the Great Wall was a fascinating experience.*

fascination /ˌfæsə'neɪʃən/ [noun] great interest in something: *The spectators looked on **in fascination.***

fashion * /'fæʃən/ [noun] a style of clothes, hair, etc., or a way of doing something, that is very popular at a particular time: *Fur coats have **gone out of fashion** (=are no longer fashionable).* | *She only wears the latest fashions.*

fashionable * /'fæʃənəbəl/ [adjective; more fashionable, most fashionable] popular, usually only for a short period of time; *opposite* UNFASHIONABLE: *Short coats are very fashionable.*

fast[1] * 〒 /fæst/ [adjective; faster, fastest]
1 able to move or do something very quickly: *He's the fastest 400-meter runner at our college.* | *a fast car* | *a fast worker*
2 happening in a short period of time: *The new freeway makes the trip much faster.*
3 a clock or watch that is fast shows a time that is later than the actual time: *It isn't 10 yet—your watch is fast.*
↪ *Compare* SLOW[1].

fast[2] * 〒 /fæst/ [adverb; faster, fastest]
1 moving or doing something quickly: *I can't walk fast.* | *He's driving too fast.*

2 done quickly or happening in a short period of time: *Children grow up so fast!*
↪ *Compare* SLOWLY.
━━ PHRASE ━━
3 **fast asleep** completely asleep and not likely to wake up easily: *The baby was fast asleep.*
↪ *Compare* **wide awake** *at* WIDE[2].

fast[3] [verb; fasted, fasting] to not eat for a period of time, especially for religious or health reasons: *My friend Jessica fasts once a month.*

fasten * /'fæsən/ [verb; fastened, fastening]
1 to close something or join two parts of something together; *opposite* UNFASTEN: *Please fasten your seat belts before takeoff.*
2 to attach something firmly to something else: *He **fastened** the pin **to** his lapel.*

fastener /'fæsənɚ/ [noun] an object that closes or joins two parts of something together: *The fastener on my purse is broken.*

fast-food /'fæst 'fud/ [adjective; no comparative] a fast-food restaurant makes and serves food very quickly. You can eat the food there or take it away with you: *There are lots of fast-food places at the mall.*

fat[1] * /fæt/ [adjective; fatter, fattest]
1 weighing much more than you should; *opposite* THIN: *If you eat too much, you'll **get fat**.* | *a small, fat man*
2 used to emphasize that something is wide or thick: *a big fat slice of cake*

SYNONYMS   fat, heavy, large, plump, overweight
It is not polite to say that someone is **fat**. If you want to describe someone who is fat in a more polite way, use **heavy** or **large**: *She's a little heavier than the last time I saw her.* | *A large man entered the room.*

Plump is a way of talking about someone, especially a woman or a child, who is a little fat in an attractive way: *His wife was a plump, pretty woman.*

Overweight is neither polite nor impolite, and is a way of saying that someone weighs more than he or she should: *I'm a little overweight.* | *Over 40% of the population is overweight.*

fat[2] * [*noun*]
  1 an oily substance which is used in cooking and is naturally present in many foods: *Butter is high in fat.* | *low-fat yogurt*
  2 a substance under the skin of people and animals that helps to keep them warm: *Remove all the fat from the meat.*

fatal /'feɪtəl/ [*adjective; no comparative*] causing someone's death: *a fatal accident*

fate /feɪt/ [*noun*]
  1 the things that will happen to someone: *Disease and death was the fate of many of the prisoners.*
  2 a power that some people believe controls the events in your life: *We met again after 30 years—it must be fate.*

father * /'fɑðɚ/ [*noun,name*]
  1 a male who has a child: *My father works in a bank.* | *He's the father of twin boys.*
  ⇨ See the picture at FAMILY TREE.
  2 Father the title for a priest in some religions: *Father Brown*

father-in-law /'fɑðɚ ɪn ˌlɔ/ [*noun; plural* **fathers-in-law**] the father of your husband or wife
  ⇨ See the picture at FAMILY TREE.

faucet /'fɔsɪt/ [*noun*] an object that is used to get water from a pipe, that has one or two handles to control the water and a curved metal pipe: *The faucet's dripping.*
  ⇨ Compare TAP[2] (definition 2). ⇨ See the picture at SINK[2].

fault * /fɔlt/ [*noun*]
  1 a problem that stops something from working correctly: *There was a fault in the car's design.*

2 a bad or weak part of someone's character: *Her worst fault is jealousy.*
  ━ PHRASE ━
  3 be someone's fault if something bad that happens is someone's fault, he or she is responsible for it: *It's not my fault.* | *It's his fault she's so upset.*

faultless /'fɔltlɪs/ [*adjective; no comparative*] without any mistakes: *a faultless performance*

faulty /'fɔlti/ [*adjective; no comparative*] having a problem that stops something from working correctly: *a faulty lamp*

favor ⊤ /'feɪvɚ/ [*noun*]
  1 something that you do to help someone: *Would you do me a favor and feed the cat?* | *Can I ask a favor?*
  ━ PHRASE ━
  2 be in favor of something to think that something is a good idea: *Most people are in favor of the plan.*

favorable * /'feɪvərəbəl/ [*adjective;* **more favorable, most favorable**] good for a person or a situation; opposite UNFAVORABLE: *Rick's teacher made some favorable comments about his work.* | *Low taxes have a favorable effect on business.*

favorite[1] * /'feɪvərɪt/ [*adjective; no comparative*] your favorite person or thing is the one you like more than any others: *Who's your favorite baseball player?* | *Blue is my favorite color.*

favorite[2] [*noun*]
  1 the person or thing that you like more than other people or things: *That song has always been one of my favorites.* | *He was the boss's favorite.*
  2 the person or team that is expected to win a race, game, or competition: *Brazil was the favorite to win the World Cup.*

fax /fæks/ [*noun; plural* **faxes**]
  1 also **fax machine** /'fæks məˌʃin/ a machine that is used to send a copy of a letter, picture, etc., somewhere else: *Do you have a fax at home?* | *She sent the letter to the bank by fax.*
  ⇨ See the picture at OFFICE.
  2 a copy of a letter, document, etc., that is sent using a fax machine: *They sent a fax with their arrival information.*

— PHRASE —

3 fax number the set of numbers that you press to connect to someone's fax machine

fear[1] * /fɪr/ [noun] the feeling that you have when you are afraid or are worried about something: *I have a fear of heights* (=fear of being in high places). | *He talked about his hopes and fears.*

fear[2] [verb; feared, fearing] to feel afraid or to be worried about something: *I fear that I'll lose my job.*

fearless /'fɪrlɪs/ [adjective; more fearless, most fearless] FORMAL not afraid: *fearless soldiers*

feast[1] /fist/ [noun] a large meal that is eaten on a special occasion: *a wedding feast*

feast[2] [verb; feasted, feasting] to eat a large amount, especially at a celebration: *We feasted on turkey and roasted vegetables.*

feather * /'fɛðɚ/ [noun] one of the things that cover a bird's body, that look like sticks with soft hairs: *Seagulls have gray-white feathers.*

feature * /'fitʃɚ/ [noun]
1 a part of something that seems typical, interesting, or important: *The car has new safety features.*
2 part of your face, such as your nose or eyes: *Her smile is her best feature.*

Feb. the written abbreviation of FEBRUARY

February * /'fɛbyu,ɛri/ [noun] the second month of the year: *The exhibit starts on February 10th.* | *St. Valentine's Day is in February*
⇨ See the usage note at MONTH.

fed * /fɛd/ [verb] the past tense and past participle of FEED[1]

federal T /'fɛdərəl/ [adjective; no comparative] relating to the central government of a country such as the U.S., rather than its separate states: *federal laws* | *the federal government*

fed up /'fɛd 'ʌp/ [adjective; no comparative] feeling unhappy, bored, or annoyed because something has continued too long: *I'm fed up with all this rain.*

fee /fi/ [noun; plural fees] money that you pay for a special reason or a particular kind of work: *Lawyers' fees are very high.*
⇨ See the synonym note at COST[2].

feed[1] * /fid/ [verb; fed, feeding]
1 to give food to an animal or person: *Don't forget to feed the fish.* | *How often do you have to feed the baby?*
2 when animals feed, they eat: *The puppies are feeding.*

— PHRASAL VERB —

feed on [phrasal verb]
3 if animals feed on a particular food, that is the main thing they eat: *Sheep feed on grass.*

feed[2] [noun] food for animals: *pig feed* | *cattle feed*

feel * /fil/ [verb; felt, feeling]
1 [linking] to experience a feeling: *How are you feeling today?* | *She felt sad after they left.* | *I feel as if I should help.*
2 [linking] if something feels cold, soft, etc., you have that feeling when you touch it: *Your hands feel really cold.*
3 to have an opinion that is based on your feelings: **feel (that)** ▸ *We felt that he wasn't being honest.* | *How do you feel about pizza for lunch?*
4 to touch something with your fingers to find out what it is like: *Feel how hot his forehead is.*

— PHRASES —

5 feel like something to want something: *I feel like a nice hot bath.*
6 feel like doing something to want to do something: *Do you feel like going to the movies?*
7 feel free used to tell someone that he or she may do or have something: **feel free to do something** ▸ *Feel free to make yourself something to eat.*
8 feel (bad) for someone to have sympathy for someone: *I feel for her, but what can I do?*

/i/ see /ɪ/ big /eɪ/ day /ɛ/ get /æ/ hat /ɑ/ father, hot /ʌ/ up /ə/ about /ɔ/ saw /oʊ/ hope /ʊ/ book /u/ too /aɪ/ I /aʊ/ how /ɔɪ/ boy /ɚ/ bird /ɚ/ teacher /ɪr/ ear /ɛr/ air /ɑr/ far /ɔr/ more /ʊr/ tour /aɪr/ fire /aʊɚ/ hour /θ/ nothing /ð/ mother /ʃ/ she /ʒ/ measure /tʃ/ church /dʒ/ jump /ŋ/ long

feeling * /'filɪŋ/ [noun]
1 an emotion: *feelings of joy*
2 an opinion about something that is based on your emotions: *I had a feeling that I might see you here.* | *What are your feelings about the team?*
3 something that you feel in your body, such as pain, heat, etc.: *I had a strange feeling in my stomach.*

feet * /fit/ [noun]
1 the plural of FOOT (definitions 1 and 2)
2 a plural of FOOT (definition 4)

fell * /fɛl/ [verb] the past tense of FALL¹

fellow [adjective; no comparative] like you in some way, or doing the same thing you do: *our fellow citizens*

felony /'fɛləni/ [noun; plural **felonies**] a serious crime for which someone must go to prison: *Robbery is a felony in this country.*

felt * /fɛlt/ [verb] the past tense and past participle of FEEL

felt-tip pen /'fɛlt ˌtɪp 'pɛn/ [noun] a pen with a thick, soft writing end

female¹ * /'fimeɪl/ [adjective; no comparative] belonging to the sex that can have babies: *a female monkey*
➪ Compare MALE¹.

female² * [noun] a person or animal that belongs to the sex that can have babies: *The females are less colorful than the males.*
➪ Compare MALE².

feminine /'fɛmənɪn/ [adjective; more feminine, most feminine] relating to women, or typical of women: *a feminine hairstyle*
☛ Do not use "feminine" to talk about the sex of a person or animal. Use **female**. For example, do not say "a feminine dog." Say **a female dog**.
➪ Compare MASCULINE.

feminism /'fɛməˌnɪzəm/ [noun] the belief that women should have the same rights as men

fence * /fɛns/ [noun] a structure made of wood or metal that surrounds a piece of land: *She climbed over the fence.* | *A high wire fence surrounded the camp.*

fender /'fɛndɚ/ [noun] the part of a CAR or bicycle that covers its wheels

fern /fɝn/ [noun] a kind of plant that has green leaves that look like feathers, but has no flowers

ferocious /fə'roʊʃəs/ [adjective; more ferocious, most ferocious] fierce and violent: *a ferocious attack*

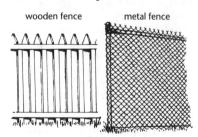
a fern

ferry /'fɛri/ [noun; plural **ferries**] a boat that takes people or vehicles across a river or part of a sea

fertile ⊤ /'fɝtəl/ [adjective; more fertile, most fertile] fertile soil produces a lot of crops because plants grow well in it: *a rich, fertile valley*

fertilizer /'fɝtəˌlaɪzɚ/ [noun] a substance that is put onto soil to help plants and crops grow: *She sprinkled fertilizer on the flower beds.*

festival /'fɛstəvəl/ [noun]
1 an occasion when there are a lot of organized events such as concerts or movies in a particular place: *a film festival* | *a music festival*
2 an occasion when a lot people celebrate something such as a religious or national event: *Every year they **hold a festival** to celebrate independence.*

fetch /fɛtʃ/ [verb; fetches, fetched, fetching]
1 to go to get something and bring it back to a place; <u>synonym</u> GET: **fetch someone something** ▸ *Could you fetch me my glasses?*
2 to be sold for a particular amount of

wooden fence   metal fence

fences

money: *I'm hoping the car will fetch at least $3,000.*

fever * /ˈfivɚ/ [*noun*] a very high body temperature caused by an illness or a disease: *She woke up with a fever.*

few[1] * /fyu/ [*determiner, pronoun*] not very many things or people: *Few cats live past the age of 20.* | *They have a gym, but few use it.*
↪ *See also* FEWER, FEWEST.

USAGE few, a few

Do not confuse **few** and **a few**. **Few** is used mainly in written English to mean "not many": *Few people attended the event.* **A few** is less formal and means "a small number": *A few people arrived late.* | *We'll start in a few minutes.*

Do not use **few** or **a few** with uncountable nouns. Use **a little, not much,** or **not a lot of**: *There's a little bread left.* | *There's not much bread.* | *We don't have a lot of time.*

few[2] * [*noun*]
━━ PHRASES ━━━
1 a few a small number: *I have a few things to do before I leave.* | *Could I borrow a few of these books?* | *He hasn't been feeling very well for the last few days* (=the days just before today). | *"Are there any tickets left?" "A few."*
2 quite a few a large enough number to be noticeable or surprising: *Quite a few people left the party early.*

fewer * /ˈfyuɚ/ [*determiner, pronoun*]
1 not as many; *opposite* MORE: *They're giving fewer concerts than last year.* | *Few people came, and even fewer stayed to the end.*
☛ Only use the determiner **fewer** before a countable noun.
↪ *Compare* LESS[1].
━━ PHRASE ━━━
2 fewer and fewer used to say that something is becoming smaller in number: *Fewer and fewer people are moving here.*
↪ *See also* **less and less** *at* LESS[2]. ↪ *Compare* **more and more** *at* MORE[2].

fewest * /ˈfyuɪst/ [*determiner, pronoun*]
the fewest fewer than all other things or people; *opposite* MOST: *Our class has*

the fewest students. | *I have a lot of freckles, my sister has fewer, and my brother has the fewest.*
☛ Only use the determiner **the fewest** before a countable noun.
↪ *Compare* LEAST[1].

fiancé /ˌfianˈseɪ/ [*noun; plural* **fiancés**] the man that a woman is going to marry: *Her fiancé's name is John.*

fiancée /ˌfianˈseɪ/ [*noun; plural* **fiancées**] the woman that a man is going to marry: *Let me introduce my fiancée, Sarah.*

fib /fɪb/ [*noun*] a lie, especially one that is not very serious: *Stop telling fibs!*

fiber /ˈfaɪbɚ/ [*noun*] natural or artificial threads that are used for making cloth, rope, etc.: *man-made fibers*

fiction /ˈfɪkʃən/ [*noun*] books about imaginary people and events: *Do you enjoy reading fiction?*

field * /fild/ [*noun*]
1 a piece of land where crops are grown or where farm animals are kept: *Sheep were grazing in the field.* | *fields of wheat*
2 a piece of land used for playing an outdoor sport such as baseball, soccer, etc.: *a football field*

fierce * /firs/ [*adjective;* **fiercer, fiercest**] a fierce animal is angry and ready to attack: *That dog looks very fierce!*

fifteen * /ˈfɪfˈtin/ [*number*] 15: *My daughter will be fifteen next month.*

fifteenth * /ˈfɪfˈtinθ/ [*adverb, adjective; no comparative*] coming after fourteen other people, things, or events; sometimes written as "15th": *the fifteenth day of the month* | *I finished fifteenth in the race.*
↪ *See the usage note at* SECOND[2].

fifth[1] * /fɪfθ/ [*adverb, adjective; no comparative*] coming after four other people, things, or events; sometimes

/i/ see	/ɪ/ big	/eɪ/ day	/ɛ/ get	/æ/ hat
/ɑ/ father, hot	/ʌ/ up	/ə/ about	/ɔ/ saw	
/oʊ/ hope	/ʊ/ book	/u/ too	/aɪ/ I	/aʊ/ how
/ɔɪ/ boy	/ɝ/ bird	/ɚ/ teacher	/ɪr/ ear	/ɛr/ air
/ɑr/ far	/ɔr/ more	/ʊr/ tour	/aɪr/ fire	
/aʊɚ/ hour	/θ/ nothing	/ð/ mother	/ʃ/ she	
/ʒ/ measure	/tʃ/ church	/dʒ/ jump	/ŋ/ long	

written as "5th": *My little sister is in fifth grade.* | *I finished fifth in the contest.*

fifth[2] * [*noun, pronoun*] one of five equal parts: *Twenty is a fifth of a hundred.*
  ⇨ *See the usage note at* SECOND[2].

fiftieth * /'fɪftiɪθ/ [*adjective, adverb; no comparative*] coming after 49 other people, things, or events; sometimes written as "50th": *It's Dad's fiftieth birthday tomorrow.*
  ⇨ *See the usage note at* SECOND[2].

fifty * /'fɪfti/ [*number, noun; plural* **fifties**]
  1 50: *Over fifty people came to the party.*
    ⇨ *See the usage note at* TEENS.
  2 a piece of paper money worth $50: *Can you give me two fifties and five twenties, please?*

fig /fɪg/ [*noun*] a purple or green fruit with a lot of small seeds

fight[1] * /faɪt/ [*verb;* **fought, fighting**]
  1 to use weapons or a part of your body in order to hurt or kill someone: *Two men fought in the street.* | *The army has been fighting the rebels for months.*
  2 to take part in a war or battle: *Her grandfather fought in the last war.*
  3 to argue loudly and angrily: *They're always fighting about money.* | *Don't fight with your brother.*
    ⇨ *See the synonym note at* ARGUE.

fight[2] * [*noun*]
  1 an occasion when people fight each other: *There was a fight at the dance on Friday night.*
  2 a loud, angry argument: *We had a big fight last night.* | *I left after a fight with my sister.*

fighter /'faɪtɚ/ [*noun*] someone who tries hard to do something, even when this is difficult: *Jim is a real fighter.*

figure[1] * /'fɪgyɚ/ [*noun*]
  1 a number written as a sign rather than as a word: *She was adding up columns of figures.*
  2 a number that is an amount or total: *a high figure* | *What figure did you end up with?*
  3 the shape of a person's body, especially a woman's: *My cousin has a great figure* (=she looks attractive).
  4 a shape in mathematics: *A pentagon is a figure that has five sides.*

figure[2] [T] [*verb;* **figured, figuring**]
  1 INFORMAL to think something: **figure (that)** ▸ *I figured that you might be worried.* | *They figured you'd be late.*
  — PHRASAL VERB —
  figure out [*phrasal verb*]
  2 to gradually understand something or to solve a problem by thinking about it: **figure out something** ▸ *Did you figure out the instructions?* | **figure something out** ▸ *Sorry, I can't figure this out.* | **figure out how/why/etc.** ▸ *I can't figure out why she was angry.*

file[1] /faɪl/ [*noun*]
  1 a large stiff paper envelope or other container in which information about someone or something is kept
    ⇨ *See the picture at* OFFICE.
  2 a collection of information that is kept together and has one name in a computer: *Why can't I print this file?* | *We keep files on each student.*
  3 a metal tool with a rough surface, used to make wood, metal, or fingernails smooth: *a nail file*
    ⇨ *See also* **(in) single file** *at* SINGLE[1].

file[2] [*verb;* **filed, filing**]
  1 to put files, documents, etc., in a special order so that you can find them at a later time: *File those papers in that drawer.*
  2 to make a surface smooth using a file: *She was filing her nails.*

file cabinet /'faɪl ˌkæbənɪt/ [*noun*] a piece of OFFICE furniture in which files are kept: *Look in the top drawer of that file cabinet.*

fill * /fɪl/ [*verb;* **filled, filling**]
  1 to make something full, or to become full: **fill something with something** ▸ *Fill the pan with water.* | *The kitchen was filled with smoke.* | *The theater slowly filled up* (=with people). | *Please fill the gas tank up.*
  — PHRASAL VERB —
  fill in or **fill out** [*phrasal verb*]
  2 to write the information that you are asked for in the spaces on a document: **fill in/out something** ▸ *Fill in your name on line one.* | **fill something in/out** ▸ *It took over an hour to fill it out.*

filling /ˈfɪlɪŋ/ [noun]
1 a substance used to fill a hole in a tooth, or the filled place: *The dentist gave her six fillings.*
2 the food that is put inside baked dough, a sandwich, etc.: *fruit filling*

film[1] * /fɪlm/ [noun]
1 the thin flat length of material that is put inside a camera and used for taking photographs or recording moving pictures: *I need film for my camera.* | *a roll of film* (=film in a metal container)
2 a story or a set of events shown in the form of moving pictures on a screen; synonym MOVIE: *She is discussing her latest film on TV tonight.*
3 a very thin layer of a substance on a surface: *There was a film of grease on the stove.*

film[2] * [verb; **filmed, filming**] to use a camera to make a movie or television show: *The movie was filmed in Argentina.* | *When do we start filming?*

filter[1] /ˈfɪltɚ/ [noun] an object used to remove unwanted things from a liquid or gas that is passed through it: *a coffee filter*

filter[2] [verb; **filtered, filtering**]
1 to put a liquid or gas through a filter: *I filter the tap water to remove lead.*
2 when something filters somewhere, it happens slowly or in a small amount: **filter in/into/through/etc. something** ▶ *The crowd began to filter into the theater.* | *Sunlight filtered through the thin curtains.*

filthy /ˈfɪlθi/ [adjective; **filthier, filthiest**] very dirty: *I have to wash this filthy floor.*

fin /fɪn/ [noun] one of the thin parts on the body of a FISH that it uses to swim

final[1] * /ˈfaɪnəl/ [adjective; no comparative]
1 last in a series of events, actions, or parts of something: *Don't miss the final game next week.* | *In the final chapter, the hero returns home.*
2 not able to be changed: *Is that your final offer?* | *You're not going out, and that's final!*

final[2] [noun]
1 the last and most important game in

a competition: *Tickets for the final are already sold out.*
2 an examination that high school and college students take at the end of a period of study: *When's your history final?* | *Finals begin May 12.*

finally * /ˈfaɪnəli/ [adverb]
1 after a long time: *The bus has finally arrived.*
↪ See also **at last** at LAST[3].
2 used before the last thing you say or write: *Finally, let's all work to make next year more successful.*

finance[1] Ⓣ /ˈfaɪnæns/ [noun] the activity of managing money, especially money belonging to a company or large organization: *The finance committee meets on Tuesdays.*

finance[2] Ⓣ /fɪˈnæns/ [verb; **financed, financing**] to provide money for something: *All the research will be financed by the company.*

financial * /fɪˈnænʃəl/ [adjective; no comparative] relating to money: *We provide expert financial advice.*

financially /fɪˈnænʃəli/ [adverb] in a way that relates to money: *The company is financially strong.*

find * /faɪnd/ [verb; **found, finding**]
1 to see or get something that you have been looking for: *Did you find the keys?* | *We still haven't found a place to live.*
↪ Compare LOSE.
2 to learn or discover something by studying it or experiencing it: **find (that)** ▶ *I find that a hot bath helps me relax.*
3 to have a particular opinion or feeling about someone or something: **find someone/something to be something** ▶ *I've always found her to be very nice.* | *He finds the idea of flying terrifying.*
4 if something such as a plant or animal is found somewhere, it exists

/i/ **see**	/ɪ/ **big**	/eɪ/ **day**	/ɛ/ **get**	/æ/ **hat**
/ɑ/ **father, hot**	/ʌ/ **up**	/ə/ **about**	/ɔ/ **saw**	
/oʊ/ **hope**	/ʊ/ **book**	/u/ **too**	/aɪ/ **I**	/aʊ/ **how**
/ɔɪ/ **boy**	/ɝ/ **bird**	/ɚ/ **teacher**	/ɪr/ **ear**	/ɛr/ **air**
/ɑr/ **far**	/ɔr/ **more**	/ʊr/ **tour**	/aɪr/ **fire**	
/aʊɚ/ **hour**	/θ/ **nothing**	/ð/ **mother**	/ʃ/ **she**	
/ʒ/ **measure**	/tʃ/ **church**	/dʒ/ **jump**	/ŋ/ **long**	

in that place: *Cactuses are found in desert climates.*

☛ This meaning of **find** is nearly always used in the passive tense.

━━ PHRASAL VERB ━━

find out [*phrasal verb*]
5 to learn or discover something: **find out (that)** ▸ *I found out later that they'd tried to contact me.* I **find out something** ▸ *Did you find out what the problem was?*

fine[1] ∗ T /faɪn/ [*adjective*; **finer, finest**]
1 SPOKEN all right or good enough: *"Did you have good seats for the concert?" "Yes, they were fine."*
2 SPOKEN healthy or happy: *"How are you feeling?" "I'm fine, thanks."*
3 of a very good quality: *This is the band's finest album.* I *He's a fine athlete.*
4 very thin or delicate: *Look at the fine detail in this picture!*
5 weather that is fine is bright and without rain: *a fine, sunny day*

━━ PHRASE ━━

6 that's fine (with me) or **it's fine (with me)** SPOKEN used to say "yes" when someone asks or suggests something: *"Is it OK if I leave early today?" "That's fine."*

fine[2] T [*adverb*]
1 in a way that is good or satisfactory: *Everything's **going fine** (=happening in a good way).*

━━ PHRASE ━━

2 do fine to do something well or in a satisfactory way: *He's doing fine at school.*

fine[3] T [*noun*] money that you pay as a punishment: *The fine for littering is $50.*

fine[4] T [*verb*; **fined, fining**] to make someone pay an amount of money as a punishment: *The library fines you for returning books late.*

finger ∗ /ˈfɪŋgɚ/ [*noun*] one of the four long parts at the end of your hand
⇨ *See the picture at* BODY.

fingernail /ˈfɪŋgɚˌneɪl/ [*noun*] the hard flat part at the end of each of your fingers; synonym NAIL
⇨ *See the picture at* BODY.

fingerprint /ˈfɪŋgɚˌprɪnt/ [*noun*] the pattern of lines on the end of a finger,

or the mark made by this on a surface: *Whose dirty fingerprints are on my book?*

fingertip /ˈfɪŋgɚˌtɪp/ [*noun*] the end of a finger: *He could just touch the top shelf with his fingertips.*

finish[1] ∗ /ˈfɪnɪʃ/ [*verb*; **finishes, finished, finishing**]
1 to do all of something to the end or until it is complete; opposite START: *Have you finished that book yet?* I **finish doing something** ▸ *Did you finish the ironing?* I *I thought you'd **be finished** (=have finished) by now.*
2 to eat or drink all of something: *He didn't finish his dinner.* I **Finish up** *your milk, please.*

━━ PHRASAL VERBS ━━

finish off or **finish up** [*phrasal verb*]
3 to eat or drink the last of something: **finish off/up something** ▸ *He finished off his coffee.* I **finish something off/up** ▸ *Who finished the pizza up?*

finish up [*phrasal verb*]
4 to end an event, situation, or period of time by doing one final thing: *You leave—I'll finish up.* I **finish up something** ▸ *We finished up the evening at a restaurant.*

finish with [*phrasal verb*]
5 to no longer need something that you have been using: **be finished with something** ▸ *Are you finished with those scissors?*

finish[2] [*noun*] the end or the last part of something, especially in a competition; opposites BEGINNING, START: *a fight **to the finish*** I *the finish line*

finished ∗ /ˈfɪnɪʃt/ [*adjective*; no comparative] completely done; opposite UNFINISHED: *Is the game finished yet?* I *Put your finished tests on my desk.*

fir /fɝ/ [*noun*] a tall tree with thin leaves like needles, which do not fall off in winter

fire[1] ∗ /faɪr/ [*noun*]
1 flames and heat that can burn and destroy things: *A **forest fire** was started by lightning.* I *The kitchen was **on fire** (=burning).* I *The carpet **caught fire** (=began to burn).* I *Firefighters **put out the fire** (=stopped it).* I *A **fire broke out** (=started) at the warehouse.* I *Enemy*

soldiers *set fire to* the barn (=made it start burning).

2 a pile of wood or coal that you burn in order to provide heat: *A log fire burned in the fireplace.* | *We lit a fire.*

fire² * [*verb; fired, firing*]

1 to shoot bullets from a gun: *We heard shots being fired.* | *The man fired at the deer.*

2 to make someone leave his or her job: *He was fired.*

fire alarm /'faɪr ə,larm/ [*noun*] a thing that makes a loud noise to warn people when there is a fire in a building: *If you hear the fire alarm, go quickly to the nearest exit.*

firecracker /'faɪr,krækəʳ/ [*noun*] a small container that explodes loudly and is used during a celebration

fire department /'faɪr dɪ,partmənt/ [*noun*] an organization that is responsible for preventing and stopping fires: *the Kansas City Fire Department*

fire drill /'faɪr ,drɪl/ [*noun*] an occasion when people practice what they should do if there is a fire in a building

fire engine /'faɪr ,ɛndʒən/ [*noun*] a vehicle with special equipment used by the fire department when they have to stop a fire

fire escape /'faɪr ɪ,skeɪp/ [*noun*] metal stairs on the outside of a building that people use to escape if there is a fire

fire extinguisher /'faɪr ɪk,stɪŋgwɪʃəʳ/ [*noun*] a metal container with water or chemicals inside used for stopping fires

firefighter /'faɪr,faɪtəʳ/ [*noun*] someone whose job is to stop fires: *Four teams of firefighters fought the blaze.*

fireman /'faɪrmən/ [*noun; plural* **firemen** /'faɪrmən/] a man whose job is to stop fires; *synonym* FIREFIGHTER

fireplace /'faɪr,pleɪs/ [*noun*] a space in a wall where a fire can be lit to warm a room

fire station /'faɪr ,steɪʃən/ [*noun*] the place where firefighters and their equipment stay until they are needed to stop a fire

firewood /'faɪr,wʊd/ [*noun*] wood that is cut and used for burning on fires

fireworks /'faɪr,wɜ˞ks/ [*plural noun*] containers that explode to produce colored lights and noise, and are used during a celebration: *a fireworks display*

firm¹ * /fɜ˞m/ [*adjective;* **firmer, firmest**]

1 not completely hard, but not easy to bend or press; <u>opposite</u> SOFT: *a firm mattress*

2 speaking or behaving in a way that shows that you will not change your opinions or plans: *You need to be firm with these kids.* | *I'd like a firm answer.*

══ PHRASE ══

3 **a firm hold/grip** if you have a firm hold on something, you are holding it tightly in your hand: *She took a firm grip on the ladder.*

firm² * [*noun*] a business or small company: *She works for a law firm.*

firmly * Ⓣ /'fɜ˞mli/ [*adverb*] in a way that shows you are not going to change your opinions or plans: *"No, you can't stay up late," she said firmly.*

first¹ * /fɜ˞st/ [*adverb*]

1 before anyone or anything else; <u>opposite</u> LAST: *Who came first in the race?* | *Let's do the dishes first.*

2 for the first time: *We first met in the summer of 1987.*

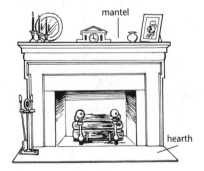

a fireplace

/i/ **see**	/ɪ/ **big**	/eɪ/ **day**	/ɛ/ **get** /æ/ **hat**
/a/ **father, hot**	/ʌ/ **up**	/ə/ **about**	/ɔ/ **saw**
/oʊ/ **hope**	/ʊ/ **book**	/u/ **too**	/aɪ/ **I** /aʊ/ **how**
/ɔɪ/ **boy**	/ɝ/ **bird**	/ɚ/ **teacher**	/ɪr/ **ear** /ɛr/ **air**
/ɑr/ **far**	/ɔr/ **more**	/ʊr/ **tour**	/aɪr/ **fire**
/aʊɚ/ **hour**	/θ/ **nothing**	/ð/ **mother**	/ʃ/ **she**
/ʒ/ **measure**	/tʃ/ **church**	/dʒ/ **jump**	/ŋ/ **long**

══ PHRASE ══

3 first (of all)

  a *SPOKEN* used before mentioning the first or most important thing you are going to talk about: *First of all, decide how much money you need.*

  b before doing anything else or before anything else happens: *First, put your seat belt on.*

first² ✱ [*adjective; no comparative*]

  1 coming or happening at the beginning; <u>opposite</u> LAST: *Your sister was the first person I met after I moved here.* I *the first week of May* I *It's **the first time** I've been abroad.*

══ PHRASE ══

  2 in the first place used to emphasize something that you say during an argument or a discussion: *If you were worried, why didn't you call me in the first place?*

first³ ✱ [*pronoun, noun*]

  1 the first the person or thing that comes before all the others; sometimes written as "1st": *Bill was **the first to** arrive.* I *She was **one of the first** to congratulate me.* I *the 1st of Aug.* (=the first day of August)

══ PHRASE ══

  2 at first used to talk about what happened at the beginning of a period of time or situation: *He was shy at first.* ⇨ *Compare* LAST³.

first aid /ˈfɝst ˈeɪd/ [*noun*] simple medical treatment that you give to someone who is sick or injured before a doctor can treat him or her: *I was able to **give him first aid.***

first-aid kit /ˌfɝst ˈeɪd ˌkɪt/ [*noun*] a small box containing things used for simple medical treatments

first-class /ˈfɝst ˈklæs/ [*adjective; no comparative*]

  1 first-class seats on a plane, train, etc., are the best and the most expensive: *a first-class seat*

  2 of the best kind: *a first-class health care system*

first class [*adverb*] if you travel somewhere first class, you travel using the most expensive seats on a plane, train, etc.: *He always flies first class.*

first floor /ˈfɝst ˈflɔr/ [*noun*] the part of a building that is at the level of the ground or street; <u>synonym</u> GROUND FLOOR: *The elevator was stuck **on the first floor.***

first lady /ˈfɝst ˈleɪdi/ [*noun; plural* **first ladies**] the wife of the president of the U.S.: *The first lady spoke at our school.*

first name /ˈfɝst ˈneɪm/ [*noun*] the name that you do not share with other members of your family, which in English comes before your family name; <u>synonym</u> GIVEN NAME: *Mr. Brown's first name is Sam.*

USAGE   first name, given name, last name, surname

In the U.S. and many other Western countries, your **first name** or **given name** is the part of your name that is not the same as those of the other people in your family.

The name you share with the other members of your family is your **last name**: *"What's Charles's last name?" "I think it's Ball."* A **surname** is a last name, but this word is more formal.

If you do not know someone well, especially someone who is in authority or someone who is a lot older than you, do not use his or her first name unless he or she says you may.

A more formal and polite way of talking to him or her is to use a title such as **Mr.**, **Mrs.**, **Professor**, etc., with his or her last name: *"Good morning, Mr. Green."*

---

first person ✱ /ˈfɝst ˈpɝsən/ [*noun*] *GRAMMAR* the form of a verb or pronoun used to show that you are the person who is speaking or writing: *"I," "me," "we,"* and *"us"* are first person pronouns. I *The first person singular of "be" is "am."*

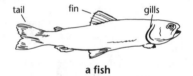

tail   fin   gills

a fish

fish¹ ✱ /fɪʃ/ [*noun; plural* **fish** *or* **fishes**]

  1 an animal that lives in water and uses its tail to swim: *Look—you can see fish in the water.* I *He caught a fish.*

2 the meat of a fish: *I love fresh fish, especially when it's grilled.*

fish[2] [*verb;* **fishes, fished, fishing**] to try to catch fish: *She is **fishing for** trout.*

fisherman /'fɪʃɚmən/ [*noun; plural* **fishermen** /'fɪʃɚmən/] a man who catches fish as a job or for pleasure

fishing /'fɪʃɪŋ/ [*noun*] the business or sport of catching fish: *the fishing industry* | *He likes to **go fishing** (=catch fish for pleasure).*

fishing rod /'fɪʃɪŋ ˌrad/ [*noun*] a long thin pole with a long string hanging from one end, used to catch fish: *Dad gave me his old fishing rod.*

fist /fɪst/ [*noun*] a hand with the fingers bent tightly inward: *She hit the table with her fists.*

fit[1] * /fɪt/ [*verb;* **fits, fit** or **fitted, fit, fitting**]

1 if clothes fit, they are the right size and shape for someone: *These jeans don't fit too well.* | *That skirt should still fit me.*

☛ Do not say "It is fitting me." Say **It fits me**.

2 to be the right size or shape for a particular space, or to put something into a space of the right size or shape: *The dresser won't **fit in** that corner.* | *You'll never **fit** all those clothes **into** one suitcase.*

━ PHRASAL VERB ━

fit in [*phrasal verb*]

3 to be accepted by other people in a group because you are similar to them: *She doesn't fit in at school.*

fit[2] [*noun*]

━ PHRASES ━

1 have a fit or **throw a fit** to get very angry and shout: *Mom will throw a fit if I'm late.*

2 be a good fit or **be a perfect fit** to fit a person or an amount of space well: *That suit is a really good fit.*

fit[3] * [*adjective;* **fitter, fittest**]

1 healthy and active; *opposite* UNFIT: *I'm not as physically fit as I used to be.* | *She stays fit (=remains healthy and active) by swimming regularly.*

☼ *See also* **in shape** *at* SHAPE.

2 suitable or good enough; *opposite*

UNFIT: *This water isn't **fit to drink**!* | *He's **in no fit state** to drive* (=not able to drive).

fitness /'fɪtnɪs/ [*noun*] the fact of being healthy and active, or the things you do to stay that way: *Physical fitness is important to him.*

five * /faɪv/ [*number, noun*]

1 5: *Each team has five players.*

2 a piece of paper money worth $5: *She gave me two fives and a ten.*

fix * /fɪks/ [*verb;* **fixes, fixed, fixing**]

1 to repair something that is broken or not working: *Could you fix this lock?*

2 to prepare a meal or drinks: *It's time to start fixing lunch.*

3 to decide on something and not change it or not allow it to change: *Have they fixed a time for the meeting?*

━ PHRASAL VERB ━

fix up [*phrasal verb*]

4 to make something look neat or attractive by cleaning, repairing, painting, etc.: *I want to fix up my room.*

fixed /fɪkst/ [*adjective; no comparative*] decided on, and unable to be changed: *a fixed-price menu* (=a complete meal in a restaurant for one price) | *You can only travel on fixed dates for cheap fares.*

fizz /fɪz/ [*noun*] very small bubbles (=balls of gas) making a soft continuous "s" sound as they rise to the top of a liquid: *This soda doesn't have any fizz.*

flag * /flæg/ [*noun*] a piece of cloth with a special design on it that represents a country or organization: *the flag of the U.S.* | *The ship flew the flag of Liberia.*

flagpole /'flæg,poʊl/ [*noun*] a tall pole to which a flag can be attached

flake /fleɪk/ [*noun*] a small, flat, thin piece of something: *Flakes of plaster were coming off the wall.*

☼ *See also* SNOWFLAKE.

/i/ **see** /ɪ/ **big** /eɪ/ **day** /ɛ/ **get** /æ/ **hat**
/ɑ/ **father, hot** /ʌ/ **up** /ə/ **about** /ɔ/ **saw**
/oʊ/ **hope** /ʊ/ **book** /u/ **too** /aɪ/ **I** /aʊ/ **how**
/ɔɪ/ **boy** /ɝ/ **bird** /ɚ/ **teacher** /ɪr/ **ear** /ɛr/ **air**
/ɑr/ **far** /ɔr/ **more** /ʊr/ **tour** /aɪr/ **fire**
/aʊɚ/ **hour** /θ/ **nothing** /ð/ **mother** /ʃ/ **she**
/ʒ/ **measure** /tʃ/ **church** /dʒ/ **jump** /ŋ/ **long**

flame * /fleɪm/ [noun]
  1 the hot, bright gas that you see when something is burning: *a candle flame*
  ══ PHRASES ══
  2 in flames burning in an uncontrolled way: *The house was in flames.*
  3 go up in flames or **burst into flames** to suddenly start burning in an uncontrolled way: *The car burst into flames.*

flap[1] /flæp/ [noun] a flat piece of cloth or paper that is attached to or hangs from a surface at one side: *He opened the flap of his jacket pocket.*

flap[2] [verb; flaps, flapped, flapping]
  1 if a piece of cloth or paper flaps, it moves around quickly and makes noise: *The flag was **flapping around** in the wind.*
  2 if a bird flaps its wings, it moves them up and down: *The geese were flapping their wings.*

flash[1] * /flæʃ/ [noun; plural **flashes**]
  1 a bright light that shines suddenly for a short time: *a **flash of lightning***
  2 a light on a camera that you use when you are taking a photograph indoors or when there is not much light: *The flash didn't **go off** (=didn't work).*
  ══ PHRASE ══
  3 in a flash or **quick as a flash** very quickly: *I'll be back in a flash.*

flash[2] * [verb; flashes, flashed, flashing] to suddenly shine brightly for a short time, or to make something do this: *Lights were **flashing on and off**.*

flashlight /'flæʃ,laɪt/ [noun] a small electric light that you carry in your hand

flat[1] * /flæt/ [adjective; flatter, flattest]
  1 without sloping or raised parts, or without hills or mountains: *You need a flat surface to work on.* | *The country around here is very flat.*
  2 a flat tire has no air inside it: *Your left rear tire is almost flat.*

flat[2] [adverb] in a straight or flat position: *He lay flat on his back.*

flat[3] [noun] a tire that has no air inside it: *My bike has a flat.*

flatten /'flætən/ [verb; flattened, flattening] to make something flat, or to become flat: *He unfolded the letter and flattened it out.*

flatter /'flætɚ/ [verb; flattered, flattering] to say nice things to someone in order to please him or her, or to get an advantage for yourself: *He's just trying to flatter you, that's all.*

flattered /'flætɚd/ [adjective; more flattered, most flattered] feeling pleased because someone has said nice things about you: *I'm **flattered that** you like my work.*

flavor /'fleɪvɚ/ [noun]
  1 the taste that a kind of food or drink has: *Our jellies come in six flavors.*
  2 the pleasant or strong taste that food or drink has: *Herbs **add flavor** to food.*

flavored /'fleɪvɚd/ [adjective; no comparative] having a particular taste: *fruit-flavored candy* | *onion-flavored potato chips*

flea /fli/ [noun; plural **fleas**] a very small jumping insect that feeds on the blood of animals and people

flee /fli/ [verb; flees, fled /flɛd/, fleeing] FORMAL to leave somewhere quickly in order to escape from danger: *Refugees are **fleeing from** the war zone.* | *Forest fires have made people flee the area.*

fleece /flis/ [noun] the wool from a sheep, or a thick soft material: *I have a warm fleece vest.*

fleet /flit/ [noun] all the ships in a navy: *The fleet was destroyed in the battle.*

flesh * /flɛʃ/ [noun] the soft part of the body of a person or animal that covers the bones: *Cut the flesh from the bone carefully.*
  ⇨ Compare SKIN.

flew * /flu/ [verb] the past tense of FLY[1]

flexible Ⓣ /'flɛksəbəl/ [adjective; more flexible, most flexible]
  1 able to bend or be bent easily; *opposite* RIGID: *a doll made of flexible plastic*
  2 able or willing to change or be changed; *opposite* RIGID: *Dad's pretty **flexible about** our bedtime.* | *My schedule is flexible.*

flight * /flaɪt/ [noun]
1 a trip on a plane, or a plane that is making a trip: *a 12-hour flight* | *They will be on flight TA684.*
2 an act of flying: *It's amazing to see an eagle in flight* (=flying).
3 a set of STAIRS between the different levels of a building: *You have to climb five flights of stairs.*

flight attendant /'flaɪt ə,tɛndənt/ [noun] someone who takes care of the passengers on a plane

fling /flɪŋ/ [verb; flung, flinging] to throw something quickly and with a lot of force: *He flung his jacket on the sofa.*

flip /flɪp/ [verb; flips, flipped, flipping]
1 to throw something such as a coin into the air so that it turns over: *They flipped a coin to see who would start.*
2 to start or stop a piece of electrical equipment by pressing a button: *Just flip the switch to turn off the power.*

flipper /'flɪpɚ/ [noun]
1 a flat part on the body of some large sea animals, such as a WALRUS, that helps them to move through the water: *Seals use their flippers to swim.*
2 a large rubber shoe that you use in order to swim faster: *a pair of flippers*

flirt /flɝt/ [verb; flirted, flirting] to behave and talk to someone as if you are attracted to him or her, but not in a very serious way: *Bill is always flirting with my sister.*

float * /floʊt/ [verb; floated, floating] to stay or move on the surface of a liquid without sinking: *She turned over in the water and floated on her back.*

flock /flak/ [noun] a group of sheep or birds

flood¹ * /flʌd/ [noun] a large amount of water that covers an area that is usually dry: *Floods damaged crops in the region.* | *We've had a flood in the bathroom.*

flood² * [verb; flooded, flooding]
1 to cover a place with water, or to become covered with water: *Heavy rain flooded the valley.* | *The river flooded and destroyed hundreds of homes.*
2 to arrive somewhere in large numbers: *Letters came flooding in.* |

We've been flooded with requests (=have received a lot of requests).

floodlight /'flʌd,laɪt/ [noun] a bright light used to light outside areas at night

floor * /flɔr/ [noun]
1 the flat surface that you stand on indoors: *She slipped on the polished floor.* | *You're spilling coffee on the floor.*
 ⊃ See the usage note at GROUND¹.
2 one of the levels in a building: *I live on the top floor.* | *a first-floor apartment*
▬▬ **PHRASE** ▬▬
3 **the ocean floor** the land at the bottom of the ocean: *Many interesting creatures live on the ocean floor.*

floorboard /'flɔr,bɔrd/ [noun] one of the long narrow pieces of wood used to make a floor: *oak floorboards*

flop /flap/ [verb; flops, flopped, flopping] to sit or lie down by letting your body fall in a relaxed way: *I flopped down on the sofa to watch TV.*

floppy /'flapi/ [adjective; floppier, floppiest] soft and hanging down loosely: *a rabbit with long floppy ears*

floppy disk /'flapi 'dɪsk/ or **floppy** [noun; plural floppy disks, floppies] a piece of square plastic with a round, flat object inside it, used for storing computer information; synonyms DISK, DISKETTE: *Save your work on a floppy disk.*
 ⊃ Compare HARD DISK.

florist /'flɔrɪst/ [noun] someone who sells flowers and small plants

flour * /'flaʊɚ/ [noun] a powder made from grain, that is used for making bread, cakes, etc.: *a bag of flour* | *wheat flour*

flow¹ * /floʊ/ [verb; flowed, flowing]
1 if a liquid flows, it moves steadily from one place to another: *A narrow river flows through the valley.*
2 if hair or clothing flows, it hangs loosely in an attractive way: *Her long hair flowed behind her.*

/i/ **see**	/ɪ/ **big**	/eɪ/ **day**	/ɛ/ **get**	/æ/ **hat**
/ɑ/ **father, hot**	/ʌ/ **up**	/ə/ **about**	/ɔ/ **saw**	
/oʊ/ **hope**	/ʊ/ **book**	/u/ **too**	/aɪ/ **I**	/aʊ/ **how**
/ɔɪ/ **boy**	/ɝ/ **bird**	/ɚ/ **teacher**	/ɪr/ **ear**	/ɛr/ **air**
/ɑr/ **far**	/ɔr/ **more**	/ʊr/ **tour**	/aɪr/ **fire**	
/aʊɚ/ **hour**	/θ/ **nothing**	/ð/ **mother**	/ʃ/ **she**	
/ʒ/ **measure**	/tʃ/ **church**	/dʒ/ **jump**	/ŋ/ **long**	

flow² * [*noun*] a continuous movement of something from one place to another: *a constant **flow of traffic***

flower¹ * /'flaʊɚ/ [*noun*]
1 the colored part of a plant or tree that produces seeds or fruit: *a bush with yellow flowers* | *a bouquet of flowers*
2 a plant with a colored part that produces seeds or fruit: *What kind of flowers did you plant?*

daffodil   violet   lily   tulip   daisy   rose   iris   carnation   orchid

common flowers

flower² [*verb*; **flowered, flowering**] to produce flowers: *Cherry trees flower in April.*

flowerbed /'flaʊɚ-ˌbɛd/ [*noun*] an area of ground where flowers are grown

flowerpot /'flaʊɚ-ˌpat/ [*noun*] a pot in which you grow plants

flown * /floʊn/ [*verb*] the past participle of **FLY**¹

flu /flu/ [*noun*]
the flu influenza; a common illness that is like a very bad cold, that gives you a fever, and can make your stomach feel sick: *Mom **has the flu**.* | *He's home in bed **with the flu**.*

fluent /'fluənt/ [*adjective*; **more fluent, most fluent**] able to speak a language very well: *He is **fluent in** Arabic.* | *fluent English/Italian/Japanese/etc.* ▸ *She speaks fluent Chinese.*

fluff /flʌf/ [*noun*] small, light pieces of feathers, fur, or cloth: *a ball of fluff*

fluffy /'flʌfi/ [*adjective*; **fluffier, fluffiest**] looking or feeling soft, light, and full: *fluffy white clouds* | *a nice fluffy pillow*

fluid /'fluɪd/ [*noun*] a liquid: *Make sure you drink plenty of fluids.* | *cleaning fluid*

flung /flʌŋ/ [*verb*] the past tense and past participle of **FLING**

flush /flʌʃ/ [*verb*; **flushes, flushed, flushing**]
1 if you flush a toilet, or if a toilet flushes, you make water go through it to clean it: *Please do not flush paper towels down these toilets.*
2 to become red in the face: *He **flushed with embarrassment** when he saw me.*

flushed /flʌʃt/ [*adjective*; **more flushed, most flushed**] red in the face: *You look a little flushed.*

flute /flut/ [*noun*] a MUSICAL INSTRUMENT that is a long, thin, metal tube, with an end you blow into and buttons you press: *She's learning to **play the flute**.*

fly¹ * /flaɪ/ [*verb*; **flies, flew, flown, flying**]
1 to move through the air from one place to another: *Everyone stopped to watch the planes flying overhead.* | *A pigeon flew down onto the roof.*
2 to travel by plane: *Is this the first time you've flown?* | **fly from a place to a place** ▸ *We're flying from New York to Seattle.*
3 to move in the air or make something move in the air: *Flags flew all around the stadium.* | *Children were **flying kites** in the park.*
4 to go somewhere very quickly: *He flew downstairs to answer the door.*
5 if a period of time flies, it passes very quickly: *The hours **flew by**.* | *The afternoon just **flew past**.*

fly² * [*noun*; **plural flies**] a small insect that flies: *Flies carry disease.*

a fly

foal /foʊl/ [*noun*] a young horse

foam /foʊm/ [noun] small white bubbles that form on the surface of a liquid

focus[1] /'foʊkəs/ [verb; **focuses, focused, focusing**]
1 to give attention to one person or thing rather than others: *Try to focus on what you're doing, please.*
2 to turn the part that light travels through on a camera, telescope, etc., until you can see clearly through it: *Be sure to focus the camera correctly.*

focus[2] [noun]
1 a situation, person, or event that people talk or write about a lot: *The Olympics have been the focus of attention worldwide.*
2 how clear the things are that you see in a photograph or through a camera, telescope, etc.: *Are the binoculars in focus? | This shot is a little out of focus.*

fog /fɑg/ [noun] thick clouds that are close to the ground and very difficult to see through: *I hate driving in fog.*

foggy /'fɑgi/ [adjective; **foggier, foggiest**] foggy weather is when there are a lot of thick clouds close to the ground: *a foggy November evening*

fold[1] * /foʊld/ [verb; **folded, folding**]
1 to bend a piece of paper or cloth by putting one part over another: *She folded the letter carefully. | Would you help me fold these sheets?*
2 if something such as furniture folds or you fold it, it becomes smaller when you close or bend it: *The couch folds out into a bed. | If you fold the chairs up, I'll put them away.*

— PHRASE —
3 fold your arms to bend one arm over the other across your chest: *He leaned back and folded his arms.*
⇒ *See also* **cross your arms/legs/fingers** *at* CROSS[1].

fold[2] * [noun] a line that is made in paper or cloth when you fold it: *Cut along the fold.*

folder /'foʊldɚ/ [noun]
1 a large folded piece of thick strong paper that you use for keeping pieces of paper together: *File folders were*

scattered over the desk. | *Arrange your papers neatly inside a folder.*
⇒ *See the picture at* OFFICE.
2 a picture on a computer screen that shows you where information is stored: *Open the folder marked "My Documents."*

folk /foʊk/ [adjective; *no comparative*] folk art, dance, songs, etc., are traditional and typical of the people who live in an area: *Irish folk dancing*
☞ Only use **folk** before a noun.

folks /foʊks/ [plural noun]
1 INFORMAL your parents or family: *She went to call her folks.*
2 SPOKEN used when you are talking to a group of people in a friendly way: *Nice to see you again, folks.*

follow * /'fɑloʊ/ [verb; **followed, following**]
1 to walk, drive, etc., behind someone else: *If you follow me, I'll show you to your room. | The principal walked in, followed by her secretary.*
2 to go in a particular direction: *Turn left, then follow the road to the lake.*
3 to happen immediately after something else: *We heard loud voices, followed by a door slamming.*
4 to understand something: *I'm sorry, I don't follow you. | The plot of the movie was a little difficult to follow.*

— PHRASES —
5 follow instructions/the rules/ orders/etc. to do something according to a set of instructions, rules, etc.: *Why didn't you follow my instructions?*
6 as follows used to introduce a list of names, instructions, etc., that come next: *The winners of the awards are as follows: 1st prize, John Hill; 2nd prize, Brenda Snow.*
7 follow in someone's footsteps to do the same thing that someone else

/i/ see	/ɪ/ big	/eɪ/ day	/ɛ/ get	/æ/ hat
/ɑ/ father, hot	/ʌ/ up	/ə/ about	/ɔ/ saw	
/oʊ/ hope	/ʊ/ book	/u/ too	/aɪ/ I	/aʊ/ how
/ɔɪ/ boy	/ɝ/ bird	/ɚ/ teacher	/ɪr/ ear	/ɛr/ air
/ɑr/ far	/ɔr/ more	/ʊr/ tour	/aɪr/ fire	
/aʊɚ/ hour	/θ/ nothing	/ð/ mother	/ʃ/ she	
/ʒ/ measure	/tʃ/ church	/dʒ/ jump	/ŋ/ long	

did before you: *He followed in his brother's footsteps and became an actor.*

following /'faloʊɪŋ/ [*adjective; no comparative*]

═══ PHRASE ═══

the following day/month/page/ etc. the next day, month, page, etc.: *He called me the following day. | See the following page for more details.*

fond /fand/ [*adjective; fonder, fondest*]

═══ PHRASE ═══

be fond of to like someone or something very much: *I'm very fond of your mother.*

food * /fud/ [*noun*] something that you eat: *Chocolate and bananas are two of my favorite foods. | a **health food** store | People eat too much **junk food** (=food that is not healthy).*

food court /'fud ˌkɔrt/ [*noun*] a part of a shopping area where there are several places to buy food, and a place in the middle with tables where you can eat

food processor /'fud ˌprɑsɛsɚ/ [*noun*] an electric machine used in the kitchen to cut or mix food very quickly
⇨ *See the picture at* APPLIANCE.

fool[1] /ful/ [*noun*]

1 a stupid or silly person: *I felt like a **fool** afterwards for getting so mad.*

═══ PHRASE ═══

2 make a fool of yourself to do something that makes you seem stupid or silly: *They made fools of themselves at the party.*

fool[2] [*verb; fooled, fooling*]

1 to make someone do or believe something by deceiving him or her: *Don't let him fool you—he's not really hurt. | **fool someone into doing something** ▸ She was fooled into giving them a lot of money.*

═══ PHRASAL VERB ═══

fool around [*phrasal verb*]

2 to behave in a silly way: *Would you two stop fooling around?*

foolish /'fulɪʃ/ [*adjective; more foolish, most foolish*] not sensible: *It was **foolish** of her to invite him. | She felt very foolish.*

foolishly /'fulɪʃli/ [*adverb*] in a stupid or silly way: *He'd behaved foolishly.*

foot * /fʊt/ [*noun*]

1 [*plural* **feet**] the part of your BODY at the end of your leg that you stand on: *She hurt her foot. | What size feet do you have?*

2 [*plural* **feet**] the part at the end of the legs of BIRDS and of some animals: *a bird's foot | pigs' feet*
⇨ *Compare* PAW.

3 [*no plural*] the bottom end, or lowest part of something: *a town **at the foot of** the mountain | She dropped her jacket on the foot of the bed.*

4 [*plural* **feet** or **foot**] a unit for measuring length, equal to 12 inches or 0.3048 meters: *Most of the players on the team are over six feet tall. | a five-foot-long board*

═══ PHRASES ═══

5 on foot if you go somewhere on foot, you walk there: *They traveled the last ten kilometers on foot.*

6 be on your feet

a to be standing or walking: *I've been on my feet all day.*

b to be feeling well after an illness: *He was happy to be on his feet again.*

football * /'fʊtˌbɔl/ [*noun*]

1 a sport or game played by two teams, in which players carry, throw, or kick a ball to one end of a field in order to get points: *My brother **plays football**. | a **football field***
⇨ *Compare* SOCCER.

2 the BALL that is used in this game

footprint /'fʊtˌprɪnt/ [*noun*] a mark that is made on a surface by a foot or shoe: *The kids left dirty footprints all over the floor.*

footstep /'fʊtˌstɛp/ [*noun*] the sound made by someone's feet as he or she walks: *We heard footsteps coming down the corridor.*
⇨ *Compare* STEP[1] (definition 1).

for * /fɔr/ [*preposition*]

1 intended to be given to a person or used in a particular situation: *She brought some candy for us. | Did you get tickets for the show? | a knife for chopping vegetables*

2 if you work for an organization, play for a sports team, etc., that is the organization or team in which you work or play: *He plays for the Miami Dolphins.* | *How long have you worked for the company?*

3 used to show a length of time or a distance: *They've lived here for over 30 years.* | *We drove for miles.*

▷ *See the usage notes at* AGO *and* DURING.

4 used to show the place where someone or something is going: *The plane for Miami leaves from Gate 23.*

5 used to show a price: *We sold the truck for $7,000.*

6 meaning something: *What's the Korean word for "window"?*

7 in order to help someone: *I can type that letter for you.*

8 relating to someone or something: *sales figures for each month*

9 in order to get or do something: *Let's go for a swim.* | *What are you doing that for* (=why are you doing that)?

10 used to show the time at which something will happen: *I reserved a table for 8 o'clock.* | *Are you going home for the holidays?*

11 because of or as a result of something: *She was fined for speeding.*

forbid * T /fɚ'bɪd/ [*verb;* **forbids, forbade** *or* **forbid, forbid** *or* **forbidden, forbidding**] FORMAL

1 to tell someone not to do something: **forbid someone to do something** ▷ *I forbid you to use the car.*

━━ PHRASE ━━

2 be forbidden to not be allowed: *Smoking is **strictly forbidden*** (=definitely not allowed).

force¹ * /fɔrs/ [*noun*]

1 the natural power that something produces when it hits something: *The ground shook from the **force of** the explosion.* | *A hurricane struck **with great force.***

2 an organized group of people who are trained to fight together: *He served in the Air Force for 20 years.* | *the **armed forces*** (=military organizations such as the Army, Navy, etc.)

3 the use of strength or violence to get or do something: *The police **used force** to enter the house.* | *Troops entered the town **by force*** (=by using violence).

force² * [*verb;* **forced, forcing**]

1 to make someone do something, especially by threatening him or her: **force someone to do something** ▷ *Don't force her to eat if she's not hungry.*

2 to move something or go somewhere using physical strength: *Burglars had **forced** the window **open.*** | *She had to **force her way** through the crowd.*

forecast /'fɔr,kæst/ [*noun*] a statement that describes what is likely to happen in the future: *Did you hear the **weather forecast**?*

forefinger /'fɔr,fɪŋgɚ/ [*noun*] the finger that is next to your thumb

forehead /'fɔr,hɛd/ [*noun*] the part of your face that is above your eyes

▷ *See the picture at* BODY.

foreign * T /'fɔrɪn/ [*adjective; no comparative*] belonging to or coming from a country that is not your own: *foreign languages* | *foreign imports* (=goods from other countries)

▷ *See the usage note at* FOREIGNER.

foreigner * /'fɔrənɚ/ [*noun*] someone who comes from a country that is not your own: *There is a limited number of work permits for foreigners.*

USAGE   foreigner, foreign

Do not use "foreigner" or "foreign" when you are talking about people from a country that is not your own—it is not polite. Use another expression, such as **They come from abroad** or **They come from China/Canada/Brazil/etc.**

foreman /'fɔrmən/ [*noun; plural* **foremen** /'fɔrmən/] someone in charge of a group of workers or a jury

forest * /'fɔrɪst/ [*noun*] a large area of land that is covered with trees: *Bears live in the forest.* | *an area of thick forest*

forever * /fɔr'ɛvɚ/ [*adverb*] continuing for all time in the future: *"I'll love you forever," she said.*

/i/ **see**	/ɪ/ **big**	/eɪ/ **day**	/ɛ/ **get**	/æ/ **hat**
/ɑ/ **father, hot**	/ʌ/ **up**	/ə/ **about**	/ɔ/ **saw**	
/oʊ/ **hope**	/ʊ/ **book**	/u/ **too**	/aɪ/ **I**	/aʊ/ **how**
/ɔɪ/ **boy**	/ɝ/ **bird**	/ɚ/ **teacher**	/ɪr/ **ear**	/ɛr/ **air**
/ɑr/ **far**	/ɔr/ **more**	/ʊr/ **tour**	/aɪr/ **fire**	
/aʊɚ/ **hour**	/θ/ **nothing**	/ð/ **mother**	/ʃ/ **she**	
/ʒ/ **measure**	/tʃ/ **church**	/dʒ/ **jump**	/ŋ/ **long**	

forgave * /fəˈgeɪv/ [verb] the past tense of FORGIVE

forge /fɔrdʒ/ [verb; forged, forging] to make an illegal copy of something such as a document or painting: *Her passport had been forged.*

forgery /ˈfɔrdʒəri/ [noun; plural **forgeries**]
1 the crime of illegally copying something such as a document or painting: *He went to prison for forgery.*
2 an illegal copy of something such as a document or painting: *The painting is now thought to be a forgery.*

forget * /fəˈget/ [verb; **forgot, forgotten, forgetting**]
1 to not remember information or facts: *I've forgotten most of the French I learned.* | *I forgot that you were a vegetarian.* | *They had forgotten all about their argument.* | *forget what/ where/how/etc.* ▸ *He's always forgetting where he put his keys.*
2 to not remember to do or bring something: *They forgot all about the meeting.* | *I forgot my pen.* | **forget to do something** ▸ *Don't forget to buy some milk.*

forgetful /fəˈgetfəl/ [adjective; **more forgetful, most forgetful**] likely to forget things: *She can be very forgetful.*

forgive * /fəˈgɪv/ [verb; **forgave, forgiven** /fəˈgɪvən /, **forgiving**] to decide not to be angry with someone when he or she has done something wrong: *Please forgive me.* | **forgive someone for something** ▸ *She never forgave him for what he'd done.*

forgot * /fəˈgɑt/ [verb] the past tense of FORGET

forgotten * /fəˈgɑtən/ [verb] the past participle of FORGET

fork[1] * /fɔrk/ [noun]
1 an object that you use for eating that has three or four sharp points that pick up food: *a knife and fork*
⇨ *See the picture at PLACE SETTING.*
2 the place where a road or river begins to go in two different directions: *They came to a fork in the road.*

fork[2] [verb; **forked, forking**] if a road or river forks, it begins to go in two

different directions: *The river forks just beyond the bridge.*

form[1] * T /fɔrm/ [verb; **formed, forming**]
1 to begin to exist, or to make something begin to exist: *Ice had started to form on the windshield.* | *The valleys were formed by rivers.*
2 to make a shape: *The dancers formed a circle.* | *Could you all form a line* (=stand together in a line) *please?*
3 to make something such as an organization or a relationship start to exist: *The club was formed almost ten years ago.*
4 to make something by combining two or more parts: *You form the plural of most nouns by adding "s" or "es."*

form[2] * T [noun]
1 a kind of something: *he has a rare form of cancer.*
2 the way in which something is made, produced, or designed: *a sculpture in the form of a large ring* | *The medicine comes in either pill or liquid form.*
3 a document on which there are spaces for you to write information such as your name, address, etc.: *They e-mailed me an application form.*

formal * /ˈfɔrməl/ [adjective; **more formal, most formal**]
1 suitable for official or serious occasions; *opposite* INFORMAL: *The language she uses is very formal.*
2 a formal speech, statement, etc., is made officially or publicly: *I intend to write a formal letter of complaint.*

formally * /ˈfɔrməli/ [adverb] in a way that is official, public, or suitable for serious occasions; *opposite* INFORMALLY: *They have formally announced that they are getting married.*

former[1] * /ˈfɔrmɚ/ [adjective; no comparative] existing before, but not now: *Our former director has agreed to attend the meeting.*
☛ Only use **former** before a noun.

former[2] [noun] FORMAL
the former used to talk about the first of two things or people that have just been mentioned; *opposite* LATTER: *She runs in the 200 and 400 meter races, but she's faster in the former.*

formerly /'fɔrmə·li/ [*adverb*] at a time in the past, but not now: *Sri Lanka was formerly known as Ceylon.*

formula /'fɔrmyələ/ [*noun; plural* **formulas**] a group of numbers or letters that represent a rule in math or science: *a chemical formula*

fort /fɔrt/ [*noun*] a large strong building that soldiers used in the past to defend a place: *A fort stood at the top of the hill.*

fortieth * /'fɔrtiɪθ/ [*adjective, adverb; no comparative*] coming after 39 other people, things, or events; sometimes written as "40th": *Our fortieth wedding anniversary is in June.*
  ⇨ *See the usage note at* SECOND[2].

fortunate * /'fɔrtʃənɪt/ [*adjective;* **more fortunate, most fortunate**] FORMAL
1 if you are fortunate, good things happen to you by chance: *I am fortunate to have survived the accident*
2 something that is fortunate is a good thing to have happen; *opposite* UNFORTUNATE: *It was fortunate that no one was in the building when the fire broke out.*

fortunately /'fɔrtʃənɪtli/ [*adverb*] used to say that an event or situation is good; *opposite* UNFORTUNATELY: *Fortunately, I arrived on time.*

fortune /'fɔrtʃən/ [*noun*]
1 a large amount of money: *Her dream is to win a fortune in the lottery.*
2 luck and the influence that it has on someone's life: *We have the **good fortune** to be healthy.*

━━ PHRASE ━━━━━━

3 tell someone's fortune to tell someone what will happen in his or her life by using special cards, looking at his or her hand, etc.: *Did you ever have your fortune told?*

forty * /'fɔrti/ [*number, noun; plural* **forties**] 40: *He's forty years old.*
  ⇨ *See the usage note at* TEENS.

forward * /'fɔrwə·d/ or **forwards** /'fɔrwə·dz/ [*adverb*]
1 toward a place that is in front of you; *opposite* BACKWARD: *He ran forward and caught the ball.*
2 toward more progress or a better position: *The peace talks cannot go forward until the fighting ends.*

fought * /fɔt/ [*verb*] the past tense and past participle of FIGHT[1]

foul[1] /faʊl/ [*adjective;* **fouler, foulest**] very dirty, or smelling or tasting extremely unpleasant: *a foul smell* | *The water is foul.*

foul[2] [*verb;* **fouled, fouling**] to do something that is against the rules while playing a sport: *Gardener fouled Hill on that play.*

foul[3] [*noun*] something that someone does that is against the rules while playing a sport: *He **committed a foul** (=did something that is a foul).*

found * ⊤ /faʊnd/ [*verb*] the past tense and past participle of FIND

foundation /faʊn'deɪʃən/ [*noun*] the supporting base of a building: *After the flood, our foundation needed repair.*

fountain /'faʊntən/ [*noun*] a specially built structure from which water rises into the air, that you see in gardens or parks: *There's a fountain in the park.*
  ⇨ *See also* DRINKING FOUNTAIN.

four * /fɔr/ [*number, noun*] 4: *Four people were sitting at each table.*

fourteen * /'fɔr'tin/ [*number*] 14: *The group has fourteen members.*

fourteenth * /'fɔr'tinθ/ [*adverb, adjective; no comparative*] coming after thirteen other people, things, or events; sometimes written as "14th": *the fourteenth day of the month* | *I finished 14th in the race.*
  ⇨ *See the usage note at* SECOND[2].

fourth[1] * /fɔrθ/ [*adverb, adjective; no comparative*] coming after three other people, things or events; sometimes written as "4th": *He finished the race in 4th place.* | *I came in fourth in the race.*

fourth[2] * [*noun, pronoun*] one of four equal parts into which something is divided; *synonym* QUARTER: *A **fourth** of 100 is 25.* | *Three-fourths (=3/4) of the pie was gone.*
  ⇨ *See the usage note at* SECOND[2].

/i/ **see**	/ɪ/ **big**	/eɪ/ **day**	/ɛ/ **get**	/æ/ **hat**
/ɑ/ **father, hot**	/ʌ/ **up**	/ə/ **about**	/ɔ/ **saw**
/oʊ/ **hope**	/ʊ/ **book**	/u/ **too**	/aɪ/ **I**	/aʊ/ **how**
/ɔɪ/ **boy**	/ɝ/ **bird**	/ɚ/ **teacher**	/ɪr/ **ear**	/ɛr/ **air**
/ɑr/ **far**	/ɔr/ **more**	/ʊr/ **tour**	/aɪr/ **fire**
/aʊə·/ **hour**	/θ/ **nothing**	/ð/ **mother**	/ʃ/ **she**
/ʒ/ **measure**	/tʃ/ **church**	/dʒ/ **jump**	/ŋ/ **long**

fox /faks/ [*noun; plural* **foxes**] an animal like a dog with red-brown fur, a pointed face, and a long thick tail

fraction /'frækʃən/ [*noun*] a smaller part of a whole number, for example ¾ or ½: *It's easy to multiply fractions.*

fragile ⊤ /'frædʒəl/ [*adjective;* **more fragile, most fragile**] easily broken or damaged: *Be careful with those glasses—they're fragile.*

fragment ⊤ /'frægmənt/ [*noun*] a small piece of something that has broken off a larger object: *Fragments of glass lay all over the road.*

fragrance /'freɪɡrəns/ [*noun*]
1 a pleasant smell, especially of flowers: *The room was filled with the fragrance of lilies.*
 ⇨ *See the synonym note at* SMELL[1].
2 a liquid with a pleasant smell that you put on your skin: *The store sells men's and women's fragrances*
 ⇨ *Compare* PERFUME.

fragrant /'freɪɡrənt/ [*adjective;* **more fragrant, most fragrant**] smelling pleasant: *The sheets were cool and fragrant.*

frail ⊤ /freɪl/ [*adjective;* **frailer, frailest**] not strong or healthy: *a frail old man*

frame[1] * /freɪm/ [*noun*]
1 the part that surrounds the edge of a picture, window, etc., and that is often shaped like a square: *a photograph in a silver frame*
2 a structure made of wood or metal that supports or holds something: *The frame of the car was rusting badly.*
3 frames [*plural*] the plastic or metal part of a pair of glasses: *Which frames look better on me?*

frame[2] [*verb;* **framed, framing**] to put a frame around a picture: *I want to frame this photo.*

frank /fræŋk/ [*adjective;* **franker, frankest**] honest, especially when you are talking about problems or difficulties: *a frank discussion*

frankly /'fræŋkli/ [*adverb*]
1 SPOKEN used before saying what you honestly think and feel about something: *Frankly, I'm surprised they offered her the job.*
2 in an honest and sincere way: *She spoke frankly about her divorce.*

fraternity /frə'tɝnɪti/ [*noun;* **fraternities**] a club at an American college that is only for male students, who usually live together in the club's house
 ⇨ *Compare* SORORITY.

fraud /frɔd/ [*noun*] the crime of obtaining money from a person or organization in a dishonest way: *tax fraud*

freak[1] /frik/ [*noun*]
1 a person or animal whose appearance or behavior is very strange: *They all stared at me as if I were a freak.*
2 INFORMAL someone who is very interested in an activity or subject and cannot stop thinking about it or doing it: *a fitness freak*

freak[2] [*adjective; no comparative*] extremely unusual: *a freak accident* | *a freak storm*
 ☛ Only use **freak** before a noun.

freckle /'frɛkəl/ [*noun*] a small brown spot on someone's skin: *She has red hair and freckles.*

free[1] * ⊤ /fri/ [*adjective;* **freer, freest**]
1 without a lot of controls or rules: *a free society* | **free to do something** ▸ *We're free to come and go as we please.*
2 not costing any money: *Entrance to the museum is free on Thursdays.*
3 having the time to do something because you are not busy: *We could go to the movies Tuesday if you're free.* | *What do you do in your free time?* (=time when you are not working)
4 not being used: *The phone's free now.*
5 not in prison or being kept in a place: *The four hostages were set free* (=given their freedom) *yesterday.*
 ⇨ *See also* feel free *at* FEEL.
 — PHRASE —
6 sugar-free/fat-free/salt-free/etc. not containing sugar, fat, salt, etc.: *a salt-free diet*

free[2] * ⊤ [*verb;* **frees, freed, freeing**]
1 to let someone leave a place where he or she has been kept as a prisoner: *He was freed from jail last year.*

2 to help someone or something to move from a place or position where he, she, or it is unable to move: *Firefighters worked to free the people who were trapped inside the building.*

free[3] * [T] [adverb]
1 without costing or spending any money: *He got the tickets for free.* | *You can visit the museum free of charge.*
2 not stuck, and able to move: *The boat was stuck in the mud and we couldn't get it free* (=move it).

freedom * /'fridəm/ [noun] when you are not controlled or are able to do what you want; synonym LIBERTY:
freedom to do something ▸ *We have the freedom to believe whatever we want.*

freely [T] /'frili/ [adverb]
1 without feeling afraid to say what you want: *The students are encouraged to express their opinions freely.*
2 without being controlled or restricted: *We traveled freely within the country.*

freeway /'fri,weɪ/ [noun; plural freeways] a wide road on which vehicles can travel very fast

freeze * /friz/ [verb; froze, frozen, freezing]
1 if a liquid freezes or something freezes in, it becomes solid because it is very cold: *Keep the heat on so the pipes don't freeze.* | *Temperatures in the twenties froze the lake.* | *What is the freezing point of gasoline?*
2 to keep food fresh by putting it in a very cold place, or to stay fresh in this way: *I'll freeze the rest of the soup.* | *Fruit doesn't always freeze well.*
3 to stop moving or working, or to make someone or something do this: *My computer froze.* | *A program error froze the system.*

freezer /'frizɚ/ [noun] a piece of electrical equipment used for keeping food frozen: *The ice cream's in the freezer.*

freezing[1] /'frizɪŋ/ [adjective; no comparative]
1 so cold that things begin to freeze: *freezing temperatures*

━━ PHRASES ━━━━━━━━━
2 it's freezing SPOKEN used to say that the temperature is very cold: *It's freezing in here.*

3 be freezing SPOKEN to feel very cold: *My feet are freezing.*
⇨ *See the synonym note at* COLD[1].

freezing[2] [noun] thirty-two degrees Fahrenheit or zero degrees Celsius: *The temperature will drop below freezing tonight.*

French fries /'frɛntʃ 'fraɪz/ [plural noun] thin sticks of potato that have been cooked in oil; synonym FRIES

frequent * [T] /'frikwənt/ [adjective; more frequent, most frequent] happening often: *I have frequent colds.*

frequently * /'frikwəntli/ [adverb] often; opposite RARELY: *They call each other frequently.*

fresh * /frɛʃ/ [adjective; fresher, freshest]
1 fresh food has been picked or made recently and tastes good: *Try to eat plenty of fresh fruit and vegetables.* | *I love the smell of fresh bread.*
⇨ *Compare* STALE.
2 smelling or looking clean: *Open the window and let in some fresh air* (=clean air from outside).
3 not used, or not seen, done, or known before; synonym NEW: *The house needs a fresh coat of paint* (=a new layer of paint). | *fresh ideas*

freshly [T] /'frɛʃli/ [adverb] made, picked, done, etc., very recently: *freshly made coffee*

freshman /'frɛʃmən/ [noun; plural freshmen /'frɛʃmən/] someone in his or her first year at a college or high school
⇨ *Compare* SOPHOMORE, JUNIOR[2], SENIOR[2].

Fri. the written abbreviation of FRIDAY

Friday * /'fraɪdeɪ/ [noun; plural **Fridays**] the day of the week that is after Thursday and before Saturday: *We're going out on Friday.* | *We finish school early on Fridays.*
⇨ *See the usage note at* DAY.

/i/ **see**	/ɪ/ **big**	/eɪ/ **day**	/ɛ/ **get** /æ/ **hat**
/ɑ/ **father, hot**	/ʌ/ **up**	/ə/ **about**	/ɔ/ **saw**
/oʊ/ **hope**	/ʊ/ **book**	/u/ **too**	/aɪ/ **I** /aʊ/ **how**
/ɔɪ/ **boy**	/ɝ/ **bird**	/ɚ/ **teacher**	/ɪr/ **ear** /ɛr/ **air**
/ɑr/ **far**	/ɔr/ **more**	/ʊr/ **tour**	/aɪr/ **fire**
/aʊɚ/ **hour**	/θ/ **nothing**	/ð/ **mother**	/ʃ/ **she**
/ʒ/ **measure**	/tʃ/ **church**	/dʒ/ **jump**	/ŋ/ **long**

fridge /frɪdʒ/ [noun] the short form of REFRIGERATOR: *Put the milk back in the fridge, please.*

fried[1] * /fraɪd/ [verb] the past tense and past participle of FRY

fried[2] * [adjective; no comparative] fried food has been cooked in hot oil: *fried chicken.*

friend * /frɛnd/ [noun]
1 someone who you know well and like a lot: *Tom's my best friend* (=the friend I like most). | *We were friends when we were little.* | *The book was given to me by a friend of mine.*
☛ Do not say "a friend of me." Say **a friend of mine.**
═ PHRASE ═
2 **make friends with someone** to become friendly with someone: *He quickly made friends with Dan and Chris.*
☛ Do not say "I made a friend with him." Say **I made friends with him.**

friendly * /'frɛndli/ [adjective; friendlier, friendliest] behaving in a way that shows you like someone and want to talk to him or her; opposite UNFRIENDLY: *She's such a cheerful, friendly girl.* | *Are you friendly with the neighbors?* (=are they your friends)

friendship /'frɛndʃɪp/ [noun] a relationship that exists between friends: *A close friendship soon developed between the two men.*

fries /fraɪz/ [plural noun] thin sticks of potato that have been cooked in oil; synonym FRENCH FRIES: *I'd like a burger and an order of fries.*

fright /fraɪt/ [noun] a sudden feeling of fear: *We got a real fright when we heard someone downstairs.*

frighten * /'fraɪtən/ [verb; frightened, frightening]
1 to make someone feel afraid; synonym SCARE: *Stop shouting! You'll frighten the children.*
═ PHRASAL VERB ═
frighten away or **frighten off** [phrasal verb]
2 to make a person or animal so frightened that he, she, or it goes away: *frighten someone away/off* ▸ *A sudden noise will frighten the deer off.*

| **frighten away/off someone** ▸ *The sound of the car must have frightened away the thieves.*

frightened * /'fraɪtənd/ [adjective; more frightened, most frightened] afraid or worried; synonym SCARED: *Don't be frightened of the dog.*

frightening * ⊤ /'fraɪtənɪŋ/ [adjective; more frightening, most frightening] making you feel afraid or worried; synonym SCARY: *The thought of traveling alone was frightening.*

frog /frag/ [noun] a small animal that lives in water and on land and uses its legs for jumping
⇨ Compare TOAD.

a frog

from * /frʌm/ [preposition]
1 used to show the place where something starts: *We drove here from Boston.*
2 used before the first of two times to show how long something continues: *The meeting will last from 2:30 to 7:30.*
☛ Do not say that something "starts from 7 p.m." Say that it **starts at 7 p.m.**
3 used to say who gave or sent something: *a present from Mom*
4 used to show a distance: *We live about 20 miles from the airport.*
5 used when people or things are moved or taken away from something or someone else: *She got a book from the top shelf.* | *Mom took the bag of candy away from me.*
6 because of something: *I'm tired from lack of sleep.*
7 used to show where someone was born or lives: *I come from Cleveland, Ohio.* | *I'm from Hong Kong.*
═ PHRASES ═
8 **from now on** starting now, and continuing in the future: *From now on, I expect your work to improve.*
9 **from time to time** sometimes, but not often; synonym OCCASIONALLY: *She visits us from time to time.*

front[1] * /frʌnt/ [noun]
1 **the front** the forward part of something: *He was standing at the front of the line.* | *The living room is in*

the front of the house. I *Could you all come and sit* **at the front**, *please?*
↳ *Compare* **the back** *at* BACK².

2 the side or surface of something that is in the same direction that it faces; *opposite* BACK: *The front of the building has two arches.* I *There was a picture of a cat* **on the front** *of the card.*

══ PHRASE ══

3 in front (of) ahead, or in the part of something that is the farthest forward: *Let's meet in front of the hotel.* I *I want to ride in front* (=in the front of a car). I *Jack was sitting two rows in front of us.*
☛ Do not say "in the front of us." Say **in front of us**.
↳ *Compare* BEHIND² (definition 1). ↳ *See the picture at* PREPOSITION.

front² ✱ [*adjective; no comparative*] at or in the front of something; *opposite* BACK: *The story was on the front page of the paper.* I *We had seats in the front row.*
☛ Only use **front** before a noun.

frontier /frʌn'tɪr/ [*noun*] an area near the border or edge of something, especially one that people do not know much about: *the frontiers of science*

frost¹ /frɔst/ [*noun*] a layer of ice that looks like white powder and covers things outside when the weather is very cold: *The windshield was covered in frost.*

frost² [*verb; frosted, frosting*] to cover a cake or other sweet food with frosting: *Let the cupcakes cool completely before you frost them.*

frosting [*noun*] a mixture of sugar, butter, and liquids that you spread on a cake; *synonym* ICING: *chocolate frosting*

frown¹ /fraʊn/ [*verb; frowned, frowning*] to look as if you are annoyed or unhappy, with the corners of your mouth turned down: *Why do you keep frowning at me?*
↳ *See the picture at* EMOTION.

frown² [*noun*] the expression on your face when you frown

froze ✱ /froʊz/ [*verb*] the past tense of FREEZE

frozen¹ ✱ /'froʊzən/ [*verb*] the past participle of FREEZE

frozen² ✱ [*adjective; no comparative*]
1 covered with ice and very hard: *The lake was completely frozen.*
2 to be very cold: *frozen vegetables* I *Can I sit by the fire? I'm frozen.*

fruit ✱ /frut/ [*noun; plural* **fruits** *or* **fruit**]
1 food that grows on trees or other plants and usually tastes sweet: *Would anyone like* **a piece of fruit?**
↳ *Compare* VEGETABLE.
2 a kind of fruit: *The store sells many different fruits and vegetables.*

1. apples
2. bananas
3. kiwis
4. grapes
5. cherries
6. lemon
7. lime
8. grapefruit
9. oranges
10. strawberries
11. plum
12. apricot
13. peach
14. pears
15. pineapple

kinds of fruits

frustrated /'frʌstreɪtɪd/ [*adjective;* **more frustrated, most frustrated**] annoyed and upset because something is stopping you from doing or getting what you want: *She was frustrated because no one would believe her.*

fry * /fraɪ/ [*verb;* **fries, fried, frying**] to cook food in hot oil or butter: *I'll fry some potatoes.*
  ⇨ *See the synonym note at* COOK[1].

frying pan /'fraɪɪŋ ˌpæn/ [*noun*] a flat pan used for frying food
  ⇨ *See the picture at* POT.

ft. the written abbreviation of FOOT or FEET when they are used as measurements: *a 10-ft. cord*

fuel * T /'fyuəl/ [*noun*] something such as coal or gas that produces heat or energy when it is burned

fulfill /fʊl'fɪl/ [*verb;* **fulfilled, fulfilling**] to do what you said you would do: *Few elected officials fulfill all their promises.*

full * /fʊl/ [*adjective;* **fuller, fullest**]
  1 containing as much of something or as many things or people as possible; *opposite* EMPTY: *a full glass of juice* I *a wallet full of money* I *All the restaurants are usually full by eight o'clock.*
  2 unable to eat any more; *opposite* HUNGRY: *"Would you like a dessert?" "No thanks, I'm full."*
  3 including all details or features; *synonym* COMPLETE: *Please write your full address, including ZIP code.*
  ━ PHRASE ━
  4 **be full of** to contain a lot of people or things of the same kind: *Miami is always full of tourists at this time of year.*

full moon /'fʊl 'mun/ [*noun*] the MOON when it looks completely round: *There's a full moon tonight.*

full-time[1] /'fʊl 'taɪm/ [*adverb*]
  ━ PHRASE ━
  work/study full-time to work or study for the number of hours that people usually work or study: *My mother works full-time in a factory.*
  ⇨ *Compare* PART-TIME[1].

full-time[2] /'fʊl ˌtaɪm/ [*adjective; no comparative*] working or studying for the number of hours that people usually work or study: *a full-time student*
  ⇨ *Compare* PART-TIME[2].

fully /'fʊli/ [*adverb*] completely: *Her children are now fully grown.*

fumes /fyumz/ [*plural noun*] unpleasant gas, smoke, or chemical smells: *The car exhaust fumes made me cough.*

fun * /fʌn/ [*noun*]
  1 enjoyment or pleasure, or an activity that provides this: *Swimming is fun.* I *We all had fun* (=enjoyed ourselves).
  ━ PHRASE ━
  2 **make fun of someone/something** to make jokes about someone or something in an unkind way: *The other kids made fun of him.*
  ☞ Do not say "make fun to someone" or "make fun with someone." Say **make fun of someone**.

function[1] T /'fʌŋkʃən/ [*noun*] the job that something or someone does: *The function of the kidneys is to clean the blood.*

function[2] T [*verb;* **functioned, functioning**] to work in a particular way: *The brain functions like a complex computer.*

fund T /fʌnd/ [*noun*]
  1 an amount of money saved for a particular purpose: *a fund to help students from poor families*
  2 **funds** [*plural*] money that is collected for a particular purpose: *We're collecting funds for the homeless.*

funding /'fʌndɪŋ/ [*noun*] money provided by a government or other organization for a particular purpose: *government funding for sports activities*

funeral * /'fyunərəl/ [*noun*] a formal ceremony that takes place when someone has died

fungus /'fʌŋgəs/ [*noun; plural* **fungi** /'fʌndʒaɪ/ *or* **funguses**] a plant without leaves that grows in dark wet places

funny * /'fʌni/ [*adjective;* **funnier, funniest**]
  1 making you laugh or smile; *synonym* AMUSING: *It was the funniest movie I ever saw.* I *He kept making funny faces.*
  2 strange or unusual; *synonym* ODD: *Jenny's a funny girl—I don't understand her.* I *That's funny, I'm sure I left the keys on my desk.*

━━ PHRASE ━━

3 very funny! SPOKEN used when other people are laughing to show that you do not think something is amusing: *Very funny! Where did you hide my keys?*

fur * /fɜ˞/ [noun]

1 the soft hair that covers the bodies of some animals: *Bears have brown, black, or white fur.*

2 a piece of clothing made from an animal's skin and soft hair: *a fur coat*

furious /ˈfyʊriəs/ [adjective; **more furious, most furious**] extremely angry: *She was furious with him for not calling her.*

➪ *See also* FURY. ➪ *See the synonym note at* ANGRY.

furnace /ˈfɜ˞nɪs/ [noun] a container used to heat a building or for heating things at very high temperatures: *Our furnace is broken.* | *The metal is melted in a furnace.*

furnish /ˈfɜ˞nɪʃ/ [verb; **furnishes, furnished, furnishing**]

1 to put furniture into a room or building: *How much did it cost to furnish the apartment?*

━━ PHRASE ━━

2 be furnished with to contain a particular kind of furniture: *The living room was furnished with antiques.*

furniture * /ˈfɜ˞nɪtʃə˞/ [noun] things in a room such as tables, chairs, etc.: *a piece of antique furniture*

☛ Do not say "a furniture." Say **a piece of furniture.**

furry * /ˈfɜ˞ri/ [adjective; **furrier, furriest**] covered in fur or soft hairs: *He was holding a furry little mouse.*

further¹ * /ˈfɜ˞ðə˞/ [adverb]

1 more than was mentioned, done, etc., before: *I don't wish to discuss this any further.*

☛ Do not say "We considered the matter farther." Say **We considered the matter further.**

2 more distant in time or space: *The bridge is about a mile further down the road.*

➪ *See the usage note at* FARTHER.

further² * [adjective; no comparative] more or additional: *Does anyone have any further comments?*

furthest¹ * /ˈfɜ˞ðɪst/ [adverb]

1 at or from the longest distance in space or time: *Who'll have to travel furthest?*

2 to the greatest limit or amount: *Dr. White has gone furthest in his research.*

furthest² * [adjective; no comparative] at or from the longest distance in space or time: *Their house was at the furthest limit of the town.*

fury /ˈfyʊri/ [noun] an extremely strong feeling of anger; synonym RAGE: *He was almost white with fury.*

➪ *See also* FURIOUS.

fuss¹ /fʌs/ [noun]

1 when people become very excited or anxious about something, especially something that is not important: *There's a lot of fuss about the new law.*

━━ PHRASES ━━

2 make a fuss (about something) to become very angry or anxious about something that is not important: *Stop making such a fuss!*

3 make a fuss over someone to give someone too much attention: *They always make a fuss over their kids.*

fuss² [verb; **fusses, fussed, fussing**] to worry and complain too much about things that are not important: *Just stop fussing—everything will be fine.*

fussy /ˈfʌsi/ [adjective; **fussier, fussiest**] too concerned about small details or things that are not important: *The boss is very fussy about how things are done.* | *a fussy eater* (=someone who does not like many kinds of food)

future * /ˈfyutʃə˞/ [noun]

1 the things that will happen or the things that someone will do in the time after now: *a young man with a bright future* (=a successful future)

/i/ **see**	/ɪ/ **big**	/eɪ/ **day**	/ɛ/ **get**	/æ/ **hat**
/ɑ/ **father, hot**	/ʌ/ **up**	/ə/ **about**	/ɔ/ **saw**	
/oʊ/ **hope**	/ʊ/ **book**	/u/ **too**	/aɪ/ **I**	/aʊ/ **how**
/ɔɪ/ **boy**	/ɜ˞/ **bird**	/ə˞/ **teacher**	/ɪr/ **ear**	/ɛr/ **air**
/ɑr/ **far**	/ɔr/ **more**	/ʊr/ **tour**	/aɪr/ **fire**	
/aʊə˞/ **hour**	/θ/ **nothing**	/ð/ **mother**	/ʃ/ **she**	
/ʒ/ **measure**	/tʃ/ **church**	/dʒ/ **jump**	/ŋ/ **long**	

2 the future
  a the time that will come and the things that will happen during this time: *I'm not worried about the future.* | *What will happen in the future?*
  b GRAMMAR the FUTURE TENSE

future continuous /'fyutʃɚ kən'tɪnyuəs/ [*noun*] GRAMMAR
the future continuous the form of a verb that shows what will be happening or be true at a time in the future. It is formed with the future tense of "be" and a present participle: *In the sentence "We will be driving home tomorrow," the verb is in the future continuous.*
  ⇨ *See the usage note at* CONTINUOUS².

future perfect /'fyutʃɚ 'pɝfɪkt/ [*noun*] GRAMMAR
the future perfect the form of a verb that shows an action or state that will be complete by or before a particular time in the future. It is formed with the

future tense of "have" and a past participle: *In the sentence "On August 17th, we will have been married one year," the verb is in the future perfect.*
  ⇨ *See the usage note at* PERFECT².

future tense * /'fyutʃɚ 'tɛns/ [*noun*] GRAMMAR
the future tense the form of a verb that you use to talk about the future. It is formed by putting "will" in front of the main verb: *The sentence "They will arrive tomorrow" is in the future tense.*
  ☛ Do not use "to" with a verb in the future tense. For example, do not say "I will to see you on Saturday." Say **I will see you on Saturday.**
  ⇨ *Compare* PAST TENSE, PRESENT TENSE.

fuzzy /'fʌzi/ [*adjective;* **fuzzier, fuzziest**]
  1 having many thin, soft threads or hairs: *a fuzzy sweater*
  2 not clear or easy to understand: *The picture on my TV is fuzzy.*

G

G * or **g** /dʒi/ [*noun; plural* **Gs** or **G's, g's**] the seventh letter of the English alphabet
  ⇨ *See the usage note at* ALPHABET.

PRONUNCIATION   The letter "g"

The letter **g** can be pronounced in English in two ways, as a "hard" sound or as a "soft" sound, usually depending on the letter that follows.

  Hard "g" (/g/) **is easy.** When **g** is followed by *a, o,* or *u,* the **g** is always hard, as in *gap, go,* and *gum,* pronounced /gæp/, /goʊ/, and /gʌm/.
  When a **g** is followed by another consonant, the **g** is hard, as in *glass* and *grow* (/glæs/, /groʊ/).
  The letter **g** at the end of a word is also hard: *bag, leg,* and *fog* (/bæg/, /lɛg/, /fɑg/).

  Soft "g" (/dʒ/) **is not easy.** A beginning **g** that is followed by *e* or *i* may be either hard or soft. It is hard in *get* and *giggle* (/gɛt/, /gɪgəl/), and soft in *gem* and *ginger* (/dʒɛm/, /'dʒɪndʒɚ/). Each of these words has to be learned.

In the middle of a word, when a single **g** is followed by an *i* or *e,* the sound of that **g** is almost always soft. Examples are *fragile, magic,* and *danger* (/'frædʒəl/, /'mædʒɪk/, /'deɪndʒɚ/).

g the written abbreviation of GRAM or GRAMS: *12 g of fat*

gadget /'gædʒɪt/ [*noun*] a useful tool or small machine: *He has a special gadget for peeling garlic.*

gain * Ⓣ /geɪn/ [*verb;* **gained, gaining**]
  1 to get something that is good or useful: *Five students from our school gained admission to Harvard University.*
  2 to increase your weight or speed: *She's gaining weight.* | *He gained 12 pounds.* | *The train was gaining speed.*

SYNONYMS   gain, earn, win

Each of these words means "to get something." **Gain** means to get more of a useful skill or quality: *This course will help you gain confidence.* **Earn** means to get money by working: *You can earn a lot of* money being a lawyer. **Win** means to get a prize in a game or competition: *She won second prize in a singing competition.*

gal. the written abbreviation of GALLON or GALLONS: *Milk: $1.89/gal.*

galaxy /'gæləksi/ [*noun; plural* **galaxies**] a very big group of stars in space: *a star at the edge of our galaxy*

gale /geɪl/ [*noun*] a very strong wind ⇨ *Compare* CYCLONE.

gallery /'gæləri/ [*noun; plural* **galleries**] a room or building where pictures or other kinds of art are shown: *We visited an **art gallery** this afternoon.*

gallon * /'gælən/ [*noun*] a unit for measuring liquids, equal to 4 quarts or 3.78 liters: *a gallon of gas*

gallop[1] /'gæləp/ [*verb;* **galloped, galloping**] if a horse or its rider gallops, the horse moves very fast: *She galloped across the meadow.*

She's **galloping.**

gallop[2] [*noun*] the fastest way that a horse can move: *She rode **at a gallop**.*

gamble[1] /'gæmbəl/ [*verb;* **gambled, gambling**] to risk money in an attempt to get more, by playing card games, guessing the result of a race, etc.: *He **gambled away** all his money.*

gamble[2] [*noun*] a risk that you take in an attempt to gain something: *Quitting your job is a gamble you shouldn't take.*

gambler /'gæmblɚ/ [*noun*] someone who gambles

gambling /'gæmblɪŋ/ [*noun*] the activity of risking money in an attempt to get more: *Gambling is legal in this state.*

game * /geɪm/ [*noun*]
1 an activity with rules that you play for enjoyment or to win, such as a sport or cards: *They spent the afternoon playing **computer games.** | I went to the **football game** on Saturday. | We play a **game of** tennis every Sunday.*
2 games [*plural*] a large sports competition with many events: *the Olympic games*

— PHRASE —
3 play games to treat someone in an unfair or dishonest way: *Stop playing games, and tell me what's happening.*

game show /'geɪm ˌʃoʊ/ [*noun*] a show on television in which people try to win money or prizes by answering questions or playing a game

gander /'gændɚ/ [*noun*] a male goose

gang[1] /gæŋ/ [*noun*]
1 a group of young people who fight other groups and cause trouble: *two **rival gangs** (=gangs that do not like each other)*
2 a group of people who do things together: *Most of **the gang** (=your group of friends) will be at the party. | a **gang of** car thieves (=a group of criminals who steal cars)*

gang[2] [*verb;* **ganged, ganging**]
— PHRASAL VERB —
gang up on [*phrasal verb*]
if several people gang up on someone, they all attack or annoy that person: **gang up on someone** ▸ *The other kids gang up on her and tease her.*

gap /gæp/ [*noun*]
1 an empty space in something or between two things: *I could see them through a **gap in** the fence. | a **gap between** two teeth*
2 a difference between two things or two groups of people: *There's a three-year **age gap** between our children. | a huge **gap between** the rich and the poor*

a **gap** in a fence

3 something that ought to exist or be present: *There are big **gaps in** my knowledge of literature.*
4 a short time when talk or an activity stops: *She tried to **fill the gap in** the conversation.*

/i/ **see** /ɪ/ **big** /eɪ/ **day** /ɛ/ **get** /æ/ **hat** /ɑ/ **father, hot** /ʌ/ **up** /ə/ **about** /ɔ/ **saw** /oʊ/ **hope** /ʊ/ **book** /u/ **too** /aɪ/ **I** /aʊ/ **how** /ɔɪ/ **boy** /ɝ/ **bird** /ɚ/ **teacher** /ɪr/ **ear** /ɛr/ **air** /ɑr/ **far** /ɔr/ **more** /ʊr/ **tour** /aɪr/ **fire** /aʊɚ/ **hour** /θ/ **nothing** /ð/ **mother** /ʃ/ **she** /ʒ/ **measure** /tʃ/ **church** /dʒ/ **jump** /ŋ/ **long**

garage * /gəˈrɑʒ/ [noun]
  1 a room or small building beside a HOUSE where a car is kept
  2 a place where cars are repaired: *My car is at the garage.*

garbage /ˈgɑrbɪdʒ/ [noun]
  1 kitchen waste and other things that people throw away, or a container you put this in: *He took out the garbage* (=put it in a container outside the house). | *Throw that in the garbage.*
  ➪ Compare TRASH.
  2 something that someone says or writes that is not true or sensible: *They print a lot of garbage in that newspaper.*

garbage can /ˈgɑrbɪdʒ ˌkæn/ [noun] a large container for waste that is usually kept outside; synonym TRASH CAN

garbage collector /ˈgɑrbɪdʒ kəˌlɛktɚ/ [noun] someone whose job is to remove waste from containers outside people's houses

garbageman /ˈgɑrbɪdʒˌmæn/ [noun; plural **garbagemen** /ˈgɑrbɪdʒˌmɛn/] a man who works as a garbage collector

garbage truck /ˈgɑrbɪdʒ ˌtrʌk/ [noun] a truck in which waste is put to be taken away

garbled /ˈgɑrbəld/ [adjective; **more garbled, most garbled**] garbled speech or writing is confused and not clear or complete: *The message was garbled.*

garden * /ˈgɑrdən/ [noun] a piece of land where flowers and other plants are grown: *a rose garden* | *a vegetable garden*

gardener /ˈgɑrdənɚ/ [noun] someone who grows and cares for flowers and other plants

gardening /ˈgɑrdənɪŋ/ [noun] the activity of growing and caring for flowers and other plants

gargle /ˈgɑrgəl/ [verb; **gargled, gargling**] to hold a liquid in the back of your mouth and breathe out through it, as a way of cleaning your mouth and throat or using a medicine: *The doctor told me to gargle with salty water.*

garlic /ˈgɑrlɪk/ [noun] the round white part of a plant that has a strong smell and

garlic

taste, and is used in cooking: *First fry the onions, garlic, and ginger together.*

garment /ˈgɑrmənt/ [noun] FORMAL a piece of clothing: *Wash dark-colored garments separately.*

gas * /gæs/ [noun; plural **gases**]
  1 the liquid that is burned in the engines of vehicles, ships, and planes to make them work; synonym GASOLINE: *Do we have enough gas in the car to get home?* | *We're nearly out of gas* (=there is not much left).
  2 a substance like air that is burned for cooking and for heating buildings: *He turned off the gas and took the pot off the stove.*
  3 any substance that is like air: *a cloud of poisonous gas* | *Nitrogen is the main gas in Earth's atmosphere.*
  ➪ Compare LIQUID¹, SOLID².

gasoline * /ˌgæsəˈlin/ [noun] the liquid that is burned in the engines of vehicles, ships, and planes to make them work; synonym GAS: *She filled the tank of the car with gasoline.*

gasp¹ /gæsp/ [verb; **gasped, gasping**]
  1 to suddenly breathe in hard, because you are shocked or surprised: *The crowd gasped when the rider fell.*
  2 to breathe hard because breathing is difficult: *The runner was exhausted and was gasping for breath.*

gasp² [noun] the action or sound of breathing in quickly: *She gave a little gasp when she saw me.*

gas station /ˈgæs ˌsteɪʃən/ [noun] a place where you can buy gas for a car

gate * /geɪt/ [noun]
  1 a thing in a fence or wall that you open and close like a door in order to

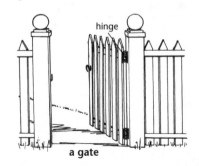

a gate

go through: *Please shut the gate, or the dog will get out.*

2 a place at an airport where people leave or enter the building to get on or off a plane: *Flight 84 to Hong Kong is now boarding at gate 15.*

gather * ⊤ /ˈgæðɚ/ [*verb;* **gathered, gathering**]
1 to come together and form a group: *Everyone **gathered around** the table.* | *Clouds were gathering in the sky.*
⇨ *See the synonym note at* MEET[1].
2 to collect things or facts and put them together: *My job is to gather information about our sales.* | **gather up something** ▸ *She gathered up the papers.*

gathering /ˈgæðɚrɪŋ/ [*noun*] a group or meeting: *He stood up to address the gathering.*

gauge /geɪdʒ/ [*noun*] a piece of equipment that shows how much of something there is: *Look at the gas gauge—the tank's nearly empty.* | *a pressure gauge*

gave * /geɪv/ [*verb*] the past tense of GIVE

gaze /geɪz/ [*verb;* **gazed, gazing**]
to look at someone or something for a long time, especially because you are interested or attracted: *He sat gazing out of the window.*

SYNONYMS **gaze, stare**

Gaze and **stare** both mean to look at something or someone for a long time. Use **gaze** to talk about looking at something or someone you like very much or think is impressive: *She stood by the shore and gazed at the ocean.* Use **stare** to talk about something or someone you think is strange or surprising: *She tried not to stare at his strange clothes.*

---

gear[1] /gɪr/ [*noun*]
1 the machinery in a vehicle that connects the engine to the wheels and makes them move: *The car **changes gears** (=changes the position of the machinery) automatically.*
2 the special clothes or equipment that you need for a sport or activity: *She packed her skiing gear into the trunk.*

gear[2] [*verb;* **geared, gearing**]
— PHRASE —
be geared to if a process or activity is geared to something, it is designed to be right for that thing: *The course is geared to the needs of part-time students.*

gearshift /ˈgɪr.ʃɪft/ [*noun*] a long handle that controls the gears of a car: *The gearshift is stuck.*

geese /gis/ [*noun*] the plural of GOOSE

gel /dʒɛl/ [*noun*] a clear, soft, thick substance, especially one that you use on your hair or skin: *a **hair gel** (=for making your hair keep its shape)* | *a **shower gel** (=for washing your skin)*

gem /dʒɛm/ [*noun*] a valuable stone that is shaped to be used in jewelry: *The gems in her necklace sparkled.*

gender /ˈdʒɛndɚ/ [*noun*] the fact of being male or female: *a study of **gender differences** (=differences between men and women)*

gene /dʒin/ [*noun*] one of the cell parts that are passed on to living things from their parents, and that control their growth and development: *a gene for eye color*

general[1] * /ˈdʒɛnərəl/ [*adjective;* **more general, most general**]
1 containing the main facts about something, but not all the details: *This book is a general introduction to chemistry.* | *I have a **general idea** of how the song goes.*
2 involving or shared by most people: *The information is not available to **the general public** (=most people).*

general[2] [*noun*]
1 [*name*] also **General;** an officer with the highest rank in the Army, Air Force, or Marine Corps
— PHRASE —
2 **in general** usually or in most cases: *In general, delivery takes two weeks.*

/i/ **see**	/ɪ/ **big**	/eɪ/ **day**	/ɛ/ **get**	/æ/ **hat**	
/ɑ/ **father, hot**	/ʌ/ **up**	/ə/ **about**	/ɔ/ **saw**		
/oʊ/ **hope**	/ʊ/ **book**	/u/ **too**	/aɪ/ **I**	/aʊ/ **how**	
/ɔɪ/ **boy**	/ɚ/ **bird**	/ɪr/ **ear**	/ɛr/ **air**		
/ɑr/ **far**	/ɔr/ **more**	/ʊr/ **tour**	/aɪr/ **fire**		
/aʊɚ/ **hour**	/θ/ **nothing**	/ð/ **mother**	/ʃ/ **she**		
/ʒ/ **measure**	/tʃ/ **church**	/dʒ/ **jump**	/ŋ/ **long**		

general election /'dʒɛnərəl ɪ'lɛkʃən/ [noun] an election to choose government officials, in which all the people in a country vote: *A general election is held every four years.*

generally * ⊤ /'dʒɛnərəli/ [adverb]
1 in most cases or by most people: *Airports generally have restaurants in them.* | *He is generally considered to be a good writer.*
2 usually: *The bus is generally late.*

general store /'dʒɛnərəl 'stɔr/ [noun] a store that sells many different things, usually in a country area where there are not many other stores

generate ⊤ /'dʒɛnə,reɪt/ [verb; generated, generating] to produce electricity: *Some electricity is generated by wind power.* | *a generating plant*

generation ⊤ /,dʒɛnə'reɪʃən/ [noun]
1 all the people in a family or a society who were born at around the same time: *There were four generations in the photo—my grandmother, mother, daughter, and me.* | *Most of the guests were of my father's generation.*
2 the time it takes for one group of people born at about the same time to become adults and have children: *This house was built to last for generations.*

generator /'dʒɛnə,reɪtɚ/ [noun] a machine for producing electricity: *The hospital has an emergency generator.*

generosity /,dʒɛnə'rasɪti/ [noun] when you are kind and willing to give things to people or help them; *opposite* SELFISHNESS: *I'd like to thank you for your generosity to my family.*

generous * /'dʒɛnərəs/ [adjective; more generous, most generous] kind and willing to give things to people or to help them; *opposite* SELFISH: *"I'll buy you lunch." "That's very generous of you."*
↷ See the synonym note at KIND².

generously /'dʒɛnərəsli/ [adverb] in a generous way; *opposite* SELFISHLY: *She generously offered to drive us home.*

genetic /dʒə'nɛtɪk/ [adjective; no comparative] involving or relating to the special cell parts that are passed on to a living thing by its parents: *She works in*

genetic engineering (=changing plants or animals by changing their genes).

genetics /dʒə'nɛtɪks/ [noun] the study of how special cell parts control the qualities and development of living things: *He has a degree in genetics.*
☛ Only use **genetics** with a singular verb.

genie /'dʒini/ [noun; plural **genies**] an powerful spirit in old Arabic stories who will use magic to help the person who can control it: *When the boy rubbed the lamp, a genie appeared.*

genius /'dʒinyəs/ [noun; plural **geniuses**] someone whose intelligence or ability is very much greater than other people's: *a musical genius*

gentle * /'dʒɛntəl/ [adjective; gentler, gentlest]
1 careful and kind in the way you deal with people or things; *opposite* ROUGH: *She's a very gentle, kind person.* | *The nurses are very gentle with the patients.*
2 not hard, strong, or using force: *A gentle breeze was blowing.*
3 not steep: *a gentle slope*

gentleman * /'dʒɛntəlmən/ [noun; plural **gentlemen** /'dʒɛntəlmən/]
1 a polite word meaning MAN: *Are you the gentleman who ordered coffee?*
2 a man who is polite and behaves well toward other people: *He was a perfect gentleman all evening.*

USAGE gentleman, man, lady, woman

Use the words **gentleman** and **lady** as a polite way of talking about a man or woman, especially when you do not know his or her name: *Will you get this gentleman his coat, please?* | *The lady at the desk said I could wait here.*

At other times, use the words **man** or **woman**: *My uncle is a very kind man.* | *Who's the woman in the green coat?*
↷ See also the warning at MISTER.

---

gently * /'dʒɛntli/ [adverb] in a gentle way; *opposite* ROUGHLY: *He gently picked up the bird's egg.*

genuine /'dʒɛnyuɪn/ [adjective; more genuine, most genuine]
1 a feeling that is genuine is real and is

not pretended: *She shows a genuine concern for her employees.*
2 something that is genuine really is what it seems to be: *Is that a genuine Rolex watch?*

geography /dʒi'agrəfi/ [*noun*] the study of the lands and oceans of Earth, and of its countries, cities, etc.

geologist /dʒi'alədʒɪst/ [*noun*] someone who studies geology and knows a lot about it

geology /dʒi'alədʒi/ [*noun*] the study of the structure and history of Earth, and of the rocks and other minerals that it is made of

geometry /dʒi'amɪtri/ [*noun*] the part of mathematics that deals with shapes, lines, and angles and the relationships between them

germ /dʒɝm/ [*noun*] an extremely small living thing that causes illness

gesture[1] /'dʒɛstʃɚ/ [*noun*] a movement of your hand, arms, or head that you make in order to show how you feel or to tell someone something: *Sign language uses gestures.*

gesture[2] [*verb*; **gestured, gesturing**] to make a movement with your hand in order to show or tell someone something: *She gestured toward the door and said, "Please leave."*

get * /gɛt/ [*verb*; **got, gotten, getting**]
1 to obtain or buy something: *Where did you get that shirt?* I *He got us tickets for the game.*
2 to receive or be given something: *He gets $300 a week, plus overtime.* I *What grade did you get on the test?*
3 [*linking*] to become: *It's getting hot in here.* I *Don't get upset.*
↪ See the synonym note at **BECOME**.
4 to bring someone or something from another place: *Dad's gone to get Mom from the airport.* I **get someone something** ▸ *Can I get you a soda?*
5 to reach a place or position: *How do I get to the station from here?* I *By the time we got home, we were exhausted.*
6 to make someone or something reach a place, position, or state: *You can't get eight people into that car.*
7 to become ill or have pain: *I was beginning to get a headache.*

— **PHRASES** —
8 get to know someone to learn more about someone: *I'd like to get to know her better.*
9 get away with something to avoid being caught or punished for doing something wrong: *I can't believe you got away with that lie.*

— **PHRASAL VERBS** —
get along [*phrasal verb*]
10 to have a good relationship: *She doesn't get along with her roommate.* I *We get along because we like the same things.*
get away [*phrasal verb*]
11 to leave a place, especially the place where you work: *You ought to get away for a few days.*
12 to escape from someone who is trying to catch you: *The fish got away.*
get back [*phrasal verb*]
13 to return to a place: *What time will you get back?*
14 to receive or have something again: **get something back** ▸ *Did you get your money back?*
get by [*phrasal verb*]
15 to manage to do what you need to do with what you have: *I can't get by on a part-time salary.*
get in [*phrasal verb*]
16 if a plane, train, or bus gets in, it arrives: *Her train gets in at five.*
get into [*phrasal verb*]
17 to be admitted to a college or university: *You need good grades to get into college.*
get off [*phrasal verb*]
18 to leave a bus, train, or plane: *Get off at Main Street.*
19 to finish the time that you work at your job: *I get off at six.* I *What time do you get off work?*
get on [*phrasal verb*]
20 to go onto a bus, train, or plane: *Where did you get on?*

/i/ **see** /ɪ/ **big** /eɪ/ **day** /ɛ/ **get** /æ/ **hat**
/a/ **father, hot** /ʌ/ **up** /ə/ **about** /ɔ/ **saw**
/oʊ/ **hope** /ʊ/ **book** /u/ **too** /aɪ/ **I** /aʊ/ **how**
/ɔɪ/ **boy** /ɝ/ **bird** /ɚ/ **teacher** /ɪr/ **ear** /ɛr/ **air**
/ɑr/ **far** /ɔr/ **more** /ʊr/ **tour** /aɪr/ **fire**
/aʊɚ/ **hour** /θ/ **nothing** /ð/ **mother** /ʃ/ **she**
/ʒ/ **measure** /tʃ/ **church** /dʒ/ **jump** /ŋ/ **long**

get out [*phrasal verb*]
21 to leave a place: *Come on, let's get out of here.*

get through [*phrasal verb*]
22 to manage to speak to someone on the phone: *I called him this morning, but I didn't get through.*
23 to succeed in dealing with a difficult situation: *I don't know how I got through the meeting.*

get together [*phrasal verb*]
24 to meet someone in order to talk and spend time together: *We're getting together with some friends tonight.*
⇨ *See the synonym note at* MEET¹.

get up [*phrasal verb*]
25 to wake up and get out of bed in the morning, or to make someone to this: *I usually get up at six o'clock.* | **get someone up** ▸ *You get the kids up and I'll fix breakfast.*
26 to stand after sitting or lying: *He got up from the couch and stretched.*

get-together /'gɛt tə,gɛðɚ/ [*noun*] an informal party or occasion when people spend time together: *We're having a get-together Friday evening.*

ghetto ⊤ /'gɛtoʊ/ [*noun; plural* **ghettos** or **ghettoes**] a part of a city where poor people live in bad and crowded conditions

ghost /goʊst/ [*noun*] the spirit of someone who has died, that is believed to be seen or heard in the place where that person lived: *They say the ghost of an old woman is in this house.*

giant¹ /'dʒaɪənt/ [*noun*] a very big man, especially a man in a story who is bigger than a real man could be: *Have you read the story of the friendly giant?*

giant² [*adjective; no comparative*] very big: *a giant roller coaster*

gift * /gɪft/ [*noun*]
1 something nice that you give to someone; *synonym* PRESENT: *a birthday gift* | *This watch was a gift from a friend.*
2 a natural ability to do something well; *synonym* TALENT: *a gift for singing*

gifted /'gɪftɪd/ [*adjective;* **more gifted, most gifted**] having a special skill or ability; *synonym* TALENTED: *a gifted young*

musician | *I teach gifted children* (=children who are very intelligent).

gigabyte /'gɪgə,baɪt/ [*noun*] a unit for measuring computer information, equal to 1,024 megabytes: *a ten-gigabyte hard drive*

gigantic ⊤ /dʒaɪ'gæntɪk/ [*adjective;* **more gigantic, most gigantic**] extremely large or great; *synonym* HUGE: *The wedding was held inside a gigantic tent.* | *Her play was a gigantic success.*

giggle¹ /'gɪgəl/ [*verb;* **giggled, giggling**] to laugh quietly in a high voice, often without being able to stop: *Some of the children were giggling.*

giggle² [*noun*] a high quiet laugh: *She handed me her poem **with a nervous giggle**.*

gills /gɪlz/ [*plural noun*] the breathing organs of a FISH, which are inside two curved holes behind its head

ginger /'dʒɪndʒɚ/ [*noun*] a root that has a strong taste and is used in cooking: *First, peel the ginger.*

a piece of
ginger root

giraffe /dʒə'ræf/ [*noun; plural* **giraffes** or **giraffe**] an animal with long legs and a very long neck, that lives in Africa

girl * /gɜrl/ [*noun*] a female child: *There are more girls than boys in my class.* | *My sister just had a **little girl**.*

a giraffe

girlfriend
/'gɜrl,frɛnd/ [*noun*]
1 a girl or young woman with whom someone has a romantic relationship: *Does your brother have a girlfriend?*
2 a girl or young woman who is a woman's friend: *She went to the movies with her girlfriends.*

Girl Scout /'gɜrl ,skaʊt/ [*noun*]
1 the Girl Scouts an organization for girls that teaches skills they will need

in life: *The Girl Scouts teaches young girls many skills that are very useful.*

☛ Only use **the Girl Scouts** with a singular verb in this meaning.

2 a girl who is a member of the Girl Scouts: *She became a Girl Scout in fourth grade.*

give * /gɪv/ [*verb; gave, given, giving*]

1 to provide someone with something: **give someone something** ▸ *My parents gave me a new CD for my birthday.* | *He wouldn't give us any information about the exam.* | **give something to someone** ▸ *She gives piano lessons to children.* | *He gave me some advice on finding an apartment* (=told me how to do this).

2 to pass something to someone: *Give me the map, please.* | **give something to someone** ▸ *I already gave the photos to her.*

3 to perform an action: *I should give Patricia a call* (=phone her).

4 to do something for a group of people to hear, see, or enjoy: *He gave a talk on the history of the town.* | *The choir will give a concert on Wednesday.*

— PHRASAL VERBS

give away [*phrasal verb*]

5 to let someone else have something, especially because you no longer want it: **give something away** ▸ *I gave my old records away.*

give back [*phrasal verb*]

6 to return something to the person who had it first: **give someone back something** ▸ *He gave me back the money he borrowed.* | **give someone something back** ▸ *Hey, give me my pen back!*

give in [*phrasal verb*]

7 to stop arguing or fighting, and do what someone else wants you to do: *He finally gave in and agreed to go.*

give out [*phrasal verb*]

8 to give something to each of a group of people: **give out something** ▸ *She gave out forms to be filled in.* | **give something out** ▸ *I will give the test papers out when everyone is seated.*

9 to start to become weak, or to stop working correctly: *The engine gave out when we were halfway home.*

give up [*phrasal verb*]

10 to stop doing or having something, especially when it was a habit: **give up doing something** ▸ *I'm trying to give up smoking.* | **give up something** ▸ *She had to give up her car when she moved to the city.*

given¹ * /'gɪvən/ [*verb*] the past participle of GIVE

given² [*adjective; no comparative*]

— PHRASE —

any given or **a given** used to talk about a time or thing as an example: *At any given moment it is raining somewhere.*

given³ [*preposition*] considering: *Given the rain, we'll stay home.*

given name /'gɪvən 'neɪm/ [*noun*] the name that you do not share with other members of your family, which in English comes before your family name; *synonym* FIRST NAME: *Her given name is Susan.*

➪ *See the usage note at* FIRST NAME.

glacier /'gleɪʃɚ/ [*noun*] a large, long mass of ice that moves very slowly, especially on a mountain: *The stream flows from a mountain glacier.*

glad * /glæd/ [*adjective; gladder, gladdest*]

1 happy because something good has happened: **glad (that)** ▸ *I'm glad that you could come today.* | *They seemed really glad to see me.*

— PHRASE —

2 be glad to do something to be willing and happy to do something: *Thanks for the invitation—I'd be glad to come.*

gladly /'glædli/ [*adverb*] in a willing way: *I'll gladly lend you a tennis racket.*

glamor /'glæmɚ/ [*noun*] another spelling of GLAMOUR

glamorous /'glæmərəs/ [*adjective; more glamorous, most glamorous*]

1 used about a woman who is very attractive, wears beautiful clothes, and

/i/ see	/ɪ/ big	/eɪ/ day	/ɛ/ get	/æ/ hat
/ɑ/ father, hot	/ʌ/ up	/ə/ about	/ɔ/ saw	
/oʊ/ hope	/ʊ/ book	/u/ too	/aɪ/ I	/aʊ/ how
/ɔɪ/ boy	/ɝ/ bird	/ɚ/ teacher	/ɪr/ ear	/ɛr/ air
/ɑr/ far	/ɔr/ more	/ʊr/ tour	/aɪr/ fire	
/aʊɚ/ hour	/θ/ nothing	/ð/ mother	/ʃ/ she	
/ʒ/ measure	/tʃ/ church	/dʒ/ jump	/ŋ/ long	

is usually rich or successful: *She looked really glamorous at the ceremony.*
2 attractive, exciting, and interesting: *A journalist's job seems glamorous to me.*

glamour /'glæmɚ/ [*noun*] the quality of being attractive, exciting, interesting, and often famous or fashionable: *There's a lot of glamour in working in TV.*

glance[1] /glæns/ [*verb*; **glanced, glancing**] to look quickly at someone or something: *I glanced at the bulletin board on my way past.*

glance[2] [*noun*] a quick look at someone or something: *A glance at the screen showed nothing was happening.*

glare[1] /glɛr/ [*verb*; **glared, glaring**]
1 to shine very brightly, and be unpleasant or difficult to look at: *cars with glaring headlights*
2 to look at someone in an angry way: *He glared at the noisy students.*

glare[2] [*noun*]
1 very bright light that is unpleasant or difficult to look at: *She shielded her eyes from the glare of the sun.*
2 an angry look: *He gave me a glare from behind his desk.*

glass[1] ✱ /glæs/ [*noun*; *plural* **glasses**]
1 a hard clear substance used for making windows, bottles, etc.: *He cut the glass to fit the window frame.* I *These beads are made of glass.*
2 a container for drinking from, made of glass or plastic and with no handle: *a glass of water* I *I need a clean glass.*
3 **glasses** [*plural*] a pair of curved pieces of plastic or glass in a frame, that you wear in front of your eyes so that you can see better: *I only wear glasses for reading.*

glass[2] ✱ [*adjective; no comparative*] made of glass: *Be careful—those glass jars could break.*

gleam /glim/ [*verb*; **gleamed, gleaming**] to shine, especially by being smooth and clean: *He polished the car until it gleamed.*

glide /glaɪd/ [*verb*; **glided, gliding**] to move very smoothly: *The dancers glided across the floor.*

glider /'glaɪdɚ/ [*noun*] a small aircraft without an engine: *We launched the glider from the edge of the cliff.*

glimmer[1] /'glɪmɚ/ [*verb*; **glimmered, glimmering**] to shine with a faint light, especially in a way that is not steady: *The candles glimmered on the table.*

glimmer[2] [*noun*] a faint light, especially one that is not steady: *A glimmer of moonlight showed us the road.*

glimpse[1] /glɪmps/ [*verb*; **glimpsed, glimpsing**] to see something for a very short time: *He glimpsed a face at the window.*

glimpse[2] [*noun*] a sight of something that is seen for a very short time: *We caught a glimpse of the movie star.*

glisten /'glɪsən/ [*verb*; **glistened, glistening**] to shine and look wet: *The snow glistened in the moonlight.*

glitter[1] /'glɪtɚ/ [*verb*; **glittered, glittering**] to shine with small points of light; *synonym* SPARKLE: *Silver decorations glittered in the sunlight.* I *She wore a glittering gold and red jacket.*

glitter[2] [*noun*] very small pieces of shiny material: *lipstick with glitter in it*

global /'gloʊbəl/ [*adjective; no comparative*] happening in or affecting the whole world: *a global media network*
☛ Only use **global** before a noun.

global warming /'gloʊbəl 'wɔrmɪŋ/ [*noun*] the slow warming of the world that may be caused by gases from cars, factories, etc.

globe /gloʊb/ [*noun*]
1 a ball with a map of Earth on its surface: *She turned the globe to point out New York.*
2 **the globe** the planet Earth: *The news had traveled to every part of the globe.*

gloomy /'glumi/ [*adjective*; **gloomier, gloomiest**]
1 dark and making you feel sad and quiet: *She hated being alone in the gloomy old house.*
2 sad and without hope: *My news made them even gloomier.*

glorious /'glɔriəs/ [*adjective*; **more glorious, most glorious**] very pleasant, beautiful, or enjoyable; *synonym* WONDERFUL: *We had glorious weather.*

glory /'glɔri/ [noun] when someone is famous, admired, and respected for something that he or she has achieved: *The director of the movie gets all the glory.*

gloss /glas/ [noun; plural **glosses**] a short explanation of a word or a group of words: *Difficult words in these examples are given a gloss.*

glossary /'glasəri/ [noun; plural **glossaries**] a list of unusual or technical words and their meanings: *There is a glossary at the back of the book.*

glossy /'glasi/ [adjective; **glossier, glossiest**] smooth and shiny: *the table's glossy surface*

glove * /glʌv/ [noun] a piece of clothing that you wear on your hand, with parts that cover each finger: *a pair of gloves*

ski gloves

mittens

winter gloves

a baseball glove

gloves

glow[1] /gloʊ/ [verb; **glowed, glowing**] to shine with a light that looks warm: *The lamp glowed in the corner.*

glow[2] [noun] light that looks warm: *a fire's red glow*

glue[1] * /glu/ [noun] a substance that is used to stick things together

glue[2] * [verb; **glues, glued, gluing**] to stick things together with glue: *He glued the pieces of the vase together.*

gnaw /nɔ/ [verb; **gnawed, gnawing**] to keep biting something that is hard: *The dog was gnawing a bone.*

go[1] * /goʊ/ [verb; **goes, went, gone, going**]

1 to move or travel toward a place: *Where are you going?* | *I have to go to the grocery store.* | *She went home.* | **have gone somewhere** ▸ *He's gone to Texas for a week.*
 ➪ See the usage note at GONE.

2 to leave a place or a person: *Come on, let's go.* | *Please go away and leave me alone.* | *I'm going out to get a newspaper.*

3 to move or travel somewhere in order to do something: *I went down to the store for some milk.* | **go to do something** ▸ *We went to visit my grandparents.* | **go (and) do something** ▸ *He went and got the car.* | *I'll go walk the dog.* | **go swimming/shopping/fishing/etc.** ▸ *Let's go swimming tomorrow.* | **go to the movies/theater/opera/etc.** ▸ *We went to the movies last night.* | **go for a swim/ride/walk/etc.** ▸ *We went for a walk along the beach.*

4 [linking] to become: **go gray/white** ▸ *His hair is going gray.* | **go bad/stale/sour** ▸ *These apples have all gone bad.*
 ➪ See the synonym note at BECOME.

=== PHRASES ===

5 be going to do something
 a to intend to do something: *I'm going to write to her tonight.*
 b to be about to do something: *Do you think they're going to win?* | *Careful—you're going to drop those plates.*

6 go well/wrong/fine/etc. to happen and have a particular result: *His speech went very well.* | *Everything was going wrong that day.*

7 go to school/college to study at a school or college: *Where do you go to school?* | *My daughter goes to college.*

8 to go SPOKEN used to say that you will take food away from a restaurant and eat it somewhere else: *Do you want that for here or to go?* | *Two coffees to go.*

=== PHRASAL VERBS ===

go back [phrasal verb]
9 to return to a place or position where you were before: *Let's go back to the house and talk.* | *Go back to the beginning and read the chapter again.*

/i/ **see** /ɪ/ **big** /eɪ/ **day** /ɛ/ **get** /æ/ **hat** /ɑ/ **father, hot** /ʌ/ **up** /ə/ **about** /ɔ/ **saw** /oʊ/ **hope** /ʊ/ **book** /u/ **too** /aɪ/ **I** /aʊ/ **how** /ɔɪ/ **boy** /ɚ/ **bird** /ɚ/ **teacher** /ɪr/ **ear** /ɛr/ **air** /ɑr/ **far** /ɔr/ **more** /ʊr/ **tour** /aɪr/ **fire** /aʊɚ/ **hour** /θ/ **nothing** /ð/ **mother** /ʃ/ **she** /ʒ/ **measure** /tʃ/ **church** /dʒ/ **jump** /ŋ/ **long**

go by [phrasal verb]
10 if time goes by, it passes: *Ten days went by with no news of my brother.*

go off [phrasal verb]
11 to explode or be fired: *The bomb was set to go off at 5:30. | His gun went off when he fell.*
12 to make a loud noise as a warning: *My alarm clock went off at 7:15.*
13 if a machine or light goes off, it stops operating: *The heat goes off at night.*

go on [phrasal verb]
14 to continue: *Please go on with your story. | The party went on for hours. |* **go on doing something** ▸ *He went on painting the fence.*
15 to be happening: *What's going on? Why aren't you all in bed?*

go out [phrasal verb]
16 to leave your house in order to meet friends or do something that you enjoy: *Do you want to go out tonight? | We usually go out for dinner on Fridays.*
17 if a light goes out, it stops shining: *I was in the tub when the light went out.*
18 to have a romantic relationship with someone: *He's going out with a girl he met in Boston. | They've been going out for a year.*

go up [phrasal verb]
19 to become greater in amount, level, or degree; synonym INCREASE: *My salary went up 3% this year.*

go² [noun]
━ PHRASE ━
on the go very active and busy: *He's on the go all the time.*

goal * /goʊl/ [noun]
1 what you want to achieve; synonym AIM: *Our goal is to sell more computers than any other company.*
2 a point that you get in a game by making a ball go into a particular area, in sports such as soccer and hockey: *Ericson scored the first goal.*
3 the area where a ball must go in order to get a point, for example in soccer: *He kicked the ball into the goal.*

goalie /'goʊli/ [noun; plural **goalies**] a short form of GOALKEEPER

goalkeeper /'goʊl,kipɚ/ [noun] the player who tries to stop the ball from going into the goal, in sports such as soccer and hockey; synonym GOALIE

goalpost /'goʊl,poʊst/ [noun] one of the two upright posts that form the sides of the goal, in sports such as football and soccer: *The ball went straight through the goalposts.*

goat * /goʊt/ [noun] an animal with horns and long hair, that is kept by farmers for its meat and milk: *A **herd of goats** grazed on the side of the hill.*
➪ *See the picture at SHEEP.*

gobble /'gabəl/ [verb; gobbled, gobbling] to eat something quickly and not politely: *The kids sat at the table gobbling up pancakes.*

god * /gad/ [noun] a male spirit that lives forever, and controls the world or a part of it: *The ancient Greeks worshiped many gods.*

God * [name] the spirit that Jewish people and Christians believe is the only god: *Let us pray to God for help.*

goddess /'gadɪs/ [noun; plural **goddesses**] a female spirit that lives forever, and controls the world or part of it: *the moon goddess*

goggles /'gagəlz/ [plural noun] a pair of thick curved pieces of plastic in a tight frame, worn to protect the eyes: *swimming goggles*

goggles

gold¹ * /goʊld/ [noun]
1 a valuable, soft, yellow metal, used in jewelry: *a ring made of gold*
2 a shiny, deep yellow color: *The curtains were cream and gold.*

gold² * [adjective; no comparative]
1 made of gold: *She wore a gold necklace. | a **gold medal** (=a medal given as first prize in a competition)*
2 of the color gold: *a gold dresss*

golden /'goʊldən/ [adjective; no comparative]
1 of a deep yellow color: *golden hair*
2 made of gold: *a golden chain*

goldfish /'goʊld̩fɪʃ/ [noun; plural **goldfish**] a yellow or orange fish, often kept in a pool or in a bowl

golf /galf/ [noun] a sport or game in which people hit a small ball a long way over grass, until they can hit it into a small hole: *Dad likes to play golf on weekends.* I *a golf ball* (=a small white ball used for golf)

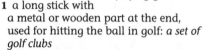

playing **golf**

golf club /'galf ˌklʌb/ [noun]
1 a long stick with a metal or wooden part at the end, used for hitting the ball in golf: *a set of golf clubs*
2 an organization that people join in order to play golf, that has its own building and golf course

golf course /'galf ˌkɔrs/ [noun] a large area of land that is covered in grass, specially designed for people to play golf on

gone * /gɔn/ [verb] the past participle of GO¹

USAGE   gone, been

If you say that someone **has gone** somewhere, you mean that he or she is there now: *My boss has gone to Hong Kong, but he'll be back tomorrow.*

If you say that someone **has been** somewhere, you mean that he or she went there in the past, but is not there now: *My sister has been to Hong Kong several times.*

gong /gɔŋ/ [noun] a hanging, flat or hollow piece of metal, that is hit with a stick to make a loud noise: *He banged the gong to signal it was time for dinner.*

good¹ * /gʊd/ [adjective; **better, best**]
1 of a high quality or standard: *This is a very good piece of work.* I *You need a better camera.*
2 giving pleasure or an advantage:

Have a good trip. I *That's a good idea.* I *I have some good news!*
3 useful or right for someone or for a purpose: *This is a good place for a picnic.* I *This paper is no good for drawing* (=it is not useful). I *Exercise is good for you* (=it helps your health).
4 SPOKEN used to show pleasure or approval: *"Rachel's coming for dinner." "Oh good!"*
5 morally acceptable or right: *It's good to be honest with your children.*
6 helpful and kind, or behaving well: *We have good neighbors.* I *My wife's parents have been good to us.* I *Be a good boy and eat your dinner.*
7 skillful at doing or dealing with something: *She was the best actress I've ever seen.* I *My brother is really good at baseball.* I *I'm not good with plants* (=I cannot make them grow).
8 food that is good is fresh enough to eat: *Is that milk still good?*
⇨ See also **good luck** at LUCK.
⇨ Compare BAD.

USAGE   good, well

Do not confuse **good** and **well**. **Good** is an adjective that is used to talk about the quality of someone or something: *It is a really good book.* **Well** is an adverb that is used to talk about the way that someone or something does something: *You write very well.*

good² [noun]
1 things that are helpful and kind, or that make a situation better: *He spent his life doing good for others.*
2 **goods** [plural] things that are produced and sold: *electrical goods* I *household goods*
━━ **PHRASES** ━━
3 **do someone good** to have a good effect on someone's health or character: *Come out for a walk—it'll do you good.*

---

4 do no good or **not do any good** to have no useful result: *I complained to the company, but it didn't do any good.*

5 for good forever: *I'm home again, and I'm staying for good.*

6 good for you/her/them/etc. SPOKEN used to say you are happy that someone has had a success: *Your sister won? Good for her!*

good afternoon /ˌgʊd ˌæftɚˈnun/ [*interjection*] used as a polite greeting when you meet someone in the afternoon: *Good afternoon. How are you?*

goodbye * /ˌgʊdˈbaɪ/ [*interjection*] used when you are leaving someone: *Goodbye. Have a good trip.* I *Say goodbye to Grandma.*

good evening /ˌgʊd ˈivnɪŋ/ [*interjection*] said as a polite greeting when you meet someone in the evening: *Good evening, Professor.*

good-looking /ˈgʊd ˈlʊkɪŋ/ [*adjective;* **more good-looking, most good-looking**] a good-looking man or woman is attractive to look at; *opposite* UNATTRACTIVE: *Her brother was good-looking, but not very nice.*

⇨ *See the synonym note at* BEAUTIFUL.

good morning /ˌgʊd ˈmɔrnɪŋ/ [*interjection*] said as a polite greeting when you meet someone in the morning: *Good morning, how are you?*

goodness /ˈgʊdnɪs/ [*noun*]

1 the quality of being morally good, or helpful and kind to other people: *I believe in the basic goodness of people.*

══ PHRASES ══

2 thank goodness SPOKEN used when you are very glad about something: *Thank goodness you noticed the leak.*

3 (my) goodness SPOKEN used when you are surprised or annoyed: *My goodness, what a mess!*

good night /ˌgʊd ˈnaɪt/ [*interjection*] used when you leave someone at night, or when you go to bed: *Good night, I'll see you tomorrow.*

goose /gus/ [*noun; plural* **geese**] a bird like a large DUCK with a long neck

goosebumps /ˈgus,bʌmps/ [*plural noun*] a condition of your skin when you are cold or afraid, in which it rises up in

many small points, and feels rough: *The wind was giving me goosebumps.*

gopher /ˈgoʊfɚ/ [*noun*] a small animal like a big rat, with a thin tail and big teeth, that lives in the ground

a gopher

gorgeous /ˈgɔrdʒəs/ [*adjective;* **more gorgeous, most gorgeous**] very beautiful: *What gorgeous flowers!* I *Who's that gorgeous girl in the red dress?*

gorilla /gəˈrɪlə/ [*noun; plural* **gorillas**] a very large animal like a monkey, with no tail

⇨ *See the picture at* APE.

gospel /ˈgaspəl/ [*noun*]

1 a kind of loud music and singing used in some churches: *a gospel choir*

2 one of the four books of the Bible that are about the life of Jesus

gossip[1] /ˈgasəp/ [*verb;* **gossiped, gossiping**] to talk about other people and the things they do, for amusement or in an unkind way: *Don't stand there gossiping—we have work to do.*

gossip[2] [*noun*] things that people say about other people, especially unkind things: *Don't pay attention to their gossip.*

got * /gat/ [*verb*] the past tense of GET

gotten * /ˈgatən/ [*verb*] the past participle of GET

govern * /ˈgʌvɚn/ [*verb;* **governed, governing**] to have political control over a country: *The Liberal Democratic Party governed Japan for over 40 years.*

government * /ˈgʌvɚnmənt/ [*noun*] the group of people who have political control over a country

governor * or **Governor** /ˈgʌvɚnɚ/ [*noun, name*] someone who has political power in one area or state of a large country: *the governor of Arkansas*

gown /gaʊn/ [*noun*]

1 a woman's long dress for a formal occasion: *a silk evening gown*

2 a piece of clothing that is long and loose, and is usually worn over other clothes: *All the students wear gowns at the graduation ceremony.*

grab /græb/ [*verb*; **grabs, grabbed, grabbing**] to take hold of something suddenly and with force; *synonym* SEIZE: *He came up to me and grabbed my arm.*

grace /greɪs/ [*noun*]
1 a smooth, beautiful way of moving: *She has the grace of a dancer.*
2 a prayer said before a meal: *Don't eat until we say grace.*

graceful * /'greɪsfəl/ [*adjective*; **more graceful, most graceful**] moving in a way that is smooth and beautiful; *opposite* AWKWARD: *He is an extremely graceful dancer.*

gracefully /'greɪsfəli/ [*adverb*] smoothly and beautifully; *opposite* AWKWARDLY: *She moved gracefully across the stage.*

grad /græd/ [*adjective*; *no comparative*] a short form of GRADUATE³: *a grad student*

grade¹ * /greɪd/ [*noun*]
1 one of twelve levels in a U.S. school: *She's in the same grade as my sister.* | **third/seventh/eighth/etc. grade** ▸ *We studied that play in ninth grade.*
2 a number or letter (A, B, C, D, or F) that is put on a student's work to show how good it is: *What grade did you get on the math test?* | *His grades have been very good this semester.*
3 a level of size or quality: *U.S. grade A meat*

grade² [*verb*; **graded, grading**]
1 if a teacher grades a student or a student's work, he or she decides what grade the student receives for the work: *It will take me all weekend to grade these papers.*
2 to arrange things into groups according to their size or quality: *The eggs are graded according to size.*

grade school /'greɪd ˌskul/ [*noun*] a school in the U.S. for children in their first five or six years of education; *synonym* ELEMENTARY SCHOOL: *What grade school did you go to?* | *We've been friends for years, ever since we were in grade school.*

gradual * ⊤ /'grædʒuəl/ [*adjective*; **more gradual, most gradual**] happening slowly during a period of time; *opposite* SHARP: *a gradual increase in temperature*

gradually * ⊤ /'grædʒuəli/ [*adverb*] slowly over a period of time; *opposite* SHARPLY: *Her playing has gradually improved.*

graduate¹ * ⊤ /'grædʒuˌeɪt/ [*verb*; **graduated, graduating**]
1 to get a degree from a college or university: *What are you going to do after you graduate?* | *She graduated from Smith College last year.*
2 to finish your final year at high school, middle school, or grade school: *After graduating from high school, he worked in his father's business.*

graduate² ⊤ /'grædʒuɪt/ [*noun*]
1 someone who has a degree from a university: *He's a graduate of Yale.*
2 someone who has completed a course of study at a school or college: *We need a high school graduate for this job.*

graduate³ /'grædʒuɪt/ [*adjective*; *no comparative*] relating to university studies that you do after your first degree: *I'm in graduate school* (=studying for a second degree). | *a graduate student* (=someone who is studying for a second degree)

graduation /ˌgrædʒu'eɪʃən/ [*noun*]
1 when a student graduates from a school, college, or university: *Her job started one week after graduation.*
2 the official end of a course of study, when there is often a special ceremony for the students who have completed it: *We're going to my sister's graduation.*

graffiti /grə'fiti/ [*plural noun*] things that are illegally written or drawn on walls in public places: *The station walls were covered in graffiti.*

grain * /greɪn/ [*noun*]
1 wheat and other crops with seeds that are used as food: *Only the best grain is used in our bread.*
2 one of the very small pieces that sand, salt, etc., is made of: *grains of sugar* | *grains of rice*

/i/ **see**	/ɪ/ **big**	/eɪ/ **day**	/ɛ/ **get**	/æ/ **hat**
/ɑ/ **father, hot**	/ʌ/ **up**	/ə/ **about**	/ɔ/ **saw**
/oʊ/ **hope**	/ʊ/ **book**	/u/ **too**	/aɪ/ **I**	/aʊ/ **how**
/ɔɪ/ **boy**	/ɝ/ **bird**	/ɚ/ **teacher**	/ɪr/ **ear**	/ɛr/ **air**
/ɑr/ **far**	/ɔr/ **more**	/ʊr/ **tour**	/aɪr/ **fire**
/aʊɚ/ **hour**	/θ/ **nothing**	/ð/ **mother**	/ʃ/ **she**
/ʒ/ **measure**	/tʃ/ **church**	/dʒ/ **jump**	/ŋ/ **long**

gram * /græm/ [noun] a unit for measuring weight, one thousand of which make one kilogram: *The necklace weighs 350 grams.*

grammar * /'græmɚ/ [noun] the rules for making words and sentences in a language: *English grammar* | *a grammar lesson*

grammatical /grə'mætɪkəl/ [adjective; more grammatical, most grammatical] correct according to the rules of grammar: *I still make a lot of grammatical errors.*

grammatically /grə'mætɪkli/ [adverb] according to the rules of grammar: *That sentence is not grammatically correct.*

grand * /grænd/ [adjective; grander, grandest]
1 best or first: *the winner of the grand prize* | *a store's grand opening* (=when it opens for the first time)
2 very large and impressive: *the Grand Canyon*

grandchild * /'græn,tʃaɪld/ [noun; plural grandchildren /'græn,tʃɪldrən'/] a child of your son or daughter

granddaughter * /'græn,dɔtɚ/ [noun] a daughter of your son or daughter
⇨ *See the picture at* FAMILY TREE.

grandfather * /'græn,faðɚ/ [noun] the father of your father or mother
⇨ *See the picture at* FAMILY TREE.

grandfather clock /'græn,faðɚ ,klak/ [noun] a big clock in a tall wooden frame: *I heard the grandfather clock in the hall strike five.*

grandma or **Grandma** /'græn,ma/ [noun, name; plural grandmas] grandmother: *I'm going to stay with my grandma.* | *Can I have another cookie, Grandma?*
⇨ *See the usage note at* CAPITAL.

grandmother * /'græn,mʌðɚ/ [noun] the mother of your father or mother
⇨ *See the picture at* FAMILY TREE.

grandpa or **Grandpa** /'græn,pa/ [noun, name; plural grandpas] grandfather: *My grandpa took me to the circus last Saturday.* | *Where are you going, Grandpa?*
⇨ *See the usage note at* CAPITAL.

grandparent * /'græn,pɛrənt/ [noun] a grandfather or grandmother: *I'm taking the kids to see their grandparents.*

grandson * /'græn,sʌn/ [noun] a son of your son or daughter
⇨ *See the picture at* FAMILY TREE.

granola /grə'noʊlə/ [noun] a kind of breakfast food made from grains and dried fruit, eaten with milk

grant¹ /grænt/ [verb; granted, granting]
1 FORMAL to officially allow someone to have or do something: *We were finally granted permission to interview the chairman.*
═ PHRASE ═══
2 **take something for granted** to be sure that something is true or will happen, when you should not be so sure: *I took it for granted that they'd agree to my plan.*

grant² [noun] money that is given to a person or group for a special purpose, especially by a government: *They have applied for a research grant.*

grape /greɪp/ [noun] a small FRUIT that is used for making wine: *a bunch of grapes*

grapefruit /'greɪp,frut/ [noun; plural grapefruit] a large, round, sour FRUIT with a thick yellow skin, which grows on trees

graph /græf/ [noun] a picture that shows the way two things are related, for example the amount of something at different times: *This graph shows the relationship of time to distance traveled.*
⇨ *Compare* CHART, TABLE (definition 2).

graphics /'græfɪks/ [plural noun] designs or pictures, especially on a computer: *You can produce excellent graphics with this program.*

grasp /græsp/ [verb; grasped, grasping]
1 to take hold of something firmly: *He grasped the rope and began to climb.*
2 to understand something: *It was hard to grasp what she was saying.*

grass * /græs/ [noun] a plant that has thin leaves and covers large areas of land, for example in parks or people's yards: *Don't walk on the grass.*
⇨ *See also* LAWN.

grasshopper /'græs,hapɚ/ [*noun*] an insect with long back legs, that can jump high and make loud sounds

grassy /'græsi/ [*adjective*; **grassier, grassiest**] grassy land has grass growing on it: *We saw a herd of deer feeding in a grassy meadow.*

grate[1] /greɪt/ [*verb*; **grated, grating**] to cut food into many small thin pieces, by rubbing it against something sharp: *Grate a little cheese over the pasta.* | *grated carrots*

grater

grating cheese

grate[2] [*noun*] a cover for an opening in a street, wall, floor, etc., that is made of metal bars: *I dropped a quarter and it fell through the grate.*

grateful * /'greɪtfəl/ [*adjective*; **more grateful, most grateful**] wanting to thank someone for help, a kind action, or a gift; *opposite* UNGRATEFUL: *We are very grateful to you for your advice.*

grater /'greɪtɚ/ [*noun*] a kitchen tool that you rub food against to cut it into small thin pieces: *a cheese grater* ➪ *See the picture at GRATE*[1].

gratitude /'grætɪ,tud/ [*noun*] the feeling that you want to thank someone who has helped you or given you something: *How can we express our gratitude for all your hard work?*

grave[1] * /greɪv/ [*noun*] a place in the ground where a dead person is buried: *She put flowers on her mother's grave.* ➪ *Compare* TOMB.

grave[2] [*adjective*; **more grave, most grave**] very serious: *They were in grave danger.*

gravel /'grævəl/ [*noun*] small stones that are used to cover a path, or to make road surfaces: *a gravel driveway*

gravestone /'greɪv,stoʊn/ [*noun*] a block of stone on a grave that shows the name of the person who is buried there

graveyard /'greɪv,yard/ [*noun*] a piece of land where dead people are buried; *synonym* CEMETERY: *The graveyard was on a hill above the town.*

gravity /'grævɪti/ [*noun*] the force that makes things fall to the ground, and makes the earth move around the sun

gravy /'greɪvi/ [*noun*] a liquid made from meat juice and flour: *He poured gravy over his meat and potatoes.*

gray[1] * /greɪ/ [*noun*] the color between black and white. It is the color of ash and smoke: *Gray is a good color for a business suit.*

gray[2] * [*adjective*; **grayer, grayest**]
1 of the color gray: *Big gray clouds covered the sky.*
━ PHRASES ━
2 go gray to begin to have gray hair: *Her mother was going gray.*
3 turn gray to change to a gray color: *My hair is turning gray.*

graze /greɪz/ [*verb*; **grazed, grazing**]
1 if an animal grazes, it eats grass or leaves: *Cows were grazing in the field.*
2 to touch someone's skin or the surface of something while moving across it, in a way that can harm it: *The plane flew so low that it grazed the tops of the trees.*

grease[1] /gris/ [*noun*]
1 thick oil that is put on a machine so that its parts move well: *His overalls were covered with grease.*
2 fat that comes from a piece of meat when you cook it: *I need to clean this grease off the stove.*

grease[2] [*verb*; **greased, greasing**] to put grease or fat on something: *Men were greasing the wheels of the train.* | *Grease the baking pan with butter.*

greasy /'grisi/ [*adjective*; **greasier, greasiest**] covered in grease, or full of grease: *He wiped his greasy hands on a cloth.* | *This hand lotion feels greasy.*

great * /greɪt/ [*adjective*; **greater, greatest**]
1 INFORMAL very good or enjoyable: *I saw a great movie last night.* | *We had a great time at the beach yesterday.*

/i/ **see**	/ɪ/ **big**	/eɪ/ **day**	/ɛ/ **get**	/æ/ **hat**
/a/ **father, hot**	/ʌ/ **up**	/ə/ **about**	/ɔ/ **saw**
/oʊ/ **hope**	/ʊ/ **book**	/u/ **too**	/aɪ/ **I**	/aʊ/ **how**
/ɔɪ/ **boy**	/ɝ/ **bird**	/ɚ/ **teacher**	/ɪr/ **ear**	/ɛr/ **air**
/ɑr/ **far**	/ɔr/ **more**	/ʊr/ **tour**	/aɪr/ **fire**
/aʊɚ/ **hour**	/θ/ **nothing**	/ð/ **mother**	/ʃ/ **she**
/ʒ/ **measure**	/tʃ/ **church**	/dʒ/ **jump**	/ŋ/ **long**

2 extreme in degree, or very large in size or amount: *We had great difficulty hearing him.* | *She lives alone in that* **great big** *house.* | *It's a great pleasure to meet you.*

3 famous and admired for being extremely good: *He was one of the greatest scientists of all time.* | *a great work of art*

— PHRASES —

4 a great deal a lot: *You've caused us a great deal of trouble.*

5 great-grandmother/great-grandfather/great-aunt/great-uncle the grandmother, grandfather, etc., of one of your parents: *My great-uncle was the first to come to America.*
⇨ *See the picture at* FAMILY TREE.

6 great-grandson/great-granddaughter/great-nephew/great-niece the grandson, granddaughter, etc., of one of your children

Great Britain ✳ /ˌgreɪt ˈbrɪtən/ [*name*] the island in the north of Europe that includes England, Scotland, and Wales: *The U.K. includes Great Britain and Northern Ireland.*

greatly /ˈgreɪtli/ [*adverb*] FORMAL to a very large degree or amount: *I was greatly impressed by what he said.*

greed /grid/ [*noun*] the feeling of wanting more food or money than you need: *His* **greed** *for money made him steal from his employer.*

greedy /ˈgridi/ [*adjective*; **greedier, greediest**] wanting more food or money than you need: *Try not to be greedy when you fill your plate.*

green[1] ✳ /grin/ [*noun*] the color of grass and leaves: *Green means "go," red means "stop."*

green[2] ✳ [*adjective*; **greener, greenest**]
1 of the color green: *The room had a green carpet.*
2 having trees, grass, and other plants: *a green valley*

green card /ˈgrin ˌkard/ [*noun*] an official document that allows someone from another country to live and work in the U.S.

☛ A green card is not green any longer, but it is still called a green card.

greenhouse /ˈgrin‚haʊs/ [*noun; plural* **greenhouses** /ˈgrin‚haʊzɪz/] a building, usually made from glass, for growing plants: *Keep the young plants in the greenhouse until spring.*

green onion /ˈgrin ˈʌnyən/ [*noun*] a small white onion with long green leaves, often eaten raw

greet ✳ /grit/ [*verb*; **greeted, greeting**] to say hello to someone: *She waited by the door to greet the guests.*

greeting ✳ /ˈgritɪŋ/ [*noun*]
1 something that you say or do when you meet or welcome someone: *His greeting was warm and affectionate.* | *She raised a hand* **in greeting.**
2 greetings [*plural*] a message of good wishes that you send to someone, for example on a birthday or on a special holiday: *Brian can't come to the party, but he* **sends** *his* **greetings.**

grew ✳ /gru/ [*verb*] the past tense of GROW

grid /grɪd/ [*noun*] a pattern of lines that cross each other to form squares: *The city's streets are laid out in a grid.*

griddle /ˈgrɪdəl/ [*noun*] a thick flat pan used for cooking over direct heat: *pancakes cooked on a griddle*

grief /grif/ [*noun*] a feeling of great sadness, especially because someone has died: *The whole nation felt* **grief** *over the president's death.*

grieve /griv/ [*verb*; **grieved, grieving**] to feel very sad, especially because someone has died: *She is still* **grieving for** *her husband.*

grill[1] /grɪl/ [*verb*; **grilled, grilling**] to cook food directly over a fire, or to be cooked in this way: *Grill the burgers for about ten minutes.*
⇨ *See the synonym note at* COOK[1].

grill[2] [*noun*] a metal object used for cooking food, that has a bottom part where a fire is lit and a top part like a frame with thick metal bars across it: *Will you light the grill?* | *We just bought a new barbecue grill.*

grim /grɪm/ [*adjective*; **grimmer, grimmest**]
1 making you feel sad and serious: *He received the grim news in silence.*

2 serious, and either sad or not friendly: *He hung up the phone with a grim look on his face.*

grime /graɪm/ [*noun*] a layer of dirt on a surface: *The tables were black with grime.*

grimy /'graɪmi/ [*adjective;* **grimier, grimiest**] covered with a layer of dirt: *The hotel furniture was old and grimy.*

grin[1] /grɪn/ [*verb;* **grins, grinned, grinning**] to give a big smile: *My brother was **grinning** at me.*

grin[2] [*noun*] a big smile: *He welcomed us with a **broad grin** (=a very big smile).*

grind ⊤ /graɪnd/ [*verb;* **ground, grinding**]
1 to crush food into extremely small pieces or into a powder: *Wheat is **ground into** flour.*

— PHRASE —
2 grind to a halt to become slower and finally stop: *The evening traffic had ground to a halt.*

grip[1] /grɪp/ [*verb;* **grips, gripped, gripping**] to hold something very tightly: *He gripped the handle and pulled.*

grip[2] [*noun*] a tight hold on something: *The policeman **tightened his grip** on the boy's arm.*

grizzly bear /'grɪzli ˌbɛr/ or **grizzly** /'grɪzli/ [*noun; plural* **grizzly bears** or **grizzlies**] a large brown bear that lives in North America

groan[1] /groʊn/ [*verb;* **groaned, groaning**] to make a low, deep noise because you are feeling pain or do not like something: *The wounded man was **groaning** in pain.* I *She **groaned** at the thought of extra English lessons.*

groan[2] [*noun*] a low, deep noise made by someone who is in pain or does not like something: *We could hear the groans of the trapped miners.*

grocer /'groʊsɚ/ [*noun*] someone who sells groceries: *His father was a grocer in a small town.*

groceries /'groʊsəriz/ [*plural noun*] food and other things that you need in your home and have to buy often: *We buy our groceries at the supermarket.*

grocery store ⊤ /'groʊsəri ˌstɔr/ [*noun*] a store that sells food and other things

that you need in your home: *Mom went to the grocery store over an hour ago.*

groom /grum/ [*noun*] the man who is getting married at a wedding, or has just gotten married
▷ Compare **BRIDE**.

groove /gruv/ [*noun*] a long narrow cut made in the surface of something: *The shelf fits into grooves in the sides of the cabinet.*

grope /groʊp/ [*verb;* **groped, groping**] to try to find something using your hands because you cannot see very well: *She **groped** under the bed **for** her other shoe.*

gross /groʊs/ [*adjective;* **grosser, grossest**] INFORMAL extremely unpleasant; synonym DISGUSTING: *The tea tastes gross.*

ground[1] ✴ /graʊnd/ [*noun*]
1 the ground the surface of the earth outdoors: *There's a little snow **on the ground**.* I *He dug a hole **in the ground**.*
2 a piece of land used for a particular activity: *the parade ground*
3 an area of land: *The house is built on high ground above the river.*
4 grounds [*plural*] the land around a large building: *They hire gardeners to take care of the grounds.*

USAGE   ground, floor

Do not confuse **ground** and **floor**. The **ground** is the surface of the land outside. The **floor** is the surface that you walk on, inside a building.

---

ground[2] [*verb*]
1 the past tense and past participle of **GRIND**
2 [**grounded, grounding**] to punish your child by not allowing him or her to do things with friends for a period of time: *If you come home late again, I'm grounding you for a week!*

ground beef /'graʊnd 'bif/ [*noun*] meat that has been cut into extremely

---

/i/ **see**	/ɪ/ **big**	/eɪ/ **day**	/ɛ/ **get**	/æ/ **hat**
/ɑ/ **father, hot**	/ʌ/ **up**	/ə/ **about**	/ɔ/ **saw**
/oʊ/ **hope**	/ʊ/ **book**	/u/ **too**	/aɪ/ **I**	/aʊ/ **how**
/ɔɪ/ **boy**	/ɝ/ **bird**	/ɚ/ **teacher**	/ɪr/ **ear**	/ɛr/ **air**
/ɑr/ **far**	/ɔr/ **more**	/ʊr/ **tour**	/aɪr/ **fire**
/aʊɚ/ **hour**	/θ/ **nothing**	/ð/ **mother**	/ʃ/ **she**
/ʒ/ **measure**	/tʃ/ **church**	/dʒ/ **jump**	/ŋ/ **long**

small pieces, and can be shaped before it is cooked: *Buy a pound of ground beef.*

ground floor /ˈgraʊnd ˈflɔr/ [*noun*] the part of a building that is at the level of the ground or street; synonym FIRST FLOOR: *There is a café on the ground floor of the hotel.*

group[1] * /grup/ [*noun*]
1 several people or things that are together: *A group of tourists waited outside the palace. | The children were put in groups by age.*
2 a small number of musicians who play or sing music together: *They formed a rock group.*

group[2] [*verb*; **grouped, grouping**]
1 to put things or people into groups: *They are grouped according to age.*
2 to come together and form a group for a particular reason: *Several schools have grouped together to buy new equipment.*

grow * T /groʊ/ [*verb*; **grew, grown, growing**]
1 to become older and bigger or taller: *That puppy will grow into a big dog. | You've grown six inches since I saw you.*
2 if plants grow or if people grow plants, the plants develop from seeds: *They grow flowers in a garden behind the house. | Rice grows well in this area.*
3 if your hair grows or you grow your hair, it gets longer: *Should I let my hair grow longer? | I'm letting my bangs grow out* (=grow to the length of the rest of my hair).
4 to increase: *Our profits have grown steadily. | A growing number of schools use computers in the classroom.*
5 [*linking*] to become: *The wind was growing stronger.*
⇨ See the synonym note at BECOME.

— PHRASAL VERBS
grow out of [*phrasal verb*]
6 to become too big for your clothes because you are growing: **grow out of something** ▸ *The kids have grown out of their winter coats.*

grow up [*phrasal verb*]
7 to become older and gradually change from a child to an adult: *I want to be an astronaut when I grow up. | I grew up in a small town in Utah.*

growl[1] /graʊl/ [*verb*; **growled, growling**] if an animal growls, it makes a low, angry sound in its throat: *Their dog growled at me when I came near the gate.*

growl[2] [*noun*] a low, angry sound made by an animal: *The bear gave a deep growl.*

grown[1] * /groʊn/ [*verb*] the past participle of GROW

grown[2] [*adjective; no comparative*]
— PHRASE
a grown man/woman someone who is an adult: *She's a grown woman who can take care of herself.*

grown up or **grown-up** /ˈgroʊn ˈʌp/ [*adjective; no comparative*] completely developed and independent as an adult: *Our children are grown up. | I have two grown-up nephews.*

grownup /ˈgroʊnˌʌp/ [*noun*] a word meaning an adult, used especially by or to children: *She sat with the grownups.*

growth * T /groʊθ/ [*noun*] the process of developing and getting bigger: *The growth of the town was slow at first. | Use fertilizer to increase plant growth.*

grumble /ˈgrʌmbəl/ [*verb*; **grumbled, grumbling**] to complain in an unhappy but not very angry way: *They were grumbling about the food, as usual.*

grumpy /ˈgrʌmpi/ [*adjective*; **grumpier, grumpiest**] not cheerful or friendly, and complaining a lot: *a grumpy old man*

grunt /grʌnt/ [*verb*; **grunted, grunting**]
1 to make a short, low noise or say a few short words, in a way that is not friendly: *I said hello but she just grunted.*
2 to make the low noise that a pig makes: *Pigs were grunting and squealing in the barn.*

guarantee[1] T /ˌgærənˈti/ [*verb*; **guarantees, guaranteed, guaranteeing**]
1 to promise that something will happen, be true, or be done: **guarantee (that)** ▸ *I guarantee you'll like the movie. | We can't guarantee that we'll be there on time.*
2 to promise to return someone's money if something is wrong with

your product or service: *We guarantee our refrigerators for two years.* | **guarantee to do something** ▶ *They guarantee to refund your money if the trip is canceled.*

guarantee[2] [*noun; plural* **guarantees**]
1 a written promise to return someone's money if something is wrong with your product or service: *These knives come with a five-year guarantee.*
⇨ *Compare* WARRANTY.
2 a promise that something will happen, be true, or be done: *I can't give you a guarantee that we'll finish by Friday.*
3 something that makes it certain that something will happen: *There's no guarantee that she can help you.*

guard[1] /gɑrd/ [*noun*]
1 someone who watches a place or person, in order to protect him, her, or it: *a security guard*
2 someone who watches a prisoner so that he or she does not escape: *You'll never get past the guards.*
3 a piece of equipment that protects part of your body: *mouth guards*

guard[2] * [*verb;* **guarded, guarding**] to watch a place or person in order to give protection or prevent an escape: *We left three men to guard the prisoners.* | *Three soldiers were guarding the gate.*

guardian /'gɑrdiən/ [*noun*] someone who is legally responsible for taking care of another person, especially a child: *After my parents died, my uncle became my guardian.*

guerrilla /gə'rɪlə/ [*noun; plural* **guerrillas**] a member of a group that fights a government by attacking suddenly and then hiding: *The guerrillas control the north of the country.*

guess[1] * /gɛs/ [*verb;* **guesses, guessed, guessing**]
1 to try to give the right answer, when you do not know the facts: *Don't tell me—let me guess what he said.* | **guess something** ▶ *I had to guess most of the answers.* | **guess who/what/where/ etc.** ▶ *Guess who I saw in town today?*
2 to succeed in giving the right answer, when you do not know the facts: *No one told me about the party—I guessed.*

— PHRASE —
3 I guess SPOKEN used when you are giving your opinion about something, especially in answer to a question: *"Is Meg coming too?" "I guess so* (=I think she is).*"* | *"Do we need our books?" "I guess not* (=I do not think so).*"* | *I guess she won't have time to meet us for dinner before the movie.*

guess[2] * [*noun; plural* **guesses**] an attempt to guess something: **a good/ lucky/correct guess** ▶ *That was a good guess—you're right.* | **take/make a guess** ▶ *Just take a guess at the answer.*

guest * /gɛst/ [*noun*]
1 someone who visits your house: *We have guests staying this weekend.*
2 someone you invite to a restaurant, theater, club, etc., or for a special event: *wedding guests*
3 someone who is staying in a hotel: *The other guests have complained that your TV is too loud.*

guidance /'gaɪdəns/ [*noun*] advice and help: *She worked as a guidance counselor* (=someone whose job is to give advice to students).

guide[1] * /gaɪd/ [*noun*]
1 someone who tells people about a place and shows them the way through it: *a museum guide* | *Our tour guide* (=guide leading a group of tourists) *told us to go back to the bus.*
2 a book that gives information about a place or a subject: *He has written an excellent guide to the islands.*

guide[2] * [*verb;* **guided, guiding**]
1 to show someone the correct way to go: *She guided us to our seats.*
2 to show someone the way through a place and give information about it: *I'll give you a guided tour of the city.*

guidebook /'gaɪd,bʊk/ [*noun*] a book that gives information about a place: *She had left the guidebook at the hotel.*

guidelines /'gaɪd,laɪnz/ [*plural noun*] instructions that tell you how you should behave or do something, especially official written instructions: *Please read the new **safety guidelines**.*

guide word /'gaɪd ,wɜ˞d/ [*noun*] a word at the top of a page in a dictionary that shows the first or last word that is explained on a page: *Guide words help you find the words you need faster.*

guilt /gɪlt/ [*noun*]
1 a feeling of shame because you have done something wrong: *She doesn't feel any **guilt about** taking the money.*
2 the fact that someone has done something wrong, especially something illegal; <u>opposite</u> INNOCENCE: *He has **admitted his guilt** (=said he did something wrong).*

guilty * /'gɪlti/ [*adjective*; **guiltier, guiltiest**]
1 ashamed because you have done something wrong or treated someone badly: *I **felt guilty about** lying to her.*
↪ *Compare* ASHAMED, EMBARRASSED.
2 responsible for doing something illegal; <u>opposite</u> INNOCENT: *He is **guilty of** theft. | The jury declared that he was **not guilty** (=not responsible for a crime).*

guinea pig /'gɪni ,pɪg/ [*noun*] a small furry animal without a tail, that is often kept as a pet

guitar /gɪ'tɑr/ [*noun*] a MUSICAL INSTRUMENT with six strings and a long neck, that you play with your fingers: *He is learning to **play the guitar**. | an **electric guitar** (=one with the sound increased by electricity)*

gulf /gʌlf/ [*noun*] a large part of an ocean that has land on two or three sides of it: *the Gulf of Mexico*

gully /'gʌli/ [*noun*; *plural* **gullies**] an area like a small narrow valley where water often flows: *The stream had formed a gully in the side of the hill.*

gulp[1] /gʌlp/ [*verb*; **gulped, gulping**] to swallow something quickly: *He gulped his coffee and stood up to go. | **gulp down something** ▸ I was gulping down*

soup. | **gulp something down** ▸ *She gulped the hot soup down too fast.*

gulp[2] [*noun*] an act of swallowing: *She finished her drink **in one gulp**.*

gum /gʌm/ [*noun*]
1 soft candy that you chew but do not swallow; <u>synonym</u> CHEWING GUM: *a piece of gum | Don't **chew gum** in class.*
2 **gums** [*plural*] the parts of your mouth from which your teeth grow: *Brushing your teeth also keeps your gums healthy.*

gun * /gʌn/ [*noun*] a weapon from which bullets are fired: *Do the police here carry guns? | a **loaded gun** (=a gun with bullets in it)*

gunfire /'gʌn,faɪr/ [*noun*] the sound or fact of guns firing: *We could hear gunfire from across the river.*

gunman /'gʌnmən/ [*noun*; *plural* **gunmen** /'gʌnmən/] someone who uses a gun illegally: *The gunman fired three shots at the police.*

gunpowder /'gʌn,paʊdə˞/ [*noun*] a substance that explodes, and is used to shoot bullets from a gun: *a barrel of gunpowder*

gunshot /'gʌn,ʃɑt/ [*noun*] the firing of a gun: *We heard a gunshot. | a **gunshot wound***

gush[1] /gʌʃ/ [*verb*; **gushes, gushed, gushing**] to flow quickly and in large amounts: *Water was **gushing through** a hole in the boat.*

gush[2] [*noun*; *plural* **gushes**] a quick, strong flow of liquid: *a **gush of** blood*

gust /gʌst/ [*noun*] a sudden, strong rush of wind: *A **gust of** wind caught his hat.*

guts /gʌts/ [*plural noun*]
1 the stomach and other organs inside a person or animal: *She cleaned the guts out of the fish.*
2 INFORMAL courage: *I didn't **have the guts** to say no.*

gutter /'gʌtə˞/ [*noun*]
1 a narrow, low area along the side of a road for carrying water away: *The gutters were full of leaves and trash.*
2 a long, narrow, curved piece of metal at the edge of a roof for carrying water away: *Water dripped from the leaking gutter.*

guy /gaɪ/ [noun; plural **guys**]
1 INFORMAL a man: *I know a guy who could fix your stereo.*
2 guys [plural] SPOKEN used when you are talking to or about people you know well: *Are you guys coming too?*
☛ In the plural, **guys** is used for both men and women.

gym /dʒɪm/ [noun]
1 gymnasium; a room or building with equipment for physical exercise: *I usually go to the gym on my lunch hour.*
2 organized physical exercise: *We have gym class once a week.*

gymnasium /dʒɪm'neɪziəm/ [noun] a GYM (definition 1): *We spent an hour in the gymnasium.*

gymnast /'dʒɪmnəst/ [noun] someone who regularly does gymnastics, in competitions or for fun

gymnastics /dʒɪm'næstɪks/ [noun] the sport or activity of doing physical exercises that need strength and control and often use special equipment: *Last year our team won two gold medals in gymnastics.*
☛ Only use **gymnastics** with a singular verb.

H

H ∗ or **h** /eɪtʃ/ [noun; plural **Hs** or **H's**, **h's**] the eighth letter of the English alphabet
⇨ *See the usage note at* ALPHABET.

habit ∗ /'hæbɪt/ [noun] something you do regularly: *Smoking is a bad habit.* | *He has a habit of reading before going to sleep.*
☛ Do not say that someone "has a habit to do something." Say that he or she **has a habit of doing something**.

USAGE   habit, custom

Do not confuse **habit** and **custom**. A **habit** is something that someone does often, because he or she has done it many times before: *Biting your nails is a bad habit.* A **custom** is a way of doing something that people in a particular country usually do: *It's an American custom to shake hands when you first meet someone.*

hack /hæk/ [verb; **hacked, hacking**]
1 to cut something in a rough and violent way: *She went first, hacking at the branches.*

—— **PHRASAL VERB** ——

hack into [phrasal verb]
2 to get into a computer system in an illegal way: **hack into something** ▸ *Someone had hacked into the company's computer system.*

hacker /'hækɚ/ [noun] INFORMAL someone who is extremely good at writing computer programs, especially someone who gets into computer systems in an illegal way

had ∗ /hæd/ [verb]
1 the past tense and past participle of HAVE¹ and HAVE²
2 used with a past participle to form the past perfect tense: *He had locked the door.* | *She had lived there all her life.*

hadn't ∗ /'hædənt/ the short form of "had not": *I hadn't met him before.*

hail¹ /heɪl/ [noun] hard balls of ice that fall from clouds

hail² [verb; **hailed, hailing**] if it hails, hard balls of ice fall from clouds: *Then it started to hail.*

hair ∗ /hɛr/ [noun]
1 the mass of thin threads that grow on your head or on the bodies of some animals: *She has beautiful hair.* | *You've had your hair cut!* | *a hair salon* (=a place where you go to have your hair cut) | *There's cat hair all over the couch.*
☛ Do not say that someone "has long hairs." Say that he or she **has long hair**.
2 one of the threads that grows on someone's head or other part of his or her body: *She found a hair on her plate.*

hairbrush /'hɛr,brʌʃ/ [noun; plural **hairbrushes**] a BRUSH for your hair

haircut /'hɛr,kʌt/ [noun]
1 when someone cuts your hair: *I need a haircut.*

2 the shape your hair has when it has been cut: *I got a new haircut.*

hairdresser /'hɛr‚drɛsɚ/ [noun] someone whose job is to cut people's hair

hair dryer /'hɛr ‚draɪɚ/ [noun] a piece of electrical equipment that you sit under or hold, that produces warm air to dry your hair
⇨ *See the picture at* APPLIANCE.

hair spray /'hɛr ‚spreɪ/ [noun; plural **hair sprays**] a liquid used to keep hair in place that comes out of a bottle or a can in very small drops

hairstyle /'hɛr‚staɪl/ [noun] the way in which someone's hair is arranged: *That hairstyle looks good on you.*

hairy * /'hɛri/ [adjective; **hairier, hairiest**]
1 having a lot of hair on your body: *a hairy man*

2 covered with something that looks like hair: *a hairy coconut shell*

half[1] * /hæf/ [noun; plural **halves**]
1 one of two equal parts of something: *I didn't like the second **half of** of the movie.* | *My homework took me two **and a half** hours.*
☛ Do not say "three days and a half" or "two dollars and a half." Say **three and a half days** or **two and a half dollars**.
⇨ *See also* HALVE.

━ PHRASES ━
2 in half into two equal pieces or parts: *Cut the sandwich **in half**.*
3 half past one/two/etc. if it is half past one, two, etc., the time is 30 minutes after one, two, etc.: *It's half past four.*
⇨ *See the usage note at* TIME[1].

half[2] * [pronoun] part of a thing or group which is equal to the other part:

He has **sideburns**.

He has a **mustache**.

He has a **beard**.

He is **bald**.

Her hair is in **braids**.

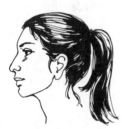

Her hair is in a **ponytail**.

She has **short curly** hair.

She has **long straight** hair with **bangs**.

talking about hair

They painted **half** of the wall blue. | **Half** of them didn't know any English at all.

☞ When using **half of**, use a singular verb with a singular noun and a plural verb with a plural noun. For example, do not say "Half of the seats was empty." Say **Half of the seats were empty.**

half³ * [determiner]

1 used to talk about part of a thing or group which is equal to the other part: *She ate half the ice cream.* | *Add half a cup of sugar.*

══ PHRASE ══

2 half an hour 30 minutes: *We're leaving in half an hour.*

half⁴ * [adverb]

1 used to say that something is exactly in the middle between two conditions: *The window was half-open.* | *The bridge is half-finished.*

2 used to say that something is equal to half of something in size, amount, etc.: *I got only* **half as much** *juice as she did.* | *Their house is* **half the size** *of ours.*

half brother /'hæf ,brʌðɚ/ [noun] a boy or man who has the same mother as you but a different father, or the same father but a different mother

half sister /'hæf ,sɪstɚ/ [noun] a girl or woman who has the same mother as you but a different father, or the same father but a different mother

halftime /'hæf,taɪm/ [noun] the period of time between the two halves of a sports game: *At halftime the score was tied.*

halfway /'hæf'weɪ/ [adverb]

1 at a point exactly in the middle between two things or places: *He'll be* **halfway** *to Australia by now.*

2 in the middle of a time or activity: *An actor forgot his lines* **halfway through** *the show.* | *We're* **halfway there** (=we've finished half of what we're doing).

hall * /hɔl/ [noun]

1 a narrow room that connects other rooms in a house or other building; *synonym* HALLWAY: *The walls in their hall are full of family photos.*

2 the room that you first enter when you come into a building; *synonym* HALLWAY: *Leave your umbrella in the hall.*

3 a large room or building for public events: *a concert hall*

Halloween /ˌhælə'win/ [noun] a holiday on the evening of October 31, when children dress like witches, ghosts, story characters, etc., and go to people's houses asking for candy

hallway /'hɔl,weɪ/ [noun; plural **hallways**] a passageway in a building, or the room that you first enter when you come in; *synonym* HALL: *She waited in the hallway.*

halt¹ Ⓣ /hɔlt/ [verb; **halted, halting**] to stop or to stop something: *He ordered the soldiers to halt.*

halt² Ⓣ [noun]

══ PHRASE ══

to a halt if something comes to a halt, it stops: *The car suddenly came to a halt.*

halve /hæv/ [verb; **halved, halving**]

1 to become half as big or make something half as big: *The number of new members has halved this year.* | *We halved the time taken to build each car.*

2 to cut something such as a fruit into two equal pieces: *Halve the peaches and remove the pits.*

halves * /hævz/ [noun] the plural of HALF¹

ham /hæm/ [noun] salty meat from the back leg of a pig: *a ham sandwich*

hamburger /'hæm,bɚgɚ/ [noun] ground beef formed into a flat round shape, often eaten as a sandwich between two thick round pieces of bread: *I'll have a hamburger and a Coke.*

hammer¹ * /'hæmɚ/ [noun] a TOOL with a long handle which is used for hitting things, especially for hitting nails into walls, wood, etc.

hammer² [verb; **hammered, hammering**] to hit something hard with a hammer or with your hand: *Finish* **hammering** *these nails* **in.** | *She* **hammered on** *the door.*

/i/ see /ɪ/ big /eɪ/ day /ɛ/ get /æ/ hat
/a/ father, hot /ʌ/ up /ə/ about /ɔ/ saw
/oʊ/ hope /ʊ/ book /u/ too /aɪ/ I /aʊ/ how
/ɔɪ/ boy /ɝ/ bird /ɚ/ teacher /ɪr/ ear /ɛr/ air
/ɑr/ far /ɔr/ more /ʊr/ tour /aɪr/ fire
/aʊɚ/ hour /θ/ nothing /ð/ mother /ʃ/ she
/ʒ/ measure /tʃ/ church /dʒ/ jump /ŋ/ long

hamster /'hæmstɚ/ [noun] an animal like a mouse with no tail, that is often kept as a pet

hand[1] * /hænd/ [noun]
1 the part of your BODY at the end of your arm, that has fingers: *Wash your hands before dinner.* | *He had a letter in his hand* (=was holding a letter).
2 a long thin piece of metal or plastic on a clock or watch that points to a number to show you what time it is: *the hour hand* (=that shows which hour it is) | *the minute hand* (=that shows which minute it is) | *the second hand* (=that shows which second it is)

— PHRASES —

3 **give someone a hand** or **lend someone a hand** help with doing something: *Can you give me a hand with this ladder?*
4 **by hand** without using a machine: *These purses are made by hand.*
5 **(on the one hand) . . . on the other hand** used when you are comparing two different facts, situations, etc.: *On the one hand, this computer costs less, but on the other hand, it may not have enough memory.*
6 **get out of hand** to become very difficult to control: *The situation was getting out of hand.*
7 **on hand** near and ready to help or be used: *Do you have any ice on hand?*
8 **hand in hand** holding each other's hand: *They walked hand in hand.*
⇨ See also **hold hands** at HOLD[1].

hand[2] [verb; handed, handing]
1 to give something you are holding to someone: **hand someone something** ▸ *She handed me the book.* | **hand something to someone** ▸ *Will you hand those tickets to Jennifer?*

— PHRASAL VERBS —

hand in [phrasal verb]
2 to give something to someone, especially someone in authority such as a teacher: **hand in something** ▸ *Have you all handed in your essays?*

hand out [phrasal verb]
3 to give a number of things to a group of people, so that each person has one: **hand out something** ▸ *Could you hand out the books, please?*

handbag /'hænd,bæg/ [noun] a small bag in which a woman carries money and personal things; <u>synonym</u> PURSE: *She took a pen from her handbag.*

handbook /'hænd,bʊk/ [noun] a book that tells you what you should do or how to do something: *All new employees must read the company handbook.*

handcuffs /'hænd,kʌfs/ [plural noun] metal rings that the police use to hold a prisoner's wrists together: *The thief was led away in handcuffs.*

handful /'hændfʊl/ [noun; plural **handfuls**]
1 as much of something as you can hold in one hand: *She picked a handful of berries.*
2 a small number of things or people: *Only a handful of people were there.*

handgun /'hænd,gʌn/ [noun] a small gun that is held in one hand

handicap /'hændi,kæp/ [noun] a condition that affects a part of a person's body or mind so that it does not work in the usual way: *a physical handicap*

handicapped /'hændi,kæpt/ [adjective; no comparative] unable to use part of your body or mind in the usual way; <u>synonym</u> DISABLED: *She works with handicapped children.*
☛ **Disabled** is the word that many people prefer to use.

handkerchief /'hæŋkɚtʃɪf/ [noun] a square piece of cloth used to dry your nose or eyes

handle[1] * ⊤ /'hændəl/ [noun] the part of a tool, container, etc., that you hold when you use it: *he handle of a cup* | *He pulled on the door handle.*

handle[2] * ⊤ [verb; handled, handling]
1 to deal with something or someone: *I wasn't sure how to handle the situation.*
2 to touch or hold something: *He handled the snake with great care.*

handlebars /'hændəl,barz/ [plural noun] the parts of a MOTORCYCLE or BICYCLE that you hold when you ride it

handmade /'hænd'meɪd/ [adjective; no comparative] made by a person or people, without using machines: *Their house is full of handmade furniture.*

handshake /'hænd,ʃeɪk/ [*noun*] when you shake someone's hand, as a polite greeting: *a firm handshake*

handsome /'hænsəm/ [*adjective;* **more handsome, most handsome**] a handsome man is attractive; <u>synonym</u> GOOD-LOOKING: *She thought he was very handsome.*

⇨ *See the synonym note at* BEAUTIFUL.

handwriting /'hænd,raɪtɪŋ/ [*noun*] the style of someone's writing when he or she uses a pen or pencil: *She has beautiful handwriting.*

My name is James.

handwriting

handwritten /'hænd,rɪtən/ [*adjective; no comparative*] written with a pen or pencil: *a handwritten note*

handy /'hændi/ [*adjective;* **handier, handiest**]
1 useful: *The purse has a handy pocket at the front.* | *You never know when a pen will* ***come in handy*** (=be useful).
2 near and available to be used: ***Keep*** *a pencil and paper* ***handy.***

hang[1] * /hæŋ/ [*verb;* **hung, hanging**]
1 to put something somewhere so that it is only supported at the top: *She hung the washing on the line.* | *You can* ***hang up*** *your coats in here.*
2 to be supported only at the top: *There were icicles* ***hanging from*** *the roof.*

== PHRASAL VERBS ==

hang around [*phrasal verb*]
3 INFORMAL to spend time somewhere or with someone, not doing very much: *They* ***kept us hanging around*** *for hours.* | *He* ***hangs around with*** *a group of older boys.*

hang on [*phrasal verb*]
4 SPOKEN used to tell someone to wait: *Hang on! I'm not ready yet!*
5 to hold something tightly: *The boy* ***hung on to*** *his mother's hand.*

hang out [*phrasal verb*]
6 INFORMAL to spend time somewhere or with someone in a relaxed way: *He likes just* ***hanging out with*** *his kids.*

hang up [*phrasal verb*]
7 to end a phone call by putting the phone down: *I called him to apologize and he* ***hung up on*** *me!*

hang[2] [*verb;* **hanged, hanging**] to kill someone by putting a rope around his or her neck and then taking the support from under his or her feet: *The murderer was hanged.*
☛ Do not use **hanged** about things. Use **hung.**

hang[3] [*noun*] INFORMAL
== PHRASE ==
get the hang of to learn how to do or use something: *I think I've got the hang of this game now.*

hangar /'hæŋɚ/ [*noun*] a building where aircraft are kept

hanger /'hæŋɚ/ [*noun*] an object with a hook in the middle, on which you hang a shirt, dress, etc., when you are not wearing it

Hanukkah /'hanəkə/ [*noun*] a Jewish celebration that takes place for eight days in December

happen * /'hæpən/ [*verb;* **happened, happening**]
1 if something happens, a person or thing does or experiences something: *What happened next?* | *So many things have happened this week.* | *It's the best thing that ever* ***happened*** *to me.*
== PHRASE ==
2 happen to do something to do something without planning to: *If you happen to see him, say hi for me.*

SYNONYMS happen, occur, take place

Use **happen** to talk about events, especially ones that are not planned: *I don't know what will happen now.* **Occur** is a formal word, and you use it to talk only about past events: *The fire occurred last week.* Use **take place** to talk about an event that is planned: *When will the meeting take place?*

/i/ **see**	/ɪ/ **big**	/eɪ/ **day**	/ɛ/ **get**	/æ/ **hat**	
/a/ **father, hot**	/ʌ/ **up**	/ə/ **about**	/ɔ/ **saw**		
/oʊ/ **hope**	/ʊ/ **book**	/u/ **too**	/aɪ/ **I**	/aʊ/ **how**	
/ɔɪ/ **boy**	/ɚ/ **bird**	/ɚ/ **teacher**	/ɪr/ **ear**	/ɛr/ **air**	
/ɑr/ **far**	/ɔr/ **more**	/ʊr/ **tour**	/aɪr/ **fire**		
/aʊɚ/ **hour**	/θ/ **nothing**	/ð/ **mother**	/ʃ/ **she**		
/ʒ/ **measure**	/tʃ/ **church**	/dʒ/ **jump**	/ŋ/ **long**		

happily * /'hæpəli/ [adverb]
1 in a happy way; _opposite_ SADLY: *She was singing happily to herself.*
2 used to say that someone is willing to do something: *I'll happily do the dishes.*

happiness * /'hæpinis/ [noun] the feeling of pleasure you have when you are in a good situation and are not worried; _opposites_ SADNESS, UNHAPPINESS: *Money can't bring you happiness.*

happy * /'hæpi/ [adjective; **happier, happiest**]
1 feeling pleasure because you are in a good situation and are not worried; _opposites_ SAD, UNHAPPY: *I just want to make you happy.* | *a happy childhood* | *She was **happy to be** home again.*
↪ *See the picture at* EMOTION.
2 thinking that something is acceptable: *My teacher is **happy with** my progress.*
☛ Do not use **happy** before a noun in this meaning.
↪ *See also* HAPPILY, HAPPINESS.

━━ PHRASES ━━
3 **be happy to do something** to be very willing to do something: *I'd be happy to show you around.*
4 **Happy Birthday!** or **Happy New Year!** used to greet someone on a special day: *Happy Birthday, Mary!*

SYNONYMS   happy, cheerful, pleased, in a good mood
There are lots of ways of saying that someone is **happy**.
Use **cheerful** when someone shows he or she is happy by smiling and being friendly, especially when he or she is always like this: *He's a cheerful boy.*
Use **pleased** when someone is happy because something good has happened: *She's pleased about her science project.*
Use **in a good mood** when someone is behaving in a happy, friendly way, and he or she is often not like this: *I hope he's in a good mood today.*

harass /hə'ræs/ [verb; **harasses, harassed, harassing**] to keep annoying someone again and again: *The athletes want reporters to stop harassing them.*

harbor T /'harbɚ/ [noun] a sheltered area of water next to a coast, where boats can stop safely

hard[1] * /hard/ [adjective; **harder, hardest**]
1 a hard substance or object does not change shape when it is pressed; _opposite_ SOFT: *a hard, stone floor* | *The ice isn't hard enough to skate on.*
↪ *See also* HARDEN.
2 needing a lot of effort, experience, or skill to understand or do; _synonym_ DIFFICULT; _opposites_ EASY, SIMPLE: *These questions are too hard.* | **hard to do something** ▸ *Some languages are harder to learn than others.* | *It's **hard for him** to pay attention.*
3 involving a lot of effort: *Thank you for all your **hard work**.*

hard[2] * [adverb]
1 with a lot of effort: *They worked hard all day.* | *He tried hard not to laugh.*
2 with a lot of force: *Push harder!* | *It rained so hard that the river flooded.*

USAGE   hard, hardly
Do not confuse the adverbs **hard** and **hardly. Hard** is used to say that someone does something with a lot of effort or force: *I hope you're working hard.* **Hardly** means "almost not at all": *We could hardly hear you.*

hard disk /'hard 'dɪsk/ [noun] the part in a computer that can store a lot of programs and information
↪ *Compare* FLOPPY DISK.

harden /'hardən/ [verb; **hardened, hardening**] to become hard or to make something hard, so that it does not change shape when it is pressed; _opposite_ SOFTEN: *Wait until the glue has hardened.*

hardly * T /'hardli/ [adverb]
1 almost not at all, almost none at all, etc.; _synonyms_ BARELY, SCARCELY: *I could hardly breathe.* | *I hardly knew him.* | *He had **hardly any** hair.* | ***Hardly anyone** else had heard of the book.*
2 used to mean "not," when you think that what you are saying is very clear: *It's hardly surprising that she's late—she always is.*
☛ Do not use "hardly" with another negative, such as "no" or "nothing." For

example, do not say "He hardly did nothing." Say **He hardly did anything.**

━━ PHRASE ━━

3 hardly ever almost never: *She hardly ever goes out.*

⋄ *See the usage note at* HARD².

hardware /'hard,wɛr/ [*noun*]
1 tools and other objects that are used for building or fixing things: *a hardware store*
2 computers and the physical parts inside them: *Can we use the new software with our old hardware?*

⋄ *Compare* SOFTWARE.

hardworking /'hard'wɜ·kɪŋ/ [*adjective;* **more hardworking, most hardworking**] always working very hard; *opposite* LAZY: *a hardworking employee*

hare /hɛr/ [*noun*] an animal that looks like a large rabbit

harm¹ * /harm/ [*noun*]
1 damage to something or someone: *Chemicals can **cause harm to** the environment.* I *We didn't **mean her any harm*** (=we did not want to harm her).

━━ PHRASE ━━

2 there's no harm in asking/ trying/etc. used to say that something may help you and will not harm anyone: *Maybe there are more tickets—there's no harm in asking.*

harm² * [*verb;* **harmed, harming**] to damage something or someone: *He's a friendly dog—he won't harm you.*

harmful * Ⓣ /'harmfəl/ [*adjective;* **more harmful, most harmful**] causing damage, or able to damage someone or something: *Looking at the sun is harmful to your eyes.*

harmless /'harmlɪs/ [*adjective;* **more harmless, most harmless**] not causing any damage, or not likely to damage someone or something: *Although the spider looks scary, it is totally harmless.*

harsh /harʃ/ [*adjective;* **harsher, harshest**]
1 cruel or severe; *opposite* KIND: *He didn't deserve such harsh treatment.*
2 very unpleasant to experience; *opposite* PLEASANT: *Many animals did not survive the harsh winter.*

harvest¹ Ⓣ /'harvɪst/ [*noun*]
1 when crops are gathered because they are ready to be eaten, sold, or stored: *the fall harvest*
2 a crop that has been gathered: *a good corn harvest*

harvest² Ⓣ [*verb;* **harvested, harvesting**] to gather crops when they are ready to be eaten, sold, or stored: *The wheat is ready to be harvested.*

has * /hæz/ [*verb*] the present form of HAVE, that is used with "he," "she," "it," and names: *She has a nice smile.*

hasn't * /'hæzənt/ the short form of "has not": *He hasn't come back yet.*

hassle¹ /'hæsəl/ [*verb;* **hassled, hassling**] INFORMAL to annoy someone by causing problems, asking too many questions, speaking to him or her when this is not welcome, etc.: *Two boys kept hassling her when she walked to school.*

hassle² [*noun*] INFORMAL a situation that involves a lot of small problems and annoys you: *It's such a hassle trying to get everything ready.*

haste /heɪst/ [*noun*] when you do something quickly, sometimes too quickly: *In her haste, she knocked over her coffee.*

hasty /'heɪsti/ [*adjective;* **hastier, hastiest**] done quickly, especially because there is not much time: *They left at seven after a hasty breakfast.*

hat * /hæt/ [*noun*] a piece of CLOTHING that you wear on your head

eggshell

hatch /hætʃ/ [*verb;* **hatches, hatched, hatching**] if an egg, bird, or insect hatches,

The chick is **hatching.**

the young bird or insect comes out of the egg: *Have all the eggs hatched?*

/i/ **see** /ɪ/ **big** /eɪ/ **day** /ɛ/ **get** /æ/ **hat** /ɑ/ **father, hot** /ʌ/ **up** /ə/ **about** /ɔ/ **saw** /oʊ/ **hope** /ʊ/ **book** /u/ **too** /aɪ/ **I** /aʊ/ **how** /ɔɪ/ **boy** /ɝ/ **bird** /ɚ/ **teacher** /ɪr/ **ear** /ɛr/ **air** /ɑr/ **far** /ɔr/ **more** /ʊr/ **tour** /aɪr/ **fire** /aʊɚ/ **hour** /θ/ **nothing** /ð/ **mother** /ʃ/ **she** /ʒ/ **measure** /tʃ/ **church** /dʒ/ **jump** /ŋ/ **long**

hate[1] * /heɪt/ [*verb;* **hated, hating**]
1 to not like someone or something in any way; *opposite* LOVE: *Sometimes she hated him for being so rude.* | *I hate it when I can't remember someone's name.* | **hate doing something** ▸ *He hates driving at night.*
↪ Compare DISLIKE.

▬▬ PHRASE ▬▬
2 **would hate** used to emphasize that someone does not want to do something: *I would hate to live there.*

hate[2] [*noun*] the strong feeling of not liking someone or something in any way; *opposite* LOVE: *His love for her had turned to hate.*

USAGE   hate, hatred

Use **hate** to talk about this feeling in general: *Hate is a dangerous emotion.* Use **hatred** to say that someone has this feeling: *His hatred of us was clear.*

hatred * /'heɪtrɪd/ [*noun*] a strong feeling that you do not like someone or something in any way; *opposite* LOVE: *I don't understand his hatred of school.*
↪ See the usage note at HATE[2].

haul /hɔl/ [*verb;* **hauled, hauling**] to pull or carry something heavy: *A truck hauled away the old refrigerator.*

haunted /'hɔntɪd/ [*adjective; no comparative*] a haunted place is one where people think that the spirit of a dead person lives: *The old cemetery is said to be haunted.*

have[1] * /hæv/ [*verb*]
1 used to say that someone owns something, or that something can be used: *He has a big house.* | *We don't have much money.* | *We'll have time to go shopping.*
2 used to describe someone or something, or say what condition or place someone or something is in: *She has brown hair.* | *He has a fever.* | *He still had his coat on* (=was still wearing his coat). | *The car has a dent in it.*
3 used to say that someone does something: *I had a long talk with him.* | *Have you had lunch yet?*
4 used to say that someone experiences something: *We all had a great time.* | *She has trouble with spelling.*
5 to get something: *You have two messages.*
↪ See also HAVE TO.

have[2] * [*auxiliary verb*] used with a past participle to form the present perfect tense: *He has made good progress.* | *Have you ever visited Japan?*

USAGE   Short forms of the auxiliary verb "have"

You can use a short form of **have** or **has** or **had**, such as **you've** or **he's** or **they'd**, at the beginning of a sentence: *We've never seen a Broadway play.* You can also use a short form in the middle of a sentence | *I think she's seen one.*

However, at the end of a sentence, you must use **have** or **has** or **had**: *We'd never seen a Broadway play before last night, but she **had*** (=not "she'd").

You must use **have** or **has** or **had**, not a short form, at the beginning of a question: *Have you seen my new car?*

Forms of *have*				
	present tense		past tense	
singular	I **have** he/she/it **has** you **have**		I **had** he/she/it **had** you **had**	
plural	we **have** they **have** you **have**		we **had** they **had** you **had**	
negatives	I **haven't** or **don't have** he/she/it **hasn't** or **doesn't have** you/we/they **haven't** or **don't have**		I **hadn't** or **didn't have** he/she/it **hadn't** or **didn't have** you/we/they **hadn't** or **didn't have**	
participles	**having**		**had**	

haven't * /'hævənt/ the short form of "have not": *I haven't seen her for years.*

have to * /'hæv ˌtu/ or **have got to** /ˌhæv 'gɑt ˌtu/ [*modal verb*] used with a main verb to say that something is necessary or must be done: *He has to do his homework.* | *I have to go now.* | *We have got to get home by ten o' clock.*

hawk /hɔk/ [*noun*] a bird that kills and eats small birds and animals

hay /heɪ/ [*noun*] dried grass used for feeding animals

hazard /'hæzɚd/ [*noun*] something that might be dangerous: *These piles of paper are a fire hazard* (=might cause a fire).

hazardous 🔵 /'hæzɚdəs/ [*adjective; more hazardous, most hazardous*] dangerous and involving risk: *a very hazardous road*

haze /heɪz/ [*noun*] dust, mist, or smoke in the air: *The haze over the city could be seen from the bridge.*

hazelnut /'heɪzəlˌnʌt/ [*noun*] a small round **NUT**: *a candy bar with hazelnuts*

hazy /'heɪzi/ [*adjective; hazier, haziest*] if it is hazy, there is dust, mist, or smoke in the sky so that things in the distance are not clear: *It's too hazy to see the mountains today.*

he * /he/ [*pronoun*] used to talk about a man, boy, or male animal, as the subject of a verb: *He said he was waiting for his son.* | *He's a very friendly dog.*
⇨ *See also* **HIM**.

head¹ * /hɛd/ [*noun*]
1 the top part of your **BODY**, where your brain and face are: *Her head ached.* | *My head's too big for this hat.*
2 your mind: *Use your head* (=think clearly)! | *I can't get that song out of my head* (=I keep thinking about it).
3 the person in charge of a group or organization: *a head of state* (=a government leader)
4 the front or most important part of something: *Who's that at the head of the line?* | *My son is at the head of his class* (=has the best grades).
══ **PHRASE** ══
5 keep your head to stay calm in a difficult or dangerous situation: *He kept his head and got everyone outside.*
⇨ *See also* **shake your head** at **SHAKE**.

head² [*verb; headed, heading*]
1 to go toward a place or thing, or to go in a particular direction: *They headed for the door.* | *I'm heading east.*
2 to be in charge of a group or organization: *The rebels are headed by a former army officer.*

head³ [*adjective; no comparative*] used in the title of someone who is in charge of other people at work: *the head waiter*
☛ Only use **head** before a noun.

headache /'hɛdˌeɪk/ [*noun*] a continuous pain in your head: *I have a terrible headache.*

headfirst /hɛd'fɚst/ [*adverb*] if you go somewhere headfirst, you go there with your head leading: *She fell headfirst into the bushes.*

heading /'hɛdɪŋ/ [*noun*] the words above a piece of writing, that say what it is about: *Each section needs a heading.*

headlight /'hɛdˌlaɪt/ [*noun*] a bright light at the front of a **CAR**, truck, etc.

headline /'hɛdˌlaɪn/ [*noun*]
1 the big words above a newspaper story that tell you what it is about
══ **PHRASE** ══
2 be in the headlines to be written about in newspapers a lot: *It's a story that's been in the headlines all week.*

headphones /'hɛdˌfoʊnz/ [*plural noun*] a piece of electrical equipment with a band that goes over your head and parts that cover each ear, used for listening privately to music, people speaking to you, etc.
⇨ *Compare* **EARPHONES**.

He's listening to music on his **headphones**.

headquarters /'hɛdˌkwɔrtɚz/ [*plural noun*] the main place where an organization is controlled from

---

/i/ **see**	/ɪ/ **big**	/eɪ/ **day**	/ɛ/ **get**	/æ/ **hat**
/ɑ/ **father, hot**	/ʌ/ **up**	/ə/ **about**	/ɔ/ **saw**	
/oʊ/ **hope**	/ʊ/ **book**	/u/ **too**	/aɪ/ **I**	/aʊ/ **how**
/ɔɪ/ **boy**	/ɚ/ **bird**	/ɚ/ **teacher**	/ɪr/ **ear**	/ɛr/ **air**
/ɑr/ **far**	/ɔr/ **more**	/ʊr/ **tour**	/aɪr/ **fire**	
/aʊɚ/ **hour**	/θ/ **nothing**	/ð/ **mother**	/ʃ/ **she**	
/ʒ/ **measure**	/tʃ/ **church**	/dʒ/ **jump**	/ŋ/ **long**	

heal * /hil/ [*verb;* **healed, healing**]
if an injury heals, or if someone or
something heals it, it becomes healthy
again: *His broken leg took a long time to
heal.* | *This plant was used to heal burns.*

health * /hɛlθ/ [*noun*]
1 the condition of how well or sick
you are: *Fried foods are **bad for your
health**.* | *He has been **in poor health**
for some time.*
☛ Do not say that someone "has a bad
health." Say that he or she **has bad
health** or **is in bad health**.
2 the condition of being healthy: *I want
to travel while I still **have my health**.*

healthy * /'hɛlθi/ [*adjective;* **healthier,
healthiest**]
1 well, not sick; *opposite* UNHEALTHY:
She's a normal, healthy teenager.
2 healthy food, activities, etc., keep you
well; *opposite* UNHEALTHY: *Make sure you
eat a healthy diet.*

heap¹ /hip/ [*noun*] a pile of things that
is not very neat: *He left his clothes **in a
heap** on the bed.*

heap² [*verb;* **heaped, heaping**] to put a
lot of things or a lot of a substance onto
something: *He heaped rice onto his plate.*

hear * /hɪr/ [*verb;* **heard** /hɚd/,
hearing]
1 if you hear something, sound reaches
your ears and you notice it: *I could
hear voices in the next room.* | *What did
he say? I couldn't hear.* | **hear someone
do something** ▸ *I heard him lock the
door.* | **hear someone doing
something** ▸ *She heard her mother
coming up the stairs.*
2 to be told some news or information:
*I've **heard a lot about** you.* | *I've **heard
of** him, but I haven't read his book.*

— **PHRASAL VERB** —

hear from someone [*phrasal verb*]
3 to receive a letter or phone call from
someone: *I haven't heard from him yet.*

USAGE   hear, listen

Do not confuse **hear** and **listen**. If you
can **hear** a sound, you are able to notice
it: *I can't hear you.* If you **listen** to a
sound, you pay attention so that you can
hear it: *Are you listening to me?*

---

hearing /'hɪrɪŋ/ [*noun*] the ability to
hear: *Her hearing was getting worse.*

hearing aid /'hɪrɪŋ ˌeɪd/ [*noun*] a small
object worn in the ear, that makes
someone who cannot hear well able to
hear better

heart * /hart/ [*noun*]
1 the organ in your chest that makes
blood move around your body: *Her
heart was beating very fast.*
2 used to talk about someone's feelings
or character: *He's a good person **at
heart** (=this is his real character).* | *She
has always had a generous heart.*
3 a shape a little like a
heart, used to represent
love
4 the middle of a place or
thing: *They live in **the
heart of** the city.*

heart

— **PHRASES** —

5 **learn by heart** or **know by heart**
to learn or know a piece of writing or
song so well that you can remember
it: **learn/know something by heart** ▸
I knew the poem by heart.
6 **lose heart** to stop feeling confident,
cheerful, or eager: *After their fourth
defeat, the team lost heart.*
7 **your heart sinks** if your heart
sinks when you see or realize
something, you suddenly feel
unhappy or worried: *My heart sank
when I saw all that work.*
8 **break someone's heart** to make
someone feel extremely sad or
disappointed: *It broke her father's
heart when she left home.*
↪ *See also* HEARTBROKEN.

heart attack /'hart əˌtæk/ [*noun*] when
your heart suddenly stops working: *He
had a heart attack and died.*

heartbeat /'hartˌbit/ [*noun*] the
movement or sound of your heart:
I ran so hard I could feel my heartbeat.

heartbroken /'hartˌbroʊkən/ [*adjective;
no comparative*] extremely sad or
disappointed: *When her dog died, she
was heartbroken.*

hearth /harθ/ [*noun*] the floor under or
around a FIREPLACE

heat[1] * /hit/ [*noun*]
1 energy that makes things hot: *The heat of the sun soon dried the ground.*
2 the heat hot weather: *I love the heat.*

heat[2] * [*verb*; **heated, heating**]
to become hotter or make something hotter: *When glass is heated, it melts. | a heated swimming pool | He waited for the water to **heat up**.*

heated /'hitɪd/ [*adjective*; **more heated, most heated**] a heated discussion or argument is one in which people get angry or excited: *After a heated argument, Thomas left.*

heater /'hitɚ/ [*noun*] a piece of equipment used for heating a room or water: *Can you turn the heater off?*

heating /'hitɪŋ/ [*noun*] a system used to heat a building: *Is the heating on?*

heave /hiv/ [*verb*; **heaved, heaving**] to move something heavy somewhere with a lot of effort: *They heaved the sacks onto the truck.*

heaven * /'hɛvən/ [*noun*]
1 the place where God and the spirits of good people who have died are believed to be

— PHRASES —
2 for heaven's sake SPOKEN used when you are annoyed or surprised: *For heaven's sake, why didn't you call?*
3 good heavens! SPOKEN used when you are surprised or annoyed: *Good heavens! How did you get so dirty?*

heavily /'hɛvəli/ [*adverb*] with a lot of force or weight, or in large amounts; *opposite* LIGHTLY: *It is raining more heavily now.*

heavy * /'hɛvi/ [*adjective*; **heavier, heaviest**]
1 weighing a lot: *The box was too heavy to lift. | a heavy man*
   ⇨ *See the synonym note at* FAT[1].
2 used to say that there is a lot of something: *Heavy snow was expected. | There is heavy traffic on all the roads.*
3 used to say that something is very large, very serious, etc.; *synonym* BIG: *a heavy meal | a heavy responsibility | a heavy fine*
4 done with a lot of force: *He received a heavy blow to the head.*
   ⇨ *Compare* LIGHT[2].

— PHRASES —
5 a heavy sleeper someone who does not wake easily when there is noise: *Dad's always been a heavy sleeper.*
6 a heavy drinker/smoker/etc. someone who drinks a lot of alcohol, smokes a lot, etc.: *He was a **heavy smoker** and died young.*

he'd * /hid/
1 the short form of "he had": *He'd seen the movie before.*
   ☛ Do not use "he'd" for **he had** when **have** is the main verb. For example, don't say "He'd a good job." Say **He had a good job.**
2 the short form of "he would": *He'd like to come with us.*

hedge /hɛdʒ/ [*noun*] a row of bushes that form a fence: *His neighbor was cutting the hedge.*

heel * /hil/ [*noun*]
1 the back part of your foot
   ⇨ *See the picture at* BODY.
2 the part of a shoe or sock at the back: *I can't walk in shoes with high heels.*
   ⇨ *See the picture at* CLOTHING.

height * /haɪt/ [*noun*]
1 used to talk about how tall something or someone is: *The bookcase is four feet in height. | He was about my height* (=was about as tall as me).

He's of medium height.

He's tall.   He's short.

height

/i/ **see**	/ɪ/ **big**	/eɪ/ **day**	/ɛ/ **get**	/æ/ **hat**
/ɑ/ **father, hot**	/ʌ/ **up**	/ə/ **about**	/ɔ/ **saw**	
/oʊ/ **hope**	/ʊ/ **book**	/u/ **too**	/aɪ/ **I**	/aʊ/ **how**
/ɔɪ/ **boy**	/ɝ/ **bird**	/ɚ/ **teacher**	/ɪr/ **ear**	/ɛr/ **air**
/ɑr/ **far**	/ɔr/ **more**	/ʊr/ **tour**	/aɪr/ **fire**	
/aʊɚ/ **hour**	/θ/ **nothing**	/ð/ **mother**	/ʃ/ **she**	
/ʒ/ **measure**	/tʃ/ **church**	/dʒ/ **jump**	/ŋ/ **long**	

2 used to talk about how far above the ground something is: *The plane was traveling at a height of 30,000 feet.*

heir /ɛr/ [*noun*] a person who will get someone's property or money when he or she dies: *He's the heir to a fortune.*

heiress /ˈɛrɪs/ [*noun; plural* **heiresses**] a woman who will get someone's property or money when he or she dies

held * /hɛld/ [*verb*] the past tense and past participle of HOLD[1]

helicopter /ˈhɛlɪˌkɑptɚ/ [*noun*] an aircraft with long blades on the top which move quickly around: *The helicopter hovered over the trees.*

helium /ˈhiliəm/ [*noun*] a gas that is very light and makes things float

hell /hɛl/ [*noun*] a place where bad people are believed to be punished after they die

he'll * /hil/ the short form of "he will": *He'll be back soon.*

hello * /hɛˈloʊ/ [*interjection*] used as a greeting when you meet someone or answer the telephone; *synonym* HI: *Hello! I didn't expect to see you here! | Go over and say hello. | Come say hello to Grandma.*

helmet /ˈhɛlmɪt/ [*noun*] a hard hat worn to protect your head from injury: *He put on his helmet and rode off.*

bicycle helmet

visor

football helmet

motorcycle helmet

helmets

help[1] * /hɛlp/ [*verb;* **helped, helping**]
1 to do things to make an activity or situation easier for someone: *I'll help in any way I can. | Can I help you?* (=used especially to a customer in a store) | **help someone with something** ▸ *Mom*

helps me with my homework. | **help someone do something** ▸ *I helped him pack.* | **help (to) do something** ▸ *Tom helped clean up the mess.*

=== PHRASES ===

2 help yourself (to) to take any food or other things that you want: *Help yourself to the vegetables. | We have plenty—please help yourself.*

3 can't help doing to be unable to stop yourself from doing something, or to stop something from happening: **can't help doing something** ▸ *I can't help worrying about him. | I'm sorry I was late—I couldn't help it.*

=== PHRASAL VERB ===

help out [*phrasal verb*]
4 to do things for someone who has a lot of work or is in a difficult situation: *I help out in Dad's store on weekends.*

help[2] * [*noun*]
1 when you do things for someone: *Thanks for all your help.*
2 when you do something for someone in a difficult situation: *He shouted for help when the boat began to sink.*

=== PHRASE ===

3 be a help or **be a lot of help** to make an activity or situation easier for someone: *"I could set the table." "That would be a big help." | You've been a lot of help today.*

help[3] * [*interjection*] used to tell people that you are in danger and want to be saved: *Help! I can't get out!*

help desk /ˈhɛlp ˌdɛsk/ [*noun*] a place that a business provides for you to telephone or visit to get help with special questions or problems, for example if your computer is not working: *A full help desk is available with 24-hour support.*

helpful * /ˈhɛlpfəl/ [*adjective;* **more helpful, most helpful**] making an activity or situation easier for someone; *opposite* UNHELPFUL: *The sales clerk was very helpful. | helpful advice*

helping /ˈhɛlpɪŋ/ [*noun*] an amount of food that is put on your plate at one time: *He ate two helpings of potatoes.*

helpless /ˈhɛlplɪs/ [*adjective; no comparative*] not able to protect yourself or do anything to make a situation better: *When my mother got sick, I felt totally helpless.*

hem /hɛm/ [*noun*] the bottom edge of a piece of clothing: *a skirt hem*

hen /hɛn/ [*noun*] a female CHICKEN

her[1] * /hɝ/ [*determiner*] belonging to or connected with a particular girl, woman, or female animal: *She wiped her hands on her skirt.* | *She doesn't talk about her parents.*

☛ Only use the determiner **her** before a noun.

her[2] * [*pronoun*] used to talk about a particular girl, woman, or female animal, as the object of a verb or preposition: *He called his wife and told her the news.* | *They just laughed at her.*

➪ *See also* SHE, HERSELF, HERS.

herb /ɝb/ [*noun*] a plant that is used to add a pleasant taste to food or to make medicine

herbal /'ɝbəl/ [*adjective; no comparative*] made from herbs: *a cup of herbal tea*

herd[1] /hɝd/ [*noun*] used as the name for a group of particular animals, such as cattle, deer, or elephants: *They saw a small **herd of** deer.*

herd[2] [*verb; herded, herding*] to make a group of animals or people move somewhere: *They herded the sheep into the truck.*

here[1] * /hɪr/ [*adverb*]
1 in, at, or to this place: *She's not here right now.* | *I'm **over here**! | We moved here two years ago.*
➪ *Compare* THERE[2] (definition 1).
2 used to say that something or someone has just arrived or has just been found: *Here's Lisa!* | *Where's my key? Oh, here it is.*

━━ **PHRASES** ━━
3 here is or **here are** *SPOKEN* used when you are giving something to someone: *Here's the money I owe you.* | *Here are your gloves.*
4 here you are *SPOKEN* used when you are giving something to someone: *"Can I borrow your pen?" "Here you are."*
5 here and there in several different

places: *We stopped here and there on our way to Atlanta.*

USAGE here and there

The difference between **here** and **there** can be very confusing. **Here** is used to talk about a place where you are: *How long have you lived here?* **There** is used to talk about a place that you are not in: *"I used to live in Los Angeles." "How long did you live there?"*

Here and **there** can also be used to talk about things that are close to you or farther from you: *You sit here in this chair, and I'll sit there in that one.*

here[2] * [*interjection*] used when you are giving something to someone: *Here— take this.*

hero ⊤ /'hɪroʊ/ [*noun; plural* **heroes**]
1 someone who has done something brave, good, or impressive: *The first men in space were real heroes.*
2 the most important person in a story, play, or movie

heroic /hɪ'roʊɪk/ [*adjective; more heroic, most heroic*] very brave; *opposite* COWARDLY: *He made a **heroic** attempt to rescue the children.*

heroine /'hɛroʊɪn/ [*noun*]
1 a woman who has done something brave, good, or impressive: *The woman who saved the boy was a heroine.*
2 the most important woman in a story, play, or movie

hers * /hɝz/ [*pronoun*] something that belongs to or is connected with a particular woman or girl: *My sister's dress was prettier, so I wore hers.* | *These books are hers.*
➪ *See also* HER[2].

herself * /hɝ'sɛlf/ [*pronoun*]
1 used to say that the person affected by an action is the woman or girl doing it: *She locked herself in her room.*
2 used to emphasize a name, title, or

/i/ **see**	/ɪ/ **big**	/eɪ/ **day**	/ɛ/ **get**	/æ/ **hat**
/ɑ/ **father, hot**	/ʌ/ **up**	/ə/ **about**	/ɔ/ **saw**	
/oʊ/ **hope**	/ʊ/ **book**	/u/ **too**	/aɪ/ **I**	/aʊ/ **how**
/ɔɪ/ **boy**	/ɝ/ **bird**	/ɚ/ **teacher**	/ɪr/ **ear**	/ɛr/ **air**
/ɑr/ **far**	/ɔr/ **more**	/ʊr/ **tour**	/aɪr/ **fire**	
/aʊɚ/ **hour**	/θ/ **nothing**	/ð/ **mother**	/ʃ/ **she**	
/ʒ/ **measure**	/tʃ/ **church**	/dʒ/ **jump**	/ŋ/ **long**	

the word "she": *The principal dealt with the problem herself.* I *She herself didn't want to see the movie.*

☛ Do not use **herself** as a subject. For example, do not say "Herself had not been to college." Say **She herself had not been to college.**

━ PHRASES ━

3 by herself alone or without any help: *She's old enough to travel by herself.* I *Did she do this **all by herself**?*

4 to herself not sharing something with anyone else: *She finally had an apartment **all to herself**.*

he's * /hiz/
1 the short form of "he is": *He's smart.*
2 the short form of "he has": *He's failed his English test again.*

☛ Do not use "he's" for **he has** if **have** is the main verb. For example, do not say "He's a green jacket." Say **He has a green jacket.**

hesitate /'hɛzɪˌteɪt/ [*verb;* **hesitated, hesitating**] to wait for a short time before doing something because you are not sure whether you should do it or not: **hesitate to do something** ▶ *If you need something, don't hesitate to ask.*

☛ Do not say "hesitate doing something." Say **hesitate to do something.**

hesitation /ˌhɛzɪ'teɪʃən/ [*noun*] when you hesitate: *After a moment's hesitation, he agreed.*

hey /heɪ/ [*interjection*] used to get someone's attention or when you are interested, surprised, or annoyed: *Hey, come back!*

hexagon /'hɛksəˌgɑn/ [*noun*] a shape with six sides of equal length
⇨ *See* Shapes *in the Smart Study section.*

hi /haɪ/ [*interjection*] an informal way to say HELLO: *Hi! Great to see you!*

hiccup /'hɪkʌp/ [*noun*]
the hiccups [*plural*] if you have the hiccups, you get a series of uncontrolled movements in your throat: *He ate too quickly and **got the hiccups**.*

hide¹ * Ⓣ /haɪd/ [*verb;* **hid** /hɪd/, **hidden** /'hɪdən/, **hiding**]
1 to put something where it cannot be seen or found: *She hid his birthday present under her bed.*

2 to go to or stay in a place where you cannot be seen or found: *I hid behind a tree.*
3 to not show your feelings: *He tried to hide his disappointment.*

hide² [*noun*] an animal skin, usually used to make leather: *Their tents were made from buffalo hides.*

hide-and-seek /'haɪd ən 'sik/ [*noun*] a children's game in which several children hide and one child tries to find them: *They're **playing hide-and-seek**.*

high¹ * /haɪ/ [*adjective;* **higher, highest**]
1 measuring a lot from top to bottom, or a long way above the ground: *a high wooden fence* I *The rooms have high ceilings.*

☛ Do not say "a high person." Say **a tall person.**

2 used to talk about how much something measures from top to bottom, or how far something is above the ground: *The box was **30 inches high**.* I ***How high** is the wall?*

☛ Do not use **high** before a noun in this meaning. Use it after an amount or in questions after "how."

3 very good or important: *She got high grades in math.* I *a high rank in the army*
4 great in amount or level: *The price is too high.* I *The car was traveling at a high speed.*
5 near the top end of the range of musical sounds: *She sang even the highest notes perfectly.*
⇨ *See also* HEIGHT, HIGHLY. ⇨ *Compare* LOW¹.

high² * [*adverb;* **higher, highest**] a long way above the ground; <u>opposite</u> LOW: *The bird flew higher and higher.* I *These monkeys live **high up** in the trees.*
⇨ *Compare* HIGHLY.

USAGE   high, highly

Use the adverb **high** to talk about distance: *He can jump very high.* The adverb **highly** is only used with some adjectives to emphasize a quality: *highly toxic* (=extremely poisonous) I *highly regarded* (=extremely well-liked)

higher education /ˈhaɪər ˌedʒʊˈkeɪʃən/ [noun] education at a college or university: *Most of the students here go on to higher education.*

highlight[1] T /ˈhaɪˌlaɪt/ [noun] the best part of an event, performance, or experience: *The highlight of the day was the boat trip.*

highlight[2] T [verb; highlighted, highlighting] to mark parts of a piece of writing so that you can find them again easily: *Highlight the parts you want me to read.*

highlighter /ˈhaɪˌlaɪtɚ/ [noun] a pen with brightly colored ink, used to mark parts of a piece of writing

highly T /ˈhaɪli/ [adverb]
1 used with some adverbs to mean "very": *I think it's highly unlikely that she'll pass.*
   ➪ See the usage note at HIGH[2].
━━ PHRASE ━━
2 **think/speak highly of** to think or say that someone or something is very good: *They all think very highly of her.*

high school /ˈhaɪ ˌskul/ [noun] a school for children between the ages of 14 or 15 and 18: *He did pretty well in high school.* | *We went to the same high school.*

high-tech /ˈhaɪ ˈtɛk/ [adjective; more high-tech, most high-tech] using very modern machines, scientific methods, or materials: *high-tech lab equipment*

highway /ˈhaɪˌweɪ/ [noun; plural highways] a main road that goes between and through towns and cities

hijack /ˈhaɪˌdʒæk/ [verb; hijacked, hijacking] to take control of a plane or vehicle by force: *A plane carrying 200 passengers has been hijacked.*

hijacker /ˈhaɪˌdʒækɚ/ [noun] someone who takes control of a plane or vehicle by force

hike[1] /haɪk/ [verb; hiked, hiking] to go for a long walk in the country: *We hiked through the woods.*

hike[2] [noun] a long walk in the country: *They went on a hike in the mountains.*

hiking /ˈhaɪkɪŋ/ [noun] the activity of going for a long walk in the country: *They used to go hiking on weekends.*

hilarious /hɪˈlɛriəs/ [adjective; more hilarious, most hilarious] extremely funny: *a hilarious movie*

hill * /hɪl/ [noun] a raised area of ground: *Their house is up on that hill.*
   ➪ Compare MOUNTAIN.

hilly /ˈhɪli/ [adjective; hillier, hilliest] a hilly area has a lot of hills: *It's very hilly around where I live.*

him * /hɪm/ [pronoun] used to talk about a particular man, boy, or male animal, as the object of a verb or preposition: *I asked him what he was doing.* | *We couldn't have done it without him.*
   ➪ See also HE.

himself * /hɪmˈsɛlf/ [pronoun]
1 used to say that the person affected by an action is the man or boy doing it: *He tried to keep himself warm.* | *He made himself a sandwich.*
2 used to emphasize a name, title, or the word "he": *Grandpa built the house himself.* | *He himself didn't care who won the game.*
   ☛ Do not use **himself** as a subject. For example, do not say "Himself did it." Say **He did it himself.**
━━ PHRASES ━━
3 **by himself** alone or without any help: *He prefers being by himself.* | *Did he make that model all by himself?*
4 **to himself** not sharing something with anyone else: *He has a bedroom all to himself.*

Hindu[1] /ˈhɪndu/ [noun; plural Hindus] someone who believes in the Indian religion of Hinduism

Hindu[2] [adjective; no comparative] relating to the Indian religion of Hinduism: *We visited a Hindu temple.*

Hinduism /ˈhɪnduˌɪzəm/ [noun] an Indian religion which includes the belief that you are born again after you have died

/i/ **see**	/ɪ/ **big**	/eɪ/ **day**	/ɛ/ **get** /æ/ **hat**
/ɑ/ **father, hot**	/ʌ/ **up**	/ə/ **about**	/ɔ/ **saw**
/oʊ/ **hope**	/ʊ/ **book**	/u/ **too**	/aɪ/ **I** /aʊ/ **how**
/ɔɪ/ **boy**	/ɝ/ **bird**	/ɚ/ **teacher**	/ɪr/ **ear** /ɛr/ **air**
/ɑr/ **far**	/ɔr/ **more**	/ʊr/ **tour**	/aɪr/ **fire**
/aʊɚ/ **hour**	/θ/ **nothing**	/ð/ **mother**	/ʃ/ **she**
/ʒ/ **measure**	/tʃ/ **church**	/dʒ/ **jump**	/ŋ/ **long**

hinge /hɪndʒ/ [*noun*] an object attached to the edge of a door, lid, or **GATE**, that makes it able to swing open and shut: *The cabinet hinges are loose.*

hint[1] /hɪnt/ [*verb;* **hinted, hinting**] to say something in a way that is not direct: *He **hinted that** he had some news.*

hint[2] [*noun*]
  1 something that is said in a way that is not direct: *He kept **dropping hints** (=giving people hints) about what he wanted for his birthday.* | *Eventually she **took the hint** (=did what someone hinted she should do) and left us alone.*
  2 a piece of advice about how to do something: *She **gave** me a few **hints on** applying makeup.*

hip /hɪp/ [*noun*] the side of your **BODY** between your waist and the top of your leg: *She stood with her hands on her hips.*

hippo /ˈhɪpoʊ/ [*noun; plural* **hippos**] a short form of **HIPPOPOTAMUS**

a hippopotamus

hippopotamus /ˌhɪpəˈpɑtəməs/ [*noun; plural* **hippopotamuses**] a large African animal with a very big mouth and gray skin, that spends a lot of its time in water; *synonym* **HIPPO**

hire Ⓣ /haɪr/ [*verb;* **hired, hiring**] to start paying someone to work for you: *The company hired more workers.*

his[1] * /hɪz/ [*determiner*] belonging to or connected with a particular man, boy, or male animal: *He took off his shoes.*
  ☛ Only use **his** before a noun.

his[2] * [*pronoun*] something that belongs to or is connected with a particular man or boy: *She put her hand on his.* | *That car is his.*

Hispanic [*adjective; no comparative*] belonging or relating to Spain or Latin America, or to people who speak Spanish or Portuguese: *They live in a Hispanic neighborhood.*
  ▷ Compare **LATINO**.

hiss[1] /hɪs/ [*verb;* **hisses, hissed, hissing**] to make a noise like a continuous "s" sound: *The snake hissed at him.*

hiss[2] [*noun; plural* **hisses**] a noise like a continuous "s" sound: *There was a hiss of steam from the engine.*

historic /hɪˈstɔrɪk/ [*adjective;* **more historic, most historic**] very important as a part of history: *a historic speech*

historical * /hɪˈstɔrɪkəl/ [*adjective; no comparative*] having happened in the past, or relating to the past: *a historical novel*

history * /ˈhɪstəri/ [*noun*]
  1 events and situations in the past up to the present, or the time in which they happened: *She told me **the history of** the building.* | ***Throughout history**, people have studied the stars.*
  2 the school or college subject which involves learning about the past: *She got an A in history.* | *my history teacher*

hit[1] * /hɪt/ [*verb;* **hits, hit, hit, hitting**]
  1 to touch someone or something with a lot of force, or to do this with an object: *He hit the ball hard.* | *The truck hit a tree.* | *I **got hit on** the head.*
  ▷ See the picture at **PLAY**[1].
  ══ PHRASE ══
  2 hit the roof or **hit the ceiling** INFORMAL to become very angry: *When I came home late, Dad hit the roof.*

hit[2] * [*noun*]
  1 something such as a record or a movie that is successful and popular: *Do you think this movie will be a hit?* | *The band had many **hit records**.*
  2 the act of touching someone or something with a lot of force: *One hit with a hammer broke open the lock.*

hitchhike /ˈhɪtʃˌhaɪk/ [*verb;* **hitchhiked, hitchhiking**] to travel by getting free rides in people's cars: *He hitchhiked all the way from St. Louis to Chicago.*

hitchhiker /ˈhɪtʃˌhaɪkɚ/ [*noun*] someone who travels somewhere by getting free rides in people's cars

hitter /'hɪtɚ/ [*noun*] someone who hits the ball in baseball or hits someone in boxing: *He's the team's best hitter.*

hive /haɪv/ [*noun*] a kind of box where bees are kept, or a structure which the bees make themselves; *synonym* BEEHIVE: *The bees were buzzing around the hive.*

hmm /hmm/ [*interjection*] used to show that someone is thinking about something or is not sure about something: *Hmm, what tie should I wear?*

hoard¹ /hɔrd/ [*verb*; **hoarded, hoarding**] to gather and hide a large amount of something to be used later: *When the banks failed, people started hoarding cash.*

hoard² [*noun*] a large amount of something that is hidden to be used later: *a squirrel's hoard of nuts*

hoarse /hɔrs/ [*adjective*; **hoarser, hoarsest**] if you are hoarse, your voice is rough and quiet, for example because you are sick or you have been talking a lot: *She was hoarse from cheering at the game.*

hobby ⊤ /'hɑbi/ [*noun*; *plural* **hobbies**] an activity that you do in your free time because you enjoy it: *My main hobby is playing computer games.*

hockey /'hɑki/ [*noun*] a sport or game played on ice in which two teams use sticks to try to hit a puck into the other team's goal: *Can you play hockey?* | *a hockey rink* (=where hockey is played) | *He's on the college ice hockey team.*

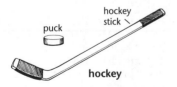

puck   hockey stick

hockey

hoe /hoʊ/ [*noun*; *plural* **hoes**] a TOOL with a long handle used to remove small unwanted plants from the ground

hog /hɔg/ [*noun*] a large pig

hoist /hɔɪst/ [*verb*; **hoisted, hoisting**] to lift or pull something or someone up, especially by using ropes or equipment: *They hoisted the building material up to the roof.*

hold¹ * /hoʊld/ [*verb*; **held, holding**]
1 to have something in your hand or arms: *He held a letter.* | *I held the baby.*
⇨ *See the synonym note at* CARRY.
2 to keep something in a particular position or place: *I held the door open for him.* | *Hold up your hand if you know the answer.*
3 to contain something or to be able to contain something: *The hall can hold 500 people.*
4 to have a meeting, party, etc.: *The concert will be held in the opera house.*
5 to have a document or a job: *You must hold a valid passport.* | *He holds a high position in the government.*
6 to wait during a phone call until the person you want can speak to you: *Please hold.* | *Hold the line, please.*

━ PHRASES ━

7 hold hands if people hold hands, one person's right hand holds another person's left hand: *They sat holding hands and watched the sunset.*
8 hold your breath to not breathe for a short time: *She held her breath and dove into the water.*

━ PHRASAL VERBS ━

hold back [*phrasal verb*]
9 to stop someone or something from going forward or making progress: **hold someone/something back** ▸ *The police held the crowd back.*

hold on [*phrasal verb*]
10 SPOKEN used to tell someone to wait: *Hold on, I'm not finished.* | *Hold on and I'll see if she can speak with you.*
11 to hold something and not stop holding it; *synonym* GRIP: *He held on to the side of the boat.*

hold up [*phrasal verb*]
12 to delay someone or something: **hold up someone/something** ▸ *Come on. You're holding up dinner.* | **hold someone/something up** ▸ *What's holding things up?*

/i/ **see** /ɪ/ **big** /eɪ/ **day** /ɛ/ **get** /æ/ **hat**
/ɑ/ **father, hot** /ʌ/ **up** /ə/ **about** /ɔ/ **saw**
/oʊ/ **hope** /ʊ/ **book** /u/ **too** /aɪ/ **I** /aʊ/ **how**
/ɔɪ/ **boy** /ɝ/ **bird** /ɚ/ **teacher** /ɪr/ **ear** /ɛr/ **air**
/ɑr/ **far** /ɔr/ **more** /ʊr/ **tour** /aɪr/ **fire**
/aʊɚ/ **hour** /θ/ **nothing** /ð/ **mother** /ʃ/ **she**
/ʒ/ **measure** /tʃ/ **church** /dʒ/ **jump** /ŋ/ **long**

hold² * [*noun*]
1 an action of holding something: *He loosened his **hold on** my arm.*
2 the part of a ship or plane in which goods are carried
▬ PHRASES ▬
3 take/grab/get/catch hold of to start holding something in your hand: *He took hold of the door handle.*
4 get hold of to manage to find something or speak to someone: *I've been trying to get hold of you all day.*
5 on hold waiting on the telephone to speak to someone: *They **kept** me **on hold** for twenty minutes!*

holder /'hoʊldɚ/ [*noun*]
1 someone who owns or has something: *This is the line for ticket holders.*
2 an object that is used to hold something: *a candle holder*
⇨ *See the picture at* CANDLE.

holdup /'hoʊld,ʌp/ [*noun*] INFORMAL when something does not start as early as it should; *synonym* DELAY: *Sorry about the holdup, folks!*

hole * /hoʊl/ [*noun*]
1 a space in something solid, especially the ground: *They're are **digging a hole** for a new well.*
2 an open space in something: *There's a **hole in** my sock.*
☛ Do not say "a hole on something." Say **a hole in something**.

holiday * /'halɪ,deɪ/ [*noun*] a special day on which people do not have to go to work: *Veteran's Day is a **national holiday** (=that the whole country celebrates).*

hollow * /'haloʊ/ [*adjective; no comparative*] having an empty space inside: *The statue is hollow.*

holly /'hali/ [*noun*] a tree that has red berries and shiny green leaves with sharp points, used as a decoration in the winter: *a holly wreath*

holy * 🔲 /'hoʊli/ [*adjective;* **holier, holiest**]
1 connected with God or gods and therefore respected by people; *synonym* SACRED: *a holy book*
2 very religious and good, and respected for this: *a holy woman*

home¹ * /hoʊm/ [*noun*]
1 the building or place in which you live: *I've never been to his home.* I *I left my calculator at home.*
2 a place where a group of people who need special care live: *a **nursing home*** (=for old people)
▬ PHRASES ▬
3 leave home to stop living in your family's home: *He left home when he was eighteen.*
4 feel at home to feel comfortable and welcome in a place: *You always make me feel at home.*

home² * [*adverb*] to or in the place where you live: *When I **got home**, my parents were out.* I *They'd rather **stay home** and watch TV.*
☛ Do not say "go to home" or "get to home." Say **go home** or **get home**.

home³ [*adjective; no comparative*]
1 relating to the place where you live: *What's your **home address**?*
2 used to talk about a game played in a team's own town or area: *I go to all their **home games**.* I *the **home team***
☛ Only use **home** before a noun.

homecoming /'hoʊm,kʌmɪŋ/ [*noun*] a time each year when former students visit the college or high school they graduated from

homeless /'hoʊmlɪs/ [*noun*]
the homeless people who do not have a place to live: *a shelter for the homeless*
☛ Only use **the homeless** with a plural verb.

homemade /'hoʊm'meɪd/ [*adjective; no comparative*] made by someone in his or her home: *homemade cookies*

home page /'hoʊm ,peɪdʒ/ [*noun*] a document on the Internet that is the main page on a website

homeroom /'hoʊm,rum/ [*noun*] a class, usually at the beginning of the school day, where the teacher counts the students and gives school information: *Where's your homeroom?* I *We have to be **in homeroom** by 7:45.*

home run /'hoʊm 'rʌn/ [*noun*] when a baseball player hits the ball and runs around all the bases, scoring a run

homesick /'hoʊm,sɪk/ [adjective; **more homesick, most homesick**] sad because you are away from home: *When she went away to college she was very homesick.*

hometown /'hoʊm'taʊn/ [noun] the town or city where you grew up: *My parents still live in my hometown.*

homework /'hoʊm,wɜ·k/ [noun] work for school, such as studying, writing, etc., that students do at home: *I'd better go do my homework now.*
↪ Compare CLASSWORK.

USAGE   homework, housework

Do not confuse **homework** and **housework**. **Homework** is the studying you do at home after school. **Housework** is work such as cleaning, washing clothes, etc., that you do in your home.

---

honest * /'ɑnɪst/ [adjective; **more honest, most honest**]
1 someone who is honest does not lie or steal; *opposite* DISHONEST: *He's a good, honest worker.*
2 true, or telling someone the truth, even though it might be upsetting; *synonym* FRANK: *She is always honest with me.* I *I want an honest answer.*

honestly * /'ɑnɪstli/ [adverb]
1 in an honest way: *He spoke honestly about his feelings.*
2 used to emphasize that you are telling the truth: *I honestly don't know.*

honesty /'ɑnɪsti/ [noun] the quality of being honest: *Honesty is important in a relationship.*

honey /'hʌni/ [noun]
1 a sweet substance made by bees, that you can eat: *a jar of honey*
2 SPOKEN used instead of a name for someone you love or like very much: *Thanks, honey.*

honeymoon /'hʌni,mun/ [noun] a vacation taken by a man and a woman who have just been married: *They went to Hawaii on their honeymoon.*

honk /hank/ [verb; honked, honking] to make a loud sound with a horn or like a horn: *Drivers were honking their horns and shouting.* I *a goose honking*

honor[1] * /'ɑnɚ/ [noun]
1 great respect that people have for a person, country, or organization: *They fought for the honor of England.* I *the honor society* (=a club for students who have good grades)
2 something that makes you feel pleased and proud: *It would be an honor to work with you.*

=== PHRASES ===
3 in honor of in order to show respect for someone or something: *They gave a party in honor of the professor.*
4 his/her/your Honor used when you are talking to or mentioning a judge or mayor: *Yes, your Honor.*

honor[2] [verb; honored, honoring] to do something special that makes someone feel pleased and proud: *They honored him with a special dinner.*

hood /hʊd/ [noun]
1 part of a coat at the back of the neck, which can be pulled over your head: *It was raining, so she put her hood up.*
2 the part of a CAR that covers the engine, that can be lifted up

a hood

hoof /hʊf/ [noun; plural **hoofs** or **hooves**] the hard base of the foot of some animals, such as a HORSE or BULL

hook * /hʊk/ [noun]
1 a thin curved piece of metal or plastic, used for hanging things on
↪ See the picture at RACK.
2 a thin curved piece of metal with a sharp point, used for catching fish

=== PHRASE ===
3 off the hook if a telephone is off the hook, the part you hold is not in its usual place, so it cannot receive calls: *He left his phone off the hook.*

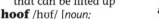

/i/ **see** /ɪ/ **big** /eɪ/ **day** /ɛ/ **get** /æ/ **hat**
/ɑ/ **father, hot** /ʌ/ **up** /ə/ **about** /ɔ/ **saw**
/oʊ/ **hope** /ʊ/ **book** /u/ **too** /aɪ/ **I** /aʊ/ **how**
/ɔɪ/ **boy** /ɝ/ **bird** /ɚ/ **teacher** /ɪr/ **ear** /ɛr/ **air**
/ɑr/ **far** /ɔr/ **more** /ʊr/ **tour** /aɪr/ **fire**
/aʊɚ/ **hour** /θ/ **nothing** /ð/ **mother** /ʃ/ **she**
/ʒ/ **measure** /tʃ/ **church** /dʒ/ **jump** /ŋ/ **long**

hooked /hʊkt/ [*adjective; no comparative*] *INFORMAL* enjoying something so much that you cannot stop doing it: *He's* ***hooked on*** *computer games.*
☛ Do not use **hooked** before a noun.

hoop /hup/ [*noun*] a large ring of metal or wood: *a basketball hoop*

hooray /hʊ'reɪ/ [*interjection*] shouted to show happiness or approval: *Hooray—we won!*

hoot[1] /hut/ [*noun*] a loud short sound: *a* ***hoot of laughter*** | *the hoot of a car horn*

hoot[2] [*verb;* **hooted, hooting**] to make a loud short sound: *the hooting of an owl*

hooves /hʊvz/ [*noun*] a plural of HOOF

hop /hap/ [*verb;* **hops, hopped, hopping**]
1 to make short jumps on one foot or two feet: *He hopped over to a bench.* | *She* ***hopped up and down.***
➪ *See the picture at* MOVEMENT.
2 if a bird or animal hops somewhere, it jumps there: *The bird hopped around, looking for crumbs.*
3 *INFORMAL* to get into a vehicle: *Hop in. I'll give you a ride.* | *He hopped a train to New York.*

hope[1] * /hoʊp/ [*verb;* **hoped, hoping**] to want something to happen or to be true: *I'm* ***hoping for*** *good grades this semester.* | *"Will he be OK?"* ***"I hope so."*** | *"Do your parents know how late you got back?"* ***"I hope not!"*** | **hope to do something** ▸ *I hope to hear from them soon.*
☛ Do not say "I don't hope." For example, do not say "I don't hope I lose." Say **I hope I don't lose**.

hope[2] * [*noun*]
1 the belief that something you want is possible: *We never* ***lost hope*** (=stopped hoping). | *He* ***had hopes of*** *becoming a writer.*
2 a possibility of doing something: *He* ***has no hope of*** *winning.*
☛ Use **of**, not "to," with the noun **hope**. For example, do not say "I have no hope to win." Say **I have no hope of winning**.
— PHRASE —
3 **have high hopes** to believe that someone or something may be very successful: *The company* ***has high hopes for*** *its latest product.*

hopeful * /'hoʊpfəl/ [*adjective;* **more hopeful, most hopeful**] believing that something you want to happen is likely: *She seemed* ***hopeful that*** *she would get better.*

hopefully /'hoʊpfəli/ [*adverb*]
1 used to say that you hope something will happen: *Hopefully, we can fix it.*
2 in a hopeful way: *The dog was looking hopefully at the bone.*

hopeless /'hoʊplɪs/ [*adjective; no comparative*]
1 very bad and unable to be improved: *The situation seemed hopeless.*
2 *INFORMAL* very bad at doing something: *I was* ***hopeless at*** *math.*
3 not successful, or not likely to be successful: *We tried to make him change his mind, but* ***it was hopeless.***

hopelessly /'hoʊplɪsli/ [*adverb*] used to say that a situation is very bad: *I got hopelessly lost.*

horizon /hə'raɪzən/ [*noun*]
the horizon the line in the distance where the sky and the earth or ocean seem to meet: *There were dark clouds* ***on the horizon.***

horizontal /ˌhɔrə'zantəl/ [*adjective; no comparative*] flat and level, with no end or side higher than the other: *The picture was not quite horizontal.*
➪ *Compare* VERTICAL.

hormone /'hɔrmoʊn/ [*noun*] a chemical in the body that makes it grow and work correctly

horn * /hɔrn/ [*noun*]
1 one of the two hard sharp parts that grow out of the head of some animals, such as a BULL or RHINOCEROS
2 an object in a vehicle that the driver uses to make a noise as a warning: *The bus driver* ***honked his horn.***
3 a kind of MUSICAL INSTRUMENT in the form of a metal tube that you blow into: *Trumpets and trombones are horns.*

horrible /'hɔrəbəl/ [*adjective;* **more horrible, most horrible**] very bad or unpleasant; synonym TERRIBLE: *What's that horrible smell?*

horrified /'hɔrəˌfaɪd/ [*adjective; no comparative*] extremely shocked: *I was horrified when I saw the damage.*

horror[1] /'hɔrɚ/ [noun] a feeling of great shock or fear: *We watched **in horror** as the fire spread.*

horror[2] [adjective; no comparative] a horror story or horror movie is very frightening: *They stayed up watching a **horror movie.***

☞ Only use **horror** before a noun.

a horse

horse * /hɔrs/ [noun]
1 a large animal with four legs which people ride or use to pull vehicles

━ PHRASE ━

2 **hold your horses** used to tell someone to slow down or wait: *Hold your horses—I'm not ready yet.*

horseback /'hɔrs,bæk/ [noun]

━ PHRASE ━

on horseback riding a horse: *A group of men on horseback rode toward us.*

horseback riding /'hɔrs,bæk ,raɪdɪŋ/ [noun] the activity of riding a horse: *She loves to **go horseback riding.***

horseshoe /'hɔrs,ʃu/ [noun; plural **horseshoes**] a piece of metal in the shape of a "U," attached to the bottom of a horse's foot

a horseshoe

hose /hoʊz/ [noun] a long plastic tube that can be attached to a pipe so that water can flow through it to another place: *a garden hose*
⇨ See the picture at LEAKY.

hospital * /'hɑspɪtəl/ [noun] a building where sick and injured people are treated: *I was **in the hospital** for a week.*

hospitality /,hɑspɪ'tælɪti/ [noun] friendly treatment of guests or visitors: *Thanks again for your hospitality.*

host /hoʊst/ [noun] the person who invites people to his or her home, or who organizes a social event

hostage /'hɑstɪdʒ/ [noun] someone who is kept as a prisoner by a person or group in order to force other people to do something: *The plane's passengers have been **taken hostage** (=made to stay in a place as prisoners).*

hostess /'hoʊstɪs/ [noun; plural **hostesses**] a woman who invites people to her home, or who organizes a social event

hostile Ⓣ /'hɑstəl/ [adjective; **more hostile, most hostile**] against someone or something, in a very angry way: *a hostile reaction* | *They were **hostile to** us.*

hot * /hɑt/ [adjective; **hotter, hottest**]
1 having a high temperature; <u>opposite</u> COLD: *nice hot soup* | *I'm hot—may I open a window?* | *The weather's hotter today than it was yesterday.*
2 making your mouth feel very hot; <u>opposite</u> MILD: *a hot sauce made with chili peppers*

hot chocolate /'hɑt 'tʃɔkəlɪt/ [noun] a hot drink made from cocoa, sugar, and milk, or a cup of this: *I'll have a cup of hot chocolate, please.* | *I'd like three hot chocolates to go.*

hot dog /'hɑt ,dɔg/ [noun] a long round piece of meat eaten in a thick piece of bread

a hot dog

hotel * /hoʊ'tɛl/ [noun] a building where people pay to stay for a short time, for example on vacation

hour * /'aʊɚ/ [noun]
1 a period of 60 minutes: *The flight takes five hours.* | *I'll be back **in an***

/i/ see	/ɪ/ big	/eɪ/ day	/ɛ/ get	/æ/ hat
/ɑ/ father, hot	/ʌ/ up	/ə/ about	/ɔ/ saw	
/oʊ/ hope	/ʊ/ book	/u/ too	/aɪ/ I	/aʊ/ how
/ɔɪ/ boy	/ɝ/ bird	/ɚ/ teacher	/ɪr/ ear	/ɛr/ air
/ɑr/ far	/ɔr/ more	/ʊr/ tour	/aɪr/ fire	
/aʊɚ/ hour	/θ/ nothing	/ð/ mother	/ʃ/ she	
/ʒ/ measure	/tʃ/ church	/dʒ/ jump	/ŋ/ long	

hour. | *They left **an hour ago*** (=one hour before now). | *The city is **an hour's** drive from here.*
↪ *See also* **half an hour** *at* HALF[3].
2 a particular time: *Why are you still awake **at this hour**? | Call me, **any hour** of the day or night.*
3 hours [*plural*]
a the period of time during which a place is open or work is done: ***Office hours** are nine to five* (=the office is open then). | *I **work long hours*** (=for longer than the usual working time).
b INFORMAL a long time | *We stood in line **for hours**. | This will **take hours** to fix.*

— PHRASES

4 on the hour at the start of each hour, at one o'clock, two o'clock, etc.: *Trains to Boston leave on the hour.*
5 all hours during all of the 24 hours in a day, especially the night hours: *a store that's open all hours*

hourly /'aʊɚli/ [*adverb, adjective; no comparative*] happening once every hour: *Planes fly to New York hourly. | There are hourly flights to New York.*

house * ⊤ /haʊs/ [*noun; plural* **houses** /'haʊzɪz/]
1 a building in which people live, especially just one family: *They lived in a big old house on Fir Street.*
2 all the people who are in a house: *Quiet! The **whole house** can hear you.*

household[1] ⊤ /'haʊs,hoʊld/ [*adjective; no comparative*] used in or relating to the home: *household cleaning products | She helps with all the **household** chores.*
☛ Only use **household** before a noun.

household[2] ⊤ [*noun*] all the people living in a house: *How many are there in your household?*

housing /'haʊzɪŋ/ [*noun*] buildings for people to live in: *The college provides housing for all freshmen.*

housekeeper /'haʊs,kipɚ/ [*noun*] someone who does the cooking and cleaning in someone else's house as a job

House of Representatives /'haʊs əv rɛprɪ'zɛntətɪvz/ [*noun*] one of the two groups in the U.S. Congress that make laws
↪ *Compare* SENATE (definition 1).

housewife /'haʊs,waɪf/ [*noun; plural* **housewives** /'haʊs,waɪvz/] a woman who takes care of her home and family and does not have a paid job

housework ⊤ /'haʊs,wɜrk/ [*noun*] work done in the home, such as cleaning, washing clothes, etc.: *We **do the housework** on Saturdays.*
↪ *See the usage note at* HOMEWORK.

hover /'hʌvɚ/ [*verb;* **hovered, hovering**] to stay in one place in the air while flying: *The helicopter **hovered over** the ground.*

how[1] * /haʊ/ [*adverb*]
1 used to ask about something or say the way to do something: *How do you spell your name? | I asked her how she spelled her name. | He showed me **how to** use the computer.*
2 used to ask about an amount, quantity, or degree: ***How many** students are there in your class? | How old are you? | How much does this cost? | How far is it to the station? | He asked me how long I had been waiting.*
3 used to emphasize an amount, quantity, or degree: *I was amazed at how big the school was. | How awful! You must have been really upset!*
☛ Do not use **how** to emphasize a noun phrase. For example, do not say "How mean thing to do!" Say **What a mean thing to do!**
4 used to ask about someone's health or situation: *"Hello! How are you?" "I'm fine!" | How are you doing?*
5 used to ask what something is like: *How was your trip? | How is the weather in Dallas? | How did you like New York?*

— PHRASES

6 how do you do? SPOKEN, FORMAL used as a polite way of greeting someone you have not met before: *"This is Mr. Gardener." "How do you do?"*
7 how about . . . ? SPOKEN used to make a suggestion: *How about a pizza?*

how[2] [*conjunction*] used before you mention a fact or event: *Remember how he fell asleep during the movie? | I know how you like cherries.*

however * /haʊ'ɛvɚ/ [*adverb*]
1 used when you are saying something that is different from what you have

a house with a yard

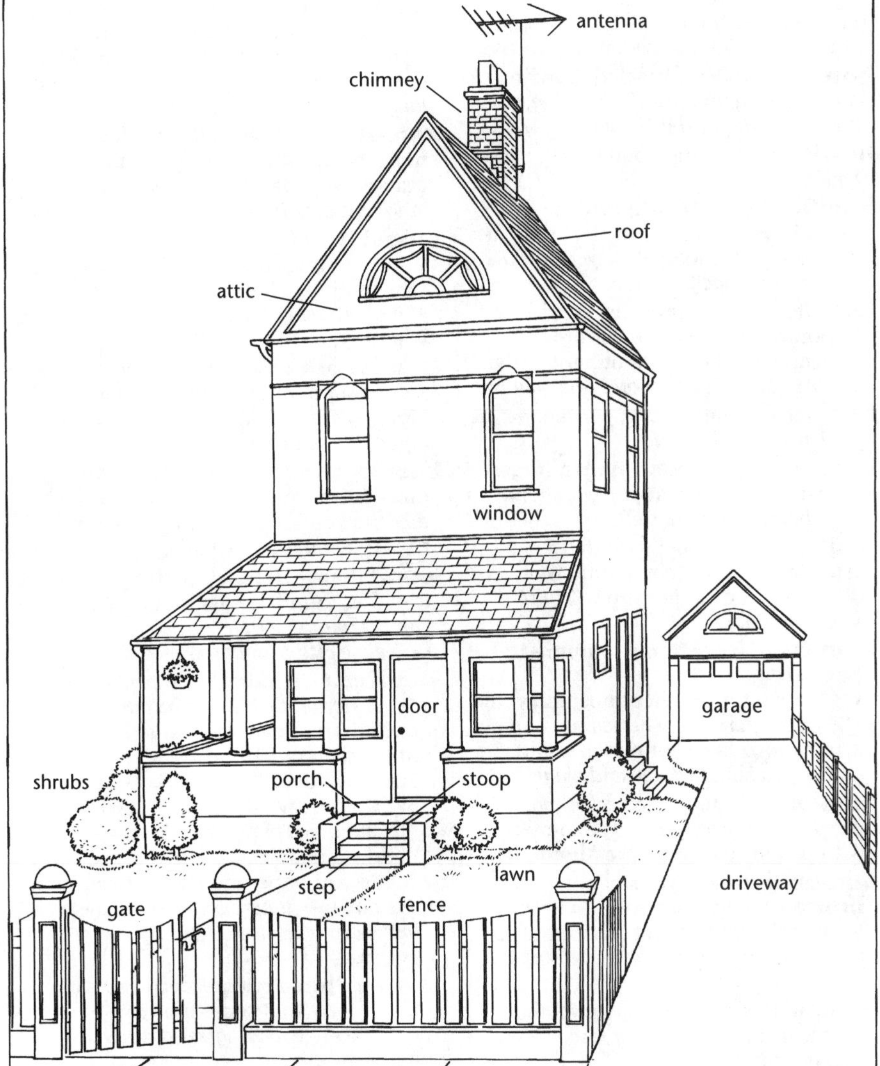

antenna

chimney

roof

attic

window

garage

door

shrubs

porch

stoop

gate

step

fence

lawn

driveway

sidewalk

curb

just said: *That's a problem. However, I think I can help.* | *Most of the kids were okay; Matt, however, was injured.*
2 used to say that the amount, quantity, or degree of something does not matter: *However old you are, you can always learn something new.*

howl¹ /haʊl/ [*verb*; **howled, howling**] to make a long, loud noise: *The dog was howling in the yard.* | *the howling wind*

howl² [*noun*] a long, loud noise: *a baby's howls*

huddle /ˈhʌdəl/ [*verb*; **huddled, huddling**] to stand or sit close together in a group: *The football players **huddled around** the coach.*

hug¹ /hʌg/ [*verb*; **hugs, hugged, hugging**] to put your arms around someone and hold him or her tightly: *She hugged her mother and said goodbye.*

hug² [*noun*] when you hug someone: *He gave his son **a big hug**.*

huge /hyudʒ/ [*adjective*; **huger, hugest**] extremely large or great; *opposite* TINY: *a huge building* | *a huge effort*

huh /hʌ/ [*interjection*] used to ask someone to repeat something that you did not hear or understand: *"Huh?" "I said I'm hungry."*

hum /hʌm/ [*verb*; **hums, hummed, humming**]
1 to sing a tune without opening your lips: *She hummed to herself as she drove.*
2 to make a low continuous sound: *The machines hummed day and night.*

human * /ˈhyumən/ [*adjective*; *no comparative*] belonging to or connected with people: *a book on **the human body***

human being /ˈhyumən ˈbiɪŋ/ or **human** [*noun*; *plural* **human beings** or **humans**] a person, not an animal or a machine: *Human beings are related to the apes.*

humanity /hyuˈmænɪti/ [*noun*] the people in the world: *Their research will help all of humanity.*

humble /ˈhʌmbəl/ [*adjective*; **humbler, humblest**]
1 not rich, important, or impressive: *His father was a humble farm worker.*
2 not too proud: *She made a humble speech accepting the prize.*

humid /ˈhyumɪd/ [*adjective*; **more humid, most humid**] air that is humid is wet and warm: *This plant needs hot, humid conditions.*

humiliated /hyuˈmɪli,eɪtɪd/ [*adjective*; **more humiliated, most humiliated**] feeling embarrassed and that you have done something stupid or bad: *Everyone laughed, and I felt humiliated.*

humiliating /hyuˈmɪli,eɪtɪŋ/ [*adjective*; **more humiliating, most humiliating**] making you feel stupid or weak and embarrassed: *It was a humiliating defeat.*

humor * T /ˈhyumɚ/ [*noun*]
1 funny things that are said or done, or the quality of being funny: *There's a lot of humor in the book.*
═ PHRASE ═
2 **sense of humor** the ability to know when something is funny and to laugh at it: *Our history teacher **has a great sense of humor**.*

humorous * /ˈhyumərəs/ [*adjective*; **more humorous, most humorous**] making you laugh or smile; *synonym* FUNNY: *a humorous remark*

hump /hʌmp/ [*noun*] a round part that is higher than the area around it: *a camel's hump*
⇨ *See the picture at* CAMEL.

hundred * /ˈhʌndrɪd/ [*number, noun*]
1 100: *Her brother lives **a hundred** miles away.* | *There were **five hundred** people at the concert.* | ***Hundreds of** (=over 200, or a lot of) tickets have been sold.*
☛ Do not say "six hundreds people" or "six hundreds of people." Say **six hundred people**.
2 a piece of paper money worth $100: *She had two hundreds and a twenty in her wallet when it was stolen.*
═ PHRASE ═
3 **a/one hundred percent** SPOKEN used to say that something is completely true: *I agree with you a hundred percent.*

hundredth * /ˈhʌndrɪdθ/ [*adjective*, *adverb*; *no comparative*] coming after 99 other people, things, or events; sometimes written as "100th": *It's her hundredth birthday today.*
⇨ *See the usage note at* SECOND².

hung * /hʌŋ/ [verb] the past tense and past participle of HANG[1]: *She hung the clothes on the line to dry.*
☛ Do not use "hanged" about things. Use **hung**.

hunger * /'hʌŋgɚ/ [noun] the feeling that you want or need to eat: *People in the region are dying of hunger* (=they do not have enough to eat).
☛ Do not say "I have hunger." Say **I'm hungry**.

hungry * /'hʌŋgri/ [adjective; **hungrier, hungriest**] wanting or needing to eat something; *opposite* FULL: *By lunchtime, I was pretty hungry.*

hunt[1] * /hʌnt/ [verb; **hunted, hunting**]
1 to try to find and kill wild animals: *They were out hunting rabbits.*
2 to try to find something or someone by looking carefully in a place; *synonym* SEARCH: *She hunted in her purse for a pen.*

hunt[2] [noun]
1 when people try to find and kill wild animals: *They took us on a deer hunt.*
2 when a person or a group of people try to find someone or something; *synonym* SEARCH: *The hunt for the missing child continues.*

hunter /'hʌntɚ/ [noun] someone who tries to find and kill wild animals

hurl /hɝl/ [verb; **hurled, hurling**] to throw something with a lot of force: *He hurled the book across the room.*

hurricane /'hɝɪˌkeɪn/ [noun] a violent storm with very strong spinning winds and rain that comes in from the Atlantic Ocean
⇨ *Compare* CYCLONE, TORNADO, TYPHOON.

hurriedly /'hɝɪdli/ [adverb] something that is done hurriedly is done quickly, especially because there is not enough time: *I got dressed hurriedly.*

hurry[1] * /'hɝi/ [verb; **hurries, hurried, hurrying**]
1 to go somewhere or do something quickly, or to make someone do this; *synonym* RUSH: *I hurried back to my seat.* | *She hurried me into the store.*

━━ PHRASAL VERB ━━
hurry up [phrasal verb]
2 to go somewhere or do something

more quickly, or to make someone do this: *Hurry up—we're going to be late.* | **hurry someone up** ▸ *Can you try to hurry them up?*

hurry[2] * [noun]
━━ PHRASES ━━
1 **in a hurry** quickly, or needing to do something quickly: *He left in a hurry.* | *He seemed in a hurry to leave.*
2 **in no hurry** not needing to do anything quickly: *I'm in no hurry.*

hurt[1] * /hɝt/ [verb; **hurts, hurt, hurt, hurting**]
1 if a part of your body hurts, you feel pain there: *My stomach hurts.*
2 to make someone feel pain: *Let go— you're hurting me!*
3 to damage someone's body, or your own body; *synonym* INJURE: *She fell and hurt her arm.* | *Be careful not to hurt yourself.*
4 to make someone unhappy and upset: *I didn't want to hurt their feelings.*

hurt[2] [adjective; **more hurt, most hurt**]
1 physically injured: *Luckily, she wasn't seriously hurt.*
2 unhappy and upset because of something that someone has done: *I was hurt by their attitude.*

USAGE   hurt
  When you use the meaning of **hurt** that means "injured," you can say that someone is **slightly hurt, badly hurt**, or **seriously hurt**.
  Do not use these adverbs with the meaning of **hurt** that means "upset by someone's behavior." Say **a little hurt, very hurt**, or **deeply hurt** instead.

husband * /'hʌzbənd/ [noun] the man that a woman is married to: *I'd like you to meet my husband.*
⇨ *Compare* WIFE. ⇨ *See the picture at* FAMILY TREE.

/i/ **see**	/ɪ/ **big**	/eɪ/ **day**	/ɛ/ **get**	/æ/ **hat**	
/ɑ/ **father, hot**	/ʌ/ **up**	/ə/ **about**	/ɔ/ **saw**		
/oʊ/ **hope**	/ʊ/ **book**	/u/ **too**	/aɪ/ **I**	/aʊ/ **how**	
/ɔɪ/ **boy**	/ɝ/ **bird**	/ɚ/ **teacher**	/ɪr/ **ear**	/ɛr/ **air**	
/ɑr/ **far**	/ɔr/ **more**	/ʊr/ **tour**	/aɪr/ **fire**		
/aʊɚ/ **hour**	/θ/ **nothing**	/ð/ **mother**	/ʃ/ **she**		
/ʒ/ **measure**	/tʃ/ **church**	/dʒ/ **jump**	/ŋ/ **long**		

hush /hʌʃ/ [*interjection*] used to tell someone, especially a child, to be quiet: *Hush—the show is starting.*

hut /hʌt/ [*noun*] a small, simple building, usually with only one room: *a hut in the woods*

hydrogen /'haɪdrədʒən/ [*noun*] a very light gas

hyena /haɪ'inə/ [*noun; plural* **hyenas**] a wild animal that looks like a dog and makes a laughing noise: *a pack* (=group) *of hyenas*

hymn /hɪm/ [*noun*] a song of praise, usually to God

hyphen /'haɪfən/ [*noun*] a mark used in writing. It looks like this: -
➪ *See* Punctuation *in the Smart Study section.*

hyphenated /'haɪfə,neɪtɪd/ [*adjective; no comparative*] a hyphenated word always has a hyphen between its two parts: *Is it hyphenated or is it written as two words?*

hysterical /hɪ'stɛrɪkəl/ [*adjective;* **more hysterical, most hysterical**] very excited or upset, and behaving in an uncontrolled way: *She was hysterical and couldn't tell us what had happened.*

I

I * or **i** /aɪ/ [*noun; plural* **Is** or **I's, i's**] the ninth letter of the English alphabet
➪ *See the usage note at* ALPHABET.

I * /aɪ/ [*pronoun*] used to talk about yourself, as the subject of a verb: *I saw her yesterday.* | *I am sixteen.*
➪ *See also* ME.

ice * /aɪs/ [*noun*]
1 frozen water: *The pond was covered with ice.* | *Do you want ice in your soda?*
— **PHRASE** —
2 break the ice to make people who have not met before feel comfortable with each other: *We played a game to break the ice.*

iceberg /'aɪsbɚg/ [*noun*] a very large block of ice floating in the ocean

ice cream /aɪs ˌkrim/ [*noun*] a sweet frozen food made with cream or milk: *There's vanilla ice cream for dessert.*

ice-cream cone /'aɪs ˌkrim ˌkoʊn/ [*noun*] a thin cookie shaped like a cone and filled with ice cream

an ice-cream cone

ice cube /'aɪs ˌkyub/ [*noun*] a small square piece of ice that you put in a cold drink

iced /aɪst/ [*adjective; no comparative*] an iced drink is very cold or has pieces of ice in it: *a glass of iced tea*

ice skate /'aɪs ˌskeɪt/ [*noun*] a boot with a metal blade underneath that you wear to move across ice; *synonym* SKATE: *I need a new pair of ice skates.*

ice-skating /'aɪs ˌskeɪtɪŋ/ [*noun*] the sport or activity of moving across ice wearing ice skates. In the sport, you do special jumps and movements: *As a child, I loved to go ice-skating.* | *an ice-skating rink* (=where people go ice-skating)

icicle /'aɪsɪkəl/ [*noun*] a long pointed piece of ice made by water falling slowly from something and freezing

icing /'aɪsɪŋ/ [*noun*] a mixture of sugar, butter, and liquids that you spread on a cake; *synonym* FROSTING: *vanilla icing*

icon /'aɪkɑn/ [*noun*] a small picture on a computer screen that can be used to make the computer do something: *The scissors icon means "cut."*

icy /'aɪsi/ [*adjective;* **icier, iciest**]
1 covered with ice: *She slipped on the icy sidewalk.*
2 extremely cold; *synonym* FREEZING: *The icy wind made his ears hurt.*

I'd * /aɪd/
1 the short form of "I had": *I'd met them before.*
☞ Do not use "I'd" for **I had** when **had** is the main verb. For example, do not say "I'd the flu." Say **I had the flu.**

2 the short form of "I would": *I'd like some juice, please.*

ID /ˈaɪˈdi/ [*noun; plural* **IDs** *or* **ID's**] identification; a document or card that shows who you are: *Please have your IDs ready.* | *a student ID card*

idea * /aɪˈdiə/ [*noun; plural* **ideas**]
 1 a thought about what should happen or how something should be done: *I* **have an idea**—*let's ask Dad.* | *That's a* **good idea.**
 2 an opinion or belief: *He has some strange* **ideas about** *health.*
 3 knowledge about a subject or about how to do something: *"Where's Mom?"* *"I* **have no idea**" (=I do not know). | *I* **have some idea** *what she means, but I'm not sure.*
 ☛ Do not say "I have no idea of what she means." Say **I have no idea what she means.**

ideal Ⓣ /aɪˈdiəl/ [*adjective; no comparative*] exactly what is needed or wanted; <u>synonym</u> PERFECT: *Florida is an ideal place for a vacation.*

identical /aɪˈdɛntɪkəl/ [*adjective; no comparative*] if two or more things are identical, they look or seem exactly the same: *They wore identical dresses.* | *Eric and Brian are* **identical twins.**

identification /aɪˌdɛntəfɪˈkeɪʃən/ [*noun*] a document or card that shows who you are; <u>synonym</u> ID: *The police officer asked if we had any identification.*

identify /aɪˈdɛntəˌfaɪ/ [*verb*; **identifies, identified, identifying**] to recognize or say who someone is or what something is: *How many kinds of flowers can you identify?*

identity Ⓣ /aɪˈdɛntɪti/ [*noun; plural* **identities**] the identity of a person is who he or she is: *The identity of the painter is not known.*

idiom /ˈɪdiəm/ [*noun*] two or more words that are used together with a special meaning: *"Hit the roof" is an idiom meaning "to get very angry."*

idiomatic /ˌɪdiəˈmætɪk/ [*adjective;* **more idiomatic, most idiomatic**] when language is idiomatic, it sounds natural and correct to people who have spoken

the language from birth: *"Get upset" is more idiomatic than "become upset."*

idiot /ˈɪdiət/ [*noun*] someone who does stupid things: *He's such an idiot—he bought the wrong tickets!*

i.e. /ˌaɪˈi/ an abbreviation meaning "that is," used before an explanation of words you have used: *I drink my coffee black, i.e., without milk.*

if * /ɪf/ [*conjunction*]
 1 used to mention something that happens or that might happen: *If I go to bed late, I'm tired the next day.* | *I'll fix your bicycle if you want.* | *Do you* **mind if** *I sit here* (=may I sit here)?
 2 used to mention something that did not happen or is not true: *If I had caught the bus, I would have been here on time.* | *If I were taller, I could see the stage better.*
 ☛ Use **were**, not "was," with singular subjects in this meaning. For example, do not say "if he was." Say **if he were.**
 3 used to talk about something you are not sure about: *I asked if I was in the right room.* | *I didn't know if he liked me.*
 ⇨ Compare WHETHER.

═ PHRASES ═
 4 as if used to say how someone or something appears or seems: *He acted as if he hadn't heard what I said.*
 ⇨ See also **as though** at THOUGH[1].
 5 even if used to say that something that may happen will not affect a situation: *We'll have the party even if it rains.*
 6 if I were you used to make a suggestion: *If I were you, I'd leave now.*
 7 if only used to mention something that you wish had happened: *If only I'd asked her for her phone number.*

ignorance /ˈɪgnərəns/ [*noun*] when someone does not know about something; <u>opposite</u> KNOWLEDGE: *I was amazed at his* **ignorance** *of literature.*

/i/ **see** /ɪ/ **big** /eɪ/ **day** /ɛ/ **get** /æ/ **hat**
/ɑ/ **father, hot** /ʌ/ **up** /ə/ **about** /ɔ/ **saw**
/oʊ/ **hope** /ʊ/ **book** /u/ **too** /aɪ/ **I** /aʊ/ **how**
/ɔɪ/ **boy** /ɝ/ **bird** /ɚ/ **teacher** /ɪr/ **ear** /ɛr/ **air**
/ɑr/ **far** /ɔr/ **more** /ʊr/ **tour** /aɪr/ **fire**
/aʊə/ **hour** /θ/ **nothing** /ð/ **mother** /ʃ/ **she**
/ʒ/ **measure** /tʃ/ **church** /dʒ/ **jump** /ŋ/ **long**

ignorant /'ɪgnərənt/ [adjective; **more ignorant, most ignorant**] not knowing about something; _opposite_ KNOWLEDGEABLE: _He was **ignorant about** geography and economics._

ignore * ⊤ /ɪg'nɔr/ [verb; **ignored, ignoring**] to not show that you have noticed someone or something: _The phone rang, but she ignored it._ | _Why are you ignoring me?_

ill * /ɪl/ [adjective; **more ill, most ill**] having an illness or disease; _synonym_ SICK; _opposite_ WELL: _He is **seriously ill**._ | _She's even more ill than she was last week._
☛ Do not use **ill** before a noun.

I'll * /aɪl/ the short form of "I will" or "I shall": _I'll see you tomorrow._

illegal * /ɪ'ligəl/ [adjective; no comparative] not allowed by the law; _opposite_ LEGAL: _It's **illegal to** drive a car without a license._ | _illegal drugs_

illegally * /ɪ'ligəli/ [adverb] in a way that is not allowed by the law; _opposite_ LEGALLY: _Her car was illegally parked._

illegible /ɪ'lɛdʒəbəl/ [adjective; **more illegible, most illegible**] illegible writing is not clear enough to read: _Her handwriting is nearly illegible._

illiterate /ɪ'lɪtərɪt/ [adjective; no comparative] unable to read or write: _Too many adults in this country are illiterate._

illness * /'ɪlnɪs/ [noun; plural **illnesses**] when someone is sick from a disease, an infection, or any other physical condition: _He died after a **long illness**._ | _I missed a lot of school because of illness._
⇨ _See the synonym note at_ DISEASE.

illustrate /'ɪlə,streɪt/ [verb; **illustrated, illustrating**]
1 to show something by giving or being an example: _He showed charts to illustrate his point._
⇨ _Compare_ DEMONSTRATE (definition 1).
2 to provide a picture or pictures to go with some writing: _an illustrated children's book._

illustration ⊤ /,ɪlə'streɪʃən/ [noun] a picture in a book, magazine, etc.

I'm * /aɪm/ the short form of "I am": _I'm hungry._ | _Go on, I'm listening._

image * ⊤ /'ɪmɪdʒ/ [noun]
1 people's opinion or idea of someone or something: _The president wants to improve his image._
2 a picture, especially a photograph or a moment in a movie: _My favorite image was a little boy playing in the rain._
3 a picture you see in your mind: _The image of her father's face never left her._

imaginary * /ɪ'mædʒə,nɛri/ [adjective; no comparative] not existing in the real world; _opposite_ REAL: _The story is about an imaginary place where animals talk._

SYNONYMS   imaginary, made-up
   Use **imaginary** to talk about events or people in stories: _an imaginary creature._ Use **made-up** to emphasize that someone is pretending that something is true: _a made-up excuse_

imagination * /ɪ,mædʒə'neɪʃən/ [noun] the ability to think of new ideas or things that are not real: _She **has a vivid imagination** (=is good at imagining things)._ | _We need employees with imagination._

imaginative /ɪ'mædʒənətɪv/ [adjective; **more imaginative, most imaginative**]
1 able to think of new ideas or things that are not real: _an imaginative child_
2 new and different: _imaginative ideas_
⇨ _Compare_ CREATIVE.

imagine * /ɪ'mædʒɪn/ [verb; **imagined, imagining**]
1 to produce a picture or idea of something in your mind: _I can't imagine a nicer place to live._ | _**Imagine what** it would be like to be really rich._ | **imagine doing something** ▸ _He imagined winning the competition._
☛ Do not say "I can't imagine to be rich." Say **I can't imagine being rich.**
2 to think something: _I imagine that she will want to come too._

imam /ɪ'mam/ [noun] a Muslim religious leader, especially one who performs religious ceremonies and duties in a mosque

imitate /'ɪmɪ,teɪt/ [verb; **imitated, imitating**] to do what someone else does in exactly the same way; _synonym_

COPY: *He is good at imitating the way people speak.*

imitation /ˌɪmɪˈteɪʃən/ [*noun*]
1 something that has been made to look like something else: *The painting isn't genuine, but it's a good imitation.*
2 when someone deliberately does exactly what someone else does: *He does a good imitation of our teacher.*

immature /ˌɪməˈtʃʊr/ [*adjective;* **more immature, most immature**]
1 behaving like a child or in a way that is not sensible; <u>opposite</u> MATURE: *You're so immature—act your age!*
2 not yet completely grown; <u>opposite</u> MATURE: *Immature plants should be protected from frost.*

immediate /ɪˈmidiɪt/ [*adjective; no comparative*]
1 happening without any delay after something: *My immediate reaction was anger.*
━ PHRASE ━
2 **immediate family** your close relations, especially your parents, brothers and sisters, and children: *Everyone in my immediate family is coming to my graduation.*

immediately * T /ɪˈmidiɪtli/ [*adverb*] very soon, with no delay: *Get in the house immediately!*
⭢ *See also* at once *at* ONCE[1] (definition 7).

─────────────────────────
USAGE   immediately
If you tell someone to do something **immediately**, it can sound rude: *Come here immediately!* Use **as soon as possible** instead: *I'd like you to come as soon as possible.*
─────────────────────────

immense T /ɪˈmɛns/ [*adjective;* **more immense, most immense**] extremely large or great; <u>synonym</u> HUGE: *The ship was immense.*

immensely /ɪˈmɛnsli/ [*adverb*] to a very great degree: *She was immensely glad to see him.*

immigrant T /ˈɪmɪɡrənt/ [*noun*] someone from a foreign country who comes to live in a country: *Many Polish immigrants settled in Chicago.*
⭢ *Compare* EMIGRANT.

immigrate T /ˈɪmɪˌɡreɪt/ [*verb;* **immigrated, immigrating**] to enter a new country in order to live there permanently: *Thousands of East Europeans immigrated to the U.S.*
⭢ *Compare* EMIGRATE.

immigration /ˌɪmɪˈɡreɪʃən/ [*noun*]
1 when people from foreign countries come to live in a country: *A new law has been passed to control immigration.*
⭢ *Compare* EMIGRATION.
2 **Immigration** the place at an airport, port, or border where people coming into a country must show their official travel documents: *He was stopped at Immigration.*

immoral T /ɪˈmɔrəl/ [*adjective;* **more immoral, most immoral**] immoral behavior is not good or acceptable because it harms other people; <u>synonym</u> WRONG; <u>opposite</u> MORAL: *Lying is immoral.*

immortal /ɪˈmɔrtəl/ [*adjective; no comparative*] living forever; <u>opposite</u> MORTAL: *No one is immortal.*

immunize /ˈɪmyəˌnaɪz/ [*verb;* **immunized, immunizing**] to put a substance in someone's body that makes him or her unable to be harmed by a disease; <u>synonym</u> VACCINATE: *Babies are immunized against childhood diseases.*

impact /ˈɪmpækt/ [*noun*]
1 the effect that something has on something or someone: *What impact will the new law have?* | *His speech made a great impact on me.*
2 when one thing hits another, or the force involved: *The rock hit the ground with a great impact.* | *The cars burst into flames on impact.*

impatient /ɪmˈpeɪʃənt/ [*adjective;* **more impatient, most impatient**] wanting something to happen or be done more quickly: *The play hadn't started, and we were getting impatient.*

─────────────────────────
/i/ **see** /ɪ/ **big** /eɪ/ **day** /ɛ/ **get** /æ/ **hat**
/ɑ/ **father, hot** /ʌ/ **up** /ə/ **about** /ɔ/ **saw**
/oʊ/ **hope** /ʊ/ **book** /u/ **too** /aɪ/ **I** /aʊ/ **how**
/ɔɪ/ **boy** /ɝ/ **bird** /ɚ/ **teacher** /ɪr/ **ear** /ɛr/ **air**
/ɑr/ **far** /ɔr/ **more** /ʊr/ **tour** /aɪr/ **fire**
/aʊɚ/ **hour** /θ/ **nothing** /ð/ **mother** /ʃ/ **she**
/ʒ/ **measure** /tʃ/ **church** /dʒ/ **jump** /ŋ/ **long**

imperative /ɪmˈpɛrətɪv/ or
imperative form /ɪmˈpɛrətɪv ˌfɔrm/
[*noun*] GRAMMAR the form of a verb that
is used to tell someone to do something:
*In the sentence "Be quiet!," "be" is in the
imperative.*

impersonal T /ɪmˈpɜrsənəl/ [*adjective;*
more impersonal, most impersonal]
not friendly or not treating you as
though you are important: *It was a cold,
impersonal letter.* | *Large organizations
can be impersonal.*

imply /ɪmˈplaɪ/ [*verb;* implies, implied,
implying] to suggest something but not
say it directly: *What are you implying?* |
She implied that she had traveled a lot.

impolite /ˌɪmpəˈlaɪt/ [*adjective;* more
impolite, most impolite] behaving in a
rude way; *opposite* POLITE: *It is impolite
to ask people how old they are.*

import[1] /ɪmˈpɔrt/ [*verb;* imported,
importing] to buy and bring in goods
from another country; *opposite* EXPORT:
This fruit was imported from Peru.

import[2] /ˈɪmpɔrt/ [*noun*] something
that is sold that was made or produced
in another country; *opposite* EXPORT:
People are buying cheap imports.
☛ The noun **import** is usually used in
the plural.

importance * /ɪmˈpɔrtəns/ [*noun*]
when something is important: *She
knows the importance of hard work.*

important * /ɪmˈpɔrtənt/ [*adjective;*
more important, most important]
1 having great value or meaning, or
being very useful; *opposite*
UNIMPORTANT: *This is an important
document—do not lose it.* | *It is
important to eat the right food.*
2 having a high rank: *An important
visitor is coming to the school today.*

importer /ɪmˈpɔrtər/ [*noun*] a company
or country that buys things from
foreign countries; *opposite* EXPORTER: *an
importer of manufactured goods*

impossible * /ɪmˈpɑsəbəl/ [*adjective; no
comparative*] not able to happen or be
done; *opposite* POSSIBLE: *an impossible
task* | *It was impossible to hear what
they were saying.*

impressed /ɪmˈprɛst/ [*adjective;* more
impressed, most impressed] thinking
that someone or something is very
good: *I'm very impressed with your work.*

impression T /ɪmˈprɛʃən/ [*noun*]
1 an opinion about something that you
have because of what you have seen
or heard: *She gave the impression
that she wasn't very interested.* | *I made
a good impression in the interview*
(=gave people a good opinion of me).

━━━ PHRASE ━━━

2 be under the impression that to
believe something, usually something
that is not correct: *I was under the
impression that he was rich.*

impressive * T /ɪmˈprɛsɪv/ [*adjective;*
more impressive, most impressive] if
someone or something is impressive,
people admire him, her, or it a lot: *The
palace is a very impressive building.* |
You've done an impressive job.

imprison /ɪmˈprɪzən/ [*verb;*
imprisoned, imprisoning] to put
someone in prison as an official
punishment: *He was imprisoned for ten
years.*
⇨ *Compare* JAIL[2].

imprisonment /ɪmˈprɪzənmənt/ [*noun*]
when someone is put or kept in prison:
He was sentenced to life imprisonment
(=he had to stay in prison for the rest of
his life).

improve * /ɪmˈpruv/ [*verb;* improved,
improving]
1 to become better or make something
better: *The teacher said my work had
improved.* | *They want to improve the
transportation system.*
2 to become well again after an illness:
Her condition continues to improve.
⇨ *See the synonym note at* RECOVER.

improvement * /ɪmˈpruvmənt/ [*noun*]
1 when something becomes better or is
made better: *They have made some
improvements to the product.* | *There's
been much improvement in her health.*
2 something that is better than a
previous thing: *The new system is an
improvement on the old one.*

impulse /'ımpʌls/ [*noun*] a sudden wish to do something: *On impulse, she cut her hair* (=suddenly, without planning).

impulsive /ım'pʌlsıv/ [*adjective;* **more impulsive, most impulsive**] done without planning, or tending to do things without planning: *an impulsive decision* | *He's always been impulsive.*

The rice is **in** the bowl.

The rice is **on** a plate.

in *and* **on**

in¹ * /ın/ [*preposition*]

1 used to talk about where someone or something is or where something happens: *She put the letter in a drawer.* | *Get in the car.* | *My parents live in New York.* | *an earthquake in California*
☛ Do not say that food is "in a plate." Say that it is **on a plate**.

2 used to talk about how something happens: *Two men were speaking in English.* | *He spoke in a loud voice.* | *They were paid in dollars.*

3 used to say when something happened or will happen: *They're getting married in September.* | *In the past, things were very different.* | *I'll be ready in ten minutes* (=ten minutes from now).

4 if you are in a situation, condition, kind of work, etc., it is what you do or what is happening to you: *He's in banking.* | *We're in trouble.* | *Are you still in school?*

5 if something is in a letter, book, movie, etc., it is part of it: *What does he say in his letter?* | *This is the best scene in the play.*

6 used to say what someone is wearing: *Who's the girl in the blue dress?*

7 used to say what a difference or change involves: *The fruit varied in size.* | *There has been a sharp increase in prices recently.*

━━ PHRASE ━━

8 in all including everyone or everything: *There were 25 students in all taking the test.*

in² * [*adverb*]

1 into a container, vehicle, place, etc.; *opposite* OUT: *I opened the door and went in.*

2 indoors; *opposite* OUT: *You can let the dog in now.*

in³ [*adjective; no comparative*]

1 at home or at the place where you work; *opposite* OUT: *"Can I speak to your father?" "I'm afraid he's not in."*

2 *INFORMAL* fashionable; *opposite* OUT: *Short skirts are in this year.*

in. the written abbreviation of INCH or INCHES: *Calculate the area of a circle that is 3 in. in diameter.*

inaccurate /ın'ækyərıt/ [*adjective;* **more inaccurate, most inaccurate**] not exactly right; *opposite* ACCURATE: *Their estimate of the cost was inaccurate.*

inadequate /ın'ædıkwıt/ [*adjective; no comparative*] not enough, or not good enough; *opposite* ADEQUATE: *The time allowed was inadequate.* | *That is an inadequate excuse.*

inappropriate Ⓣ /,ınə'prouprııt/ [*adjective;* **more inappropriate, most inappropriate**] not right or suitable for a situation or a person; *opposite* APPROPRIATE: *He was wearing* **inappropriate** *clothes* **for** *the office.*

incapable /ın'keıpəbəl/ [*adjective;* **more incapable, most incapable**] not able to do something; *synonym* UNABLE; *opposite* CAPABLE: *He seemed* **incapable of** *understanding the simplest requests.*
☛ Do not use **incapable** before a noun.

inch¹ * /ıntʃ/ [*noun; plural* **inches**] a unit for measuring length, equal to 2.54 centimeters: *There are 12 inches in a foot.* | *The insect was three inches long.*

inch² [verb; inches, inched, inching] to move somewhere very slowly, a short distance at a time: *He inched toward the door.* | *A caterpillar **inched its way** along the branch.*

incident /'ɪnsɪdənt/ [noun] FORMAL an event, especially an unusual or unpleasant one: *The police are investigating the incident.* | *an amusing incident*

inclined ⊤ /ɪn'klaɪnd/ [adjective; **more inclined, most inclined**]

━ PHRASE ━━━━

be inclined to do something to be likely to do something, or want to do something: *I'm inclined to believe her.*
☛ Do not use **inclined** before a noun.

include * ⊤ /ɪn'klud/ [verb; included, including]
1 if something includes a particular thing or things, it or they are part of it: *The English course includes reading and listening skills.*
2 to make someone or something part of a larger group or thing; *opposite* EXCLUDE: **include someone/something in something** ▸ *You should include your sister in your game.*

including * /ɪn'kludɪŋ/ [preposition] used to mention something or someone that is part of a group or thing: *I like most vegetables, including cabbage.*

income * ⊤ /'ɪnkʌm/ [noun] the money that you get for working or from other activities: *She has **an income of $50,000** a year.* | *Do you have any other **source of income**?*
↪ See the usage note at PAY².

income tax /'ɪnkʌm ˌtæks/ [noun; plural **income taxes**] money you pay to the government out of the money you earn: *We pay federal and state income taxes.*

incomplete /ˌɪnkəm'plit/ [adjective; no comparative] not complete or finished: *Our plans are incomplete.* | *an incomplete jigsaw puzzle*

inconsiderate /ˌɪnkən'sɪdərɪt/ [adjective; **more inconsiderate, most inconsiderate**] not caring about how your actions could cause problems or upset people; *opposite* CONSIDERATE: *How could you be so inconsiderate?*
↪ Compare THOUGHTLESS.

inconvenient /ˌɪnkən'vinyənt/ [adjective; **more inconvenient, most inconvenient**] causing you slight problems; *opposite* CONVENIENT: *I hope I haven't called at an inconvenient time.*

incorrect ⊤ /ˌɪnkə'rɛkt/ [adjective; no comparative] not correct; *synonym* WRONG; *opposite* RIGHT: *That's an incorrect answer.*

incorrectly /ˌɪnkə'rɛktli/ [adverb] in a way that is not correct; *synonym* WRONG: *He wrote the address incorrectly.*

increase¹ * ⊤ /ɪn'kris/ [verb; increased, increasing] to become greater, or to make something greater in amount, level, or degree; *opposite* DECREASE: *In time, my interest increased.* | *Science has increased our knowledge of the world.*

increase² * ⊤ /'ɪnkris/ [noun] when an amount, level, or degree becomes greater; *opposite* DECREASE: *There's been a big **increase in** the number of jobs.* | *an **increase of** 40 percent* | *a 40% increase*

increasingly /ɪn'krisɪŋli/ [adverb] used to say that something happens more and more, as time passes: *She became increasingly worried.*

incredible /ɪn'krɛdəbəl/ [adjective; **more incredible, most incredible**] very surprising, great, or good: *We had some incredible luck.*

indeed ⊤ /ɪn'did/ [adverb] FORMAL used to emphasize that something happened or is true: *If he has indeed lied, that is a serious matter.*
↪ Compare REALLY.

indefinite /ɪn'dɛfənɪt/ [adjective; no comparative]
1 without a fixed end or limit: *He will be off work for an **indefinite period**.*
2 not clear or not completely certain; *opposite* DEFINITE: *His plans are still indefinite.*

indefinite article /ɪn'dɛfənɪt 'ɑrtɪkəl/ [noun] GRAMMAR the word A or AN: *Use the indefinite article with countable nouns.*
↪ Compare DEFINITE ARTICLE.

indefinitely /ɪn'dɛfənɪtli/ [adverb] until some time in the future that has not been fixed, and perhaps forever: *She will be staying with us indefinitely.*

independence /ˌɪndɪˈpɛndəns/ [*noun*]
1 when you can make your own decisions and take care of yourself without help from anyone else: *Teenagers want greater independence.*
2 when a country stops being ruled by another country: *The country is celebrating its independence.*

Independence Day /ˌɪndɪˈpɛndəns ˌdeɪ/ [*noun*] a U.S. holiday on July 4th, celebrating the signing of the Declaration of Independence in 1776: *an Independence Day parade*

independent * T /ˌɪndɪˈpɛndənt/ [*adjective*; **more independent, most independent**]
1 able to make your own decisions and take care of yourself without help from anyone else: *I want to be financially independent* (=not needing anyone to give me money).
2 not ruled by another country: *The country has been independent for fifty years.*

index /ˈɪndɛks/ [*noun; plural* **indexes**] a list at the back of a book that tells you on what page things are mentioned or dealt with: *Look up "whales" in the index.*

index finger /ˈɪndɛks ˌfɪŋɡɚ/ [*noun*] your first finger, next to your thumb
↪ *See the picture at* **BODY.**

Indian[1] /ˈɪndiən/ [*noun*]
1 a member of the original group of people of North or South America
↪ *Compare* **AMERICAN INDIAN, NATIVE AMERICAN.**
2 someone who comes from India

Indian[2] [*adjective; no comparative*]
1 relating to the original group of people of North or South America: *Indian arts and crafts*
2 belonging to, from, or relating to India: *He's interested in Indian music.*

Indian Ocean /ˈɪndiən ˈoʊʃən/ [*name*]
the Indian Ocean a sea to the south of India

indicate /ˈɪndɪˌkeɪt/ [*verb;* **indicated, indicating**]
1 to show something: *These figures indicate that our sales are increasing.*
2 to point to something: *She indicated a photograph on the wall.*

indication /ˌɪndɪˈkeɪʃən/ [*noun*] a sign that something is happening or is true: *He gave no indication that he was upset.*

indignant /ɪnˈdɪɡnənt/ [*adjective;* **more indignant, most indignant**] angry about something you think is unfair or wrong: *She was indignant at being ignored by the sales assistant.*

indirect /ˌɪndəˈrɛkt/ [*adjective;* **more indirect, most indirect**] not going the straightest way to a place; *opposite* DIRECT: *They took an indirect route to avoid the flooded area.*

indirect object * /ˈɪndərɛkt ˈɑbdʒɛkt/ [*noun*] GRAMMAR a word or group of words that refers to the person or thing that something is given to, done to, said to, or done for: *In the sentence, "She gave me a book," "me" is the indirect object.*
↪ *Compare* **DIRECT OBJECT.**

individual[1] T /ˌɪndəˈvɪdʒuəl/ [*noun*] a person, separately from other people: *The amount of sleep needed varies from individual to individual.*

individual[2] T [*adjective; no comparative*] relating to or intended for just one person or thing: *We try to meet the needs of each individual child.* | *an individual serving of cereal*
☛ Only use the adjective **individual** before a noun.

individually /ˌɪndəˈvɪdʒuəli/ [*adverb*] separately or one at a time: *The teacher spoke to each student individually.*

indoor * /ˈɪnˌdɔr/ [*adjective; no comparative*] inside, or used or happening inside; *opposite* OUTDOOR: *an indoor tennis court* | *an indoor barbecue grill* | *indoor games*
☛ Only use **indoor** before a noun.

indoors * /ɪnˈdɔrz/ [*adverb*] inside a house or other building; *opposites* OUT, OUTDOORS: *He stayed indoors all day.*

/i/ **see** /ɪ/ **big** /eɪ/ **day** /ɛ/ **get** /æ/ **hat**
/ɑ/ **father, hot** /ʌ/ **up** /ə/ **about** /ɔ/ **saw**
/oʊ/ **hope** /ʊ/ **book** /u/ **too** /aɪ/ **I** /aʊ/ **how**
/ɔɪ/ **boy** /ɚ/ **bird** /ɚ/ **teacher** /ɪr/ **ear** /ɛr/ **air**
/ɑr/ **far** /ɔr/ **more** /ʊr/ **tour** /aɪr/ **fire**
/aʊɚ/ **hour** /θ/ **nothing** /ð/ **mother** /ʃ/ **she**
/ʒ/ **measure** /tʃ/ **church** /dʒ/ **jump** /ŋ/ **long**

industrial * /ɪnˈdʌstriəl/ [adjective; no comparative] relating to or having a lot of industry: Industrial production has increased. | a big industrial city

industry * /ˈɪndəstri/ [noun; plural **industries**]
1 a business that makes or does something of a particular kind: the computer industry | the music industry
2 businesses that make goods in factories: She works in industry.

inefficient /ˌɪnɪˈfɪʃənt/ [adjective; **more inefficient, most inefficient**] not using your time, money, or effort in the best possible way; opposite EFFICIENT: This water heater is inefficient.

inexperienced /ˌɪnɪkˈspɪriənst/ [adjective; **more inexperienced, most inexperienced**] not having done something very often; opposite EXPERIENCED: an inexperienced driver

infant /ˈɪnfənt/ [noun] FORMAL a baby: These car seats are designed for infants. | She was carrying her infant son.

infect * /ɪnˈfɛkt/ [verb; **infected, infecting**] to give someone a disease by causing bacteria or a virus to enter his or her body: **infect someone with something** ▸ Stay home, or you'll infect other students with the flu.

infected * /ɪnˈfɛktɪd/ [adjective; no comparative] full of dangerous bacteria or a virus: The cut became infected.

infection * /ɪnˈfɛkʃən/ [noun]
1 a disease caused by bacteria or a virus: She has a lung infection.
2 when a disease is given to someone: Clean the cut well to prevent infection.

infectious * /ɪnˈfɛkʃəs/ [adjective; **more infectious, most infectious**] an infectious disease can easily be passed from one person to another: It is a **highly infectious** virus.
⇨ See the synonym note at CONTAGIOUS.

inferior /ɪnˈfɪriɚ/ [adjective; no comparative] FORMAL less good; synonym WORSE: His work is **inferior to** yours. | The material was of an inferior quality.
☛ Do not say "inferior than something." Say **inferior to something**.
⇨ Compare SUPERIOR[1].

infinite /ˈɪnfənɪt/ [adjective; no comparative] having no end or limit: an infinite number of stars

infinitive * /ɪnˈfɪnɪtɪv/ [noun] GRAMMAR the basic form of a verb, which is often used after "to." Examples are "go," "write," and "be": You can use an infinitive with "to" after "want."

inflate T /ɪnˈfleɪt/ [verb; **inflated, inflating**] to push a gas or air into something such as a tire: They used helium to inflate the balloon.
⇨ See also **blow up** at BLOW[1] (definition 10).

inflation T /ɪnˈfleɪʃən/ [noun] when prices get higher: The **rate of inflation** is now 9 percent.

influence[1] /ˈɪnfluəns/ [noun]
1 the ability to make someone do something or to make something happen: I don't have much **influence with** the club management.
2 someone or something that affects what someone does or what happens: Her mother was **a great influence on** her. | His friend Jason is **a bad influence on** him.

influence[2] * T [verb; **influenced, influencing**] to affect what someone does or what happens: What influenced your career choice?

influential /ˌɪnfluˈɛnʃəl/ [adjective; **more influential, most influential**] able to make someone do something or make something happen: She got the job because she has influential friends.

influenza /ˌɪnfluˈɛnzə/ [noun] a common illness that is like a very bad cold, that gives you a fever, and can make your stomach feel sick; synonym FLU

inform * /ɪnˈfɔrm/ [verb; **informed, informing**] FORMAL to tell someone something: **inform someone that** ▸ He informed me that the play had already started. | **inform someone of something** ▸ They informed her of the change of schedule.

informal * /ɪnˈfɔrməl/ [adjective; **more informal, most informal**] friendly and relaxed, or suitable for times when you are not doing anything special; opposite

FORMAL: *You shouldn't wear informal clothes to an interview.* | *"Hi" is an informal greeting.*

informally /ɪnˈfɔrməli/ [*adverb*] in a way that is friendly and relaxed, or suitable for occasions that are not serious; *opposite* FORMALLY: *He was informally dressed in jeans and a T-shirt.*

information * /ˌɪnfɚˈmeɪʃən/ [*noun*] facts about something: *Could you give me some information about yourself?* | *That's a useful piece of information.*
☛ Do not say "some informations."

information technology /ˌɪnfɚˈmeɪʃən tɛkˌnɑlədʒi/ [*noun*] the use of computers to store and show information

informative /ɪnˈfɔrmətɪv/ [*adjective; more informative, most informative*] giving you a lot of information about something: *a very informative book*

ingredient 𝕋 /ɪnˈgridiənt/ [*noun*] something that is mixed with other things to make something, especially food: *Fry the onion, then add the other ingredients.*

inhabit /ɪnˈhæbɪt/ [*verb; inhabited, inhabiting*] FORMAL if people or animals inhabit a place, they live there: *Many kinds of snakes inhabit the forest.*

inhabitant /ɪnˈhæbɪtənt/ [*noun*] FORMAL someone who lives in a particular town or area: *The local inhabitants were very friendly.*

inherit /ɪnˈhɛrɪt/ [*verb; inherited, inheriting*]
1 to get property or money from someone who has died, because he or she wanted you to have it: **inherit something from someone** ▸ *He inherited the house from his father.*
2 to get the way you look or behave, or an illness, from one of your parents: *She inherited her mother's dark hair.*

inheritance /ɪnˈhɛrɪtəns/ [*noun*] property or money that you get from someone who has died: *He used his inheritance to buy a business.*

initial[1] /ɪˈnɪʃəl/ [*adjective; no comparative*] used to describe something that happens first, or at the beginning of something: *Her initial response was to

laugh.* | *The initial stages of the competition begin Monday.*
☛ Only use **initial** before a noun.

initial[2] [*noun*] the first letter of a name: *His initials—R.J.S.—were on his luggage.*

initially /ɪˈnɪʃəli/ [*adverb*] at the beginning: *Initially, he wasn't sure the idea would work.*

inject /ɪnˈdʒɛkt/ [*verb; injected, injecting*] to put a liquid such as a medicine into someone's body using a hollow needle: **inject someone with something** ▸ *She was injected with an anesthetic.*

injection /ɪnˈdʒɛkʃən/ [*noun*] a drug or medicine put into your body with a hollow needle, for example to prevent a disease; *synonym* SHOT: *The doctor said the injection might make my arm feel sore.* | *The vaccine is given by injection.*

injure * /ˈɪndʒɚ/ [*verb; injured, injuring*] to hurt someone's body, or your own body: *He was badly injured in the crash.* | *She injured her leg skiing.*

injury * /ˈɪndʒəri/ [*noun; plural injuries*] damage to someone's body: *Her injuries were not severe.* | *Wear a helmet to avoid injury.*

injustice /ɪnˈdʒʌstɪs/ [*noun*] something that is wrong and unfair, or a state in which things are unfair: *We must correct this obvious injustice.* | *There is still injustice in the legal system.*
↪ Compare JUSTICE.

ink * /ɪŋk/ [*noun*] a black or colored liquid used for writing, drawing, or printing: *a drawing in colored inks* | *Please fill out this form in ink.*

inland[1] /ˈɪnlənd/ [*adjective; no comparative*] not near the ocean or a coast: *an inland town*
☛ Only use **inland** before a noun.

inland[2] /ˈɪnˌlænd/ [*adverb*] in or toward an area that is not near the ocean or a coast: *The explorers headed inland.*

/i/ see	/ɪ/ big	/eɪ/ day	/ɛ/ get	/æ/ hat
/ɑ/ father, hot	/ʌ/ up	/ə/ about	/ɔ/ saw	
/oʊ/ hope	/ʊ/ book	/u/ too	/aɪ/ I	/aʊ/ how
/ɔɪ/ boy	/ɝ/ bird	/ɚ/ teacher	/ɪr/ ear	/ɛr/ air
/ɑr/ far	/ɔr/ more	/ʊr/ tour	/aɪr/ fire	
/aʊɚ/ hour	/θ/ nothing	/ð/ mother	/ʃ/ she	
/ʒ/ measure	/tʃ/ church	/dʒ/ jump	/ŋ/ long	

in-line skate /'ɪn
laɪn 'skeɪt/ [*noun*]
a boot with wheels in
a line from front to
back; *synonym*
ROLLERBLADE
▷ Compare ROLLER
SKATE.

in-line skates/
Rollerblades

inmate /'ɪn‚meɪt/
[*noun*] someone who
is being kept in a prison; *synonym*
PRISONER

inn /ɪn/ [*noun*] a small hotel: *a charming
country inn*

inner * /'ɪnɚ/ [*adjective; no comparative*]
near the center of something, or on the
inside of it; *opposite* OUTER: *He led me
through to an inner room.* | *an inner wall*
☞ Only use **inner** before a noun.

innocence /'ɪnəsəns/ [*noun*] the fact
that someone has not committed a
particular crime; *opposite* GUILT: *She was
convinced of her son's innocence.*

innocent /'ɪnəsənt/ [*adjective;* **more
innocent, most innocent**]
1 not having committed a particular
crime; *opposite* GUILTY: *Do you think he's
guilty or innocent?*
2 not knowing about bad things that
happen in the world: *an innocent child*

input /'ɪn‚pʊt/ [*noun*]
1 someone's ideas, information, and
suggestions: *We would welcome your
input on this.*
2 information put into a computer: *The
input is stored in files.*

inquire /ɪn'kwaɪr/ [*verb;* **inquired,
inquiring**] FORMAL to ask for
information: *We inquired about rooms.*
| *"Are you hungry?" he inquired.*

inquiry /'ɪnkwəri/ [*noun; plural*
inquiries] a question to get
information: *She made some inquiries
about plane tickets.*

inquisitive /ɪn'kwɪzɪtɪv/ [*adjective;*
more inquisitive, most inquisitive]
eager to find out about things: *His
mother was inquisitive about his friends.*

insane /ɪn'seɪn/ [*adjective;* **more insane,
most insane**]
1 seriously mentally ill; *opposite* SANE:

*He went insane and was put in a
mental hospital.*
2 INFORMAL not at all sensible, or very
strange; *synonym* CRAZY: *What an
insane idea!*

insect * /'ɪnsɛkt/ [*noun*] a very small
creature with six legs: *Cover the food to
protect it from insects.*

insensitive /ɪn'sɛnsɪtɪv/ [*adjective;* **more
insensitive, most insensitive**] not
considering whether your behavior may
upset someone, or not noticing that
someone is upset; *opposite* SENSITIVE: *He's
so insensitive—why did he say that?*

insert /ɪn'sɝt/ [*verb;* **inserted, inserting**]
FORMAL to put one thing into another,
especially into a hole in a machine:
insert something in/into something ▸
*Insert a quarter in the coin slot, then dial
the number.*

inside[1] * /‚ɪn'saɪd/ [*preposition*]
surrounded by a building, container,
etc.; *opposite* OUTSIDE: *Inside the box were
some letters.* | *Ten people were trapped
inside the building.*

The boy
is **inside**
the house.

The peas
are **inside**
the pod.

inside[2] * /‚ɪn'saɪd/ [*adverb*]
1 surrounded by a building, container,
etc.; *opposite* OUTSIDE: *When he opened
the envelope, he found a check inside.* |
Let's go inside—I'm cold.
═══ PHRASE ═══
2 inside of in less than: *I'll be there
inside of an hour.*

inside[3] * /'ɪn‚saɪd/ [*noun*]
1 the inside the part or surface of
something that is facing the center or
at the center; *opposite* OUTSIDE: *The*

inside of the box was painted black. |
The door was locked on the inside.

— PHRASE

2 inside out if a piece of clothing is
inside out, the inside is facing out: He
had put his sweater on inside out.

inside[4] * /'ɪn,saɪd/ [adjective; no
comparative] an inside wall, room, etc.,
is in something or further in it than
other things; opposite OUTSIDE: He works
in an inside office with no window.
☛ Only use **inside** before a noun.

insist ⊤ /ɪn'sɪst/ [verb; insisted,
insisting]
1 to say very firmly that something is
true, even though people do not
believe you: **insist (that)** ▸ I insisted
that I had not taken the money.
2 to say very firmly that something
must happen: **insist on doing
something** ▸ She insisted on taking me
to the hospital. | **insist (that)** ▸ Her
parents insisted she tell the truth.
☛ Do not say that someone "insisted
to do something." Say that he or she
insisted on doing something.

inspect /ɪn'spɛkt/ [verb; inspected,
inspecting] to look at something
carefully to find anything that is wrong
with it: **inspect something for
something** ▸ He inspected the car for
signs of rust.

inspection /ɪn'spɛkʃən/ [noun] a careful
examination of something to find
anything that is wrong with it: a safety
inspection | Please have your passports
ready for inspection.

inspector /ɪn'spɛktɚ/ [noun] someone
whose job is to officially check that
businesses are not dangerous: A health
inspector visited the restaurant today.

inspire ⊤ /ɪn'spaɪr/ [verb; inspired,
inspiring] to make someone want to do
or make something: His father's example
inspired him. | **inspire someone to do
something** ▸ What inspired you to
become a painter?

inspiring /ɪn'spaɪrɪŋ/ [adjective; more
inspiring, most inspiring] exciting
and making you want to achieve
something: This inspiring book changed
my life.

install /ɪn'stɔl/ [verb; installed,
installing]
1 to put a piece of equipment into the
place where it can be used: Someone is
coming to install our new dryer today.
2 to put computer programs into a
computer: Installing the software is easy.

installment /ɪn'stɔlmənt/ [noun]
1 one of several payments that you
make to buy something or pay back
what you owe: The **first installment** is
due today. | He paid **in installments**.
2 one of several parts of a story in a
magazine, on television, etc.: I can
hardly wait for the next installment.

instance /'ɪnstəns/ [noun]

— PHRASE

for instance used to give an example:
She sings when she's alone—in the shower,
for instance.
⇨ See also E.G., **for example** at EXAMPLE.

instant[1] ⊤ /'ɪnstənt/ [adjective; no
comparative]
1 happening immediately: an instant
response
2 instant food or drinks are made
quickly, for example by just adding
water: a jar of instant coffee | instant
pudding
☛ Only use **instant** before a noun.

instant[2] ⊤ [noun]
1 a very short period of time; synonyms
MOMENT, SECOND: For an instant she
couldn't remember his name. | He was
back in an instant.
☛ The noun **instant** is usually used in
the singular.

— PHRASE

2 the instant (that) as soon as: He
ran off the instant I saw him.

instantly ⊤ /'ɪnstəntli/ [adverb]
immediately: I recognized her instantly.

instead * /ɪn'stɛd/ [adverb] in the place
of someone or something: If you don't
like swimming, you can play tennis

/i/ **see**	/ɪ/ **big**	/eɪ/ **day**	/ɛ/ **get**	/æ/ **hat**	
/ɑ/ **father, hot**	/ʌ/ **up**	/ə/ **about**	/ɔ/ **saw**		
/oʊ/ **hope**	/ʊ/ **book**	/u/ **too**	/aɪ/ **I**	/aʊ/ **how**	
/ɔɪ/ **boy**	/ɝ/ **bird**	/ɚ/ **teacher**	/ɛr/ **air**		
/ɑr/ **far**	/ɔr/ **more**	/ʊr/ **tour**	/aɪr/ **fire**		
/aʊɚ/ **hour**	/θ/ **nothing**	/ð/ **mother**	/ʃ/ **she**		
/ʒ/ **measure**	/tʃ/ **church**	/dʒ/ **jump**	/ŋ/ **long**		

instead. | *Lisa drove* **instead of** *Carlos.* | *I walk to school* **instead of** *taking the bus.*
☛ Do not say "Can I instead you to do it?" Say **Can I do it instead of you?**

instinct /'ɪnstɪŋkt/ [*noun*] a natural wish, feeling, or action, rather than one that is the result of thinking about it: *My first instinct was to hide.* | *Birds know* **by instinct** *when to fly south.*

institute Ⓣ /'ɪnstɪ,tut/ [*noun*] an organization for research or education: *He works for a medical research institute.*

institution * Ⓣ /,ɪnstɪ'tuʃən/ [*noun*] an organization such as a university, bank, or hospital: *a large* **financial institution**

instruct /ɪn'strʌkt/ [*verb*; **instructed, instructing**]
1 to teach someone how to do something: **instruct someone in something** ▸ *He instructed them in horseback riding.*
2 to tell someone to do something: **instruct someone to do something** ▸ *She instructed her secretary to send the letters.*

instructions * /ɪn'strʌkʃənz/ [*plural noun*] an explanation of how to do something, especially one that comes with a piece of equipment: *I couldn't understand the instructions for the VCR.*

instructor /ɪn'strʌktɚ/ [*noun*] someone who teaches people how to do something: *a skiing instructor*
⇨ Compare TEACHER.

instrument * /'ɪnstrəmənt/ [*noun*]
1 a tool used in science or medicine: *The dentist had his instruments laid out.*
2 something that is used to make music, such as a violin or flute: *The musicians put their instruments away.*
⇨ See the picture at MUSICAL INSTRUMENT.

instrumental /,ɪnstrə'mɛntəl/ [*adjective*; *no comparative*] written for or played by musical instruments only and not voices: *The concert began with two instrumental pieces.*

insult[1] * /ɪn'sʌlt/ [*verb*; **insulted, insulting**] to say something rude to someone or do something that shows you have a bad opinion of him or her: *He insulted the umpire and was thrown out of the game.*

insult[2] /'ɪnsʌlt/ [*noun*] a rude remark or an action which shows you have a bad opinion of someone: *A group of boys shouted insults at us.*

insulting * /ɪn'sʌltɪŋ/ [*adjective*; **more insulting, most insulting**] rude and offensive: *an* **insulting remark**

insurance * Ⓣ /ɪn'ʃʊrəns/ [*noun*] when you pay money to a company so that it gives you the money you need if something bad happens to you or to something you own: *health insurance* | *He couldn't afford to pay the* **insurance on** *his house.*

insure * /ɪn'ʃʊr/ [*verb*; **insured, insuring**] to pay money to a company so that it will give you the money you need if something bad happens to you or to something you own: *She insured her antique table for $7,000.* | **insure something against something** ▸ *Is the building insured against fire?*

intelligence * /ɪn'tɛlɪdʒəns/ [*noun*] the ability to understand and learn things quickly: *a man of great intelligence*

intelligent * /ɪn'tɛlɪdʒənt/ [*adjective*; **more intelligent, most intelligent**] able to understand and learn things quickly; <u>synonym</u> SMART; <u>opposites</u> DUMB, STUPID: *a very intelligent child*

intend * /ɪn'tɛnd/ [*verb*; **intended, intending**]
1 to have an action planned in your mind; <u>synonym</u> PLAN: **intend to do something** ▸ *I don't intend to stay long.*
⇨ See also **mean to** at MEAN[1].
2 to plan that something will have a particular use or result: **be intended for someone** ▸ *This playground is intended for children under 12.* | **be intended to do something** ▸ *The prizes were intended to make students work harder.*
⇨ See also INTENTION.

intense Ⓣ /ɪn'tɛns/ [*adjective*; **more intense, most intense**] very great or strong; <u>opposite</u> MILD: *The intense heat melted the metal door.*

intensive /ɪn'tɛnsɪv/ [*adjective*; **more intensive, most intensive**] involving a lot of work and attention: *I took an intensive English course last summer.*

intention * /ɪnˈtɛnʃən/ [noun]
something you plan to do or plan to make happen: *I believe his intentions are good.* | *He **had no intention of** repaying the money.*
⇨ See also INTEND.

intentional ⊤ /ɪnˈtɛnʃənəl/ [adjective; no comparative] if an action was intentional, the person who did it meant to do it; synonym DELIBERATE; opposite ACCIDENTAL: *He tripped me, but it wasn't intentional.*

interactive /ˌɪntərˈæktɪv/ [adjective; no comparative] an interactive computer program is one that allows the user to decide what happens: *interactive video games*

interest[1] * /ˈɪntərɪst/ [noun]
1 the feeling you have when you want to continue finding out about something or doing something: *People with an **interest** in history will enjoy this book.* | *He began collecting stamps but soon **lost interest**.*
2 something you do or find out about because you enjoy it: *Her wide range of interests include skating and jazz.*
3 money that you pay regularly to an organization because it has lent you money, or money paid regularly to you by an organization that is keeping your money: *I can't afford to **pay the interest on** the loan.* | *My savings account **earns 3% interest**.*
══ PHRASE ══
4 of interest interesting: *This article might be of interest to you.*

interest[2] * [verb; interested, interesting] if something interests you, it makes you want to continue finding out about it or doing it: *Sports didn't interest him at all.*

interested * /ˈɪntrəstɪd/ [adjective; **more interested, most interested**] someone who is interested wants to learn more about something, or wants to do something: *Daniel's always been very interested in birds.* | *I'm **interested in** buying that picture.*
☛ Do not say "I am interested to buy it." Say **I am interested in buying it.**
☛ Do not use **interested** before a noun.

USAGE   interested, interesting
Do not confuse **interested** and **interesting. Interested** is used about people: *I'm interested in ancient history.* **Interesting** is used about things: *Ancient history is interesting.*

interesting * /ˈɪntərəstɪŋ/ [adjective; **more interesting, most interesting**] something that is interesting makes you want to learn more about it or continue doing it; opposite BORING: *I was watching an interesting program about tigers.*
⇨ See the usage note at INTERESTED.

interfere /ˌɪntəˈfɪr/ [verb; interfered, interfering]
1 to involve yourself in someone else's life, work, etc., when he or she does not want you to: *She was making a mistake, but I didn't want to interfere.*
══ PHRASAL VERB ══
interfere with [phrasal verb]
2 to prevent something from continuing as it should: **interfere with something** ▸ *Mrs. Green's interruptions interfered with the meeting.*

interior[1] /ɪnˈtɪriə/ [noun] FORMAL the inside of a building, vehicle, etc.; opposite EXTERIOR: *The interior of the car is black.*

interior[2] [adjective; no comparative] FORMAL an interior wall, door, decoration, etc., is inside a building, vehicle, etc.; opposite EXTERIOR: *The interior hallways are painted white.*
☛ Only use **interior** before a noun.

interjection * /ˌɪntəˈdʒɛkʃən/ [noun] a word that expresses a complete thought. It is used to show feelings such as surprise or anger, or to get someone's attention: *"Wow" and "hey" are interjections.*

intermediate /ˌɪntəˈmidiɪt/ [adjective; no comparative] in the middle between beginning and advanced: *The course is*

/i/ see	/ɪ/ big	/eɪ/ day	/ɛ/ get	/æ/ hat
/ɑ/ father, hot	/ʌ/ up	/ə/ about	/ɔ/ saw	
/oʊ/ hope	/ʊ/ book	/u/ too	/aɪ/ I	/aʊ/ how
/ɔɪ/ boy	/ɚ/ bird	/ɚ/ teacher	/ɪr/ ear	/ɛr/ air
/ɑr/ far	/ɔr/ more	/ʊr/ tour	/aɪr/ fire	
/aʊɚ/ hour	/θ/ nothing	/ð/ mother	/ʃ/ she	
/ʒ/ measure	/tʃ/ church	/dʒ/ jump	/ŋ/ long	

appropriate for intermediate learners. | an intermediate-level exam

intermission /ˌɪntɚˈmɪʃən/ [*noun*]
a period of time between parts of a performance: *There was a brief intermission between acts. | I spoke with a friend during intermission.*

internal /ɪnˈtɜ˞nəl/ [*adjective; no comparative*] inside, or happening inside; *opposite* EXTERNAL: *He died as a result of* **internal injuries** (=injuries inside his body).

international * ⊤ /ˌɪntɚˈnæʃənəl/ [*adjective; no comparative*] involving two or more countries: *This is his first international competition. | a busy international airport*
➪ Compare NATIONAL.

Internet /ˈɪntɚˌnɛt/ [*noun*]
the Internet a network that connects computers all over the world, so that information can be gotten or sent: *We have access to the Internet.*
➪ See also **the Net** at NET. ➪ Compare WORLD WIDE WEB.

interpret ⊤ /ɪnˈtɜ˞prɪt/ [*verb; interpreted, interpreting*] to repeat the words that one person speaks in another language, so that someone else can understand them: *She interpreted the president's greeting.*
➪ Compare TRANSLATE.

interpretation /ɪnˌtɜ˞prɪˈteɪʃən/ [*noun*]
someone's decision about how to understand an event or what something means: *Many people disagree with the mayor's interpretation of the law.*

interpreter /ɪnˈtɜ˞prɪtɚ/ [*noun*]
someone who repeats the words that one person speaks in another language, so that someone else can understand them: *The interpreter made few mistakes.*
➪ Compare TRANSLATOR.

interracial /ˌɪntɚˈreɪʃəl/ [*adjective; no comparative*] involving people of different races: *an interracial couple*

interrupt * /ˌɪntəˈrʌpt/ [*verb; interrupted, interrupting*] to say or do something while someone is speaking or doing something, so that he or she has to stop: *He interrupted her to ask a*

question. | *I'm sorry to interrupt, but there's a telephone call for you.*

interruption /ˌɪntəˈrʌpʃən/ [*noun*]
when someone says or does something while someone else is speaking or doing something, so that he or she has to stop: *I don't want any more interruptions. | She worked all day without interruption.*

intersection /ˌɪntɚˈsɛkʃən/ [*noun*]
a place where roads meet: *There's a grocery store at* **the intersection of** *Third and Peach Streets.*

interstate[1] /ˈɪntɚˌsteɪt/ [*adjective; no comparative*] involving more than one state, especially in the U.S.: *a new* **interstate highway**
☞ Only use **interstate** before a noun.

interstate[2] [*noun*] a main road that connects big cities in the U.S.

interval /ˈɪntɚvəl/ [*noun*]
1 a period of time between two events: *After a short interval he opened the door.*
━━ PHRASE ━━
2 **at intervals** with spaces or periods of time between each thing or occasion: *You should visit the dentist* **at regular intervals**. | *The trees were planted* **at intervals of** *20 feet.*

interview[1] ⊤ /ˈɪntɚˌvyu/ [*noun*]
1 when an employer or teacher meets someone to decide if he or she is good enough for a job or a course of study: *I have a job interview on Tuesday.*
2 a conversation in which a writer or someone on television, radio, etc., asks someone questions: *The magazine contains* **interviews with** *famous actors. | He never* **gives interviews** (=lets these people ask him questions).

interview[2] ⊤ [*verb; interviewed, interviewing*] to ask someone questions to find out if he or she is good enough for a job or a course of study, or to find out information about him or her: *She was* **interviewed for** *the job of office manager. | He has interviewed many famous people.*

intestine /ɪnˈtɛstɪn/ [*noun*] a tube in your body through which food goes when it leaves your stomach

into * /'ɪntu/ [preposition]
1 to or toward the inside of a place, container, etc.: *He jumped into the river.* | *Her books were packed into boxes.*
2 used with verbs such as "drive" and "walk" to show that you hit something: *He drove into a lamppost.*
3 used to talk about a new situation or state: *I'm worried that he might get into trouble.* | *They got into debt.* | *She crumpled the paper into a ball.*
4 used when one number is divided by another: *Two goes into twelve six times.*
5 INFORMAL if you are into something, you are interested in it: *I'm not really into sports.*

lamppost

She's pouring batter **into** a pan.

The truck crashed **into** a lamppost.

intransitive * /ɪn'trænsɪtɪv/ [adjective; no comparative] GRAMMAR an intransitive verb does not have an object. Examples are "sleep" and "wait": *In the sentence "She sings in a choir," "sings" is intransitive.*
↪ Compare TRANSITIVE.

introduce * T /ˌɪntrə'dus/ [verb; introduced, introducing]
1 to formally tell someone the name of another person he or she has not met before: *Let me **introduce myself** (=tell you who I am).* | **introduce someone to someone** ▸ *I introduced him to my friend.*
2 to start using a new system or method: *The new library system will be introduced next month.*
3 to say what is going to be next in a television or radio program: *The show was introduced by Mary Winters.*

introduction * /ˌɪntrə'dʌkʃən/ [noun]
1 when a new system or method starts

being used: *This technique has saved thousands of lives since its introduction.*
2 the part at the beginning of a book or piece of writing, that explains what it is about: *I've just started reading the introduction.*

invade /ɪn'veɪd/ [verb; invaded, invading] if one country invades another, its army enters it to take control of it: *Our country has never been invaded.*

invalid /'ɪnvəlɪd/ [noun] someone who is very sick and weak: *She has been an invalid for many years.*

invasion /ɪn'veɪʒən/ [noun] when one country's army enters another country to take control of it: *Napoleon's **invasion** of Russia failed.*

invent * T /ɪn'vɛnt/ [verb; invented, inventing]
1 to think of a new idea for a machine, way of doing something, etc.: *Printing was invented in China.*
2 to think of a story or of something to say that is not true: *I invented an excuse about being sick.*
↪ See also **make up** at MAKE[1] (definition 14).

SYNONYMS invent, discover

When you **invent** something, you think of a new idea yourself: *Who invented the telephone?*
When you **discover** something, you find it for the first time, but it already existed or was already true: *Who discovered the first dinosaur bones?*

---

invention T /ɪn'vɛnʃən/ [noun]
1 a new machine, way of doing something, etc.: *He is trying to sell his invention to a large company.*
2 when someone thinks of a new idea for a machine, way of doing something, etc.: ***The invention of** trains made travel much easier.*

/i/ **see** /ɪ/ **big** /eɪ/ **day** /ɛ/ **get** /æ/ **hat**
/ɑ/ **father, hot** /ʌ/ **up** /ə/ **about** /ɔ/ **saw**
/oʊ/ **hope** /ʊ/ **book** /u/ **too** /aɪ/ **I** /aʊ/ **how**
/ɔɪ/ **boy** /ɜ/ **bird** /ɚ/ **teacher** /ɪr/ **ear** /ɛr/ **air**
/ɑr/ **far** /ɔr/ **more** /ʊr/ **tour** /aɪr/ **fire**
/aʊɚ/ **hour** /θ/ **nothing** /ð/ **mother** /ʃ/ **she**
/ʒ/ **measure** /tʃ/ **church** /dʒ/ **jump** /ŋ/ **long**

inventor /ɪn'vɛntɚ/ [*noun*] the person who invented something new: *Who was the inventor of the steam engine?*

invest /ɪn'vɛst/ [*verb*; **invested, investing**] to buy something or lend money in order to make a profit: *Is it sensible to invest in diamonds?* | **invest something in something** ▸ *He invested all his money in the company.*
➪ *See also* INVESTMENT.

investigate Ⓣ /ɪn'vɛstɪˌgeɪt/ [*verb*; **investigated, investigating**] to try to find information about something, especially a crime: *The police are investigating the incident.*

investigation /ɪnˌvɛstɪ'geɪʃən/ [*noun*] the activity of finding information about something, especially a crime: *a police investigation*

investment /ɪn'vɛstmənt/ [*noun*]
1 something that you buy in order to make or save money: *Property is always a good investment.*
2 when people buy something or lend money in order to make a profit: *an investment account* at a bank

invisible Ⓣ /ɪn'vɪzəbəl/ [*adjective*; no comparative] not able to be seen; *opposite* VISIBLE: *Gravity is an invisible force.*

invitation * /ˌɪnvɪ'teɪʃən/ [*noun*] a request to come to an event: *I got an invitation to their party.*

invite * /ɪn'vaɪt/ [*verb*; **invited, inviting**] to ask someone to come to an event or to do something with you: *How many people are you inviting?* | **invite someone to something** ▸ *They invited 150 people to the wedding.* | **invite someone to do something** ▸ *Should I invite her to join us?*
☛ Do not say "I invite you to come." say **Would you like to come?**

inviting /ɪn'vaɪtɪŋ/ [*adjective*; **more inviting, most inviting**] something that is inviting makes you want to get in it, go to it, or do it: *The swimming pool looked very inviting.*

involve * Ⓣ /ɪn'vɑlv/ [*verb*; **involved, involving**]
1 if an event or situation involves someone or something, that person or thing is part of it: *The project involved two companies.*
2 to allow someone to take part in something or be connected with it: **involve someone in something** ▸ *The other kids don't involve her in their games.*

involved /ɪn'vɑlvd/ [*adjective*; **more involved, most involved**] including someone or something, or taking part in something: *My kids are really involved in sports.*

involvement Ⓣ /ɪn'vɑlvmənt/ [*noun*] when someone takes part in something or is included in it: *He had no involvement in planning the party.*

inward * /'ɪnwɚd/ or **inwards** /'ɪnwɚdz/ [*adverb*] toward the inside, or into a place; *opposite* OUTWARD: *The door opens inward.*

iodine /'aɪəˌdaɪn/ [*noun*] a chemical substance that is often in salt, or is mixed in water and used to clean wounds

IOU /ˌaɪoʊ'yu/ [*noun*] a short form of "I owe you"; a promise, often written, to pay money you have borrowed: *Will you take an IOU? I can pay you next week.*

iris /'aɪrɪs/ [*noun; plural* **irises**] a large blue-purple FLOWER with a long stem

iron¹ * /'aɪɚn/ [*noun*]
1 a heavy heated object you press over clothes to make them smooth and ready to wear
➪ *See the picture at* APPLIANCE.
2 a hard metal used for making tools: *There were iron bars over the window.*

iron² [*verb*; **ironed, ironing**] to press an iron over clothes to make them smooth: *She washed and ironed her dress.*

ironing /'aɪɚnɪŋ/ [*noun*]
1 when you press an iron over clothes to make them smooth: *I hate ironing!* | *Will you **do the ironing** for me?*
2 clothes that are ready to be ironed or have just been ironed: *I have a pile of ironing to do.*

ironing board /'aɪɚnɪŋ ˌbɔrd/ [*noun*] a long board on which clothes are pressed with an iron to make them smooth

irregular * /ɪˈrɛgyələ-/ [adjective; no comparative] GRAMMAR an irregular form of a word is not formed in the usual way; opposite REGULAR: The noun "child" has the irregular plural "children." | "Have" and "eat" are **irregular verbs**.

irrigate /ˈɪrɪˌgeɪt/ [verb; irrigated, irrigating] to bring water into a field for crops: Those hoses irrigate the wheat.

irrigation /ˌɪrɪˈgeɪʃən/ [noun] the process of bringing water into a field for crops: an irrigation system

irritable /ˈɪrɪtəbəl/ [adjective; more irritable, most irritable] easily made angry: He seems very irritable today.

irritate /ˈɪrɪˌteɪt/ [verb; irritated, irritating]
1 if something irritates you, it makes you a little angry, especially because it happens often or all the time; synonym ANNOY: The noise of the TV irritated her.
2 to make a part of your body sore: Wool sweaters irritate my skin.

is * /ɪz/ [verb] the present form of BE that is used with "he," "she," "it," and names: She is five years old. | Is it time to leave?

Islam /ɪsˈlɑm/ [noun] a religion that teaches that there is only one God, called Allah
➪ See also MUSLIM[1].

Islamic /ɪsˈlæmɪk/ [adjective; no comparative] belonging to or connected with the religion that teaches that there is only one God, called Allah; synonym MUSLIM: Islamic law

island * /ˈaɪlənd/ [noun] an area of land that is completely surrounded by water: They live **on an island** near the coast.

isn't * /ˈɪzənt/ the short form of "is not": Mom isn't here right now. | Isn't it hot?

isolate /ˈaɪsəˌleɪt/ [verb; isolated, isolating] to keep someone or something away or separate from others: We must isolate the infected plants.

isolated ⊤ /ˈaɪsəˌleɪtɪd/ [adjective; more isolated, most isolated] a long way from other places; synonym REMOTE: He lives on an isolated farm.

issue[1] /ˈɪʃu/ [noun; plural issues] something that needs to be discussed or dealt with: This issue concerns us all. | **the issue of** racism | He decided to **raise the issue** with his boss (=suggest that it be discussed).

issue[2] [verb; issues, issued, issuing]
1 to make an official statement: The weather service has issued a flood warning.
2 to officially give something to someone: Tickets are issued by mail. | **issue something to someone** ▸ The tour leader issued maps to everyone.

it * /ɪt/ [pronoun]
1 used to talk about something, as the subject of a verb: If you sit on that table, it will break. | "What's that sound?" "It's my beeper."
2 used to talk about something, as the object of a verb or preposition: I picked up the shell and put it in my pocket. | Let me think about it.
3 used to talk about the time, the weather, or the light, as the subject of a verb: It's nearly two o'clock. | It was snowing. | It was dark in the cave.
4 used to describe a fact or situation, as the subject or object of a verb: It was great to be back home. | She found it hard to forgive him.
➪ See also ITS.

IT /ˌaɪˈti/ [noun] information technology; the use of computers to store and show information: an IT department

itch[1] /ɪtʃ/ [verb; itches, itched, itching] if a part of your body itches, you feel that you want to rub or scratch it: My legs itched where the mosquitoes bit me.

itch[2] [noun] a feeling in a part of your body that makes you want to rub or scratch it

itchy /ˈɪtʃi/ [adjective; itchier, itchiest] if a part of your body is itchy, you feel that you want to rub or scratch it: The shirt made her skin itchy.

/i/ see /ɪ/ big /eɪ/ day /ɛ/ get /æ/ hat
/ɑ/ father, hot /ʌ/ up /ə/ about /ɔ/ saw
/oʊ/ hope /ʊ/ book /u/ too /aɪ/ I /aʊ/ how
/ɔɪ/ boy /ɝ/ bird /ɚ/ teacher /ɪr/ ear /ɛr/ air
/ɑr/ far /ɔr/ more /ʊr/ tour /aɪr/ fire
/aʊɚ/ hour /θ/ nothing /ð/ mother /ʃ/ she
/ʒ/ measure /tʃ/ church /dʒ/ jump /ŋ/ long

it'd * /ˈɪtəd/ SPOKEN
  1 the short form of "it had": *It'd rained during the night.*
  ☛ Do not use "it'd" for **it had** when **had** is the main verb. For example, do not say "It'd a funny color." Say **It had a funny color.**
  2 the short form of "it would": *It'd be nice to see you again.*

item ⊤ /ˈaɪtəm/ [*noun*]
  1 used to refer to a single object or thing: *What's the most important item of equipment?* | *an item of clothing*
  2 FORMAL one of a group of things: *She made a list of items to buy.*

it'll * /ˈɪtəl/ SPOKEN the short form of "it will": *It'll be nice to see her again.*

its * /ɪts/ [*determiner*] belonging to or connected with a particular thing, animal, or group: *The town is famous for its fall festival.* | *Look, its wing is broken.*
  ☛ Only use **its** before a noun.
  ⇨ *See the usage note at* IT'S.

it's * /ɪts/
  1 the short form of "it is": *It's great to see you again.* | *It's ten to four.*
  2 the short form of "it has": *It's been very cold lately.*
  ☛ Do not use "it's" for **it has** when **has** is the main verb. For example, do not say "I like this flower. It's a nice smell." Say **It has a nice smell.**

USAGE   it's, its

  Do not confuse **it's** and **its**. **It's** is the short form of **it is** or **it has**: *It's still raining.* | *It's been a great day.* **Its** is the possessive form of **it**: *The tree had lost its leaves.*

---

itself * /ɪtˈsɛlf/ [*pronoun*]
  1 used to say that the animal or thing affected by an action is the animal or thing doing it: *The monkey was scratching itself.*
  ☛ Do not use **itself** as a subject. For example, do not say "Itself climbed the tree." Say **It climbed the tree itself.**
  2 used to emphasize a particular thing: *The garage needed repairs, but the house itself was in good condition.*

══ PHRASE ══
  3 by itself without any help, or without needing a person to do something: *A baby horse can walk by itself.* | *The alarm will stop by itself.*

I've * /aɪv/ the short form of "I have": *I've never been in an airplane.*
  ☛ Don't use "I've" for **I have** if **have** is the main verb. For example, do not say "I've a ticket to the concert." Say **I have a ticket to the concert.**

ivory /ˈaɪvəri/ [*noun*] the hard cream-colored substance that an elephant's long teeth are made of: *a carved figure made of ivory*

J

J * or **j** /dʒeɪ/ [*noun; plural* Js or J's, j's] the tenth letter of the English alphabet
  ⇨ *See the usage note at* ALPHABET.

jab[1] /dʒæb/ [*verb;* **jabs, jabbed, jabbing**] to push someone or something quickly with your finger or a pointed object: **jab someone/ something with something** ▸ *She jabbed me with her umbrella.*

jab[2] [*noun*] a sudden, hard push with a pointed object: *I felt a jab in my arm.*

jack /dʒæk/ [*noun*] an object used to lift something heavy, such as a car, off the ground: *I need the jack to change the tire.*

jacket * /ˈdʒækɪt/ [*noun*]
  1 a short coat, or the top part of a suit: *She was wearing a denim jacket.*

collar   lapel

denim jacket   sports jacket

jackets

2 a paper cover on the outside of a book which protects it: *Try not to tear the jacket.*

jack-o'-lantern /'dʒæk ə ˌlæntə-n/ [*noun*] a pumpkin with a face cut into it and a lit candle inside, used as a decoration at Halloween: *Do you want to help carve the jack-o'-lantern?*

jackpot /'dʒæk,pat/ [*noun*] a large amount of money that you win in a game of chance: *The lottery jackpot is now $5 million.*

jade /dʒeɪd/ [*noun*] a green stone used for making jewelry and attractive objects: *a jade necklace*

jagged /'dʒægɪd/ [*adjective;* **more jagged, most jagged**] having a rough, sharp edge: *She cut her hand on a jagged piece of glass.*

jail¹ /dʒeɪl/ [*noun*] a place where people are locked in as an official punishment for a crime: *He was in jail because he robbed a store.* | *They are moving her from the local jail to a large prison.*
↪ *Compare* PRISON.

jail² [*verb;* **jailed, jailing**] to put someone in jail as an official punishment: *He was jailed for theft.*
↪ *Compare* IMPRISON.

jailer /'dʒeɪlə-/ [*noun*] someone who guards people in a jail or keeps someone in a jail: *His jailers treated him badly.*

jam¹ /dʒæm/ [*noun*]
1 a thick, sweet food made from boiled fruit and sugar, that has pieces of fruit in it: *Do you want some strawberry jam on your toast?*
↪ *Compare* JELLY.
2 when a large number of people or things fill a place so tightly that they cannot move: *a traffic jam*

jam² [*verb;* **jams, jammed, jamming**]
1 to push something into a small space using a lot of force: *I jammed the things into the box and shut the lid.*
2 to fill a space with people or things until there is no more room: *Times Square was jammed with people.*
3 if a machine jams or if you jam it, it stops working because something is preventing it from moving: *The fax*

machine has jammed again. | *I had somehow jammed the lock.*

jammed /dʒæmd/ [*adjective; no comparative*] stuck between two surfaces and very difficult to move: *My foot was jammed in the door.*

Jan. the written abbreviation of JANUARY

jangle /'dʒæŋgəl/ [*verb;* **jangled, jangling**] if metal things jangle or if you jangle them, they make a sound when they hit each other: *The coins in his pocket jangled as he walked.* | *Please stop jangling your keys.*

janitor /'dʒænɪtə-/ [*noun*] someone whose job is to take care of a building

January * /'dʒænyuˌɛri/ [*noun*] the first month of the year: *It's my birthday on January 2nd.* | *He graduated in January.*
↪ *See the usage note at* MONTH.

jar /dʒɑr/ [*noun*] a glass CONTAINER with a wide top and a lid: *a jar of peanuts*

jaw * /dʒɔ/ [*noun*] one of the two parts of your face that contain your teeth, especially the lower part
↪ *See the picture at* BODY.

jazz /dʒæz/ [*noun*] music that has a strong beat and was first played in the city of New Orleans in the U.S.: *a jazz musician*

jealous /'dʒɛləs/ [*adjective;* **more jealous, most jealous**]
1 unhappy because you do not have something that someone else has; *synonym* ENVIOUS: *She was jealous of her sister's good grades.*
2 unhappy because someone you love seems to like another person more than you: *He was jealous when his wife talked to the neighbor.*

jealousy /'dʒɛləsi/ [*noun*] the unhappy feeling you have when you wish you had what someone else has; *synonym* ENVY: *Jealousy can harm a relationship.*

jeans /dʒinz/ [*plural noun*] pants that are made of a strong, usually blue, cotton

---

/i/ **see** /ɪ/ **big** /eɪ/ **day** /ɛ/ **get** /æ/ **hat**
/ɑ/ **father, hot** /ʌ/ **up** /ə/ **about** /ɔ/ **saw**
/oʊ/ **hope** /ʊ/ **book** /u/ **too** /aɪ/ **I** /aʊ/ **how**
/ɔɪ/ **boy** /ɝ/ **bird** /ɚ/ **teacher** /ɪr/ **ear** /ɛr/ **air**
/ɑr/ **far** /ɔr/ **more** /ʊr/ **tour** /aɪr/ **fire**
/aʊɚ/ **hour** /θ/ **nothing** /ð/ **mother** /ʃ/ **she**
/ʒ/ **measure** /tʃ/ **church** /dʒ/ **jump** /ŋ/ **long**

cloth called "denim": *I don't wear jeans to school.* | *a pair of jeans*

Jeep /dʒip/ [*noun*] TRADEMARK a vehicle that is made for traveling over rough ground; synonym **SUV**: *You need a Jeep to travel in these mountain areas.*

jeer /dʒɪr/ [*verb*; **jeered, jeering**] to laugh or shout in a rude way to show that you do not like or admire someone: *They were jeering loudly at the other team.*

Jell-O /'dʒɛloʊ/ [*noun*] TRADEMARK a sweet food that tastes like fruit and that becomes solid when it is cold: *lime Jell-O*

jelly /'dʒɛli/ [*noun*; *plural* **jellies**] a thick sweet food made from boiled fruit juice and sugar without any fruit pieces in it: *a jar of grape jelly* | *They make their own jellies.*
➪ *Compare* JAM¹ (definition 1).

jellyfish /'dʒɛli,fɪʃ/ [*noun*; *plural* **jellyfish**] a soft transparent sea creature that can sting people

jerk¹ /dʒɜrk/ [*verb*; **jerked, jerking**] to pull something hard or move with a quick, sudden movement: *She jerked the door open.* | *The car jerked forward.* | *He jerked his hand away from the oven.*

jerk² [*noun*]
1 an annoying person: *Don't pay attention to that jerk.*
2 a hard, sudden pull on something: *I gave the rope a jerk.*

jersey /'dʒɜrzi/ [*noun*; *plural* **jerseys**] a soft shirt or sweater, worn especially by people playing sports: *a football jersey*

Jesus /'dʒizəs/ or **Jesus Christ** /'dʒizəs 'kraɪst/ [*name*] the man whose life and beliefs the Christian religion is based on

jet /dʒɛt/ [*noun*]
1 a kind of airplane that can go very fast: *a private jet*
2 an amount of water or gas that comes out fast from a small hole: *A jet of water shot from the fountain.*

jet lag /'dʒɛt ,læg/ [*noun*] the feeling of being tired that you have when you have flown a very long way: *I had jet lag when I came back from Europe.*

jewel * /'dʒuəl/ [*noun*] a valuable stone such as a diamond: *The jewels in her necklace sparkled.*

jeweler /'dʒuələr/ [*noun*] someone who makes or sells jewelry: *The jeweler showed them a range of rings.*

jewelry * /'dʒuəlri/ [*noun*] things such as rings and necklaces that you wear for decoration

ring
earring
bracelet
necklace

jewelry

Jewish /'dʒuɪʃ/ [*adjective*; *no comparative*] relating to the religion of Judaism or the people who have this religion: *They had a Jewish wedding ceremony.*

jigsaw puzzle /'dʒɪgsɔ ,pʌzəl/ [*noun*] a picture cut into many small pieces that you put together for fun: *I'm doing a 1,000-piece jigsaw puzzle.*

jingle /'dʒɪŋgəl/ [*verb*; **jingled, jingling**] if metal things jingle or if you jingle them, they make a pleasant sound like small bells: *Her bracelets jingled as she danced.* | *He jingled his keys.*

job * /dʒɑb/ [*noun*]
1 work that you do regularly to get money, especially in a business: *My father has a job in a factory.*
➪ *See the usage note at* WORK¹.
2 a piece of work that you must do: *I have a few jobs to do this morning.*
━━ PHRASE ━━
3 on the job working at a particular job: *He's been on the job here for a year.*

jockey /'dʒɑki/ [*noun*; *plural* **jockeys**] someone whose job is to ride horses in races: *Jockeys are usually small.*

jog¹ /dʒɑg/ [*verb*; **jogs, jogged, jogging**]
1 to run fairly slowly as a way of exercising: *She jogs around the park every morning.*
2 to push something slightly, usually by mistake: *I accidentally jogged her elbow.*

jog² [*noun*] a slow run that you do as a way of exercising, especially outdoors: *Do you want to go for a jog?*

jogger Ⓣ /'dʒɑgɚ/ [*noun*] someone who runs slowly as a way of exercising

jogging /'dʒɑgɪŋ/ [*noun*] the activity of running slowly as a way of exercising: *I like jogging and playing basketball.*

join * /dʒɔɪn/ [*verb*; **joined, joining**]
  1 to become a member of a group or organization: *She joined the school chess club.* | *I want to join the army.*
  2 to connect things together or to become connected: *The two rivers join here.* | *I wasn't sure how to join the pieces of wood together.* | *Everybody join hands* (=hold the hand of the person beside you).
  3 to do something with someone else or go to where he or she is: *Would you like to join us for coffee?* | *He joined them after a few minutes.* | *We'll join up with the others at Karen's house.*
══ PHRASAL VERB ══
join in [*phrasal verb*]
  4 to take part in an activity, play a game, etc., with other people: *The other kids are playing. Why don't you join in?* | *join in something* ▶ *We all joined in the singing.*

joint¹ * /dʒɔɪnt/ [*noun*]
  1 a place in your body where two bones meet, that bends: *the joints of the fingers*
  2 the place where two parts or pieces meet: *a pipe joint*

joint² * [*adjective*; no comparative] shared, owned, or done by two or more people: *It was a joint decision.* | *My wife and I have a joint bank account.*
☞ Only use **joint** before a noun.

jointly /'dʒɔɪntli/ [*adverb*] together, in an equal way: *Parents are jointly responsible for their children.*

joke¹ * /dʒoʊk/ [*noun*] something that you say or do in order to make someone laugh: *I know a really good joke about a frog.* | *I like to tell jokes.*

joke² * [*verb*; **joked, joking**]
  1 to say something to make someone laugh: *We were laughing and joking.*
  2 to say something that is not true, as

a joke; *synonym* KID: *Don't be angry—I was only joking!*

jolt¹ /dʒoʊlt/ [*noun*]
  1 a sudden rough movement: *There was a jolt as the plane landed.*
  2 a sudden strong feeling, especially of surprise or shock: *a jolt of excitement*

jolt² [*verb*; **jolted, jolting**] to make a sudden rough movement or many movements like this: *We jolted along the road in the old truck.*

jot /dʒɑt/ [*verb*; **jots, jotted, jotting**]
══ PHRASAL VERB ══
jot down [*phrasal verb*]
to write something quickly on a piece of paper: *jot down something* ▶ *Wait, let me jot down your address.*

journal /'dʒɝnəl/ [*noun*]
  1 a magazine for people who do a particular job or have a particular interest: *a business journal* | *a medical journal*
  2 a book in which you write what you think and feel, and what happened during the day; *synonym* DIARY: *He kept a journal while he was in India.*

journalism /'dʒɝnəl,ɪzəm/ [*noun*] the work of writing for a newspaper, magazine, or news program: *I would like to have a career in journalism.*

journalist /'dʒɝnəlɪst/ [*noun*] someone who writes for a newspaper, magazine, or news program: *He's a journalist for a local radio station.*

journey * /'dʒɝni/ [*noun*; plural **journeys**] a long trip from one place to another: *I was tired after the journey.* | *a twelve-hour journey by train*

joy /dʒɔɪ/ [*noun*; plural **joys**]
  1 when you feel extremely happy: *Their children brought them great joy.*
  2 something that makes you feel extremely happy: *My puppy is a real joy.* | *the joys of teaching*

joyful /'dʒɔɪfəl/ [*adjective*; **more joyful, most joyful**] feeling very happy, or

/i/ see	/ɪ/ big	/eɪ/ day	/ɛ/ get	/æ/ hat
/ɑ/ father, hot	/ʌ/ up	/ə/ about	/ɔ/ saw
/oʊ/ hope	/ʊ/ book	/u/ too	/aɪ/ I	/aʊ/ how
/ɔɪ/ boy	/ɝ/ bird	/ɚ/ teacher	/ɪr/ ear	/ɛr/ air
/ɑr/ far	/ɔr/ more	/ʊr/ tour	/aɪr/ fire
/aʊɚ/ hour	/θ/ nothing	/ð/ mother	/ʃ/ she
/ʒ/ measure	/tʃ/ church	/dʒ/ jump	/ŋ/ long

making people very happy: *Weddings are joyful celebrations.*

joystick /'dʒɔɪˌstɪk/ [*noun*] an upright handle that you use to change the direction in which something moves, for example in a plane or a computer game: *You play this game using a joystick.*

Jr. a written abbreviation of **JUNIOR**, used after a man's name when he has the same name as his father: *Thomas Brown, Jr.*

Judaism /'dʒudiˌɪzəm/ [*noun*] the Jewish religion, based on the first part of the Bible and other books

judge¹ * /dʒʌdʒ/ [*verb*; **judged, judging**]
1 to form an opinion about something, especially after thinking about it carefully: *I don't know enough about it to judge.* | **judge which/where/what** etc. ▸ *I can never judge when a turkey is cooked.* | **judge someone/something by something** ▸ *People often judge you by the way you look.*
2 to decide who has won a competition: *He's going to judge the art competition.*

judge² * [*noun*]
1 the person in charge of a court of law, who decides what punishment a criminal should have: *The judge sentenced him to five years in jail.*
2 someone who decides who has won a competition: *The judges gave her a 9.5.*

judgment * /'dʒʌdʒmənt/ [*noun*]
1 an opinion that you form after thinking carefully: ***In my judgment** she's a great teacher* (=I think she's a great teacher). | *It's hard to **make a judgment** without knowing all the facts.*
2 the ability to form correct opinions or make good decisions: *I'm trusting you to **use good judgment.***

judo /'dʒudoʊ/ [*noun*] a Japanese fighting sport in which people try to throw each other onto the ground
▷ See also **MARTIAL ART.**

jug /dʒʌg/ [*noun*] a container with a narrow top and a small handle, for holding liquids: *We keep a big **jug of** water in the car.*

handle

a jug

juggle /'dʒʌgəl/ [*verb*; **juggled, juggling**] to keep three or more things moving through the air by throwing and catching them many times: *He was juggling three balls.*

He's **juggling** balls.

juggler /'dʒʌglɚ/ [*noun*] someone who juggles objects to entertain people: *The juggler was very skillful.*

juice * T /dʒus/ [*noun*] liquid from fruit or vegetables: *a glass of orange juice* | *Could I have some juice, please?* | *a drink made from different fruit juices*

juicy * /'dʒusi/ [*adjective*; **juicier, juiciest**] fruits or vegetables that are juicy have a lot of liquid in them: *a nice juicy peach*

Jul. the written abbreviation of **JULY**

July * /dʒʊˈlaɪ/ [*noun*] the seventh month of the year: *It's Will's birthday **on** July 8th.* | *We're going to Europe **in** July.*
▷ See the usage note at **MONTH.**

jumble /'dʒʌmbəl/ [*noun*] a lot of things mixed together without being organized: *a **jumble of** toys in the closet*

jumbo /'dʒʌmboʊ/ [*adjective*; no comparative] extremely large: *Buy the jumbo box of detergent.*

jump¹ * /dʒʌmp/ [*verb*; **jumped, jumping**]
1 to push yourself up into the air using your legs: *She **jumped across** the stream.* | *He **jumped over** the gate.* | *The kids **were jumping up and down** with excitement* (=jumping a lot of times in one place).
▷ See the picture at **MOVEMENT.**
2 if you jump when something happens suddenly, your body makes a sudden movement: *A loud noise made me jump.*
3 to suddenly move on or off, or in or out of something: *He **jumped off** the wall.* | ***Jump in** and I'll give you a ride home.* | *They **jumped out of** the car.* | *We **jumped onto** the train.*

4 to suddenly increase in amount or size: *Home sales jumped in May.*

— PHRASE —

5 **jump rope** to keep jumping over a rope which is being moved up over your head and down again: *The kids were jumping rope in the playground.*

She's **jumping rope**.

jump² * [*noun*] when you jump: *a very high jump*

jumper /'dʒʌmpɚ/ [*noun*] a dress without sleeves which is worn over a shirt or sweater

▷ *See the picture at* CLOTHING.

jump rope /'dʒʌmp ˌroʊp/ [*noun*] a piece of rope that children jump over when it is moving, as a game: *The girls were playing with a jump rope.*

Jun. the written abbreviation of JUNE

June * /dʒun/ [*noun*] the sixth month of the year: *Their wedding is on June 28th.* | *We moved here in June.*

▷ *See the usage note at* MONTH.

jungle /'dʒʌŋgəl/ [*noun*] a forest where a lot of plants grow closely together, especially in a warm, wet place: *Many rare animals live in jungles.* | *an area of jungle*

▷ *See the usage note at* RAIN FOREST.

junior¹ /'dʒunyɚ/ [*adjective; no comparative*]

1 having a fairly low rank in an organization; *opposite* SENIOR: *junior employee*

2 relating to the third year of high school or college: *He's in his junior year.*

junior² [*noun*] a student who is in the year before the last year of high school or college: *She is a junior this year.*

▷ *Compare* FRESHMAN, SOPHOMORE, SENIOR².

Junior [*adjective*] used after the name of a man who has the same name as his father, often in the form "Jr.": *Thomas Brown, Junior*

▷ *Compare* SENIOR.

junior college /'dʒunyɚ 'kɑlɪdʒ/ [*noun*] a college in the U.S. where students study for two years

junior high school /'dʒunyɚ 'haɪ ˌskul/ or **junior high** [*noun*] a school in the U.S. for students between the ages of 12 and 13 or 14

▷ *Compare* MIDDLE SCHOOL.

junk /dʒʌŋk/ [*noun*] things that you do not want because they are old or not useful: *an attic full of junk*

junk food 🔲 /'dʒʌŋk ˌfud/ [*noun*] food that is not good for you because it has a lot of sugar or fat in it

junk mail /'dʒʌŋk ˌmeɪl/ [*noun*] advertisements that you get in the mail

Jupiter /'dʒupɪtɚ/ [*name*] the planet that is fifth from our sun

juror /'dʒʊrɚ/ [*noun*] one of the people who decide whether someone is guilty in a court of law: *a juror in a murder trial*

jury 🔲 /'dʒʊri/ [*noun; plural* **juries**] a group of people who decide whether someone is guilty in a court of law: *The jury decided that he was not guilty.*

just¹ * /dʒʌst/ [*adverb*]

1 a short time ago: *He just left.*

2 not more than a particular number or amount; *synonym* ONLY: *We have just enough money for the train fare.*

3 involving one thing or person and nothing more; *synonym* ONLY: *The movie is just for adults.* | *I'm not just interested in his money.*

4 used to emphasize that something is exactly right, exactly the same, etc.: *The picture looks just right in this room.* | *She looks just like her mother!* | *That's just what I said!*

5 used to emphasize that something or someone is not at all serious, important, dangerous, etc.; *synonyms* MERELY, ONLY: *I just called to see how you are* | *He's just a delivery boy.* | *It's just a cold, not the flu.*

6 used to say that something is nearly not possible or nearly did not happen: *I can just reach the top shelf.* | *He arrived just in time to catch the plane.*

/i/ **see**	/ɪ/ **big**	/eɪ/ **day**	/ɛ/ **get** /æ/ **hat**
/a/ **father, hot**	/ʌ/ **up**	/ə/ **about**	/ɔ/ **saw**
/oʊ/ **hope**	/ʊ/ **book**	/u/ **too**	/aɪ/ **I** /aʊ/ **how**
/ɔɪ/ **boy**	/ɝ/ **bird**	/ɚ/ **teacher**	/ɪr/ **ear** /ɛr/ **air**
/ɑr/ **far**	/ɔr/ **more**	/ʊr/ **tour**	/aɪr/ **fire**
/aʊɚ/ **hour**	/θ/ **nothing**	/ð/ **mother**	/ʃ/ **she**
/ʒ/ **measure**	/tʃ/ **church**	/dʒ/ **jump**	/ŋ/ **long**

7 used to emphasize that something should not be hard to do: *Wait—I'll just see if he's here.* | *Will you just listen for a minute?*

═══ PHRASES ═══

8 be just doing something to be doing something at this moment: *I'm just eating dinner. I'll call you later.*

9 be just about to do something to be going to do something very soon: *We're just about to go out.*

10 just about almost: *I'm just about ready to go.*

11 just a minute/second/moment used to tell someone to wait for a short time: *Just a minute—I'll go see if I can find it.*

12 just before/after/under/etc. a little before, after, less than, etc.: *The*

flight was just under three hours.* | *I saw him just before he went on vacation.*

13 just now a short time ago, or at this moment: *Jack called just now to see if you were home yet.*

just^2 [*adjective; no comparative*] fair or morally right: *a just cause* (=something you believe in and work for because it is right)

justice * /'dʒʌstɪs/ [*noun*]
  1 a state in which things are right and fair: *Justice can be difficult to achieve.*
  ⇨ Compare INJUSTICE.
  2 the legal system in a country: *The country has a good justice system.*

juvenile /'dʒuvənaɪl/ [*adjective; no comparative*] FORMAL relating to children or young people: *juvenile crime* (=illegal things done by children)

K

K * or **k** /keɪ/ [*noun; plural* **Ks** or **K's, k's**] the 11th letter of the English alphabet
⇨ See the usage note at ALPHABET.

kangaroo /ˌkæŋgə'ru/ [*noun; plural* **kangaroos**] a large Australian animal that has very strong back legs for jumping and a pocket for its baby on its front: *A baby kangaroo is called a "joey."*

karate /kə'rɑti/ [*noun*] a kind of fighting sport in which you attack with your hands and feet
⇨ See also MARTIAL ART.

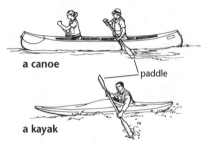

a canoe

paddle

a kayak

kayak /'kaɪæk/ [*noun*] a long, narrow boat that is usually built for one person

KB the written abbreviation of KILOBYTE or KILOBYTES: *The document is 78KB.*

a kangaroo

keep * /kip/ [*verb;* **kept, keeping**]
  1 to continue to have something or not give something back: *You can keep that book—I have another copy.*
  2 [*linking*] to stay in a particular condition or position: *I can't take your picture unless you keep still.* | *There's been an accident—**keep back** (=don't come any closer).* | ***Keep in touch!*** (=call or write to me sometime)
  ⇨ See also STAY^1 (definition 2).
  3 to make someone or something stay in a particular condition or position: *He kept his hands in his pockets.* | *A fan kept the room cool.* | *Keep that cat away from me!* | **keep someone up** ▸ *Their loud music kept me up* (=made me stay awake) *all night.*

place or container: *Where do you keep your envelopes?*

5 if food keeps, it stays fresh enough to be eaten: *Will the fish keep until tomorrow?*

— **PHRASES** —

6 keep (on) doing something to repeat an action a lot of times or to continue doing something: *You keep making the same mistakes in your math.* | *He just kept on driving.*

7 keep a secret to not tell anyone about something that is secret: *My sister can't keep a secret.*

8 keep a promise or **keep your word** to do what you have promised to do: *I know he'll keep his word.*

9 keep out used to tell people not to enter a place: *Private property. Keep out.* | *Keep out of here! This is my room!*

▷ *See also* **lose/keep your temper** *at* TEMPER *and* **keep your head** *at* HEAD[1].

— **PHRASAL VERBS** —

keep off [*phrasal verb*]

10 to prevent water, dust, or light from touching or damaging something: **keep something off something** ▸ *Wear a hat to keep the sun off your head.* | **keep off something** ▸ *They used a plastic sheet to keep off the rain.*

keep out [*phrasal verb*]

11 to prevent someone or something from getting into a place: **keep someone/something out** ▸ *An alarm may help keep burglars out.* | **keep out someone/something** ▸ *You need a heavier coat to keep out the cold.*

keep up [*phrasal verb*]

12 to continue doing something: **keep up something** ▸ *Keep up the good work.* | **keep something up** ▸ *I can't keep this up much longer.*

13 to move or do things as quickly as other people: *It was hard to **keep up with** the other students.*

kennel /'kɛnəl/ [*noun*] a place where dogs are kept while their owners are away from home: *Our dog stayed in the kennel when we went away.*

kept * /kɛpt/ [*verb*] the past tense and past participle of KEEP

ketchup /'kɛtʃəp/ [*noun*] a thick red sauce made from tomatoes: *Would you like some ketchup on your burger?*

kettle /'kɛtəl/ [*noun*] a container with a handle and a lid, used for boiling water: *I'll **put the kettle on** (=boil water in a kettle) and make some coffee.*

key[1] * /ki/ [*noun; plural* **keys**]

1 a shaped piece of metal used to open or lock a door, start a car, etc.: *Do you remember where I put my house keys?*

keys

2 one of the small buttons on a computer or typewriter that you press when you are using it: *What does this key do?*

3 one of the thin black or white bars on a piano that you press when you are playing it: *Don't hit the keys so hard.*

4 a set of musical notes that starts on a particular note: *This piece of music is* **in the key of** *G.*

key[2] ⊤ [*adjective; no comparative*] very important or most important: *These are the key words you need to know.*

☛ Only use **key** before a noun.

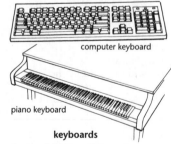

computer keyboard

piano keyboard

keyboards

keyboard /'ki,bɔrd/ [*noun*]

1 a row or several rows of keys on a computer: *Is the keyboard connected to the computer correctly?*

2 the part of a piano, organ, etc., where the keys are

/i/ **see** /ɪ/ **big** /eɪ/ **day** /ɛ/ **get** /æ/ **hat**
/ɑ/ **father, hot** /ʌ/ **up** /ə/ **about** /ɔ/ **saw**
/oʊ/ **hope** /ʊ/ **book** /u/ **too** /aɪ/ **I** /aʊ/ **how**
/ɔɪ/ **boy** /ɝ/ **bird** /ɚ/ **teacher** /ɪr/ **ear** /ɛr/ **air**
/ɑr/ **far** /ɔr/ **more** /ʊr/ **tour** /aɪr/ **fire**
/aʊɚ/ **hour** /θ/ **nothing** /ð/ **mother** /ʃ/ **she**
/ʒ/ **measure** /tʃ/ **church** /dʒ/ **jump** /ŋ/ **long**

3 any musical instrument, such as a piano, electric piano, organ, etc., that you play by pressing keys: *She plays keyboards in a band.*

keyhole /'ki,hoʊl/ [*noun*] the small hole in a lock that you put a key into: *She looked through the keyhole.*

key ring /'ki ,rɪŋ/ [*noun*] a small metal ring that you keep your KEYs on

kg the written abbreviation of KILOGRAM or KILOGRAMS: *1 kg of sugar*

khaki[1] /'kæki/ [*noun*] a pale yellow-brown color: *The socks come in green, brown, and khaki.*

khaki[2] [*adjective; no comparative*] of the color khaki: *He wore a khaki shirt and a brown tie*

khakis /'kækiz/ [*plural noun*] pants made of yellow-brown cloth: *He wore a plaid shirt and khakis.*

kick[1] * /kɪk/ [*verb; kicked, kicking*]
1 to hit something or someone with your foot: *Kevin, stop kicking! | Mom, David kicked me. | He kicked the ball across the yard.*
⇨ *See the picture at* PLAY[1].

━━ PHRASAL VERBS ━━

kick off [*phrasal verb*]
2 INFORMAL to start doing something such as a sports game or event, or to make it start: *The celebrations will kick off at noon.*

kick out [*phrasal verb*]
3 INFORMAL to make someone leave a place: **kick out someone** ▸ *They kicked out anyone causing trouble at the dance. | **kick someone out** ▸ The school kicked him out again.*

kick[2] * [*noun*]
1 when you kick something: *Italy scored with the last kick of the ball.*
2 INFORMAL a feeling of excitement or pleasure: *Some kids try stealing just* **for kicks.** *| She gets a real* **kick out of** *playing golf.*

kickoff /'kɪk,ɔf/ [*noun*] when a game of football or soccer starts: *The crowd was waiting for the kickoff. | Kickoff will be at three o'clock.*

kid[1] /kɪd/ [*noun*]
1 INFORMAL a child or young person: *The*

kids are out playing in the yard. | You can't blame Lisa—she's just a kid.
⇨ *See the synonym note at* CHILD.
2 a young goat, or the leather made from its skin: *a goat and its kid | kid gloves*

kid[2] [*verb; kids, kidded, kidding*]
INFORMAL
1 to say something that is not true, as a joke: *He said everyone left, but he was just kidding. | You're kidding me!*

━━ PHRASE ━━

2 kid yourself to allow yourself to believe something is true when it is not true: *Don't kid yourself. She'll never change.*

kidnap /'kɪdnæp/ [*verb; kidnaps, kidnapped, kidnapping*] to take someone away illegally and keep him or her until money or something else is given: *The son of a rich businessman has been kidnapped.*

kidnapper /'kɪdnæpɚ/ [*noun*] someone who takes someone away illegally: *His kidnappers are demanding $100,000.*

kidney /'kɪdni/ [*noun; plural kidneys*] one of the two organs in your body that remove waste from your blood

kill * /kɪl/ [*verb; killed, killing*] to make a person or other living thing die: *His mother was killed in a car crash. | Frost killed my tomato plant.*
⇨ *Compare* MURDER[1].

killer /'kɪlɚ/ [*noun*] a person, animal, or disease that kills: *Heart disease is a major killer.*

kilo * /'kiloʊ/ [*noun; plural kilos*] the short form of KILOGRAM: *four kilos of rice*

kilobyte /'kɪlə,baɪt/ [*noun*] a unit for measuring computer information, equal to 1024 bytes: *The file is 27 kilobytes.*

kilogram * /'kɪlə,græm/ [*noun*] a unit for measuring weight, equal to 1,000 grams: *My luggage weighs twenty kilograms.*

kilometer * /kɪ'lɑmɪtɚ/ [*noun*] a unit for measuring distance, equal to 1,000 meters: *There's a gas station a few kilometers down the road.*

kimono /kə'moʊnə/ [*noun; plural* **kimonos**] a long loose coat with a wide belt and wide sleeves, traditionally worn in Japan

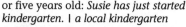

kin /kɪn/ [*noun*] family members: *a dead person's next of kin* (=closest relative)
☛ Only use **kin** with a plural verb.
⇨ *See also* RELATION (definition 1), RELATIVE[1].

kind[1] * /kaɪnd/ [*noun*] a member of a group of people or things that are similar in some way; *synonym* TYPE: *What kind of music do you like?* | *There were all kinds of people in the restaurant* (=many different kinds). | *Dogs of this kind are usually friendly.*
⇨ *See also* KIND OF. ⇨ *See the usage note at* TYPE[1].

a kimono

kind[2] * [*adjective;* **kinder, kindest**] helpful and nice toward other people; *opposites* MEAN, UNKIND: *Thank you for your kind offer of help.* | *It was very kind of you to let us borrow your car.* | *Her mother has been very kind to us.*
⇨ *See also* KINDLY, KINDNESS.

SYNONYMS   kind, considerate, generous

If someone is **kind**, he or she tries to help people or make them happy: *Thank you for being so kind.*

If someone is **considerate**, he or she thinks about people's feelings and is careful not to upset them: *I wish you'd be more considerate.*

If someone is **generous**, he or she often helps people by giving them money or gifts: *It was very generous of you to pay for my ticket.*

---

kind of * /'kaɪnd əv/ [*adverb*] SPOKEN a little; *synonym* SLIGHTLY: *I was feeling kind of shy.* | *"Are you tired?" "Kind of."*

kindergarten /'kɪndɚˌgɑrtən/ [*noun*] a class or school for children who are four

or five years old: *Susie has just started kindergarten.* | *a local kindergarten*

kindhearted /'kaɪnd'hɑrtɪd/ [*adjective; no comparative*] always ready to be helpful and nice: *She's always been a kindhearted woman.*

kindly /'kaɪndli/ [*adverb*]
1 done in a friendly and helpful way: *Peter kindly offered me a ride.*
2 SPOKEN FORMAL used to mean "please" when you are annoyed: *Would you kindly stop doing that?*

kindness /'kaɪndnɪs/ [*noun*] kind behavior or a kind action: *I'll never forget your kindness to me.*

king * /kɪŋ/ [*noun*] the male ruler of a country: *King Henry VIII* | *the king of Spain*

kingdom /'kɪŋdəm/ [*noun*] the country ruled by a king or queen: *the kingdom of Thailand*

king-size /'kɪŋ ˌsaɪz/ or **king-sized** /'kɪŋ ˌsaɪzd/ [*adjective; no comparative*] very large: *a king-size bed*
☛ Only use **king-size** and **king-sized** before a noun.

kiss[1] * /kɪs/ [*verb;* **kisses, kissed, kissing**] to touch someone with your lips to show your love or as a greeting: *The child kissed her on the cheek.* | *She kissed me goodbye* (=said goodbye by kissing me).

kiss[2] * [*noun; plural* **kisses**] when you touch someone with your lips: *He gave her a kiss on the cheek.*

kit /kɪt/ [*noun*]
1 a set of tools or pieces of equipment that you need to do a particular activity: *He got a screwdriver from his tool kit.* | *Where's the first-aid kit?* (=things for treating small injuries)
2 something that is sold in parts which you put together yourself: *We made the model airplane from a kit.*

---

kitchen * /'kɪtʃən/ [*noun*] the room in which food is prepared and cooked: *We usually eat in the kitchen.* | *a kitchen table*

kite /kaɪt/ [*noun*] a toy that can fly in the air on the end of a long string, made of a light frame covered with paper or plastic: *Let's fly our kites.*

tail

kitten /'kɪtən/ [*noun*] a young cat: *Our cat just had three kittens.*

a kite

kiwi fruit /'kiwi ˌfrut/ [*noun; plural* **kiwi fruits** or **kiwi fruit**] a FRUIT that is green inside and has a hairy brown skin

Kleenex /'klinɛks/ [*noun; plural* **Kleenex**] TRADEMARK a piece of soft thin paper used especially for drying your nose and eyes; *synonym* TISSUE

km the written abbreviation of KILOMETER or KILOMETERS: *Toronto—48 km*

knead /nid/ [*verb;* **kneaded, kneading**] to press a soft material, such as clay or a mixture of flour and water, with your hands to make it smooth: *Knead the dough for ten minutes.*

knee * /ni/ [*noun; plural* **knees**]
1 the joint in the middle of your leg where it bends: *Bend your knees when you lift something heavy.* | *He got down on his knees* (=knelt down).
— PHRASE —
2 on someone's knee on the top part of someone's leg, when he or she is sitting down: *Come, sit on my knee.* ↪ *Compare* LAP¹ (definition 1).

kneecap /'niˌkæp/ [*noun*] the round bone at the front of the knee

knee-deep /'ni 'dip/ [*adjective; no comparative*] deep enough to reach from the ground to your knees: *The water here is only knee-deep.*

kneel * /nil/ [*verb;* **knelt** /nɛlt/ or **kneeled, kneeling**] to be in or move into a position in which your knees are on the ground: *A man was kneeling by the injured boy.* | *We knelt down to pray.*

knew * /nu/ [*verb*] the past tense of KNOW

knife * /naɪf/ [*noun; plural* **knives**] a tool with a short handle and a sharp flat part, which is used for cutting things or as a weapon: *He picked up his knife and fork and started to eat.* | *a bread knife* | *a carving knife*
↪ *See the picture at* PLACE SETTING.

knight /naɪt/ [*noun*] a man of high rank in the Middle Ages, who fought while riding a horse: *One of the king's knights rode forward.*

knit /nɪt/ [*verb;* **knits, knitted** or **knit, knitting**] to make clothes out of thick thread or wool, using thick needles or a machine: *Can you knit?* | **knit someone something** ▸ *She's knitting me a sweater.*

knitting needle /'nɪtɪŋ ˌnidəl/ [*noun*] one of the two long sticks that you use to knit something: *a pair of knitting needles*
↪ *See the picture at* NEEDLE.

knives * /naɪvz/ [*noun*] the plural of KNIFE

knob /nab/ [*noun*]
1 a round handle on a door, drawer, or lid: *The knob came off the top drawer.*
2 a round button that you turn to use a machine or piece of equipment: *This knob controls the volume.*

knock¹ * /nak/ [*verb;* **knocked, knocking**]
1 to hit a door, window, or other surface with your closed hand in order to get someone's attention: *Is someone knocking at the door?* | *She knocked loudly on the window.*
2 to hit someone or something hard enough to make it move or fall: *He kept knocking my arm when I was trying to draw.* | *You knocked my glass over.* | *A bike rider knocked that woman down.*
— PHRASE —
3 knock it off INFORMAL used to tell someone to stop doing something you do not like, such as making too much noise: *Knock it off! I'm trying to read.*

— PHRASAL VERBS —

knock into [*phrasal verb*]
4 to hit someone by accidentally walking into him or her: **knock into someone** ▸ *That man knocked right into me.*

knock off [*phrasal verb*]
5 to lower the price of something: **knock something off something** ▸ *He knocked $250 off the price.* I **knock off something** ▸ *He knocked off $250.*

knock out [*phrasal verb*]
6 to hit someone so hard that he or she is not conscious, usually for a short time: **knock out someone** ▸ *He knocked out his opponent two minutes into the fight.*

knock² * [*noun*] the act of hitting something hard, or the sound this makes: *There was a **knock on** the door.*

knockout /'nɑk,aʊt/ [*noun*] when someone is hit so hard in a boxing match that he cannot get up again: *The fight ended in a knockout.*

knot¹ * /nɑt/ [*noun*]
1 a place where string, rope, etc., has been tied: *Thread the needle, then tie the ends in a knot.*

a knot

2 a place in your hair where many hairs have become twisted together: *Mommy, can you comb this knot out of my hair?*
3 a unit for measuring the speed of a ship, equal to about 1.15 miles per hour: *The ship was traveling at around 12 knots.*

knot² * [*verb; knots, knotted, knotting*] to tie together two ends or pieces of string, rope, etc.: *She had a silk scarf knotted around her neck.*

know * /noʊ/ [*verb; knew, known, knowing*]
1 to have information about something or be sure about something: *I don't know the answer to question six.* I *What do you know about Shakespeare's poetry?* I *He knew that she liked him.* I *Does anyone know what time it is?* I *I know just what you mean.*

2 to be familiar with a person, place, or thing: *I've known Mr. and Mrs. Green for over twenty years.* I *The best way to get to know the city* (=become familiar with it) *is on foot.*
3 to have learned something and be good at doing it: *Do you know Spanish?* I **know how to do something** ▸ *I know how to set the VCR.*
↪ *See the usage note at* TEACH.

— PHRASES —

4 you know SPOKEN used when you are explaining something: *It's the building next to the bank—you know, the new brick one.*
5 I know SPOKEN used when you have just had an idea, or when you agree with someone: *I know, let's ask Donna to help.* I *"Kevin's so bossy!" "I know. He's awful."*
6 as far as I know used when you think that something is true, but you are not sure: *As far as I know, the whole class has been invited.*
7 know better to have enough experience not to do something wrong: *Don't spit, Jordan, you're old enough to know better.*
8 you never know used to say that it is possible that something good might happen: *You never know, you might win.*

knowledge * /'nɑlɪdʒ/ [*noun*]
1 the fact that you know something, or what you know; *opposite* IGNORANCE: *He has an amazing **knowledge of** history.* I *She went to the dance **without her parents' knowledge*** (=without them knowing).

— PHRASE —

2 to the best of someone's knowledge used to say that someone thinks that something is true, but cannot be certain: *To the best of my knowledge, that is correct.*

/i/ **see** /ɪ/ **big** /eɪ/ **day** /ɛ/ **get** /æ/ **hat**
/ɑ/ **father, hot** /ʌ/ **up** /ə/ **about** /ɔ/ **saw**
/oʊ/ **hope** /ʊ/ **book** /u/ **too** /aɪ/ **I** /aʊ/ **how**
/ɔɪ/ **boy** /ɝ/ **bird** /ɚ/ **teacher** /ɪr/ **ear** /ɛr/ **air**
/ɑr/ **far** /ɔr/ **more** /ʊr/ **tour** /aɪr/ **fire**
/aʊɚ/ **hour** /θ/ **nothing** /ð/ **mother** /ʃ/ **she**
/ʒ/ **measure** /tʃ/ **church** /dʒ/ **jump** /ŋ/ **long**

knowledgeable ⊤ /'nɑlɪdʒəbəl/ [adjective; **more knowledgeable, most knowledgeable**] knowing a lot; opposite IGNORANT: *She's very knowledgeable about classical music.*

known[1] * /noʊn/ [verb] the past participle of KNOW

known[2] * [adjective; no comparative] known about, especially by a lot of people: *The disease has no known cure.* | *A secret known to more than one person will not be a secret for long.*
↪ *See also* WELL-KNOWN.

knuckle /'nʌkəl/ [noun] one of the joints in your fingers: *She knocked lightly on the window with her knuckles.*

koala /koʊ'ɑlə/ [noun; plural **koalas**] a small Australian animal that lives in trees and eats leaves

Koran /kə'rɑn/ [noun] **the Koran** the holy book of Islam

kosher /'koʊʃɚ/ [adjective; no comparative] kosher food is prepared according to Jewish law: *kosher meat*

a koala

kung fu /'kʌŋ 'fu/ [noun] a Chinese fighting sport in which you attack with your hands and feet
↪ *See also* MARTIAL ART.

L

L * or **l** /ɛl/ [noun; plural **Ls** or **L's, l's**] the 12th letter of the English alphabet
↪ *See the usage note at* ALPHABET.

l 1 the written abbreviation of LITER or LITERS: *a 2-l bottle of cola*
2 also **L**; the written abbreviation of LARGE, especially relating to clothes size: *Labels are marked either s, m, or l.*

lab /læb/ [noun] the short form of LABORATORY: *the chemistry lab*

label[1] /'leɪbəl/ [noun] a small piece of paper or cloth that gives information about the thing it is attached to: *The label says the shirt is washable.*

label[2] [verb; **labeled, labeling**] to attach a label to something: *They labeled all the bottles clearly.* | **be labeled something** ▸ *The jar was labeled "Poison."*

labor[1] /'leɪbɚ/ [noun]
1 hard work: *They were pleased with the results of their labor.*
2 workers as a group: *There is a shortage of skilled labor.*
3 the period of time just before a woman gives birth to a baby: *She was in labor for ten hours.*

labor[2] [verb; **labored, laboring**] to do hard work: *The students labored over their assignments.*

laboratory /'læbərə,tɔri/ [noun; plural **laboratories**] a place where scientific tests are done; synonym LAB: *He set up an experiment in his laboratory.*

Labor Day /'leɪbɚ ,deɪ/ [noun] a U.S. holiday to honor workers on the first day in September

laborer /'leɪbərɚ/ [noun] someone who does hard physical work: *farm laborers*

labor union /'leɪbɚ ,yunyən/ [noun] an organized group of workers who try to make sure that their pay, working conditions, etc., are acceptable; synonym UNION: *Is he a member of a labor union?*

lace[1] /leɪs/ [noun]
1 a kind of cloth in which the thread forms a pattern of small holes: *a collar made of lace*
2 a thick string used to fasten a shoe or boot: *His laces had come undone.*

lace[2] [verb; **laced, lacing**]
━━ PHRASAL VERB ━━
lace up [phrasal verb]
to fasten something with laces: **lace up something** ▸ *I'll help you lace up your boots.*

lack[1] * ⊤ /læk/ [noun] if there is a lack of something, there is none of it or there is not enough of it: *Our main problem was a lack of money.* | *Lack of confidence is his main problem.*

lack[2] * ⊤ [*verb; lacked, lacking*] to not have something or not have enough of something: *The team lacks skill.*

ladder /'lædɚ/ [*noun*] a piece of equipment used to climb up to high places, made of two long pieces of wood or metal connected with short bars

rung

a ladder

laden /'leɪdən/ [*adjective; no comparative*] carrying a lot of heavy things: *She arrived home **laden** with bags.* | *a **heavily laden** truck*

ladies' room /'leɪdiz ˌrum/ [*noun*] a room containing public toilets for women

ladle /'leɪdəl/ [*noun*] a large deep spoon with a long handle

lady * /'leɪdi/ [*noun; plural* **ladies**] a polite word meaning WOMAN: *This lady wants to know the time of the next bus.* | *Good evening, **ladies and gentlemen**!*
⇨ *See the usage note at* GENTLEMAN. ⇨ *See the warning at* MISTER.

laid * /leɪd/ [*verb*] the past tense and past participle of LAY[1]

lain * /leɪn/ [*verb*] the past participle of LIE[1]

lake * /leɪk/ [*noun*] a large area of fresh water surrounded by land: *Chicago is on the shores of Lake Michigan.*

lamb * /læm/ [*noun*] a young SHEEP or its meat: *roast leg of lamb*

lame /leɪm/ [*adjective; no comparative*] not able to walk well, for example because of an injury: *Her horse **went lame**.*

lamp * /læmp/ [*noun*] a light that uses electricity, oil, or gas, that you can carry from one place to another

lampshade

switch

base

a lamp

lamppost /'læmpˌpoʊst/ [*noun*] a tall pole in the street with a light at the top
⇨ *See the picture at* INTO.

lampshade /'læmpˌʃeɪd/ [*noun*] a cover for an electric LAMP

land[1] * /lænd/ [*noun*]
1 ground that is not covered by water: *They're building a supermarket on that land over there.*
2 FORMAL a country: *We must protect this beautiful land of ours.*

land[2] * [*verb; landed, landing*] to come to the ground from the air or the water: *The plane lands at 4:30.* | *The ball landed near the fence.* | *Their ship landed in a small bay.*

landing /'lændɪŋ/ [*noun*]
1 a flat area at the top of a set of stairs: *She waited on the landing.*
2 when a plane or boat arrives on land: *The plane **made an emergency landing** (=landed suddenly to avoid danger).*

landlady /'lændˌleɪdi/ [*noun; plural* **landladies**] a woman who owns and is paid rent for a house, apartment, etc.: *The landlady is raising my rent.*
⇨ *Compare* TENANT.

landlord ⊤ /'lændˌlɔrd/ [*noun*] a man who owns and is paid rent for a house, apartment, etc.: *The landlord lives downstairs.*
⇨ *Compare* TENANT.

landmark /'lændˌmark/ [*noun*] something such as a building, a statue, a mountain, etc., that can be easily seen and recognized: *He pointed out all the famous landmarks.*

landscape ⊤ /'lændˌskeɪp/ [*noun*]
1 what an area of land looks like: *I love the desert landscape of Arizona.*
2 a picture of an area of land: *She paints both landscapes and portraits.*

landslide /'lændˌslaɪd/ [*noun*] when rocks and earth fall down the side of a hill or mountain: *The road had been blocked by a landslide.*

lane /leɪn/ [*noun*]
1 one of the parts into which a big road

/i/ **see**	/ɪ/ **big**	/eɪ/ **day**	/ɛ/ **get**	/æ/ **hat**
/ɑ/ **father, hot**	/ʌ/ **up**	/ə/ **about**	/ɔ/ **saw**	
/oʊ/ **hope**	/ʊ/ **book**	/u/ **too**	/aɪ/ **I**	/aʊ/ **how**
/ɔɪ/ **boy**	/ɚ/ **bird**	/ɚ/ **teacher**	/ɪr/ **ear**	/ɛr/ **air**
/ɑr/ **far**	/ɔr/ **more**	/ʊr/ **tour**	/aɪr/ **fire**	
/aʊɚ/ **hour**	/θ/ **nothing**	/ð/ **mother**	/ʃ/ **she**	
/ʒ/ **measure**	/tʃ/ **church**	/dʒ/ **jump**	/ŋ/ **long**	

is divided, which is wide enough for one vehicle: *I was in the outside lane.*
2 a narrow road, usually in the country: *I rode my horse down the lane.*

language * /'læŋgwɪdʒ/ [*noun*] words, especially the words used by the people in a particular country: *She speaks two foreign languages.* | *He often uses old-fashioned language.*

language laboratory /'læŋgwɪdʒ ,læbrə,tɔri/ [*noun; plural* **language laboratories**] a room in a school where you learn a foreign language by listening to tapes, working on computers, etc.: *This week's lesson will be in the language laboratory.*

lantern /'læntə·n/ [*noun*] a small lamp, usually with a handle: *We'll take the gas lantern on our camping trip.*

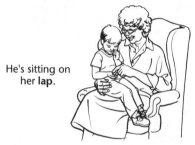

He's sitting on her **lap**.

lap[1] /læp/ [*noun*]
1 the top part of your legs when you are sitting down: *She held the child on her lap.*
2 when someone goes around a race track once, or from one side of a pool to the other: *After three laps, Jason was in the lead.*

lap[2] [*verb;* **laps, lapped, lapping**] to drink something by moving it into your mouth with your tongue: *The dog quickly lapped up the water.*

lapel /lə'pɛl/ [*noun*] one of the two parts of a JACKET or coat that are folded back on each side above the buttons

laptop /'læp,tap/ [*noun*] a small computer that can be carried around: *I used my laptop on the plane.*

large[1] * /lardʒ/ [*adjective;* **larger, largest**]
1 big in size, or high in number or amount; *opposites* LITTLE, SMALL: *I wish I*

lived in a larger house. | *He sold the painting for a large amount of money.*
2 a large person weighs a lot; *synonym* HEAVY: *They sell clothes for large women.*
▷ *See the synonym note at* FAT[1].

large[2] * [*noun*] a size of clothing that is fairly big: *I don't know if he wears a large or an extra large.* | *The shirt comes in small, medium, and large.*
▷ *Compare* SMALL[2], MEDIUM[2], EXTRA LARGE.

largely /'lardʒli/ [*adverb*] used to show that you are mentioning the main reason for something; *synonym* MAINLY: *His bad grades were largely the result of his long illness.*

laser /'leɪzə·/ [*noun*] a piece of equipment that produces a narrow beam of very bright light, used, for example, to cut things: *The surgery was performed using a laser.* | *a laser beam*

lash /læʃ/ [*noun; plural* **lashes**] a short form of EYELASH: *long dark lashes*

lasso /'læsoʊ/ [*noun; plural* **lassos**] a rope tied in a large circle, that can be pulled tight and is used to catch cattle and horses

last[1] * /læst/ [*adverb*]
1 after all the other people or things; *opposite* FIRST: *Jenny was seen by the teacher last.*
2 most recently: *When did you last go on vacation?*

USAGE last, at last

Do not confuse **last** and **at last**. Use **last** when you are mentioning the final thing in a list: *First, I have math class, then English, then biology. Last, I have geography.* Use **at last** to say that something happened after a very long wait: *At last, the bus came.*

---

last[2] * [*adjective; no comparative*]
1 coming or remaining after all the other people or things have come or gone; *opposite* FIRST: *Who ate the last cookie?* | *The last people to arrive were Tom and Cynthia.*
2 most recent: *What was the last movie you saw?* | *I saw him last week.*
☛ Do not say "They arrived on last Friday." Say **They arrived last Friday.**

— PHRASE —

3 the last straw a bad thing that happens after a lot of other bad things, and makes a situation impossible to bear any more: *When he was late to work again, that was the last straw.*

last³ * [*pronoun, noun*]

1 the last the person, thing, or part that comes or remains after all the others: *I was the last to leave.* | *He ate the last of the bread.*

— PHRASE —

2 at last after a long time; synonym FINALLY: *At last dinner was ready.*
⇨ *See the usage note at* LAST¹.
⇨ *Compare* FIRST³.

last⁴ * [*verb;* lasted, lasting]

1 to continue: *The movie **lasted** for three hours.* | *The pain only lasted a few seconds.*

2 to remain, or to remain able to be used: *This table should last a lifetime.* | *The box of cereal lasted him two weeks.*

lasting T /'læstɪŋ/ [*adjective;* **more lasting, most lasting**] existing or continuing for a long time: *a lasting peace agreement*

last name /'læst 'neɪm/ [*noun*] the name that you share with other members of your family, which in English comes last
⇨ *See the usage note at* FIRST NAME.

latch /lætʃ/ [*noun; plural* **latches**] a small object on the edge of a window, door, gate, etc., that keeps it closed: *We need a new latch for that gate.*

late¹ * /leɪt/ [*adjective;* **later, latest**]

1 after the usual, expected, or right time; opposite EARLY: *He was **late** for the interview.* | *The train was 20 minutes late.* | *You're late. What happened?*

2 near the end of a period of time; opposite EARLY: *The school was built in the late 1950s.* | *It's late—we should be getting back.* | *It's later than I thought.*

3 having recently died: *There was a photo of **her late husband** by her bed.*
☛ Only use **late** before a noun in this meaning.

late² * [*adverb;* **later, latest**]

1 after the usual, expected, or right time; opposite EARLY: *Her birthday card arrived late.* | *It's too late to change your mind!* (=there is no time left)

2 near the end of a period of time; opposite EARLY: *He called me late last night.* | *The party lasted until late in the evening.*

lately * /'leɪtli/ [*adverb*] in recent days or months: *She's a lot happier lately.*

USAGE **lately, recently**

These words mean the same thing when they are used with the present perfect tense: *He's been acting odd lately.* | *He's been acting odd recently.*

However, you cannot use **lately** with the past tense. For example, do not say "I saw your father lately." Say **I saw your father recently.**

later¹ /'leɪtɚ/ [*adverb*] at a time after the present time, or after a time or event in the past: *I'll finish it later.* | *They got married three weeks later.* | *We'll see you later on at the party.*
☛ Do not say "I'll be back ten minutes later." Say **I'll be back in ten minutes.**

later² [*adjective; no comparative*]

1 happening or coming after something else: *This can be discussed at a later date.*

2 more recent: *Some of her later poems have just been published*
☛ Only use **later** before a noun.

latest /'leɪtɪst/ [*adverb, adjective; no comparative*] most recent: *Have you heard their latest song?*

Latin /'lætən/ [*noun*] the language used by the people of ancient Rome: *The writing on the stone was in Latin.*

Latin America /'lætɪn ə'mɛrɪkə/ [*name*] the countries south of the U.S. where Spanish, Portuguese, or French is spoken: *the music of Latin America*

Latin American¹ /'lætɪn ə'mɛrɪkən/ [*noun*] someone who comes from Latin America

/i/ **see**	/ɪ/ **big**	/eɪ/ **day**	/ɛ/ **get**	/æ/ **hat**	
/ɑ/ **father, hot**	/ʌ/ **up**	/ə/ **about**	/ɔ/ **saw**	
/oʊ/ **hope**	/ʊ/ **book**	/u/ **too**	/aɪ/ **I**	/aʊ/ **how**	
/ɔɪ/ **boy**	/ɝ/ **bird**	/ɚ/ **teacher**	/ɪr/ **ear**	/ɛr/ **air**	
/ɑr/ **far**	/ɔr/ **more**	/ʊr/ **tour**	/aɪr/ **air**	
/aʊɚ/ **hour**	/θ/ **nothing**	/ð/ **mother**	/ʃ/ **she**	
/ʒ/ **measure**	/tʃ/ **church**	/dʒ/ **jump**	/ŋ/ **long**	

Latin American[2] [adjective; no comparative] belonging to, from, or relating to Latin America: Latin American dances

Latino /lə'tinoʊ/ [adjective; no comparative] belonging or relating to a Latin American country, or to people who speak Spanish or Portuguese: In my class, 40% of the students are Latino. ⟹ Compare HISPANIC.

latitude /'lætɪ,tud/ [noun] a position to the north or south measured from a line around the middle of the earth

latter /'lætɚ/ [noun] FORMAL
the latter used to talk about the second of two things or people that have just been mentioned; opposite FORMER: She plays both piano and violin, but she prefers the latter.

laugh[1] * /læf/ [verb; laughed, laughing] to make a sound that shows you think something is funny or silly: When he fell off his chair, we laughed. | The kids laugh at his jokes. | She burst out laughing (=started to laugh).

laugh[2] * [noun] the sound you make when you laugh: Daddy has a loud laugh.

laughter * /'læftɚ/ [noun] when someone laughs, or the sound he or she makes: They could hear laughter coming from the classroom.

launch ⊤ /lɔntʃ/ [verb; launches, launched, launching]
1 to put a boat in the water or send a space vehicle, bomb, etc., into the air: They launched the shuttle at 7 a.m.
2 to begin producing or doing something new: The store launched its fall fashions this week.

Laundromat /'lɔndrə,mæt/ [noun] TRADEMARK a place where people pay to wash and dry clothes in machines

laundry ⊤ /'lɔndri/ [noun] clothes, sheets, etc., that need to be washed or have just been washed: His mom did his laundry for him.

lava /'lavə/ [noun] hot liquid rock that explodes from a mountain and becomes hard when it cools

lavatory /'lævə,tɔri/ [noun; plural lavatories] a room with a toilet in it; synonym BATHROOM: Where's the lavatory?

law * /lɔ/ [noun]
1 an official statement about what is or is not allowed in a country: tax laws | a law against drunk driving
2 the profession of being a lawyer: She decided to go into law. | a law degree
3 **the law** the laws of a country: Theft is against the law (=is a crime). | He broke the law (=committed a crime).

lawn /lɔn/ [noun] an area of grass that is cut short: His dad was mowing the lawn (=was cutting it). ⟹ See the picture at HOUSE.

lawn mower /'lɔn ,moʊɚ/ [noun] a machine for cutting grass; synonym MOWER: The lawn mower is out of gas. ⟹ See the picture at MOW.

lawsuit /'lɔ,sut/ [noun] a complaint made by one person or organization about another, that is dealt with in a court of law: He brought a lawsuit against the company.

lawyer * /'lɔɪɚ/ [noun] someone whose job involves helping people with legal matters: She went to see her lawyer to change her will.

lay[1] * /leɪ/ [verb; lays, laid, laying]
1 to put something that can lie flat on top of something else: He laid a red cloth on the table. ⟹ Compare LIE[1]. ⟹ See the usage note at PUT.
2 if a bird, insect, or other animal lays or lays eggs, it produces eggs from its body: The bird in our tree laid four eggs. | Something's wrong with this chicken. It's not laying.
3 to put a baby or small child in a place where he or she can lie down: She laid the baby in his crib. ⟹ See the chart at LIE[1]

── PHRASAL VERB ──
lay out [phrasal verb]
4 to put a number of things on something, arranged so they can all be seen: lay out something ▸ She laid out all her paints. | lay something out ▸ Lay the photos out on the table.

lay[2] * [verb] the past tense of LIE[1]

layer * /'leɪɚ/ [*noun*] an amount of a substance that covers something or is between things: *There was a thick layer of snow on the ground.* I *He drilled through many layers of rock.*

lazy * /'leɪzi/ [*adjective;* **lazier, laziest**] not doing things, especially things you should do: *He's too lazy to walk home.*

lb. the written abbreviation of POUND or POUNDS: *Mix together 1 lb. cooked rice and 2 lb. chopped meat.*

lead¹ * /lid/ [*verb;* **led, leading**]
1 to go somewhere with someone, showing him or her where to go: *He led them into a large room.*
2 to go toward or show the way to a place: *This hallway leads to the gym.* I *There are signs to lead you to the exit.*
3 to be winning or doing better than another person or group: *Which team is leading?* I *Our country leads the world in exports.*
4 to be in charge of something: *Is he the right person to lead the country?*
5 to have a particular kind of life: *I just want to lead a quiet life.*

   ━━ PHRASAL VERB ━━

lead to [*phrasal verb*]
6 to cause something: **lead to something** ▸ *Smoking can lead to health problems.*

lead² /lid/ [*noun*]
1 the amount by which a person or group is winning: *They now have a lead of 10 points.*
2 the lead a winning position: *Andrew was in the lead.*

lead³ /lɛd/ [*noun*]
1 a soft, heavy metal that can poison you: *a lead pipe*
2 the dark or colored substance in the middle of a pencil

leader * /'lidɚ/ [*noun*] the person who is in charge of a group: *The party is about to choose a new leader.*

leadership /'lidɚʃɪp/ [*noun*] the position or actions of a leader: *The country got richer under his leadership.*

leading /'lidɪŋ/ [*adjective; no comparative*] important or most successful: *a leading expert on physics*
☞ Only use **leading** before a noun.

leaf * /lif/ [*noun; plural* **leaves**] one of the flat green parts that grow on a tree or other plant

leaflet /'liflɪt/ [*noun*] a piece of paper that gives information about something: *a leaflet about tooth care*

league /lig/ [*noun; plural* **leagues**] a group of people or organizations that share an aim or activity, especially a group of sports teams: *Their baseball team is leading the league.*

leak¹ /lik/ [*verb;* **leaked, leaking**]
1 if something leaks, liquid or gas comes through it by accident: *The roof is leaking.*
2 if a liquid or gas leaks into or out of something, it comes through it by accident: *Water leaked into the boat.*

leak² [*noun*] when a liquid or gas comes through something by accident: *The explosion was caused by a gas leak.*

leaky /'liki/ [*adjective;* **leakier, leakiest**] having a crack, hole, or small opening that liquid or gas can come through: *a leaky faucet*

a leaky hose

lean¹ * /lin/ [*verb;* **leaned, leaning**]
1 to move into a less upright position: *I leaned back in my chair.* I *He leaned over and whispered "Who's that?"*
2 to rest against something, or to rest something against something else: *She stood leaning against the wall.* I **lean something against something** ▸ *He leaned his bicycle against the fence.*

lean² [*adjective;* **leaner, leanest**] very thin, or having little fat: *Marcus has a lean face.* I *I prefer lean meat.*

leap¹ /lip/ [*verb;* **leaped** or **leapt, leaping**] to jump with one leg in front of the other: *He leaped over the stream.*
➪ See the picture at MOVEMENT.

/i/ **see**	/ɪ/ **big**	/eɪ/ **day**	/ɛ/ **get**	/æ/ **hat**
/ɑ/ **father, hot**	/ʌ/ **up**	/ə/ **about**	/ɔ/ **saw**	
/oʊ/ **hope**	/ʊ/ **book**	/u/ **too**	/aɪ/ **I**	/aʊ/ **how**
/ɔɪ/ **boy**	/ɚ/ **bird**	/ɚ/ **teacher**	/ɪr/ **ear**	/ɛr/ **air**
/ɑr/ **far**	/ɔr/ **more**	/ʊr/ **tour**	/aɪr/ **fire**	
/aʊɚ/ **hour**	/θ/ **nothing**	/ð/ **mother**	/ʃ/ **she**	
/ʒ/ **measure**	/tʃ/ **church**	/dʒ/ **jump**	/ŋ/ **long**	

leap[2] [*noun*] when someone jumps with one leg in front of the other: *She took a big leap over the hedge.*

leap year /'lip ˌyɪr/ [*noun*] a year that has an extra day, February 29, that happens every four years

learn * /lɜ˞n/ [*verb*; **learned, learning**]
1 to gain knowledge or an ability: *She learned English in school.* | *We're learning about American history.* | **learn (how) to do something** ▸ *I learned to swim when I was seven.*
➪ *See the usage notes at* STUDY[1] *and* TEACH
2 to hear or find out a fact: *When did you learn that you'd won?* | *I was shocked to learn of his death.*

learner /'lɜ˞nə˞/ [*noun*] someone who is learning how to do something or learning about something: *English spelling is difficult for many learners.*

learning /'lɜ˞nɪŋ/ [*noun*] the process of gaining knowledge: *Learning can be fun.*

lease /lis/ [*noun*] a contract allowing someone to use another person's property for a particular period of time and amount of money: *a two-year lease*

leash /liʃ/ [*noun*; *plural* **leashes**] a long piece of leather, chain, etc., which is attached to a dog's collar and held so that the dog cannot move far away

least[1] * /list/ [*determiner, pronoun*]
1 less than any other person, thing, amount, etc.; *opposite* MOST: *I like art class because it's the least amount of work.* | *No one wants to stay here, least of all me.*
☛ Only use the determiner **the least** before an uncountable noun.
➪ *Compare* FEWEST.
━━ PHRASES ━━
2 **at least**
  a used to say that an amount or number is the smallest possible or allowed: *Her dress must have cost at least a thousand dollars.*
  ➪ *Compare* **at (the) most** *at* MOST[1].
  b used to mention a good part of a situation that is mostly bad: *At least it didn't rain.*
3 **not in the least** not in any way, or not at all: *He wasn't in the least upset.*

least[2] * [*adverb*] less than anything or anyone else; *opposite* MOST: *I bought the least expensive radio I could find.* | *That was the movie I liked least.*

leather * /'lɛðə˞/ [*noun*] the skin of an animal, used to make shoes, bags, etc.: *a leather jacket*

leave[1] * /liv/ [*verb*; **left, leaving**]
1 to go away from a place, person, or organization: *When does the next bus leave?* | *He left for New York (=went away to go to New York) last week.* | *I left home when I turned 18.* | *She left the company last year.*
2 to not take something or someone with you when you go somewhere: *I accidentally left my coat at school.* | *We left the kids at home.*
3 to let something stay in a particular state or condition: *I left the door open.*
4 to put or keep something in a place for someone to find or have: *I left your lunch in the fridge.*
5 to say that someone should have something that you own after you die: **leave someone something** ▸ *His aunt left him her house in her will.* | **leave something to someone** ▸ *He left all his money to his children.*
━━ PHRASES ━━
6 **be left (over)** to still be available after part has been used: *There's some pizza left.* | *These sodas are left over from the party.*
7 **leave someone alone** to stay away from someone and not annoy or harm him or her: *Leave me alone—I don't want to talk.*
8 **leave something alone** to not touch something or stop touching it: *Leave that vase alone!*
━━ PHRASAL VERB ━━
leave out [*phrasal verb*]
9 to not include something or someone: **leave out someone/something** ▸ *You left out a word here.* | **leave someone/something out** ▸ *Did I leave anyone out?*

leave[2] [*noun*] one or more days when someone has special permission to be away from his or her work: *Captain Brown is away on leave.*

leaves * /livz/ [noun] the plural of LEAF

lecture[1] /'lɛktʃɚ/ [noun] a formal talk about a subject, given to a group of students or other people: *She gave a lecture on 19th-century poetry.*

lecture[2] [verb; lectured, lecturing] to give a formal talk about a subject: *He lectures on economics.*

led * /lɛd/ [verb] the past tense and past participle of LEAD[1]

ledge /lɛdʒ/ [noun] a narrow shelf on the side of a mountain or under a window: *He climbed up onto the ledge.* | *There were plants on the window ledge.*

leek /lik/ [noun] a vegetable like a very tall white onion with thick green leaves, that is eaten cooked

left[1] * [adjective; no comparative] on the left; *opposite* RIGHT: *His left leg was injured in the accident.*
☞ Only use **left** before a noun.

left[2] * [adverb] toward the left; *opposite* RIGHT: *Turn left at the next intersection.*

left[3] * /lɛft/ [noun] the side that is toward the west when you are facing north; *opposite* RIGHT: *Their house was on the left.* | *To your left is the oldest building in the town.*

left[4] * [verb] the past tense and past participle of LEAVE[1]

left-hand /'lɛft 'hænd/ [adjective; no comparative] on or toward the left; *opposite* RIGHT-HAND: *Stay in the left-hand lane.* | *a left-hand turn*
☞ Only use **left-hand** before a noun.

left-handed /'lɛft 'hændɪd/ [adjective; no comparative] someone who is left-handed writes, uses tools, etc. with his or her left hand; *opposite* RIGHT-HANDED: *How many of your friends are left-handed?*

leftovers /'lɛft,oʊvɚz/ [plural noun] food that has not been eaten at a meal and can be eaten later: *She heated up some leftovers for supper.*

leg * /lɛg/ [noun]
1 one of the long parts of the BODY on which a person or animal stands and walks: *The cat rubbed against my leg.*
2 one of the long parts that a chair, table, etc. stands on: *The table has one leg that's too short.*

legal * /'ligəl/ [adjective; no comparative]
1 allowed by the law; *opposite* ILLEGAL: *The legal age for voting is 18.*
2 relating to laws: *the legal system*

legalize /'ligə,laɪz/ [verb; legalized, legalizing] to make something legal: *Should this drug be legalized?*

legally * /'ligəli/ [adverb] in a way that is allowed by the law; *opposite* ILLEGALLY: *You can get legally married in a church or a court.*

legend /'lɛdʒənd/ [noun]
1 an old story which is probably not completely true: *According to legend, there was a great city there.*
2 someone who is very famous and admired: *a baseball legend*

legislation /,lɛdʒɪs'leɪʃən/ [noun] FORMAL laws that are being created or have just been created: *Congress is expected to pass legislation* (=approve laws) *that reduces taxes.*

legislator /'lɛdʒɪs,leɪtɚ/ [noun] a member of the group of people who make the laws in a government

legislature /'lɛdʒɪs,leɪtʃɚ/ [noun] the group of people who make the laws in a government

leisure /'liʒɚ/ [noun] time when you are not working or studying: *We don't have a lot of leisure time.*

lemon /'lɛmən/ [noun] a sour yellow FRUIT that grows on trees in hot places

lemonade /,lɛmə'neɪd/ [noun] a drink made from lemons or tasting of lemons, or a glass of this: *a glass of lemonade* | *I'd like a lemonade with that burger.*

lend * /lɛnd/ [verb; lent, lending] to give money or something you own to someone for a period of time; *synonym* LOAN: **lend someone something** ▸ *He lent me ten dollars.* | **lend something to someone** ▸ *She lent her bike to a friend.*

/i/ see	/ɪ/ big	/eɪ/ day	/ɛ/ get	/æ/ hat
/ɑ/ father,	hot	/ʌ/ up	/ə/ about	/ɔ/ saw
/oʊ/ hope	/ʊ/ book	/u/ too	/aɪ/ I	/aʊ/ how
/ɔɪ/ boy	/ɝ/ bird	/ɚ/ teacher	/ɪr/ ear	/ɛr/ air
/ɑr/ far	/ɔr/ more	/ʊr/ tour	/aɪr/ fire	
/aʊɚ/ hour	/θ/ nothing	/ð/ mother	/ʃ/ she	
/ʒ/ measure	/tʃ/ church	/dʒ/ jump	/ŋ/ long	

USAGE lend, borrow

Do not confuse **lend** and **borrow**. If you **lend** something that is yours, you allow someone to use it: *Will your father lend you his car?* If you **borrow** something, you use something that is owned by someone else: *Can I borrow a pen?*

length * /lɛŋkθ/ [noun]
1 used to talk about how long something is: *The table is five feet in length.* | *The pieces of wood were all different lengths.*
2 the amount of time something lasts: *The classes vary in length from 30 minutes to 2 hours.*

lengthen /'lɛŋkθən/ [verb; lengthened, lengthening] to become longer or to make something longer: *The daytime lengthens in the spring.* | *She lengthened her blue skirt.*

lengthy /'lɛŋkθi/ [adjective; lengthier, lengthiest] continuing for a long time or for many pages: *a lengthy discussion* | *a lengthy article*

lens /lɛnz/ [noun; plural lenses] a curved piece of glass or plastic which makes things appear larger, smaller, or clearer: *She had thick lenses in her glasses.* | *a camera lens*
⇨ *See also* CONTACT LENS.

lent * /lɛnt/ [verb] the past tense and past participle of LEND

lentils /'lɛntəlz/ [plural noun] small round seeds that can be cooked and eaten: *a package of dried lentils*

leopard /'lɛpərd/ [noun] a large wild cat that is yellow-brown with black spots

a leopard

less¹ * /lɛs/ [determiner, pronoun]
1 a smaller amount; *opposite* MORE: *They get less homework than we do.* | *You should eat less.* | *Under the new plan, less of the forest will be destroyed.*

☛ Only use the determiner **less** before an uncountable noun.
⇨ *See also* LEAST¹ *and see* **more or less** *at* MORE¹. ⇨ *Compare* FEWER.

— PHRASE —
2 less and less used to say that something is becoming smaller in degree or amount: *I spend less and less time exercising.*
⇨ *See also* **fewer and fewer** *at* FEWER.
⇨ *Compare* **more and more** *at* MORE¹.

less² * [adverb] to a smaller degree or amount; *opposite* MORE: *The second program was less interesting than the first.* | *I see her less often than I used to.*
⇨ *See also* LEAST².

lessen /'lɛsən/ [verb; lessened, lessening] to become less, or to make something less in amount, level, or degree; *synonym* DECREASE: *This medicine will lessen the pain.*

lesson * /'lɛsən/ [noun] a period of time in which a teacher teaches a person or group of people something: *My mother gives music lessons.* | *She's taking driving lessons* (=being taught how to drive). | *The kids have swimming lessons on Saturday mornings.*
⇨ *Compare* CLASS (definition 2).

let * /lɛt/ [verb; lets, let, let, letting]
1 to allow something to happen or be done: **let someone/something do something** ▸ *My parents let me stay up late.* | *Let the soup boil for two minutes.*
☛ Do not say "I'll let him to do it." Say **I'll let him do it.**
☛ Do not say "He will be let to do it." Say **He will be allowed to do it.**
⇨ *See also* LET'S.
2 to allow someone or something to go into or out of a place: *He banged on the door and yelled "Let me out!"* | *Will you let the dog in?*

— PHRASES —
3 let me used to offer to do something: *Let me help you with that.*
4 let go (of) to stop holding something or someone; *synonym* RELEASE: *He wouldn't let go of her hand.*
5 let go to allow a person or animal to leave or go free; *synonym* RELEASE: **let someone/something go** ▸ *We caught three fish, but we let them all go.*

6 let alone used to mention something greater, more difficult, etc., than the thing just mentioned: *I couldn't stand up, let alone walk.*

7 let someone know to tell someone something at some time in the future: *If you need any more help, let me know.*

— PHRASAL VERB ▬▬▬▬

let down [*phrasal verb*]

8 to not do what someone wanted and expected you to do; <u>synonym</u> DISAPPOINT: **let someone down** ▸ *He felt he'd let the team down.*

lethal /'liθəl/ [*adjective; no comparative*] a lethal substance or weapon can cause death: *Taking too much of that medicine can be lethal.*

let's * /lɛts/ the short from of "let us," used to make a suggestion about what you and someone else should do: *Let's get something to eat.*

letter * /'lɛtɚ/ [*noun*]

uppercase

1 a shape used to represent a sound, such as "a" or "b": *The letter E is not always pronounced.*

A / lowercase a /

kinds of **letters**

2 a written message that you send to someone by mail: *I got a **letter from** my boyfriend today.*

letter carrier /'lɛtɚ ˌkæriɚ/ [*noun*] someone whose job is to deliver mail

lettuce /'lɛtɪs/ [*noun*] a large VEGETABLE with green leaves that are eaten raw: *a lettuce and tomato salad*

level[1] * /'lɛvəl/ [*noun*] a height or amount: *The **water level** had risen.* | *There's a **high level of** crime in the area.*

level[2] * [*adjective*]

1 [**more level, most level**] with no part higher than any other part: *That painting isn't level.*

2 [*no comparative*] at the same height or position or someone else: *My sister's head is **level with** my chin.*

level[3] [*verb; leveled, leveling*] to make something level: *They leveled the ground before planting the grass.*

lever /'lɛvɚ; 'livɚ/ [*noun*]

1 a long handle that is used to operate a machine: *You pull that lever to start the machine.*

2 a bar that can be used to move something by putting one end under the thing and pushing on the other end: *He managed to open the window, using a screwdriver as a lever.*

liable /'laɪəbəl/ [*adjective; **more liable, most liable**]

— PHRASE ▬▬▬▬

be liable to do something to be likely to do something: *If you don't wear a helmet, you're liable to get hurt.*

liar /'laɪɚ/ [*noun*] someone who tells lies: *Liar! I know that's not true!*

liberal T /'lɪbərəl/ [*adjective; **more liberal, most liberal**] believing that people should not be limited too much: *Many voters did not approve of his liberal views.*

liberty /'lɪbɚti/ [*noun*] when you are not controlled or are able to do what you want; <u>synonym</u> FREEDOM: *After ten years in prison, he was enjoying his liberty.*

librarian /laɪ'brɛriən/ [*noun*] someone who works in a library

library * T /'laɪˌbrɛri/ [*noun; plural* **libraries**] a place where books are kept, especially a place used by the public or students: *She borrowed the book from the college library.*

lice /laɪs/ [*plural noun*] very small creatures that can live on people and animals, especially in their hair

license[1] /'laɪsəns/ [*noun*] a document showing that you have official permission to do or have something: *a driver's license* | *a gun license*

license[2] [*verb; licensed, licensing*] to give someone official permission to do or have something: *Lawyers have to be licensed by the state they work in.*

license plate /'laɪsəns ˌpleɪt/ [*noun*] a small sign attached to the front and back of a CAR that makes it legal to be driven: *Don't you remember your license plate number?*

/i/ **see** /ɪ/ **big** /eɪ/ **day** /ɛ/ **get** /æ/ **hat**
/ɑ/ **father, hot** /ʌ/ **up** /ə/ **about** /ɔ/ **saw**
/oʊ/ **hope** /ʊ/ **book** /u/ **too** /aɪ/ **I** /aʊ/ **how**
/ɔɪ/ **boy** /ɝ/ **bird** /ɚ/ **teacher** /ɪr/ **ear** /ɛr/ **air**
/ɑr/ **far** /ɔr/ **more** /ʊr/ **tour** /aɪr/ **fire**
/aʊɚ/ **hour** /θ/ **nothing** /ð/ **mother** /ʃ/ **she**
/ʒ/ **measure** /tʃ/ **church** /dʒ/ **jump** /ŋ/ **long**

lick

lick /lɪk/ [verb; licked, licking] to move
your tongue over something: *The dog
jumped up and licked her face.*

lid * /lɪd/ [noun] a part that covers the
top of a CONTAINER: *I can't get the lid off
this jar.*

lie[1] * /laɪ/ [verb; lies, lay, lain, lying]
1 to be in a flat position somewhere:
*John was lying on the floor watching TV.
I There was a book lying on the table.*
☞ Do not say "I was laying in the sun."
Say **I was lying in the sun.**
⇨ Compare LAY[1].

— PHRASAL VERB —

lie down [phrasal verb]
2 to move so that you are in a flat
position, especially so you can rest:
I lay down on the couch.
☞ Do not say "I'm going to lay down."
Say **I'm going to lie down.**

Forms of lie[1]

	present tense	past tense
singular and plural	I **lie** he/she/it **lies** you/we/they **lie**	I **lay** he/she/it **lay** you/we/they **lay**
participles	**lying**	**lain**

Forms of lay

	present tense	past tense
singular and plural	I **lay** he/she/it **lay** you/we/they **lay**	I **laid** he/she/it **laid** you/we/they **laid**
participles	**laying**	**laid**

lie[2] * [verb; lies, lied, lying]
to deliberately say something that is
not true: *Why did you lie to me? I He lied
about the money.*

lie[3] * [noun; plural lies] something that
someone says, knowing it is not true:
That's a lie! I Stop telling lies.

lieutenant or **Lieutenant** /luˈtɛnənt/
[noun, name] an officer with a middle
rank in the Army, Air Force, Navy,
Marine Corps, or police force

life * /laɪf/ [noun; plural lives]
1 the period of time when someone is
alive, or the fact of being alive: *I've*

*lived here all my life. I The firefighters
saved the children's lives* (=prevented
them from dying).
2 what people do or what happens
when they are alive: *Life was hard in
the 1930s. I Our daily lives are very busy.*
3 the quality of having a lot of energy:
She is full of life.
4 growth or activity: *The garden has
come back to life* (=is growing again).
5 living things: *Scientists came to study
the island's animal life.*

— PHRASE —
6 for life for all of the rest of your life:
Win $50,000 a year for life!

lifeboat * /ˈlaɪfˌboʊt/ [noun] a boat that
is used to save people from danger on
the ocean: *We all got into the lifeboats.*

lifeguard * /ˈlaɪfˌgɑrd/ [noun] someone
whose job is to save people from danger
when they are swimming: *Don't go
swimming if there are no lifeguards.*

life jacket /ˈlaɪf ˌdʒækɪt/ [noun] a
special piece of clothing that keeps
someone floating in water, for example
after falling from a boat: *Everyone has to
wear a life jacket on board.*
⇨ Compare LIFE PRESERVER. ⇨ See the
picture at ROWBOAT.

lifeless /ˈlaɪflɪs/ [adjective; no comparative]
seeming dead, or no longer alive: *His
lifeless body was found in the valley.*

lifelike /ˈlaɪfˌlaɪk/ [adjective; more
lifelike, most lifelike] a lifelike picture,
model, etc., looks very much like a real
person or animal: *The doll looks so
lifelike!*

life preserver /ˈlaɪf prɪˌzɜrvər/ [noun] a
ring that keeps someone floating in
water, for example after falling from a
boat: *They threw a life preserver to him.*
⇨ Compare LIFE JACKET.

life sentence /ˈlaɪf ˈsɛntɪns/ [noun] the
punishment of being in prison for life:
Both men received life sentences.

life-size /ˈlaɪf ˌsaɪz/ or **life-sized** /ˈlaɪf
ˌsaɪzd/ [adjective; no comparative] a life-
size model, picture, etc., is the same size
as the person or thing it looks like: *a
life-size statue of a general*

lifestyle 🔊 /ˈlaɪfˌstaɪl/ [noun] where you
live, what you do for your work and for

fun, and how much money you spend: *Having a baby changes your lifestyle.*

lifetime /'laɪf,taɪm/ [*noun*] the period of time during which someone is alive: *I have seen many changes during my lifetime.*

lift[1] * /lɪft/ [*verb*; **lifted, lifting**] to move someone or something to a higher position: *Can you help me lift this box?* ⇨ *See the synonym note at* CARRY.

lift[2] * [*noun*] a ride in a car or other vehicle: *She gave me a lift to the airport.*

liftoff /'lɪft,ɔf/ [*noun*] the moment when a space vehicle's engines send it into the air: *Liftoff is scheduled for 10 a.m.*

light[1] * /laɪt/ [*noun*]
1 the energy from a lamp or the sun, that lets you see things: *There wasn't enough light to read.*
2 something that produces this energy, especially using electricity: *I turned the kitchen light on.*
3 a set of red, yellow, and green lights on a street that control traffic, or one of these lights: *Go right at the next light.* | *Wait for the green light.*

light[2] * [*adjective*; **lighter, lightest**]
1 pale in color; *opposite* DARK: *a light blue dress*
2 not much in weight, amount, or force: *He gave me the lightest suitcase to carry.* | *A light rain was falling.* | *a light breeze*
3 food that is light does not make you feel like you have eaten a lot, or has been specially made to contain less fat: *a light lunch* | *a light yogurt* ⇨ *Compare* HEAVY.

—— PHRASES ——
4 a light sleeper someone who wakes easily if there is noise: *Older people are often light sleepers.*
5 a light drinker/smoker/etc. someone who does not drink much alcohol, does not smoke much, etc.: *My parents are light drinkers.*

light[3] * [*verb*; **lit, lighting**]
1 to make something start burning: *She lit the fire.*
2 to make something bright: *The room was lit with candles.*

—— PHRASAL VERB ——
light up [*phrasal verb*]
3 to make something very bright: **light up something** ▸ *The fireworks lit up the sky.* | **light something up** ▸ *A big lamp lit the room up.*

light bulb /'laɪt ,bʌlb/ [*noun*] a glass object that fits into a lamp and produces light: *A light bulb in the bedroom has burned out.*

lighten /'laɪtən/ [*verb*; **lightened, lightening**]
1 to make something brighter or paler: *I'm going to lighten my hair.*
2 to make something weigh less: *Removing the drawers will lighten the desk so we can move it.*

lighter /'laɪtɚ/ [*noun*] an object used to light cigarettes: *She borrowed his cigarette lighter.*

lighthouse /'laɪt,haʊs/ [*noun*; *plural* **lighthouses** /'laɪt,haʊzɪz/] a tall building with a light at the top, which is built near the ocean and warns ships of danger

a lighthouse

lighting /'laɪtɪŋ/ [*noun*] the lights in a place: *We need to improve the lighting in the kitchen.*

lightly * /'laɪtli/ [*adverb*] with very little force or weight, or in a very small amount; *opposite* HEAVILY: *lightly falling snow*

lightning /'laɪtnɪŋ/ [*noun*] a sudden bright flash of light that appears from the sky in a storm: *The children were frightened of the thunder and lightning.*

likable /'laɪkəbəl/ [*adjective*; **more likable, most likable**] pleasant and easy to like: *a likable young woman*

/i/ **see** /ɪ/ **big** /eɪ/ **day** /ɛ/ **get** /æ/ **hat**
/ɑ/ **father, hot** /ʌ/ **up** /ə/ **about** /ɔ/ **saw**
/oʊ/ **hope** /ʊ/ **book** /u/ **too** /aɪ/ **I** /aʊ/ **how**
/ɔɪ/ **boy** /ɝ/ **bird** /ɚ/ **teacher** /ɪr/ **ear** /ɛr/ **air**
/ɑr/ **far** /ɔr/ **more** /ʊr/ **tour** /aɪr/ **fire**
/aʊɚ/ **hour** /θ/ **nothing** /ð/ **mother** /ʃ/ **she**
/ʒ/ **measure** /tʃ/ **church** /dʒ/ **jump** /ŋ/ **long**

like[1] * /laɪk/ [verb; liked, liking]
1 to think that someone or something is good, pleasant, or fun; _opposite_ DISLIKE: _I really liked him._ | _like doing something_ ▸ _I like watching TV._

━━ PHRASES ━━

2 would like to want something or want to do something: _Would you like some coffee?_ | _I'd like to visit Europe some day._

☛ Do not say "Would you like coming too?" Say **Would you like to come too?**

3 if you like if this is what you would like: _We can have ice cream for dessert, if you like._

like[2] * [preposition]
1 similar to someone or something, or in the same way as someone or something: _She is very much like her mother._ | _He cried like a baby._
2 used to give an example of something: _Don't say things like that._
3 used to describe someone or something: _He seems like a nice person._ | _What was the concert like?_ | _She dances like an angel._

like[3] * [conjunction] INFORMAL
1 in the same way as someone or something: _He can't play the guitar like I can._
2 used to say how someone or something appears or seems: _It looks like it's going to rain._

↪ _See also_ **as if** _at_ IF _and_ **as though** _at_ THOUGH[1].

likely * /ˈlaɪkli/ [adjective; likelier, likeliest] if something is likely, it will probably happen or be done; _opposite_ UNLIKELY: _"He might apologize." "That's not likely."_ | _likely to do something_ ▸ _Is she likely to win?_

likes /laɪks/ [plural noun] things that someone likes: _I know all his **likes and dislikes.**_

likewise /ˈlaɪkˌwaɪz/ [adverb] the same thing, or in the same way: _He worked hard, and expected his employees to do likewise._

liking /ˈlaɪkɪŋ/ [noun] if you have a liking for something, you like it: _I remembered his **liking for** old movies._

lilac[1] /ˈlaɪlək/ [noun]
1 a tall bush with bunches of small white or purple flowers: _There's a lilac growing behind the house._
2 a pale purple color: _The walls are lilac._

lilac[2] [adjective; no comparative] of the color lilac: _a lilac scarf_

lily /ˈlɪli/ [noun; plural lilies] a plant with large FLOWERs: _The bride carried a bouquet of white lilies._

limb /lɪm/ [noun]
1 one of the large branches on a tree: _They hung a swing from a high limb._
2 an arm or leg: _The cold made his limbs numb._

lime /laɪm/ [noun] a sour green FRUIT that grows on trees in hot places

limit[1] * /ˈlɪmɪt/ [noun]
1 the greatest, or sometimes smallest, amount that is allowed or possible: _He was stopped for driving over **the speed limit.**_ | _There is no **limit to** what you can achieve._
2 the farthest point or edge of something: _Our house is outside the **city limits.**_

↪ _See also_ OFF-LIMITS.

limit[2] * [verb; limited, limiting] to prevent something from being greater than a particular amount: _We'll have to limit our spending._ | _limit something to something_ ▸ _They limited the number of hours he could watch television to fifteen a week_

limited * /ˈlɪmɪtɪd/ [adjective; **more limited, most limited**] a limited number or amount is not at all large; _opposite_ UNLIMITED: _The store sells a limited range of goods._

limo /ˈlɪmoʊ/ [noun; plural limos] limousine; a large comfortable car, usually one in which an important person is driven: _Many of the guests arrived in limos._

limousine /ˈlɪməˌzin/ [noun] a LIMO: _The movie star arrived in a limousine._

limp[1] /lɪmp/ [verb; limped, limping] to walk in an uneven way because your foot or leg hurts or is injured: _Why are you limping?_

limp[2] [noun] an uneven way of walking because of an injury: _He's had a limp ever since the accident._

limp³ [*adjective;* **limper, limpest**] not stiff or firm: *The carrots have gotten limp.*

line¹ * /laɪn/ [*noun*]
  1 a long thin mark: *Write your address on the line below.*
  2 a number of people or things next to or behind each other in one row: *There was a long line outside the entrance.* | *Please* **form a line** (=stand in a line) *behind the ticket window.* | *a* **line** *of cars*
  3 a long piece of wire, string, etc.: *It is dangerous to go near* **power lines.** | *a* **telephone line**
  4 some words of a song, poem, or play that are written on one line: *Under the picture were a couple of lines of poetry.*

  ═ **PHRASES** ═
  5 **in line** in a line of people: *We had to* **wait in line** *to buy the tickets.* | *Go* **stand in line** *over there.*
  6 **out of line** no longer standing in a line: *If you get out of line, you'll lose your place.*
  ⟳ *See also* ON-LINE.

line² [*verb;* **lined, lining**]
  1 if people or things line a road or area, they are along the edges of it: *People lined the streets to see the parade.*
  2 to put a layer of paper, cloth, etc., on the inside of something: *She lined the suit with silk.*
  ⟳ *See also* LINING.

═ **PHRASAL VERB** ═
line up [*phrasal verb*]
  3 if people line up or are lined up, they stand in a line: *All the children lined up outside the school.* | **line someone/ something up** ▸ *The police officer lined the men up against the wall.*

linen /ˈlɪnən/ [*noun*]
  1 sheets: *Make sure there is clean linen on the beds.*
  2 a kind of cloth like cotton: *a linen suit*

lining /ˈlaɪnɪŋ/ [*noun*] a layer of paper, cloth, etc., on the inside of something: *The jacket had a silk lining.*

link¹ /lɪŋk/ [*noun*]
  1 the fact that two things or people are related; *synonym* CONNECTION: *They found a* **link between** *the two crimes.*
  2 one of the rings that connect together to form a CHAIN: *My bracelet fell off because one of the links broke.*

link² [*verb;* **linked, linking**] to connect one thing or person with another: *Many bridges link the two parts of the city.*

linking verb * /ˈlɪŋkɪŋ ˌvɚb/ [*noun*] GRAMMAR a verb such as "be," "become," or "seem" that connects the subject of a sentence to the adjective that describes it: *In the sentence "You seem tired," "seem" is a linking verb.*
  ☞ The linking verbs "be" and "become" can also connect nouns to a subject: **He is a student. He became a doctor.**

Eric is **at the front of** the line. He is **first** in line.

Sarah is **behind** Eric and **in front of** Brian. She is **next** in line.

Brian is **after** Sarah and **ahead of** Joseph.

Joseph is **at the back of** the line. He is **last** in line.

Eric   Sarah   Brian   Joseph

waiting in line: positions

lint /lɪnt/ [*noun*] very small pieces of thread or cloth: *There's lint all over my black jacket.*

lion * /'laɪən/ [*noun*] a large, wild, yellow-brown cat. The male has long thick hair around its head: *The lion moved quietly through the grass.*

lioness /'laɪənɪs/ [*noun; plural* **lionesses**] a female lion: *a lioness and her cub*

lip * /lɪp/ [*noun*] one of the dark soft parts along the top and bottom edges of your mouth: *He kissed her on the lips.*

lipstick /'lɪp,stɪk/ [*noun*] a substance used to color a woman's lips: *She was wearing bright red lipstick.*

liquid[1] * /'lɪkwɪd/ [*noun*] any substance that has a form like water: *Make sure you drink enough liquids when you're sick.*
 ⇨ *Compare* GAS (definition 3), SOLID[2].

liquid[2] * [*adjective; no comparative*] in the form of a liquid: *liquid soap*

liquor /'lɪkɚ/ [*noun*] a strong alcoholic drink: *He doesn't drink liquor.*

list[1] * /lɪst/ [*noun*] a number of things written down on separate lines: *What's the next item on the list?* | *I'll make a list of what we need.* | *a shopping list*

list[2] [*verb;* **listed, listing**] to write a number of things down in a list, or to mention a number of things: *He listed all the places he had visited on vacation.*

listen * /'lɪsən/ [*verb;* **listened, listening**] to pay attention to a sound or to what someone is saying: *I was listening to the radio.* | *She was still talking to him, but he wasn't listening.*
 ⇨ *See the usage note at* HEAR.

lit[1] * /lɪt/ [*verb*] the past tense and past participle of LIGHT[3]

lit[2] [*adjective; no comparative*] burning, or giving off light: *a lit match*

liter * /'litɚ/ [*noun*] a unit for measuring liquids, equal to 33.8 ounces: *a liter of milk*

literally /'lɪtərəli/ [*adverb*] used to emphasize that you are telling the exact truth about something: *He has literally hundreds of comic books.*

literature * /'lɪtərətʃɚ/ [*noun*] serious books, poetry, and plays: *We've been studying African literature.*

litter[1] /'lɪtɚ/ [*noun*] pieces of paper, empty cans, etc., that are dropped on the ground: *The streets were full of litter.*

litter[2] [*verb;* **littered, littering**] to drop waste on the ground instead of throwing it away properly: *Keep Our Parks Green—Don't Litter!*

little[1] * /'lɪtəl/ [*adjective;* **littler, littlest**]
 1 small in size; <u>opposites</u> BIG, LARGE: *My feet are little.* | *There was a little smile on her face.*
 2 small and young: *a little girl* | *I was afraid of the dark when I was little.*

little[2] * [*determiner*]
 1 not much: *We have so little time left!*
 ☛ Only use **little** before an uncountable noun in this meaning.
 ⇨ *See the usage note at* FEW[1].
 ══ **PHRASES** ══
 2 a little some, but not very much: *Add a little water to the mixture.*
 3 a little bit a very small amount: *I'd like just a little bit of milk.*

little[3] * [*adverb*]
 1 not much: *They worry little about what could happen.*
 ══ **PHRASE** ══
 2 a little slightly: *I'm feeling a little better now.*

little[4] * [*pronoun*]
 1 not much: *He said little at dinner.*
 ══ **PHRASES** ══
 2 a little some, but not very much: *I know a little about it.* | *I'll have a little of the apple pie.*
 3 little by little gradually: *Little by little, she became more confident.*

live[1] * /lɪv/ [*verb;* **lived, living**]
 1 to have your home in a particular place: *"Where do you live?" "I live in Denver."* | *He still lives with his parents.*
 2 to stay alive and not die: *Some of these trees live for two hundred years.*
 ⇨ *See also* LIFE.
 ══ **PHRASAL VERBS** ══
live on [*phrasal verb*]
 3 to eat, do, or use something to stay alive: **live on something** ▸ *He lived on soup when he was a student.* | *I had only $75 a week to live on.*
live up to [*phrasal verb*]
 4 to do or achieve what someone

expects: **live up to something** ▸ *She tries to live up to her own high standards.*

live² /laɪv/ [*adjective; no comparative*]
  1 a live broadcast or performance is made when the show happens or when people are watching: *a live talk show on the radio*
  2 live animals or plants are not dead or artificial: *The lab does experiments on live rats.*
  ☛ Only use **live** before a noun in this meaning.

liveliness /'laɪvlinɪs/ [*noun*] the quality of being active and having a lot of energy: *I love the liveliness of puppies.*

lively /'laɪvli/ [*adjective;* **livelier, liveliest**] very active and with a lot of energy: *He's a very lively little boy.*

liver /'lɪvɚ/ [*noun*]
  1 an important organ in the body which cleans the blood
  2 the liver of an animal, eaten as meat: *I like chicken livers.* | *Liver is good for you.*

lives * /laɪvz/ [*noun*] the plural of LIFE

living¹ /'lɪvɪŋ/ [*adjective; no comparative*] someone who is living is still alive: *He's the world's most famous living artist.*

living² [*noun*] the money that you need to buy things: *It's a strange way to* **make a living** (=earn money). | *What do you do* **for a living** (=as your job)?

living room /'lɪvɪŋ ,rum/ [*noun*] the main room in a home where people can sit and read, talk, watch television, etc.: *We were playing in the living room.*

lizard /'lɪzɚd/ [*noun*] an animal like a small snake with four short legs

a lizard

'll /l/ the short form of WILL¹: *She'll be late.* | *It'll take a long time.*

load¹ * /loʊd/ [*noun*] things that are being carried, for example in a vehicle: *a load of grain*

load² * [*verb;* **loaded, loading**]
  1 to put a lot of things on or into a vehicle, ship, etc.; *opposite* UNLOAD: *They loaded the cartons onto the truck.*

2 to put something into a piece of equipment so it can be used: *How do you load the program onto your computer?* | *I forgot to* **load the camera** (=put film in it).

— **PHRASAL VERB** ——

load up [*phrasal verb*]
  3 to put a lot of things into or onto something: **load up something** ▸ *Will you help me load up the van?* | **load something up** ▸ *Jim loaded his plate up with food.*

loaf /loʊf/ [*noun; plural* **loaves**] bread in one whole piece, that is usually cut into smaller pieces: *She bought a* **loaf of bread** *and some cheese.*

loan¹ /loʊn/ [*noun*] money that someone lends you: *Maybe we could get a loan from the bank.*

loan² [*verb;* **loaned, loaning**] to lend someone something: **loan someone something** ▸ *Could you loan me $20?* | **loan something to someone** ▸ *He loaned his bike to a friend.*

loaves /loʊvz/ [*noun*] the plural of LOAF

lobby /'labi/ [*noun; plural* **lobbies**] the room you walk into when you enter a large building such as a hotel

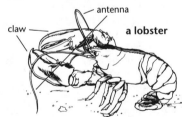
antenna
claw
a lobster

lobster /'labstɚ/ [*noun*] a sea creature that you can eat, that has ten legs, the front two of which have large claws

local¹ * /'loʊkəl/ [*adjective; no comparative*]
  1 in or near the area you are talking about or where you live: *the local hospital* | *local residents*

/i/ **see** /ɪ/ **big** /eɪ/ **day** /ɛ/ **get** /æ/ **hat** /ɑ/ **father, hot** /ʌ/ **up** /ə/ **about** /ɔ/ **saw** /oʊ/ **hope** /ʊ/ **book** /u/ **too** /aɪ/ **I** /aʊ/ **how** /ɔɪ/ **boy** /ɚ/ **bird** /ɚ/ **teacher** /ɪr/ **ear** /ɛr/ **air** /ɑr/ **far** /ɔr/ **more** /ʊr/ **tour** /aɪr/ **fire** /aʊɚ/ **hour** /θ/ **nothing** /ð/ **mother** /ʃ/ **she** /ʒ/ **measure** /tʃ/ **church** /dʒ/ **jump** /ŋ/ **long**

2 a local train or bus stops at many places: *Only the local trains run on weekends.*
⇨ *Compare* EXPRESS².
☛ Only use **local** before a noun.

local² [*noun*]
1 a train or bus that stops at many places: *the Sixth Avenue local*
⇨ *Compare* EXPRESS³.
2 someone who lives in a particular place: *When I'm traveling, I like talking to the locals.*

locate /'loʊkeɪt/ [*verb;* **located, locating**] FORMAL to find out where something or someone is: *They were unable to locate the missing painting.*

located Ⓣ /'loʊkeɪtɪd/ [*adjective; no comparative*]
══ PHRASE ══
be located somewhere to be somewhere; used about things that cannot move, such as cities, buildings, or rooms: *The town is located on a lake.*

location Ⓣ /loʊ'keɪʃən/ [*noun*] where something is: *The hotel was in a beautiful location.*

lock¹ * /lak/ [*verb;* **locked, locking**]
1 to fasten or close something with a lock; *opposite* UNLOCK: *He locked the front door.* | *Did you lock the garage?*
══ PHRASAL VERBS ══
lock in [*phrasal verb*]
2 to put someone or something into a place and lock it: **lock someone/ something in something** ▸ *Oh no, I locked my keys in the car.*
lock out [*phrasal verb*]
3 to make someone unable to enter a place, by locking its door: **lock someone out** ▸ *I accidentally locked myself out of my apartment.*
lock up [*phrasal verb*]
4 to close and lock all the doors and windows in a building: *The office was already locked up for the night.*
5 to put someone in prison: **lock someone up** ▸ *They should lock people like him up.*

lock² * [*noun*] an object that is used to fasten or close something, and that is usually opened with a key: *You should put a better lock on your bicycle.*

locker /'lakɚ/ [*noun*] a small closet that can be locked and in which people can leave clothes and other things while they play sports, work, or study: *He put his clothes and wallet in a locker.*

locker room /'lakɚ ˌrum/ [*noun*] a room in a place where people play sports, where you can change clothes, wash, and leave your things in lockers: *I left my towel in the locker room.*

locksmith /'lakˌsmɪθ/ [*noun*] someone who repairs and attaches locks and makes keys: *The locksmith came and installed the new door locks.*

locust /'loʊkəst/ [*noun*] an insect like a large grasshopper that eats crops: *A swarm of locusts destroyed the wheat.*

loft /lɔft/ [*noun*] a large room or an upper level at the top of a building: *a hay loft* (=for storing food for animals in a barn)

log¹ /lɔg/ [*noun*] a thick piece of a tree: *She put another log on the fire.*

log² [*verb;* **logs, logged, logging**]
══ PHRASAL VERBS ══
log on or **log in** [*phrasal verb*]
1 to start using a computer system, often by typing a secret word: *She logged on and read her e-mail messages.*
log off or **log out** [*phrasal verb*]
2 to stop using a computer system: *I found the information I wanted and logged off.*

logging /'lɔgɪŋ/ [*noun*] the activity of cutting down trees to use them in industry, or to use the land they are on: *Logging can hurt the environment.*

loneliness /'loʊnlinɪs/ [*noun*] the feeling of being unhappy because you are alone: *After her children grew up, she felt great loneliness.*

lonely * /'loʊnli/ [*adjective;* **lonelier, loneliest**] unhappy because you are alone: *I felt very lonely when I first moved here.*
⇨ *See the synonym note at* ALONE².

long¹ * /lɔŋ/ [*adjective;* **longer** /'lɔŋgɚ/, **longest** /'lɔŋgɪst/]
1 measuring a lot from one end to the other; *opposite* SHORT: *She had long hair.*
2 measuring a particular amount from

one end to the other: *The table was six feet long.* | *How long is the room?*
☞ Do not use **long** before a noun in this meaning. Use it after an amount or in questions after "how."
3 lasting for or taking a lot of time; *opposites* BRIEF, SHORT: *He took a long vacation.*
➪ *See also* LENGTH, LENGTHEN.

long[2] * [*adverb;* **longer, longest**]
1 for a lot of time: *I haven't been waiting too long.* | *How long will you be staying?* | *The pork has cooked long enough.*
☞ The adverb **long** is used mainly in negative sentences and questions, and with "too" and "enough."
2 used to emphasize that a lot of time has passed: *I arrived home long after the others.* | *They're already long gone* (=they left many hours ago). | *Our family settled here long ago* (=many years ago).
— PHRASE ══════
3 as long as or **so long as** used to say that one thing can happen only if another thing happens first: *You can watch TV as long as you've finished your homework.*
➪ *See also* **no longer** *at* LONGER.

long[3] * [*noun*]
1 used in questions and negative sentences to mean "a lot of time": *Will it take long?* | *I haven't known him for long.*
— PHRASE ══════
2 before long after only a short time; *synonym* SOON: *Before long they had fallen in love.*

long[4] [*verb;* **longed, longing**] to want something very much: *She was longing for news.* | **long to do something** ▸ *He longed to see his son again.*

long-distance /'lɔŋ 'dɪstəns/ [*adjective; no comparative*] going a long way, or between places that are far apart: *a long-distance runner* | *a long-distance phone call*

longer /'lɔŋgɚ/ [*adverb*]
— PHRASE ══════
no longer or **not any longer**
if something no longer happens or is no longer true, it used to happen or be true

but does not happen or is not true now: *He no longer wants to be an actor.*

longitude /'lɑndʒɪtud/ [*noun*] a position to the east or west measured from a line around the earth that crosses the North and South Poles

look[1] * /lʊk/ [*verb;* **looked, looking**]
1 to turn your eyes toward something or someone and pay attention: *Look at this!* | *She looked out of the window.*
➪ *See the usage note at* SEE.
2 [*linking*] to seem to be true, or seem to have a particular quality: *She looked unhappy.* | *Their house looked exactly like ours.*
☞ Do not use an adverb with this meaning. For example, do not say "He looked angrily." Say **He looked angry.**
3 to consider something: *They are looking at some new ideas.*
— PHRASES ══════
4 look out! SPOKEN used to warn someone about danger: *Look out— there's a car coming!*
5 it looks like or **it looks as if** used to say what you think is likely to happen or be true: *It looks like it's going to rain.*
— PHRASAL VERBS ══════
look after [*phrasal verb*]
6 to take care of someone or something: **look after someone/something** ▸ *There was no one to look after the children.*
look ahead [*phrasal verb*]
7 to consider and decide things about the future: *Looking ahead, we plan to build a new factory in two years.*
look around [*phrasal verb*]
8 to go around a place to see all of it and learn more about it: *I visited the campus and looked around.* | **look around something** ▸ *We want to look around the school again.*
look for [*phrasal verb*]
9 to try to find something or someone:

/i/ **see**	/ɪ/ **big**	/eɪ/ **day**	/ɛ/ **get**	/æ/ **hat**
/ɑ/ **father, hot**	/ʌ/ **up**	/ə/ **about**	/ɔ/ **saw**	
/oʊ/ **hope**	/ʊ/ **book**	/u/ **too**	/aɪ/ **I**	/aʊ/ **how**
/ɔɪ/ **boy**	/ɚ/ **bird**	/ə/ **teacher**	/ɪr/ **ear**	/ɛr/ **air**
/ɑr/ **far**	/ɔr/ **more**	/ʊr/ **tour**	/aɪr/ **fire**	
/aʊɚ/ **hour**	/θ/ **nothing**	/ð/ **mother**	/ʃ/ **she**	
/ʒ/ **measure**	/tʃ/ **church**	/dʒ/ **jump**	/ŋ/ **long**	

look for someone/something ▶ *I'm looking for my hat—have you seen it?*

look forward to [*phrasal verb*]
10 to be thinking happily and eagerly about something that you are going to do or experience: **look forward to something** ▶ *She was looking forward to the trip.* I **look forward to doing something** ▶ *I look forward to meeting you.*
☛ Do not say "I look forward to do it." Say **I look forward to doing it**.

look over [*phrasal verb*]
11 to look at every part of something: **look something over** ▶ *He came with us to look the place over.* I **look over something** ▶ *Will you look over the report I've written?*

look up [*phrasal verb*]
12 to find a particular piece of information in a book or on a computer: **look something up** ▶ *If you don't know a word, look it up in the dictionary.* I **look up something** ▶ *He looked up her phone number.*

look² * [*interjection*]
1 used when you are annoyed and are trying to explain something: *Look, I don't want to buy any magazines!*
2 used when you want someone to look at something: *Hey, look! There's a deer next to the road.*

look³ * [*noun*]
1 when someone looks at something or someone: *Take a look at this.*
2 the appearance of something: *They're giving the mall a new look.*
3 an expression on someone's face: *There was a look of surprise on his face.*
4 looks [*plural*] your looks are your appearance, especially when this is attractive: *He was proud of his looks.*

loom /lum/ [*noun*] a piece of equipment used to make cloth: *The rugs are made on a giant loom.*

loop /lup/ [*noun*] a shape formed when string, a rope, etc., is bent around so that it touches or crosses itself: *He tied the end of the rope into a loop.*

loose * /lus/ [*adjective;* **looser, loosest**]
1 not close against something or not firmly attached; *opposite* TIGHT: *Wear loose clothing when it's hot.* I *One of the screws is loose on the lid of the pot.*
2 if an animal is loose it is not in a locked or enclosed area, or not tied: *Her dog got loose and ran off.*

USAGE loose, lose
Do not confuse **loose** and **lose**. **Loose** means that something is not tight: *a loose jacket.* **Lose** means to no longer have something: *Don't lose your mittens.*

loosely * /'lusli/ [*adverb*] in a way that is not close against something or not firmly attached; *opposites* TIGHT, TIGHTLY: *His scarf hung loosely around his neck.*

loosen /'lusən/ [*verb;* **loosened, loosening**] to make something looser, or to become looser; *opposite* TIGHTEN: *He loosened his tie.* I *The knot had loosened.*

lord * /lɔrd/ [*noun*]
1 the Lord another name for God or Jesus: *Let us pray to the Lord.*
2 a man who had a high social rank in past times: *The land used to belong to a great lord.*

lose * /luz/ [*verb;* **lost, losing**]
1 to no longer have an object with you and not know where it is: *I've lost my gloves.*
↪ *Compare* FIND.
2 to no longer have something or someone you used to have: *He had lost their respect.* I *You've lost weight* (=become thinner). I *Many people lost their lives* (=were killed) *in the disaster.* I *I lost my mother last year* (=she died).
3 to do worse than the other person or team in a game, competition, fight, etc.; *opposite* WIN: *We can't lose this game.* I *The team had lost again.*
↪ *See the usage note at* LOOSE.

━ PHRASE ━
4 lose your hearing/sight/etc. to no longer be able to hear, see, etc.: *Grandpa began to lose his hearing two years ago.*
↪ *See also* **lose/keep your temper** *at* TEMPER.

loser /'luzɚ/ [*noun*] the person or team that loses a game or competition; *opposite* WINNER: *The winners shook hands with the losers.*

loss * /lɔs/ [*noun; plural* **losses**]
1 when you lose something or someone: *He was very upset about the* **loss of** *his dog.*
2 when a person or team loses a game, competition, etc.; *opposite* WIN: *They ended the season with eleven wins and five losses.*
3 when a company earns less money than it spends; *opposite* PROFIT: *The factory* **made a loss** *this year.*

lost[1] * /lɔst/ [*verb*] the past tense and past participle of LOSE

lost[2] * [*adjective; no comparative*] if you are lost, you do not know where you are: *I think we're lost.* | *Bring a map, so we don't* **get lost.**

lost-and-found /'lɔst ən 'faʊnd/ [*noun*] a place in a school, office building, station, etc., where things people have lost are kept: *Why don't you see if your hat is* **in the lost-and-found?**

lot[1] * /lat/ [*determiner*]
═══ PHRASE ═══
a lot of or **lots of** very many or very much: *It cost a lot of money.* | *She has lots of friends.*

USAGE   **a lot of, lots of**
If the object of **a lot of** or **lots of** is plural, use a plural verb: *A lot of people* **were** *there.* If the object is singular, use a singular verb: *Lots of time* **was** *wasted.*

lot[2] * [*adverb*]
═══ PHRASE ═══
a lot or **lots**
1 very much: *She seems a lot happier now.* | *I love you lots and lots.*
2 many times; *synonyms* FREQUENTLY, OFTEN: *I visit my grandmother a lot.*
↪ *Compare* MUCH[1].

lot[3] * [*noun*]
1 a piece of land in a town that does not have a building on it: *People planted gardens in many empty city lots.*
↪ *See also* PARKING LOT.
═══ PHRASE ═══
2 **a lot** or **lots** very many or very much: *"How much do those shoes cost?" "A lot."* | *"How much did you spend?" "Lots—much too much, in fact."*

lotion /'loʊʃən/ [*noun*] a thick liquid that you put on your skin to protect it, clean it, or make it softer: *She rubbed the lotion into her hands.* | *Use some* **suntan lotion** (=lotion that protects skin from the sun).

lottery /'latəri/ [*noun; plural* **lotteries**] a game in which people buy tickets, and prizes are given to the people with tickets whose numbers match the ones that are chosen

loud[1] * /laʊd/ [*adjective;* **louder, loudest**] easily heard because of the large amount of sound; *opposites* QUIET, SOFT: *"Hello!" he said in a loud voice.* | *The noise from the street was getting louder and louder.*

loud[2] * [*adverb;* **louder, loudest**] in a loud way: *She asked him to speak louder.*

loudly * /'laʊdli/ [*adverb*] in a loud way; *opposites* QUIETLY, SOFTLY: *He used to play records very loudly.*

loudspeaker /'laʊd,spikɚ/ [*noun*] a piece of electrical equipment that makes voices louder: *They make school announcements* **over the loudspeakers**.

lounge /laʊndʒ/ [*noun*] a room for people to sit or wait in, in a hotel or airport: *The* **departure lounge** *was full.*

lousy /'laʊzi/ [*adjective;* **lousier, lousiest**] INFORMAL very bad: *I've had a lousy day.*

lovable /'lʌvəbəl/ [*adjective;* **more lovable, most lovable**] easy to love or like very much: *He's such a lovable baby.*

love[1] * /lʌv/ [*verb;* **loved, loving**]
1 to have very strong good feelings about someone, sometimes romantic feelings; *opposite* HATE: *Do you love me?* | *He loves his kids very much.*
2 to like something very much; *opposite* HATE: *I love chocolate.* | **love doing something** ▸ *He loves playing chess.*
☛ Do not say "How would you love your eggs cooked?" Say **How would you like your eggs cooked?**

/i/	**see**	/ɪ/	**big**	/eɪ/	**day**	/ɛ/	**get**	/æ/ **hat**
/ɑ/	**father, hot**	/ʌ/	**up**	/ə/	**about**	/ɔ/	**saw**
/oʊ/	**hope**	/ʊ/	**book**	/u/	**too**	/aɪ/	**I**	/aʊ/ **how**
/ɔɪ/	**boy**	/ɝ/	**bird**	/ɚ/	**teacher**	/ɪr/	**ear**	/ɛr/ **air**
/ɑr/	**far**	/ɔr/	**more**	/ʊr/	**tour**	/aɪr/ **fire**
/aʊɚ/	**hour**	/θ/	**nothing**	/ð/	**mother**	/ʃ/ **she**
/ʒ/	**measure**	/tʃ/	**church**	/dʒ/	**jump**	/ŋ/ **long**

3 would love to want something very much: *"Would you like to come over for dinner tomorrow?" "I'd love to!"*

love[2] * [*noun*]
1 very strong good feelings about someone, sometimes romantic feelings; *opposites* HATE, HATRED: *Her love for her children is very deep.*
2 a strong feeling that you like something very much; *opposite* HATRED: *Her parents encouraged her love of art.*
— PHRASES —
3 in love (with) loving someone in a romantic way: *He was in love with her.* | *I fell in love with him* (=started loving him).
4 Love, used at the end of a letter to a friend or family member before the name of the person who wrote it: *He signed the letter "Love, Steve."*

lovely /'lʌvli/ [*adjective;* **lovelier, loveliest**] very pleasant or attractive: *I had a lovely time.* | *You look lovely.*

lover /'lʌvɚ/ [*noun*] someone who likes something very much: *an art lover* | *a lover of classical music*

loving /'lʌvɪŋ/ [*adjective;* **more loving, most loving**] showing love for someone: *They're such loving parents.*

low[1] * /loʊ/ [*adjective;* **lower, lowest**]
1 measuring a small amount from top to bottom: *The house was surrounded by a low wall.*
2 near the ground: *She put the bowl on the lowest shelf.*
3 not very good or important: *He got low grades in school.* | *a low rank in the army*
4 small in amount or level: *It's not easy living on low pay.*
5 a low sound is deep or quiet: *She spoke in a very low voice.*
▷ *Compare* HIGH[1].

low[2] * [*adverb;* **lower, lowest**] toward or near the ground; *opposite* HIGH: *The plane was flying too low.*

lower[1] * /'loʊɚ/ [*verb;* **lowered, lowering**] to move something to a lower level, position, or amount; *opposite* RAISE: *They lowered the crates onto the ship.* | *She lowered her eyes*

(=looked downward). | *Please lower the volume on the stereo.*

lower[2] * [*adjective; no comparative*] used to describe a thing or part that is below another thing or part; *opposite* UPPER: *The fire had started on one of the lower floors.*
☛ Only use **lower** before a noun.

lowercase /'loʊɚ-'keɪs/ [*adjective; no comparative*] a lowercase LETTER of the alphabet has the form "a," "b," "c," etc., rather than "A," "B," "C," etc.; *opposites* UPPERCASE, CAPITAL: *Names do not begin with a lowercase letter.*

loyal * /'lɔɪəl/ [*adjective;* **more loyal, most loyal**] always supporting a person, group, or belief; *synonym* FAITHFUL; *opposite* DISLOYAL: *He remained loyal to his friend.* | *a loyal sports fan*

loyalty * /'lɔɪəlti/ [*noun*] when someone is loyal: *He knew he could depend on their loyalty.*

luck * T /lʌk/ [*noun*]
1 something good that happens by chance: *Did you have any luck finding your keys?* | *With luck* (=if the things that happen are good), *we won't have to wait long.*
2 the way in which good or bad things happen to people, by chance: *I've had a lot of bad luck recently.*
— PHRASE —
3 good luck! SPOKEN used to wish someone success: *"I have an English test today." "Well, good luck!"*

luckily /'lʌkəli/ [*adverb*] used to say that an event or situation is lucky: *Luckily, I'd brought a map with me.*

lucky * /'lʌki/ [*adjective;* **luckier, luckiest**]
1 if you are lucky, good things happen to you by chance; *opposite* UNLUCKY: *Who will be the lucky winner?*
2 something that is lucky is a good thing to have happen or makes good things happen; *opposite* UNLUCKY: *She wears a bracelet she thinks is lucky.*

luggage /'lʌgɪdʒ/ [*noun*] cases and bags that you take with you when you travel somewhere; *synonym* BAGGAGE: *She put her luggage onto the train.*

lukewarm /'luk'wɔrm/ [*adjective; no comparative*] a little warm: *The water in the bathtub was only lukewarm.*

lumber /'lʌmbɚ/ [*noun*] cut pieces of wood used for building: *The lumber for the deck was delivered today.*

lump /lʌmp/ [*noun*]
1 a piece of something, usually one without a neat shape: *He threw another lump of coal onto the fire.*
2 a swelling under the skin: *The doctor looked at that lump on my neck.*

lumpy ⊤ /'lʌmpi/ [*adjective;* **lumpier, lumpiest**] filled or covered with lumps: *This sauce is lumpy.*

lunar /'lunɚ/ [*adjective; no comparative*] relating to the moon: *The first lunar landing took place in 1969.*
☛ Only use **lunar** before a noun.
↪ Compare SOLAR.

lunatic /'lunətɪk/ [*noun*] someone who does things that are not at all reasonable: *Only a lunatic would do something as risky as that!*

lunch /lʌntʃ/ [*noun; plural* **lunches**] a meal that is eaten in the middle of the day: *Have you had lunch yet?*

lunchtime /'lʌntʃ,taɪm/ [*noun*] the time when people have lunch: *It's almost lunchtime.*

lung * /lʌŋ/ [*noun*] one of the two large parts inside your chest which are used in breathing: *Smoking harms your lungs.*

luxurious /lʌkˈʃʊriəs/ [*adjective;* **more luxurious, most luxurious**] very comfortable and expensive: *a luxurious apartment*

luxury /'lʌkʃəri/ [*noun; plural* **luxuries**]
1 something that is not necessary and usually expensive, but pleasant to have: *I can't afford to buy any luxuries.*
2 when you have a comfortable life with a lot of expensive things: *They live in luxury.*

lying * /'laɪɪŋ/ [*verb*] the present participle of LIE[1] and LIE[2]

lyrics /'lɪrɪks/ [*plural noun*] the words of a song: *I couldn't hear all of the lyrics.*

M

M * or **m** /ɛm/ [*noun; plural* **Ms** or **M's, m's**] the 13th letter of the English alphabet
↪ See the usage note at ALPHABET.

m 1 the written abbreviation of METER or METERS: *a room 3m by 4m* | *She is 1.67m in height.*
2 also **M;** the written abbreviation of MEDIUM, especially relating to clothes sizes: *Clothing labels are marked s, m, l, or xl.*

M.A. /'ɛm'eɪ/ [*noun; plural* **M.A.s** or **M.A.'s**] Master of Arts; a degree in a subject such as history or English that you can study for after your first degree: *He has an M.A. in math.* | *Lisa Bell, M.A.*
↪ Compare **B.A., B.S., M.S., PH.D.**

ma'am /mæm/ [*name*] SPOKEN the short form of MADAM; used to speak politely to a woman, especially someone you do not know or someone who is in a position of authority: *I'm sorry, ma'am, could you repeat your question?* | *"Do you*

like your new school?" "Yes, ma'am."
↪ Compare MISS (definition 1). ↪ See the warning at MISTER.

macaroni /,mækəˈrouni/ [*noun*] dough in the shape of small tubes that is boiled and eaten with sauce: *Mom makes great macaroni and cheese.*

machine * /məˈʃin/ [*noun*] a piece of equipment made of several different parts, that does a particular job: *Put your money in the machine and it will give you a ticket.* | *a sewing machine*

machine gun /məˈʃin ,gʌn/ [*noun*] a gun that shoots bullets very quickly

machinery * /məˈʃinəri/ [*noun*] a collection of machines, or the parts of a machine: *There's some very expensive machinery in this factory.* | *Something's wrong with the machinery.*

mad /mæd/ [*adjective;* **madder, maddest**]
1 angry: *He made me so mad I almost hit him.* | *Dad's really mad at you.*

☞ Do not say that someone "becomes mad." Say that he or she **gets mad**.
⇨ See the synonym note at ANGRY.
2 not at all controlled: *Everyone made a mad rush for the front seats.*

═ PHRASES ═

3 do something like mad to do something with a lot of speed or energy: *I had to run like mad to catch up with her.*

4 be mad about something/ someone to like someone or something very much: *He's mad about my cousin Rose.*

madam /ˈmædəm/ [*name*] FORMAL used to speak or write politely to a woman, especially someone you do not know or someone who is in a position of authority: *Please come this way, madam.* | *Dear Madam, I am writing to request some information.*
⇨ Compare MISS (definition 1), SIR.

made * /meɪd/ [*verb*] the past tense and past participle of MAKE

made-up /ˈmeɪd ˈʌp/ [*adjective; no comparative*] not true or real, and often intended to deceive people: *It's obvious that his excuse is made-up.*
⇨ See the synonym note at IMAGINARY.

madly /ˈmædli/ [*adverb*] in an uncontrolled or extremely excited way: *She's madly in love with my brother.*

magazine *
/ˌmægəˈzin/ [*noun*] a thin book with a paper cover that you can bend, containing stories and pictures about news, fashion, etc., that is sold every week or month: *In my spare time I like reading sports magazines.*

a magazine

magic[1] * /ˈmædʒɪk/ [*noun*] a power that makes strange or unusual things happen, or something that is done using this power: *I like to do magic.* | *The house wasn't cleaned by magic!*

magic[2] * [*adjective; no comparative*] using magic or seeming to be caused by

magic: *Let me show you a magic trick.* | *I was the assistant in a magic show.*

magical /ˈmædʒɪkəl/ [*adjective;* more magical, most magical] strange, exciting, and attractive: *The dancers gave a magical performance.*

magician /məˈdʒɪʃən/ [*noun*] someone who does things that seem like magic, especially to entertain people: *The magician did card tricks.*

magnesium /mægˈniziəm/ [*noun*] a light silver-white metal that burns with a bright white flame

magnet /ˈmægnɪt/ [*noun*] a piece of metal that attracts iron or steel: *Using a magnet, he lifted the key off the floor.*

magnetic /mægˈnɛtɪk/ [*adjective; no comparative*] having the power of a magnet: *Credit cards have a magnetic strip on the back.*

magnificent /mægˈnɪfəsənt/ [*adjective;* more magnificent, most magnificent] extremely good or impressive: *Her tennis has been magnificent this year.* | *We visited a magnificent golden temple.*

magnify /ˈmægnəˌfaɪ/ [*verb;* magnifies, magnified, magnifying] to make something seem bigger than it really is: *This is a photo of a single drop of water, magnified 100 times.*

magnifying glass /ˈmægnəfaɪɪŋ ˌglæs/ [*noun; plural* magnifying glasses] a special piece of glass that you look through, that makes very small things look bigger

It's easy to read small print with a magnifying glass.

a magnifying glass

maid /meɪd/ [*noun*] a female servant or worker in a hotel, big house, etc.: *The maid hasn't cleaned the room yet.*

maiden name /ˈmeɪdən ˈneɪm/ [*noun*] the name a woman has before she is married and starts using her husband's name: *Mom's maiden name is Green.*

maid of honor /'meɪd əv 'anɚ/ [*noun; plural* **maids of honor**] a woman who has been specially chosen by another woman who is getting married, to take part in the wedding and make some of the arrangements

mail¹ * /meɪl/ [*verb;* **mailed, mailing**] to send a letter or package by putting it in a mailbox or taking it to a post office: **mail someone something** ▸ *I've just mailed you a long letter.* I **mail something to someone** ▸ *If you find my scarf, will you mail it to me?*

mail² * [*noun*]
1 the system for sending and receiving letters and packages: *Your birthday present is **in the mail**. I I sent your invitation **by mail** yesterday.*
2 letters or packages sent by mail: *Has the mail come yet? I I don't get much mail.*

mailbox /'meɪl,baks/ [*noun; plural* **mailboxes**]
1 a container in a public place where you put letters that you want to send: *Can you put this in the mailbox on your way to school?*
2 a box outside someone's home where his or her mail is delivered: *Please check the mailbox when you get home.*

mailboxes

mailman /'meɪl,mæn/ [*noun; plural* **mailmen** /'meɪl,mɛn/] a man whose job is to deliver mail

main * /meɪn/ [*adjective; no comparative*] the biggest, most important, most serious, etc.: *Meet me at the main station. I Who played the main part in the movie? I The main reason she's unhappy is that she's lonely.*
☛ Only use **main** before a noun.

mainland /'meɪn,lænd/ [*noun*] the main part of an area or country, and not its islands: *There's a ferry service between the island and **the mainland**.*

mainly * /'meɪnli/ [*adverb*] used to say that something is true most of the time or that it is true of most of a group; *synonym* MOSTLY: *Mainly I read science fiction books. I Tourists come mainly in June and July.*

maintain Ⓣ /meɪn'teɪn/ [*verb;* **maintained, maintaining**]
1 to keep something in good condition: *Cars can be very expensive to maintain.*
2 to make something continue: *They've maintained contact for 30 years.*

maintenance /'meɪntənəns/ [*noun*] work done to keep something in good condition: *The museum has closed for building maintenance.*

majestic /mə'dʒɛstɪk/ [*adjective;* **more majestic, most majestic**] big and impressive: *a majestic mountain range*

major¹ Ⓣ /'meɪdʒɚ/ [*adjective; no comparative*] very important, very serious, etc.; *opposite* MINOR: *He's already had a major heart attack. I You made one major mistake.*
☛ Only use **major** before a noun.

major² [*noun*]
1 the main subject a student studies at a college or university: *My major is English literature.*
↪ Compare MINOR² (definition 2).
2 [*name*] also **Major;** an officer with a fairly high rank in the Army, the Air Force, or the Marine Corps

major³ [*verb;* **majored, majoring**]
══ PHRASAL VERB ══
major in [*phrasal verb*]
to study a particular subject as your major: **major in something** ▸ *She majored in computer science.*
↪ Compare MINOR³.

/i/ see /ɪ/ big /eɪ/ day /ɛ/ get /æ/ hat
/ɑ/ father, hot /ʌ/ up /ə/ about /ɔ/ saw
/oʊ/ hope /ʊ/ book /u/ too /aɪ/ I /aʊ/ how
/ɔɪ/ boy /ɝ/ bird /ɚ/ teacher /ɪr/ ear /ɛr/ air
/ɑr/ far /ɔr/ more /ʊr/ tour /aɪr/ fire
/aʊɚ/ hour /θ/ nothing /ð/ mother /ʃ/ she
/ʒ/ measure /tʃ/ church /dʒ/ jump /ŋ/ long

majority /mə'dʒɔrɪti/ [*noun*] the largest part of a group of people or things; *opposite* MINORITY: *A majority of students do well on their final exams.* | *Voters who want lower taxes are in the majority.*

make * /meɪk/ [*verb; made, making*]
1 to produce something: *We make all our own clothes.* | *Those kids are making a lot of noise.* | *This vase was made in Hungary.* | **make someone something** ▸ *I made you a present.*
2 used before some nouns to show that someone does something: *It's very easy to make a mistake.* | *Have you made your decision yet?*
3 to cause a situation or an action: *Snow makes driving dangerous.* | *Poison mushrooms can make you extremely sick.* | **make someone do something** ▸ *This song always makes me cry.* | *You made me spill my drink!*
4 to force someone to do something, especially something he or she does not want to do: *Dad made me finish my homework before dinner.* | *I didn't want to do it. Alice made me.*
☛ Don't say "He made me to do it." Say **He made me do it.**
5 to earn money: *He makes a lot of money selling things to tourists.* | *One week I made $200.*
6 if two numbers added together make another number, that is their total: *Seven plus three makes ten.*

━ PHRASES ━
7 **(be) made of something** to be built or formed of a particular thing or things: *a desk made of oak*
8 **make a bed** to arrange the bed covers neatly on a bed, after you have slept in it: *You're not going out to play until you've made your bed.*
9 **make it** to succeed in arriving somewhere or doing something: *The weather was awful, but we made it home.* | *Only a small number of actors make it in Hollywood.*
10 **make do** to manage with whatever is available: *We've run out of pens—can you make do with a pencil?*
11 **make believe** to pretend that something is real or true, especially as

a children's game: *Let's make believe we're cowboys.*
➪ *See also* **make up your mind** *at* MIND[1] *and* **make sure** *at* SURE[1].

━ PHRASAL VERBS ━
make out [*phrasal verb*]
12 to write someone's name on a check so that the money is paid to him or her: **make a check out** ▸ *Please make the check out to Gary Brown.* | **make out a check** ▸ *I made out the check to my sister.*
13 to be able to understand something that is seen, heard, or done: **make something out** ▸ *I can't make the words out.* | **make out something** ▸ *Could you make out what she said?*
make up [*phrasal verb*]
14 to invent a story or account of something: **make up something** ▸ *He's always making up stories to tell the kids.* | **make something up** ▸ *It can't be true, you're making it up!*
15 if two or more things make up another, they combine to form it: *The choir is made up of children from three schools.*

makeup or **make-up** /'meɪk,ʌp/ [*noun*] colored powders, creams, etc., that women and actors put on their faces: *You're too young to wear makeup.*

malaria /mə'lɛriə/ [*noun*] a serious illness caused by the bite of a mosquito

male[1] * /meɪl/ [*adjective; no comparative*]
1 belonging to the sex that cannot have babies: *Most of our students are male.* | *a male dog*
➪ *Compare* FEMALE[1].
2 relating to men, boys, and animals that are not female: *Football is traditionally a male sport.*

male[2] * [*noun*] a person or animal that belongs to the sex that cannot have babies: *All adult males served in the army.*
➪ *Compare* FEMALE[2].

mall /mɔl/ [*noun*] a place where there are many stores and restaurants, either in one building or built closely together

mammal /'mæməl/ [*noun*] a kind of animal, including humans, whose babies develop inside their bodies and who produce milk to feed them: *Dogs, cats, and pigs are all mammals.*

man * /mæn/ [*noun; plural* **men**]
1 an adult male person: *A man in a blue suit walked toward me.* | *Most of the teachers at my school are men.*
⇨ *See the usage note at* GENTLEMAN.
2 men and women considered as a group: *When did man first travel in space?*

manage * T /'mænɪdʒ/ [*verb; managed, managing*]
1 to succeed in doing something, especially something difficult: **manage to do something** ▶ *I finally managed to get the lid off the bottle.* | *"I got her to lend me some money." "How did you manage that?"*
2 to be in charge of a group of people, an organization, or an area of business: *I manage a team of twelve workers.* | *She manages our accounts.*

management T /'mænɪdʒmənt/ [*noun*]
1 the activity or process of being in charge of people, an organization, etc.: *This is his first job in management.*
2 the people who are in charge of a company: *The management will make a decision later today.* | *A sign on the restaurant door read "Under New Management."*

manager * T /'mænɪdʒɚ/ [*noun*] someone who is in charge of a group of people, an organization, etc.: *He's a manager with a large shipping company.* | *The band fired its manager last month.*

mane /meɪn/ [*noun*] the long, thick hair around the neck and head of a lion, a HORSE, etc.

mango /'mæŋgoʊ/ [*noun; plural* **mangoes** or **mangos**] an orange fruit with red skin and a big seed inside, which grows on trees in hot places

man-made /'mæn 'meɪd/ [*adjective; no comparative*] made by people rather than being natural; *synonym* ARTIFICIAL: *man-made fabric* | *a man-made lake*

manner /'mænɚ/ [*noun*]
1 FORMAL the way something is done: *He was walking in a very strange manner.*
2 **manners** [*plural*] the way you

behave: *Your kids have very good manners.* | *It's bad manners to interrupt when someone's speaking.*

mansion /'mænʃən/ [*noun*] a very big and impressive house: *the governor's mansion*

manslaughter /'mæn,slɔtɚ/ [*noun*] the crime of killing someone without intending to
⇨ *Compare* MURDER².

mantel /'mæntəl/ [*noun*] a shelf above a FIREPLACE in a house

manual¹ /'mænyuəl/ [*noun*] a book that gives you instructions about how something works or how to do something: *To find out how to delete files, look at your manual.* | *a car manual*

manual² [*adjective; no comparative*] done by a person or people, not by machines: *a car with a manual gearshift* | *hard manual labor*

manufacture /,mænyə'fæktʃɚ/ [*verb; manufactured, manufacturing*] to produce something in large quantities, especially in a factory: *Cars have been manufactured at this factory for 40 years.*

manufacturer /,mænyə'fæktʃərɚ/ [*noun*] a person or company that manufactures something: *If there is a problem, return the product to the manufacturer.*

manuscript /'mænyə,skrɪpt/ [*noun*] a written document, especially one containing a play, a book, etc., before it is printed: *He checked the manuscript for errors.*

many * /'mɛni/ [*determiner, pronoun*]
1 used especially in questions and negative sentences to mean a large amount of things or people; *opposite* FEW: *Does she have many friends?* | *I don't have many books of my own.* | *Many of them decided to go.*
☛ Only use the determiner **many** before countable nouns.
⇨ *Compare* MUCH².

/i/ see /ɪ/ big /eɪ/ day /ɛ/ get /æ/ hat
/ɑ/ father, hot /ʌ/ up /ə/ about /ɔ/ saw
/oʊ/ hope /ʊ/ book /u/ too /aɪ/ I /aʊ/ how
/ɔɪ/ boy /ɝ/ bird /ɚ/ teacher /ɪr/ ear /ɛr/ air
/ɑr/ far /ɔr/ more /ʊr/ tour /aɪr/ fire
/aʊɚ/ hour /θ/ nothing /ð/ mother /ʃ/ she
/ʒ/ measure /tʃ/ church /dʒ/ jump /ŋ/ long

— PHRASE —

2 how many used to talk or ask about the number of things or people: *How many eggs are left?* | *I don't know how many people are coming.*

☞ Do not use **how many** with uncountable nouns. Say **how much**. For example, do not say "How many time do you need?" Say **How much time do you need?**

map * /mæp/ [*noun*] a picture of the parts of an area such as a country or town: *We were lost and didn't have a map.* | *a map of the world*
➭ *See the picture at* CLASSROOM.

maple /ˈmeɪpəl/ [*noun*] a tree that produces a thick, sweet substance, or the wood from this tree: *a maple leaf* | *a maple bookcase*

maple syrup /ˈmeɪpəl ˈsɪrəp/ [*noun*] a sweet food made by boiling the liquid from a maple tree: *I love pancakes with maple syrup.*

Mar. the written abbreviation of MARCH

marble /ˈmɑrbəl/ [*noun*]
1 a kind of hard rock, often white in color, used to make buildings, statues, etc.: *a beautiful marble staircase* | *Most of his sculptures were made of marble.*
2 a small colored glass ball used by children in games: *Her brother was outside playing marbles.*

march[1] * /mɑrtʃ/ [*verb*; **marches, marched, marching**] to walk with regular, formal steps, especially as a group: *Soldiers marched into the town.* | *Their band is marching in the parade.*

march[2] * [*noun; plural* **marches**] a public event at which people walk together to show that they support something or are against it: *Women went on marches to win the right to vote.*

March * [*noun*] the third month of the year: *I was born on March 16th.* | *Their wedding is sometime in March.*
➭ *See the usage note at* MONTH.

margarine /ˈmɑrdʒərɪn/ [*noun*] a soft food like butter, made from vegetable oil

margin /ˈmɑrdʒɪn/ [*noun*] the space around the writing on a page: *Leave a margin of about an inch on the left side of the page.*

marine[1] /məˈrin/ [*adjective; no comparative*] relating to the ocean: *a book about marine life* (=the plants, fish, etc., that live in the ocean)

marine[2] [*noun*]
1 a member of the Marine Corps
2 the Marines [*plural*] the MARINE CORPS: *She joined the Marines.* | *He's in the Marines.*

Marine Corps /məˈrin ˌkɔr/ [*noun*] the part of the U.S. military forces whose members are trained to fight on land or at sea: *He spent five years in the Marine Corps.* *

mark[1] * T /mɑrk/ [*noun*]
1 a dirty line, spot, or damaged area on a surface: *What's that mark on your shirt?*
2 a small letter or other sign you write or print on a page: *a question mark*

SYNONYMS   mark, stain, spot, smudge

    A **mark** is a dirty or damaged area on something: *You have an ink mark on your sleeve.* A **stain** is larger than a mark, and is difficult to remove: *I can't get the juice stain out of my shirt.* A **spot** is a small round mark: *Oh no, I got grease spots on my pants.* A **smudge** is a mark made by accidentally rubbing a liquid such as paint or ink: *There were smudges of ink all over the page.*

---

mark[2] * [*verb*; **marked, marking**]
1 to put a word or sign on something, for example to give information about it: **mark something something** ▸ *Mark the letter "air mail."* | **mark something with something** ▸ *On the map, I've marked our hotel with an X.*
2 if a teacher marks a student's work, he or she gives it a grade: *I'll mark your homework tonight.*

— PHRASAL VERB —

mark down
3 to reduce the price of something: **mark down something** ▸ *Their umbrellas are marked down 50 percent.* | **mark something down** ▸ *Have they marked the sweaters down yet?*

market * /ˈmɑrkɪt/ [*noun*]
1 a place where people buy and sell

goods, especially outdoors: *There's a large fruit and vegetable market in the middle of the town.*

2 a country or area where goods are sold: *Europe is an important market for Indian products.*

━━ PHRASE ━━

3 on the market offered or available for sale: *She said they've put the beach house on the market.*

marketing /'markɪtɪŋ/ [*noun*]
the activity of deciding how to sell a product, for example how to advertise it and what its price should be: *Companies spend a lot of money on marketing.*

marketplace /'markɪt,pleɪs/ [*noun*]
1 the part of business that involves buying and selling: *the international marketplace*
2 an outdoor area in a town where a market usually is

marmalade /'marmə,leɪd/ [*noun*]
a thick sweet food made from boiled oranges and sugar
⇨ Compare JAM[1], JELLY.

marriage * /'mærɪdʒ/ [*noun*]
1 when a man and woman become husband and wife: *a marriage ceremony*
2 the whole time that two people are married, or the relationship they have: *She has two children from her first marriage.* | *He is enjoying marriage.*

married * /'mærid/ [*adjective; no comparative*] having a wife or husband; *opposites* SINGLE, UNMARRIED: *My husband and I have been married for ten years.* | *Do you think they will ever get married* (=marry)?
☛ Do not say "He has married for five years." Say **He has been married for five years.**

USAGE　Getting married

If you say that two people **marry**, it can sound a little formal. It is more usual to say that they **get married**. The event where this happens is a **wedding**. The woman getting married is the **bride** and the man is the **groom**.

marry * /'mæri/ [*verb; marries, married, marrying*] to become someone's husband or wife, or to make

two people husband and wife in a wedding ceremony: *Will you marry me?* | *This is the priest who married us.*

Mars /marz/ [*name*] the planet that is fourth from our sun

marsh /marʃ/ [*noun; plural marshes*] an area of soft, wet land: *People come to these marshes to see the wildlife.*

martial art /'marʃəl 'art/ [*noun*] a kind of traditional Asian fighting sport, in which you use your hands and feet to attack and to defend yourself: *He taught karate, judo, and other martial arts.*

marvelous /'marvələs/ [*adjective; more marvelous, most marvelous*]
extremely good; *synonym* WONDERFUL: *The weather was marvelous.* | *a marvelous garden*

masculine /'mæskyəlɪn/ [*adjective; no comparative*] relating to men, or typical of men: *a deep masculine voice.*
☛ Do not use "masculine" to talk about the sex of a person or animal. Use **male**. For example, do not say "a masculine cat." Say **a male cat.**
⇨ Compare FEMININE.

mash /mæʃ/ [*verb; mashes, mashed, mashing*] to press or crush something, usually food, into a soft mixture: *mashed potatoes* (=mixed with milk and butter)

costume masks

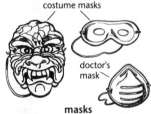

doctor's mask

masks

mask /mæsk/ [*noun*] something you wear over your face, for example for protection or so that people do not know who you are: *a doctor's face mask* | *A man wearing a mask robbed the store.*

/i/ **see**	/ɪ/ **big**	/eɪ/ **day**	/ɛ/ **get**	/æ/ **hat**
/a/ **father, hot**	/ʌ/ **up**	/ə/ **about**	/ɔ/ **saw**	
/oʊ/ **hope**	/ʊ/ **book**	/u/ **too**	/aɪ/ **I**	/aʊ/ **how**
/ɔɪ/ **boy**	/ɝ/ **bird**	/ɚ/ **teacher**	/ɪr/ **ear**	/ɛr/ **air**
/ɑr/ **far**	/ɔr/ **more**	/ʊr/ **tour**	/aɪr/ **fire**	
/aʊɚ/ **hour**	/θ/ **nothing**	/ð/ **mother**	/ʃ/ **she**	
/ʒ/ **measure**	/tʃ/ **church**	/dʒ/ **jump**	/ŋ/ **long**	

mass * /mæs/ [*noun; plural* **masses**]
1 a large amount of something: *There was a mass of clouds above the hills.*
2 a word used especially in science meaning the amount of material in a substance: *Calculate the mass of this piece of metal.*

massacre[1] /ˈmæsəkɚ/ [*noun*] the violent killing of a large number of people

massacre[2] [*verb;* **massacred, massacring**] to kill a large number of people violently: *Thousands of innocent people were massacred during the war.*

massage /məˈsɑʒ/ [*verb;* **massaged, massaging**] to rub someone's body so that he or she feels relaxed or stops feeling pain: *Will you massage my shoulders for me?*

massive Ⓣ /ˈmæsɪv/ [*adjective;* **more massive, most massive**] extremely large or great: *a massive ship* | *He had a massive heart attack.* | *It was a massive earthquake.*

mast /mæst/ [*noun*] a tall pole that the sails on a ship are attached to

master[1] /ˈmæstɚ/ [*noun*]
1 a man who is in control of someone or something: *The dog followed its master everywhere.*
2 someone who is very skillful at something: *He is considered a master of Chinese cooking.*

master[2] [*verb;* **mastered, mastering**] to learn to do something well: *Hungarian is a very difficult language to master.* | *Once you've mastered the basics, dancing is fun.*

masterpiece /ˈmæstɚˌpis/ [*noun*] an extremely good painting, piece of music, or other piece of work: *Masterpieces from many great painters are in the museum.*

mat /mæt/ [*noun*] a piece of thick material that you put on the floor: *an exercise mat* | *Wipe your feet on the mat before you come in.*
⇨ *Compare* CARPET, RUG.

match[1] * /mætʃ/ [*noun; plural* **matches**]
1 a small piece of wood or thick paper with a special substance on the end, that produces a flame: *He struck a match and held it up in the darkness.*

I *a book of matches* (=20 paper matches in a folded paper cover)
2 the word used for an organized game between two people or teams in some sports: *The chess match lasted almost a week.*
I *We have a tennis match this weekend.*

a matchbox
matches
a book of matches

match[2] * [*verb;* **matches, matched, matching**]
1 if two things match, they look good when they are put together, because they are similar in color or style: *The curtains and cushions match perfectly.* | *I need shoes that match my purse.*
2 to find the connection between two or more things: *Match these photographs with the names written on the list.*

matchbox /ˈmætʃˌbɑks/ [*noun; plural* **matchboxes**] a box that holds wooden MATCHes

mate[1] /meɪt/ [*noun*] one of a pair of animals or birds that produce young together: *A male penguin will sit on its mate's egg.*

mate[2] [*verb;* **mated, mating**] if animals mate, they have sex: *Deer mate at this time of year.*

material * /məˈtɪriəl/ [*noun*]
1 cloth used to make clothes, curtains, etc.; *synonym* FABRIC: *How much material will you need for your dress?* | *a blouse made from a light material*
2 the things you need to build or make something: *They sell building materials.*

math * /mæθ/ [*noun*] mathematics; the study of numbers, quantities, shapes, etc.: *Math is my least favorite subject.*

mathematical /ˌmæθəˈmætɪkəl/ [*adjective; no comparative*] relating to mathematics: *We had to answer some difficult mathematical questions.*

mathematics * /ˌmæθəˈmætɪks/ [*noun*] the study of numbers, quantities, shapes, etc.; *synonym* MATH: *Our students study six subjects including mathematics and science.*

☛ Only use **mathematics** with a singular verb.

matinee /ˌmætəˈneɪ/ [noun; plural matinees] an afternoon performance of a play, or an afternoon movie: *Our tickets are for the Wednesday matinee.*

matter[1] * /ˈmætɚ/ [verb; mattered] to be important: *Does it matter if I arrive early?* | *"I forgot to bring a sleeping bag." "It doesn't matter, we have a spare bed."*
☛ Do not say "It is mattering" or "It is not mattering." Say **It matters** or **It doesn't matter.** There is no continuous form of this verb.

matter[2] * [noun]
1 a subject or situation that has to be dealt with: *Stop laughing, this is a serious matter.*
2 the material that objects and substances are made from: *Do not put solid matter down the sink.*
━ **PHRASES** ━
3 what's the matter? used to ask someone why he or she is worried, sad, etc.: *"What's the matter?" "I can't find my keys."*
4 no matter what/why/how/etc. used to say that something will not affect a situation or decision: *No matter how hard I scrub, the bathtub still looks dirty.*
5 as a matter of fact SPOKEN used to add information or to emphasize something: *He's been playing very well. As a matter of fact, he's one of our best players.*
6 something is the matter or **nothing is the matter** used to say that you think something is wrong, or that there is nothing wrong: *Something's the matter, but she won't tell me what.* | *There's absolutely nothing the matter with your bicycle.*

mattress /ˈmætrɪs/ [noun; plural mattresses] a large flat object put on a bed to make it comfortable to sleep on

mature[1] /məˈtʃʊr/ [adjective; more mature, most mature]
1 behaving in a sensible way, like an adult; *opposite* IMMATURE: *She's very mature for her age.*
2 completely grown; *opposite* IMMATURE: *A mature crocodile can grow up to 20 feet long.*

mature[2] [verb; matured, maturing]
1 to begin behaving in a sensible way, like an adult, or to make someone do this: *She matured when she went away to college.* | *William's summer job has matured him.*
2 to become completely grown: *This species of tree matures quickly.*

max. the abbreviation of MAXIMUM: *Operating temperature: max. 425° F.*

maximum[1] /ˈmæksəməm/ [determiner, adverb] biggest, highest, most, etc.; *opposite* MINIMUM: *This car has a maximum speed of 120 miles per hour.* | *The maximum yearly fee is $50.*
☛ Only use the determiner **maximum** before a noun.

maximum[2] [noun] the biggest, highest, most, etc., possible; *opposite* MINIMUM: *The elevator holds a maximum of five people.* | *She scored ten points, which is the maximum you can get.*

may * /meɪ/ [modal verb]
1 used to show that something is possible: *I may need you to help me.* | *He may have caught a later train.*
↪ Compare MIGHT[1] (definition 1).
2 used to ask politely for permission to do something: *May we speak with you for a moment?*
↪ Compare CAN[1] (definition 3).
3 used to tell someone politely that he or she is allowed to do something: *You may now board the plane.*

May * [noun] the fifth month of the year: *Our party is on May 7th.* | *We moved here in May.*
↪ See the usage note at MONTH.

maybe * /ˈmeɪbi/ [adverb] used to say that something may happen, may be true, or may be right; *synonyms* POSSIBLY, PERHAPS: *Maybe you left your sweater in the car.* | *"Do you think she'll call?" "Maybe."*
☛ Do not use **maybe** in formal writing. Use **perhaps.**

/i/ **see**	/ɪ/ **big**	/eɪ/ **day**	/ɛ/ **get**	/æ/ **hat**
/ɑ/ **father, hot**	/ʌ/ **up**	/ə/ **about**	/ɔ/ **saw**
/oʊ/ **hope**	/ʊ/ **book**	/u/ **too**	/aɪ/ **I**	/aʊ/ **how**
/ɔɪ/ **boy**	/ɚ/ **bird**	/ɚ/ **teacher**	/ɪr/ **ear**	/ɛr/ **air**
/ɑr/ **far**	/ɔr/ **more**	/ʊr/ **tour**	/aɪr/ **fire**
/aʊɚ/ **hour**	/θ/ **nothing**	/ð/ **mother**	/ʃ/ **she**
/ʒ/ **measure**	/tʃ/ **church**	/dʒ/ **jump**	/ŋ/ **long**

mayonnaise /ˌmeɪəˈneɪz/ [noun] a thick white sauce made from eggs and oil: *Would you like mayonnaise on your sandwich?*

mayor or **Mayor** /ˈmeɪɚ/ [noun, name] the most important official in a city or town: *He was the first black mayor of Atlanta.*

MB the written abbreviation of MEGABYTE or MEGABYTES: *a computer with 128MB of RAM*

M.B.A. /ˌɛmˈbiˈeɪ/ [noun; plural M.B.A.s or M.B.A.'s] Master of Business Administration; a degree in subjects relating to business that you can study for after your first degree

me * /mi/ [pronoun] used to talk about yourself, as the object of a verb or preposition: *Give that book to me.* | *Will you lend me $20?* | *Please listen to me.* | *I waved, but he didn't see me.* | *"I'll have a cup of coffee." "Me too"* (=so will I). ➪ *See also* I.

meadow /ˈmɛdoʊ/ [noun] a field with grass and flowers in it

meal * /mil/ [noun] an occasion when you sit down and eat food at a particular time of day, or the food that you eat: *Sit down and eat your meal with the rest of the family.* | *It's not good for you to miss meals.*

mean[1] * /min/ [verb; meant, meaning]
1 to have a particular meaning: *Do you know what the word "merchant" means?* | *When I blow the whistle, it means the game is over.*
☛ In this use of **mean**, do not use the form "meaning." For example, do not say that something "is meaning something." Say that it **means something**.
— PHRASES
2 **mean to** to intend to do something: *I'm sorry—I didn't mean to hurt her.* | *Do you really think he meant to leave the door open?*
☛ Do not say that someone "is meaning to do something." Say that someone **means to do something**.
3 **mean something/nothing/a lot/ etc. to someone** to be important or not important to someone: *It would mean a lot to me if you could come.* | *You know she means nothing to me.*

4 **I mean it!** used to say angrily that you are serious about something: *Get in here right now. I mean it!*

mean[2] [adjective; meaner, meanest] unkind or cruel; opposites KIND, NICE: *The kids are always being mean to each other.* | *Don't be mean to your little brother, let him play with you.*

meaning * /ˈminɪŋ/ [noun] the idea or thing that is represented by a word or sign: *Some English words have many different meanings.* | *What's the meaning of this symbol?*

means * ⊤ /minz/ [noun; plural means]
1 a method or object that you use to do something: *Without a key, we had no means of getting into the house.* | *She'll use any means she can to win.* | *Flying is the fastest means of transportation.* | *The equation can't be solved by this means* (=using this method). | *We crossed the river by means of a narrow wooden bridge* (=using one).
— PHRASES
2 **by all means** used to tell someone that you are happy for them to do something: *If you need me, by all means call.* | *Yes, you can borrow the car, by all means.*
3 **by no means** used to say that something is definitely not a fact: *This discussion is by no means finished.*

meant * /mɛnt/ [verb] the past tense and past participle of MEAN[1]

meantime /ˈminˌtaɪm/ [noun]
— PHRASE
in the meantime between now and a time in the future, or between two past events: *I'll buy you a new bicycle, but in the meantime you can borrow mine.*

meanwhile /ˈminˌwaɪl/ [adverb] between now and a time in the future or between two past events: *Your teacher will be back soon. Meanwhile, get on with your work.*

measles /ˈmizəlz/ [noun] a disease, often caught by children, that gives you small red spots on your skin: *She got the measles and had to stay home for two weeks.*
☛ Only use **measles** with a singular verb.

measure[1] * /'mɛʒɚ/ [verb; measured, measuring]
1 to discover the length, amount, size, etc., of something: *The nurse weighed me and measured my height.*
2 to be a particular length, amount, size, etc.: *The boat measures 15 feet across.*

measure[2] * [noun]
1 something you do in order to achieve a result: *We **took measures to** stop this from happening again.*
2 a method of measuring something: *The meter is a unit of measure.*

measurement * /'mɛʒɚmənt/ [noun]
1 a number representing a length, size, amount, etc.: *We need to know the measurements of the room.*
2 the process of measuring: *Accurate measurement is important.*

meat * /mit/ [noun] the flesh of animals eaten as food, or a kind of this food: *She hasn't eaten meat for three years.* I *The table was filled with meats and cheeses.*

USAGE   Kinds of meats
The meat from a pig is **pork**. The meat from a cow is **beef**, or if it is from a calf, **veal**. The meat from a young sheep is **lamb**.

---

meatball /'mit,bɔl/ [noun] meat cut up into very small pieces and made into the shape of a ball: *We're having spaghetti and meatballs for supper.*

mechanic /mə'kænɪk/ [noun] someone who repairs vehicles and machinery as a job

mechanical /mə'kænɪkəl/ [adjective; no comparative]
1 relating to a machine: *The plane crash was caused by a mechanical failure.*
2 using only machine parts rather than electricity: *a mechanical clock*

mechanism /'mɛkə,nɪzəm/ [noun] a set of moving parts in an object that make something happen: *The locking mechanism seems to be broken.*

medal /'mɛdəl/ [noun] a flat piece of metal with a design on it, given as a reward for courage or as a prize for winning a race, competition, etc.: *He*

was awarded a medal for bravery. I *Our team is expected to win the gold medal.*

medals

media /'midiə/ [noun]
the media
newspapers, magazines, television, etc., considered as a group: *This story has been widely reported **in the media**.*
☛ Only use **the media** with a plural verb.

medical * /'mɛdɪkəl/ [adjective; no comparative] relating to illnesses or their treatment, or to the job of treating sick people: *Do you have any medical problems?* I *the medical profession*

medically /'mɛdɪkli/ [adverb] relating to illness or its treatment: *The surgery is not medically necessary.*

medication /,mɛdɪ'keɪʃən/ [noun] drugs taken to treat an illness or other medical problem: *Are you **on any medication** at the moment?*
☛ The word **medication** is usually used by doctors. Use the words **drugs, pills,** or **medicine** instead.

medicine * /'mɛdəsɪn/ [noun]
1 a drug that you take to treat an illness or other medical problem: *Have you **taken your medicine** this morning?* I *I need some medicine for my sore throat.*
2 the study or job of treating sick people: *She's **studying medicine** in Canada.* I *What made you decide on a career in medicine?*

medieval /,midi'ivəl/ [adjective; no comparative] relating to the Middle Ages, the historical period between about 500 and 1500 A.D.: *The castle dates back to medieval times.* I *a tiny medieval church*

meditate /'mɛdɪ,teɪt/ [verb; meditiated, meditating] to try to make yourself

/i/ see	/ɪ/ big	/eɪ/ day	/ɛ/ get	/æ/ hat
/ɑ/ father, hot	/ʌ/ up	/ə/ about	/ɔ/ saw	
/oʊ/ hope	/ʊ/ book	/u/ too	/aɪ/ I	/aʊ/ how
/ɔɪ/ boy	/ɚ/ bird	/ɚ/ teacher	/ɪr/ ear	/ɛr/ air
/ɑr/ far	/ɔr/ more	/ʊr/ tour	/aɪr/ fire	
/aʊɚ/ hour	/θ/ nothing	/ð/ mother	/ʃ/ she	
/ʒ/ measure	/tʃ/ church	/dʒ/ jump	/ŋ/ long	

completely calm, by thinking carefully about one thing and taking deep breaths: *I try to meditate for at least thirty minutes each day.*

medium[1] ⊤ /'midiəm/ [*adjective; no comparative*] of a size or amount that is not small and not large; *synonym* AVERAGE: *The man is blond and of medium height.* | *a medium-sized saucepan*

medium[2] ⊤ [*noun*] a size of clothing that is not small and not large: *There aren't any mediums left.* | *This dress is too big. Do you have it in medium?*
⊃ *Compare* SMALL[2], LARGE[2], EXTRA LARGE.

meet[1] * /mit/ [*verb;* **met, meeting**]
1 to see and speak with someone for the first time: *Where did you two meet?* | *They met each other in college.* | *Karen has a sister but I've never met her.* | *It was nice meeting you* (=used when you are saying goodbye to someone).
2 to arrange to be in the same place as someone at a particular time so that you can do something together: *Meet me at seven at my place.* | *Do you know a good place to meet?* | *Can I meet with you tomorrow?*

SYNONYMS meet, get together, bump into, run into, gather, assemble

When two people arrange to **meet** each other, you can say that they **get together**: *Would you like to get together some time?*

If you meet someone accidentally, you **bump into** or **run into** him or her: *I bumped into John at the grocery store.* | *We ran into our neighbors at the mall.*

If a lot of people meet in a place, they **gather** there: *A crowd was gathering around the fight.* If they gather as part of an organized plan, they **assemble** there: *We will assemble in the main square at 5:00 p.m.*

---

meet[2] [*noun*] a competition in some sports, involving all the members of several teams: *He missed two **track meets.***

meeting * /'mitɪŋ/ [*noun*] an occasion when a group of people meet to discuss something, especially at work: *I have a meeting at two o'clock.* | *She's in a meeting at the moment.*

megabyte /'mɛgə,baɪt/ [*noun*] a unit for measuring computer information, equal to 1,024 kilobytes: *This program will use up about 100 megabytes of your hard disk.*

megahertz /'mɛgə,hɜˈts/ [*noun; plural* **megahertz**] a unit for measuring how fast something happens, used especially to show the speeds of computer parts

megaphone /'mɛgə,foʊn/ [*noun*] a piece of equipment you speak into to make your voice heard by a lot of people

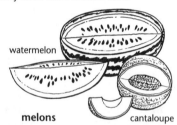
a megaphone

melody /'mɛlədi/ [*noun; plural* **melodies**] the musical sounds that make a tune: *This melody is easy to remember.*

melon /'mɛlən/ [*noun*] a large, round, juicy fruit with a hard skin

watermelon

melons   cantaloupe

melt * /mɛlt/ [*verb;* **melted, melting**] to turn into a liquid or become soft because of heat, or to make something do this: *The snow melted, causing many floods.* | *Melt some chocolate in a pan.*

member * /'mɛmbɚ/ [*noun*] someone who forms part of a group, club, organization, etc.: *She is a member of the Girl Scouts.* | *This is a private club and only members are allowed in.*

membership /'mɛmbɚ,ʃɪp/ [*noun*] the right to be a member of a group, club, organization, etc.: *I renewed my membership in the tennis club.* | *Membership costs $150 per year.*

memo /'mɛmoʊ/ [*noun; plural* **memos**] a written message sent between people in a company: *She sent everyone a memo about the meeting.*

memorial /mə'mɔriəl/ [noun]
something such as a stone structure that reminds people of someone who has died or of something that happened in the past: *There's a war memorial in the center of town.* I *He made the movie as a memorial to his father.*

memorize /'mɛmə,raɪz/ [verb; memorized, memorizing] to learn words or numbers completely so that you can say or remember them without reading them: *Before the test, Jessica and I memorized ten English verbs.*

memory * /'mɛməri/ [noun; plural memories]
1 your ability to remember things: *I have a terrible memory.* I *He repeated the whole list from memory.*
2 a thought about the past that you have in your mind: *I have good memories of my childhood.* I *She had a vague memory* (=one that is not very clear) *of her grandmother.*
3 the part inside a computer that stores information: *I need to put more memory in my computer.*

men * /mɛn/ [noun] the plural of MAN

mend /mɛnd/ [verb; mended, mending] to repair something that is damaged, especially clothes: *The hem of my skirt needs mending.*

men's room /'mɛnz ,rum/ [noun] a room containing public toilets for men

mental * /'mɛntəl/ [adjective; no comparative]
1 relating to the mind rather than the body or spirit; *opposite* PHYSICAL: *He studies the mental processes involved in learning.*
2 relating to illness of the mind: *a mental institution* (=where mentally ill people are treated) I *mental illness*

mentally * /'mɛntəli/ [adverb] in a way that uses or affects the mind: *mentally ill* (=not able to think in a normal way)

mention * T /'mɛnʃən/ [verb; mentioned, mentioning]
1 to talk or write about something for a short time: **mention something to someone** ▸ *Did he mention anything to you about his plans?* I *She doesn't mention her daughter in her will.*

☛ Do not say "mention about something." Say **mention something.**

═══ PHRASES ═══
2 **don't mention it** SPOKEN used as a polite reply to someone who has just thanked you: *"Thanks for the advice." "Don't mention it."*
➪ *See also* **you're welcome** *at* WELCOME[1].
3 **not to mention ....** used to add extra information to what you are saying: *She's smart and nice, not to mention beautiful.*

menu /'mɛnyu/ [noun; plural menus]
1 a list of all the food that is available in a restaurant: *May I please see the menu?* I *What's on the menu* (=what is available to eat) *today?*
2 a list of things to choose from on a computer: *Pull down the menu and click on the file you want.*

meow[1] /mi'aʊ/ [verb; meowed, meowing] to make the sound a cat makes: *Didn't you hear the cat meowing?*

meow[2] [noun] the sound that a cat makes

merchant /'mɚtʃənt/ [noun] someone who buys and sells things as a business: *They belong to a merchants' association.*

mercury /'mɚkyəri/ [noun] a silver-white substance that is used in thermometers and is liquid at room temperature

Mercury [name] the planet that is closest to our sun

mercy /'mɚsi/ [noun] kind or gentle actions, especially from an enemy or a judge: *The soldiers will show no mercy if they catch you.* I *Your Honor, I beg you for mercy.*

merely /'mɪrli/ [adverb] used to emphasize that something or someone is not at all serious, important, dangerous, etc.; *synonyms* JUST, ONLY: *I merely said she might be wrong, and she got mad at me.*

/i/ **see** /ɪ/ **big** /eɪ/ **day** /ɛ/ **get** /æ/ **hat**
/ɑ/ **father, hot** /ʌ/ **up** /ə/ **about** /ɔ/ **saw**
/oʊ/ **hope** /ʊ/ **book** /u/ **too** /aɪ/ **I** /aʊ/ **how**
/ɔɪ/ **boy** /ɚ/ **bird** /ɚ/ **teacher** /ɪr/ **ear** /ɛr/ **air**
/ɑr/ **far** /ɔr/ **more** /ʊr/ **tour** /aɪr/ **fire**
/aʊɚ/ **hour** /θ/ **nothing** /ð/ **mother** /ʃ/ **she**
/ʒ/ **measure** /tʃ/ **church** /dʒ/ **jump** /ŋ/ **long**

merit[1] /'mɛrɪt/ [noun] a good quality or feature of something: *Each of these methods has its merits.*

merit[2] [verb; merited, meriting] to deserve something: *It's a good movie but I don't think it merits an Oscar.*

mermaid /'mɝˌmeɪd/ [noun] an imaginary sea creature with the body of a woman and a fish's tail

merry /'mɛri/ [adjective; merrier, merriest]

— PHRASE —

Merry Christmas used as a greeting at Christmas time: *I wish you all a Merry Christmas and a Happy New Year.*

merry-go-round /'mɛri goʊ ˌraʊnd/ [noun] a machine that goes around and around that children ride on for fun: *Can I go on the merry-go-round, Mom?*

mess[1] /mɛs/ [noun; plural messes]
1 a group of things, especially dirty things, spread around in a careless way: *Don't leave the kitchen in a mess. | Who's going to clean up this mess? | What a mess!*
2 a situation full of problems and trouble: *How am I going to get myself out of this mess?*

mess[2] [verb; messes, messed, messing]

— PHRASAL VERBS —

mess up [phrasal verb]
1 to make something dirty or less organized: **mess up something** ▸ *Don't mess up those clothes. I've just ironed them. |* **mess something up** ▸ *My little brother messed my room up.*
2 INFORMAL to make a big mistake or cause a lot of trouble: *You really messed up this time. |* **mess something up** ▸ *He messed things up for the whole team.*

mess around [phrasal verb]
3 to behave in a silly way, not thinking about the things you should be doing: *Stop messing around and listen to what I'm saying.*

message ✻ /'mɛsɪdʒ/ [noun] a written or spoken piece of information that you leave for someone when you cannot speak to him or her directly: *If I'm not in, leave a message on the answering machine. | Did you get my message? |*

Chris isn't here right now. Can I take a message for him? (=used in phone calls)

messenger /'mɛsəndʒɚ/ [noun] someone who takes messages or packages containing business papers to people: *He sent it by messenger.*

messy /'mɛsi/ [adjective; messier, messiest] not organized, and often dirty; <u>opposite</u> NEAT: *Do you have a comb? My hair's all messy. | a messy house*

met ✻ /mɛt/ [verb] the past tense and past participle of MEET[1]

metal[1] ✻ /'mɛtəl/ [noun] a solid, usually shiny substance such as steel or silver: *Gold is a fairly soft metal. | The staircase is made of metal.*

metal[2] [adjective; no comparative] made of metal: *The money is stored in a huge metal safe. | Are those earrings metal or plastic?*

metallic /mə'tælɪk/ [adjective; no comparative] made of metal, or similar to metal: *a metallic object*

meter ✻ /'mitɚ/ [noun]
1 a unit for measuring length, equal to one hundred centimeters: *I weigh 55 kilograms and am 1.67 meters tall. | This fabric costs $20 per meter.*
2 a machine or tool for measuring how much of something has been used, for example gas, electricity, or water: *The guy from the gas company is here to read the meter.*
⇨ See also PARKING METER.

method ✻ T /'mɛθəd/ [noun] a way of doing something; <u>synonym</u> TECHNIQUE: *This is the easiest method of cooking rice. | the latest teaching methods*

metric /'mɛtrɪk/ [adjective; no comparative] based on the system of measurement that uses meters, liters, and grams: *Americans don't use metric measurements.*

mg the written abbreviation of MILLIGRAM or MILLIGRAMS: *a 50-mg dose twice a day*

MHz the written abbreviation of MEGAHERTZ: *a 550 MHz processor*

mi. a written abbreviation of MILE or MILES: *Next exit 5 mi.*

mice ✻ /maɪs/ [noun] the plural of MOUSE (definition 1).

microchip /'maɪkroʊ,tʃɪp/ [*noun*] a very small object with electronic connections on it, used to make computers or other electronic equipment work: *My computer uses the most up-to-date microchip technology.*

microphone
/'maɪkrə,foʊn/
[*noun*] a piece of
equipment you use
to make your voice
heard, for example
when you sing or
give a speech;
synonym MIKE

a microphone

microprocessor /'maɪkroʊ,prɑsɛsɚ/ [*noun*] a microchip containing a very small system of electronic parts, that makes computers or other electronic equipment work

microscope
/'maɪkrə,skoʊp/
[*noun*] a piece of
equipment used to
look at extremely
small things: *A
scientist examines the
samples of blood
under a microscope.*

microwave[1]
/'maɪkroʊ,weɪv/ or
microwave oven
/'maɪkroʊweɪv ,ʌvən/
[*noun*] a small oven
that cooks food very
quickly: *Cook the broccoli in the
microwave for five minutes.*
⇨ *See the picture at* APPLIANCE.

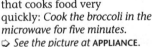
slide
a microscope

microwave[2] [*verb*; **microwaved, microwaving**] to cook food in a microwave: *Microwave the chicken on "high" for four minutes.*

midday /'mɪd'deɪ/ [*noun*] 12 o'clock in the middle of the day; *synonym* NOON: *Now it's time for the midday news.*
⇨ *Compare* MIDNIGHT.

middle[1] * /'mɪdəl/ [*noun*]
the middle the central point or part of something: *You sit here, and I'll sit **in the middle**. | He got hit right **in the middle** of the back.*
⇨ *See the usage note at* CENTER.

middle[2] * [*adjective; no comparative*] in or near the center of something: *She was sitting in the middle row of seats. | I put the ring on my middle finger.*
☞ Only use **middle** before a noun.

middle-aged /'mɪdəl 'eɪdʒd/ [*adjective; no comparative*] between the ages of around 45 and 65: *A middle-aged man in a gray suit approached us.*

Middle Ages /'mɪdəl 'eɪdʒɪz/ [*noun*]
the Middle Ages the time in European history from about 500 to about 1500 A.D.: *The drawings date back to the Middle Ages.*

middle class /'mɪdəl 'klæs/ [*noun*]
the middle class the people in a society who are neither extremely rich nor extremely poor: *The middle class is the largest group in the population.*
⇨ *Compare* UPPER CLASS.

middle-class [*adjective; no comparative*] belonging to or typical of the middle class: *She grew up in a middle-class home.*
⇨ *Compare* UPPER-CLASS.

Middle East /'mɪdəl 'ist/ [*name*]
the Middle East the area including Iran, Egypt, and all the Asian countries to the west and southwest of Iran: *He has worked as a journalist in the Middle East for two years.*

middle school /'mɪdəl ,skul/ [*noun*] a school in the U.S. for students between the ages of 10 or 11 and 13: *There's a middle school in our neighborhood. | She starts middle school next week.*
⇨ *Compare* JUNIOR HIGH SCHOOL.

midnight /'mɪd,naɪt/ [*noun*] 12 o'clock in the middle of the night; *opposite* NOON: *I try to be in bed before midnight. | All the lights are turned off at midnight.*

midterm /'mɪd,tɝm/ [*noun*] an examination taken by students in the middle of a school year period: *I have my midterms in two weeks.*

might[1] * /maɪt/ [*modal verb*]
1 used to show that something is

/i/ **see**	/ɪ/ **big**	/eɪ/ **day**	/ɛ/ **get**	/æ/ **hat**
/ɑ/ **father, hot**	/ʌ/ **up**	/ə/ **about**	/ɔ/ **saw**
/oʊ/ **hope**	/ʊ/ **book**	/u/ **too**	/aɪ/ **I**	/aʊ/ **how**
/ɔɪ/ **boy**	/ɝ/ **bird**	/ɚ/ **teacher**	/ɪr/ **ear**	/ɛr/ **air**
/ɑr/ **far**	/ɔr/ **more**	/ʊr/ **tour**	/aɪr/ **fire**
/aʊɚ/ **hour**	/θ/ **nothing**	/ð/ **mother**	/ʃ/ **she**
/ʒ/ **measure**	/tʃ/ **church**	/dʒ/ **jump**	/ŋ/ **long**

possible but not certain: *We might come by and see you tomorrow.* I *"Are you going to Ben's party?" "I'm not sure. I might."*
⇨ Compare MAY (definition 1).
2 FORMAL the past tense of MAY: *I asked if I might speak with her.*

might² [noun] strength, force, or effort: *She tried **with all her might** to change their minds.*

mighty /'maɪti/ [adjective; **mightier, mightiest**] very powerful: *Napoleon was once the mightiest man in Europe.* I *the mighty force of a volcano*

migrant /'maɪgrənt/ [noun] someone who moves from one place to another to live or work: *migrant farm workers*

migrate /'maɪgreɪt/ [verb; **migrated, migrating**]
1 if birds migrate, they fly from one place to another in large numbers, at a particular time of the year: *Geese migrate south for the winter.*
2 if people migrate, they move from one area to another, especially to find work or good weather: *Many people have migrated to Florida from the north.*

migration /maɪ'greɪʃən/ [noun] when birds or people migrate from one place to another: *The ducks had begun their winter migration.*

mike /maɪk/ [noun] a short form of MICROPHONE: *Anna took the mike and began to sing.*

mild /maɪld/ [adjective; **milder, mildest**]
1 not very bad, serious, or dangerous: *a mild headache*
2 mild food does not have a hot, strong, or sharp taste: *Is this a mild or a hot chili?*
3 mild weather is neither extremely hot nor extremely cold: *It's been a very mild winter.*

mildly /'maɪldli/ [adverb] in a mild way, without being extreme: *I think Andrew was mildly annoyed.*

mile * /maɪl/ [noun]
1 a unit for measuring distance, equal to 1.609 kilometers: *How many miles is it to town?* I *I **ran a mile** in six minutes.*
2 **miles** [plural] a long way: *We'd traveled **miles** and were very tired.*

☞ Do not say "The hotel is 20 miles far from here." Say **The hotel is 20 miles from here** or **The hotel is 20 miles away.**

military¹ * /'mɪlɪˌtɛri/ [adjective; no comparative] from or belonging to an army, navy, or air force: *He attended a military academy for three years.* I *a soldier wearing a military uniform*

military² [noun]
the military an army, navy, or air force: *My father was **in the military** for 20 years.*

milk¹ * /mɪlk/ [noun] the white liquid that female animals produce to feed their babies: *Do you take milk in your coffee?* I *a **glass of milk***

milk² [verb; **milked, milking**] to get milk from a cow: *Farmers have to get up early to milk the cows.*

milkshake /'mɪlkˌʃeɪk/ [noun] a drink made from milk, ice cream, and fruit or chocolate: *a strawberry milkshake*

mill /mɪl/ [noun]
1 an object or machine used to crush small hard solid pieces into a powder: *Please pass me the pepper mill.*
2 a factory, especially one where flour, metal, or cloth is produced: *a steel mill*

millennium /mɪ'lɛniəm/ [noun] a period of a thousand years: *Printing was the most important invention of the last millennium.*

milligram * /'mɪlɪˌgræm/ [noun] a unit for measuring weight, equal to one-thousandth of a gram: *Take one 4-milligram tablet three times a day.*

milliliter * /'mɪləˌlitɚ/ [noun] a unit for measuring liquids, equal to one-thousandth of a liter: *35 milliliters of medicine*

millimeter * /'mɪləˌmitɚ/ [noun] a unit for measuring length, equal to one-thousandth of a meter or one-tenth of a centimeter: *My little finger is 55 millimeters long.*

million * /'mɪlyən/ [number] 1,000,000: *Two million people live in this city.* I *Millions of dollars have already been spent on the project.*

☞ Do not say "three millions dollars" or

"three millions of dollars." Say **three million dollars.**

millionaire /ˌmɪlyə'nɛr/ [*noun*] someone who has more than a million dollars

millionth * /'mɪlyənθ/ [*adjective; no comparative*] coming after 999,999 other people, things, or events; sometimes written as "1,000,000th": *The store gave $1,000 to their millionth customer.*
   ⇨ *See the usage note at* SECOND².

mimic¹ /'mɪmɪk/ [*verb*; **mimics, mimicking, mimicked**] to pretend to be someone by copying his or her actions or behavior: *He's always mimicking the teachers.*

mimic² [*noun*] someone who is good at copying the way people move or behave: *an actor who is a great mimic*

min. the written abbreviation of MINUTE or MINUTES: *Bake for 25 min. at 375°.*

mince /mɪns/ [*verb*; **minced, mincing**] to cut food into very small pieces: *minced onion*

mind¹ * /maɪnd/ [*noun*]
1 the part of you that you use to think, feel, judge, etc.: *She has a brilliant mind.* | *Tell me what's **on your mind*** (=what you are thinking about).

— PHRASES —
2 change your mind to change your decision about what you want to do: *I've changed my mind. I'll go shopping tomorrow instead.*
3 make up your mind to decide what you are going to do or choose, after thinking about it for a while: *I can't make up my mind what to wear to the party.*
4 take your mind off something to stop thinking about something: *Maybe going to the movies will take your mind off your worries.*
5 out of your mind INFORMAL not thinking clearly at all; *synonym* CRAZY: *You're going swimming in this weather? You must be out of your mind.*

mind² * [*verb*; **minded, minding**]
1 to feel annoyed or worried about something: *Do you think she'll mind if I borrow some money?* | *Come as often as you like. I don't mind at all.*

— PHRASES —
2 never mind
  a used to comfort someone who is upset or who has made a mistake or done something wrong: *"I spilled my milk." "Oh, never mind, we can clean it up."*
  ⇨ *See the usage note at* **you're welcome** *at* WELCOME¹.
  b used to say that you do not want to repeat something or talk about it any more: *"What's wrong?" "Oh, never mind."*
3 do you mind or **would you mind** used to ask someone for permission or help in a polite way: *Do you mind if I sit here?* | *Would you mind helping me with my suitcase?*

mine¹ * /maɪn/ [*pronoun*] belonging to or connected with me: *That CD is mine.* | *Mine is the blue house on the left.* | *Sam is a good friend **of mine**.*
  ⇨ *See also* MY.

mine² * [*noun*]
1 a place where coal, metal, oil, etc., is taken from under the ground: *Her father worked in a coal mine.*
2 a bomb hidden in the ground or under water that explodes when it is touched

mine³ [*verb*; **mined, mining**]
1 to take iron, coal, silver, etc., out of the ground: *They've recently begun mining for copper.* | *People here mined coal for decades.*
2 to hide mines in the ground or under water: *The decision was made to mine the harbor.*

miner /'maɪnɚ/ [*noun*] someone who works in a mine

mineral * /'mɪnərəl/ [*noun*] a substance that forms naturally, especially under the ground: *Coal, salt, tin, and iron are all minerals.*

/i/ **see**	/ɪ/ **big**	/eɪ/ **day**	/ɛ/ **get**	/æ/ **hat**

/i/ **see** /ɪ/ **big** /eɪ/ **day** /ɛ/ **get** /æ/ **hat** /ɑ/ **father, hot** /ʌ/ **up** /ə/ **about** /ɔ/ **saw** /oʊ/ **hope** /ʊ/ **book** /u/ **too** /aɪ/ **I** /aʊ/ **how** /ɔɪ/ **boy** /ɚ/ **bird** /ɚ/ **teacher** /ɪr/ **ear** /ɛr/ **air** /ɑr/ **far** /ɔr/ **more** /ʊr/ **tour** /aɪr/ **fire** /aʊɚ/ **hour** /θ/ **nothing** /ð/ **mother** /ʃ/ **she** /ʒ/ **measure** /tʃ/ **church** /dʒ/ **jump** /ŋ/ **long**

mineral water /'mınərəl ˌwɔtɚ/ [noun]
water that you buy in bottles and that
often has bubbles in it

miniature /'mıniətʃɚ/ [adjective; no
comparative] used to describe something
that is smaller than usual for that
thing: *He likes to play with his miniature
railroad.*

minimum[1] /'mınəməm/ [determiner,
adverb] smallest, lowest, least, etc.;
opposite MAXIMUM: *Sixty percent is the
minimum score to pass the test.*
☛ Only use the determiner **minimum**
before a noun.

minimum[2] [noun] the smallest, lowest,
least, etc. possible; opposite MAXIMUM: *I'll
sell it to you for $400, that's the
minimum.* | *We're expecting a minimum
of six hundred people at the conference.*

minimum wage /'mınəməm 'waıdʒ/
[noun] the lowest amount of money that
an employer is legally able to pay
someone for an hour of work: *She's only
paid the minimum wage.*

miniskirt /'mıniˌskɚt/ [noun] a very
short skirt

minister * /'mınəstɚ/ [noun]
1 someone whose job is to perform
religious ceremonies and duties in
some Christian churches
2 someone who has an important job
in the government of some countries:
*Ministers from all the European countries
met to discuss the crisis.*

minivan /'mıniˌvæn/ [noun] a vehicle
that looks like a small bus, with more
seats than a car has and room in the
back for camping things: *Minivans are
popular family vehicles.*
⇨ See also VAN.

minor[1] /'maınɚ/ [adjective; no
comparative] not very important,
serious, etc.; opposite MAJOR: *You made a
few minor mistakes, but nothing serious.* |
It's just a minor illness.
☛ Only use **minor** before a noun.

minor[2] [noun]
1 someone who is below the age of a
legal adult: *We cannot sell liquor to
minors.*
2 a subject that a student studies at a
college or university that is not his or

her main subject: *My minor is chemistry.*
⇨ Compare MAJOR[2] (definition 1).

minor[3] [verb; minored, minoring]
━━ PHRASAL VERB ━━
minor in [phrasal verb]
to study a particular subject as your
minor: **minor in something** ▸ *She
minored in math.*
⇨ Compare MAJOR[3].

minority [T] /mı'nɔrıti/ [noun; plural
minorities]
1 a group of people who belong to a
different race or religion or speak a
different language than most of the
other people in a country or area:
Minorities must be treated equally.
2 the smallest part of a group of people
or things; opposite MAJORITY: *A minority
of students get a Ph.D.* | *Some people
want change, but they're in the
minority.*

mint /mınt/ [noun]
1 a plant that smells sweet and tastes
slightly hot: *I like to put mint in summer
drinks.*
2 a candy that tastes like mint: *Would
you like a mint?*

minus[1] /'maınəs/ [preposition]
1 used when one number is taken
away from another; opposite PLUS: *125
minus 35 equals 90 (125 − 35 = 90).*
⇨ See also SUBTRACT.
2 used to show a negative number: *The
answer is minus 4 (−4).*

minus[2] [adjective; no comparative]
━━ PHRASE ━━
A−/B−/C− a mark given to student for
their work; spoken as "A minus," etc.
An A− is lower than an A, and a B− is
lower than a B: *I got a B− in English.*
⇨ Compare PLUS[2].

minute[1] * /'mınıt/ [noun]
1 a unit of time equal to sixty seconds:
*The baby was born at twelve minutes
past seven.* | *It takes about ten minutes
to drive from my house to the airport.* |
I'll be with you in a few minutes.
2 a very short period of time: *This will
only take a minute.* | *I'll do it in a
minute.* | *Wait a minute and I'll come
with you.* | *Minutes afterward, her father
came home.*

⮑ *See also* **just a minute/second/ moment** *at* JUST[1].

3 a particular point in time: *Come here this minute!* (=now) | *The minute we left, the dog started barking.*

━ PHRASE ━

4 any minute (now) SPOKEN very soon: *The movie will start any minute.* | *Any minute now, the bus should come.*

minute[2] /maɪˈnut/ [*adjective;* **more minute, most minute**] extremely small; *synonym* TINY; *opposite* HUGE: *The printing is minute. I can hardly read it.*

miracle /ˈmɪrəkəl/ [*noun*]
1 something extremely good that happens that you would never expect to happen: *It'll be a miracle if he manages to finish in time.*
2 something that happens which people believe was caused by God: *She prayed for a miracle to save her daughter's life.*

miraculous /mɪˈrækyələs/ [*adjective;* **more miraculous, most miraculous**] extremely good and surprising: *He made a miraculous recovery* (=he was extremely ill, but he got well).

mirror ✱ ⊤ /ˈmɪrɚ/ [*noun*] a piece of glass with a special substance on the back, that you look at to see yourself: *He's always looking in the mirror and admiring himself.*

reflection
a mirror

misbehave /ˌmɪsbɪˈheɪv/ [*verb;* **misbehaved, misbehaving**] if someone, especially a child, misbehaves, he or she behaves badly: *If you misbehave, you won't get any dessert.*

mischief /ˈmɪstʃɪf/ [*noun*] behavior, especially by children, that is bad and annoys other people but is not very serious: *Go out to play, but don't get into any mischief.*

mischievous /ˈmɪstʃəvəs/ [*adjective;* **more mischievous, most mischievous**] badly behaved, but in a way that is not very serious: *a mischievous child*

PRONUNCIATION mischievous
Some people may say /mɪsˈtʃiviəs/. However, this is not correct. You should say /ˈmɪstʃəvəs/.

---

miserable /ˈmɪzərəbəl/ [*adjective;* **more miserable, most miserable**] unhappy or making you unhappy: *Why are you looking so miserable?* | *We had a really miserable time.*

misery /ˈmɪzəri/ [*noun*] a feeling of being extremely unhappy: *To add to her misery, it started to rain.*

mislead /mɪsˈlid/ [*verb;* **misled** /mɪsˈlɛd/, **misleading**] to make someone think that something is true when it is not: *I was misled into thinking he was honest.*

SCHOOL BUS

He **missed** the bus.

miss[1] ✱ [*verb;* **misses, missed, missing**]
1 to fail to do something or go somewhere: *I'm sorry I missed your party.* | *This concert is too good to miss.*
2 to arrive somewhere too late, so you do not see something or cannot do something: *We missed the start of the show.* | *If you miss your flight, there isn't another one until tomorrow.*
3 to feel sad because someone is not with you: *I'll miss you when you go away.*
4 to not manage to hit or catch something: *He shot at the goal but missed.* | *It's important not to miss the target.*
5 to fail to notice or hear something: *I missed the weather report this morning.*

/i/ **see**	/ɪ/ **big**	/eɪ/ **day**	/ɛ/ **get**	/æ/ **hat**
/ɑ/ **father, hot**	/ʌ/ **up**	/ə/ **about**	/ɔ/ **saw**
/oʊ/ **hope**	/ʊ/ **book**	/u/ **too**	/aɪ/ **I**	/aʊ/ **how**
/ɔɪ/ **boy**	/ɝ/ **bird**	/ɚ/ **teacher**	/ɪr/ **ear**	/ɛr/ **air**
/ɑr/ **far**	/ɔr/ **more**	/ʊr/ **tour**	/aɪr/ **fire**
/aʊɚ/ **hour**	/θ/ **nothing**	/ð/ **mother**	/ʃ/ **she**
/ʒ/ **measure**	/tʃ/ **church**	/dʒ/ **jump**	/ŋ/ **long**

miss[2] [*noun; plural* **misses**] a failure to hit or catch something, usually a ball: *His first swing was a miss.*

Miss /mɪs/ [*name*]
  1 usually **miss;** used to speak politely to a young woman, especially one you do not know: *Excuse me, miss, is this seat taken?*
    ⇨ *Compare* MA'AM, MADAM.
  2 used before the name of a woman who is not married: *This is Miss Brown.* | *Miss Mary Brown*
    ⇨ *Compare* MRS., MS.

missile /ˈmɪsəl/ [*noun*] a weapon that is fired into the air, can travel a long way, and explodes like a bomb: *These planes can fire missiles from 1000 meters.*

missing /ˈmɪsɪŋ/ [*adjective; no comparative*] someone or something that is missing cannot be found: *Did you ever find your missing shoe?* | *a missing child*

missionary /ˈmɪʃəˌnɛri/ [*noun; plural* **missionaries**] someone who goes to a foreign country to teach people about his or her religion

mist * /mɪst/ [*noun*] very small drops of water in the air that make it look pale: *An early morning mist covered the fields.* | *The valley was still full of mist.*
  ⇨ *See also* MISTY.

mistake * /mɪˈsteɪk/ [*noun*]
  1 something that is wrong or done in the wrong way; *synonym* ERROR: *This essay is full of mistakes.* | *I think I made a mistake. I should have turned left.*
  — PHRASE
  2 **by mistake** if you do something by mistake, you do it but you do not want to or intend to; *synonym* ACCIDENTALLY: *I took your coat home by mistake.*

mistaken ⊤ /mɪˈsteɪkən/ [*adjective;* **more mistaken, most mistaken**] wrong about something: *I think you're mistaken. No one by that name lives here.* | *a mistaken belief*

mister /ˈmɪstɚ/ [*name*] the spoken form of **Mr.**, used when you are talking to a man in an informal way: *Hey mister, you left your wallet on the table.*
  ☛ Using **mister** or **lady** instead of **sir** or **ma'am** is not very polite. For example, do

not say "Excuse me, mister" or "Pardon me, lady." Say **Excuse me, sir** and **Pardon me, ma'am.**
  ⇨ *Compare* SIR.

misty /ˈmɪsti/ [*adjective;* **mistier, mistiest**]
  1 misty weather has a lot of mist: *a cold misty morning*
  2 not clear or bright: *The windows were all misty.*

mitten /ˈmɪtən/ [*noun*] a piece of clothing you wear on your hand that covers your four fingers and has a separate part to cover your thumb
  ⇨ *See the picture at* GLOVE.

mix * /mɪks/ [*verb;* **mixes, mixed, mixing**]
  1 to combine two or more things: *Oil and water don't mix.* | **mix something with something** ▸ *If you mix blue with yellow, you get green.*
  — PHRASAL VERB
  mix up [*phrasal verb*]
  2 to put things together in the wrong order: **mix up something** ▸ *Don't mix up all my important papers.* | **mix something up** ▸ *My sister tried to help me, but she mixed my notes up.*

mixed /mɪkst/ [*adjective; no comparative*] combined with other things: *a can of mixed nuts*

mixer /ˈmɪksɚ/ [*noun*] an electric machine used for mixing food: *Put all the ingredients in a mixer.*

mixture * /ˈmɪkstʃɚ/ [*noun*] two or more things mixed together: *Pour the mixture into the dish.* | *Our music is a mixture of rock and jazz.*

ml a written abbreviation of MILLILITER or MILLILITERS: *200ml of water*

mm a written abbreviation of MILLIMETER or MILLIMETERS: *a 35mm camera*

moan /moʊn/ [*verb;* **moaned, moaning**] to make a long low sound, especially because you are in pain: *He fell down, moaning and holding his side.*

mobile home /ˈmoʊbəl ˈhoʊm/ [*noun*] a small house that can be moved but is usually kept in one place; *synonym* TRAILER

mock /mak/ [verb; mocked, mocking]
FORMAL to laugh at someone and make
him or her feel stupid, especially by
copying his or her voice or behavior:
The older kids often mocked him.

modal verb * /'moʊdəl 'vɜ˞b/ [noun]
GRAMMAR a verb such as "can," "may,"
"might," "should," and "would," that is
used before an auxiliary verb or a main
verb: *This chapter deals with modal verbs.*

model[1] * T /'madəl/ [noun]
1 a copy of something that is smaller
than the real thing: *The children were
busy making model airplanes.* I *This is
a model of the castle.*
2 someone whose job is to show or
advertise clothes, shoes, etc., to people
by wearing them: *She's so beautiful she
could be a model.* I *He always wanted to
be a fashion model.*

model[2] [verb; modeled, modeling] to
wear clothes in a fashion show, or to do
this as your job: *She models for a French
designer.* I *He is modeling a wool suit.*

modem /'moʊdəm/ [noun] a piece of
electronic equipment used to make
information pass from a computer
through a telephone line: *To use the
Internet you will need a modem.*

moderate T /'madərɪt/ [adjective; more
moderate, most moderate] not large
or small, but somewhere in between: *He
earns a moderate amount of money.*

modern * T /'madə˞n/ [adjective; more
modern, most modern] in the newest
style or using the newest methods;
opposite OLD-FASHIONED: *Our school is in a
modern building.* I *modern technology*
➪ *See also* UP-TO-DATE.

modest /'madɪst/ [adjective; more
modest, most modest] not acting in a
proud way about the things you
achieve or are good at; *opposite*
ARROGANT: *He's too modest to tell you he's
the champion.*

modesty /'madɪsti/ [noun] the quality of
being modest: *What I like best about him
is his modesty.*

moist /mɔɪst/ [adjective; moister,
moistest] slightly wet: *The cake should
be light and moist.*

moisture /'mɔɪstʃə˞/ [noun] tiny drops of
water in a substance, on a surface, or in
the air: *Hot weather takes most of the
moisture out of the soil.*

molasses /məˈlæsɪz/ [noun] a thick dark
brown liquid with a strong sweet taste,
produced when sugar is made purer:
molasses candy

mold[1] /moʊld/
[noun]
1 a hollow container
you pour liquid
into, so that when
the liquid becomes
firm or hard, it is a
particular shape:
*She lifted the mold
off the Jell-O.*

a mold

2 an unpleasant green or brown
substance that grows on old food, wet
material, etc.: *The sauce was covered in
mold.*

mold[2] [verb; molded, molding] to form
a soft material into a shape: *She molds
her statues from the local red clay.*

moldy /'moʊldi/ [adjective; moldier,
moldiest] covered in mold: *This cheese
is moldy.* I *moldy bread*

mole /moʊl/ [noun]
1 a small animal with black fur that
lives under the ground: *Dad's trying to
get rid of the moles in the lawn.*
2 a small, dark, raised spot on
someone's skin: *She has a small mole
on her right arm.*

molecule /'malə,kyul/ [noun] the
smallest unit of a substance or living
thing that can exist without becoming
something different: *Atoms of hydrogen
and oxygen combine to form water
molecules.*
➪ *Compare* ATOM.

mom or **Mom** /mam/ [noun, name]
mother: *I'll ask my mom if that's OK.* I
Where's my baseball cap, Mom?
➪ *See the usage note at* CAPITAL.

/i/ **see** /ɪ/ **big** /eɪ/ **day** /ɛ/ **get** /æ/ **hat**
/ɑ/ **father, hot** /ʌ/ **up** /ə/ **about** /ɔ/ **saw**
/oʊ/ **hope** /ʊ/ **book** /u/ **too** /aɪ/ **I** /aʊ/ **how**
/ɔɪ/ **boy** /ɜ˞/ **bird** /ə˞/ **teacher** /ɪr/ **ear** /ɛr/ **air**
/ɑr/ **far** /ɔr/ **more** /ʊr/ **tour** /aɪr/ **fire**
/aʊə˞/ **hour** /θ/ **nothing** /ð/ **mother** /ʃ/ **she**
/ʒ/ **measure** /tʃ/ **church** /dʒ/ **jump** /ŋ/ **long**

moment * /'moʊmənt/ [*noun*]

1 a very short period of time: *Wait a moment, I'm busy.* | *I'll be with you in a moment.* | *Moments later, the police arrived.* | *He just left a moment ago.*
 ⇨ *See also* just a minute/second/moment *at* JUST¹.

2 a particular point in time: *At that moment, there was a knock at the door.* | *The moment the teacher left, everyone started talking.*
 ☞ Do not say "the moment he will arrive." Say the moment he arrives.

═ PHRASES ═

3 **at the moment** at the present time: *Can I call you back? I'm busy at the moment.*
 ⇨ *See also* right now *at* RIGHT².

4 **for the moment** used to say that something is true now but could change in the future: *We're done for the moment, but I'll call you later.*
 ⇨ *See also* for now *at* NOW.

mommy or **Mommy** /'mami/ [*noun, name; plural* **mommies**] a word meaning MOTHER, used especially by children: *I want my mommy!*
 ⇨ *See the usage note at* CAPITAL.

Mon. the written abbreviation for MONDAY

monarch /'manɚk/ [*noun*] one person who rules a country, such as a king or queen

monarchy /'manɚki/ [*noun; plural* **monarchies**] a country or system that has a monarch: *a democratic monarchy*

monastery /'manə,stɛri/ [*noun; plural* **monasteries**] a place where monks live

Monday * /'mʌndeɪ/ [*noun; plural* **Mondays**] the day of the week that is after Sunday and before Tuesday: *I'll go to the bank on Monday.* | *On Mondays I visit my grandmother.*
 ⇨ *See the usage note at* DAY.

money * ⊤ /'mʌni/ [*noun*]

1 coins and bills used to pay for things: *Can I borrow some money?* | *How much money do you have?*
 ☞ Don't say "How much money is this bag?" Say How much is this bag? or How much does this bag cost?

2 wealth: *His family has money.*

monitor¹ /'manɪtɚ/ [*noun*] the part of a computer that you look at to see what you are writing, how the computer is operating, etc.: *I need a bigger monitor.*
 ⇨ *See the picture at* OFFICE.

monitor² [*verb; monitored, monitoring*] to watch someone or something closely: *We monitor students' progress throughout the year.* | *a machine to monitor water levels*

monk /mʌŋk/ [*noun*] a man who belongs to a religious group of men who live together and usually do not marry: *The monks take care of the monastery's gardens.*
 ⇨ *Compare* NUN.

monkey * /'mʌŋki/ [*noun; plural* **monkeys**] an animal with a long tail and a body similar to that of a human, that climbs trees

a monkey

monotonous ⊤ /mə'natənəs/ [*adjective; more monotonous, most monotonous*] if something is monotonous, it is boring because it continues in the same way without changing: *This is such monotonous work.* | *a monotonous song*

monsoon /man'sun/ [*noun*] the season of heavy rain in southern Asia, or the wind that brings this rain

monster /'manstɚ/ [*noun*] a frightening creature, especially in stories: *My little sister was afraid that a monster lived under the bed.*

month * /mʌnθ/ [*noun*]

1 one of the twelve periods into which a year is divided, for example January or February: *I'm going to college next month.* | *It was my birthday last month.* | *She's going on a two-month vacation to Africa.*

2 a period of time lasting about four weeks: *One of these bottles should last about a month.*
⇨ See also **all day/night/week/ month/year** at ALL¹.

USAGE **Talking about months**

Use **in** to talk about what happens, happened, or will happen during a particular month of the year: *I always take a vacation in August.* | *We got married in June.* | *The children will start school in September.*

Use **this** to talk about the month you are in now: *I have a lot to do this month.* | *Oh, your trip to Hong Kong is this month, isn't it?*

Use **last** to talk about the month before this one, or any month in the year before this month: *I got a new car last month.* | *Last February, we went on a cruise.*

Use **next** to talk about the month after this one, or any month in the year after this month: *We're going skiing next month.* | *Their wedding is next April.*

Use **on** to talk about what happens, happened, or will happen on a particular day of the month: *There are fireworks on the 4th of July.* | *She arrived in Miami on May 6th.* | *The play starts on March 15th.*

If it is clear which month you are talking about, you can use only the number of the day: *Have you made any plans yet for the fourth?*
⇨ See the usage note at SECOND².

monthly¹ ∗ /'mʌnθli/ [*adjective; no comparative*] happening, done, or produced every month: *It was time for our monthly meeting.* | *a monthly magazine*
☛ Only use **monthly** before a noun.

monthly² ∗ [*adverb*] every month: *She visits her grandmother monthly.*

monument /'manyəmənt/ [*noun*] something such as a statue built to make people remember a person or event: *The statue is a monument to those who died in war.*

moo /mu/ [*verb*; **moos**, **mooed**, **mooing**] if a cow moos, it makes a long low sound: *You could hear the cows mooing in the barn.*

mood /mud/ [*noun*] the way you are feeling at a particular time: *I'm not in the mood for a party.* | *She's been in a great mood all day.*
⇨ See the synonym note at HAPPY.

moody /'mudi/ [*adjective*; **moodier**, **moodiest**] often becoming annoyed or upset: *He's always been a moody child.*

moon ∗ /mun/ [*noun*] a natural object that travels around a planet. You can see Earth's moon shining in the sky at night: *Some day, anyone will be able to travel to the moon.* | *the moons of Jupiter*

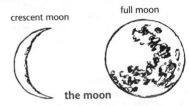

crescent moon   full moon

the moon

moonlight /'mun,laɪt/ [*noun*] the light from Earth's moon: *The lake shone in the moonlight.*

mop¹ /map/ [*noun*] an object with a long handle that you use for washing floors: *The mop and bucket are in this closet.*

mop² [*verb*; **mops**, **mopped**, **mopping**] to clean a floor with a mop: *We mop all the floors on Saturdays.*

moral¹ ∗ /'mɔrəl/ [*adjective*; **more moral**, **most moral**] moral behavior or ideas are considered right and good; *opposite* IMMORAL: *You have a moral duty to take care of your family.*

moral² [*noun*]
1 a main point in a story or event that teaches what behavior is right or wrong: *Can anyone tell me the moral of this fairy tale?*
2 morals [*plural*] ideas about right and wrong that make someone behave in the right way: *Some people say he has no morals.*

morally * /'mɔrəli/ [adverb] in a way that follows or does not follow what is considered right and good: *I think it's* **morally wrong** *to wear fur* (=it is not the right thing to do).

more[1] * /mɔr/ [determiner, pronoun]
1 a greater amount or number; *opposites* FEWER, LESS: *More teachers are needed in the school.* I **More than a** *million people visit the museum every year.* I *More of the money should be invested.*
   ⇨ *See also* MOST[1].
2 an additional amount or number: *Would you like more coffee?* I *There's room for two more people in the car.* I *Thanks for the cookies. Can I have one more?*

━━ PHRASES ━━

3 more or less used to say that an amount, number, etc., is not exact: *He's more or less the same age as me.*
4 more and more used to say that something is increasing: *More and more people are using the Internet.*
   ⇨ *Compare* **fewer and fewer** *at* FEWER *and* **less and less** *at* LESS[1].

more[2] * [adverb]
1 to a greater degree, amount, etc.; *opposite* LESS: *Our math classes are becoming more difficult.* I *I drive much more slowly than you.*
   ⇨ *See also* MOST[2].
2 used to say that something is repeated or that something continues for a longer time: *I'm going to call him* **once more.** I *Can we talk* **some more** *tomorrow?* I *You should go out more.*

━━ PHRASE ━━

3 not . . . any more used to say that something no longer happens: *I used to be very good at gymnastics, but not any more.* I *Why don't you come and see me any more?*

morning * /'mɔrnɪŋ/ [noun] the first part of the day, until around noon: *Can I come* **tomorrow morning?** I *I'm going to see the doctor* **on Friday morning.** I *He hates to get up* **in the morning.**
   ☛ Do not say "last morning." Say **yesterday morning.**

mortal /'mɔrtəl/ [adjective; no comparative] if you say that people are

mortal, you mean that one day they will die; *opposite* IMMORTAL: *You cannot escape the fact that we are all mortal.*

mortgage /'mɔrgɪdʒ/ [noun] an amount of money that a bank lends someone so that he or she can buy a house: *He didn't have enough money to* **pay the mortgage.**

mosque ⊤ /mask/ [noun; plural **mosques**] a building where Muslims meet and pray to Allah

mosquito /mə'skitoʊ/ [noun; plural **mosquitoes**] a very small flying insect that bites you and can spread disease

moss /mɔs/ [noun] a tiny green or brown plant that grows in a soft, thick bunch in wet places

a mosquito

most[1] * /moʊst/ [determiner, pronoun]
1 more than any other person, thing, amount, etc.; *opposites* FEWEST, LEAST: *Most parks close at sunset.* I *This was* **the most** *fun I've ever had!* I *Most of my friends live in the city.* I *Some students don't go on to college, but most do.*

━━ PHRASES ━━

2 at (the) most used to say that an amount or number is the largest possible or allowed: *I'll only be away for a couple of days at most.*
   ⇨ *Compare* **at least** *at* LEAST[1].
3 for the most part most of the time: *Emma's grades are very good for the most part.*

most[2] * [adverb] more than anything or anyone else; *opposite* LEAST: *Who is the most intelligent in your class?* I *I enjoy many kinds of music, but I like jazz most.*
   ☛ Do not say "Most the children sat quietly" or "The most children sat quietly." Say **Most of the children sat quietly.**

mostly * ⊤ /'moʊstli/ [adverb] used to say that something is true most of the time or that it is true of most of a group; *synonym* MAINLY: *I mostly do my homework in the evenings.* I *Our clients are mostly women.*

motel /moʊ'tɛl/ [noun] a cheap hotel designed for people traveling by car

moth /mɔθ/ [noun; plural **moths** /mɔðz/] an insect with wings that flies at night and is attracted to light
⇨ See the picture at CATERPILLAR.

mother * /'mʌðɚ/ [noun] a female who had a child: My mother is a teacher. | She's **the mother of** two girls.
⇨ See the picture at FAMILY TREE.

mother-in-law /'mʌðɚ ɪn ˌlɔ/ [noun; plural **mothers-in-law**] the mother of your husband or wife
⇨ See the picture at FAMILY TREE.

motion T /'moʊʃən/ [noun] the action or process of moving; synonym MOVEMENT: You should throw the ball in one smooth motion. | The motion of the waves put her to sleep.

motionless /'moʊʃənlɪs/ [adjective; no comparative] not moving at all: The runners waited motionless for the start signal.

motion picture /'moʊʃən 'pɪktʃɚ/ [noun] a story or a set of events shown in the form of moving pictures on a screen; synonyms MOVIE, FILM: the motion picture industry

motive /'moʊtɪv/ [noun] a reason for doing something serious: What were your **motives** for leaving your job?

motor * /'moʊtɚ/ [noun] a small engine that makes a vehicle or machine move or work: There's something wrong with the boat's motor. | an electric motor

motorbike /'moʊtɚˌbaɪk/ [noun] a bicycle with an engine, or a small motorcycle; synonym BIKE: A policeman on a motorbike sped past me.

motorboat /'moʊtɚˌboʊt/ [noun] a small boat with a motor that makes it go fast

motorcycle * /'moʊtɚˌsaɪkəl/ [noun] a vehicle with a motor and two wheels: Motorcycle riders must wear helmets.

motor home /'moʊtɚ ˌhoʊm/ [noun] a vehicle with a part you can live in, used for camping or taking long trips; synonym R.V.: My parents bought a motor home and traveled across the U.S.

motorist /'moʊtərɪst/ [noun] someone who is driving a car

motto /'matoʊ/ [noun; plural **mottoes** or **mottos**] a few words that a person or group uses to express what they believe in: Our team's motto is "Be the Best."

mound /maʊnd/ [noun] a pile of earth, sand, stones, etc.: The car was buried under a mound of snow.

mount [verb; **mounted, mounting**]
1 to increase in number, size, or amount: mounting excitement | These bills are beginning to **mount up**.
2 to climb on or up to something: You mount a horse from its left side.

Mount /maʊnt/ [name] used in some names of mountains: Mount Rainier is a volcano in Washington State.

mountain * /'maʊntən/ [noun] an extremely high hill, especially one that rises to a point: They climbed right to the top of the mountain. | I like camping **in the mountains** (=in an area where there are a lot of mountains).

mountain bike /'maʊntən ˌbaɪk/ [noun] a strong bicycle with thick tires, for riding on rough land

mountainous /'maʊntənəs/ [adjective; more **mountainous**, most **mountainous**] having a lot of mountains: a mountainous area | It's very mountainous along the border.

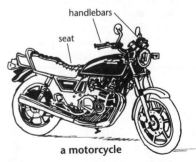

handlebars

seat

a motorcycle

/i/ **see**	/ɪ/ **big**	/eɪ/ **day**	/ɛ/ **get**	/æ/ **hat**
/a/ **father, hot**	/ʌ/ **up**	/ə/ **about**	/ɔ/ **saw**	
/oʊ/ **hope**	/ʊ/ **book**	/u/ **too**	/aɪ/ **I**	/aʊ/ **how**
/ɔɪ/ **boy**	/ɚ/ **bird**	/ɚ/ **teacher**	/ɪr/ **ear**	/ɛr/ **air**
/ɑr/ **far**	/ɔr/ **more**	/ʊr/ **tour**	/aɪr/ **fire**	
/aʊɚ/ **hour**	/θ/ **nothing**	/ð/ **mother**	/ʃ/ **she**	
/ʒ/ **measure**	/tʃ/ **church**	/dʒ/ **jump**	/ŋ/ **long**	

mourn /mɔrn/ [*verb;* **mourned, mourning**] to feel sad because someone you know has died: *She is still mourning the death of her father.*

mourning /'mɔrnɪŋ/ [*noun*] sadness caused by someone's death: *The whole family is in mourning.*

mouse * /maʊs/ [*noun*]
1 [*plural* **mice**] a very small animal with a long tail: *A little gray mouse ran across the kitchen floor.*
2 [*plural* **mouses**] a small object attached to a computer that you move around and press to make the computer do things: *You can move text using the mouse or the keyboard.*
⤷ *See the picture at* OFFICE.

a mouse

moustache /'mʌstæʃ/ [*noun*] another spelling of MUSTACHE

mouth * /maʊθ/ [*noun; plural* **mouths** /maʊðz/]
1 the opening in your face that contains your tongue and teeth: *The doctor asked me to open my mouth wide.*
⤷ *See the picture at* BODY.
2 a place or a part of an object that lets people or things go out or in: *the mouth of a cave* | *a jar with a wide mouth* | *at the mouth of the river* (=where it joins the ocean)
━ PHRASE ━
3 **keep your mouth shut** INFORMAL to be quiet or to not tell anyone about something: *Will he keep his mouth shut about all this?*

mouthful /'maʊθ,fʊl/ [*noun; plural* **mouthfuls**] as much of something as your mouth can hold: *a mouthful of cake*

move * ⊤ /muv/ [*verb;* **moved, moving**]
1 to go and live in a new home: *We moved to the city ten years ago.* | *I'm hoping to move next month.*
2 to change to another place or position, or to make something do

this: *Stay here and don't move.* | *Help me move the TV into that corner.*
3 to make someone have a strong feeling: *The book moved him to tears.*
━ PHRASAL VERBS ━
move in [*phrasal verb*]
4 to put all your possessions into a new home and start living there: *Is it OK if I move in on Thursday?*
move out [*phrasal verb*]
5 to take all your possessions out of a home and stop living there: *My roommate asked me to move out.*

movement * ⊤ /'muvmənt/ [*noun*] when someone or something moves: *He made a movement toward the door.* | *the movement of waves on a beach*

movie * /'muvi/ [*noun; plural* **movies**] a story or a set of events shown in the form of moving pictures on a screen; *synonym* FILM: *That was a really romantic movie.* | *Let's go to the movies* (=see a movie at a theater). | *They're at the movies* (=at a theater seeing a movie).

movie star /'muvi ,star/ [*noun*] someone who is very famous because he or she has appeared in a lot of movies

movie theater /'muvi ,θiətɚ/ [*noun*] a place where you go to watch movies: *I'll meet you at the movie theater at six.*

moving /'muvɪŋ/ [*adjective;* **more moving, most moving**] making people feel strong emotions, especially sadness: *He made a very moving speech at the funeral.*

mow /moʊ/ [*verb;* **mowed, mowing**] to cut grass using a machine that you push: *In the summer, I mow the lawn every Saturday.*

He's **mowing** the lawn.

lawn mower

He's **ducking** under the pipe.

He's **stooping** under the pipe.

She's **bending** over.

He's **slumped** in the chair.

She's **crouching**.

She's **squatting**.

He's **reaching** for the apple.

She's **stretching**.

He's **slouching**.

She's **jumping**.

She's **hopping**.

She's **leaping**.

movements and positions

mower /'mouɚ/ [noun] a machine for cutting grass; <u>synonym</u> LAWN MOWER: *a noisy old mower*

mpg /'ɛm'pi'dʒi/ the abbreviation of "miles per gallon"; used to show how much gas a vehicle uses: *The car gets around 40 mpg.*

mph the written abbreviation of "miles per hour"; used to show how fast a vehicle travels: *a car with a top speed of 120 mph.*

Mr. /'mɪstɚ/ [name] the written form of MISTER, used before a man's name: *I'd like to speak to Mr. White, please.* | *Mr. John White*

Mrs. /'mɪsɪz/ [name] used before a married woman's name: *Have you met Mrs. West?* | *Mrs. Emily West*
↪ Compare MISS, Ms.

M.S. /'ɛm'ɛs/ [noun; plural **M.S.s** or **M.S.'s**] Master of Science; a degree in a science subject such chemistry that you can study for after your first degree: *I'm studying for an M.S. in marine biology.*
↪ Compare **B.A., B.S., M.A., Ph.D.**

Ms. /mɪz/ [name] used before a woman's name: *The letter was addressed to Ms. Rivers.* | *Ms. Susan Rivers*
↪ Compare MISS, MRS.

Mt. the written abbreviation of MOUNT: *Mt. Everest*

much¹ * /mʌtʃ/ [adverb]
1 used before the word "too" and words such as "bigger," "slower," and "happier," to mean "a lot": *I'm feeling much better today.* | *You must work much harder to pass your tests.* | *I can't afford that. It's much too expensive.*
☛ Do not say "It is too much expensive." Say **It is much too expensive.**
2 used to emphasize the degree of something: *She says that I talk too much* (=more than I should). | *I can't believe how much you eat!* (=you eat a lot) | *Thanks very much* (=a lot) *for your letter.*
— PHRASE —
3 not much
  a not very often: *I don't watch TV much. I prefer to read.*

  b only a very small amount: *I don't like him much.*

much² * [determiner, pronoun]
1 used especially in questions and negative sentences to mean a lot of something; <u>opposite</u> LITTLE: *I don't have much time for sports.* | *Was there much gas in the car?* | *Much of her day was spent cooking and cleaning.*
☛ Only use the determiner **much** before uncountable nouns.
↪ Compare MANY.
2 used to emphasize the size, amount, etc., of something: *I put too much salt in the food.* | *Why is there so much violence in the world?*
☛ Only use the determiner **much** before uncountable nouns.
— PHRASES —
3 how much used to talk or ask about an amount or price: *How much pie is left?* | *I don't know how much it costs.* | *How much is that dress?*
☛ Do not use **how much** with countable nouns. For example, do not say "How much CDs do you have?" Say **How many CDs do you have?**
4 not much
  a not very often: *"How often do you go swimming?" "Not much."*
  b only a very small amount: *"Is there any food left?" "Not much."*

mud * /mʌd/ [noun] wet soft dirt that sticks to your shoes, to floors, etc.: *Be careful not to walk in the mud.*

muddy /'mʌdi/ [adjective; **muddier, muddiest**] covered in mud: *Don't come into the house with muddy shoes.*

muffin /'mʌfɪn/ [noun] a kind of bread that is small and sweet: *We had blueberry muffins for breakfast.*

mug /mʌg/ [noun] a cup for drinking hot drinks that has a handle and straight sides: *a mug of coffee*

a mug

Muhammad /mʊ'hæməd/ [name] the man on whose ideas and beliefs Islam is based

mule /myul/ [noun] an animal that is the child of a female horse and a male donkey: *He loaded up his mule and set off for the market.*

multicolored /'mʌltiˌkʌlɚd/ [*adjective; no comparative*] having many different colors: *a multicolored sweater*

multicultural /ˌmʌlti'kʌltʃərəl/ [*adjective; no comparative*] including the cultures of many different races of people: *We live in a multicultural society.*

multimedia /ˌmʌlti'midiə/ [*adjective; no comparative*] using different ways of giving information, for example pictures, writing, and movies, especially on a computer: *a multimedia presentation*

multiplication /ˌmʌltəplɪ'keɪʃən/ [*noun*] when you increase a number by a particular number of times; *opposite* DIVISION: *You need to do more practice in multiplication.*

multiply * /'mʌltəˌplaɪ/ [*verb; multiplies, multiplied, multiplying*] to increase a number by a particular number of times; *opposite* DIVIDE: *Seven multiplied by two equals fourteen* (7 × 2 = 14).
↪ *See also* TIMES.

mumble /'mʌmbəl/ [*verb; mumbled, mumbling*] to say something in a low voice that is difficult for other people to hear: *Take your hand away from your mouth and stop mumbling.*

mumps /mʌmps/ [*noun*] a disease, often caught by children, that makes your neck, mouth, and throat become sore and swollen: *She has the mumps.*
☛ Only use **mumps** with a singular verb.

murder[1] * /'mɝdɚ/ [*verb; murdered, murdering*] to kill someone deliberately: *A man was murdered in the park last night.*

murder[2] * [*noun*] the crime of killing someone deliberately: *There have been three murders in the area this month.* I *What makes someone commit murder?*
☛ Do not confuse **murder** and **murderer**. **Murder** is a crime and a **murderer** is the criminal who kills someone.

murderer /'mɝdərɚ/ [*noun*] a criminal who has killed someone

deliberately: *Police are still trying to find the murderer.*

muscle * /'mʌsəl/ [*noun*] part of your body under your skin that connects your bones and that you use when you move: *If you don't warm up before you run, you can pull a muscle* (=injure it).

museum T /myu'ziəm/ [*noun*] a building where statues, paintings, old beautiful objects, etc., are kept for people to see: *There are many museums to visit in Paris.* I *a museum of modern art*

mushrooms

mushroom /'mʌʃrum/ [*noun*] a fungus that is eaten raw or cooked as a vegetable

mushy /'mʌʃi/ [*adjective; mushier, mushiest*] a mushy mixture is soft, wet, and thick: *If you boil the rice too long, it will get mushy.*

music * /'myuzɪk/ [*noun*]
1 notes from instruments or the human voice, arranged to have a pleasant sound: *I could hear music coming from behind the door.* I *What's your favorite kind of music?* I *I got a new piece of music to play at my piano lesson.*
☛ Do not say "I can play many musics." Say **I can play many pieces of music.**
2 printed or written notes, used to represent a tune: *Do you read music?* (=can you play a tune by looking at written music)

musical * /'myuzɪkəl/ [*adjective; no comparative*] sounding like music, or relating to music: *a musical performance*

/i/ **see** /ɪ/ **big** /eɪ/ **day** /ɛ/ **get** /æ/ **hat**
/ɑ/ **father, hot** /ʌ/ **up** /ə/ **about** /ɔ/ **saw**
/oʊ/ **hope** /ʊ/ **book** /u/ **too** /aɪ/ **I** /aʊ/ **how**
/ɔɪ/ **boy** /ɝ/ **bird** /ɚ/ **teacher** /ɪr/ **ear** /ɛr/ **air**
/ɑr/ **far** /ɔr/ **more** /ʊr/ **tour** /aɪr/ **fire**
/aʊɚ/ **hour** /θ/ **nothing** /ð/ **mother** /ʃ/ **she**
/ʒ/ **measure** /tʃ/ **church** /dʒ/ **jump** /ŋ/ **long**

musical instrument /'myuzɪkəl 'ɪnstrəmənt/ [*noun*] an object that makes musical sounds when you blow into it, press parts of it, hit it, etc.

musician * /myu'zɪʃən/ [*noun*] someone who plays a musical instrument, especially to a high standard: *My brother is a very good musician.* | *a famous jazz musician*

Muslim[1] /'mʌzlɪm/ [*noun*] someone who follows the religion of Islam

Muslim[2] [*adjective; no comparative*] belonging to or connected with the religion of Islam; <u>synonym</u> ISLAMIC: *The Koran is the Muslim holy book.*

mussel /'mʌsəl/ [*noun*] a creature with two shells that close around it, that lives in oceans and lakes: *steamed mussels in wine sauce*

must * /mʌst/ [*modal verb*]
1 used to say that something has to happen or that someone has to do something, for example because a rule or law says that he or she should: *You must not wear shorts in school.* | *I must do my homework before I go out.* | *"Must I go to bed now?" "Yes, you must."*
2 used to say that something is very likely to be true: *He must be almost finished by now.* | *I must have dropped my purse getting out of the car.*

mustache /'mʌstæʃ/ [*noun*] the HAIR that grows on a man's upper lip: *Dad grew a mustache.*

mustard /'mʌstəd/ [*noun*] a yellow or brown sauce that tastes hot, which you put on some foods: *Do you want mustard on your hot dog?*

mustn't * /'mʌsənt/ the short form of "must not": *You mustn't go out without telling me where you're going.*
☛ **Mustn't** does not mean "don't have to." Do not say "You mustn't go if you don't want to." Say **You don't have to go if you don't want to.**

must've /'mʌstəv/ SPOKEN the short form of "must have": *He must've forgotten he was supposed to meet me.*

mutter /'mʌtə/ [*verb; muttered, muttering*] to say something not very clearly, so that people cannot hear or

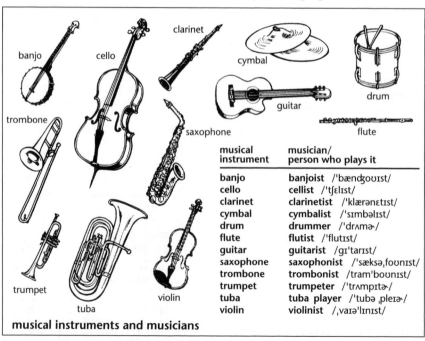

musical instrument	musician/ person who plays it
banjo	banjoist /'bændʒoʊɪst/
cello	cellist /'tʃɛlɪst/
clarinet	clarinetist /'klærənɛtɪst/
cymbal	cymbalist /'sɪmbəlɪst/
drum	drummer /'drʌmə/
flute	flutist /'flutɪst/
guitar	guitarist /gɪ'tarɪst/
saxophone	saxophonist /'sæksə,foʊnɪst/
trombone	trombonist /tram'boʊnɪst/
trumpet	trumpeter /'trʌmpɪtə/
tuba	tuba player /'tubə ,pleɪə/
violin	violinist /,vaɪə'lɪnɪst/

musical instruments and musicians

understand you: *Stop muttering and tell me what you want to say.*

my * /maɪ/ [*determiner*] belonging to or connected with me: *Give me my book.* | *My head hurts.*

☞ Only use **my** before a noun.

➪ See also MINE¹.

myself * /maɪˈsɛlf/ [*pronoun*]
1 used as the object of a verb or preposition when the subject is "I": *I calmed myself and went back into the room.* | *I looked at myself in the mirror.*
2 used to emphasize the word "I": *I myself never liked Lee.* | *I carried all the baggage myself.*

☞ Do not use **myself** as a subject. For example, do not say "Myself will tell her." Say **I will tell her myself.**

━━ PHRASES ━━
3 **by myself** alone or without any help: *I live by myself.* | *I can't possibly do this work all by myself.*
4 **to myself** not sharing something with anyone else: *I kept my thoughts to myself* (=did not say them out loud).

mysterious * T /mɪˈstɪriəs/ [*adjective; more mysterious, most mysterious*] secret, unknown, or not clear: *Something very mysterious is going on.* | *Mysterious noises were coming from the cave.*

mystery * /ˈmɪstəri/ [*noun; plural* **mysteries**] something that is secret, unknown, or not clear: *It's a mystery to me how she stays so thin.*

myth /mɪθ/ [*noun*] a traditional story, especially one with gods and heroes: *an ancient Greek myth*

mythology /mɪˈθɑlədʒi/ [*noun*] myths generally: *the heroes of Roman mythology*

N

N * or **n** /ɛn/ [*noun; Ns or N's, n's*] the 14th letter of the English alphabet

➪ See the usage note at ALPHABET.

N. or **N** a written abbreviation of NORTH: *N. America* | *250 N Main Street*

➪ Compare E., S., W.

nag /næg/ [*verb; nagged, nagging*] to complain a lot to someone until he or she does what you want: **nag someone to do something** ▸ *My mom keeps nagging me to clean my room.*

nail¹ * /neɪl/ [*noun*]
1 a thin pointed piece of metal that you hit into something, used to fasten pieces of wood together, to hang pictures on walls, etc.
➪ See the picture at TOOL.
2 one of the hard parts at the ends of your fingers or toes: *I need to cut my nails.*
➪ See also FINGERNAIL, TOENAIL.

nail² * [*verb; nailed, nailing*] to fasten something to something else with a pointed piece of metal: *He nailed the sign to a tree.*

nail file /ˈneɪl ˌfaɪl/ [*noun*] a piece of rough metal or plastic that you use to clean and shape your fingernails

nail polish /ˈneɪl ˌpɑlɪʃ/ [*noun*] colored or clear liquid that you put on your nails to make them look more attractive: *She wore red nail polish.*

naked /ˈneɪkɪd/ [*adjective; no comparative*] not wearing any clothes: *Kids were swimming completely naked.*

name¹ * /neɪm/ [*noun*]
1 the word you use for a person or thing: *My name is Anne. What's your name?* | *I forgot the name of the street she lives on.*
2 the opinion that people have about someone, based on what they have heard; *synonym* REPUTATION: *He got a bad name when he was young.*

name² * [*verb; named, naming*]
1 to give someone or something a name: *They named the baby Karen.*
2 to say what the name of something is: *Can you name all 50 U.S. states?*

namely /ˈneɪmli/ [*adverb*] used to show exactly who or what you are talking about: *Two people, namely Katie and Joey, did very well.*

nanny /ˈnæni/ [*noun; plural* **nannies**] someone who is paid to live with a family and take care of the children

nap /næp/ [noun] when you sleep for a short time during the day: *Mom's taking a nap* (=sleeping for a short time) *right now.*

napkin /'næpkɪn/ [noun] a piece of cloth or paper that you use while you are eating to keep your mouth, hands, and clothes clean
↪ *See the picture at* PLACE SETTING.

narrow¹ * T /'næroʊ/ [adjective; narrower, narrowest] having only a small amount of space from one side to the other; *opposite* WIDE: *The road is very narrow.* | *a narrow river*

narrow² [verb; narrowed, narrowing] to become less wide; *opposite* WIDEN: *The path narrows as it goes through the woods.*

nasty * /'næsti/ [adjective; nastier, nastiest]
1 unpleasant to see, taste, etc.: *There's a nasty smell in here.*
2 unpleasant and unkind; *synonym* MEAN; *opposite* NICE: *a nasty boy*

nation * /'neɪʃən/ [noun]
1 a country and all the people who belong to it: *The whole nation is mourning the death of the president.*
↪ *See the synonym note at* COUNTRY.
2 all the people who belong to a particular group that are the same race, and often have their own laws: *the Cherokee Nation* (=of Native Americans)

national * /'næʃənəl/ [adjective; no comparative] relating to or belonging to a country: *a national holiday* | *national borders*
↪ *Compare* INTERNATIONAL.

national anthem /'næʃənəl 'ænθəm/ [noun] the official song of a country

nationalism /'næʃənəl‚ɪzəm/ [noun] the love and loyalty that people have for their own land and people, especially when they want their own country or do not want strangers in their country: *Feelings of nationalism are increasing.*

nationality /‚næʃə'nælɪti/ [noun; plural nationalities] the fact of belonging to a particular country: *Students of many nationalities study here.* | *He has British nationality.*

national park /'næʃənəl 'pɑrk/ [noun] an interesting or beautiful area that a government takes care of so that people can visit it: *Grand Canyon National Park*

native¹ T /'neɪtɪv/ [adjective; no comparative] relating to the place where someone was born or where something grows naturally: *My native language is English.* | *a plant that is native to Asia*

native² T [noun] someone who was born in a particular place: *Dan's a native of New York.*

Native American /'neɪtɪv ə'mɛrɪkən/ [noun] someone from one of the groups of people who lived in North America before Europeans arrived; *synonym* AMERICAN INDIAN
↪ *Compare* INDIAN¹ (definition 1).

native speaker /'neɪtɪv 'spikɚ/ [noun] someone who learned a particular language as his or her first language: *a native speaker of Korean*

natural * T /'nætʃərəl/ [adjective]
1 not made by machines or people; *opposite* ARTIFICIAL: *natural fibers such as wool and silk*
2 normal or usual; *opposite* UNNATURAL: *It's natural to be sad when your pet dies.*

natural history /'nætʃərəl 'hɪstəri/ [noun] the study of animals, plants, rocks, and other natural objects: *a natural history museum*

naturally * /'nætʃərəli/ [adverb]
1 used to say that something is what you would expect: *Naturally, he was tired after such a long trip.*
2 not resulting from something that a machine or person does: *She has naturally curly hair* (=it grows that way).

nature * T /'neɪtʃɚ/ [noun]
1 plants, animals, weather, and all the other things that machines or people have not made: *We should do more to protect nature.*
2 the character that someone or something has: *It's not in his nature to steal.* | *She's very quiet by nature.*

naughty /'nɔti/ [adjective; naughtier, naughtiest] a naughty child is behaving badly: *Emily's been very naughty today.*

nausea /'nɔziə/ [*noun*] a feeling of sickness in your stomach

nauseous /'nɔʃəs/ [*adjective; no comparative*] feeling sick in your stomach: *I **get nauseous** when I ride in cars.*

naval /'neɪvəl/ [*adjective; no comparative*] relating to ships or a navy: *a naval officer*

☛ Only use **naval** before a noun.

navigate /'nævɪˌgeɪt/ [*verb*; **navigated, navigating**] to decide which way a plane, ship, or car should go by using a map or special instruments: *You drive and I'll navigate.*

navigation /ˌnævɪ'geɪʃən/ [*noun*] the act of planning which way a plane, ship, or car should go, and guiding it there: *The river pilot is responsible for navigation through the channel.*

navigator /'nævɪˌgeɪtɚ/ [*noun*] the person who decides which way a plane, ship, or car should go: *The crew included the pilot and a navigator.*

navy[1] * /'neɪvi/ [*noun; plural* **navies**]
1 also **Navy;** the part of a country's military that fights at sea: *Her son's **in the Navy**.*
2 also **navy blue;** a dark blue color: *a navy business suit*

navy[2] * or **navy blue** /'neɪvi 'blu/ [*adjective*] of the color navy: *navy blue shoes*

N.E. or **NE** the written abbreviation for NORTHEAST: *Their address is 803 N.E. 179th Street.*

near[1] * /nɪr/ [*preposition*] close to something: *Is there a lake near here?*

USAGE   near, nearly

Do not confuse **near** and **nearly**. **Near** is used to talk about short distances: *He lives near Shanghai. | We couldn't get near the stage.* **Nearly** means "almost": *I nearly fell over. | Dinner's nearly ready.*

---

near[2] * [*adverb*] close or closer in distance or time: *There wasn't a bank anywhere near. | The date of the wedding was drawing near* (=coming close).

near[3] * [*adjective; nearer, nearest*] close in distance: *The nearest mall is in the next town.*

nearby Ⓣ /nɪr'baɪ/ [*adverb, adjective; no comparative*] close to somewhere: *My grandparents live nearby. | We asked for help at a nearby house.*

nearly * /'nɪrli/ [*adverb*] almost or close to: *I'm nearly 13. | Their car is nearly the same as ours. | She's **not nearly** finished with her homework* (=not even close to being finished).

⇨ See the usage note at NEAR[1].

nearsighted /'nɪrˌsaɪtɪd/ [*adjective; no comparative*] unable to see things clearly if they are a long way from you; *opposite* FARSIGHTED: *Liz wears glasses because she is nearsighted.*

neat * /nit/ [*adjective; neater, neatest*] with nothing out of place or out of order; *opposite* MESSY: *His clothes and hair always look very neat and clean.*

neatly * /'nitli/ [*adverb*] in a careful way with nothing out of place: *The sheets were neatly folded and put away.*

neatness /'nitnɪs/ [*noun*] the quality of being neat or doing things neatly: *Neatness is important in doing math.*

necessary * /'nɛsəˌsɛri/ [*adjective; more necessary, most necessary*] something that is necessary needs to be done, had, said, etc.; *opposite* UNNECESSARY: *A good education is **necessary for** a good job. | **necessary to do something** ▸ Is it really necessary to fill out these forms?*

necessity /nə'sɛsɪti/ [*noun; plural* **necessities**] something that you must have or that must be done: *A computer is a necessity nowadays.*

neck * /nɛk/ [*noun*]
1 the part of your BODY between your head and shoulders
2 a narrow piece that is part of or connected to something: *the neck of a bottle | the neck of a guitar*

— PHRASES
3 **be up to your neck in something** INFORMAL to be in a situation that is

---

/i/ see	/ɪ/ big	/eɪ/ **day**	/ɛ/ get	/æ/ **hat**
/ɑ/ **father, hot**	/ʌ/ **up**	/ə/ **about**	/ɔ/ **saw**	
/oʊ/ hope	/ʊ/ **book**	/u/ **too**	/aɪ/ **I**	/aʊ/ **how**
/ɔɪ/ **boy**	/ɚ/ **bird**	/ɚ/ teacher	/ɪr/ **ear**	/ɛr/ **air**
/ɑr/ **far**	/ɔr/ **more**	/ʊr/ **tour**	/aɪr/ **fire**	
/aʊɚ/ **hour**	/θ/ **nothing**	/ð/ mother	/ʃ/ **she**	
/ʒ/ measure	/tʃ/ **church**	/dʒ/ **jump**	/ŋ/ **long**	

difficult to deal with: *She's been up to her neck in paperwork all week.*

4 neck and neck if two people are neck and neck in a race, it is so close that you cannot be sure who will win: *It was neck and neck, but Jim won.*

necklace /'nɛklɪs/ [*noun*] a piece of JEWELRY that you wear around your neck: *She was wearing a silver necklace.*

necktie /'nɛk,taɪ/ [*noun; plural* **neckties**] a long thin piece of cloth which is tied around a man's shirt collar and hangs down at the front; *synonym* TIE

nectarine /ˌnɛktə'rin/ [*noun*] a fruit that looks like a smooth peach and tastes similar

need[1] * /nid/ [*verb;* **needed, needing**]
  1 if you need something, you must have it: *She needs a new pair of shoes.* | *I don't need any help.*
  ☛ Do not say "I am needing," "he is needing," etc. Say **I need, he needs,** etc.
  2 if something needs to be done, it must be done: *I need to finish my homework.* | *The house needs to be repaired.*
  ☛ Do not say that something "needs being done." Say that it **needs doing** or **needs to be done.**
  ▬ PHRASE ▬
  3 do not need to do something used to say that something is not necessary: *You don't need to send a letter—just call her.*

need[2] * [*noun*]
  1 something that you must have: *In business, it's important to **meet the needs** of clients* (=give them what they need).
  2 when something must be done or is extremely important: *There is a real need to expand the library.*
  ▬ PHRASE ▬
  3 in need of needing something: *This room is in need of a coat of paint.*

needle * /'nidəl/ [*noun*]
  1 a thin, pointed piece of metal or plastic, often with a hole in one end, used for sewing: *a needle and thread* | *knitting needles*
  2 a thin, hollow, pointed piece of metal

that can be put in someone's body to put medicine in or take liquid out: *a syringe with a long needle*
  3 a small, thin, pointed leaf from some trees: *pine needles*

needless /'nidlɪs/ [*adjective*]
  1 not necessary: *It's a needless waste of food to cook so much pasta.*
  ▬ PHRASE ▬
  2 needless to say used before you tell someone something that he or she already expects or knows: *We played the champions and, needless to say, we lost.*

needlework /'nidəl,wɜ·k/ [*noun*] the skill or process of sewing, or things that are made by sewing: *Look at the beautiful needlework in this quilt.*

negative[1] * T /'nɛgətɪv/ [*adjective*]
  1 [*no comparative*] a negative answer or statement means or uses "no" or "not": *a negative reply* | *"Does not" is the negative form of "does."*
  2 [**more negative, most negative**] bad or harmful: *The divorce had a negative effect on the kids.*
  3 [**more negative, most negative**] believing that a situation will have a bad result: *I don't like your negative attitude.*
  4 [*no comparative*] a negative number is less than 0: *The result, –2, is a negative number.*
  5 [*no comparative*] a negative electrical charge is the kind of charge carried by an electron: *This molecule has a negative charge.*
  ↪ *Compare* POSITIVE.

negative[2] * T [*noun*]
  1 a word or expression that means "no": *"Not" is used to form negatives.*
  2 a piece of film that a photograph is made from: *I'll get a copy of the photograph if you give me the negative.*

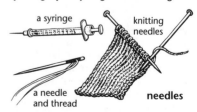

a syringe   knitting needles

a needle and thread   **needles**

neglect[1] T /nɪˈglɛkt/ [*verb;* **neglected, neglecting**] to not give enough attention or care to someone or something: *She neglected her health by not eating properly.*

neglect[2] T [*noun*] when someone does not give enough care or attention to someone or something: *The dog was suffering from serious neglect.*

neglected /nɪˈglɛktɪd/ [*adjective;* **more neglected, most neglected**] not given enough care or attention: *The garden had been neglected for years.*

negotiate T /nɪˈgouʃiˌeɪt/ [*verb;* **negotiated, negotiating**] to talk about something in order to reach an agreement, especially in business or politics: *It's better to negotiate than to argue.* | *They're negotiating a new contract.*

neigh /neɪ/ [*verb;* **neighed, neighing**] if a horse neighs, it makes a loud noise: *The horse neighed and trotted toward her.*

neighbor /ˈneɪbɚ/ [*noun*] someone who lives in a house or apartment next to you or very near you

neighborhood /ˈneɪbɚˌhʊd/ [*noun*] an area in a town and the people who live there: *There are some very good schools in the neighborhood.*

neighboring /ˈneɪbərɪŋ/ [*adjective; no comparative*] near to a particular place: *The hospital serves the neighboring towns.*
☛ Only use **neighboring** before a noun.

neither[1] * /ˈniðɚ/ [*determiner, pronoun*] not one and not the other of two people or things: *Neither of her sons goes to college.* | *Neither book looked interesting.*
➪ *Compare* BOTH[1], EITHER[1].

neither[2] * [*adverb*] used to add to another negative statement, or to agree with it: *He can't swim, and neither can I.* | *"I don't really like him." "Neither do I."*

neither[3] * [*conjunction*]
━ PHRASE ━

neither . . . nor FORMAL used to say that two or more negative things are true: *Neither John nor his father can play the piano.* | *She speaks neither French nor German.*
➪ *See the usage note at* EITHER[2].

nephew /ˈnɛfyu/ [*noun*]
1 a son of your brother or sister
2 a son of your wife's or husband's brother or sister
➪ *See the picture at* FAMILY TREE.

Neptune /ˈnɛptun/ [*name*] the planet that is eighth from our sun

nerd /nɝd/ [*noun*] someone who is awkward in social situations and usually is very interested in science or computers: *He may be smart, but he's a real nerd.*

nerve * /nɝv/ [*noun*]
1 a thin thread that carries messages of feeling or movement between your brain and other parts of your body: *The pain in her back is caused by a pinched nerve.*
2 the courage to do something: *She did not have the nerve to phone him.*
━ PHRASES ━
3 lose your nerve to suddenly be not brave enough to do something: *He lost his nerve and wouldn't try the dive.*
4 get on someone's nerves to annoy someone: *She really gets on my nerves.*

nervous * /ˈnɝvəs/ [*adjective;* **more nervous, most nervous**] worried and a little afraid: *I'm really nervous about my job interview.*

USAGE   nervous, anxious

If you are **nervous**, you feel worried and a little frightened about something that is going to happen or something new or difficult you have to do: *I always get nervous before going on stage.* | *He makes me feel nervous.*

If you are **anxious**, you feel worried about something that might happen, and you feel that you have no control over it: *My mother gets anxious when I'm not home on time.*

---

nervous system /ˈnɝvəs ˌsɪstəm/ [*noun*] the parts of your body that make

/i/ **see**	/ɪ/ **big**	/eɪ/ **day**	/ɛ/ **get**	/æ/ **hat**
/ɑ/ **father, hot**	/ʌ/ **up**	/ə/ **about**	/ɔ/ **saw**	
/oʊ/ **hope**	/ʊ/ **book**	/u/ **too**	/aɪ/ **I**	/aʊ/ **how**
/ɔɪ/ **boy**	/ɝ/ **bird**	/ɚ/ **teacher**	/ɪr/ **ear**	/ɛr/ **air**
/ɑr/ **far**	/ɔr/ **more**	/ʊr/ **tour**	/aɪr/ **fire**	
/aʊɚ/ **hour**	/θ/ **nothing**	/ð/ **mother**	/ʃ/ **she**	
/ʒ/ **measure**	/tʃ/ **church**	/dʒ/ **jump**	/ŋ/ **long**	

you feel pain, heat, etc., and control how you move: *The nervous system includes your brain and nerves.*

nest * /nɛst/ [*noun*] the home that a bird makes to keep its eggs and to care for young birds in

a nest

net * /nɛt/ [*noun*]
1 a piece of material made from threads tied together, with spaces in between: *a volleyball net* | *a fishing net*
2 **the Net** the Internet; a network that connects computers all over the world, so that information can be gotten or sent: *Millions of people now use the Net regularly.*

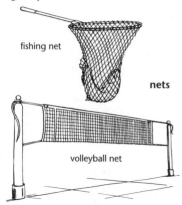

fishing net

nets

volleyball net

network * /'nɛt,wɜk/ [*noun*]
1 a system of things or people that are connected: *a computer network* | *a road network*
2 a group of television or radio stations that show many of the same programs in different places, and the company that supplies the programs: *All the major networks have news programs.*

neutron /'nutrɑn/ [*noun*] a part of an atom that has no electrical charge: *Neutrons and protons are at the center of an atom.*
↪ Compare **ELECTRON, PROTON**.

never * /'nɛvɚ/ [*adverb*]
1 not at any time in the past, present,

or future: *I have never been to Canada.* | *He felt he would never pass the test.*
☛ Do not say "This is one of the best books I have never read." Say **This is one of the best books I have ever read.**

━━ PHRASE ━━

2 **you never know** used to say that something might happen even if it is not likely: "*Do you think we'll win the competition?*" "*You never know.*"

new * /nu/ [*adjective*; **newer, newest**]
1 recently made or bought; *opposite* OLD: *Are you going to wear your new dress tonight?*
↪ Compare **SECOND-HAND, USED**[1].
2 not seen, done, or known before: *Anna has a new friend.* | *We're happy to listen to new ideas.*

new shoes   old shoes

new *and* **old**

newborn /'nu,bɔrn/ [*adjective*; no *comparative*] recently born: *a newborn baby*
☛ Only use **newborn** before a noun.

newcomer Ⓣ /'nu,kʌmɚ/ [*noun*] someone who has recently arrived in a place or recently started doing something: *Let's welcome the newcomers to our school.*

newly /'nuli/ [*adverb*] recently: *a newly painted room*

news * /nuz/ [*noun*]
1 new information about a person or about something that has recently happened: *Have you heard any news about Jenny's father?* | *We were delighted by the news of her new baby.*
2 things that have happened recently in the world that you read about in newspapers or see on television: *a news report*
3 **the news** a program on radio or television that tells you what has happened recently in the world: *I*

heard about the accident **on the news.** I
The news was not very interesting today
☛ Only use **news** or **the news** with a
singular verb.

newspaper * /'nuz,peɪpɚ/ [*noun*] a set
of large pieces of paper containing
news and pictures, that you buy every
day or every week: *He usually reads a
newspaper on the train.* I *I read about the
crash* **in the newspaper.**

newsstand /'nuz,stænd/ [*noun*] a place
on a street or in a building where you
can buy newspapers, magazines, candy,
etc.

New Year /'nu 'yɪr/ [*noun*] the time
when people celebrate the beginning
of a year: *New Year celebrations*

New Year's Day /'nu ,yɪrz 'deɪ/ [*noun*]
January 1st, a day that is a holiday in
the U.S. and many other countries: *We
visited my parents on New Year's Day.*

New Year's Eve /'nu ,yɪrz 'iv/ [*noun*]
the evening of December 31st, when
people in the U.S. and many other
countries celebrate before the beginning
of the year: *a New Year's Eve party*

next¹ * /nɛkst/ [*adverb*]
1 immediately or very soon afterward:
I was not sure what to do next.
━ PHRASES ━
2 next to very close to someone or
something; *synonym* BESIDE: *She was
sitting next to Jim on the sofa.*
⟡ *See the picture at* POSITION.
3 next to nothing a very small
amount: *This scarf cost next to nothing.*

next² * [*adjective; no comparative*]
1 coming or happening after the
present thing, day, person, etc.: *What
is the next item on the list?* I *It's my
birthday next Monday.* I *The clerk called
out, "Who's next?"*
2 nearest to where you are now: *He
lives on the next street.*

next³ [*pronoun, noun*]
the next the person or thing that
comes after another one: *Their band was
the next to perform.* I *The next I heard,
she had gotten married.*

next-door /'nɛkst ,dɔr/ [*adjective; no
comparative*] living in the closest house,

apartment, etc., to your own: *Our **next-
door neighbors** have a dog.*

next door /'nɛkst 'dɔr/ [*adverb*] to, at,
or in the next house, apartment, etc.:
They live next door.

nibble /'nɪbəl/ [*verb;* nibbled, nibbling]
to eat food by biting very small
amounts: *The rabbit was nibbling a
carrot.*

nice * /naɪs/ [*adjective;* nicer, nicest]
1 good and pleasant: *Did you have a
nice vacation?* I *a nice meal*
2 kind and friendly; *opposites* MEAN,
NASTY: *My teacher is very nice.*
━ PHRASE ━
3 (it's) nice to meet you SPOKEN used
when you meet someone for the first
time: *Hello, Mr. Gray, nice to meet you.*

nickel /'nɪkəl/ [*noun*]
1 a COIN used in the U.S. that is equal
to 5 cents
2 a hard white metal: *Nickel is often
blended with other metals.*

nickname /'nɪk,neɪm/ [*noun*] a name
that your friends call you that is not
your real name: *Her nickname is
"Brains" because she is very smart.*

niece /nis/ [*noun*]
1 a daughter of your brother or sister
2 a daughter of your wife's or
husband's brother or sister
⟡ *See the picture at* FAMILY TREE.

night * /naɪt/ [*noun*]
1 the time when it is dark and most
people are sleeping; *opposite* DAY: *That
night, I had a very strange dream.* I *You
can see the stars in the sky* **at night.**
2 the time during the evening: *We went
to see a movie **last night** (=yesterday
evening).* I *He spends most nights
watching TV.*
☛ Do not say "yesterday night." Say
yesterday evening or **last night.**
⟡ *See also* **all day/night/week/
month/year** *at* ALL¹. *See also* **the other
day/night** *at* OTHER¹.

/i/	**see**	/ɪ/	**big**	/eɪ/	**day**	/ɛ/ **get** /æ/ **hat**

/i/ **see** /ɪ/ **big** /eɪ/ **day** /ɛ/ **get** /æ/ **hat**
/ɑ/ **father, hot** /ʌ/ **up** /ə/ **about** /ɔ/ **saw**
/oʊ/ **hope** /ʊ/ **book** /u/ **too** /aɪ/ **I** /aʊ/ **how**
/ɔɪ/ **boy** /ɝ/ **bird** /ɚ/ teacher /ɪr/ **ear** /ɛr/ **air**
/ɑr/ **far** /ɔr/ **more** /ʊr/ **tour** /aɪr/ **fire**
/aʊɚ/ **hour** /θ/ **nothing** /ð/ **mother** /ʃ/ **she**
/ʒ/ **measure** /tʃ/ **church** /dʒ/ **jump** /ŋ/ **long**

nightgown
/'naɪt,gaʊn/ [*noun*] a piece of clothing like a loose dress that women and girls wear in bed

a nightgown

nightie /'naɪti/ [*noun; plural* **nighties**] INFORMAL the short form of NIGHTGOWN

nightingale /'naɪtən,geɪl/ [*noun*] a small bird that sings beautifully, especially at night

nightmare /'naɪt,mɛr/ [*countable noun*]
1 a frightening dream that you have while you are sleeping: *I had a nightmare about monsters last night.*
2 a very unpleasant or frightening situation: *The trip was a nightmare because the weather was so bad.*

night school /'naɪt ,skul/ [*noun*] classes in the evening that people can go to if they work during the day

nighttime /'naɪt,taɪm/ [*noun*] the time when it is dark: *a nighttime TV show*

nine * /naɪn/ [*number, noun*] 9: *Nine students got A's.*

nineteen * /naɪn'tin/ [*number*] 19: *We had nineteen cups but we needed twenty.*

nineteenth * /naɪn'tinθ/ [*adverb, adjective; no comparative*] coming after 18 other people, things, or events; sometimes written as "19th": *I live on the nineteenth floor.* | *I finished nineteenth in the race.*
⇨ *See the usage note at* SECOND[2].

ninetieth * /'naɪntiθ/ [*adjective, adverb; no comparative*] coming after 89 other people, things, or events; sometimes written as "90th": *Grandma's ninetieth birthday*
⇨ *See the usage note at* SECOND[2].

ninety * /'naɪnti/ [*number, noun; plural* **nineties**] 90: *My grandfather is ninety years old.*
⇨ *See the usage note at* TEENS.

ninth[1] * /naɪnθ/ [*adverb, adjective, no comparative*] coming after eight other people, things, or events; sometimes written as "9th": *September is the ninth month of the year.* | *I finished ninth in the race.*

ninth[2] * [*noun*] one of nine equal parts: *A ninth of eighteen is two.*
⇨ *See the usage note at* SECOND[2].

nip /nɪp/ [*verb;* **nips, nipped, nipping**] to bite someone quickly: *The turtle nipped me on the finger.*

nitrogen /'naɪtrədʒən/ [*noun*] a gas that forms most of Earth's air: *Air is about 78% nitrogen.*

no[1] * /noʊ/ [*adverb*]
1 used to refuse something or say that something is not true; <u>opposite</u> YES: *"Would you like a cup of coffee?" "No, thanks."* | *"You like soccer, don't you?" "No, I prefer baseball."*
2 used to disagree with a statement; <u>opposite</u> YES: *"He must be about 60 years old." "No, he's only 50."*
⇨ *See the usage note at* QUESTION[1].

no[2] * [*determiner*]
1 not any: *There's no milk.* | *There was no furniture in the room.*
2 used on signs to say you must not do something: *The sign said "No Smoking."*
⇨ *See also* **no way** *at* WAY[1].

no[3] * [*noun; plural* **noes**] a negative reply: *She responded with a definite no.*

no. a written abbreviation for NUMBER: *See picture no. 15 on p. 56.*

nobody /'noʊ,badi/ [*pronoun*] not anyone; <u>synonym</u> NO ONE: *I went to the house but there was nobody there.*

nod /nad/ [*verb;* **nods, nodded, nodding**]
1 to move your head up and down to show that you agree with something or understand it: *I asked him if he was tired and he nodded.*
⇨ *Compare* **shake your head** *at* SHAKE.
━━ PHRASAL VERB ━━
nod off [*phrasal verb*]
2 to fall asleep when you do not intend to: *I nodded off and missed the last part of the program.*

noise * /nɔɪz/ [*noun*] a sound, especially when it is loud, unpleasant, or sudden: *I heard a noise in the next room.* | *The children were making a lot of noise.*
⇨ *See the usage note at* SOUND[1].

noisily /'nɔɪzəli/ [*adverb*] in a way that makes a lot of noise: *They were playing noisily.*

noisy /'nɔɪzi/ [adjective; noisier, noisiest] making a lot of noise; opposite QUIET: The engine was noisy. | Mom told us not to be so noisy.

nomad /'noʊmæd/ [noun] someone who has no permanent home but moves around from place to place: a tribe of nomads

nominate /'nɑməˌneɪt/ [verb; nominated, nominating] to formally suggest that someone should receive a prize, be given a particular position, etc.: **nominate someone for something** ▸ She was nominated for the school's science prize.

none * /nʌn/ [pronoun] not any: None of the class did very well on the test.

nonalcoholic /ˌnɑnælkəˈhɔlɪk/ [adjective; no comparative] a nonalcoholic drink has no alcohol in it: They only serve nonalcoholic drinks such as apple juice and tea.

nonfat /'nɑn'fæt/ [adjective; no comparative] nonfat food has had the fat removed from it: nonfat milk

nonfiction /nɑn'fɪkʃən/ [noun] books that are about real facts that are not imagined: Books about plants and animals are in the nonfiction section of the library.

nonsense * /'nɑnsɛns/ [noun] ideas, opinions, or words that are stupid or have no meaning: His speech was complete nonsense.

nonsmoker /nɑn'smoʊkɚ/ [noun] someone who does not smoke; opposite SMOKER: Nonsmokers have the right to work in a smoke-free environment.

nonstandard /'nɑn'stændɚd/ [adjective] nonstandard words and expressions are often used, but most people think they are not correct: "Could of" is a nonstandard way of saying "could have."

nonstop[1] /'nɑn'stɑp/ [adjective; no comparative] not stopping: a nonstop flight to Detroit

nonstop[2] [adverb] all the time, without stopping; synonym CONTINUOUSLY: The baby cried nonstop.

noodle /'nudəl/ [noun] one of many long thin pieces of dough that are boiled: rice noodles (=made with rice) | chicken noodle soup (=chicken soup with noodles in it)

noon * /nun/ [noun] 12 o'clock in the middle of the day; opposite MIDNIGHT: She eats lunch at noon.

no one * /'noʊ ˌwʌn/ [pronoun] not anyone; synonym NOBODY: No one wants dessert.

nor * /nɔr/ [conjunction] used to add a negative statement to another negative statement: I'm not lying to you, nor have I ever lied.
  ⇨ See also neither . . . nor at NEITHER[3].

normal * /'nɔrməl/ [adjective; more normal, most normal] usual and expected: **it is normal to do something** ▸ It's normal to feel nervous before a test.

normally * ⊤ /'nɔrməli/ [adverb]
  1 in the usual and expected way: The baby seems to be developing normally.
  2 used to say what usually happens: He normally arrives late for class.

north[1] * /nɔrθ/ [noun]
  the north the direction or area that is on your left when you look at the rising sun: There's a river to the north of here. | They live in the north of the state.
  ⇨ See the usage note at DIRECTION.

north[2] * [adjective; no comparative] in, toward, or coming from the north: The hotel is at the north end of the park. | the north side of the building | a north wind
  ☛ Only use north before a noun.

north[3] * [adverb] toward or in the north: We're traveling north tomorrow. | The capital is north of here.

North America * /'nɔrθ ə'mɛrɪkə/ [name] the large area of land between the Atlantic Ocean and the Pacific Ocean, south of the Arctic and including the southern part called Central America

---

/i/ see	/ɪ/ big	/eɪ/ day	/ɛ/ get	/æ/ hat
/ɑ/ father, hot	/ʌ/ up	/ə/ about	/ɔ/ saw
/oʊ/ hope	/ʊ/ book	/u/ too	/aɪ/ I	/aʊ/ how
/ɔɪ/ boy	/ɝ/ bird	/ɚ/ teacher	/ɪr/ ear	/ɛr/ air
/ɑr/ far	/ɔr/ more	/ʊr/ tour	/aɪr/ fire
/aʊɚ/ hour	/θ/ nothing	/ð/ mother	/ʃ/ she
/ʒ/ measure	/tʃ/ church	/dʒ/ jump	/ŋ/ long

North American[1] * /ˈnɔrθ əˈmɛrɪkən/ [*name*] someone who comes from North America

North American[2] * [*adjective; no comparative*] belonging to, from, or relating to North America: *North American exports*

northeast[1] * /ˌnɔrθˈist/ [*noun*]
the northeast the direction or area that is between north and east: *Most of the farming is in the northeast.*
➪ See the usage note at DIRECTION.

northeast[2] * [*adjective; no comparative*] in, toward, or coming from the northeast: *the northeast part of Ohio* | *the northeast corner of the house* | *a northeast wind*
☛ Only use **northeast** before a noun.

northeast[3] * [*adverb*] toward or in the northeast: *The plane turned and went northeast.* | *Her house is northeast of mine.*

northeastern * /ˌnɔrθˈistən/ [*adjective; no comparative*] in or from the northeast: *There are many good universities in the northeastern U.S.*

northern * /ˈnɔrðən/ [*adjective; no comparative*] in or from the north: *She comes from a town in northern France.* | *a northern accent*

Northerner /ˈnɔrðənə/ [*noun*] someone who comes from the north of a country: *She married a Northerner and moved to Chicago.*

North Pole /ˌnɔrθ ˈpoʊl/ [*name*]
the North Pole the point on Earth that is the farthest north: *They are doing scientific experiments at the North Pole.*

northward /ˈnɔrθwəd/ or **northwards** /ˈnɔrθwədz/ [*adverb*] toward the north: *They hiked northward for two days.*

northwest[1] * /ˌnɔrθˈwɛst/ [*noun*]
the northwest the direction or area that is between north and west: *There are many factories in the northwest.*
➪ See the usage note at DIRECTION.

northwest[2] * [*adjective; no comparative*] in, toward, or coming from the northwest: *the northwest frontier* | *the northwest side of town* | *a northwest wind*
☛ Only use **northwest** before a noun.

northwest[3] * [*adverb*] toward or in the northwest: *The train was traveling northwest.* | *There's a large lake just northwest of here.*

northwestern * /ˌnɔrθˈwɛstən/ [*adjective; no comparative*] in or from the northwest: *There are a lot of apples grown in the northwestern U.S.*

nose * /noʊz/ [*noun*]
1 the part of your face that you use for breathing and smelling: *He broke his nose playing football.* | *Here's a tissue. Blow your nose* (=blow through it into a cloth or paper to clean it). | *My nose is running* (=liquid is coming out of it).
➪ See the picture at BODY.
━━ PHRASES ━━
2 under someone's nose if something is under your nose, it is so close to you that you should see it or notice it, but do not: *I spent an hour looking for the CD and it was right under my nose all the time.*
3 poke/stick your nose into to show too much interest in what other people are doing: *Don't poke your nose into other people's business.*

nosebleed /ˈnoʊzˌblid/ [*noun*] when blood comes out of your nose: *I had a nosebleed this morning.*

nostril /ˈnɑstrəl/ [*noun*] one of the two open parts at the bottom end of a nose
➪ See the picture at BODY.

nosy /ˈnoʊzi/ [*adjective; nosier, nosiest*] showing too much interest in what other people are doing: *Our neighbors are very nosy.*

not * /nɑt/ [*adverb*] used to give a word or statement an opposite meaning: *I'm not tired.* | *Are you coming or not?* | *Not many people were there.* | *There was not much hope of his winning the race.*

note[1] * /noʊt/ [*noun*]
1 a short message that you write: *I wrote her a note to thank her.*
2 something you write down so you will remember it: *Let me make a note of that book title.* | *Taking good notes in class helps you study better.*
3 a particular sound in music, or this sound represented by a written sign: *It's difficult to sing the high notes.*

note² * [*verb;* noted, noting]
1 to notice something or pay attention to it: *She **noted that** the room was very clean.* | *He noted my comments.*
2 to write something on a piece of paper so you will remember it: *He noted the meeting time in his calendar.*

notebook
/'noʊt,bʊk/ [*noun*] a set of pieces of paper fastened together like a book, for writing in: *a school notebook*

notepad
/'noʊt,pæd/ [*noun*] a set of pieces of **notebooks** paper fastened together at the top, for writing on

notepaper /'noʊt,peɪpɚ/ [*noun*] paper that you write letters or notes on

nothing * /'nʌθɪŋ/ [*pronoun*]
1 not anything: *There's nothing in that trunk.* | *I have nothing more to say.*
━ PHRASES ━
2 **for nothing**
 a without paying any money: *He gave us an extra ticket for nothing.*
 b without achieving what you were trying to do: *The store was closed, so we'd gone all that way for nothing.*
3 **have nothing to do with** to not be related to a fact or situation: *His illness has nothing to do with his job.*

notice¹ * Ⓣ /'noʊtɪs/ [*verb;* noticed, noticing] to see or hear something: *She noticed a small tear in the fabric.* | *He noticed that Ben looked unhappy.* | *I waved at her, but she didn't notice.* | *They drove by **without noticing** us.*
☛ Do not say "I was noticing." Say I noticed.

notice² * [*noun*]
1 a written message in a public place that gives you information or tells you not to do something: *There was a notice in the cafeteria about the meeting.*
━ PHRASE ━
2 **take no notice** to not listen to or not do what someone is telling you: *I told him to wait but he took no notice.*

noticeable * /'noʊtɪsəbəl/ [*adjective;* more noticeable, most noticeable] easy to see or recognize: *Don't worry. The stain on your tie isn't noticeable.*

notorious /noʊ'tɔriəs/ [*adjective; no comparative*] famous for something that people think is bad: *a notorious art thief* | *The mayor is **notorious for** being late.*
↪ See the synonym note at **FAMOUS**.

noun * /naʊn/ [*noun*] GRAMMAR a word that is the name of a thing, person, place, etc.: *"Dog," "table," and "girl" are all nouns.*

Nov. the written abbreviation of NOVEMBER

novel Ⓣ /'nɑvəl/ [*noun*] a book that tells an imagined story: *The novel is about a boy with magical powers.*

novelist /'nɑvəlɪst/ [*noun*] someone who writes novels: *a famous novelist*

November * /noʊ'vɛmbɚ/ [*noun*] the eleventh month of the year: *Our flight is on November 12th.* | *Thanksgiving is in November.*
↪ See the usage note at **MONTH**.

now * /naʊ/ [*adverb*]
1 at the present time: *We're going swimming now. Do you want to come?* | *One of my old students is now a doctor.* | *I'm going to be on time **from now on** (=starting from the present time).*
2 used to get someone's attention: *Now, can everyone listen, please?*
━ PHRASES ━
3 **for now** until a little later: *Leave the dishes in the sink for now*
4 **now and then** sometimes, but with a fairly long time in between: *I still see her now and then.*

nowadays /'naʊə,deɪz/ [*adverb*] used to say what the situation is now compared with the past: *Nowadays, children need to learn how to use a computer.*

/i/ **see**	/ɪ/ **big**	/eɪ/ **day**	/ɛ/ **get**	/æ/ **hat**
/ɑ/ **father, hot**	/ʌ/ **up**	/ə/ **about**	/ɔ/ **saw**	
/oʊ/ **hope**	/ʊ/ **book**	/u/ **too**	/aɪ/ **I**	/aʊ/ **how**
/ɔɪ/ **boy**	/ɝ/ **bird**	/ɚ/ **teacher**	/ɪr/ **ear**	/ɛr/ **air**
/ɑr/ **far**	/ɔr/ **more**	/ʊr/ **tour**	/aɪr/ **fire**	
/aʊɚ/ **hour**	/θ/ **nothing**	/ð/ **mother**	/ʃ/ **she**	
/ʒ/ **measure**	/tʃ/ **church**	/dʒ/ **jump**	/ŋ/ **long**	

nowhere * /'nou,wɛr/ [adverb]
 1 not to or in any place: *"Where did you go last weekend?" "Nowhere. We stayed home."*
— PHRASE —
 2 get nowhere to have no success with what you are trying to do: *I tried to convince him to come with us, but I got nowhere.*

nuclear /'nukliɚ/ [adjective; no comparative] relating to the power or explosive force made by splitting or joining atoms: *The U.S. has many of its nuclear weapons in Europe.* I *a nuclear power plant*

nucleus /'nukliəs/ [noun; plural nuclei /'nukli,aɪ/]
 1 the central part inside an atom: *The nucleus is made up of neutrons and protons.*
 2 the part of a plant or animal cell that controls the cell: *Scientists have developed methods for moving the nucleus into a different cell.*

nude[1] /nud/ [adjective; no comparative] without any clothes on: *a painting of a nude figure*

nude[2] [noun]
— PHRASE —
 in the nude not wearing any clothes; synonym NAKED: *My cousin walked into the room while I was in the nude.*

nudge[1] /nʌdʒ/ [verb; nudged, nudging] to push someone or something gently, especially with your elbow: *Just nudge me if I fall asleep.*

nudge[2] [noun] a gentle push, usually with your elbow: *Sandy gave me a nudge and said, "Look over there!"*

nugget /'nʌgɪt/ [noun] a small piece of something rough and hard: *a nugget of iron ore* I *gold nuggets*

nuisance /'nusəns/ [noun] someone or something that annoys you or makes a situation difficult: *She's a complete nuisance, always asking me questions.* I *"I have to leave my car with the mechanic for a week." "What a nuisance!"*

numb /nʌm/ [adjective; no comparative] unable to feel anything: *It was so cold that my hands were numb.*

number[1] * /'nʌmbɚ/ [noun]
 1 a figure such as 1, 2, 13, 49, etc., or a word that represents this: *Think of a number between one and twenty.* I *Open your books to page number 26.* I *apartment number 314*
 2 a telephone number: *Give me your number and I'll call you.*
— PHRASE —
 3 a number of several: *A number of people were watching them play tennis.*
 ⤳ *See the usage note at* AMOUNT.

number[2] [verb; numbered, numbering] to give several things a number to put them in order: *He numbered all the photographs.*

numbered /'nʌmbɚd/ [adjective; no comparative] having a number that is part of a particular order: *The tickets are numbered.*

numeral /'numərəl/ [noun] a figure used instead of a word to represent a number: *You don't need to spell out these numbers, just write the numerals.*

numerous /'numərəs/ [adjective; no comparative] many in number: *I've spoken with him numerous times.*

nun /nʌn/ [noun] a woman who belongs to a religious group of women who live together and do not marry: *The nuns lived in a small convent.*
 ⤳ *Compare* MONK.

nurse[1] * /nɝs/ [noun] someone who takes care of people when they are sick, especially in a hospital: *Just press that button to call the nurse.*

nurse[2] * [verb; nursed, nursing] to take care of someone when he or she is sick: *He nursed his father, who had cancer.*

nursery /'nɝsəri/ [noun; plural nurseries]
 1 a room or place where very young children are taken care of: *The church has a nursery where you can leave your daughter.*
 2 a place where plants are grown: *We bought these tomato plants at the nursery on South Street.*

nursery rhyme /'nɝsəri ,raɪm/ [noun] a short song or poem for young children

nursery school /'nɜ˞səri ˌskul/ [*noun*]
a school for very young children

nursing home T /'nɜ˞sɪŋ ˌhoʊm/
[*noun*] a place where old people live
and are taken care of

nut * /nʌt/ [*noun*]
1 a dry fruit with a hard shell that
grows on a tree, which can be eaten:
Add chopped nuts to the batter. |
Almonds and cashews are types of nuts.
2 a small piece of metal with a hole in
it that is used with a bolt to fasten
things together: *The metal plate was
fastened with a small nut and bolt.*
↪ *See the picture at* TOOL.

nuts

1. peanuts
2. cashews
3. almonds
4. walnuts
5. hazelnuts
6. pecans

nutrition /nu'trɪʃən/ [*noun*] the study
or process of getting the right kinds of
food that are needed for good health:
Good nutrition is important.

nutritious /nu'trɪʃəs/ [*adjective;* **more
nutritious, most nutritious**] food that
is nutritious contains things that your
body needs to stay healthy: *a nutritious
drink*

nuts /nʌts/ [*adjective; no comparative*]
INFORMAL
1 not at all sensible, or very strange;
synonym CRAZY: *You must be nuts to work
18 hours a day!*
━━ PHRASE ━━
2 **go nuts** to become very angry or
excited: *My dog goes nuts whenever the
doorbell rings.*

N.W. or **NW** the written abbreviation
for NORTHWEST: *I live at 302 N.W. 12th
Street.*

nylon /'naɪlɑn/ [*noun*] an artificial
material used for making clothes and
some kinds of plastics: *a nylon bag* |
nylon stockings

O

O * or **o** /oʊ/ [*noun; plural* **Os** or **O's, o's**]
the 15th letter of the English alphabet
↪ *See the usage note at* ALPHABET.

o * /oʊ/ [*number*] SPOKEN the number zero:
apartment number 108 (=said as "one o
eight")

oak /oʊk/ [*noun*] a large tree that grows
mainly in northern countries, or the
wood from this tree: *an oak table*

oar * /ɔr/ [*noun*] a thick long stick with a
wide flat end, used to make a boat
move through water
↪ *See the picture at* ROWBOAT.

oasis /oʊ'eɪsɪs/ [*noun; plural* **oases**
/oʊ'eɪsiz/] a place with water and plants
in the desert

oath /oʊθ/ [*noun; plural* **oaths** /oʊðz/] a
formal and serious promise: *She swore
an oath to tell the truth in court.*

oatmeal /'oʊtˌmil/ [*noun*] a hot food
made from cooked oats, usually eaten
for breakfast: *a bowl of oatmeal*

oats /oʊts/ [*plural noun*] a grain that
people and animals can eat

obedience /oʊ'bidiəns/ [*noun*] when
you do what you are told to do and
obey rules, laws, etc.; opposite
DISOBEDIENCE: *He expects total obedience
from his children.*

obedient /oʊ'bidiənt/ [*adjective;* **more
obedient, most obedient**] willing to do
what people or laws tell you to do;
opposite DISOBEDIENT: *She was a quiet,
obedient, little girl.*

obey * /oʊ'beɪ/ [*verb;* **obeys, obeyed,
obeying**] to do what someone tells you
to do, or what the law says you must
do; opposite DISOBEY: *Soldiers must always
obey their orders.* | *We must all obey the
traffic laws.*

object[1] * /'ɑbdʒɪkt/ [*noun*]
1 a thing that you can see or touch:
*The shop was full of extremely beautiful
and highly unusual objects.*

2 an aim or purpose, for example of an activity or game: *The object of the game is to win the most points.*
3 GRAMMAR the person or thing that a verb affects: *In the sentence "I baked a cake," "a cake" is the object.*
↪ *See also* DIRECT OBJECT, INDIRECT OBJECT. ↪ *Compare* SUBJECT (definition 3).

object[2] /əb'dʒɛkt/ [*verb;* objected, objecting] to say that you do not like or agree with something: *I strongly object to your suggestion.* | *I'll leave now, if no one objects.*

objection [T] /əb'dʒɛkʃən/ [*noun*] a reason why you do not like or agree with something: *I have no objection to the plan.* | *Several people raised objections* (=said they disagreed).

objective /əb'dʒɛktɪv/ [*noun*] something that you are working to achieve: *Our main objective is to increase sales.*

obligation /ˌablɪ'geɪʃən/ [*noun*] something that you must do: *I have obligations to my family.* | *You're under no obligation to come.*

obliged [T] /ə'blaɪdʒd/ [*adjective; no comparative*]
═══ PHRASE ═══
be/feel obliged to do something to know or feel that you must do something, especially because it is your duty: *I feel obliged to help her, since I said I would.*

observation /ˌabzɚ'veɪʃən/ [*noun*]
1 when you watch someone or something carefully over a period of time: *The doctor wants to keep her under observation* (=watch her carefully).
2 a remark or statement about something that you have noticed: *May I make an observation about your writing style?*

observe [T] /əb'zɝv/ [*verb;* observed, observing] to watch someone or something carefully: *Detectives have been observing the house for weeks.*

obstacle /'abstəkəl/ [*noun*] something that is in your way or makes it difficult for you to succeed: *The cars are steered around obstacles on the track.* | *Lack of education can be an obstacle to success.*

obstruct [T] /əb'strʌkt/ [*verb;* obstructed, obstructing] to block someone's way or make it difficult for someone to do something: *A car had broken down and was obstructing traffic.*

obstruction /əb'strʌkʃən/ [*noun*] something that blocks your way forward: *A major accident has caused an obstruction on the freeway.*

obtain * [T] /əb'teɪn/ [*verb;* obtained, obtaining] FORMAL to get something that you want: *Where can I obtain a copy of the report?*

obtuse /əb'tus/ [*noun*] an obtuse ANGLE is greater than 90 degrees

obvious [T] /'abviəs/ [*adjective;* more obvious, most obvious] very easy to notice or be certain about; *synonym* CLEAR: *There were some obvious mistakes in your paper.* | *It's obvious that you didn't study for this test.*

obviously [T] /'abviəsli/ [*adverb*]
1 in a way that is easily noticed or understood: *He was obviously annoyed.*
2 used to emphasize that what you are saying is clearly true: *Obviously, we need time to learn the new software.*

occasion * /ə'keɪʒən/ [*noun*]
1 a particular time when something happens: *I've met with them on several occasions.*
2 an important event: *I only drink champagne on special occasions.*

occasional /ə'keɪʒənəl/ [*adjective; no comparative*] happening sometimes but not often: *This afternoon will be sunny with occasional showers.*

occasionally [T] /ə'keɪʒənəli/ [*adverb*] sometimes but not often: *We meet for lunch occasionally.*

occupation /ˌakyə'peɪʃən/ [*noun*] a job or profession: *State your name and occupation.*

occupied /'akyə,paɪd/ [*adjective;* more occupied, most occupied] busy doing something: *She's very occupied with work right now.* | *It was hard to keep the boys occupied.*

occupy /'akyə,paɪ/ [*verb;* occupies, occupied, occupying]
1 to live in or fill a particular place or area: *The apartment hasn't been*

occupied yet (=no one is living in it). |
*A health store occupies the first floor of
the building.*
2 to be something that you spend time
doing: *Studying occupies all of her time.*

occur T /ə'kɜ˞/ [*verb;* **occurs, occurred,
occurring**]
1 FORMAL used about past events to
mean "to happen": *What exactly
occurred on the night of the crime?*
➪ *See the synonym note at* HAPPEN.
━━ **PHRASAL VERB** ━━━━━
occur to [*phrasal verb*]
2 to come into someone's mind
suddenly: *It never occurred to me that
she might be lying.*

ocean * /'oʊʃən/ [*noun*]
1 a large area of salt water that covers
the earth's surface, each with its own
name
2 the ocean the salt water that covers
most of the earth's surface: *Have you
ever been swimming in the ocean?*

SYNONYMS   ocean, sea

     Ocean is used about the largest areas of
salt water on the earth: *the Pacific Ocean* |
Have you ever sailed on the ocean? | *They
have a house on a hill above the ocean.*
     Sea is used about smaller areas of salt
water, or sometimes about the ocean: *the
Mediterranean Sea* | *the Baltic Sea* | *The
hotel is by the sea.*
     Sea is also used in many expressions
about both oceans and seas: *He **went to
sea*** (=became a sailor) *at the age of 18.* |
*People came west **by land and by sea***
(=traveling on land or the ocean).

---

o'clock * /ə'klɑk/ [*adverb*] used after a
number from one to twelve to show
what hour of the day it is: *He gets up at
six o'clock every morning.*
➪ *See the usage note at* TIME[1].

Oct. the written abbreviation of
OCTOBER

octagon /'ɑktə,gɑn/ [*noun*] a flat shape
with eight sides and eight angles
➪ *See* Shapes *in the Smart Study section.*

October * /ɑk'toʊbə˞/ [*noun*] the tenth
month of the year: *The concert is **on**
October 19th.* | *The party is **in** October.*
➪ *See the usage note at* MONTH.

octopus /'ɑktəpəs/ [*noun; plural*
octopuses] a soft sea creature that you
can eat, that has eight long arms

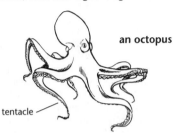

an octopus

tentacle

odd * T /ɑd/ [*adjective*]
1 [**odder, oddest**] different from what is
usual or expected; *synonym* STRANGE:
It's odd that she hasn't called.
2 [*no comparative*] an odd number
cannot be divided by two; *opposite*
EVEN: *There's an odd number of students,
so one team will have three.*

odds /ɑdz/ [*plural noun*] the chance or
possibility that something will happen:
What are the odds that he'll come?

odds and ends /'ɑdz ən 'ɛndz/ [*plural
noun*] many different small things,
especially ones that do not have much
value: *He searched through the odds and
ends in the drawer for a pen.*

odor /'oʊdə˞/ [*noun*] an unpleasant or
strong smell: *There was an odor of mold
in the hallway.*
➪ *See the synonym note at* SMELL[1].

of * /ʌv/ [*preposition*]
1 used to show a quality or feature that
something has: *I love the color of your
suit.* | *Look at the size of that fish!*
2 used to show that something is part
of something else: *the back of the chair*
3 used to show that something belongs
to or is connected with someone or
something else: *a friend of Bob's* | *She
was wearing a shirt of her husband's.*
4 used to show measurements or

/i/ **see** /ɪ/ **big** /eɪ/ **day** /ɛ/ **get** /æ/ **hat**
/ɑ/ **father, hot** /ʌ/ **up** /ə/ **about** /ɔ/ **saw**
/oʊ/ **hope** /ʊ/ **book** /u/ **too** /aɪ/ **I** /aʊ/ **how**
/ɔɪ/ **boy** /ɜ˞/ **bird** /ə˞/ **teacher** /ɪr/ **ear** /ɛr/ **air**
/ɑr/ **far** /ɔr/ **more** /ʊr/ **tour** /aɪr/ **fire**
/aʊə˞/ **hour** /θ/ **nothing** /ð/ **mother** /ʃ/ **she**
/ʒ/ **measure** /tʃ/ **church** /dʒ/ **jump** /ŋ/ **long**

amounts: *two tablespoons of sugar* | *a piece of cake* | *a cup of coffee*

5 used to show that something belongs to a particular group or set: *a flock of sheep* | *a pack of gum*

6 used to say what something is caused by or results from: *I'm afraid of heights.* | *She died of a heart attack.*

7 used to say where something is in relation to something else: *The university campus is just outside of town.* | *They live east of Princeton.*

8 used to show the name of something: *the city of Boston*

9 used in dates: *the 4th of July*

off¹ ＊ /ɔf/ [*preposition*] not on or touching something: *Take your shoes off the table!* | *He took a book off the shelf.*

She's taking a book **off** the shelf.　　She's putting the book **on** the shelf.

off *and* on

off² ＊ [*adverb*]

1 away from or out of a place or position: *He slammed the door and drove off.* | *Oh no, my button's come off!*

2 so that something is not operating; *opposite* ON: *Turn off the television set now.* | *Please turn the heaters off before you leave.*

3 used to say that you are not wearing something; *opposite* ON: *She took her jacket off.*

4 not at work or school because you are on vacation: *I'm taking two weeks off in August.*

5 below the usual price: *They're taking 15% off everything in the store.*

6 out of a bus, train, or plane; *opposite* ON: *The bus stopped to let her off.*

7 out of a bus, train, or plane; *opposite* ON: *The bus stopped to let her off.*

off³ [*adjective; no compararative*]

1 not operating; *opposite* ON: *Please make sure the lights are off.*

2 not at work or school because you are on vacation: *I was off for three days last week.*

☞ Do not use **off** before a noun.

offend ＊ /əˈfɛnd/ [*verb; offended, offending*] to make someone feel angry and upset: *I'm sorry if I offended you.* | *People were offended by his remarks.*

offense ＊ /əˈfɛns for definitions 1 and 2; ˈɔfɛns for definition 3/ [*noun*]

1 something that is against the law or is a crime: *a minor traffic offense* | *Stealing is a **criminal offense**.*

2 the feeling of being angry and upset: *I couldn't tell him without **causing offense** (=making him upset).* | *She **takes offense** (=gets upset) very easily.*

3 the part of the team that tries to score in football, soccer, basketball, etc.; *opposite* DEFENSE: *They had a great offense last year.* | *I like playing offense.*

offensive ＊ /əˈfɛnsɪv for definition 1; ˈɔfɛnsɪv for definition 2/ [*adjective*]

1 [*more offensive, most offensive*] insulting and likely to upset people: *She found his remarks deeply offensive.*

2 [*no comparative*] used for attacking someone or something: *offensive weapons*

☞ Only use this meaning of **offensive** before a noun.

offer¹ ＊ /ˈɔfɚ/ [*verb; offered, offering*] to say that you are willing to give something to someone or do something for someone: *He **offered to** help with the cleaning.* | **offer someone something** ▸ *She offered him a ride into town.* | *I was offered $50 for my old bicycle.*

USAGE　Ways of offering

A polite way of offering something is to say **Would you like . . . ?**: *Would you like to sit down?* If you want to offer someone food or a drink, you can say **Can I get you . . . ?**: *Can I get you some more tea?* A polite way of offering to do something is to say **Should I . . . ?**: *Should I ask him for you?* If you want to offer to do something in a more firm, but kind and friendly way, you can say **Let me . . . .**: *Let me get you a drink.* | *Let me take your coat.*

To accept an offer, say **yes, please** or **thank you**: *"Would you like a cookie?"*

"Yes, please." | *"Let me take your luggage."* *"Oh, thank you."* To refuse an offer, say **no, thank you** or **no, thanks:** *"Can I get you something to eat?"* *"No thank you. I'm fine."*

offer[2] * [*noun*] a statement that you are willing to give something to someone or do something for someone: *She has two job offers.* | *Thank you very much for your offer of help.* | *He made me an offer of $250 for my old computer.*

office * /ˈɔfɪs/ [*noun*] room or building with desks, computers, telephones, etc., where people work or do business: *I have to be in the office early tomorrow.* | *a private office (=for one person)* | *the dentist's office*

officer * /ˈɔfəsɚ/ [*noun*]
  1 someone who has a position of authority in an army, a navy, or an air force: *the commanding officer*
  2 [*name*] also **Officer;** a member of a police force: *Officer Brown*
  3 someone with an important position in a company: *the chief financial officer*

official[1] * /əˈfɪʃəl/ [*adjective; no comparative*] approved of or done by someone in authority, or by a government; *opposite* UNOFFICIAL: *There was an official investigation into school safety.*

official[2] * [*noun*] someone with a position of authority in an organization, especially someone who works for a government: *Immigration officials stopped him at the airport.*

officially * /əˈfɪʃəli/ [*adverb*] used to say that something is approved of or done by someone in authority: *The mayor officially opened the new library today.*

off-limits /ˈɔf ˈlɪmɪts/ [*adjective; no comparative*] if a place is off-limits, you are not allowed to go there: *This part of the museum is off-limits to the public.*

often * /ˈɔfən/ [*adverb*]
  1 many times: *We often go to the movies on Saturdays.*
  ▬ **PHRASE** ▬
  2 how often used to ask how many times or how frequently something happens or is done: *How often did you visit her?* | *How often does it rain here?*

oh /oʊ/ [*interjection*] something you say when you are surprised, annoyed, etc.: *"She got the job." "Oh, that's great!"* | *Oh no! I can't find my camera.*

oil[1] * /ɔɪl/ [*noun*]
  1 a thick dark liquid used for burning or for making machines run smoothly: *motor oil (=for cars)*
  2 a smooth thick liquid produced by plants that is used in cooking: *Fry the onions in a little olive oil.*

oil[2] [*verb; oiled, oiling*] to put oil into or onto something to make it work more smoothly: *The door hinge is squeaking and needs to be oiled.*

oil painting /ˈɔɪl ˌpeɪntɪŋ/ [*noun*] a painting done with paints that contain oil.

oil well /ˈɔɪl ˌwɛl/ [*noun*] a deep hole through which oil is taken out of the ground

oily * /ˈɔɪli/ [*adjective; oilier, oiliest*] full of oil or covered with oil: *This salad dressing is too oily.* | *an oily rag*

ointment /ˈɔɪntmənt/ [*noun*] an oily cream that you rub on your skin, especially as a medical treatment

OK[1] or **okay** /oʊˈkeɪ; ˌoʊˈkeɪ/ [*adjective; no comparative*] SPOKEN
  1 used to say that there are no problems, or that something is satisfactory; *synonym* ALL RIGHT: *"I'm sorry I'm late." "That's OK."* | *The plans look okay.*
  2 well, or not hurt; *synonym* ALL RIGHT: *She was in an accident, but she's okay.*

OK[2] or **okay** [*adverb*] SPOKEN
  1 used to say yes, or when you agree with something: *"I think we should go now." "Okay."*
  2 used when you start talking; *synonym* ALL RIGHT: *OK, let's start.*
  3 in a way that is satisfactory but not excellent; *synonym* ALL RIGHT: *I didn't win, but I did okay.*

/i/ **see** /ɪ/ **big** /eɪ/ **day** /ɛ/ **get** /æ/ **hat**
/ɑ/ **father, hot** /ʌ/ **up** /ə/ **about** /ɔ/ **saw**
/oʊ/ **hope** /ʊ/ **book** /u/ **too** /aɪ/ **I** /aʊ/ **how**
/ɔɪ/ **boy** /ɝ/ **bird** /ɚ/ **teacher** /ɪr/ **ear** /ɛr/ **air**
/ɑr/ **far** /ɔr/ **more** /ʊr/ **tour** /aɪr/ **fire**
/aʊɚ/ **hour** /θ/ **nothing** /ð/ **mother** /ʃ/ **she**
/ʒ/ **measure** /tʃ/ **church** /dʒ/ **jump** /ŋ/ **long**

OK[3] or **okay** [verb; OK's, OK'd, OK'ing
or okays, okayed, okaying] INFORMAL to
say yes, or to agree to something: *The
bank has finally OK'd our loan.*

okra /'oʊkrə/ [noun] a small green
vegetable that is eaten cooked

old * T /oʊld/ [adjective; older, oldest]
 1 having lived or existed for a long
time: *an old man with white hair* | *a
bookstore that sells old books* | *It was the
oldest house on the block.* | *He's an old
friend of mine* (=he has been my friend
for a long time).
 ☛ It is not polite to call someone **old**
directly.
 ➪ See the warning at ELDER. ➪ Compare
YOUNG[1].
 2 having been used a lot; *opposite* NEW:
an old pair of shoes
 3 used to describe someone or
something that you had before but no
longer have now: *I met my old math
teacher yesterday.* | *Do you ever regret
leaving your old job?*

━━ PHRASES ━━
 4 **3/70/21/etc. years old** being a
particular age: *My grandfather is 75
years old.* | *How old are you?*
 ☛ It is not polite to ask an adult how
old he or she is.
 5 **five-year-old/six-year-old/etc.**
someone who is a particular age: *My
four-year-old is already learning to read.*

old-fashioned * T /'oʊld 'fæʃənd/
[adjective; more old-fashioned, most
old-fashioned] not modern or
fashionable any more: *an old-fashioned
hat* | *old-fashioned ideas*

olive /'ɑlɪv/ [noun] a small black or
green fruit that grows on trees and is
used to make oil, or is kept in salty
water so it can be eaten

olive oil /'ɑlɪv ˌɔɪl/ [noun] oil made from
olives that is used in cooking: *a salad
dressing of vinegar and olive oil*

Olympic Games /ə'lɪmpɪk 'geɪmz/ or
Olympics /ə'lɪmpɪks/ [plural noun] an
international sports event that takes
place every four years in a different
country

omelet or **omelette** /'ɑmlɪt/ [noun] a
mixture of eggs beaten together and
cooked in hot fat, and often filled with
other foods: *a mushroom omelet*

omit T /oʊ'mɪt/ [verb; omits, omitted,
omitting] FORMAL to not include
something, either deliberately or by
mistake: *You omitted a comma in this
sentence.*
 ➪ See also **leave out** at LEAVE[1].

on[1] * /ɑn/ [preposition]
 1 touching the top or surface of
something, or hanging from
something: *An empty bottle was on the
table.* | *You have some food on your tie.* |
There was a mirror on the wall.
 ➪ See the pictures at IN[1], OFF[3] and on
page 346.
 2 in a particular place, area, or
position: *I live on Sixth Avenue.* | *a hotel
on the river* | *Stand here, on my left.*
 3 used with days or dates, to show
when something happens: *We went
swimming on Friday.* | *I was born on
June 4th.*
 4 being broadcast by a television or
radio station: *There's a good movie on
TV tonight.*
 5 inside a bus, train, or plane: *I can
never sleep on a plane.*
 ☛ Do not say "on a car." Say **in a car.**

on[2] * [adverb]
 1 so that something is operating;
opposite OFF: *Could you turn the light
on, please?* | *He turned on the radio.*
 2 used to say that you are wearing
something; *opposite* OFF: *He put his
coat on.* | *She had a red dress on.*
 3 forward or ahead: *They drove on for
another ten miles.*
 4 used to say that something continues
or can continue: *She kept on talking for
another hour.* | *Go on, tell me about it.*
 5 into a bus, train, or plane; *opposite*
OFF: *They aren't letting the passengers
on the plane yet.*

/i/ see /ɪ/ big /eɪ/ day /ɛ/ get /æ/ hat
/ɑ/ father, hot /ʌ/ up /ə/ about /ɔ/ saw
/oʊ/ hope /ʊ/ book /u/ too /aɪ/ I /aʊ/ how
/ɔɪ/ boy /ɝ/ bird /ɚ/ teacher /ɪr/ ear /ɛr/ air
/ɑr/ far /ɔr/ more /ʊr/ tour /aɪr/ fire
/aʊɚ/ hour /θ/ nothing /ð/ mother /ʃ/ she
/ʒ/ measure /tʃ/ church /dʒ/ jump /ŋ/ long

— PHRASE —

6 and so on and other things of the same type: *The teachers discussed homework, tests, grading, and so on.*

on³ [*adjective; no comparative*]
1 being broadcast, or shown in a theater: *The news will be on next.* I *What's on at the movies tonight?*
2 operating, or ready to operate; *opposite* OFF: *Do you know if the fax machine is on?*

once¹ * /wʌns/ [*adverb*]
1 one time or on one occasion: *I've only met him once.*
2 at some time in the past, but not any more: *She must have been rich once.*

— PHRASES —

3 once a week/day/etc. one time every week, day, etc.: *We usually eat out once a week.*
4 once in a while sometimes, but with a fairly long time in between: *We only call them once in a while.*
5 once more one more time: *Can I have another ride, Daddy—just once more?*
6 at once
a all at the same time: *Don't everyone talk at once.*

b immediately: *Get this mess cleaned up at once!*
7 all at once suddenly: *All at once, the rain stopped.*
8 once upon a time an expression used in children's stories meaning "a long time ago.": *Once upon a time there was a little princess with long black hair.*

once² [*conjunction*] from the moment something happens: *Once you've tried some, you'll want more.*

one¹ * /wʌn/ [*number, noun*]
1 1: *He has one brother and two sisters.*
2 a piece of paper money worth $1.00; *synonym* SINGLE: *Here's your change— two dimes, a quarter, and three ones.*

one² * [*pronoun*]
1 used to talk about someone or something that has already been mentioned: *"Do you have a computer?" "No, but I'm getting one soon."* I *"Which one is your sister?" "The one in the red dress."*
2 FORMAL used to talk about people in general; *synonym* YOU: *What should one do in such a situation?*

the preposition "on"

Joey is sitting **on** the chair.

The chair and table are **on** the rug.

There is a stain **on** Joey's shirt.

The books are **on** the table.

There is a picture **on** the cover of the book.

A picture is hanging **on** the wall.

Joey

━━ **PHRASES** ━━

3 one another each other: *They spoke to one another yesterday.*

4 one by one if people do something one by one, the first one does it, then the next one, etc.: *The people came into the room one by one.*

5 one . . . after another if things happen one after the other, they happen without much time passing between them: *This year we've had one problem after another.*

one³ ✷ [*determiner*]

1 a particular person or thing: *One thing I like about her is that she is kind.* | *One guest went home early.*

━━ **PHRASE** ━━

2 one morning/day/night/etc. on any morning, day, etc., it does not matter which: *Let's go out for lunch one day soon.*

oneself /wʌnˈsɛlf/ [*pronoun*] FORMAL used as the object of a verb or preposition when the subject is "one": *Sometimes one has to put oneself first.*

one-way /ˈwʌn ˈweɪ/ [*adjective; no comparative*]

1 moving or allowing movement in only one direction: *a one-way street* | *one-way traffic*

2 for going to a place, but not back again: *a one-way ticket to Boston* ⇨ *Compare* ROUND TRIP².

onion ✷ /ˈʌnyən/ [*noun*] a round VEGETABLE that is white, yellow, or red, has a strong smell and taste, and is made up of many layers

on-line or **online** /ˈɑn ˈlaɪn/ [*adverb, adjective; no comparative*]

1 directly connected to or controlled by a computer: *an on-line printer*

2 connected to the Internet: *Much of our work is done on-line.* | *All our schools will be online by early next year.*

only¹ ✷ /ˈoʊnli/ [*adverb*]

1 not more than a particular amount or number; *synonym* JUST: *I can't drive yet—I'm only 15.* | *It's only $10 for a large pizza.*

2 involving one thing or person and nothing more; *synonym* JUST: *She only has one good suit.* | *This cafeteria is for company employees only.*

3 used to emphasize that something or someone is not at all serious, important, dangerous, etc.; *synonyms* JUST, MERELY: *I was only kidding.* | *He's only a clerk, you know.* | *Don't worry, the dogs are only playing.*

━━ **PHRASE** ━━

4 only just

a almost not: *It was so noisy, I could only just hear her.*

b since a very short time ago: *He's only just started playing the trumpet.*

only² ✷ [*adjective; no comparative*]

1 with no others of the same kind: *She's the only person I feel I can really trust.* | *The only vegetable I don't like is celery.*

2 an only child does not have any brothers or sisters: *My husband and I are both only children.*

USAGE   only

The position of the adjective **only** in a sentence can change the meaning. Always put **only** before the word it describes. *Only Sarah kissed Paul* means that Sarah kissed Paul, but no one else kissed him. *Sarah only kissed Paul* means that Sarah kissed Paul, and she did nothing else. *Sarah kissed only Paul* means that Sarah kissed him, but she kissed no one else.

---

only³ ✷ [*conjunction*] used to give a reason that something is wrong, cannot be done, etc.; *synonym* BUT: *We were going to have a picnic, only it started to rain.*

onto ✷ /ˈɑntu/ [*preposition*] used with verbs of movement to mean "on a particular place": *He climbed onto the table to fix the light.* | *Their camera fell down onto some rocks below.*

onward /ˈɑnwərd/ [*adverb*] continuing forward in time: *The course covers philosophy from 1700 onward.*

/i/ **see**	/ɪ/ **big**	/eɪ/ **day**	/ɛ/ **get** /æ/ **hat**
/ɑ/ **father, hot**	/ʌ/ **up**	/ə/ **about**	/ɔ/ **saw**
/oʊ/ **hope**	/ʊ/ **book**	/u/ **too**	/aɪ/ **I** /aʊ/ **how**
/ɔɪ/ **boy**	/ɝ/ **bird**	/ɚ/ **teacher**	/ɪr/ **ear** /ɛr/ **air**
/ɑr/ **far**	/ɔr/ **more**	/ʊr/ **tour**	/aɪr/ **fire**
/aʊɚ/ **hour**	/θ/ **nothing**	/ð/ **mother**	/ʃ/ **she**
/ʒ/ **measure**	/tʃ/ **church**	/dʒ/ **jump**	/ŋ/ **long**

ooze /uz/ [verb; oozed, oozing] to flow out of something very slowly: *Blood was oozing from under his bandage.*

open[1] * /'oʊpən/ [adjective; no comparative]
1 if something with parts that can move is open, its parts are not together; *opposites* CLOSED, SHUT: *an open door* | *A book was open on his desk.*
2 ready for business; *opposites* CLOSED, SHUT: *Is the store still open?*
3 available for people to do or take part in; *opposite* CLOSED: *The program is open to children ages six to nine.* | *The gallery is open to the public.*
4 if a computer document or program is open, you can see it and use it: *Don't keep too may files open at the same time.*
5 willing to consider what other people say or think: *She's open to new ideas.*
6 not surrounded by things or covered by buildings: *It's all open country from here to the mountains.*

open[2] * [verb; opened, opening]
1 to become open, or to make something open; *opposites* CLOSE, SHUT: *That jar doesn't open very easily.* | *Open your eyes now.*
2 to be ready for business; *opposites* CLOSE, SHUT: *Most stores open at about 9 a.m.* | *Does the museum open on Sundays?*
3 to make a computer document or program appear so you can use it: *Why won't this folder open?*
4 to start a business: *He wants to open his own restaurant.* | *There's a new movie theater opening up near us.*
5 to take the paper or other cover off a gift to see what it is: *Can I open my presents now, Mom?*

opener /'oʊpənɚ/ [noun] a tool used to open something: *Did you bring a can opener?*

opening[1] /'oʊpənɪŋ/ [noun]
1 a hole or space in something: *They got in through an opening in the fence.*
2 when a job is available: *There's an opening in sales.*
3 an occasion when a new business, building, etc., opens: *The grand opening of the mall will be next week.*

4 the beginning of a story, program, play, etc.: *The opening of the movie was very dramatic.*

opening[2] [adjective; no comparative] done or said at the beginning of something: *The president made a few opening remarks.*

open-minded /'oʊpən 'maɪndɪd/ [adjective; more open-minded, most open-minded] willing to consider, accept, and learn about new things and ideas: *I'm looking for a doctor who's open-minded about different treatments.*

opera /'apərə/ [noun; plural operas] a musical play in which all the words are sung: *We went to see an opera last night.* | *Do you like opera?*

operate * /'apəˌreɪt/ [verb; operated, operating]
1 to work or make a machine work: *The machine operates best at high speeds.* | *We learned how to operate the equipment.*
2 to cut open someone's body to repair or remove a part that is damaged: *The surgeon operated on her for six hours.*

operating system /'apəreɪtɪŋ ˌsɪstəm/ [noun] a system in a computer that helps its programs to work together: *Which operating systems do you make software for?*

operation * /ˌapə'reɪʃən/ [noun]
1 when a doctor cuts open someone's body to remove or repair a part that is damaged: *He had an operation on his knee.*
2 a series of actions that are planned for a particular purpose: *a rescue operation*

operator /'apəˌreɪtɚ/ [noun]
1 someone who works for a telephone company and helps you make calls if you have problems: *Call the operator if you can't get the number.*
2 someone who makes a piece of equipment work: *a computer operator*

opinion * /ə'pɪnyən/ [noun] what you think about a particular subject: *What's your opinion on nuclear weapons?* | *In my opinion* (=this is what I think), *everyone should learn a foreign language.*

opossum /əˈpasəm/ [noun] a North American animal that looks like a large rat and can hang from trees by its tail; synonym POSSUM

opponent * /əˈpounənt/ [noun] someone who tries to defeat you in a competition, game, election, etc.: He knocked out his opponent.

opportunity * T /ˌapəˈtunɪti/ [noun; plural **opportunities**] an occasion when it is possible for you to do something good, enjoyable, useful, etc.; synonym CHANCE: You must take the job—it's a wonderful opportunity. | She never had the opportunity to go to college.

oppose * /əˈpouz/ [verb; **opposed, opposing**]
1 to strongly disagree with something and try to stop it: Local residents are opposing the development plan.
— PHRASE —
2 **as opposed to** used to compare two things and show that they are different: She wants to study engineering as opposed to electronics.

opposing /əˈpouzɪŋ/ [adjective; no comparative] competing, fighting, or playing against a person, team, etc.: The opposing team came onto the field.
☛ Only use **opposing** before a noun.

opposite¹ * /ˈapəzɪt/ [adjective; no comparative]
1 as different or as far as possible from something else: The car drove off in the opposite direction. | They live on the opposite side of town.
2 facing something or directly across from something: Our house is on the opposite side of the street from hers.

opposite² * [preposition] if one person or thing is opposite another, they are facing each other: The church is opposite the bookstore.

opposite³ * [noun] a person or thing that is as different as possible from another person or thing: "Full" is the opposite of "empty."

opposition * T /ˌapəˈzɪʃən/ [noun] when people strongly disagree with something and try to stop it: There is a lot of opposition to the plan.

optimist /ˈaptəmɪst/ [noun] someone who believes that good things are going to happen; opposite PESSIMIST

optimistic /ˌaptəˈmɪstɪk/ [adjective; more optimistic, most optimistic] believing that good things are going to happen; opposite PESSIMISTIC: John is very optimistic about the future.

option /ˈapʃən/ [noun] a choice that you can make in a particular situation: I have the option of working at home.

optional /ˈapʃənəl/ [adjective; no comparative] if something is optional, you can do it or have it if you want to, but you do not have to; opposite REQUIRED: Evening classes are optional.

or * /ɔr/ [conjunction]
1 used to show possibilities or choices: Would you like coffee or a soda or juice? | We could go to a movie, or we could just stay home.
☞ See also **either . . . or** at EITHER².
2 not one thing and not the other thing or things: She won't go to movies or plays or concerts.
☞ See also **neither . . . nor** at NEITHER³.
3 used to say what might happen if something else is not done: You'd better hurry or you'll miss your bus.
— PHRASE —
4 **or so** used to say that a number, figure, etc., is not exact: There's a motel a mile or so farther on.

oral /ˈɔrəl/ [adjective; no comparative]
1 spoken, not written: an oral exam
2 relating to the mouth: oral surgery

orange¹ * /ˈɔrɪndʒ/ [noun]
1 a bright yellow-red FRUIT that has sweet juice and a thick skin, and grows in hot places
2 a bright color that is a mixture of yellow and red

orange² * [adjective; no comparative]
1 of the color orange: an orange basketball
2 tasting like oranges: orange soda

/i/ **see** /ɪ/ **big** /eɪ/ **day** /ɛ/ **get** /æ/ **hat** /ɑ/ **father, hot** /ʌ/ **up** /ə/ **about** /ɔ/ **saw** /ou/ **hope** /ʊ/ **book** /u/ **too** /aɪ/ **I** /aʊ/ **how** /ɔɪ/ **boy** /ɝ/ **bird** /ɚ/ **teacher** /ɪr/ **ear** /ɛr/ **air** /ɑr/ **far** /ɔr/ **more** /ʊr/ **tour** /aɪr/ **fire** /aʊɚ/ **hour** /θ/ **nothing** /ð/ **mother** /ʃ/ **she** /ʒ/ **measure** /tʃ/ **church** /dʒ/ **jump** /ŋ/ **long**

orangutan /ɔ'ræŋʊˌtæn/ [*noun*] an animal like a large monkey with long arms and no tail, that lives in trees on islands in the Pacific
↪ See the picture at **APE**.

orbit[1] /'ɔrbɪt/ [*noun*] the path traveled in space by a planet, a moon, etc., around a bigger planet, star, etc.: *The satellite is in orbit around the earth.*

orbit[2] [*verb;* orbited, orbiting] to travel in space around a larger object: *A satellite has been sent to orbit Mars.*

The moon **orbits** the Earth.

orchard /'ɔrtʃərd/ [*noun*] a place where fruit trees are grown: *an apple orchard*

orchestra /'ɔrkəstrə/ [*noun; plural* orchestras] a large group of musicians who play formal music together and are directed by a person called a "conductor"

orchid /'ɔrkɪd/ [*noun*] a tropical **FLOWER**: *She pinned the orchid onto her dress.*

order[1] * /'ɔrdər/ [*noun*]
  1 the way in which things are arranged: *It's her job to keep her boss's files in order. | The students were listed in alphabetical order.*
  2 a request for food in a restaurant, goods from a company, etc.: *The waiter took their order. | We need to place an order* (=make a request) *for supplies.*
  3 when people obey the law or a set of rules: *People are worried about law and order in our cities.*
  4 a command from someone in authority: *Get upstairs right now! That's an order! | The general gave the order for the troops to advance.*

  — PHRASES —
  5 **out of order** if a machine is out of order, it is not working the way it should: *The telephone's out of order.*
  6 **in order to do something** or **in order for something to happen** so that someone can do something or something can happen: *She turned up*

the music in order to hear better. | *In order for the machine to work, you have to close the lid.*

order[2] * [*verb;* ordered, ordering]
  1 to ask for something in a restaurant, from a company, etc.: *We're not ready to order yet. | I ordered a necklace from their catalog.* | **order someone something** ▸ *Can I order you a drink?*
  2 if an army leader, police officer, etc., orders you to do something, he or she tells you to do it: **order someone to do something** ▸ *The general ordered his men to attack.*

orderly /'ɔrdərli/ [*adjective;* **more orderly, most orderly**] arranged in a neat way: *orderly piles of books*

ordinal /'ɔrdənəl/ or **ordinal number** /'ɔrdnəl 'nʌmbər/ [*noun*] a number that is used for putting things in order: *The ordinals are "first," "second," "third," etc.*
↪ Compare **CARDINAL**.

ordinarily Ⓣ /ˌɔrdən'ɛrɪli/ [*adverb*] usually: *I don't ordinarily eat dessert.*

ordinary * /'ɔrdənˌɛri/ [*adjective;* **more ordinary, most ordinary**]
  1 regular and usual, not special or different: *It was just an ordinary day like any other. | Use the ordinary napkins, not the fancy ones.*

  — PHRASE —
  2 **out of the ordinary** unusual or unexpected: *Was there anything out of the ordinary about the man?*

ore /ɔr/ [*noun*] rock or earth that has metal inside it: *iron ore*

organ * /'ɔrgən/ [*noun*]
  1 a part of the body, such as the heart or the lungs, that has a particular purpose
  2 a large musical instrument with keys like a piano and long pipes, that is often played in churches: *My mother plays the organ.*

organic /ɔr'gænɪk/ [*adjective; no comparative*]
  1 relating to living things or the study of living things: *organic matter | organic chemistry*
  2 growing or producing food without

using artificial chemicals, or grown by this method: *organic farming* | *Organic vegetables are often more expensive.*

organism /'ɔrgə,nɪzəm/ [*noun*] a living thing: *The pond is full of tiny organisms.*

organization * ⊤ /,ɔrgənə'zeɪʃən/ [*noun*]
1 a group that has been formed for a particular purpose, for example a club or a company: *We're glad you've joined our organization.*
2 the way in which things are planned and arranged: *Your files need better organization.*

organize * /'ɔrgə,naɪz/ [*verb*; organized, organizing] to plan or arrange something: *I'm organizing a party for her birthday.*

organized * /'ɔrgə,naɪzd/ [*adjective*; more organized, most organized]
1 neat or carefully arranged; *opposite* DISORGANIZED: *Her office is always well organized.*
2 good at planning or arranging things; *opposite* DISORGANIZED: *He's always very organized and never misses an appointment.*

Oriental /,ɔri'ɛntəl/ [*adjective; no comparative*] coming from or relating to the Eastern countries of the world, especially China, Korea, and Japan: *Oriental art*
☞ Do not use "Oriental" to talk about a person. Use **Asian**.

origin * /'ɔrɪdʒɪn/ [*noun*] the place or situation that something comes from, or where it began: *What is the origin of this saying?* | *a word of Greek origin*

original[1] * ⊤ /ə'rɪdʒənəl/ [*adjective*]
1 [*no comparative*] the first or earliest: *The car still has its original paint.* | *Our original plan was to take the train.*
2 [*more original, most original*] completely new and different: *This book has original ideas for making gifts.*

original[2] [*noun*] the real thing, not a copy: *The painting was definitely an original, not a fake.*

originally * /ə'rɪdʒənəli/ [*adverb*] at or in the beginning: *We originally lived on Second Street.*

ornament /'ɔrnəmənt/ [*noun*] an object that is interesting or beautiful to look at, especially one that you use to decorate your home: *Delicate china ornaments were displayed on the shelves.*

a Christmas tree **ornament**

orphan /'ɔrfən/ [*noun*] a child whose parents are dead

orphanage /'ɔrfənɪdʒ/ [*noun*] a building in which children who have no parents live

ostrich /'ɔstrɪtʃ/ [*noun; plural* ostriches] a very large bird with long legs, which runs very fast but cannot fly

an ostrich

other[1] * /'ʌðɚ/ [*determiner, adjective; no comparative*]
1 used to talk about a thing, person, or group that is not the one you have already mentioned or the one you are talking to: *I've found one sock, but where's the other one?* | *Go play in the yard with the other children.*
2 different from or in addition to someone or something else: *Put your other shoes on—those are dirty.* | *There are other people you could ask.*

━ PHRASES ━
3 **other than** except for: *I couldn't find a pan other than this one.*
4 **the other day/night** not long ago; *synonym* RECENTLY: *I saw Michael the other day.*

other[2] * [*pronoun*]
1 a thing, person, or group that is not the one you have already mentioned: *Kay and I came by bus but the others are driving.* | *I've found one shoe, but where's the other?*

/i/ **see** /ɪ/ **big** /eɪ/ **day** /ɛ/ **get** /æ/ **hat**
/ɑ/ **father, hot** /ʌ/ **up** /ə/ **about** /ɔ/ **saw**
/oʊ/ **hope** /ʊ/ **book** /u/ **too** /aɪ/ **I** /aʊ/ **how**
/ɔɪ/ **boy** /ɝ/ **bird** /ɚ/ **teacher** /ɪr/ **ear** /ɛr/ **air**
/ɑr/ **far** /ɔr/ **more** /ʊr/ **tour** /aɪr/ **fire**
/aʊɚ/ **hour** /θ/ **nothing** /ð/ **mother** /ʃ/ **she**
/ʒ/ **measure** /tʃ/ **church** /dʒ/ **jump** /ŋ/ **long**

2 a different or additional thing or person: *I don't like this book. Do you have any others I could read?*

otherwise /'ʌðɚ,waɪz/ [adverb]
   1 used to say that something will happen if another thing does not happen first: *Do your homework, otherwise you'll get into trouble.*
   2 apart from or differently from what you have just mentioned: *My throat's still a little sore, otherwise I feel OK.* | *We all wanted to go to the movies, but Dad decided otherwise.*

otter /'ɑtɚ/ [noun] a small animal with brown fur that lives near water, swims, and eats fish

an otter

ouch /aʊtʃ/ [interjection] something you say when something hurts you: *Ouch! You stepped on my foot.*

ought to * /'ɔt ,tə/ [modal verb] used to say what you think someone should do: *You ought to apologize to her.*

ounce * /aʊns/ [noun] a unit for measuring weight and liquids, equal to 28.35 grams or 29.5 milliliters: *There are 16 ounces in one pound.*

our * /'aʊɚ/ [determiner] belonging to or connected with us: *That's our new car.* | *We wrote our names in our new books.*
   ☛ Only use **our** before a noun.

ours * /'aʊɚz/ [pronoun] something that belongs to or is connected with us: *Their house isn't as big as ours.*

ourselves * /aʊɚ'sɛlvz/ [pronoun]
   1 used as the object of a verb or preposition when the subject is "we": *We bought ourselves some new clothes.*
   2 used to emphasize the word "we": *Do you like the cabin? We built it ourselves.*
   ☛ Do not use **ourselves** as a subject. For example, do not say "Ourselves did it." Say **We did it ourselves.**

— PHRASES
   3 by ourselves alone or without any help: *We're not allowed to stay home by ourselves.* | *We made breakfast for Mom all by ourselves.*
   4 to ourselves not sharing something with anyone else: *It was nice to have the whole house to ourselves.*

out¹ * [preposition]
   1 from inside something, or through something: *She looked out the window.*
— PHRASE
   2 out of
      a from a particular place: *He took the key out of his pocket.*
      b from a larger group of the same kind: *Two out of three people voted no.*
      c having none of something: *We're almost out of gas.*

out² * [adverb]
   1 away from the inside of a container, vehicle, place, etc.; *opposite* IN: *Close the door as you go out.* | *She opened the box and took some books out.*
   2 outside; *opposites* IN, INDOORS: *Why don't you go out and get some air?*
   3 used with verbs and adjectives to mean "completely": *Rinse out your glass and put it in the sink.* | *Wow, I'm tired out.*

out³ * /aʊt/ [adjective; no comparative]
   1 outside, or away from home or work; *opposite* IN: *I'm sorry, Joe's out right now.* | *The children are out in the yard.*
   2 not burning or shining: *The lights were all out and no one was home.*
   3 if a product is out, it is available to be bought or used: *When will their new CD be out?*
   4 no longer fashionable; *opposite* IN: *Wearing fur is out.*

outcome /'aʊt,kʌm/ [noun] the result of a meeting or process: *No one knows what the outcome of the talks will be.*

outdated /,aʊt'deɪtɪd/ [adjective; no comparative] no longer useful or modern: *Computers become outdated very quickly.*

outdoor * /'aʊt,dɔr/ [adjective; no comparative] outside, or used or happening outside; *opposite* INDOOR: *an*

outdoor swimming pool | *warm outdoor clothing* | *outdoor activities*
☛ Only use **outdoor** before a noun.

outdoors ✴ /ˌaʊtˈdɔrz/ [*adverb*] outside, not in a house or other building; *opposite* INDOORS: *Let's have our supper outdoors tonight.*

outer ✴ /ˈaʊtɚ/ [*adjective; no comparative*] far from the center of something, or on the outside of it; *opposite* INNER: *They live in the outer suburbs.* | *Throw away the tough outer leaves of the cabbage.*
☛ Only use **outer** before a noun.

outer space /ˈaʊtɚ ˈspeɪs/ [*noun*] the area outside the earth's atmosphere, where the stars and planets are

outfit /ˈaʊtˌfɪt/ [*noun*] a set of clothes that are worn together: *I like your outfit.*

outgoing /ˈaʊtˌɡoʊɪŋ/ [*adjective*]
1 [**more outgoing, most outgoing**] liking to meet new people and talk to them; *opposite* SHY: *a friendly, outgoing woman*
2 [*no comparative*] leaving a place: *This tray is for the outgoing mail.*
☛ Only use this meaning of **outgoing** before a noun.

outgrow /ˌaʊtˈɡroʊ/ [*verb;* **outgrew, outgrown, outgrowing**] to grow and become too large for something: *I have to wear the clothes my brother outgrows.* | *The company has outgrown its building.*

outlet /ˈaʊtlɛt/ [*noun*] a place on a wall where you can connect something to a supply of electricity

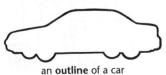

plug   cord

an electrical **outlet**

outline /ˈaʊtˌlaɪn/ [*noun*]
1 a line around the edge of something that shows its shape
2 the main parts of a plan, speech, piece of writing, etc., without the

an **outline** of a car

details: *Could you give us a* **rough outline of** (=a general description of) *the course?*

outnumber /ˌaʊtˈnʌmbɚ/ [*verb;* **outnumbered, outnumbering**] to be more in number than another group: *The boys outnumber the girls in this class* (=there are more boys than girls). | *They outnumber the girls two to one* (=there are twice as many boys).

out-of-date or **out of date** /ˈaʊt əv ˈdeɪt/ [*adjective; no comparative*] no longer useful or correct: *an out-of-date calendar* | *This schedule is out of date.*

outraged /ˈaʊtˌreɪdʒd/ [*adjective;* **more outraged, most outraged**] feeling very shocked and angry: *We were outraged by the judge's decision.*

outright /ˈaʊtˈraɪt/ [*adverb*] clearly and directly: *She told him outright that she thought his plan was stupid.*

outside¹ ✴ /ˌaʊtˈsaɪd/ [*preposition*]
1 out of a building or room but still near it; *opposite* INSIDE: *I'll meet you outside the theater at 7:30.*
2 beyond the limits of a city, state, etc: *They live just outside Chicago.*

outside² ✴ /ˌaʊtˈsaɪd/ [*adverb*]
1 not inside a building: *Mom, can we go outside and play?*
2 not in a room or building, but still near it: *She left the room but waited outside in the hall.*

outside³ ✴ /ˈaʊtˈsaɪd/ [*noun*] **the outside** the part or surface of something that is facing away from it or at the edge of it; *opposite* INSIDE: *The outside of the old cabinet was scratched.* | *On the outside, the house looked nice.*

outside⁴ ✴ /ˈaʊtˌsaɪd/ [*adjective; no comparative*] an outside part of a building is at the edge of it or on its surface; *opposite* INSIDE: *an outside wall*
☛ Only use **outside** before a noun.

/i/ **see** /ɪ/ **big** /eɪ/ **day** /ɛ/ **get** /æ/ **hat**
/ɑ/ **father, hot** /ʌ/ **up** /ə/ **about** /ɔ/ **saw**
/oʊ/ **hope** /ʊ/ **book** /u/ **too** /aɪ/ **I** /aʊ/ **how**
/ɔɪ/ **boy** /ɝ/ **bird** /ɚ/ **teacher** /ɪr/ **ear** /ɛr/ **air**
/ɑr/ **far** /ɔr/ **more** /ʊr/ **tour** /aɪr/ **fire**
/aʊɚ/ **hour** /θ/ **nothing** /ð/ **mother** /ʃ/ **she**
/ʒ/ **measure** /tʃ/ **church** /dʒ/ **jump** /ŋ/ **long**

outskirts /'aʊt,skɜⁱts/ [*plural noun*] the parts of a town or city that are farthest away from the center: *My uncle has an apartment on the outskirts of Dallas.*

outspoken /'aʊt'spoʊkən/ [*adjective; more outspoken, most outspoken*] saying what you think honestly, even if you offend or shock some people: *He is an outspoken critic of the government.*

outstanding /,aʊt'stændɪŋ/ [*adjective; more outstanding, most outstanding*] extremely good, and better than many others: *an outstanding achievement* | *Your work this year has been outstanding.*

outward¹ /'aʊtwəd/ or **outwards** /'aʊtwədz/ [*adverb*] toward the outside, or away from a place; *opposite* INWARD: *The door opens outwards.*

outward² [*adjective; no comparative*] relating to the way someone or something appears to be: *He gave no outward sign of his feelings.*
☛ Only use **outward** before a noun.

oval¹ /'oʊvəl/ [*noun*] a shape like a circle, but longer than it is wide
↪ See Shapes *in the Smart Study section.*

oval² [*adjective; no comparative*] shaped like a circle, but longer than it is wide: *an oval box*

oven * /'ʌvən/ [*noun*] a large piece of kitchen equipment in which food is cooked, shaped like a box with a door at the front: *Cook the pizza in a hot oven for 15 minutes.*
↪ See the picture at STOVE.

over¹ * /'oʊvə/ [*preposition*]
1 above something or on top of something; *opposite* UNDER: *I can't see over the heads of the people in front of me.* | *There were dark clouds over the mountains.*
↪ See the picture at POSITION.
2 above something, from one side of it to the other: *We climbed over the fence.*
3 on someone or something so that he, she, or it is covered: *She pulled the blanket over herself.*
↪ See the picture at UNDER¹.
4 more than a particular number, amount, size, or age; *opposite* UNDER: *Children over ten are allowed in the big pool.* | *Over a hundred people came to the wedding.*

5 during a particular time: *We had guests staying over the weekend.*

over² * [*adverb*]
1 used to show where someone or something is: *Peter! I'm over here!* | *Look at that painting over there.*
2 down from an upright position: *Careful! Don't knock your glass over.*
3 to a particular place: *Why don't you come over* (=come to my house) *this weekend?* | *Who's leaving cups all over the house?* (=in many places in it)
4 to a different or opposite side: *You should turn the mattress over.* | *Roll over onto your side.*
5 again: *This homework's so messy you'll have to do it over.* | *We seem to have the same argument over and over.*
6 more than a particular number, amount, size, or age; *opposite* UNDER: *Only people 18 and over can use the gym.*

over³ [*adjective; no comparative*] finished: *The game is almost over.*

overall¹ /'oʊvər,ɔl/ [*adjective; no comparative*] with everything or everyone included: *Em was the overall winner.*

overall² /,oʊvər'ɔl/ [*adverb*]
1 including everything or everyone: *What is the cost of the vacation overall?*
2 generally: *Overall, I'm happy with my grades.*

overalls /'oʊvər,ɔlz/ [*plural noun*] thick cotton pants with a piece that covers your chest and two bands that go over your shoulders

He's wearing **coveralls.**

He's wearing **overalls.**

overboard /'oʊvɚˌbɔrd/ [*adverb*] over the side of a ship and into the water: *She slipped and fell overboard.*

overcast /'oʊvɚˈkæst/ [*adjective; no comparative*] full of clouds: *an overcast day* | *The sky was dark and overcast.*

overcoat /'oʊvɚˌkoʊt/ [*noun*] a long warm coat

overcome Ⓣ /ˌoʊvɚˈkʌm/ [*verb; overcame, overcoming*] to control a feeling or problem that stops you from doing something: *He's trying to overcome his fear of flying.*

overcrowded /ˌoʊvɚˈkraʊdɪd/ [*adjective; more overcrowded, most overcrowded*] an overcrowded place or vehicle has too many people or things in it: *an overcrowded bus*

overdose /'oʊvɚˌdoʊs/ [*noun*] too much of a drug taken at one time: *Doctors think she may have taken an overdose.*

overdue /ˌoʊvɚˈdu/ [*adjective; no comparative*] not done, given, returned, etc., when expected or needed; *synonym* LATE: *overdue library books* | *An answer from the governor is long overdue.*

overflow /ˌoʊvɚˈfloʊ/ [*verb; overflowed, overflowing*] if a liquid overflows, it goes over the edges of the container or place it is in: *I forgot to turn off the faucet, and the sink overflowed.*

overgrown /ˌoʊvɚˈɡroʊn/ [*adjective; more overgrown, most overgrown*] covered with plants that are not under control: *a path overgrown with weeds*

overhead /'oʊvɚˌhɛd/ [*adverb, adjective; no comparative*] in a position above your head, or moving above your head: *an overhead cable* | *Birds flew overhead.*

overhear /ˌoʊvɚˈhɪr/ [*verb; overheard /ˌoʊvɚˈhɝd/, overhearing*] to accidentally hear what someone is saying, when he or she is not talking to you directly: *I'm sorry, I couldn't help overhearing what you said.*

overjoyed /ˌoʊvɚˈdʒɔɪd/ [*adjective; no comparative*] extremely happy: *They were overjoyed about your news.*

overlook Ⓣ /ˌoʊvɚˈlʊk/ [*verb; overlooked, overlooking*]
1 to not notice something, or not

realize that it is important: *They had overlooked a few details.*
2 to have a view of something from above: *The deck overlooks the lake.*

overnight¹ /'oʊvɚˈnaɪt/ [*adverb*] for a whole night, or during the night: *We stayed overnight at a small motel.* | *A storm came in overnight.*

overnight² /'oʊvɚˌnaɪt/ [*adjective; no comparative*] continuing or happening during the night: *an overnight flight*
☛ Only use **overnight** before a noun.

overpass /'oʊvɚˌpæs/ [*noun; plural* **overpasses**] the part of a road that goes over another road or railroad; *opposite* UNDERPASS: *When you get off the highway, turn left onto the overpass.*

overpriced /ˌoʊvɚˈpraɪst/ [*adjective; no comparative*] too expensive: *It's a nice restaurant, but the food's overpriced.*

overseas¹ Ⓣ /ˌoʊvɚˈsiz/ [*adverb*] to or in a foreign country that is separated from your country by an ocean: *Her son is working overseas.*

overseas² Ⓣ /'oʊvɚˈsiz/ [*adjective; no comparative*] to, in, or from a foreign country: *overseas students* | *an overseas trip*

oversleep /ˌoʊvɚˈslip/ [*verb; overslept, oversleeping*] to sleep for longer than you intended: *I'm sorry I'm late—I overslept.*

overtime /'oʊvɚˌtaɪm/ [*noun*] time that you spend working at your job in addition to your normal working hours: *He does ten hours a week of overtime to earn some extra money.*

overweight /'oʊvɚˈweɪt/ [*adjective; more overweight, most overweight*] weighing more than you should: *I'm about 20 pounds overweight.*
↪ See the synonym note at FAT¹.

owe * /oʊ/ [*verb; owed, owing*]
1 to have to pay someone money because you have borrowed money

/i/ **see**	/ɪ/ **big**	/eɪ/ **day**	/ɛ/ **get**	/æ/ **hat**
/ɑ/ **father, hot**	/ʌ/ **up**	/ə/ **about**	/ɔ/ **saw**
/oʊ/ **hope**	/ʊ/ **book**	/u/ **too**	/aɪ/ **I**	/aʊ/ **how**
/ɔɪ/ **boy**	/ɝ/ **bird**	/ɚ/ **teacher**	/ɪr/ **ear**	/ɛr/ **air**
/ɑr/ **far**	/ɔr/ **more**	/ʊr/ **tour**	/aɪr/ **fire**
/aʊɚ/ **hour**	/θ/ **nothing**	/ð/ **mother**	/ʃ/ **she**
/ʒ/ **measure**	/tʃ/ **church**	/dʒ/ **jump**	/ŋ/ **long**

from him or her: **owe someone something** ▸ *I still owe you $20.*
2 to feel grateful to someone or feel that you should do something for him or her, because he or she has done something for you: **owe someone something** ▸ *I'll ask Lori to help. She* ***owes me a favor*** *(=I already did something for her).*

owl /aʊl/ [*noun*] a large bird that has large eyes, a loud call, and hunts at night

own[1] * /oʊn/ [*determiner*] belonging to or done by yourself and no one else: *I want to buy my own home. | It's your own choice.*

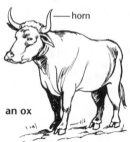

an owl

own[2] * [*pronoun*]
1 belonging to or done by yourself and no one else: *He has a room **of his own**.*
━━ PHRASE ━━
2 on your/my/his/etc. own without anyone or anything else: *Don't go into the woods on your own.*
▷ *See the synonym note at* ALONE[2].

own[3] * [*verb*; **owned, owning**] to have something that is yours because you bought it or were given it: *He owns a house in Montana.*

owner * /'oʊnɚ/ [*noun*] someone who owns something: *Who's the **owner of** that big boat?*

ox /aks/ [*noun*; *plural* **oxen** /'aksən/] a bull that is often used for work on farms

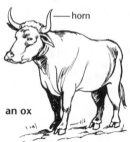

horn

an ox

oxygen * /'aksɪdʒən/ [*noun*] a gas in the air that has no color, taste, or smell, and that animals and plants need in order to live

oyster /'ɔɪstɚ/ [*noun*] a sea creature that you can eat, that has two rough shells that close around it, and that can produce pearls
▷ *See the picture at* SHELLFISH.

oz. the written abbreviation of OUNCE or OUNCES: *a 12-oz. bottle of shampoo*

ozone layer /'oʊzoʊn ˌleɪɚ/ [*noun*] a layer of gases that prevents harmful light from the sun from reaching Earth

P

P * or **p** /pi/ [*noun*; *plural* **Ps** or **P's, p's**] the 16th letter of the English alphabet
▷ *See the usage note at* ALPHABET.

p. the written abbreviation of PAGE: *See p. 34 for a list of phrasal verbs.*

pace[1] Ⓣ /peɪs/ [*noun*] the speed at which someone moves or something is done: *The runners set off at a fast pace. | We were allowed to work **at our own pace** (=at the speed we wanted to).*

pace[2] [*verb*; **paced, pacing**] to walk forward and back again many times, especially because you are worried or do not like waiting: *He paced up and*

down, hoping for news. | *She paced the floor of the waiting room.*

Pacific * /pə'sɪfɪk/ [*name*]
the Pacific (Ocean) the large ocean between North and South America on the east, and Asia on the west

pacifier /'pæsəˌfaɪɚ/ [*noun*] a rubber object given to a baby to suck on so that he or she does not cry

pack[1] * /pæk/ [*verb*; **packed, packing**]
1 to put clothes or other things into cases, bags, boxes, etc., in order to take them somewhere; *opposite* UNPACK: *I haven't finished packing yet. | You've packed your suitcase too full.*

2 to fill a place or container completely with people or things: *A huge crowd packed the stadium.*

━━ PHRASAL VERB ━━━━━

pack up [*phrasal verb*]
3 to stop working and put your things away: *It was time to pack up and go.*
⮑ *See also* PACKED, PACKING.

pack² [*noun*]
1 a number of things sold together in a package: *I'd like a pack of gum, please.*
2 a set of playing cards; *synonym* DECK: *a pack of cards*
3 a large bag made of cloth that you wear on your back, used for carrying things; *synonym* BACKPACK
4 a group of animals that hunt and stay together: *a pack of wolves*

package * Ⓣ /'pækɪdʒ/ [*noun*]
1 the bag, paper, container, etc., in which food and other things are sold: *a package of crackers*
2 something in a large envelope or wrapped in paper, that is sent by mail: *He tore the package open.*
3 a number of goods or services that are sold or given together: *Each new computer comes with a software package.*

packaging /'pækɪdʒɪŋ/ [*noun*] the kind of package that something is sold in, including its design: *We created new packaging for our toys this year.*

packed /pækt/ [*adjective; no comparative*] a place or vehicle that is packed is full of people; *synonym* CROWDED: *The concert hall was packed and I couldn't find my friends.* | *a packed bus*

packet /'pækɪt/ [*noun*] an envelope, especially one with things inside it: *My grandmother orders packets of seeds from a flower catalog.* | *an information packet*

packing /'pækɪŋ/ [*noun*] when you pack clothes and other things: *I'll do my packing in the morning.*

pact /pækt/ [*noun*] an agreement between two countries or people: *The two countries signed a peace pact in 1946.*

pad /pæd/ [*noun*]
1 a number of pieces of paper for writing on, glued together at one end: *I need a new writing pad.* | *a pad of paper*
2 a piece of soft material used for protecting a part of the body, for

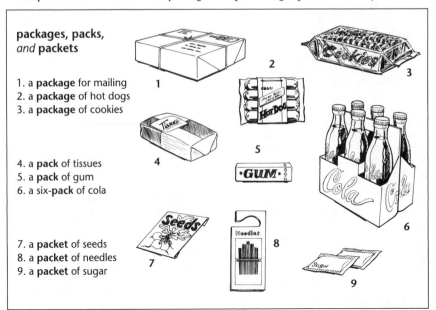

packages, packs,
and **packets**

1. a **package** for mailing
2. a **package** of hot dogs
3. a **package** of cookies

4. a **pack** of tissues
5. a **pack** of gum
6. a six-**pack** of cola

7. a **packet** of seeds
8. a **packet** of needles
9. a **packet** of sugar

making things more comfortable, etc.: *Always wear knee pads when you go roller-skating or rollerblading.*

padded /'pædɪd/ [*adjective; no comparative*] a padded object has something soft over it or in it, to protect it or make it bigger or more comfortable: *a suit jacket with padded shoulders*

paddle[1] /'pædəl/ [*noun*]
   1 a thin round piece of wood with a flat part at one end, used to make a narrow boat move along: *She stepped carefully into the canoe and picked up the paddle.*
   ➪ *See the picture at* KAYAK.
   2 a round object with a short handle, used for hitting the ball in the game of PING-PONG: *Hold your paddle like this.*

paddle[2] [*verb; paddled, paddling*] to move a narrow boat through water using a paddle: *We paddled to the other side of the lake.* | *He paddled his kayak to the shore.*

paddy /'pædi/ [*noun; plural paddies*] a field where rice is grown in water: *He worked in the rice paddies all his life.*

padlock /'pæd,lak/ [*noun*] a lock that has a U-shaped bar that fits into the main part of the lock

page * /peɪdʒ/ [*noun*] one of the pieces of paper that makes a book or newspaper: *Turn to page four in your textbooks.* | *The story was on the front page of all the newspapers.*

pager /'peɪdʒɚ/ [*noun*] a small electronic machine that you carry or wear, that makes a sound when you have a message or need to phone someone; *synonym* BEEPER: *Excuse me a minute—my pager is beeping.*

paid * /peɪd/ [*verb*] the past tense and past participle of PAY[1]

pail /peɪl/ [*noun*] a round open container with a handle over the top; *synonym* BUCKET: *The kids took their plastic pails down to the beach.*

pain * /peɪn/ [*noun*]
   1 the unpleasant physical feeling you have when your body hurts: *She was in pain* (=feeling pain). | *She felt a sharp pain in her side.*

2 the feeling you have when you are extremely sad or upset: *The pain of her mother's death was hard to bear.*
   3 used to talk about someone or something that is annoying: *My little sister is such a pain—and so are her friends!* | *I hate doing housework. It's a pain in the neck.*
   ━━ PHRASE ━━
   4 take pains to do something to make a lot of effort to do something: *They've taken great pains to find the right school for their son.*

painful * /'peɪnfəl/ [*adjective; more painful, most painful*]
   1 making you feel pain: *He has a painful knee injury.*
   2 making you feel extremely sad or upset: *Leaving their home after 35 years was painful for them.*
   ☞ **Painful** is not used to describe people. Do not say "She is very painful." Say **She is in a lot of pain** or **It is very painful for her.**

painless /'peɪnlɪs/ [*adjective; more painless, most painless*] not causing any pain: *Don't worry. The treatment is painless.*

paint[1] * /peɪnt/ [*noun*] a colored liquid that you put onto a surface with a brush: *Careful! The paint in the hallway is still wet!* | *The artist set out his paints and brushes.*

paint[2] * [*verb; painted, painting*]
   1 to put paint on a wall, door, or object: *She's outside painting the front gate.* | *Put on old clothes before you start painting.* | **paint something red/blue/yellow/etc.** ▸ *He wants to paint his bedroom green.*
   2 to make a picture using paint: *I didn't know you could paint!* | *He painted a picture of a vase of flowers.*
   ➪ *See also* PAINTING.

paintbrush /'peɪnt,brʌʃ/ [*noun; plural paintbrushes*] a BRUSH used to put paint onto a surface

painter * /'peɪntɚ/ [*noun*]
   1 someone who paints pictures; *synonym* ARTIST: *The art gallery has works by many famous painters.*
   2 someone whose job involves painting rooms, buildings, etc.

painting * /'peɪntɪŋ/ [*noun*]
1 a picture that is painted: *a painting of a beach*
2 the skill of painting pictures: *She was better at drawing than at painting.*

pair * /pɛr/ [*noun*]
1 two things that are similar and are worn or used together: *a pair of gloves* | *The shoes didn't fit, so I tried on a bigger pair.*
2 something that has two similar parts joined together: *I have three pairs of jeans.* | *This pair of scissors doesn't cut very well.*
3 two people who are doing something together: *A pair of firefighters brought out the hose.*
☞ Use a singular verb when talking about a pair of things: *This pair of pants is OK.* Use a plural verb when talking about a pair of people: *A pair of dancers have been practicing for the competition for hours.*
⇨ See the usage note at **COUPLE**.

pajamas /pə'dʒɑməz/ [*plural noun*]
loose pants and a top that you wear in bed: *He was still in his pajamas.* | *a pair of striped pajamas*

palace /'pælɪs/ [*noun*] a large beautiful building that is, or once was, the home of a king, queen, or other ruler

pale * /peɪl/ [*adjective; paler, palest*]
1 not bright or dark in color: *She wore a pale blue sweater.*
2 having skin that has little color in it: *Are you OK? You look pale.* | *She went pale when I mentioned the money.*

palm /pɑm/ [*noun*]
1 the surface of the inside of your hand: *She rubbed the cream into the palms of her hands.*
⇨ See the picture at **BODY**.
2 also **palm tree** /'pɑm ˌtri/ a tall tree with a lot of long leaves at the top, which grows in warm places

pamphlet /'pæmflɪt/ [*noun*] a short book with a paper cover, which gives information about something: *The vet has pamphlets on how to care for various common pets.*

pan * /pæn/ [*noun*]
1 a round metal container with one

long handle, used for cooking: *Melt the butter in a large pan, then add the onions and garlic.*
2 a metal container used for baking: *a cake pan* | *a square baking pan*
⇨ See also **DUSTPAN, FRYING PAN.** ⇨ See the picture at **POT.**

pancake Ⓣ /'pæn,keɪk/ [*noun*] a flat round cake made from flour, eggs, and milk, that is fried on both sides

panda /'pændə/ [*noun; plural pandas*] a large black and white animal that looks like a bear

a panda

pane /peɪn/ [*noun*] a single piece of glass in a window or door: *There was frost on the window panes.* | *She cleaned every pane of glass.*

panel /'pænəl/ [*noun*]
1 a flat piece of wood on a wall or in a door: *One of the door panels is cracked.*
2 a group of people who discuss a subject, answer questions, judge a competition, etc., especially in public: *Are there questions for the members of our panel?* | *a panel of experts*

panic[1] /'pænɪk/ [*verb; panics, panicked, panicking*] to suddenly feel great fear and be unable to be sensible: *When I saw the test questions, I just panicked.*

/i/ **see**	/ɪ/ **big**	/eɪ/ **day**	/ɛ/ **get**	/æ/ **hat**
/ɑ/ **father, hot**	/ʌ/ **up**	/ə/ **about**	/ɔ/ **saw**	
/oʊ/ **hope**	/ʊ/ **book**	/u/ **too**	/aɪ/ **I**	/aʊ/ **how**
/ɔɪ/ **boy**	/ɝ/ **bird**	/ɚ/ **teacher**	/ɪr/ **ear**	/ɛr/ **air**
/ɑr/ **far**	/ɔr/ **more**	/ʊr/ **tour**	/aɪr/ **fire**	
/aʊɚ/ **hour**	/θ/ **nothing**	/ð/ **mother**	/ʃ/ **she**	
/ʒ/ **measure**	/tʃ/ **church**	/dʒ/ **jump**	/ŋ/ **long**	

panic[2] [*noun*] a sudden feeling of great fear that makes you unable to be sensible: *The earthquake caused panic across the city.*

pant /pænt/ [*verb; panted, panting*] to breathe quickly through your mouth, for example because you have been exercising: *By the end of our run, we were both panting.*

panties /ˈpæntiz/ [*plural noun*] a short piece of underwear that a woman or girl wears between her waist and her legs; synonym UNDERPANTS: *a pair of panties*

pantry /ˈpæntri/ [*noun; plural* **pantries**] a small room near a kitchen, used for storing food, dishes, etc.: *Get me some rice from the pantry.*

pants * /pænts/ [*plural noun*] a piece of CLOTHING that covers your legs with a separate part for each leg; synonym TROUSERS: *a pair of pants* | *These pants are too long.*

pantyhose /ˈpæntiˌhoʊz/ [*plural noun*] a thin piece of clothing that covers the whole of a woman's feet, legs, and lower body: *a pair of pantyhose* ⇨ Compare STOCKING.

papaya /pəˈpaɪə/ [*noun; plural* **papayas**] a yellow fruit with a yellow-green skin, which grows on trees in hot places

paper * /ˈpeɪpɚ/ [*noun*]
1 thin sheets used for writing on, for making the pages of a book, etc.: *Do you have any **writing paper**?* (=for letters or notes) | *wrapping paper* (=for covering packages) | *a paper bag* ☛ Do not say "a paper" for this meaning. Say **a piece of paper** or **a sheet of paper**.
2 a newspaper: *Be quiet. I'm trying to read the paper.*
3 a piece of writing you do for school, college, etc.: *I wrote a **paper on Hamlet.***
4 **papers** [*plural*] pieces of paper containing important or official information: *She keeps all her important papers in one file.* | *immigration papers*

paperback /ˈpeɪpɚˌbæk/ [*noun*] a book with a cover made of thick paper: *I'll take a paperback with me on the plane.*

paper clip /ˈpeɪpɚ ˌklɪp/ [*noun*] a flat, curled piece of wire used to hold pieces of paper together: *Her desk drawer was full of paper clips.*

paperwork /ˈpeɪpɚˌwɝk/ [*noun*] work that involves such things as writing letters and keeping records

parachute /ˈpærəˌʃut/ [*noun*] a large piece of cloth that opens when someone jumps out of a plane, so that he or she falls slowly

parade /pəˈreɪd/ [*noun*] when a group of people walk through the streets together, sometimes dressed in special clothes or playing music, in order to celebrate something: *The Thanksgiving Day Parade goes down Fifth Avenue.*

paradise /ˈpærəˌdaɪs/ [*noun*] a place or situation where everything is perfect: *Sitting by the pool all day—now, that's paradise!*

paragraph /ˈpærəˌgræf/ [*noun*] a part of a piece of writing that begins on a new line, deals with one particular idea, and usually consists of several sentences

parallel * ⊤ /ˈpærəˌlɛl/ [*adjective; no comparative*] parallel lines, roads, etc., are the same distance apart at every point: *Draw a line **parallel to** the base of the triangle.* | *His street **runs parallel to** ours.*

paralysis /pəˈræləsɪs/ [*noun*] when you cannot move and have no feeling in your body, especially because of a serious accident: *Back injuries can result in paralysis.*

paralyzed /ˈpærəˌlaɪzd/ [*adjective; no comparative*] unable to move and having no feeling in your body, especially because of a serious accident: *The car crash left him paralyzed from the waist down.*

pardon[1] /ˈpardən/ [*interjection*]
━ PHRASES ━
1 pardon me
 a used to get someone's attention: *Pardon me, is this seat taken?*
 b used to say politely that you are

sorry for doing something that is slightly wrong or not polite, or that may annoy someone: *Pardon me, I didn't mean to push you.*

⇨ *See the usage note at* APOLOGIZE.

2 pardon (me) used to ask someone politely to repeat something: *Pardon? Did you say "thirteen" or "thirty"?*

⇨ *See also* **excuse me** *at* EXCUSE[1].

pardon[2] [*noun*] when you forgive someone: *Oh, I beg your pardon* (=I'm sorry).

parent * ⊤ /'pɛrənt/ [*noun*] a mother or father

parentheses /pə'rɛnθəˌsiz/ [*noun*] a pair of marks used in writing. They look like this: ( )

⇨ *See* Punctuation *in the Smart Study section.*

park[1] * /park/ [*noun*] a public area of land with grass and trees, and sometimes areas for sports: *I like to jog in the park.* | *We live near Central Park.*

⇨ *See also* NATIONAL PARK.

park[2] * [*verb; parked, parking*] to stop your car somewhere and leave it there for a period of time: *You can park right outside our house.* | *He parked the car and got out.*

parking /'parkɪŋ/ [*noun*] when you stop your car somewhere and leave it there for a period of time: *Many new drivers have problems with parking.* | *Across the gate was a sign saying "No Parking."*

parking lot /'parkɪŋ ˌlat/ [*noun*] an area where cars can be left for a period of time: *The store's parking lot was full.*

parking meter /'parkɪŋ ˌmitɚ/ [*noun*] a machine on a street that you put money into so that you can leave your car next to it for a period of time: *How much time is left on the parking meter?*

parkway /'parkˌweɪ/ [*noun; plural* **parkways**] a wide road with grass and trees along its sides: *Turn onto the parkway at the next traffic light.*

parochial school /pə'roʊkiəl ˌskul/ [*noun*] a private school that is run by a religious organization

parrot /'pærət/ [*noun*] a brightly colored bird that lives in hot countries and can sometimes be trained to talk

parsley /'parsli/ [*noun*] a plant that is used to add taste or to decorate food: *The soup was sprinkled with fresh parsley.*

parsnip /'parsnɪp/ [*noun*] a thin white root with a sweet taste that is cooked and eaten as a vegetable

part[1] * /part/ [*noun*]

1 one piece or area of something: *Part of my tooth broke off when I fell.* | *The front part of the house is gray.* | *Listen carefully, this is the important part.*

2 one of the pieces that makes a vehicle, tool, or machine: *I'm waiting for a new part for my computer.*

3 the person that an actor plays in a movie, play, etc.; *synonym* ROLE: *She's hoping to get a part in the school play.* | *Who played the part of Juliet?*

━ PHRASES ━

4 play a part in or **have a part in** to be involved in something: *New drugs played a big part in her recovery from cancer.*

5 in part used to say that something is one of the ways, reasons, etc., but not the only one: *They moved here in part to be nearer their grandchildren.*

⇨ *See also* **take part (in)** *at* TAKE.

part[2] [*verb; parted, parting*]

1 to separate hair using a comb so that it falls in two directions: *I usually part my hair on the left.*

2 to separate into parts: *The clouds parted, revealing the full moon.*

━ PHRASAL VERB ━

part with [*phrasal verb*]

3 to give something away: **part with something** ▸ *She'll never part with her old dolls.*

partial /'parʃəl/ [*adjective; no comparative*] not total or complete: *A partial tuition payment is due in June.*

partially ⊤ /'parʃəli/ [*adverb*] not completely: *The door was partially blocked by a chair.*

/i/ **see** /ɪ/ **big** /eɪ/ **day** /ɛ/ **get** /æ/ **hat**
/a/ **father, hot** /ʌ/ **up** /ə/ **about** /ɔ/ **saw**
/oʊ/ **hope** /ʊ/ **book** /u/ **too** /aɪ/ **I** /aʊ/ **how**
/ɔɪ/ **boy** /ɝ/ **bird** /ɚ/ **teacher** /ɪr/ **ear** /ɛr/ **air**
/ar/ **far** /ɔr/ **more** /ʊr/ **tour** /aɪr/ **fire**
/aʊɚ/ **hour** /θ/ **nothing** /ð/ **mother** /ʃ/ **she**
/ʒ/ **measure** /tʃ/ **church** /dʒ/ **jump** /ŋ/ **long**

participant /par'tɪsəpənt/ [noun]
FORMAL someone who takes part in an activity or event: *He was a willing participant in all their games.*

participate T /par'tɪsə‚peɪt/ [verb; participated, participating] FORMAL to take part in an activity or event: *She was invited to participate in a television debate.*

participle * /'partə‚sɪpəl/ [noun] GRAMMAR a form of a verb used as an adjective or noun, or after another verb: *"Working" is a participle of "work."*
➪ See also PAST PARTICIPLE, PRESENT PARTICIPLE.

particular[1] * T /pɚ'tɪkyələ‑/ [adjective; no comparative] used to talk about a single thing or person that is special in some way; synonym SPECIFIC: *Do you want any particular color?* | *He was talking about this one particular girl.*
☛ Only use **particular** before a noun.

particular[2] T [noun]
━━━ PHRASE ━━━
in particular used to say that something is especially true of one thing or person: *I like all kinds of music, but rock in particular.*

particularly /pɚ'tɪkyələ‑li/ [adverb] especially: *I love dance, particularly modern dance.*

partly * /'partli/ [adverb] not completely: *The accident was partly my fault.* | *The cabin was partly hidden by bushes.*

partner * /'partnɚ/ [noun]
1 someone you do a particular activity with, for example dancing or playing a game: *She missed the ball, but her partner hit it.*
2 one of the owners of a business: *He was one of six partners in the company.*
3 one of the two people in a relationship, for example in a marriage: *Have you met my partner, Cathy?*

part of speech * /'part əv 'spitʃ/ [noun; plural **parts of speech**] GRAMMAR the class of a word that describes how it is used, for example a noun, verb, or adjective: *What part of speech is the word "quickly"?*

part-time[1] /'part 'taɪm/ [adverb]
━━━ PHRASE ━━━
work/study part-time to work or study for fewer than the number of hours that people usually work or study: *He teaches part-time at the local college.*
➪ Compare FULL-TIME[1].

part-time[2] /'part ‚taɪm/ [adjective; no comparative] working or studying for fewer than the number of hours that people usually work or study: *a part-time job* | *She's a part-time student.*
➪ Compare FULL-TIME[2].

party * /'parti/ [noun; plural **parties**]
1 an occasion when people meet to enjoy themselves eating, drinking, and dancing: *I'm **throwing a party** (=giving a party) next month.* | *Please come to my birthday party.*
2 an organization of people with the same political aims and opinions: *The U.S. only has two main political parties.*

pass[1] * T /pæs/ [verb; **passes, passed, passing**]
1 to go past someone or something: *The car slowed down as it passed.* | *A runner passed them very fast.*
2 to move from one place to another, going in a particular direction: *We'll pass through my hometown on the way.*
3 to give something that is near you or that you are holding to someone: *Please pass the sugar.*
4 to succeed in a test or course; opposite FAIL: *I passed! I can't believe it!* | *Did you pass your math test?*
5 if time passes, it goes by, and if you pass time, you spend it doing something: *Seven years passed before she saw her mother again.* | *He passed the time until dinner reading in his room.*
6 to kick, throw, or hit a ball to another member of your team: *Ben passed to Nick, who scored.* | *Today we're going to practice passing the ball.*
7 to approve or accept something such as a law or rule, usually by voting: *The school budget passed by a large margin.* | *Congress is not likely to pass that law.*
➪ See the usage note at PAST[4].

— PHRASAL VERBS —

pass away [phrasal verb]
8 to die: My aunt has just passed away.

pass on [phrasal verb]
9 to give or tell something to someone: **pass something on** ▶ Would you pass the news on to your family?

pass out [phrasal verb]
10 to suddenly not be conscious, usually for a short time; synonym FAINT: I was so excited I nearly passed out.

pass² T [noun; plural **passes**]
1 an official document that shows that you can enter a place, or that you do not need to pay: I have two passes to the theater tonight.
2 a road across or between mountains
3 when you kick, throw, or hit the ball to another member of your team: That was a beautiful pass.

passage * /'pæsɪdʒ/ [noun] a short piece of writing in a book: She read a passage from her favorite novel.

passageway * /'pæsɪdʒ,weɪ/ [noun; plural **passageways**] a narrow place that connects other places, such as a hall or a small street: Your cabin is down that passageway, on the left.

passenger * /'pæsəndʒɚ/ [noun] someone who is traveling in a bus, train, car, etc., but is not driving it

passerby /'pæsɚ-'baɪ/ [noun; plural **passersby** /'pæsɚz-'baɪ/] someone who is walking past a place by chance: Police are asking about passersby who might have seen the accident.

passing /'pæsɪŋ/ [adjective; no comparative] moving past: I saw her waving from a passing bus.

passion /'pæʃən/ [noun] a very strong emotion, especially of love, hate, or anger: He always sings **with** great passion.

passionate /'pæʃənɪt/ [adjective; **more passionate, most passionate**] with very strong feelings: She delivered a passionate appeal for help. | passionate commitment

passionately /'pæʃənɪtli/ [adverb; **more passionately, most passionately**] in a way that shows very strong feelings: She spoke passionately.

passive¹ * /'pæsɪv/ [noun] GRAMMAR
the passive in the passive, the action of the verb has an effect on the subject of the sentence: In the sentence, "The house was built in the 1920s," the verb "build" is in the passive.

passive² * [adjective; no comparative] GRAMMAR a passive sentence or verb has as its subject the person or thing that the action is done to: "A speech was given by the president" is a passive sentence.
◇ Compare ACTIVE (definition 2).

passport /'pæspɔrt/ [noun] a small book that has your photograph and information about you in it, and that you must show if you travel abroad

password /'pæs,wɚd/ [noun] a secret word or phrase that you must use or say before you can enter a place, or use a computer system: You must type in your password to pick up your e-mail.

past¹ * /pæst/ [noun]
1 the past
  a the time that has passed: Life was much simpler in the past.
  b GRAMMAR the PAST TENSE
2 all the things that have happened to someone, or that he or she has done: She wanted to forget her past.

past² * [adjective; no comparative] having happened, existed, or been experienced before now: He wanted to make up for his past mistakes. | She knew from past experience that he wouldn't change.

past³ * [preposition]
1 farther than: The school is just past the church.
2 up to and beyond: He walked straight past me without speaking.
3 after a particular time: It's already past six o'clock. | It's nearly ten past two (=ten minutes after two o'clock).

past⁴ * [adverb] up to and beyond a particular place: The cars sped past.

/i/ **see** /ɪ/ **big** /eɪ/ **day** /ɛ/ **get** /æ/ **hat**
/ɑ/ **father, hot** /ʌ/ **up** /ə/ **about** /ɔ/ **saw**
/oʊ/ **hope** /ʊ/ **book** /u/ **too** /aɪ/ **I** /aʊ/ **how**
/ɔɪ/ **boy** /ɚ/ **bird** /ɚ/ **teacher** /ɪr/ **ear** /ɛr/ **air**
/ɑr/ **far** /ɔr/ **more** /ʊr/ **tour** /aɪr/ **fire**
/aʊɚ/ **hour** /θ/ **nothing** /ð/ **mother** /ʃ/ **she**
/ʒ/ **measure** /tʃ/ **church** /dʒ/ **jump** /ŋ/ **long**

USAGE   past, passed

Do not confuse **past** and **passed**. **Past** is a preposition or adverb: *I walked past your house this morning.* | *She smiled as she walked past.* **Passed** is the past tense and past participle of the verb **pass**: *I passed your house this morning.*

pasta /'pɑstə/ [*noun*] an Italian food made of dough that is cut into many different shapes, then boiled: *My favorite meal is pasta with tomato sauce.*

past continuous /'pæst kən'tɪnyuəs/ [*noun*] GRAMMAR
the past continuous the form of a verb that shows what was happening or was true at a time in the past. It is formed with the past tense of "be" and a present participle: *In the sentence "We were driving home when it started raining," the verb "drive" is **in the past continuous**.*
⊃ *See the usage note at* CONTINUOUS².

paste¹ /peɪst/ [*verb*; **pasted, pasting**] to stick something to something else with glue: *The children were pasting pictures into a scrapbook.*

paste² [*noun*] a kind of thick glue that is used for sticking paper together, or sticking it to other things: *Don't put too much paste on your brush.*

past participle * /'pæst 'pɑrtəsɪpəl/ [*noun*] GRAMMAR the form of a verb that is usually formed by adding "-ed" to the verb. It is used to make the perfect tenses: *The past participle of "look" is "looked."* | *The past participle of "go" is irregular: "gone."*

past perfect /'pæst 'pɜfɪkt/ [*noun*] GRAMMAR
the past perfect the form of a verb that shows an action or state that was completed by or before a particular time in the past. It is formed with the past form of "have" and a past participle: *In the sentence "She had already finished by five o'clock," the verb "finish" is **in the past perfect**.*
⊃ *See the usage note at* PERFECT².

pastry /'peɪstri/ [*noun*; *plural* **pastries**]
1 a small cake or other kind of sweet food: *They ordered a pot of coffee and some pastries for the meeting.*
2 a mixture of flour, fat, and water that you fill with another food and bake in an oven: *Line the dish with **pastry dough**, then pour the fruit mixture in.*

past tense * /'pæst 'tɛns/ [*noun*] GRAMMAR **the past tense** the form of a verb that shows that an action started or happened in the past. It is usually formed by adding "-ed" to the verb: *The past tense of "look" is "looked."* | *The past tense of "go" is irregular: "went."*
⊃ *Compare* PRESENT TENSE, FUTURE TENSE.

pasture /'pæstʃɚ/ [*noun*] an area of land with grass on it that farm animals eat: *Their goats are in the west pasture.*

pat¹ /pæt/ [*verb*; **pats, patted, patting**] to touch someone or something lightly several times with your hand flat: *He bent down and patted the dog.*

pat² [*noun*] a light touch with your hand flat: *a pat on the head*

patch¹ /pætʃ/ [*noun*; *plural* **patches**]
1 a small piece of material used to cover a hole in something: *There were patches on both knees of his jeans.*
2 a small area that looks or is different from the area around it: *There's a damp patch on the ceiling.*

patch² [*verb*; **patches, patched, patching**] to fill or cover a hole: *I need to patch those pants.*

path * /pæθ/ [*noun*; *plural* **paths** /pæðz/]
1 a track for walking along: *a path through the forest*
2 where someone or something is moving or is meant to move: *A tornado destroys everything in its path.* | *Planes follow particular flight paths.*

patience * /'peɪʃəns/ [*noun*] the ability to wait for a long time or to deal with problems without becoming angry or worried: *One quality a teacher must have is patience.* | *I lost my patience (=became angry) and shouted at him.*

patient¹ * /'peɪʃənt/ [*adjective*; **more patient, most patient**] able to wait for a long time or to deal with problems without becoming angry or worried: *Please be patient—the doctor will see you*

soon. I *You should be more **patient with**
your brother—he's only four years old.*

patient[2] [*noun*] someone who is being
cared for by a doctor: *There were many
patients in the waiting room.*

patio /'pætioʊ/ [*noun; plural* **patios**] an
outdoor area with a hard surface next
to a house: *Let's eat out on the patio.*
⇨ Compare TERRACE (definition 1).

patriotic /ˌpeɪtriˈɑtɪk/ [*adjective;* **more
patriotic, most patriotic**] loving your
country and very proud of it, or showing
that you feel this way: *Seeing our flag
makes me feel patriotic.* I *patriotic songs*

patrol[1] /pəˈtroʊl/ [*noun*]
  1 a group of police or soldiers who
  move around an area in order to
  protect it: *the Highway Patrol*
— PHRASE —
  2 on patrol regularly moving around
  an area in order to protect it: *Guards
  are on patrol here 24 hours a day.*

patrol[2] [*verb;* **patrols, patrolled,
patrolling**] to regularly go around an
area in order to watch it and to prevent
problems from happening: *Police patrol
the streets throughout the night.*

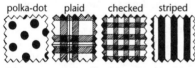
polka-dot   plaid   checked   striped

patterns

pattern * ⊤ /'pætərn/ [*noun*]
  1 a design made from shapes, colors,
  lines, etc., arranged in a regular way:
  a tablecloth with a checked pattern
  2 the regular way something happens
  or is done: *All his novels follow the same
  pattern.*

pause[1] * /pɔz/ [*verb;* **paused, pausing**]
to stop doing something for a short
time before starting again: *At the top of
the hill we paused to admire the view.* I
*She paused for a moment, then went on
with her story.*

pause[2] * [*noun*] a short time when you
stop doing something: *After a pause he
said, "OK, I agree."*

pave /peɪv/ [*verb;* **paved, paving**] to
cover a street or other piece of ground
with a hard material: *The men will pave
the driveway on Thursday.*

pavement /'peɪvmənt/ [*noun*] a hard
material covering a street or other area:
*Most city sidewalks are covered with
pavement.*

paw /pɔ/ [*noun*] the foot of an animal
such as a dog or a CAT

pay[1] * /peɪ/ [*verb;* **pays, paid, paying**]
  1 to give money for something in order
  to buy it, or for someone's work or a
  service: *I get paid monthly.* I *We have to
  pay the electricity bill by Saturday.* I **pay
  for something** ▸ *I'll pay for the
  groceries.* I **pay someone something** ▸
  We paid the painter $300. I **pay
  someone for something** ▸ *Did you pay
  me for last week's piano lesson?* I **pay
  someone to do something** ▸ *I'll pay
  you to wash my car.*
  ⇨ Compare SPEND (definition 1).
— PHRASES —
  2 pay attention to watch or listen to
  someone carefully: *Stop talking and pay
  attention.*
  3 pay someone a visit to visit
  someone: *My uncle paid us a visit.*
— PHRASAL VERBS —
pay back [*phrasal verb*]
  4 to give someone back the money that
  you owe him or her: **pay someone
  back** ▸ *Can I borrow $10 and pay you
  back on Friday?*
pay off [*phrasal verb*]
  5 to finish paying you owe for
  something: **pay off something** ▸ *We'll
  have paid off the car loan by August.* I
  pay something off ▸ *It will take two
  years to pay the loan off.*

pay[2] * [*noun*] money that you receive for
work that you have done: *The pay's
better at his new job.*

/i/ s**ee** /ɪ/ b**i**g /eɪ/ d**ay** /ɛ/ g**e**t /æ/ h**a**t
/ɑ/ f**a**ther, h**o**t /ʌ/ **u**p /ə/ **a**bout /ɔ/ s**a**w
/oʊ/ h**o**pe /ʊ/ b**oo**k /u/ t**oo** /aɪ/ **I** /aʊ/ h**ow**
/ɔɪ/ b**oy** /ɝ/ b**ir**d /ɚ/ teach**er** /ɪr/ **ear** /ɛr/ **air**
/ɑr/ f**ar** /ɔr/ m**ore** /ʊr/ t**our** /aɪr/ f**ire**
/aʊɚ/ **hour** /θ/ **n**o**th**ing /ð/ **m**o**th**er /ʃ/ **sh**e
/ʒ/ mea**s**ure /tʃ/ **ch**urch /dʒ/ **j**ump /ŋ/ lo**ng**

SYNONYMS　　pay, salary, wage, income

　Pay is a general word meaning the money you get from your employer for doing your job: *What's the pay like?*
　People who are lawyers, doctors, office workers, etc., usually receive their pay once or twice a month and it is called their **salary**: *He earns a salary of $40,000 a year.*
　Factory workers and other workers usually are paid by the hour and it is called their **wage** or **wages**: *Her wage is $14 an hour.*
　Your **income** is the money that you receive from anywhere: *What is your monthly income?*

paycheck /'peɪˌtʃɛk/ [*noun*] money paid regularly to someone for his or her job: *I usually get my paycheck on Fridays.*

payment * /'peɪmənt/ [*noun*]
　1 an amount of money that is paid, especially as part of a larger amount: *How much is the monthly payment?*
　2 the act of paying for something: *A check in payment for your work is in the envelope.*

pay phone /'peɪ ˌfoʊn/ [*noun*] a public telephone into which you have to put coins or a card before you can use it

PC /'piˈsi/ [*noun; plural* **PCs** *or* **PC's**] personal computer; a small computer that is used by one person: *We use our PC for writing letters and homework.*

PE /'piˈi/ [*noun*] physical education; sports and exercises taught at school: *We have two hours of PE each week.*

pea /pi/ [*noun; plural* **peas**] a very small, round, green VEGETABLE

peace * /pis/ [*noun*]
　1 when everything is calm and nothing annoys you: *What I'd really like is a little peace and quiet.* | *Let your brother do his homework in peace.*
　2 when there is no war or fighting: *The two countries are finally at peace* (=not fighting).

peaceful * /'pisfəl/ [*adjective;* more **peaceful, most peaceful**]
　1 calm and not making you annoyed or worried: *a peaceful, quiet afternoon*

　2 not fighting a war or being violent: *a peaceful nation* | *The march was a peaceful protest against the reforms.*

peach /pitʃ/ [*noun; plural* **peaches**] a round FRUIT with a rough, pale orange skin, that has one large seed and grows on trees

peacock /'piˌkɑk/ [*noun*] a large bird that has long blue and green tail feathers that it can raise and spread out: *The peacock is India's national bird.*

peak /pik/ [*noun*]
　1 the biggest, highest, most successful, etc., point: *He won't reach his athletic peak for several years.* | *She's at the peak of her career.*
　2 the pointed top of a hill or mountain: *mountain peaks covered with snow*

peanut /'piˌnʌt/ [*noun*] a small NUT that you can eat and that has a soft, light brown shell: *a bag of salted peanuts*

peanut butter /'piˌnʌt ˌbʌtɚ/ [*noun*] a soft food made from crushed peanuts: *a peanut butter and jelly sandwich*

pear /pɛr/ [*noun*] a green, yellow, brown, or red FRUIT that is white inside and grows on trees

pearl /pɝl/ [*noun*] a small, round, white stone that forms inside the shell of some oysters, and is used to make expensive jewelry: *a pearl necklace*

peasant /'pɛzənt/ [*noun*] someone who lives in the country and works on a farm, especially for someone else: *The peasants had no land of their own.*

pebble /'pɛbəl/ [*noun*] a small smooth stone found near water: *The children collected pebbles on the beach.*

pecan /pɪˈkæn/ [*noun*] a small NUT that you can eat and that has a smooth, hard, brown shell

peck /pɛk/ [*verb;* **pecked, pecking**] when a bird pecks, it takes small bites or hits something with its beak: *That bird is pecking outside the window again.* | *A bird pecked a hole in our tree.*

peculiar 🔲 /pɪˈkyulyɚ/ [*adjective;* more **peculiar, most peculiar**] strange, especially in a way that is worrying or surprising: *A very peculiar smell was coming from the kitchen.*

pedal[1] /'pɛdəl/ [noun]
1 one of the two flat parts of a BICYCLE that you push around with your foot to make it move
2 a flat part of a machine, car, etc., that you press with your foot to make something happen: *She put her foot down hard on the gas pedal.*

pedal[2] [verb; pedaled, pedaling] to move a bicycle by pushing on the pedals: *A man pedaled slowly up the hill.*

pedestrian /pə'dɛstriən/ [noun] someone who is walking rather than driving a car or riding a bicycle: *This area is for pedestrians only.*

peel[1] /pil/ [verb; peeled, peeling] to remove the outer skin from a fruit or vegetable: *Would you peel the potatoes?*

peeling a potato

peel[2] [noun] the outer skin of some kinds of fruit: *Add some sliced lemon peel.*

peep /pip/ [verb; peeped, peeping] to look quickly at something without anyone seeing you do it: *She peeped at the audience from behind the curtain.*

peer /pɪr/ [verb; peered, peering] to look very hard at something, especially because you cannot see it clearly: *He drove on, **peering into** the fog.*

peg /pɛg/ [noun]
1 a piece of wood or metal fastened to a wall, on which you can hang coats, bags, etc.
2 a wooden or metal stick used to keep a tent fastened to the ground: *They gathered up the **tent pegs**.*

pen * /pɛn/ [noun]
1 a long thin object used for writing in ink: *Could I borrow a pen, please?* | *Please complete the form **in pen** (=using a pen).*
2 a small area of land with a fence around it, in which farm animals are kept

penalty /'pɛnəlti/ [noun; plural penalties] a punishment for not obeying a law or rule: *The **penalty for** speeding is a $120 fine.*

pencil * /'pɛnsəl/ [noun] a long thin wooden object filled with a stick of a black or colored substance, used for writing or drawing: *Have you seen my new colored pencils?* | *Do your homework **in pencil** (=using a pencil).*

a pencil

pencil sharpener /'pɛnsəl ˌʃɑrpənɚ/ [noun] a small object with a sharp blade inside, used to give pencils a sharp point

penetrate /'pɛnɪˌtreɪt/ [verb; penetrated, penetrating] FORMAL to go through or into something, especially when this is difficult: *The sun could not penetrate the thick clouds.*

penguin /'pɛŋgwɪn/ [noun] a large black and white bird that lives in the Antarctic and cannot fly but can swim

penknife /'pɛnˌnaɪf/ [noun; plural penknives /'pɛnˌnaɪvz/] a small knife with a blade that folds into the handle; *synonym* POCKETKNIFE

a penguin

penny /'pɛni/ [noun; plural pennies]
1 a COIN worth one cent in the U.S. or Canada: *A couple of pennies fell out of his pocket.*

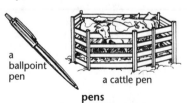
a ballpoint pen

a cattle pen

pens

/i/ **see**	/ɪ/ **big**	/eɪ/ **day**	/ɛ/ **get**	/æ/ **hat**
/ɑ/ **father, hot**	/ʌ/ **up**	/ə/ **about**	/ɔ/ **saw**	
/oʊ/ **hope**	/ʊ/ **book**	/u/ **too**	/aɪ/ **I**	/aʊ/ **how**
/ɔɪ/ **boy**	/ɝ/ **bird**	/ɚ/ **teacher**	/ɪr/ **ear**	/ɛr/ **air**
/ɑr/ **far**	/ɔr/ **more**	/ʊr/ **tour**	/aɪr/ **fire**	
/aʊɚ/ **hour**	/θ/ **nothing**	/ð/ **mother**	/ʃ/ **she**	
/ʒ/ **measure**	/tʃ/ **church**	/dʒ/ **jump**	/ŋ/ **long**	

━━ **PHRASE** ━━

2 every penny all of a particular amount of money: *She borrowed $500 and paid back every penny.*

pen pal /'pɛn ˌpæl/ [noun] someone in another country that you have never met, but who you have become friends with by writing regular letters: *I'd like to have a South American pen pal.*

pension /'pɛnʃən/ [noun] money that the government or a company pays to someone when he or she is too old or too sick to work: *a retirement pension*

pentagon /'pɛntəˌgɑn/ [noun] a flat shape with five sides
↪ *See* Shapes *in the Smart Study section.*

people * /'pipəl/ [noun] the plural of PERSON: *Thousands of people came to the concert.* | *If you're rude, people won't like you.*
☛ Only use **people** with a plural verb. For example, do not say "People was worried." Say **People were worried**.

pepper * /'pɛpɚ/ [noun]
1 a powder that is used in cooking to make food taste hot: *Would you like **salt and pepper**?*
2 a hollow red, green, or yellow VEGETABLE

peppermint /'pɛpɚˌmɪnt/ [noun]
1 a plant with a sweet hot taste that is used to make medicine, candy, and tea: *peppermint-flavored toothpaste*
2 a candy with a peppermint taste: *Would you like a peppermint?*

per * /pɚ/ [preposition] for each: *Oranges—only 50¢ per pound.*

percent * /pɚ'sɛnt/ [noun] used to talk about hundredths of an amount; for example, "fifty percent" means "half": *Sixty-nine **percent of** U.S. teenagers have used the Internet.* | *The bank currently charges interest at thirteen percent (13%).*
☛ The written sign for **percent** is **%**.

USAGE   Using verbs with "percent"

Use a plural verb if you are talking about a number of people or things: *Sixty percent of the students are male.* Use a singular verb if you are talking about part of one thing: *Sixty percent of the population is male.*

---

percentage ⊤ /pɚ'sɛntɪdʒ/ [noun] a particular amount out of every hundred or out of a whole: *What **percentage of** households have two cars?* | *Only a small **percentage of** the crop was harmed.*

perch[1] /pɚtʃ/ [verb; perches, perched, perching] if a bird perches somewhere, it sits there: *A robin **perched on** the windowsill.*

perch[2] [noun; plural perches] a branch or stick that a bird sits on: *A parrot was sitting on a perch near the window.*

perfect[1] * ⊤ /'pɚfɪkt/ [adjective; **more perfect, most perfect**]
1 the best possible, with no faults or mistakes: *She speaks perfect Spanish.* | *The jeweler made a perfect copy of my earring.* | *Well, **nobody's perfect** (=everyone makes mistakes).*
2 completely suitable or right for a particular situation or person: *Turkey is the perfect place for a vacation.*
3 used to emphasize a noun: *She was dancing with a perfect stranger.* | *You have a perfect right to be angry.*
☛ Only use **perfect** before a noun in this meaning.

perfect[2] [noun] GRAMMAR
the perfect the PRESENT PERFECT

USAGE   Perfect tenses

A perfect tense is the form of a verb used to show conditions or complete actions in the past, present, or future. Perfect verbs are formed with the past, present, or future tense of "have" and a past participle.

the past perfect: *We had returned from shopping before Mom got home.*
the present perfect | *We have just returned from shopping.*
the future perfect | *We will have returned from shopping by the time Mom gets home.*

---

perfect[3] ⊤ /pɚ'fɛkt/ [verb; perfected, perfecting] to make something perfect or as good as you can: *She's spending a year in the U.S. to perfect her English.*

perfection /pɚ'fɛkʃən/ [noun] the condition of being perfect: *The beef was cooked **to perfection** (=so that it was perfect).*

perfectly * /'pɜˈfɪktli/ [adverb]
1 extremely well, without any mistakes: *She sang the song perfectly.*
2 used to mean "very" or "completely," especially when you are annoyed about something: *He knows perfectly well I didn't mean it.* | *Let me make myself perfectly clear.*

perform * /pəˈfɔrm/ [verb; performed, performing]
1 to do something to entertain people, for example to act, sing, dance, or play a musical instrument: *Which band is performing this evening?* | *His plays are performed all over the world.*
2 to do a particular action or piece of work: *A local priest performed the wedding ceremony.*

performance * /pəˈfɔrməns/ [noun]
1 when people act, sing, etc., in order to entertain people: *The performance begins at 8:30.*
2 how well or badly a person or machine works or does something: *The car's performance is superb.*

performer * /pəˈfɔrmə/ [noun] someone who does something to entertain people: *Some of the performers seemed a little nervous.*

perfume /'pɜˈfyum/ [noun] a liquid with a strong pleasant smell that you put on your skin: *I don't often **wear perfume**.* | *They have several different perfumes on sale.*
   ▷ Compare FRAGRANCE. ▷ See the synonym note at SMELL¹.

perhaps * /pəˈhæps/ [adverb] maybe; <u>synonym</u> POSSIBLY: *Perhaps I'll see him at the party.* | *"Do you think I should buy this?" "**Perhaps not**."*

period * /'pɪriəd/ [noun]
1 a length of time: *Camels can go for long periods without water.* | *a **period of** two weeks*
2 a particular length of time in history, in someone's life, in a school day, etc.: *The castle was built in the medieval period.* | *It was an unhappy period in my life.* | *I have math first period, and geography second period.*
3 a mark (.) used in writing
   ▷ See Punctuation *in the Smart Study section.*

perish /'pɛrɪʃ/ [verb; perishes, perished, perishing] to die: *Many of the animals and plants perished in the drought.*

perm /pɜm/ [noun] a chemical treatment to make hair have curls

permanent * /'pɜmənənt/ [adjective; more permanent, most permanent] lasting for a long time or for all time; <u>opposite</u> TEMPORARY: *a permanent job* | *Write the labels in permanent ink.*

permanently * 🔲 /'pɜmənəntli/ [adverb] for a long time or for all time; <u>opposite</u> TEMPORARILY: *He was permanently disabled when he fell from his horse.*

permission * /pəˈmɪʃən/ [noun] when someone tells you that you may do something: *He took the book **without permission**.* | *I **asked permission** to leave early.* | *Did Mom **give you permission** to borrow the car?*

permit¹ * 🔲 /pəˈmɪt/ [verb; permits, permitted, permitting] FORMAL to allow something to happen or be done: *Smoking is not permitted on the plane.* | **permit someone to do something** ▶ *They were not permitted to enter the building.*
   ▷ Compare LET *(definition 1).*

permit² /'pɜmɪt/ [noun] an official document that says that you are allowed to do something: *He didn't have a **work permit**.* | *You need a permit to park here.*

person * /'pɜsən/ [noun; plural **people**]
1 a man, woman, or child: *She's such a helpful person.* | *Is he the right person for the job?*

━━ PHRASE ━━
2 **in person** if you do something in person, you do it yourself rather than sending a letter or another person: *I spoke to him in person.*

personal * 🔲 /'pɜsənəl/ [adjective; more personal, most personal]
1 belonging to you and no one else: *Passengers are responsible for their*

/i/ **see**	/ɪ/ **big**	/eɪ/ **day**	/ɛ/ **get**	/æ/ **hat**	
/ɑ/ **father, hot**	/ʌ/ **up**	/ə/ **about**	/ɔ/ **saw**		
/oʊ/ **hope**	/ʊ/ **book**	/u/ **too**	/aɪ/ **I**	/aʊ/ **how**	
/ɔɪ/ **boy**	/ɝ/ **bird**	/ɚ/ **teacher**	/ɪr/ **ear**	/ɛr/ **air**	
/ɑr/ **far**	/ɔr/ **more**	/ʊr/ **tour**	/aɪr/ **fire**		
/aʊɚ/ **hour**	/θ/ **nothing**	/ð/ **mother**	/ʃ/ **she**		
/ʒ/ **measure**	/tʃ/ **church**	/dʒ/ **jump**	/ŋ/ **long**		

personal property. | *My personal opinion is that you shouldn't trust him.*

2 private and concerning only you: *I don't want to talk about it—it's personal.* | *He had some personal matters to deal with.*

➪ See also **PERSONALLY**.

personality T /ˌpɝsəˈnælɪti/ [*noun; plural* **personalities**]
1 someone's character, especially the way he or she behaves toward other people: *She has a great personality.* | *In this job, personality is more important than experience.*
2 a famous person who works in sports or entertainment: *a radio personality*

personally T /ˈpɝsənəli/ [*adverb*] used to emphasize that you are giving your own opinion: *Personally, I hate him.*

personal pronoun /ˈpɝsənəl ˈproʊnaʊn/ [*noun*] GRAMMAR a pronoun used for the person who is speaking or being spoken to, or the person or thing being spoken about, such as "I," "you," or "them"

personnel /ˌpɝsəˈnɛl/ [*plural noun*] the people who work for a company or other organization: *All personnel are given a security badge.*

perspective T /pɚˈspɛktɪv/ [*noun*]
1 a particular way of thinking about or judging something: *You should look at the issue from your sister's perspective.*
━━━ PHRASE ━━━
2 in perspective if you have something in perspective, you do not think that it is more important than it really is: *Let's keep everything in perspective here.*

persuade * T /pɚˈsweɪd/ [*verb;* **persuaded, persuading**] to give someone good reasons for doing something so that he or she decides to do it: **persuade someone to do something** ▸ *I managed to persuade my brother to come too.*

persuasion /pɚˈsweɪʒən/ [*noun*] when you try to persuade someone to do something: *After some persuasion, he agreed to join us.*

pessimist /ˈpɛsəmɪst/ [*noun*] someone who believes that bad things are going to happen; *opposite* OPTIMIST

pessimistic /ˌpɛsəˈmɪstɪk/ [*adjective;* **more pessimistic, most pessimistic**] believing that bad things are going to happen; *opposite* OPTIMISTIC: *He has a pessimistic view of life.*

pest /pɛst/ [*noun*]
1 an insect or small animal that destroys crops: *a chemical that kills garden pests*
2 an annoying person: *That kid next door is a real pest.*

pester /ˈpɛstɚ/ [*verb;* **pestered, pestering**] to annoy someone, especially by asking too many questions: *Stop pestering me while I'm cooking.*

pet[1] * /pɛt/ [*noun*] a small animal such as a cat or a dog that you have at home and take care of: *Do you have any pets?* | *We aren't allowed to keep pets in our apartment.*

pet[2] [*verb;* **pets, petted, petting**] to gently move your hand over an animal's head or back: *Can I pet the kitten?*

petal /ˈpɛtəl/ [*noun*] one of the colored parts that makes a flower: *a rose with red petals*

petition T /pəˈtɪʃən/ [*noun*] a piece of paper that is signed by a lot of people and sent to people in authority to ask them to do something: *Would you sign our petition against the new freeway?*

petroleum /pəˈtroʊliəm/ [*noun*] thick oil taken out of the ground and used to make gasoline and many other things: *Petroleum is refined here for heating oil.*

petty /ˈpɛti/ [*adjective;* **more petty, most petty**] not important: *These are petty concerns that can be taken care of later.*

pew /pyu/ [*noun*] a long, narrow, wooden seat with a back on which several people can sit in a church

pharmacist /ˈfɑrməsɪst/ [*noun*] someone whose job is to prepare medicines in a store or hospital

pharmacy /ˈfɑrməsi/ [*noun; plural* **pharmacies**] a store or part of a store where medicines are prepared and sold
➪ Compare **DRUGSTORE**.

phase /feɪz/ [noun] a particular part of a process or series of events: *Phase one of the project is information gathering.*

Ph.D. /ˈpi ˌeɪtʃ ˈdi/ [noun; plural **Ph.D.**s or **Ph.D.**'s] Doctor of Philosophy; the highest university degree, or someone who has this degree: *Bob has a Ph.D. in American literature.* | *Bob Green, Ph.D.*
➪ Compare **B.A., B.S., M.A., M.S.**

philosopher /fɪˈlasəfɚ/ [noun] someone who studies philosophy

philosophy /fɪˈlasəfi/ [noun; plural **philosophies**]
1 the study of what it means to be alive, what knowledge is, and how people should live: *She teaches philosophy at a university.*
2 a set of rules that you follow in living your life: *Enjoy yourself while you're young, that's my philosophy.*

phone[1] * /foʊn/ [noun] a piece of equipment that you use to talk to someone who is in another place; *synonym* TELEPHONE: *Could someone answer the phone, please?* | *I have to make a long-distance phone call.* | *We reserved tickets by phone.* | *She's been on the phone* (=making a phone call) *for twenty minutes.*

phone[2] * [verb; **phoned, phoning**] to use a telephone to talk to someone; *synonyms* CALL, TELEPHONE: *Did anyone phone while I was out?* | *I must phone Dad to tell him the news.*
☛ Do not say "I phoned to her last week." Say **I phoned her last week.**
➪ See the synonym note at CALL[1].

phone book /ˈfoʊn ˌbʊk/ [noun] a book with a list of the names, addresses, and phone numbers of all the people and companies in a particular area; *synonym* TELEPHONE BOOK: *I got your number out of the phone book.*

phone booth /ˈfoʊn ˌbuθ/ [noun; plural **phone booths** /ˈfoʊn ˌbuðz/] a structure containing a public telephone; *synonym* TELEPHONE BOOTH: *There's a phone booth in the hotel lobby.*

phone call /ˈfoʊn ˌkɔl/ [noun] when you talk to someone using a phone; *synonyms* CALL, TELEPHONE CALL: *I need to make a phone call.*

phone number /ˈfoʊn ˌnʌmbɚ/ [noun] the number you need to use when you want to speak to someone on the telephone; *synonym* TELEPHONE NUMBER: *Have I given you our new phone number?*

phonetic /fəˈnɛtɪk/ [adjective; no comparative] relating to the sounds people make when they are speaking: *The International Phonetic Alphabet shows you how to pronounce words.*

phony /ˈfoʊni/ [adjective; **phonier, phoniest**] not true or real; *synonym* FAKE: *He gave the bank a phony address.*

photo /ˈfoʊtoʊ/ [noun; plural **photos**] photograph; a picture made using a camera: *I took photos of my dog.*

photocopier /ˈfoʊtəˌkapiɚ/ [noun] a machine that quickly makes copies of documents by photographing them: *A piece of paper is stuck in the photocopier.*
➪ See the picture at OFFICE.

photocopy[1] /ˈfoʊtəˌkapi/ [noun; plural **photocopies**] a copy of a document made on a special machine: *Make two photocopies of the agreement.*

photocopy[2] [verb; **photocopies, photocopied, photocopying**] to copy a document on a special machine: *I photocopied the article.*

photograph[1] * /ˈfoʊtəˌgræf/ [noun] a picture made using a camera; *synonym* PHOTO: *He took some beautiful photographs of the lake.*

photograph[2] * [verb; **photographed, photographing**] to make a picture of someone or something using a camera: *I don't like being photographed.*

photographer * /fəˈtagrəfɚ/ [noun] someone who takes photographs, especially as his or her job

photography /fəˈtagrəfi/ [noun] the art or profession of taking photographs

phrasal verb * /ˈfreɪzəl ˈvɚb/ [noun] GRAMMAR a verb that is made up of two or more words: *"Give up" and "put up with" are phrasal verbs.*

/i/ **see**	/ɪ/ **big**	/eɪ/ **day**	/ɛ/ **get**	/æ/ **hat**
/ɑ/ **father, hot**	/ʌ/ **up**	/ə/ **about**	/ɔ/ **saw**	
/oʊ/ **hope**	/ʊ/ **book**	/u/ **too**	/aɪ/ **I**	/aʊ/ **how**
/ɔɪ/ **boy**	/ɝ/ **bird**	/ɚ/ **teacher**	/ɪr/ **ear**	/ɛr/ **air**
/ɑr/ **far**	/ɔr/ **more**	/ʊr/ **tour**	/aɪr/ **fire**	
/aʊɚ/ **hour**	/θ/ **nothing**	/ð/ **mother**	/ʃ/ **she**	
/ʒ/ **measure**	/tʃ/ **church**	/dʒ/ **jump**	/ŋ/ **long**	

phrase * /freɪz/ [noun] GRAMMAR a group of words that forms part of a sentence: *In the sentence "We ran down the hill," "down the hill" is a phrase.*

physical * /'fɪzɪkəl/ [adjective; no comparative]
1 relating to your body rather than your mind or spirit; *opposites* MENTAL, SPIRITUAL: *She likes doing physical work.*
2 relating to real things that you can see and touch: *The physical conditions in the prison were awful.*
☛ Only use **physical** before a noun in this meaning.

physically * /'fɪzɪkli/ [adverb] relating to your body: *She tries to keep herself physically fit* (=in good health).

physician /fɪ'zɪʃən/ [noun] a doctor of medicine

physicist /'fɪzəsɪst/ [noun] someone who studies physics

physics /'fɪzɪks/ [noun] the study of movement and of things such as heat, light, and electricity
☛ Only use **physics** with a singular verb.

pianist /'piənɪst/ [noun] someone who plays the piano: *His mother was a concert pianist.*

piano * /pi'ænoʊ/ [noun; plural **pianos**] a large musical instrument that you sit at and play by pressing small black and white bars with your fingers: *Can you play the piano?* | *I have a piano lesson every Friday.*

pick¹ * /pɪk/ [verb; **picked, picking**]
1 to choose something or someone from a group of things or people: *Pick a card from the deck.* | **pick someone as something** ▸ *The team picked him as their captain.*
2 to pull a flower, fruit, or leaf from a plant or branch: *Let's pick some flowers for Mom.*
3 to take small pieces from something with your finger: *He picked a hair off my sweater.* | *Don't pick your nose* (=clean inside it with your finger).
━ PHRASE ━
4 pick a fight to make someone angry so he or she will fight with you: *He's just trying to pick a fight.*

━ PHRASAL VERBS ━
pick on [phrasal verb]
5 to be unfair or unkind to a particular person: **pick on someone** ▸ *The other boys are always picking on him.*
pick out [phrasal verb]
6 to choose something: **pick out something** ▸ *Did you pick out a dress to wear?* | **pick something out** ▸ *I picked this one out.*
pick up [phrasal verb]
7 to take something from the ground or another flat surface: **pick something up** ▸ *Pick your coat up and hang it properly.* | **pick up something** ▸ *She picked up a book and began to read.*
8 to get someone or something from a place in order to take that person or thing somewhere: **pick someone/something up** ▸ *I'll pick you up at about 7 o'clock.* | **pick up someone/something** ▸ *She picked up her mail.*

pick² [noun] a choice someone makes: *I'm giving away these books, so **take your pick*** (=choose the ones you want).

pickle /'pɪkəl/ [noun] a thin piece of cucumber that has been preserved in salty, sour liquid: *Our sandwiches are served with a pickle and potato chips.*

pickpocket /'pɪk,pɑkɪt/ [noun] someone who steals things from people's pockets and bags, especially in crowded places: *Beware of pickpockets on the subway.*

pickup truck /'pɪkʌp ,trʌk/ [noun] a small truck with a large open area at the back for carrying things

a pickup truck   cab   tailgate

picnic¹ /'pɪknɪk/ [noun] a meal that you eat outdoors, usually sitting on the ground: *It's a lovely day—let's **have a picnic**.* | *On Sunday we **went for a picnic** in the country.*

picnic² [verb; **picnics, picnicked, picnicking**] to have a meal outdoors, usually sitting on the ground: *We picnicked under a shady tree.*

picture[1] * ⊤ /'pɪktʃɚ/ [*noun*]
1 a drawing, painting, or photograph: *Draw a picture of a house.* | *Will you take a picture* (=take a photograph) *of us?*
2 the things that can be seen on a screen: *What's wrong with the TV? The picture's all blurred.*

USAGE   Kinds of pictures

There are many ways to make a **picture**.

A **painting** is done with paints: *They bought a big oil painting.*

A **drawing** is done using a pen or pencil: *She did a drawing of her house.*

A **sketch** is a very simple drawing done very quickly: *Can you do a quick sketch of the kitchen?*

A **portrait** is a painting or drawing of a person: *The portraits of many kings and queens hang in the National Gallery.*

A **photograph** or **photo** is taken with a camera: *I have some very old photos of my mother's grandparents.*

---

picture[2] ⊤ [*verb*; **pictured, picturing**]
to imagine something by making a picture of it in your mind: *I just can't picture myself in a wedding dress.*

picture book /'pɪktʃɚ ,bʊk/ [*noun*]
a children's book with a lot of pictures in it: *She loves to look at picture books.*

pie * /paɪ/ [*noun*; *plural* **pies**] fruit or other sweet food baked in dough: *For dessert we had apple pie and ice cream.*

piece * /pis/ [*noun*]
1 a part of something that has been cut, separated, or broken off from the rest of it: *Would you like a piece of cheese?* | *The glass fell and broke into pieces on the floor.*
2 a single thing, often part of a set: *Please could I have another piece of paper?* | *Make sure*

a **piece** of cheese

that each **piece of** clothing is marked with your name. | *a piece of music*

pier /pɪr/ [*noun*] a structure built in the shallow water next to the shore, where boats can stop; synonym WHARF

pierce /pɪrs/ [*verb*; **pierced, piercing**] to make a hole in or through something using an object with a sharp point: *She's getting her ears pierced today.*

pig * /pɪg/ [*noun*]
1 a fat farm animal with no fur and a tail that curls
  ▷ Compare PORK.
2 INFORMAL someone who is not at all neat or clean, or eats too much: *Don't be a pig—leave some food for others!*

a pig

pigeon /'pɪdʒən/ [*noun*] a fat gray bird with short legs that is common in cities

piglet /'pɪglɪt/ [*noun*] a baby pig: *Look at the cute piglets!*

pigpen /'pɪg,pɛn/ [*noun*] a place where pigs are kept on a farm

pigtails /'pɪg,teɪlz/ [*plural noun*] hair that is worn in two parts that are tied on each side of the head: *She usually wears her hair in pigtails.*
  ▷ Compare PONYTAIL.

pile[1] * /paɪl/ [*noun*] a number of things put one on top of the other: *She put her clothes in a pile on the bed.* | *There's a pile of dirty dishes in the sink.*

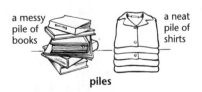

a messy pile of books   a neat pile of shirts

piles

/i/ see	/ɪ/ big	/eɪ/ day	/ɛ/ get	/æ/ hat	
/ɑ/ father, hot	/ʌ/ up	/ə/ about	/ɔ/ saw		
/oʊ/ hope	/ʊ/ book	/u/ too	/aɪ/ I	/aʊ/ how	
/ɔɪ/ boy	/ɝ/ bird	/ɚ/ teacher	/ɪr/ ear	/ɛr/ air	
/ɑr/ far	/ɔr/ more	/ʊr/ tour	/aɪr/ fire		
/aʊɚ/ hour	/θ/ nothing	/ð/ mother	/ʃ/ she		
/ʒ/ measure	/tʃ/ church	/dʒ/ jump	/ŋ/ long		

pile² [*verb;* **piled, piling**] to make a pile by putting things on top of each other: *They piled the laundry in a corner.* | *a plate piled up with food*

pilgrim /'pɪlgrɪm/ [*noun*] someone who travels a long way to visit a holy place

pill /pɪl/ [*noun*] a small solid piece of medicine that you swallow: *sleeping pills* | *Don't forget to take your pill.*

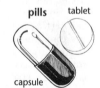

pills   tablet

capsule

pillar /'pɪlɚ/ [*noun*] a large post that supports part of a building; <u>synonym</u> COLUMN: *There were beautiful stone pillars on either side of the door.*
↪ *See the picture at ARCH.*

pillow /'pɪloʊ/ [*noun*] a cloth bag filled with a soft material, which you put your head on when you are in bed

pillowcase /'pɪloʊ,keɪs/ [*noun*] a cloth cover that you put on a pillow: *a cotton pillowcase*

pilot * /'paɪlət/ [*noun*] someone who flies an aircraft or guides a ship

pimple /'pɪmpəl/ [*noun*] a small, painful, raised area on your skin, containing an unpleasant liquid: *Teenagers often get pimples.*

pin¹ * /pɪn/ [*noun*]
1 a thin piece of metal with a sharp point, used to fasten things such as pieces of cloth together: *Be careful! I've dropped a pin on the floor.*
2 a piece of jewelry with a pin on the back that you fasten to your clothes: *She wore a diamond pin.*

pin² * [*verb;* **pins, pinned, pinning**] to fasten things together or attach one thing to another with a pin: *Pin the front and back together before sewing them.* | *He pinned the announcement up on the bulletin board.*

PIN /pɪn/ [*noun*] personal identification number; a number that only you know and that you use to get money from a bank machine

pinch¹ /pɪntʃ/ [*verb;* **pinches, pinched, pinching**] to press something between your finger and thumb very tightly, for

example someone's flesh: *Ouch! You pinched me!*

pinch² [*noun; plural* **pinches**] a small amount of something that you put in food: *a pinch of salt*

pine /paɪn/ [*noun*] a tall tree with long thin leaves like needles, which do not fall off in winter, or the wood from this tree: *She planted three little pines behind the house.* | *a pine table*

pineapple /'paɪ,næpəl/ [*noun*] a large, yellow, sweet-sour FRUIT with rough skin and stiff leaves that stick out at the top, which grows in hot places

Ping-Pong /'pɪŋ ,pɑŋ/ [*noun*] TRADEMARK an indoor sport or game for two or four players in which a small white ball is hit across a net on a table; <u>synonym</u> TABLE TENNIS: *Let's play Ping-Pong.* | *a Ping-Pong ball*

a **Ping-Pong** paddle

pink¹ * /pɪŋk/ [*noun*] a pale red color: *Her favorite color is pink.*

pink² * [*adjective;* **pinker, pinkest**] of the color pink: *Cynthia was wearing bright pink lipstick.*

pint * /paɪnt/ [*noun*] a unit for measuring liquids, equal to 16 ounces or 0.47 liters: *Grandma went to the grocery store for a **pint of** milk.*

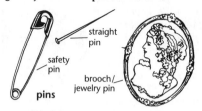

straight pin

safety pin

brooch/ jewelry pin

pins

pioneer 🅣 /,paɪə'nɪr/ [*noun*] one of the first people to go to a new place or do something new: *the **pioneers of** space travel*

pipe * /paɪp/ [*noun*]
1 a tube through which water or gas flows: *A pipe burst in the kitchen.* | *a gas pipe*
2 a thin tube with a small bowl at one end, used for smoking: *Grandpa used to enjoy smoking his pipe.*

pirate /'paɪrət/ [noun] someone who sails on the ocean, attacking other ships and stealing from them

pistol /'pɪstəl/ [noun] a small gun

pit /pɪt/ [noun]
1 the large hard seed in the center of some fruits: *an olive pit* | *a peach pit*
2 a deep hole dug in the ground: *a garbage pit*

pitch[1] /pɪtʃ/ [verb; **pitches, pitched, pitching**]
1 to throw the ball toward the person with the bat in a game of baseball: *I used to pitch for my high school team.* | *He pitched a great game.*
2 to put up a tent: *It took him about fifteen minutes to pitch his tent.*
3 to throw something with a lot of force: *He pitched the can into the trash.*

pitch[2] [noun; plural **pitches**]
1 how high or low a sound or musical note is: *Dogs can hear sounds of a higher pitch than people can.*
2 a throw of the ball toward the person with the bat in baseball: *His first pitch was a little low.*

pitcher /'pɪtʃɚ/ [noun]
1 a container with a handle, for holding and pouring liquids: *a **pitcher** of water*
2 someone who throws the ball toward the person with the bat in a game of baseball

pity[1] * /'pɪti/ [noun]
1 the sympathy that you feel for someone who is hurt, unhappy, or having problems: *Pity is not enough; we must provide practical help.* | *A woman took pity on (=felt sorry for) me and gave me a ride.*
☛ Do not say "feel pity on someone." Say **take pity on someone** or **feel pity for someone**.

━━ PHRASE ━━
2 **What a pity** or **It's a pity** used to say that you are sorry about a situation: *It's a pity she didn't get accepted to medical school.* | *"I can't go to the wedding." "Oh, what a pity!"*

pity[2] * [verb; **pities, pitied, pitying**] to feel sympathy for someone because he or she is hurt, unhappy, or in a difficult

situation: *I pity your having to work so hard all the time.*
☛ Do not say "I am pitying you." Say **I pity you.**

pizza /'pitsə/ [noun; plural **pizzas**] a flat round piece of bread baked with tomato sauce, cheese, and meat or vegetables on top

place[1] * /pleɪs/ [noun]
1 an area, point, or position in space: *Keep your keys in a safe place.* | *The fabric of the chair was worn in some places.* | *He traveled **from place to place** looking for work.*
2 a particular building, town, or business: *I want to buy a place (=home) in the country.* | *Have you tried the new Mexican place (=restaurant) yet?* | *Our town is a pretty friendly place.* | *They all came over to my place (=my house).*
3 a seat somewhere, or a position in a line: *Is this place taken?* | *Could you save my place while I buy a hot dog?*
☛ Do not say "Is there place for me on the bus? Say **Is there room for me on the bus?**
4 the position, authority, or condition that someone or something has: *It's not your place to tell the others what to do.* | *The computer has taken the place of the typewriter.*

━━ PHRASES ━━
5 **in place of** instead of someone or something: *A special program is being shown in place of tonight's movie.*
☛ Do not say "in place of doing something." Say **instead of doing something**.
6 **first/second/third/etc. place** first, second, third, etc., position in a race or competition: *She took first place in the diving competition.*
⇨ See also **take place** at TAKE.

place[2] * [verb; **placed, placing**]
1 to put something somewhere

/i/ **see** /ɪ/ **big** /eɪ/ **day** /ɛ/ **get** /æ/ **hat**
/ɑ/ **father, hot** /ʌ/ **up** /ə/ **about** /ɔ/ **saw**
/oʊ/ **hope** /ʊ/ **book** /u/ **too** /aɪ/ **I** /aʊ/ **how**
/ɔɪ/ **boy** /ɝ/ **bird** /ɚ/ **teacher** /ɪr/ **ear** /ɛr/ **air**
/ɑr/ **far** /ɔr/ **more** /ʊr/ **tour** /aɪr/ **fire**
/aʊɚ/ **hour** /θ/ **nothing** /ð/ **mother** /ʃ/ **she**
/ʒ/ **measure** /tʃ/ **church** /dʒ/ **jump** /ŋ/ **long**

carefully; _synonym_ SET: _He placed the vase in the middle of the table._

━━━ PHRASE ━━━

2 place an order to ask a store or business to get you something that you want to buy: _I'd like to **place an order** for 25 striped umbrellas._

place setting /'pleɪs ˌsetɪŋ/ [_noun_] an arrangement of plates, knives, forks, spoons, and glasses on a table for one person to use: _Can you make room for another place setting?_

place setting

1. dinner fork   4. butter knife   7. glass
2. salad fork   5. bread plate   8. knife
3. napkin   6. dinner plate   9. spoon

plaid /plæd/ [_adjective; no comparative_] with a PATTERN of lines that form squares in several colors: _a plaid skirt_

plain¹ * /pleɪn/ [_adjective; plainer, plainest_]
1 simple and without any pattern or decoration; _opposite_ FANCY: _Bob likes plain home cooking._ | _a plain black dress_
2 very clear or easy to see, hear, or understand: _**It was plain that** she wanted to be alone._ | _Just tell me what you want **in plain English** (=clearly and simply)._

plain² * [_noun_] a large flat area of land: _the grassy plains of Argentina_

plain³ * [_adverb_] INFORMAL clearly and completely: _That kid is just plain rude._

plainly /'pleɪnli/ [_adverb_] in a way that is easy to see, hear, or understand; _synonym_ CLEARLY: _He was plainly angry._

plan¹ * /plæn/ [_noun_]
1 something that you have decided or arranged to do: _My plan is to finish school and then travel for a year._ | _Do_

you **have** any **plans for** this evening? | _a_ **plan to do something** ▸ _There's a plan to build a new stadium._
2 a drawing of a room, building, machine, etc., as it would be seen from above, showing all its parts: _He was studying a **plan of** the house._

━━━ PHRASE ━━━

3 go according to plan to happen in the way that has been arranged or intended: _Everything went according to plan._

plan² * [_verb; plans, planned, planning_]
1 to think carefully about something you want to do and decide how you are going to do it: _They've been planning their wedding for months._ | _We must **plan for** the future._
2 to intend to do something: **plan to do something** ▸ _He's planning to go to graduate school._ | **plan on doing something** ▸ _We plan on staying in Italy for a week._

plane * /pleɪn/ [_noun_]
1 a vehicle that flies, that has an engine and wings; _synonym_ AIRPLANE: _Her plane lands at about 11 o'clock._
2 a completely flat surface, for example in a mathematical figure: _Squares and circles are planes._ | _plane geometry_

planet * /'plænɪt/ [_noun_]
1 a large round object in space that goes around the sun or another star: _Jupiter is the largest planet._ | _here on planet Earth_
2 the planet the world: _Pollution is a threat to the planet._

plank /plæŋk/ [_noun_] a long flat piece of wood: _The floor was made of six-inch planks._

plant¹ * /plænt/ [_noun_]
1 a living thing with leaves and roots that grows in earth: _a tomato plant_
2 a place such as a factory where something is made, produced, or treated: _a steel plant_

plant² * [_verb; planted, planting_] to put seeds or plants into the ground to grow: _I'm going to plant peas this year._

plantation /plæn'teɪʃən/ [_noun_] a large area of land where plants producing tea, coffee, sugar, cotton, or rubber are grown: *He owns a coffee plantation.*

plaster[1] /'plæstɚ/ [*noun*] a substance used to cover walls and ceilings, that gets hard when it dries: *Let the plaster dry completely before painting it.*

plaster[2] [*verb*; **plastered, plastering**] to cover a wall or ceiling with plaster: *The builders have finished plastering the den.*

plastic[1] * /'plæstɪk/ [*adjective*; no comparative] made of plastic: *a plastic bag*

plastic[2] * [*noun*] a strong light material made by a chemical process and used to make many things: *Lots of toys are made of plastic.* | *modern plastics*

plate * /pleɪt/ [*noun*] a flat round dish that you eat from or serve food on: *He put some more vegetables on his plate.* | *a dinner plate*

☛ Do not say "in a plate." Say **on a plate.**

↪ *See the pictures at IN[1] and PLACE SETTING[1].*

platform /'plætfɔrm/ [*noun*]
1 a raised structure that people can stand or work on: *The senator spoke to the crowd from a platform.*

2 the place beside a railroad track where you get on and off a train: *The next train to Baltimore leaves from platform 21.*

play[1] * /pleɪ/ [*verb*; **plays, played, playing**]
1 to take part in a game or sport: *The kids are in the yard playing basketball.* | *He **plays on** the tennis team.* | *Who will they **play against** in their next game?*

2 if children play, they enjoy themselves with their toys and games or by pretending things: *She sat on the floor, **playing with** her doll.* | *The kids were playing checkers.*

3 to perform a piece of music on a musical instrument: *I'm learning to play the guitar.* | *A band usually plays here on Saturdays.*

4 if you play something on a piece of electrical equipment, or if it plays, that is what you hear or see: *What's the song that's playing on the radio?* | *Something's wrong. The videotape won't play.* | *She played that same CD three times today.*

He's **bouncing** the ball to her.   She's **hitting** the ball.

He's **kicking** the ball.   He's **throwing** the ball and she's **catching** it.

playing games

5 to pretend to be a particular person in a movie, play, or TV program: *I really wanted to play that part.*

=== PHRASAL VERB ===

play with [phrasal verb]
6 to touch something a lot or move it around a lot: *Stop playing with your food and eat it.*

play[2] * [noun; plural **plays**]
1 a story that is performed by actors in a theater: *They went to see a play.* I *The school puts on a play* (=organizes and performs a play) *every spring.*
2 when people take part in a sport or game: *Rain stopped play at 3:25 this afternoon.* I *We've seen some excellent play here today.*

player * /'pleɪɚ/ [noun] someone who plays a game, a sport, or a musical instrument: *a chess player*

playful /'pleɪfəl/ [adjective; more **playful, most playful**] full of fun and enjoyment: *playful children*

playground /'pleɪˌgraʊnd/ [noun] an area of land next to a school or in a park where children can play

plaza /'plazə/ [noun; plural **plazas**] an outdoor place with a lot of stores and businesses: *The biggest branch of the store is in Central Plaza.*

plead /plid/ [verb; **pleaded** or **pled**, **pleaded** or **pled**, **pleading**]
1 to ask for something in an emotional, anxious way, because you want it very much: *"Don't leave me!" she pleaded.* I **plead with someone to do something** ▸ *He pleaded with his father to allow him to go.*

=== PHRASE ===

2 plead guilty or **plead not guilty** to say in a court of law that you are or are not guilty of a crime: *She pled not guilty to the charge of theft.*

pleasant * /'plɛzənt/ [adjective; more **pleasant, most pleasant**] nice or enjoyable; *opposite* UNPLEASANT: *What a pleasant surprise!* I *a pleasant vacation*

pleasantly * /'plɛzəntli/ [adverb] in a nice and enjoyable way: *The weather was pleasantly warm.*

please[1] * /pliz/ [adverb] used when you are asking for something or accepting something someone offers you: *May I*

please have a drink of water? I *"Would you like a ride?" "Yes, please."* I *Please don't make so much noise.*

please[2] * [verb; **pleased, pleasing**] to make someone feel happy or satisfied: *His gift really pleased her.*

pleased * /plizd/ [adjective; more **pleased, most pleased**]
1 happy or satisfied because something good has happened: *The teacher's very pleased with your work.* I *She was pleased that he remembered her.*
⇨ *See the synonym note at* HAPPY.

=== PHRASE ===

2 (I'm) pleased to meet you SPOKEN something you say to be polite when you meet someone for the first time: *How do you do, Mr. Gray? Pleased to meet you.*

pleasure * /'plɛʒɚ/ [noun]
1 the feeling of happiness or satisfaction that you get from doing something you enjoy: *Cooking gives me great pleasure.*
☛ Do not say "I read for my pleasure." Say **I read for pleasure**.
☛ Do not say "have the pleasure to do something." Say **have the pleasure of doing something**.

=== PHRASE ===

2 It's a pleasure or **It's my pleasure** SPOKEN used as a polite reply when someone thanks you for doing something: *"Thank you so much for your help." "It was a pleasure."*

plenty * /'plɛnti/ [pronoun] a large quantity or amount that is enough or more than enough: *"Do you want some more pie?" "No, thanks, I've had plenty."* I *There's no hurry; we have plenty of time.*
☛ **Plenty** can be used with a singular or a plural verb. For example, you should say **There is plenty of time** but **There are plenty of seats**.
⇨ *See the synonym note at* ENOUGH[1].

pliers /'plaɪɚz/ [plural noun] a small metal TOOL used for bending wire, removing nails, etc.: *He fixed the chain with a pair of pliers.*

plot[1] /plat/ [noun]
1 the main story of a book, movie, or play: *The plot is pretty boring.*

2 a secret plan to do something wrong or illegal: **a plot to do something** ▸ *They had discovered a plot to bomb the post office.*

3 a small piece of ground: *a plot of land* | *a garden plot*

plot[2] [*verb; plots, plotted, plotting*] to secretly plan to do something wrong or illegal: **plot to do something** ▸ *They plotted to take over the government.*

plow[1] /plaʊ/ [*noun*]

1 a large piece of equipment used on farms to break up the ground so that seeds can be planted: *Farmers used to use horses to pull the plows.*

2 a large curved piece of equipment that attaches to the front of a vehicle and is used to push snow off roads

plow[2] [*verb; plowed, plowing*] to use a plow to break up the ground: *He's out plowing the north field.*

pluck /plʌk/ [*verb; plucked, plucking*] to remove something by pulling it quickly: *plucking a chicken* (=removing its feathers)

plug[1] /plʌg/ [*noun*]

1 the small thing on the end of a wire that connects a piece of electrical equipment to the electricity supply: *He pulled the plug out of the socket.*
⇨ *See the picture at* OUTLET.

2 a small round piece of rubber that stops water from flowing out of a bathtub, SINK, etc.

plug[2] [*verb; plugs, plugged, plugging*]

1 to fill or cover a hole with something: *She plugged her ears with her fingers.*

═══ PHRASAL VERB ═══

plug in [*phrasal verb*]

2 to connect a piece of electrical equipment to the electricity supply; *opposite* UNPLUG: **plug in something** ▸ *He plugged in the toaster.* | **plug something in** ▸ *Could you plug the TV in, please?*

plum /plʌm/ [*noun*] a soft purple, red, or yellow FRUIT that has a smooth skin and one large seed, and grows on trees

plumber /ˈplʌmɚ/ [*noun*] someone whose job is to repair or connect water and toilet pipes

plumbing /ˈplʌmɪŋ/ [*noun*] the system of water pipes in a building: *They've had a lot of problems with their plumbing.*

plump /plʌmp/ [*adjective; plumper, plumpest*] round or fat, in an attractive way: *a plump juicy peach* | *the baby's plump little legs*
⇨ *See the synonym note at* FAT[1].

plunge /plʌndʒ/ [*verb; plunged, plunging*] to move suddenly forward and downward, or to push something suddenly downward: *A hawk plunged from the sky and snatched a rabbit.* | *He plunged his hands into his pockets and walked off.*

plural[1] ✳ /ˈplʊrəl/ [*noun*] GRAMMAR the form of a noun that is used to talk about more than one person or thing: *"Children" is the plural of "child."*

plural[2] ✳ [*adjective; no comparative*] GRAMMAR a plural verb, noun, or pronoun is used to talk about more than one person or thing: *The plural form of the verb "to be" is "are."*
⇨ *Compare* SINGULAR.

plus[1] /plʌs/ [*preposition*] used when one number is added to another; *opposite* MINUS: *Six plus two equals eight* (6 + 2 = 8).
⇨ *See also* ADD (definition 3).

plus[2] [*adjective; no comparative*]

═══ PHRASE ═══

A+/B+/C+ a mark given to students for their work; spoken as "A plus," etc. An A+ is higher than an A, and a B+ is higher than a B: *I got a B+ in history.*
⇨ *Compare* MINUS[2].

Pluto /ˈplutoʊ/ [*name*] the planet that is farthest away from our sun

p.m. or **P.M.** /ˈpiˈɛm/ an abbreviation used to show that a time is in the afternoon or evening, after 12 o'clock noon: *I get off work at 6 p.m.*
⇨ *Compare* A.M.

/i/ **see**	/ɪ/ **big**	/eɪ/ **day**	/ɛ/ **get**	/æ/ **hat**
/ɑ/ **father, hot**	/ʌ/ **up**	/ə/ **about**	/ɔ/ **saw**	
/oʊ/ **hope**	/ʊ/ **book**	/u/ **too**	/aɪ/ **I**	/aʊ/ **how**
/ɔɪ/ **boy**	/ɝ/ **bird**	/ɚ/ **teacher**	/ɪr/ **ear**	/ɛr/ **air**
/ɑr/ **far**	/ɔr/ **more**	/ʊr/ **tour**	/aɪr/ **fire**	
/aʊɚ/ **hour**	/θ/ **nothing**	/ð/ **mother**	/ʃ/ **she**	
/ʒ/ **measure**	/tʃ/ **church**	/dʒ/ **jump**	/ŋ/ **long**	

pneumonia /nʊˈmoʊnyə/ [*noun*] a serious disease of the lungs, which makes it difficult for people to breathe

PO Box /ˈpiˈoʊ ˌbɑks/ [*noun*] post office box; a private box in a post office where mail can be sent for you: *PO Box 2550*

pocket * /ˈpɑkɪt/ [*noun*] a piece of material sewn onto or into CLOTHING to make a small bag where you can keep things: *I lost the key because there was a hole in my pocket.*

pocketknife /ˈpɑkɪtˌnaɪf/ [*noun; plural* **pocketknives** /ˈpɑkɪtˌnaɪvz/] a small knife with a blade that folds into the handle; *synonym* PENKNIFE

pod /pɑd/ [*noun*] a long narrow part on some plants, that the seeds grow inside: *a pea pod*
↪ See the picture at INSIDE.

poem * /ˈpoʊəm/ [*noun*] a piece of writing arranged in lines, which expresses feelings and ideas in carefully chosen, often beautiful, language

He's **pointing** at something.

poet * /ˈpoʊɪt/ [*noun*] someone who writes poems

poetry * /ˈpoʊɪtri/ [*noun*] poems in general: *I especially enjoy reading poetry.*

point¹ * /pɔɪnt/ [*noun*]
1 a single fact or idea in a discussion or argument: *She made an interesting point.*
2 a particular moment in time, or a part of a process: *By that point, I had decided to leave.* | *They have reached the halfway point in the race.*
3 the point the most important part of what someone is saying or of a situation: *Get to the point!* (=start talking about what is most important) | *The point is that I can't afford it.*

4 an exact place or position: *The two lines cross at point A.*
5 a mark that you win in a sport or a game: *A goal in soccer is worth one point.*
6 a mark (.) used to separate a whole number from the decimal after it: *thirty-three point two percent (33.2%)*
7 a sharp end of something: *Use a brush with a very fine point.* | *the point of a needle*
8 the purpose or use of something: *What is the point of studying when I can't afford college?* | *There's no point in arguing with him.*
☛ Do not say "There's no point to do something." Say **There's no point in doing something.**

══ PHRASE ══
9 up to a point to some degree but not completely: *I understand his concern up to a point.*
↪ See also POINT OF VIEW.

point² * [*verb;* **pointed, pointing**]
1 to show someone where something is by stretching your finger out toward it: *"That's her," he said, pointing to a tall woman.* | *He pointed at the balloon in the sky.*
2 to hold something straight toward someone: **point something at someone** ▸ *Never point a gun at anyone.*

══ PHRASAL VERB ══
point out [*phrasal verb*]
3 to tell someone something important that he or she had not thought of: **point out something** ▸ *She pointed out that it was getting late.* | **point something out** ▸ *Thanks for pointing that out.*

pointed * /ˈpɔɪntɪd/ [*adjective; no comparative*] with a point at the end: *The bird had a long pointed beak.*

pointless /ˈpɔɪntlɪs/ [*adjective;* **more pointless, most pointless**] with no use or purpose: *It's pointless to keep working —it's too dark.*

point of view /ˈpɔɪnt əv ˈvyu/ [*noun; plural* **points of view**] a particular way of thinking about or judging something: *Look at it from my point of view.*

poison[1] * /'pɔɪzən/ [noun] a substance that can kill you or make you sick if it gets into your body: *They put poison in the cellar to kill the rats.*

poison[2] * [verb; poisoned, poisoning]
1 if food or another substance poisons you, you become sick or die after eating or drinking it: *Many types of mushrooms can poison you.*
2 to kill a person or an animal by giving poison to him, her, or it: *The king was poisoned by his enemies*

poisonous * T /'pɔɪzənəs/ [adjective; more poisonous, most poisonous] containing or producing poison: *The fruit of this tree is very poisonous.* | *a poisonous snake*

poke /poʊk/ [verb; poked, poking]
1 to push someone or something quickly with a pointed object such as your finger or a stick: *Be careful! You nearly poked me in the eye.*
2 to push something into or out of something: *She poked her head out of the window.*

poker /'poʊkɚ/ [noun] a card game that people often play for money: *He won $200 in a poker game.*

polar /'poʊlɚ/ [adjective; no comparative] near or relating to the North Pole or the South Pole: *the polar ice caps*

polar bear /'poʊlɚ ˌbɛr/ [noun] a large white bear that lives near the North Pole: *Polar bears eat fish and seals.*

a polar bear

pole * /poʊl/ [noun] a long smooth stick or post: *Two wooden poles held up the tent.*
  ➪ *See also* NORTH POLE, SOUTH POLE.

police * /pə'lis/ [plural noun] the group of men and women whose job is to protect people and their property and make sure they obey the law: *A neighbor*

heard noises and called **the police**. | *We saw two police cars with flashing lights.*

police department /pə'lis dɪˌpɑrtmənt/ [noun] the official police organization in an area: *You should call the police department to report a theft.*

police force /pə'lis ˌfɔrs/ [noun] all of the police officers who work for a particular police organization: *a member of the local police force*

policeman /pə'lismən/ [noun; plural policemen /pə'lismən/] a male police officer

police officer /pə'lis ˌɔfəsɚ/ [noun] a member of the police

police station /pə'lis ˌsteɪʃən/ [noun] the local office of the police in a town or city

policewoman /pə'lisˌwʊmən/ [noun; plural policewomen /pə'lisˌwɪmən/] a female member of the police

policy T /'pɑləsi/ [noun; plural policies] a way of doing things that has been decided by an organization, a government, etc.: *What's the company's policy on travel expenses?*

polish[1] * /'pɑlɪʃ/ [verb; polishes, polished, polishing] to make something shine by rubbing it with a cloth: *His shoes need polishing.* | *She polished the silver until it shone.*

polish[2] [noun] a soft substance that you rub onto surfaces to make them shine: *Don't use too much furniture polish.*

polite * /pə'laɪt/ [adjective; politer, politest] things that you say or do that are polite show that you respect someone; *opposites* RUDE, IMPOLITE: *What a polite little boy!* | *a polite request* | *It's not polite to ask a lady how old she is.*

politely * /pə'laɪtli/ [adverb] in a way that shows respect for someone; *opposite* RUDELY: *She asked politely for a glass of water.*

/i/ **see**	/ɪ/ **big**	/eɪ/ **day**	/ɛ/ **get**	/æ/ **hat**
/ɑ/ **father**, **hot**	/ʌ/ **up**	/ə/ **about**	/ɔ/ **saw**	
/oʊ/ **hope**	/ʊ/ **book**	/u/ **too**	/aɪ/ **I**	/aʊ/ **how**
/ɔɪ/ **boy**	/ɝ/ **bird**	/ɚ/ **teacher**	/ɪr/ **ear**	/ɛr/ **air**
/ɑr/ **far**	/ɔr/ **more**	/ʊr/ **tour**	/aɪr/ **fire**	
/aʊɚ/ **hour**	/θ/ **nothing**	/ð/ **mother**	/ʃ/ **she**	
/ʒ/ **measure**	/tʃ/ **church**	/dʒ/ **jump**	/ŋ/ **long**	

political * /pə'lɪtɪkəl/ [adjective; no comparative] relating to the government and the people who have power in a country: *The U.S. has two main political parties.* | *a period of great political change*

politically * /pə'lɪtɪkli/ [adverb] in a way that relates to politics: *He became politically active in his community.*

politician * /ˌpɑlɪ'tɪʃən/ [noun] someone who works in politics, especially in a government: *Politicians from both parties support the new law.*

politics * /'pɑlɪtɪks/ [noun] ideas and actions that are concerned with gaining and using power in a government: *Politics is an interesting subject.* | *She hopes to go into politics* (=start working as a politician).

☛ Only use **politics** with a singular verb.

polka-dot /'poʊkə ˌdɑt/ [adjective; no comparative] polka-dot material or paper has a PATTERN of colored spots all over it: *a polka-dot blouse*

poll /poʊl/ [verb; polled, polling]
1 to ask a large number of people to answer a question or give their opinion, especially in an election: *Let's poll the committee.*
2 to vote in an election: *Not all the districts have finished polling.*

polls ⊤ /poʊlz/ [plural noun]
the polls the places where people vote: *Voters are going to the polls* (=voting) *next Tuesday.*

pollute ⊤ /pə'lut/ [verb; polluted, polluting] to put dangerous, harmful substances in the air, water, or soil: *Smoke from factories pollutes the air.*

polluted /pə'lutɪd/ [adjective; more polluted, most polluted] dirty and dangerous to use: *This is one of the most polluted rivers in the country.*

pollution ⊤ /pə'luʃən/ [noun]
1 the process of putting dangerous, harmful substances in the air, water, or soil: *Air pollution is a serious problem.*
2 substances that make the air, water, or soil dirty and dangerous to use: *Our rivers are full of pollution.* | *Pollution levels in the city are high.*

pond /pɑnd/ [noun] an area of water that is smaller than a lake: *There were ducks swimming on the pond.*

pony /'poʊni/ [noun; plural ponies] a small horse: *When she was little, she wanted to have a pony.*

ponytail /'poʊniˌteɪl/ [noun] HAIR that is tied together at the back of your head and hangs down: *She tied her hair back in a ponytail.*
➪ Compare PIGTAILS.

pool * /pul/ [noun]
1 a structure filled with water that people can swim in; synonym SWIMMING POOL: *an indoor pool*
2 a small area of still water or other liquid, for example in a hollow place in the ground: *He was searching for crabs in the rock pools.*
3 an indoor game played on a table, in which you hit a ball with a long stick so that it hits other balls into holes around the table: *Do you play pool?* | *a game of pool*

poor[1] * /pʊr/ [adjective]
1 [poorer, poorest] not having much money or many possessions; opposites RICH, WEALTHY: *My father was too poor to go to college.* | *one of the poorest countries in the world*
2 [poorer, poorest] not of a high standard or good quality; synonym BAD; opposite GOOD: *The soil in this area is very poor.* | *As she grew older her eyesight got poorer.*
3 [no comparative] used to show that you feel sympathy for someone: *The poor man was lost and confused.*
☛ Only use **poor** before a noun in this meaning.

poor[2] * [noun]
the poor people who have very little money: *The new laws will do nothing to help the poor.*
☛ Only use **the poor** with a plural verb.

poorly * /'pʊrli/ [adverb; no comparative] not at all well; synonym BADLY: *The houses were poorly built.*

pop[1] /pɑp/ [verb; pops, popped, popping] to burst open with a short loud sound, or to make something do

this: *Hey, that boy popped my balloon!* |
I love the smell of popcorn popping.

pop² [*noun*]
1 popular modern music: *She likes rock
and pop.* | *a pop record*
2 a sudden short sound like a very
small explosion: *The cork came out with
a loud pop.*

popcorn /'pɑp,kɔrn/ [*noun*] a kind of
corn that swells and bursts when it is
cooked

pope or **Pope** /poʊp/ [*noun, name*] the
leader of one of the main groups of
Christian churches

popular * /'pɑpyələ/ [*adjective;* **more
popular, most popular**] liked by a lot
of people; *opposite* UNPOPULAR: *He's the
most popular boy in the class.* | *Music
videos are very **popular with** kids.*

popularity /,pɑpyə'lerɪti/ [*noun*] the
quality of being liked by many people:
*The president's popularity has increased
over the last year.*

populated /'pɑpyə,leɪtɪd/ [*adjective;*
more populated, most populated] if a
place or area is populated, people live
there: *The northern part of Canada is
thinly populated.*

population * /,pɑpyə'leɪʃən/ [*noun*] the
people in a country, area, or town, or
the number of people there: *Most of the
population lived in rural areas.* | *What is
the population of Australia?*

porch /pɔrtʃ/ [*noun; plural* **porches**] a
structure built onto a HOUSE at the front
or back door, with a floor and roof but
no walls

pork /pɔrk/ [*noun*] the meat from pigs:
pork chops (=pieces of meat from the
side of a pig)

port * /pɔrt/ [*noun*] a place where ships
stop so that people can get on, goods
can be taken on and off, etc.: *a busy
port* | *The boat will be **in port** for two
days.*

portable /'pɔrtəbəl/ [*adjective; no
comparative*] light and easy to carry: *a
portable TV*

porter /'pɔrtə/ [*noun*] someone whose
job is to carry people's bags at a station,
airport, or hotel

porthole /'pɔrt,hoʊl/ [*noun*] a small
round window in the side of a ship or
plane

portion /'pɔrʃən/ [*noun*]
1 an amount of food that is enough for
one person: *This restaurant serves very
big portions.*
2 a part of something: *It's smart to save
a **portion of** your salary every month.*

portrait /'pɔrtrɪt/ [*noun*] a painting,
drawing, or photograph of someone:
*a **portrait of** my father*

position * Ⓣ /pə'zɪʃən/ [*noun*]
1 the way in which someone is
standing or sitting, or the direction in
which an object is pointing: *He kept
turning over, trying to find a comfortable
position.* | *Keep the bottle in an upright
position.*
2 the situation that someone is in: *The
company is **in a difficult position**
financially.* | *If I were **in your position**,
I think I'd quit.*
3 FORMAL a job: *I am writing to apply for
the **position of** secretary.*
4 a place where someone or something
is, especially in relation to something
else: *We found a good position for
watching the parade.*

━━ PHRASE ━━━━━━
5 **in/into position** in or into the
right place: *It was easy to slot the
shelves into position.*

positive * Ⓣ /'pɑzɪtɪv/ [*adjective*]
1 [*no comparative*] sure that something
is true; *synonym* CERTAIN: *Are you
positive that it was Maria you saw?*
2 [**more positive, most positive**] good
or useful: *Living abroad has been a
positive experience for me.*
3 [**more positive, most positive**]
believing that a situation will be all
right and problems will be solved: *Try
to be **positive about** your future.*
4 [*no comparative*] a positive number is
greater than 0: *When you multiply −2 by
−4, the result is the positive number 8.*

/i/ **see** /ɪ/ **big** /eɪ/ **day** /ɛ/ **get** /æ/ **hat**
/ɑ/ **father, hot** /ʌ/ **up** /ə/ **about** /ɔ/ **saw**
/oʊ/ **hope** /ʊ/ **book** /u/ **too** /aɪ/ **I** /aʊ/ **how**
/ɔɪ/ **boy** /ɜ/ **bird** /ə/ **teacher** /ɪr/ **ear** /ɛr/ **air**
/ɑr/ **far** /ɔr/ **more** /ʊr/ **tour** /aɪr/ **fire**
/aʊə/ **hour** /θ/ **nothing** /ð/ **mother** /ʃ/ **she**
/ʒ/ **measure** /tʃ/ **church** /dʒ/ **jump** /ŋ/ **long**

5 [no comparative] a positive electrical charge is the kind of charge carried by a proton: *This molecule has a positive charge.*
↪ Compare NEGATIVE[1].

possess * /pə'zɛs/ [verb; possesses, possessed, possessing] FORMAL to have or own something: *He possesses many fine qualities.*

possessions * /pə'zɛʃənz/ [plural noun] things that you own: *You don't need a lot of possessions to be happy.*

possibility * /ˌpɑsə'bɪləti/ [noun; plural possibilities] something that might happen or be true: *Is there any possibility that you could be mistaken?* | *We discussed the possibility of leaving earlier.*
☛ Do not say "the possibility to do something." Say **the possibility of doing something.**

possible * Ⓣ /'pɑsəbəl/ [adjective; no comparative]
1 able to happen or be done; *opposite* IMPOSSIBLE: *Would it be possible for me to see the doctor this morning?* | *I'd like you to do it as soon as possible* (=as soon as you can).
☛ Do not say "It can be possible." Say **It is possible,** or, when you are talking about the future, **It may/might be possible.**
2 used to say that something may be true: *It's possible that she's forgotten her appointment.*

possibly * Ⓣ /'pɑsəbli/ [adverb]
1 used to say that something may happen, may be true, or may be right; *synonyms* MAYBE, PERHAPS: *"Are you going to Sam's party?" "Possibly—I might have to work."*
2 used to emphasize "can" or "could": *What could he possibly mean?* | *I can't possibly do it now.*

possum /'pɑsəm/ [noun] INFORMAL opossum; a North American animal that looks like a large rat and can hang from trees by its tail

a possum

post[1] * /poʊst/ [noun]
1 a thick straight piece of wood, metal, or stone that is fixed into the ground: *He tied the dog's leash to a fence post.*
2 a job, especially an important one: *He has taken up the post of ambassador to France.*

post[2] * [verb; posted, posting] to put a sign or a notice about something in a place where people can see it: *"No Parking" signs were posted along the street.* | *They posted the results of their study on their Web page.*

postage /'poʊstɪdʒ/ [noun] the money you pay to send a letter or package by mail: *My letter came back because there wasn't enough postage on it.*

postal service /'poʊstəl ˌsɝvɪs/ [noun] the system of sending letters and packages from one part of a country or the world to another: *the U.S. Postal Service*

postcard /'poʊstˌkɑrd/ [noun] a small card, often with a picture on the front, that you can send through the mail without using an envelope: *Did you get my postcard from Mexico?*

poster /'poʊstɚ/ [noun] a large notice or picture, put up on a wall to advertise something or as a decoration: *She had several posters on her bedroom walls.*

postmark /'poʊstˌmɑrk/ [noun] an official mark made with a machine on a letter or package, which shows when and from where it was sent: *According to the postmark, it was sent on March 23.*

post office /'poʊst ˌɔfɪs/ [noun] a place where you can buy stamps, send letters and packages, etc.

postpone Ⓣ /poʊst'poʊn/ [verb; postponed, postponing] to change the time of an event to a later time or date: *I'm afraid we'll have to postpone our meeting.*

pot * /pɑt/ [noun]
1 a deep round container used for cooking: *There was a huge pot of soup on the stove.*
2 a container with a handle and a part for pouring the liquid out, used for

making or serving tea or coffee: *I'll
make a fresh* **pot of** *coffee.*
⇨ *See the picture at* TEAPOT.
3 a container for a plant: *This plant
needs a larger pot.*
⇨ *See also* FLOWERPOT.

lid

casserole

soup pot

frying pan

baking pan

rack

saucepan

roasting
pan

pots and pans

potato * /pə'teɪtoʊ/ [*noun; plural*
potatoes] a round white root with
brown skin that is cooked and eaten as
a VEGETABLE: **baked potatoes** (=cooked in
an oven with their skins on) | **mashed
potatoes** (=peeled, boiled, and mixed
with milk and butter)

potato chip /pə'teɪtoʊ ˌtʃɪp/ [*noun*] a
very thin piece of potato that is cooked
in oil: *He opened a bag of potato chips.*
⇨ *See the picture at* CHIP¹.

pottery /'patəri/ [*noun*]
1 containers, dishes, and other objects
made of baked clay: *The museum has a
display of Native American pottery.*
2 the activity of making things out of
baked clay: *a pottery class*

poultry /'poʊltri/ [*plural noun*] chickens
and other birds that are kept on a farm
to provide eggs and meat: *a poultry farm*

pounce /paʊns/ [*verb*; **pounced,
pouncing**] to suddenly jump at
something and take hold of it: *The wolf
pounced, quickly killing the sheep.*

pound¹ * /paʊnd/ [*noun*] a unit for
measuring weight, equal to 16 ounces

or 0.454 kilograms: *Two pounds of
carrots and a pound of tomatoes, please.*
⇨ *See also* LB.

pound² [*verb*; **pounded, pounding**] to
hit something very hard again and
again: *He pounded on the door.*

pour * /pɔr/ [*verb*; **poured, pouring**]
1 to make a liquid flow out of a
container: *Pour the batter into a baking
pan.* | **pour someone something** ▸
Can I pour you some tea?
2 to rain with a lot of force: *I'm not
going out—it's pouring!*

poverty Ⓣ /'pavərti/ [*noun*] the situation
of having very little or no money:
Millions of families live **in poverty.**

powder * /'paʊdər/ [*noun*] a dry
substance in the form of extremely
small pieces: **baby powder** (=to keep a
baby's skin dry) | *dried milk powder*

power * /'paʊər/ [*noun*]
1 the ability or right to control people
or events: *How did the emperor* **come to
power?** (=become a ruler)
2 energy such as electricity that is used
to make machines work: *The country
depends too much on nuclear power.* |
solar power (=from the sun)
3 the ability or right to do a particular
thing: **the power to do something** ▸
Congress has the power to make laws.
4 a strong and important country: *a
meeting of the major* **world powers**
(=the strongest countries in the world)

powerful * Ⓣ /'paʊərfəl/ [*adjective*;
more powerful, most powerful]
1 able to control or influence people or
events: *It is one of the most powerful
nations in the world.*
2 having a lot of strength or force: *He
was a big, powerful man.* | *Her speech
had a powerful effect on the audience.*

powerless /'paʊərlɪs/ [*adjective*; *no
comparative*] unable to control
something or stop it from happening:

/i/ see /ɪ/ big /eɪ/ day /ɛ/ get /æ/ hat
/a/ father, hot /ʌ/ up /ə/ about /ɔ/ saw
/oʊ/ hope /ʊ/ book /u/ too /aɪ/ I /aʊ/ how
/ɔɪ/ boy /ɝ/ bird /ɚ/ teacher /ɪr/ ear /ɛr/ air
/ar/ far /ɔr/ more /ʊr/ tour /aɪr/ fire
/aʊɚ/ hour /θ/ nothing /ð/ mother /ʃ/ she
/ʒ/ measure /tʃ/ church /dʒ/ jump /ŋ/ long

powerless to do something ▸ *We were powerless to stop them.*

power plant /'pɑʊɚ ˌplænt/ [*noun*] a building or part of a building where electricity is produced

pp. the written abbreviation of "pages": *See pp. 29–30.*

practical ✱ T /'præktɪkəl/ [*adjective*; more **practical**, most **practical**]
1 relating to real situations: *She has a college degree, but not much **practical** experience.*
2 practical ideas, plans, etc., are sensible and likely to work or be useful: *a practical suggestion*
3 a practical person is sensible and thinks about what is really possible: *She's a good artist, but she's not very practical.*

practically /'præktɪkli/ [*adverb*]
1 almost: *Practically all my friends were at the party.*
2 in a sensible way: *"Let's clear this mess up first," he suggested practically.*

practice[1] ✱ /'præktɪs/ [*noun*]
1 when you do something, or do it a lot of times, in order to improve your skill at it: *I need more practice speaking English.*
2 something that people often do: *This practice should be made illegal.* I *It's **normal practice** for budgets to be done once a year.*

━━ PHRASES ━━
3 **be out of practice** to be unable to do something well because you have not done it for a long time: *I play the guitar, but I'm out of practice.*
4 **in practice** used to say what is actually true or what actually happens: *In practice, goals are often hard to achieve.*
    ➪ Compare **in theory** at THEORY.

practice[2] ✱ [*verb*; **practiced**, **practicing**] to do something often in order to improve your skill at it: *You'll have to practice hard if you want to be a professional.* I *She's practicing the piano.*

SYNONYMS practice, rehearse, train

If you **practice** something, you do it often in order to improve your skill: *I practice my violin every evening.* If you

rehearse, you prepare for a play or concert so that you will be ready to perform it: *This is the last time we will rehearse before the show opens.* If you **train**, you prepare for a sports event by exercising: *He's training hard for the Olympic Games.*

─────────

prairie /'prɛri/ [*noun*; plural **prairies**] a large flat area of land that has no trees and is covered with grass or crops

praise[1] ✱ T /preɪz/ [*verb*; **praised**, **praising**] to say that you admire someone or what he or she has done: *The police officer **was praised for** his bravery.*

praise[2] ✱ T [*noun*] words that say how much you admire someone or what he or she has done: *The principal was **full of praise for** the school.*

prawn /prɔn/ [*noun*] a pink sea creature like a large SHRIMP, that you can eat

pray ✱ /preɪ/ [*verb*; **prays**, **prayed**, **praying**] to speak to God or a god in order to ask for help or to show your thanks: *Let us pray.* I *I **prayed that** he would be all right.*

prayer ✱ /prɛr/ [*noun*] words that you say when you speak to God or a god: *They **said a prayer for** world peace.* I *His head was bowed **in prayer**.*

preach /pritʃ/ [*verb*; **preaches**, **preached**, **preaching**] to give a talk about a religious subject, especially in a church: *The minister **preached a sermon** about forgiving people.* I *He **preached to** people all over the country.*

preacher /'pritʃɚ/ [*noun*] someone who gives religious talks, especially in churches

precaution /prɪ'kɔʃən/ [*noun*] something that you do to stop something bad from happening: *He **took the precaution of** buckling his seat belt.* I *You should insure your camera **as a precaution**.*

precinct /'prisɪŋkt/ [*noun*] a part of a city that has its own police force and some local government officials: *There has been a series of robberies in the 42nd Precinct.*

precious ⊤ /'prɛʃəs/ [adjective; **more precious, most precious**]
1 rare and valuable: *Precious metals like gold and silver are used to make jewelry.*
2 very important or special to you: *Her privacy is very **precious** to her.*

precipitation /prɪˌsɪpɪ'teɪʃən/ [noun] rain or snow

precise ⊤ /prɪ'saɪs/ [adjective; **more precise, most precise**]
1 exact and correct: *The precise details of the deal are still a secret.* | *I'm sorry I can't be more precise.*

▬▬ PHRASE ▬▬

2 to be precise used to add exact details about something: *He was born in Italy; Rome, to be precise.*

precisely /prɪ'saɪsli/ [adverb]
1 exactly: *I don't know precisely how old she is.*
2 used to say that what someone has said or suggested is true: *"So you don't believe her?" "Precisely."*

predict ⊤ /prɪ'dɪkt/ [verb; **predicted, predicting**] to guess and say that something is going to happen before it happens: *They're **predicting that** we will have another hot summer.*

prediction /prɪ'dɪkʃən/ [noun] a statement in which you say what you guess is going to happen: *I wouldn't like to **make** any **predictions about** his test results.*

prefer * /prɪ'fɝ/ [verb; **prefers, preferred, preferring**]
1 to like one thing more than another: *Do you prefer coffee or tea?* | **prefer to do something** ▸ *Would you prefer to go to a restaurant or eat at home?* | **prefer something to something** ▸ *I prefer football to baseball.*
☞ Do not say "I prefer football than baseball." Say **I prefer football to baseball**.

▬▬ PHRASE ▬▬

2 I'd prefer it if used to ask someone politely to do or not do something: *I'd prefer it if we left now.* | *I'd prefer it if you didn't smoke.*

preferable /'prɛfərəbəl/ [adjective; no comparative] better or more suitable: *Anything is preferable to a nuclear war.*

preferably /'prɛfərəbli/ [adverb] used to show which you think is the best choice, method, etc.: *Bring along two, or preferably three, changes of clothing.*

preference /'prɛfərəns/ [noun] when you like one thing more than another: *I **have a preference for** bright colors.*

prefix * /'prifɪks/ [noun; plural **prefixes**] GRAMMAR a group of letters that is added to the beginning of a word and changes its meaning: *The prefix "un-" makes a word mean the opposite, as in "unhappy."*
➪ Compare SUFFIX. ➪ See Prefixes and Suffixes *in the Smart Study section.*

pregnancy ⊤ /'prɛgnənsi/ [noun; plural **pregnancies**] when a baby is developing inside a woman's body: *These pills must not be taken **during pregnancy**.* | *This is my first pregnancy.*

pregnant /'prɛgnənt/ [adjective; no comparative] having a baby developing inside your body: *She's **pregnant with** her third child.*

prejudice ⊤ /'prɛdʒədɪs/ [noun] an unfair feeling of not liking someone, especially because of his or her race, sex, or religion: *Laws alone cannot get rid of **racial prejudice**.* | *There is still **prejudice against** foreigners.*

prejudiced /'prɛdʒədɪst/ [adjective; **more prejudiced, most prejudiced**] not liking someone unfairly, especially because of his or her race, sex, or religion: *Why are you so **prejudiced against** Mexicans?*

premature /ˌprimə'tʃʊr/ [adjective; no comparative] happening earlier than expected or before the right time: *a premature baby* (=one born before the usual time)

preparation * /ˌprɛpə'reɪʃən/ [noun]
1 the process of getting ready for something: *The hall had been cleared **in preparation for** the concert.*
2 preparations [plural] arrangements

/i/ see	/ɪ/ big	/eɪ/ day	/ɛ/ get	/æ/ hat
/ɑ/ father, hot	/ʌ/ up	/ə/ about	/ɔ/ saw
/oʊ/ hope	/ʊ/ book	/u/ too	/aɪ/ I	/aʊ/ how
/ɔɪ/ boy	/ɝ/ bird	/ɚ/ teacher	/ɪr/ ear	/ɛr/ air
/ɑr/ far	/ɔr/ more	/ʊr/ tour	/aɪr/ fire
/aʊɚ/ hour	/θ/ nothing	/ð/ mother	/ʃ/ she
/ʒ/ measure	/tʃ/ church	/dʒ/ jump	/ŋ/ long

for something that is going to happen:
*How are the **preparations for** the
meeting going?*

prepare * ⊤ /prɪ'pɛr/ [verb; prepared,
preparing]
  1 to make something ready to be used:
  Who prepared all this delicious food?
  2 to get ready for something: *She was
  out by the track, **preparing for** the next
  race.* | **prepare to do something** ▸ *He
  prepared to jump from the plane.*

prepared /prɪ'pɛrd/ [adjective; **more
prepared, most prepared**]
  1 ready to do something or deal with a

situation: *Christopher wasn't at all
prepared for the job interview.*
☛ Do not use **prepared** before a noun.

━━ PHRASE ━━
2 be prepared to do something to
be willing to do something if it is
necessary: *Would you be prepared to
make that statement in court?*

preposition * /ˌprɛpə'zɪʃən/ [noun] a
word such as "to," "at," "in," or "for"
that is used before a noun or pronoun,
and shows place, time, direction,
method, etc.

The hats are on the shelf **above** the purses.

The purses are on the shelf **between** the
dresses and the hats.

The dresses are hanging **under** the shelves.

The shoes are on the floor **under/below**
the dresses.

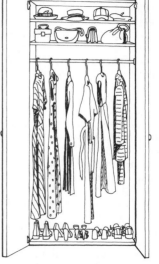

Mr. and Mrs. Ruiz and Maria are
standing **behind** the couch.

Maria is standing **between**
her parents.

Jimmy is sitting **next to/beside** Rick.

Grandma is sitting **in front of**
Mrs. Ruiz.

The baby is sitting **on** Grandma's lap.

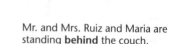

prepositions of position

prep school /'prɛp ˌskul/ [noun] a private school that prepares students for college

prescribe /prɪ'skraɪb/ [verb; prescribed, prescribing] if a doctor prescribes a particular medicine or treatment, he or she says that a sick person should have it: *Doctors should not prescribe antibiotics to treat viruses.*

prescription /prɪ'skrɪpʃən/ [noun] instructions from a doctor, usually written on a piece of paper, that say what medicine a sick person should have: *The doctor gave me a prescription for some pills.*

presence /'prɛzəns/ [noun]
1 when someone is in a place or with a person or group: *The children seemed nervous in our presence.*
2 FORMAL the fact that something is in a place or exists: *We want to strengthen our firm's presence in the market.*

present[1] * /'prɛzənt/ [adjective; no comparative] in a place or with a particular person or group; *opposite* ABSENT: *He was not present at the meeting.*
☛ Do not use **present** before a noun.

present[2] * /'prɛzənt/ [noun]
1 something nice that you give to someone; *synonym* GIFT: *I had lots of birthday presents.* | *The book was a present from my mother.*
2 the present
  a the time that is happening now: *Stop worrying about the past and live for the present.*
  b GRAMMAR the PRESENT TENSE

present[3] /prɪ'zɛnt/ [verb; presented, presenting] to give something to someone, usually at an official ceremony: **present someone with something** ▸ *The winning team was presented with a trophy.* | **present something to someone** ▸ *The mayor presented the prizes to the top students.*

presentation /ˌprɛzən'teɪʃən/ [noun]
1 a formal talk using pictures, charts, etc., that is given to a group: *We gave a presentation on our new products.*
2 when something is given to someone, especially a prize at a ceremony: *The*

presentation of this year's awards will take place after dinner.

present continuous /'prɛzənt kən'tɪnyuəs/ [noun] GRAMMAR
the present continuous the form of a verb that shows what is happening or is true at this moment. It is formed with the present tense of "be" and a present participle: *In the sentence "She is playing tennis," the verb is in the present continuous.*
↪ See the usage note at CONTINUOUS[2].

present participle * /'prɛzənt 'partəsɪpəl/ [noun] GRAMMAR the form of a verb ending in "-ing." It is used to form continuous tenses and as an adjective or noun: *"Hitting" is the present participle of the verb "hit."*

present perfect /'prɛzənt 'pɚfɪkt/ [noun] GRAMMAR
the present perfect the form of a verb that shows time up to and including the present. It is formed with the present tense of "have" and the past participle: *In the sentence "She has gone to Rome," the verb is in the present perfect.*
↪ See the usage note at PERFECT[2].

present tense * /'prɛzənt 'tɛns/ [noun] GRAMMAR
the present tense the form of a verb that shows what the situation is now, or what usually happens: *In the sentence "We usually eat dinner at 7," the verb is in the present tense.*
↪ Compare PAST TENSE, FUTURE TENSE.

preservation Ⓣ /ˌprɛzɚ'veɪʃən/ [noun] when people keep something safe from being destroyed or changed too much: *The preservation of our wildlife is important.*

preserve * Ⓣ /prɪ'zɚv/ [verb; preserved, preserving] to prevent something from being destroyed or changed too much: *They want to preserve the historic center of*

/i/ **see**	/ɪ/ **big**	/eɪ/ **day**	/ɛ/ **get** /æ/ **hat**

/i/ **see** /ɪ/ **big** /eɪ/ **day** /ɛ/ **get** /æ/ **hat**
/ɑ/ **father, hot** /ʌ/ **up** /ə/ **about** /ɔ/ **saw**
/oʊ/ **hope** /ʊ/ **book** /u/ **too** /aɪ/ **I** /aʊ/ **how**
/ɔɪ/ **boy** /ɝ/ **bird** /ɚ/ **teacher** /ɪr/ **ear** /ɛr/ **air**
/ɑr/ **far** /ɔr/ **more** /ʊr/ **tour** /aɪr/ **fire**
/aʊɚ/ **hour** /θ/ **nothing** /ð/ **mother** /ʃ/ **she**
/ʒ/ **measure** /tʃ/ **church** /dʒ/ **jump** /ŋ/ **long**

the city. I *Store the coffee in a cool, dark place to preserve its flavor.*

president ∗ or **President** /ˈprɛzɪdənt/ [*noun, name*]
1 the leader of a country and often of its government: *President Kennedy was shot in 1963.* I *the president of France*
2 someone who is in charge of a college, business, club, etc.: *The president of the college spoke first.*

press[1] /prɛs/ [*noun*]
the press newspapers and magazines, or the people who write reports for them: *Members of the press questioned the lawyer outside the court.* I *His picture was all over the press* (=in many newspapers). I *The press is here, Mr. President.*
☞ Only use **the press** with a singular verb.

press[2] ∗ [*verb*; presses, pressed, pressing]
1 to press a button or key in order to make a machine do something: *She pressed the wrong key on the computer.*
2 to push something firmly against something else: *I was pressed against the wall of the elevator.*

pressure ∗ T /ˈprɛʃɚ/ [*noun*]
1 conditions in your work or your life that give you problems or worry you: *I couldn't cope with the pressures of my job.* I *I'm under a lot of pressure right now.*
2 when someone tries to make someone do something: *The boss is putting pressure on him to work later.*
3 a physical force or weight that affects something: *The changes in air pressure in a plane hurt my ears.*

pretend ∗ /prɪˈtɛnd/ [*verb*; pretended, pretending] to behave as if something is true, when it is not: *You're not sick. You're just pretending.* I *He pretended that he hadn't heard.* I **pretend to do something** ▸ *She pretended to be interested in his story.*

pretty[1] ∗ /ˈprɪti/ [*adjective*; prettier, prettiest] attractive and pleasant to look at: *a pretty girl* I *I think this dress is prettier than that one.*
↪ See the synonym note at BEAUTIFUL.

pretty[2] [*adverb*] INFORMAL fairly, but not extremely: *He comes from a pretty wealthy family.*

pretzel /ˈprɛtsəl/ [*noun*] a piece of bread baked in the shape of a knot or stick, usually with salt on it

prevent ∗ T /prɪˈvɛnt/ [*verb*; prevented, preventing] to stop something from happening, or stop someone from doing something: *Could the accident have been prevented?* I **prevent someone from doing something** ▸ *His injury will prevent him from playing in today's game.*

prevention /prɪˈvɛnʃən/ [*noun*] things that you do to stop something from happening: *The whole community can help with crime prevention.* I *the prevention of forest fires*

previous ∗ T /ˈpriviəs/ [*adjective*; no comparative*] happening or coming before now, or before the time you are talking about; synonym EARLIER: *I already studied this in my previous school.* I *In previous years, they had a party on New Year's Eve.*
☞ Only use **previous** before a noun.

previously /ˈpriviəsli/ [*adverb*] before now, or before the time you are talking about: *The position was previously held by the new chairman.*

prey /preɪ/ [*noun*] an animal's prey is an animal that it hunts and eats: *The lioness crept slowly toward her prey.* I *birds of prey* (=birds that kill and eat other animals)

price[1] ∗ /praɪs/ [*noun*] the exact amount of money you must pay to buy something in a store, restaurant, etc.: *I'd like to buy it, but the price is too high.* I *What's the price of this clock?*
☞ Do not say "an expensive price." Say **a high price.**
↪ See the synonym note at COST[2].

price[2] [*verb*; priced, pricing] to give something a price in order to sell it: *Priced at only $30, these sweaters are a bargain.*

priceless /ˈpraɪslɪs/ [*adjective*; no comparative*] extremely valuable: *His apartment is full of priceless antiques.*

prick /prɪk/ [verb; pricked, pricking] to make a small hole in something with a sharp point: Roses have thorns that can prick you.

pride /praɪd/ [noun] the feeling of being pleased about something you have done, or about someone or something you are connected with: He looked around his home **with pride**. I She takes great **pride in** her work.
⇨ Compare PROUD.

priest * /prist/ [noun] someone who can officially perform religious ceremonies and duties

primary Ⓣ /'praɪmɛri/ [adjective; no comparative] most important: Her primary aim is to get into medical school.
☛ Only use **primary** before a noun.

primary school /'praɪmɛri ˌskul/ [noun] a school for children in their first five or six years of education; synonyms ELEMENTARY SCHOOL, GRADE SCHOOL

prime minister or **Prime Minister** /praɪm 'mɪnɪstɚ/ [noun, name] the leader of the government in some countries

primitive /'prɪmɪtɪv/ [adjective; more primitive, most primitive] belonging to an early part of human history: These cave paintings were done by primitive people long ago.

prince * or **Prince** /prɪns/ [noun, name] the son or other close male relative of a king or queen

princess or **Princess** /'prɪnsɪs/ [noun, name; plural princesses] the daughter or other close female relative of a king or queen, or the wife of a prince

principal[1] Ⓣ /'prɪnsəpəl/ [adjective; no comparative] main or most important: What's your principal reason for quitting?
☛ Only use **principal** before a noun.

principal[2] [noun] the person in charge of a school: The teacher sent the boy to the principal's office.

principally /'prɪnsəpli/ [adverb] mainly: Some test scores have improved, principally among the girls.

principle * /'prɪnsəpəl/ [noun] an idea or rule that you believe is right: Equality is a principle we all agree upon. I My father doesn't gamble **on principle** (=because of his moral opinions).

print[1] * /prɪnt/ [verb; printed, printing]
1 to put words and pictures onto paper or other surfaces using a machine: This book was printed in Italy. I Something's wrong; the printer won't print.
2 to write words by hand without joining the letters together: Print your answers neatly.

print[2] * [noun]
1 words that have been printed in books, newspapers, etc.: Children's books have larger print. I She was excited when she saw her name **in print**.
2 a mark in a surface made by pressing something into it: Those paw prints were made by a bear.

printer * /'prɪntɚ/ [noun]
1 a machine that copies documents from a computer onto paper
2 a company that prints books or magazines, or a large machine that does this: Her latest novel is now **at the printer's**.

printout /'prɪntˌaʊt/ [noun] a sheet or long length of paper with information from a computer printed on it

prison * /'prɪzən/ [noun] a building, especially a large one, where people are locked in as an official punishment for a crime: The judge sent him to a prison in Texas. I She has been **in prison** before.
⇨ Compare JAIL[1].

prisoner * /'prɪzənɚ/ [noun] someone who is being kept in a prison or being kept somewhere and forced to stay there: The prisoners walked slowly around the exercise yard. I He **was taken prisoner** (=was caught by the enemy) near the end of the war.

privacy Ⓣ /'praɪvəsi/ [noun] a situation in which other people do not see you or know details of your personal life: It's hard for movie stars to keep their privacy.

/i/ see	/ɪ/ big	/eɪ/ day	/ɛ/ get	/æ/ hat
/ɑ/ father, hot	/ʌ/ up	/ə/ about	/ɔ/ saw	
/oʊ/ hope	/ʊ/ book	/u/ too	/aɪ/ I	/aʊ/ how
/ɔɪ/ boy	/ɚ/ bird	/ɚ/ teacher	/ɪr/ ear	/ɛr/ air
/ɑr/ far	/ɔr/ more	/ʊr/ tour	/aɪr/ fire	
/aʊɚ/ hour	/θ/ nothing	/ð/ mother	/ʃ/ she	
/ʒ/ measure	/tʃ/ church	/dʒ/ jump	/ŋ/ long	

private[1] * /'praɪvɪt/ [*adjective*]
1 [**more private, most private**] only for one particular person or group, not for everyone; opposite PUBLIC: *One of the rooms can be rented for private parties.* | *Private Land—Keep Out!*
2 [*no comparative*] concerning only yourself and not being something that other people have a right to know about: *How dare you read my private mail?* | *Please don't tell anyone else about this. It's private.*

private[2] [*noun*]
1 [*name*] also **Private;** a soldier in the Army or Marine Corps of the lowest rank
— PHRASE —
2 **in private** in a place where other people cannot see or hear you: *Can we talk somewhere in private?*

privately * /'praɪvɪtli/ [*adverb*] in a way that involves only you, or does not involve many people: *I'd like to talk to you privately.*

private school /'praɪvɪt ˌskul/ [*noun*] in the U.S., a school that people pay to send their children to
➪ *Compare* PUBLIC SCHOOL.

privilege /'prɪvəlɪdʒ/ [*noun*] an advantage that is given to only one person or group of people: *Some of the prisoners are given special privileges.*

prize * /praɪz/ [*noun*] something that you win by being successful in a competition, game, or race: *There are lots of prizes to be won!* | *Dad* ***won first prize*** *in the contest.*

pro /proʊ/ [*noun; plural* **pros**] INFORMAL someone who is a professional or is very good at doing something: *I love watching him play—he's a real pro.*

probable /'prabəbəl/ [*adjective;* **more probable, most probable**] likely to happen or be true: *The most probable explanation is that there was a computer error.*

probably * /'prabəbli/ [*adverb*] likely to happen or be true: *I invited her to the party but she probably won't come.* | *"Do you think it'll rain today?" "Probably."* | *This is probably the best vacation they've ever had.*
☛ Use **probably** after the verb "be," not before it.

problem * /'prabləm/ [*noun*]
1 a difficult situation or person that someone has to deal with: *Are you* ***having*** *any* ***problems*** *at home?* | *Crime is a* ***serious problem*** *in this city.* | *A new battery should* ***solve the problem****.*
☛ Do not say "have problems to do something." Say **have problems doing something**.
— PHRASE —
2 **no problem** SPOKEN
a used to say that you are very willing to do something: *"Could you help load the car?" "Sure, no problem."*
b used to reply to someone who has thanked you or said that he or she is sorry: *"Thanks for your help." "No problem!"*

proceed /prə'sid/ [*verb;* **proceeded, proceeding**] to continue doing something that has been started: *Work on the new hospital is proceeding according to plan.*

process[1] * /'prasɛs/ [*noun; plural* **processes**]
1 a series of actions, changes, or developments: *Learning English was a difficult process for me.* | *Boys' voices change by a natural process.*
— PHRASE —
2 **be in the process of doing something** to have started doing something and still be doing it: *We're in the process of buying a house.*

process[2] [*verb;* **processes, processed, processing**]
1 to deal with information or instructions using a particular method: *They're still processing the research data.*
2 to use heat or a special machine to prepare or preserve food: *processed cheese*

processor /'prasɛsɚ/ [*noun*] a computer program or a part of a computer that manages the information in a computer: *a word processor* (=a program that lets you create documents on a computer) | *How fast is your computer's processor?*
➪ *See also* **CPU**.

produce[1] * T /prə'dus/ [*verb;* **produced, producing**]

1 to grow something or make it naturally: *The apple tree didn't produce much fruit this year.*

2 to make something happen or have a particular result: *Their business school has produced many company leaders.*

3 to make things in large quantities: *The factory produces 800 cars a week.*

4 to be in charge of making a movie, play, or television or radio program: *The movie was produced and directed by the same man.*

produce[2] /'proʊdus/ [*noun*] plants grown for food, especially fruits and vegetables: *the produce section of a supermarket*

producer /prə'dusɚ/ [*noun*]

1 a person or organization that produces something: *We buy most of our goods from local producers.*

2 someone who is in charge of making a movie, play, or television or radio program: *Her father's a famous movie producer.*

product * /'prɑdəkt/ [*noun*] something that is made in a factory or is grown: *That store has a large selection of beauty products.* | *My son is allergic to all* **dairy products** (=milk, cheese, etc.).

production * T /prə'dʌkʃən/ [*noun*]

1 the process of making or growing things, or the amount that is produced: *The factory will increase its production next year.* | *Iron helps in the* **production of** *red blood cells.*

2 a play, movie, or program that is done or made by a particular group of people: *The school does three productions each year.*

Prof. the written abbreviation of PROFESSOR: *Prof. White*

profession * T /prə'fɛʃən/ [*noun*] a job that needs a lot of special education and training, for example in law, medicine, or science

professional[1] /prə'fɛʃənəl/ [*adjective; no comparative*]

1 relating to jobs in law, medicine, science, etc., or to someone who has this kind of job: *It's best to get*

professional advice about your taxes. | *For that job, you'll need a professional license.*

2 doing something such as a sport as your main job; *opposite* AMATEUR: *He wanted to be a professional boxer.*

professional[2] T [*noun*] someone whose main job is doing a sport or whose job is in in law, medicine, etc.: *He signed as a professional with the team in 1992.*

professor or **Professor** /prə'fɛsɚ/ [*noun, name*] a teacher at a university or college: *Professor Black will be teaching the European Literature course.* | *a math professor* | *a* **professor of** *physics*

profit * /'prɑfɪt/ [*noun*] the money you gain by selling something or doing business; *opposite* LOSS: *They* **made a** *huge* **profit** *when they sold their house.* | *Is there much profit in second-hand books?*

☛ Do not say "gain a profit." Say **make a profit.**

profitable /'prɑfɪtəbəl/ [*adjective;* **more profitable, most profitable**] making or resulting in a profit: *We're looking for ways to make the store more profitable.*

program[1] * /'proʊgræm/ [*noun*]

1 a show broadcast on radio or television: *What's your favorite TV program?* | *Did you see that* **program about** *the rain forests last night?*

2 a set of instructions that is given to a computer to make it do something: *a computer program*

3 printed information about what will happen or who will take part in a concert, play, football game, etc.: *Let's buy a program.*

program[2] * T [*verb;* **programs, programmed, programming**] to give a computer instructions to make it do a particular job: **program something to do something** ▶ *They can now program computers to recognize your voice.*

/i/ **see**	/ɪ/ **big**	/eɪ/ **day**	/ɛ/ **get** /æ/ **hat**
/ɑ/ **father, hot**	/ʌ/ **up**	/ə/ **about**	/ɔ/ **saw**
/oʊ/ **hope**	/ʊ/ **book**	/u/ **too**	/aɪ/ **I** /aʊ/ **how**
/ɔɪ/ **boy**	/ɚ/ **bird**	/ɚ/ **teacher**	/ɪr/ **ear** /ɛr/ **air**
/ɑr/ **far**	/ɔr/ **more**	/ʊr/ **tour**	/aɪr/ **fire**
/aʊɚ/ **hour**	/θ/ **nothing**	/ð/ **mother**	/ʃ/ **she**
/ʒ/ **measure**	/tʃ/ **church**	/dʒ/ **jump**	/ŋ/ **long**

programmer /ˈproʊɡræmɚ/ [noun] someone whose job is to write programs for computers

progress[1] * /ˈprɑɡrɛs/ [noun] the process of getting better at something or getting nearer to finishing something: *She's made good progress in math this year.*

progress[2] /prəˈɡrɛs/ [verb; **progresses, progressed, progressing**]
1 to develop or improve over a period of time: *How's the work progressing?* | *The doctor says that Grandpa is progressing well.*
2 to move forward or continue: *As the evening progressed, I began to feel better.*

prohibit /proʊˈhɪbɪt/ [verb; **prohibited, prohibiting**] to officially not allow an activity, or to say that it is illegal: *Smoking in the hallways is prohibited.* | **prohibit someone from doing something** ▸ *The law prohibits stores from selling fireworks.*
☛ Do not say "prohibit someone to do something." Say **prohibit someone from doing something**.

project /ˈprɑdʒɛkt/ [noun]
1 the process of planning and building or producing: *They are working on a new museum project.*
2 a part of a student's course that involves collecting information about a particular subject: *We're doing a project on volcanoes.*

projector /prəˈdʒɛktɚ/ [noun] a piece of equipment for showing movies or pictures on a screen or wall: *He set up the movie projector.*

promise[1] * /ˈprɑmɪs/ [verb; **promised, promising**] to say that you will definitely do or provide something: *Promise that you won't tell anyone!* | *I'll be there, I promise.* | **promise someone something** ▸ *I promised him a bike for his birthday.* | **promise to do something** ▸ *I promise to be home early.*
☛ Do not say that you "promised doing something." Say that you **promised to do something**.

promise[2] * [noun] a statement that you will definitely do or provide something: *The mayor made a lot of promises to the*

people. | *He made a promise that he would never lie to her again.* | *He kept his promises* (=did what he promised). | *You broke your promise* (=did not do what you promised).

promote [T] /prəˈmoʊt/ [verb; **promoted, promoting**]
1 to support something and help it become successful or more important: *The organization promotes cancer research.*
2 to give someone a job of a higher level: *My goal is to be promoted next year.* | **promote someone to something** ▸ *He's been promoted to Assistant Manager.*

promotion /prəˈmoʊʃən/ [noun] a move to a job of a higher level: *She got a promotion to Sales Manager.*

prompt [T] /prɑmpt/ [adjective; **more prompt, most prompt**] done quickly or at the right time: *Prompt payment of bills is important.*

pronoun * /ˈproʊˌnaʊn/ [noun] GRAMMAR a word such as "he," "it," or "everyone" that is used instead of a noun

pronounce * /prəˈnaʊns/ [verb; **pronounced, pronouncing**] to say a word using particular sounds: *How do you pronounce your name?*

pronunciation * /prəˌnʌnsiˈeɪʃən/ [noun] the way in which a word or language is pronounced: *Her grammar is good, but her pronunciation is terrible.* | *The noun "address" has two possible pronunciations.*

proof * /pruf/ [noun] facts or documents that prove that something is true: *Do you have any proof that this is your purse?* | *He was asked to provide proof of his identity.*

propeller /prəˈpɛlɚ/ [noun] a piece of equipment with blades that spin very fast, which moves a boat or aircraft: *a helicopter's propellers*

proper * [T] /ˈprɑpɚ/ [adjective; no comparative] correct or right for a particular purpose: *It's dangerous to ski without the proper equipment.* | *Please put the books back on the proper shelves.*
☛ Only use **proper** before a noun.

properly * /'prɑpə-li/ [adverb] correctly, or in the way people think is right: *He's ten but he still can't read properly.*

property * Ⓣ /'prɑpə-ti/ [noun; plural properties]
1 something that someone owns: *Most stolen property is never found.*
2 FORMAL a building or piece of land: *There are some beautiful properties near the park.* | *Keep out! This is private property.*

prophet /'prɑfɪt/ [noun] someone who tells people what will happen in the future, especially a religious leader

proportion Ⓣ /prə'pɔrʃən/ [noun] part of an amount or quantity compared to the rest of it: *The proportion of fat in your diet should be low.*

proposal * /prə'poʊzəl/ [noun] a plan or idea that is formally suggested by someone: *They sent us a proposal for a new TV show.* | **proposal to do something** ▶ *The school board put forward a proposal to build a new gym.*
☛ Do not say "a proposal of doing something." Say **a proposal to do something.**

propose Ⓣ /prə'poʊz/ [verb; proposed, proposing]
1 to make a formal suggestion that something should be done: *I propose that we accept their offer.*
2 to ask someone to marry you: *He proposed to me in a restaurant.*

prosperous Ⓣ /'prɑspərəs/ [adjective; more prosperous, most prosperous] rich and successful: *His father was a prosperous businessman.*

protect * Ⓣ /prə'tɛkt/ [verb; protected, protecting] to prevent someone or something from being hurt or damaged: *Thick walls protected the castle.* | *Vaccines help protect against diseases.* | **protect someone/something from something** ▶ *Wear sunglasses to protect your eyes from sunlight.*

protection * Ⓣ /prə'tɛkʃən/ [noun] when someone or something is prevented from being hurt or damaged: *The penguin's feathers give it protection against the weather.*

protein Ⓣ /'proʊtin/ [noun] a substance in some foods, for example meat and eggs, that helps your body grow and stay healthy

protest[1] * /'proʊtɛst/ [noun] a strong public complaint about an action, situation, or plan: *Hundreds of people joined the protest against the new freeway.* | *They went on a protest march* (=when many people march to protest something).

protest[2] * /'proʊtɛst; prə'tɛst/ [verb; protested, protesting] to say or do something to show that you think an action, situation, or plan is wrong: *Many people wrote letters to protest against the tax.* | *Many parents protested the closing of the school.*

proton /'proʊtɑn/ [noun] a part of an atom that has a positive charge: *An atom of hydrogen has one proton.*
↪ Compare ELECTRON, NEUTRON.

protractor /proʊ'træktə-/ [noun] a flat piece of clear plastic, shaped like half a circle, that is used to draw or measure angles

proud * /praʊd/ [adjective; prouder, proudest]
1 feeling pleased about something you have done, or about someone or something you are connected with: *He wanted his parents to be proud of him.* | **proud to do something** ▶ *We are proud to announce the birth of our son.*
2 thinking that you are too good or important to do something: *He was too proud to borrow money.*
↪ See also PRIDE.

proudly * /'praʊdli/ [adverb] in a way that shows you are proud: *He proudly showed us his garden.*

prove * Ⓣ /pruv/ [verb; proves, proved, proven or proved, proving] to show that something is definitely true: *The police think he is guilty but they can't*

/i/ see /ɪ/ big /eɪ/ day /ɛ/ get /æ/ hat
/ɑ/ father, hot /ʌ/ up /ə/ about /ɔ/ saw
/oʊ/ hope /ʊ/ book /u/ too /aɪ/ I /aʊ/ how
/ɔɪ/ boy /ɝ/ bird /ɚ/ teacher /ɪr/ ear /ɛr/ air
/ɑr/ far /ɔr/ more /ʊr/ tour /aɪr/ fire
/aʊə-/ hour /θ/ nothing /ð/ mother /ʃ/ she
/ʒ/ measure /tʃ/ church /dʒ/ jump /ŋ/ long

prove it. | *This video **proves that** he was in the building at the time of the murder.*

proverb /'pravə-b/ [*noun*] a short statement that most people know, which often contains advice about life: *Remember the proverb: "Silence is golden"* (=it is often good not to speak).

provide * /prə'vaɪd/ [*verb*; **provided, providing**] to give or supply something to someone: *You bring the drinks, and I'll provide the food.* | **provide something for someone** ▸ *The city should provide play areas for children.* | **provide someone with something** ▸ *The library can provide you with more information.*

provided /prə'vaɪdɪd/ [*conjunction*] used to say that something will happen or be possible only if something else happens: *I'll lend you the money **provided that** you pay it back next week.*

province /'pravɪns/ [*noun*] one of the large areas that some countries are divided into: *Canada has 10 provinces and 3 territories.*

provoke /prə'voʊk/ [*verb*; **provoked, provoking**] to deliberately annoy someone so that he or she gets angry: *What did you do to provoke him?*

prowl /praʊl/ [*verb*; **prowled, prowling**] to move quietly so you will not be heard or seen: *I think I heard someone prowling in the yard.* | *Cougars prowl the mountains here.*

P.S. /'pi'ɛs/ the abbreviation of the word "postscript" (/'poʊst,skrɪpt/), which is written before a sentence that is added at the end of a letter: *P.S. Let me know how you do on your test.*

psalm /sam/ [*noun*] a religious poem that is often sung: *The concert program includes two psalms.*

psychological /,saɪkə'ladʒɪkəl/ [*adjective*; no comparative] relating to the way people think and how this affects their behavior: *His unhappy childhood left him with psychological problems.*

pt. the written abbreviation of PINT or PINTS: *a 1-pt. bottle*

public¹ * T /'pʌblɪk/ [*adjective*; no comparative]
1 available to be used by anyone; *opposite* PRIVATE: *I borrowed the book from the public library.* | *Smoking is now banned in many public places.*
2 relating to the ordinary people in a country: *The law has been changed due to public pressure.*
☛ Only use **public** before a noun.

public² * [*noun*]
1 the public the ordinary people in a country: *The gallery is **open to the public** in the summer.* | *The video will not be sold to **the general public**.* | *The public has the right to know what the government is doing.*
☛ Only use **the public** with a singular verb.

═══ PHRASE ═══

2 in public in a place where people can see or hear you: *It was the first time she had sung in public.*

publication /,pʌblɪ'keɪʃən/ [*noun*] when a book, magazine, etc., is produced and available to buy: *She stopped writing after the **publication of** her third novel.*

publicity /pʌ'blɪsɪti/ [*noun*] the amount of time or space given to someone or something in newspapers, on television, etc.: *Her film received a lot of publicity.*

publicly * /'pʌblɪkli/ [*adverb*] in such a way that everyone can see, hear, or know about something: *The information was not known publicly.*

public school /'pʌblɪk ,skul/ [*noun*] in the U.S., a school that is paid for by the government
⇨ Compare PRIVATE SCHOOL.

publish /'pʌblɪʃ/ [*verb*; **publishes, published, publishing**] to arrange for a book, magazine, or newspaper to be printed and sold: *His first book of poetry was published in 1956.*

publisher /'pʌblɪʃə-/ [*noun*] a person or company that arranges the writing, printing, and sale of books, magazines, or newspapers: *She sent her stories to a small publisher.*

puck /pʌk/ [*noun*] a small, round, hard, flat object used in the sport of HOCKEY

pudding /'pʊdɪŋ/ [*noun*] a sweet food made with eggs, sugar, and milk: *Would you like some more chocolate pudding?*

puddle /'pʌdəl/ [*noun*] a small area of water on the ground: *Kids love splashing through puddles when it rains.*

puff[1] /pʌf/ [*noun*] a short breath or movement of air, smoke, wind, etc.: *He took another puff on his pipe.*

puff[2] [*verb*; **puffed, puffing**] to breathe in quick short breaths: *I was puffing because I ran to catch the train.*

pull[1] ✱ /pʊl/ [*verb*; **pulled, pulling**]
1 to use your hands to make something move toward you; <u>opposite</u> PUSH: *Pull your chair closer to the fire.* | *When she **pulled on** the rope, a bell rang.* | **pull something open/shut** ▸ *He pulled the door shut behind him.*
2 if a vehicle or animal is pulling something, that thing is attached behind it and is being made to move along: *We saw a horse pulling a plow.*

pull[2] ✱ [*noun*] when you pull something or someone: *Give the line **a pull** when you feel a fish bite.*

pulse T /pʌls/ [*noun*] the regular beats of your heart as it pumps blood around your body, which can be felt in your wrist or neck: *The nurse is going to **take your pulse*** (=count the beats).

pump[1] /pʌmp/ [*noun*] a machine that forces liquid or gas into or out of something: *She borrowed my bicycle pump because her tires were flat.*

pump[2] ✱ [*verb*; **pumped, pumping**] to force liquid or gas into or out of something using a machine: *The cellar flooded, so we pumped the water out.*

pumpkin /'pʌmpkɪn/ [*noun*] a large, round, orange VEGETABLE with a hard skin, that is eaten cooked

punch[1] /pʌntʃ/ [*verb*; **punches, punched, punching**]
1 to hit someone or something with your closed hand: *I was so angry I could have punched him.*

─── PHRASE ───
2 **punch a hole** to make a hole in something by pushing something into it: *My brother got mad and punched a hole in the wall.*

punch[2] [*noun*; *plural* **punches**]
1 a drink made of fruit juice mixed

with other things: *There's some fresh punch in the fridge for the kids.*
2 a quick strong hit with your closed hand: *I gave him a **punch on the** nose.*

punctual /'pʌŋktʃuəl/ [*adjective*; **more punctual, most punctual**] arriving at exactly the time that was arranged: *Please be more punctual in the future.*

punctuate /'pʌŋktʃu,eɪt/ [*verb*; **punctuated, punctuating**] to add commas, periods, etc., to a piece of writing: *The assignment is to punctuate these sentences.*

punctuation /,pʌŋktʃu'eɪʃən/ [*noun*] the use of commas, periods, etc., in a piece of writing: *Be more careful with punctuation.* | *a **punctuation mark*** (=a comma, period, etc.)
⇨ See Punctuation *in the Smart Study section.*

puncture /'pʌŋktʃɚ/ [*verb*; **punctured, puncturing**] to make a small hole in something using a sharp object: *a punctured tire*

punish ✱ /'pʌnɪʃ/ [*verb*; **punishes, punished, punishing**] to do something unpleasant to someone because he or she has done something wrong: **punish someone for something** ▸ *His parents punished him for coming home late.*

punishment ✱ /'pʌnɪʃmənt/ [*noun*] the way in which someone is punished for doing something wrong: *The boy had to stand in the corner as a punishment.* | *the **punishment for** a crime*
☛ Do not say "a strong punishment." Say **a harsh punishment** or **a severe punishment**.

pupil ✱ /'pyupəl/ [*noun*]
1 someone who is taught, especially a student in a school: *All pupils must wear uniforms.*
2 the round black part in the middle of your eye: *His pupils were larger than usual.*

/i/ **see** /ɪ/ **big** /eɪ/ **day** /ɛ/ **get** /æ/ **hat** /ɑ/ **father, hot** /ʌ/ **up** /ə/ **about** /ɔ/ **saw** /oʊ/ **hope** /ʊ/ **book** /u/ **too** /aɪ/ **I** /aʊ/ **how** /ɔɪ/ **boy** /ɝ/ **bird** /ɚ/ **teacher** /ɪr/ **ear** /ɛr/ **air** /ɑr/ **far** /ɔr/ **more** /ʊr/ **tour** /aɪr/ **fire** /aʊɚ/ **hour** /θ/ **nothing** /ð/ **mother** /ʃ/ **she** /ʒ/ **measure** /tʃ/ **church** /dʒ/ **jump** /ŋ/ **long**

puppet /'pʌpɪt/ [noun] a model of a person or animal that you can move by pulling strings attached to it or by putting your hand inside it: *The kids put on a **puppet show** (=when a story is told using puppets).*

puppy /'pʌpi/ [noun; plural **puppies**] a young dog

purchase[1] /'pɜˈtʃəs/ [verb; **purchased, purchasing**] to buy something: *The company has purchased new computers.*

purchase[2] [noun] the act of buying something, or something that you buy: *The clerk put her purchases in a bag.*

pure * /pyʊr/ [adjective; **purer, purest**]
 1 not mixed with anything else: *This coat is 100% pure wool.*
 2 without anything dirty or harmful in it: *pure mountain air*

purely /'pyʊrli/ [adverb] only and completely: *I met him purely by chance.*

purple[1] * /'pɜˈpəl/ [noun] a dark color made by mixing red and blue: *That's a beautiful shade of purple.*

purple[2] * [adjective; **more purple, most purple**] of the color purple: *purple grapes*

purpose * /'pɜˈpəs/ [noun]
 1 what you hope to achieve by doing something: *The **purpose of** these tests is to find out who may need extra help.*
 — PHRASE
 2 **on purpose** deliberately; *opposite* ACCIDENTALLY: *I'm sorry—I didn't do it on purpose!*

purposely /'pɜˈpəsli/ [adverb] done deliberately: *We purposely arrived early to set up the chairs.*

purr /pɜˈ/ [verb; **purred, purring**] if a cat purrs, it makes a soft low sound in its throat: *The cat lay on her lap, purring.*

purse /pɜˈs/ [noun] a small bag in which a woman carries money and personal things; *synonym* HANDBAG: *She bought some navy shoes and a matching purse.*

push[1] * /pʊʃ/ [verb; **pushes, pushed, pushing**]
 1 to use your hands to make something move away from you or move along in front of you; *opposite* PULL: *Stop pushing! I **Push** harder **on** the door—it's stuck. I He **pushed** her **into** the pool.*
 2 to press part of a machine to make it do something: *Push the green button to start the fax machine.*

push[2] * [noun; plural **pushes**] when you push something or someone: *She **gave** him **a push** on his sled.*

put * /pʊt/ [verb; **puts, put, put, putting**]
 1 to move something in a particular place or position: *She put her bag down by the door. I Do you remember where I put the scissors? I They put up a painting over the fireplace.*
 2 to change the situation someone is in or the way he or she feels: *The use of computers may put people out of work. I Music always puts me in a good mood.*
 3 to write or print something somewhere: *What answer did you put for question five?*
 — PHRASAL VERBS
 put away [phrasal verb]
 4 to put something in the place where you usually keep it: **put away something** ▸ *Could you help me put away all these books? I* **put something away** ▸ *You can play with the train set, but put it away afterward.*
 put back [phrasal verb]
 5 to put things in the place they were in before: **put something back** ▸ *Please put the CDs back in their boxes.*
 put off [phrasal verb]
 6 to not do something, and intend to do it later: **put something off** ▸ *I had homework to do, but I kept putting it off. I* **put off doing something** ▸ *You shouldn't put off paying your bills.*
 put on [phrasal verb]
 7 to put a piece of clothing on your body: **put something on** ▸ *I put my pajamas on. I* **put on something** ▸ *She put on her best dress.*
 ⇨ *Compare* **take off** *at* TAKE (definition 15). ⇨ *See the synonym note at* DRESS[2].
 8 to put a substance on a surface; *synonym* APPLY: *Wait, let me put my lipstick on.*
 put out [phrasal verb]
 9 to stop a fire, cigarette, etc., from burning: **put something out** ▸ *She put*

the candles out. | **put out something** ▸
He put out the fire by stamping on it.
put together [phrasal verb]
10 to make or build something that has
many pieces: **put something
together** ▸ Dad and I put my new bike
together.
put up [phrasal verb]
11 to build a structure: **put up
something** ▸ They're putting up a new
office building there.
put up with [phrasal verb]
12 to accept someone's bad behavior or
a bad situation and not try to change
it: **put up with something** ▸ I don't
know how you put up with him!

USAGE   put, set, lay

Use **put** to talk in general about leaving
something in a place or on an object: She
put her coat in the closet. | Put the book
back on the shelf.

Use **set** to talk about putting something
somewhere carefully or slowly: She set the
vase on the table. | He set his book down
and looked at her.

Use **lay** especially for clothes and other
things that lie flat: She laid a quilt over her
daughter.

---

puzzle Ⓣ /'pʌzəl/ [noun] a game or toy
in which you have to solve a problem: I
like doing **crossword puzzles**. | The
jigsaw puzzle had 500 pieces.
puzzled /'pʌzəld/ [adjective; **more
puzzled, most puzzled**] confused and
unable to understand something: She
read the letter, looking puzzled.
pyramid /'pɪrəmɪd/ [noun] a solid
shape with a square flat base and sides
shaped like triangles that meet at a
point at the top, or a large stone
building in this shape
▷ See **Shapes** in the Smart Study section.

Q

Q * or **q** /kyu/ [noun; plural Qs or Q's, q's]
the 17th letter of the English alphabet
▷ See the usage note at **ALPHABET**.
qt. the written abbreviation of **QUART** or
QUARTS: a 2-qt. saucepan
quack /kwæk/ [verb; **quacked,
quacking**] if a duck quacks, it makes a
rough sound from its throat: We heard
ducks quacking on the pond.
quake /kweɪk/ [verb; **quaked, quaking**]
FORMAL to shake violently: Suddenly, the
earth began to quake.
qualification Ⓣ /ˌkwɑləfɪ'keɪʃən/
[noun] something you achieve or learn
that gives you the right skills for
something: He doesn't have the right
qualifications to work in a bank.
☛ This word is usually used in the plural.
qualified Ⓣ /'kwɑləˌfaɪd/ [adjective;
more qualified, most qualified]
having the skills or knowledge you
need for something: She's a **highly
qualified** lawyer. | **qualified to do/be
something** ▸ I'm not really qualified to
answer that.

qualify /'kwɑləˌfaɪ/ [verb; **qualifies,
qualified, qualifying**] to pass a test or
gain the skills that you need in order to
do something: The team has **qualified
for** a place in the finals.
quality * Ⓣ /'kwɑlɪti/ [noun; plural
qualities]
1 used to talk about how good or bad
something is: The quality of her work
has improved recently. | They used **poor
quality** (=bad quality) materials. |
These paintings are **of** very **high quality**
(=very good quality).
2 a basic feature of someone or
something, especially a good feature:
He has all the qualities of a good
teacher.
quantity * /'kwɑntɪti/ [noun; plural
quantities] an amount of something:
You only need a small **quantity of** flour. |
They sell large **quantities of** oil.
quarrel[1] /'kwɔrəl/ [verb; **quarreled,
quarreling**] to argue with someone,
especially about something that is
not important: You two are always
quarreling about something.

☛ Do not say that people "quarrel something" or "quarrel for something." Say that they **quarrel about it** or **quarrel over it**.

quarrel[2] [*noun*] an angry disagreement with someone: *They're having another quarrel.*

quarry /ˈkwɔri/ [*noun; plural* **quarries**] a large hole in the ground from which stone is dug: *My father worked in the quarry for twenty years.*

quart * /kwɔrt/ [*noun*] a unit for measuring liquids, equal to two pints or 0.95 liters: *We need two quarts of milk.*

quarter * /ˈkwɔrtɚ/ [*noun*]
1 one of four equal parts into which something is divided; *synonym* FOURTH: *Cut the sandwiches into quarters for the kids.* | *A quarter of the land belongs to her brother.*
2 a COIN equal to one fourth of a dollar (25 cents): *The candy machine takes quarters or dollar bills.*
3 one of the four parts into which the year is divided in some schools and colleges; *synonym* TERM: *I got a B in chemistry this quarter.*
➪ Compare SEMESTER.
━━ PHRASES ━━
4 **a quarter of an hour** or **a quarter hour** fifteen minutes: *I'll be ready in a quarter of an hour.*
5 **a quarter to six/ten/twelve/etc.** or **a quarter of six/ten/twelve/etc.** used when telling the time to mean fifteen minutes before six, ten, twelve, etc.: *"I'll meet you at a quarter to three." "Can we meet at quarter of four instead?"*
6 **a quarter after six/ten/twelve/etc.** or **a quarter past six/ten/twelve/etc.** used when telling the time to mean fifteen minutes past six, ten, twelve, etc.: *It's a quarter after five.* | *The train is due at a quarter past seven.*

quarterly[1] /ˈkwɔrtɚli/ [*adjective; no comparative*] happening, done, or produced every three months: *a quarterly journal* | *a company's quarterly profits*
☛ Only use **quarterly** before a noun.

quarterly[2] [*adverb*] every three months: *You can pay your bills quarterly.*

quartet /kwɔrˈtɛt/ [*noun*] four musicians or singers who perform together, or music for this: *a string quartet* (=played on violin, cello, etc.)

queen * /kwin/ [*noun*] the female ruler of a country, or the wife of a king: *She became queen in 1952.* | *Queen Elizabeth*

quench /kwɛntʃ/ [*verb;* **quenches, quenched, quenching**]
━━ PHRASE ━━
quench your thirst to drink something so that you no longer feel thirsty: *Alcoholic drinks don't really quench your thirst.*

question[1] * /ˈkwɛstʃən/ [*noun*]
1 a sentence that is used to ask someone something: *Please answer my question.* | *Bobby asks questions all the time.*
☛ Do not say "question someone a question." Say **ask someone a question**.
━━ PHRASES ━━
2 **out of the question** if something is out of the question, it definitely cannot happen: *No, you can't go to the party. It's out of the question.*
3 **be a question of money/trust/ etc.** used when you are giving an important reason for not doing something, or an important point that must be considered: *I'd like a bigger apartment; it's just a question of money.*

USAGE Asking questions

In English, questions end with a question mark (?).

Simple questions put the auxiliary verb before the subject: *Does he want to come with us?*

If you think something is true but you are not sure, you can make a statement, then add a short question at the end of it. Short questions use only the auxiliary and the subject. A negative statement gets a positive question, and a positive statement gets a negative question: *He doesn't want to come with us, does he?* | *He wants to come with us, doesn't he?*

You can also answer a question with a short statement. To say that what someone says is true, use the same positive or negative form of the verb that the question has: *"Does he want to come?" "Yes, he does."* | *"Doesn't he want to come?" "No, he doesn't."*

To disagree or say that the opposite is true, use the opposite form of the verb: *"Does he want to come?" "No, he doesn't."* | *"Doesn't he want to come?" "Yes, he does."*

☛ Do not say "Yes, he doesn't" or "No, he does."

question² * [*verb*; **questioned, questioning**]
1 to ask someone questions in order to find out what he or she knows about something, or as part of a test: *The police want to **question** him **about** a robbery.* | *Students will be **questioned on** all five subjects.*
☛ Do not say "question someone history." Say **question someone on history**.
2 to say that you are not certain whether something is correct or reasonable: *I question the truth of his statement.*

question mark /'kwɛstʃən ˌmɑrk/ [*noun*] a mark used in writing. It looks like this: **?**
➪ *See* Punctuation *in the Smart Study section.*

questionnaire /ˌkwɛstʃə'nɛr/ [*noun*] a list of questions given to a large number of people to find out their opinions, habits, etc.: *I had to **fill out a** a **questionnaire** in health class.*

quick¹ * /kwɪk/ [*adjective*; **quicker, quickest**]
1 taking a very short amount of time; *opposite* SLOW: *Let's have a quick swim before dinner.* | *It will be quicker if you do the work yourself.* | **be quick to do something** ▸ *He is very quick to learn.*
2 moving fast; *opposite* SLOW: *She worked with quick movements of her hands.*
═══ PHRASE ═══
3 be quick used to tell someone to come quickly or do something faster: *Be quick—the taxi will be here soon.*

quick² [*adverb*] moving or happening fast: *Come quick! There's been an accident.*

quickly * ⊤ /'kwɪkli/ [*adverb*] moving or happening fast; *opposite* SLOWLY: *She ran down the stairs as quickly as she could.* | *You can learn this exercise very quickly.*

───────────────────
USAGE quickly, soon

Use **quickly** to talk about how fast someone does something: *He dressed quickly and left the house.* Use **soon** to talk about time: *He will be here soon.*
───────────────────

quiet¹ * /'kwaɪt/ [*adjective*; **quieter, quietest**]
1 without any sound or with very little sound; *opposite* NOISY: *The house was quiet.* | *It got quiet when the teacher entered the room.*
2 making no sound or very little sound, or not talking very much; *opposite* LOUD: *We have very quiet neighbors.* | *You're very quiet today—are you OK?* | *Please be quiet—I have a headache.*
3 without much activity; *opposite* BUSY: *The stores are very quiet in the afternoon.*

quiet² * [*noun*]
the quiet when there is very little sound: *He likes the quiet of the countryside.*

quietly * /'kwaɪtli/ [*adverb*] if you do something quietly, you do it without making any sound or with very little sound; *opposite* LOUDLY: *He quietly closed the door behind him.* | *Please speak quietly so you don't wake the baby.*

quilt /kwɪlt/ [*noun*] a thick soft cover for a bed: *She pulled the quilt up around her shoulders.*

quintet /kwɪn'tɛt/ [*noun*] five musicians or singers who perform together, or music for this: *a brass quartet* (=played on trumpets, trombones, etc.)

quit /kwɪt/ [*verb*; **quits, quit, quit, quitting**] to stop happening or to stop doing something: *I don't want to play anymore. I quit!* | *It would be silly to quit*

───────────────────
/i/ **see** /ɪ/ **big** /eɪ/ **day** /ɛ/ **get** /æ/ **hat**
/ɑ/ **father, hot** /ʌ/ **up** /ə/ **about** /ɔ/ **saw**
/oʊ/ **hope** /ʊ/ **book** /u/ **too** /aɪ/ **I** /aʊ/ **how**
/ɔɪ/ **boy** /ɜ/ **bird** /ɚ/ **teacher** /ɪr/ **ear** /ɛr/ **air**
/ɑr/ **far** /ɔr/ **more** /ʊr/ **tour** /aɪr/ **fire**
/aʊɚ/ **hour** /θ/ **nothing** /ð/ **mother** /ʃ/ **she**
/ʒ/ **measure** /tʃ/ **church** /dʒ/ **jump** /ŋ/ **long**

your job. | **quit doing something** ▸ *Quit bothering us!*

quite * /kwaɪt/ [*adverb*]
1 used to make an adjective, adverb, or noun stronger: *This is quite interesting.* | *You gave us quite a shock.* | *We had to wait quite a long time.*

═══ PHRASES ═══

2 not quite not completely: *I haven't quite finished.* | *"Is dinner ready yet?" "Not quite."*
☛ Do not say "I'm not very finished." Say **I'm not quite finished.**

3 quite a few a fairly large number: *We had quite a few complaints.* | *Quite a few of my friends have computers.*

quiver /'kwɪvɚ/ [*verb*; **quivered, quivering**] to shake, especially because you are afraid or excited: *His lip was quivering, then he started to cry.*

quiz /kwɪz/ [*noun*; *plural* **quizzes**]
1 a short test given by a teacher: *We have a math quiz every Friday.*

2 a short test done for fun: *I won a CD in a quiz run by the local radio station.*

quotation /kwoʊ'teɪʃən/ [*noun*] a phrase or a few sentences taken from a book or speech and repeated somewhere else; <u>synonym</u> QUOTE: *Her speech was full of famous quotations.*

quotation marks /kwoʊ'teɪʃən ˌmɑrks/ [*plural*] a pair of marks used in writing. They look like this: " "
↪ *See also* QUOTE² (definition 2).
↪ *See* Punctuation *in the Smart Study section.*

quote¹ /kwoʊt/ [*verb*; **quoted, quoting**] to repeat a phrase or a few sentences from a book, speech, etc.: *I can't quote exactly what she said.* | *He's always quoting from other writers.*

quote² [*noun*]
1 the short form of QUOTATION: *What's that famous quote about fear?*
2 quotes [*plural*] the short form of QUOTATION MARKS: *The words "Keep Out" were written **in quotes**.*

▬ R ▬

R * or **r** /ɑr/ [*noun*; *plural* **Rs** or **R's, r's**] the 18th letter of the English alphabet
↪ *See the usage note at* ALPHABET.

rabbi 🔊 /'ræbaɪ/ [*noun*; *plural* **rabbis**] a Jewish religious leader, especially one who performs religious ceremonies and duties in a synagogue

rabbit * /'ræbɪt/ [*noun*] an animal that has long ears and two long front teeth, which lives in a hole under the ground

race¹ * /reɪs/ [*noun*]

a rabbit

1 a competition in which runners, drivers, etc., try to be the fastest to travel a particular distance: *He **won** the **race** easily.* | *a bicycle race*
2 one of the groups of human beings that have the same physical features,

skin color, etc.: *People of many different races live in the U.S.* | *a discussion about race and religion*

race² * [*verb*; **raced, racing**] to take part in a race: *She will be **racing against** the world champion tomorrow.* | *I'll race you to the end of the street.*

racehorse /'reɪsˌhɔrs/ [*noun*] a horse that runs in races.

racetrack /'reɪsˌtræk/ [*noun*] a wide flat path or road where races take place; <u>synonym</u> TRACK

racial 🔊 /'reɪʃəl/ [*adjective*; *no comparative*] relating to someone's race: *There are some racial differences between the two communities.*

racism /'reɪsɪzəm/ [*noun*] the belief that your own race is better than others, especially when you show this by treating people of other races unfairly: *Racism will not be tolerated in this school.*

racist¹ /'reɪsɪst/ [*adjective*; **more racist, most racist**] treating people of other races in a cruel or unfair way, or believing that they are not as good as you: *He's so racist.* | *a racist remark*

racist[2] [*noun*] someone who is racist: *He accused me of being a racist.*

rack /ræk/ [*noun*]
1 a shelf made of bars, usually metal ones: *a luggage rack on a car* | *an oven rack*
↪ See the picture at **STOVE**.
2 an object that has several parts that things can hang from: *a coat rack*

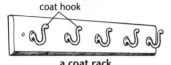

coat hook

a coat rack

racket * /'rækɪt/ [*noun*]
1 an object used for hitting the ball in games such as **TENNIS**: *Can I borrow your tennis racket?*
2 INFORMAL a lot of loud, unpleasant noise: *Stop making that racket!*

radar /'reɪdar/ [*noun*] a way of finding the position or speed of an object that cannot be seen, by using radio waves: *The ship was on our radar screen.*

radiation /ˌreɪdi'eɪʃən/ [*noun*] a kind of energy that comes from the sun, from some substances, or from bombs and can be dangerous to people, animals, and plants

radiator /'reɪdiˌeɪtɚ/ [*noun*]
1 a metal object that hot water runs through, used for heating a room
2 the part of a car that cools the water to prevent the engine from getting too hot.

a radiator

radio * /'reɪdiˌoʊ/ [*noun; plural* **radios**]
1 a piece of electronic equipment that is used to listen to music and programs that are broadcast: *Turn the radio up* (=increase the sound).
2 the system of broadcasting programs for the radio, or the programs themselves: *a radio show* | *Dad's upstairs **listening to the radio**.* | *What's that song they're playing **on the radio**?*

radish /'rædɪʃ/ [*noun; plural* **radishes**] a small white or red root with a hot taste that is eaten raw as a vegetable

radius /'reɪdiəs/ [*noun; plural* **radii** /'reɪdiaɪ/] the distance from the center of a circle to the edge of it, measured in a straight line: *What is the **radius of** this circle?*
↪ See the picture at **DIAMETER**.

radishes

raft /ræft/ [*noun*] a simple boat made of rubber or of pieces of wood joined together.

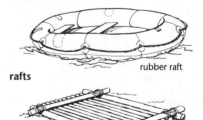

rafts

rubber raft

wooden raft

rag /ræg/ [*noun*]
1 an old or torn piece of cloth, used especially for cleaning things: *These rags are for polishing shoes.*
━━ PHRASE ━━
2 **in rags** if someone's clothes are in

/i/ **see** /ɪ/ **big** /eɪ/ **day** /ɛ/ **get** /æ/ **hat**
/ɑ/ **father, hot** /ʌ/ **up** /ə/ **about** /ɔ/ **saw**
/oʊ/ **hope** /ʊ/ **book** /u/ **too** /aɪ/ **I** /aʊ/ **how**
/ɔɪ/ **boy** /ɝ/ **bird** /ɚ/ **teacher** /ɪr/ **ear** /ɛr/ **air**
/ɑr/ **far** /ɔr/ **more** /ʊr/ **tour** /aɪr/ **fire**
/aʊɚ/ **hour** /θ/ **nothing** /ð/ **mother** /ʃ/ **she**
/ʒ/ **measure** /tʃ/ **church** /dʒ/ **jump** /ŋ/ **long**

rags, they are old, torn, and dirty: *The children were dressed in rags.*

rage /reɪdʒ/ [*noun*]
1 an extremely strong feeling of anger; *synonym* FURY: *Her face went red with rage.*
— PHRASE —
2 **in a rage** extremely angry: *He was in a rage because someone hit his car.*

raid[1] /reɪd/ [*verb*; **raided, raiding**] to suddenly enter a place to attack it, to search for something, or to steal something: *The police raided the house, looking for stolen goods.*

raid[2] [*noun*] when soldiers, police, or thieves suddenly enter a place to attack it, search for something, or steal something: *an air raid* (=when a place is attacked by planes) | *a bank raid*

rail /reɪl/ [*noun*]
1 one of the two metal bars on the ground on which a train travels: *They had to clear snow from the rails.*
2 travel by train: *The town is easy to reach by rail or road.* | *the rail network*
3 a wood or metal bar along a wall that you can hold so that you do not fall: *She walked down the steps, holding onto the rail.*
⤷ *See the picture at* STAIR.

railing /'reɪlɪŋ/ [*noun*] a wood or metal bar supported by posts that stops people from falling: *A car went through the railing at the side of the road.*
⤷ *See the picture at* STAIR.

railroad * /'reɪl,roʊd/ [*noun*]
1 a track made of metal bars over which a train travels: *A bridge carries the railroad across the valley.* | *a railroad track*
2 a company that owns and uses a system of rail tracks for trains: *My father works for the railroad.*

rain[1] * /reɪn/ [*noun*]
1 water that falls in drops from clouds: *We've had a lot of rain this spring.*
☛ Do not say "big rain." Say **heavy rain**.
— PHRASE —
2 **look like rain** if it looks like rain, it will probably rain because there are dark clouds: *It looked like rain so we brought our umbrellas.*

☛ Do not say "It looks like raining." Say **It looks like rain**.

rain[2] * [*verb*; **rained, raining**] if it rains, water falls in drops from clouds: *It rained all day.* | *It's still raining.*
☛ Do not say "It rained big." Say **It rained heavily** or **It rained hard**.

rainbow /'reɪn,boʊ/ [*noun*] a curve of colors that appears in the sky when light from the sun passes through drops of rain.

a rainbow

raincoat /'reɪn,koʊt/ [*noun*] a long coat that stops you from getting wet when it is raining.

raindrop /'reɪn,drɑp/ [*noun*] one drop of rain: *Raindrops ran down the window.*

rainfall /'reɪn,fɔl/ [*noun*] the rain that falls at a particular time and place: *There was a heavy rainfall this morning.* | *Rainfall for this month was below average.*

rain forest /'reɪn ,fɔrɪst/ [*noun*] a thick forest where it rains a lot: *Much of Latin America's rain forest has been destroyed.*

USAGE   rain forest, jungle

Both these words mean "a wet forest with many trees growing close together." Use **rain forest** when you are talking about the environment.

rainy /'reɪni/ [*adjective*; **rainier, rainiest**]
1 when there is a lot of rain: *On rainy days, the children play indoors.*
— PHRASE —
2 **save something for a rainy day** to save money for a time in the future when you will need it: *I've got some cash that I've been saving for a rainy day.*

raise[1] * ⊤ /reɪz/ [*verb*; **raised, raising**]
1 to move something to a higher position; *opposite* LOWER: *Raise your arms above your head.* | *You'll need to raise the shelf about an inch.*
⤷ *See the usage note at* RISE[1].

2 to increase the level or amount of something; *opposite* LOWER: *The store raised the price of many of its goods.* | *The teacher had to* **raise his voice** (=speak louder) *to be heard.*
3 to collect money to give to someone: *He raised $4,000 for charity.*
4 to take care of a child from a young age until he or she is grown: *Mom died and my Dad raised me by himself.*

raise[2] [*noun*] an increase in the amount of money you get for the work that you do: *I'm going to* **ask** *my boss* **for a raise.**

raisin /'reɪzɪn/ [*noun*] a small dried grape that you can eat.

rake[1] /reɪk/ [*noun*] a garden TOOL with a long handle and long thin flat parts at the end, used to gather leaves from the ground, make the earth level, etc.

rake[2] [*verb;* **raked, raking**] to use a rake to gather leaves together, make the earth level, etc.: *She's outside raking the lawn.*

ram /ræm/ [*verb;* **rams, rammed, ramming**] to hit or push something with a lot of force: *The truck rammed a telephone pole.*

RAM [*noun*] the part of a computer where information is kept only while it is being used: *My computer has 128 megabytes of RAM.*

ramp /ræmp/ [*noun*]
1 a long sloping path or structure that you walk along to go from one level to another: *a ramp for wheelchair users*
2 a road leading on or off a highway: *the* **on ramp** | *the* **off ramp**

ran * /ræn/ [*verb*] the past tense of RUN[1]

ranch /ræntʃ/ [*noun; plural* **ranches**] a large area of land where horses, cattle, or sheep are raised.

rang * /ræŋ/ [*verb*] the past tense of RING[2]

range[1] * /reɪndʒ/ [*noun*]
1 the limits between which something can change or be different: *a range in temperature of between five and ten degrees Celsius*
2 a number of similar products or other things; *synonym* SELECTION: *The store stocks a* **wide range of** *children's books.*

3 a group of mountains that form a line: *We've been hiking in that mountain range before*

range[2] [*verb;* **ranged, ranging**] to change or be different within particular limits: *Book prices* **range from** $5.00 **to** $100.

rank[1] * /ræŋk/ [*noun*] the official position of someone in the police force or in the army, navy, etc.: *He quickly rose to the rank of captain.*

rank[2] [*verb;* **ranked, ranking**]
1 to have or be given a particular place or position in a group: *She ranks in the top 5 percent of her graduating class.*
2 to place someone or something in order as part of a group: *The students are ranked by ability.*

ransom /'rænsəm/ [*noun*] money that is paid to a person or group so they will let a prisoner go: *The kidnappers* **demanded a ransom** *of a million dollars.*

rap /ræp/ [*noun*] popular music in which words are spoken to a strong beat.

rape[1] /reɪp/ [*verb;* **raped, raping**] to force someone to have sex: *Soldiers raped women in the village.*

rape[2] [*noun*] the crime of forcing someone to have sex.

rapid * /'ræpɪd/ [*adjective;* **more rapid, most rapid**] moving, happening, or being done quickly; *synonym* FAST: *Her heartbeat became more rapid.* | *He is making rapid progress in his studies.*

rapidly * Ⓣ /'ræpɪdli/ [*adverb*] quickly: *The temperature was rising rapidly.*

rapper /'ræpɚ/ [*noun*] someone who performs rap music: *Who's your favorite rapper?*

rare * Ⓣ /rɛr/ [*adjective;* **rarer, rarest**] not happening very often, or not existing in many places; *synonym* UNCOMMON; *opposite* COMMON: *The zoo contains many rare animals.*

/i/ **see**	/ɪ/ **big**	/eɪ/ **day**	/ɛ/ **get**	/æ/ **hat**
/ɑ/ **father, hot**	/ʌ/ **up**	/ə/ **about**	/ɔ/ **saw**	
/oʊ/ **hope**	/ʊ/ **book**	/u/ **too**	/aɪ/ **I**	/aʊ/ **how**
/ɔɪ/ **boy**	/ɝ/ **bird**	/ɚ/ **teacher**	/ɪr/ **ear**	/ɛr/ **air**
/ɑr/ **far**	/ɔr/ **more**	/ʊr/ **tour**	/aɪr/ **fire**	
/aʊɚ/ **hour**	/θ/ **nothing**	/ð/ **mother**	/ʃ/ **she**	
/ʒ/ **measure**	/tʃ/ **church**	/dʒ/ **jump**	/ŋ/ **long**	

USAGE rare, scarce

Do not confuse **rare** and **scarce**. Use **rare** to talk about things that are valuable or unusual because there are not very many of them: *Paintings like this are very rare.* Use **scarce** to talk about things that are difficult to get at a particular time: *In times of drought, food is scarce.*

rarely T /ˈrɛrli/ [*adverb*] not at all often; *opposite* FREQUENTLY: *I'm rarely sick.*

rash /ræʃ/ [*noun; plural* **rashes**] an area of spots or redness on your skin, especially one that appears when you are ill.

raspberry /ˈræzˌbɛri/ [*noun; plural* **raspberries**] a small, soft, red fruit that grows on bushes

rat * /ræt/ [*noun*] an animal that looks like a big mouse and has a long tail.

a rat

rate * T /reɪt/ [*noun*]
1 the number of times that something happens, or the number of people affected by something, in a particular period of time: *a low rate of unemployment* I *This method has a good success rate* (=is very often successful).
2 the speed at which something happens or is done: *Children learn to read at different rates.*
3 an amount of money: *They are working for very low rates of pay.*

rather * /ˈræðɚ/ [*adverb*]
1 a little, but not very or not completely; *synonym* FAIRLY: *Aren't you driving rather fast?*
═══ PHRASES ═══
2 **would rather** if you would rather do one thing than another, you prefer to do the first thing: *I'd rather stay in bed than get up early.* I *He'd rather you came by another day.*
3 **rather than** instead of: *Rather than taking the bus, I decided to walk.*

rattle¹ /ˈrætəl/ [*verb;* **rattled, rattling**] to make a noise by shaking and hitting something, or to shake something so that it makes this noise: *The shutters rattled in the storm.* I *Stop rattling your bracelets!*
⇨ *See the synonym note at* SHAKE.

rattle² [*noun*]
1 a baby's toy that makes a noise when you shake it
2 the noise of something rattling: *Do you hear that rattle in the engine?*

a baby's **rattle**

raw * /rɔ/ [*adjective; no comparative*] raw food is not cooked: *Raw vegetables are good for you.*

ray /reɪ/ [*noun; plural* **rays**] a narrow beam of light: *A ray of light shone through a crack in the door.*

razor /ˈreɪzɚ/ [*noun*] an object used for cutting hair off your body: *Dad shaves with a disposable razor* (=one you can throw away). I *an electric razor*

razor blade /ˈreɪzɚ ˌbleɪd/ [*noun*] a sharp, narrow blade in a razor

Rd. the written abbreviation of ROAD: *Her address is 101 Station Rd.*

're /r/ the short form of ARE: *You're early.* I *We're going shopping.*

reach¹ * /ritʃ/ [*verb;* **reaches, reached, reaching**]
1 to arrive at a place: *When you reach the end of the block, turn left.*
☛ Do not use "reach to" in this meaning. For example, do not say "The boat reached to the shore." Say **The boat reached the shore.**
2 to manage to touch or get something by stretching your arm: *Put medicines where children can't reach them.*
3 to stretch your arm to try and touch or get something: *I reached out and touched her face.* I *He reached for his glass but knocked it over.*
⇨ *See the picture at* MOVEMENT.
4 to be tall or long enough to touch something: *Her dress reached the floor.* I *I can't wash the top windows because my ladder doesn't reach.*

5 to become a particular level or amount: *The rate of inflation reached 10%.* | *The river has reached flood level.*

reach² *[noun]*

═══ **PHRASES** ═══

1 **in reach** or **within reach** close enough to be reached easily: *The stores are in easy reach of the hotel.* | *I keep a flashlight within reach of my bed.*

2 **out of reach** far away and difficult for you to reach: *The box was on the top shelf, out of reach.*

react * [T] /riˈækt/ *[verb; reacted, reacting]* to say or do something after you hear about something, when something happens, etc.: *How did he react to your suggestion?*

reaction * [T] /riˈækʃən/ *[noun]* what you say or do when you hear about something, when something happens, etc.: *What was his reaction when he won?* | *Public reaction to the plan has been positive.*

read * /rid/ *[verb; reads, read /rɛd/, read /rɛd/, reading]*

1 to look at written or printed words and understand them: *I'm reading the newspaper.* | *She can't read yet—she's only three years old.*

2 to say written or printed words out loud: *I have to read the poem aloud in class* (=read it so that everyone can hear). | **read someone something** ▸ *Will you read me a story?*

☛ Do not say "read to someone something." Say **read someone something** or **read something to someone.**

═══ **PHRASAL VERB** ═══

read through/over *[phrasal verb]*

3 to read something to check if there are any mistakes or to get a general idea of what it is about: **read something through/over** ▸ *Will you read my paper through for me?* | **read through/over something** ▸ *I read over the instructions before starting.*

PRONUNCIATION   read

When **read** is a present tense form, it is pronounced /rid/. When it is a past tense form or a past participle, it is pronounced /rɛd/.

---

reader /ˈridɚ/ *[noun]*

1 someone who reads: *a good reader*

2 someone who reads a particular magazine, book, etc.: *Readers of The Daily News have been following this story with interest.*

readily [T] /ˈrɛdəli/ *[adverb]*

1 quickly and easily: *The information is readily available.*

2 in a willing way: *He readily agreed to help us.*

ready * /ˈrɛdi/ *[adjective; no comparative]*

1 prepared or in a suitable condition to do something or be used: **ready to do something** ▸ *Are you ready to leave?* | **be ready for something** ▸ *The children were ready for bed by 7 o'clock.* | **get ready** ▸ *She is still getting ready.* | **get something ready** ▸ *I'll get dinner ready.*

2 willing to do something: **ready to do something** ▸ *He is always ready to help.*

real * /ˈriəl/ *[adjective; no comparative]*

1 existing, not pretended or imagined; *opposites* IMAGINARY, MADE-UP: *It's a true story about a real person.* | *That never happens in real life.*

2 actual, not a copy: *Are those real diamonds?*

☛ Do not say "true gems" or "true gold." Say **real gems** or **real gold.**

3 true, not made up: *Is that his real name?*

4 INFORMAL used to emphasize a noun: *You've made a real mess of this.*

▷ *See also* REALLY.

real estate /ˈriəl ɪˌsteɪt/ *[noun]* land and buildings: *I don't own any real estate.*

real estate agent /ˈriəl ɪˌsteɪt ˌeɪdʒənt/ *[noun]* someone who sells land and buildings; *synonym* REALTOR: *The real estate agent showed us four houses today.*

reality /riˈælɪti/ *[noun]*

1 real things, facts, events, etc.: *It's nice to read a book and escape from reality for a while.*

/i/ **see** /ɪ/ **big** /eɪ/ **day** /ɛ/ **get** /æ/ **hat**
/ɑ/ **father, hot** /ʌ/ **up** /ə/ **about** /ɔ/ **saw**
/oʊ/ **hope** /ʊ/ **book** /u/ **too** /aɪ/ **I** /aʊ/ **how**
/ɔɪ/ **boy** /ɝ/ **bird** /ɚ/ **teacher** /ɪr/ **ear** /ɛr/ **air**
/ɑr/ **far** /ɔr/ **more** /ʊr/ **tour** /aɪr/ **fire**
/aʊɚ/ **hour** /θ/ **nothing** /ð/ **mother** /ʃ/ **she**
/ʒ/ **measure** /tʃ/ **church** /dʒ/ **jump** /ŋ/ **long**

— PHRASE —
2 in reality used to say what the real situation is, not the imagined or pretended one: *She said she's a doctor, but in reality she's still in training.*

realization /ˌriələˈzeɪʃən/ [*noun*] when someone realizes something: *I've come to the realization that I need a new job.*

realize * /ˈriəˌlaɪz/ [*verb*; **realized, realizing**] to suddenly understand or notice something: *I realized my mistake right away.* | **realize (that)** ▸ *Did you realize your zipper was undone?* | **realize what/why/how/when/etc.** ▸ *Now I realize why she was so angry.*

really * /ˈriəli/ [*adverb*]
1 very: *The store was really busy.*
2 used to give the actual truth about a situation: *She's not really angry—she's just pretending.* | *Is he really that old?*
— PHRASES —
3 really? SPOKEN used to reply to someone who has told you something surprising: *"I have ten cats." "Really?"*
4 not really SPOKEN used to answer no: *"Did you enjoy the meal?" "Not really."*

Realtor /ˈriəltɚ/ [*noun*] TRADEMARK someone who sells land and buildings; *synonym* REAL ESTATE AGENT: *Ellie was the best Realtor we'd met.*

reappear /ˌriəˈpɪr/ [*verb*; **reappeared, reappearing**] to be somewhere again or to happen again: *He went into the building and reappeared an hour later.* | *The same old problems keep reappearing.*

rear[1] /rɪr/ [*adjective*; *no comparative*] used to talk about the back part of something; *synonym* BACK: *Please use the rear door.* | *The rear seat belts are broken.*
☛ Only use **rear** before a noun.

rear[2] [*noun*]
the rear the back part of something: *The kitchen is at the rear of the house.*
➪ See also **the back** at BACK[2].

rear[3] [*verb*; **reared, rearing**]
1 to take care of a child or animal from a young age until he or she is grown up: *Bears are more fierce when they are rearing their young.*
2 if a horse rears, it lifts its front legs and stands on its back ones: *Sudden noises can make a horse rear.*

rearrange /ˌriəˈreɪndʒ/ [*verb*; **rearranged, rearranging**]
1 to move things so that they are in different positions: *I decided to rearrange the furniture.*
2 to change the times or order of events: *This afternoon's classes have been rearranged.*

reason * /ˈrizən/ [*noun*]
1 why something happens or is done: *Do you know **the reason** she left early?* | *There are good **reasons for** exercising.* | *He just hit me **for no reason** (=I did not do anything to make him do it).*
☛ Do not say "the reason of." Say **the reason for.**
➪ See the usage note at CAUSE[2].
2 good judgment and understanding: *She refuses to **listen to reason** (=listen to sensible advice).* | *I wish you'd **see reason** (=start behaving in a sensible way).*

SYNONYMS reason, explanation, excuse

A **reason** for something is why you do it: *The reason I'm calling is to tell you about the party.* An **explanation** is when you explain to someone why you have done something, why something happened, etc.: *Will you please listen to my explanation?* An **excuse** is a reason you give for doing something wrong or bad: *She says she's tired, but that's just an excuse for not working.*

reasonable * /ˈrizənəbəl/ [*adjective*; **more reasonable, most reasonable**]
1 sensible and fair; *opposite* UNREASONABLE: *My boss is a reasonable woman.* | **it is reasonable to do something** ▸ *It's not reasonable to expect us to do so much work.*
2 fairly good but not very good: *The apartment is in reasonable condition.*
3 not too cheap or expensive: *What is a **reasonable price** for a new car?*

reasonably /ˈrizənəbli/ [*adverb*]
1 in a sensible and fair way: *You're not acting reasonably.*
2 more than a little, but not completely: *You have a **reasonably good** chance of winning.*

3 at a price that is not too expensive: *a store selling **reasonably priced** clothes*

reassure /ˌriəˈʃʊr/ [*verb*; **reassured, reassuring**] to make someone feel less worried about something: **reassure someone that** ▸ *He reassured me that everything would be all right.*

reassuring /ˌriəˈʃʊrɪŋ/ [*adjective*; **more reassuring, most reassuring**] making you feel less worried: *It is reassuring to know that you are nearby.* | *He gave her a reassuring hug.*

rebel[1] /ˈrɛbəl/ [*noun*] someone who fights against people in authority or who refuses to behave correctly: *A group of rebels have taken over the airport.* | *a teenage rebel*

rebel[2] /rɪˈbɛl/ [*verb*; **rebels, rebelled, rebelling**] to fight against people in authority or refuse to behave in the way you are expected to: *She's **rebelling against** her parents.*

rebellion /rɪˈbɛlyən/ [*noun*] when a group of people start fighting against their government or ruler: *Soldiers came to **crush the rebellion*** (=stop it).

rebellious [T] /rɪˈbɛlyəs/ [*adjective*; **more rebellious, most rebellious**] behaving in a way that parents and other people in authority do not approve of, especially by refusing to obey them: *She had always been a rebellious child.*

recall /rɪˈkɔl/ [*verb*; **recalled, recalling**] to remember something: *I don't recall her name.* | **recall someone's doing something** ▸ *Do you recall his saying anything about this?*

receipt /rɪˈsit/ [*noun*] a note that shows someone has received goods or money: *When you pay, remember to get a receipt.*

receive * /rɪˈsiv/ [*verb*; **received, receiving**]
1 to get something from someone: *He received a lot of support from the public.*
2 to get a letter, telephone call, message, etc., from someone: *I never received your message.*

receiver /rɪˈsivər/ [*noun*] the part of a TELEPHONE that you pick up and hold to have a conversation with someone

recent * [T] /ˈrisənt/ [*adjective*; **more recent, most recent**] happening not long ago: *a recent death in the family*

recently * [T] /ˈrisəntli/ [*adverb*] not long ago: *I recently bought a new boat.* | *They got married recently.*
↪ *See the usage note at* LATELY.

reception /rɪˈsɛpʃən/ [*noun*]
1 a party, for example one after a wedding ceremony: *There will be 98 guests at the reception.*
2 the quality of the pictures or sound on a television or radio: *The reception isn't very good in bad weather.*

receptionist /rɪˈsɛpʃənɪst/ [*noun*] someone whose job is to answer the telephone, welcome customers, etc., in an office

recess /ˈrisɛs/ [*noun*; *plural* **recesses**]
1 a break in the school day when children can play: *I fell off the swings during recess.*
2 a break between meetings or in a meeting, especially in a court of law: *The court will take a short recess.* | *Congress is now on its summer recess.*

recipe /ˈrɛsəpi/ [*noun*] a set of instructions for preparing a particular dish or kind of food: *Do you have the **recipe for** those muffins?*

recite /rɪˈsaɪt/ [*verb*; **recited, reciting**] to say something that you have learned, remembering the words without reading them: *She loves to recite poetry.*

reckless /ˈrɛklɪs/ [*adjective*; **more reckless, most reckless**] dangerous and careless: *He's a very reckless driver.*

recognition /ˌrɛkəgˈnɪʃən/ [*noun*]
1 when you recognize someone: *There was no sign of recognition on his face.*
2 when people realize that someone has achieved something or done something good: *He never received any **recognition for** his work.* | *This medal is **in recognition of** your bravery.*

/i/ **see**	/ɪ/ **big**	/eɪ/ **day**	/ɛ/ **get**	/æ/ **hat**
/ɑ/ **father, hot**	/ʌ/ **up**	/ə/ **about**	/ɔ/ **saw**	
/oʊ/ **hope**	/ʊ/ **book**	/u/ **too**	/aɪ/ **I**	/aʊ/ **how**
/ɔɪ/ **boy**	/ɝ/ **bird**	/ɚ/ **teacher**	/ɪr/ **ear**	/ɛr/ **air**
/ɑr/ **far**	/ɔr/ **more**	/ʊr/ **tour**	/aɪr/ **fire**	
/aʊɚ/ **hour**	/θ/ **nothing**	/ð/ **mother**	/ʃ/ **she**	
/ʒ/ **measure**	/tʃ/ **church**	/dʒ/ **jump**	/ŋ/ **long**	

recognize * T /ˈrɛkəgˌnaɪz/ [verb; recognized, recognizing]
1 to realize who someone is or what something is when you see him, her or it: *I recognized her immediately.* | *Someone recognized the stolen car.*
2 to realize that someone has achieved something or done something good: **recognize that** ▸ *I recognize that you have worked very hard.*

recommend /ˌrɛkəˈmɛnd/ [verb; recommended, recommending]
1 to say that you think someone or something is good, suitable, etc.: *Can you recommend a good dentist?* | **recommend someone/something to someone** ▸ *My friend recommended this restaurant to me.*
2 to say that you think someone should do something: **recommend (that)** ▸ *The doctor recommended that she rest.*

recommendation /ˌrɛkəmɛnˈdeɪʃən/ [noun] when someone recommends someone or something: *We went to that movie **on her recommendation**.* | *The report makes several recommendations.*

reconsider /ˌrikənˈsɪdɚ/ [verb; reconsidered, reconsidering] to change a decision that you have made, after thinking about it again: *I wish you would reconsider.* | *We will not reconsider our decision.*

record[1] * /rɪˈkɔrd/ [verb; recorded, recording]
1 to write down information or put it into a computer, so you can see it when you need it: *The computer records each player's score.*
2 to put sounds or pictures onto tape, film, a disc, etc., so that they can be heard or seen later: *They're recording their next album right now.* | *Many top TV shows are recorded at this studio.*

record[2] * T /ˈrɛkɚd/ [noun]
1 information about something that is written down or put into a computer: *I **kept a record of** everything I ate for a week.* | *He **checked his records** to see if the payment had been made.* | *We have **no record of** Mr. Green* (=he does not appear in our records).
2 the highest or best score, rate, level, etc., ever achieved, especially in

sports: *Who **holds the record** for the 100m race?* | *She easily **beat the world record**.* | *He **set a new speed record** (=went faster than anyone else before).*
3 a flat black circular object on which music or speech has been recorded: *I love **listening to** old **records**.*

record[3] /ˈrɛkɚd/ [adjective; no comparative] a record level, amount, etc., is the highest or best ever: *Record amounts of rain have fallen.*
☛ Only use **record** before a noun.

recorder /rɪˈkɔrdɚ/ [noun] a machine that records sounds or pictures: *a tape recorder*
↪ See also **VCR**.

recording /rɪˈkɔrdɪŋ/ [noun] sounds or pictures stored on tape, film, a disc, etc.: *I phoned, but all I got was a recording.* | *a video recording*

record player /ˈrɛkɚd ˌpleɪɚ/ [noun] a piece of equipment used for playing records: *He turned on the record player.*

recover T /rɪˈkʌvɚ/ [verb; recovered, recovering]
1 to become well again after an illness: *It took me a long time to recover.* | *He is **recovering from** cancer.*
2 to get back something that you lost or that was taken away from you: *The police helped us recover our money.*

SYNONYMS recover, get better, improve

All of these words mean "to become well again after an illness." **Recover** is a slightly formal word, and is often used about serious illness: *It may take him a while to recover.* Use **get better** in normal conversation: *When is she going to get better?*

If someone who is ill is becoming less ill, you can say that he or she **is improving** or **is getting better**: *She's still in the hospital, but she's improving.* | *I'm glad he's finally getting better.*

recovery /rɪˈkʌvəri/ [noun; plural recoveries] when someone becomes well again after being sick: *She **made a quick recovery** (=got well again fast).* | *What are his chances of recovery?*

recreation /ˌrɛkriˈeɪʃən/ [*noun*] activities you do for enjoyment: *For recreation, I like to watch movies.*

recreational /ˌrɛkriˈeɪʃənəl/ [*adjective; no comparative*] relating to things you do for enjoyment: *recreational activities*

recruit[1] /rɪˈkrut/ [*verb; recruited, recruiting*] to persuade someone to start working for you or to join your organization: *We will be recruiting again in the spring.* | *The army recruited 10,000 new soldiers.*

recruit[2] [*noun*] a new member of an army, navy, etc.: *a training course for new recruits*

rectangle /ˈrɛkˌtæŋgəl/ [*noun*] a shape like a square but with two opposite sides longer than the other two sides ⇨ *See* Shapes *in the Smart Study section.*

rectangular /rɛkˈtæŋgyələ/ [*adjective; no comparative*] like a rectangle in shape: *The houses are built around a rectangular courtyard.*

recycle /riˈsaɪkəl/ [*verb; recycled, recycling*] to treat waste materials so they can be used again, or to use something again: *Most cans and bottles can be recycled.* | *This notepaper is made from recycled paper.*

This symbol means you can **recycle** something.

red[1] * /rɛd/ [*noun*] the color of blood: *Red means "stop," green means "go."*

red[2] * [*adjective; redder, reddest*]
1 of the color red: *Why don't you wear your red dress?* | *Her face went bright red* (=she was embarrassed).
2 red hair is a dark orange color: *Everyone in my family has red hair.*

red-hot /ˈrɛd ˈhɑt/ [*adjective; no comparative*] extremely hot and becoming red: *Don't touch that pan—it's red-hot.* | *a red-hot burner*

redness /ˈrɛdnɪs/ [*noun*] the condition of being red: *Insect bites can cause redness and swelling.*

reduce * /rɪˈdus/ [*verb; reduced, reducing*] to make something less in amount, level, or degree; *synonym* DECREASE: *Yoga can reduce stress.* | *He reduced his speed as he drove through the town.*

reduction * /rɪˈdʌkʃən/ [*noun*] when an amount, level, or degree becomes less; *synonym* DECREASE: *a reduction in taxes*

reed /rid/ [*noun*] a kind of tall strong grass that grows in or near water

reef /rif/ [*noun*] an area of rock or sand, that is near the surface of the ocean

reel /ril/ [*noun*] a round object on which movie film, wire, etc., is wound: *a reel of film* | *the reel of a fishing rod*

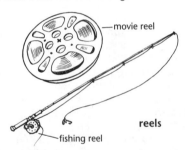

movie reel

reels

fishing reel

refer * /rɪˈfɚ/ [*verb; refers, referred, referring*]

━━━ **PHRASAL VERB** ━━━

refer to [*phrasal verb*]
1 to mention someone or something: **refer to someone/something** ▸ *What's the "secret project" he keeps referring to?*
2 to look at a book, map, etc., to find information that you need: *For details, refer to page 200.* | *During her speech she never once referred to her notes.*

referee /ˌrɛfəˈri/ [*noun; plural referees*] someone who makes sure that players obey the rules in a game, especially in

/i/ **see**	/ɪ/ **big**	/eɪ/ **day**	/ɛ/ **get**	/æ/ **hat**
/ɑ/ **father, hot**	/ʌ/ **up**	/ə/ **about**	/ɔ/ **saw**	
/oʊ/ **hope**	/ʊ/ **book**	/u/ **too**	/aɪ/ **I**	/aʊ/ **how**
/ɔɪ/ **boy**	/ɚ/ **bird**	/ɚ/ **teacher**	/ɪr/ **ear**	/ɛr/ **air**
/ɑr/ **far**	/ɔr/ **more**	/ʊr/ **tour**	/aɪr/ **fire**	
/aʊɚ/ **hour**	/θ/ **nothing**	/ð/ **mother**	/ʃ/ **she**	
/ʒ/ **measure**	/tʃ/ **church**	/dʒ/ **jump**	/ŋ/ **long**	

a sports game: *The referee blew three short blasts on his whistle.*
⇨ Compare UMPIRE.

reference /ˈrɛfərəns/ [*noun*]
1 when you look at a book, map, etc., in order to find information that you need: *You may use an encyclopedia for reference.*
2 a letter written by someone who knows you, saying that you are suitable for a new job, a course of study, etc.: *You will need a reference from your teacher.*
3 when someone mentions someone or something: *His writing is full of references to his family.*

reference book /ˈrɛfərəns ˌbʊk/ [*noun*] a book such as an encyclopedia or dictionary that you look at to find information

refill /ˈriˌfɪl/ [*noun*] the act of filling a container again, or the substance that is put into the container again: *Hand me your cup and I'll give you a refill.*

refine /rɪˈfaɪn/ [*verb*; **refined, refining**] to treat a raw substance so that it is more pure: *Beets are refined into sugar.*

reflect T /rɪˈflɛkt/ [*verb*; **reflected, reflecting**]
1 if a surface reflects light, an image, etc., it throws it back: *She could see her face reflected in the window.*
2 to think about something, especially something that has happened: *When I reflect on my life, I feel content.*

reflection T /rɪˈflɛkʃən/ [*noun*]
1 an image which can be seen in a MIRROR, smooth water, etc.: *He studied his reflection in the mirror.*
2 when you think about something for a while: *After some reflection, I admitted I was wrong.*

reflexive /rɪˈflɛksɪv/ [*adjective; no comparative*] GRAMMAR a reflexive verb has an object (a reflexive pronoun) that refers to the same person as the subject: *In the sentence "I cut myself," "cut" is a reflexive verb and "myself" is a reflexive pronoun.*

reform[1] /rɪˈfɔrm/ [*verb*; **reformed, reforming**] to change a system or

organization so that it becomes better: *People want to reform the legal system.*

reform[2] [*noun*] when a system or organization is changed so that it becomes better: *political reforms | a period of economic reform*

refresh /rɪˈfrɛʃ/ [*verb*; **refreshes, refreshed, refreshing**] to make someone feel cooler, or to give someone more energy: *A good night's sleep should refresh you.*

refreshed /rɪˈfrɛʃt/ [*adjective; no comparative*] feeling cooler or that you have energy again: *I was refreshed after taking a short nap.*

refreshing /rɪˈfrɛʃɪŋ/ [*adjective; **more refreshing, most refreshing**] making you feel cooler or more active: *We had a refreshing drink of lemonade.*

refreshments /rɪˈfrɛʃmənts/ [*plural noun*] things to eat and drink, especially at an event or when traveling

refrigerator /rɪˈfrɪdʒəˌreɪtɚ/ [*noun*] a piece of electrical equipment used for storing food at low temperatures; synonym FRIDGE: *Put the butter back in the refrigerator.*

refuge /ˈrɛfyudʒ/ [*noun*] protection from something dangerous, such as the weather or violence: *When the storm began, they **took refuge** in a cave* (=went into it for protection).

refugee /ˌrɛfyʊˈdʒi/ [*noun; plural* **refugees**] someone who leaves his or her country because of danger, especially when there is a war

refund[1] /ˈrifʌnd/ [*noun*] money given back to someone when he or she returns something to a store: *This radio doesn't work—I'm asking for a refund.*

refund[2] /rɪˈfʌnd/ [*verb*; **refunded, refunding**] to give someone a refund: *The store refused to refund my money.*

refusal * /rɪˈfyuzəl/ [*noun*] when someone refuses to do or accept something: **refusal to do something** ▸ *I don't understand her refusal to eat meat.*

refuse * T /rɪˈfyuz/ [*verb*; **refused, refusing**] to say that you will not do or accept something: *I asked him to tell me but he refused. | Rob always refuses any* *offer of help.* | **refuse to do something** ▸ *She refused to put on her coat.*

☛ Do not say that someone "refused me to do it." Say that he or she **refused to let me do it** or **refused to allow me to do it.**

regard[1] ✻ /rɪˈgɑrd/ [*verb;* **regarded, regarding**] to have a particular opinion or feeling about someone or something: **regard someone/ something as something** ▸ *I regard you as my closest friend.* | **regard someone/ something with something** ▸ *She regards any kind of change with suspicion.*

regard[2] [*noun*]
▬ PHRASES ▬
1 have regard for someone to have a good opinion about someone: *I have great regard for her abilities.*
2 have no regard for someone/ something to not think or care about someone or something at all, especially when you should: *She seems to have no regard for her own safety.*
3 give your regards to send someone your good wishes, either in a letter or through someone else: **give your regards to someone** ▸ *Give my regards to your mother.* | **give someone your regards** ▸ *Give her my regards.*

regarding /rɪˈgɑrdɪŋ/ [*preposition*] FORMAL used to say what you are talking about: *I wrote to him a week ago regarding the check.*

regardless /rɪˈgɑrdlɪs/ [*adverb*]
1 without taking any notice of advice, criticism, etc.; synonym ANYWAY: *I told her it was a mistake, but she continued regardless.*
▬ PHRASE ▬
2 regardless of used to say that something does not or will not affect a situation: *I like her, regardless of what you say.*

reggae /ˈrɛgeɪ/ [*noun*] a kind of popular music with a strong regular beat

region Ⓣ /ˈridʒən/ [*noun*] a large area of a country, part of the body, etc.: *There is rain in southern regions of the country.* | *She felt pain in the shoulder region.*

regional /ˈridʒənəl/ [*adjective; no comparative*] relating to a particular

area of a country or of the world: *She has a strong regional accent.*

register[1] Ⓣ /ˈrɛdʒəstɚ/ [*noun*] an official list or record of names, events, etc.: *a voting register* | *a class register*
⇨ See also CASH REGISTER.

register[2] [*verb;* **registered, registering**]
1 to put your name on an official list so you can start doing something: *She registered for Judo.* | **register to do something** ▸ *She registered to vote.*
2 to put a name or other information on an official list: *You have to register your car every year.*
3 if an instrument registers a level or amount, it shows that level or amount: *That package weighs too little to register on these scales.* | *The thermometer registered 40 degrees.*

registration /ˌrɛdʒəˈstreɪʃən/ [*noun*]
1 when you put a name or other information on an official list: *Please have your student number ready for registration.*
2 a document that gives information about a car or other vehicle and the name of its owner

regret[1] Ⓣ /rɪˈgrɛt/ [*verb;* **regrets, regretted, regretting**] to wish you had not done something you did: *I do not regret my decision.* | *If you quit your job, you'll regret it.* | **regret doing something** ▸ *Do you ever regret getting married so young?*

☛ Do not say "I regret to do something." Say **I regret doing something** or **I regret having done something.**

regret[2] [*noun*] a feeling of being sorry and sad about something you did or something you did not do: *I have no regrets about my past.*

regular ✻ /ˈrɛgyələr/ [*adjective*]
1 [**more regular, most regular**] with the same amount of time or space between each event, sound,

---

/i/ **see** /ɪ/ **big** /eɪ/ **day** /ɛ/ **get** /æ/ **hat**
/ɑ/ **father, hot** /ʌ/ **up** /ə/ **about** /ɔ/ **saw**
/oʊ/ **hope** /ʊ/ **book** /u/ **too** /aɪ/ **I** /aʊ/ **how**
/ɔɪ/ **boy** /ɚ/ **bird** /ɚ/ **teacher** /ɪr/ **ear** /ɛr/ **air**
/ɑr/ **far** /ɔr/ **more** /ʊr/ **tour** /aɪr/ **fire**
/aʊɚ/ **hour** /θ/ **nothing** /ð/ **mother** /ʃ/ **she**
/ʒ/ **measure** /tʃ/ **church** /dʒ/ **jump** /ŋ/ **long**

movement, etc.: *I have regular health checkups.* | *a regular heartbeat*

2 [*no comparative*] usual or normal; <u>synonym</u> ORDINARY; <u>opposite</u> SPECIAL: *Just wear your regular clothes.*

☛ Only use **regular** before a noun in this meaning.

3 [*no comparative*] of a standard size, not large or small: *I'd like a large soda and regular fries.*

☛ Only use **regular** before a noun in this meaning.

4 [*no comparative*] GRAMMAR a regular form of a word is changed in a standard way when its tense, number, or subject changes, for example by adding "-ed"; <u>opposite</u> IRREGULAR: *"Wish" is a regular verb.*

regularity /ˌrɛgyəˈlærɪti/ [*noun*] the fact that something happens regularly: *I'm grateful for the regularity of his visits.*

regularly * /ˈrɛgyələli/ [*adverb*] often, with similar periods of time between each event: *I write to my uncle regularly.*

regulation T /ˌrɛgyəˈleɪʃən/ [*noun*] a law, rule, or other order made by someone in authority: *There are **regulations against** smoking in public buildings.*

rehearsal /rɪˈhɜsəl/ [*noun*] when you practice a play, speech, piece of music, etc.: *It was the final rehearsal before the concert.*

rehearse /rɪˈhɜs/ [*verb*; rehearsed, rehearsing] to practice a play, speech, piece of music, etc., that you are going to perform: *The band rehearses once a week.* | *All the actors are busy rehearsing their parts.*

⇨ *See the synonym note at* PRACTICE².

reign¹ /reɪn/ [*noun*] a period of time during which a particular king or queen rules a country: *She was born during the **reign of** Queen Victoria.*

reign² [*verb*; reigned, reigning] if a king or queen reigns, he or she rules a country: *He reigned for 37 years.*

rein /reɪn/ [*noun*] a long thin piece of leather attached to bands around a horse's head, which the rider moves to control the HORSE

reindeer /ˈreɪnˌdɪr/ [*noun; plural* reindeer] a large deer that lives in northern parts of the world. Both the male and female reindeer have horns.

a reindeer

reject T /rɪˈdʒɛkt/ [*verb*; rejected, rejecting]

1 to not accept or allow something: *He rejected their offer.* | *I hope they don't reject our idea completely.*

2 to say or show that you do not want someone; <u>opposite</u> ACCEPT: *The college rejected her application.*

rejection /rɪˈdʒɛkʃən/ [*noun*] when someone does not accept or want something or someone: *She was upset by the rejection of her suggestion.* | *His book had five rejections before it was published.*

relate * T /rɪˈleɪt/ [*verb*; related, relating]

1 if two facts, events, etc., relate to each other, they are connected in some way: *The graph shows how profits **relate to** sales.*

2 to tell someone a story or to describe a series of events to him or her: **relate something to someone** ▸ *She related the story to her mother.*

related * /rɪˈleɪtɪd/ [*adjective; no comparative*]

1 if two people are related, they are in the same family: *Are you two **related to** each other?*

2 related facts, events, or subjects are connected in some way; <u>opposite</u> UNRELATED: *The two bomb attacks could be related.*

relation * /rɪˈleɪʃən/ [*noun*]

1 someone who is a member of your family, for example an aunt, uncle, or cousin; <u>synonym</u> RELATIVE: *All our **friends and relations** came to the wedding.*

2 a connection between two or more facts, events, etc.: *There's a **relation between** poverty and crime.*

3 relations [*plural*] connections or relationships between countries, groups, or people: *Relations between the two countries have always been good.*

━━━ PHRASE ━━━

4 in relation to used when you are comparing something to something else: *My house is tiny in relation to his.*

relationship * /rɪˈleɪʃənˌʃɪp/ [*noun*]
1 the way two people or groups feel and behave toward each other: *He has a good relationship with his dad.* | *The relationship between the government and the media is difficult.*
2 when two people are friends, especially in a romantic way: *Do you think they're having a relationship?*
3 the way in which two things or people are connected: *There is a relationship between smoking and cancer.* | *"What's your relationship to him?" "He's my brother-in-law."*

relative[1] * /ˈrɛlətɪv/ [*noun*] someone who is a member of your family, for example an aunt, uncle, or cousin; *synonym* RELATION: *She didn't even tell her close relatives she was ill.*

relative[2] [*adjective; no comparative*] compared with something else: *What are the relative benefits of public school and private school?*

relatively [T] /ˈrɛlətɪvli/ [*adverb*] fairly, or compared to something else: *The dress was relatively cheap.* | *It's a relatively good school.*

relax * /rɪˈlæks/ [*verb*; **relaxes, relaxed, relaxing**]
1 to stop worrying, or to do things that make you feel calm and comfortable: *Relax—you'll be fine!* | *You need to find time to relax.*
☛ Do not say that you "relax yourself." Say that you **relax**.
2 to make your muscles less stiff, or to become less stiff: *Relax your shoulders.* | *Let all your muscles relax.*

relaxation /ˌrilækˈseɪʃən/ [*noun*] when you do things that make you feel calm and comfortable: *I read for relaxation.*

relaxed /rɪˈlækst/ [*adjective*; **more relaxed, most relaxed**] calm and comfortable: *You look more relaxed now.*

relay /ˈrileɪ/ [*noun; plural* **relays**] a race in which each member of a team runs,

swims, etc., part of the way: *She will be running the first leg of the relay* (=part of the relay). | *a relay race*

release[1] /rɪˈlis/ [*verb*; **released, releasing**]
1 to let a prisoner or animal go free: *He will be released from jail next year.* | *We released fish into our new pond.*
➪ *See also* **let go** *at* LET.
2 to stop holding something or someone: *He suddenly released my hand.*
➪ *See also* **let go (of)** *at* LET.
3 to make a new record or movie available for people to buy or see: *The band has just released its fourth album.*

release[2] [*noun*]
1 when a prisoner is released: *His family is waiting eagerly for his release.*
2 a record or movie that has recently been released: *The local radio station plays all the new releases.*

reliability /rɪˌlaɪəˈbɪlɪti/ [*noun*] when something or someone is reliable: *An important quality in a friend is reliability.*

reliable /rɪˈlaɪəbəl/ [*adjective*; **more reliable, most reliable**]
1 always working well or doing things in the way you expect, and therefore easy to trust; *synonym* DEPENDABLE; *opposite* UNRELIABLE: *She's a good, reliable worker.* | *The car is old and not very reliable.*
2 reliable information is very likely to be true: *Some of the evidence may not be reliable.*

relief /rɪˈlif/ [*noun*] the feeling you get when you can stop worrying about something, or when you stop suffering: *To her relief, the store was still open.* | *What a relief!* (=said when you know you do not have to worry)

relieve /rɪˈliv/ [*verb*; **relieved, relieving**] to make an unpleasant feeling or situation less severe; *synonym* EASE: *Aspirin may relieve the pain.*

/i/ **see** /ɪ/ **big** /eɪ/ **day** /ɛ/ **get** /æ/ **hat** /ɑ/ **father, hot** /ʌ/ **up** /ə/ **about** /ɔ/ **saw** /oʊ/ **hope** /ʊ/ **book** /u/ **too** /aɪ/ **I** /aʊ/ **how** /ɔɪ/ **boy** /ɚ/ **bird** /ə/ **teacher** /ɪr/ **ear** /ɛr/ **air** /ɑr/ **far** /ɔr/ **more** /ʊr/ **tour** /aɪr/ **fire** /aʊɚ/ **hour** /θ/ **nothing** /ð/ **mother** /ʃ/ **she** /ʒ/ **measure** /tʃ/ **church** /dʒ/ **jump** /ŋ/ **long**

relieved /rɪ'livd/ [adjective; more relieved, most relieved] happy or calm again because you no longer need to worry about something: *We were relieved to hear she was safe.*

religion * /rɪ'lɪdʒən/ [noun] a set of beliefs about God or gods: *There are many religions in the world.* I *We always disagree about religion.*

religious * T /rɪ'lɪdʒəs/ [adjective]
1 [no comparative] relating to religion: *He and I have different religious beliefs.*
2 [more religious, most religious] a religious person has strong religious beliefs and shows this in his or her behavior: *My mother is very religious and goes to church every day.*

reluctant T /rɪ'lʌktənt/ [adjective; more reluctant, most reluctant] not wanting to do something: **reluctant to do something** ▸ *He seemed reluctant to speak with me.*

reluctantly T /rɪ'lʌktəntli/ [adverb] if you do something reluctantly, you do it but you are not happy about it: *Mom reluctantly allowed me to go to the party.*

rely /rɪ'laɪ/ [verb; relies, relied, relying]
—— PHRASAL VERB ——
rely on [phrasal verb]
to trust someone or something, and know that he, she, or it will help you or do things for you: **rely on someone/something** ▸ *You can always rely on her.* I *I can't rely on this watch.* I **rely on someone/something to do something** ▸ *He relies on friends to drive him places.*

remain * T /rɪ'meɪn/ [verb; remained, remaining]
1 [linking] to stay in a particular position, state, or situation: *Please remain standing.* I *She remained certain that she was right.*
2 FORMAL to stay somewhere rather than leaving: *He remained at work while the others went out.*

remainder /rɪ'meɪndɚ/ [noun]
the remainder the part of something that remains when the rest has gone, been dealt with, etc.: *She'll do the remainder of the work.*
⇨ *See also* **the rest (of)** *at* REST[1].

remains /rɪ'meɪnz/ [plural noun] what is left when the rest of something has been eaten, used, etc.: *I gave the remains of my dinner to the dog.*

remark[1] * /rɪ'mark/ [noun] something that you say about someone or something; synonym COMMENT: *He kept making remarks about my hair.*

remark[2] [verb; remarked, remarking] to say something about someone or something; synonym COMMENT: *She remarked that I looked like a rock star.* I *No one remarked on his absence.*

remarkable T /rɪ'markəbəl/ [adjective; more remarkable, most remarkable] unusual, especially in a good way; synonym AMAZING: *a remarkable woman* I *a remarkable achievement*

remarkably /rɪ'markəbli/ [adverb] used to talk about something that is remarkable: *Remarkably, no one was injured.* I *He seemed remarkably calm.*

remarry /ri'mæri/ [verb; remarries, remarried, remarrying] to get married again: *Mom remarried when I was four.*

remedy /'rɛmɪdi/ [noun; plural remedies] a cure for an illness or medical condition: *a remedy for a sore throat*

remember * /rɪ'mɛmbɚ/ [verb; remembered, remembering]
1 to bring a fact or event into your mind again after a period of time, or to be able to do this: *I'm sorry, I don't remember your name.* I *"What was the name of the movie?" "I can't remember."* I **remember (that)** ▸ *I suddenly remembered that I had an appointment.* I **remember how to do something** ▸ *Do you remember how to get to John's house?* I **remember doing something** ▸ *I don't remember telling you that.*
☛ Do not say "I don't remember to do something." Say **I don't remember doing something.**
2 to do something you intended to do, bring something you intended to bring, etc.: *Did you remember your keys?* (=did you bring them) I **remember to do something** ▸ *I must remember to phone her.*

USAGE   remember, remind

Do not confuse **remember** and **remind**. If you **remember** something, a fact or event from the past comes into your mind: *I don't remember where I bought that dress.* If you **remind** someone about something, you tell him or her to remember it: *Remind me to return his book.*

---

remind * /rɪ'maɪnd/ [*verb*; **reminded, reminding**]
1 to tell someone to remember to do something: **remind someone to do something** ▸ *I reminded him that he owed me money.* | **remind someone about something** ▸ *Thanks for reminding me about it.*
☛ Do not say "Remind me of doing something." Say **Remind me to do something**.
⊃ *See the usage note at* REMEMBER.
2 to make someone remember a fact or event: **remind someone of something** ▸ *She reminded him of his promise.* | **remind someone (that)** ▸ *I reminded her that we had to leave soon.*

— PHRASE —
3 remind someone of someone/ something to be like another person or thing, and make someone think of that person or thing: *You remind me of my daughter.*
☛ Do not say that someone "remind you someone." Say that he or she **reminds you of someone**.

remote ⊤ /rɪ'moʊt/ [*adjective*; **remoter, remotest**] far away from most places: *He lives in the remotest part of the island.*

remote control /rɪ'moʊt kən'troʊl/ [*noun*] a piece of equipment used to control something such as a television from a distance: *He kept changing channels using the remote control.*

a remote control

remotely /rɪ'moʊtli/ [*adverb*]
— PHRASE —
not remotely not at all: *She wasn't remotely concerned about her health.*

removable /rɪ'muvəbəl/ [*adjective; no comparative*] easy to remove: *a coat with a removable hood*

remove * /rɪ'muv/ [*verb*; **removed, removing**] to take something away from a place, position, or thing: *Ink stains are hard to remove.* | **remove something from something** ▸ *Please remove your bicycle from the hallway.*

remover /rɪ'muvɚ/ [*noun*] a substance that can remove another substance: *nail polish remover* | *paint remover*

rename /ri'neɪm/ [*verb*; **renamed, renaming**] to give something a new name: *He showed me how to rename a computer file.*

renew /rɪ'nu/ [*verb*; **renewed, renewing**] if you renew an official document or agreement, you officially increase the amount of time it is legal or can be used: *I renewed my passport.*

rent[1] * /rɛnt/ [*noun*]
1 a regular payment you make to someone who owns a building, so you can live in it or use it: *I haven't **paid the rent** yet.* | *Office rents are quite high in this area.*

— PHRASE —
2 for rent available to be rented: *Are there any houses for rent around here?*

rent[2] * [*verb*; **rented, renting**]
1 to pay money to use a building, vehicle, or piece of equipment: *I rented a small apartment.* | *There's a place in the park where you can rent bicycles.*
2 to allow someone to use something in return for money: **rent something to someone** ▸ *I rent my loft to an artist.*

rental /'rɛntəl/ [*noun*] an amount of money paid in order to rent a vehicle or

---

/i/ **see** /ɪ/ **big** /eɪ/ **day** /ɛ/ **get** /æ/ **hat**
/ɑ/ **father, hot** /ʌ/ **up** /ə/ **about** /ɔ/ **saw**
/oʊ/ **hope** /ʊ/ **book** /u/ **too** /aɪ/ **I** /aʊ/ **how**
/ɔɪ/ **boy** /ɝ/ **bird** /ɚ/ **teacher** /ɪr/ **ear** /ɛr/ **air**
/ɑr/ **far** /ɔr/ **more** /ʊr/ **tour** /aɪr/ **fire**
/aʊɚ/ **hour** /θ/ **nothing** /ð/ **mother** /ʃ/ **she**
/ʒ/ **measure** /tʃ/ **church** /dʒ/ **jump** /ŋ/ **long**

piece of equipment: *How much is the car rental per day?* | *What's the weekly rental?*

repaid /rɪ'peɪd/ [*verb*] the past tense and past participle of REPAY

repair[1] * /rɪ'pɛr/ [*verb*; **repaired, repairing**] to fix something that is broken: *Can you repair my watch?*

repair[2] * [*noun*] when someone fixes something that is broken: *They **made** some **repairs to** the roof.* | *The car is badly **in need of repair.***

repay /rɪ'peɪ/ [*verb*; **repays, repaid, repaying**] to pay money that you owe: *I always repay my debts.*

repeat * T /rɪ'pit/ [*verb*; **repeated, repeating**]
1 to say something again: *Could you repeat the instructions?*
2 to do something again: *Repeat the exercise five times.*

repeated /rɪ'pitɪd/ [*adjective*; no comparative] happening many times: *He made repeated attempts to call them.*
☞ Only use **repeated** before a noun.

repeatedly /rɪ'pitɪdli/ [*adverb*] if you do something repeatedly, you do it many times: *She repeatedly warned us about the dangers of fireworks.*

repetition /ˌrɛpɪ'tɪʃən/ [*noun*] when someone says or does the same thing more than once: *We learn verbs through repetition.*

replace * T /rɪ'pleɪs/ [*verb*; **replaced, replacing**]
1 if one thing or person replaces another, that thing or person starts being used or doing a job instead of the other one: *Do you think computers will replace books in the future?* | **replace someone as something** ▶ *Who will replace him as head of the company?*
2 to put something new in the place of something else: *We replaced our old rug.*
3 to put something back where it was before it was moved: *He replaced the book on the shelf.*

replacement /rɪ'pleɪsmənt/ [*noun*] someone who starts doing a job that used to be done by someone else, or something that starts being used

instead of something else: *His replacement will start work on Monday.* | *replacement parts for cars*

replay[1] /ri'pleɪ/ [*verb*; **replays, replayed, replaying**]
1 to play something that was recorded again: *To replay the message, press 2. To erase it, press 3.*
2 to play a game again, because neither team won: *The game will be replayed on Tuesday.*

replay[2] /'ri,pleɪ/ [*noun*; plural **replays**] when part of a videotape is played again: *They watched the replay to see if the referee was right.*

reply[1] * /rɪ'plaɪ/ [*verb*; **replies, replied, replying**] to say or write something as an answer: *I wrote to them last week, but they haven't replied.* | *Have you **replied to** their invitation?* | *"No," the man replied.* | *She **replied that** it was impossible.*
☞ Do not say "reply a letter." Say **reply to a letter.**

reply[2] * [*noun*; plural **replies**]
1 what you say or write to someone who has said or written something to you; synonym ANSWER: *I shouted "Hello!" but there was no reply.*
═══ PHRASE ═══
2 **in reply (to)** as a reply: *In reply to their questions, he said he knew nothing.*

report[1] * /rɪ'pɔrt/ [*verb*; **reported, reporting**]
1 to tell people about something important that has happened: *The event was reported on the evening news.* | **report something to someone** ▶ *Have you reported this to the police?*
2 to tell someone in authority about someone who has done something wrong: *I'm going to report those boys!* | **report someone to someone** ▶ *She reported him to the principal.*

report[2] * [*noun*]
1 a document that gives official information about something that happened or is happening: *He gave the **report on** sales to his boss.*
2 an article in a newspaper or a part of a broadcast that gives news about something: *Did you hear the weather report?*
3 when someone tells people about

something important that has happened: *There have been **reports** of fighting in the west of the country.*

report card /rɪ'pɔrt ˌkard/ [*noun*] a document that shows a student's grades for his or her classes

reporter /rɪ'pɔrtɚ/ [*noun*] someone whose job is to report news for a newspaper, television company, etc.; *synonym* CORRESPONDENT: *He works as a sports reporter.*

represent * /ˌrɛprɪ'zɛnt/ [*verb*; represented, representing]
1 to officially speak or do something for a person or a group: *I'm the lawyer representing Mr. Green.*
2 if you represent your country, you take part in an international competition: *I am proud to be representing my country in the Olympics.*

representative * /ˌrɛprɪ'zɛntətɪv/ [*noun*]
1 someone who has been chosen to officially speak or do something for a person or a group: *Please leave your number, and a sales representative will call you.*
2 [*name*] also **Representative**; someone who is a member of the House of Representatives in the U.S. Congress, or who is a member of a state's government

reproduce /ˌriprə'dus/ [*verb*; reproduced, reproducing]
1 to produce babies, eggs, seeds, etc.: *These birds are not yet old enough to reproduce.*
2 to make a copy of something: *Photocopiers don't reproduce photos very well.*

reproduction /ˌriprə'dʌkʃən/ [*noun*]
1 a copy of a picture, piece of furniture, etc.: *This painting is a reproduction.*
2 the producing of babies, eggs, seeds, etc.: *different methods of reproduction*

reptile /'rɛptaɪl/ [*noun*] an animal such as a snake, lizard, or turtle that has no fur and lays eggs: *Alligators are reptiles.*

republic /rɪ'pʌblɪk/ [*noun*] a country whose leader is chosen by its people: *the Republic of South Africa*

Republican /rɪ'pʌblɪkən/ [*noun*] someone who belongs to or supports the Republican Party (=a political party in the U.S.)

reputation /ˌrɛpyə'teɪʃən/ [*noun*] the opinion people have about someone or something, based on what they have heard: *The school **has a good reputation**. | a reputation for honesty*

request[1] * /rɪ'kwɛst/ [*noun*] when someone asks for something, or asks for something to be done, in a polite or formal way: *May I **make a request**? | The letter contained a **request for** money.*

request[2] [*verb*; requested, requesting] FORMAL to ask for something, or ask for something to be done, in a polite or formal way: *He **requested that** his name not be given in the article.*

require ⊤ /rɪ'kwaɪr/ [*verb*; required, requiring]
1 to need something: *This game requires some skill.*
2 FORMAL to say officially that people must do something: **require someone to do something** ▶ *Students are required to buy their own uniforms.*

required /rɪ'kwaɪrd/ [*adjective*; no comparative] necessary or officially asked for; *opposites* OPTIONAL, UNNECESSARY: *This is **required reading** for the course.*

requirement /rɪ'kwaɪrmənt/ [*noun*] something that is needed or officially asked for: *She has all the requirements for this job.*

rescue[1] /'rɛskyu/ [*verb*; rescues, rescued, rescuing] to save someone who is in a dangerous place or situation: *They were **rescued from** the burning house.*

rescue[2] [*noun*; plural rescues]
1 when someone is saved from danger: *There seemed to be no hope of rescue. | a brave rescue*

/i/ **see** /ɪ/ **big** /eɪ/ **day** /ɛ/ **get** /æ/ **hat**
/ɑ/ **father, hot** /ʌ/ **up** /ə/ **about** /ɔ/ **saw**
/oʊ/ **hope** /ʊ/ **book** /u/ **too** /aɪ/ **I** /aʊ/ **how**
/ɔɪ/ **boy** /ɝ/ **bird** /ɚ/ **teacher** /ɪr/ **ear** /ɛr/ **air**
/ɑr/ **far** /ɔr/ **more** /ʊr/ **tour** /aɪr/ **fire**
/aʊɚ/ **hour** /θ/ **nothing** /ð/ **mother** /ʃ/ **she**
/ʒ/ **measure** /tʃ/ **church** /dʒ/ **jump** /ŋ/ **long**

2 come to the rescue or **come to someone's rescue** to help someone who is in a dangerous or difficult situation: *He came to my rescue when my computer stopped working.*

research[1] * /'risɜⁿtʃ/ [*noun*] when you study something to find out facts about it, especially facts that no one knows: *Scientists are doing research on the causes of cancer.* | *She did a lot of research into the writer's early life.*

research[2] /rɪ'sɜⁿtʃ/ [*verb*; **researches, researched, researching**] to try to find out facts about something by studying it: *I researched the subject thoroughly.*

resemblance /rɪ'zɛmbləns/ [*noun*] the fact that two things or people look similar: *The resemblance between the statue and the copy is remarkable.*

resemble /rɪ'zɛmbəl/ [*verb*; **resembled, resembling**] to look or act like someone or something else: *I resemble my aunt.*

resent /rɪ'zɛnt/ [*verb*; **resented, resenting**] to feel angry and unhappy about something you think is unfair or wrong: *He resents being told what to do by someone younger.* | *I resent it that I always have to wait for you.*

resentment /rɪ'zɛntmənt/ [*noun*] the feeling you have when you resent something: *She still feels resentment about the way she was treated.*

reservation [T] /ˌrɛzɚ'veɪʃən/ [*noun*] an arrangement that a restaurant table, hotel room, etc., will be kept available for you: *I'd like to **make a reservation for** two people, please.*

reserve[1] /rɪ'zɜⁿv/ [*verb*; **reserved, reserving**] to arrange for a restaurant table, a hotel room, etc., to be kept available for you; *synonym* BOOK: *I reserved a table for 8 o'clock.*

reserve[2] [*noun*]
1 an amount of something that is kept until it is needed: *The president has not released the oil reserves.*
2 an area of land that is kept for a particular purpose: *We visited a **wildlife reserve** (=where wild animals are protected).*

3 in reserve available to be used in the future if necessary: *We kept some money in reserve.*

reservoir /'rɛzɚˌvwɑr/ [*noun*] a natural or artificial lake where water is stored

residence [T] /'rɛzɪdəns/ [*noun*] FORMAL a house: *The meeting was held at the governor's residence.*

resident [T] /'rɛzɪdənt/ [*noun*] someone who lives in a particular place: *The local residents don't want the factory to be built here.* | *Are you a **resident of** the U.S.?*

resign /rɪ'zaɪn/ [*verb*; **resigned, resigning**] to formally say that you are leaving your job: *He **resigned from** his job as sales manager.*

resignation /ˌrɛzɪg'neɪʃən/ [*noun*] when you formally say that you are leaving your job: *His boss accepted his resignation.* | *a **letter of resignation***

resist [T] /rɪ'zɪst/ [*verb*; **resisted, resisting**]
1 to fight against an attack or a change: *It was useless to resist.* | *The staff resisted the new working methods.*
2 if you cannot resist something, you cannot stop yourself from doing or taking it: *She couldn't **resist the temptation** to have dessert.* | **resist doing something** ▸ *I couldn't resist stopping to take a look.*

resistance [T] /rɪ'zɪstəns/ [*noun*] when someone fights against an attack or a change: *The proposals **met with some resistance** (=were resisted by some people).*

resolution /ˌrɛzə'luʃən/ [*noun*]
1 a formal decision or statement of opinion, made by a group of people after a vote: *a United Nations resolution*
2 a promise to yourself that you will do something: *I made a **New Year's resolution** to get more exercise.*

resolve /rɪ'zɑlv/ [*verb*; **resolved, resolving**] to decide firmly to do something: **resolve to do something** ▸ *She resolved to spend more time studying.*

resort /rɪ'zɔrt/ [*noun*] a place where a lot of people go on vacation, especially one that is by a beach or in the mountains: *a popular ski resort*

resource /'risɔrs/ [*noun*] something that can be used if it is needed: *The country has many natural resources* (=trees, minerals, oil, etc.).
☛ This word is usually used in the plural.

respect[1] * T /rɪ'spɛkt/ [*verb*; **respected, respecting**] to have a good opinion of someone: *He is respected by all his colleagues.* | *a highly respected writer*

respect[2] * T [*noun*]
1 the good opinion that you have of someone, and the way this makes you treat him or her: *He has a lot of respect for his employees.*
— PHRASE —
2 in some/many respects in some ways, or in many ways: *In some respects, his plan was a good one.*

respectable /rɪ'spɛktəbəl/ [*adjective*; **more respectable, most respectable**]
1 not involved in doing anything wrong, so that people have a good opinion of you: *Her father was a respectable businessman.*
2 fairly good: *That's a respectable score.*

respectful /rɪ'spɛktfəl/ [*adjective*; **more respectful, most respectful**] showing respect: *They listened to the speech in respectful silence.*

respond T /rɪ'spand/ [*verb*; **responded, responding**] to say or do something after you hear about something, when something happens, etc.; *synonym* REACT: *He responded by shaking his head.* | *How did they respond to the news?* | *Thank goodness the firefighters were quick to respond* (=came quickly).

response T /rɪ'spans/ [*noun*]
1 what you say or do when you hear about something, when something happens, etc.; *synonym* REACTION: *Her response to his criticism was to work harder.* | *I tried writing to the company but got no response.*
— PHRASE —
2 in response (to) as a response: *In response to my call, I received a letter of apology.*

responsibility T /rɪ,spansə'bɪlɪti/ [*noun; plural* **responsibilities**]
1 a duty to take care of something or to deal with someone or something: *As a*

manager, she has a lot of responsibility.* | *It is your responsibility to keep your room clean.*
2 the fact that a particular person did or caused something bad: *The boy admitted responsibility for the fire.*

responsible * /rɪ'spansəbəl/ [*adjective*]
1 [**more responsible, most responsible**] someone who is responsible can be trusted to do sensible things: *Is she responsible enough to be left in charge?*
2 [*no comparative*] someone who is responsible for something bad that happened either did it or caused it: *Who was responsible for the accident?*
☛ Do not use **responsible** before a noun in this meaning.
3 [*no comparative*] having a duty to take care of something or to deal with something: *You're responsible for buying the sodas.*
☛ Do not use **responsible** before a noun in this meaning.

rest[1] * /rɛst/ [*noun*]
1 a period of time when you do nothing or you sleep, especially after doing a lot: *You can take a rest now.* | *She just needs some rest.*
— PHRASE —
2 the rest (of) all the other things, people, or parts of something: *They cleaned the kitchen first, and then the rest of the house.* | *She's a better athlete than all the rest.*

rest[2] * [*verb*; **rested, resting**]
1 to stop doing an activity for a period of time, or to sleep: *He needs to rest for a few days.* | *Sit down and rest a while.*
2 to put something somewhere so that it is supported by something: *She rested her chin on her hands.*
3 to be supported by something: *His hand rested on hers for a moment.*

/i/ **see**	/ɪ/ **big**	/eɪ/ **day**	/ɛ/ **get**	/æ/ **hat**	
/ɑ/ **father, hot**	/ʌ/ **up**	/ə/ **about**	/ɔ/ **saw**		
/oʊ/ **hope**	/ʊ/ **book**	/u/ **too**	/aɪ/ **I**	/aʊ/ **how**	
/ɔɪ/ **boy**	/ɝ/ **bird**	/ɚ/ **teacher**	/ɪr/ **ear**	/ɛr/ **air**	
/ɑr/ **far**	/ɔr/ **more**	/ʊr/ **tour**	/aɪr/ **fire**		
/aʊɚ/ **hour**	/θ/ **nothing**	/ð/ **mother**	/ʃ/ **she**		
/ʒ/ **measure**	/tʃ/ **church**	/dʒ/ **jump**	/ŋ/ **long**		

restaurant * /'rɛstərənt/ [*noun*] a building or room where people eat meals they pay for: *a French restaurant*

restless /'rɛstlɪs/ [*adjective;* **more restless, most restless**] not willing to stay in one place or to continue doing the same thing: *After a few months with the company, he began to get restless.*

restore Ⓣ /rɪ'stɔr/ [*verb;* **restored, restoring**] to fix a building, piece of furniture, etc., so that it is in good condition again: *They spent two years restoring the house.*

restrain /rɪ'streɪn/ [*verb;* **restrained, restraining**] to stop someone or yourself from doing something: *He wanted more cake, but he managed to restrain himself.*

restrict * /rɪ'strɪkt/ [*verb;* **restricted, restricting**] to carefully limit something so that it does not involve too many activities or people: *The law restricts trade between the two countries.* | *The pool is restricted to club members only.*

restricted /rɪ'strɪktɪd/ [*adjective;* **more restricted, most restricted**] carefully limited to particular people, a particular purpose, or particular activities: *This is a restricted area.* | *a restricted diet*

restriction /rɪ'strɪkʃən/ [*noun*] a rule controlling what people do or the amount of something: *The restrictions on imports have been lifted* (=have been removed).

restroom Ⓣ /'rɛst,rum/ [*noun*] a room with toilets and sinks in a public place ➪ *Compare* BATHROOM.

result[1] * /rɪ'zʌlt/ [*noun*]
1 something that happens because something else happened: *She stopped studying and failed as a result.*
2 the information given by a test: *We'll send you results of your blood test.*

result[2] * [*verb;* **resulted, resulting**]
1 to be caused by something: *Terrible damage resulted from the earthquake.*
— PHRASAL VERB
result in [*phrasal verb*]
2 to cause something: **result in something** ▸ *This disease can result in blindness.*

resume /rɪ'zum/ [*verb;* **resumed, resuming**] FORMAL to start again after stopping for a period of time: *Work on the new airport has resumed.*

retake /ri'teɪk/ [*verb;* **retook, retaken** /ri'teɪkən/, **retaking**] to take an exam again, because you failed it: *I had to retake my driving test.*

retire Ⓣ /rɪ'taɪr/ [*verb;* **retired, retiring**] to stop having a job, when you have reached the end of your normal working life: *He retired from his job as a professor last year.* | *Most people retire at 65* (=when they are 65).

retired /rɪ'taɪrd/ [*adjective; no comparative*] no longer working because you have reached the end of your working life: *My parents are both retired.* | *a retired doctor*

retirement /rɪ'taɪrmənt/ [*noun*] when you retire, or the period of time after you retire: *Are you looking forward to retirement?* | *They wished him a long and happy retirement.*

retook /ri'tʊk/ [*verb*] the past tense of RETAKE

retreat[1] /rɪ'trit/ [*verb;* **retreated, retreating**] to move back or away from an enemy, or from something you are afraid of: *The soldiers retreated to the other side of the river.*

retreat[2] [*noun*] when soldiers move away from an enemy: *Their forces are now in retreat.*

return[1] * /rɪ'tɜrn/ [*verb;* **returned, returning**]
1 to go back to a place, activity, or condition: *After college, he returned to New York.* | *She returned home at 10:00.* | *He'll return to work next week.* | *A polluted lake may never return to normal.*
2 to give something back: *He hasn't returned the book he borrowed.* | **return something to someone** ▸ *If you find the papers, please return them to me.*

return[2] * [*noun*]
1 when you go back to a place: *She made a sudden return to the U.S. from Australia.* | *a return flight* (=coming back from the place you went to)
2 when you give something back: *The*

store accepts *returns* (=you can bring back something you bought and get your money back).

═══ PHRASE ═══

3 in return (for) if you do something for someone in return, you do it because of what that person did for you: *He gave me a ride to school in return for my help.* | *If you're nice to people, they'll be nice in return.*

reunion /rɪ'yunyən/ [*noun*] when people who have not seen each other for a long time meet together: *We're having a big **family reunion** next week.*

Rev. the written abbreviation of REVEREND: *Rev. Brown*

reveal Ⓣ /rɪ'vil/ [*verb; revealed, revealing*]
1 to tell people something they do not know: *They refused to reveal their plans.*
2 to show something that was hidden: *She took off her coat to reveal an amazing evening dress.*

revenge /rɪ'vɛndʒ/ [*noun*] when you hurt or harm someone who has hurt or harmed you or someone you care about: *Gangs keep attacking each other in revenge for other attacks.*

Reverend /'rɛvərənd/ [*name*] used as the title of a Christian priest or minister: *Reverend Brown*

reverse¹ /rɪ'vɜ˞s/ [*verb; reversed, reversing*]
1 if a vehicle or its driver reverses, it goes backward: *He reversed down the driveway.*
2 to make a condition, decision, or situation the opposite of what it was: *If our situations were reversed, what would you do?*

reverse² Ⓣ [*noun*]
1 the reverse the opposite: *In fact, the reverse is true.*

── PHRASE ──

2 in reverse if a vehicle is in reverse, it is going backward or is ready to go backward: *I put the car in reverse.*

review¹ /rɪ'vyu/ [*verb; reviewed, reviewing*]
1 to look carefully at facts or a situation again: *Review chapters one*

through five for the test (=study them again) *next Monday.*
2 to write an article or make a broadcast giving your opinion of a book, movie, etc.: *He reviews books for the New York Times.*

review² [*noun*]
1 when you look carefully at facts or a situation again: *Every month, we have a review of the project.* | *For review, read chapter nine.*
2 an article or part of a broadcast in which someone gives his or her opinion of a book, movie, etc.: *Her first book got very good reviews.*

revise /rɪ'vaɪz/ [*verb; revised, revising*] to change something that is written by adding to it or correcting it: *a revised edition of a dictionary*

revive /rɪ'vaɪv/ [*verb; revived, reviving*] to become conscious again, or to make someone do this: *They pulled him out of the water and tried to revive him.*

revolt /rɪ'voʊlt/ [*noun*] when the people of a country start fighting against their government or ruler: *The army was brought in to stop the revolt.* | *The whole country was in revolt.*

revolting /rɪ'voʊltɪŋ/ [*adjective; more revolting, most revolting*] extremely unpleasant: *This food is revolting!*

revolution /ˌrɛvə'luʃən/ [*noun*]
1 when there are great changes in the way that something is done: *There has been a revolution in technology.*
2 when people remove the government or ruler of their country by force: *the French Revolution*

revolutionary /ˌrɛvə'luʃəˌnɛri/ [*adjective*]
1 [*more revolutionary, most revolutionary*] something new that is revolutionary is very different and will change the way that something is done: *a revolutionary new drug*
2 [*no comparative*] involved in a

/i/ **see**	/ɪ/ **big**	/eɪ/ **day**	/ɛ/ **get**	/æ/ **hat**	
/a/ **father, hot**	/ʌ/ **up**	/ə/ **about**	/ɔ/ **saw**		
/oʊ/ **hope**	/ʊ/ **book**	/u/ **too**	/aɪ/ **I**	/aʊ/ **how**	
/ɔɪ/ **boy**	/ɝ/ **bird**	/ɚ/ **teacher**	/ɪr/ **ear**	/ɛr/ **air**	
/ɑr/ **far**	/ɔr/ **more**	/ʊr/ **tour**	/aɪr/ **fire**		
/aʊɚ/ **hour**	/θ/ **nothing**	/ð/ **mother**	/ʃ/ **she**		
/ʒ/ **measure**	/tʃ/ **church**	/dʒ/ **jump**	/ŋ/ **long**		

political revolution: *They were arrested for revolutionary activities.*
☛ Only use **revolutionary** before a noun in this meaning.

revolve /rɪ'valv/ [*verb;* **revolved, revolving**] to go or turn around: *The earth **revolves around** the sun.* | *The earth revolves every 24 hours.*

revolver /rɪ'valvɚ/ [*noun*] a small gun

reward[1] * /rɪ'wɔrd/ [*noun*] something that someone is given for doing something good or helpful: *They are offering a $2,000 **reward for** information on the robbery.*

reward[2] * [*verb;* **rewarded, rewarding**] to give someone a reward: *If you help, I promise you'll be rewarded.*

rewarding ⊤ /rɪ'wɔrdɪŋ/ [*adjective;* **more rewarding, most rewarding**] a rewarding job or activity makes you feel happy because you are doing something useful: *Being a nurse is a rewarding job.*

rewind /ri'waɪnd/ [*verb;* **rewound** /ri'waʊnd/, **rewinding**] if you rewind a tape or a tape rewinds, it goes backward: *Please rewind the videotape when you're done.* | *He waited while the cassette rewound.*

rewrite /ri'raɪt/ [*verb;* **rewrote** /ri'roʊt/, **rewritten** /ri'rɪtən /, **rewriting**] to make a lot of changes to a piece of writing: *You need to rewrite your paper.*

rhinoceros /raɪ'nasərəs/ [*noun; plural* **rhinoceroses**] a large animal with thick skin and one or two large horns on its nose

a rhinoceros

rhyme[1] /raɪm/ [*verb;* **rhymed, rhyming**] if words rhyme, they end in the same sound: *"You" **rhymes with** "do."*

rhyme[2] [*noun*] a short poem in which pairs or groups of lines end in the same sound

rhythm ⊤ /'rɪðəm/ [*noun*]
1 a pattern of sounds in music or poetry: *The music had an unusual rhythm.*
2 a pattern of movements that you can hear: *the **rhythm of** waves on the beach*

rib /rɪb/ [*noun*] one of the curved bones around your chest
↪ See the picture at **SKELETON**.

ribbon /'rɪbən/ [*noun*] a long narrow piece of cloth: *I tied a ribbon around the present.* | *She had ribbons in her hair.*

rice * /raɪs/ [*noun*] the seeds of a plant that grows in wet ground, which can be cooked and eaten: *a bowl of rice* | *a **grain of rice** (=one small piece of rice)*

rich[1] * ⊤ /rɪtʃ/ [*adjective;* **richer, richest**]
1 having a lot of money and possessions; <u>opposite</u> **POOR**: *He is one of the richest men in the world.*
2 food that is rich contains a lot of fat: *I felt a little sick after eating all that rich food.*

rich[2] [*noun*]
the rich people who are rich: *Only the rich can afford to live there.*
☛ Only use **the rich** with a plural verb.

riches /'rɪtʃɪz/ [*plural noun*] a large amount of money and possessions; <u>synonym</u> **WEALTH**: *A career in teaching won't bring you riches.*

rid * /rɪd/ [*adjective;* no comparative]
═══ PHRASE ═══
get rid of to remove or throw away something that you do not want: *I opened a window to get rid of the smell.*

ridden * /'rɪdən/ [*verb*] the past participle of **RIDE**[1]

riddle /'rɪdəl/ [*noun*] a question that has an unusual or funny answer that you try to guess: *She asked me a riddle: "What's the difference between a jeweler and a jailer?" (Answer: One sells watches and the other watches cells.)*

ride[1] * /raɪd/ [*verb;* **rode, ridden, riding**]
1 to go somewhere on a horse, bicycle, motorcycle, etc.: *a man **riding on** a horse* | *He rode off down the road.* | *I learned to ride a bicycle when I was five.*
2 to be taken somewhere in a car or truck: *I got to ride in his big car.*

USAGE ride

You **ride** or **ride on** things you can sit on: *Can I ride on your motorcycle?* | *I want to ride the roller coaster.*

You can also **ride** a bus or train: *I ride the bus to work.*

You **ride in** a car or truck: *You can ride in Grandma's car.*

☛ Do not say "ride a car" or "ride on a car."

ride² ✱ [noun]
1 a trip in a vehicle or on a bicycle, motorcycle, horse, etc.: *He gave me a ride into town* (=drove me in his car). | *We went for a ride in my new car.* | *She lives a short bus ride from the school.*
2 a large machine that carries a number of people, which people ride on for fun and excitement: *I want to go on every ride at the carnival.*

rider ✱ /ˈraɪdɚ/ [noun] someone who is riding a bicycle, motorcycle, HORSE, etc.: *Bicycle riders should stay off the sidewalks.*

ridge Ⓣ /rɪdʒ/ [noun]
1 a long narrow hill or part of a mountain: *They walked along the top of the ridge.*
2 a line that is higher than the surface around it: *The soles of the boots have rubber ridges.*

ridiculous Ⓣ /rɪˈdɪkyələs/ [adjective; more ridiculous, most ridiculous] very silly: *It's a ridiculous idea!*

riding /ˈraɪdɪŋ/ [noun] the activity of riding on a horse: *It's a nice day—let's go riding.*

rifle /ˈraɪfəl/ [noun] a long gun, often used to hunt

right¹ ✱ /raɪt/ [adjective; no comparative]
1 correct or suitable; *opposites* INCORRECT, WRONG: *I think you made the right decision.* | *Is he the right person for the job?* | *I said it wouldn't work, and I was right.*
2 acceptable, fair, or moral; *opposite* WRONG: *I couldn't lie to him—it wouldn't be right.* | *It's not right that I should have to pay for it all.*

☛ Do not use **right** before a noun in this meaning.

3 on the right; *opposite* LEFT: *She had a pain in her right side.*

☛ Only use **right** before a noun in this meaning.

4 SPOKEN used to ask for or to show agreement: *"That's OK, right?" "Right."*
— PHRASE —
5 get something right to do something correctly: *I'll get it right eventually!*

➪ See also ALL RIGHT.

right² ✱ [adverb]
1 exactly in a particular position: *He was standing right in front of me.* | *It's right here.*
2 all the way: *He hit the ball right into the crowd.*
3 correctly; *opposite* WRONG: *I guessed right.*
4 toward the right; *opposite* LEFT: *Turn right at the light.*
— PHRASES —
5 right now or **right away** immediately, or at this moment: *I'm going to call him right now.* | *Please come right away.*
6 right after immediately following the person, thing, or event mentioned: *I'll do it right after I've finished my lunch.* | *I went home right after school.*

right³ ✱ [noun]
1 the fact that someone should be allowed to do or have something: *I know my rights.* | *He has a right to a share of the money.* | **right to do something** ▸ *He has a right to be here.*
2 the side that is toward the east when you are facing north; *opposite* LEFT: *On your right is the library.* | *We sat to the right of the stage.*
3 actions that are acceptable or fair; *opposite* WRONG: *Children should be taught the difference between right and wrong.*

/i/ **see** /ɪ/ **big** /eɪ/ **day** /ɛ/ **get** /æ/ **hat** /ɑ/ **father, hot** /ʌ/ **up** /ə/ **about** /ɔ/ **saw** /oʊ/ **hope** /ʊ/ **book** /u/ **too** /aɪ/ **I** /aʊ/ **how** /ɔɪ/ **boy** /ɝ/ **bird** /ɚ/ **teacher** /ɪr/ **ear** /ɛr/ **air** /ɑr/ **far** /ɔr/ **more** /ʊr/ **tour** /aɪr/ **fire** /aʊɚ/ **hour** /θ/ **nothing** /ð/ **mother** /ʃ/ **she** /ʒ/ **measure** /tʃ/ **church** /dʒ/ **jump** /ŋ/ **long**

right angle /'raɪt 'æŋgəl/ [noun] an ANGLE of 90 degrees, like the corner of a square

right-hand /'raɪt ˌhænd/ [adjective; no comparative] on or toward the right; _opposite_ LEFT-HAND: *His house is on the right-hand side of the road.* | *a right-hand turn*

☞ Only use **right-hand** before a noun.

right-handed /'raɪt 'hændɪd/ [adjective; no comparative] someone who is right-handed writes, uses tools, etc., with his or her right hand; _opposite_ LEFT-HANDED: *Most people are right-handed.*

rigid Ⓣ /'rɪdʒɪd/ [adjective; **more rigid, most rigid**]
1 stiff and not easily bent; _opposite_ FLEXIBLE: *It's important to keep a broken arm rigid until it heals.*
2 if there is a rigid rule, system, etc., people must do what has been stated and nothing else is ever allowed; _opposite_ FLEXIBLE: *The school had rigid rules about attendance.*

rim /rɪm/ [noun] the top or outside edge of something: *There was lipstick on the **rim of** one of the cups.*

rind /raɪnd/ [noun] the hard outside of a fruit such as an orange, or of cheese or some meats: *grated lemon rind*

ring¹ * /rɪŋ/ [noun]
1 a piece of JEWELRY that you wear on your finger: *a diamond ring* | *a wedding ring*
2 a circle: *We danced around in a ring.*
3 the sound that a bell makes: *Did you hear that ring? Someone's at the door.*

ring² * [verb; **rang, rung, ringing**]
1 if a phone or bell rings, it produces a sound: *Suddenly the phone rang.*
2 to make a bell produce a sound: *She rang the doorbell.*

rink /rɪŋk/ [noun] a large flat area with a special surface for skating on: *an ice rink* | *a roller-skating rink*

rinse /rɪns/ [verb; **rinsed, rinsing**] to wash something using water but not soap: *She rinsed her hands under the faucet.* | **rinse something off** ▸ *Rinse the soap off.* | **rinse off something** ▸ *Rinse off the lettuce first.*

riot¹ /'raɪət/ [noun] when a lot of people behave in a violent and uncontrolled way in a public place: *There have been riots in the streets of the capital.*

riot² [verb; **rioted, rioting**] if a group of people riot, they behave in a violent and uncontrolled way in a public place: *When their exercise time was reduced, the prisoners rioted.*

rip¹ /rɪp/ [verb; **rips, ripped, ripping**] to tear quickly or to tear something quickly: *He pulled at her coat and it ripped.* | *She **ripped open** the envelope.*

rip² [noun] a tear in cloth: *You have a **rip** in your jeans.*

ripe /raɪp/ [adjective; **riper, ripest**] if a fruit or crop is ripe, it is ready to eat or be cut: *This pear doesn't feel ripe yet.* | *ripe wheat*

ripple /'rɪpəl/ [noun] a little wave on the surface of water: *The breeze made ripples on the lake.*

rise¹ * /raɪz/ [verb; **rose, risen, rising**]
1 to increase; _opposite_ FALL: *Prices have risen in the past year.*
2 to move to a higher position: *The helicopter rose into the air.* | *The level of the river is rising.* | *There was smoke **rising up** from a fire in the distance.*
3 if the sun rises, it appears at the beginning of the day; _opposite_ SET: *He woke before the sun had risen.*
4 FORMAL to stand up; _opposite_ SIT: *She rose slowly **to her feet.***

⇨ See also **get up** at GET (definition 26).

USAGE rise, raise

Do not confuse **rise** and **raise**. **Rise** is used to say that something moves by itself to a higher position: *We got up early to watch the sun rise.* **Raise** is used to say that someone moves something to a higher position: *Raise your hand if you have a question.*

rise² * [noun] an increase; _opposite_ FALL: *a rise in students' test scores*

risen * /'rɪzən/ [verb] the past participle of RISE¹

risk¹ * /rɪsk/ [noun]
1 a possibility that something bad will happen: *There's **a risk that** the patient*

might die. I *He's **running the risk of
losing money** (=he may lose it).* I *No
investment is without risk.*

2 an action that may be dangerous or
not successful: *I know it's a risk, but we
have no choice.* I *He's **taking a big risk**.*

━ PHRASE ━

3 at risk (of) in danger: *He **put** other
people **at risk**.*

risk^2 * [*verb;* risked, risking]

1 to do something even though
something bad might result: **risk
doing something** ▸ *I decided not to risk
driving in the snow.*

☛ Do not say "risk to do something."
Say **risk doing something**.

2 to put something in danger of being
harmed or lost: *Firefighters **risk their
lives** all the time.*

risky /ˈrɪski/ [*adjective;* riskier, riskiest]
a risky action may be dangerous or not
successful: *Rock climbing is a risky sport.*

rival /ˈraɪvəl/ [*noun*] a person, group, or
company that is competing strongly
with another for something: *He beat his
two main rivals in the 200-meter race.* I
*He now works for a **rival company**.*

rivalry /ˈraɪvəlri/ [*noun*] when people,
groups, or companies are competing
strongly: *There is fierce rivalry between
the two soft drink companies.*

river * 🖼 /ˈrɪvɚ/ [*noun*] water that flows
continuously along a course through
land: *A boat was traveling down the river.*
I *the Mississippi River*

roach /roʊtʃ/ [*noun; plural* roaches] a
COCKROACH

road * or **Road** /roʊd/ [*noun*]

1 a hard flat surface that vehicles
travel on: *the **main road** through town
(=the biggest one)* I *a **road accident*** I *I
live on Maple Road.*

━ PHRASE ━

2 on the road traveling: *His job keeps
him on the road a lot.*

roadside [*adjective; no comparative*]
beside the road: *a roadside café*

☛ Only use **roadside** before a noun.

roam /roʊm/ [*verb;* roamed, roaming]
to go to many places or parts of a place,
with no particular purpose; *synonym*

WANDER: *He spent three years **roaming
around** the U.S.*

roar^1 /rɔr/ [*verb;* roared, roaring]

1 to make a long loud noise: *The lion
roared.*

━ PHRASE ━

2 roar with laughter to laugh very
loudly: *We all roared with laughter.*

roar^2 [*noun*] a long or continuous loud
noise: *The roar of traffic kept me awake.*

roast^1 /roʊst/ [*verb;* roasted, roasting]
to cook meat or vegetables in an oven,
without water but sometimes with a
little fat or oil: *The turkey was already
roasting in the oven.*

⇨ *See the synonym note at* COOK^1.

roast^2 [*adjective; no comparative*] cooked
in an oven: *We had roast lamb for dinner.*

☛ Only use **roast** before a noun.

rob * /rab/ [*verb;* robs, robbed, robbing]
to steal something from a person or
place: *Two men robbed him.* I *They tried
to rob a jewelry store.*

☛ You say that someone **robs** a person
or place, not money or property.

⇨ *Compare* STEAL.

robber /ˈrabɚ/ [*noun*] someone who
goes into a place and steals things: *The
police caught the **bank robbers**.*

robbery /ˈrabəri/ [*noun; plural*
robberies] when a person or group of
people steals things from a person or
place: *There's been an **armed robbery**
(=the robber used a gun).*

robe /roʊb/ [*noun*]

1 a piece of CLOTHING like a long loose
coat, which people wear in their
homes, for example before getting
dressed; *synonym* BATHROBE: *She put on
her robe and went to make breakfast.*

2 a long loose piece of clothing worn
by someone taking part in a
ceremony: *The priest put on his robe.*

robin /ˈrabɪn/ [*noun*] a small brown bird
with a red breast

/i/ **see**	/ɪ/ **big**	/eɪ/ **day**	/ɛ/ **get**	/æ/ **hat**		
/a/ **father, hot**	/ʌ/ **up**	/ə/ **about**	/ɔ/ **saw**			
/oʊ/ **hope**	/ʊ/ **book**	/u/ **too**	/aɪ/ **I**	/aʊ/ **how**		
/ɔɪ/ **boy**	/ɝ/ **bird**	/ɚ/ **teacher**	/ɪr/ **ear**	/ɛr/ **air**		
/ɑr/ **far**	/ɔr/ **more**	/ʊr/ **tour**	/aɪr/ **fire**			
/aʊɚ/ **hour**	/θ/ **nothing**	/ð/ **mother**	/ʃ/ **she**			
/ʒ/ **measure**	/tʃ/ **church**	/dʒ/ **jump**	/ŋ/ **long**			

robot /'roʊbət/ [*noun*] a machine that can move and do things without someone operating it: *Robots are now used in many car factories.*

rock[1] * /rak/ [*noun*]
1 the hard substance of which land is made: *You can see different layers of rock in a canyon.*
2 a piece of rock: *The boat hit a rock just below the surface.*
3 also **rock music** /'rak ,myuzɪk/ a kind of popular music with a strong beat, typically played on guitars and drums: *a rock concert*

rock[2] [*verb; rocked, rocking*] to move gently backward and forward or from side to side: *The train rocked from side to side.* | *She rocked the baby until he stopped crying.*

rocket /'rakɪt/ [*noun*]
1 a long tube that burns fuel and lifts space vehicles or weapons into the air: *Rockets are used to launch satellites.*
2 a container that goes high into the air and explodes with a lot of bright lights: *The rocket exploded with a loud bang.*

rocking chair /'rakɪŋ ,tʃɛr/ [*noun*] a chair with two curved pieces on the bottom, that can move gently backward and forward

rocky /'raki/ [*adjective; rockier, rockiest*] consisting of rock, or having a lot of rocks: *a rocky coastline*

rod /rad/ [*noun*] a long thin piece of something, especially metal or wood: *a curtain rod* (=that curtains hang from)

rode * /roʊd/ [*verb*] the past tense of RIDE[1]

rodeo /'roʊdi,oʊ/ [*noun; plural rodeos*] a show in which people show their skills in riding horses and using a rope to catch animals

role ⊤ /roʊl/ [*noun*]
1 the person that an actor plays in a movie, play, etc.; *synonym* PART: *He plays the role of the hero's brother.*
2 what is done by someone or something in an event, situation, system, etc.: *Stress plays a role in many diseases* (=it is involved in causing them).

roll[1] * /roʊl/ [*verb; rolled, rolling*]
1 to move by turning over and over, or to make something do this: *The dog rolled over* (=turned over once). | *She rolled the ball to him.* | *The car rolled down the hill* (=on wheels).
2 to make something into the shape of a ball or tube: *Roll the clay into a ball.* | **roll up something** ▸ *He rolled up the map and put it away.*

━━ **PHRASAL VERBS** ━━

roll out [*phrasal verb*]
3 to make something flat by moving a tube over it: *Roll out the dough to half an inch thick.*

roll up [*phrasal verb*]
4 to turn the ends of your sleeves or pants back on themselves several times: **roll something up** ▸ *We rolled our sleeves up and got to work.* | **roll up something** ▸ *He rolled up his pants and waded into the water.*

roll[2] [*noun*]
1 something that is wrapped into the shape of a tube: *I need a roll of film for my camera.*
2 bread that has been baked in a small round shape
3 an official list of the names of the people who are in a class or other group: *I'm on the honor roll* (=a list of the students with the best grades).

Rollerblade /'roʊlɚ,bleɪd/ [*noun*] TRADEMARK a boot with wheels underneath in a line from front to back; *synonym* IN-LINE SKATE: *a pair of Rollerblades*

rollerblading /'roʊlɚ,bleɪdɪŋ/ [*noun*] the activity of moving along wearing Rollerblades: *Let's go rollerblading tomorrow.*

roller coaster /'roʊlɚ ,koʊstɚ/ [*noun*] a curved track with very high and very low parts that people ride on in open cars for fun

roller skate /'roʊlɚ ,skeɪt/ [*noun*] a boot with two sets of wheels underneath; *synonym* SKATE: *a girl on roller skates* | *a pair of roller skates* ➪ *Compare* IN-LINE SKATE.

roller skates

roller-skating /ˈroʊlɚ ˌskeɪtɪŋ/ [*noun*] the activity of moving along wearing roller skates: *There's a track around the lake where you can go roller-skating.*

romance /roʊˈmæns/ [*noun*] a relationship between two people who are in love, especially a relationship that is short or exciting: *a summer romance* (=it only lasted for the summer)

romantic * /roʊˈmæntɪk/ [*adjective;* **more romantic, most romantic**] showing strong love between two people in a relationship: *He does romantic things like buying her flowers.*

roof * /ruf/ [*noun*]
1 the top surface of a building
⇨ *See the picture at* HOUSE.
2 the top surface of a CAR, bus, etc.

room[1] * /rum/ [*noun*]
1 one of the areas inside a building that are separated from each other by walls: *How many rooms does your house have?* | *She went into the dining room.*
2 space in which something can be done or put: *There wasn't much room for furniture in the apartment.* | **room to do something** ▸ *You'll have lots of room to play.* | *The others made room for him on the sofa* (=moved so that there was space).
⇨ *See the warning at* PLACE[1] (definition 3).

room[2] [*verb;* **roomed, rooming**]
━━ PHRASAL VERB ━━
room with [*phrasal verb*]
to live in the same room or apartment as someone: **room with someone** ▸ *I used to room with him in college.*

roommate [T] /ˈrumˌmeɪt/ [*noun*] someone who lives in the same room or apartment as someone else: *I'd like you to meet my roommate.*

roomy /ˈrumi/ [*adjective;* **roomier, roomiest**] having a lot of space: *This is a very roomy apartment.*

rooster /ˈrustɚ/ [*noun*] an adult male CHICKEN: *a rooster's crow* (=loud sound it makes)

root * /rut/ [*noun*] the part of a plant that is in the ground: *The roots of some plants are good to eat.*

rope * /roʊp/ [*noun*] threads twisted together to form a thick strong line: *He tied a piece of rope to the back of the car.*

rose[1] * /roʊz/ [*noun*] a FLOWER that has a sweet smell and is often given as a gift

rose[2] * [*verb*] the past tense of RISE[1]

rot /rɑt/ [*verb;* **rots, rotted, rotting**]
1 to be slowly destroyed by natural chemicals, or to destroy something in this way; *synonym* DECAY: *Some of the apples had fallen on the ground and rotted.* | *Candy can rot your teeth.*
⇨ *See also* ROTTEN. ⇨ *Compare* RUST[2].
━━ PHRASAL VERB ━━
rot away [*phrasal verb*]
2 if something rots away, it rots until there is none of it left: *Part of the boat had rotted away.*

rotate /ˈroʊteɪt/ [*verb;* **rotated, rotating**] FORMAL to turn around and around; *synonym* SPIN: *An electric fan has a rotating blade.*

rotation /roʊˈteɪʃən/ [*noun*] when something turns around completely: *Earth makes one rotation in 24 hours.*

rotten /ˈrɑtən/ [*adjective*]
1 [*no comparative*] having rotted: *She threw the rotten vegetables away.*
2 [**more rotten, most rotten**] very bad or unpleasant: *I had a rotten day.*

rough * [T] /rʌf/ [*adjective;* **rougher, roughest**]
1 not at all smooth on the surface; *opposite* SOFT: *Her skin felt rough and dry.* | *a rough country road*
2 not exact or complete; *synonym* APPROXIMATE: *He gave me a rough estimate of the cost.* | *I have a rough idea of what the job involves.*
3 unkind, or using too much force; *opposite* GENTLE: *He gave the boy a rough push.*
4 if an ocean or lake is rough, there are a lot of big waves; *opposite* CALM: *The sea was too rough to launch the boat.*

/i/ **see** /ɪ/ **big** /eɪ/ **day** /ɛ/ **get** /æ/ **hat**
/ɑ/ **father, hot** /ʌ/ **up** /ə/ **about** /ɔ/ **saw**
/oʊ/ **hope** /ʊ/ **book** /u/ **too** /aɪ/ **I** /aʊ/ **how**
/ɔɪ/ **boy** /ɝ/ **bird** /ɚ/ **teacher** /ɪr/ **ear** /ɛr/ **air**
/ɑr/ **far** /ɔr/ **more** /ʊr/ **tour** /aɪr/ **fire**
/aʊɚ/ **hour** /θ/ **nothing** /ð/ **mother** /ʃ/ **she**
/ʒ/ **measure** /tʃ/ **church** /dʒ/ **jump** /ŋ/ **long**

roughly /'rʌfli/ [adverb]
 1 possibly a little more or less, a little later or earlier, etc.; *opposite* EXACTLY: *The hall holds roughly 800 people.*
 2 without all the details; *opposite* EXACTLY: *That's roughly what the conversation was about.*
 3 with too much force; *opposite* GENTLY: *Don't play so roughly with your brother.*

round¹ * /raʊnd/ [adjective; **rounder, roundest**] shaped like a circle or a ball: *a round window* | *People used to believe the world was flat, not round.*

round² [adverb]
 ━ PHRASE ━
 all year round in every part of the year: *The park is open all year round.*

round³ [noun] a number of connected events: *Which players will reach the next round?* (=in a sports competition) | *The two leaders will have another round of talks.*

round trip¹ /'raʊnd 'trɪp/ [noun] a trip to a place and back again: *The round trip takes four hours.*

round trip² [adverb, adjective; no comparative] going to a place and back again: *It's two hours round trip.* | *a round-trip ticket*
 ➪ Compare ONE-WAY (definition 2).

route /rut/ [noun] a way of getting from one place to another: *What's the quickest route to your house from here?* | *a bus route*

routine¹ /ru'tin/ [noun] things that are regularly done in the same way or at the same time: *Jogging was part of his daily routine.* | *You can get bored with office routine.*

routine² [adjective; no comparative] a routine action is done because it is usual: *He did a routine check on the truck's tires.*

row¹ * /roʊ/ [noun]
 1 a number of things or people beside each other in a line: *He planted two rows of carrots.* | *The kids sat in a row.* | *We had front row seats at the concert.*
 ━ PHRASE ━
 2 in a row happening one after the other, with nothing else in between: *He won three games in a row.*

row² * [verb; **rowed, rowing**] to make a boat move along using oars: *She rowed across the lake.* | *I had never rowed a boat before.*

rowboat /'roʊ,boʊt/ [noun] a small boat which you move by rowing

a rowboat

royal * /'rɔɪəl/ [adjective; no comparative] belonging to or connected with a king or queen: *a royal palace*
 ☛ Only use **royal** before a noun.

royalty ⊤ /'rɔɪəlti/ [noun] kings, queens, and their close relatives: *a member of the British royalty*

rub * /rʌb/ [verb; **rubs, rubbed, rubbing**]
 1 to move your hand or a cloth over something several times, pressing on it: *He rubbed his chin thoughtfully.* | *She rubbed at the stain with a sponge.* | *Rub the lotion into your face and neck.*
 2 to move over something several times, pressing on it: *Her shoes rubbed her feet.* | *The wall was dirty where the cat had rubbed against it.*

rubber * /'rʌbɚ/ [noun] a natural or artificial substance that goes back to its original shape after it is pressed: *These boots have rubber soles.* | *a rubber ball*

rubber band /'rʌbɚ 'bænd/ [noun] a small ring of rubber that is put around things to keep them together

ruby /'rubi/ [noun; plural **rubies**] a valuable red stone that is used to make jewelry: *a pair of ruby earrings*

rude * /rud/ [adjective; **ruder, rudest**] things that you say or do that are rude show that you do not respect someone; *synonym* IMPOLITE; *opposite* POLITE: *What a rude young woman!* | *She made rude remarks about him.* | *He was rude to the salesclerk.*

rudely * /'rudli/ [*adverb*] in a way that shows you do not respect someone; *opposite* POLITELY: *"Go away," she said rudely.*

rudeness * /'rudnɪs/ [*noun*] rude words or behavior: *He apologized for his rudeness.*

rug /rʌg/ [*noun*] a piece of cloth or fur which covers part of a floor: *She lay on the rug in front of the fire.*
↪ Compare CARPET.

ruin * ⊤ /'ruɪn/ [*verb*; ruined, ruining] to destroy something or damage it very badly: *The storm had ruined their crops.* I *I cooked the meat too long and ruined it.*

ruined /'ruɪnd/ [*adjective*; no comparative] a ruined building is old and in very bad condition, so that it is no longer used: *an old ruined castle*
☛ Only use **ruined** before a noun.

ruins /'ruɪnz/ [*plural noun*] the parts of something that remain when it has been very badly damaged: *We saw the ruins of an ancient castle.*

rule[1] * /rul/ [*noun*]
1 an official statement that says what can or cannot be done: *I taught him the rules of the game.* I *He broke the rules* (=did something that is not allowed). I *It's against the rules* (=not allowed) *to touch the ball with your hands.*
2 political control over a country: *They have had 30 years of military rule.*

rule[2] * [*verb*; ruled, ruling]
1 to have political control over a country: *The Ming emperors ruled China for nearly 300 years.*
2 to make an official decision as a judge in a court or a competition: *The judge ruled in favor of my client.*

ruler * /'rulɚ/ [*noun*]
1 a long flat straight object with regular marks on it, used to measure things or draw straight lines
↪ See the picture at Measurement *in the Smart Study section.*
2 someone such as a king who has complete political control over a country: *a military ruler*

rumble[1] /'rʌmbəl/ [*noun*] continuous low sounds: *the rumble of thunder*

rumble[2] [*verb*; rumbled, rumbling] to make continuous low sounds, or to move making these sounds: *He couldn't sleep because of the trucks rumbling past.*

rumor /'rumɚ/ [*noun*] something that people are saying, which might or might not be true: *There's a rumor that she was caught stealing.* I *I don't want to listen to rumors about his private life.*

run[1] * /rʌn/ [*verb*; ran, run, running]
1 to move quickly along on your feet: *She ran down the corridor.* I *Her brother came running upstairs.*
↪ See also RUNNING[1].
2 to be in charge of a company or other organization: *He runs a car repair business.*
3 if a machine runs, it operates: *He left the car engine running.* I *The toy runs on batteries* (=uses batteries to operate). I *How late do the buses run?* (=carry passengers)
4 to go somewhere quickly and not stay there long: *I need to run to the bank.*
5 to flow, or to make a liquid flow somewhere: *Tears were running down her face.* I *She ran some more hot water into the sink.*
↪ See also **running water** at RUNNING[2].
6 if a road, wire, etc., runs somewhere, it is in that place or goes in that direction: *They took the road that ran through the forest.*
7 to try to be elected, especially to a political position: *He's running for governor.*

═══ **PHRASAL VERBS** ═══

run after [*phrasal verb*]
8 if you run after someone who is moving along ahead of you, you run and try to reach him or her: **run after someone** ▸ *He ran after her, shouting "Hey! Wait a minute!"*

run away [*phrasal verb*]
9 to leave the place where you are living without telling anyone where

/i/ **see**	/ɪ/ **big**	/eɪ/ **day**	/ɛ/ **get**	/æ/ **hat**
/ɑ/ **father**	/ɑ/ **hot**	/ʌ/ **up**	/ə/ **about**	/ɔ/ **saw**
/oʊ/ **hope**	/ʊ/ **book**	/u/ **too**	/aɪ/ **I**	/aʊ/ **how**
/ɔɪ/ **boy**	/ɚ/ **bird**	/ɚ/ **teacher**	/ɪr/ **ear**	/ɛr/ **air**
/ɑr/ **far**	/ɔr/ **more**	/ʊr/ **tour**	/aɪr/ **fire**
/aʊɚ/ **hour**	/θ/ **nothing**	/ð/ **mother**	/ʃ/ **she**
/ʒ/ **measure**	/tʃ/ **church**	/dʒ/ **jump**	/ŋ/ **long**

you are going: *He **ran away from home** at the age of fifteen.*

run into [*phrasal verb*]

10 to meet someone by chance: **run into someone** ▸ *I was out shopping when I ran into an old friend.*
↪ *See the synonym note at* MEET[1].

11 to hit something or someone with a vehicle: **run into something/ someone** ▸ *We ran into the back of the car in front of us.*

run off [*phrasal verb*]

12 to leave or go away very quickly, or to make someone do this: *He ran off all of a sudden.* | **run someone/ something off something** ▸ *She ran him off her property.*

run out [*phrasal verb*]

13 to no longer have any of something: *We've **run out of** pasta.*

14 to be used up so that there is none left: *What will we do when the money **runs out**?*

run over [*phrasal verb*]

15 to hit and drive over a person or animal: **run over someone/ something** ▸ *We ran over a rabbit.*

run[2] * [*noun*]

1 when someone runs somewhere, for exercise: *She **goes for a run** every day.*

2 a trip somewhere: *I **made a quick run** to the store.*

3 a point scored in baseball by getting to all the bases and back: *How many runs has he scored this season?*

═ PHRASE ═

4 in the long run or **in the short run** used when you are considering what will happen a long or short time in the future: *If you go to college, you will be better off in the long run.*

runaway /'rʌnəˌweɪ/ [*noun; plural* **runaways**] a young person or child who has left home without telling anyone where he or she has gone: *The church runs a shelter for runaways.*

rung[1] * /rʌŋ/ [*verb*] the past participle of RING[2]

rung[2] [*noun*] one of the narrow steps of a LADDER

runner * /'rʌnɚ/ [*noun*] someone who is running in a race: *One of the runners tripped and fell.*

running[1] /'rʌnɪŋ/ [*noun*] the activity of running as a sport or exercise: *He started running five years ago.*

running[2] [*adjective; no comparative*]
═ PHRASE ═
running water water that comes from a pipe: *The camp is supplied with running water.*

running[3] [*adverb*]
═ PHRASE ═
for two days/four years/etc. running for a specific period of time, with nothing else happening in between: *It has rained here for five days running.*
↪ *See also* **in a row** *at* ROW[1].

runny /'rʌni/ [*adjective;* **runnier, runniest**]

1 containing too much liquid: *The icing was runny and dripped down the cake.* | *runny paint*

2 a runny nose has liquid coming out of it, usually because you are ill: *My nose is runny and my throat hurts.*

runway /'rʌnˌweɪ/ [*noun; plural* **runways**] the place where planes take off and land

rural /'rʊrəl/ [*adjective; no comparative*] in or connected with the country, as opposed to cities or towns: *People are moving from rural areas to the big cities.*
↪ *Compare* URBAN.

rush[1] * /rʌʃ/ [*verb;* **rushes, rushed, rushing**]

1 to go somewhere or do something very quickly; *synonym* HURRY: *I rushed home to tell Mom.* | **rush to do something** ▸ *We rushed to finish the report.*

2 to take someone somewhere very quickly: *He was rushed to the hospital.*

rush[2] [*noun*]

1 when people move somewhere or do something suddenly and quickly: *The crowd **made a rush for** the exits.*
═ PHRASE ═
2 in a rush quickly, or needing to do something quickly: *If you do things in a rush, you make mistakes.*

rush hour /'rʌʃ ˌaʊɚ/ [*noun*] the time when roads, trains, etc., are full of vehicles or crowds because people are going to work or going home: *He left the office early to avoid rush hour.*

rust[1] /rʌst/ [*noun*] the orange-brown substance that forms on iron and steel when they get wet: *The old tools were covered with rust.*
> See also RUSTY.

rust[2] [*verb; rusted, rusting*] if metal rusts, it becomes covered with rust or changes into rust: *The screws had rusted and were hard to turn.*
> Compare ROT.

rustle[1] /ˈrʌsəl/ [*verb; rustled, rustling*] if things such as papers, leaves, or pieces of material rustle, they make a soft sound as they move: *Her dress rustled as she walked.*

rustle[2] [*noun*] a soft sound made by something moving: *the rustle of leaves*

rusty /ˈrʌsti/ [*adjective; rustier, rustiest*] covered with rust: *a rusty old gate*

rut /rʌt/ [*noun*]
1 a deep line made along a road by the wheel of a vehicle: *The road to the farm was full of ruts.*

— PHRASE —

2 **in a rut** always doing the same thing or behaving the same way and not changing: *She said she's in a rut and needs a change.*

R.V. /ˈɑr ˈvi/ [*noun; plural* **R.V.s** *or* **R.V.'s**] recreational vehicle; a vehicle with a part you can live in, used for camping or taking long trips; *synonym* MOTOR HOME

rye bread /ˈraɪ ˈbrɛd/ *or* **rye** /raɪ/ [*noun*] dark bread that tastes slightly sour: *I'll have turkey on rye, please.*

S

S * *or* **s** /ɛs/ [*noun; plural* **Ss** *or* **S's, s's**] the 19th letter of the English alphabet
> See the usage note at ALPHABET.

S. *or* **S** a written abbreviation for SOUTH: *I live at 505 S. Main Street.*
> Compare E., N., W.

s *or* **S** the written abbreviation of SMALL, especially relating to clothes size: *Labels are marked s, m, or l.*

's * /z/
1 used at the end of names and other singular nouns to show that something belongs to a person, organization, place, etc.: *This is Sam's bike.* | *the store's parking lot* | *Is this anyone's coat?*
2 the short form of IS: *That's hers.* | *Tom's still at school.*
3 the short form of the auxiliary verb HAS: *It's got to get better.* | *She's seen that movie already.*
> See the usage note at HAVE[2].

s' * /z/ used at the end of plural nouns to show that something belongs to a group: *Those are the girls' bikes.*

sack /sæk/ [*noun*] a large strong bag with no handle, usually made of rough cloth: *three sacks of potatoes*

sacred /ˈseɪkrɪd/ [*adjective;* **more sacred, most sacred**] connected with God or gods and therefore respected by people; *synonym* HOLY: *sacred texts* | *a sacred temple*

sacrifice[1] /ˈsækrəˌfaɪs/ [*noun*]
1 when you stop doing something that you enjoy so that something more important can happen: *My parents* **made** *a lot of* **sacrifices** *to pay for my education.*
2 a living thing that is killed and offered to God or a god in a ceremony: *The goat was killed as a* **sacrifice to** *the gods.*

sacrifice[2] ⊤ [*verb;* **sacrificed, sacrificing**]
1 to stop doing something that you enjoy so that something more important can happen: **sacrifice something to do something** ▸ *I'd sacrifice my vacation to play in the championship.*
2 to kill a living thing and offer it to God or a god in a ceremony: *They sacrificed a lamb on the altar.*

sad * /sæd/ [*adjective;* **sadder, saddest**] unhappy, or making you feel unhappy;

opposite HAPPY: *Why are you looking so sad?* | *This is the saddest song I've ever heard.*

⇨ *See the picture at* EMOTION.

saddle /'sædəl/ [*noun*] a seat for someone riding a HORSE

sadly /'sædli/ [*adverb*]
1 in a sad way; _opposite_ HAPPILY: *He sadly waved goodbye to his mother.*
2 used to show that what you are going to say is sad: *Sadly, my grandmother died last month.*

sadness * /'sædnɪs/ [*noun*] the feeling of being sad; _opposite_ HAPPINESS: *She had a look of great sadness on her face.*

safari /sə'fari/ [*noun; plural* **safaris**] a trip to discover wild animals, especially in Africa: *We went **on safari** in Kenya.*

safe[1] * /seɪf/ [*adjective;* **safer, safest**]
1 not in danger of harm or damage: *I just want to know that you're safe.* | *Please **keep** this letter **safe** for me.* | *The castle was on a hill, where it was **safe from** attack.*
2 not causing harm or damage: *Flying is the safest form of travel.* | *Is he a safe driver?* | *Put your money in **a safe place** (=where it cannot be lost or stolen).*

safe[2] [*noun*] a strong metal box with a lock, used for storing money or other valuable things

safely * /'seɪfli/ [*adverb*] without being harmed or damaged or without harming or damaging anything: *The pilot landed the plane safely.* | *The snake is now safely back in its cage.*

safety * /'seɪfti/ [*noun*] when someone or something is safe from harm or damage: *Your safety is my main concern.* | *The family escaped **to safety**.*

☞ The word **safety** is a noun, not an adjective, but you can use it before some nouns. You can talk about **safety measures**, a **safety rope**, a **safety rail**, etc.

safety pin /'seɪfti ,pɪn/ [*noun*] a PIN bent to form a spring, with a part to cover the point: *I attached the ribbon to my dress with a safety pin.*

sag /sæg/ [*verb;* **sags, sagged, sagging**] to bend, drop, or hang lower than something should: *a sagging hem*

said * /sɛd/ [*verb*] the past tense and past participle of SAY

sail[1] * /seɪl/ [*verb;* **sailed, sailing**]
1 to travel somewhere on a boat or ship: *We sailed up and down the river.* | *A ship sailed into the harbor.*
2 to guide a boat or ship using its sails or controls: *Many people were out sailing their yachts.*

sail[2] * [*noun*]
1 a large piece of cloth on a boat that catches the wind and makes the boat move: *One of the boat's sails was torn.*
2 a trip in a boat or ship: *Ray took us for a sail in his boat.*

sailboat /'seɪl,boʊt/ [*noun*] a boat that has one or more sails: *On sunny days, the bay is full of sailboats.*

sailor /'seɪlɚ/ [*noun*] someone who works on a ship or is in a country's navy: *My sister is married to a sailor.*

saint or **Saint** /seɪnt/ [*noun, name*] someone who people remember for living a very religious life, especially someone who has died: *She was made a saint recently.* | *Saint Christopher*

sake /seɪk/ [*noun*]

══ PHRASES ══
1 **for someone's sake** to help someone or to make him or her happier: *You should come home for Christmas, for your father's sake.*
2 **for goodness' sake** used to show that you are annoyed or surprised: *For goodness' sake, stop following me around!*

salad * /'sæləd/ [*noun*] a mixture of raw vegetables such as tomatoes and lettuce: *Would you like some salad?* | *I'm going to make a salad.*

salad dressing /'sæləd ,drɛsɪŋ/ [*noun*] a mixture of oil, vinegar, salt, and pepper that you pour over salad: *There's too much salad dressing on these tomatoes.* | *a creamy salad dressing*

salary Ⓣ /'sæləri/ [*noun; plural* **salaries**] an amount of money paid regularly to someone for doing his or her job: *His salary is $35,000 a year.*

⇨ *Compare* WAGE. ⇨ *See the usage note at* PAY[2].

sale * /seɪl/ [*noun*]
1 when a person or company sells something: *Our sales have been good this year.* | *The state controls the sale of alcohol.*
2 when a store sells its goods at lower prices than usual: *There's a sale on sheets at the department store.*
━━ PHRASES ━━
3 **for sale** available to be bought: *The car's not for sale.*
4 **on sale**
a being sold in a store at a lower price than usual: *I got these shoes on sale.*
b available in stores to be bought: *The band's latest album is now on sale.*

salesclerk /'seɪlz,klɜˑk/ [*noun*] someone who sells goods in a store: *Ask the salesclerk if they have these pants in brown.*

salesman /'seɪlzmən/ [*noun; plural* **salesmen** /'seɪlzmən/] a man who sells things as his job: *My uncle is a furniture salesman.*

salesperson /'seɪlz,pɜˑsən/ [*noun; plural* **salespeople** /'seɪlz,pipəl/] someone who sells things as his or her job: *One of our salespeople will assist you.*

sales representative /'seɪlz rɛprɪ'zɛntətɪv/ *also* **sales rep** /'seɪlz ,rɛp/ [*noun*] someone who travels from place to place, selling his or her company's products

saleswoman /'seɪlz,wʊmən/ [*noun; plural* **saleswomen** /'seɪlz,wɪmən/] a woman who sells things as her job

salmon /'sæmən/ [*noun; plural* **salmon**] a kind of fish with pink flesh that you can eat: *Do you like salmon?*

salon /sə'lɑn/ [*noun*] a place where you can get your hair cut or have beauty treatments: *a hair salon* | *a beauty salon*

salt * /sɔlt/ [*noun*] a white substance used to improve the taste of food such as vegetables, meat, or fish: *There's too much salt in this soup.* | *a pinch of salt* (=a very small amount)

salted /'sɔltɪd/ [*adjective; no comparative*] covered in salt, or preserved with salt: *salted nuts* | *salted fish*

salty * /'sɔlti/ [*adjective;* **saltier, saltiest**] containing salt, or containing a lot of salt: *These chips are too salty.* | *Salty foods make you thirsty.*

salute[1] /sə'lut/ [*verb;* **saluted, saluting**] to raise your hand to your head as a formal sign of respect for someone: *They all saluted as the general drove past.*

salute[2] [*noun*] the action of saluting someone: *His hand was raised in a salute.*

same[1] * /seɪm/ [*adjective; no comparative*]
1 **the same** having all the features or qualities that something else has; *opposite* DIFFERENT: *I have the same dress in red.* | *He is the same height as I am.*
▷ *Compare* SIMILAR.
━━ PHRASES ━━
2 **the/this/that/these/those same** the person, thing, etc., that is mentioned, not a different one: *You'll be having the same teacher as last year.* | *I've lived in this same house all my life.* | *She moved in March, and moved again that same year.*
☛ Do not use **same** without a determiner. For example, do not say "same color" or "same person." Say **the same color** or **the same person.**
3 **do the same thing** to do exactly what another person does: *Whatever I do, my brother wants to do the same thing.*

same[2] * [*pronoun*]
the same not at all different: *You and your sister look exactly the same.* | *Your cars are just the same.* | *That dress is the same as mine.*

same[3] * [*adverb*]
━━ PHRASE ━━
the same (as) exactly like someone or something else; *opposite* DIFFERENTLY: *"Oh" is pronounced the same as "owe."*

sample[1] /'sæmpəl/ [*noun*] a small amount or example that shows what

---

/i/ **see** /ɪ/ **big** /eɪ/ **day** /ɛ/ **get** /æ/ **hat**
/ɑ/ **father, hot** /ʌ/ **up** /ə/ **about** /ɔ/ **saw**
/oʊ/ **hope** /ʊ/ **book** /u/ **too** /aɪ/ **I** /aʊ/ **how**
/ɔɪ/ **boy** /ɜˑ/ **bird** /ɚ/ **teacher** /ɪr/ **ear** /ɛr/ **air**
/ɑr/ **far** /ɔr/ **more** /ʊr/ **tour** /aɪr/ **fire**
/aʊɚ/ **hour** /θ/ **nothing** /ð/ **mother** /ʃ/ **she**
/ʒ/ **measure** /tʃ/ **church** /dʒ/ **jump** /ŋ/ **long**

something is like: *A free sample of a new perfume came in the mail.*

sample[2] [*verb;* **sampled, sampling**] to taste or use a small amount of something to find out what it is like: *The deli lets you sample the cheeses.*

sand * /sænd/ [*noun*] a substance on the ground on beaches and in deserts, that is made of tiny pieces of rock: *The hot sand burned my feet.*

sandal /'sændəl/ [*noun*] a light, open shoe that you wear in warm weather: *He was wearing **a pair of sandals**.*

sandwich * /'sændwɪtʃ/ [*noun; plural* **sandwiches**] a small meal consisting of two pieces of bread with food between them: *I'll just have a sandwich. | tuna fish sandwiches*

sandy /'sændi/ [*adjective;* **sandier, sandiest**] covered with sand: *a sandy beach*

sane /seɪn/ [*adjective;* **saner, sanest**] not mentally ill; *opposite* INSANE: *The doctors said that he was completely sane.*

sang * /sæŋ/ [*verb*] the past tense of SING

sank * /sæŋk/ [*verb*] the past tense of SINK[1]

Santa Claus /'sæntə ˌklɔz/ or **Santa** [*name*] an imaginary man with a long white beard who wears a red suit and brings children presents at Christmas: *What did Santa Claus bring you?*

sap /sæp/ [*noun*] a liquid inside a tree or other plant: *The branches were sticky with sap.*

sapphire /'sæfaɪr/ [*noun*] a valuable blue stone that is used to make jewelry: *sapphire earrings*

sarcastic /sar'kæstɪk/ [*adjective;* **more sarcastic, most sarcastic**] if you say something that is sarcastic, you say the opposite of what you mean in order to annoy someone: *a sarcastic remark*

sardine /sar'din/ [*noun*] a small fish that you can eat: *a can of sardines*

sat * /sæt/ [*verb*] the past tense and past participle of SIT

Sat. the written abbreviation of SATURDAY

satellite /'sætəˌlaɪt/ [*noun*] a piece of equipment sent into space, for example

to send signals from one part of the earth to another: *a communications satellite | The concert will be broadcast live by satellite.*

satin /'sætən/ [*noun*] smooth shiny cloth: *a beautiful satin dress*

satisfaction * /ˌsætɪs'fækʃən/ [*noun*] the feeling of happiness that you get when something happens the way you want it to: *I get a lot of satisfaction from my job.*
☛ Do not say that something "is a satisfaction." Say that it **gives you satisfaction**.

satisfactory * /ˌsætɪs'fæktəri/ [*adjective;* **more satisfactory, most satisfactory**] good enough; *synonym* ACCEPTABLE; *opposite* UNSATISFACTORY: *Her schoolwork is satisfactory.*
↪ *See the warning at* SATISFYING.

satisfied * /'sætɪsˌfaɪd/ [*adjective;* **more satisfied, most satisfied**] feeling happy because something has the results you want; *opposite* DISSATISFIED: *She had a satisfied expression on her face. | I'm not satisfied with this essay.*

satisfy * /'sætɪsˌfaɪ/ [*verb;* **satisfies, satisfied, satisfying**] to make someone feel happy because something has the results he or she wants: *Nothing I do seems to satisfy her.*

satisfying [T] /'sætɪsˌfaɪɪŋ/ [*adjective;* **more satisfying, most satisfying**] making you feel happy because something has the results you want: *It is satisfying to know that you've done a job well.*
☛ Do not confuse **satisfying** and **satisfactory**. The word **satisfying** is used about things that make you happy, and **satisfactory** is used about things that are just good enough.

Saturday * /'sætərˌdeɪ/ [*noun; plural* **Saturdays**] the day of the week that is after Friday and before Sunday: *I'm going home on Saturday. | On Saturdays, I go shopping.*
↪ *See the usage note at* DAY.

Saturn /'sætərn/ [*name*] the planet that is sixth from our sun

sauce * /sɔs/ [*noun*] a liquid that you pour over food or cook food in: *Can I* *have chocolate sauce on my ice cream?* I *chicken in a sweet-and-sour sauce*

saucepan /'sɔsˌpæn/ [*noun*] a metal cooking POT with a handle and sometimes a lid

saucer /'sɔsɚ/ [*noun*] a small plate for holding a cup: *Where do you keep the* **cups and saucers?**

⇨ *See the picture at* TEAPOT.

sauna /'sɔnə/ [*noun; plural* **saunas**] a room with wooden walls that is full of hot steam, where people sit for a short time for their health

sausage /'sɔsɪdʒ/ [*noun*] meat that is ground and mixed with salt and spices, often formed into long, thin, round pieces: *a pound of sausage* I *Do you want sausages or bacon with your eggs?*

savage /'sævɪdʒ/ [*adjective;* **more savage, most savage**] fierce and wild: *The sheep were killed by a savage dog.*

save * /seɪv/ [*verb;* **saved, saving**]
   1 to stop a person or animal from being harmed or killed; *synonym* RESCUE: *Dr. Brown* **saved** *my life.* I **save someone from doing something** ▸ *She saved me from making a big mistake.*
   2 to keep money somewhere and not spend it, so that you can use it later: *I'm* **saving for** *a new bicycle.* I *I saved $2,000 last year.* I *We're* **saving up** *for our vacation.*
   3 to use something carefully or in small amounts, so you do not waste it: *To save energy, turn off the light when you leave a room.*
   4 to prevent computer information from being lost, for example by pressing a particular key on the keyboard: *Save your work often.*

savings /'seɪvɪŋz/ [*plural noun*] the money that you have saved, or the bank account this is in: *He has a lot of money* **in savings.**

savings account /'seɪvɪŋ əˌkaʊnt/ [*noun*] a bank account in which you keep the money you want to save to use later: *I'd like to open a savings account.*

⇨ *Compare* CHECKING ACCOUNT.

saw[1] * /sɔ/ [*verb*] the past tense of SEE

saw[2] [*noun*] a TOOL used for cutting wood, metal, etc., by pushing it backward and forward over the material's surface: *You'll need a saw to cut that board.*

saw[3] [*verb;* **sawed, sawed** or **sawn, sawing**] to cut something with a saw: *He's sawing some wood to make a desk.*

sawdust /'sɔˌdʌst/ [*noun*] tiny pieces of wood produced when sawing: *The bottom of the mouse's cage was covered in sawdust.*

saxophone /'sæksəˌfoʊn/ [*noun*] a MUSICAL INSTRUMENT that is a long curved metal tube, with an end you blow into and buttons you press: *He* **plays the saxophone** *with a jazz band.*

say[1] * /seɪ/ [*verb;* **says, said, saying**]
   1 to express something in words: *I said hello.* I **say something to someone** ▸ *What did you say to her?* I **say (that)** *. . .* ▸ *She said in her letter that she'd come.* I **say where/how/when/etc.** ▸ *I wish you'd say what's bothering you.*
   ☞ Do not say "I said her to do something." Say **I told her to do something.**
   2 if some writing, a picture, an instrument, etc., says something, it gives that information: *The clock said ten-thirty.* I **say to do something** ▸ *The recipe said to put in one cup of sugar.*

⇨ *See the usage note at* SPEAK.

USAGE say, tell

Use **say** about the words someone uses: *She said, "Yes, I'll come."* You can also use **say** to report words: *She said that she would come.* Use **tell** to report what someone said: *She told us that she would come.* Do not say "She said us that she would come."

Be careful when you use "to" with **say** and **tell**. These sentences are correct: *What did she say to you?* and *What did she tell you?* Do not say "What did she tell to you?"

Use **tell** about information, facts, or stories: *He told them about his new bike.* | *He told the children a story.* | *He told a story to the children.* Do not say "He told to the children a story."

say[2] [*noun*] a chance to give your opinion or help to make a decision: *Don't I get any say in this?* | *You will all have a say in the matter.*

saying /'seɪɪŋ/ [*noun*] a sentence with a particular meaning, that people often say to each other: *We have a saying, "Good things come to those who wait."*

scab /skæb/ [*noun*] a hard layer of skin that forms over a cut on your body

scaffold /'skæfəld/ [*noun*] a temporary structure that workers stand on to reach areas high above the ground: *A scaffold was put up around the building.*

scale * /skeɪl/ [*noun*]
1 a piece of equipment used for weighing: *She put the package on the scale.*
2 a particular method of measuring things: *The model is on a scale of one inch to one foot.*
3 a series of musical notes, arranged in order: *She practiced scales on her violin.*
4 one of the thin, flat, hard pieces of skin that cover some animals, such as fish: *He scraped the scales off the fish.*

scallop /'skæləp/ [*noun*] a sea creature that you can eat, that has two colorful shells that close around it
⇨ *See the picture at* SHELLFISH.

scalp /skælp/ [*noun*] the skin covering the top of your head, under your hair: *Use this shampoo if your scalp itches.*

scanner /'skænɚ/ [*noun*] a piece of equipment attached to a computer that passes over a picture or document in order to copy it: *Put the document in the scanner, then press "Start."*

scandal /'skændəl/ [*noun*] a situation that shocks people, and makes them start talking to everyone about it: *The government has been hurt by a series of scandals.*

scar /skɑr/ [*noun*] a mark left on your skin by a wound after it heals: *Will the operation leave a scar?*

scarce /skɛrs/ [*adjective*; **scarcer, scarcest**] not available in large amounts, and difficult to get: *Jobs have become scarcer in this region.*
⇨ *See the usage note at* RARE.

scarcely Ⓣ /'skɛrsli/ [*adverb*] almost not at all, almost none at all, etc.; synonyms BARELY, HARDLY: *I lost scarcely any weight.*

scare[1] /skɛr/ [*verb*; **scared, scaring**] to make someone feel afraid; synonym FRIGHTEN: *Stop it, you're scaring me!*

scare[2] [*noun*]
1 the feeling you have when you are afraid and worried: *Her illness gave us a scare.*
2 something that frightens or worries you or a number of people, which often does not actually happen: *a bomb scare*

scarecrow /'skɛrˌkroʊ/ [*noun*] a figure in the shape of a person in old clothes, put in a field of crops to frighten birds away

scared /skɛrd/ [*adjective*; **more scared, most scared**] afraid or worried about something or someone; synonym FRIGHTENED: *Are you scared of the dark?* | **be scared of doing something** ▸ *I'm scared of making a mistake.* | **be scared (that)** ▸ *She was scared that her father would disapprove.*

scarf /skɑrf/ [*noun*; **plural scarfs** or **scarves** /skɑrvz/] a large piece of cloth that you wear around your neck or shoulders to stay warm or to look nice
⇨ *See the picture at* CLOTHING.

scary /'skɛri/ [*adjective*; **scarier, scariest**] making you feel afraid; synonym FRIGHTENING: *We watched a scary horror movie.*

scatter * Ⓣ /'skætɚ/ [*verb*; **scattered, scattering**] if you scatter things somewhere, or if they scatter there, they fall in many places all around the area: *Scatter the seeds evenly over the ground.* | *Her papers scattered in all directions.*

scene * /sin/ [*noun*]
1 a place where something such as an accident happens: *Reporters were soon at the scene of the crash.*
2 a view or picture of something and

what is happening there: *She likes to paint beach scenes.*

3 a short part of a play or movie in which the action happens: *In the first scene, the two main characters meet each other.* | *Act II Scene III*
⇨ *See the warning at* SCENERY.

scenery T̄ /ˈsinəri/ [*noun*] the fields, trees, mountains, etc., that you see in a place, especially when these are attractive: *Relax. Enjoy the scenery.*
☛ Do not confuse **scenery** and **scene**. Use **scenery** to talk about what the land in a place looks like. Use **scene** to talk about what is happening in a place.

scent /sɛnt/ [*noun*] the smell of something, especially the smell that a plant or animal produces: *the scent of roses* | *The dog followed the fox's scent.*
⇨ *See the synonym note at* SMELL[1].

schedule[1] /ˈskɛdʒul/ [*noun*]
1 a plan of the things you intend to do and when you intend to do them: *I have a very busy schedule this week.*
2 a list of the times at which buses, trains, etc., arrive and leave: *Can I look at your bus schedule?*

━━ PHRASES ━━
3 ahead of schedule earlier than planned: *The plane landed ahead of schedule.*
4 on schedule running or happening as planned: *All the subways are on schedule this morning.*
5 behind schedule later than planned: *Work on the new building is already behind schedule.*

schedule[2] [*verb*; **scheduled, scheduling**] to plan when something will happen or be done: *Our flight is scheduled to leave at 7:00 a.m.*

scholarship /ˈskɑlə˞ˌʃɪp/ [*noun*] a gift of money from an organization to help a student with his or her studies: *He won a scholarship to go to college.*

school * /skul/ [*noun*]
1 a place where children and young people are taught: *My school is very close to my home.* | *David's still at school* (=he is still in the school building). | *the school bus* (=the bus that takes students to school)

2 the time during the day when students are taught, or the time someone spends being a student: *Why don't you come over to my house after school?* | *Where did you go to school?* | *David's still in school* (=he has not graduated yet).
3 the time when college classes happen: *School starts in September.*

schoolwork /ˈskulˌwɜ˞k/ [*noun*] the work that students do for school, in the class and at home: *Her schoolwork is excellent.*

science * /ˈsaɪəns/ [*noun*]
1 the study of the natural world, especially of how things grow, work, or are made: *a science laboratory*
2 a subject such as physics, chemistry, or biology: *I like the arts more than the sciences.*

science fiction /ˈsaɪəns ˈfɪkʃən/ [*noun*] movies and books about the future that show how scientific knowledge could change life

scientific * /ˌsaɪənˈtɪfɪk/ [*adjective; no comparative*] relating to science: *scientific discoveries*

scientist * /ˈsaɪəntɪst/ [*noun*] someone whose job is to study science

scissors * /ˈsɪzə˞z/ [*plural noun*] a cutting TOOL that you hold in your hand, which consists of two joined blades: *These scissors aren't very sharp.* | *I need a pair of scissors.*

scold /skoʊld/ [*verb*; **scolded, scolding**] to tell someone in an angry way that he or she did something wrong: *Mom will scold you for getting your dress all dirty.*

scoop[1] /skup/ [*noun*] a deep spoon used for serving food, or the amount this spoon holds: *an ice-cream scoop* | *I'd like two scoops of vanilla.*

scoop[2] [*verb*; **scooped, scooping**] to use a spoon or your curved hand to pick up

/i/ see /ɪ/ big /eɪ/ day /ɛ/ get /æ/ hat
/ɑ/ father, hot /ʌ/ up /ə/ about /ɔ/ saw
/oʊ/ hope /ʊ/ book /u/ too /aɪ/ I /aʊ/ how
/ɔɪ/ boy /ɝ/ bird /ə˞/ teacher /ɪr/ ear /ɛr/ air
/ɑr/ far /ɔr/ for /ʊr/ tour /aɪr/ fire
/aʊə˞/ hour /θ/ nothing /ð/ mother /ʃ/ she
/ʒ/ measure /tʃ/ church /dʒ/ jump /ŋ/ long

or remove something: *He scooped up some water and splashed it on his face.*

score[1] * /skɔr/ [*noun*] the number of points or marks you get in a game or on a test: *She got the highest score on the test.* | *The **final score** (=the score at the end of the game) was 4–0.* | *Who's **keeping score?*** (=recording the number of points)

score[2] * [*verb*; **scored, scoring**] to get a point or mark in a game or on a test: *The team from India was the first to score (=the first team to get a point). | I scored seventeen points out of twenty on the test.*

scorer /'skɔrɚ/ [*noun*] the person who scores a point in a sports game: *She is our **top scorer** (=the person who has scored the most points) this season.*

scorpion /'skɔrpiən/ [*noun*] a small animal with a poisonous sting in its tail, that lives mostly in hot areas

Scotch tape /'skɑtʃ 'teɪp/ [*noun*] TRADEMARK a kind of clear TAPE that is used to fasten pieces of paper, packages, etc.: *I fixed the torn page with a piece of Scotch tape.*

scrambled eggs /'skræmbəld 'ɛgz/ [*plural noun*] a dish made of eggs that have had their yellow and clear parts mixed together before being cooked

scrap /skræp/ [*noun*] a small piece of something: *She wrote her phone number on a **scrap** of paper. | The dog was eating scraps left over from dinner.*

scrapbook /'skræp,bʊk/ [*noun*] a book in which you can put pictures, newspaper articles, etc.

scrape /skreɪp/ [*verb*; **scraped, scraping**] to damage a surface or to remove a substance from it by rubbing it with something rough or sharp: *He fell down and scraped his knees. | I scraped the mud off my boots.*

scratch[1] * /skrætʃ/ [*verb*; **scratches, scratched, scratching**]
  1 to damage or mark the surface of something with something sharp: *I scratched my hand on the roses. | The cat was **scratching at** the door.*
  2 to rub something, for example a part of your body, with your fingernails:

Scratching an insect bite will only make it itch worse.

scratch[2] [*noun; plural* **scratches**] a small wound or long thin mark on something: *Stop crying—it's only a little scratch!*

scream[1] /skrim/ [*verb*; **screamed, screaming**] to make a loud cry when you are very afraid or upset: *She screamed when she saw the rat. | "Get out of here," he screamed.*

scream[2] [*noun*] a loud cry, made when you are very afraid or upset: *No one heard their screams.*

screen * /skrin/ [*noun*]
  1 a surface that you can see pictures or information on: *She sat staring at the TV screen. | The screen in that movie theater is very big.*
  2 a structure that can be moved, and is used to stop someone or something from being seen, or to stop insects from getting through an open door or window: *You can leave the window open, but keep the screen closed.*

screw[1] * /skru/ [*noun*] a small nail that you twist into a hole to fasten things together
  ⇨ *See the picture at* TOOL.

screw[2] * [*verb*; **screwed, screwing**]
  1 to fasten something in place with screws; *opposite* UNSCREW: *Screw the top of the table **to** the base.*
  2 to attach two parts by twisting them together; *opposite* UNSCREW: *Screw the lid back **on** the jar.*

screwdriver /'skru,draɪvɚ/ [*noun*] a TOOL used for fastening or removing screws

scribble /'skrɪbəl/ [*verb*; **scribbled, scribbling**] to write or draw something quickly and carelessly: *He scribbled a note for her, then left.*

scripture or **Scripture** /'skrɪptʃɚ/ [*noun*] the holy books of a religion, especially the Bible: *a reading from Scripture* | *We're studying scriptures from several sources in my literature class.*

scroll /skroʊl/ [*verb*; **scrolled, scrolling**] to make the information on a computer screen move up or down so you can see it: *Scroll down to the next paragraph.*

scrub /skrʌb/ [*verb;* **scrubs, scrubbed, scrubbing**] to rub something hard with a brush or cloth when you are washing it: *She made me scrub the floor.* | *I scrubbed hard, but the stain wouldn't come out.*

sculptor /'skʌlptɚ/ [*noun*] someone who makes figures from wood, stone, metal, etc.: *the famous sculptor, Michelangelo*

sculpture /'skʌlptʃɚ/ [*noun*] a figure or figures made from wood, stone, etc., or the art of making them: *A small sculpture stood in the garden.* | *The museum displays modern sculpture.*

S.E. or **SE** the written abbreviation for SOUTHEAST: *He lives at 160 S.E. 3rd Avenue.* | *the countries of SE Asia*

sea * /si/ [*noun; plural* **seas**] an area of salt water that covers the earth's surface: *The whales headed back out to sea.* | *the Black Sea*
⇨ *See the synonym note at* OCEAN.

seafood /'si,fud/ [*noun*] fish and other creatures that live in the ocean and can be eaten: *Lobster is my favorite type of seafood.*

seagull /'si,gʌl/ [*noun*] a kind of large bird that lives near the ocean

a seagull

seal[1] /sil/ [*noun*]
1 an animal with short fur that eats fish and lives partly on the land and partly in the ocean, especially in cold parts of the world
2 something that makes a bottle or other container close tightly, protecting what is inside: *The seal on the jar was broken.*

seal[2] [*verb;* **sealed, sealing**]
1 to close something firmly or tightly, protecting what is inside it: *The bottle was sealed with a cork.*
2 to close an envelope by sticking down the sticky part at the back: *The name of the winner was in a sealed envelope*

seam /sim/ [*noun*] a line in a piece of clothing where two pieces of material have been sewn together: *The seam down the front of the dress isn't straight.*

search[1] * /sɝtʃ/ [*verb;* **searches, searched, searching**] to try to find something or someone by looking carefully in a place; *synonym* HUNT: *I've searched the house but I still can't find my watch.* | *He spent a long time searching for his glasses.*
☛ You **search** a place, but you **search for** a person or thing. For example, do not say "He searched his keys." Say **He searched for his keys.**

search[2] [*noun; plural* **searches**] when a person or a group of people try to find someone or something; *synonym* HUNT: *Many people have joined the search for the missing child.*

seashell /'si,ʃɛl/ [*noun*] a shell you find on a beach that once covered a sea creature

seashore /'si,ʃɔr/ [*noun*] the land next to the ocean: *a rocky seashore*

seasick /'si,sɪk/ [*adjective;* **more seasick, most seasick**] feeling sick because of the movement of a boat you are traveling in: *I got seasick on the cruise.*

season * 🔲 /'sizən/ [*noun*]
1 one of the four main periods of the year: spring, summer, fall, or winter: *What is your favorite season?*
2 the time of year when something usually happens: *During the tourist season, many people visit the Great Wall.* | *It's the baseball season again.*

USAGE Talking about seasons

You can use several different phrases to talk about the seasons.
Use **in the** to talk about what happens during a season: *It snows in the winter.*
Use **this** to talk about the season right now or a season that is coming: *This spring has been very warm.* | *I'm going to college this fall.*
Use **next** to talk about a season the year

/i/ **see**	/ɪ/ **big**	/eɪ/ **day**	/ɛ/ **get**	/æ/ **hat**
/ɑ/ **father, hot**	/ʌ/ **up**	/ə/ **about**	/ɔ/ **saw**	
/oʊ/ **hope**	/ʊ/ **book**	/u/ **too**	/aɪ/ **I**	/aʊ/ **how**
/ɔɪ/ **boy**	/ɝ/ **bird**	/ɚ/ **teacher**	/ɪr/ **ear**	/ɛr/ **air**
/ɑr/ **far**	/ɔr/ **more**	/ʊr/ **tour**	/aɪr/ **fire**	
/aʊɚ/ **hour**	/θ/ **nothing**	/ð/ **mother**	/ʃ/ **she**	
/ʒ/ **measure**	/tʃ/ **church**	/dʒ/ **jump**	/ŋ/ **long**	

after the one now, and **last** to talk about a season the year before the one now: *Last summer we went to Canada, this summer we're going to Mexico, and next summer we're going to Europe.*

You can use a season as a countable noun or an uncountable noun: *We got married two summers ago.* | *I can't wait for summer.* | *We go camping every summer.*

spring   summer
the seasons
fall/autumn   winter

seasoned /'sizənd/ [*adjective; no comparative*] with salt, pepper, etc., added: *Roll the chicken pieces in seasoned flour, then fry them.* | *a well-seasoned stew*

season ticket /'sizən 'tıkıt/ [*noun*] a ticket you can use to go to as many sports games, concerts, etc., as you like in one season: *We have season tickets to the opera.*

seat[1] * /sit/ [*noun*]
1 a place where you can sit, or an object you sit on: *There are 28 seats on the bus.* | *a bicycle seat* | *I'd like to reserve a seat for tonight's concert.*
▬ PHRASE ▬
2 have a seat or **take a seat** used to tell someone politely to sit down: *Have a seat. I will tell Mr. Green you're here.*

seat[2] [*verb; seated, seating*]
1 to make someone sit somewhere, or to give someone a particular place to sit: *The host seated me next to his wife.*
▬ PHRASE ▬
2 be seated FORMAL to be sitting somewhere: *The children were seated at their desks.* | *Please be seated* (=please sit down).

seat belt or **seatbelt** /'sit ˌbɛlt/ [*noun*] a band of material that you fasten across your body to keep you safely in your seat in a car, plane, etc.: *Please fasten your seat belts.*

seaweed /'si,wid/ [*noun*] a green plant that grows in the ocean: *The beach was covered in seaweed.*

second[1] * /'sɛkənd/ [*adverb, adjective; no comparative*] coming after the first person, thing, or event; sometimes written as "2nd": *Take the second turn on the left.* | *That's the second time you've asked.* | *I came in second in the race.*

second[2] * [*noun*]
1 one-sixtieth of a minute: *The page will take 5 seconds to print.* | *I finished the race in 7 minutes 36 seconds.*
2 a very short period of time: *Wait a second, I'm busy.* | *Will you help me? It'll only take a second.*
↪ See also **just a minute/second/ moment** at JUST[1].

USAGE second, third, fourth, etc.
All the numbers that show order can be pronouns: *I tried on five dresses, but I like the third best.* They can also be singular nouns when used to talk about dates | *the 2nd of July* (=the second day of July)

secondary school /'sɛkənˌdɛri ˌskul/ [*noun*] a school that children go to after elementary school and before college ↪ *Compare* HIGH SCHOOL.

second-hand /'sɛkənd 'hænd/ [*adjective; no comparative*] owned by someone else before you; *synonym* USED; *opposite* NEW: *She wears a lot of second-hand clothes.*

second person * /'sɛkənd 'pɜˈsən/ [*noun*] GRAMMAR the form of a verb or pronoun used to show who is being spoken to: *"You" is the second person* *pronoun.* | *The second person plural of the verb "be" is "are."*

secret[1] ∗ T /'sikrɪt/ [*noun*] something you do not or should not tell anyone about: *"Who gave you that?" "I can't tell you, it's a secret."* | *Can you keep a secret?* (=not tell anyone about something)

secret[2] ∗ T [*adjective;* **more secret, most secret**] only known about by one person or a small number of people: *We had a secret meeting.* | *Type in your secret password.*

secretary ∗ T /'sɛkrɪˌtɛri/ [*noun; plural* **secretaries**]
1 someone whose job is to work in an office, answering the telephone, writing letters, etc.
2 also **Secretary**; someone whose job is to manage a part of a government: *the Secretary of Labor*

secretly ∗ /'sikrɪtli/ [*adverb*] in a way that is secret: *She was secretly in love with him.*

section ∗ /'sɛkʃən/ [*noun*] a part of something: *There is heavy traffic on some sections of the freeway.* | *The last section of your paper needs more work.*

secure T /sɪ'kyʊr/ [*adjective;* **securer, securest**] safe and with no danger of something being stolen or moved: *Locks on the windows will make your house more secure.*

security T /sɪ'kyʊrɪti/ [*noun*]
1 when there is no danger or risk to someone or something: *We cannot guarantee the security of things you leave in your hotel room.*
2 things that are done to protect someone or something from crime or attack: *Security has been tightened at the airport.*

see ∗ /si/ [*verb;* **sees, saw, seen, seeing**]
1 to notice someone or something by using your eyes: *She was the most beautiful woman I had ever seen.* | *He could see that she was upset.* | *Grandpa doesn't see very well any more.* | *I see someone do something* ▸ *She saw me hide the book.* | *I see someone doing something* ▸ *A man was seen acting suspiciously.*

2 used to talk about watching a television program, movie, game, etc.: *Did you see that TV show about UFOs?*
☛ Use **watch**, not "see," to talk about watching something while you are doing it. For example, do not say "I'm seeing the game right now." Say **I'm watching the game right now.**

3 to understand something: *I see your point* (=I understand what you mean). | *I see what/why/how/etc.* ▸ *Now do you see why I was worried?*

4 to visit someone: *I go to see my uncle on Mondays.* | *You should see a doctor about that cough.*

5 to find out about something: **see if/ how/what/etc.** ▸ *Let's see if there's anything to eat.*

━━ PHRASES ━━

6 **I'll see/we'll see** SPOKEN used to tell someone that you will consider something but will not definitely agree to it: *"Can I go swimming tomorrow?" "We'll see."*

7 **see you** or **see you later/ tomorrow/next week/etc.** SPOKEN used to say goodbye to someone, or to say when you will meet again: *See you—have a good vacation!* | *I have to go now. See you tomorrow.*

8 **let's see** SPOKEN used when you are trying to remember or think about something: *She lived here, let's see, twenty-five years ago.*

━━ PHRASAL VERB ━━

see to [*phrasal verb*]
9 to deal with or take care of something: **see to something** ▸ *Don't worry—I'll see to everything.*

USAGE see, watch, look

Do not confuse these verbs. If you **see** something, you notice it with your eyes: *I saw a man walking toward us.*

You **watch** things such as television shows, movies, games, races, and other events that involve things moving or

---

/i/ **see**	/ɪ/ **big**	/eɪ/ **day**	/ɛ/ **get**	/æ/ **hat**
/ɑ/ **father, hot**	/ʌ/ **up**	/ə/ **about**	/ɔ/ **saw**	
/oʊ/ **hope**	/ʊ/ **book**	/u/ **too**	/aɪ/ **I**	/aʊ/ **how**
/ɔɪ/ **boy**	/ɝ/ **bird**	/ɚ/ **teacher**	/ɪr/ **ear**	/ɛr/ **air**
/ɑr/ **far**	/ɔr/ **more**	/ʊr/ **tour**	/aɪr/ **fire**	
/aʊɚ/ **hour**	/θ/ **nothing**	/ð/ **mother**	/ʃ/ **she**	
/ʒ/ **measure**	/tʃ/ **church**	/dʒ/ **jump**	/ŋ/ **long**	

happening: *I usually watch the evening news after dinner.*

If you **look at** people or things that are still, you pay attention to them: *Why are you looking at me like that?*

---

seed * /sid/ [*noun*] a small hard part of a plant that grows into a new plant

seek /sik/ [*verb;* **sought, seeking**] FORMAL to try to find or get something: *She finally sought help for her problem.*
↪ *See also* **look for** *at* LOOK¹.

seem * /sim/ [*linking verb;* **seemed, seeming**] if something seems nice, impossible, etc., it has qualities or behavior that make you think it is nice, impossible, etc.: *She seems to be much happier now.* | *He seems like a nice guy.* | *It seemed as if no one cared.* | **seem to do something** ▸ *The car seemed to suddenly go out of control.*

seen * /sin/ [*verb*] the past participle of SEE

seesaw /'si,sɔ/ [*noun*] a piece of equipment for children to play on, consisting of a long piece of wood supported in the middle so that it balances

seize * /siz/ [*verb;* **seized, seizing**] to take hold of something suddenly and with force; *synonym* GRAB: *She seized the boy's arm and pulled him out of the street.*

seldom /'sɛldəm/ [*adverb*] not at all often; *synonym* RARELY: *I seldom go to the movies.*

select /sɪ'lɛkt/ [*verb;* **selected, selecting**] FORMAL to choose one or something: *The winner can select from a number of prizes.*

selection /sɪ'lɛkʃən/ [*noun*] a collection of different things: *There was a huge selection of leather goods.*

self /sɛlf/ [*noun; plural* **selves**] the person who you are and your character: *The baby is his usual happy self.*

self-confidence /,sɛlf 'kɑnfɪdəns/ [*noun*] the feeling of confidence in your abilities: *He is full of self-confidence.*

self-confident /,sɛlf 'kɑnfɪdənt/ [*adjective;* **more self-confident, most self-confident**] confident about your

abilities: *a self-confident young woman* | *You should learn to be more self-confident.*

self-control /'sɛlf kən'troʊl/ [*noun*] the ability to stop yourself from doing things or showing your feelings: *He gets angry too easily and has no self-control.*

self-defense /'sɛlf dɪ'fɛns/ [*noun*] things you do to protect yourself when you are attacked

selfish /'sɛlfɪʃ/ [*adjective;* **more selfish, most selfish**] only thinking or caring about yourself, not about other people; *opposite* GENEROUS: *Don't be selfish. Share your toys with her.*

selfishly /'sɛlfɪʃli/ [*adverb*] in a selfish way; *opposite* GENEROUSLY: *He selfishly ate all the cake himself.*

selfishness /'sɛlfɪʃnɪs/ [*noun*] selfish behavior; *opposite* GENEROSITY: *She had few friends because of her selfishness.*

self-service /'sɛlf 'sɝvɪs/ [*adjective; no comparative*] a self-service restaurant, store, etc., is one where you serve yourself: *The gas station was self-service.*

sell * /sɛl/ [*verb;* **sold, selling**]
1 to give something to someone in exchange for money: *I sold my computer for $600.* | **sell someone something** ▸ *He sold me his bicycle.*
↪ *Compare* BUY.
2 to make things available for people to buy: *The bookstore also sells magazines.*

━━━ **PHRASAL VERB** ━━━

sell out [*phrasal verb*]
3 if a store sells out of something, it sells all of it so there is no more available to be bought: *Music stores* **sold out of** *the CD in a day.* | *"I'd like a loaf of bread." "Sorry, we're sold out."*

selves /sɛlvz/ [*noun*] the plural of SELF

semester /sɪ'mɛstɚ/ [*noun*] one of the two parts into which a school year is divided; *synonym* TERM: *I only went to that school for three semesters.*
↪ *Compare* QUARTER (definition 3).

semicircle /'sɛmɪ,sɝkəl/ [*noun*] a shape that is the same as half a circle: *There was one row of seats, arranged in a semicircle.*

semicolon /'sɛmɪ,koʊlən/ [*noun*] a mark used in writing. It looks like this: ;

⇨ *See* Punctuation *in the Smart Study section.*

semifinal /ˌsɛmiˈfaɪnəl/ [*noun*] one of the two games in a competition that decide who will take part in the final: *Our team got through to the semifinals.*

Senate or **senate** /ˈsɛnɪt/ [*noun*]
1 the Senate one of the two groups in the U.S. Congress that make laws
⇨ *Compare* HOUSE OF REPRESENTATIVES.
2 a group of politicians who are part of a government: *the ancient Roman senate*

senator or **Senator** /ˈsɛnətɚ/ [*noun, name*] a member of a senate

send * /sɛnd/ [*verb*; **sent, sending**]
1 to put something in the mail so that someone can receive it; *synonym* MAIL: *She sent the package yesterday.* | **send someone something** ▸ *I sent him a long letter.*
2 to tell or order someone to go somewhere: **send someone to do something** ▸ *I sent her to the store to get more coffee.*
☛ Do not say "Send someone doing something." Say **Send someone to do something.**
3 to use a computer to make an electronic message go somewhere: *I sent her an e-mail but she hasn't replied.*
4 to give someone a greeting through someone else: *Rachel sends her best wishes.*
5 to make something or someone move or go in a particular direction: *The satellite sends signals back to earth.*

━━ PHRASAL VERBS ━━
send for [*phrasal verb*]
6 to ask someone to come to you or for something to be brought to you: **send for someone/something** ▸ *I think we should send for the doctor.*
send in [*phrasal verb*]
7 to mail something to a place where it can be dealt with: **send in something** ▸ *Send in your competition entries by May 30th.* | **send something in** ▸ *I forgot to send my application in.*

senior¹ /ˈsinyɚ/ [*adjective*; **more senior, most senior**]
1 having a high rank or position in an

organization; *opposite* JUNIOR: *He has a senior position in a bank.*
2 relating to the final year of high school or college: *She's in her senior year.*

senior² T [*noun*] a student in the final year of high school or college
⇨ *Compare* FRESHMAN, SOPHOMORE, JUNIOR².

Senior /ˈsinyɚ/ [*adjective; no comparative*] used after the name of a man who has the same name as his son, often in the form "Sr.": *Thomas Brown, Senior*
⇨ *Compare* JUNIOR.

senior citizen T /ˈsinyɚ ˈsɪtəzən/ [*noun*] someone over the age of 60 or 65: *We offer special discounts to senior citizens.*

sensation * /sɛnˈseɪʃən/ [*noun*] a feeling in a part of your body: *I had no sensation in my toes.* | *a burning sensation*

sense¹ * T /sɛns/ [*noun*]
1 intelligence and good judgment: *She had the **good sense** to save some money every month.*
2 the ability to see, hear, smell, taste, or feel things: *A dog's **sense of** hearing is better than a person's.*
3 one of the meanings of a word: *This word has three different senses.*

━━ PHRASES ━━
4 a sense of guilt/pride/loss/etc. a particular feeling: *Painting gives me a sense of achievement.*
5 make sense to seem clear and sensible: *Why would he want to leave? It didn't make sense.*

sense² T [*verb*; **sensed, sensing**] to have a particular feeling about something: **sense (that)** ▸ *I could sense that something was wrong.*

sensible * /ˈsɛnsəbəl/ [*adjective*; **more sensible, most sensible**] showing good judgment and doing things that will

/i/ see	/ɪ/ big	/eɪ/ day	/ɛ/ get	/æ/ hat
/ɑ/ father, hot		/ʌ/ up	/ə/ about	/ɔ/ saw
/oʊ/ hope	/ʊ/ book	/u/ too	/aɪ/ I	/aʊ/ how
/ɔɪ/ boy	/ɝ/ bird	/ɚ/ teacher	/ɪr/ ear	/ɛr/ air
/ɑr/ far	/ɔr/ more	/ʊr/ tour	/aɪr/ fire	
/aʊɚ/ hour	/θ/ nothing	/ð/ mother	/ʃ/ she	
/ʒ/ measure	/tʃ/ church	/dʒ/ jump	/ŋ/ long	

have good results; _opposite_ FOOLISH: _She's a very sensible girl._ | _sensible advice_

sensitive * ⊤ /ˈsɛnsɪtɪv/ [_adjective;_ **more sensitive, most sensitive**]
  1 easily offended or upset: _Don't be so sensitive—I was only joking!_
  2 able to understand other people's feelings, or to notice when they are upset; _opposite_ INSENSITIVE: _He's a very sensitive and caring young man._

sent * /sɛnt/ [_verb_] the past tense and past participle of SEND

sentence¹ * /ˈsɛntəns/ [_noun_]
  1 a group of words used to state something, ask a question, or tell someone to do something: _Start all sentences with a capital letter._ | _The first sentence of the novel is very famous._
  2 the punishment that a court gives someone for a crime: _He **is serving a life sentence** for murder_ (=has to stay in prison for the rest of his life). | _She could receive a **death sentence**_ (=could be legally killed as a punishment).

sentence² [_verb;_ **sentenced, sentencing**] if a judge sentences someone for a crime, he or she says what punishment that person will have: **be sentenced to something** ▸ _He was sentenced to five years in prison._

separate¹ * /ˈsɛpərɪt/ [_adjective; no comparative_] not joined or connected to something: _The garage is **separate from** the house._ | _She likes to keep her work and her private life separate._ | _The tests will be given on three separate_ (=different) _days._

separate² * /ˈsɛpəˌreɪt/ [_verb;_ **separated, separating**]
  1 to make two things become separate or no longer together, or to move away from something: _Separate the white and the yolk of the egg._ | _A small number of children **separated from** the main group._ | **separate someone from someone** ▸ _The teacher separated him from his brother._
  2 if a husband and wife separate, they stop living together: _My parents separated two years ago._

separated /ˈsɛpəˌreɪtɪd/ [_adjective; no comparative_] no longer living with your

wife or husband: _Many of the women were divorced or separated._

separation ⊤ /ˌsɛpəˈreɪʃən/ [_noun_]
  1 when two things separate or are separated: _The separation of the two departments will be completed in May._
  2 when a husband and wife live apart for a period of time

separately * /ˈsɛpərɪtli/ [_adverb_] not together: _He and his girlfriend arrived at the party separately._

Sept. the written abbreviation of SEPTEMBER

September * /sɛpˈtɛmbɚ/ [_noun_] the ninth month of the year: _He was born **on September 8th, 1998.**_ | _The new store will open **in September**._
  ⇨ See the usage note at MONTH.

sequence /ˈsikwəns/ [_noun_] a series of things or the order things are arranged in: _a **sequence of events**_ (=related events that had a result) | _The photos are **out of sequence**_ (=not in the right order).

sergeant or **Sergeant** /ˈsardʒənt/ [_noun, name_] an officer with a fairly low rank in the Army, Air Force, Marine Corps, or police force

series * /ˈsɪriz/ [_noun; plural_ **series**]
  1 a number of similar events happening one after the other: _There has been a **series of** thunderstorms in Georgia this week._
  2 a set of television or radio programs which have the same subject or name: _This program is the last in the series._ | _a new TV series about space_

serious * /ˈsɪriəs/ [_adjective;_ **more serious, most serious**]
  1 bad and making you worried or afraid; _synonym_ MAJOR; _opposite_ MINOR: _He is recovering from a serious illness._ | _Air pollution is a serious problem._
  2 important and needing a lot of attention: _Don't laugh. This is serious._
  3 not joking or pretending: _Are you serious? Will you really move to the city?_ | _He looked very serious._

seriously * /ˈsɪriəsli/ [_adverb_]
  1 in a way that shows you think something is important and you are not joking: _He spoke very seriously._

2 take someone/something seriously to consider someone or something to be important: *You never take my ideas seriously.*

3 seriously ill extremely ill: *She was worried about her father, who was seriously ill.*

sermon /'sɜrmən/ [noun] a talk given by a religious leader, usually during a religious service: *What was today's sermon about?*

servant * /'sɜrvənt/ [noun] someone who works in someone else's home and cleans, cooks, etc.

serve[1] * /sɜrv/ [verb; served, serving]
1 to give food or drinks to people at a meal, party, etc.: *This pie can be served hot or cold.* | *Could you help me serve?*
2 to do work for an organization: *He served in the army for many years.*
3 to start playing tennis by throwing the ball high in the air and hitting it toward your opponent: *It's my turn to serve.*

— PHRASE —

4 it serves someone right used when you think someone deserved something bad that happened to him or her: *"I failed the test." "It serves you right for not studying!"*

serve[2] * [noun] when a player serves the ball in tennis: *That was a great serve!*

service * T /'sɜrvɪs/ [noun]
1 the help given to customers in a restaurant, store, etc.: *The food was good but the service was terrible.*
2 work done for someone: *You may need the services of a lawyer.* | *He retired after 40 years of service with the bank.*
3 an occasion when people gather for a religious meeting to pray, sing, etc.: *Will you be at the service on Sunday?*
4 an organization or system that provides something for the public: *the United States Postal Service* | *There is a regular bus service into town.*

sesame /'sɛsəmi/ [noun] a tropical plant with small seeds that are used in cooking: *sesame oil* (=from the seeds)

session /'sɛʃən/ [noun] a period of time used for a particular purpose: *The band*

has practice sessions twice a week. | *The court is still in session* (=still meeting).

set[1] * /sɛt/ [verb; sets, set, set, setting]
1 to do something that other people will try to copy or achieve: *She has set a new world record.* | *You need to set an example for your brother* (=behave well so that he will too).
2 to put something somewhere carefully; synonym PLACE: *He set the vase on the table.*
3 to decide something such as a rule, a goal, a date something will happen, etc.: *They set very high standards for their workers.*
4 if the sun sets, it goes down at the end of the day; opposite RISE: *The sun sets over the western mountains.*
☛ Do not say "The sun sets down." Say **The sun sets.**
5 to press or turn part of a machine to make it ready to do what you want: *I set the alarm clock for six o'clock.*

— PHRASES —

6 set the table to put plates, glasses, etc., on a table before a meal: *Could you set the table for dinner?*
↪ See the picture at PLACE SETTING.
7 set something on fire to make something start burning: *Someone had set the barn on fire.*
8 set someone free to allow a prisoner to leave a prison: *Should he ever be set free?*

— PHRASAL VERBS —

set off or **set out** [phrasal verb]
9 to begin a trip; synonym LEAVE: *They set out early in the morning.* | *What time do you set off for work?*

set off [phrasal verb]
10 to make something explode: **set off something** ▸ *You shouldn't set off fireworks near buildings.*

set up [phrasal verb]
11 to make preparations so that something can be used or started: **set**

/i/ **see**	/ɪ/ **big**	/eɪ/ **day**	/ɛ/ **get**	/æ/ **hat**
/ɑ/ **father, hot**	/ʌ/ **up**	/ə/ **about**	/ɔ/ **saw**	
/oʊ/ **hope**	/ʊ/ **book**	/u/ **too**	/aɪ/ **I**	/aʊ/ **how**
/ɔɪ/ **boy**	/ɜr/ **bird**	/ɚ/ **teacher**	/ɪr/ **ear**	/ɛr/ **air**
/ɑr/ **far**	/ɔr/ **more**	/ʊr/ **tour**	/aɪr/ **fire**	
/aʊɚ/ **hour**	/θ/ **nothing**	/ð/ **mother**	/ʃ/ **she**	
/ʒ/ **measure**	/tʃ/ **church**	/dʒ/ **jump**	/ŋ/ **long**	

something up ▸ *He's busy setting the computer up.* | **set up something** ▸ *She set up her own business.*

set² * [*noun*]
1 a group of related things: *You will need two **sets** of clothing.* | *a chess set*
2 a piece of equipment you look at to watch television programs: *a TV set*

set³ [*adjective; no comparative*]
1 ready: *Okay, are we all set?*
2 fixed: *The test is given on set dates.*

settle * ⊤ /'sɛtəl/ [*verb*; **settled, settling**]
1 to sit or rest somewhere in a comfortable way: *He settled back against the pillows.* | *The puppy settled himself by the door.*
2 if snow or dust settles, it falls on the ground and stays there: *The snow quickly began to settle.*
3 to end an argument or disagreement, or to make a decision: *Have you settled on which movie you want to see?*
4 to start living in a new area or country: *My grandmother's family moved west and settled in Idaho.*

— PHRASAL VERBS —
settle down [*phrasal verb*]
5 to become calm after being very active or excited: *Settle down and go to sleep.*
settle for [*phrasal verb*]
6 to accept less than you originally wanted: **settle for something** ▸ *You may have to settle for a smaller house.*
settle in [*phrasal verb*]
7 to become more comfortable in a new home, job, etc.: *It took a while for us to really settle in.*

seven * /'sɛvən/ [*number, noun*] 7: *My sister is seven years old.*

seventeen * /'sɛvən'tin/ [*number*] 17: *Seventeen people came to my party.*

seventeenth * /'sɛvən'tinθ/ [*adverb, adjective; no comparative*] coming after 16 other people, things, or events; sometimes written as "17th": *her seventeenth birthday* | *I finished seventeenth in the race.*
⇨ *See the usage note at* SECOND².

seventh¹ * /'sɛvənθ/ [*adverb, adjective; no comparative*] coming after six other

people, things, or objects; sometimes written as "7th": *July is the seventh month of the year.* | *I finished seventh in the race.*

seventh² * [*noun*] one of seven equal parts: *Seven is a **seventh** of forty-nine.*
⇨ *See the usage note at* SECOND².

seventieth * /'sɛvəntɪθ/ [*adjective, adverb; no comparative*] coming after 69 other people, things, or objects; sometimes written as "70th": *It is my grandfather's seventieth birthday.*
⇨ *See the usage note at* SECOND².

seventy * /'sɛvənti/ [*number, noun; plural* **seventies**] 70: *My family moved here seventy years ago.*
⇨ *See the usage note at* TEENS.

several¹ * /'sɛvərəl/ [*determiner*] more than two but fewer than many: *Several kids in our class are sick.* | *For dessert, there are several choices.*
☛ Use **several** with plural nouns and verbs. For example, do not say "There was several people there." Say **There were several people there.**

several² * [*pronoun*] more than two but fewer than many things or people: *I checked her work for mistakes and found several.* | ***Several of** my friends speak Japanese.*

severe * ⊤ /sə'vɪr/ [*adjective*; **more severe, most severe** or **severer, severest**]
1 very bad or serious: *It was the most severe storm this year.* | *He has a severe case of the flu.*
2 very strict, and not at all pleasant or friendly: *The judge was very severe.* | *a severe tone of voice*

sew * /soʊ/ [*verb*; **sewed, sewn** or **sewed, sewing**] to make or repair something using a needle and thread or a special machine: *My mother taught me to sew.* | *I sewed the button back on my jacket.*

sewing /'soʊɪŋ/ [*noun*] the activity of sewing, or the thing that you sew: *I love sewing.* | *She put down her sewing.*

sewing machine /'soʊɪŋ mə,ʃin/ [*noun*] a machine for sewing

sewn * /soʊn/ [*verb*] a past participle of SEW

sex * /sɛks/ [noun; plural **sexes**]
1 the quality of being male or female: *What sex is the kitten?*
2 kissing, touching, and other close physical activity, especially the kind that can produce babies: *He's always talking about sex.* | *You're too young to* **have sex** (=do this activity).

sexist /'sɛksɪst/ [adjective; **more sexist, most sexist**] treating women in a cruel or unfair way, or believing that they are not as good as men: *There are still many laws that are sexist.* | *sexist language*

sexual * /'sɛkʃuəl/ [adjective; no comparative] relating to sex: *sexual activity*

sexually /'sɛkʃuəli/ [adverb] in a way that relates to sex: *sexually attractive*

shabby /'ʃæbi/ [adjective; **shabbier, shabbiest**] looking old and in bad condition: *a shabby old overcoat*

shade[1] * /ʃeɪd/ [noun]
1 a place where something gives you protection from the sun: *I always stay in the shade when it's very hot.* | *There is no shade anywhere in this garden.*
⊃ *See the usage note at* SHADOW.
2 a piece of material rolled onto a bar at the top of a window, that can be pulled down to cover the window: *We bought new shades for the dining room.*
⊃ *Compare* BLIND[3] (definition 2).
3 a particular kind of a color: *I love this shade of blue.*

shade[2] * [verb; **shaded, shading**] to stop light from reaching something: *This hat will shade your face.*

shadow * /'ʃædoʊ/ [noun] a dark shape you see on a surface when someone or something blocks the sun or another light: *I could see my shadow on the ground.* | *the shadow of a tall building*

USAGE shadow, shade

Do not confuse **shadow** and **shade**. A **shadow** is the dark shape made by something when it blocks the sun: *The tree's shadow spread across the lawn.* **Shade** is used to talk about the protection from the sun that a shadow gives: *It was cooler in the shade of the tree.*

shady /'ʃeɪdi/ [adjective; **shadier, shadiest**] a shady outdoor place is protected from the sun: *It's shadier on the back porch.*

shake * /ʃeɪk/ [verb; **shook, shaken, shaking**]
1 to move quickly from side to side in small movements, or to make something or someone do this: *Her hands were shaking as she opened the letter.* | *The earthquake shook the house.*

━━ PHRASES ━━
2 **shake hands (with)** to hold someone's hand and move it up and down slightly as a greeting: *The two men shook hands with each other.*
3 **shake your head** to move your head from side to side, in order to say no to someone: *When I asked him to stay, he just shook his head.*
⊃ *Compare* NOD (definition 1).

SYNONYMS shake, rattle, wobble, vibrate

If something **shakes**, it moves quickly from side to side: *The car shook as we went over the bumps.* If something **rattles**, it shakes and hits against something, making a noise: *What's that rattling in the trunk of the car?* If something **wobbles**, it is not steady and moves from side to side: *That chair wobbles when you sit on it.* If something **vibrates**, it shakes with very small, fast, regular movements: *You could feel the machines in the factory vibrate.*

---

shall * /ʃæl/ [modal verb]
1 sometimes used with "I" and "we" to talk about the future: *I shall tell you tomorrow.* | *We shall never give up.*
⊃ *Compare* WILL[1] (definition 1).
2 FORMAL used in questions to offer to do something, ask for advice, or make a suggestion: *Shall I tell him you're here?* | *What shall we do?*
☛ Do not use "will" instead of **shall** in this meaning.

/i/ **see** /ɪ/ **big** /eɪ/ **day** /ɛ/ **get** /æ/ **hat**
/ɑ/ **father, hot** /ʌ/ **up** /ə/ **about** /ɔ/ **saw**
/oʊ/ **hope** /ʊ/ **book** /u/ **too** /aɪ/ **I** /aʊ/ **how**
/ɔɪ/ **boy** /ɝ/ **bird** /ɚ/ **teacher** /ɪr/ **ear** /ɛr/ **air**
/ɑr/ **far** /ɔr/ **more** /ʊr/ **tour** /aɪr/ **fire**
/aʊɚ/ **hour** /θ/ **nothing** /ð/ **mother** /ʃ/ **she**
/ʒ/ **measure** /tʃ/ **church** /dʒ/ **jump** /ŋ/ **long**

shallow * T /'ʃæloʊ/ [adjective; shallower, shallowest] measuring only a short distance from top to bottom; opposite DEEP: The lake is shallowest here. | a shallow dish

shame * /ʃeɪm/ [noun]
1 an unpleasant feeling you get when you have done something wrong and people think you are bad: He seemed to feel no shame for what he did. | You have **brought shame on** your family. ⇨ See also ASHAMED. ⇨ Compare GUILT.

━━ PHRASES ━━
2 shame on you SPOKEN used to say that a person should feel ashamed, usually said to a child: Did you take all the cookies? Shame on you!
3 it's/what a shame SPOKEN used to say that you think something is sad or disappointing: What a shame you're leaving! | It's a shame he didn't tell us sooner.

shampoo /ʃæm'pu/ [noun; plural shampoos] a liquid soap for washing your hair

shape * /ʃeɪp/ [noun]
1 the form that an object or area has: squares, circles, triangles, and other shapes | She made a cake **in the shape of** a cat. | The swimming pool was round **in shape**.

━━ PHRASES ━━
2 in shape in good physical condition: She jogs to stay in shape.
3 out of shape not in good physical condition: He's out of shape and needs to lose weight.

shaped * /ʃeɪpt/ [adjective; no comparative] used to describe the shape of something: a V-shaped mark | The pin was **shaped like** a butterfly.

share¹ * T /ʃer/ [verb; shared, sharing]
1 if two people share something, they both use it: There aren't enough books. Some of you will have to share. | **share something with someone** ▸ I share a room with my brother.
2 to divide something and give an equal part of it to each member of a group: **share something between/among people** ▸ The money he left was shared among his children.

share² * [noun] a part of something that has been divided between a group of people: I want my **share of** the money.

shark /ʃark/ [noun] a large fish that has many sharp teeth

sharp¹ * /ʃarp/ [adjective; sharper, sharpest]
1 having a thin cutting edge or a small point; opposites BLUNT, DULL: I need a sharper knife than this. | a sharp pencil
2 happening quickly or suddenly; opposite GRADUAL: There has been a sharp increase in the price of gas.
3 quick to understand: She has a sharp mind.

sharp² [adverb]
━━ PHRASE ━━
six o'clock/two-thirty/etc. sharp exactly six o'clock, two-thirty, etc.: Meet me at eight o'clock sharp.

sharpen /'ʃarpən/ [verb; sharpened, sharpening] to make something sharp: Bring two sharpened pencils with you for the test.

sharply /'ʃarpli/ [adverb] quickly and suddenly; opposite GRADUALLY: The price of gasoline increased sharply.

sharpener /'ʃarpənɚ/ [noun] a tool for making things sharp: a pencil sharpener | a knife sharpener

shatter /'ʃætɚ/ [verb; shattered, shattering] to break into many pieces, or to make something do this: The glass shattered when it hit the floor. | The explosion shattered windows all along the street.

shave¹ /ʃeɪv/ [verb; shaved, shaving] to cut hair very close to the skin using a sharp blade: He washed and shaved. | **shave off something** ▸ You shaved off your mustache!

shave² [noun] when a man shaves: I need a shave.

shaver /'ʃeɪvɚ/ [noun] a small electrical tool used for cutting hair very close to the skin

she * /ʃi/ [pronoun] used to talk about a particular woman, girl, or female animal, as the subject of a verb: "How's your mother?" "She's fine, thanks." | She was a beautiful cat. ⇨ See also HER.

shears /ʃɪrz/ [*plural noun*] large scissors or a TOOL that cuts like scissors

she'd * /ʃid/
1 the short form of "she had": *She'd already finished.*
☛ Do not use "she'd" for **she had** when **have** is the main verb. For example, do not say "She'd red hair." Say **She had red hair.**
2 the short form of "she would": *She'd like to talk to you.*

shed[1] 🔲 /ʃed/ [*verb*; **sheds, shed, shed, shedding**] to drop or lose small pieces, such as hair or leaves: *Our cat sheds a lot.* | *The trees had shed their leaves.*

shed[2] [*noun*] a small building used for storing things

sheep * /ʃip/ [*noun*; *plural* **sheep**] a farm animal with thick hair that curls, which is used to make cloth: *Wool comes from sheep.* | *A flock of sheep was grazing in the field.*

a goat

a sheep

sheer /ʃɪr/ [*adjective*; *no comparative*] without any other feeling or condition involved: *It was sheer luck that no one got hurt.*
☛ Only use **sheer** before a noun.

sheet * /ʃit/ [*noun*]
1 a piece of paper: *Her letter filled four sheets of paper.*
2 a large piece of thin cloth which is put over a bed

shelf * /ʃelf/ [*noun*; *plural* **shelves**] a flat piece of wood or metal attached to a wall or other object, on which you put

things: *She took a book from the middle shelf.* | *The shelves were empty.*

shell * /ʃel/ [*noun*] the hard covering of a snail, sea creature, egg, or nut: *an oyster shell* | *Here's a bowl to put the peanut shells in.*

she'll * /ʃil/ the short form of "she will": *She'll be here in a minute.*

shellfish /'ʃel,fɪʃ/ [*noun*; *plural* **shellfish**] a sea creature that has a shell, especially one that is used for food: *"Do you eat clams?" "Yes. I love shellfish."*

clam   oyster   scallop

shellfish

shelter[1] * 🔲 /'ʃeltər/ [*noun*]
1 a structure that protects you from bad weather or danger: *They stayed in the shelter until the hurricane passed.*
2 protection from bad weather or danger: *They tried to find shelter from the storm.*

shelter[2] * 🔲 [*verb*; **sheltered, sheltering**] to give or find protection from bad weather or danger: *They sheltered in the barn until the rain stopped.*

shelves * /ʃelvz/ [*noun*] the plural of SHELF

shepherd /'ʃepərd/ [*noun*] someone whose job is to take care of sheep

sheriff /'ʃerɪf/ [*noun*] someone who is in charge of police work in a county

she's * /ʃiz/
1 the short form of "she is": *She's a great kid.*
2 the short form of "she has": *She's had an accident.*
☛ Do not use "she's" for **she has** if **have** is the main verb. For example, do not say "She's a sweater." Say **She has a sweater.**

/i/ see /ɪ/ big /eɪ/ day /ɛ/ get /æ/ hat
/ɑ/ father, hot /ʌ/ up /ə/ about /ɔ/ saw
/oʊ/ hope /ʊ/ book /u/ too /aɪ/ I /aʊ/ how
/ɔɪ/ boy /ɝ/ bird /ɚ/ teacher /ɪr/ ear /ɛr/ air
/ɑr/ far /ɔr/ more /ʊr/ tour /aɪr/ fire
/aʊɚ/ hour /θ/ nothing /ð/ mother /ʃ/ she
/ʒ/ measure /tʃ/ church /dʒ/ jump /ŋ/ long

shield[1] /ʃild/ [*noun*] something that protects you from being hit or injured: *Roman soldiers used to carry large shields.*

shield[2] [*verb;* **shielded, shielding**] to protect someone or something from being hit or injured: *She pulled up her scarf to* **shield** *her face* **from** *the wind.*

shift[1] Ⓣ /ʃift/ [*verb;* **shifted, shifting**] to move from one place or position to another: *The boxes in the back of the truck had shifted forward.*

shift[2] Ⓣ [*noun*]
1 one of several periods during the day and night when a group of people work: *I'm on the late shift this week.*
2 a change in how a person or group does something or thinks about something: *There's been a* **shift** *in the public's attitude toward gun control.*

shin /ʃin/ [*noun*] the front of the lower part of your leg
↪ *See the picture at* BODY.

shine * /ʃain/ [*verb;* **shined** or **shone, shining**]
1 to produce light: *The sun shone brightly.*
2 to look smooth and bright: *This shampoo will make your hair shine.*
3 to make a light shine somewhere: *He shined his flashlight into the bushes.*

shiny * /'ʃaini/ [*adjective;* **shinier, shiniest**] smooth and bright; opposite DULL: *He was proud of his shiny new car.*

ship[1] * /ʃip/ [*noun*] a large boat: *They could see a ship sailing toward the harbor.* | *The goods were transported by ship.*

ship[2] [*verb;* **ships, shipped, shipping**] to move goods by boat, train, truck, or plane: *How do you want to ship these books?*

shipment /'ʃipmənt/ [*noun*] a set of goods being moved by boat, train, etc.: *The latest shipment of toys has just arrived.*

shirt * /ʃɜ˞t/ [*noun*] a piece of CLOTHING with sleeves that you wear on the upper half of your body: *He always wears a* **shirt and tie** *to work.*

shiver /'ʃivə˞/ [*verb;* **shivered, shivering**] to shake because you are cold or afraid: *It was so cold I couldn't stop shivering.*

shock[1] * /ʃak/ [*noun*]
1 the feeling you get when something surprising and unpleasant happens: *The news* **gave** *her quite* **a shock***.* | *She stood there* **in shock***.*
2 a sudden feeling of pain you get when electricity passes through your body: *I* **got a shock** *when I touched the wire.*

shock[2] * [*verb;* **shocked, shocking**] to say or do something that makes someone feel very surprised and upset: *He shocked his mother by telling her he was leaving home.*

shocked /ʃakt/ [*adjective;* **more shocked, most shocked**] very upset and surprised by something unpleasant: *I was shocked to hear he'd been fired.*

shocking * /'ʃakiŋ/ [*adjective;* **more shocking, most shocking**] surprising and very unpleasant: *shocking news*

shoe * /ʃu/ [*noun; plural* **shoes**] one of the two things you wear on your feet to protect them outdoors: *a* **pair of shoes**
↪ *See the picture at* CLOTHING.

shoelace /'ʃu,leis/ [*noun*] a thick string used to fasten a shoe; synonym LACE
↪ *See the picture at* SNEAKER.

shone * /ʃoʊn/ [*verb*] a past tense and past participle of SHINE

shook * /ʃʊk/ [*verb*] the past tense of SHAKE

shoot[1] * /ʃut/ [*verb;* **shot, shooting**]
1 to fire a weapon, or to hurt someone with a gun: *Someone shot him in the arm.* | *She was* **shot dead***.* | *He was* **shooting at** *a target on a tree.*
2 to throw or kick a ball to get points in a sports game: *He shot and scored.*
3 to move very quickly: *The car just shot out in front of us.*

shoot[2] [*noun*] a small new part growing from a plant: *One tiny new shoot showed the plant wasn't dead.*

shop[1] * /ʃap/ [*noun*] a small store, especially one that sells a particular kind of thing: *She works in a card shop.*

shop[2] * [*verb;* **shops, shopped, shopping**] to visit stores in order to buy things: *She loves to shop.*

shopping /'ʃapiŋ/ [*noun*] when you visit stores in order to buy things: *I have* *a lot of shopping to do today.* | *We're going shopping for a new TV.*

shopping bag /'ʃɑpɪŋ ˌbæg/ [noun] a large BAG with handles, which stores give to customers for carrying things they buy

shore * /ʃɔr/ [noun] the land along the edge of the ocean or a lake
⮑ Compare BEACH.

short * /ʃɔrt/ [adjective; **shorter, shortest**]
1 measuring a small amount from one end to the other; *opposite* LONG: *The beach is only a short distance away.* | *She has very short hair.*
2 continuing for a small amount of time; *synonym* BRIEF; *opposite* LONG: *Let's take a short break.* | *My vacation was too short.*
3 small in HEIGHT; *opposite* TALL: *I'm shorter than my brother.*
━ PHRASE ━
4 be short (of) to not have as much of something as you need: *We're two chairs short.* | *I'm a little **short of cash** right now.*

shortage 🔲 /'ʃɔrtɪdʒ/ [noun] when there is not enough of something: *a **shortage of** water* | *a **food shortage***

shortcut /'ʃɔrtˌkʌt/ [noun] a quicker way to a place than the usual way: *I **took a shortcut** through the park.*

shorten /'ʃɔrtən/ [verb; **shortened, shortening**] to make something shorter: *My new pants need to be shortened.*

shortly /'ʃɔrtli/ [adverb] soon: *He will be here shortly.* | *She arrived **shortly after** ten o'clock.*

shorts /ʃɔrts/ [plural noun]
1 pants which do not cover your legs below your knees
⮑ See the picture at CLOTHING.
2 a piece of men's underwear that looks like shorts

shot¹ * /ʃɑt/ [noun]
1 the firing of a gun, or the sound made by this: *Someone **took a shot at** us.* | *I heard two shots and then silence.*
2 a photograph: *We **took** some good **shots** of the bay.*
3 when someone throws or kicks a ball

to get points in a sports game: *That was a great shot!*
4 a drug or medicine put into your body with a hollow needle, for example to prevent a disease; *synonym* INJECTION: *I get **a flu shot** every year.*

shot² * [verb] the past tense and past participle of SHOOT

shotgun /'ʃɑtˌgʌn/ [noun] a long gun, often used to hunt

should * /ʃʊd/ [modal verb]
1 used for giving someone advice or giving your opinion: *You should check the bus schedule before leaving.* | *He shouldn't eat so much candy.*
2 used to say what you expect to happen or what you think will be true: *He should be home soon.* | *The trip shouldn't take long.*
3 used in questions to offer to do something, ask for advice, or make a suggestion: *Should I start supper now?* | *What should we do tonight?*
━ PHRASE ━
4 should have used to talk about something good, sensible, etc., that was not done, or something expected that did not happen: *You should have made sure the gate was shut.* | *I should have been home by eleven.*

shoulder * /'ʃoʊldɚ/ [noun] one of the parts on either side of your neck where your arms join the rest of your BODY

shouldn't * /'ʃʊdənt/ the short form of "should not": *You shouldn't fight with your sister.* | *The doctor shouldn't be long.*

should've /'ʃʊdəv/ SPOKEN the short form of "should have": *You should've worn a coat.* | *She should've called by now.*

shout¹ * /ʃaʊt/ [verb; **shouted, shouting**]
1 to say something in a very loud voice; *opposite* WHISPER: *There's no need to shout. I can hear you.* | *He shouted my name.*

/i/ see /ɪ/ big /eɪ/ day /ɛ/ get /æ/ hat
/ɑ/ father, hot /ʌ/ up /ə/ about /ɔ/ saw
/oʊ/ hope /ʊ/ book /u/ too /aɪ/ I /aʊ/ how
/ɔɪ/ boy /ɝ/ bird /ɚ/ teacher /ɪr/ ear /ɛr/ air
/ɑr/ far /ɔr/ more /ʊr/ tour /aɪr/ fire
/aʊɚ/ hour /θ/ nothing /ð/ mother /ʃ/ she
/ʒ/ measure /tʃ/ church /dʒ/ jump /ŋ/ long

— PHRASAL VERB —

shout at [phrasal verb]

2 to talk in a loud angry way to someone, especially because he or she did something wrong: **shout at someone** ▸ *His mother shouted at him to come inside.*

shout² ✳ [noun] a loud cry; <u>opposite</u> WHISPER: *a shout for help*

shove /ʃʌv/ [verb; **shoved, shoving**] to push someone or something with force: *Someone in the crowd was shoving.* | *We shoved the bookcase against the wall.*

shovel¹ ✳ /'ʃʌvəl/ [noun] a TOOL with a long handle and a wide curved metal part at one end, used for moving dirt, snow, etc.

↪ Compare SPADE.

shovel² [verb; **shoveled, shoveling**] to move dirt, snow, etc., with a shovel: *Dad's outside shoveling the driveway.*

show¹ ✳ /ʃoʊ/ [verb; **showed, shown** or **showed, showing**]

1 to let someone see something: *Please show your tickets at the door.* | **show something to someone** ▸ *Show the video to your mother.* | **show someone something** ▸ *She showed me the bruise on her leg.*

2 to make something clear: *Tests* **showed that** *he had cancer.*

3 to behave in a particular way or let people see your feelings: *She has shown great courage.* | *He showed no emotion.*

4 to explain something to someone in a way that can be seen: *Will you* **show** *me* **where** *to park my car?* | *A diagram* **showed how** *to put the table together.*

☛ Do not say "show someone to do something." Say **show someone how to do something.**

5 if a picture or map shows something, that thing can be seen in the picture or on the map: *The video showed a man entering a house.*

— PHRASE —

6 **show someone somewhere** to guide someone into or out of a place, especially a home or office: *"Mr. Brown is here." "Please* **show him in."** | *Will you* **show** *our guests* **to the door?** | *The maid will* **show** *you out.*

— PHRASAL VERBS —

show around [phrasal verb]

7 to take someone around a place, so that he or she can see what it is like: **show someone around something** ▸ *One of the students showed him around the school.*

show off [phrasal verb]

8 to try to make people admire you, in a way that is annoying to other people: *He always shows off when there are girls around.*

9 to make sure people will see something so they will admire it: **show off something** ▸ *He rode around the neighborhood, showing off his new bike.*

show up [phrasal verb]

10 to arrive, especially at a place where you are expected: *Do you think he'll show up for school today?*

show² ✳ [noun]

1 a play in a theater, or a program on television or radio: *We went to see a show on Saturday.* | *a TV show*

2 an event where many things of the same type are shown for people to look at or buy: *a flower show* | *a boat show*

shower ✳ /'ʃaʊɚ/ [noun]

1 a place in a bathroom where you can stand under falling water to wash yourself, or the piece of equipment that makes the water fall: *When I* **turned on the shower,** *the water was cold.*

2 when you wash yourself in a shower: *I'm going to* **take a shower.**

3 a short period of rain or snow: *In the morning, there were* **heavy showers** (=there was a lot of rain).

shown ✳ /ʃoʊn/ [verb] a past participle of SHOW¹

show-off /'ʃoʊ ˌɔf/ [noun] someone who tries too hard to make people admire what he or she has or can do: *Don't be such a show-off.*

shrank /ʃræŋk/ [verb] the past tense of SHRINK

shredded /'ʃrɛdɪd/ [adjective; no comparative] torn or cut into small, thin pieces: *shredded coconut* | *shredded cabbage*

shrimp /ʃrɪmp/ [*noun; plural* **shrimp**] a small sea creature you can eat, that has a curved body and is pink when it is cooked

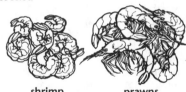

shrimp   prawns

shrine /ʃraɪn/ [*noun*] a place where people pray, which is connected with a god or a holy person

shrink /ʃrɪŋk/ [*verb;* **shrank, shrunk, shrinking**] to become smaller: *My sweater shrank when I washed it.*

shrub /ʃrʌb/ [*noun*] a plant like a very small tree
↪ *See the picture at* HOUSE.

shrug /ʃrʌg/ [*verb;* **shrugs, shrugged, shrugging**] to raise your shoulders and then lower them to show that you do not know the answer to a question or do not care about something: *Don't just shrug your shoulders. Answer my question.*

shrunk /ʃrʌŋk/ [*verb*] the past participle of SHRINK

shut¹ * /ʃʌt/ [*verb;* **shuts, shut, shut, shutting**]
1 to close something or become closed; *opposite* OPEN: *I shut the box and locked it.* | *Shut your eyes and relax.* | *The door shut behind him.*
2 if a store, office, etc., shuts or if someone shuts it, it is no longer open; *synonym* CLOSE: *The store shuts at 6:30.* | *They sometimes shut the museum without notice.*

━ **PHRASAL VERBS** ━

shut down [*phrasal verb*]
3 if a piece of electrical equipment shuts down or is shut down, it is turned off: **shut something down** ▸ *Don't forget to shut your computer down.*

shut up [*phrasal verb*]
4 *INFORMAL* to stop talking: *I wish he'd shut up!* | *Shut up, Mark!*
☞ Saying "shut up" is rude. Use **be quiet** instead.

shut² * [*adjective; no comparative*] closed; *opposite* OPEN: *Make sure all the windows are shut.*

shutter /ˈʃʌtɚ/ [*noun*] one of a set of covers on the outside of a window that can swing together to protect it: *a white house with green shutters*

shuttle /ˈʃʌtəl/ [*noun*]
1 a bus, plane, or train that travels between two places regularly: *She caught a shuttle to Washington, D.C.*
2 a vehicle that can travel into space and come back again: *the space shuttle*

shy * /ʃaɪ/ [*adjective;* **shyer, shyest**] afraid to talk to people because you become nervous and embarrassed; *opposite* OUTGOING: *He was very shy when he was young.* | *Don't be shy—tell us all about it.*
↪ *Compare* TIMID.

sick * /sɪk/ [*adjective;* **sicker, sickest**]
1 uncomfortable or in pain, usually because you have an illness; *synonym* ILL; *opposite* WELL: *She was too sick to go out.* | *He is a very sick man.*

━ **PHRASES** ━

2 be sick (to your stomach) to bring food up from your stomach, out of your mouth; *synonym* VOMIT: *I think I'm going to be sick.*
3 feel sick to not feel well, or feel as though you are going to bring food up from your stomach: *Traveling on boats makes me feel sick.*
4 make someone sick to make someone feel very angry or disappointed: *You make me sick!*
5 be sick of to be annoyed, because something keeps happening or because you spend too much time with someone: *I'm sick of hearing you complain all the time.*

sickness * /ˈsɪknɪs/ [*noun*] when you feel sick or have an illness that is not

---

/i/ **see** /ɪ/ **big** /eɪ/ **day** /ɛ/ **get** /æ/ **hat**
/ɑ/ **father, hot** /ʌ/ **up** /ə/ **about** /ɔ/ **saw**
/oʊ/ **hope** /ʊ/ **book** /u/ **too** /aɪ/ **I** /aʊ/ **how**
/ɔɪ/ **boy** /ɝ/ **bird** /ɚ/ **teacher** /ɪr/ **ear** /ɛr/ **air**
/ɑr/ **far** /ɔr/ **more** /ʊr/ **tour** /aɪr/ **fire**
/aʊɚ/ **hour** /θ/ **nothing** /ð/ **mother** /ʃ/ **she**
/ʒ/ **measure** /tʃ/ **church** /dʒ/ **jump** /ŋ/ **long**

very serious: *He stayed home from work because of sickness.*
⇨ *See the synonym note at* DISEASE.

side * /saɪd/ [*noun*]
1 one of the surfaces forming the outside of something, but not the bottom or the top: *There was a lock on* **the side of** *the box.*
2 the left or right part of something: *He is paralyzed on one* **side of** *his body.* | *Do you want to sit on the right or left* **side**?
3 a part of an area that is far from the middle of it; *synonym* EDGE: *I stood at* **the side of** *the field.* | *Their house is* **on the other side of** *the lake* (=on the opposite side).
4 a surface of a piece of paper, a door, etc.: *Write on both* **sides of** *the paper.*
5 one of the two people or groups involved in a war, competition, argument, etc.: *Our* **side** *won the baseball game.* | *Whose* **side** *are you on?* (=whom do you support) | *Why do you always* **take her side**? (=support her)
— PHRASES
6 **at/by someone's side** next to someone: *Her dog is always at her side.*
7 **side by side** next to each other: *The girls walked side by side.*

sideburns /'saɪdˌbɜˑnz/ [*plural noun*] HAIR that grows down the sides of a man's face

sidewalk * /'saɪdˌwɔk/ [*noun*] a hard path by the side of a street for people to walk on: *He was sweeping the sidewalk in front of his store.*
⇨ *See the picture at* HOUSE.

sideways * /'saɪdˌweɪz/ [*adverb*]
1 with the front or back facing the side: *She sat sideways in her mother's lap.*
2 in the direction of one side or the other: *We need to move the bookcase sideways a few inches.*

sigh[1] /saɪ/ [*verb*; **sighed, sighing**] to let your breath out slowly with a small sound, for example because you are not happy about something: *When I asked her about her boyfriend, she just sighed.*

sigh[2] [*noun*] when you let your breath out with a small sound: *He gave a* **sigh of relief**.

sight * /saɪt/ [*noun*]
1 the ability to see things; *synonyms* EYESIGHT, VISION: *He lost his sight in an accident.*
2 something you see: *It was a frightening sight.* | *I want to see* **the sights of** *Tokyo* (=the interesting things to see in Tokyo).
— PHRASES
3 **out of sight** if something is out of sight, you cannot see it: *We watched until the plane flew out of sight.*
4 **catch sight of** to suddenly see someone or something: *I caught sight of something moving in the bushes.*
5 **in/within sight** close enough to be seen: *The finish line was soon in sight.*

sightseeing /'saɪtˌsiɪŋ/ [*noun*] the activity of visiting interesting places, especially when you are on vacation: *In the afternoon, we* **did some sightseeing**.

sign[1] * /saɪn/ [*noun*]
1 a board with writing or pictures on it, used to give a warning, directions to a place, etc.: *A sign on the door read, "No Smoking."* | *a road sign*
2 something that shows that something else happened or will happen, or that something is true or exists: *Black clouds are a* **sign of** *rain.* | *He gave no* **sign that** *he was upset.*
3 a mark that has a particular meaning: *a multiplication sign* (×)
⇨ *Compare* SIGNAL.

sign[2] * [*verb*; **signed, signing**] to write your name on something: *Please sign here.* | *I forgot to sign the letter.*

signal[1] * /'sɪgnəl/ [*noun*] a light, sound, or action that warns you or orders you to do something: *The runners waited for the starting signal.*
⇨ *Compare* SIGN[1].

signal[2] [*verb*; **signaled, signaling**] to make a movement or another kind of sign to show what you are going to do or what someone should do: *That driver didn't signal that he was turning.*

signature /'sɪgnətʃɚ/ [*noun*] someone's name that he or she writes on a letter or an official document: *The contract is ready for your signature.*

significant ⊤ /sɪg'nɪfɪkənt/ [*adjective*; **more significant, most significant**] big or important enough to be noticed or mentioned: *There has been a significant increase in pollution.*

sign language /'saɪn ˌlæŋgwɪdʒ/ [*noun*] language that uses hand movements instead of speech, used for speaking with people who cannot hear

signpost /'saɪnˌpoʊst/ [*noun*] a road sign that tells you where or how far a place is

silence * /'saɪləns/ [*noun*] when there is no noise at all: *We all listened **in silence**.*

silent * /'saɪlənt/ [*adjective; no comparative*] making no noise at all: *Please **remain silent** until the end of the concert.*

silk * /sɪlk/ [*noun*] a shiny material made from soft, thin threads: *an expensive silk blouse*

silly * /'sɪli/ [*adjective; sillier, silliest*] not sensible: *a silly idea* | *a silly child*

silver[1] * /'sɪlvɚ/ [*noun*]
1 a shiny gray-white metal used for making jewelry, coins, etc.: *The knives and forks were made of silver.*
2 a shiny gray-white color: *The gowns are available in silver or gold.*

silver[2] * [*adjective; no comparative*]
1 made of silver: *a silver necklace* | *a silver medal* (=a medal given as second prize in a competition)
2 of the color silver: *a silver bicycle*

silverware /'sɪlvɚˌwɛr/ [*noun*] knives, forks, and spoons for eating with: *She got out the plates and silverware.*

similar * T /'sɪmələr/ [*adjective; more similar, most similar*] having most of the features or qualities that someone or something else has: *My brother and I are very similar in character.* | *Your ring is **similar to** mine.*
☛ Do not say one thing is "similar with" another. Say it is **similar to** it.
⇨ *Compare* DIFFERENT, SAME[1].

similarity * /ˌsɪmə'lærɪti/ [*noun; plural similarities*] when something is similar to another thing, or the thing that makes it similar: *Her **similarity to** the girl in the photograph was remarkable.* | *What are the **similarities between** Chinese and Thai cooking?*
⇨ *Compare* DIFFERENCE.

simple * /'sɪmpəl/ [*adjective; simpler, simplest*]
1 easy to understand or do, or not complicated; opposites HARD, DIFFICULT: *Just follow these simple directions.* | *Anyone can cook rice—it's simple.* | *The answer is simple.*
2 not decorated; opposite FANCY: *We live in a simple farmhouse.*

simply * /'sɪmpli/ [*adverb*]
1 in a way that is easy to understand: *How can I explain this to you simply?*
2 used to emphasize that something should not be hard to do; synonym JUST: *If you want more information, simply call this number.*
3 used to emphasize something: *He simply doesn't understand how I feel.*

sin /sɪn/ [*noun*] an action or way of behaving that breaks a moral or religious law: *the sin of lying*

since[1] * /sɪns/ [*preposition*]
1 from an event or time in the past until now: *I've been waiting since 2:30.* | *Since leaving college, he's lived with his parents.*
☛ Do not say "I've been waiting from 2:30." Say **I've been waiting since 2:30.**
⇨ *See the usage note at* AGO.
2 during the time between a past event or time and now: *He has written to me twice since I saw him.*

since[2] * [*adverb*] from an event or time in the past until now: *He moved to Ohio in 1998, and has lived there **ever since**.*

since[3] * [*conjunction*]
1 from an event or time in the past until now: *She's wanted to be a dancer since she was a child.*
2 at a particular time between a past event or time and now: *We've made some good friends since we moved here.*
3 because: *Since it was raining, we didn't go out.*
☛ Do not say "Since it was raining, so we didn't go out." Say **Since it was**

/i/ **see** /ɪ/ **big** /eɪ/ **day** /ɛ/ **get** /æ/ **hat**
/ɑ/ **father, hot** /ʌ/ **up** /ə/ **about** /ɔ/ **saw**
/oʊ/ **hope** /ʊ/ **book** /u/ **too** /aɪ/ **I** /aʊ/ **how**
/ɔɪ/ **boy** /ɝ/ **bird** /ɚ/ **teacher** /ɪr/ **ear** /ɛr/ **air**
/ɑr/ **far** /ɔr/ **more** /ʊr/ **tour** /aɪr/ **fire**
/aʊɚ/ **hour** /θ/ **nothing** /ð/ **mother** /ʃ/ **she**
/ʒ/ **measure** /tʃ/ **church** /dʒ/ **jump** /ŋ/ **long**

raining, we didn't go out or It was raining, so we didn't go out.

sincere * /sɪn'sɪr/ [adjective; **more sincere, most sincere** or **sincerer, sincerest**] expressing your true feelings, not pretending: I don't know if he was being sincere. I Please accept my sincerest apologies (=I am very sorry).

sincerely * /sɪn'sɪrli/ [adverb]
1 used to say that someone is not pretending: He sincerely believed he did nothing wrong.

── PHRASE ──

2 Sincerely (yours) used at the end of a formal letter before signing your name: He ended the letter, "Sincerely, Matthew Brown."

sing * /sɪŋ/ [verb; **sang, sung, singing**] to make music with your voice: I could hear someone singing. I **sing someone something** ▶ Sing us a song, Grandma! ☛ You can also say that birds sing.

singer * /'sɪŋɚ/ [noun] someone who sings: You're a very good singer.

single¹ * Ⓣ /'sɪŋɡəl/ [adjective; no comparative]
1 used to emphasize that a thing or person is the only one: There was a single rose left on the bush. I Not a single person came to visit her.
☛ Only use **single** before a noun in this meaning.
2 not married: My sister is married and my brother is single.
3 for one person only: What is the price of a single room?
☛ Only use **single** before a noun in this meaning.
↪ Compare DOUBLE¹ (definition 3).

── PHRASE ──

4 (in) single file with one person behind the next in one line: Everybody line up single file, please.

single² [noun]
1 a piece of paper money worth $1.00: Do you have a couple of singles I can borrow until tomorrow?
2 a song produced as a recording by a band: Three singles from their album are selling really well.

singular * /'sɪŋɡyələr/ [adjective; no comparative] GRAMMAR a singular verb,

noun, or pronoun is used to talk about one person or thing: The article "a" is used before singular nouns. I a verb in the singular form
↪ Compare PLURAL².

sink¹ * /sɪŋk/ [verb; **sank, sunk, sinking**]
1 to go under the surface of water, fall to the bottom, and not come up again: The boat was beginning to sink. I His watch came off and sank to the bottom of the river.
2 to go down to a lower level: I watched the sun sink behind the trees.

sink² [noun] an object in a kitchen or bathroom that holds water so you can wash your hands, dishes, etc.

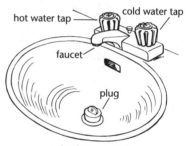

a bathroom sink

sip¹ /sɪp/ [verb; **sips, sipped, sipping**] to drink something gradually in small amounts: He sipped his coffee.

sip² [noun] a small amount of a drink: Would you like a sip of my water?

sir or **Sir** /sɜr/ [name] used to speak or write politely to a man, especially someone you do not know or someone who is in a position of authority: Excuse me, sir, you left your wallet on the table. I "Sit down, young man." "Yes, Sir." I The letter began, "Dear Sir."
↪ Compare MADAM. ↪ See the warning at MISTER.

siren /'saɪrən/ [noun] a piece of equipment on a fire truck, police car, etc. that makes a loud noise to warn people: an ambulance siren

sister * /'sɪstər/ [noun] a girl or woman who has the same parents as you: a younger sister
↪ See the picture at FAMILY TREE.

sister-in-law /'sɪstə- ɪn ˌlɔ/ [*noun; plural* **sisters-in-law** /'sɪstə-z ɪn ˌlɔ/] your brother's wife, or the sister of your husband or wife
⇨ *See the picture at* FAMILY TREE.

sit * /sɪt/ [*verb;* **sat, sitting**]
1 to lower yourself from a standing position so that your bottom rests on something: *The teacher told us all to sit.* | *Don't sit on my newspaper!* | *I wanted to sit down and rest.*
2 to have your bottom resting on a seat: *He was sitting at his desk writing a letter.* | *They sat on the ground in a circle.* | *I sit next to Lisa in math class.*
━━ **PHRASAL VERBS** ━━
sit around [*phrasal verb*]
3 to spend time sitting without doing anything useful: *Are you just going to sit around indoors on this beautiful day?*
sit up [*phrasal verb*]
4 to sit with your back straight, or to move from lying flat to a sitting position: *Sit up straight!* | *He's still sick, but he can sit up in bed now.*

site /saɪt/ [*noun*]
1 the place where something happened: *He took us to the site of the old Roman wall.*
2 a place where something will be built or is being built: *We're visiting the building site tomorrow.*

situation * Ⓣ /ˌsɪtʃu'eɪʃən/ [*noun*] the conditions in a particular place at a particular time, or what is happening then: *He is in a very difficult situation.* | *What can we do to improve the situation?*

six * /sɪks/ [*number, noun; plural* **sixes**] 6: *Six people live in our house.* | *We moved here when I was six.*

sixteen * /'sɪks'tin/ [*number*] 16: *I will be sixteen years old tomorrow.*

sixteenth * /'sɪks'tinθ/ [*adjective, adverb; no comparative*] coming after 15 other people, things, or events; sometimes written as "16th": *the sixteenth day of the month*
⇨ *See the usage note at* SECOND².

sixth¹ * /sɪksθ/ [*adverb, adjective; no comparative*] coming after five other people, things, or events; sometimes written as "6th": *June is the sixth month of the year.* | *I finished sixth in the contest.*

sixth² * [*noun*] one of six equal parts: *A sixth of 24 is four.*
⇨ *See the usage note at* SECOND².

sixtieth * /'sɪkstɪɪθ/ [*adjective, adverb; no comparative*] coming after 59 other people, things, or events; sometimes written as "60th": *their sixtieth wedding anniversary*
⇨ *See the usage note at* SECOND².

sixty * /'sɪksti/ [*number, noun; plural* **sixties**] 60: *Sixty people were killed.*
⇨ *See the usage note at* TEENS.

size * /saɪz/ [*noun*]
1 used to talk about how big or small something or someone is: *What size is your apartment?* | *People come in all shapes and sizes.*
2 one of a particular set of measurements for clothes and other goods that are sold: *They didn't have the dress in my size.* | *What size shoes do you take?*
⇨ *See* Prefixes and Suffixes *in the Smart Study section.*

USAGE   **Talking about size**

The usual way of asking about the **size** of something is to use **how big**: *I don't know how big my waist is.* | *How big is your school?*
When you are asking about someone's clothes or shoe size, you can say **What size are you?** or **What size do you wear?** The person would then reply **I'm a size 8** or **I wear a size 11.**

---

skate¹ /skeɪt/ [*verb;* **skated, skating**] to move over a surface on skates: *She skated across the ice.*

skate² [*noun*] a boot with a blade underneath for moving on ice, or with small wheels underneath: *a pair of skates*
⇨ *See also* ICE SKATE, IN-LINE SKATE, ROLLER SKATE.

/i/ **see** /ɪ/ **big** /eɪ/ **day** /ɛ/ **get** /æ/ **hat**
/ɑ/ **father, hot** /ʌ/ **up** /ə/ **about** /ɔ/ **saw**
/oʊ/ **hope** /ʊ/ **book** /u/ **too** /aɪ/ **I** /aʊ/ **how**
/ɔɪ/ **boy** /ɚ/ **bird** /ɚ/ **teacher** /ɪr/ **ear** /ɛr/ **air**
/ɑr/ **far** /ɔr/ **more** /ʊr/ **tour** /aɪr/ **fire**
/aʊɚ/ **hour** /θ/ **nothing** /ð/ **mother** /ʃ/ **she**
/ʒ/ **measure** /tʃ/ **church** /dʒ/ **jump** /ŋ/ **long**

skateboard /'skeɪtˌbɔrd/ [*noun*] a board with small wheels attached underneath which you stand on to ride: *Kids were riding skateboards in the street.*

skateboarding /'skeɪtˌbɔrdɪŋ/ [*noun*] the sport or activity of riding a skateboard: *Let's go skateboarding on Saturday.*

skater /'skeɪtɚ/ [*noun*] someone who skates, in competitions or for fun

skating /'skeɪtɪŋ/ [*noun*] the activity of moving on skates: *In winter, we go skating on the frozen lake.*

skeleton /'skɛlɪtən/ [*noun*] the set of bones of a person or animal: *There is a human skeleton in our biology classroom.*

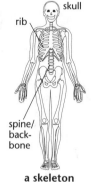

a skeleton

sketch[1] /skɛtʃ/ [*noun; plural* **sketches**] a simple drawing, usually done quickly: *He did a quick sketch of the building.*

sketch[2] [*verb;* **sketches, sketched, sketching**] to do a simple drawing: *I quickly sketched the man's face.*

ski[1] /ski/ [*verb;* **skis, skied, skiing**] to move on snow wearing skis: *There are great places to ski in these mountains.*

ski[2] [*noun; plural* **skis**] one of two long thin pieces of wood or plastic that you wear on your feet to move on snow: *a pair of skis*

skier /'skiɚ/ [*noun*] someone who skis, in competitions or for fun

skid /skɪd/ [*verb;* **skids, skidded, skidding**] to accidentally slide across or along a road, for example because there is ice or water on it: *The car skidded into the fence.*

skiing /'skiɪŋ/ [*noun*] the sport or activity of moving on snow wearing skis: *We go skiing every year.*

skill * /skɪl/ [*noun*] the ability to do something well after you are taught how to do it: *He plays football with great skill.* | *My computer skills are improving.*
↪ *See the synonym note at* ABILITY.

skilled /skɪld/ [*adjective;* **more skilled, most skilled**] having skill, or specially trained to do something; *opposite* UNSKILLED: *These vases are made by skilled craftsmen.* | **skilled in/at** doing something ▸ *He is skilled at playing the piano.*
☛ Do not say that someone is "skilled to do something." Say that he or she is **skilled at doing something**.

skillful * /'skɪlfəl/ [*adjective;* **more skillful, most skillful**] good at doing something: *He is a very skillful artist.*

skin * /skɪn/ [*noun*]
1 the outer covering of a person's or animal's body: *The wind was cold on my skin.* | *a tent made of animal skins*
↪ *Compare* FLESH.
2 the outer covering of a fruit or vegetable: *a banana skin*

skinny /'skɪni/ [*adjective;* **skinnier, skinniest**] INFORMAL thin in a way that is not attractive: *a skinny teenager*
↪ *See the synonym note at* THIN.

skip /skɪp/ [*verb;* **skips, skipped, skipping**]
1 to move forward with little jumps between each step: *The children skipped down the sidewalk.*
↪ *See the picture at* MOVEMENT.
2 to not do something when you should: *He skipped class again today* (=did not go to class).

skirt * /skɝt/ [*noun*] a piece of CLOTHING for a woman that hangs down from her waist

skull /skʌl/ [*noun*] the bones of a person's or an animal's head: *She cracked her skull in an accident.*

sky * /skaɪ/ [*noun*] the area above the earth that contains clouds: *There was a plane in the sky above us.* | *There's a patch of blue sky between the clouds.*

skyscraper /'skaɪˌskreɪpɚ/ [*noun*] an extremely tall building: *His office is on the 40th floor of a skyscraper.*

slab /slæb/ [*noun*] a thick flat piece of something: *The path was made of stone slabs.* | *a slab of meat*

slam /slæm/ [*verb;* **slams, slammed, slamming**]
1 to close with a loud noise, or to make

something do this: *The window*
slammed shut. | *Please don't slam the
car doors.*
2 to hit something hard with
something else and make a loud
noise: *He slammed his hand on the desk.*

slang /slæŋ/ [*noun*] very informal words
and phrases, for example the ones used
by young people: *I couldn't understand
the slang they used in the movie.*

slant /slænt/ [*verb;* **slanted, slanting**] to
lean to one side: *Her handwriting slants
to the left.*

slap[1] /slæp/ [*verb;* **slaps, slapped,
slapping**] to hit someone or something
with your hand open: *She **slapped** him
across the face. | He slapped my back
and said, "You did great!"*

slap[2] [*noun*] a hit with your hand open:
*I wanted to **give** him **a slap.***

slash[1] /slæʃ/ [*noun; plural* **slashes**]
a mark (/) used in writing to show
choices, or to mean "for each": *In this
dictionary, phrases such as "be based in/
on/at" have slashes to show different
words you can use.* | *Tomatoes: $1.29/lb.*

slash[2] [*verb;* **slashes, slashed, slashing**]
to cut something with a knife, blade,
etc., with a quick movement: *Someone
had slashed the painting from top to
bottom.*

slaughter /ˈslɔtɚ/ [*verb;* **slaughtered,
slaughtering**] to kill an animal, for its
meat or because it has a disease: *The
sick animals were slaughtered.*

slave * ⊤ /sleɪv/ [*noun*] someone who is
owned by another person and is forced
to work for him or her: *His ancestors
were African slaves.* | *I'm not your slave—
wash your own clothes!*

slavery /ˈsleɪvəri/ [*noun*] when people
are owned by other people: *Slavery is
now illegal.*

sled /slɛd/ [*noun*] a small flat vehicle
with long metal parts instead of wheels,
used for traveling on snow: *We jumped
on the sled and went down the hill.*

sleep[1] * /slip/ [*verb;* **slept, sleeping**] to
be in the state in which your eyes are
closed, your body is completely relaxed,
and you do not know what is

happening around you: *Did you sleep
well last night?* | *Quiet! The baby's
sleeping.* | *I had to sleep on the floor.*
⇨ *See also* ASLEEP.

sleep[2] * [*noun*]
1 the state of sleeping: *Children need
plenty of sleep.*
2 a period of sleeping: *Soon, she fell into
a deep sleep (=she slept very well).*

━ PHRASES ━

3 go to sleep to start to sleep: *Shut
your eyes and go to sleep.*
☛ Do not say "I slept around 11 o'clock."
Say **I went to sleep around 11 o'clock.**
⇨ *Compare* **wake up** *at* WAKE. ⇨ *See the
usage note at* BED.
4 get some sleep used to tell
someone to go to bed and try to sleep:
I think we should all get some sleep.

sleeping bag /ˈslipɪŋ ˌbæg/ [*noun*] a
long bag, usually made of cloth, that
you sleep in outdoors or in a tent

sleepy /ˈslipi/ [*adjective;* **sleepier,
sleepiest**] tired and close to falling
asleep: *As the evening went on, I felt
sleepier and sleepier.*
⇨ *Compare* ASLEEP.

sleet[1] /slit/ [*noun*] freezing rain falling
from clouds: *Soon the snow turned to
sleet.*

sleet[2] [*verb;* **sleeted, sleeting**] if it sleets,
freezing rain falls from clouds: *It started
to sleet.*

sleeve * /sliv/ [*noun*] one of the two
parts of a piece of CLOTHING that cover
your arms: *She **rolled** her **sleeves up.***

slender /ˈslɛndɚ/ [*adjective;* **slenderer,
slenderest**] narrow or thin, in an
attractive way; synonym SLIM: *She was
proud of her slender waist.*
⇨ *See the synonym note at* THIN.

slept * /slɛpt/ [*verb*] the past tense and
past participle of SLEEP[1]

/i/ **see**	/ɪ/ **big**	/eɪ/ **day**	/ɛ/ **get**	/æ/ **hat**
/ɑ/ **father, hot**	/ʌ/ **up**	/ə/ **about**	/ɔ/ **saw**
/oʊ/ **hope**	/ʊ/ **book**	/u/ **too**	/aɪ/ **I**	/aʊ/ **how**
/ɔɪ/ **boy**	/ɝ/ **bird**	/ɚ/ **teacher**	/ɪr/ **ear**	/ɛr/ **air**
/ɑr/ **far**	/ɔr/ **more**	/ʊr/ **tour**	/aɪr/ **fire**
/aʊɚ/ **hour**	/θ/ **nothing**	/ð/ **mother**	/ʃ/ **she**
/ʒ/ **measure**	/tʃ/ **church**	/dʒ/ **jump**	/ŋ/ **long**

slice[1] /slaɪs/ [*noun*] a piece of food cut from a larger thing: *thick **slices** of bread*

a **slice** of cake

slice[2] [*verb;* **sliced, slicing**] to cut something into slices, or to cut through something: *Next, slice the onions. | He sliced the orange in half.*

slide[1] * /slaɪd/ [*verb;* **slid** /slɪd/, **sliding**] to move smoothly across a surface, or to make something move like this: *In the winter, we slide down that hill on sleds. | He slid his desk drawer shut.*

slide[2] [*noun*]
1 a piece of children's play equipment which has a long smooth surface to slide down
2 a small piece of film in a frame which you can shine light through to make a picture on a screen: *Let me show you the slides of my vacation.*
3 a small piece of glass that things or substances are put on so that they can be seen through a MICROSCOPE

slight * T /slaɪt/ [*adjective;* **slighter, slightest**] a slight change, problem, chance, etc., is a very small one: *There's a slight chance of rain today. | The slightest sound wakes her.* (=even a very quiet sound wakes her).

slightly * /'slaɪtli/ [*adverb*] a little: *I'm feeling slightly better now.*

slim /slɪm/ [*adjective;* **slimmer, slimmest**]
1 thin in an attractive way; <u>synonym</u> **SLENDER**: *Most girls want to be slim.*
  ↪ *See the synonym note at* **THIN**.
2 very small in amount: *He has only a slim chance of being elected.*

slime /slaɪm/ [*noun*] a smooth, wet, thick substance that is unpleasant

sling /slɪŋ/ [*noun*] a piece of material that holds an injured arm and ties around the neck to support it: *My arm was in a sling for a month.*

slip[1] * /slɪp/ [*verb;* **slips, slipped, slipping**]
1 to slide suddenly and accidentally: *I slipped and fell. | The vase slipped out of her hands.*
2 to go somewhere quickly and quietly: *No one noticed her **slip out** of the room.*
3 to put something somewhere quickly and quietly: *He slipped a note under her door.*

slip[2] [*noun*]
1 a small piece of paper: *Write your address on this **slip of paper**.*
2 a piece of women's underwear worn under a dress or skirt: *a satin slip*

slipper /'slɪpɚ/ [*noun*] a soft shoe you wear indoors: *a **pair of slippers***

slippery * /'slɪpəri/ [*adjective;* **slipperier, slipperiest**] covered in water, ice, etc., and therefore easy to slip on: *Heavy rain made the roads slippery.*

slit[1] /slɪt/ [*noun*] a long thin cut in something

slit[2] [*verb;* **slits, slit, slit, slitting**] to make a long cut in something: *I slit open the envelope.*

slogan /'sloʊgən/ [*noun*] a phrase used by a company, organization, etc., that is easy to remember: *Our campaign needs a slogan.*

slope[1] * /sloʊp/ [*noun*] ground that is higher at one end than the other, for example the side of a hill: *grassy mountain slopes*

slope[2] * [*verb;* **sloped, sloping**] if a surface or area of land slopes, one end or side of it is higher than the other: *The fields slope down to the river.*

sloppy /'slapi/ [*adjective;* **sloppier, sloppiest**] careless and not neat: *You're such a sloppy eater!*

slot /slat/ [*noun*] a narrow hole in a machine or container, for example for putting coins into

slouch /slaʊtʃ/ [*verb;* **slouches, slouched, slouching**] to stand or sit with your back slightly bent and your shoulders forward: *Stand up straight and stop slouching*
  ↪ *See the picture at* **MOVEMENT**.

slow[1] * /sloʊ/ [*adjective;* **slower, slowest**]
1 not fast or quick: *Why is this train so slow?* | *My car is slower than his.* | *Ticket sales have been very slow.* | **slow to do something** ▸ *He was slow to realize what he had done.*
2 a clock that is slow shows an earlier time than the real time; *opposite* FAST: *Her watch was a few minutes slow.*

slow[2] * [*verb;* **slowed, slowing**]
▬▬ **PHRASAL VERB** ▬▬
slow down [*phrasal verb*]
to become slower or to make someone or something slower: *The train slowed down as it approached the station.* | **slow someone/something down** ▸ *My heavy bags were slowing me down.* | **slow down someone/something** ▸ *What do you think is slowing down our progress?*
▷ *Compare* **speed up** *at* SPEED[2].

slowly * /'sloʊli/ [*adverb*] not fast or quickly: *He closed the door slowly behind him.* | *Try to speak more slowly.*

slug /slʌg/ [*noun*] a small animal with a soft body and no legs, that moves very slowly

slum /slʌm/ [*noun*] a house or an area of a city that is dirty and in bad condition: *He was born in **the slums**.*

slumped /slʌmpt/ [*adjective; no comparative*] sitting or lying with your body resting against something because you are tired, weak, sad, etc.: *He sat slumped on the couch, staring at the TV.*
▷ *See the picture at* MOVEMENT.

smack[1] /smæk/ [*verb;* **smacked, smacking**] to hit someone or something with your hand open: *He smacked the table and yelled at them.*

smack[2] [*noun*] a hit with your hand open: *She **gave** him **a smack**.*

small[1] * /smɔl/ [*adjective;* **smaller, smallest**]
1 not big; *synonym* LITTLE; *opposite* LARGE: *My brother is a lot smaller than me.* | *I'd rather live in a small town than a big city.*
2 not important or serious; *synonym* MINOR; *opposites* BIG, MAJOR: *You only made one small mistake.* | *There's one small thing we need to fix.*
3 a small child is very young; *synonym*

LITTLE: *Many movies are not suitable for small children.*

small[2] * [*noun*] a size of clothing that is not very big: *I think Mom wears a small.* | *Ask if they have this blouse in small.*
▷ *Compare* MEDIUM[2], LARGE[2], EXTRA LARGE.

smart[1] * /smart/ [*adjective;* **smarter, smartest**] intelligent; *opposites* STUPID, DUMB: *He's the smartest kid in my class.*

smash /smæʃ/ [*verb;* **smashes, smashed, smashing**] to break into a lot of small pieces, or to make something break in this way: *The vase smashed into tiny pieces.* | *She dropped and smashed a pile of plates.*

smear /smɪr/ [*verb;* **smeared, smearing**] to spread a soft substance on something: *You've smeared jelly all over your face.*

smell[1] * /smɛl/ [*noun*] the quality something has that you notice with your nose: *What's that strange smell?* | *The smell of garlic was coming from the kitchen.*

SYNONYMS   smell, odor, stink, aroma, scent, fragrance, perfume

    A **smell** is a quality you notice with your nose: *I like the smell of freshly cut grass.* If you use **smell** alone and do not say what kind of smell it is, it usually means an unpleasant smell: *I can't get rid of that smell.*
    Use **odor** to talk about a strong or unpleasant smell: *the odor of a fish market.* You can also use **stink** to refer to an unpleasant smell, especially one that is extremely strong and unpleasant: *What's that awful stink?*
    Use **aroma** and **scent** to talk about pleasant smells. **Aroma** is especially used about the smell of food or drink: *This coffee has a wonderful aroma.* **Scent** is especially used about the smell that plants or animals produce: *The scent of lilacs filled the house.*
    Use **fragrance** to talk about the smell of

/i/ **see**	/ɪ/ **big**	/eɪ/ **day**	/ɛ/ **get**	/æ/ **hat**
/a/ **father, hot**	/ʌ/ **up**	/ə/ **about**	/ɔ/ **saw**	
/oʊ/ **hope**	/ʊ/ **book**	/u/ **too**	/aɪ/ **I**	/aʊ/ **how**
/ɔɪ/ **boy**	/ɝ/ **bird**	/ɚ/ **teacher**	/ɪr/ **ear**	/ɛr/ **air**
/ɑr/ **far**	/ɔr/ **tour**	/ʊr/ **tour**	/aɪr/ **fire**	
/aʊə/ **hour**	/θ/ **nothing**	/ð/ **mother**	/ʃ/ **she**	
/ʒ/ **measure**	/tʃ/ **church**	/dʒ/ **jump**	/ŋ/ **long**	

flowers, or of a liquid that people use to smell nice: *These lilies have a lovely fragrance.* | *What's that fragrance you're wearing?* **Perfume** is a fragrance that a woman wears: *He bought her a bottle of perfume.*

smell[2] * [*verb;* **smelled, smelling**]
1 [*linking*] to have a particular kind of smell: *That coffee smells good!* | *Her perfume* **smells like** *roses.*
2 to have an unpleasant smell; *synonym* **STINK:** *His feet smell.*
3 to notice or try to discover a smell: *I can smell something burning.* | *He smelled the milk to see if it was fresh.*

smelly /'smɛli/ [*adjective;* **smellier, smelliest**] having an unpleasant smell: *Are these your smelly socks?*

smile[1] * /smaɪl/ [*verb;* **smiled, smiling**] if you smile, the corners of your mouth turn upward because you are happy or are being friendly: *She* **smiled at** *me.*
☛ Do not say "What are you smiling?" Say **What are you smiling at?** or **Why are you smiling?**
↪ *See the picture at* **EMOTION**.

smile[2] * [*noun*] the expression on your face when you smile: *Her face* **broke into a smile** (=she began to smile).

smoke[1] * /smoʊk/ [*noun*] the white, gray, or black gases you see when something burns

smoke[2] * [*verb;* **smoked, smoking**] to breathe smoke into your lungs from a cigarette: *I don't smoke.* | *The man was smoking a cigarette.*

smoker /'smoʊkɚ/ [*noun*] someone who smokes; *opposite* **NONSMOKER:** *Smokers get sick more often than nonsmokers.*

smoking /'smoʊkɪŋ/ [*noun*] the activity of smoking cigarettes: *She's trying to stop smoking.*

smoky /'smoʊki/ [*adjective;* **smokier, smokiest**] full of smoke: *The room was very smoky.*

smooth[1] * /smuð/ [*adjective;* **smoother, smoothest**] having an even surface, without things sticking up from it; *opposite* **ROUGH:** *The sea was very smooth that day.* | *the smooth surface of a table* | *a cream to make your skin smoother*

smooth[2] [*verb;* **smooths, smoothed, smoothing**] to make something have an even surface: *They say this stuff will* **smooth away** *the wrinkles.* | *She smoothed the sheets on the bed.*

smoothly * /'smuðli/ [*adverb*]
— PHRASE —
go smoothly to happen without any problems: *Did your meeting go smoothly?*

smother /'smʌðɚ/ [*verb;* **smothered, smothering**]
1 to prevent someone from breathing: *The thick smoke from a fire can smother people.*
2 to cover something with a large amount of another substance: *He smothered his steak and potatoes in gravy.*

smudge[1] /smʌdʒ/ [*noun*] a dirty mark on something, made by rubbing or touching: *You have a* **smudge of** *paint on your cheek.*
↪ *See the synonym note at* **MARK**[1].

smudge[2] [*verb;* **smudged, smudging**] if ink or another substance smudges or is smudged, it is no longer clear or neat because someone has rubbed or touched it: *The edges of the pages were smudged and hard to read.*

smuggle /'smʌgəl/ [*verb;* **smuggled, smuggling**] to take things or people somewhere secretly, when it is illegal to do this: *They were arrested for smuggling drugs into the country.*

smuggler /'smʌglɚ/ [*noun*] someone who takes things from one place to another secretly and illegally

snack[1] /snæk/ [*noun*] a small meal or piece of food you have between your main meals: *I usually* **have a snack** *at around 4:30.*

snack[2] [*verb;* **snacked, snacking**] to eat a small meal or piece of food between your main meals: *Give your kids healthy food to* **snack on**, *such as fruit.*

snack bar /'snæk ˌbɑr/ [*noun*] an informal restaurant where you can buy small meals: *We had lunch in the snack bar across the street.*

snail /sneɪl/ [*noun*] a small animal with a soft body, no legs, and a round shell on its back, that moves very slowly

snake * /sneɪk/ [noun] a long thin animal without legs that moves by sliding on surfaces or swimming

snap /snæp/ [verb; **snaps, snapped, snapping**]
1 to break with a quick loud noise, or to make something do this: *Twigs snapped as I walked through the woods.*
2 to suddenly speak in an angry way to someone: *I didn't mean to snap at you.*
3 if an animal snaps, it tries to bite you: *His dog snapped at me.*

— PHRASE —

4 **snap your fingers** to make a noise by moving your thumb and middle finger firmly together and across each other: *She was snapping her fingers in time to the music.*

snatch /snætʃ/ [verb; **snatches, snatched, snatching**] to suddenly take something from someone: **snatch something from someone** ▶ *He snatched the photo from me.*

sneak /snik/ [verb; **sneaked** or **snuck**, **sneaking**]
1 to go somewhere quietly and secretly: *I sneaked out when no one was looking.*
2 to take or put something somewhere quietly and secretly: *I sneaked the dog into my bedroom.*

sneaker /'snikɚ/ [noun] a light shoe with a rubber bottom, worn for sports or with informal clothes; synonym TENNIS SHOE: *a pair of sneakers*

shoelace

sneakers/ tennis shoes

sneeze[1] /sniz/ [verb; **sneezed, sneezing**] to suddenly force air loudly out of your nose and mouth, for example when you have a cold: *I couldn't stop sneezing.*

sneeze[2] [noun] the action or sound of sneezing: *I could hear his sneezes from the next room.*

sniff /snɪf/ [verb; **sniffed, sniffing**] to breathe in hard through your nose, for example to smell something or when you have a cold: *She sniffed the drink suspiciously.* | *He sniffed and tried to find his handkerchief.*

snob /snab/ [noun] someone who admires people of a high social rank and tries to be like them: *Don't be such a snob—there's nothing wrong with this restaurant.*
☛ The word **snob** is used to show that you do not approve of someone's attitude.

snooze /snuz/ [verb; **snoozed, snoozing**] INFORMAL to sleep lightly or for a short time; synonym DOZE: *Mom is snoozing on the couch.*

snore /snɔr/ [verb; **snored, snoring**] to make a loud noise when you breathe during your sleep: *He snored all night long.*

snoring /'snɔrɪŋ/ [noun] the sound you make when you snore: *Your snoring keeps me awake.*

snow[1] * /snoʊ/ [noun] white pieces of frozen water that fall from clouds when it is very cold

snow[2] * [verb; **snowed, snowing**] if it snows, white pieces of frozen water fall from clouds: *It's been snowing all night.*

snowball /'snoʊ,bɔl/ [noun] snow that someone has made into a ball: *The children **threw snowballs** at each other.*

snowboarding /'snoʊ,bɔrdɪŋ/ [noun] the sport or activity of moving across snow with both your feet on a special board: *I'd love to go snowboarding.*

snowflake /'snoʊ,fleɪk/ [noun] a small soft white piece of frozen water that forms snow

snowman /'snoʊ,mæn/ [noun; plural **snowmen** /'snoʊ,mɛn/] a model of a person made from large balls of snow

snowy /'snoʊi/ [adjective; **snowier, snowiest**] with a lot of snow falling: *a snowy day* | *It's snowy in the mountains.*

snuck /snʌk/ [verb] a past tense and past participle of SNEAK

/i/ **see** /ɪ/ **big** /eɪ/ **day** /ɛ/ **get** /æ/ **hat**
/ɑ/ **father, hot** /ʌ/ **up** /ə/ **about** /ɔ/ **saw**
/oʊ/ **hope** /ʊ/ **book** /u/ **too** /aɪ/ **I** /aʊ/ **how**
/ɔɪ/ **boy** /ɝ/ **bird** /ɚ/ **teacher** /ɪr/ **ear** /ɛr/ **air**
/ɑr/ **far** /ɔr/ **more** /ʊr/ **tour** /aɪr/ **fire**
/aʊɚ/ **hour** /θ/ **nothing** /ð/ **mother** /ʃ/ **she**
/ʒ/ **measure** /tʃ/ **church** /dʒ/ **jump** /ŋ/ **long**

so[1] * /soʊ/ [adverb]
1 to that degree: *I didn't know she was so upset.* | *Don't walk so fast!* | **so . . . that** ▸ *The dresses were so cheap that I bought two.*
➪ Compare SUCH (definition 1).
2 SPOKEN very: *It's so hot!*
3 also: *If he's going, then so am I.* | *I had a bad cold and so did he.*
☛ Don't say "I'm so" or "He did so" in this meaning. Say **So am I** or **So did he.**
4 used before a question or to get someone's attention: *So, what should we do next?*

— PHRASES —

5 or so used after a number or amount to show that it is not exact: *There were seven or so people there.*
6 so far up to this moment: *So far, things are going well.*
7 so long goodbye: *So long—I'll see you tomorrow.*
8 say/think/hope/etc. so to say, think, hope, etc., what has just been mentioned: *I know he likes you because he said so.* | *"Are you OK?" "I think so."*
➪ See also **and so on** at ON[2].

so[2] * [conjunction]
1 for the reason that has been mentioned: *The store was closed, so we came home.*
➪ Compare THEREFORE. ➪ See the warning at BECAUSE (definition 1).
2 used before mentioning the purpose of an action: **so (that)** ▸ *I moved nearer the front so I could see better.*

soak /soʊk/ [verb; **soaked, soaking**]
1 to leave something in a liquid, or to be in a liquid for a period of time: *I left the dishes to soak a while.*
2 to make something completely wet: *It started to rain and we got soaked.*

soap * /soʊp/ [noun] a substance used with water for washing yourself: *a bar of soap*

soap opera /'soʊp ˌɑpərə/ [noun] a television or radio program that is shown every day, about the lives of a group of characters

soar /sɔr/ [verb; **soared, soaring**]
1 to go up high and fly through the air: *A plane soared by overhead.*

2 to quickly increase to a very high level: *The price of heating oil is expected to soar this month.*

sob[1] /sɑb/ [verb; **sobs, sobbed, sobbing**] to cry with short loud breaths because you are extremely upset: *She ran out of the room, sobbing.*

sob[2] [noun] a short loud breath you take when you are sobbing: *I could hear his sobs from my bedroom.*

sober /'soʊbɚ/ [adjective; **more sober, most sober**] having not drunk any alcohol, or not affected by alcohol; *opposite* DRUNK: *You must stay sober if you are driving.*

soccer * /'sɑkɚ/ [noun] a sport or game played by two teams, in which players try to score goals by kicking a BALL into a net: *Some boys were playing soccer in the school yard.* | *a soccer field*
➪ Compare FOOTBALL.

sociable /'soʊʃəbəl/ [adjective; **more sociable, most sociable**] liking to spend time with people and talk to them: *She used to be very shy, but now she's more sociable.*

social * T /'soʊʃəl/ [adjective; no comparative]
1 relating to human society: *We are going through a period of social change.*
2 relating to things you do with other people: *I have a pretty active social life* (=I do many fun things).
☛ Only use **social** before a noun.

Social Security T /'soʊʃəl sɪ'kyʊrɪti/ [noun] a U.S. government program that provides money for people who are old or are no longer able to work: *Social Security benefits*

society * /sə'saɪti/ [noun; plural **societies**]
1 all the people in a particular country or group, who share the same ways of living: *Families are important in our society.*
☛ Do not say "in the society." Say **in society** or **in our/their/this/that society.**
2 an organization whose members share an interest or activity; *synonym* CLUB: *She's a member of the school honor society.*

sock * /sak/ [*noun*] a piece of CLOTHING that you wear on your foot, inside your shoe: *a pair of socks*

socket /'sakɪt/ [*noun*] a hollow part that something fits into: *a light bulb socket* | *The keyboard cord plugs into a socket at the back of the computer.*

soda /'soʊdə/ [*noun; plural* **sodas**]
1 a cold sweet drink that has bubbles in it: *I like grape soda.* | *Can I buy you a soda?*
2 also **soda water** /'soʊdə ˌwɔtər/ water that has bubbles in it, or a glass or bottle of this; *synonym* CLUB SODA: *I'd like a glass of soda with lemon.*

sofa /'soʊfə/ [*noun; plural* **sofas**] a long soft chair for two or more people to sit on; *synonym* COUCH: *I fell asleep on the sofa after dinner.*

soft * /sɔft/ [*adjective;* **softer, softest**]
1 easy to press; *opposites* FIRM, HARD: *This is a very soft bed.* | *When it rains, the ground becomes softer.*
2 smooth and nice to touch; *opposite* ROUGH: *A baby's skin is very soft.*
3 quiet and pleasant to hear; *opposite* LOUD: *Soft music was playing in the background.*
↪ See also SOFTEN, SOFTLY.

softball /'sɔftˌbɔl/ [*noun*] a game similar to baseball, played on a smaller playing field with a bigger, softer ball

soft drink T /'sɔft 'drɪŋk/ [*noun*] a drink that does not contain alcohol and usually contains bubbles

soften /'sɔfən/ [*verb;* **softened, softening**] to become softer or to make something softer; *opposite* HARDEN: *a cream that softens dry skin*

softener /'sɔfənər/ [*noun*] a substance that is used to remove minerals from water or to make clothes soft when you wash them: *liquid fabric softener*

softly * /'sɔftli/ [*adverb*] quietly and in a way that is nice to hear; *opposite* LOUDLY: *"Listen," he said softly.*

software /'sɔftˌwɛr/ [*noun*] the programs or instructions that make a computer do a particular job: *My company bought new e-mail software*
↪ Compare HARDWARE (definition 2).

soggy /'sagi/ [*adjective;* **soggier, soggiest**] completely wet, in an unpleasant way: *The roof leaked, and now the carpet's all soggy.*

soil * /sɔɪl/ [*noun*] the earth in which plants grow: *The soil is fertile in this valley.*

solar /'soʊlər/ [*adjective; no comparative*] relating to the sun: *solar energy*
☛ Only use **solar** before a noun.
↪ Compare LUNAR.

solar system /'soʊlər ˌsɪstəm/ [*noun*] a sun and all the planets that go around it: *Jupiter is the biggest planet in our solar system.*

sold * /soʊld/ [*verb*] the past tense and past participle of SELL

soldier * /'soʊldʒər/ [*noun*] a member of an army: *Soldiers marched through the streets.*

sole[1] /soʊl/ [*noun*] the bottom of your foot or shoe: *The soles of my feet were sore.* | *shoes with rubber soles*
↪ See the picture at BODY.

sole[2] [*adjective; no comparative*] being the only one: *He was the sole student to receive a perfect score.*

solely /'soʊli/ [*adverb*] alone or only: *No individual is solely responsible for the company's success.*

solid[1] * T /'salɪd/ [*adjective;* **more solid, most solid**]
1 firm and hard: *The pond had frozen solid.*
— PHRASE —
2 **solid silver/gold/etc.** silver, gold, etc., that contains no other substance: *a solid gold ring*

solid[2] [*noun*] any substance that has a shape: *Solids can be hard, like rock, or soft, like clay.*
↪ Compare GAS (definition 3), LIQUID[1].

solo /'soʊloʊ/ [*noun; plural* **solos**] a piece of music, song, or dance, for one performer: *I'm going to sing a solo in the school concert.*

/i/ **see**	/ɪ/ **big**	/eɪ/ **day**	/ɛ/ **get**	/æ/ **hat**
/ɑ/ **father, hot**	/ʌ/ **up**	/ə/ **about**	/ɔ/ **saw**	
/oʊ/ **hope**	/ʊ/ **book**	/u/ **too**	/aɪ/ **I**	/aʊ/ **how**
/ɔɪ/ **boy**	/ɝ/ **bird**	/ɚ/ **teacher**	/ɪr/ **ear**	/ɛr/ **air**
/ɑr/ **far**	/ɔr/ **more**	/ʊr/ **tour**	/aɪr/ **fire**	
/aʊə/ **hour**	/θ/ **nothing**	/ð/ **mother**	/ʃ/ **she**	
/ʒ/ **measure**	/tʃ/ **church**	/dʒ/ **jump**	/ŋ/ **long**	

soloist /'soulouɪst/ [noun] a performer who plays, sings, or dances to music alone

solution * T /sə'luʃən/ [noun]
1 something that will stop a problem; synonym ANSWER: *They are still trying to find a solution to the crisis.*
2 the answer to a math problem: *The solution to this equation is –3.*

solve * T /salv/ [verb; solved, solving] to find the answer to a problem or a math question: *I can't solve your problems for you.* | *Solve the following problem: 2x + 6x = 24.*

some * /sʌm/ [determiner, pronoun]
1 used when you are not being exact about an amount or number: *Would you like some coffee?* | *There were some books on the table.* | *If you can't get paper from school, buy some yourself.*
  ⇨ Compare ANY[1].
2 part of a group or amount, but not all: *Some people hate going on vacation, but most like it.* | *She needs to work harder in some subjects.* | *Some of the money was missing.*
3 a fairly large amount of something, or a fairly large number of things: *He said he had been waiting some time.* | *She had been in bad health for some years.*
4 used to talk about someone or something when you do not know exactly who the person is or what the thing is: *For some reason, the computer wasn't working.* | *"Who told her that?" "Some boy in school."*
  ☛ Do not say "a some boy." Say **some boy.**

somebody * /'sʌm,badi/ [pronoun] used to talk about a person when you do not know who the person is, or when you are not being exact; synonym SOMEONE: *There's somebody at the door.*
  ☛ Do not say "somebodies." Say **some people.**

someday /'sʌm,deɪ/ [adverb] at some time in the future: *I hope to go to college someday.*

somehow * /'sʌm,haʊ/ [adverb] in some way: *Can you get a message to her somehow?*

someone * /'sʌm,wʌn/ [pronoun] used to talk about a person when you do not know who the person is, or when you are not being exact; synonym SOMEBODY: *She could hear someone crying.* | *If you move over, someone else* (=another person) *can sit down.*
  ☛ Do not say "someones." Say **some people.**

somersault /'sʌmɚ,sɔlt/ [noun] a movement in which you turn your body completely over on the ground or in the air: *He did somersaults on the lawn.*

something * /'sʌm,θɪŋ/ [pronoun] used to talk about a thing, subject, event, etc., when you do not know what it is, or when you are talking generally: *Something is wrong with the TV.* | *I did something really stupid.*

sometime /'sʌm,taɪm/ [adverb] used to talk about a time when you do not know when it is, or when you are not being exact: *We're getting married sometime next year.* | *You should come visit us sometime!*
  ⇨ See the warning at SOMETIMES.

sometimes * T /'sʌm,taɪmz/ [adverb] on some occasions: *I sometimes go swimming after school.* | *Sometimes I don't feel like doing my homework.*
  ☛ Do not confuse **sometimes** and **sometime. Sometimes** is used to talk about how often something happens. **Sometime** is used to talk about the time of one particular event.

somewhere * /'sʌm,wɛr/ [adverb, pronoun] used to talk about a place when you do not know where the place is, or when you are not being exact: *I left my purse somewhere.* | *I want to live somewhere better.*
  ⇨ Compare ANYWHERE.

son * /sʌn/ [noun] someone's male child
  ⇨ See the picture at FAMILY TREE.

song * /sɔŋ/ [noun] a short piece of music that is sung: *We sat around singing songs.* | *This is my favorite song.*

son-in-law /'sʌn ɪn ,lɔ/ [noun; plural **sons-in-law** /'sʌnz ɪn ,lɔ/] the husband of your daughter
  ⇨ See the picture at FAMILY TREE.

soon * /sun/ [*adverb;* **sooner, soonest**]
1 in a short time from now: *I'll be home soon.* I *Friday is the soonest I can come.*
⇨ *See the usages notes at* EARLY[2] *and* QUICKLY.

=== PHRASES ===

2 **as soon as** used to say that one thing happens immediately after another: *As soon as I saw her, I knew who she was.* I *Please call as soon as possible* (=the earliest time you can). ☛ Do not say "I came soon when I could." Say **I came as soon as I could.**

3 **sooner or later** used to say that something will definitely happen, although it may not happen soon: *She'll find out sooner or later.*

4 **soon after** a short time after: *She arrived soon after 10 o'clock.*

5 **too soon** too early or too quickly: *It's too soon to take the turkey out of the oven.*

soot /sʊt/ [*noun*] a dirty black substance produced when something burns

soothe /suð/ [*verb;* **soothed, soothing**]
1 to make someone feel calm and less worried: *She soothed the crying baby.*
2 to make something hurt less: *I need something to soothe my sunburn.*

sophisticated /sə'fɪstɪ,keɪtɪd/ [*adjective;* **more sophisticated, most sophisticated**]
1 having a lot of knowledge and experience of life: *a sophisticated young woman from the city*
2 a sophisticated machine is complicated and can do difficult jobs: *a sophisticated control system*

sophomore /'safə,mɔr/ [*noun*] a student who is in the second year of college or high school
⇨ *Compare* FRESHMAN, JUNIOR[2], SENIOR[2].

sore[1] * /sɔr/ [*adjective;* **sorer, sorest**] a sore part of your body is painful, for example because you have injured it: *I had walked miles and my feet were getting sore.* I *She has a sore throat.*

sore[2] [*noun*] a painful area on your skin or inside your mouth, often caused by a disease: *I'm seeing a doctor about the sores on my hand.*

sorority /sə'rɔrɪti/ [*noun;* plural **sororities**] a club at an American college that is only for female students, who usually live together in the club's house
⇨ *Compare* FRATERNITY.

sorry * /'sari/ [*adjective;* **sorrier, sorriest**]
1 ashamed or unhappy about something wrong you have done: **sorry (that)** ▸ *I'm sorry I lied.* I *She said some awful things and she's not even sorry.* I *"You're standing on my foot." "Oh, sorry."* I **sorry for doing something** ▸ *We're very sorry for breaking your window.*
⇨ *See the usage note at* APOLOGIZE.
2 sad or disappointed about something: *I'm sorry I missed the concert.* I *We're sorry about your father* (=sad that he died, had bad luck, is sick, etc.).
☛ Do not use **sorry** before a noun.

=== PHRASE ===

3 **feel sorry for someone** to feel pity for someone because something bad has happened to him or her: *I feel sorry for him, but there's nothing I can do to help.*
☛ Do not say "I feel sorry to someone." Say **I feel sorry for someone.**

sort[1] * /sɔrt/ [*noun*]
1 a particular type or kind of something: *There are many sorts of rice.*

=== PHRASES ===

2 **sort of** SPOKEN a little; synonym SLIGHTLY: *I'm sort of busy right now.*

3 **all sorts of** many different kinds of: *All sorts of people go to night school.*

sort[2] [*verb;* **sorted, sorting**]
1 to separate a group of things into smaller groups of similar things: *He's downstairs sorting the laundry* (=separating the dark and light clothes).

/i/ **see**	/ɪ/ **big**	/eɪ/ **day**	/ɛ/ **get**	/æ/ **hat**
/ɑ/ **father, hot**	/ʌ/ **up**	/ə/ **about**	/ɔ/ **saw**
/oʊ/ **hope**	/ʊ/ **book**	/u/ **too**	/aɪ/ **I**	/aʊ/ **how**
/ɔɪ/ **boy**	/ɝ/ **bird**	/ɚ/ **teacher**	/ɪr/ **ear**	/ɛr/ **air**
/ɑr/ **far**	/ɔr/ **more**	/ʊr/ **tour**	/aɪr/ **fire**
/aʊɚ/ **hour**	/θ/ **nothing**	/ð/ **mother**	/ʃ/ **she**
/ʒ/ **measure**	/tʃ/ **church**	/dʒ/ **jump**	/ŋ/ **long**

— PHRASAL VERB —

sort out [phrasal verb]
2 to organize or arrange something, or solve a problem: **sort out something** ▸ *You need to sort out the clothes you want to take.* | **sort something out** ▸ *I knew Dad would sort things out.*

so-so /'soʊ ˌsoʊ/ [adjective; no comparative] INFORMAL not very good, and not very bad: *It was a so-so performance.*

sought /sɔt/ [verb] the past tense and past participle of SEEK

soul ✱ /soʊl/ [noun] the part of you that contains your feelings, mind, and character, which many people believe does not die when you die; *synonym* SPIRIT: *the souls of the dead*

sound[1] ✱ /saʊnd/ [noun] something that can be heard: *I could hear the sound of music.* | *There was no sound at all.*

USAGE   sound, noise

A **sound** is something you can hear: *I like the sound of waves on the beach.* | *She didn't make a sound.* A **noise** is a kind of sound, especially a loud, unpleasant, or sudden one: *the noise of airplanes taking off* | *Stop making that noise.*

sound[2] ✱ [verb, linking verb; **sounded, sounding**] if something sounds funny, sad, stupid, etc., it seems funny, sad, stupid, etc., when you hear it or hear about it: *His voice sounded strange.* | *She sounds like a nice woman.*

sound[3] ✱ [adjective; **sounder, soundest**]
1 good, and showing careful thought: *I trust her—she has sound judgment.*
2 strong and in good condition: *a sound roof* | *sound health*

sound[4] [adverb]
— PHRASE —
sound asleep completely asleep: *He was sound asleep in front of the TV.*

soup ✱ /sup/ [noun] a liquid food made by boiling vegetables or meat in water: *a bowl of hot chicken soup*

sour ✱ /'saʊɚ/ [adjective; **sourer, sourest**]
1 sour food is not sweet, and tastes similar to lemons or vinegar: *These apples are a little sour.*
2 sour milk or cream is no longer fresh

and tastes extremely unpleasant: *The milk has **gone sour**.*

sourdough /'saʊɚˌdoʊ/ [noun] white bread that tastes slightly sour

source ⊤ /sɔrs/ [noun] the place that something comes from: *We tried to find the **source of** the stream.* | *He got the same information from several sources.*

south[1] ✱ /saʊθ/ [noun]
the south the direction or area that is on your right when you look at the rising sun: *He grew up **in the south**.* | *an island **to the south of** China*
⇨ See the usage note at DIRECTION.

south[2] ✱ [adjective; no comparative] in, toward, or coming from the south: *The south part of the island is much warmer.* | *the south side of the house* | *a south wind*
☛ Only use **south** before a noun.

south[3] ✱ [adverb] toward or in the south: *The plane headed south.* | *Their farm is just **south of** here.*

South America ✱ /'saʊθ əˈmɛrɪkə/ [name] the large area of land between the Atlantic Ocean and the Pacific Ocean, north of Antarctica

South American[1] /'saʊθ əˈmɛrɪkən/ [noun] someone who comes from South America

South American[2] [adjective; no comparative] belonging to, from, or relating to South America: *South American coffee*

southeast[1] ✱ /ˌsaʊθ'ist/ [noun]
the southeast the direction or area that is between south and east: *There are storms **in the southeast**.*
⇨ See the usage note at DIRECTION.

southeast[2] ✱ [adjective; no comparative] in, toward, or coming from the southeast: *the southeast shores of the island* | *the southeast side of the building* | *a southeast wind*
☛ Only use **southeast** before a noun.

southeast[3] ✱ [adverb] toward or in the southeast: *They sailed southeast.* | *The factory is **southeast of** us.*

southeastern ✱ /ˌsaʊθ'istɚn/ [adjective; no comparative] in or from the southeast: *the southeastern states of the U.S.*

southern * /'sʌðə˞n/ [adjective; no comparative] in or from the south of a place: a small southern town | He had a southern accent.

Southerner /'sʌðə˞nə˞/ [noun] someone who comes from the south of a country: Southerners speak with a different accent.

South Pole /'saʊθ 'poʊl/ [name]
the South Pole the point on Earth that is the farthest south: They went on an expedition to the South Pole.

southward /'saʊθwə˞d/ or **southwards** /'saʊθwə˞dz/ [adverb] toward the south: If you look southward, you can see the volcano.

southwest[1] * /ˌsaʊθ'wɛst/ [noun]
the southwest the direction or area that is between south and west: There isn't much rain in the southwest.
▷ See the usage note at DIRECTION.

southwest[2] * [adjective; no comparative] in, toward, or coming from the southwest: the southwest region of India | the southwest wall of the house | a southwest wind
☞ Only use the adjective **southwest** before a noun.

southwest[3] * [adverb] toward or in the southwest: We'll drive southwest for two days. | The canyon is two miles **southwest** of here.

southwestern * /ˌsaʊθ'wɛstə˞n/ [adjective; no comparative] in or from the southwest: I've never visited the southwestern part of the country.

souvenir ⊤ /ˌsuvə'nɪr/ [noun] something that you bring back with you from a place or event to remind you of it: I got a T-shirt at the **souvenir shop**.

sow[1] /soʊ/ [verb; sowed, sown /soʊn/, sowing] to spread seeds over an area so that they can grow into plants: Sow the grass seeds in the spring.

soy sauce /'sɔɪ ˌsɔs/ [noun] a brown salty sauce used in Asian cooking: Add ginger and soy sauce to the vegetables.

space * /speɪs/ [noun]
1 an empty area: The painting is too big for that space on the wall. | We need more space to set up our equipment.

2 the area beyond the Earth, where there are planets and stars: The astronauts have been **in space** for two weeks.
☞ Do not say "in the space." Say in space.

spacecraft /'speɪsˌkræft/ [noun; plural **spacecraft** or **spacecrafts**] a vehicle that can travel in space

spaceship /'speɪsˌʃɪp/ [noun] a vehicle in which people travel in space: She claimed to have seen an alien spaceship.

space shuttle /'speɪs ˌʃʌtəl/ [noun] a vehicle with wings that carries people and equipment into space and can fly back to Earth and be used again

spacious ⊤ /'speɪʃəs/ [adjective; **more spacious, most spacious**] large, with a lot of space: a spacious apartment

spade /speɪd/ [noun] a tool with a long handle and a wide square metal part at one end, used for cutting and digging earth
▷ Compare SHOVEL[1].

spaghetti /spə'gɛti/ [noun] dough in the shape of long strings that is boiled and eaten with sauce: We're having spaghetti and clam sauce for dinner.

span[1] /spæn/ [noun] a period of time, or the length of something: In the **span of** two years we've lived in three cities.

span[2] ⊤ [verb; singular **spans, spanned, spanning**] to include a particular time or distance: Three bridges span the river.

spank /spæŋk/ [verb; **spanked, spanking**] to hit a child on the bottom with the inside of your hand: If you do that again, I'll spank you.

spare[1] /spɛr/ [adjective; no comparative]
1 spare things are ones that are still available to be used: Do you have any spare stamps? | a **spare tire**
▷ Compare EXTRA[1].

/i/ see	/ɪ/ big	/eɪ/ day	/ɛ/ get	/æ/ hat	
/ɑ/ father, hot	/ʌ/ up	/ə/ about	/ɔ/ saw		
/oʊ/ hope	/ʊ/ book	/u/ too	/aɪ/ I	/aʊ/ how	
/ɔɪ/ boy	/ɚ/ bird	/ə˞/ teacher	/ɪr/ ear	/ɛr/ air	
/ɑr/ far	/ɔr/ more	/ʊr/ tour	/aɪr/ fire		
/aʊə˞/ hour	/θ/ nothing	/ð/ mother	/ʃ/ she		
/ʒ/ measure	/tʃ/ church	/dʒ/ jump	/ŋ/ long		

— PHRASE —

2 spare time time when you are not working, studying, etc.: *She spends most of her spare time reading.*

spare[2] [*verb;* **spared, sparing**]
1 to be able to use some of your time or to lend some of your money: *I want to go on vacation, but I can't spare the time.* | **spare someone something** ▸ *Can you spare me the subway fare?*

— PHRASE —

2 to spare if you have something to spare, it is left when you have used all that you need: *He arrived at the bus station with two minutes to spare* (=he was two minutes early for his bus).

spark /spark/ [*noun*] a small, bright, hot piece of fire: *Sparks flew from the fire.*

sparkle /'sparkəl/ [*verb;* **sparkled, sparkling**] to shine with small points of light; *synonym* GLITTER: *The jewels in her ring sparkled.* | *a sparkling stream*

sparrow /'spærou/ [*noun*] a small gray-brown bird

spat /spæt/ [*verb*] a past tense and past participle of SPIT

speak * /spik/ [*verb;* **spoke, spoken, speaking**]
1 to say words out loud, or to discuss something; *synonym* TALK: *He was too frightened to speak.* | *Can I speak to you for a minute?*
2 to be able to talk using a particular language: *Do you speak Swedish?*
☛ Do not say "Do you speak in English?" Say **Do you speak English?**

— PHRASAL VERBS —

speak out [*phrasal verb*]
3 to say what you think about something, in a brave way: *He was the only one to speak out against what was happening.*

speak up [*phrasal verb*]
4 to speak loudly enough for people to hear: *Speak up. I can't understand you.*

USAGE   speak, say

Use **speak** about words that you say out loud: *Speak louder, please. I can't hear you.* Use **say** about words that are spoken or written: *The teacher said I did well on my test.* | *The newspaper says that it will rain tomorrow.*

---

speaker * /'spikɚ/ [*noun*]
1 someone who gives a speech, or who speaks a particular language: *He was one of the main speakers at the conference.* | *a Spanish speaker*
2 a part of a music system that the sound comes out of

spear /spɪr/ [*noun*] a long wooden weapon with a pointed blade at the end: *They catch fish using spears.*

special * /'spɛʃəl/ [*adjective; no comparative*]
1 better or more important than other things or people of the same kind: *He wanted the evening to be special.* | *She's a special friend.* | *Are you doing anything special tonight?*
2 different from what is usual, for a particular reason; *opposite* REGULAR: *The subway runs on a special schedule on holidays.*

specialist ⊤ /'spɛʃəlɪst/ [*noun*] someone who works with or studies one particular thing, and therefore knows a lot about it: *My father had to visit an ear specialist.*

specialize /'spɛʃəˌlaɪz/ [*verb;* **specialized, specializing**] to work with or study one particular thing more than others: *The company specializes in leather chairs.*

specially * /'spɛʃəli/ [*adverb*] for a particular purpose: *This chair is specially designed for people with back pain.*

specialty ⊤ /'spɛʃəlti/ [*noun; plural* **specialties**]
1 a kind of food that is always very good in a particular area, restaurant, etc.: *Beef is a specialty of this restaurant.*
2 the thing that you know most about or are best at: *My specialty is math.*

species /'spiʃiz/ [*noun; plural* **species**] a group of animals or plants that are alike and can breed with each other: *We should protect rare species of animals* (=ones that are not common on Earth).

specific * ⊤ /spɪ'sɪfɪk/ [*adjective;* **more specific, most specific**]
1 clear and exact: *Can you be more specific—what kind of car was it?* | *He gave us very specific instructions on what to do.*

2 used to talk about a single thing or person that is special in some way; synonym PARTICULAR: *I asked you to come here for a specific reason.* | *Their research will deal with* **one specific** *area.*
☞ Only use **specific** before a noun in this meaning.

specifically /spɪˈsɪfɪkli/ [*adverb*]
1 clearly and exactly: *I specifically asked you not to tell anyone.*
2 used to say that something is intended for or deals with only particular people or things: *This magazine is aimed specifically at men.*

specify /ˈspɛsəˌfaɪ/ [*verb;* **specifies, specified, specifying**] to say exactly what you want, what will happen, etc.: *Did he specify a time when he'd call?* | *The company specified that computer skills are required for the job.*

speck /spɛk/ [*noun*] a very small piece of something: *There's never a single speck of dust in her house.*

spectacular /spɛkˈtækyələ-/ [*adjective;* **more spectacular, most spectacular**] extremely impressive: *The new drug has had spectacular results.*

spectator /ˈspɛkteɪtə-/ [*noun*] someone who watches a sports event or other public performance: *A tennis ball hit one of the spectators.*

sped /spɛd/ [*verb*] a past tense and past participle of SPEED[2]

speech * /spitʃ/ [*noun;* plural **speeches**]
1 a talk given to a group of people: *He stood up to* **make a speech.** | *She gave a speech at graduation.*
2 spoken words or the action of speaking: *This grammatical pattern is rarely used in speech.* | **freedom of speech** *(=the right to say or write any opinion you have)*

speed[1] * /spid/ [*noun*] used to talk about how fast someone or something moves or works: *The gears operate at different speeds.* | *His speed and strength make him a great football player.* | *The car was traveling* **at full speed** *(=as fast as it could).*

speed[2] [*verb;* **sped** or **speeded, speeding**]
1 to go somewhere very fast, or to take

someone or something somewhere very fast: *He sped off on his bicycle.* | *They sped him away in an ambulance.*
2 to drive faster than you are allowed to by law: *Slow down—you're speeding.*
☞ Do not say that a car, bus, etc., "is overspeeding." Say that it **is speeding.**

=== PHRASAL VERB ===

speed up [*phrasal verb*]
3 to start moving or doing something faster than before, or to make something do this: *The car speeded up after it turned the corner.*
⇨ Compare **slow down** at SLOW[2].

speed limit /ˈspid ˌlɪmɪt/ [*noun*] the fastest speed that cars are allowed to travel on a particular road: *You must not* **exceed the speed limit** *(=go faster than the speed limit).*

spell[1] * /spɛl/ [*verb;* **spelled, spelling**]
1 to write a word using the right letters in the right order: *People always spell my name wrong.* | *I don't spell too well.*
2 if letters spell a word, they form that word: *Y-e-s spells yes.*
☞ Do not say "Y-e-s spell yes." Say **Y-e-s spells yes.**

spell[2] * [*noun*] a piece of magic or the words used to make it happen: *The witch* **cast a spell on** *him (=said a spell that affected him).*

spelling * /ˈspɛlɪŋ/ [*noun*]
1 the way in which a word is spelled: *Some words have different spellings in British and American English.*
☞ Do not say that words have "different spelling." Say that they have **different spellings.**
2 the skill of spelling words in the right way: *The teacher pointed out my spelling mistakes.*

spend * /spɛnd/ [*verb;* **spent** /spɛnt/, **spending**]
1 to use money for buying things: *Did you spend all your money?* | **spend**

/i/ see	/ɪ/ big	/eɪ/ day	/ɛ/ get	/æ/ hat
/ɑ/ father, hot	/ʌ/ up	/ə/ about	/ɔ/ saw	
/oʊ/ hope	/ʊ/ book	/u/ too	/aɪ/ I	/aʊ/ how
/ɔɪ/ boy	/ɚ/ bird	/ə-/ teacher	/ɪr/ ear	/ɛr/ air
/ɑr/ far	/ɔr/ more	/ʊr/ tour	/aɪr/ fire	
/aʊə-/ hour	/θ/ nothing	/ð/ mother	/ʃ/ she	
/ʒ/ measure	/tʃ/ church	/dʒ/ jump	/ŋ/ long	

something on something ▸ *I spent a lot on that dress.*
 ⟳ Compare PAY¹ (definition 1).
2 to use time or effort doing something: spend something on something ▸ *I spent a lot of time on this paper.* I spend something doing something ▸ *We spent the day fishing.*
3 to stay somewhere for a particular period of time: *Is it OK if I spend the night at Grandma's house?*

sphere /sfɪr/ [*noun*] a shape or object like a ball: *A globe is a map of the world in the shape of a sphere.*
 ⟳ See Shapes in the Smart Study section.

spice /spaɪs/ [*noun*] a substance that is added to food to make it taste more interesting: *She uses a lot of herbs and spices in her cooking.*

spicy /'spaɪsi/ [*adjective;* spicier, spiciest] having a hot taste: *I like spicy food.*

spider /'spaɪdɚ/ [*noun*] a small creature with eight legs that makes structures out of thin threads for catching insects

spied /spaɪd/ [*verb*] the past tense and past participle of SPY²

spike /spaɪk/ [*noun*] a pointed object that sticks up from something or out of something

spill /spɪl/ [*verb;* spilled, spilling] if a liquid or another substance spills or you spill it, it accidentally comes out of its container: *I spilled juice on the tablecloth.* I *The package broke open and pasta spilled everywhere.*

spin * /spɪn/ [*verb;* spun, spinning] to turn around and around fast, or to make something do this: *One wheel on the car isn't spinning right.* I *I spun a coin on the table.*

spinach /'spɪnɪtʃ/ [*noun*] a vegetable with large, dark green leaves

spine /spaɪn/ [*noun*] the line of bones down the center of your back; *synonym* BACKBONE
 ⟳ See the picture at SKELETON.

spiral /'spaɪrəl/ [*noun*] a shape or object that curls around and around: *A tornado cloud moves in a spiral.*

spirit * /'spɪrɪt/ [*noun*]
1 the part of you that contains your feelings, mind, and character, that

many people believe does not die when you die; *synonym* SOUL: *His spirit continues to live in his writing.*
2 spirits [*plural*] strong alcoholic drinks; *synonym* LIQUOR: *The store sells a variety of wines and spirits.*
— PHRASE —
3 team/public/community spirit a feeling of loyalty to a group: *Their team spirit was the reason they won.*

spiritual /'spɪrɪtʃuəl/ [*adjective;* more spiritual, most spiritual]
1 relating to the spirit or a religion rather than the body or mind; *opposite* PHYSICAL: *People have spiritual needs as well as physical ones.*
2 relating to people's religious beliefs: *a great spiritual leader*

spit /spɪt/ [*verb;* spits, spit or spat, spit or spat, spitting] to force a small amount of liquid, food, etc., out of your mouth: *Never, never spit at someone.* I *Spit out your gum.*

spite * /spaɪt/ [*noun*]
1 the feeling of wanting to be unkind to someone: *He ruined my drawing out of spite.*
— PHRASE —
2 in spite of used to say that something happens even though something else, which you would expect to prevent it, also happens; *synonym* DESPITE: *We had a great vacation in spite of the weather.*
 ☛ Do not say "in spite of it rained." Say in spite of the rain.

splash¹ /splæʃ/ [*verb;* splashes, splashed, splashing] to make water fly up, especially by jumping in it or hitting it: *Most kids like to splash around in puddles.* I *A passing car splashed water all over me.*

splash² [*noun; plural* splashes] a sound made when something falls or moves in water: *The stone landed in the stream with a splash.*

splinter /'splɪntɚ/ [*noun*] a very small, thin, sharp piece of something such as wood or glass: *I got a splinter in my finger.*

split[1] * /splɪt/ [*verb;* **splits, split, split, splitting**]
1 if something splits or you split it, it tears or divides into two parts: *Oh no— the bag split!* | *He's in the backyard, splitting logs.*
2 to divide something into two or more parts and share it between people: *We decided to split the profits.*

— PHRASAL VERB ——

split up [*phrasal verb*]
3 if people split up, they stop living, traveling, or doing things together: *The band split up after ten years together.*

split[2] [*noun*] a long thin tear in a piece of clothing, material, etc.: *Do you know there's a split in your jeans?*

spoil * /spɔɪl/ [*verb;* **spoiled, spoiling**]
1 to harm something so that it cannot be used or enjoyed: *The rain spoiled our picnic.*
2 if food spoils, it is no longer fresh and cannot be eaten: *We should eat these tomatoes before they spoil.*
3 to be too kind to someone, especially a child, and give him or her too much: *You're spoiling that kid!*

spoiled /spɔɪld/ [*adjective;* **more spoiled, most spoiled**] a spoiled child is rude and unpleasant because he or she has always been given everything he or she wants: *You're acting like a spoiled six-year-old!*

spoke[1] * /spoʊk/ [*verb*] the past tense of SPEAK

spoke[2] [*noun*] one of many thin metal bars that reach from the center to the outside of a wheel
⇨ *See the picture at* BICYCLE.

spoken * /'spoʊkən/ [*verb*] the past participle of SPEAK

sponge /spʌndʒ/ [*noun*] a light soft block full of holes that can hold liquid, used for cleaning things: *a sponge mop* (=a tool with a sponge on the end for cleaning floors)

spool /spul/ [*noun*] a kind of wide wheel that thread, wire, rope, etc., can be wound on: *a spool of black thread*

spoon * /spun/ [*noun*] an object used for eating that has a handle and a bowl-shaped part at one end
⇨ *See the picture at* PLACE SETTING.

spoonful /'spunfʊl/ [*noun;* plural **spoonfuls**] as much of something as a spoon can hold: *He put a large spoonful of sugar in his coffee.*

sport * /spɔrt/ [*noun*] a physical activity or game, such as baseball, basketball, or tennis: *Swimming is my favorite sport.* | *She likes playing sports.*

sports car /'spɔrts ˌkar/ [*noun*] a fast low car that usually has room for only two people: *I want to own a sports car.*

sports jacket /'spɔrts ˌdʒækɪt/ [*noun*] a man's informal suit coat
⇨ *See the picture at* JACKET.

spot[1] * /spat/ [*noun*]
1 a small round colored area on something: *His tie was green with white spots.* | *What's that spot on your shirt?*
⇨ *See the synonym note at* MARK[1].
2 a place, usually outdoors: *This is the spot where I fell in the creek.*

spot[2] [*verb;* **spots, spotted, spotting**] to notice someone or something, especially one that is difficult to see: *I spotted a deer moving in the bushes.*

spouse /spaʊs/ [*noun*] FORMAL your husband or wife: *You have to give the name of your spouse on the form.*

spout /spaʊt/ [*noun*] a part of a container shaped like a tube, through which liquid can be poured
⇨ *See the picture at* TEAPOT.

sprain /spreɪn/ [*verb;* **sprained, spraining**] to twist and injure part of your arm or leg: *I sprained my ankle jumping off a rock.*

sprang * /spræŋ/ [*verb*] the past tense of SPRING[2]

spray[1] /spreɪ/ [*verb;* **sprays, sprayed, spraying**] to send out a liquid in very small drops, or to be sent out in this way: *When he opened the can, the soda sprayed out all over him.* | *Someone sprayed paint on the wall.*

/i/ **see**	/ɪ/ **big**	/eɪ/ **day**	/ɛ/ **get**	/æ/ **hat**
/ɑ/ **father, hot**	/ʌ/ **up**	/ə/ **about**		/ɔ/ **saw**
/oʊ/ **hope**	/ʊ/ **book**	/u/ **too**	/aɪ/ **I**	/aʊ/ **how**
/ɔɪ/ **boy**	/ɚ/ **bird**	/ɚ/ **teacher**	/ɪr/ **ear**	/ɛr/ **air**
/ɑr/ **far**	/ɔr/ **more**	/ʊr/ **tour**	/aɪr/ **fire**	
/aʊɚ/ **hour**	/θ/ **nothing**	/ð/ **mother**	/ʃ/ **she**	
/ʒ/ **measure**	/tʃ/ **church**	/dʒ/ **jump**	/ŋ/ **long**	

spray[2] [noun; plural **sprays**] liquid sent out of a container in a particular direction in very small drops: *This hair spray is sticky.*

spread * /sprɛd/ [verb; **spreads, spread, spread, spreading**]
1 to open or stretch something so that it covers an area or becomes larger: *We spread our blanket under the tree.* | *The bird spread its wings and flew off.*
2 if something spreads or you spread it, it passes from one person or place to another so that it then affects a larger area or more people: *Once it starts, fire spreads very quickly.*
3 to cover a surface with a soft substance: *This butter isn't spreading very easily.*

spreadsheet /'sprɛd,ʃit/ [noun] a large amount of information, usually numbers, that is organized by a computer program

spring[1] * /sprɪŋ/ [noun]
1 the season between winter and summer
⇨ See the usage note at SEASON.
2 a thin strong piece of twisted metal that returns to its shape after being pulled or pushed: *The springs creaked every time I turned over in bed.*
⇨ See the picture at COIL.

spring[2] * [verb; **sprang, sprung, springing**] to move or jump somewhere suddenly: *The lock sprang open.* | *The tiger looked ready to spring.*

sprinkle /'sprɪŋkəl/ [verb; **sprinkled, sprinkling**]
1 to scatter drops of a liquid or small pieces of something onto something: *Sprinkle sugar onto the cake.*
2 when it sprinkles, rain falls very lightly: *It's only sprinkling outside.*

sprinkler /'sprɪŋklɚ/ [noun] an object that turns and sends out water over a large area of grass and plants

sprout[1] /spraʊt/ [verb; **sprouted, sprouting**] to begin growing: *The bulbs we planted are now sprouting.*

sprout[2] [noun] a plant or a new part of a plant that has just begun to grow: *Bean sprouts are eaten as a vegetable.*

sprung * /sprʌŋ/ [verb] the past participle of SPRING[2]

spun * /spʌn/ [verb] the past tense and past participle of SPIN

spurt /spɚt/ [verb; **spurted, spurting**] if a liquid spurts out from somewhere, or if something spurts it, it comes out in short strong bursts: *Water was spurting from a broken pipe.*

spy[1] /spaɪ/ [noun; plural **spies**] someone who is employed by a government to get secret information about another country: *They accused him of being a spy.*

spy[2] [verb; **spies, spied, spying**]
━ PHRASAL VERB ━
spy on [phrasal verb]
to secretly watch someone: **spy on someone** ▸ *Have you been spying on me?*

squad /skwɑd/ [noun] a small group of people who do a particular activity or job: *a bomb squad* (=a group of people who take bombs apart and make them safe)

square[1] * /skwɛr/ [noun]
1 a shape with four straight sides of the same length, and with equal angles: *a square of cloth* | *arranged in a square*
⇨ See Shapes in the Smart Study section.
2 an open public area in a town with buildings around it: *There were many tourists in Market Square.*
3 the number you get when you multiply a number by itself: *The square of four is sixteen.*

square[2] * [adjective; no comparative]
1 having the shape of a square: *a square table*
━ PHRASE ━
2 a square foot/yard/meter/etc. a square whose sides are a foot, yard, meter, etc., long: *an area of 20 square yards*

squared /skwɛrd/ [adjective; no comparative] used to describe a number that is multiplied by itself: *2 squared is 4.*

square root /'skwɛr 'rut/ [noun] the square root of a number is the number that you multiply by itself to produce the first number: *4 is the square root of 16.*

squash[1] /skwaʃ/ [*noun*]
  1 a VEGETABLE that grows close to the ground, usually has a hard skin, and is usually cooked
  2 a game that involves hitting a small rubber ball hard against four walls in a room using a racket: *Do you play squash?*

squash[2] [*verb;* **squashes, squashed, squashing**]
  1 to press something very hard so that it is damaged or changes shape: *Be careful not to squash the tomatoes.*
  2 to press into a small space, or to make people or things press into a small space: *Six of us squashed into my car.*

squat /skwat/ [*verb;* **squats, squatted, squatting**] to sit very near to the ground, resting on your feet with your knees apart: *He squatted down and looked under the bed.*
  ⇨ *See the picture at* MOVEMENT.

squeak[1] /skwik/ [*verb;* **squeaked, squeaking**] to make a short sharp high sound: *The door squeaked as it opened.*

squeak[2] [*noun*] a short sharp high sound: *a mouse's squeak*

squeal[1] /skwil/ [*verb;* **squealed, squealing**] to make a long sharp high sound: *The kids were squealing with excitement.*

squeal[2] [*noun*] a long sharp high sound: *a pig's squeal*

squeeze[1] /skwiz/ [*verb;* **squeezed, squeezing**]
  1 to press each side of something with your hand: *Squeeze hard to get all the water out of the sponge.*

  ━━ PHRASAL VERB ━━
squeeze into [*phrasal verb*]
  2 to make someone or something fit in a space or an object: **squeeze into something** ▸ *I'm too fat to squeeze into these jeans.*

squeeze[2] [*noun*] when you press each side of something with your hand: *She gave my hand a squeeze.*

squid /skwɪd/ [*noun; plural* **squid** or **squids**] a sea creature with ten arms and a long body, which can be eaten

squint /skwɪnt/ [*verb;* **squinted, squinting**] to look at something with

your eyes partly closed: *The sun was so bright she had to squint to see.*

squirrel /ˈskwɜrəl/ [*noun*] a small animal with a thick furry tail that lives in trees and eats nuts

a squirrel

squirt /skwɜrt/ [*verb;* **squirted, squirting**] if a liquid squirts somewhere, or if you squirt it there, it goes there suddenly and with a lot of force: *He squirted water at me from the hose.*

Sr. the written abbreviation of SENIOR, used after a man's name when he has the same name as his son: *Thomas Brown, Sr.*

St. 1 the written abbreviation of STREET: *I live at 101 35th St.*
  2 the written abbreviation of SAINT: *St. Christopher is often associated with traveling.*

stab /stæb/ [*verb;* **stabs, stabbed, stabbing**] to stick a pointed weapon into someone: *She stabbed him with a kitchen knife.*

stable[1] /ˈsteɪbəl/ [*noun*] a building where horses are kept: *We clean the stables every day.*

stable[2] [*adjective;* **stabler, stablest**] not likely to fall, move, or change: *Make sure the ladder is stable.* | *a stable relationship*

stack[1] /stæk/ [*noun*] a neat pile of things: *There was a **stack of** magazines on his desk.*

stack[2] [*verb;* **stacked, stacking**] to put things in a neat pile: *Stack those boxes in the corner.*

/i/ see	/ɪ/ big	/eɪ/ day	/ɛ/ get	/æ/ hat
/a/ father,	hot	/ʌ/ up	/ə/ about	/ɔ/ saw
/oʊ/ hope	/ʊ/ book	/u/ too	/aɪ/ I	/aʊ/ how
/ɔɪ/ boy	/ɝ/ bird	/ɚ/ teacher	/ɪr/ ear	/ɛr/ air
/ɑr/ far	/ɔr/ more	/ʊr/ tour	/aɪr/ fire	
/aʊɚ/ hour	/θ/ nothing	/ð/ mother	/ʃ/ she	
/ʒ/ measure	/tʃ/ church	/dʒ/ jump	/ŋ/ long	

stadium /'steɪdiəm/ [noun] a structure with a large area for sports games and other events, surrounded by rows of seats: We went to a rock concert at the stadium.

staff /stæf/ [noun] a group of people who do the work of a company or organization: The school's staff is one of the best in the area. | The memo was sent to all staff members.

☛ Staff refers to a group of people, not to one person. Do not say "There are ten staffs at the school." Say **There are ten staff members at the school** or **The school has a staff of ten.**

stage ✶ 🔳 /steɪdʒ/ [noun]
1 a raised area in a theater where actors perform, singers sing, etc.: He walked to the front of the stage. | Everyone cheered when the band came **on stage.**
2 a part of a process or of the development of something: She is still in the early **stages of** her career.

stagger /'stægə·/ [verb; staggered, staggering]
1 to walk in a way that is not steady: The horse staggered and fell.
2 to arrange events or activities so that they happen one after the other, not at the same time: My boss and I usually **stagger** our lunch hours.

stain[1] /steɪn/ [noun] a dirty mark that is difficult to remove: I can't get this stain out of my dress. | food stains
⇨ See the synonym note at MARK[1].

stain[2] [verb; stained, staining] to make a dirty mark on something that is difficult to remove: I spilled coffee on the carpet and stained it.

stainless steel /'steɪnlɪs 'stil/ [noun] a kind of steel that stays bright and does not become weak: a stainless steel sink

stair ✶ /stɛr/ [noun]
1 one step in a set of steps inside a house: I tripped

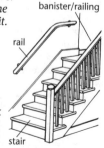

banister/railing
rail
stair

a flight of stairs

on the top stair. | Our apartment is up four **flights of stairs** (=sets of stairs).
2 **the stairs** [plural] a set of steps inside a house: Her husband was standing at the bottom of the stairs. | She slowly **climbed the stairs.**
⇨ See also DOWNSTAIRS, UPSTAIRS.

staircase /'stɛr,keɪs/ [noun] a set of steps inside a house: The carpet on the staircase was worn.

stale /steɪl/ [adjective; staler, stalest] stale food or air is old and not fresh: These cookies are stale.

stalk /stɔk/ [noun] the tall thin part of a plant from which flowers and branches grow; synonym STEM: a celery stalk

stall[1] /stɔl/ [noun]
1 a small private area containing a toilet or shower: There are five stalls in the ladies' room.
2 a part of a market where someone shows and sells his or her goods: I bought these apples from the fruit stall.

stall[2] [verb; stalled, stalling] if a car stalls or you stall it, the engine suddenly stops working: The car stalled right in the middle of a busy street.

stammer /'stæmə·/ [verb; stammered, stammering] to repeat the first parts of words when you speak; synonym STUTTER: He stammers when he's nervous.

stamp[1] ✶ /stæmp/ [verb; stamped, stamping]
1 to put your foot down with a lot of force on the ground: I **stamped on** the insect. | When she gets angry she **stamps her feet.**
2 to put an official mark on something with a tool than can hold ink: The immigration official stamped his passport.

stamp[2] ✶ [noun] a small piece of paper that you stick on an envelope or package to show you have paid for it to be mailed: Put a stamp on the letter.

stand[1] ✶ /stænd/ [verb; stood, standing]
1 to be in an upright position on your feet: She stood watching the children. | Don't just stand there. Help me! | **Stand still!** (=do not move)
2 to get into an upright position on your feet: Please stand to sing the

national anthem. I *The students all stood up when the principal entered.*

3 to be in a particular place or position: *A large statue stands in the center of the square.*

— PHRASE —

4 can't stand to hate or be unable to deal with something or someone: *I can't stand waiting any longer.* I *He can't stand her.*

— PHRASAL VERBS —

stand by [*phrasal verb*]

5 to wait and be ready to do something: *A nurse was standing by with oxygen.*

6 to continue to support and help someone in a difficult situation: **stand by someone** ▸ *I'll always stand by you.*

stand for [*phrasal verb*]

7 if letters stand for a word, name, etc., they are a short form of it: **stand for something** ▸ *The letters "U.S." stand for "United States."*

stand up for [*phrasal verb*]

8 to say things in support of someone or something: **stand up for someone/ something** ▸ *He should learn to stand up for himself.*

stand² [*noun*] a piece of furniture that holds something: *an umbrella stand*

standard¹ * /'stændəd/ [*noun*] a level of quality that is acceptable or normal: *We have very **high standards** in this school.* I *This work isn't **up to standard** (=it is not as good as it should be).*

standard² [*adjective; no comparative*] normal or usual: *Air conditioning is a standard feature of this car.*

standstill /'stænd,stɪl/ [*noun*]

— PHRASES —

1 at a standstill not moving or making any progress: *Production at the factory is at a standstill.*

2 come to a standstill to stop moving or making progress: *The traffic came to a standstill.*

stank /stæŋk/ [*verb*] the past tense of STINK¹

staple¹ /'steɪpəl/ [*noun*] a short piece of wire put through pieces of paper and bent to keep them together: *Please use staples, not paper clips.*

staple² [*verb; stapled, stapling*] to attach pieces of paper together with a staple: *Staple the pages together.*

stapler /'steɪplə/ [*noun*] an object used for putting staples in pieces of paper
▷ *See the picture at* OFFICE.

star¹ * /star/ [*noun*]

1 a ball of burning gas that appears as a small bright light in the sky at night: *You can see the stars more clearly in the country.*

2 a shape with five or six points: *He was wearing a badge in the shape of a star.*

star shapes

3 a very famous actor, singer, etc.: *Los Angeles is where many movie stars live.*

star² [*verb; stars, starred, starring*] if an actor stars in a movie or a movie stars an actor, he or she has an important part in it: *Who **starred in** "Titanic"?* I *a movie starring Julia Roberts*

stare /stɛr/ [*verb; stared, staring*] to look at someone or something for a long time, especially when he, she, or it is strange or surprising: *What are you **staring at**?*
▷ *See the synonym note at* GAZE.

starfish /'star,fɪʃ/ [*noun; plural **starfish**] a sea creature with legs that come out of its body like a star

start¹ * /start/ [*verb; started, starting*]

a starfish

1 to begin happening or to begin doing something: *What time does the movie start?* I *I haven't started my homework yet.* I **start to do something** ▸ *Suddenly she started to laugh.* I **start doing something** ▸ *You should start making dinner soon.*
▷ *See the usage note at* BEGIN.

2 to begin in a particular place: *The fire started in the kitchen.*

3 if a car starts or you start it, you

/i/ see	/ɪ/ big	/eɪ/ day	/ɛ/ get	/æ/ hat
/ɑ/ father, hot	/ʌ/ up	/ə/ about	/ɔ/ saw
/oʊ/ hope	/ʊ/ book	/u/ too	/aɪ/ I	/aʊ/ how
/ɔɪ/ boy	/ɚ/ bird	/ə/ teacher	/ɪr/ ear	/ɛr/ air
/ɑr/ far	/ɔr/ more	/ʊr/ tour	/aɪr/ fire
/aʊə/ hour	/θ/ nothing	/ð/ mother	/ʃ/ she
/ʒ/ measure	/tʃ/ church	/dʒ/ jump	/ŋ/ long

make the engine begin working: *This car always starts the first time.*

⇨ Compare END², FINISH¹, STOP¹.

— PHRASE ——

4 to start with used to say what happens first or in the first part of something: *He wasn't very interested in the idea to start with.*

⇨ See also **to begin with** at BEGIN.

— PHRASAL VERBS ——

start off [*phrasal verb*]
5 to begin something in a particular way: **start something off** ▸ *I usually start my day off with a swim.*

start out [*phrasal verb*]
6 to begin a trip: *We started out at dawn.*

start over [*phrasal verb*]
7 to begin doing something again because you did something wrong the first time: *Let me start over and try to explain it better.*

start² * [*noun*] the first part of something; *synonym* BEGINNING; *opposite* END: *We missed **the start of** the race.* | *I knew **from the start** I was going to enjoy the course.*

⇨ Compare FINISH².

startle /'stɑrtəl/ [*verb*; **startled, startling**] to make someone feel surprised and slightly frightened for a short time: *You startled me, coming in without knocking.*

starvation /stɑr'veɪʃən/ [*noun*] when someone becomes weak and sick because he or she has no food to eat: *Many animals **died of starvation** in the drought.*

starve /stɑrv/ [*verb*; **starved, starving**] to become weak or die because you have no food to eat: *They **starved to death.***

starving /'stɑrvɪŋ/ [*adjective*; *no comparative*] INFORMAL very hungry: *Let's get something to eat. I'm starving!*

state¹ * /steɪt/ [*noun, name*]
1 the condition that something or someone is in: *He asked me about **the state of** the project.* | *She's **in a terrible state** (=she is very upset).*
2 one of the political areas into which

some countries are divided: *The U.S.A. has 50 states.* | *the **state of** Texas*
3 a country or nation, or its government: *It became an independent state in 1992.* | *Education is paid for by the state.*

⇨ See the synonym note at COUNTRY.

state² * [*verb*; **stated, stating**] to say or write something officially or in a formal situation: *Please state your name and address.*

statement * /'steɪtmənt/ [*noun*] something that someone says or writes which gives information or an opinion: *I don't agree with your last statement.*

States /steɪts/ [*name*] INFORMAL
the States the UNITED STATES: *I'd love to visit the States.*

⇨ See the synonym note at AMERICA.

statesman /'steɪtsmən/ [*noun*; *plural* **statesmen** /'steɪtsmən/] an important politician: *a portrait of a famous statesman*

station * /'steɪʃən/ [*noun*]
1 a place where buses or trains arrive and leave: *Where's the nearest **bus station**?* | *a **subway station*** | *a **train station***
2 a building or place that is the center of a kind of work or activity: *Please come with me to the **police station**.* | *a **polling station** (=where people vote)*

⇨ See also GAS STATION.

3 a company that makes radio or television broadcasts, or its building: *Fans waited outside the **TV station**.* | *a country music station*

stationary /'steɪʃəˌnɛri/ [*adjective*; *no comparative*] FORMAL not moving: *a stationary bicycle (=used for exercising)*

stationery [*noun*] writing paper, cards, and envelopes: *a stationery store (=that sells paper, pens, pencils, etc.)*

station wagon /'steɪʃən ˌwægən/ [*noun*] a vehicle with an area behind the seats into which you can load things from a door at the back: *We put the bags of groceries in the station wagon.*

statistic ⊤ /stə'tɪstɪk/ [*noun*] a number that represents a fact or measurement: *Statistics prove that you are safer in a plane than in a car.*

statue * /'stætʃu/ [noun; plural **statues**] a figure of a person or animal made of stone, metal, etc.: *a **statue of** a famous general*

stay[1] * /steɪ/ [verb; **stays, stayed, staying**]
1 to remain in a place: *Stay there— I want to show you something.*
2 [linking] to continue to be in a particular position, state, or situation; synonym REMAIN: *I hope the weather stays fine.* | *I stayed perfectly still.*
  ⇨ See also KEEP (definition 2).
3 to live or sleep somewhere for a short time: *I'm staying at the Park Hotel.*

━━ PHRASAL VERB ━━
stay up [phrasal verb]
4 to go to bed late: *Dad let me stay up on Friday night.*

stay[2] * [noun] when someone visits or lives somewhere for a short time: *I hope you enjoy your stay in Dallas.*

steadily * Ⓣ /'stɛdəli/ [adverb] without any sudden changes: *Prices have been rising steadily.*

steady * Ⓣ /'stɛdi/ [adjective; **steadier, steadiest**]
1 firm and not moving or shaking; opposite UNSTEADY: *She tried to hold the camera steady.*
2 without any sudden changes: *a steady rise in temperature*

steak /steɪk/ [noun] a large thick piece of meat or fish: *How do you like your steak cooked?* | *a tuna steak*

steal * /stil/ [verb; **stole, stolen, stealing**] to take something that does not belong to you, secretly or using force: *Someone stole my wallet.* | **steal something from someone/ something** ▸ *She was caught stealing money from her employer.*
  ⇨ Compare ROB.

steam[1] * /stim/ [noun] the mist that rises from very hot water: *The bathroom was full of steam.*

steam[2] [verb; **steamed, steaming**] to cook food over very hot water: *Steam the asparagus for five minutes.* | *I steamed carrots*
  ⇨ See the synonym note at COOK[1].

steel * /stil/ [noun] a strong metal made from iron and other materials: *This bridge is made of steel.*
  ⇨ See also STAINLESS STEEL.

steep * /stip/ [adjective; **steeper, steepest**] a steep hill, road, etc., goes up at a high angle: *It was the steepest mountain I had ever climbed.*

steeple /'stipəl/ [noun] a pointed tower on a church

steer /stɪr/ [verb; **steered, steering**] to make a vehicle, boat, or plane go in a particular direction: *Trucks can be difficult to steer.*

steering wheel /'stɪrɪŋ ˌwil/ [noun] the round object in a CAR, bus, etc., that you turn to change its direction

stem * /stɛm/ [noun] the tall thin part of a plant from which flowers and branches grow; synonym STALK: *red roses with long stems*

step[1] * /stɛp/ [noun]
1 a movement made by putting one foot in front or in back of the other: *Look! The baby's starting to take her first steps.*
  ⇨ Compare FOOTSTEP.
2 one of a series of things that you do in order to achieve something: *We are **taking steps** to solve the problem.*
3 a flat piece of wood or stone used for walking from one level to another: *There are three steps leading into the garden.*
  ⇨ Compare STAIR.

━━ PHRASE ━━
4 step by step slowly, doing one thing first and then the next: *Follow the instructions step by step.*

step[2] * [verb; **steps, stepped, stepping**] to move forward or backward with one foot: *She stepped back to look at the painting.* | *I think I just **stepped on** a bug.*

/i/ **see**	/ɪ/ **big**	/eɪ/ **day**	/ɛ/ **get**	/æ/ **hat**
/ɑ/ **father, hot**	/ʌ/ **up**	/ə/ **about**	/ɔ/ **saw**	
/oʊ/ **hope**	/ʊ/ **book**	/u/ **too**	/aɪ/ **I**	/aʊ/ **how**
/ɔɪ/ **boy**	/ɚ/ **bird**	/ə/ **teacher**	/ɪr/ **ear**	/ɛr/ **air**
/ɑr/ **far**	/ɔr/ **more**	/ʊr/ **tour**	/aɪr/ **fire**	
/aʊə/ **hour**	/θ/ **nothing**	/ð/ **mother**	/ʃ/ **she**	
/ʒ/ **measure**	/tʃ/ **church**	/dʒ/ **jump**	/ŋ/ **long**	

stepbrother /'stɛp,brʌðɚ/ [noun] the son of your stepmother or stepfather

stepfather /'stɛp,faðɚ/ [noun] a man who is married to your mother but is not your father

stepmother /'stɛp,mʌðɚ/ [noun] a woman who is married to your father but is not your mother

stepsister /'stɛp,sɪstɚ/ [noun] the daughter of your stepfather or stepmother

stereo /'stɛri,oʊ/ [noun; plural **stereos**] a piece of equipment for playing recorded music such as tapes and CDs

stew /stu/ [noun] meat and vegetables cooked slowly in thick liquid

stewardess /'stuɚdɪs/ [noun; plural **stewardesses**] a woman who takes care of the passengers on a plane; synonym FLIGHT ATTENDANT

stick[1] * /stɪk/ [verb; **stuck, sticking**]
1 to attach something with a substance such as glue, or to become attached: *Stick a stamp on the envelope.* | *Her wet hair stuck to her face.*
2 to push something long and pointed into something: **stick something into/in something** ▶ *She stuck her finger into the batter to taste it.*
3 to become fixed and impossible to move or change: *The door's stuck—I can't open it.*
4 SPOKEN to put something somewhere: *Just stick your coat on that rack.*

━━ PHRASAL VERBS ━━

stick out [phrasal verb]
5 to come out further than a surface, or to make something do this: *Do you think my ears stick out?* | **stick something out** ▶ *He keeps sticking his tongue out at me.*

stick to something [phrasal verb]
6 to do what you have been already doing, or what you have decided or promised to do: *You should stick to the kind of work you like.*

stick[2] * [noun]
1 a long thin piece of wood: *We gathered sticks to build a fire.*
2 a long thin object: *a **stick** of gum* | *a **stick of** dynamite*

3 a long thin object used in some sports ▷ *See the picture at* HOCKEY.
▷ *See also* CANDLESTICK, CHOPSTICK, LIPSTICK.

sticker /'stɪkɚ/ [noun] a small piece of paper with a sticky substance on the back so you can attach it to something: *a price sticker*

sticky * /'stɪki/ [adjective; **stickier, stickiest**] easily sticking to things, or covered with a substance that does this: *sticky syrup* | *The jelly made my fingers all sticky.*

stiff * ⊤ /stɪf/ [adjective; **stiffer, stiffest**]
1 firm and difficult to bend: *a box made of stiff cardboard*
2 a handle, door, etc., that is stiff is difficult to move: *The drawer is sometimes a little stiff.*

still[1] * /stɪl/ [adverb]
1 used to say that a situation that has existed for a while exists now: *I'm still waiting for her to call.* | *He's still in school.*
▷ *Compare* YET.
2 used to say that something that has been true for a while is true now: *That's still not the right answer.*
3 used to say that something is true even though something else is also true: *He ran fast, but he still lost the race.*
☛ Use **still** before the main verb, unless the main verb is "be" or is negative.

still[2] [adjective; **stiller, stillest**] quiet or not moving: *Keep still—there's a bee on your back.* | *The night was warm and still.*
▷ *Compare* CALM[1] (definition 2).

sting * /stɪŋ/ [verb; **stung, stinging**] to make someone feel a sharp pain: *I've been stung by a bee!* | *It might sting when I clean your cut.*

stink[1] /stɪŋk/ [verb; **stank, stunk, stinking**] INFORMAL to smell extremely unpleasant: *Your feet stink!*

stink[2] [noun] an extremely strong and unpleasant smell
▷ *See the synonym note at* SMELL[1].

stir * /stɚ/ [verb; **stirs, stirred, stirring**]
1 to mix a liquid or mixture with a spoon: *Gently stir the flour into the batter.*
2 to move slightly: *The baby didn't stir when I looked into the crib.*

stirrup /'stɜrəp/ [*noun*] one of the two metal objects into which you put your feet when riding a horse

stitch[1] * /stɪtʃ/ [*noun; plural* **stitches**] one of the short pieces of thread that can be seen along the line where something has been sewn: *Some of the stitches had come undone.*

stitch[2] [*verb;* **stitches, stitched, stitching**] to sew something, especially by hand: *I stitched a patch on over the tear.*

stock[1] /stak/ [*noun*]
1 a supply of something: *Their **stocks** of fuel were getting low.* | *The store has many sizes **in stock*** (=there are supplies available to be sold). | *I'm afraid that book is **out of stock*** (=there are no supplies available to be sold).
2 the shares that people can buy to own part of a company, that can have a higher or lower value depending on how well the company does: *We have **stock in** a computer company.*

stock[2] [*verb;* **stocked, stocking**]
1 if a store stocks a particular thing, it keeps a supply of it to sell: *They stock a lot of imported foods.*
━ PHRASAL VERB ━
stock up [*phrasal verb*]
2 to buy a lot of something at one time so that you can use it later: *She stocked up on canned food.*

stocking /'stakɪŋ/ [*noun*] a thin piece of women's clothing that covers the foot and most of the leg: *a pair of stockings* ⇨ Compare PANTYHOSE.

stole * /stoʊl/ [*verb*] the past tense of STEAL

stolen * /'stoʊlən/ [*verb*] the past participle of STEAL

stomach * /'stʌmək/ [*noun*]
1 the organ in your body where your food goes when you swallow it
2 the front part of the body of a person or animal between the chest and the legs: *a bald man with a fat stomach*
━ PHRASE ━
3 **on an empty stomach** without eating anything: *You shouldn't go to school on an empty stomach.*

stomachache /'stʌmək,eɪk/ [*noun*] pain in the stomach: *Don't eat so fast or you'll get a stomachache.*

stone * /stoʊn/ [*noun*]
1 a small piece of rock, especially a smooth one
2 a hard substance from the ground, used especially for building: *The statue is made of stone.* | *a set of stone steps*

stony /'stoʊni/ [*adjective;* **stonier, stoniest**] covered with stones: *a stony river bottom*

stood * /stʊd/ [*verb*] the past tense and past participle of STAND[1]

stool /stul/ [*noun*] a seat with no back or arms, for one person to sit on

stoop[1] /stup/ [*noun*] a set of steps going from a sidewalk to the door of a HOUSE: *On summer nights, people sit on their stoops and talk.*

a stool

stoop[2] [*verb;* **stooped, stooping**] to bend your head and shoulders in order to walk under something: *The doorway was so low he had to stoop to go in.*
⇨ See the picture at MOVEMENT.

stop[1] * T /stap/ [*verb;* **stops, stopped, stopping**]
1 to not continue, or to make someone or something not continue; <u>opposite</u> START: *Let's stop and rest.* | *Suddenly, the music stopped.* | *What can be done to stop the war?* | *stop doing something* ▸ *He never stopped talking!*
2 to prevent someone from doing something, or prevent something from happening: *I'm going home and you can't stop me.* | *stop someone/ something from doing something* ▸ *They stopped the fire from spreading.*
3 to not continue moving or traveling, or to make something do this: *The ball stopped just in front of me.* | *Stop the car. I want to get out.*

/i/ **see**   /ɪ/ **big**   /eɪ/ **day**   /ɛ/ **get**   /æ/ **hat**
/ɑ/ **father, hot**   /ʌ/ **up**   /ə/ **about**   /ɔ/ **saw**
/oʊ/ **hope**   /ʊ/ **book**   /u/ **too**   /aɪ/ **I**   /aʊ/ **how**
/ɔɪ/ **boy**   /ɚ/ **bird**   /ə/ **teacher**   /ɪr/ **ear**   /ɛr/ **air**
/ɑr/ **far**   /ɔr/ **more**   /ʊr/ **tour**   /aɪr/ **fire**
/aʊə/ **hour**   /θ/ **nothing**   /ð/ **mother**   /ʃ/ **she**
/ʒ/ **measure**   /tʃ/ **church**   /dʒ/ **jump**   /ŋ/ **long**

☛ Do not use the **to** form of a verb with **stop**. For example, do not say "It stopped to rain" or "I stopped him to go." Say It **stopped raining** or I **stopped him from going**.

— PHRASE

4 stop it or **stop that** used to tell someone not to do what he or she is doing: *Stop it, or I'll tell Mom!*

stop[2] * 🅃 [noun]
1 when something stops or you stop it: *The train came to a stop.*
2 a place where buses or trains stop to let passengers on or off: *Get off at the next stop.* | *Meet me at the bus stop.*

stoplight /'stɑp,laɪt/ [noun] a set of red, yellow, and green lights on a street, that control traffic; synonym TRAFFIC LIGHT

store[1] * /stɔr/ [noun] a place where goods are sold: *You can buy nails at the hardware store.* | *a department store*

store[2] * [verb; stored, storing]
1 to put something somewhere in order to keep it there until you need it: *We store firewood behind the house.*
2 if a computer stores information, it keeps it in its memory: *The computer stores data on all the students.*

storm * /stɔrm/ [noun] weather with strong winds and heavy rain: *A tree fell onto our house in the storm.*

stormy /'stɔrmi/ [adjective; stormier, stormiest] having storms, or affected by storms: *In stormy weather, I stay inside the house.* | *stormy seas*

story * 🅃 /'stɔri/ [noun; plural stories]
1 something you write or say that tells about a real or imaginary event: *I'm reading a story about a pirate.* | *a love story* | *He told stories of life in the army.*
2 a report written in a newspaper or broadcast on radio or television: *The story was on the front page of all the newspapers.*
3 one of the levels of a building; synonym FLOOR: *My apartment building has has twenty stories.* | *a ten-story building*

stove /stoʊv/ [noun] a piece of equipment on which food is cooked, which is usually on the top of an oven

a stove

straight[1] * /streɪt/ [adjective; straighter, straightest]
1 without any bends or curves; opposites BENT, CURVED: *He drew a straight line using a ruler.* | *a straight road*
2 straight HAIR has no curls: *She has long, straight hair.*
3 even or level; opposite CROOKED: *She had to wear braces to make her teeth straighter.*
4 honest, even when this makes someone upset or offended: *I wish you'd give me a straight answer.* | **be straight with someone** ▸ *I'll be straight with you—your work isn't good enough.*
5 one after the other: *She got straight A's in high school* (=an A grade in every subject).

straight[2] * [adverb]
1 in a straight line: *He couldn't even walk straight.* | *The car was coming straight toward me.*
2 directly, or without stopping: *Come straight home after school.* | *It rained for five days straight.*

— PHRASES

3 stand up/sit up straight to stand or sit with your back upright and your head held high: *Sit up straight and pay attention!*
4 straight on continuing in the

direction you are going, without
turning: *Go straight on at the traffic
lights.*

☞ Do not say "straightly," because this
word does not exist. The adverb and the
adjective are both **straight**.

straighten /'streɪtən/ [*verb*;
straightened, straightening]
1 to become straight or to make
something straight: *The road
straightened as we entered the valley.* |
He straightened his tie.

— PHRASAL VERB ——————

straighten up [*phrasal verb*]
2 to make a place neat: **straighten up
something** ▸ *Have you straightened up
your room?*

strain[1] /streɪn/ [*noun*]
1 worry that is the result of being in a
difficult situation: *He's been **under a
lot of strain** recently.*
2 an injury to a part of your body
caused by stretching it too much:
*A knee strain forced him to leave the
competition.*

strain[2] [*verb*; strained, straining]
1 to injure a part of your body by
stretching it too much: *Be careful not
to strain your back.*
2 to try hard to do something: *She was
straining to see the parade from the
middle of the crowd.*
3 to pour food into an object that
separates the liquid part from the solid
pieces: *Please strain the vegetables.*

strainer /'streɪnɚ/ [*noun*] a piece of
kitchen equipment that looks like a
metal net, used for separating liquid
from solid pieces of food: *a tea strainer*

strait /streɪt/ [*noun*] a narrow area of
water connecting two large areas of
water

strand /strænd/ [*noun*] a single piece of
something long and thin such as hair
or wire: *a strand of hair*

stranded /'strændɪd/ [*adjective; no
comparative*] unable to leave a place: *I
missed the last train and was left stranded
at the station overnight.*

strange * T /streɪndʒ/ [*adjective;
stranger, strangest*]
1 different from what is usual or
expected; *synonym* ODD; *opposite*

NORMAL: *A **strange thing** happened
yesterday.* | *It's **strange that** no one
noticed him.*

↪ *See the usage note at* STRANGER.
2 a strange situation or place is one
that you have never been in before;
synonym UNFAMILIAR: *She was all alone in
a strange town.*

strangely * /streɪndʒli/ [*adverb*] in an
unusual way; *opposite* NORMALLY: *He's
been acting strangely recently.*

stranger * /'streɪndʒɚ/ [*noun*]
1 someone you do not know: *a
complete stranger* (=someone you
have never seen before)
2 someone who has not been in a place
long and does not know it well: *It is
easy for a stranger to get lost around
here.*

USAGE   stranger, strange

A **stranger** is someone you do not
know: *My parents told me not to talk to
strangers.* A **strange** person is someone
who behaves in an unusual way: *There are
some strange people in this town.*

---

strangle /'stræŋgəl/ [*verb*; strangled,
strangling] to kill someone by pressing
your hands or a rope around his or her
throat so that he or she cannot breathe:
She had been strangled with a silk scarf.

strap /stræp/ [*noun*] a long narrow piece
of material, especially leather, used for
carrying something or fastening
something: *The strap on my shoulder bag
broke.*

straw[1] /strɔ/ [*noun*]
1 dried stems from wheat or other
grains, used as a bed or food for
animals
2 a narrow tube through which you
suck a drink

— PHRASE ——————

3 the last straw the thing that makes
you finally become very angry: *When
she lied to me, that was the last straw.*

/i/ see /ɪ/ big /eɪ/ **day** /ɛ/ get /æ/ h**a**t
/ɑ/ f**a**ther, h**o**t /ʌ/ up /ə/ **a**bout /ɔ/ s**a**w
/oʊ/ hope /ʊ/ book /u/ too /aɪ/ I /aʊ/ how
/ɔɪ/ boy /ɝ/ bird /ɚ/ teacher /ɪr/ ear /ɛr/ air
/ɑr/ far /ɔr/ more /ʊr/ tour /aɪr/ fire
/aʊɚ/ hour /θ/ nothing /ð/ mother /ʃ/ she
/ʒ/ measure /tʃ/ church /dʒ/ jump /ŋ/ long

straw[2] [*adjective; no comparative*] made from straw: *a straw hat* | *a straw basket*

strawberry /'strɔ,bɛri/ [*noun; plural* **strawberries**] a small red FRUIT that grows on plants close to the ground

stray[1] /streɪ/ [*noun; plural* **strays**] a dog or cat that has no owner: *I think this dog is a stray.* | *a stray cat*

stray[2] [*verb;* **strays, strayed, straying**] to move away from the place where you should be: *Stay together and don't stray from the trail.*

streak /strik/ [*noun*] a long narrow area of color: *He has **streaks of** gray in his hair.*

stream[1] * ⊤ /strim/ [*noun*] a narrow river: *A small stream runs through the woods.*

stream[2] [*verb;* **streamed, streaming**] if liquid or a crowd of things or people streams somewhere, it moves there quickly in a continuous line: *Tears were streaming down her face.* | *The traffic streamed past.*

street * or **Street** /strit/ [*noun*] a road in a town or city, with houses, stores, or offices along it: *The store is over there, just across the street.* | *Don't drop litter **in** the street.* | *I live at 42 West 48th Street.*

streetlight /'strit,laɪt/ [*noun*] one of the lights on tall poles along a street or road: *As it began to get dark outside, the streetlights came on.*

strength * /strɛŋkθ/ [*noun*]
1 the quality of being strong or having power: *He did exercises to increase his strength.* | *the strength of their love*
2 a good quality or ability; *opposite* WEAKNESS: *One of her strengths is that she learns quickly.*

strengthen ⊤ /'strɛŋkθən/ [*verb;* **strengthened, strengthening**] to become stronger, or to make someone or something stronger; *opposite* WEAKEN: *This experience has strengthened our relationship.*

stress[1] /strɛs/ [*noun; plural* **stresses**]
1 worry caused by having too much work to do or being in a difficult situation: *Many managers suffer from stress.* | *the **stresses and strains** of everyday life*

2 extra force that you give to part of a word when you say it: *Put the stress on the first syllable.*

stress[2] [*verb;* **stresses, stressed, stressing**]
1 to talk about something in a way that shows you think it is important; *synonym* EMPHASIZE: *She **stressed that** everyone had to be on time.*
2 to put extra force on part of a word when you say it: *Stress the end of the word.*

stressed /strɛst/ [*adjective;* **more stressed, most stressed**] worried and unable to relax: *I'm **stressed about** my job.*

stressful /'strɛsfəl/ [*adjective;* **more stressful, most stressful**] making you feel worried and unable to relax: *Taking care of children can be stressful.*

stretch[1] * /strɛtʃ/ [*verb;* **stretches, stretched, stretching**]
1 to move your body or part of your body as far as it will go: *The boy yawned and stretched.* | *He sat down and **stretched out** his legs.*
⊃ *See the picture at* MOVEMENT.
2 to become bigger or looser, or to make something do this: *The jeans should stretch with time.* | *Don't pull my sweater—you'll stretch it.*
3 to cover a large area: *Their farm stretches for miles.*

stretch[2] [*noun; plural* **stretches**] a continuous length of road, land, or water: *This is a very dangerous stretch of road.*

stretcher /'strɛtʃɚ/ [*noun*] a frame covered with cloth, used for carrying a sick or injured person: *He was carried off the football field on a stretcher.*

stricken * /'strɪkən/ [*verb*] a past participle of STRIKE[1]

strict * /strɪkt/ [*adjective;* **stricter, strictest**] having many rules and expecting them to be obeyed: *My father is **very strict with** us.*
☛ Do not say that someone is "strict to you." Say that he or she is **strict with you.**

strictly * /'strɪktli/ [adverb] in a limited or exact way: *This phone number is strictly for emergencies.* | *Strictly speaking, a tomato is a fruit, not a vegetable.*

stride /straɪd/ [verb; strode, stridden /'strɪdən/, striding] to walk quickly with long steps: *He strode down the hall.*

strike[1] * /straɪk/ [verb; struck, struck or stricken, striking]
1 to hit someone or something: *Their barn was struck by lightning.*
☛ **Strike** is used more often in formal speech and writing than **hit**.
2 if workers strike or they strike a company, they stop working in order to get better pay, working conditions, etc.: *The pilots have been striking for two months.*
3 if an idea or thought strikes you, you have it: *It suddenly struck me that I'd forgotten Mom's birthday.* | *She strikes me as an honest person.*
4 if a clock strikes, it makes a loud sound when it is a particular time: *The clock struck two* (=it was two o'clock).
5 to light a match by quickly pulling the end of it across a rough or hard surface: *He struck a match and lit the candles.*

strike[2] [noun]
1 a period when workers stop working in order to get better pay, conditions, etc.: *The strike completely closed the factory.*
═══ PHRASE ═══
2 **be/go on strike** to not work or to stop working as a protest: *They have been on strike for two weeks.*

string * /strɪŋ/ [noun]
1 strong thread used for tying things, or a piece of this thread: *a package tied with a piece of string*
2 one of the long wires on a musical instrument such as a guitar or violin

strip[1] /strɪp/ [noun] a long thin piece of something: *He tore off a strip of paper.* | *Grapes are grown along this strip of land.*

strip[2] [verb; strips, stripped, stripping]
1 to remove something from a surface: *Could you strip the sheets off the bed?*

2 to remove your clothes: *The doctor told me to strip down to my shorts.*

stripe /straɪp/ [noun] a narrow band which is a different color than the rest of something: *Her dress is blue with green stripes.*

striped /straɪpt/ [adjective; no comparative] having stripes: *a striped sweater*
↪ See the picture at PATTERN.

strode /stroʊd/ [verb] the past tense of STRIDE

stroke[1] /stroʊk/ [noun]
1 a sudden, serious medical condition that affects your brain: *My grandfather had a stroke two years ago.*
2 a movement made by someone's arm when he or she does an activity such as hitting a ball, swimming, or rowing: *You need to practice the basic tennis strokes.*

stroke[2] [verb; stroked, stroking] to move your hand lightly over something: *She gently stroked his head.*

stroll[1] /stroʊl/ [verb; strolled, strolling] to walk somewhere in a slow, relaxed way for pleasure: *We strolled down to the beach.*

stroll[2] [noun] a slow, relaxed walk taken for pleasure: *Let's go for a stroll.*

stroller /'stroʊlɚ/ [noun] a chair on four wheels in which a baby or small child can be pushed along

strong * Ⓣ /strɔŋ/ [adjective; stronger, strongest]
1 having a lot of physical power or force: *Are you strong enough to carry both suitcases?* | *The strong winds caused a lot of damage.*
2 difficult to break, harm, or damage: *The tent was made of strong cloth.* | *They have a strong friendship.*
3 having power over other people or in particular situations: *a strong leader* | *a strong company*

/i/ see	/ɪ/ big	/eɪ/ day	/ɛ/ get	/æ/ hat
/ɑ/ father, hot	/ʌ/ up	/ə/ about	/ɔ/ saw
/oʊ/ hope	/ʊ/ book	/u/ too	/aɪ/ I	/aʊ/ how
/ɔɪ/ boy	/ɝ/ bird	/ɚ/ teacher	/ɪr/ ear	/ɛr/ air
/ɑr/ far	/ɔr/ more	/ʊr/ tour	/aɪr/ fire
/aʊɚ/ hour	/θ/ nothing	/ð/ mother	/ʃ/ she
/ʒ/ measure	/tʃ/ church	/dʒ/ jump	/ŋ/ long

4 a strong feeling or opinion is one that you feel or have to a great degree: *He has strong views on the subject.*
5 a strong taste or smell is one that you notice easily: *Garlic has a strong flavor.* I **strong coffee** (=coffee with a strong taste)
⤷ *See also* STRENGTH, STRENGTHEN.
⤷ *Compare* WEAK.

strongly * /'strɔŋli/ [*adverb*] very much, or to a very great degree: *I strongly disagree with you.* I *The room smelled strongly of smoke.*

struck * /strʌk/ [*verb*] the past tense and a past participle of STRIKE¹

structure * /'strʌktʃɚ/ [*noun*]
1 a building, bridge, or other large thing that has been built: *What's that large structure at the end of the street?*
2 the way in which something is built, organized, or put together: *Their houses are very simple in structure.* I *the structure of the human body*

struggle¹ * /'strʌgəl/ [*verb*; **struggled, struggling**]
1 to try very hard to do something difficult: **struggle to do something** ▸ *She struggles to pay the bills.*
2 to try to get free from someone who is holding you: *My son struggles every time I dress him.*

struggle² * [*noun*]
1 a situation in which you have to try very hard to do or get something: *Every day was a **struggle to** survive.* I *the people's **struggle for** freedom*
2 when you fight or try to get free from someone who is holding you: *A man was injured after a struggle with police.*

stubborn /'stʌbɚn/ [*adjective*; **stubborner, stubbornest**] not willing to change your opinion or to do what someone wants you to do: *Stop being stubborn, and apologize.*

stuck¹ * [*verb*] the past tense and past participle of STICK¹

stuck² /stʌk/ [*adjective*; *no comparative*]
1 unable to move or be moved: *Help—I'm stuck!* I *I can't open the door—the key's stuck.* I *The car got stuck in the snow.*

2 unable to do something because it is too difficult: *I'm **stuck on** question ten.*
☛ Do not use **stuck** before a noun.

student * /'studənt/ [*noun*] someone who is studying at a school or college: *She's a medical student* (=studying to become a doctor).

studio /'studi,oʊ/ [*noun*; *plural* **studios**]
1 a place where films or television or radio programs are made: *a movie studio*
2 a room or office where an artist works: *a photography studio*
3 an apartment with only one main room

study¹ * /'stʌdi/ [*verb*; **studies, studied, studying**] to learn about something by taking classes, reading books, etc.: *She's studying hard for her final exams.* I *I want to study French in college.* I **study to be something** ▸ *My brother is studying to be a doctor.*

USAGE   study, learn

Study is usually used to talk about the activity of trying to know about a subject: *I studied Spanish in college* (=I may or may not have learned it very well). I *I studied music for a while.*
Learn is usually used to show that someone knows about a subject or has an ability: *I learned Spanish in college* (=I was able to speak it). I *I learned how to play the piano.*

study² * [*noun*; *plural* **studies**]
1 the activity of studying: *The **study** of history can teach us a lot.*
2 a report that is the result of studying something: *They've done several **studies** on water pollution.*
3 a room in a house in which you study, write things, etc.
4 studies [*plural*] the work a student does in a school or college: *He would like to continue his studies at Yale.*

stuff¹ /stʌf/ [*noun*] INFORMAL
1 a substance: *What's that black stuff coming out of the engine?*
2 a group of things, especially things belonging to someone: *He leaves his stuff all over the house.*

stuff[2] [*verb*; **stuffed, stuffing**]
  1 to fill something with something else: *a pillow* **stuffed with** *feathers* | *He stuffed his mouth full of food.*
  2 to push something into something else in a quick, rough way: *I stuffed my clothes into a suitcase.*

stuffing /'stʌfɪŋ/ [*noun*]
  1 bread mixed with spices and meat or vegetables that is put inside a chicken or other large bird before it is cooked
  2 soft material that fills the inside of a piece of furniture, soft toy, etc.: *The stuffing was coming out of a hole in the car seat.*

stumble /'stʌmbəl/ [*verb*; **stumbled, stumbling**] to almost fall as you walk: *Grandpa stumbled a few times on the beach.*

stump /stʌmp/ [*noun*] the part of something that remains after most of it has been cut off: *a tree stump*

stung * /stʌŋ/ [*verb*] the past tense and past participle of STING

stunk /stʌŋk/ [*verb*] the past participle of STINK[1]

stunned /stʌnd/ [*adjective*; **more stunned, most stunned**] extremely surprised and shocked: *I'm stunned. I had no idea you felt that way.*

stunning /'stʌnɪŋ/ [*adjective*; **more stunning, most stunning**] extremely beautiful: *The view from here is absolutely stunning.*

stupid * /'stupɪd/ [*adjective*; **stupider, stupidest**] not intelligent or sensible; *synonym* DUMB; *opposite* SMART: *How can I have been so stupid?* | *That's a stupid idea.* | *a stupid mistake*

stupidity /stu'pɪdɪti/ [*noun*] stupid behavior, or a lack of intelligence: *Because of your stupidity, we lost the game.*

sturdy Ⓣ /'stɜrdi/ [*adjective*; **sturdier, sturdiest**] a sturdy object or structure is strong and does not break easily: *I put the books in the sturdiest box I could find.*

stutter /'stʌtər/ [*verb*; **stuttered, stuttering**] to repeat the first parts of words when you speak; *synonym* STAMMER: *He stuttered when he spoke.* | *She stuttered her thanks.*

style * /staɪl/ [*noun*]
  1 a way of behaving or doing something: *an author's* **style of** *writing* | *a painting* **in** *a 19th-century* **style**
  2 a design of hair or clothes, especially one that is popular: *He tried on several* **styles of** *hats.* | *Short hair is* **in style** *now.*
  3 an impressive way of doing things: *He arrived* **in style**—*in a limousine.*

subject * /'sʌbdʒɪkt/ [*noun*]
  1 an area of study in school such as history, math, or English: *My favorite subject is chemistry.* | *Which subjects are you taking this semester?*
  2 something that someone writes or talks about; *synonym* TOPIC: *What is the* **subject of** *the book?* | *I'm tired of talking about sports. Can we* **change the subject**? (=talk about something different)
  3 GRAMMAR the word or phrase in a sentence that is used to mention the person or thing that does something or that is being described: *In the sentence "I ate an apple," "I" is the subject.* | *In the sentence "The weather is stormy," "weather" is the subject.*
  ⇨ *Compare* OBJECT[1] (definition 3).

submarine /ˌsʌbmə'rin/ [*noun*] a kind of ship that can travel under water

substance * /'sʌbstəns/ [*noun*] a particular kind of solid or liquid: *They work with some dangerous substances in the lab.* | *The leaves were covered with a sticky substance.*

substitute[1] Ⓣ /'sʌbstɪˌtut/ [*verb*; **substituted, substituting**] to use one thing or person instead of another one: **substitute something for something** ▸ *You can substitute honey for sugar.*

substitute[2] [*noun*] someone who does another person's job for a short time: *a substitute teacher*

subtitle /'sʌbˌtaɪtəl/ [*noun*] words in one language that are shown at the bottom

---

/i/ see	/ɪ/ big	/eɪ/ day	/ɛ/ get	/æ/ hat
/ɑ/ father, hot	/ʌ/ up	/ə/ about	/ɔ/ saw	
/oʊ/ hope	/ʊ/ book	/u/ too	/aɪ/ I	/aʊ/ how
/ɔɪ/ boy	/ɝ/ bird	/ɚ/ teacher	/ɪr/ ear	/ɛr/ air
/ɑr/ far	/ɔr/ more	/ʊr/ tour	/aɪr/ fire	
/aʊɚ/ hour	/θ/ nothing	/ð/ mother	/ʃ/ she	
/ʒ/ measure	/tʃ/ church	/dʒ/ jump	/ŋ/ long	

of a movie that is in another language, which explain what is being said: *an American movie with French subtitles*

subtract * /səb'trækt/ [*verb;* **subtracted, subtracting**] to take one number away from another and get a smaller number as the result; *opposite* ADD: **subtract something from something** ▸ *Subtract what you've spent from the total.*
↪ *See also* MINUS.

subtraction /səb'trækʃən/ [*noun*] when you take one number away from another; *opposite* ADDITION: *You made a mistake in your subtraction.*

suburb Ⓣ /'sʌbɚb/ [*noun*] an area just outside a city where a lot of people live: *I grew up in* **a suburb** *of Dallas.* | *the Phoenix suburbs*

subway /'sʌb,weɪ/ [*noun;* plural **subways**] a system of electric trains that travel under the ground: *I'll* **take the subway** *home.* | *a subway station*

succeed * Ⓣ /sək'sid/ [*verb;* **succeeded, succeeding**] to manage to do or achieve something; *opposite* FAIL: *You must work hard if you want to succeed.* | **succeed in doing something** ▸ *He finally succeeded in getting a job interview.*
☛ Do not say "succeed to do something." Say **succeed in doing something**.

success * /sək'sɛs/ [*noun;* plural **successes**]
1 when you manage to do or achieve something: *I don't have much* **success** *with cooking.* | *Only a few bands have* **success in** *the music business.*
☛ Do not say "success on something." Say **success in something**.
2 a person, thing, or event that achieves what was wanted or intended; *opposite* FAILURE: *I just want to be a success.* | *His book was a* **big success.**

successful * /sək'sɛsfəl/ [*adjective;* **more successful, most successful**] achieving what was wanted or intended; *opposite* UNSUCCESSFUL: *He is a successful writer.* | *The movie was very successful.* | **successful in doing something** ▸ *Were you successful in persuading him to come?*

☛ Do not say that someone is "successful to do something." Say that he or she is **successful in doing something**.

successfully * /sək'sɛsfəli/ [*adverb*] in the way you wanted or intended: *Have you successfully installed the software?*

such * Ⓣ /sʌtʃ/ [*determiner, adverb*]
1 used to emphasize how good, bad, big, etc., something is: *Learning English is such hard work.* | *He's such an idiot!* | **such . . . that** ▸ *They were such fun that I spent the whole day with them.*
☛ Do not say "He is such a good boy." Say **He is such a good boy**.
↪ *Compare* SO¹ (definition 1).
2 used to talk about the thing or person just mentioned: *Quit school? Where did you get such an idea?*

— PHRASES —
3 such as used to give examples: *I like sports such as basketball, soccer, and tennis.*
4 not such (. . . as) used to say that one thing has less of a quality than another: *It wasn't such a good movie as his first one.*
5 there is no such thing (as) used to say that something does not exist: *There's no such thing as ghosts.*

suck * /sʌk/ [*verb;* **sucked, sucking**] to hold something in your mouth and pull on it with your lips and tongue: *She was sucking lemonade through a straw.* | *He sucked on his pen.*

sudden * Ⓣ /'sʌdən/ [*adjective; no comparative*]
1 happening quickly when you do not expect it: *He was caught in a sudden storm.* | *a sudden death*

— PHRASE —
2 all of a sudden quickly and without being expected; *synonym* SUDDENLY: *All of a sudden, she started to cry.*

suddenly * /'sʌdənli/ [*adverb*] quickly and without being expected: *I suddenly felt very afraid.* | *Suddenly, it started raining.*

sue /su/ [*verb;* **sues, sued, suing**] to make a legal claim that a person or organization has harmed you and should give you money: *They were **sued** for breaking their contract.*

suede /sweɪd/ [*noun*] a kind of leather with a soft, slightly rough surface: *brown suede shoes*

suffer * ⊤ /'sʌfɚ/ [*verb;* **suffered, suffering**] to experience something bad such as pain or sadness: *The town suffered a lot of damage from the storm.* | *She is **suffering from** a knee injury.*

suffering /'sʌfərɪŋ/ [*noun*] when someone experiences something bad: *The doctors are trying to ease his suffering.*

sufficient ⊤ /sə'fɪʃənt/ [*adjective; no comparative*] FORMAL enough: *There wasn't sufficient money to complete the work.*
➪ *See the synonym note at* ENOUGH[1].

suffix * /'sʌfɪks/ [*noun; plural* **suffixes**] GRAMMAR a group of letters that is added to the end of a word and changes its meaning slightly: *Adding the suffix "-or" to the verb "act" creates the noun "actor."*
➪ *Compare* PREFIX. ➪ *See* Prefixes and Suffixes *in the Smart Study section.*

suffocate /'sʌfə,keɪt/ [*verb;* **suffocated, suffocating**] to die because you are unable to breathe, or to kill someone in this way: *Babies can suffocate if they sleep on their stomachs.*

sugar * /'ʃʊgɚ/ [*noun*] a white or brown substance that is added to food to make it taste sweet: *Do you take sugar in your coffee?*

suggest * ⊤ /səg'dʒɛst/ [*verb;* **suggested, suggesting**] to mention something that could be done or that might be a solution, explanation, etc.: *I suggested that she see a doctor.* | **suggest doing something** ▸ *Someone suggested going to see a movie.*
☛ Do not say "I suggest you to call him." Say **I suggest that you call him.**
☛ Do not say "suggest someone something." For example, do not say "I suggested her an idea." Say **I suggested an idea to her.**

suggestion * ⊤ /səg'dʒɛstʃən/ [*noun*] a possible action, explanation, choice, etc., that someone mentions: *May I **make a suggestion**? | Does anyone have any other suggestions?*

suicide ⊤ /'suə,saɪd/ [*noun*] when someone kills himself or herself: *What reason did she have to **commit suicide**?* (=kill herself)

suit[1] * /sut/ [*noun*]
1 a set of clothes, usually a jacket and pants or a skirt, made of the same material: *You look great in a suit and tie.* | *a business suit*
➪ *See the picture at* CLOTHING.
2 a piece of clothing worn for a particular activity: *a diving suit*
➪ *See also* SWIMSUIT.

suit[2] * [*verb;* **suited, suiting**]
1 if a color or a piece of clothing suits you, you look good when you wear it: *I'm not sure if pink suits me.*
2 to be convenient or easy for you: *"Is 10:30 OK?" "Yes, that suits me fine."*
☛ Do not say that something "suits for" or "suits to" someone. Say that it **suits** him or her.

suitable * ⊤ /'sutəbəl/ [*adjective;* **more suitable, most suitable**] good or acceptable for a particular person, job, use, etc.; *synonym* APPROPRIATE; *opposite* UNSUITABLE: *This TV show isn't **suitable for** children.* | *They don't think he's a **suitable** husband **for** their daughter.*

suitcase /'sut,keɪs/ [*noun*] a bag with straight sides, used for carrying clothes and other things when you are traveling: *I haven't **packed my suitcase** yet* (=put things in it).

suite /swit/ [*noun*] a set of rooms to be used together, for example in a hotel

sum * /sʌm/ [*noun*] an amount of money: *She left her family a large **sum of money** when she died.*

summary /'sʌməri/ [*noun; plural* **summaries**] a report about something that includes the main things but does not give every detail: *Can you give me a **summary of** what you learned?*

/i/ see	/ɪ/ big	/eɪ/ day	/ɛ/ get	/æ/ hat		
/ɑ/ father, hot	/ʌ/ up	/ə/ about	/ɔ/ saw			
/oʊ/ hope	/ʊ/ book	/u/ too	/aɪ/ I	/aʊ/ how		
/ɔɪ/ boy	/ɚ/ bird	/ɚ/ teacher	/ɪr/ ear	/ɛr/ air		
/ɑr/ far	/ɔr/ more	/ʊr/ tour	/aɪr/ fire			
/aʊɚ/ hour	/θ/ nothing	/ð/ mother	/ʃ/ she			
/ʒ/ measure	/tʃ/ church	/dʒ/ jump	/ŋ/ long			

summer * /'sʌmɚ/ [noun] the warm season between spring and fall
⇨ See the usage note at SEASON.

summer school /'sʌmɚ ˌskul/ [noun] classes taught in the summer at a school or college: I learned a lot in summer school.

summertime /'sʌmɚˌtaɪm/ [noun] the time of the year when it is summer: In the summertime we often eat outside.

summer vacation /'sʌmɚ veɪ'keɪʃən/ [noun] a period of time during the summer when schools and colleges are closed: Every summer vacation, we go camping.

summit /'sʌmɪt/ [noun] the highest point of a mountain

sun * /sʌn/ [noun]
1 the nearest star to earth, which gives it light and warmth: The sun was already high in the sky.
2 light or warmth from the sun; synonym SUNSHINE: You might get burned if you sit in the sun.
☛ Do not say "sit under the sun." Say sit in the sun.

Sun. the written abbreviation of SUNDAY

sunbathe /'sʌnˌbeɪð/ [verb; sunbathed, sunbathing] to sit or lie in the sun, especially in order to make your skin darker

sunburn /'sʌnˌbɚn/ [noun] red sore skin that has been burned by the sun: I had a bad sunburn.

sunburned /'sʌnˌbɚnd/ [adjective; more sunburned, most sunburned] having red sore skin that has been burned by the sun: Wearing sunscreen stops you from getting sunburned.

Sunday * /'sʌndeɪ/ [noun; plural Sundays] the day of the week that is after Saturday and before Monday: Are you going to church on Sunday? | I don't work on Sundays.
⇨ See the usage note at DAY.

sung * /sʌŋ/ [verb] the past participle of SING

sunglasses /'sʌnˌglæsɪz/ [plural noun] dark-colored glasses worn to protect your eyes from the sun: I got a new pair of sunglasses.

sunk * /sʌŋk/ [verb] the past tense and past participle of SINK[1]

sunlight /'sʌnˌlaɪt/ [noun] the light that comes from the sun: Bright sunlight was coming through the trees.

sunny /'sʌni/ [adjective; sunnier, sunniest] having a lot of sunlight; synonym BRIGHT: It was one of the sunniest days of the year. | a sunny room

sunrise /'sʌnˌraɪz/ [noun] when the sun appears at the beginning of the day; opposite SUNSET: He gets up at sunrise every morning.

sunscreen /'sʌnˌskrin/ [noun] cream you put on your skin to stop it from being burned by the sun: Don't go out without putting sunscreen on.

sunset /'sʌnˌsɛt/ [noun] when the sun disappears at the end of the day; opposite SUNRISE: They arrived just before sunset.

sunshine /'sʌnˌʃaɪn/ [noun] light or warmth from the sun; synonym SUN: The kids were playing out in the sunshine.

suntan /'sʌnˌtæn/ [noun] the darker color of skin that someone gets after he or she has been in the sun; synonym TAN: I got a suntan.

superb /sʊ'pɚb/ [adjective; no comparative] extremely good; synonym EXCELLENT: You get a superb view of the lake from here.

superior[1] /sə'pɪriɚ/ [adjective; no comparative] higher in rank, quality, skill, etc., than someone or something else: These paintings are superior to his earlier works.
☛ Do not "superior than something." Say superior to something.
⇨ Compare INFERIOR.

superior[2] [noun] someone who has a higher rank or position than you: She is my superior at work.

superlative * /sə'pɚlətɪv/ [noun] GRAMMAR the form of an adjective or adverb used when comparing three or more things or people, and saying that one has the most of that quality:

*"Smallest" is the superlative of "small." |
a superlative form*
☞ Superlatives are almost always used
with **the**: *He's the smallest boy in the class.*
| *I'm the tallest of all of us.*
▷ *See the usage note at* COMPARATIVE.

supermarket /'supɚ,markɪt/ [*noun*] a
large store that sells food and other
goods for the house, in which you serve
yourself

superstition /,supɚ'stɪʃən/ [*noun*] a
belief that a particular event or object
will make something bad or good
happen: *They say that breaking a mirror
causes bad luck, but it's just a superstition.*

superstitious /,supɚ'stɪʃəs/ [*adjective;*
**more superstitious, most
superstitious**] believing in
superstitions: *Are you superstitious?*

supervise /'supɚ,vaɪz/ [*verb;*
supervised, supervising] to make sure
that students or workers are doing
things right: *His job was to supervise the
men's work.*

supervision /,supɚ'vɪʒən/ [*noun*] the
activity of making sure that someone is
doing things right: *The children will be
under my supervision during the class
trip.*

supervisor /'supɚ,vaɪzɚ/ [*noun*]
someone who is responsible for making
sure that other people are doing things
right

supper * /'sʌpɚ/ [*noun*] a meal you eat
in the evening: *What time are we having
supper?*
▷ *Compare* DINNER.

supply[1] * /sə'plaɪ/ [*verb;* **supplies,
supplied, supplying**] to give someone
something that he or she needs;
synonym PROVIDE: **supply someone with
something** ▸ *Can you supply me with 40
copies of the book?* | **supply something
to someone** ▸ *The Middle East supplies
oil to most of the world.*
☞ Do not say "supply someone
something." Say **supply something to
someone** or **supply something to
someone.**

supply[2] * [*noun; plural* **supplies**] an
amount of something that is available
to be used: *We have a large supply of*

firewood. | *Supplies are running low*
(=there is not much left).

support[1] * ⊤ /sə'pɔrt/ [*verb;* **supported,
supporting**]
1 to help someone by showing
sympathy, giving him or her money,
etc.: *I will support you in anything you
do.* | *He earns enough money to support
his family.*
2 if something supports something that
is resting or leaning on it, it holds it
up: *Two huge pillars support the ceiling.*
3 to agree with a particular person,
political party, or idea: *Most voters still
support the president.*

support[2] * ⊤ [*noun*]
1 when someone helps another person
by showing sympathy, giving advice,
etc.: *My friends **have given** me a lot of
support.*
2 when someone agrees with a
particular person, political party, or
idea: *Which candidate has the most
support?*

supporter ⊤ /sə'pɔrtɚ/ [*noun*] someone
who agrees with a particular person,
political party, or idea: *I'm a supporter of
gun control.*

suppose[1] * /sə'pouz/ [*verb;* **supposed,
supposing**]
1 to think or believe something: *I
suppose we should visit your mother.* |
What do you suppose he meant? | *"Is
this the right place?" "I suppose so."* |
*"I don't think it's a good idea." "No, I
suppose not."*
— PHRASE —
2 be supposed to do something if
you are supposed to do something, or
if something is supposed to happen,
you should do it or it should happen:
*I'm supposed to go to bed before ten, but
I usually don't.* | *You weren't supposed to
tell her.*

/i/ see /ɪ/ big /eɪ/ day /ɛ/ get /æ/ hat
/a/ father, hot /ʌ/ up /ə/ about /ɔ/ saw
/ou/ hope /ʊ/ book /u/ too /aɪ/ I /aʊ/ how
/ɔɪ/ boy /ɝ/ bird /ɚ/ teacher /ɪr/ ear /ɛr/ air
/ar/ far /ɔr/ more /ʊr/ tour /aɪr/ fire
/aʊɚ/ hour /θ/ nothing /ð/ mother /ʃ/ she
/ʒ/ measure /tʃ/ church /dʒ/ jump /ŋ/ long

suppose[2] * [*conjunction*] used to mention a possible situation: *Suppose I were rich, would you marry me then?*

supreme /sə'prim/ [*adjective; no comparative*] highest in authority, importance, or degree: *the Supreme Court*
☞ Only use **supreme** before a noun.

sure[1] * /ʃʊr/ [*adjective; surer, surest*]
1 having no doubts about something; *synonym* CERTAIN; *opposite* UNSURE: *Are you sure that you saw a deer? | Are you sure about that? | I'm sure of it.*
☞ Do not use **sure** before a noun.

━━ PHRASES ━━
2 **make sure**
  a to take special care so that something happens or is done: **make sure (that)** ▸ *Make sure that the volume isn't too high. | Make sure you save some cake for me!*
  b to check that something is true: *Go make sure you turned off the iron.*
3 **be sure to do something** if something is sure to happen, it will definitely happen: *It's sure to rain. | He's sure to win.*
☞ Do not say "It's sure of raining." Say **It's sure to rain.**
☞ Do not say "It's sure he'll win." Say **He's sure to win.**

sure[2] * [*adverb*] SPOKEN
1 used to say yes: *"Can I have some more tea?" "Sure. Help yourself."*
2 used to accept someone's thanks: *"Thanks for helping me." "Sure, no problem."*
3 used to emphasize what you are saying; *synonym* CERTAINLY: *I sure don't want that to happen again.*

sure[3] * [*noun*]
━━ PHRASE ━━
know for sure to be completely certain about something: *We don't know for sure that he's leaving.*

surely /'ʃʊrli/ [*adverb*] used to show that you think or hope something is true: *Surely she knows what she's doing.*

surf /sɜrf/ [*verb; surfed, surfing*]
1 to ride on ocean waves while standing on a long narrow board: *Come on, I'll teach you to surf.*

━━ PHRASE ━━
2 **surf the Net** to go from place to place on the Internet: *I surfed the Net to find information for a school report.*

surface * /'sɜrfɪs/ [*noun*] the extreme outside or top of something: *the **surface** of the earth | Whales come up to the surface for air.*

surfboard /'sɜrf,bɔrd/ [*noun*] a long narrow board you can stand on to ride on waves

surfing /'sɜrfɪŋ/ [*noun*] the sport or activity of riding on a surfboard: *Let's go surfing.*

surge /sɜrdʒ/ [*verb; surged, surging*] to suddenly move forward in large amounts or numbers: *The crowd surged forward. | The dam burst and water surged out.*

surgeon /'sɜrdʒən/ [*noun*] a doctor who does medical operations: *Dr. Bell is a **brain surgeon**.*

surgery /'sɜrdʒəri/ [*noun; plural surgeries*] the performing of an operation by a doctor: *He **had surgery on** a lump on his neck. | heart surgery*

surname /'sɜr,neɪm/ [*noun*] a more formal word for LAST NAME: *Women in the U.S. usually use their husband's surname.*
⇨ *See the usage note at* FIRST NAME.

surprise[1] * /sə'praɪz/ [*noun*]
1 the feeling you get when something that is unusual or that you did not expect happens: *He raised his eyebrows **in surprise**. | **To my surprise**, I enjoyed the play.*
2 an event, gift, etc., that you were not expecting: *I want the party to be a surprise for her. | I love surprises!*

surprise[2] * [*verb; surprised, surprising*] to do something special or unusual that someone was not expecting: *He surprised me by buying me flowers. | **It surprises me that** (=I am surprised) you don't like him.*

surprise[3] * [*adjective; no comparative*] not expected: *a surprise birthday party*

surprised /sə'praɪzd/ [*adjective; more surprised, most surprised*] feeling surprise because something unexpected or unusual has happened: **be surprised**

(that) ▸ *I'm surprised you don't like him.* | **surprised to do something** ▸ *I was surprised to hear he was married.*
↪ *See the warning at* SURPRISING.

surprising * /sɚ'praɪzɪŋ/ [*adjective; more surprising, most surprising*] making you feel surprised: *She gave us some very surprising news.*
☛ Do not confuse **surprised** and **surprising**. A person is surprised: *I was surprised by the news.* Facts and events are surprising: *That's surprising news!*

surround * ⊤ /sə'raʊnd/ [*verb; surrounded, surrounding*] to be all around something, or to move into this position: *A high wall surrounds the garden.* | *A group of pigeons suddenly surrounded me.*

surroundings ⊤ /sə'raʊndɪŋz/ [*plural noun*] the area around a place or person: *The house is set in beautiful surroundings.*

survey ⊤ /'sɚveɪ/ [*noun; plural surveys*] when you ask a group of people a set of questions to find out their opinions, habits, etc.: *They did a survey on people's computer use.*

survival ⊤ /sɚ'vaɪvəl/ [*noun*] when someone or something survives: *The survival of a baby depends on its parents.*

survive ⊤ /sɚ'vaɪv/ [*verb; survived, surviving*] to stay alive or to continue to exist, in spite of bad events or dangers: *Only the strongest animals survive.* | *They all survived the crash.*
☛ Do not say that someone "survives from something." Say that he or she **survives it.**

suspect[1] ⊤ /sə'spɛkt/ [*verb; suspected, suspecting*] to believe something is true, even though you cannot prove it: **suspect (that)** ▸ *I suspect she's lying.* | **suspect someone of doing something** ▸ *They suspect him of stealing.*

suspect[2] /'sʌspɛkt/ [*noun*] someone who the police think may be responsible for a crime

suspend /sə'spɛnd/ [*verb; suspended, suspending*]
1 to stop an activity from continuing:

The game was suspended for almost ten minutes.
2 to stop a student from returning to school for a period of time: *They suspended him for fighting on the playground.*

suspenders /sə'spɛndɚz/ [*plural noun*] two pieces of cloth that go over your shoulders and stop your pants from falling down

He's wearing **suspenders.**

suspense /sə'spɛns/ [*noun*] the excited nervous feeling you get when you are waiting to find out or see something: *Don't keep me in suspense—tell me what happened!*

suspicion /sə'spɪʃən/ [*noun*] when you believe that something is true, even though you cannot prove it: *Her suspicions turned out to be correct.*

suspicious /sə'spɪʃəs/ [*adjective; more suspicious, most suspicious*] feeling that someone should not be trusted or that there is something wrong: *I was suspicious from the minute he approached me.* | *He was always suspicious of strangers.*

suspiciously /sə'spɪʃəsli/ [*adverb*] in a way that makes you feel that someone should not be trusted or that there is something wrong: *A man was seen behaving suspiciously just before the robbery.*

SUV /'ɛs,yu'vi/ [*noun; plural SUVs*] sport utility vehicle; a vehicle that is made for traveling over rough ground

S.W. or **SW** the written abbreviation for SOUTHWEST: *I live at 50 S.W. Lake Street.*

swallow * /'swɑloʊ/ [*verb; swallowed, swallowing*] to make something go down your throat when you are eating

/i/ **see**	/ɪ/ **big**	/eɪ/ **day**	/ɛ/ **get**	/æ/ **hat**
/ɑ/ **father, hot**	/ʌ/ **up**	/ə/ **about**	/ɔ/ **saw**
/oʊ/ **hope**	/ʊ/ **book**	/u/ **too**	/aɪ/ **I**	/aʊ/ **how**
/ɔɪ/ **boy**	/ɚ/ **bird**	/ɚ/ **teacher**	/ɪr/ **ear**	/ɛr/ **air**
/ɑr/ **far**	/ɔr/ **more**	/ʊr/ **tour**	/aɪr/ **fire**
/aʊɚ/ **hour**	/θ/ **nothing**	/ð/ **mother**	/ʃ/ **she**
/ʒ/ **measure**	/tʃ/ **church**	/dʒ/ **jump**	/ŋ/ **long**

or drinking: *My throat hurts when I swallow.* I *I find it difficult to swallow pills.*

swam * /swæm/ [*verb*] the past tense of SWIM[1]

swamp /swɑmp/ [*noun*] an area of land that is covered in water that is not very deep, especially in a hot country or area

swampy /'swɑmpi/ [*adjective*; **swampier, swampiest**] covered in a swamp: *a swampy area near a river*

swan /swɑn/ [*noun*] a large white bird that has a long neck and swims on water

swap /swɑp/ [*verb*; **swaps, swapped, swapping**] to give someone something in exchange for something he or she gives you; <u>synonym</u> TRADE: **swap something for something** ▸ *I'll swap my orange for your apple.*

swarm[1] /swɔrm/ [*noun*] a large group of insects: *a swarm of bees*

swarm[2] [*verb*; **swarmed, swarming**] to move together in a large group: *People swarmed into the stadium.*

sway /sweɪ/ [*verb*; **sways, swayed, swaying**] to move or swing from side to side: *trees swaying in the wind*

swear * /swɛr/ [*verb*; **swore, sworn, swearing**]
1 to make a serious promise: *I swear I won't lie to you.* I **swear to do something** ▸ *She swore to keep the secret.*
2 to use rude and offensive words: *He swore at the taxi driver.*

sweat[1] /swɛt/ [*noun*]
1 water that your skin produces when you are very hot, worried, or sick: *His sheets were damp with sweat.*
  ⇨ See also SWEATY.
2 **sweats** [*plural*] loose pants and a loose shirt, made of soft cloth, worn especially for relaxing or exercising
  ⇨ See the picture at CLOTHING.

sweat[2] [*verb*; **sweated, sweating**] if you sweat, your skin produces sweat: *She was sweating after her long hot walk.*

sweater * /'swɛtɚ/ [*noun*] a piece of warm CLOTHING that you wear on the top half of your body

sweatpants /'swɛtˌpænts/ [*plural noun*] loose pants made of soft cloth, worn especially for relaxing or exercising: *She was wearing a **pair of** old, dark gray sweatpants.*
  ⇨ See the picture at CLOTHING.

sweatshirt /'swɛtˌʃɚt/ [*noun*] a loose shirt made of soft cloth, worn especially for relaxing or exercising
  ⇨ See the picture at CLOTHING.

sweaty /'swɛti/ [*adjective*; **sweatier, sweatiest**] covered in sweat: *Your hands are all sweaty.*

sweep * /swip/ [*verb*; **swept, sweeping**] to remove dust, dirt, etc., from the floor or ground using a brush with a long handle: *I just swept the floor. Don't drop crumbs!*

sweet * /swit/ [*adjective*; **sweeter, sweetest**]
1 tasting of sugar; <u>opposite</u> SOUR: *It was the sweetest fruit I've ever tasted.*
2 having a pleasant character or appearance: *a sweet little girl*

sweet potato /'swit pəˌteɪtoʊ/ [*noun*; *plural* **sweet potatoes**] a dark orange root that is cooked and eaten as a vegetable: *Matt's favorite meal is ham with sweet potatoes.*

sweets /swits/ [*plural noun*] sweet foods in general: *Sweets are bad for your teeth.*

swell * /swɛl/ [*verb*; **swelled, swollen, swelling**] to become bigger: *My feet swell when they get hot.*
  ⇨ See also SWOLLEN[1].

swept * /swɛpt/ [*verb*] the past tense and past participle of SWEEP

swim[1] * /swɪm/ [*verb*; **swam, swum, swimming**] to move your body through water using your arms and legs: *I can't swim.* I *I swam a mile yesterday.*

swim[2] * [*noun*] when you swim: *Let's **go for a swim**.* I *We **had a swim** in the lake before lunch.*

swimmer /'swɪmɚ/ [*noun*] someone who is swimming or who knows how to swim: *I'm a good swimmer.*

swimming /'swɪmɪŋ/ [*noun*] the sport or activity of swimming: *We **went swimming** every day.*

swimming pool /'swɪmɪŋ ˌpul/ [*noun*] a structure filled with water that people can swim in

swimsuit /'swɪmˌsut/ [*noun*] a piece of CLOTHING that you wear for swimming; *synonym* BATHING SUIT: *We all changed into our swimsuits.*

swing[1] * /swɪŋ/ [*verb*; **swung, swinging**] if something with one end or side that is attached to something swings or is swung, the other end of it moves once or several times: *He swings his arms when he walks.* | *The gate swung open.*

swing[2] [*noun*] a seat hanging from ropes or chains, on which you can swing backward and forward: *Let's go play on the swings.*

switch[1] ⊤ /swɪtʃ/ [*verb*; **switches, switched, switching**]
1 to change from one place, job, activity, etc., to another: *Mom sang and I played piano, then we switched.* | *They switched seats.*

— PHRASAL VERBS —

switch off [*phrasal verb*]
2 to make a piece of electrical equipment stop working by pressing or moving a switch: **switch something off** ▸ *Did you switch the TV off?*

switch on [*phrasal verb*]
3 to make a piece of electrical equipment start working by pressing or moving a switch: **switch something on** ▸ *Can someone switch the light on?*

switch[2] [*noun; plural* **switches**] a small part of a piece of electrical equipment that you move to make it start or stop working: *a light switch*
⇨ *See the picture at* LAMP.

swollen[1] * /'swoʊlən/ [*verb*] the past participle of SWELL

swollen[2] [*adjective; more* **swollen,** *most* **swollen**] bigger than usual: *a swollen river* | *a swollen ankle*

sword * /sɔrd/ [*noun*] a weapon with a long sharp blade and a short handle

swore * /swɔr/ [*verb*] the past tense of SWEAR

sworn * /swɔrn/ [*verb*] the past participle of SWEAR

swum * /swʌm/ [*verb*] the past participle of SWIM[1]

swung * /swʌŋ/ [*verb*] the past tense and past participle of SWING[1]

syllabi /'sɪləˌbaɪ/ [*noun*] a plural form of SYLLABUS

syllable /'sɪləbəl/ [*noun*] one of the parts into which a word can be divided, each containing a vowel: *The word "window" has two syllables.*

syllabus /'sɪləbəs/ [*noun; plural* **syllabuses** or **syllabi**] a list of the things to be included in a course of study at a school or college: *That topic's not on the syllabus.*

symbol ⊤ /'sɪmbəl/ [*noun*] an object, picture, shape, etc., that represents something: *The dove is a symbol of peace.* | *The "P" symbol on the map means "parking."*

sympathetic * /ˌsɪmpə'θɛtɪk/ [*adjective; more* **sympathetic,** *most* **sympathetic**] understanding someone's problems and wanting to help or listen to him or her: *She wasn't very sympathetic about my accident.*

sympathy * ⊤ /'sɪmpəθi/ [*noun*] a feeling of understanding someone else's problems and being sorry about them: *I have a lot of sympathy for people who have to work all night.*

symptom /'sɪmptəm/ [*noun*] a physical condition that is the result of an illness and is also a sign of it: *She showed all the symptoms of an allergy.*

synagogue ⊤ /'sɪnəˌgag/ [*noun; plural* **synagogues**] a place where Jewish people meet and pray to God

synonym * /'sɪnənɪm/ [*noun*] a word that means the same thing as another word: *"Nearly" is a synonym of "almost."*

/i/ **see** /ɪ/ **big** /eɪ/ **day** /ɛ/ **get** /æ/ **hat**
/ɑ/ **father, hot** /ʌ/ **up** /ə/ **about** /ɔ/ **saw**
/oʊ/ **hope** /ʊ/ **book** /u/ **too** /aɪ/ **how**
/ɔɪ/ **boy** /ɚ/ **bird** /ɚ/ **teacher** /ɪr/ **ear** /ɛr/ **air**
/ɑr/ **far** /ɔr/ **more** /ʊr/ **tour** /aɪr/ **fire**
/aʊə/ **hour** /θ/ **nothing** /ð/ **mother** /ʃ/ **she**
/ʒ/ **measure** /tʃ/ **church** /dʒ/ **jump** /ŋ/ **long**

synthetic /sɪn'θɛtɪk/ [*adjective; no comparative*] made of chemicals that are mixed or changed by people, rather than being natural: *Nylon is a synthetic fiber.*

syringe /sə'rɪndʒ/ [*noun*] a medical tool with a NEEDLE at one end and a hollow plastic part on the other, used for putting medicine in your body or for taking liquids out: *The nurse used a syringe to take blood from my arm.*

syrup /'sɪrəp/ [*noun*] a thick sweet liquid: *She poured some maple syrup on her pancakes.*

system * /'sɪstəm/ [*noun*]
   1 a group or number of things that work together: *the city's transportation system* | *The drug may affect your digestive system.*
   2 an organized way of doing something: *I have a new system for doing my homework.*

T

T * or **t** /ti/ [*noun; plural* Ts or T's, t's] the 20th letter of the English alphabet
   ↪ *See the usage note at* ALPHABET.

T or **T.** a written abbreviation of TABLESPOON or TABLESPOONS; synonyms TBS, TBSP: *Add 2 T milk to 3 eggs, and stir.*

t or **t.** a written abbreviation of TEASPOON or TEASPOONS; synonym TSP: *Mix 2 c flour, 1 c sugar, and 1 t salt.*

table * /'teɪbəl/ [*noun*]
   1 a piece of furniture with a flat surface and four legs: *You left your book on the table.* | *He sat at the table studying.*
   2 information such as names, numbers, or dates arranged in rows
   ↪ *Compare* CHART, GRAPH.
   — PHRASES
   3 **set the table** to put plates, knives, forks, etc., on a table before a meal: *Could you set the table for me, please?*
   4 **clear the table** to remove the dirty dishes, cups, etc., from a table after a meal: *He started clearing the table.*

tablecloth /'teɪbəl,klɔθ/ [*noun; plural* tablecloths /'teɪbəl,klɔðz/ 'teɪbəl,klɔθs/] a piece of cloth used to cover and protect a table

tablespoon /'teɪbəl,spun/ [*noun*] a large spoon, or the amount of something it holds: *Add two tablespoons of flour.*
   ↪ *Compare* TEASPOON.

tablet /'tæblɪt/ [*noun*] a small, round, solid piece of medicine medicine that you swallow: *an aspirin tablet*
   ↪ *See the picture at* PILL.

table tennis /'teɪbəl ,tɛnɪs/ [*noun*] an indoor sport or game for two or four players in which a small white ball is hit across a net on a table; synonym PING-PONG: *Who wants to play table tennis?*

tack[1] /tæk/ [*noun*] a short pin with a round flat top, used for attaching things to a wall or board; synonym THUMBTACK

tack[2] [*verb;* tacked, tacking] to attach something to a wall or board using a tack: *She had some photos tacked on her bulletin board.*

tackle[1] /'tækəl/ [*verb;* tackled, tackling]
   1 to deal with a difficult problem: *I think our leaders are afraid to tackle tough issues.*
   2 to stop someone who is carrying the ball in a game such as football by pulling that person to the ground: *He got tackled at the 25-yard line.*

tackle[2] [*noun*] when one player tackles another player in a game such as football

tact /tækt/ [*noun*] the ability to deal with difficult situations without offending anyone: *Tact and patience will be needed to resolve the problem.*

tactful /'tæktfəl/ [*adjective;* more tactful, most tactful] careful not to say or do anything that will offend people; opposite TACTLESS: *Yes, she's wrong, but be tactful when you tell her.*

tactfully /ˈtæktfəli/ [adverb] without offending anyone: *He deals with difficult customers tactfully but firmly.*

tactic /ˈtæktɪk/ [noun] a deliberate plan or a way of behaving that is intended to achieve a result: *The team needs to change tactics if it's going to win the championship.*

tactless /ˈtæktlɪs/ [adjective; **more tactless, most tactless**] likely to offend or embarrass people; *opposite* TACTFUL: *a tactless remark*

tadpole /ˈtædpoʊl/ [noun] a small creature that swims in water and later becomes a frog or toad

tag[1] /tæg/ [noun] a small piece of paper or metal attached to something to show a price, name, etc.: *Everyone at the conference wore a **name tag**.*

tag[2] [verb; **tags, tagged, tagging**]
1 to attach a small piece of paper or metal to something to show its price, name, etc.: *The animals were tagged to make them easier to identify.*

— PHRASAL VERB —
tag along [phrasal verb] INFORMAL
2 to go somewhere with someone: *Do you mind if I tag along?*

tai chi /ˈtaɪ ˈtʃi/ [noun] a set of special exercises done to gain control over your mind and body and to make you calm: *She does tai chi every morning at 6:00.*

tail * /teɪl/ [noun]
1 the long thin part at the back of an animal's body: *The dog ran up to us wagging its tail.*
⇨ *See the picture at* CAT.
2 the back or end part of something: *the tail of a plane* | *the tail of a kite*
⇨ *See the pictures at* AIRPLANE *and* KITE.

tailgate /ˈteɪlˌgeɪt/ [noun] a large door at the back of a station wagon (=a kind of car) or certain trucks that you open in order to load or remove goods
⇨ *See the picture at* PICKUP TRUCK.

taillight /ˈteɪlˌlaɪt/ [noun] one of two red lights at the back of a CAR, truck, etc.

tailor /ˈteɪlɚ/ [noun] someone whose job is to make clothes, especially high-quality men's clothes

take * /teɪk/ [verb; **took, taken, taking**]
1 to move something or someone to another place or position: *Don't forget to take your umbrella.* | *He took her home after the party.* | *I'll take the kids to the park this afternoon.*
⇨ *See the usage note at* BRING.
2 used with some nouns to show an action: *He took a great photo of the cathedral.* | *She's taking her math test today.* | *Do I have time to take a shower?* | *Hey, take a look at this.*
3 to need or use something: *The radio takes three batteries.* | *How long does it take to fly to Miami?* | *It will take me hours to do all this work.*
4 to steal something: *Someone took my purse.*
5 to accept something: *The restaurant doesn't take credit cards.* | *You should take her advice.*
6 to use a particular vehicle or road in order to go somewhere: *We took a cab back to the hotel.* | *Take Third Avenue to 135th Street.*
7 to swallow medicine: *Take these pills three times a day.*
8 to study a subject: *I'm taking piano lessons.* | *He took two years of French in high school.*
9 to remove something from a place, person, or position: *She took a map out of her bag.* | *Stop playing with that ball indoors, or I'll take it away.* | *It's time to take down the holiday decorations.*
10 used to say what you are going to buy: *I'll take a cup of coffee, please.*
11 INFORMAL to deal with something difficult without becoming upset; *synonym* BEAR: *I can't take any more of this hot weather.*

— PHRASES —
12 take part (in) to do something with other people: *She likes to take part in student activities.*
⇨ *See also* **join in** *at* JOIN.

/i/ **see** /ɪ/ **big** /eɪ/ **day** /ɛ/ **get** /æ/ **hat** /ɑ/ **father, hot** /ʌ/ **up** /ə/ **about** /ɔ/ **saw** /oʊ/ **hope** /ʊ/ **book** /u/ **too** /aɪ/ **I** /aʊ/ **how** /ɔɪ/ **boy** /ɝ/ **bird** /ɚ/ **teacher** /ɪr/ **ear** /ɛr/ **air** /ɑr/ **far** /ɔr/ **more** /ʊr/ **tour** /aɪr/ **fire** /aʊɚ/ **hour** /θ/ **nothing** /ð/ **mother** /ʃ/ **she** /ʒ/ **measure** /tʃ/ **church** /dʒ/ **jump** /ŋ/ **long**

13 take place a fairly formal word meaning "to happen": *The parade will take place on Friday.*
⇨ *See the synonym note at* HAPPEN.

— PHRASAL VERBS —

take back [*phrasal verb*]
14 to return something you bought to a store, and get back your money: **take something back** ▸ *I had to take the dress back—it was too small.*
⇨ *Compare* EXCHANGE[1].

take off [*phrasal verb*]
15 to remove a piece of clothing: **take off something** ▸ *She took off her shoes.* | **take something off** ▸ *Do you mind if I take my jacket off?*
⇨ *Compare* **put on** *at* PUT.
16 if a plane takes off, it leaves the ground; *opposite* LAND: *We will be taking off in five minutes.*

take out [*phrasal verb*]
17 to invite someone and go with him or her to a restaurant, concert, etc.: **take someone out** ▸ *He's taking his girlfriend out Friday night.*

take over [*phrasal verb.*]
18 to begin to control something: *You've been driving a long time—let me take over.* | **take over something** ▸ *He took over the family business when his father died.*

take up [*phrasal verb*]
19 to start doing an activity: **take up something** ▸ *You should take up tennis—it's a great game.*
⇨ *See also* **take care of** *at* CARE[2].

taken * /'teɪkən/ [*verb*] the past participle of TAKE

takeoff /'teɪkˌɔf/ [*noun*] when a plane leaves the ground; *opposite* LANDING: *Please fasten your seat belts before takeoff.*

takeout[1] /'teɪkˌaʊt/ [*noun*] a meal that you buy in a restaurant and take somewhere else to eat: *Let's get takeout tonight.*

takeout[2] [*adjective; no comparative*] a takeout restaurant is one that sells meals you can take somewhere else to eat: *Let's get something from the takeout Chinese place.*

tale /teɪl/ [*noun*] a story about imaginary events: *He told us a tale about a magic book.*
⇨ *See also* FAIRY TALE.

talent /'tælənt/ [*noun*] a natural ability to do something well; *synonym* GIFT: *You have a lot of talent.* | *Her greatest talent was singing.*
⇨ *See the synonym note at* ABILITY.

talented /'tæləntɪd/ [*adjective;* **more talented, most talented**] having a special skill or ability; *synonym* GIFTED: *a talented musician*

talk[1] * /tɔk/ [*verb;* **talked, talking**]
1 to say something to someone or to discuss something; *synonym* SPEAK: *We sat for hours just talking.* | *He doesn't **talk about** his family very often.* | *Are you **talking to** me?* | *I need to **talk with** you for a few minutes.*
☛ Do not say "I talk English." Say I speak English.

— PHRASAL VERBS —

talk into [*phrasal verb*]
2 to persuade someone to do something: **talk someone into doing something** ▸ *I talked him into coming shopping.* | **talk someone into something** ▸ *How did you manage to talk her into it?*

talk out of [*phrasal verb*]
3 to persuade someone not to do something: **talk someone out of doing something** ▸ *We talked her out of leaving college.* | **talk someone out of something** ▸ *You won't talk me out of this.*

talk over [*phrasal verb*]
4 to discuss something seriously: **talk something over** ▸ *If you're worried, you should talk it over with someone.*

talk[2] * [*noun*]
1 a conversation: *Call me if you want to **have a talk**.* | *We **had a long talk about** our relationship.*
2 a speech: *Professor Black **gave a** very interesting **talk on** India.*
3 things that you hear people saying that may or may not be true: *There is **talk of** a new highway being built.* | *You shouldn't worry about what she says—**it's only talk**.*

4 talks [*plural*] when two governments or organizations meet in order to discuss something important: *the Middle East peace talks*

talkative /'tɔkətɪv/ [*adjective;* **more talkative, most talkative**] talking a lot; opposite QUIET: *My husband's never been very talkative.*

talk show /'tɔk ˌʃoʊ/ [*noun*] a radio or television program in which many different subjects are discussed, sometimes with famous people: *He has appeared on many talk shows.*

tall * /tɔl/ [*adjective;* **taller, tallest**]
1 having a HEIGHT that is more than average; opposite SHORT: *New York has many tall buildings.* I *She's just a little taller than her sister.*
⇨ *See the warning at* HIGH[1] (definition 1).
━━ PHRASE ━━
2 150cm/100m/6 feet/etc. tall 150 centimeters, 100 meters, 6 feet, etc., in height: *I am 5 feet, 3 inches tall.*

tambourine /ˌtæmbə'rin/ [*noun*] a musical instrument, made of a round wooden frame with bells attached, that you shake or hit: *I learned to play the tambourine.*

a tambourine

tame[1] /teɪm/ [*adjective;* **tamer, tamest**] a tame animal is trained to live with people; opposite WILD: *Don't worry. These birds are very tame.*

tame[2] [*verb;* **tamed, taming**] to train a wild animal to live with or work for people and not attack them: *How long did it take to tame the bear?*

tan[1] /tæn/ [*noun*]
1 the darker skin color that someone gets after he or she has been in the sun; synonym SUNTAN: *Where did you get that tan?*
2 a light brown color: *Do you have those shoes in tan?*

tan[2] [*adjective;* **tanner, tannest**]
1 having skin that is darker from being in the sun: *Wow! You're so tan!*
2 of the color tan: *tan pants*

tan[3] [*verb;* **tans, tanned, tanning**] if your skin tans or if the sun tans it, it becomes darker in color: *He tans easily.*

tangerine /ˌtændʒə'rin/ [*noun*] a fruit that looks like a small orange

tangle /'tæŋgəl/ [*noun*] threads or hairs that are twisted together: *Sit still while I comb the tangles out of your hair.*

tangled /'tæŋgəld/ [*adjective;* **more tangled, most tangled**] tangled hair, thread, etc., is twisted together: *Try to keep your computer cords from getting tangled.*

tank /tæŋk/ [*noun*]
1 a large container for liquid or gas: *A fish tank stood in the corner of the room.* I *a gas tank* (=the part of a vehicle that holds gasoline)
2 a large strong vehicle with guns on it that is used by an army in battles

tanker /'tæŋkɚ/ [*noun*] a large ship or truck that can carry oil or gas

tantrum /'tæntrəm/ [*noun*] when a young child suddenly starts to shout or cry and behave very badly: *He threw a tantrum in the middle of the store.* I *a temper tantrum*
⇨ *Compare* TEMPER.

tap[1] /tæp/ [*verb;* **taps, tapped, tapping**] to hit someone or something gently with your finger or foot: *I began tapping my feet to the music.* I *She tapped lightly on his arm.*

tap[2] [*noun*]
1 when you hit someone or something gently with your finger: *She gave him a gentle tap on his back.*
2 an object that you turn to stop or start a flow of liquid from a pipe or a container: *I forgot to turn off the tap and flooded the bathroom.* I *the hot water tap*
⇨ *Compare* FAUCET. ⇨ *See the picture at* SINK[2].

/i/ see	/ɪ/ big	/eɪ/ day	/ɛ/ get	/æ/ hat
/ɑ/ father, hot	/ʌ/ up	/ə/ about	/ɔ/ saw	
/oʊ/ hope	/ʊ/ book	/u/ too	/aɪ/ I	/aʊ/ how
/ɔɪ/ boy	/ɚ/ bird	/ɚ/ teacher	/ɪr/ ear	/ɛr/ air
/ɑr/ far	/ɔr/ more	/ʊr/ tour	/aɪr/ fire	
/aʊɚ/ hour	/θ/ nothing	/ð/ mother	/ʃ/ she	
/ʒ/ measure	/tʃ/ church	/dʒ/ jump	/ŋ/ long	

tap dancing /'tæp ˌdænsɪŋ/ [noun] a kind of dancing in which you wear shoes with metal underneath, that make a noise when you step: *a tap dancing competition*

tape[1] * /teɪp/ [noun]
1 a long thin piece of plastic material used for recording sounds or pictures, or the case that contains this material: *We have the whole concert on tape* (=recorded on tape). I *She keeps her tapes in alphabetical order.*
  ⇨ See also VIDEOTAPE[1], CASSETTE.
2 a long thin piece of sticky material used for fastening pieces of paper together; synonym SCOTCH TAPE: *Do you have any tape? I need to wrap a present.*

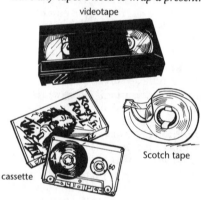

videotape

cassette

Scotch tape

kinds of tapes

tape[2] [verb; taped, taping]
1 to record sound or images on a tape: *I'll tape the movie and watch it later.*
  ⇨ See also VIDEOTAPE[2].
2 to stick a piece of paper or material onto something using tape: *Posters of movie stars were taped on her bedroom walls.*

tape deck /'teɪp ˌdɛk/ [noun] a piece of electronic equipment for playing or recording music tapes, that is part of a larger music system

tape measure /'teɪp ˌmɛʒɚ/ [noun] a long rolled piece of plastic or metal marked in inches or centimeters, that is used for measuring

tape recorder /'teɪp rɪˌkɔrdɚ/ [noun] a piece of equipment used for recording or listening to music or voices on tape

tar /tɑr/ [noun] a black sticky substance used for making road surfaces

target /'tɑrgɪt/ [noun]
1 an object that you aim at when firing a weapon: *He hit the target from a distance of 20 meters.*
2 someone or something that people choose to attack or criticize: *a target for a military attack* I *She became the target of most of our jokes.*

task /tæsk/ [noun] a piece of work that you must do; synonym JOB: *This is going to be a difficult task.*

taste[1] * /teɪst/ [noun]
1 the feeling that you have in your mouth when you eat or drink something: *Kids love the taste of sweet food.* I *The soup had an unusual taste.*
2 a small amount of food or drink that you put in your mouth to find out if you like it: *Have a taste of this fish— it's delicious!*
3 the kind of thing that someone usually likes: *What are her tastes in music?* I *He has terrible taste* (=likes things that are not attractive, good, etc.).

taste[2] * [verb; tasted, tasting]
1 [linking] to have a particular taste: *The chicken tasted good.* I *What does the sauce taste like?*
  ☛ Do not say that something "tastes well." Say that it **tastes good**.
2 to notice a particular taste: *Can you taste the garlic in your stew?*

tasteful /'teɪstfəl/ [adjective; more tasteful, most tasteful] designed or decorated in an attractive way: *The hotel was furnished in a very tasteful way.*
  ⇨ See the warning at TASTY.

tasteless /'teɪstlɪs/ [adjective; more tasteless, most tasteless]
1 designed or decorated in a way that is not attractive: *I don't want any cheap tasteless souvenirs. I want something nice.*
2 not right for any occasion: *a tasteless joke*
  ⇨ Compare OFFENSIVE (definition 1).
3 not having any taste and therefore not enjoyable to eat; opposite TASTY: *The vegetables were fairly tasteless.*

tasty /'teɪsti/ [adjective; tastier, tastiest] having a good taste: *It was the tastiest food I had ever eaten.*

☛ Do not confuse **tasty** and **tasteful**. **Tasty** is used to describe food that tastes good. **Tasteful** is used to describe things that are decorated or designed in an attractive way.

tattoo /tæ'tu/ [noun; plural tattoos] a picture or word that is put permanently on someone's skin using special ink

taught * /tɔt/ [verb] the past tense and past participle of TEACH

tax¹ * /tæks/ [noun; plural taxes] money that you must pay to a government from the money you earn, when you buy goods, etc.: *How much do you pay in taxes a year? | There will be an increase in the tax on gasoline.*

tax² * [verb; taxes, taxed, taxing] to make people pay tax: *The government taxes people to pay for things like roads.*

taxi * /'tæksi/ [noun; plural taxis] a car with a driver whom you pay to take you somewhere; *synonym* CAB: *Let's take a taxi to the station. | The taxi driver will tell you where to get out.*

a taxi/a cab

taxi stand /'tæksi ˌstænd/ [noun] a place where taxis wait for people: *There's a taxi stand behind the station.*

tbs or **tbsp** a written abbreviation of TABLESPOON or TABLESPOONS; *synonyms* T, T.: *Add 3 tbs milk to 5 eggs, and stir well.*

tea * /ti/ [noun; plural teas]
1 an Asian plant that is used to make traditional tea: *a blend of Indian teas*
2 a drink made by pouring hot water onto the dry leaves of the tea plant or another plant: *Would you like tea or coffee? | herbal tea* (=made from other plants besides tea plants) *| Two teas, please* (=we would like two cups of tea).

teach * /titʃ/ [verb; teaches, taught, teaching]
1 to give lessons in a subject, especially in a school or college: *She teaches math at the high school. | I'd like to teach when I leave college.*
2 to show someone how to do something: *I can't swim. Will you teach me? |* **teach someone (how) to do something** ▸ *Mom's teaching me to sew.*
☛ Do not say "teach someone doing something." Say **teach someone to do something** or **teach someone how to do something.**

━━ PHRASE ━━
3 **teach someone a lesson** to stop someone from doing something that is wrong or annoying by punishing him or her: *He needs to be taught a lesson.*

USAGE   teach, learn, know

If you **teach** someone, you give lessons or show how to do something: *Will you teach me to dance?*

The person who is being taught **learns** something: *I'm learning how to dance.*

After you learn something, you **know** it: *I know how to dance.*

---

teacher * /'titʃɚ/ [noun] someone who teaches as his or her job: *I like my math teacher. | a teacher in a middle school*
☛ Do not say "He is a teacher of a school." Say **He is a teacher in a school** or **He is a teacher at a school.**
↪ *See the picture at* CLASSROOM.

teaching /'titʃɪŋ/ [noun]
1 the profession or work of being a teacher: *Teaching takes a lot of patience.*
2 **teachings** [plural] the things that a religious or political leader taught people about, such as what God is like or how people should behave: *the teachings of Jesus*

teacup /'ti,kʌp/ [noun] a small cup used for drinking tea and other hot drinks
↪ *See the picture at* TEAPOT.

/i/ **see** /ɪ/ **big** /eɪ/ **day** /ɛ/ **get** /æ/ **hat**
/ɑ/ **father, hot** /ʌ/ **up** /ə/ **about** /ɔ/ **saw**
/oʊ/ **hope** /ʊ/ **book** /u/ **too** /aɪ/ **I** /aʊ/ **how**
/ɔɪ/ **boy** /ɝ/ **bird** /ɚ/ **teacher** /ɪr/ **ear** /ɛr/ **air**
/ɑr/ **far** /ɔr/ **more** /ʊr/ **tour** /aɪr/ **fire**
/aʊɚ/ **hour** /θ/ **nothing** /ð/ **mother** /ʃ/ **she**
/ʒ/ **measure** /tʃ/ **church** /dʒ/ **jump** /ŋ/ **long**

team¹ * /tim/ [*noun*] a group of people who play a sport together against other groups, or a group of people who work together: *He's on the college football team.* | *a team of scientists*
☛ Only use **team** with a singular verb. For example, do not say "The team have lost." Say **The team has lost.**

team² [*verb; teamed, teaming*]
— PHRASAL VERB —
team up [*phrasal verb*]
to join with other people in order to do something: *Neighbors teamed up with city workers to clean the park.*

teammate /'tim,meɪt/ [*noun*] someone who is on the same sports team as you

teamwork /'tim,wɜ·k/ [*noun*] when a group of people work together as a team: *Teamwork is the secret of our success.*

teapot /'ti,pat/ [*noun*] a container in which tea is made that has a handle and a part for pouring

a teapot
spout
teacup
saucer

tear¹ * /tɛr/ [*verb; tore, torn, tearing*]
1 if you tear paper or cloth or if it tears, you make a hole in it or make it divide into two or more parts; *synonym* RIP: *Be careful not to tear any of the pages.* | *She tore the envelope open* (=opened it in a quick and careless way). | *This material tears easily.*
— PHRASAL VERBS —
tear down [*phrasal verb*]
2 to destroy a wall, building, or other structure: *We tore down the old barn.*
tear up [*phrasal verb*]
3 to destroy something made of paper by pulling it into small pieces: **tear up something** ▸ *He tore up the note in anger.* | **tear something up** ▸ *Why did you tear the picture up?*

tear² * /tɛr/ [*noun*] a long hole in paper or cloth: *There was a tear in the back of her jacket.*
☼ See also RIP².

tear³ * /tɪr/ [*noun*] a drop of salty water that forms in your eye when you cry: *She walked out of the room in tears* (=crying). | *He burst into tears* (=suddenly started crying).

tease /tiz/ [*verb; teased, teasing*] to embarrass or annoy someone, especially by making jokes about him or her: *Stop teasing your brother!* | *Don't get so upset—I was only teasing.*

teaspoon /'ti,spun/ [*noun*] a small spoon, or the amount of something it holds: *Add two teaspoons of salt.*
☼ Compare TABLESPOON.

technical * /'tɛknɪkəl/ [*adjective*]
1 [*no comparative*] relating to the special knowledge or skills used in science or industry: *He showed me a technical diagram.*
2 [**more technical, most technical**] technical words or phrases are connected with a particular profession or activity and are difficult for most people to understand: *The article was full of technical terms.*

technique /tɛk'nik/ [*noun; plural techniques*]
1 a way of doing something; *synonym* METHOD: *Scientists are developing new techniques for treating cancer.*
2 the way you do something that needs skill to do well: *He has worked hard to improve his tennis technique.*

technology Ⓣ /tɛk'nalədʒi/ [*noun*] scientific knowledge or skill, and the way it is used to make new equipment and machinery: *New technology means that computers keep getting faster.*

teddy bear /'tɛdi/ [*noun*] a toy for young children that looks like a small bear

teen /tin/ [*noun*] INFORMAL a short form of TEENAGER: *We specialize in clothes for teens.*
☼ See also TEENS.

teenage /'tin,eɪdʒ/ [*adjective; no comparative*] between the ages of 13 and 19: *I have two teenage sons.*
☛ Only use **teenage** before a noun.

teenager ⊤ /'tin,eɪdʒɚ/ [noun] someone who is between the ages of 13 and 19: *The mall was full of teenagers.*

SYNONYMS   teenager, adolescent, youth

These words are all used to talk about young people.

A **teenager** is someone who is between 13 and 19 years old: *That song is popular with teenagers.*

An **adolescent** is someone who is at the age when he or she is changing from a child into an adult. This word is often used when talking about the problems young people have at this age: *As an adolescent, he was rude and difficult.*

Youth is a little old-fashioned, and is used to talk about young men who are between around 15 and 25 years old, especially when they behave badly: *She was robbed by a group of youths.*

teens /tinz/ [plural noun]

1 the teens the years between 1910 and 1919, or a temperature between 10 and 19 degrees: *Our house was built sometime during the teens.*

━ PHRASE ━

2 in your teens between the ages of 13 and 19: *Many professional tennis players are only in their teens.*

USAGE   teens, twenties, thirties, forties, etc.

Use **the teens, the twenties**, etc., to talk about the years between 1910 and 1919, 1920 and 1929, etc.: *She was born in the sixties.* You can also talk about temperature this way: *The temperature will drop into the teens tonight.*

Use **your teens, your twenties**, etc., to talk about age: *My grandfather is in his nineties.*

teeth * /tiθ/ [noun] the plural of TOOTH

telecommunications /ˌtɛlɪkəˌmyunɪ'keɪʃənz/ [plural noun] the activity of sending and receiving messages over long distances by telephone, radio, television, etc.

telegram /'tɛlɪ,græm/ [noun] a message sent using a system of electrical or radio

signals: *My aunt and uncle sent us a telegram on our wedding day.*

telegraph /'tɛlɪ,græf/ [noun] a system of sending messages using electrical or radio signals: *The messages were sent by telegraph.*

telephone[1] * /'tɛlə,foʊn/ [noun] a piece of equipment that you use to talk to someone who is in another place; *synonym* PHONE: *The telephone kept ringing in the office.* | *Could you **answer the telephone**, please?* | *She spends a lot of time **on the telephone*** (=talking to people using the telephone). | *You can contact me **by telephone** if you need to.*
☛ Do not say "I gave her a telephone." Say **I gave her a call** or **I called her**.

receiver

button

cord

a telephone/
a phone

base

telephone[2] * [verb; telephoned, telephoning] to use a telephone to talk to someone; *synonyms* CALL, PHONE: *He promised to telephone if he heard any news.* | *I've been trying to telephone you all evening.*
☛ Do not say "I will telephone to him tomorrow." Say **I will telephone him tomorrow**.
↪ See the synonym note at CALL[1].

telephone book /'tɛləfoʊn ,bʊk/ [noun] a book with a list of the names, addresses, and phone numbers of all the people and companies in a particular area; *synonym* PHONE BOOK: *Their number isn't in the telephone book.*

/i/ **see** /ɪ/ **big** /eɪ/ **day** /ɛ/ **get** /æ/ **hat** /ɑ/ **father, hot** /ʌ/ **up** /ə/ **about** /ɔ/ **saw** /oʊ/ **hope** /ʊ/ **book** /u/ **too** /aɪ/ **I** /aʊ/ **how** /ɔɪ/ **boy** /ɝ/ **bird** /ɚ/ **teacher** /ɪr/ **ear** /ɛr/ **air** /ɑr/ **far** /ɔr/ **more** /ʊr/ **tour** /aɪr/ **fire** /aʊɚ/ **hour** /θ/ **nothing** /ð/ **mother** /ʃ/ **she** /ʒ/ **measure** /tʃ/ **church** /dʒ/ **jump** /ŋ/ **long**

telephone booth
/'tɛləfoʊn ˌbuθ/
[*noun; plural*
telephone booths
/'tɛləfoʊn ˌbuðz/]
a structure
containing a
public telephone;
synonym PHONE
BOOTH

telephone call
/'tɛləfoʊn ˌkɔl/
[*noun*] when you
talk to someone
using a telephone;
synonyms CALL,
PHONE CALL: *May I make a quick
telephone call?*

*a telephone booth/
a phone booth*

telephone number /'tɛləfoʊn
ˌnʌmbɚ/ [*noun*] the number you need to
use when you want to speak to
someone on the telephone; *synonym*
PHONE NUMBER: *She gave me your
telephone number.*

telescope ⊤ /'tɛləˌskoʊp/ [*noun*] a long
metal tube you look through to see
things such as the stars that are far
away

televise /'tɛləˌvaɪz/ [*verb;* **televised,
televising**] to broadcast something on
television: *The ceremony will be televised.*

television * /'tɛləˌvɪʒən/ [*noun*]
1 a piece of electronic equipment that
has a screen on which you watch
programs that are broadcast; *synonym*
TV: *A large television stood in one corner
of the living room.*
2 the system of broadcasting programs
for the television, or the programs
themselves; *synonym* TV: *We spent all
evening **watching television**. | Is there
anything good **on television**?* (=being
broadcast on the television)

tell * /tɛl/ [*verb;* **told, telling**]
1 to speak to someone in order to give
him or her facts or information: **tell
someone something** ▶ *Tell me your
name.* | **tell someone (that)** ▶ *Did I tell
you that your brother called?* | *They told
us the meeting was canceled.* | **tell
someone about something** ▶ *Did you
tell him about the party?* | **tell someone**

what/how/why/etc. ▶ *Calm down and
tell me what happened.*
2 to order or advise someone to do
something: **tell someone to do
something** ▶ *The doctor told her to stop
smoking.* | **tell someone what/how/**
etc. ▶ *Don't tell me what to do!* | **tell
someone (that)** ▶ *I told her that she
needs a pet.* | *She keeps telling me I
should quit my job.*
☛ Do not say "tell someone doing
something." Say **tell someone to do
something**.
3 to be able to recognize something
because of what you see, hear, etc.:
*You're upset about something—I can tell.
| How can you **tell when** the cake is
done? | The twins are so alike I can't **tell
the difference between** them* (=know
which one is which).

━━━ PHRASES ━━━

4 tell the truth to say things that are
true, not made up: *I hope you're telling
the truth.*
5 I told you so SPOKEN used after
something happens that you warned
someone about: *See? I told you so. You
should have listened.*

━━━ PHRASAL VERB ━━━

tell off [*phrasal verb*]
6 to speak to someone in an angry way
because he or she has done something
wrong or something you do not like:
tell someone off ▶ *My mother's always
telling me off for something.*

temper * /'tɛmpɚ/ [*noun*]
1 the way you feel and behave,
especially when things make you
angry: *He has a terrible temper. | She
just can't seem to control her temper.*

━━━ PHRASE ━━━

2 lose/keep your temper to
suddenly become very angry, or to
succeed in staying calm: *I lost my
temper and told them to shut up. | She
managed to keep her temper.*

temperature * /'tɛmprətʃɚ/ [*noun*]
1 how hot or cold something is: *The
temperature was already over 80 degrees.
| There will be a sharp **fall in
temperature** during the night.*
↪ See the usage note at TEENS.

2 how hot or cold someone's body is, that shows whether he or she is healthy or not: *She's running a temperature* (=has a temperature that is higher than normal). I *Let me take your temperature* (=measure it). I *I don't have a temperature* (=my temperature is not higher than normal).

☞ Do not say "measure someone's temperature." Say **take someone's temperature.**

degrees **Celsius**   degrees **Fahrenheit**

boiling point 100°C/ 212° F.

freezing point 0°C/ 32° F.

A **thermometer** measures **temperature.**

temple /'tempəl/ [*noun*]
  1 a building in some religions where people meet and pray: *a Buddhist temple*
  2 one of the flat parts at the side of your head just above and a little in front of your ear: *He had gray hair at his temples.*
  ⇨ *See the picture at* BODY.

temporarily * /ˌtempəˈrerəli/ [*adverb*] for a short time, not for all time; *opposite* PERMANENTLY: *We agreed that he could stay here temporarily.*

temporary * /'tempəˌreri/ [*adjective;* **more temporary, most temporary**] continuing, existing, or available for only a short time, not for all time; *opposite* PERMANENT: *The company mainly employs temporary workers.*

tempt Ⓣ /tempt/ [*verb;* **tempted, tempting**]
  1 to try to make someone do something, especially something that is wrong or that may not be good for him or her: *"Would you like more pie?" "Don't tempt me!"*
  — PHRASE —
  2 be tempted to do something to want to do something, especially something you should not do: *I was tempted to stop studying and go swimming.*

temptation /tempˈteɪʃən/ [*noun*] the feeling of wanting to have or do something, especially something that is wrong or harmful: *I resisted the temptation to open the box of candy.*

ten * /ten/ [*number, noun*]
  1 10: *Ten plus ten equals twenty.*
  2 a piece of paper money worth $10: *Can you lend me a ten, Mom?*

tenant /'tenənt/ [*noun*] someone who pays money to the owner of an apartment or house in order to live there: *Tenants are responsible for their phone and electricity bills.*
  ⇨ *Compare* LANDLADY, LANDLORD.

tend * Ⓣ /tend/ [*verb;* **tended, tending**]
  1 to take care of someone or something: *A team of gardeners tends the grounds.*
  — PHRASE —
  2 tend to do something to usually do something or react in a particular way: *It tends to be rainy at this time of year.* I *He tends to get mad if you criticize him.*

tendency * /'tendənsi/ [*noun; plural* **tendencies**]
  1 a part of your character that makes you likely to behave in a particular way: **have a tendency to do something** ▸ *She has a tendency to lose her temper.*
  2 when something is usually done or usually happens: *There's a tendency nowadays for people to marry later.*

tender /'tendɚ/ [*adjective;* **tenderer, tenderest**]
  1 meat or other food that is tender is soft and easy to chew; *opposite* TOUGH: *The steak was beautifully tender.*
  2 showing love in a gentle way: *She gave her son a tender kiss.*
  3 a part of your body that is tender feels painful when it is touched: *My elbow still feels tender from where I hit it.*

/i/ **see**	/ɪ/ **big**	/eɪ/ **day**	/ɛ/ **get**	/æ/ **hat**
/ɑ/ **father,**	**hot**	/ʌ/ **up**	/ə/ **about**	/ɔ/ **saw**
/ou/ **hope**	/ʊ/ **book**	/u/ **too**	/aɪ/ **I**	/aʊ/ **how**
/ɔɪ/ **boy**	/ɚ/ **bird**	/ə/ **teacher**	/ɪr/ **ear**	/ɛr/ **air**
/ɑr/ **far**	/ɔr/ **more**	/ʊr/ **tour**	/aɪr/ **fire**
/aʊɚ/ **hour**	/θ/ **nothing**	/ð/ **mother**	/ʃ/ **she**
/ʒ/ **measure**	/tʃ/ **church**	/dʒ/ **jump**	/ŋ/ **long**

tennis ∗ /'tɛnɪs/ [noun] a sport or game for two or four people in which a ball is hit over a net using a racket: *Would you like to play tennis on Saturday?* | *a tennis court* | *a tennis racket*
⇨ See also TABLE TENNIS.

a tennis racket

tennis shoe /'tɛnɪs ˌʃu/ [noun; plural **tennis shoes**] a light shoe with a rubber bottom, worn for sports or with informal clothes; *synonym* SNEAKER: *a pair of tennis shoes*

tense[1] /tɛns/ [adjective; **tenser, tensest**]
1 unable to relax, especially because you are worried: *What's the matter? You seem tense.*
2 tense muscles are stiff and uncomfortable: *My neck feels really tense.*

tense[2] ∗ [noun] GRAMMAR a form of a verb that shows when an action takes place, or whether an action is finished: *The story is written in the present tense.* | *"Went" is the past tense of "go."*

tense[3] [verb; **tensed, tensing**] to become stiff and uncomfortable, or to make someone's body do this: *I always tense up a little before a race.*

tension Ⓣ /'tɛnʃən/ [noun]
1 the feeling that you have when you are worried and unable to relax: *Walking helps me get rid of tension.*
2 when something such as a muscle, rope, or wire is stiff or tight: *Working at a computer can cause tension in the shoulders.*
3 a relationship between two people, groups, or countries that is not friendly and may cause an argument or war: *There's been some tension at work lately.*

tent ∗ /tɛnt/ [noun] a large piece of material supported by poles, used as a shelter: *It took an hour to put up the tent.*

tentacle /'tɛntəkəl/ [noun] one of the long thin parts of a sea creature that it uses for holding things
⇨ See the picture at OCTOPUS.

tenth[1] ∗ /tɛnθ/ [adverb, adjective; no comparative] coming after nine other people, things, or events; sometimes written as "10th": *October is the tenth month of the year.* | *I finished tenth in the race.*

tenth[2] ∗ [noun] one of ten equal parts: *He gives away a tenth of what he earns.*
⇨ See the usage note at SECOND[2].

term /tɜrm/ [noun]
1 a word or a group of words with a special meaning: *The contract was full of legal terms I didn't understand.*
2 a limited period of time in which someone has a position: *U.S. Senators have six-year term.*
3 a period into which a school year is divided; *synonyms* SEMESTER, QUARTER: *I'll graduate at the end of next term.* | *My term paper is due next Friday.*
4 **terms** [plural] the things which must be done, according to a contract or other legal arrangement: *What are the terms of the contract?*

— PHRASES

5 **in terms of** if you judge a situation or event in terms of something, you are considering that part, quality, feature, etc.: *It has been a successful year in terms of profit.*
6 **be on good terms (with)** or **be on bad terms (with)** to have a good or bad relationship with someone: *We're on very good terms with our neighbors.*

terminal /'tɜrmənəl/ [noun]
1 a large building where a plane, bus, ship, etc., begins or ends its journey: *All international flights leave from Terminal C.*
2 a screen and keyboard connected to a computer somewhere else: *Each desk had its own computer terminal.*

a tent

termite /'tɜ·maɪt/ [*noun*] a small insect that eats wood

terrace /'tɛrəs/ [*noun*]
1 an outdoor area with a hard surface next to a house, restaurant, or other building: *The tables on the terrace were all full.*
⇨ Compare PATIO.
2 a flat area on the side of a hill that has been specially made for growing crops: *Tea is grown there on terraces.*

terrible * /'tɛrəbəl/ [*adjective*; **more terrible, most terrible**]
1 very bad or unpleasant; *synonym* AWFUL: *His spelling is terrible.*
2 very severe and often causing harm or damage: *I had terrible stomach pains all night.* | *a terrible storm*

terribly /'tɛrəbli/ [*adverb*]
1 very badly: *They played terribly, and lost the game 5–0.*
2 extremely: *She seemed terribly nervous during the interview.*

terrific /tə'rɪfɪk/ [*adjective*; *no comparative*] INFORMAL very good or enjoyable: *There was a terrific atmosphere at the concert.*

terrified /'tɛrə,faɪd/ [*adjective*; **more terrified, most terrified**] extremely frightened: *I'm terrified of flying.*
⇨ See also TERROR.

terrify /'tɛrə,faɪ/ [*verb*; **terrifies, terrified, terrifying**] to make someone feel extremely frightened: *The thought of giving a speech terrifies her.*
⇨ See also TERROR.

territory /'tɛrɪ,tɔri/ [*noun*; *plural* **territories**]
1 land that belongs to a particular country or organization: *You are now entering Canadian territory.*
2 an area that an animal considers to be its own: *Lions will attack other lions who enter their territory.*

terror * /'tɛrə·/ [*noun*] a feeling of extreme fear: *She screamed in terror.*
⇨ See also TERRIFIED, TERRIFY.

terrorism Ⓣ /'tɛrə,rɪzəm/ [*noun*] the use of violence to achieve political aims: *We strongly oppose all forms of terrorism.*

terrorist /'tɛrərɪst/ [*noun*] someone who uses violence to achieve political aims:

The terrorists who bombed the embassy were jailed for life.

test[1] * /tɛst/ [*noun*]
1 a set of questions or activities intended to measure someone's knowledge or skill: *When do you take your driver's test?* | *He passed the geography test easily.* | *I have a math test tomorrow.*
2 a process for measuring how healthy someone is, whether something works correctly, etc.: *You need a blood test.* | *Each car is put through many safety tests.*

test[2] * [*verb*; **tested, testing**]
1 to use or examine something in order to discover something about it: *All equipment should be tested regularly.* | *The city's water is tested for bacteria.*
2 to make someone answer questions or do an activity in order to measure his or her skill or knowledge: *You will be tested on both written and spoken English.*

testify /'tɛstə,faɪ/ [*verb*; **testifies, testified, testifying**] to state publicly that something is true, especially in a court of law: *Are you willing to testify that these men attacked you?* | *She did not want to testify against her son.*

test tube /'tɛst ,tub/ [*noun*] a small tube-shaped glass container used in a science laboratory

text /tɛkst/ [*noun*]
1 the writing in a book, newspaper, etc., rather than the pictures: *The text was so small I could hardly read it.*
2 a book that students must read during a course of study: *Her book is now a required text in universities.*

textbook /'tɛkst,bʊk/ [*noun*] a book that students use which contains information about a subject: *a biology textbook*

textile /'tɛkstaɪl/ [*noun*] cloth, or goods made from cloth: *a textile factory*

/i/ **see**	/ɪ/ **big**	/eɪ/ **day**	/ɛ/ **get**	/æ/ **hat**
/ɑ/ **father, hot**	/ʌ/ **up**	/ə/ **about**	/ɔ/ **saw**
/oʊ/ **hope**	/ʊ/ **book**	/u/ **too**	/aɪ/ **I**	/aʊ/ **how**
/ɔɪ/ **boy**	/ɚ/ **bird**	/ə·/ **teacher**	/ɪr/ **ear**	/ɛr/ **air**
/ɑr/ **far**	/ɔr/ **more**	/ʊr/ **tour**	/aɪr/ **fire**
/aʊɚ/ **hour**	/θ/ **nothing**	/ð/ **mother**	/ʃ/ **she**
/ʒ/ **measure**	/tʃ/ **church**	/dʒ/ **jump**	/ŋ/ **long**

texture /'tɛkstʃɚ/ [noun] the way that something feels when you touch it: *The leaves have a rough texture.*

than[1] * /ðɛn/ [conjunction] used after a comparative form of an adjective to compare two facts, situations, etc.: *He could run much faster than I could.* | *They arrived sooner than I expected.*

than[2] * [preposition] used after a comparative form of an adjective to compare two people, things, etc.: *My sister is ten years older than me.* | *That book costs more than this one.*

thank * /θæŋk/ [verb; **thanked, thanking**]
1 to tell someone that you are grateful and happy about something he or she has given you or done for you: **thank someone for something** ▸ *I thanked him for the present.*
⇨ See also THANK YOU.
━ PHRASE ━
2 thank God or **thank goodness** or **thank heavens** SPOKEN used when you are pleased that a situation is not as bad as it could have been: *Thank God no one was badly injured.*

thankful /'θæŋkfəl/ [adjective; no comparative] feeling grateful and happy about something, especially because you no longer have to worry about it: *We're just **thankful that** he's home again.* | *I'm **thankful for** any help I can get.*

thanks[1] /θæŋks/ [interjection] INFORMAL
1 used to tell someone that you are grateful or happy about something he or she has given you or done; **synonym** THANK YOU: *"I'll give you a ride to school." "Thanks, Dad."* | ***Thanks for** calling—it was good to talk.*
━ PHRASE ━
2 no, thanks SPOKEN used to refuse something politely: *"Have some more ice cream." "No, thanks."*
⇨ See the usage note at OFFER[1].

thanks[2] [plural noun]
1 the things that you say to show that you are grateful for something that someone has given you or done: *We'd like to **express our thanks** to everyone who's helped us.*

━ PHRASE ━
2 thanks to
a used to say that someone or something made something good happen or be possible: *Thanks to his hard work, the event was a success.*
b used to show that you are annoyed because someone or something made something bad happen: *Thanks to her, we were over half an hour late.*

Thanksgiving /,θæŋks'gɪvɪŋ/ [noun] a public holiday in the U.S. in November that celebrates the first English people in America, when families have a special meal together. A similar holiday is celebrated in Canada in October: *We're going to my parents' house for Thanksgiving.*

thank you * /'θæŋk ,yu/ [interjection]
1 used to tell someone that you are grateful or happy about something he or she has given you or done: *"You can use my computer if you need to." "Thank you."* | ***Thank you very much for** the presents.* | ***Thank you all for** coming.*
━ PHRASE ━
2 no, thank you used to refuse something politely: *"Can I get you more coffee?" "No, thank you."*
⇨ See the usage note at OFFER[1].

that[1] * /ðæt/ [determiner; plural **those**]
1 used to talk about someone or something that is not near in space: *Who's that man over there by the door?* | *Why are those books on the floor?*
⇨ See the usage note at THIS[1].
2 used to talk about someone or something that has just been mentioned or is already known about: *I must remember to give that book back to my cousin.*
3 used to talk about something that is not near in time: *I'll never forget that night a few years ago.*

that[2] * [pronoun; plural **those**]
1 used to talk about something or someone that has just been mentioned or is already known about: *Don't say that—you're making me nervous.* | *We used to have a dog just like that.* | *"You should come visit." "I'd like that."*
2 used to talk about something or

someone that is not near in space or time: *Those were the happiest days of my life.*

⇨ *See the usage note at* THIS[1].

3 used before you mention something that makes it clear what person or thing you are talking about: *There's the woman that I was telling you about. | The shoes that he wanted were too expensive.*

☛ In this meaning, **that** can be singular or plural.

⇨ *See also* WHICH[1] (definition 2), WHO.

— PHRASES —

4 that is used to give more information about something you just said: *We leave at ten, that is, if the taxi is here then.*

5 that's it SPOKEN

  a used to tell someone that he or she is doing something correctly: *Take your foot off the pedal slowly. That's it.*

  b used to say angrily that you will not let a situation continue or will no longer be involved in it: *That's it! I'm never going to speak to her again.*

  c used to say that something is finished or that there is no more of something: *I think that's it. We can go home now. | "Is there any more pie?" "No, that's it."*

6 that's that SPOKEN used to say something has finished or will not be changed: *I said no, and that's that!*

that[3] * [*conjunction*]

1 used after a verb, adjective, noun, etc., to give information about it: *I think that she's still feeling a little upset. | He was sure that he locked the door. | The idea that he would lie to you is ridiculous.*

☛ The word **that** is often left out after verbs and adjectives, especially in spoken English. For example, you can say **I'm sure that I'm right** or **I'm sure I'm right**.

2 used after "it" to talk about a fact that you are describing: *It's odd that she didn't call. | He finds it funny that people think he's handsome.*

3 used after "so" and "such" to talk about the result of something: *I was so*

tired **that** *I fell asleep immediately. | He was gone* **such** *a long time* **that** *she got worried.*

that[4] [*adverb*]

— PHRASE —

not that bad/much/etc. not as bad, large, etc., as something might be or was said to be: *We don't have that much time. | "Well, I think it's a terrible song." "Oh, it's not that bad."*

that'd /ðætəd/ SPOKEN

1 the short form of "that would": *That'd be a silly thing to do, wouldn't it?*

2 the short form of "that had": *That'd always been his problem.*

that'll /ðætəl/ SPOKEN the short form of "that will": *That'll be a big help.*

that's * /ðæts/ the short form of "that is": *That's a great idea!*

thaw /θɔ/ [*verb;* **thawed, thawing**]

1 if frozen food thaws or you thaw it, it becomes soft and ready to cook: *Let the cake* **thaw out** *for two hours before serving.*

2 if ice or snow thaws or is thawed, it becomes water again: *The lake didn't thaw until late in the spring.*

⇨ *Compare* MELT.

the * /ðə; ði *for definition 7*/ [*article*]

1 used before a noun or adjective to show which thing or person you are talking about: *Shut the door, please. | Mrs. Brown is the principal of our school. | When does the next train leave?*

2 used in the names of some oceans, rivers, areas, and other places: *an island in the Pacific Ocean | The capital is in the north of the country. | We visited the Museum of Modern Art.*

3 used before a singular noun to show that you are talking about that thing in general: *Can you play the piano? | Many animals, such as the panda and the tiger, may soon die out.*

4 used with the superlative forms of adjectives: *It's the best book I ever read.*

/i/ **see** /ɪ/ **big** /eɪ/ **day** /ɛ/ **get** /æ/ **hat**
/ɑ/ **father, hot** /ʌ/ **up** /ə/ **about** /ɔ/ **saw**
/oʊ/ **hope** /ʊ/ **book** /u/ **too** /aɪ/ **I** /aʊ/ **how**
/ɔɪ/ **boy** /ɝ/ **bird** /ɚ/ **teacher** /ɪr/ **ear** /ɛr/ **air**
/ɑr/ **far** /ɔr/ **more** /ʊr/ **tour** /aɪr/ **fire**
/aʊɚ/ **hour** /θ/ **nothing** /ð/ **mother** /ʃ/ **she**
/ʒ/ **measure** /tʃ/ **church** /dʒ/ **jump** /ŋ/ **long**

5 used to talk about a particular period of time: *My mother grew up in **the fifties*** (=the 1950s). | *the month of June*
➪ *See the usage note at* TEENS.
6 for or in each or every one: *There are 16 ounces **to the** pound.* | *My car gets 24 miles **to the** gallon.*
7 used to say that someone or something is more important or popular than anyone or anything else: *It's become the restaurant to go to in town.*
☛ Pronounce **the** as /ði/ in this meaning.

— PHRASES —

8 the rich/the sick/the British/ etc. used to talk about a particular group of people: *He spent his life helping the poor and the sick.* | *a school for the deaf* | *The British speak English.*
☛ Only use a plural verb after phrases like this.
9 the more . . . the more used to show that two things are connected and that one affects and changes the other: *The more she saw of him, the more she liked him.* | *The quicker you work, the sooner you'll be finished.*

theater * /ˈθiətɚ/ [*noun*] a place where you go to watch a play: *I always **go to the theater** when I'm in New York.*
➪ *See also* MOVIE THEATER.

theft /θɛft/ [*noun*] when someone steals something: *There's been an increase in car thefts.* | *We reported the **theft of** the jewelry to the police.*

their * /ðɛr/ [*determiner*]
1 belonging to or connected with particular people or things: *They said their son was in college.* | *We're studying the different chemicals and their properties.*
☛ Only use **their** before a noun.
2 used after words like "everyone," "anyone," etc., to avoid saying "his or her": *Everyone is responsible for looking after their own luggage.*
☛ Some people consider this use of **their** to be wrong.

theirs * /ðɛrz/ [*pronoun*]
1 something that belongs to or is connected with particular people or things: *The yellow suitcase is ours and the black one is theirs.* | *We have our opinions and they have theirs.*
2 used after words like "everyone," "anyone," etc., to avoid saying "his or hers": *We don't have a car, so if anyone could lend us theirs, we'd be grateful.*
☛ Some people consider this use of **theirs** to be wrong.

them * /ðɛm/ [*pronoun*]
1 used to talk about particular people or things, as the object of a verb or preposition: *I promised Mom and Dad I'd go see them this weekend.* | *"Are those shoes new?" "Yes, do you like them?"* | *Both of them were good at sports.*
2 used after words like "everyone," "anyone," "someone," etc., to avoid saying "him or her": *Someone called but I told them you were out.*
☛ Some people consider this use of **them** to be wrong.
➪ *See also* THEY.

theme /θim/ [*noun*] the main idea or subject in a book, play, movie, etc.: *The **theme of** the novel is friendship.*

theme park /ˈθim ˌpark/ [*noun*] a large park with many kinds of entertainment that are all connected with one subject, such as space travel or water: *Thousands of tourists visit theme parks every year.*

themselves * /ˌðɛmˈsɛlvz/ [*pronoun*]
1 used to say that the people affected by an action are the people doing it: *The kids washed and dressed themselves.*
2 used to emphasize a plural subject or the word "they": *Mr. and Mrs. Gray started the business themselves.* | *They paid for the wedding themselves.*
☛ Do not use **themselves** as a subject. For example, do not say "Themselves bought it." Say **They bought it themselves**.

— PHRASES —

3 by themselves alone or without any help: *All the people in this building live by themselves.* | *They started the business **all by themselves**.*
4 to themselves not sharing something with anyone else: *They had the whole beach **all to themselves**.*

then * /ðɛn/ [*adverb*]
1 at a time in the past or future but not

now: *I was 25 then and had just gotten married.* | *Hopefully we'll have found somewhere to live by then.*

2 after something has happened: *She took a shower, then went to bed.*

3 used to say that if one thing is true, something else should also happen or be true: *If he's not feeling well, then he should stay home.*

theology /θiˈaləʤi/ [noun] the study of religions: *She has a degree in theology.*

theoretical /ˌθiəˈrɛtɪkəl/ [adjective; no comparative] a theoretical situation could exist but is not yet proven or is not likely to exist: *What he suggested is just a theoretical possibility.*

theoretically 🔲 /ˌθiəˈrɛtɪkli/ [adverb] used to say that a situation might happen or be true, but that it is not yet proven to be true or is not likely to happen: *Theoretically, the president could be forced to resign.*

theory /ˈθiəri/ [noun; plural **theories**]

1 an idea or set of ideas about something that has not yet been definitely proven true: *the **theory of** evolution* | *The police have a **theory that** the woman was kidnapped.*

— PHRASE ——————

2 in theory used to say that something could be true or possible, but may not actually be true or possible: *In theory, the plan should work.*

▷ *Compare* **in practice** *at* **PRACTICE**[1].

therapist /ˈθɛrəpɪst/ [noun] someone who treats emotional or physical problems: ***Physical therapists** help people with injuries.*

therapy /ˈθɛrəpi/ [noun; plural **therapies**]

1 the treatment of an injury or illness: *I've been having therapy for my shoulder for several months.*

2 the treatment of emotional or mental illness by listening to someone talk about his or her problems: *He has been **in therapy** for his depression.*

there[1] ✱ /ðɛr/ [pronoun] used before some verbs, especially the verb "be," to say that something exists or happens, or that someone or something is somewhere: *There's a strange smell in*

this room. | *There was a loud explosion.* | *There seems to be a lot of confusion about the rules.*

☛ Use a plural verb if the noun or pronoun after the verb is plural: *There were two cups on the table.*

there[2] ✱ [adverb]

1 in, at, or to a place that is not near: *"Where's my key?" "It's there, on the table."* | *I've never been to Washington but I'd like to go there.*

▷ *See the usage note at* **HERE**[1].

2 at a particular point during a process: *Finish the first ten questions, then stop there and we'll check the answers.*

— PHRASES ——————

3 Hello there or **Hi there** SPOKEN used as an informal greeting: *Hi there! How are you?*

4 be there for someone INFORMAL to be willing to help and support someone: *I'll always be there for you, you know that.*

there'd /ðɛrd/ SPOKEN

1 the short form of "there had": *There'd been a fire in the building next door.*

2 the short form of "there would": *There'd be a party every time our team won.*

therefore ✱ /ˈðɛrˌfɔr/ [adverb] FORMAL for the reason that has been mentioned: *This equipment is complicated and therefore expensive.*

▷ *Compare* **SO**[2] (definition 1).

there'll /ðɛrl/ SPOKEN the short form of "there will": *There'll be lots of dancing and plenty of food.*

there's ✱ /ðɛrz/

1 the short form of "there is": *There's a phone call for you.*

2 SPOKEN the short form of "there has": *There's been a terrible accident.*

there've /ðɛrv/ SPOKEN the short form of "there have": *There've been some nasty rumors about her fiancé.*

/i/ **see** /ɪ/ **big** /eɪ/ **day** /ɛ/ **get** /æ/ **hat**
/ɑ/ **father, hot** /ʌ/ **up** /ə/ **about** /ɔ/ **saw**
/oʊ/ **hope** /ʊ/ **book** /u/ **too** /aɪ/ **I** /aʊ/ **how**
/ɔɪ/ **boy** /ɝ/ **bird** /ɚ/ **teacher** /ɪr/ **ear** /ɛr/ **air**
/ɑr/ **far** /ɔr/ **more** /ʊr/ **tour** /aɪr/ **fire**
/aʊɚ/ **hour** /θ/ **nothing** /ð/ **mother** /ʃ/ **she**
/ʒ/ **measure** /tʃ/ **church** /dʒ/ **jump** /ŋ/ **long**

thermometer /θəˈmɑmɪtə/ [noun]
an object that is used for measuring
TEMPERATURE: *an outdoor thermometer* |
*The nurse put a thermometer in my
mouth.*

Thermos /ˈθɜˈməs/ [noun; plural
Thermoses] TRADEMARK a kind of bottle
that will keep a hot liquid inside it hot
or keep a cold liquid cold

thesaurus /θɪˈsɔrəs/ [noun; plural
thesauruses] a kind of dictionary that
contains groups of words with similar
meanings: *I often use a thesaurus when
I'm writing.*

these * /ðiz/ [determiner, pronoun] the
plural of THIS: *Where did you buy these
apples?* | *I'll take these, please.*

thesis /ˈθisɪs/ [noun; plural **theses** /ˈθisiz/]
a long piece of writing about a subject
that you do in order to get an advanced
university degree: *He did his **thesis on**
genetics.*

they * /ðeɪ/ [pronoun]
1 used to talk about particular people
or things, as the subject of a verb: *My
parents met when they were in college.* |
The paintings are beautiful, aren't they?
2 used to talk about people in general:
They say it's never too late to change.
3 used after words like "everyone,"
"anyone," "someone," etc., to avoid
saying "he or she": *If anyone is going
on the trip, they should see me.*
☛ Some people consider this use of
they to be wrong.
⇨ *See also* THEM.

they'd * /ðeɪd/
1 the short form of "they had": *They'd
left before I got there.*
☛ Do not use "they'd" for **they had**
when **have** is the main verb. For
example, do not say "They'd a lot of
money." Say **They had a lot of money.**
2 the short form of "they would":
They'd be interested in the idea.

they'll * /ðeɪl/ the short form of "they
will": *They'll need some help.*

they're * /ðɛr/ the short form of "they
are": *They're nice people.*

they've * /ðeɪv/ the short form of "they
have": *They've never been to Mexico.*
☛ Do not use "they've" for **they have**

when **have** is the main verb. For example,
do not say "They've two cars." Say **They
have two cars.**

thick * ⊤ /θɪk/ [adjective; **thicker,
thickest**]
1 having a large distance between two
opposite surfaces or edges; *opposite*
THIN: *a thick wool blanket* | *a thick slice
of bread* | *a thick line*
2 measuring a particular amount
between two opposite surfaces: *a
wooden board **an inch thick***
⇨ *See also* THICKNESS.
3 a thick liquid does not have much
water in it and does not flow easily;
opposite THIN: *She gave us bowls of thick
vegetable soup.*
4 thick smoke, cloud, etc., fills the air
and is difficult to see through; *synonym*
DENSE: *Thick fog is making driving
conditions difficult.*
5 with many things or parts very close
together; *opposite* THIN: *He had thick
brown hair.*

a **thin** slice of bread

a **thick** slice of bread

thick dough

thin soup

thick *and* **thin**

thicken /ˈθɪkɪn/ [verb; **thickened,
thickening**] to become thicker or to
make something thicker: *Heat the sauce
gently until it begins to thicken.*

thickly * /ˈθɪkli/ [adverb]
1 in a way that produces something
with a large distance between two
opposite surfaces: *thickly sliced bread*
2 in a way that covers an area with
little space in between: *Trees grew
thickly in this part of the forest.*

3 in a thick layer: *The cake was thickly covered with chocolate frosting.*
⇨ Compare THINLY.

thickness /'θɪknɪs/ [*noun; plural* **thicknesses**] the distance between the opposite surfaces of an object: *She measured the thickness of the table top.*

thief * /θif/ [*noun; plural* **thieves** /θivz/] someone who steals things: *Several people tried to stop the thieves from getting away.*

thigh /θaɪ/ [*noun*] the top part of your leg above your knee
⇨ See the picture at BODY.

thimble /'θɪmbəl/ [*noun*] a small hard cover that you put on your finger to protect it when you are sewing

thin * ⊤ /θɪn/ [*adjective;* **thinner, thinnest**]
1 having only a small distance between two opposite surfaces or edges; *opposite* THICK: *She was wearing only a thin cotton dress.* | *thin slices of cheese*
2 not having much fat on your body; *opposite* FAT: *She's much thinner now than she used to be.* | *He had a long, thin face.*
3 a thin liquid has a lot of water in it and flows easily; *opposite* THICK: *I don't like this gravy. It's too thin.*
4 with a lot of space between things or parts; *opposite* THICK: *As he got older, his hair got thinner.*
⇨ See also THINLY. ⇨ See the picture at THICK.

SYNONYMS thin, slim, slender, skinny

If you are **thin**, you do not have much fat on your body: *You're looking very thin —are you okay?* **Slim** and **slender** mean "thin in an attractive way": *I wish I were as slim as you.* | *My sister is tall and slender.* **Skinny** means "thin in a way that is not attractive": *His legs are too skinny.*

---

thing * /θɪŋ/ [*noun*]
1 an object, not a person or animal: *"What's that thing?" "It's the switch for the fan."* | *Could you help me move this thing, please?*

2 something that happens, exists, or is said: *Strange things have been happening recently.* | *What an awful thing to say!*
3 things [*plural*]
  a life in general or a particular situation: *Things at work have been difficult recently.* | *"How are things with you?" "Oh, OK."*
  b clothes or objects that belong to you; *synonym* BELONGINGS | *I'll check that I haven't forgotten any of my things.*

— PHRASES ———
4 not know/see/hear/etc. a thing to not know, see, hear, etc., anything at all: *Our car was stolen from our driveway but we didn't hear a thing.*
5 there's no such thing (as) used to emphasize that something does not exist: *There's no such thing as a perfect marriage.*
6 the thing is SPOKEN used to show that you are about to say something important: *The thing is, I don't think she understands the problem.*
7 first thing at the beginning of the day: *I'll call you first thing tomorrow.*

think * /θɪŋk/ [*verb;* **thought, thinking**]
1 to have an opinion or belief about something: *What do you think I should do?* | *What did you think of the movie?* | *I thought, "That's weird."* | *I think (that)* ▸ *She thought he was handsome.* | *I don't think we've met* (=I believe we have not met).
2 to use your mind to produce a plan, explanation, answer, etc.: *Be quiet and let me think!* | *He tried to think of something to say.* | *I can't think why she invited him.*
3 to have a particular person or thing in your mind: *Hi! I was just thinking about you.* | *She often thought of her old friends.*

/i/ **see**	/ɪ/ **big**	/eɪ/ **day**	/ɛ/ **get**	/æ/ **hat**
/ɑ/ **father, hot**	/ʌ/ **up**	/ə/ **about**	/ɔ/ **saw**
/oʊ/ **hope**	/ʊ/ **book**	/u/ **too**	/aɪ/ **I**	/aʊ/ **how**
/ɔɪ/ **boy**	/ɝ/ **bird**	/ɚ/ **teacher**	/ɪr/ **ear**	/ɛr/ **air**
/ɑr/ **far**	/ɔr/ **more**	/ʊr/ **tour**	/aɪr/ **fire**
/aʊɚ/ **hour**	/θ/ **nothing**	/ð/ **mother**	/ʃ/ **she**
/ʒ/ **measure**	/tʃ/ **church**	/dʒ/ **jump**	/ŋ/ **long**

━━ PHRASE ━━

4 I think so used when you think that the answer to a question is "yes" but you are not sure: *"Is your mom at work?" "I think so."*

━━ PHRASAL VERBS ━━

think back [*phrasal verb*]
5 to think of or remember something that happened in the past: *I like to* **think back on** *all the fun we had together.*

think of [*phrasal verb*]
6 to consider something that you might decide to do: **think of doing something** ▸ *We're thinking of moving to Arizona.*

think over [*phrasal verb*]
7 to consider something carefully: **think something over** ▸ *Think it over—you don't have to decide now.*

think through [*phrasal verb*]
8 to consider the possible results of something: **think something through** ▸ *They obviously hadn't thought the plan through.*

think up [*phrasal verb*]
9 to produce a reason or a new idea by thinking hard: **think up something** ▸ *Can't we think up an excuse for not going?*

thinker /'θɪŋkɚ/ [*noun*] someone who thinks about serious things or thinks in a particular way: *a creative thinker*

thinly ✴ /'θɪnli/ [*adverb*]
1 in a way that produces something with only a small distance between two opposite surfaces: *thinly sliced cheese*
2 in a way that covers an area but leaves a lot of space in between; *opposite* DENSELY: *a thinly populated area*
3 in a thin layer: *Thinly butter each slice of bread.*
▷ *Compare* THICKLY.

third[1] ✴ /θɚd/ [*adverb, adjective; no comparative*] coming after two other people, things, or events; sometimes written as "3rd": *His third wife was an actress.* | *I came in third in the race.*

third[2] ✴ [*noun*] one of three equal parts: *A third of 90 is 30.* | *He had already*

spent two-thirds (=2/3) of the money.
▷ *See the usage note at* SECOND[2].

third person ✴ /'θɚd 'pɚsən/ [*noun*]
GRAMMAR
the third person words or forms of words used to talk about a particular thing or about a person that is not speaking or being spoken to: *Any sentence beginning with "he," "she," "it," or "they" is in the third person.*

Third World /'θɚd 'wɚld/ [*noun*]
the Third World an expression used to talk about the poor countries of the world: *We should do more to help people in the Third World.*
☞ Some people think this expression is offensive.

thirst /θɚst/ [*noun*] the feeling that you have when you need to drink something: *He woke with a terrible thirst.*
☞ Do not say "I have thirst." Say **I'm thirsty.**

thirsty ✴ /'θɚsti/ [*adjective;* **thirstier, thirstiest**] needing or wanting to drink something: *Let's have some iced tea—I'm thirsty.*

thirteen ✴ /'θɚ'tin/ [*number*] 13: *There were thirteen players on each team.*

thirteenth ✴ /'θɚ'tinθ/ [*adverb, adjective; no comparative*] coming after 12 other people, things, or events; sometimes written as "13th": *It's my thirteenth birthday tomorrow.* | *I finished thirteenth in the race.*
▷ *See the usage note at* SECOND[2].

thirtieth ✴ /'θɚtiɪθ/ [*adjective, adverb; no comparative*] coming after 29 other people, things, or events; sometimes written as "30th": *her thirtieth birthday*
▷ *See the usage note at* SECOND[2].

thirty ✴ /'θɚti/ [*number, noun; plural* **thirties**] 30: *"How old are you?" "I'm thirty."*
▷ *See the usage note at* TEENS.

this[1] ✴ /ðɪs/ [*determiner; plural* **these**]
1 used to talk about someone or something that is near in space: *Is it all right if I borrow this book?* | *I like this dress better than that one.*
2 used to talk about someone or something that has just been

mentioned or is already known about: *This information is secret.*

3 used to talk about something that is near in time: *Why were you late for school this morning?* | *We're going to the coast this weekend.*

4 SPOKEN used to mention a person or thing for the first time in a story: *I was waiting for the bus when this guy came up to me.*

USAGE   this, that

The difference between **this** and **that** can be very confusing. **This** is used about things that are near to you or that you are holding or showing. **That** is used about things that are farther from you or that you are pointing to. Read the dialogue below to see the difference:

"Please bring me that red book on the shelf," she said.
    "This one?" he asked, touching a book.
    "No, that one, next to it," she said.
    "Oh, this one," he said, taking it off the shelf.

---

this[2] * [*pronoun; plural* **these**]

1 used to talk about something or someone that you have just mentioned or that is already known about: *We have a chair just like this at home.* | *Please don't mention this to anyone.*

2 used to talk about something or someone that is near in space or time: *"Would you like one of these?" she said, offering us a box of chocolates.* | *This has been a really fun day.*

3 used to talk about something you are going to say or show: *OK, this is what you should do.* | *He danced like this.*

═══ PHRASE ═══

4 this is

  a used to say who you are when you call someone on the telephone: *This is Bob Green. May I speak to Mr. Black?*

  b used when you introduce someone to someone else: *Michael, this is my wife, Emily.*

this[3] [*adverb*] used to emphasize an adjective or adverb: *I didn't know you wanted to leave this early.* | *Will the cord reach this far?*

this'd /ðɪsd/ SPOKEN

1 the short form of "this had": *This'd been going on all day.*

2 the short form of "this would": *This'd mean a lot to me.*

this'll * /ðɪsl/ SPOKEN the short form of "this will": *This'll taste better with salt.*

thistle /'θɪsəl/ [*noun*] a plant with a purple flower and leaves with sharp points

thong /θɔŋ/ [*noun*] a flat shoe with a thin band that goes between your toes: *She slipped on her thongs.*
☞ This word is usually used in the plural.

thongs

thorn /θɔrn/ [*noun*] a sharp point on the stem of some plants

thorough * ⊤ /'θɜroʊ/ [*adjective;* **more thorough, most thorough**] including every part or detail: *She did a thorough job of researching her topic.*

thoroughly * ⊤ /'θɜrəli/ [*adverb*]

1 completely or very much: *We thoroughly enjoyed ourselves.*

2 in a careful way that includes every part or detail: *Make sure you clean the equipment thoroughly.*

those * /ðoʊz/ [*determiner, pronoun*] the plural of THAT[1] and THAT[2]: *Whose are those keys?* | *I like those—they're beautiful.*

though[1] * /ðoʊ/ [*conjunction*]

1 used to introduce a fact that makes another fact seem surprising in some way; <u>synonym</u> ALTHOUGH: *She wants to be a dancer, though it will be difficult.* | *Though he was small, he was very strong.*

═══ PHRASES ═══

2 as though used to say how someone or something appears or seems: *Everyone was staring at me as though I were crazy.*

/i/ **see** /ɪ/ **big** /eɪ/ **day** /ɛ/ **get** /æ/ **hat**
/ɑ/ **father, hot** /ʌ/ **up** /ə/ **about** /ɔ/ **saw**
/oʊ/ **hope** /ʊ/ **book** /u/ **too** /aɪ/ **I** /aʊ/ **how**
/ɔɪ/ **boy** /ɝ/ **bird** /ɚ/ **teacher** /ɪr/ **ear** /ɛr/ **air**
/ɑr/ **far** /ɔr/ **more** /ʊr/ **tour** /aɪr/ **fire**
/aʊɚ/ **hour** /θ/ **nothing** /ð/ **mother** /ʃ/ **she**
/ʒ/ **measure** /tʃ/ **church** /dʒ/ **jump** /ŋ/ **long**

☛ In past tense sentences, use **were**, not **was**, with singular subjects and **as though**. For example, do not say "as though I was." Say **as though I were**.
⊳ See also **as if** at IF.

3 even though used to say that something does not or did not affect a situation: *She sang in the concert even though she was feeling ill.*
⊳ Compare ALTHOUGH.

though[2] * [*adverb*] in spite of something you have just said: *We had to work pretty hard. It was fun, though.*

thought[1] * /θɔt/ [*verb*] the past tense and past participle of THINK

thought[2] * [*noun*]
1 something that you think: *I just had a thought—let's ask Dad to drive us.* | *We'd like to hear your thoughts on the subject.* | *The thought of eating made her hungry.*
2 when you think about something or consider it carefully: *I could see that he was deep in thought* (=thinking carefully). | *We'll give your idea some serious thought.*

thoughtful /'θɔtfəl/ [*adjective*; **more thoughtful, most thoughtful**]
1 showing that you are always thinking about what other people need or feel; *opposite* THOUGHTLESS: *a kind, thoughtful boy*
⊳ Compare CONSIDERATE.
2 not saying much because you are thinking a lot: *She sat at her desk, looking thoughtful.*

thoughtfully /'θɔtfəli/ [*adverb*] in a way that shows you are thinking a lot: *"Well, maybe I can help," she said thoughtfully.*

thoughtless /'θɔtlɪs/ [*adjective*; **more thoughtless, most thoughtless**] a thoughtless person or thoughtless behavior shows that the person is not thinking about what other people need or feel; *opposite* THOUGHTFUL: *That was very thoughtless of you.* | *a thoughtless remark*
⊳ Compare INCONSIDERATE.

thousand * /'θaʊzənd/ [*number*] 1,000: *It cost a thousand dollars.* | *The stadium*

can hold ten thousand people. | *He gets thousands of* (=over 2000, or a lot) *letters every week from fans.*
☛ Do not say "three thousands people" or "three thousands of people." Say **three thousand people**.

thousandth * /'θaʊzəndθ/ [*adjective; no comparative*] coming after 999 other people, things, or events; sometimes written as "1,000th": *That's the thousandth time I've told you to put away your toys!*

thread[1] * /θrɛd/ [*noun*] a long thin piece of cotton, silk, etc., used when you are sewing: *a spool of thread*

thread[2] [*verb; **threaded, threading***] to put a piece of thread, string, etc., through a hole, especially the hole in a needle: *I can't see well enough to thread the needle.*

threat * /θrɛt/ [*noun*]
1 a warning in which someone says that he or she will harm someone or cause problems: *She said he came to her house and made threats.* | *He received a death threat.*
2 the possibility that something bad will happen: *There is still a threat of flooding in some areas.*

threaten * /'θrɛtən/ [*verb; **threatened, threatening***]
1 to say that you will harm someone or cause problems: *She claimed that her neighbor had threatened her.* | **threaten to do something** ▸ *The workers have threatened to strike.*
2 to be likely to harm something: *Many animals are threatened with extinction.*

threatening * /'θrɛtənɪŋ/ [*adjective; no comparative*] intended to make someone feel afraid: *His threatening behavior frightened her.*

three * /θri/ [*number, noun; plural **threes***] 3: *They have three children.* | *Bad things come in threes.*

three-dimensional /'θri dɪ'mɛnʃənəl/ [*adjective; no comparative*] having or seeming to have height, width, and depth, rather than being flat: *He has learned to draw three-dimensional objects.*

threw * /θru/ [*verb*] the past tense of THROW¹

thrill /θrɪl/ [*noun*] a strong feeling of excitement, or something that makes you feel this: *I'll never forget **the thrill of** my son's birth.*

thrilled /θrɪld/ [*adjective;* **more thrilled, most thrilled**] very excited or pleased: *He was **thrilled with** his test score.*

thrilling /'θrɪlɪŋ/ [*adjective;* **more thrilling, most thrilling**] making you feel very excited or interested: *Brazil won a thrilling game, 4–3.*

throat * /θroʊt/ [*noun*]
1 the tube that starts at the back of your mouth that you use to swallow things: *A fish bone had gotten stuck in my throat.*
2 the front of your neck: *Someone grabbed him by the throat.*
➪ *See the picture at* BODY.

throb /θrab/ [*verb;* **throbs, throbbed, throbbing**] if a part of your body throbs, you feel a series of pains in it: *My shoulder was **throbbing with pain**.*

throne /θroʊn/ [*noun*] a large decorated chair that a king or queen sits on

through¹ * /θru/ [*preposition*]
1 from one side of a hole, passage, or area to the other: *The train goes through a long tunnel. | They pushed their way through the crowd.*
2 by doing or using something: *Their success was achieved through hard work.*
3 from the beginning of something to the end: *He worked **all through** the summer. | The exhibit will be open Tuesday through Saturday (=from Tuesday until the end of Saturday).*
➪ *See also* **get through** *at* GET.

━━ PHRASE ━━━
4 go/look through something to search something completely: *I went through everything on my desk looking for the receipt.*

through² * [*adverb*]
1 from one side of a hole, passage, or area to the other: *The gap in the fence wasn't big enough to get through.*
➪ *See also* **get through** *at* GET.

━━ PHRASE ━━━
2 read/think something through to read or think about something from the beginning to the end: *I don't think he's thought his plan through.*

through³ [*adjective; no comparative*]
━━ PHRASE ━━━
be through (with) to have finished doing or using something: *We should be through with the job by this evening. | Okay, I'm through.*

throughout /θru'aʊt/ [*adverb, preposition*]
1 in every part of an area or place: *This plant is common throughout Europe. | The apartment was painted white throughout.*
2 from the beginning of a period of time to the end: *The team did well throughout the season.*

throw¹ * /θroʊ/ [*verb;* **threw, thrown, throwing**]
1 to make something move from your hand through the air by pushing your arm forward suddenly: **throw something at someone/something** ▸ *The kids were throwing stones at a row of bottles (=in order to hit them). |* **throw something to someone** ▸ *She threw the ball to him (=so that he caught it).*
➪ *See the picture at* PLAY¹.
2 to put something somewhere quickly or violently: *He threw his coat on the chair.*
3 to suddenly move your head, hands, or arms into a different position: *She threw back her head and started to laugh.*

━━ PHRASE ━━━
4 throw (someone) a party to organize a party and invite guests: *She threw a huge party to celebrate her 50th birthday.*

━━ PHRASAL VERBS ━━━
throw away/out [*phrasal verb*]
5 to get rid of something that you do

/i/ **see**	/ɪ/ **big**	/eɪ/ **day**	/ɛ/ **get**	/æ/ **hat**
/ɑ/ **father, hot**	/ʌ/ **up**	/ə/ **about**	/ɔ/ **saw**	
/oʊ/ **hope**	/ʊ/ **book**	/u/ **too**	/aɪ/ **I**	/aʊ/ **how**
/ɔɪ/ **boy**	/ɝ/ **bird**	/ɚ/ **teacher**	/ɪr/ **ear**	/ɛr/ **air**
/ɑr/ **far**	/ɔr/ **more**	/ʊr/ **tour**	/aɪr/ **fire**	
/aʊɚ/ **hour**	/θ/ **nothing**	/ð/ **mother**	/ʃ/ **she**	
/ʒ/ **measure**	/tʃ/ **church**	/dʒ/ **jump**	/ŋ/ **long**	

not want: **throw away/out something** ▸ *Can I throw out these old magazines?* | **throw something away/out** ▸ *Do you want to throw these letters away?*

throw out [*phrasal verb*]
6 to make someone leave a place or organization: **throw out someone** ▸ *I'll throw out anyone who starts trouble!* | **throw someone out** ▸ *They threw him out of the club.*

throw up [*phrasal verb*]
7 INFORMAL if you throw up, food and liquid come up from your stomach and out of your mouth; *synonym* VOMIT: *I think I'm going to throw up.*

throw² * [*noun*] when someone throws something such as a ball: *He made a good throw to first base.*

thrown * /θroʊn/ [*verb*] the past participle of THROW¹

thrust /θrʌst/ [*verb*; **thrust, thrusting**] to put something somewhere suddenly and firmly: *She thrust a $10 bill into my hand.*

thruway /ˈθruˌweɪ/ [*noun*; *plural* **thruways**] a wide road on which vehicles can travel very fast

thud /θʌd/ [*noun*] the loud dull sound that is made when something heavy falls and hits something else: *The book hit the floor with a thud.*

thug /θʌɡ/ [*noun*] a violent man: *a gang of thugs*

thumb¹ * /θʌm/ [*noun*] the shortest and thickest of your fingers that is separated from your other fingers: *Stop sucking your thumb!*
↪ See the picture at BODY.

thumb² [*verb*; **thumbed, thumbing**]
— PHRASAL VERB —
thumb through [*phrasal verb*]
to read or look through a book or magazine quickly: **thumb through something** ▸ *She sat in the waiting room thumbing through a magazine.*

thumbtack /ˈθʌmˌtæk/ [*noun*] a short pin with a round flat top, used for attaching things to a wall or board; *synonym* TACK

thump /θʌmp/ [*verb*; **thumped, thumping**] to hit something with a loud dull sound, or to make something do this: *The ball thumped against the goalpost.*

thunder¹ /ˈθʌndər/ [*noun*] the loud noise in the sky that you sometimes hear during a storm: *The dog was frightened of the thunder and lightning.*

thunder² [*verb*; **thundered, thundering**] if it thunders, there is a loud noise in the sky during a storm: *Heavy rain fell and then it started to thunder.*

thunderstorm /ˈθʌndərˌstɔrm/ [*noun*] a storm during which there are loud noises in the sky and flashes of light

Thurs. the written abbreviation of THURSDAY

Thursday * /ˈθɜrzdeɪ/ [*noun*; *plural* **Thursdays**] the day of the week that is after Wednesday and before Friday: *I have an appointment on Thursday.* | *I play tennis on Thursdays.*
↪ See the usage note at DAY.

tick¹ /tɪk/ [*noun*]
1 the short sound that a clock or watch makes every second: *The only sound was the tick of the clock.*
2 an insect that attaches itself to your skin and can make you sick

tick² [*verb*; **ticked, ticking**] if a clock or watch ticks, it makes a short sound every second: *I lay awake, listening to the clock ticking.*

ticket * /ˈtɪkɪt/ [*noun*]
1 a small piece of paper that shows that you have paid to do something such as travel on a train or go to a movie: *How much were the theater tickets?* | *a round-trip ticket* (=a ticket for a trip to a place and back again)
2 a small piece of paper that orders you to pay money for a driving offense: *I got another parking ticket.* | *a speeding ticket*

tickle /ˈtɪkəl/ [*verb*; **tickled, tickling**]
1 to touch part of someone's body lightly with your fingers in order to make him or her laugh: *Stop tickling my feet!*
2 if something tickles or tickles you, it

touches a part of your body in a way that makes you want to rub it: *The long grass was tickling my legs.*

ticklish /'tɪklɪʃ/ [*adjective;* **more ticklish, most ticklish**] someone who is ticklish laughs easily when you touch a part of his or her body with your fingers: *Don't touch me there—I'm ticklish!*

tick-tack-toe /ˌtɪk tæk 'toʊ/ [*noun*] a children's game in which they put the marks "O" and "X" into squares and try to form a line

tidal wave /'taɪdəl ˌweɪv/ [*noun*] a very big ocean wave that destroys things on land

tide /taɪd/ [*noun*]
  1 the rise and fall of the level of the water in the ocean: *The tide was out* (=the water was at its lowest level). | *The tide is in* (=the water is at its highest level).
  ▬▬ PHRASE ▬▬
  2 high/low tide the time when the ocean reaches its highest or lowest level in a particular place: *Those rocks are covered at high tide.* | *Low tide is at 3:43 today.*

tidy[1] ∗ /'taɪdi/ [*adjective;* **tidier, tidiest**] neat: *How do you manage to keep the house so clean and tidy?*

tidy[2] ∗ [*verb;* **tidies, tidied, tidying**] to make a place look neater: *Come on, we'd better start tidying up.*

tie[1] ∗ /taɪ/ [*verb;* **ties, tied, tying**]
  1 to fasten something using string, rope, etc.; *opposite* UNTIE: **tie something to/around something** ▸ *She tied the dog's leash around the post.* | *We need to tie the boat up to the docks.*
  2 to make a knot in a piece of string, rope, etc., or to be made into a knot; *opposite* UNTIE: *She hasn't learned to tie her shoelaces yet.*
  3 to do equally well in a competition or game: *Sweden and Canada tied for first place* (=both got first position).
  ▬▬ PHRASAL VERB ▬▬
  tie up [*phrasal verb*]
  4 to put something such as rope

around someone's body to prevent him or her from escaping: *The prisoners were tied up and taken away.*

tie[2] ∗ [*noun; plural ties*]
  1 a long thin piece of cloth which is tied around a man's shirt collar and hangs down at the front; *synonym* NECKTIE
  2 when players or teams do equally well in a competition or game: *The game ended in a tie.*

bow tie

ties

tie/necktie

tiebreaker /'taɪˌbreɪkɚ/ [*noun*] a final question or game to decide who wins a competition when the players or teams have the same number of points: *The first person to answer the tiebreaker correctly wins the quiz.*

tied /taɪd/ [*adjective; no comparative*] having the same score in a game or competition: *Right now, the teams are tied.*

tier /tɪr/ [*noun*]
  1 a row of seats that is above or below other rows of seats: *We were sitting in the top tier.*
  2 one of several levels within an organization: *There are several tiers of management.*

tiger ∗ /'taɪgɚ/ [*noun*] a large wild cat that has orange and black lines on its body

tight[1] ∗ /taɪt/ [*adjective;* **tighter, tightest**]
  1 tight clothes fit your body very closely or too closely; *opposite* LOOSE: *This skirt's a little tight.*
  2 pulled or stretched firmly; *opposite* LOOSE: *Check that all the tent ropes are tight.*

/i/ **see** /ɪ/ **big** /eɪ/ **day** /ɛ/ **get** /æ/ **hat** /ɑ/ **father, hot** /ʌ/ **up** /ə/ **about** /ɔ/ **saw** /oʊ/ **hope** /ʊ/ **book** /u/ **too** /aɪ/ **I** /aʊ/ **how** /ɔɪ/ **boy** /ɝ/ **bird** /ɚ/ **teacher** /ɪr/ **ear** /ɛr/ **air** /ɑr/ **far** /ɔr/ **more** /ʊr/ **tour** /aɪr/ **fire** /aʊɚ/ **hour** /θ/ **nothing** /ð/ **mother** /ʃ/ **she** /ʒ/ **measure** /tʃ/ **church** /dʒ/ **jump** /ŋ/ **long**

tight² [adverb] very closely or firmly, with a lot of pressure; _synonym_ TIGHTLY; _opposite_ LOOSELY: _Hold on tight to my hand._ I _She had her eyes **tight** shut._

tighten /'taɪtən/ [verb; tightened, tightening]
1 to make something fit around or in something else more closely or firmly; _opposite_ LOOSEN: _These screws need to be tightened._ I _He tightened his grip on the bat._
2 to become tighter by being stretched or pulled, or to make something do this; _opposite_ LOOSEN: _You need to tighten that knot._

tightly * T /'taɪtli/ [adverb] very closely or firmly, with a lot of pressure; _synonym_ TIGHT; _opposite_ LOOSELY: _She held tightly onto the rope._

tights /taɪts/ [plural noun] a thick piece of clothing that covers a woman's or girl's feet, legs, and waist

tile /taɪl/ [noun] a square piece of baked clay or another hard material, used for covering roofs, walls, or floors

till¹ /tɪl/ [conjunction] INFORMAL used to talk about what will happen between now and a time in the future; _synonym_ UNTIL: _We waited till Dad got home before having dinner._

till² [preposition] INFORMAL used to talk about what will happen between now and a time in the future; _synonym_ UNTIL: _I'll be staying here till the end of August._

till³ [noun] a machine in a store that holds the money and shows how much each sale is; _synonym_ CASH REGISTER

tilt /tɪlt/ [verb; tilted, tilting] if something tilts or you tilt it, one end or side of it becomes higher than the other: _The boat was tilting slightly to one side._ I _He tilted his chair back._

timber /'tɪmbər/ [noun] wood cut from trees and used to build things, or the trees themselves

time¹ * /taɪm/ [noun]
1 what is measured in minutes, hours, days, etc.: _How much time do we have before the train leaves?_ I _Let's not waste time worrying about small details._ I _It_

takes **time** (=you need a lot of time) _to make new friends._
2 a point in time, as shown by a clock or watch: _"What time is it?" "It's two o'clock."_ I _He asked the **time of** the next flight._ I _Is it **time for** supper yet?_
⇨ See also DINNERTIME, LUNCHTIME.
3 an occasion when something is done or happens: _I've been to Hawaii three times._ I _Come and visit us **the next time** you're in town._ I _**The last time** I saw her, she looked well._ I _**Every time** we arrange to meet, you're late._ I _They both spoke **at the same time**._
4 an amount of time: _We waited **a long time** in line._
5 a particular period in someone's life or in history: _**At that time**, we were living in Boston._ I _This custom comes from medieval times._
6 an occasion or situation which is or is not suitable for something to be done: _When would be **a good time** to call you?_ I _**This is not the time** to start arguing._
⇨ See also TIMES.
━━ PHRASES ━━
7 it's time used to say that something should happen now: _She feels **it's time for** a change._ I _**It's time that** we had a talk._ I _I think **it's time** to go home._
8 on time at the arranged time, not late: _Please arrive on time._
9 in time early enough to do something: _Be home **in time for** dinner._ I _We got to the airport **in time to** meet them._
☛ Do not confuse **on time** and **in time**. If something happens **on time**, it happens at the arranged time (neither late nor early). If you arrive somewhere **in time**, you are not too late for the event, performance, etc.
10 in no time very quickly: _She took a shower and got dressed in no time._
11 all the time often or for a long time; _synonym_ CONTINUALLY: _She listens to the radio all the time._
12 the whole time continuously through a period: _He ignored me the whole time I was there._
13 from time to time sometimes but not often: _Grandpa comes to see us from time to time._

14 have a good/bad/wonderful/ etc. time to be happy or unhappy somewhere or at some event: *I had a good time in college.* | *Have a great time, you two!*

15 ahead of time early, or before the time when something will happen or begin: *You must study for the test ahead of time.* | *We were ready for our guests ahead of time.*

16 one/two/three/etc. at a time separately or in groups of two, three, etc.: *The children came forward, one at a time, to receive their prizes.*

17 take your time to do something carefully, without hurrying: *"Sorry, I'm not ready yet." "Don't worry, take your time."*

18 time off a period when you stop doing a job or an activity in order to rest or to do something different: *You need a vacation. When will you get some time off?* | *I took time off between high school and college.*

19 it's about time SPOKEN used to emphasize the fact that you think something should happen very soon or should already have happened: *It's about time you got a haircut!*

20 for the time being for a short time but not forever: *They're living in an apartment for the time being.*

21 in time to following the speed of a piece of music: *He tapped his feet in time to the beat.*

USAGE Talking about time

Use **it's** or **it is** to talk about the time it is now: *It's four o'clock* (=4:00). | *What time is it?* You can also use only the number: *It's four.*

Use **at** to say exactly when something happened or will happen: *The last train left at midnight.* | *The meeting is at four o'clock* (=it will happen then). Only use **o'clock** with hours. For example, do not say "it's four-fifteen o'clock."

You can say 4:15 in different ways: *It's four-fifteen.* | *It's a quarter after four.* | *It's a quarter past four.* You can say 4:30 in different ways: *It's four-thirty.* | *It's half past four.* You can say 4:45 in different ways: *It's four forty-five.* | *It's a quarter to five.* | *It's a quarter of five.*

For other parts of the hour, say: *It's four-ten* (=4:10). | *It's ten after four.* | *It's ten past four.* | *It's four-fifty* (=4:50). | *It's ten to five.* | *It's ten of five.*

time² ∗ [*verb*; **timed, timing**]
1 to measure how long something takes: *He timed each race.*
2 to arrange for something to happen at a particular time: *The fireworks display was timed to start at midnight.*

time-out /'taɪm 'aʊt/ [*noun*] when players rest during a sports game and get instructions from the person in charge of the team or get medical treatment: *The Giants will now take a two-minute time-out.*

timer /'taɪmɚ/ [*noun*] an object that measures a period of time, for example when you are cooking: *Set the oven timer for 45 minutes.*

times /taɪmz/ [*preposition*]
1 used when one number is increased by a particular number of times: *Three times three equals nine* (3 × 3 = 9).
⇨ See also MULTIPLY.

— PHRASES —
2 three/ten/fifty/etc. times used to say how much bigger, smaller, better, etc., one person or thing is than another: *The local airport is only twenty times bigger than a football field.* | *She earns three times as much as I do.*

3 at times sometimes: *He can be really annoying at times.*

time zone /'taɪm ˌzoʊn/ [*noun*] one of the 24 areas of the world that have different times: *Denver is in a different time zone from Los Angeles.*

timid /'tɪmɪd/ [*adjective*; **more timid, most timid**] afraid to talk or do something because you do not have much confidence: *She was too timid to interrupt them.*
⇨ *Compare* SHY.

/i/ **see**	/ɪ/ **big**	/eɪ/ **day**	/ɛ/ **get**	/æ/ **hat**

/i/ see /ɪ/ big /eɪ/ day /ɛ/ get /æ/ hat
/ɑ/ father, hot /ʌ/ up /ə/ about /ɔ/ saw
/oʊ/ hope /ʊ/ book /u/ too /aɪ/ I /aʊ/ how
/ɔɪ/ boy /ɝ/ bird /ɚ/ teacher /ɪr/ ear /ɛr/ air
/ɑr/ far /ɔr/ more /ʊr/ tour /aɪr/ fire
/aʊɚ/ hour /θ/ nothing /ð/ mother /ʃ/ she
/ʒ/ measure /tʃ/ church /dʒ/ jump /ŋ/ long

timing /ˌtaɪmɪŋ/ [*noun*] the time at which something happens or at which you decide to do something, and whether it is suitable or not: *With perfect timing, they arrived just as the train did.*

tin /tɪn/ [*noun*]
  1 a soft silver metal used for covering parts of buildings or for making cans: *The shed had a tin roof.*
  2 a metal CONTAINER, usually with a lid: *a tin of cookies*

tingle /ˈtɪŋɡəl/ [*verb*; **tingled, tingling**] to have a feeling like slight sharp pains in a part of your body: *My feet tingled as the fire warmed them.*

tinsel /ˈtɪnsəl/ [*noun*] long pieces of a shiny material that are used for decoration, especially at Christmas

tiny * T /ˈtaɪni/ [*adjective*; **tinier, tiniest**] very small; *opposite* HUGE: *The plant was covered with tiny insects.*

tip[1] /tɪp/ [*noun*]
  1 the pointed end of something: *the tip of a pencil* I *the tip of someone's nose*
  2 a small extra amount of money that you give to someone for a service: *We gave the taxi driver a $3 tip.*
  3 a piece of advice: *My coach **gives** me **tips on** how to improve my game.*

tip[2] [*verb*; **tips, tipped, tipping**]
  1 to fall or lean to one side, or to make something do this: *Careful—the vase nearly **tipped over**. I Don't tip your cup so far—it'll spill.*
  2 to give someone a small extra amount of money for a service: *How much should I tip the waiter?*

tiptoe /ˈtɪpˌtoʊ/ [*verb*; **tiptoes, tiptoed, tiptoeing**] to walk on your toes in order not to make a noise: *She tiptoed into the bedroom.*

tire[1] * /taɪr/ [*noun*] a round piece of rubber that goes around a wheel of a vehicle
  ⇨ *See the pictures at* BICYCLE *and* CAR.

tire[2] [*verb*; **tired, tiring**]
  ━ PHRASAL VERB ━━━━━━━━
  tire out [*phrasal verb*]
  to make someone completely tired: **tire someone out** ▸ *Shopping all day had tired them out.*

tired * /taɪrd/ [*adjective*; **more tired, most tired**]
  1 feeling as if you need to sleep or rest: *You look tired. I I'm **too** tired **to** drive.*
  ━ PHRASE ━━━━━━━━
  2 be/get tired of to be or become bored or annoyed with someone or something: *I'm getting tired of your stupid jokes.*

tiring * /ˈtaɪrɪŋ/ [*adjective*; **more tiring, most tiring**] making you feel tired: *Driving long distances can be very tiring.*

tissue /ˈtɪʃu/ [*noun*; *plural* **tissues**]
  1 a piece of soft thin paper used especially for drying your nose and eyes: *a pack of tissues*
  2 a group of cells that make up part of a person, animal, or plant: *muscle tissue*

title * /ˈtaɪtəl/ [*noun*]
  1 the name of a book, movie, play, etc.: *The title of her novel was "The Secret."*
  2 a word such as "Dr." or "Mrs." that is used in front of someone's name to show his or her profession, rank, etc.: *Write your title, initials, and last name in the boxes provided.*

to[1] * /tu/ used to form the infinitive of a verb: *I want to buy that car. I We weren't sure what to do. I I just called to see* (=in order to see) *if you were OK.*
  ☛ In some kinds of sentences, when a verb has already been used, the verb is not repeated after "to": *They asked him to come with them but he didn't want to.*

to[2] * [*preposition*]
  1 used to say where someone or something will be after traveling or moving: *She walked **over to** the window. I We always go to my aunt's house for Thanksgiving. I The flight to Orlando has been delayed.*
  ⇨ *See the usage note at* TOWARD.
  2 used to show who is intended to receive or hear something: *He gave a check for $50 to his son. I Could you give this message to her? I He never said anything to me about it.*
  3 used to say what state or situation someone or something is in after a change: *She got to sleep at midnight. I The plate was smashed to pieces.*

4 used to say where a person or thing is in relation to another: *Montreal is about 350 miles to the east of here.* | *His office is to the left.*

5 used to show the person or thing that is affected by something: *The other children were very friendly to us.* | *Many chemicals are harmful to the environment.*

6 as far as, or until: *It had rained so hard, the water came up to our ankles.* | *She usually works from 9 a.m. to 5 p.m.*

7 used to show whose opinion you are giving: *It looks OK to me.* | *The plan seemed fine to her.*

8 used to say how someone feels when he or she sees or hears something: *To her surprise, the room was empty.*

— PHRASE

9 ten to nine/five to three/etc. ten minutes, five minutes, etc., before an hour: *"What time is it?" "It's twenty to ten."*

☛ Do not say "It's thirty to ten." Say **It's nine-thirty**.

toad /toʊd/ [*noun*] an animal like a frog that lives mainly on land
↪ Compare **FROG**.

a toad

to and fro /'tu ən 'froʊ/ [*adverb*] forward and then back again: *The cat kept walking to and fro along the wall.*
↪ See also **back and forth** at **BACK**[1].

toast /toʊst/ [*noun*]
1 a piece of bread that has been cooked until it is brown and fairly hard: *a piece of toast*
2 when a group of people raise their glasses of alcohol at the same time in order to wish someone happiness or to celebrate something: *I'd like to **propose a toast** (=ask people to drink a toast) to the bride and groom.*

toaster /'toʊstɚ/ [*noun*] a machine that cooks pieces of bread to make them brown
↪ See the picture at **APPLIANCE**.

tobacco * /tə'bækoʊ/ [*noun*] the dried leaves of plants that are smoked in cigarettes or pipes

today[1] * /tə'deɪ/ [*adverb*]
1 during the day that it is now: *I won't have time to see you today—I'm busy.*
2 at this period of time in history: *Today, more and more people are living alone.*
☛ Do not say "on today." Just say **today**.

today[2] * [*noun*]
1 the day it is now: *Today is Monday.* | *Today's game will start at 3:00.*
2 this period of time in history: *The children **of today** don't seem to have much respect for adults.*

toddler /'tadlɚ/ [*noun*] a very young child who has just learned to walk
↪ See the synonym note at **CHILD**.

toe * /toʊ/ [*noun; plural* **toes**] one of the five short thick parts at the end of your foot
↪ See the picture at **BODY**.

toenail /'toʊˌneɪl/ [*noun*] the hard part covering the top of the end of your toe; synonym **NAIL**
↪ See the picture at **BODY**.

together * /tə'gɛðɚ/ [*adverb*]
1 if two or more things are put, joined, or mixed together, they are in one place or form one thing: *Mix the butter, flour, and sugar together.* | *Put all the papers together in a pile.*
2 with someone else, or with other people: *Let's all have dinner together.*
3 at the same time: *Problems always seem to come together.*

toilet * /'tɔɪlɪt/ [*noun*] the thing that you sit on when you get rid of waste from your body

toilet paper /'tɔɪlɪt ˌpeɪpɚ/ [*noun*] thin paper you use to clean yourself after using the toilet

---

token /'toʊkən/ [noun]
  1 a thing like a coin that you put in some machines instead of money: *a subway token | a bus token*
  ── PHRASE ──
  2 a token of respect/thanks/ appreciation/etc. something that you give to someone or do to show a feeling that you have: *Please accept this gift as a token of our thanks.*

told * /toʊld/ [verb] the past tense and past participle of TELL

tolerant /'talərənt/ [adjective; **more tolerant, most tolerant**] willing to accept opinions or behavior that are different from your own without criticizing them: *We must learn to be more tolerant of each other.*

tolerate /'talə,reɪt/ [verb; **tolerated, tolerating**] to accept something unpleasant and not try to stop or change it: *I will not tolerate your rude behavior any longer!*

toll /toʊl/ [noun]
  1 an amount of money you pay to use a bridge, road, etc.: *You have to pay a $2.00 toll at the bridge.*
  2 a bad result from a particular cause: *The **death toll** (=number of people killed) from the flood was very high. | Lack of sleep is **taking its toll on** her work* (=having a bad effect on it).

tomato /tə'meɪtoʊ/ [noun; plural **tomatoes**] a round, juicy, red fruit that is eaten as a VEGETABLE

tomb /tum/ [noun] a grave that is usually above the ground and made of stone

tombstone /'tum,stoʊn/ [noun] a block of stone on a tomb or grave that shows the name of the person who is buried there

tomorrow[1] * /tə'mɔroʊ/ [adverb] during the day after today: *Remind me to put some gas in the car tomorrow.*
  ☛ Do not say "on tomorrow." Just say tomorrow.

tomorrow[2] * [noun]
  1 the day after today: *What's tomorrow's date?*
  2 the future: *What kind of environment will the children of tomorrow live in?*

ton /tʌn/ [noun]
  1 a unit of weight equal to 2,000 pounds: *He ordered three **tons of** coal.*
  ── PHRASES ──
  2 tons of SPOKEN a lot of: *He got tons of presents on his birthday.*
  3 weigh a ton SPOKEN to be very heavy: *My bag weighs a ton!*

tone /toʊn/ [noun]
  1 the way in which your voice shows what you are feeling or thinking: *I could tell by his **tone of voice** that he was upset.*
  2 a sound made by a telephone or answering machine: *Leave your message after the tone.*
  3 the quality of the sound of a musical instrument or of someone's voice: *the deep rich tones of the piano | Her voice was high in tone.*

tongs /taŋz/ [plural noun] a tool used to pick up things that is made of two long pieces of metal attached together at the top or the middle: *ice tongs | Turn the meat in the pan with tongs or a large fork.*

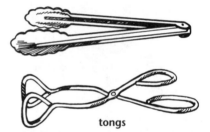

tongs

tongue * /tʌŋ/ [noun; plural **tongues**] the long, soft, pink part inside your mouth that you use to taste things

tonight[1] * /tə'naɪt/ [adverb] during the night that follows today: *You'd better go to bed early tonight.*

tonight[2] * [noun] the night that follows today: *We're all looking forward to tonight's show.*

too * /tu/ [adverb]
  1 more than is necessary, right, acceptable, etc.: *Those pants are **much too** tight for you. | There's **too much** advertising on TV. | There are **too many** players on the field. | I felt **too** tired **to** go out* (=so tired I could not go out).

2 not enough: *You're getting **too little** sleep.* | *We have **too few** theaters nearby.*
3 used at the end of a sentence to mean "also": *"We're going to the movies." "Can I come too?"*
⫸ *See also* **as well (as)** *at* AS[1]. ⫸ *See the usage note at* ALSO.
— PHRASE —
4 not too not very: *That wasn't too bad.* | *Let's hope we don't have to wait too long.*

USAGE too, very

Too is usually used about something bad: *You're driving too fast.* | *I've been waiting too long.* **Very** is used to emphasize something that may be good or bad: *It's a very good book.* | *You're being very stupid.*
You can use **too** before adjectives on their own: *These jeans are too tight.*
☛ You cannot use **too** before an adjective followed by a noun. For example, do not say "These are too tight jeans."

took * /tʊk/ [*verb*] the past tense of TAKE
tool * /tul/ [*noun*] an object that is used to build, shape, cut, remove, or repair things: *garden tools*
tooth * /tuθ/ [*noun; plural* **teeth**]
1 one of the hard white things at the top and bottom of your mouth that are used for biting and eating food: *Remember to **brush your teeth** (=clean them).*
2 one of the many pointed parts on a COMB, or on the edge of a tool used for cutting
toothache /ˈtuθˌeɪk/ [*noun*] a pain in one of your teeth: *I have a toothache.*
toothbrush /ˈtuθˌbrʌʃ/ [*noun; plural* **toothbrushes**] a small brush that you use when you clean your teeth
toothpaste /ˈtuθˌpeɪst/ [*noun*] a soft substance used for cleaning your teeth: *a tube of toothpaste*
toothpick /ˈtuθˌpɪk/ [*noun*] a small thin piece of wood used to clean food from between your teeth, or to pick up small pieces of food to eat
top[1] * /tɑp/ [*noun*]
1 the highest part or surface of

something; *opposite* BOTTOM: *The tops of the mountains were covered in snow.* | *He scratched the top of his head.* | *Write your name at the top of the page.*
2 something such as a lid that covers a box, bottle, etc.: *Please put the top back on the bottle.* | *I've lost my pen top.*
3 a piece of clothing that a woman wears on the upper part of her body: *She bought a skirt and a matching top.*
— PHRASES —
4 the top (of) the highest or best position on a list, in an organization, etc.: *It's the people **at the top** who make the decisions.* | *She's near **the top of the class** in math.*
5 on top (of) on the highest surface of something: *Don't put anything on top of your computer.* | *a dessert with whipped cream on top*
⫸ *Compare* UNDERNEATH[1].
6 on top of
a in control of a difficult situation: *There's a lot to be done, but he's on top of it.*
b in addition to something: *On top of all her other problems, she broke her leg.*
7 at the top of your voice/lungs very loudly: *I had to shout at the top of my voice to be heard.*
top[2] * [*adjective; no comparative*]
1 in the highest position; *opposite* BOTTOM: *The bowls are on the top shelf.*
2 best or most successful: *Several top rock bands will perform at the festival.*
☛ Only use **top** before a noun.
top[3] [*verb*; **tops, topped, topping**] to be more or better than something else: *I bet you can't top my score.*
topic 🔊 /ˈtɑpɪk/ [*noun*] a subject that you write or talk about: *a topic of conversation*
topping /ˈtɑpɪŋ/ [*noun*] something that you put on top of food to give it more taste or to make it look attractive: *Choose from our range of pizza toppings.*

/i/ **see** /ɪ/ **big** /eɪ/ **day** /ɛ/ **get** /æ/ **hat** /ɑ/ **father, hot** /ʌ/ **up** /ə/ **about** /ɔ/ **saw** /oʊ/ **hope** /ʊ/ **book** /u/ **too** /aɪ/ **I** /aʊ/ **how** /ɔɪ/ **boy** /ɝ/ **bird** /ɚ/ **teacher** /ɪr/ **ear** /ɛr/ **air** /ɑr/ **far** /ɔr/ **more** /ʊr/ **tour** /aɪr/ **fire** /aʊɚ/ **hour** /θ/ **nothing** /ð/ **mother** /ʃ/ **she** /ʒ/ **measure** /tʃ/ **church** /dʒ/ **jump** /ŋ/ **long**

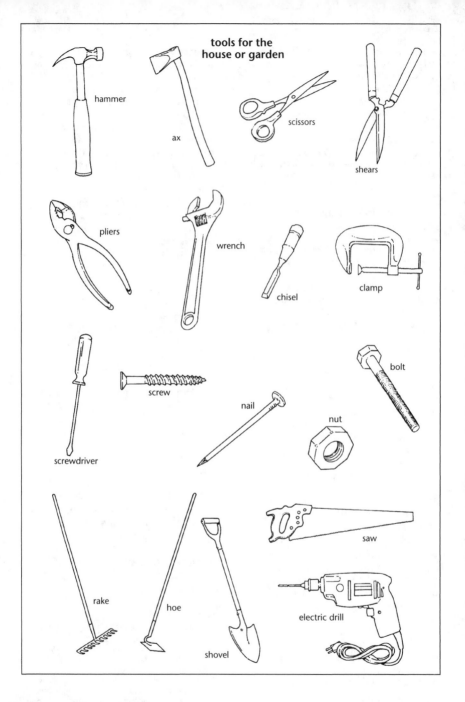

tools for the house or garden

hammer

ax

scissors

shears

pliers

wrench

chisel

clamp

screwdriver

screw

nail

bolt

nut

rake

hoe

shovel

saw

electric drill

top-secret /ˈtɑp ˈsikrɪt/ [*adjective; no comparative*] top-secret information must only be known about by very few people: *top-secret government files*

torch /tɔrtʃ/ [*noun; plural* **torches**] a long stick that burns at one end and is carried as a light: *the Olympic torch*

tore * /tɔr/ [*verb*] the past tense of TEAR[1]

torn * /tɔrn/ [*verb*] the past participle of TEAR[1]

tornado /tɔrˈneɪdoʊ/ [*noun; plural* **tornadoes** or **tornados**] a violent storm that happens over land, in which the wind spins into a tube shape that touches the ground
⭢ *Compare* CYCLONE, HURRICANE, TYPHOON.

torpedo /tɔrˈpidoʊ/ [*noun; plural* **torpedoes**] a weapon like a bomb that a ship fires under the surface of the water at another ship

torrent /ˈtɔrənt/ [*noun*] a large amount of water that flows with a lot of force: *The river bank was washed away by a torrent of water.*

tortilla /tɔrˈtiyə/ [*noun; plural* **tortillas**] a flat round bread made from ground corn or wheat flour: *Tortillas are used in Mexican cooking.*

tortoise /ˈtɔrtəs/ [*noun*] an animal with a hard round shell on its body that moves slowly and lives mainly on land
⭢ *Compare* TURTLE.

tortoiseshell /ˈtɔrtəsˌʃɛl/ [*noun*] a hard brown and yellow material, used especially for making combs and jewelry: *glasses with tortoiseshell frames*

torture[1] /ˈtɔrtʃɚ/ [*noun*] when someone deliberately hurts someone else physically in order to make him or her give information

torture[2] [*verb; tortured, torturing*] to deliberately hurt someone else physically in order to make him or her give information: *He refused to say anything, even when tortured.*

toss /tɔs/ [*verb; tosses, tossed, tossing*]
1 to throw something in a careless way: *He tossed the letter into the wastebasket.*

— PHRASE —
2 toss and turn to move a lot when you are in bed because you cannot sleep: *She spent the whole night tossing and turning.*

total[1] * /ˈtoʊtəl/ [*adjective; no comparative*]
1 including everything, or to the greatest degree that is possible: *The party was a total disaster.*
⭢ *Compare* COMPLETE[1] (definition 2).

— PHRASE —
2 total amount/number/etc. the number or amount after everything has been added together: *The total cost of the repairs was $1,000.*

total[2] * [*noun*] the number or amount after everything has been added together: *He earned a total of $30,000 last year.* | *In total, 260 people ran in the race.*

totally /ˈtoʊtəli/ [*adverb*] as much as is possible, or in every possible way; synonym COMPLETELY: *We were totally exhausted after our hike.* | *You are totally wrong!*

touch[1] * /tʌtʃ/ [*verb; touches, touched, touching*]
1 to put your hand or finger onto someone or something: *Please do not touch the photographs.* | *He touched her hand gently.*
⭢ *Compare* FEEL (definition 4).
2 if two things touch, or if one thing touches another, there is no space between them: *They sat close together, their shoulders touching.* | *When he stood up, his head almost touched the ceiling.*

touch[2] * [*noun*]
1 when someone touches someone or something: *He felt the touch of her hand on his shoulder.*

— PHRASES —
2 get in touch (with) to write to someone or to speak to someone on

/i/ **see**	/ɪ/ **big**	/eɪ/ **day**	/ɛ/ **get**	/æ/ **hat**
/ɑ/ **father, hot**	/ʌ/ **up**	/ə/ **about**	/ɔ/ **saw**	
/oʊ/ **hope**	/ʊ/ **book**	/u/ **too**	/aɪ/ **I**	/aʊ/ **how**
/ɔɪ/ **boy**	/ɚ/ **bird**	/ɚ/ **teacher**	/ɪr/ **ear**	/ɛr/ **air**
/ɑr/ **far**	/ɔr/ **more**	/ʊr/ **tour**	/aɪr/ **fire**	
/aʊɚ/ **hour**	/θ/ **nothing**	/ð/ **mother**	/ʃ/ **she**	
/ʒ/ **measure**	/tʃ/ **church**	/dʒ/ **jump**	/ŋ/ **long**	

the telephone: *I'll get in touch with you next week.*

3 be/keep/stay in touch
  a to continue to write or talk to someone although you no longer see him or her very often: *I'm still in touch with most of my college friends.*
  b to have the most recent information or knowledge about something: *It's important to keep in touch with the news.*

4 be/feel out of touch to no longer have information or knowledge of something: *It's been so long since I left home, I feel out of touch with events there.*

5 a touch of something a small amount of something: *"I wish I could go too," she said, with a touch of sadness.*

touchdown /'tʌtʃ͵daʊn/ [*noun*] when a team scores in the game of football by carrying or throwing the ball into the area at the end of the field: *Denver just scored its second touchdown of the game.*

touched /tʌtʃt/ [*adjective;* **more touched, most touched**] pleased because someone has been kind to you: *We were touched by your letter.*

touching /'tʌtʃɪŋ/ [*adjective;* **more touching, most touching**] making you feel an emotion such as sympathy or sadness: *It's a touching story of a little girl's struggle against cancer.*

touchy /'tʌtʃi/ [*adjective;* **touchier, touchiest**] easily offended or upset: *You're very touchy tonight. Is something wrong?*

tough /tʌf/ [*adjective;* **tougher, toughest**]
  1 difficult to do or deal with; synonym HARD; opposite EASY: *The journalist asked some tough questions. | This year has been tough, but we'll get through it.*
  2 able to deal with difficulties and not easily hurt or upset: *He is one of the toughest competitors I know.*
  3 difficult to bite or eat; opposite TENDER: *This steak's a little tough.*
  4 very strict: *Many people think the gun laws should be much tougher.*

— PHRASE —

5 tough (luck)! SPOKEN used to show that you do not feel any sympathy for someone: *"I'm hungry." "Tough! You should have eaten earlier."*

tour[1] /tʊr/ [*noun*]
  1 a journey during which you visit different places: *We're going on a two-week tour of Italy.*
  2 a short visit to a famous place or building: *We went on a tour of the White House. | a guided tour* (=when a guide takes you around a place and tells you about it)

tour[2] [*verb;* **toured, touring**] to visit different places within a country or area: *We're hoping to tour India next year.*

tourism /'tʊrɪzəm/ [*noun*] the business of providing places to stay and activities for people who are on vacation: *Tourism helps the island's economy.*

tourist * [T] /'tʊrɪst/ [*noun*] someone who visits or stays in a place while he or she is on vacation: *The streets were packed with tourists.*

tournament /'tʊrnəmənt/ [*noun*] a competition that involves many players or teams: *a golf tournament*

tow /toʊ/ [*verb;* **towed, towing**] to pull a vehicle or boat by attaching a rope or chain to it: *Our car broke down and we were towed to the garage.*

toward * /tɔrd/ or **towards** /tɔrdz/ [*preposition*]
  1 in the direction of someone or something: *We started driving toward Phoenix. | A woman was hurrying down the road toward us.*
  ⇨ Compare AWAY (definition 1).
  2 used to show who or what is affected by something: *You should have a better attitude toward your work. | He felt great anger toward her.*
  3 almost at a particular time: *The rain stopped toward evening. | It was getting on toward 9:00.*

USAGE   toward, to

  Toward is used to talk about a direction: *We drove toward town for a mile, then turned east.* **To** is used to talk about a direction and the place where you arrive: *We drove to town* (=we drove all the way there).

towel /'taʊəl/ [*noun*] a piece of thick material used for drying things or parts of your body: *a bath towel* | *a kitchen towel*

tower * /'taʊɚ/ [*noun*] a tall narrow building or a tall narrow part on top of a building: *We could see the castle towers in the distance.*

town * /taʊn/ [*noun*]
1 a place with houses and businesses that is smaller than a city: *She's from a small town in northern California.*
— PHRASES
2 **be out of town** to be away for a short time from a particular city or town: *I'll be out of town for a week.*
3 **be in town** to be staying for a short time in a particular city or town: *The circus is in town.*

town hall /'taʊn 'hɔl/ [*noun*] a large public building used by the government of a town

toxic 🔲 /'taksɪk/ [*adjective*; **more toxic, most toxic**] containing poisonous substances: *This is where they store toxic chemicals.*

toy * /tɔɪ/ [*noun; plural* **toys**] an object that is especially made for children to play with: *It's time to put your toys away.* | *a toy train set*

trace[1] 🔲 /treɪs/ [*verb;* **traced, tracing**]
1 to copy a drawing or design by putting a piece of thin paper on it and drawing over the lines: *Did you draw that yourself, or did you trace it?*
2 to find someone or something: *Police are still trying to trace the stolen car.*

trace[2] [*noun*] a sign that something exists or existed: *There were no traces of life on the island.*

track[1] * /træk/ [*noun*]
1 a path or road with a rough surface: *A dirt track led to the farmhouse.*
2 the metal lines along which a train travels: *a railroad track*
3 a wide flat path or road where races take place; synonym RACETRACK: *The cars kept skidding on the wet track.*

4 the sport of running: *He is on the high school track team.*
5 **tracks** [*plural*] the marks made on the ground by the feet of an animal or person or by a vehicle: *The deer tracks went right through our backyard.* | *tire tracks*
— PHRASE
6 **keep/lose track of** to know or not know something about a situation: *I always try to keep track of what's in the news.* | *I'm late—I lost track of the time.*

track[2] [*verb;* **tracked, tracking**]
— PHRASAL VERB
track down [*phrasal verb*]
to find someone or something after searching for a long time: **track someone/something down** ▸ *The police finally tracked him down in Chicago.*

track and field /'træk ən 'fild/ [*noun*] sports that consist of running, jumping, or throwing

tractor /'træktɚ/ [*noun*] a large vehicle used by farmers for pulling farm machines

trade[1] * /treɪd/ [*noun*]
1 the activity of buying and selling goods: **Trade between** *the U.S. and China is increasing.*
▷ Compare BUSINESS (definition 1).
2 a kind of business activity: *The **tourist trade** was hurt by the bad weather.* | *I'm a carpenter **by trade** (=I work as a carpenter).*

trade[2] [*verb;* **traded, trading**]
1 to buy and sell goods: *We now **trade with** countries in Eastern Europe.* | *a company that **trades in** leather goods*
2 to give someone something in exchange for something he or she gives you: *"I don't like this seat." "I'll **trade with** you."* | **trade someone something for something** ▸ *I'll trade you this shirt for your baseball cap.*

/i/ **see** /ɪ/ **big** /eɪ/ **day** /ɛ/ **get** /æ/ **hat** /ɑ/ **father, hot** /ʌ/ **up** /ə/ **about** /ɔ/ **saw** /oʊ/ **hope** /ʊ/ **book** /u/ **too** /aɪ/ **I** /aʊ/ **how** /ɔɪ/ **boy** /ɝ/ **bird** /ɚ/ **teacher** /ɪr/ **ear** /ɛr/ **air** /ɑr/ **far** /ɔr/ **more** /ʊr/ **tour** /aɪr/ **fire** /aʊɚ/ **hour** /θ/ **nothing** /ð/ **mother** /ʃ/ **she** /ʒ/ **measure** /tʃ/ **church** /dʒ/ **jump** /ŋ/ **long**

trademark /'treɪd,mɑrk/ [*noun*] a word or a sign used by a particular company on its products

trader /'treɪdɚ/ [*noun*] someone whose job is buying and selling: *Many of the early Western pioneers were fur traders. | His sister is a stock trader.*

tradition ⊤ /trə'dɪʃən/ [*noun*] a way of doing something that a group of people follow for a long time: *It's a family tradition to go to the beach each summer.*

traditional * ⊤ /trə'dɪʃənəl/ [*adjective*; more traditional, most traditional]
1 connected with the traditions of a country or group of people: *The dancers wore traditional Russian costumes.*
2 traditional methods have existed for a long time and are not influenced by modern ideas: *The teachers here use very traditional teaching methods.*

traditionally * /trə'dɪʃənəli/ [*adverb*] in a way that follows a tradition: *Traditionally, Americans eat turkey on Thanksgiving Day.*

traffic * /'træfɪk/ [*noun*] the vehicles that are moving along a road or within an area: *There's heavy traffic (=a lot of traffic) this morning.*
☛ Do not say that "Traffic is crowded." Say **There is a lot of traffic** or **The traffic is heavy**.

traffic jam /'træfɪk ,dʒæm/ [*noun*] a long line of vehicles on a road that cannot move or can only move slowly: *I was stuck in a traffic jam for over an hour.*

traffic light /'træfɪk ,laɪt/ [*noun*] a set of red, yellow, and green lights on a street, that control traffic; *synonym* STOPLIGHT

tragedy /'trædʒɪdi/ [*noun*; plural tragedies]
1 an extremely sad or terrible event: *It's a tragedy he died so young. | The voyage ended in tragedy (=many people died).*
2 a serious play about sad events in which the main character usually dies
☼ Compare COMEDY.

tragic /'trædʒɪk/ [*adjective*; more tragic, most tragic] a tragic event or situation is extremely sad, especially because someone dies: *a tragic accident*

trail¹ /treɪl/ [*verb*; trailed, trailing]
1 to be losing a game or competition: *The San Diego team is trailing Atlanta. | They're trailing 2–1.*
2 to walk more slowly than other people so that you are behind them: *The kids trailed along behind their parents.*

trail² [*noun*] a rough path through fields or a forest: *There's a nice trail around the lake.*

trailer /'treɪlɚ/ [*noun*]
1 a large structure with wheels that can be pulled behind a car, used for living in during a vacation
2 a small house that can be moved but is usually kept in one place; *synonym* MOBILE HOME: *They live in a trailer park (=a place where many trailers are).*
3 a large container or frame that is pulled behind a car and used for carrying heavy objects or large animals: *a horse trailer*

train¹ * /treɪn/ [*noun*] a set of connected railroad cars that people or goods travel on: *What time does the train leave for New York? | I rarely travel by train.*
☛ Do not say "travel by a train" or "travel by the train." Say **travel by train**.

train² * [*verb*; trained, training]
1 to teach or learn the skills to do a job or activity: **train to do something** ▸ *He's training to be an accountant. |* **train someone in something** ▸ *We train people in basic computer skills.*
☛ Do not say "We will train you a teacher." Say **We will train you to be a teacher**.
2 to prepare for a sports event by practicing or doing physical exercise, or to make someone do this: *I spent eight hours a day training for the race.*
☛ Do not say "train on a race." Say **train for a race**.
☼ See the synonym note at PRACTICE².

trainee ⊤ /treɪ'ni/ [*noun*; plural trainees] someone who is learning the skills to do a job: *a management trainee*

trainer /'treɪnɚ/ [noun] someone who helps people to practice for a sports event or to keep fit and healthy: *Most top athletes have their own personal trainer.*

training * /'treɪnɪŋ/ [noun]
1 when you do physical exercises in order to prepare for a sports event or to stay fit: *Training begins two months before the baseball season starts.*
2 when you learn the skills that are necessary to do a job: *You will need to go to the main office for training.* | *a six-week training course*

traitor /'treɪtɚ/ [noun] someone who is not loyal to his or her country or friends

trample /'træmpəl/ [verb; trampled, trampling] to walk with a lot of force on something and damage it: *Don't trample on the flowers.* | *The whole garden was trampled.*

trampoline /ˌtræmpə'lin/ [noun] a large piece of sports equipment that you jump up and down on

transfer[1] /træns'fɚ/ [verb; transfers, transferred, transferring] to move from one place to another, or to make people or things do this: **transfer to** ▸ *She's transferring to Ohio State University next year.* | **transfer something to** ▸ *Medical supplies are being transferred to the area.*

transfer[2] /'trænsfɚ/ [noun] when someone or something moves from one place, organization, or position to another: *I'm hoping to get a transfer to Michigan* (=work for the same company in Michigan).

transform /træns'fɔrm/ [verb; transformed, transforming] to change someone or something completely: *Losing weight has transformed her.*

transitive * /'trænsɪtɪv/ [adjective; no comparative] GRAMMAR a transitive verb has an object. Examples are "put" and "bring": *In the sentence, "She sang a song," "sang" is transitive.*
↪ Compare INTRANSITIVE.

translate * /'trænsleɪt/ [verb; translated, translating] to change speech or writing from one language

into another: *It's very difficult to translate poetry.* | *Translate this passage from German into English.*
↪ Compare INTERPRET.

translation /træns'leɪʃən/ [noun] a piece of writing that has the same meaning as a piece that is written in a different language: *We had to do an English translation for homework.* | *It's a good translation of the book.*

translator /'trænsleɪtɚ/ [noun] someone who translates books and documents as his or her job
↪ Compare INTERPRETER.

transparent * /træns'pɛrənt/ [adjective; more transparent, most transparent] a transparent object is easy to see through because light can pass through it: *transparent glass* | *transparent curtain*
↪ See the synonym note at CLEAR[1].

transplant /'træns,plænt/ [noun] a medical operation in which an organ from a someone's body is put into another person's body: *a heart transplant*

transport [T] /træns'pɔrt/ [verb; transported, transporting] to take goods or people from one place to another in a car, plane, train, etc.: *How will you transport all the equipment?*

transportation [T] /ˌtrænspɚ'teɪʃən/ [noun]
1 vehicles or systems that make it possible for people to travel from one place to another: *I had no means of transportation* (=I had no car, bicycle, etc.). | *The city has good public transportation.*
2 when people or goods travel from one place to another: *Transportation of goods to the island is done mainly by boat.*

trap[1] * [T] /træp/ [noun]
1 a piece of equipment for catching an animal: *a bear trap*
2 a plan that is intended to deceive or

/i/ **see**	/ɪ/ **big**	/eɪ/ **day**	/ɛ/ **get**	/æ/ **hat**	
/ɑ/ **father, hot**	/ʌ/ **up**	/ə/ **about**	/ɔ/ **saw**		
/oʊ/ **hope**	/ʊ/ **book**	/u/ **too**	/aɪ/ **I**	/aʊ/ **how**	
/ɔɪ/ **boy**	/ɚ/ **bird**	/ɚ/ teacher	/ɪr/ **ear**	/ɛr/ **air**	
/ɑr/ **far**	/ɔr/ **more**	/ʊr/ **tour**	/aɪr/ **fire**		
/aʊɚ/ **hour**	/θ/ **nothing**	/ð/ mother	/ʃ/ **she**		
/ʒ/ **measure**	/tʃ/ **church**	/dʒ/ **jump**	/ŋ/ **long**		

catch someone: *They set a trap for her to see if she was the one who was stealing.*

trap² * ⊤ [*verb*; **traps, trapped, trapping**]
1 to catch an animal in a piece of equipment: *The hunters trap animals for their fur.*
— PHRASE
2 be trapped to be in a unpleasant or dangerous situation from which you cannot escape: *A woman was trapped inside the wrecked car.*

trash /træʃ/ [*noun*]
1 waste material such as paper and empty containers, or a container you put this in: *The trash goes outside in plastic bags.* | *Put these cartons in the trash.*
↪ Compare GARBAGE.
2 INFORMAL something that is of very bad quality: *Her books are just trash.*

trash can /'træʃ ˌkæn/ [*noun*] a large container for waste material that is usually kept outside; synonym GARBAGE CAN: *The trash can's already full.*

travel¹ * /'trævəl/ [*verb*; **traveled, traveling**]
1 to go from one place to another in a vehicle, plane, etc.: *They spent three months traveling around Australia.* | *She has traveled the world in her job.*
2 to move at a particular speed or over a particular distance: *The new trains can travel at 400 km per hour.* | *I travel 50 miles to work every day.*

travel² * [*noun*] when people travel in cars, planes, etc.: *Foreign travel is an important part of the job.*
☛ Do not say "a travel." Say **a trip**.

travel agency /'trævəl ˌeɪdʒənsi/ [*noun*; *plural* **travel agencies**] a place that arranges travel and vacations for people

travel agent /'trævəl ˌeɪdʒənt/ [*noun*] someone who works in or owns a travel agency

traveler * /'trævələ·/ [*noun*] someone who is on a trip

traveler's check /'trævələ·z ˌtʃɛk/ [*noun*] a check that you can exchange for money in a foreign country

tray /treɪ/ [*noun*; *plural* **trays**] a flat object used for carrying drinks, food, etc.: *He brought me my breakfast on a tray.* | *a tray of drinks*

treason /'trizən/ [*noun*] the crime of not being loyal to your country or government

treasure¹ /'trɛʒə·/ [*noun*] gold, silver, or jewels, especially when they are found together in the same place: *a pirate's hidden treasure*

treasure² [*verb*; **treasured, treasuring**] to consider someone or something to be very valuable or important: *We treasure the time we spend together.*

treat¹ * /trit/ [*verb*; **treated, treating**]
1 to behave in a particular way toward someone: *Her husband treats her very well.* | *Stop treating me like an idiot!*
2 to deal with something in a particular way: *The problems faced by young people shouldn't be treated lightly.*
3 to try to make an illness or wound better using drugs, medical operations, etc.: *There are several ways to treat the disease.* | *He is being treated for a broken leg.*
☛ Do not say "treat someone of something." Say **treat someone for something**.
4 to buy or do something special for someone: *I'm going to treat the kids to a trip to the zoo.*

treat² [*noun*] something special that you give to someone or do for him or her: *I often buy ice cream as a treat.*

treatment * /'tritmənt/ [*noun*]
1 drugs, medical operations, etc., that are used to make an illness or wound better: *Scientists are working on new cancer treatments.* | *He received treatment for a strained leg muscle.*
2 a way of behaving toward someone: *We give all the students equal treatment* (=everyone is treated the same).

treaty /'triti/ [*noun*; *plural* **treaties**] an official agreement between two or more countries: *a new peace treaty*

tree * /tri/ [*noun*; *plural* **trees**] a very tall plant with branches, leaves, and a large trunk: *a cherry tree* | *She has always loved climbing trees.*

tremble /'trɛmbəl/ [verb; trembled, trembling] to shake, especially because you are afraid or angry: *I was so scared my legs began to tremble.* | *Bill was trembling with rage.*

tremendous ⊤ /trɪ'mɛndəs/ [adjective; more tremendous, most tremendous] used to emphasize how fast, big, loud, etc., something is: *These animals can run at a tremendous speed.*

tremor /'trɛmɚ/ [noun] a shaking movement, especially of your body or of the ground

trench /trɛntʃ/ [noun; plural trenches] a long narrow hole that has been dug into the ground

trend ⊤ /trɛnd/ [noun] the way a situation changes and develops: *There's a trend toward working from home.*

trendy /'trɛndi/ [adjective; trendier, trendiest] modern and fashionable; *synonym* IN; *opposite* OUT: *trendy clothes*

trespass /'trɛspæs/ [verb; trespasses, trespassed, trespassing] to go onto land owned by someone without his or her permission: *If I catch you trespassing again, I'll call the police.*

trespasser /'trɛspæsɚ/ [noun] someone who goes onto land owned by someone without his or her permission: *Trespassers keep out!*

trial /'traɪəl/ [noun]
1 a legal process in which a court of law decides whether someone is guilty or not guilty, and his or her punishment is decided: *a murder trial* | *He is on trial for robbery.*
2 a test to see whether something works well: *All our vehicles go through safety trials.* | *New customers can take the equipment on trial for 30 days.*
— PHRASE —
3 **trial and error** when you do something in different ways to see which way is the best: *I learned a lot of my computer skills by trial and error.*

triangle /'traɪˌæŋgəl/ [noun] a flat shape with three sides and three angles
⇨ *See* Shapes *in the Smart Study section.*

triangular /traɪ'æŋgyələ/ [adjective; no comparative] having three sides and three angles

tribe * /traɪb/ [noun] a group of people of the same race who live in a particular area and have the same customs and beliefs: *He was the leader of an African tribe.*

tributary /'trɪbyəˌtɛri/ [noun; plural tributaries] a small river that flows into a larger river

tribute /'trɪbyut/ [noun]
1 something that you say or do to praise someone or to show that you admire him or her: *At the ceremony, we will pay tribute to our veterans.*
— PHRASE —
2 **be a tribute to** to clearly show the good qualities of someone or something: *The team's success is a tribute to the coach's hard work.*

trick[1] * /trɪk/ [noun]
1 a plan to deceive someone: *It's just a trick to try to get your money.*
2 something smart and unusual that you do that looks like magic: *Dad enjoys teaching us card tricks.*
— PHRASE —
3 **play a trick on someone** to do something silly to someone in order to make people laugh: *They're always playing tricks on their little sister.*

trick[2] * ⊤ [verb; tricked, tricking] to do something in order to deceive someone: **trick someone into doing something** ▸ *She was tricked into signing the contract.*

trickle /'trɪkəl/ [verb; trickled, trickling] if a liquid trickles, it flows slowly in small drops: *Raindrops trickled down the window.*

tricky /'trɪki/ [adjective; trickier, trickiest or more tricky, most tricky] difficult or confusing: *a tricky math problem*

tricycle /'traɪsɪkəl/ [noun] a bicycle with three wheels

tried * /traɪd/ [verb] the past tense and past participle of TRY[1]

/i/ see	/ɪ/ big	/eɪ/ day	/ɛ/ get	/æ/ hat
/ɑ/ father, hot	/ʌ/ up	/ə/ about	/ɔ/ saw	
/oʊ/ hope	/ʊ/ book	/u/ too	/aɪ/ I	/aʊ/ how
/ɔɪ/ boy	/ɚ/ bird	/ə/ teacher	/ɪr/ ear	/ɛr/ air
/ɑr/ far	/ɔr/ more	/ʊr/ tour	/aɪr/ fire	
/aʊə/ hour	/θ/ nothing	/ð/ mother	/ʃ/ she	
/ʒ/ measure	/tʃ/ church	/dʒ/ jump	/ŋ/ long	

trigger /'trɪgɚ/ [noun] the part of a gun that you pull with your finger to fire it

trim /trɪm/ [verb; **trims, trimmed, trimming**] to cut small pieces off something to make it neater: *Could you trim my hair at the back?*

trio /'triou/ [noun; plural **trios**] three musicians or singers who perform together, or music for this: *He plays in a jazz trio.*

trip[1] * /trɪp/ [noun] a short journey, especially one you will return from: *We're **taking a** boat **trip** around the islands.* | *a weekly **trip to** the grocery store* | *He's away on **a business trip**.*
⇨ *See also* ROUND TRIP[1].

trip[2] * [verb; **trips, tripped, tripping**]
   1 to fall or almost fall from hitting something with your foot as you are walking or running: *He **tripped on** the hose and hurt his ankle.*
   2 to make someone fall as he or she is moving by putting your foot in front of him or her: *Sorry—I didn't mean to trip you.*

triple[1] T /'trɪpəl/ [adjective; no comparative]
   1 three times the usual amount or size: *a **triple scoop** ice-cream cone* (=with three balls of ice cream)
   2 done three times: *He did a **triple** somersault.*
   ☛ Only use **triple** before a noun.

triple[2] T [verb; **tripled, tripling**] to become three times as big, or to make something three times as big: *The number of students has tripled during the past season.* | *We tripled our profits last year.*

triplet /'trɪplɪt/ [noun] one of three children who are born to the same mother at the same time
⇨ *Compare* TWIN[1].

triumph[1] T /'traɪʌmf/ [noun] an impressive victory or success, or the feeling you get when you achieve this

triumph[2] [verb; **triumphed, triumphing**] to achieve an impressive victory or success: *It was a hard game, but Chicago eventually triumphed.*

trolley /'trali/ [noun; plural **trolleys**] a vehicle connected to electric wires that

moves along tracks on a street: *the trolleys in San Francisco*

trolley car /'trali ˌkar/ [noun] a TROLLEY

trombone /tram'boun/ [noun] a metal MUSICAL INSTRUMENT with a part you blow into and another part you push forward and backward: *I'm learning to **play the trombone**.*

troops /trups/ [plural noun] soldiers considered as a group: *The sergeant ordered his troops to fire.*

trophy /'troufi/ [noun; plural **trophies**] a special object you get when you win a competition or race

tropical * /'trapɪkəl/ [adjective; no comparative] related to the areas of the world closest to the equator (=the line around the middle of the earth), where the weather is very hot and wet: *Much of the **tropical rain forest** is being destroyed.* | *a **tropical storm***

tropics /'trapɪks/ [plural noun] **the tropics** the areas of the world closest to the middle of the earth, where the weather is very hot and wet: *Many rare animals live in the tropics.*

trot /trat/ [verb; **trots, trotted, trotting**] if a horse trots, it moves fairly quickly but does not run: *The horses trotted around the arena.*

trouble[1] * /'trʌbəl/ [noun]
   1 problems that make a situation difficult to deal with, make you worried, etc.: *I can always tell her my troubles.* | *If there's any trouble, just call the police.* | *We're **having trouble with** the computers at work.* | *Why do you always **cause trouble**?*
   2 a difficult or dangerous situation: *We **got in trouble** when the car broke down in the storm.*
   3 a physical or health problem: *heart trouble* | *Dad has trouble hearing.*
   4 the effort or work that is needed to do something: *She **went to a lot of trouble** preparing a meal for everyone.* | *They **took a lot of trouble to** make us all feel welcome.*
— PHRASES
   5 be in trouble/get into trouble to be likely to be punished because you have done something wrong or illegal:

He's always **getting into trouble with** the teacher.

6 the trouble with SPOKEN used when you are explaining what is wrong with a person or situation: *The trouble with you is that you worry too much.*

trouble[2] [*verb*; **troubled, troubling**]
FORMAL
1 to ask someone to do something that may involve an effort: *Could I trouble you for the time?* (=What time is it?)
2 to make someone worried: *What's troubling you?*

troubled /'trʌbəld/ [*adjective*; **more troubled, most troubled**] having problems that make you feel very upset and worried: *He had a troubled look on his face.*

trough /trɔf/ [*noun*] a long narrow container that animals eat or drink from

trousers * /'traʊzəz/ [*plural noun*] a piece of CLOTHING that covers your legs with a separate part for each leg; synonym PANTS: *I only have one pair of trousers.*

trout /traʊt/ [*noun; plural* **trout**] a kind of fish that lives in rivers and lakes, or the meat of the fish: *We caught three trout yesterday.*

truant /'truənt/ [*noun*] a student who stays away from school without permission: *Much daytime crime is committed by truants.*

truancy /'truənsi/ [*noun*] when students stay away from school without permission: *Truancy is not a big problem in this school.*

truck * /trʌk/ [*noun*] a large vehicle that has a motor and is used for carrying heavy goods: *He drives a big truck for a furniture company.* | *a delivery truck*
⇨ See also PICKUP TRUCK. ⇨ Compare VAN.

trudge /trʌdʒ/ [*verb*; **trudged, trudging**] to walk slowly, usually because you are tired: *He trudged up the hill carrying a heavy suitcase.*

true * T /tru/ [*adjective*; **truer, truest**]
1 based on fact and not imaginary or made up; opposites FALSE, UNTRUE: *Are the following statements true or false?* |

His book is based on *a true story.*
⇨ See also TRUTH.

━━ PHRASES ━━
2 true love/friendship/courage/ etc. love, friendship, etc., that is strong and continues for a long time: *She showed true courage in fighting her illness.*
3 come true if your dreams, hopes, etc., come true, the things you want to happen do happen: *Being on TV was a dream come true for me.*
☛ Do not say that something "turns true." Say that it **comes true.**

truly T /'truli/ [*adverb*]
1 used to emphasize that you are being sincere and honest: *I truly believe what he said.*
2 used to emphasize that what you are saying or describing is true: *She's truly one of the best athletes I've seen.*

━━ PHRASE ━━
3 Yours truly written at the end of a formal letter before you sign your name: *Yours truly, Anna Banks*

trumpet /'trʌmpɪt/ [*noun*] a metal MUSICAL INSTRUMENT with a part you blow into and three buttons that you press: *It's hard to play the trumpet.*

trunk * /trʌŋk/ [*noun*]
1 the long thick stem of a tree: *A squirrel ran up the tree trunk.*
2 the separate space at the back of a CAR where you can put large objects: *Put your suitcases in the trunk.*
3 a very large box for storing clothes, books, etc.
4 the long thin nose of an ELEPHANT
5 trunks [*plural*] short pants that a man wears when he goes swimming: *Don't forget to pack a pair of trunks.*
⇨ See also BATHING SUIT, SWIMSUIT. ⇨ See the picture at CLOTHING.

trust[1] * T /trʌst/ [*verb*; **trusted, trusting**]
1 to believe that someone is honest,

/i/ **see**	/ɪ/ **big**	/eɪ/ **day**	/ɛ/ **get**	/æ/ **hat**
/ɑ/ **father, hot**	/ʌ/ **up**	/ə/ **about**	/ɔ/ **saw**	
/oʊ/ **hope**	/ʊ/ **book**	/u/ **too**	/aɪ/ **I**	/aʊ/ **how**
/ɔɪ/ **boy**	/ɝ/ **bird**	/ɚ/ **teacher**	/ɪr/ **ear**	/ɛr/ **air**
/ɑr/ **far**	/ɔr/ **more**	/ʊr/ **tour**	/aɪr/ **fire**	
/aʊə/ **hour**	/θ/ **nothing**	/ð/ **mother**	/ʃ/ **she**	
/ʒ/ **measure**	/tʃ/ **church**	/dʒ/ **jump**	/ŋ/ **long**	

kind, etc., and will not deceive or disappoint you: *She needs to talk to someone she can trust.* | **trust someone to do something** ▸ *Can I trust you to keep a secret?*

— PHRASAL VERB —

trust in [*phrasal verb*]
2 to believe that you can depend on someone or something: **trust in someone/something** ▸ *You should trust in your own abilities more.*

trust² * [*noun*] the belief that someone is kind and honest and will not deceive or disappoint you: *You have to put your trust in your teammates* (=you must trust them).

trusting /'trʌstɪŋ/ [*adjective;* **more trusting, most trusting**] willing to trust other people: *She has a very trusting nature.*
⟳ *Compare* SUSPICIOUS.

trustworthy /'trʌst,wɜ˞ði/ [*adjective;* **more trustworthy, most trustworthy**] able to be trusted: *My father is an honest, trustworthy man.*

truth * /truθ/ [*noun*]
1 **the truth** the true facts about something: *We'll never know the truth about what happened.* | *Is she telling the truth?*
2 the quality of being based on fact, not imagined or made up: *There is no truth in the rumor that he's going to quit.*
⟳ *See also* TRUE.

truthful /'truθfəl/ [*adjective;* **more truthful, most truthful**] honest or giving the true facts about something: *He wasn't being completely truthful.*

try¹ * /traɪ/ [*verb;* **tries, tried, trying**]
1 to make an effort to do something, without knowing if you are going to be successful; *synonym* ATTEMPT: *I can't unlock this door. Will you try?* | **try (not) to do something** ▸ *She tried hard not to cry.* | **try doing something** ▸ *Try pedaling a little faster.*
2 to use or test something to discover if it works, if it is good, etc.: *Perhaps we should try out a different method.* | *Try this sauce—it's delicious.* | **try doing something** ▸ *You should try getting*

more exercise. | **try out something** ▸ *Let's try out the new equipment.*
☞ Do not say "try out it." Say **try it out.**
3 to examine someone in a court of law to discover whether he or she is guilty of a crime: *She was tried for murder.*

— PHRASE —

4 **try your best** to make the biggest effort you can: *You should always try your best, even if it's hard.*

— PHRASAL VERB —

try on [*phrasal verb*]
5 to put on a piece of clothing to find out whether it fits you: **try something on** ▸ *Would you like to try the dress on?* | **try on something** ▸ *I want to try on these shoes.*

try² [*noun; plural* **tries**] when you make an effort to do something, without knowing if you are going to be successful; *synonym* ATTEMPT: *Okay, I'll give it a try.* | *That was quite good for a first try.*

tryout /'traɪ,aʊt/ [*noun*] a test to find out if someone is good enough to do something: *He has a tryout for the school football team today.*

T-shirt or **tee shirt** /'ti,ʃɜ˞t/ [*noun*] a light cotton shirt, usually with short sleeves
⟳ *See the picture at* CLOTHING.

tsp the written abbreviation of TEASPOON or TEASPOONS; *synonyms* T, T.: *Add 2 tsp vanilla and stir well.*

tub /tʌb/ [*noun*]
1 a large container that you fill with water and sit in to wash your body; *synonym* BATHTUB: *Is she still in the tub?*
2 a small plastic food container with a lid: *a tub of margarine*

tuba /'tubə/ [*noun; plural* **tubas**] a large metal MUSICAL INSTRUMENT that makes a very low sound when you blow into it: *He's learning to play the tuba.*

tube * /tub/ [*noun*]
1 a long hollow pipe that liquids or gases go through
2 a long narrow CONTAINER that is closed at one end and that you press to push a substance out: *Is there any*

glue left in the tube? | *a **tube of toothpaste***

tuck /tʌk/ [*verb;* **tucked, tucking**]
  1 to push the edge of a piece of material firmly under something: *Tuck the sheet **under** the mattress.* | *He tucked his shirt **into** his pants.*
  2 to put something into a space where it fits tightly or is safe: *She tucked her hair up under her hat.*

  ━━ PHRASAL VERB ━━
  tuck in [*phrasal verb*]
  3 to make a child comfortable in bed by putting the covers around him or her: **tuck someone in** ▸ *I'll come upstairs soon and tuck you in.*

Tues. the written abbreviation of TUESDAY

Tuesday ∗ /'tuzdeɪ/ [*noun; plural* **Tuesdays**] the day of the week that is after Monday and before Wednesday: *Are you doing anything **on Tuesday**?* | *I have an art class **on Tuesdays**.*
  ⇨ *See the usage note at DAY.*

tug[1] /tʌg/ [*verb;* **tugs, tugged, tugging**] to pull something with a sudden quick movement: *Her son **tugged at** her arm.*

tug[2] [*noun*]
  1 also **tugboat** /'tʌg,boʊt/ a small strong boat used for pulling ships: *A tug guided the ship into the harbor.*
  2 when you suddenly pull something: *Give that rope a tug.*

tug-of-war /'tʌg əv 'wɔr/ [*noun*] a competition in which two teams pull different ends of a rope and try to pull the other team across a line between them

tuition /tu'ɪʃən/ [*noun*] what you pay to go to a university or a private school: *College tuition can be very expensive.*

tulip /'tulɪp/ [*noun*] a brightly colored FLOWER that looks like a tall cup

tumble /'tʌmbəl/ [*verb;* **tumbled, tumbling**] to fall in a series of rolling movements: *He slipped and tumbled downstairs.*

tummy /'tʌmi/ [*noun; plural* **tummies**] INFORMAL someone's stomach: *She tickled the baby's tummy.* | *You'll get a **tummy ache** if you eat too much candy.*

tumor /'tumɚ/ [*noun*] a group of cells in someone's body that grow too quickly and can make him or her very ill

tuna /'tunə/ [*noun; plural* **tunas**] a large ocean fish, or the meat of this fish: *a tuna sandwich*

tuna fish /'tunə ˌfɪʃ/ [*noun; plural* **tuna fish**] another word for TUNA: *tuna fish salad*

tune[1] ∗ /tun/ [*noun*]
  1 the notes that make up a song or a piece of music: *He whistled a little tune to himself.*

  ━━ PHRASES ━━
  2 in tune if music is in tune, it has the correct musical notes: *She doesn't sing in tune.*
  3 out of tune if music is out of tune, the notes are too high or too low: *The violins sounded out of tune.*

tune[2] [*verb;* **tuned, tuning**]
  1 to make changes to the strings of a musical instrument so that it plays notes correctly: *We must get the piano tuned.*

  ━━ PHRASAL VERB ━━
  tune in [*phrasal verb*]
  2 to make a radio or television receive a program by moving its controls: **tune in something** ▸ *We can't tune in that station.*
  3 to listen to or watch a radio or television program: *Don't forget to **tune in for** next week's final show.*

tune-up /'tun ˌʌp/ [*noun*] when someone cleans a vehicle's engine and makes sure it is operating well

tunnel /'tʌnəl/ [*noun*] a passage built under the ground for people, cars, or trains to use: *The train disappeared into a tunnel.*

turban /'tɝbən/ [*noun*] a long piece of cloth that is wound around the head, worn especially by men in parts of southern Asia

/i/ see	/ɪ/ big	/eɪ/ day	/ɛ/ get	/æ/ hat
/a/ father, hot	/ʌ/ up	/ə/ about	/ɔ/ saw	
/oʊ/ hope	/ʊ/ book	/u/ too	/aɪ/ I	/aʊ/ how
/ɔɪ/ boy	/ɝ/ bird	/ɚ/ teacher	/ɪr/ ear	/ɛr/ air
/ɑr/ far	/ɔr/ more	/ʊr/ tour	/aɪr/ fire	
/aʊɚ/ hour	/θ/ nothing	/ð/ mother	/ʃ/ she	
/ʒ/ measure	/tʃ/ church	/dʒ/ jump	/ŋ/ long	

turkey /'tɜ˞ki/ [*noun; plural* **turkeys**]
a bird that is usually raised on farms
for its meat: *We always have turkey at
Thanksgiving.*

a turkey

turn¹ * /tɜ˞n/ [*verb;* **turned, turning**]
1 to go in a different direction, or to
make something do this: *Turn right at
the next intersection.* I *She turned the car
around and went home.*
2 to move your body so that you are
facing a different direction: *Everyone
turned around when he walked in.* I
Could you all turn to face me, please? I
*Turn over onto your stomach and I'll rub
your back.*
3 to move around a central point, or to
make something do this: *The wheel
began to turn slowly.* I *Turn the key to
the left.*
4 to change from one condition to
another: *The weather has turned cold in
the last few days.* I *Age had turned his
hair completely white.* I *Mom is turning
50 this year* (=she will be 50 years old).
5 to make a different side of something
face up or down: **turn something over** ▸
*Would you help me turn the mattress
over?* I *Turn dark clothes inside out to
wash them.*
— **PHRASES** —
6 turn a/the corner to go around a
corner: *We watched until their car
turned the corner.*
7 turn a/the page to move a page in
a book or magazine in order to read
the next page: *She turned the page and
continued reading.*
— **PHRASAL VERBS** —
turn down [*phrasal verb*]
8 to reduce the amount of heat or noise
produced by a machine: **turn
something down** ▸ *Could you turn the*

volume down, please? I **turn down
something** ▸ *Turn down the oven a
little.*
9 to refuse something such as a request
or invitation: **turn down someone/
something** ▸ *How could you turn down
an offer like that?* I **turn someone/
something down** ▸ *He's afraid she'll
turn him down.*
turn in [*phrasal verb*]
10 to give something that has been lost
or borrowed to a person in authority:
turn in something ▸ *Fortunately,
someone had turned in my coat.* I **turn
something in** ▸ *Please turn your keys in
before 11 a.m.*
turn into [*phrasal verb*]
11 to become something different, or to
make someone or something different:
turn into someone/something ▸ *After
a few weeks, the tadpole turns into a
frog.* I **turn someone/something
into** ▸ *We turned the attic into an office.*
turn off [*phrasal verb*]
12 to make a machine or piece of
equipment stop working: **turn off
something** ▸ *Don't forget to turn off the
lights.* I **turn something off** ▸ *Press
this button to turn the computer off.*
turn on [*phrasal verb*]
13 to make a machine or a piece of
equipment start working: **turn
something on** ▸ *She always turns the
TV on when she gets home.* I **turn on
something** ▸ *Would you turn on that
light?*
turn out [*phrasal verb*]
14 to make an electric light stop
working: **turn something out** ▸ *I
forgot to turn the light out.* I **turn out
something** ▸ *Please turn out the lights
when you leave.*
15 to happen or be finished in a
particular way: *The poster I made
turned out really well.*
turn over [*phrasal verb*]
16 to give someone control of
something or allow him or her to have
it: **turn over something to someone** ▸
*He's turned over the management of the
company to his nephew.* I **turn
something/someone over to**

someone ▸ *We had to turn our records over to the court.*

turn to [phrasal verb]

17 to open a book, magazine, etc., at a particular page: **turn to something** ▸ *Everyone please turn to page 53.*

18 to look for help, advice, etc., from someone or something: **turn to someone/something** ▸ *You're the only one I can turn to.* | *She turned to her work to forget her grief.*

turn up [phrasal verb]

19 to increase the amount of heat or noise produced by a machine: **turn up something** ▸ *Turn up the heat and fry the meat for five minutes.* | **turn something up** ▸ *Can I turn the television up a little?*

20 if something turns up, you find it after thinking you had lost it: *Don't worry—I'm sure your keys will turn up.*

21 to arrive somewhere: *They turned up over an hour late.*

turn² * [noun]

1 when you change the direction in which you are moving: *At the next light,* **make a left turn.**

2 when it is your chance or time to do something: *She* **took** *her* **turn** *already* (=she already did it). | *It's your turn to put out the garbage.*

3 a place where you can go from one road, path, etc., onto another to travel in a different direction: *Take the second turn on the right.*

▬ PHRASE ▬

4 take turns if two or more people take turns doing something, they each do it at different times, especially in order to share work fairly: *We all take turns cleaning the apartment.*

turnip /'tɜ·nɪp/ [noun] a round, pale yellow root that is cooked and eaten as a VEGETABLE

turn signal /'tɜ·n ˌsɪgnəl/ [noun] one of two lights on the back of a car used to show that the car will turn left or right: *It's confusing when drivers don't use their turn signals.*

turntable /'tɜ·nˌteɪbəl/ [noun] the round surface on which you put a record in order to play it: *The DJ put another record on the turntable.*

turquoise¹ /'tɜ·kɔɪz/ [noun]

1 a blue-green stone used for making jewelry

2 a blue-green color: *the bright turquoise of a tropical bay*

turquoise² [adjective; no comparative] of the color turquoise: *a turquoise blouse*

turtle /'tɜ·təl/ [noun] an animal with a hard round shell on its body that lives mainly in water

↪ Compare TORTOISE.

tusk /tʌsk/ [noun] one of the two long pointed teeth of an ELEPHANT, walrus, etc.

tutor¹ /'tutɚ/ [noun] a teacher who gives special training to one student in a subject: *She has a private math tutor.*

tutor² [verb; **tutored, tutoring**] to teach a student: *I tutor after school, two days a week.* | *He is being* **tutored in** *math.*

tuxedo /tʌk'sidoʊ/ [noun; plural **tuxedos**] a man's black suit that is worn on formal social occasions: *Peter looked really good in his tuxedo.*

TV * /'ti'vi/ [noun; plural **TVs** or **TV's**]

1 television; a piece of electronic equipment that has a screen on which you watch programs that are broadcast: *a wide-screen TV*

2 television; the system of broadcasting programs for the television, or the programs themselves: *The kids* **watch** *too much* **TV.**

tweezers /'twizɚz/ [plural noun] a small tool used to pick up or pull on very small things, that is made of two narrow pieces of metal attached together at one end

tweezers

twelfth * /twɛlfθ/ [adverb, adjective; no comparative] coming after 11 other people, things, or events; sometimes

/i/ **see**	/ɪ/ **big**	/eɪ/ **day**	/ɛ/ **get**	/æ/ **hat**
/ɑ/ **father, hot**	/ʌ/ **up**	/ə/ **about**	/ɔ/ **saw**
/oʊ/ **hope**	/ʊ/ **book**	/u/ **too**	/aɪ/ **I**	/aʊ/ **how**
/ɔɪ/ **boy**	/ɝ/ **bird**	/ɚ/ **teacher**	/ɪr/ **ear**	/ɛr/ **air**
/ɑr/ **far**	/ɔr/ **more**	/ʊr/ **tour**	/aɪr/ **fire**
/aʊɚ/ **hour**	/θ/ **nothing**	/ð/ **mother**	/ʃ/ **she**
/ʒ/ **measure**	/tʃ/ **church**	/dʒ/ **jump**	/ŋ/ **long**

written as "12th": *December is the twelfth month of the year.* | *I finished 12th in the race.*

⇨ *See the usage note at* SECOND².

twelve * /twɛlv/ [*number*] 12: *Each team is made up of twelve players.*

twentieth * /'twɛntiiθ/ [*adverb, adjective; no comparative*] coming after 19 other people, things, or events; sometimes written as "20th": *Jessica's sister got married on her twentieth birthday.*

⇨ *See the usage note at* SECOND².

twenty * /'twɛnti/ [*number, noun; plural* **twenties**]
1 20: *We are a small company employing twenty people.*

⇨ *See the usage note at* TEENS.

2 a piece of paper money worth $20: *Do you have change for a $20?*

twice * /twaɪs/ [*adverb*]
1 two times: *He's been married twice.*
═══ **PHRASE** ═══
2 twice as big/long/good/etc. double the size, length, etc., of something: *My car is twice as fast as yours.*

twig /twɪg/ [*noun*] a very small thin branch that grows on a tree or brush

twin¹ /twɪn/ [*noun*] one of two children who are born to the same mother at the same time: *The boys are identical twins* (=they look exactly the same).

⇨ *Compare* TRIPLET.

twin² [*adjective; no comparative*] used about two things that are used together or considered as a pair: *a twin-engine jet plane* | *The hotel has twin towers.*

☛ Only use **twin** before a noun.

twin bed /'twɪn 'bɛd/ [*noun*] a bed that is only big enough for one person to sleep in: *My brother and I share a room with twin beds.*

twinkle /'twɪŋkəl/ [*verb;* **twinkled, twinkling**] if stars or lights twinkle, they shine with quick flashes of light: *Lights from the boats twinkled in the night.*

twist¹ * /twɪst/ [*verb;* **twisted, twisting**]
1 to turn the two ends or sides of something in opposite directions until

it curves: *He **twisted** two pieces of rope **together*** (=around each other).

2 to turn your body or a part of your body into a different position: *Ouch! You're twisting my wrist!*

3 if a river, road, or path twists, it curves a lot: *The river **twisted and turned** through the valley.*

twist² * [*noun*]
1 a curve in a river, road, or path: *After a few **twists and turns**, the road straightened out.*

2 something that has a twisted shape: *cheese twists* (=hard sticks of bread that have a cheese taste)

3 a change that you do not expect: *Each time he tells that story he adds a new twist.*

twisted /'twɪstɪd/ [*adjective;* **more twisted, most twisted**] bent or curved, with two ends turning in different directions: *All that was left of the car was a lot of twisted metal.*

twister /'twɪstɚ/ [*noun*] INFORMAL another word for TORNADO

twitch¹ /twɪtʃ/ [*verb;* **twitches, twitched, twitching**] to move with sudden small movements that you cannot control: *Her nose began to twitch and she sneezed loudly.*

twitch² [*noun; plural* **twitches**] when part of your body suddenly begins to move with small movements that you cannot control: *He developed a twitch in his eye.*

two * /tu/ [*number, noun; plural* **twos**] 2: *We have two children.* | *Cut the cake in two* (=into two pieces). | *People began to arrive, in ones and twos* (=one or two at a time).

tying * /'taɪɪŋ/ [*verb*] the present participle of TIE¹

type¹ * /taɪp/ [*noun*]
1 a member of a group of people or things that are similar in some way; synonym KIND: *A maple is **a type of** tree.* | *There are many **types of** trees.* | *He's **the type of** guy who would always help a friend.*

2 printed words or letters on a page: *The article was printed in large type.*

USAGE   type of, kind of

Use a singular noun after **type of** or **kind of**: *I like this type of book.* Use a plural noun after **types of** or **kinds of**: *I like different kinds of books.*

type² ∗ [*verb*; **typed, typing**] to write using a computer or typewriter: *I can't type very quickly.* | *Could you type a letter for me?*

typewriter /'taɪpˌraɪtɚ/ [*noun*] a machine used to write printed words or numbers: *The letter had been written on a typewriter.*

typhoon /taɪ'fun/ [*noun*] a violent storm with very strong spinning winds and rain that comes in from the Pacific Ocean
➪ Compare CYCLONE, HURRICANE, TORNADO.

typical ∗ T /'tɪpɪkəl/ [*adjective*; **more typical, most typical**] having the qualities or features you would expect of a particular thing or person: *We're just a typical American family.* | *It's typical of them to arrive late.*

typically ∗ T /'tɪpɪkli/ [*adverb*] used when something is exactly what you would expect of someone or something: *Typically, she forgot to bring her umbrella.*

typing /'taɪpɪŋ/ [*noun*] when you write using a typewriter or computer: *Would you do some typing for me?*

typist /'taɪpɪst/ [*noun*] someone whose job is to type letters and documents

tyrant /'taɪrənt/ [*noun*] someone who uses his or her power in a cruel and unfair way: *Medieval kings were often tyrants.*

U

U ∗ or **u** /yu/ [*noun*; *plural* **Us** or **U's, u's**] the 21st letter of the English alphabet
➪ See the usage note at ALPHABET.

udder /'ʌdɚ/ [*noun*] the part of a COW, goat, etc., from which milk is produced

UFO /'yuˈɛfˈoʊ/ [*noun*; *plural* **UFOs**] unidentified flying object; a strange light or shape seen in the sky, which some people think is a space vehicle from another planet

ugly ∗ /'ʌgli/ [*adjective*; **uglier, ugliest**] unpleasant to look at; *synonym* UNATTRACTIVE; *opposite* BEAUTIFUL: *He was the ugliest man I had ever seen.* | *an ugly building*

U.K. or **UK** /'yuˈkeɪ/ [*name*]
the U.K. the United Kingdom: a country that is made up of Great Britain and Northern Ireland

ulcer /'ʌlsɚ/ [*noun*] a sore area on your skin or in your mouth or stomach

ultraviolet /ˌʌltrəˈvaɪəlɪt/ [*adjective*; *no comparative*] ultraviolet light is light that cannot be seen by people but that makes your skin darker: *Ultraviolet rays can cause sunburn.* | *an ultraviolet lamp*

umbrella /ʌmˈbrɛlə/ [*noun*] a round cover on a long handle that you hold over your head when it is raining: *an open umbrella* | *a closed umbrella*
➪ See the picture at UNDER¹.

umpire /'ʌmpaɪr/ [*noun*] someone who makes sure that the players obey the rules in a game of baseball, tennis, and some other sports
➪ Compare REFEREE.

UN /'yuˈɛn/ [*noun*]
the UN the United Nations; an organization of countries that tries protect the world from war, hunger, etc.

unable ∗ /ʌnˈeɪbəl/ [*adjective*; *no comparative*] not able to do something; *synonym* INCAPABLE: **be unable to do something** ▸ *I was unable to answer his question.*
☛ Do not use **unable** before a noun.

unacceptable /ˌʌnəkˈsɛptəbəl/ [*adjective*; **more unacceptable, most unacceptable**] if something is unacceptable, it is so bad that it cannot be accepted or allowed; *opposite* ACCEPTABLE: *Your essay is totally unacceptable.*

unanimous /yuˈnænəməs/ [*adjective*; *no comparative*] if a decision, feeling, etc., is unanimous, everyone involved wants or thinks the same thing: *a unanimous vote* | *The judges were unanimous in their decision.*

unarmed /ʌnˈɑrmd/ [*adjective; no comparative*] not carrying any weapons; *opposite* ARMED: *He held his hands out to show he was unarmed.*

unattractive /ˌʌnəˈtræktɪv/ [*adjective; more unattractive, most unattractive*] not nice to look at; *synonym* UGLY; *opposite* ATTRACTIVE: *She thought her large nose was unattractive.*

unauthorized /ʌnˈɔθəraɪzd/ [*adjective; no comparative*] if something is unauthorized, official permission for it has not been given; *opposite* AUTHORIZED: *There had been several unauthorized withdrawals of money.*

unaware Ⓣ /ˌʌnəˈwɛr/ [*adjective; no comparative*] not knowing about a situation or event; *opposite* AWARE: *She seemed unaware of his feelings for her.* | *He was unaware that he was late.*
☛ Do not use **unaware** before a noun.

unbearable Ⓣ /ʌnˈbɛrəbəl/ [*adjective; more unbearable, most unbearable*] causing a lot of pain, or making someone very unhappy: *The heat is unbearable here in the summer.*

unbelievable /ˌʌnbɪˈlivəbəl/ [*adjective; more unbelievable, most unbelievable*]
1 used to emphasize that something is very good, bad, big, etc.: *The prices of her paintings are unbelievable.*
2 very surprising, or not likely to be true: *His story seemed unbelievable at first.*

uncertain /ʌnˈsɝtən/ [*adjective; more uncertain, most uncertain*]
1 not sure about something; *opposite* CERTAIN: *He was uncertain of the total cost.* | *They were uncertain what to do.*
2 not known or definite: *The country has an uncertain future.*

uncle * or **Uncle** /ˈʌŋkəl/ [*noun, name*] a brother of your father or mother, or your aunt's husband: *My uncle came to my birthday party.* | *We had dinner with Uncle Michael.*
⇨ *See the picture at* FAMILY TREE.

unclear /ʌnˈklɪr/ [*adjective; more unclear, most unclear*] not easy to understand, or not sure about something: *unclear instructions* | *I'm unclear about what to do next.*

uncomfortable * /ʌnˈkʌmfə·təbəl/ [*adjective; more uncomfortable, most uncomfortable*]
1 uncomfortable clothes, furniture, etc., are not pleasant to wear or use; *opposite* COMFORTABLE: *The theater's seats were really uncomfortable.*
2 feeling a little worry or pain, and not relaxed; *opposite* COMFORTABLE: *Meeting new people makes her feel uncomfortable.*

uncommon /ʌnˈkamən/ [*adjective; more uncommon, most uncommon*] not happening very often, or not existing in many places; *synonym* RARE; *opposite* COMMON: *Accidents of this kind are uncommon.*

unconnected /ˌʌnkəˈnɛktɪd/ [*adjective; no comparative*] not related to something; *opposite* CONNECTED: *Her headaches are unconnected to any illness.*

unconscious * /ʌnˈkanʃəs/ [*adjective; no comparative*] in a state similar to a deep sleep, because of an accident or illness; *opposite* CONSCIOUS: *He was unconscious for three hours after the accident.*

uncontrollable /ˌʌnkənˈtroʊləbəl/ [*adjective; more uncontrollable, most uncontrollable*] an uncontrollable feeling or reaction is one that you cannot stop yourself from having: *uncontrollable laughter*

uncontrolled * /ˌʌnkənˈtroʊld/ [*adjective; more uncontrolled, most uncontrolled*] not being controlled, or showing that you do not have any control: *an uncontrolled child* | *uncontrolled anger*

uncountable noun * /ʌnˈkaʊntəbəl ˈnaʊn/ [*noun*] GRAMMAR a noun that does not have a plural form, cannot be used with "a" before it, and can be used with or without "the" before it: *"Water," "money," "behavior," and "advice" are all uncountable nouns.*
⇨ *Compare* COUNTABLE NOUN.

uncover /ʌnˈkʌvɚ/ [verb; **uncovered, uncovering**]
1 to take the cover off something: *Uncover the pot and boil the sauce for two minutes.*
2 to discover something that was secret or hidden: *They uncovered the journals she had kept her whole life.*
   ↪ *Compare* REVEAL.

under¹ * /ˈʌndɚ/ [preposition]
1 under something or covered by something; *synonym* UNDERNEATH; *opposite* OVER: *She kept her slippers under her bed.* | *He swept the dust under the mat.*
   ↪ *See the picture at* POSITION.
2 less than a particular number, amount, size, or age; *opposite* OVER: *Children under five get in free.* | *All of these books cost under $20.*
3 affected by or involved in something: *I've been under a lot of stress recently.* | *He's **under** arrest* (=in jail until he goes to a court).
4 with a lower rank or position than someone else in a company, army, etc.: *How many people work under you?*

under² [adverb]
1 to a place that is below something or covered by something: *Fold the edge of the cloth under and pin it.*
2 less than a particular number, amount, size, or age; *opposite* OVER: *The competition is for children aged twelve and under.*

underfoot /ˌʌndɚˈfʊt/ [adverb] used to talk about how ground feels when you walk on it: *The grass was wet and slippery underfoot.*

undergo /ˌʌndɚˈgoʊ/ [verb; **undergoes, underwent, undergone** /ˌʌndɚˈgɔn/, **undergoing**] to experience something that is not pleasant: *She is undergoing surgery tomorrow.*

undergraduate /ˌʌndɚˈgrædʒuɪt/ [noun] a college student who is studying for his or her first degree

underground /ˈʌndɚˌgraʊnd/ [adjective; no comparative] under the surface of the ground: *an underground television cable* | *an underground tunnel*

undergrowth /ˈʌndɚˌgroʊθ/ [noun] small trees and bushes growing under big trees in a wood or forest

underline /ˈʌndɚˌlaɪn/ [verb; **underlined, underlining**] to draw or type a line under a word or number of words: *The word "Urgent" was underlined in red.*

underneath * /ˌʌndɚˈniθ/ [adverb, preposition] below something or covered by something; *synonym* UNDER: *The snow was too deep to see the path underneath.* | *Underneath her jacket she wore a black dress.*
   ↪ *Compare* **on top (of)** *at* TOP¹.

underpants /ˈʌndɚˌpænts/ [plural noun] underwear that covers your body between your waist and your legs: *a pair of underpants*

underpass /ˈʌndɚˌpæs/ [noun; plural **underpasses**] the part of a road that goes under another road or railroad;

She has a blanket **over** herself.

She's **under** the blanket.

She's holding an umbrella **over** herself.

She's **under** the umbrella.

under *and* **over**

opposite OVERPASS: *Take the first exit after the underpass.*

undershirt /'ʌndɚˌʃɜˈt/ [*noun*] a piece of underwear that covers your body above the waist

understand * /ˌʌndɚˈstænd/ [*verb;* **understood, understanding**]

1 to know what someone's words or actions mean: *The woman obviously didn't understand.* | *I'm sorry, I don't understand Spanish.*

2 to know how or why something happens or someone does something: *"I need to go home." "We understand."* | *I just don't understand computers.* | **understand what/how/why/etc.** ▸ *I understand why you left.*

☛ Do not say "I am understanding." Say I understand.

⇨ *See also* UNDERSTANDING.

understanding[1] /ˌʌndɚˈstændɪŋ/ [*adjective;* **more understanding, most understanding**] kind to someone who has problems or difficulties: *When I explained why I couldn't come, he was very understanding.*

understanding[2] [*noun*]

1 knowledge about something: *His **understanding of** the subject has improved.* | *My understanding is that he didn't want the job.*

2 sympathy you feel because you understand why someone did something or what he or she is suffering: *She just needs love and understanding.*

understood * /ˌʌndɚˈstʊd/ [*verb*] the past tense and past participle of UNDERSTAND

undertake /ˌʌndɚˈteɪk/ [*verb;* **undertook, undertaken** /ˌʌndɚˈteɪkən/, **undertaking**] FORMAL

1 to start to do something difficult: *It was brave of him to undertake this task.*

━━ PHRASE ━━

2 undertake to do something to formally promise to do something: *They undertook to deliver the goods on June 1st.*

undertaker /'ʌndɚˌteɪkɚ/ [*noun*] someone whose job is to arrange funerals

undertook /ˌʌndɚˈtʊk/ [*verb*] the past tense of UNDERTAKE

underwater[1] /'ʌndɚˌwɔtɚ/ [*adjective; no comparative*] happening, existing, or used below the surface of water: *underwater photography* | *an underwater laboratory*

☛ Only use **underwater** before a noun.

underwater[2] /'ʌndɚˈwɔtɚ/ [*adverb*] below the surface of water: *I don't like swimming underwater.*

underwear * /'ʌndɚˌwɛr/ [*noun*] clothes that you wear next to your skin under your main clothes: *Don't forget to pack enough underwear for your trip.*

underwent /ˌʌndɚˈwɛnt/ [*verb*] the past tense of UNDERGO

undo * /ʌnˈdu/ [*verb;* **undoes, undid** /ʌnˈdɪd/, **undone, undoing**]

1 to make something go back to the way it was before anything else happened: *If you made a typing error, you can undo it by pressing this key.*

2 to move the buttons or zipper on a piece of clothing, so it is no longer fastened; *synonym* UNFASTEN: *He undid the top two buttons on his shirt.*

undone /ʌnˈdʌn/ [*adjective; no comparative*]

1 not fastened: *One of your shoelaces **has come undone** (=is no longer tied).*

2 not completed; *opposite* FINISHED: *I hate leaving things undone.*

☛ Do not use **undone** before a noun.

undress /ʌnˈdrɛs/ [*verb;* **undresses, undressed, undressing**] to take your clothes off, or to take someone's clothes off; *opposite* DRESS: *I undressed quickly and got into bed.* | *His mother undressed him and gave him a bath.*

undressed /ʌnˈdrɛst/ [*adjective; no comparative*]

1 not wearing any clothes, or only wearing underwear or sleeping clothes: *The children were already undressed and in bed.*

☛ Do not use **undressed** before a noun.

━━ PHRASE ━━

2 get undressed to take your clothes off: *I was too tired to get undressed.*

uneasy /ʌnˈizi/ [adjective; **more uneasy, most uneasy**] a little worried or uncomfortable because you are afraid that something bad might happen: *The man in the corner makes me feel uneasy.*
☛ "Uneasy" does not mean "difficult."

uneducated /ʌnˈɛdʒʊˌkeɪtɪd/ [adjective; **more uneducated, most uneducated**] without much education; *opposite* EDUCATED: *If you use bad grammar, you sound uneducated.*

unemployed[1] /ˌʌnɛmˈplɔɪd/ [adjective; *no comparative*] without a job: *He has been unemployed for eight months.*

unemployed[2] [noun]
the unemployed people without jobs: *The unemployed will be offered training.*
☛ Only use **the unemployed** with a plural verb.

unemployment Ⓣ /ˌʌnɛmˈplɔɪmənt/ [noun]
1 when people do not have jobs: *Unemployment is a big problem now.*
2 money paid by a government to someone when he or she no longer has a job: *You can **get unemployment** (=be paid money) for six months here.*

uneven * /ʌnˈivən/ [adjective; **more uneven, most uneven**] not flat or smooth: *The table wasn't steady because the floor was uneven.*

unexpected * /ˌʌnɪkˈspɛktɪd/ [adjective; **more unexpected, most unexpected**] not expected, and surprising because of that: *I had an unexpected letter from an old friend.*

unfair * /ʌnˈfɛr/ [adjective; **more unfair, most unfair**] someone or something that is unfair does not treat people in an equal way or give them what they deserve; *opposite* FAIR: *The judge's decision was unfair!* | *It's unfair to test them on something they weren't taught.*

unfairly * /ʌnˈfɛrli/ [adverb] in a way that is not fair; *opposite* FAIRLY: *He thinks he has been treated unfairly.*

unfamiliar /ˌʌnfəˈmɪlyɚ/ [adjective; **more unfamiliar, most unfamiliar**]
1 if something is unfamiliar, you have not seen or heard it before; *synonym* STRANGE; *opposite* FAMILIAR: *The author's name was unfamiliar to me.*

━━ PHRASE ━━
2 be unfamiliar with to have not seen or heard something before: *I am unfamiliar with their music.*

unfashionable /ʌnˈfæʃənəbəl/ [adjective; **more unfashionable, most unfashionable**] unfashionable music, clothes, etc., are not popular; *opposite* FASHIONABLE: *an unfashionable hairstyle*

unfasten /ʌnˈfæsən/ [verb; **unfastened, unfastening**] to open something that had been fastened; *synonym* UNDO; *opposite* FASTEN: *Do not unfasten your seat belt until the plane has landed.*

unfavorable Ⓣ /ʌnˈfeɪvərəbəl/ [adjective; **more unfavorable, most unfavorable**] not good for a person or a situation; *opposite* FAVORABLE: *unfavorable weather conditions* | *Many voters have an unfavorable opinion of the senator.*

unfinished /ʌnˈfɪnɪʃt/ [adjective; *no comparative*] not yet completely done; *opposite* FINISHED: *We still have some unfinished business.*

unfit /ʌnˈfɪt/ [adjective; **more unfit, most unfit**]
1 not good enough for something; *opposite* FIT: *The water was unfit to drink.* | *He is unfit for the governor's office.*
2 not healthy, because you do not get enough exercise; *opposite* FIT: *I'm so unfit that I can hardly climb the stairs.*
⏎ *See also* **out of shape** *at* SHAPE.

unfold /ʌnˈfoʊld/ [verb; **unfolded, unfolding**] to open something that was folded: *The table unfolds easily.* | *He unfolded the note and read it.*

unforgettable /ˌʌnfɚˈgɛtəbəl/ [adjective; **more unforgettable, most unforgettable**] something that is unforgettable is so exciting, unusual, etc., that it will not be forgotten: *The trip was an unforgettable experience.*

/i/ **see** /ɪ/ **big** /eɪ/ **day** /ɛ/ **get** /æ/ **hat**
/ɑ/ **father, hot** /ʌ/ **up** /ə/ **about** /ɔ/ **saw**
/oʊ/ **hope** /ʊ/ **book** /u/ **too** /aɪ/ **I** /aʊ/ **how**
/ɔɪ/ **boy** /ɝ/ **bird** /ɚ/ **teacher** /ɪr/ **ear** /ɛr/ **air**
/ɑr/ **far** /ɔr/ **more** /ʊr/ **tour** /aɪr/ **fire**
/aʊɚ/ **hour** /θ/ **nothing** /ð/ **mother** /ʃ/ **she**
/ʒ/ **measure** /tʃ/ **church** /dʒ/ **jump** /ŋ/ **long**

unfortunate /ʌnˈfɔrtʃənɪt/ [*adjective; more unfortunate, most unfortunate*] something that is unfortunate is a bad thing to have happen; *opposite* FORTUNATE: *an unfortunate mistake* | *It was unfortunate that it rained all day.*

unfortunately /ʌnˈfɔrtʃənɪtli/ [*adverb*] used to say that an event or situation is bad; *opposite* FORTUNATELY: *Unfortunately, there were no tickets left.*

unfriendly /ʌnˈfrɛndli/ [*adjective; unfriendlier, unfriendliest*] not friendly or nice: *He was very unfriendly.*

ungrateful /ʌnˈgreɪtfəl/ [*adjective; more ungrateful, most ungrateful*] not wanting to thank someone, although you should; *opposite* GRATEFUL: *How can you be so ungrateful?*

unhappiness /ʌnˈhæpɪnɪs/ [*noun*] a feeling of sadness caused by a bad event or situation; *opposite* HAPPINESS: *He caused her a lot of unhappiness.*

unhappy * /ʌnˈhæpi/ [*adjective; unhappier, unhappiest*] feeling sad because of a bad event or situation; *opposite* HAPPY: *I was unhappy at school.*

unhealthy * T /ʌnˈhɛlθi/ [*adjective; unhealthier, unhealthiest*]
  1 not physically healthy: *He looks unhealthier than he did last year.*
  2 not good for your health; *opposite* HEALTHY: *an unhealthy diet*

unhelpful /ʌnˈhɛlpfəl/ [*adjective; more unhelpful, most unhelpful*] not helping someone; *opposite* HELPFUL: *Your criticisms are completely unhelpful.*

unidentified /ˌʌnaɪˈdɛntɪˌfaɪd/ [*adjective; no comparative*] an unidentified person or thing is one whose name or type is not known; *synonym* UNKNOWN: *The owner of the lost dog is still unidentified.*

uniform * T /ˈyunəˌfɔrm/ [*noun*] the official clothes worn at some schools or by people with a particular job, for example soldiers: *The students wear uniforms.* | *a photo of a man in uniform*

unimportant /ˌʌnɪmˈpɔrtənt/ [*adjective; more unimportant, most unimportant*] not worth anyone's worry or attention; *opposite* IMPORTANT: *The details of the story are unimportant.*

uninterrupted /ˌʌnɪntəˈrʌptɪd/ [*adjective; no comparative*] happening without changing or stopping; *synonym* CONTINUOUS: *We had ten days of uninterrupted good weather.*

union * /ˈyunyən/ [*noun*] an organized group of workers who try to make sure that their pay, working conditions, etc., are acceptable; *synonym* LABOR UNION: *He belongs to the miners' union.*

unique T /yuˈnik/ [*adjective; no comparative*]
  1 unusual and special: *I had a unique opportunity to see the animals close up.*
  2 different from anything else: *His style of writing is unique.*

unit * /ˈyunɪt/ [*noun*]
  1 one thing or organization that has many parts or members: *He's in my army unit.* | *an air conditioning unit*
  2 one person or thing that is a complete part of something else: *a power unit* (=part of a machine)
  3 an amount that is used to describe a measurement: *metric units such as meters and centimeters* | *a **unit of** length*

unite * /yuˈnaɪt/ [*verb; united, uniting*] to join together and do things as a group, or to join groups or people together: *The workers united to make their position stronger.* | *They need a leader who will unite the country.*

united /yuˈnaɪtɪd/ [*adjective; more united, most united*] if people or groups are united, they are joined or connected by having the same aims or by feeling the same things: *Everyone was united in support of the team.*

United Kingdom /yuˈnaɪtɪd ˈkɪŋdəm/ [*name*]
  the United Kingdom a country made up of Great Britain and Northern Ireland; *synonyms* U.K., UK

United Nations /yuˈnaɪtɪd ˈneɪʃənz/ [*noun*]
  the United Nations an organization of countries that tries to protect the world from war, hunger, etc.; *synonym* UN
  ☞ Only use **the United Nations** with a singular verb.

United States * /yu'naɪtɪd 'steɪts/ or
United States of America
/yu'naɪtɪd 'steɪts əv ə'mɛrɪkə/ [*name*]
the United States a country in North
America, south of Canada and north of
Mexico; *synonym* **U.S., U.S.A.**
☛ Only use **the United States** or **the
United States of America** with a singular
verb.
⇨ See the synonym note at **AMERICA.**

universal /ˌyunə'vɜ˞səl/ [*adjective;* **more
universal, most universal**] existing or
happening everywhere, or involving
everyone: *The need for love is universal.*

universe * /'yunəˌvɜ˞s/ [*noun*]
the universe space and everything in
it, including planets and stars

university * /ˌyunə'vɜ˞sɪti/ [*noun; plural*
universities] a place where you can
study for a degree, including an
advanced degree, or do research

unkind * /ʌn'kaɪnd/ [*adjective;*
unkinder, unkindest] not at all nice;
synonym **MEAN;** *opposite* **KIND:** *Don't be
unkind to your little sister.* I *an unkind
remark*

unknown * /ʌn'noʊn/ [*adjective; no
comparative*] not known: *The cause of the
fire is still unknown.*

unleaded /ʌn'lɛdɪd/ [*adjective; no
comparative*] unleaded gasoline does
not have the harmful metal lead in it:
Unleaded gas is better for people's health.

unless * /ʌn'lɛs/ [*conjunction*] used to
mention an action or situation that
another action or situation depends on:
I won't talk to her unless she apologizes.
☛ Do not use **unless** with another
negative. For example, do not say "You
can't get in unless you don't have a key."
Say **You can't get in unless you have a
key** or **You can't get in if you don't have
a key.**

unlike /ʌn'laɪk/ [*preposition*]
1 different from someone or something:
He's so unlike his brother. I *Unlike many
people, I walk to work.*
2 not typical of someone: *It was unlike
him to be late.*
☛ **Unlike** is not a verb. Do not say "I
unlike him." Say **I dislike him** or **I don't
like him.**

unlikely Ⓣ /ʌn'laɪkli/ [*adjective;* **more
unlikely, most unlikely**] if something
is unlikely, it will probably not happen;
opposite **LIKELY:** *Our team might win, but
it's unlikely.* I *It's unlikely that anybody
saw us.* I **be unlikely to do
something** ▸ *You're unlikely to get a car
for your birthday.*

unlimited /ʌn'lɪmɪtɪd/ [*adjective; no
comparative*] an unlimited amount can
be as large as you like; *opposite* **LIMITED:**
*You can borrow an unlimited number of
books from the library.*

unload /ʌn'loʊd/ [*verb;* **unloaded,
unloading**] to take things off or out of
a vehicle, ship, etc.; *opposite* **LOAD:** *We
unloaded the groceries.* I *Will you help me
unload the car?*

unlock /ʌn'lɑk/ [*verb;* **unlocked,
unlocking**] to open a lock on
something, usually with a key; *opposite*
LOCK: *He unlocked the car and got in.*

unlucky /ʌn'lʌki/ [*adjective;* **unluckier,
unluckiest**]
1 if you are unlucky, bad things
happen to you by chance; *opposite*
LUCKY: *I must be the unluckiest person in
the world!*
2 something that is unlucky is a bad
thing to have happen or makes bad
things happen; *opposite* **LUCKY:** *People
say it's unlucky to walk under a ladder.*

unmarried /ʌn'mærid/ [*adjective; no
comparative*] not married; *synonym*
SINGLE: *She was staying with her
unmarried daughter.*

unnatural /ʌn'nætʃərəl/ [*adjective;*
more unnatural, most unnatural] not
normal or usual; *opposite* **NATURAL:** *It's
unnatural to always want to be alone.*

unnecessary /ʌn'nɛsəˌsɛri/ [*adjective;*
more unnecessary, most unnecessary]
not needed; *opposites* **NECESSARY,
REQUIRED:** *Don't pack any unnecessary
clothes.* I *It seemed unnecessary to say
why I was there.*

/i/ **see** /ɪ/ **big** /eɪ/ **day** /ɛ/ **get** /æ/ **hat**
/ɑ/ **father, hot** /ʌ/ **up** /ɔ/ **about** /ɔ/ **saw**
/oʊ/ **hope** /ʊ/ **book** /u/ **too** /aɪ/ **I** /aʊ/ **how**
/ɔɪ/ **boy** /ɜ˞/ **bird** /ə˞/ **teacher** /ɪr/ **ear** /ɛr/ **air**
/ɑr/ **far** /ɔr/ **more** /ʊr/ **tour** /aɪr/ **fire**
/aʊə˞/ **hour** /θ/ **nothing** /ð/ **mother** /ʃ/ **she**
/ʒ/ **measure** /tʃ/ **church** /dʒ/ **jump** /ŋ/ **long**

unofficial /ˌʌnəˈfɪʃəl/ [adjective; no comparative] not official or definite: *Unofficial reports say 17 people were killed in the accident.*

unpack /ʌnˈpæk/ [verb; unpacked, unpacking] to take things out of a case, large box, etc.; _opposite_ PACK: *I haven't finished unpacking since my move.* I *She unpacked her suitcase.*

unpleasant * /ʌnˈplɛzənt/ [adjective; more unpleasant, most unpleasant] not pleasant to experience, look at, etc.; _synonym_ NASTY: *The whole trip was an unpleasant experience.* I *The food tasted very unpleasant.*

unplug /ʌnˈplʌg/ [verb; unplugs, unplugged, unplugging] to take a plug out of the wall to stop an electrical connection: *Don't unplug the computer.* ↪ *Compare* plug in *at* PLUG².

unpopular 🔲 /ʌnˈpɑpyələr/ [adjective; more unpopular, most unpopular] not liked by many people; _opposite_ POPULAR: *The program is **unpopular with** younger people.* I *an unpopular decision*

unpredictable /ˌʌnprɪˈdɪktəbəl/ [adjective; more unpredictable, most unpredictable] if someone or something is unpredictable, you cannot guess what he, she, or it will do next: *She had unpredictable moods.* I *The weather was unpredictable.*

unreal /ʌnˈriəl/ [adjective; no comparative] not related to things that really happen or exist: *The view was so beautiful that it seemed unreal.*

unreasonable /ʌnˈrizənəbəl/ [adjective; more unreasonable, most unreasonable] not fair or based on good reason; _opposite_ REASONABLE: *It's unreasonable to expect people to work on weekends.*

unrelated /ˌʌnrɪˈleɪtɪd/ [adjective; no comparative] not connected with something; _opposite_ RELATED: *The police say that the two robberies are unrelated.*

unreliable /ˌʌnrɪˈlaɪəbəl/ [adjective; more unreliable, most unreliable] not always doing what is needed or expected; _opposites_ RELIABLE, DEPENDABLE: *His car was unreliable and often didn't start.* I *an unreliable worker*

unroll /ʌnˈroʊl/ [verb; unrolled, unrolling] to open something that is rolled up, so that it is flat: *He unrolled the map.*

unsafe /ʌnˈseɪf/ [adjective; more unsafe, most unsafe] not safe to do or use; _synonym_ DANGEROUS: *The building is very old and unsafe.* I *It is unsafe to walk through the park late at night.*
☛ Do not use **unsafe** to describe people.

unsatisfactory /ˌʌnsætɪsˈfæktəri/ [adjective; more unsatisfactory, most unsatisfactory] not good enough; _opposite_ SATISFACTORY: *Your grades are unsatisfactory.*

unscrew /ʌnˈskru/ [verb; unscrewed, unscrewing]
1 to remove something by turning it until it is no longer attached: *I can't unscrew this lid.*
2 to remove something by taking out the screws holding it: *He unscrewed the back of the TV set.*

unskilled /ʌnˈskɪld/ [adjective; no comparative] having no skills, or not needing any special training; _opposite_ SKILLED: *Most of the workers on the site are unskilled.* I *unskilled jobs*

unsteady /ʌnˈstɛdi/ [adjective; unsteadier, unsteadiest] likely to fall over or to shake; _opposite_ STEADY: *He was very old and unsteady on his feet.* I *Be careful—that ladder's unsteady.*

unsuccessful /ˌʌnsəkˈsɛsfəl/ [adjective; more unsuccessful, most unsuccessful] not achieving what was wanted or intended; _opposite_ SUCCESSFUL: *He was **unsuccessful in** his attempt to win.*

unsuitable /ʌnˈsutəbəl/ [adjective; more unsuitable, most unsuitable] not right for a situation or a person; _synonym_ INAPPROPRIATE; _opposite_ SUITABLE: *This toy is **unsuitable for** babies.*

unsure /ʌnˈʃʊr/ [adjective; more unsure, most unsure] not knowing something or not sure about something: *She was **unsure of** the date the letter arrived.*

untangle /ʌnˈtæŋgəl/ [verb; untangled, untangling] to take the knots and twists out of string, wool, hair, etc.: *I tried to untangle the kite string.*

untie /ʌn'taɪ/ [verb; **unties, untied, untying**] to take a knot apart so that something is no longer held in place; *opposite* TIE: *I untied the ribbon that was around the box.* | *They untied the boat and rowed off.*

until[1] * /ʌn'tɪl/ [preposition]
1 if something happens until a particular time, it stops at that time: *I worked on the assignment until 11 o'clock.* | *It rained until lunchtime.*
— PHRASE —
2 not . . . until not before a particular event or time: *I didn't wake up until 10:30.*

USAGE until
Only use **until** when you are talking about time: *I stayed up until past midnight.* Do not use "until" when you are talking about a direction, place, or position. Use **to, up to,** or **as far as** instead: *He drove to the park.* | *I ran up to the end of the block.* | *You can see as far as the horizon.*

until[2] * [conjunction]
1 if something happens until a particular thing happens, it stops when that thing happens: *We stayed indoors until the rain stopped.*
— PHRASE —
2 not . . . until not before a particular event or time: *I didn't see the ocean until I was ten years old.*

untying /ʌn'taɪɪŋ/ [verb] the present participle of UNTIE

untrue /ʌn'tru/ [adjective; no comparative] not true; *synonym* FALSE: *Everything they said was untrue.*

unused /ʌn'yuʒd/ [adjective; no comparative] not being used, or never used: *His bike stood unused in the garage.*

unusual * /ʌn'yuʒuəl/ [adjective; **more unusual, most unusual**] not happening or seen often, or different from other things of its kind: *The park had many unusual plants and trees.* | *It was unusual for him to be late.*

unusually * /ʌn'yuʒuəli/ [adverb] in a way that is surprising or different from what is usual: *It has been unusually rainy this year.*

unwanted * /ʌn'wɑntɪd/ [adjective; no comparative] not wanted or needed: *She put all her unwanted clothes in boxes.*

unwilling /ʌn'wɪlɪŋ/ [adjective; **more unwilling, most unwilling**] not wanting to do something; *opposite* WILLING: **be unwilling to do something** ▸ *He was unwilling to share a room.*

unwind /ʌn'waɪnd/ [verb; **unwound, unwinding**]
1 to make thread, rope, etc., come away from the thing it is around; *opposite* WIND: *He unwound another few feet of rope.* | *The thread had become tangled as it unwound.*
2 to relax after working hard, being worried, etc.: *I unwind by watching TV.*

unwise /ʌn'waɪz/ [adjective; **more unwise, most unwise**] an action that is unwise is not sensible and may have bad results; *opposite* WISE: *It would be unwise to make a decision too quickly.*

unwound /ʌn'waʊnd/ [verb] the past tense and past participle of UNWIND

unwrap /ʌn'ræp/ [verb; **unwraps, unwrapped, unwrapping**] to take off the paper, plastic, or cloth around something; *opposite* WRAP: *The children unwrapped their presents.*

unzip /ʌn'zɪp/ [verb; **unzips, unzipped, unzipping**]
1 to open something that has been closed with a zipper; *opposite* ZIP: *She unzipped the bag and took out a comb.*
2 to open a computer file that has been made smaller using a special program; *opposite* ZIP: *I can't unzip the file you sent.*

up[1] * /ʌp/ [adverb]
1 to or in a higher place or position: *They climbed up to the top of the hill.* | *The book was up on the top shelf.* | *The boat moved **up and down** (=higher and lower), making her feel sick.*
2 to a higher rate, amount, level, etc.,

/i/ see /ɪ/ big /eɪ/ day /ɛ/ get /æ/ hat
/ɑ/ father, hot /ʌ/ up /ə/ about /ɔ/ saw
/oʊ/ hope /ʊ/ book /u/ too /aɪ/ I /aʊ/ how
/ɔɪ/ boy /ɝ/ bird /ɚ/ teacher /ɪr/ ear /ɛr/ air
/ɑr/ far /ɔr/ more /ʊr/ tour /aɪr/ fire
/aʊɚ/ hour /θ/ nothing /ð/ mother /ʃ/ she
/ʒ/ measure /tʃ/ church /dʒ/ jump /ŋ/ long

than before: *Please turn the radio up.* | *She turned the oven up.* | *Our profits went up last year.*

3 in or into an upright position: *Everyone stood up when he came into the room.* | *His collar was up so I couldn't see his face.*

4 toward or in the north: *He lives up in Maine.*

5 used to mean "completely," especially with verbs: *It's time to clean up.* | *He filled up his plate.*

▷ Compare DOWN[1].

— PHRASES —

6 up to not more than or beyond: *Up to 30 people are allowed on the bus.*

7 up against facing something that is difficult to deal with: *They're up against a team that will be hard to beat.*

8 up and down to one end of a road or place and back again: *They drove up and down looking for a place to park.*

up[2] * [*preposition*]
1 toward a higher level or position; *opposite* DOWN: *I ran up the stairs.*
2 along something or toward the far end of a place; *synonym* DOWN: *They walked slowly up the road.*

up[3] * [*adjective; no comparative*]
1 not in bed: *Dad isn't up yet.*
▷ See also **wake up** at WAKE.
2 if a number or amount is up, it is higher than before; *opposite* DOWN: *Sales are up this month.*
3 if a period of time is up, the end of it has been reached: *When the two hours were up, the students had to stop writing.*
☛ Do not use **up** before a noun.

— PHRASES —

4 be up to or **feel up to** to be or feel able to do something: *He's not up to the job.* | *I don't feel up to going out.*

5 be up to someone used to say that someone is responsible for something: *It's up to him to choose.*

6 what's up? SPOKEN used as an informal greeting: *Hi, what's up?*

upcoming /ˈʌpˌkʌmɪŋ/ [*adjective; no comparative*] an upcoming event will happen soon: *The magazine lists all the upcoming concerts.*

update /ˈʌpˌdeɪt/ [*verb; updated, updating*] to make something more

modern or to make it include the latest information: *The dictionary is updated often.*

upgrade /ʌpˈgreɪd/ [*verb; upgraded, upgrading*] to make something better or more modern: *The airline upgraded my seat from coach to business class.* | *My computer needs upgrading.*

uphill[1] /ˈʌpˈhɪl/ [*adjective; no comparative*]
1 involving going up a slope; *opposite* DOWNHILL: *The trail was mostly uphill.*

— PHRASE —

2 uphill struggle/task something that is very difficult to do: *It was an uphill struggle getting everyone to agree.*

uphill[2] [*adverb*] up a slope; *opposite* DOWNHILL: *The car went uphill slowly.*

upon /əˈpɑn/ [*preposition*] FORMAL on: *She sat down upon the ground.*

upper * /ˈʌpɚ/ [*adjective; no comparative*] used to describe a thing or part that is above another thing or part; *opposite* LOWER: *There is a good view from the upper stories of the hotel.*
☛ Only use **upper** before a noun.

uppercase /ˈʌpɚˈkeɪs/ [*adjective; no comparative*] an uppercase LETTER of the alphabet has the form A, B, C, etc., rather than a, b, c, etc.; *synonym* CAPITAL; *opposite* LOWERCASE: *Use uppercase letters for the title.*

upper class /ˈʌpɚ ˈklæs/ [*noun*] **the upper class** the people in a society who are rich and have a high social rank
▷ Compare MIDDLE CLASS.

upper-class [*adjective; no comparative*] belonging to or typical of the upper class: *She's with her upper-class friends.*
▷ Compare MIDDLE-CLASS.

upright * /ˈʌpˌraɪt/ [*adjective, adverb; no comparative*] with the head or top part as high as it can be: *Please put your seats back into their upright position before landing.* | *Babies as young as eight months old can sit upright.*

upset[1] * /ʌpˈsɛt/ [*adjective; more upset, most upset*]
1 unhappy because something bad has happened: *He was upset about his bad chemistry grade.*

2 if you have an upset stomach, you feel sick: *My stomach feels a little upset.*

upset[2] * [*verb;* **upsets, upset, upset, upsetting**]
1 to make someone feel unhappy: *The news of his accident really upset her.*
2 to stop something from happening in the way it was planned or in the usual way: *The bad weather upset our plans.*

upside down * /ˈʌpsaɪd ˈdaʊn/ [*adverb*] with the part that normally faces upward facing downward: *The painting had been hung upside down.*

upstairs[1] * /ˈʌpˈstɛrz/ [*adverb*] on or to a higher floor of a building; *opposite* DOWNSTAIRS: *"Where's Mom?" "She's upstairs." | I went upstairs to my bedroom.*
☛ Do not say that someone "went to upstairs." Say that he or she **went upstairs**.

upstairs[2] * [*adjective; no comparative*] on a floor above the main floor of a building; *opposite* DOWNSTAIRS: *He was renting one of the upstairs apartments.*
☛ Only use **upstairs** before a noun.

upstate[1] /ˈʌpˈsteɪt/ [*adjective; no comparative*] in the part of a state that is farther north: *They bought a house in upstate New York.*
☛ Only use **upstate** before a noun.

upstate[2] [*adverb*] in or to the part of a state that is farther north: *There are a lot of farms upstate. | They moved upstate.*

up-to-date /ˈʌp tə ˈdeɪt/ [*adjective;* **more up-to-date, most up-to-date**] modern or containing the latest information: *Do you have an up-to-date train schedule? | I keep my address book up-to-date.*

uptown[1] /ˈʌpˈtaʊn/ [*adverb*] in or to the part of a town or city that is farther north: *They live uptown. | Let's go uptown tonight.*
↪ Compare DOWNTOWN[1].

uptown[2] /ˈʌpˌtaʊn/ [*adjective; no comparative*] in the part of a town or city that is farther north: *an uptown store*
☛ Only use **uptown** before a noun.
↪ Compare DOWNTOWN[2].

upward * /ˈʌpwɚd/ or **upwards** /ˈʌpwɚdz/ [*adverb*] toward a higher position or level; *opposite* DOWNWARD: *The path continued upward.*

Uranus /ˈyʊrənəs; yʊˈreɪnəs/ [*name*] the planet that is the seventh from our sun

urban /ˈɚbən/ [*adjective; no comparative*] in or connected with a city or town: *People are moving from the country to urban areas. | an urban lifestyle*
↪ Compare RURAL.

urge[1] /ɚdʒ/ [*verb;* **urged, urging**] to tell someone strongly that he or she should do something: **urge someone to do something** ▸ *She urged him to stop smoking.*

urge[2] [*noun*] a strong desire to do something: **urge to do something** ▸ *He had a sudden urge to jump into the swimming pool.*

urgent * /ˈɚdʒənt/ [*adjective;* **more urgent, most urgent**] needing to be dealt with immediately: *There's an urgent phone call for you.*

urinate /ˈyʊrəˌneɪt/ [*verb;* **urinated, urinating**] FORMAL to get rid of liquid waste from your body: *A dog had urinated on the fence.*

urine /ˈyʊrɪn/ [*noun*] waste liquid from your body

us * /ʌs/ [*pronoun*] used to talk about yourself and one or more other people, as the object of a verb or preposition: *He'll never find us here! | She waved to us as she drove away.*
☛ Do not say "They are friends of us." Say **They are friends of ours.**
↪ See also WE.

U.S. * or **US** /ˈyuˈɛs/ [*name*]
the U.S. the United States: *How long have you been in the U.S.? | the U.S. government*
↪ See the synonym note at AMERICA.

U.S.A. * or **USA** /ˈyuˌɛsˈeɪ/ [*name*]
the U.S.A. the United States of America: *Soccer is becoming more popular in the U.S.A.*
↪ See the synonym note at AMERICA.

/i/ **see** /ɪ/ **big** /eɪ/ **day** /ɛ/ **get** /æ/ **hat**
/ɑ/ **father, hot** /ʌ/ **up** /ə/ **about** /ɔ/ **saw**
/oʊ/ **hope** /ʊ/ **book** /u/ **too** /aɪ/ **I** /aʊ/ **how**
/ɔɪ/ **boy** /ɚ/ **bird** /ɚ/ **teacher** /ɪr/ **ear** /ɛr/ **air**
/ɑr/ **far** /ɔr/ **more** /ʊr/ **tour** /aɪr/ **fire**
/aʊɚ/ **hour** /θ/ **nothing** /ð/ **mother** /ʃ/ **she**
/ʒ/ **measure** /tʃ/ **church** /dʒ/ **jump** /ŋ/ **long**

usage * /'yusɪdʒ/ [noun] FORMAL how words are or should be used: *There is a usage note explaining the difference between the words.*

use¹ * /yuz/ [verb; **used, using**]
1 to do something with a tool, piece of equipment, method, etc.: *He used a ladder to pick the apples.* | *Is that the best method to use?* | *What's this tool used for?*
2 to take an amount of something for a particular purpose: *I'll use some of the rice for dinner.* | *You used too much salt.*

— PHRASAL VERB

use up [phrasal verb]
3 to use all of something: **use up something** ▶ *He used up all the paint.* | **use something up** ▶ *Here, use this bottle up first.*

use² * /yus/ [noun]
1 when something is used, or a way of using something: *What do you think of the poet's **use of** language?* | *This plant has many uses.*

— PHRASES

2 **make use of** to use something for a purpose: *Can you make use of this old table?*
3 **be in use** being used: *The building is no longer in use.*
4 **be (of) no use (to)** to not be useful: *That box is no use—it has a hole in it.* | *Her advice is of no use to me.*
5 **it's no use** used to say that an action will not achieve something: *It's no use getting angry.* | *It's no use—I just can't move it.*

used¹ /yuzd/ [adjective; no comparative] owned by someone else before you; *synonym* SECOND-HAND; *opposite* NEW: *He sold **used** cars.*

used² /yust/ [adjective; no comparative]
— PHRASES
1 **be used to** to have experienced something many times or for a long time, so that you are not worried, annoyed, or surprised by it: *He was used to the noise of the city.*
2 **get/grow/become used to** to become familiar with something, so that you are not worried, annoyed, or

surprised by it: *It took me some time to get used to my new school.*

used to * /'yust ˌtə/ [modal verb] if you used to do something, you did it in the past, but you no longer do it: *I used to study judo.* | *They used to live in Texas.*
☛ Do not say "I used liking him" or "I was used to like him." Say **I used to like him.**

USAGE   used to

The negative form of **used to** is **did not use to**: *I didn't use to swim well, but now I do.* You can also say **used not to,** although it is more rare: *I used not to swim well.*
Don't say "usen't to." In questions, say **Did someone use to?**: *Did you use to go dancing often?*

useful * /'yusfəl/ [adjective; **more useful, most useful**] something that is useful is good or helpful: *She gave me some useful information.* | *The box was **useful for** storing his sports equipment.*

useless * /'yuslɪs/ [adjective; **more useless, most useless**] having no use or purpose: *Who bought that useless old car?* | *I knew **it would be useless to** argue with him.*

user * /'yuzɚ/ [noun] someone who uses a particular thing: *a computer user* | *He is a regular **user of** the library.*

usher /'ʌʃɚ/ [noun]
1 someone who works in a theater and helps people find their seats
2 a man who helps a groom and takes part in the wedding with him

usual * /'yuʒuəl/ [adjective; **more usual, most usual**]
1 happening or used nearly every time: *He wasn't home at **the usual** time.* | *She was sitting at her usual table in the café.* | *She looked much happier **than usual** (=happier than she usually did).*
— PHRASE
2 **as usual** used to say that what happened is what normally happens: *As usual, she wore a T-shirt and jeans.*

usually * /'yuʒəli/ [adverb] nearly every time: *We usually played soccer after school.* | *He is usually in bed by ten.*

utensil /yu'tɛnsəl/ [*noun*] a tool that is not electric, and is used for cooking, writing, or cleaning: *kitchen utensils* (=knives, large spoons, baking pans, etc.)

utility /yu'tɪlɪti/ [*noun; plural* **utilities**] a paid service that gives you water, electricity, gas, etc., for your home: *My rent doesn't include utilities.*

U-turn /'yu,tɜ-n/ [*noun*] when you turn in a road so that you drive back in the opposite direction: *You aren't allowed to* *make U-turns on this street.*

V

V * or **v** /vi/ [*noun*; **Vs** or **V's, v's**] the 22nd letter of the English alphabet
▷ *See the usage note at* ALPHABET.

vacancy /'veɪkənsi/ [*noun; plural* **vacancies**] a room in a hotel which is available to stay in: *I'm afraid we have no vacancies.*

vacant /'veɪkənt/ [*adjective; no comparative*] FORMAL a vacant seat, building, etc., is not being used and so is available; *synonym* EMPTY: *There were some vacant seats near the front of the train.*

vacation * /veɪ'keɪʃən/ [*noun*] a time when you are not at work or school, and often staying in a place where you do not live: *He took a short vacation.* I *She's on vacation in Italy.*

vaccinate /'væksə,neɪt/ [*verb*; **vaccinated, vaccinating**] to put a substance in someone's body that makes him or her unable to be harmed by a disease; *synonym* IMMUNIZE: **vaccinate someone for something** ▶ *Has your child been vaccinated for measles?*

vaccination /,væksə'neɪʃən/ [*noun*] when a substance is put into someone's body so that a disease cannot harm him or her: *Do I need any vaccinations to travel to Europe?*

vaccine /væk'sin/ [*noun*] a substance that is put into someone's body to make a disease unable to harm him or her: *a vaccine for the flu* I *We need more vaccine.*

vacuum[1] /'vækyum/ [*noun*]
1 a VACUUM CLEANER
2 a space with no air or other gas in it

vacuum[2] [*verb*; **vacuumed, vacuuming**] to clean a floor using a vacuum cleaner: *I did the vacuuming.*

vacuum cleaner ⊤ /'vækyum ,klinə-/ [*noun*] a piece of electrical equipment that sucks up dirt from carpets and floors; *synonym* VACUUM
▷ *See the picture at* APPLIANCE.

vague ⊤ /veɪg/ [*adjective*; **vaguer, vaguest**] without any details, and so not clear or definite: *I could see a vague shape behind the glass door.* I *She was* *vague about her plans.*

vaguely /'veɪgli/ [*adverb*] in a way that is not clear or definite: *The man's face seemed vaguely familiar* (=slightly familiar). I *"He's around somewhere,"* she said *vaguely.*

vain /veɪn/ [*adjective*; **vainer, vainest**]
1 too proud of being attractive, smart, important, etc.: *a vain man*
— PHRASE —
2 **in vain** without achieving what you wanted to achieve: *They tried in vain to get him to confess to the crime.*

valentine /'vælən,taɪn/ [*noun*] a card you give on Valentine's Day to someone you love or admire

Valentine's Day /'væləntaɪnz ,deɪ/ [*noun*] February 14th, a holiday when you give cards, flowers, or gifts to the person you love

valid /'vælɪd/ [*adjective; no comparative*] if a document or ticket is valid, it can still be used: *This ticket is valid for today only.* I *Do you have a valid passport?*

valley * /'væli/ [*noun; plural* **valleys**] a long area of low land between hills or mountains: *We lived in a valley.* I *a river valley*

valuable * /'vælyuəbəl/ [*adjective;* more valuable, most valuable]
1 worth a lot of money: *Be careful with that vase—it's valuable.*
2 extremely useful; *opposite* WORTHLESS: *He gave me some valuable advice.*

valuables /'vælyuəbəlz/ [*plural noun*] possessions that are worth a lot of money, such as jewelry: *Do not leave valuables in your hotel room.*

value[1] * T /'vælyu/ [*noun; plural* values]
1 used to talk about how much something is worth: *He was not sure of the value of the painting.* I *Their house had increased in value.*
2 used to talk about how useful or important something is: *Other scientists knew the value of his work.* I *This information will be of great value to teachers.*
3 a way of behaving or a quality that you think is right and is important to you: *Most of the people in our community share the same values.*
☛ This meaning of value is usually used in the plural.

value[2] [*verb;* values, valued, valuing]
1 to think that something is good or important: *You know how much I value your advice.*
2 to say how much something is worth: *They had their house valued.* I *The necklace was valued at $20,000.*
☛ Do not say "The watch values $80." Say **The watch is valued at $80.**

valve /vælv/ [*noun*] a part in a pipe or tube that lets liquid or air flow one way but not the other

vampire /'væmpaɪr/ [*noun*] an imaginary person who sucks blood from people's necks in order to live

van /væn/ [*noun*] a vehicle that has a motor and looks like a small bus without seats in the back, used for carrying goods: *a dry cleaner's delivery van*
➪ *See also* MINIVAN. ➪ *Compare* TRUCK.

vandal /'vændəl/ [*noun*] someone who deliberately damages property, especially public property

vandalism /'vændə,lɪzəm/ [*noun*] the crime of deliberately damaging property, especially public property

vandalize /'vændə,laɪz/ [*verb;* vandalized, vandalizing] to deliberately damage property, especially public property: *All the phone booths had been vandalized.*

vanilla /və'nɪlə/ [*noun*] a bean of a plant that is crushed or made into a liquid, and used to give food a particular taste: *vanilla ice cream*

vanish T /'vænɪʃ/ [*verb;* vanishes, vanished, vanishing] to go away suddenly in a way that is surprising or hard to explain: *When she looked again, the man had vanished.*
➪ *See also* DISAPPEAR.

vanity /'vænɪti/ [*noun*] the fact of being too proud of what you look like or what you can do

vapor /'veɪpɚ/ [*noun*] a lot of small drops of a liquid in the air: *Clouds are masses of water vapor.*

variation /,vɛri'eɪʃən/ [*noun*] when things or people of the same kind are different from each other: *Temperature variations can affect the growth of plants.* I *There is a lot of variation in the ability of the students.*

varied T /'vɛrid/ [*adjective;* more varied, most varied] consisting of a lot of different things: *The work is varied and interesting.*

variety * T /və'raɪti/ [*noun; plural* varieties]
1 when something consists of a lot of different things that make it interesting: *It is important to have variety in your job.*
2 a kind of thing, especially a plant: *They bought several different varieties of mushrooms.*

a van

— PHRASE —

3 a variety of a number of things of the same kind that are different from each other: *He has **a wide variety of** books.*

various * [T] /'vɛriəs/ [*adjective; no comparative*] several different, or many different: *I tried various times to call her.* | *various flavors of ice cream*

☛ Only use **various** before a plural noun.

varnish[1] /'varnɪʃ/ [*noun; plural* **varnishes**] a clear liquid you paint onto wood to make the surface shiny and hard: *a thick varnish*

varnish[2] [*verb;* **varnishes, varnished, varnishing**] to paint something with varnish: *a varnished table*

vary [T] /'vɛri/ [*verb;* **varies, varied, varying**]

1 to be different from other things or people of the same kind: *The musicians **vary in** their amount of experience.*

2 to change or be different: *The price of fruit varies depending on the season.*

⇨ *See also* VARIATION, VARIED.

vase /veɪs; vaz/ [*noun*] a container used to put flowers in, or as a decoration: *There was a **vase of** lilies on the table.*

vast [T] /væst/ [*adjective;* **vaster, vastest**] extremely large or great; synonym HUGE: *a vast canyon* | *There's a vast difference between their opinions.*

vault /vɔlt/ [*noun*]

1 a room with thick walls where money or valuable things are kept locked for safety: *a bank vault*

2 a large room where several people can be buried: *a family vault*

VCR /'vi'si'ar/ [*noun*] video cassette recorder; a machine that can record and play television programs, and play tapes of movies

veal /vil/ [*noun*] meat from a young cow

vegetable * /'vɛdʒtəbəl/ [*noun*] a plant or part of a plant that can be eaten and is not sweet: *They grow vegetables such as cabbages and carrots.*

⇨ *Compare* FRUIT.

vegetarian[1] [T] /ˌvɛdʒɪ'tɛriən/ [*noun*] someone who does not eat meat

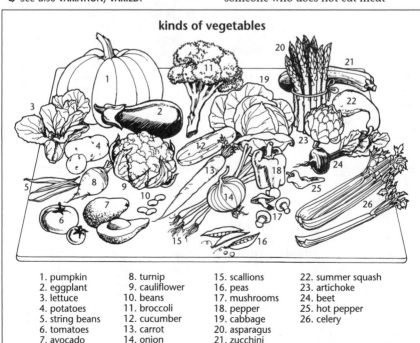

kinds of vegetables

1. pumpkin
2. eggplant
3. lettuce
4. potatoes
5. string beans
6. tomatoes
7. avocado
8. turnip
9. cauliflower
10. beans
11. broccoli
12. cucumber
13. carrot
14. onion
15. scallions
16. peas
17. mushrooms
18. pepper
19. cabbage
20. asparagus
21. zucchini
22. summer squash
23. artichoke
24. beet
25. hot pepper
26. celery

vegetarian² [adjective; no comparative] not containing or not serving any meat: *a vegetarian diet* I *a vegetarian restaurant*

vegetation /ˌvɛdʒɪ'teɪʃən/ [noun] the plants that grow in a place: *a jungle's thick vegetation*

vehicle * /'viːkəl/ [noun] something such as a car, truck, or bicycle that is used to carry people or goods: *Only* **motor vehicles** (=ones with motors) *are allowed on the highway.*

veil /veɪl/ [noun] a piece of very thin material that a woman wears over her face or head: *a bride's veil*

vein /veɪn/ [noun] a tube in your body through which blood flows to your heart
⇨ Compare ARTERY.

velvet /'vɛlvɪt/ [noun] thick, soft, shiny cloth: *a red velvet dress*

vending machine /'vɛndɪŋ məˌʃin/ [noun] a machine that gives you a drink, a candy bar, etc., when you put money in it

vendor /'vɛndɚ/ [noun] FORMAL someone who sells food or goods: *I bought the watch from a* **street vendor** (=someone who sells things on the street).

venom /'vɛnəm/ [noun] poison produced by a snake

vent /vɛnt/ [noun] a hole in a building or machine that is often connected to a pipe, and allows air, smoke, or gas to go in or out: *air vents* I *a heating vent*

ventilation /ˌvɛntəl'eɪʃən/ [noun] the flow of air in and out of a room or building: *This room has bad ventilation.*

ventilate /'vɛntəlˌeɪt/ [verb; ventilated, ventilating] to allow air to go in and out of a room or building: *Only use this paint in a* **well-ventilated** *room.*

Venus /'vinəs/ [noun] the planet that is second from our sun

veranda /və'rændə/ [noun; plural **verandas**] a structure that goes around part or all of the ground floor of a house, with a floor and roof but no walls
⇨ Compare PORCH.

verb * /vɝb/ [noun] GRAMMAR a word such as "read," "eat," or "be" that is used to talk about an action or situation: *In an ordinary sentence, the verb comes after the subject.*

verbal /'vɝbəl/ [adjective; no comparative] consisting of spoken words: *We have a* **verbal agreement**, *but not a contract.*

verdict /'vɝdɪkt/ [noun] the official decision of a court of law: *The verdict was "Not guilty."* I *The jury was unable to* **reach a verdict** (=decide).

verge /vɝdʒ/ [noun]
— PHRASE
be on the verge of to be very close to doing something: *His mother was on the verge of tears* (=almost crying). I *The team is on the verge of winning.*

verse /vɝs/ [noun]
1 one set of lines in a poem or song: *I couldn't remember the next verse.*
2 poetry: *He tried to express his feelings in verse.*

version /'vɝʒən/ [noun]
1 one form of something: *The car comes in two-door and four-door versions.* I *She has an older* **version of** *the software.*
2 one person's description of an event: *I wanted to give* **my version of** *the story.*

versus /'vɝsəs/ [preposition] used to talk about someone's opponent in a game or legal case; synonym AGAINST: *Tonight's game is Germany versus the U.S.A.*
⇨ See also VS.

vertebra /'vɝtəbrə/ [noun; plural **vertebrae** /'vɝtəˌbreɪ/] one of the bones forming a line down the middle of your back

vertical /'vɝtɪkəl/ [adjective; no comparative] with the top part directly over the bottom part, not leaning: *The walls of the old house were no longer vertical.* I *vertical stripes*
⇨ Compare HORIZONTAL.

very¹ * /'vɛri/ [adverb]
1 used to say that someone or something has a lot of a quality or feeling: *I was very pleased to see them.* I *He plays the violin very well.*
☛ Do not use **very** with words that already have a strong meaning, for example **disgusting, enormous,** or

crazy. For example, do not say "The smell was very disgusting." Say **The smell was disgusting.**

⇨ *See the usage note at* TOO.

2 used to emphasize adjectives that are superlatives or determiners: *a suit made of the **very best** cloth | They were born on the **very same** day. | Next year, I'll get my **very own** room.*

☛ Do not use "very" when you are comparing things. For example, do not say "This is very better." Say **This is much better.**

— PHRASES —

3 not very used to say that someone or something does not have much of a particular quality or feeling: *He was not very smart. | I'm not very tired.*

4 not very much not a lot, or not often: *We don't have very much time. | I don't eat meat very much.*

5 very much a lot: *I like her very much.*

☛ Do not use "very much" with nouns in positive sentences. For example, do not say "We have very much time." Say **We have a lot of time.**

very² [*adjective; no comparative*] used to emphasize that you are talking about the furthest, first, or last part of something: *We climbed to the **very top** of the hill. | The hero dies at the **very end** of the movie.*

☛ Only use **very** before a noun.

vest /vɛst/ [*noun*] a piece of CLOTHING without sleeves, worn over a shirt or for protection: *He buttoned up his vest. | a police officer's bullet-proof vest (=that bullets cannot go through)*

vet /vɛt/ [*noun*]
1 the short form of VETERINARIAN
2 the short form of VETERAN

veteran /ˈvɛtərən/ [*noun*] someone who was a soldier in a war; *synonym* VET: *Her father is a **veteran of** the Gulf War.*

Veterans Day /ˈvɛtərənz ˌdeɪ/ [*noun*] a U.S. holiday in November for remembering soldiers who have fought in wars

veterinarian /ˌvɛtərəˈnɛriən/ [*noun*] someone whose job is to give medical treatment to sick animals; *synonym* VET: *We took our dog to the veterinarian.*

veto /ˈvitoʊ/ [*verb;* **vetoes, vetoed, vetoing**] to use your official power or vote to say no to something, especially to stop a new law from being made: *The president says he will veto the bill.*

via /ˈvaɪə/ [*preposition*]
1 if you go somewhere **via** a place, you go to or through that place on the way: *We flew to Boston via New York.*
2 if you communicate **via** something, you do it using that thing; *synonym* BY: *The program was broadcast **via** satellite.*

vibrate /ˈvaɪbreɪt/ [*verb;* **vibrated, vibrating**] to shake with very small, fast, regular movements: *The washing machine began to vibrate.*

⇨ *See the synonym note at* SHAKE.

vibration /vaɪˈbreɪʃən/ [*noun*] when something shakes slightly very quickly: *The music was so loud you could feel vibrations.*

vice /vaɪs/ [*noun*]
1 a bad quality or a bad habit such as smoking; *opposite* VIRTUE: *He was a man with no vices.*
2 crimes that involve sex or drugs: *the vice squad (=police who deal with these crimes)*

vice president or **Vice President** /ˈvaɪs ˈprɛzɪdənt/ [*noun, name*] the person directly below a president in rank

vicinity /vɪˈsɪnɪti/ [*noun*] FORMAL

— PHRASE —

in the vicinity (of) near a place: *They wanted a house in the vicinity of the lake. | A bear was seen in the vicinity (=in this area) recently.*

vicious /ˈvɪʃəs/ [*adjective;* **more vicious, most vicious**] violent or nasty: *a vicious beating | a vicious rumor*

victim /ˈvɪktəm/ [*noun*] someone who has been harmed or killed by someone

/i/ **see**	/ɪ/ **big**	/eɪ/ **day**	/ɛ/ **get**	/æ/ **hat**
/ɑ/ **father, hot**	/ʌ/ **up**	/ə/ **about**	/ɔ/ **saw**	
/oʊ/ **hope**	/ʊ/ **book**	/u/ **too**	/aɪ/ **I**	/aʊ/ **how**
/ɔɪ/ **boy**	/ɝ/ **bird**	/ɚ/ **teacher**	/ɪr/ **ear**	/ɛr/ **air**
/ɑr/ **far**	/ɔr/ **more**	/ʊr/ **tour**	/aɪr/ **fire**	
/aʊɚ/ **hour**	/θ/ **nothing**	/ð/ **mother**	/ʃ/ **she**	
/ʒ/ **measure**	/tʃ/ **church**	/dʒ/ **jump**	/ŋ/ **long**	

or something: *the victim of the murderer* | *They sent food to the flood victims.*

victory * /'vɪktəri/ [noun; plural **victories**] when a person, team, or army wins; *opposite* DEFEAT: *It was their third victory in four games.*

video /'vɪdi,oʊ/ [noun; plural **videos**] a movie or television program recorded on tape: *Let's watch a video tonight.*

video game /'vɪdioʊ ,geɪm/ [noun] a game played using a computer or a similar electronic machine: *He plays video games all day.*

videotape¹ /'vɪdioʊ,teɪp/ [noun] TAPE that can have pictures and sound recorded on it, or the case that contains this material: *I put a blank videotape (=a tape used for recording) in the VCR.* | *I have the program on videotape.*

videotape² [verb; **videotaped, videotaping**] to record an event or a television program on videotape; *synonym* TAPE: *I was going out that evening, so I videotaped the game.*

view * /vyu/ [noun]
1 an opinion: *What are your views on violence in movies?*
2 the ability to see something: *We had a good view of the parade.* | *The guy in front of me is blocking my view.*
3 what you can see from a place: *Come look at the view from the balcony.* | *They waved until the car was out of view (=could not be seen).*

viewer /'vyuɚ/ [noun] someone who watches television or a particular television program: *Many viewers were upset by the program.*

vigorous Ⓣ /'vɪgərəs/ [adjective; **more vigorous, most vigorous**] using or having a lot of energy; *opposite* GENTLE: *a vigorous young man*

village * /'vɪlɪdʒ/ [noun] a very small town

villain /'vɪlən/ [noun] the main bad person in a book, movie, or play: *In the end, the hero captures the villain.*

vine /vaɪn/ [noun] a plant with long stems that spread along the ground or climb up walls: *Squash and pumpkins grow on vines.*

vinegar /'vɪnɪgɚ/ [noun] a liquid that tastes sour and is used in making or preserving food: *oil and vinegar salad dressing*

vineyard /'vɪnyɚd/ [noun] a field where grapes are grown, usually to make wine

violence * Ⓣ /'vaɪələns/ [noun]
1 actions that injure people: *I think too much violence is shown on TV.*
2 great force: *We were not prepared for the violence of the storm.*

violent * Ⓣ /'vaɪələnt/ [adjective; **more violent, most violent**]
1 injuring people, or involving actions that injure people: *a violent criminal* | *It's a very violent movie.*
2 having great force: *a violent storm*

violently * /'vaɪələntli/ [adverb]
1 in a way that injures people: *violently angry*
2 with great force: *The earthquake shook the house violently.*

violet¹ /'vaɪəlɪt/ [noun]
1 a small plant with purple or white FLOWERS
2 a blue-purple color

violet² [adjective; no comparative] of the color violet: *He loved her violet eyes.*

violin * /,vaɪə'lɪn/ [noun] a MUSICAL INSTRUMENT with four strings that you hold under your chin and play with a BOW³: *He plays the violin beautifully.*

VIP /'vi'aɪ'pi/ [noun; plural **VIPs** or **VIP's**] very important person; an important visitor, passenger, customer, etc., who is given special treatment: *The VIPs were given a special tour of the building.*

virtually /'vɝtʃuəli/ [adverb] almost: *The task seemed virtually impossible.*

virtual reality /'vɝtʃuəl ri'ælɪti/ [noun] a situation or environment made by a computer that seems completely real: *Virtual reality is used in games and to train people such as pilots.*

virtue /'vɝtʃu/ [noun; plural **virtues**] a good quality; *opposite* VICE: *He has the virtue of being honest.*

virus /'vaɪrəs/ [noun; plural **viruses**]
1 a very small living thing that can make you sick, or the illness caused by this: *The disease is caused by a virus.* | *the flu virus*

2 a computer program that destroys information or stops the computer from working correctly: *The virus got into the computer through e-mail.*

visa /'vizə/ [*noun; plural* **visas**] a mark put on your passport by an official of a foreign country which allows you to enter or leave that country

visible T /'vizəbəl/ [*adjective;* **more visible, most visible**] if something is visible, you can see it; *opposite* INVISIBLE: *The house was just visible through the trees.* | *Her embarrassment was visible to everyone.*

vision /'vɪʒən/ [*noun*]
1 your ability to see; *synonyms* EYESIGHT, SIGHT: *His vision got worse as he grew older.*
2 a picture you see in your mind about something that could happen or be true: *She has a vision of the kind of business she wants to own.*

visit¹ * /'vizit/ [*verb;* **visited, visiting**]
1 to go to see someone or go to a place for a short time: *She's away visiting relatives.* | *Have you visited them before?*
☛ Do not say "They visited to me." Say **They visited me.**
2 INFORMAL to have a conversation: *Sit down and visit for a while.* | *Grandma likes visiting with her church friends.*

visit² * [*noun*]
1 when someone stays with someone else or in a place for a short time: *I enjoyed my visit to Chicago.* | *I decided to pay him a visit* (=visit him).
2 INFORMAL when people have a conversation: *We had a nice long visit.*

visitor * /'vizitər/ [*noun*] someone who comes to see someone or comes to a place for a short time: *The city attracts visitors from all over the world.* | *We love having visitors.*

visor /'vaizər/ [*noun*]
1 the part of a cap that sticks out at the front
↪ See the picture at BASEBALL CAP.
2 the part of a HELMET that protects the face

visual /'vɪʒuəl/ [*adjective; no comparative*] connected with or involving sight: *They use a lot of visual aids in their teaching* (=things such as pictures, films, etc.).

vital T /'vaɪtəl/ [*adjective;* **more vital, most vital**] necessary or extremely important: *He had lost a vital document.* | *It is vital that you tell no one of our plans.* | *a matter of vital importance* (=that is extremely important)

vitally /'vaɪtəli/ [*adverb*] something that is vitally important is extremely important: *It is vitally important that you pass this test.*

vitamin /'vaɪtəmɪn/ [*noun*] a chemical that your body needs and that exists in small amounts in food: *Green vegetables contain a lot of vitamins.* | *Oranges are a good source of vitamin C.*

vivid /'vɪvɪd/ [*adjective;* **more vivid, most vivid**]
1 producing very clear pictures in your mind: *The book has a vivid description of a storm at sea.* | *vivid memories*
2 a vivid color is very strong and bright: *vivid red lipstick*

vocabulary * /voʊ'kæbyə,lɛri/ [*noun; plural* **vocabularies**] the words used in a language, or all the words that you know: *He has a wide vocabulary* (=knows many words).

vocal /'voʊkəl/ [*adjective; no comparative*] connected with or involving the voice: *This CD shows her amazing vocal skills.*
☛ Only use **vocal** before a noun.

voice * /vɔɪs/ [*noun*]
1 the sound produced when you speak or sing: *They could hear voices in the next room.* | *He had a very deep voice.* | *She spoke in a low voice* (=quietly).
━━ PHRASES ━━
2 lose your voice to become unable to speak: *She had a cold and lost her voice.*
3 lower your voice to speak more quietly: *Please lower your voices.*
4 raise your voice to speak more loudly, especially when you are angry: *He had never raised his voice to her before.*

/i/ **see** /ɪ/ **big** /eɪ/ **day** /ɛ/ **get** /æ/ **hat**
/ɑ/ **father, hot** /ʌ/ **up** /ə/ **about** /ɔ/ **saw**
/oʊ/ **hope** /ʊ/ **book** /u/ **too** /aɪ/ **I** /aʊ/ **how**
/ɔɪ/ **boy** /ɝ/ **bird** /ɚ/ **teacher** /ɪr/ **ear** /ɛr/ **air**
/ɑr/ **far** /ɔr/ **more** /ʊr/ **tour** /aɪr/ **fire**
/aʊɚ/ **hour** /θ/ **nothing** /ð/ **mother** /ʃ/ **she**
/ʒ/ **measure** /tʃ/ **church** /dʒ/ **jump** /ŋ/ **long**

5 at the top of your voice as loudly as you can: *He was shouting at the top of his voice.*

voice mail /'vɔɪs ˌmeɪl/ [*noun*] a system that records your spoken message when you phone someone who is not there

volcano /vɑl'keɪnoʊ/ [*noun; plural* **volcanoes**] a mountain from which ash, fire, and hot liquid rock sometimes come: *No one knows when the volcano will erupt.*

volleyball /'vɑliˌbɔl/ [*noun*]
1 a sport or game in which two teams hit a ball over a high NET using their hands, trying to prevent it from touching the ground on their side of the net: *They like playing volleyball on the beach.* | *a volleyball court*
2 the ball that is used in this game

volt /voʊlt/ [*noun*] a unit for measuring electricity: *a 9-volt battery*

voltage /'voʊltɪdʒ/ [*noun*] used to talk about the force of an electrical current: *What is the voltage of this outlet?*

volume Ⓣ /'vɑlyum/ [*noun*]
1 how loud a sound is, especially the sound of a television, radio, etc.: *Could you turn up the volume* (=make it louder), *please?*
2 the amount of space that something fills or contains: *How do you calculate the volume of a cube?*
3 a book, especially one of several that form a set: *The encyclopedia comes in four volumes.*

voluntarily /ˌvɑlən'tɛrəli/ [*adverb*] if you do something voluntarily, you do it because you choose to, not because you are forced to: *He voluntarily took his little sister to the park.*

voluntary /'vɑlənˌtɛri/ [*adjective; no comparative*] done because you choose to do it, not because you are forced to: *We get paid more for voluntary overtime work.*

volunteer[1] Ⓣ /ˌvɑlən'tɪr/ [*noun*] someone who offers to do something or works for no pay: *The teacher asked for a volunteer to carry the books.* | *volunteer fire fighters*

volunteer[2] Ⓣ [*verb;* **volunteered, volunteering**] to offer to do something: *I volunteered for the job.* | *I volunteer to*

do something ▸ *She volunteered to do the dishes.*

vomit /'vɑmɪt/ [*verb; plural* **vomited, vomiting**] if you vomit, food and liquid come up from your stomach and out of your mouth: *The smell made her want to vomit.*
↪ *See also* **be sick (to your stomach)** at SICK *and* **throw up** at THROW[1].

vote[1] ✳ /voʊt/ [*verb;* **voted, voting**] to raise your hand, put a mark on a piece of paper, etc., to show which person you want to elect, whether you agree with a plan, etc.: *I haven't decided who to vote for.* | *I voted against the proposal.* | *vote to do something* ▸ *A majority of members voted to accept the offer.*

vote[2] ✳ [*noun*] action or result of voting: *Mr. Bell won by 450 votes.* | *Let's take a vote on it.*

voter ✳ /'voʊtɚ/ [*noun*] someone who votes or is able to vote: *a registered voter* (=someone who has the right to vote in a particular place)

vow[1] /vaʊ/ [*verb;* **vowed, vowing**] FORMAL to make a serious and important promise, usually to yourself: *I vowed that I would not repeat the mistake.* | *vow to do something* ▸ *He vowed to return someday.*

vow[2] [*noun*] a serious and important promise: *wedding vows*

vowel ✳ /'vaʊəl/ [*noun*]
1 a sound that is produced when the air from your throat is not stopped at all by your lips, tongue, or teeth: *Can you hear the difference between these two vowel sounds?*
2 a letter used to represent a vowel sound: *The English vowels are "a," "e," "i," "o," and "u," and sometimes "y."*
↪ *Compare* CONSONANT.

voyage /'vɔɪdʒ/ [*noun*] a long trip in a ship or a space vehicle: *He is on a voyage around the world.* | *a voyage to the moon*

vs. the written abbreviation of VERSUS

vulgar /'vʌlgɚ/ [*adjective;* **more vulgar, most vulgar**] involving language or behavior that is very rude and usually connected with sex: *Don't be so vulgar.*

vulture /'vʌltʃɚ/ [*noun*] a large bird that eats dead animals

W

W * or **w** /ˈdʌbəlˌyu/ [*noun; plural* **Ws** or **W's, w's**] the 23rd letter of the English alphabet
➪ *See the usage note at* ALPHABET.

W or **w** the written abbreviation of WATT: *a 40W light bulb*

W. or **W** a written abbreviation of WEST: *He lives in W. Virginia.*
➪ *Compare* **E., N., S.**

wad /wad/ [*noun*] a substance or a number of things in one tight ball: *a **wad of** chewing gum* | *a **wad of** tissues*

wade /weɪd/ [*verb;* **waded, wading**] to walk through water or mud that is fairly deep: *I waded across the stream.*

wafer /ˈweɪfɚ/ [*noun*] a thin flat cookie: *vanilla wafers*

waffle /ˈwafəl/ [*noun*] a kind of flat bread that is cooked in a special pan that makes deep squares in it, eaten hot for breakfast: *We ate waffles and maple syrup.*

wag /wæg/ [*verb;* **wags, wagged, wagging**] to move a tail or a finger from side to side: *The dog was **wagging its tail** and barking.*

wage * /weɪdʒ/ [*noun*] the money that is earned by a worker who is paid by the hour: *She spends a lot of her wages on clothes.* | *the **minimum wage*** (=the lowest amount that an employer can pay per hour)
➪ *Compare* SALARY. ➪ *See the usage note at* PAY[2].

wagon /ˈwægən/ [*noun*]
1 a vehicle with four wheels that is pulled by a horse and used to carry things: *They loaded up the wagon and set off.*
2 a child's toy with four wheels and a long handle, used for carrying things: *He pulled the red wagon across the yard.*

a child's wagon

wail /weɪl/ [*verb;* **wailed, wailing**] to cry loudly, or to say something loudly and in a sad way: *"I want to go home!" wailed the child.*

waist * /weɪst/ [*noun*] the narrow part at the middle of your BODY

waistband /ˈweɪstˌbænd/ [*noun*] the part of a skirt or a pair of pants that fastens around your waist: *an elastic waistband*

wait[1] * /weɪt/ [*verb;* **waited, waiting**]
1 to stay in a place or not do anything until something happens: *Wait right there, okay?* | *I **waited** 40 minutes **for** the train.* | *She **kept** us all **waiting*** (=did not arrive at the agreed time). | **wait to do something** ▸ *I'm waiting to see the principal.* | **wait for someone to do something** ▸ *They waited for him to speak.*

— PHRASES —

2 can't wait (to do something) to be very eager to do something: *I can't wait to meet her!*
3 wait your turn to wait until other people have done something before you and it is time for you to do it: *Get in line and wait your turn.*
4 wait up! or **wait for me!** *SPOKEN* used to tell someone who is going away from you to stop: *Hey, wait up! I want to come with you.*

— PHRASAL VERBS —

wait on [*phrasal verb*]
5 to serve people food or drinks: **wait on someone** ▸ *Hotel staff waited on the guests.*
☛ Do not say "wait at someone." Say **wait on someone.**

wait up [*phrasal verb*]
6 to not go to bed until someone comes home: *His parents **waited up for** him.*

wait[2] [*noun*] when you wait for something or someone: *There's a short **wait for** the next bus.*

waiter /ˈweɪtɚ/ [*noun*] a man who serves people food and drinks in a restaurant
➪ *See also* WAITRESS.

waiting list /ˈweɪtɪŋ ˌlɪst/ [*noun*] a list of people who want to do or have something that is not available immediately: *We're **on the waiting list** for a bigger apartment.*

waiting room /'weɪtɪŋ ˌrum/ [*noun*] a room where people wait to be seen by a doctor, dentist, etc.

waitress ⊤ /'weɪtrɪs/ [*noun; plural* **waitresses**] a woman who serves people food and drinks in a restaurant
➪ *See also* WAITER.

wake * /weɪk/ [*verb;* **woke, woken, waking**]
1 to stop sleeping, or to make someone stop sleeping: *I woke early.* | *I didn't want to wake you.*
☛ Do not say that something "keeps you waking." Say that something **keeps you awake.**
➪ *See also* AWAKE. ➪ *Compare* **get up** *at* GET (definition 25).
━━ PHRASAL VERB ━━
wake up [*phrasal verb*]
2 to stop sleeping, or to make someone stop sleeping: *Wake up—it's 7:30.* | **wake someone up** ▸ *He asked me to wake him up at 6:00 a.m.* | **wake up someone** ▸ *Try not to wake up the baby.*
☛ Do not use a pronoun after **wake up.** For example, do not say "wake up her" or "wake up them." Say **wake her up** or **wake them up.**
➪ *Compare* **fall asleep** *at* ASLEEP.

walk¹ * /wɔk/ [*verb;* **walked, walking**]
1 to move along by putting one foot in front of the other: *She used to walk to school.* | *Don't walk on the wet floor.* | *He turned and walked away.*
━━ PHRASAL VERBS ━━
walk in on [*phrasal verb*]
2 to go into a place where you were not expected to be, and surprise or embarrass anyone who is there: *Don't walk in on people without knocking first!*
walk off with [*phrasal verb*]
3 to take something without asking: **walk off with something** ▸ *Someone's walked off with my calculator.*
walk out on [*phrasal verb*]
4 to leave your family, husband, wife, etc.: **walk out on someone** ▸ *One day his wife just walked out on him.*

walk² * [*noun*]
1 when you walk somewhere for pleasure or exercise: *He's gone for a*

walk *in the park.* | *I'm* **taking** *the dog* **for a walk.**
2 the way someone walks: *He has a very funny walk.*

Walkman
/'wɔkmən/ [*noun; plural* **Walkmans**] TRADEMARK a small machine for listening to music, that you can take with you anywhere

a Walkman

walk-up /'wɔk ˌʌp/ [*noun*] an apartment on the upper floor of a building that has no stairs: *a fourth floor walk-up*

wall * /wɔl/ [*noun*]
1 one of the sides of a building or a room: *They painted the walls yellow.*
2 a narrow structure made of a hard material such as brick or stone, built around or along an area: *That wall runs around the whole neighborhood.*

wallet /'wɑlɪt/ [*noun*] a small leather or cloth case where you keep paper money and plastic cards: *He took a ten-dollar bill from his wallet.*

wallpaper /'wɔlˌpeɪpɚ/ [*noun*] paper with special colors or patterns on it for decorating the walls of a room

walnut /'wɔlˌnʌt/ [*noun*] a large NUT that is often used in sweet foods, or the tree it grows on

walrus /'wɔlrəs/ [*noun; plural* **walruses** or **walrus**] a large animal that lives mostly in the ocean and has two long teeth

a walrus

wander * /'wɑndɚ/ [*verb;* **wandered, wandering**] to go to a lot of places or parts of a place, with no particular purpose: *She **wandered around** the store, but didn't buy anything.* | *Don't **wander off** (=do not leave where you are supposed to be).*

USAGE wander, wonder

Do not confuse **wander** and **wonder**. **Wander** means to go to places with no particular purpose: *We spent the afternoon wandering through the museum.* **Wonder** means to think about something that you do not know: *I wonder why the sky is blue.*

want * /wɑnt/ [*verb;* **wanted, wanting**]
1 to feel a need or desire for something: *I want some new shoes.* | **want to do something** ▸ *She wants to be a doctor.* | **want someone to do something** ▸ *He wanted me to go with him.*
➪ *See the warning at* WOULD (definition 3).

══ **PHRASE** ══
2 if you want if this is what you would like: *If you want, I'll make dinner.*

want ad /'wɑnt ˌæd/ [*noun*] a small advertisement in a newspaper or magazine asking for something: *I found my bike **through the want ads**.*

war * /wɔr/ [*noun*]
1 when two or more countries or sides fight each other: *Many soldiers were killed **in the war**.*
➪ *Compare* PEACE (definition 2).

══ **PHRASES** ══
2 be at war (with) if one country or side is at war with another, they are fighting each other: *The two countries have been at war for a year.*
3 declare war (on) to officially start fighting another country: *Then France declared war on England.*
4 go to war to become involved in a war: *Do you think we'll go to war?*

ward /wɔrd/ [*noun*] a large room or part of a hospital where there are beds for people with particular illnesses: *The cancer ward is on the fifth floor of the hospital.*

warden /'wɔrdən/ [*noun*] the person in charge of a prison

wardrobe /'wɔrˌdroʊb/ [*noun*] all the clothes you own: *She has a nice wardrobe.*

warehouse /'wɛrˌhaʊs/ [*noun; plural* **warehouses** /'wɛrˌhaʊzɪz/] a large building where goods are stored before being sold

warfare /'wɔrˌfɛr/ [*noun*] when countries or sides fight a war: *the danger of nuclear warfare*

warm[1] * /wɔrm/ [*adjective;* **warmer, warmest**]
1 having some heat, but not too hot; *opposite* COOL: *It was a warm spring day.*
2 protecting you from the cold: *Don't forget to wear your warmest clothes.*
3 very friendly; *opposite* COLD: *She was a warm and caring person.* | *We always get a **warm welcome** in Texas.*

warm[2] * [*verb;* **warmed, warming**]
1 to become warmer or make something warmer; *opposite* COOL: *I'm beginning to **warm up** now.* | *He rubbed his hands together to warm them.* | *He **warmed** the soup **up**.*

══ **PHRASAL VERB** ══
warm up [*phrasal verb*]
2 to do some easy exercises before doing more active exercise: *I watched the runners warming up for the next race.*

warmth * /wɔrmθ/ [*noun*]
1 a comfortable amount of heat: *She lay in the sun, enjoying the warmth.*
2 a friendly attitude or way of behaving: *The warmth of her smile made him feel better.*

warn * Ⓣ /wɔrn/ [*verb;* **warned, warning**] to tell someone about something bad that might happen or is going to happen: *Why didn't you warn me?* | **warn someone about someone/something** ▸ *I warned you about him.* | **warn someone (that)** ▸ *They warned us that things would get worse.*
☛ Do not say "I warned him not going." Say **I warned him not to go** or **I warned him against going.**
➪ *See also* BEWARE.

/i/ **see**	/ɪ/ **big**	/eɪ/ **day**	/ɛ/ **get**	/æ/ **hat**
/ɑ/ **father, hot**	/ʌ/ **up**	/ə/ **about**	/ɔ/ **saw**	
/oʊ/ **hope**	/ʊ/ **book**	/u/ **too**	/aɪ/ **I**	/aʊ/ **how**
/ɔɪ/ **boy**	/ɝ/ **bird**	/ɚ/ **teacher**	/ɪr/ **ear**	/ɛr/ **air**
/ɑr/ **far**	/ɔr/ **more**	/ʊr/ **tour**	/aɪr/ **fire**	
/aʊɚ/ **hour**	/θ/ **nothing**	/ð/ **mother**	/ʃ/ **she**	
/ʒ/ **measure**	/tʃ/ **church**	/dʒ/ **jump**	/ŋ/ **long**	

warning * /'wɔrnɪŋ/ [noun] when you tell someone that something bad might happen or is going to happen: He **was given** a **warning** about his bad behavior.

warrant /'wɔrənt/ [noun] an official document saying that the police are allowed to do something: They issued a **warrant for** his arrest. I a **search warrant** (=that says the police may search someone's home)

warranty /'wɔrənti/ [noun; plural **warranties**] a written agreement saying that the company that makes an object will repair or replace it free if it breaks during a particular length of time after it is sold: This washing machine comes with a two-year warranty. I Is it still **under warranty**?
⇨ Compare GUARANTEE².

warship T /'wɔr,ʃɪp/ [noun] a ship with weapons that is used in wars

was * /wʌz/ [verb] the past form of BE that is used with "I," "he," "she," "it," and names: It was very dark. I She was happy to see him.

wash¹ * /waʃ/ [verb; **washes, washed, washing**]
  1 to clean something with soap and water: He was outside washing his car.
  2 to clean your face or other parts of your body with soap and water: He washed and got dressed.
— PHRASAL VERBS —
wash away [phrasal verb]
  3 if water washes something away, it moves it from the place where it is: **wash something away** ▸ The flood had washed the bridge away.
wash off [phrasal verb]
  4 if a substance washes off, you can clean it off something else: I got ink on my fingers and it won't wash off.
wash up [phrasal verb]
  5 to wash your hands, or your hands and face: I'll go wash up.

wash² * [noun; plural **washes**]
  1 clothes and other things made of material that need to be cleaned or have just been cleaned: Will you put that **load of wash** in the dryer?

— PHRASE —
  2 in the wash being washed or ready to be washed: "Where are my blue pants?" "In the wash."

washable /'waʃəbəl/ [adjective; no comparative] washable things can be washed in water: The coat wasn't washable so I took it to the dry cleaner's.

washcloth /'waʃ,klɔθ/ [noun; plural **washcloths** /'waʃ,klɔðz; 'waʃ,klɔθs/] a piece of cloth for washing yourself

washer /'waʃɚ/ [noun] a WASHING MACHINE: Put your dirty clothes straight into the washer.

washing machine /'waʃɪŋ mə,ʃin/ [noun] a machine used to wash clothes and other things made of material; synonym WASHER

wasn't * /'wʌzənt/ the short form of "was not": She wasn't happy.

wasp /wasp/ [noun] a thin flying insect that can sting you

waste¹ * T /weɪst/ [verb; **wasted, wasting**]
  1 to use your time, money, etc., for things that are not useful: Hurry up. You're wasting time. I **waste something on something** ▸ I'm not wasting my money on candy.
  ☛ Do not say "waste money for something." Say **waste money on something**.
  2 to use more of something than you need: Don't leave all the lights on. You're wasting electricity.

waste² * T [noun]
  1 when something is not used in a useful way: The whole trip was **a waste of** money.
  2 things that are left when everything useful has been used: The factory was dumping **industrial waste** into the river.

wastebasket /'weɪst,bæskɪt/ [noun] a small container for unwanted paper and other things you want to throw away: He threw the letter in the wastebasket.
⇨ Compare TRASH CAN, GARBAGE CAN.

wasted /'weɪstɪd/ [adjective; no comparative] used for something that is not useful: My whole day was wasted waiting for the delivery.

wasteful /'weɪstfəl/ [*adjective; more wasteful, most wasteful*] using more of something than you need: *It is less wasteful to take a shower than a bath.*

watch[1] ✱ /watʃ/ [*verb; watches, watched, watching*]
  1 to look at something or someone to see what is happening: *He was watching TV.* | **watch someone do something** ▶ *She watched her father fix the bicycle.* | **watch someone doing something** ▶ *I watched the children playing.*
  ☛ Do not say "I watched them played." Say **I watched them playing** or **I watched them play.**
  ⇨ *See the usage note at SEE.*
  ━ PHRASAL VERBS ━
  watch for [*phrasal verb*]
  2 to pay attention to something so you know when something happens: *He stood at the window watching for her car.*
  watch out [*phrasal verb*]
  3 to pay attention to things around you and be prepared to deal with danger or problems: *Watch out—it's slippery.* | *He was told to **watch out for** snakes.*

watch[2] ✱ [*noun; plural watches*]
  1 a small clock that you wear on a band around your wrist
  ━ PHRASES ━
  2 keep watch to watch the area around you so that you will notice if there is danger: *I offered to keep watch.*
  3 keep a (close) watch on to watch someone or something carefully to stop something bad from happening: *His parents kept a close watch on him after the accident.*

water[1] ✱ /'wɔtɚ/ [*noun*] the liquid that is in rivers and oceans, and falls as rain: *Can I have a glass of water?* | *She dived into the water.*

water[2] ✱ [*verb; watered, watering*]
  1 to put water on plants to help them grow: *She watered the plants every day.*
  2 if your mouth or eyes water, they produce liquid: *The cold wind made his eyes water.*

watercolor /'wɔtɚˌkʌlɚ/ [*noun*] a painting done using paints mixed with water, or the paint itself

waterfall /'wɔtɚˌfɔl/ [*noun*] water falling from a higher part of a river or stream to a lower part

watering can /'wɔtərɪŋ ˌkæn/ [*noun*] a container for pouring water on plants

watermelon /'wɔtɚˌmɛlən/ [*noun*] a large green fruit that is red inside and has black seeds
  ⇨ *See the picture at MELON.*

waterproof /'wɔtɚˌpruf/ [*adjective; no comparative*] waterproof clothes or materials do not let water in: *Are these shoes waterproof?*

water-ski /'wɔtɚ ˌski/ [*verb; water-skis, water-skied, water-skiing*] to stand on two long boards and be pulled behind a boat, as an activity: *Do you know how to water-ski?*

water ski [*noun; plural water skis*] one of the two long boards that you stand on when you are water-skiing

water-skiing /'wɔtɚ ˌskiɪŋ/ [*noun*] a sport or activity that involves being pulled behind a boat while standing on two long boards: *We always go water-skiing in the summer.*

watery /'wɔtəri/ [*adjective; more watery, most watery*] containing too much water: *This sauce is watery.*

watt /wat/ [*noun*] a unit of electrical power: *You will need a 60-watt light bulb.*

wave[1] ✱ /weɪv/ [*verb; waved, waving*]
  1 to raise your hand and move it up and down or from side to side, for example to say hello or goodbye to someone who is not near you: *She waved at me.* | *They waved goodbye to us.*
  2 to move something from side to side in the air, or to move from side to side: *The children were waving flags.* | *The branches waved in the wind.*

wave[2] ✱ [*noun*]
  1 a raised amount of water in the

/i/ **see**	/ɪ/ **big**	/eɪ/ **day**	/ɛ/ **get**	/æ/ **hat**
/ɑ/ **father, hot**	/ʌ/ **up**	/ə/ **about**	/ɔ/ **saw**	
/oʊ/ **hope**	/ʊ/ **book**	/u/ **too**	/aɪ/ **I**	/aʊ/ **how**
/ɔɪ/ **boy**	/ɝ/ **bird**	/ɚ/ **teacher**	/ɪr/ **ear**	/ɛr/ **air**
/ɑr/ **far**	/ɔr/ **more**	/ʊr/ **tour**	/aɪr/ **fire**	
/aʊɚ/ **hour**	/θ/ **nothing**	/ð/ **mother**	/ʃ/ **she**	
/ʒ/ **measure**	/tʃ/ **church**	/dʒ/ **jump**	/ŋ/ **long**	

ocean: *She watched the waves crashing on the beach.*

2 a sudden increase in something such as a feeling or activity: *A wave of despair came over her.* | *The city is experiencing a crime wave.*

3 when you move your hand up and down or from side to side: *He gave a friendly wave.*

wavy /'weɪvi/ [*adjective;* **wavier, waviest**] having many gentle curves: *She had long wavy hair.* | *From the air, the river looked like a wavy line.*

wax /wæks/ [*noun*] a solid oily substance that bees make, used to make candles and other objects: *Wax dripped down the side of the candle.*

way[1] * /weɪ/ [*noun; plural* **ways**]
  1 a direction: *Which way did he go?* | *I waved, but he was looking the other way.*
  2 the path or course you take to a place: *Is this the way to the museum?* | *They were looking for the way out.*
  3 how you do something: *He was looking at me in a strange way.* | **way of doing something** ▸ *There must be an easier way of doing it.* | **way to do something** ▸ *They tried to think of a way to escape.*
  ☛ Do not say "a way doing it." Say **a way of doing it** or **a way to do it.**
  4 a distance: *He could see smoke a long way away.* | *I ran all the way here.*
  ↪ See the synonym note at FAR[1].
  5 used to talk about the direction that the front or top of something is facing: *You've hung that picture the wrong way up.* | *The plug goes in the other way around.*
  6 used to talk about an amount of time or things that need to be achieved: *You have a long way to go before you're ready to be a manager.* | *You've come a long way in the few months.*

  ━ PHRASES ━

  7 by the way SPOKEN used when you begin talking about something you have just remembered: *By the way, did you enjoy that book I lent you?*
  8 no way SPOKEN used to say that you definitely will not do something, or to show surprise: *"Tony asked me to the*

dance." "No way!" | *There's no way I am going to apologize to her.*
  9 in a way or **in some ways** used to say that something is partly true: *You're right, in a way.*
  10 get your way or **have your way** if you get or have your way, things happen in the way you want, even though someone else might want something different: *If she doesn't get her own way, she whines and complains.*
  11 in the way or **in someone's way** in a place that stops someone from going somewhere or seeing what he or she wants: *You're in the way. Go play somewhere else.* | *Someone got in my way and I couldn't take the photograph.*
  12 out of the way or **out of someone's way** away from a place so that someone can go somewhere or see what he or she wants: *Get out of the way!* | *I pushed him out of my way.*
  13 on the way or **on your way** coming to a place: *"Where's Laura?" "She's on her way."* | *On the way, we stopped for something to eat.* | *I'm on my way to the store now.*
  14 under way moving or happening: *When will the new project get under way?* (=start)
  15 make your way or **find your way** to go somewhere, usually somewhere that is a long distance away or is difficult to get to: *She made her way to the front of the crowd.*
  16 go out of your way (to do something) to make a special effort to do something: *They went out of their way to make us feel welcome.*
  17 Way to go! SPOKEN used to praise someone: *"Mom, we won our baseball game!" "Way to go!"*

way[2] * [*adverb*] very much or a long way: *That shirt's way too big for him.* | *My temperature was way above normal.*
  ☛ Use **way** before "too" or prepositions.

we * /wi/ [*pronoun*] used to talk about yourself and one or more people, as the subject of a verb: *We had a great time.* | *I think we need to have a talk.*
  ↪ See also US.

weak * T /wik/ [*adjective;* **weaker, weakest**]
1 not having much physical power or force: *She's feeling better, but she's still weak.* | *weak winter sunshine*
2 easy to break, harm, or damage: *Several of the steps were weak and dangerous.*
3 not good at a particular subject: *He was **weak in** science.* | *Math is my weakest subject* (=the subject I am least good at).
4 not having much power over other people or in particular situations: *a weak government* | *a weak economy*
5 weak drinks have a lot of water in them: *This coffee is too weak.*
➪ See also WEAKNESS. ➪ Compare STRONG.

weaken T /'wikən/ [*verb;* **weakened, weakening**] to become weaker, or to make someone or something weaker; *opposite* STRENGTHEN: *As we get older, our bones weaken.*

weakness /'wiknɪs/ [*noun; plural* **weaknesses**]
1 lack of strength or power: *A leader must not show weakness.* | *I felt a sudden weakness in my left leg.*
2 a fault or lack of ability; *opposite* STRENGTH: *You must be aware of your own weaknesses.*

wealth * /wɛlθ/ [*noun*] a large amount of money and possessions: *He was a man of great wealth.*

wealthy T /'wɛlθi/ [*adjective;* **wealthier, wealthiest**] having a lot of money and possessions; *synonym* RICH; *opposite* POOR: *She came from a wealthy family.*

weapon * /'wɛpən/ [*noun*] objects used to attack people, for example knives, guns, and bombs

wear[1] * /wɛr/ [*verb;* **wore, worn, wearing**]
1 to have clothes or jewelry on your body, especially a particular kind: *I can't decide what to wear.* | *She was wearing a black dress.*
➪ See the synonym note at DRESS[2].
2 to become thinner, weaker, or smoother because of rubbing or a lot of use, or to make something like this:

*The soles of her shoes **had worn thin**.* | *He keeps **wearing holes in** the knees of his jeans.* | *The river gradually **wore down** these rocks.*
3 to put or keep your hair in a particular style: *I like to wear my hair in a braid.*

— PHRASAL VERBS —

wear off [*phrasal verb*]
4 if a feeling or the effect of something wears off, it gradually stops: *The pain should soon wear off.*

wear out [*phrasal verb*]
5 to become unable to be used or to make something unable to be used, because it is old or has been used too much: *This type of battery wears out very quickly.* | *wear something out* ▸ *She wore her shoes out by walking everywhere.*
➪ See also WORN-OUT (definition 1).

wear[2] [*noun*]
1 damage caused by being used: *The furniture showed signs of wear.*
2 clothes for a particular kind of person or activity: *The store has a wide range of **evening wear**.* | *the men's wear department*

wearily /'wɪrəli/ [*adverb*] in a way that shows you are tired: *He wearily looked at his watch.*

weary /'wɪri/ [*adjective;* **wearier, weariest**] feeling that you need to rest or sleep; *synonym* TIRED: *She was weary after driving all day.*

weasel /'wizəl/ [*noun*] a small animal with short fur, a long thin body, and short legs

a weasel

weather * /'wɛðɚ/ [*noun*] the conditions outdoors, for example rain or sun: *The weather was pretty bad yesterday.* | *She hates hot weather.*
☛ Do not say "We had a bad weather." Say **We had bad weather.**
↪ *See the usage note at* WHETHER.

weave * /wiv/ [*verb; wove, woven, weaving*] to put threads or thin pieces of other materials under and over each other, to make cloth or a container: *The women weave the wool into rugs.* | *She was good at basket weaving.*

weave

web /wɛb/ [*noun*]
1 the net that a spider makes out of thin threads to catch insects in: *She watched a spider spinning a web.*
2 the Web all the computer documents that are connected through the system called the Internet; *synonym* WORLD WIDE WEB: *I searched the Web for information on Hong Kong.*

website or **Web site** /'wɛb,saɪt/ [*noun*] a connected group of documents on the Internet that has information about a subject, or lets you buy things: *The company set up its own website last year.*

we'd * /wid/
1 the short form of "we had": *We'd planned to start early.*
☛ Do not use "we'd" for **we had** when **have** is the main verb. For example, do not say "We'd a big house." Say **We had a big house.**
2 the short form of "we would": *We'd love to come.*

Wed. the written abbreviation of **WEDNESDAY**

wedding * /'wɛdɪŋ/ [*noun*] a ceremony in which two people get married: *They invited me to their wedding.* | *This clock was a wedding present.*

wedding ring /'wɛdɪŋ ,rɪŋ/ [*noun*] the ring that someone wears from the day that he or she gets married

wedge /wɛdʒ/ [*verb; wedged, wedging*] to put something tightly between two surfaces: *He wedged a magazine under the door.*

Wednesday * /'wɛnzdeɪ/ [*noun; plural* **Wednesdays**] the day of the week that is after Tuesday and before Thursday: *I'll see you on Wednesday.* | *I always go swimming on Wednesdays.*
↪ *See the usage note at* DAY.

weed[1] /wid/ [*noun*] a wild plant that grows in a place where it is not wanted: *The garden was full of weeds.*

weed[2] [*verb; weeded, weeding*] to remove weeds from an area: *She was weeding a flower bed.*

week * /wik/ [*noun*]
1 a period of seven days, especially one beginning on Sunday or Monday: *It's her birthday next week.* | *The course lasts six weeks.*
↪ *See also* **all day/night/week/ month/year** *at* ALL[1].
2 the days in the week when most people work, not Saturday or Sunday: *I don't go out much during the week.*

weekday /'wik,deɪ/ [*noun*] a day that is not Saturday or Sunday: *We have dinner at about 6:00 on weekdays.*

weekend /'wik,ɛnd/ [*noun*] Saturday and Sunday: *What are you doing on the weekend?* | *I sleep late on weekends.*

weekly[1] * /'wikli/ [*adjective; no comparative*] happening, done, or produced every week: *a weekly piano lesson* | *He keeps a weekly record of his expenses.*
☛ Only use **weekly** before a noun.

weekly[2] * [*adverb*] every week: *They are paid weekly.*

weeknight /'wik,naɪt/ [*noun*] any night of the week except Saturday or Sunday: *My bedtime is 9:30 on weeknights.*

weep /wip/ [*verb; wept, weeping*] FORMAL to cry: *She wept with pain.*

weigh * /weɪ/ [*verb; weighed, weighing*]
1 to be a particular amount in weight: *I weigh 130 pounds.*
↪ *See the usage note at* WEIGHT.
2 to put something on a piece of equipment to measure how heavy it is: *The clerk weighed the package.*

weight * /weɪt/ [*noun*]
1 used to talk about how heavy someone or something is: *The weight of*

the suitcase surprised her. | *She has lost weight* (=has become less heavy).
2 a heavy object, especially one that you lift in order to keep your muscles strong: *He lifts weights at the gym three times a week.*

USAGE Talking about weight

The usual way of asking about weight is to say **How much does it weigh?**: *"How much do you weigh?" "Around 110 pounds."* You can also say **What is its weight?** or **What is the weight of . . . ?**: *"How much will it cost to mail this letter?" "What's its weight?"* | *What's the weight of your luggage?* However, do not say *"How much is its weight?"*

---

weightlifting /'weɪtˌlɪftɪŋ/ [*noun*] a sport in which people lift a bar with heavy weights on each end

weird /wɪrd/ [*adjective;* **weirder, weirdest**] strange or unusual; *synonym* ODD: *I had this weird feeling that I'd met him before.*

welcome[1] * /'welkəm/ [*adjective;* **more welcome, most welcome**]
1 if you are welcome somewhere, people are happy that you are there: *You will always be welcome here.*
2 if something is welcome, people are happy that it has happened: *The rain gave us a welcome chance for a rest.* | *All suggestions are welcome.*

PHRASE

3 you're welcome SPOKEN used as a polite reply to someone who has just thanked you, to say that you were happy to do what you did: *"Thank you." "You're welcome."*

USAGE you're welcome, never mind

Do not confuse **you're welcome** and **never mind. You're welcome** is used as a reply after someone thanks you for something: *"Thanks for the coffee." "You're welcome." Never mind* is used when someone has told you about something slightly bad he or she has done, and you want to say that it does not matter: *"I broke your pen." "Never mind, I have another one."*

---

welcome[2] * [*verb;* **welcomed, welcoming**]
1 to greet someone in a way that shows you are happy he or she has come: *Hundreds of people came to the airport to welcome him.*
2 to be pleased about something, and to accept it: *The changes were not welcomed by everyone.*

welcome[3] * [*interjection*] used to greet someone and say that you are happy he or she has come: *Hello. Welcome to New York.* | *Welcome back!*

welcome[4] * [*noun*] a greeting that is given to someone when he or she arrives: *He was given a very warm welcome* (=a friendly one).

weld /weld/ [*verb;* **welded, welding**] to join pieces of metal together by heating them: *He welded the pipes together.*

welfare [T] /'welˌfer/ [*noun*]
1 money that someone who is very poor gets from the government: *He's currently on welfare* (=receiving money).
2 someone's health, happiness, and comfort: *They were concerned for the children's welfare.*

well[1] * /wel/ [*adverb;* **better, best**]
1 in a good or skillful way; *opposite* BADLY: *You played really well.* | *I don't write too well.*
 ➪ See the usage note at GOOD[1].
2 in a thorough or complete way: *Mix the paint well.*

PHRASE

3 may as well or **might as well** used to make or accept a suggestion that you are not very happy about: *We might as well go home.*
 ➪ See also **as well (as)** at AS[1].

well[2] * [*adjective;* **better, best**] not ill; *opposite* SICK: *He's not feeling very well.* | *She's a little better today.*

/i/ **see** /ɪ/ **big** /eɪ/ **day** /ɛ/ **get** /æ/ **hat**
/ɑ/ **father, hot** /ʌ/ **up** /ə/ **about** /ɔ/ **saw**
/oʊ/ **hope** /ʊ/ **book** /u/ **too** /aɪ/ **I** /aʊ/ **how**
/ɔɪ/ **boy** /ɝ/ **bird** /ɚ/ **teacher** /ɪr/ **ear** /ɛr/ **air**
/ɑr/ **far** /ɔr/ **more** /ʊr/ **tour** /aɪr/ **fire**
/aʊɚ/ **hour** /θ/ **nothing** /ð/ **mother** /ʃ/ **she**
/ʒ/ **measure** /tʃ/ **church** /dʒ/ **jump** /ŋ/ **long**

well³ [*interjection*]

1 used before saying something, or to show surprise or slight anger: *Well, I guess we ought to be getting back.* | *Well! He sure was rude.*

— PHRASE —

2 (oh) well said when you have to accept a situation that is disappointing: *Oh well, maybe you'll win next time.*

well⁴ [*noun*] a deep hole in the ground from which you get water or oil

we'll * /wil/ the short form of "we will": *We'll be there.*

well-being ⊤ /'wɛl 'biiŋ/ [*noun*] health and happiness: *Exercise can give you a feeling of well-being.*

well-known /'wɛl 'noʊn/ [*adjective; no comparative*] known about by a lot of people, especially in a particular area or in a particular group: *She married a well-known actor.* | *a well-known fact*
  ⤷ See the synonym note at FAMOUS.

well off /'wɛl 'ɔf/ [*adjective;* **better off, best off**] having enough money to buy what you want: *Generally, people are better off than they were 50 years ago.*

went * /wɛnt/ [*verb*] the past tense of GO¹

wept /wɛpt/ [*verb*] the past tense and past participle of WEEP

we're * /wɪr/ the short form of "we are": *We're late.*

were * /wɝ/ [*verb*] the past tense form of BE that is used with "you," "we," and "they": *We were glad to be home again.*

weren't * /'wɝənt/ the short form of "were not": *They weren't angry.*

west¹ * /wɛst/ [*noun*]

1 the west the direction in which the sun sets, or an area in this direction: *There were mountains to the west.* | *There are farms in the west of the country.*
  ⤷ See the usage note at DIRECTION.

2 the West countries in the western part of the world, especially North America and western Europe: *Chinese medicine is becoming more popular in the West.*

west² * [*adjective; no comparative*] in, toward, or coming from the west: *I'm from the west part of Kansas.* | *the west entrance of the building* | *a west wind*
  ☛ Only use **west** before a noun.

west³ * [*adverb*] toward or in the west: *The house faces west.* | *The town lies west of the river.*

western¹ * /'wɛstɚn/ [*adjective; no comparative*]

1 in or from the west: *California is in the western part of the U.S.* | *a western accent*

2 Western from or relating to countries in the western part of the world, especially North America and western Europe: *a meeting of Western leaders*

western² [*noun*] a movie or story about people in the western U.S. in the 19th century: *I like watching old westerns.*

Westerner /'wɛstɚnɚ/ [*noun*] someone who comes from the west of a country: *Not all Westerners are cowboys, you know!*

westward /'wɛstwɚd/ or **westwards** /'wɛstwɚdz/ [*adverb*] toward the west: *They drove westward.*

wet¹ * /wɛt/ [*adjective;* **wetter, wettest**]

1 containing or covered with a lot of liquid; *opposite* DRY: *I slipped on the wet floor.* | *It was raining hard and we got soaking wet* (=very wet).

2 if it is wet, it is raining: *It was wet, so they stayed indoors.* | *wet weather*

3 a wet substance has not yet dried: *Be careful—the paint is still wet.*

wet² * [*verb;* **wets, wetted, wetting**] to make something wet; *opposite* DRY: *Wet the cloth with warm water.*

we've * /wiv/ the short form of "we have": *We've got plenty of time.*
  ☛ Do not use "we've" when **have** is the main verb. For example, do not say "We've some good news." Say **We have some good news.**

a whale

whale /weɪl/ [*noun*] a very large sea animal that looks like a fish, and breathes through a hole in its head

wharf /wɔrf/ [noun; plural **wharves**
/wɔrvz/] a structure built in the shallow
water next to the shore, where boats
can stop; *synonym* PIER

what[1] * /wʌt/ [pronoun]
1 used to ask for information: *What did
she say?* | *You did what?* | *I asked him
what he meant.*
2 used to mean "the thing that" or "the
things that": *What we need is more
time.* | *He showed me what he'd made.*
━━ PHRASES ━━
3 **what about . . . ?** used to suggest
something or ask about something:
What about chicken for dinner? | *I'm
okay, but what about you?*
4 **what . . . for?** used to ask why
someone does something or why it
happens: *What did you do that for?*
5 **what if . . . ?** used to ask what will
happen in a particular situation: *Well,
what if she says no?*
6 **what's up?** SPOKEN used as an
informal greeting or to ask if anything
is wrong: *Hi, what's up?*

what[2] * [determiner]
1 used to ask for information: *What
time is it?* | *I asked her what kind of
music she liked.*
2 used to emphasize something: *What a
great idea!* | *What terrible news!*

USAGE   what, which

You use **what** and **which** to ask a
question about a choice you need to
make. **What** is used when you are
choosing from an unknown number of
things: *What flowers would you like in your
bouquet?* **Which** is used when you are
choosing from a limited number of things
or people: *Which dress should I wear—the
red one or the black one?*

You can use **of** after **which**: *Which of
the boys in your class do you like?* You
cannot use **of** after **what**.

---

what[3] * [interjection]
1 used to show surprise or anger: *"We
got engaged." "What?"*
2 used after someone has said your
name to get your attention, or when
you have not heard what someone

has said: *"Dad . . . ?" "What?"* | *"Can I
borrow the car?" "What?"*
☞ It is more polite to say **Pardon?** or
Pardon me? instead of "What?"

whatever[1] * /wʌt'ɛvɚ/ [pronoun,
determiner] used to mean "anything" or
"everything": *My parents let me do
whatever I like.* | *I will do whatever you
ask.* | *Come at whatever time suits you.*

whatever[2] * [conjunction] used to say
that something will happen in any
situation or every situation: *Whatever
happens, I'll always be your friend.*

whatever[3] * [interjection] used to say
that you have no opinion: *"We could
play cards, or watch TV." "Whatever."*

wheat * /wit/ [noun] a crop that
produces grain, or the grain it produces:
Wheat is used to make bread.

wheel * /wil/ [noun]
1 a round part of a vehicle, that it rolls
on: *The car's back wheels got stuck in
the mud.*
2 the round object in a CAR, bus, etc.,
that you turn to change its direction;
synonym STEERING WHEEL

wheelbarrow /'wil,bærou/ [noun] a
container with a wheel at the front and
two handles at the back that you use
for moving things outdoors: *He was
pushing a wheelbarrow full of weeds.*

wheelchair /'wil,tʃɛr/ [noun] a chair
with wheels that allows someone who
cannot walk to move around: *He has
been **in a wheelchair** for ten years.*

when[1] * /wɛn/ [adverb] at what time, on
what day, etc.: *When did you last see
him?* | *He asked when the store was open.*
☞ Do not use **when** with the present
perfect tense. For example, do not say
"When have they arrived?" Say **When did
they arrive?**

when[2] * [conjunction]
1 used to say what happens or what

/i/ **see**	/ɪ/ **big**	/eɪ/ **day**	/ɛ/ **get**	/æ/ **hat**
/ɑ/ **father, hot**	/ʌ/ **up**	/ə/ **about**	/ɔ/ **saw**
/oʊ/ **hope**	/ʊ/ **book**	/u/ **too**	/aɪ/ **I**	/aʊ/ **how**
/ɔɪ/ **boy**	/ɚ/ **bird**	/ɚ/ **teacher**	/ɪr/ **ear**	/ɛr/ **air**
/ɑr/ **far**	/ɔr/ **more**	/ʊr/ **tour**	/aɪr/ **fire**
/aʊɚ/ **hour**	/θ/ **nothing**	/ð/ **mother**	/ʃ/ **she**
/ʒ/ **measure**	/tʃ/ **church**	/dʒ/ **jump**	/ŋ/ **long**

will happen at a particular time: *You look much nicer when you smile.* | *I'll help you when I've finished this.*

☛ Do not say "I will call you when I will get back." Say **I will call you when I get back.**

2 used to give a reason why something is impossible, silly, surprising, etc.: *Why buy a new car when this one is OK?*

whenever * /wɛnˈɛvɚ/ [conjunction]
1 every time that something happens: *Whenever the phone rang, she ran to it at once.*
2 at any time: *Come whenever you like.*

where¹ * /wɛr/ [adverb] in or to what place: *Where do you live?* | *She asked me where I was going.*

where² * [conjunction] used to talk about the place in which something happens or the place something is: *This is the town where I was born.* | *There was a scar where the dog had bitten him.*

where'd /wɛrd/ SPOKEN
1 the short form of "where did": *Where'd he go?*
2 the short form of "where would": *If he's not at home, where'd he have gone?*
3 the short form of "where had": *Where'd he gone?*

where'll /ˈwɛrəl/ SPOKEN the short form of "where will": *Where'll we go shopping?*

where's /wɛrz/
1 the short form of "where is": *Where's the nearest bus stop?*
2 the short form of "where has": *Where's he gone?*

wherever /wɛrˈɛvɚ/ [conjunction]
1 used to say that something happens everywhere: *Wherever he went, people stared at him.*
2 in any place: *Sit wherever you like.*

whether * /ˈwɛðɚ/ [conjunction] used to talk about a choice, usually between two things, or a doubt about something: *I can't decide **whether** to go out **or** stay in.* | *I'm not sure **whether** it's allowed **or not**.*

USAGE whether, weather
Do not confuse **whether** and **weather**. **Whether** is used to talk about a choice

between two things: *I don't know whether or not to go to that movie.* **Weather** is used to talk about the conditions outdoors: *We had beautiful weather all week long.*

which¹ * /wɪtʃ/ [pronoun]
1 what member of a group or pair: *Which of them is the cheapest?* | *He asked me which I liked best.*
2 used to add more information about something: *I knocked on the door, which was slightly open.*

which² * [determiner] used when there is a choice between different things, to ask or say something about one of them: *Which book did you like best?* | *I couldn't decide which shoes to buy.*
↪ See the usage note at WHAT².

while¹ * /waɪl/ [conjunction]
1 at or during the time that something is happening: *He watched TV while he ate his breakfast.* | *Someone must have stolen it while they were asleep.*
2 although: *While I'd like to help you, I don't see how I can.*

while² [noun]
━ PHRASES ━
1 a while a period of time: *After a while, he got tired and stopped for a rest.* | *Let's wait a little while longer.*
↪ Compare AWHILE.
2 once in a while sometimes, but not often: *She visits me once in a while.*

whimper /ˈwɪmpɚ/ [verb; whimpered, whimpering] to cry quietly: *The baby was still whimpering a little.*

whine /waɪn/ [verb; whined, whining]
1 to complain in a high, annoying voice: *If you don't stop whining, you won't get any dessert.*
2 to make a long, high sound: *The dog was whining by the back door.*

whip¹ * /wɪp/ [noun] a short stick with a long piece of leather on the end, used for hitting animals or people: *A rider should try not to use a whip.*

whip² * [verb; whips, whipped, whipping]
1 to hit an animal or person with a

whip: *He whipped the horse to make it go faster.*

2 to stir a substance very quickly so that it becomes thick and stiff: *Whip the cream until it is thick.*

whirl /wɜrl/ [*verb;* **whirled, whirling**] to turn around and around very quickly, or to make something do this: *Snowflakes whirled to the ground.*

whisk[1] /wɪsk/ [*verb;* **whisked, whisking**]
1 to stir liquid food very quickly: *Whisk the eggs and the milk together.*
2 to take someone or something to a place very quickly: *He whisked her off to a party.*

whisk[2] [*noun*] a kitchen tool made of long wires attached to a handle, used for stirring liquid food very quickly

whisker /'wɪskɚ/ [*noun*] one of the long stiff hairs near the mouth of an animal such as a CAT

whiskey /'wɪski/ [*noun; plural* **whiskeys**] a very strong alcoholic drink, or a glass of this

whisper[1] ✳ /'wɪspɚ/ [*verb;* **whispered, whispering**] to say something in a very quiet voice; *opposite* SHOUT: *He whispered something in her ear.* | *Why are you whispering?*

whisper[2] ✳ [*noun*] a very quiet voice, or something said in a very quiet voice; *opposite* SHOUT: *They spoke in whispers.*

whistle[1] ✳ /'wɪsəl/ [*verb;* **whistled, whistling**] to make a high musical sound by blowing air through your lips or through a whistle: *He was whistling a tune.* | *Can you whistle?*

whistle[2] ✳ [*noun*]
1 a object that produces a high sound when you blow through it: *The referee* **blew** *his* **whistle.**
2 a sound produced by whistling: *There were cheers and whistles from the audience.*

white[1] ✳ /waɪt/ [*noun*]
1 the color of snow: *In the U.S., brides wear white.*
2 someone with light-colored skin: *More whites live in the suburbs.*
3 the clear part of the inside of an egg:

Add the beaten egg whites and stir them gently into the batter.

white[2] ✳ [*adjective;* **whiter, whitest**]
1 of the color white: *He wore jeans and a white shirt.* | *white walls*
2 having light-colored skin: *I was the only white kid in the class.*

White House /'waɪt ˌhaʊs/ [*noun*]
the White House the building in Washington, D.C., where the President of the United States lives and works

whiten /'waɪtən/ [*verb;* **whitened, whitening**] to become white or to make something white: *This toothpaste whitens your teeth.*

whittle /'wɪtəl/ [*verb;* **whittled, whittling**] to cut a block of wood into a shape, using a knife: *He sat on the porch, whittling a piece of oak.*

whiz or **whizz** /wɪz/ [*verb;* **whizzes, whizzed, whizzing**] INFORMAL to go somewhere very fast: *A girl on a skateboard whizzed past.*

whittling

who ✳ /hu/ [*pronoun*]
1 used to ask about a person: *Who left this magazine on my desk?* | *Who is the singer performing tonight?* | *I asked my dad who the man was.*
2 used to make it clear what person or people you are talking about: *I hate people who throw litter on the ground.*
3 used to add more information about someone: *I'm visiting my cousin, who moved here recently.*
↪ *See also* WHOM.

who'd ✳ /hud/
1 the short form of "who had": *They didn't know who'd won.*
☛ Do not use **who'd** when **had** is the main verb. For example, do not say "Who'd the best grades?" Say **Who had the best grades?**

/i/ **see** /ɪ/ **big** /eɪ/ **day** /ɛ/ **get** /æ/ **hat**
/ɑ/ **father, hot** /ʌ/ **up** /ə/ **about** /ɔ/ **saw**
/oʊ/ **hope** /ʊ/ **book** /u/ **too** /aɪ/ **I** /aʊ/ **how**
/ɔɪ/ **boy** /ɜr/ **bird** /ɚ/ **teacher** /ɪr/ **ear** /ɛr/ **air**
/ɑr/ **far** /ɔr/ **more** /ʊr/ **tour** /aɪr/ **fire**
/aʊɚ/ **hour** /θ/ **nothing** /ð/ **mother** /ʃ/ **she**
/ʒ/ **measure** /tʃ/ **church** /dʒ/ **jump** /ŋ/ **long**

2 the short form of "who would": *Who'd like to help me?*

whoever /hu'ɛvɚ/ [*pronoun*]
1 anyone who does something: *The computers were available to whoever wanted to use them.*
2 the person who does something, who is not known: *Whoever saved him was a brave man.*

whole[1] * /hoʊl/ [*noun*]
1 one complete thing or amount: *The parts fit together to form a whole.*

— PHRASES

2 on the whole used to say that something is mostly true: *On the whole, I think it's a good idea.*
3 as a whole when you consider everything: *The garden as a whole looks lovely this year.*

whole[2] * [*adjective; no comparative*] every part of something; *synonym* ENTIRE: *The whole building was destroyed.* | *I spent the whole morning practicing the piano.* | *I didn't see her again for a whole year.*
☛ Only use **whole** before a noun.

whole number /'hoʊl 'nʌmbɚ/ [*noun*] a number such as 1 or 20 that has not been divided into parts, rather than a number like ½ or 0.45 or 2.87.: *Fractions are not whole numbers.*

who'll * /hul/ the short form of "who will": *I know someone who'll help you.*

whom * /hum/ [*pronoun*] FORMAL used instead of "who" as the object of a verb or preposition: *To whom did you wish to speak?* | *She has three brothers, all of whom are doctors.*
☛ In spoken English, people often use **who** instead of **whom**.

who're * /huɚ/ the short form of "who are": *People who're interested in animals will love this book.*

who's * /huz/
1 the short form of "who is": *Who's the best soccer player in the world?*
2 the short form of "who has": *Who's taken my book?*
☛ Do not use "who's" for **who has** when **have** is the main verb. For example, do not say "Who's my book?" Say **Who has my book?**
☛ Do not confuse **who's** and **whose**.

whose * /huz/ [*determiner, pronoun*]
1 used to ask who owns something: *Whose is this bag?* | *He asked me whose sweater that was.*
2 used to make it clear who or what you are talking about: *That's the man whose car was stolen.*
3 used to add information about something belonging to a person or thing: *Jennifer, whose writing is neater than mine, wrote the labels.*

who've * /huv/ the short form of "who have": *There are lots of people who've had this problem.*
☛ Do not use "who've" for **who have** when **have** is the main verb. For example, do not say "She treats people who've cancer." Say **She treats people who have cancer.**

why * /waɪ/ [*adverb*]
1 for what reason: *Why did you lie to me?* | *"I don't like him." "Why not?"* | *I'm not sure why they left early.*

— PHRASE

2 why not . . . ? used to make a suggestion or agree to something: *Why not write him a letter?*

wicked /'wɪkɪd/ [*adjective;* **more wicked, most wicked**] OLD-FASHIONED morally bad; *synonym* EVIL: *a wicked witch*

wide[1] * Ⓣ /waɪd/ [*adjective;* **wider, widest**]
1 measuring a lot from one side to the other; *synonym* BROAD; *opposite* NARROW: *The wide streets were lined with trees.*
2 measuring a particular distance from one side to the other: *The river is 500 yards wide here.* | *How wide is the space?*
☛ Do not use **wide** before a noun in this meaning.
3 including a lot of things: *They sell a wide range of goods.*
⇨ See also WIDELY, WIDEN, WIDTH.

wide[2] * Ⓣ [*adverb*]
1 with a big space between the two parts of something: *The door was wide open.* | *The crocodile opened its mouth wide.*

— PHRASE —
2 wide awake completely awake: *Although it was after midnight, I was still wide awake.*
⇨ Compare **fast asleep** at FAST².

USAGE wide, widely
Do not confuse the adverbs **wide** and **widely**. Use **wide** when there is a big space between the two parts of something: *He opened his eyes wide.* | *She left the window wide open.* Use **widely** to say that something happens in many places, or to a great degree: *English is widely spoken.*

widely /'waɪdli/ [*adverb*]
1 in or to many parts of a country or of the world: *This medicine is now widely available.*
2 to a great degree: *Their carpets vary widely in price.*
⇨ See the usage note at WIDE².

widen /'waɪdən/ [*verb*; **widened, widening**] to become wider or to make something wider; *opposite* NARROW: *They widened the driveway.* | *The crack in the wall had widened.*

widespread Ⓣ /'waɪd'spred/ [*adjective*; **more widespread, most widespread**] existing or happening in many parts of an area: *There is widespread flooding in the region.*

widow /'wɪdoʊ/ [*noun*] a woman whose husband has died

widower /'wɪdoʊɚ/ [*noun*] a man whose wife has died

width * /wɪdθ/ [*noun*] used to talk about how wide something is: *He measured the width of the screen.*

wife * /waɪf/ [*noun*; *plural* **wives**] the woman that a man is married to: *He told his wife what had happened.*
⇨ Compare HUSBAND.

wig /wɪg/ [*noun*] an object made from hair, which someone wears on his or her head: *She sometimes wore a red wig.*

wiggle /'wɪgəl/ [*verb*; **wiggled, wiggling**] to move something with small movements, side to side or up and down: *She wiggled her toes in the water.* | *Stop wiggling and put on your seat belt.*
⇨ Compare WRIGGLE.

wild¹ * /waɪld/ [*adjective*; **wilder, wildest**]
1 wild animals and plants live in natural areas and are not taken care of by people: *She knew the names of all the wild flowers they saw.*
⇨ Compare TAME¹.
2 very excited or angry, and not controlling your behavior: *When the singer appeared, the audience went wild.*
⇨ Compare CALM¹ (definition 1).
— PHRASE —
3 be wild about INFORMAL to like something very much; *synonym* LOVE: *My son is just wild about soccer.*

wild² * [*noun*]
— PHRASE —
in the wild in a natural environment: *There aren't many tigers left in the wild.*

wilderness /'wɪldɚnɪs/ [*noun*] an area of natural land where people do not live or grow crops: *They like to camp in the wilderness.* | *A wilderness area*

wildlife /'waɪld,laɪf/ [*noun*] wild animals and plants: *The tourists hoped to see some of the local wildlife.*

wildly /'waɪldli/ [*adverb*] in an excited or angry way, without controlling your emotions: *The crowd was cheering wildly.*

will¹ * /wɪl/ [*modal verb*]
1 used to form the future tenses: *A cab will be here soon.* | *Will you stay long?* | *I'll (=I will) call you later.* | *She'll (=she will) arrive soon.* | *They'll (=they will) leave tomorrow.*
2 used to say what you are willing to do: *I will try to help you.*
3 used to say that something is possible: *My car will hold six people.*
⇨ See also CAN¹ (definition 4).
⇨ See also WON'T.
— PHRASE —
4 will you . . . ? used to ask or tell someone to do something: *Will you tell him I called, please?* | *Will you be quiet!*

/i/ see /ɪ/ big /eɪ/ **day** /ɛ/ get /æ/ **hat**
/a/ **father**, hot /ʌ/ **up** /ə/ **about** /ɔ/ **saw**
/oʊ/ hope /ʊ/ book /u/ too /aɪ/ **I** /aʊ/ how
/ɔɪ/ boy /ɝ/ **bird** /ɚ/ teacher /ɪr/ ear /ɛr/ **air**
/ɑr/ far /ɔr/ more /ʊr/ tour /aɪr/ fire
/aʊɚ/ **hour** /θ/ nothing /ð/ mother /ʃ/ **she**
/ʒ/ measure /tʃ/ **church** /dʒ/ jump /ŋ/ long

will[2] * [noun]
1 the desire or intention to do something: *He was taken there against his will* (=he did not want to go).
2 a document saying who you want to receive your money and possessions when you die: *Her father hadn't made a will.* | *She left him $50,000 in her will.*

willing * /'wɪlɪŋ/ [adjective; more willing, most willing] ready or happy to do something; opposite UNWILLING: **willing to do something** ▶ *They were willing to consider his request.* | *We had plenty of willing assistants.*

willow /'wɪloʊ/ [noun] a tree with long narrow leaves and branches that grow to the ground

wilt /wɪlt/ [verb; wilted, wilting] if a plant wilts, it becomes less upright, for example because it does not have enough water: *The flowers were wilting in the hot sun.*

win[1] * /wɪn/ [verb; won, winning]
1 to do better than the other person or team in a game, competition, fight, etc.; opposite LOSE: *The youngest boy won the race.* | *Who won?*
☛ Do not say "We will win you." Say **We will beat you.**
2 to get something because you did best in a game, competition, etc.: *She won first prize.* | *He won a TV in a competition.*
⇨ *See the synonym note at* GAIN.
⇨ *See also* WINNER.

win[2] [noun] when a person or team wins a game, competition, etc.; opposite LOSS: *The team has had only two wins this season.*

wind[1] * /wɪnd/ [noun] air that moves quickly: *The trees swayed in the wind.* | *A gust of wind blew the door shut.*
⇨ *Compare* BREEZE, GALE.

wind[2] * /waɪnd/ [verb; wound, winding]
1 to turn a key or part of a watch, clock, etc., so that it will keep working: *He'd forgotten to wind his watch.* | *Did you wind the clock up?* | *You wind up the toy and it plays a tune.*
2 if you wind a long piece of something

or if it winds, it goes around something else several times; opposite UNWIND: *The tape is still winding.* | *He wound the rope around the post.*
3 if a road or river winds somewhere, it has a lot of curves: *The road wound up the hill.* | *winding streets*

windmill /'wɪnd,mɪl/ [noun] a tall narrow structure with long, flat, wide parts on top that are turned by the wind, used for making electricity: *All their farm's power comes from windmills.*

window * /'wɪndoʊ/ [noun]
1 a space in the wall of a building or the side of a vehicle, filled by glass: *I opened the window to let some air in.*
⇨ *See the pictures at* CAR *and* HOUSE.
2 the area on a computer screen that shows the program you are using: *She shut down all the windows she was using.*

window-shopping /'wɪndoʊ ,ʃɑpɪŋ/ [noun] the activity of looking at things in store windows, but not buying anything

windowsill /'wɪndoʊ,sɪl/ [noun] the shelf at the bottom of a window

windshield /'wɪnd,ʃild/ [noun] the front window of a CAR or other vehicle

windshield wiper /'wɪndʃild ,waɪpɚ/ [noun] a rubber blade that moves over the front or back window of a CAR, clearing off rain; synonym WIPER

windy /'wɪndi/ [adjective; windier, windiest] if it is windy, there is a strong wind blowing: *It was very windy on top of the hill.* | *a windy day*

wine * /waɪn/ [noun] an alcoholic drink made from grapes: *a bottle of red wine*

wing * /wɪŋ/ [noun]
1 one of the two body parts that a BIRD uses to fly: *The bird flapped its wings* (=moved its wings up and down).
2 one of the two flat parts that stick out of the sides of an AIRPLANE
3 part of a building that sticks out from the main part: *The labs are in the science wing.*

wink /wɪŋk/ [verb; winked, winking] to close and open one eye quickly to tell someone something, for example that you are making a joke: *"That's right, isn't it?"* he said, **winking at her.**

winner * /'wɪnɚ/ [*noun*] the person or team that wins a game or competition; *opposite* LOSER

winter * /'wɪntɚ/ [*noun*] the cold season between fall and spring
⇨ *See the usage note at* SEASON.

wintertime /'wɪntɚˌtaɪm/ [*noun*] the time of the year when it is winter: *In the wintertime it can get too cold to go out.*

wipe /waɪp/ [*verb*; **wiped, wiping**]
  1 to move your hand or a cloth across a surface to remove liquid or dirt: *He wiped his face.* | *She **wiped off** the table with a sponge.* | **wipe something off (something)** ▸ *I wiped the dust off the shelf.*

— PHRASAL VERB ——————
  wipe out [*phrasal verb*] INFORMAL
  2 to destroy a group of people or things completely: **wipe something out** ▸ *Pollution will wipe whole species out.*

wiper /'waɪpɚ/ [*noun*] a rubber blade that moves over the front or back window of a car, clearing off rain; *synonym* WINDSHIELD WIPER: *He had his wipers going.*

wire * /waɪr/ [*noun*] a long thin piece of metal: *an electrical wire* | *a wire clothes hanger*

wisdom * Ⓣ /'wɪzdəm/ [*noun*] the quality of being wise: *Her grandfather was a man of great wisdom.*

wise * /waɪz/ [*adjective*; **wiser, wisest**]
  1 if something is wise, it is a good and sensible thing to do; *opposite* UNWISE: *I think that's a wise decision.* | *It would be wise to wait a few days.*
  2 having a lot of knowledge or experience, and able to judge what is best to do: *He wanted advice from someone older and wiser.*

wish[1] * /wɪʃ/ [*verb*; **wishes, wished, wishing**]
  1 to want something to happen or be true, even though it is not likely or not true: *I wish I could help you, but I can't.* | *He **wished that** he had worked harder.*
  ☛ Only use past tenses and plural

forms of verbs with **wish.** For example, do not say "I wish I have more money" or "I wish I was rich." Say **I wish I had more money** or **I wish I were rich.**

— PHRASE ——————
  2 wish someone something to say that you hope that something will happen to someone: *She wished me good luck.*

wish[2] * [*noun*; *plural* **wishes**]
  1 the fact that someone wants to do something or wants something to happen: *She respected her parents' wishes.*
  2 something that you say or think you hope will happen, especially by magic: *She closed her eyes and **made a wish.***

wit /wɪt/ [*noun*]
  1 the ability to say smart and funny things: *a writer who was famous for his wit*
  2 wits [*plural*] your mind or your ability to think: *In that kind of situation, you have to **use your wits** (=depend on quick thinking).*

witch /wɪtʃ/ [*noun*; *plural* **witches**] a woman in stories, usually an evil one, who does magic

with * /wɪθ; wɪð/ [*preposition*]
  1 near someone or something, or together: *Stay here with me.* | *He put the letter with the others.*
  2 having or including something; *opposite* WITHOUT: *a girl with black hair* | *I need a suitcase with a strong handle.* | *He did it with the help of his brother.*
  3 used to say that you use something to do something: *He tied the package with string.*
  4 used to give the reason for something: *He was shaking with fear.* | *The ground was white with snow.*
  5 used to say how someone does something: *With great care, she lifted the vase from its box.* | *She watched with*

/i/ **see** /ɪ/ **big** /eɪ/ **day** /ɛ/ **get** /æ/ **hat**
/ɑ/ **father, hot** /ʌ/ **up** /ə/ **about** /ɔ/ **saw**
/oʊ/ **hope** /ʊ/ **book** /u/ **too** /aɪ/ **I** /aʊ/ **how**
/ɔɪ/ **boy** /ɚ/ **bird** /ɚ/ **teacher** /ɪr/ **ear** /ɛr/ **air**
/ɑr/ **far** /ɔr/ **more** /ʊr/ **tour** /aɪr/ **fire**
/aʊɚ/ **hour** /θ/ **nothing** /ð/ **mother** /ʃ/ **she**
/ʒ/ **measure** /tʃ/ **church** /dʒ/ **jump** /ŋ/ **long**

amusement as he tried to open the can. |
"Yes," he said with a smile.

6 used to say what state or condition
something is in: *I always sleep with the
window open.* | *Something's wrong with
the phone.*

7 used to say who is involved in
something: *I had an argument with her.*

withdraw /wɪð'drɔ/ [*verb;* **withdrew,
withdrawn, withdrawing**]
1 to remove something, especially
money from a bank: *He withdrew $200
from his account.*
2 to leave a place, organization, or
event: *She had to* **withdraw from** *the
competition.*

withdrawal /wɪð'drɔəl/ [*noun*] when
someone removes something, especially
money from a bank: *I'd like to* **make a
withdrawal.**

withdrawn /wɪð'drɔn/ [*verb*] the past
participle of WITHDRAW

withdrew /wɪð'dru/ [*verb*] the past
tense of WITHDRAW

wither /'wɪðɚ/ [*verb;* **withered,
withering**] if a plant or part of a plant
withers, it becomes weak and dry, and
may die: *All the leaves on the tree had
withered.*

within * /wɪð'ɪn/ [*preposition*]
1 before a particular amount of time
has passed: *You should receive the goods
within ten days.*
2 no farther than a particular distance:
He stood **within 15 feet of** *the president.*
3 inside something: *Many people within
the company are worried about the
changes.*

without * /wɪð'aʊt/ [*preposition*]
1 not having something or not
including someone; opposite WITH: *I
don't like vegetables without salt.* | *I
couldn't have done it without you!*
2 used to say that something does not
happen: *She left without telling anyone.*

witness[1] * /'wɪtnɪs/ [*noun; plural*
witnesses] someone who saw a crime
or accident happen: *Were there any*
witnesses to *the robbery?*

witness[2] [*verb;* **witnesses, witnessed,
witnessing**] to see something happen:
Did anyone witness the accident?

witty /'wɪti/ [*adjective;* **wittier, wittiest**]
funny, in a smart way: *He was the
wittiest man I ever knew.* | *witty remarks*

wives * /waɪvz/ [*noun*] the plural of WIFE

wizard /'wɪzɚd/ [*noun*] a man in stories
who does magic

wobble /'wabəl/ [*verb;* **wobbled,
wobbling**] to move from side to side in
a way that is not steady: *He wobbled
and fell off his bicycle.*
↪ *See the synonym note at* SHAKE.

wok /wak/ [*noun*] a large, deep, round
pan used for cooking things in oil

woke * /woʊk/ [*verb*] the past tense of
WAKE

woken * /'woʊkən/ [*verb*] the past
participle of WAKE

wolf /wʊlf/ [*noun; plural* **wolves** /wʊlvz/]
a wild animal that looks like a large
dog

woman * /'wʊmən/ [*noun; plural*
women] an adult female person: *A
group of men and women were standing
outside the factory.*
↪ *See the usage note at* GENTLEMAN.

womb /wum/ [*noun*] the part of a
woman's body where a baby grows
before it is born

women * /'wɪmən/ [*noun*] the plural of
WOMAN

won * /wʌn/ [*verb*] the past tense and
past participle of WIN[1]

wonder[1] ⊤ /'wʌndɚ/ [*verb;* **wondered,
wondering**] to think about something
that you do not know or are surprised
by: *He* **wondered if** *she'd call.* | *I* **wonder
why** *she didn't come to the party.*
↪ *See the usage note at* WANDER.

wonder[2] [*noun*]
1 great admiration or surprise, or
something that makes you feel this:
She gazed with wonder at all the flowers.
| *It's a wonder that he wasn't hurt.*

━ PHRASE ━━━━━
2 no wonder used to say that you
are not surprised about something,
because you now know the reason for

it: *He woke up after eight? No wonder he was late for school!*

wonderful /ˈwʌndɚfəl/ [*adjective;* **more wonderful, most wonderful**] extremely good or nice: *It's a wonderful book!* | *It would be wonderful to see you again.*

won't * /woʊnt/ the short form of "will not": *I won't forget.*

wood * /wʊd/ [*noun*]
1 the substance that forms the main part of a tree, and is used for making things: *a desk made of wood* | *He's outside chopping wood for the fire.*
2 woods [*plural*] an area with trees growing near each other: *They went for a walk* **in the woods.** | *The woods around here are full of deer.*

wooden * /ˈwʊdən/ [*adjective; no comparative*] made of wood: *They sat around a large wooden table.*

woodwork /ˈwʊdˌwɜ˞k/ [*noun*] the wood around the doors, windows, etc., inside a house: *They finished painting the woodwork.*

wool[1] * /wʊl/ [*noun*] the hair that grows on sheep, or thread or cloth made from this

wool[2] * [*adjective; no comparative*] made of wool: *a wool sweater*

word * /wɜ˞d/ [*noun*]
1 a letter or a set of letters that means something and is used to make sentences: *What does the word "prairie" mean?* | *I cannot express my feelings* **in words.** | *What's the Chinese* **word for** *"people"?*
☛ In some Asian languages, words are made from characters, not letters.
2 what someone promises or says is true: *Would he* **keep his word?** (=do what he promised) | *I won't tell anyone. I* **give you my word** (=I promise). | *Are you going to* **take his word for it?** (=believe what he says)
3 something that is said or written: *He* **didn't say a word** (=did not speak). | *I can't understand a word you're saying.* | *She believed every word he said.* | *They talked so much I couldn't* **get a word in** (=could not say anything).
4 news or information about

something: *Has there been any word from the hospital?*

━ PHRASES ━
5 have a word (with someone) to speak with someone: *Could I have a word with you at the end of class?*
6 in other words used to show that you are about to say the same thing in a simpler way: *"I think it's the most boring movie ever made!" "In other words, you don't like it."*
7 in your own words without repeating what someone else has said: *Just tell us the story in your own words.*

word processing /ˈwɜ˞d ˌprɑsɛsɪŋ/ [*noun*] the activity of making documents using a computer: *He took a word processing course.*

word processor /ˈwɜ˞d ˌprɑsɛsɚ/ [*noun*] a program on a computer used for writing documents

wore * /wɔr/ [*verb*] the past tense of WEAR[1]

work[1] * /wɜ˞k/ [*noun*]
1 a job, or the place where someone does his or her job: *She enjoys her work.* | *Please don't phone me* **at work.** | *I'm having dinner with him after work.*
2 the activity of producing or achieving something: *There is a lot of building work being done in the town.* | *Thank you for all your* **hard work** (=work with a lot of effort). | *Her father was* **hard at work** (=working with effort) *in the yard.* | *Come on, let's* **get to work!** (=start working)
3 what someone does or produces as a student or at a job: *Your work is not acceptable.*
↪ *See also* HOMEWORK, CLASSWORK.
4 a book, play, picture, piece of music, etc.: *a* **work of art** (=a picture or sculpture)
━ PHRASE ━
5 out of work without a paid job: *He's been out of work for a year.*

/i/ **see**	/ɪ/ **big**	/eɪ/ **day**	/ɛ/ **get**	/æ/ **hat**
/ɑ/ **father, hot**	/ʌ/ **up**	/ə/ **about**	/ɔ/ **saw**	
/oʊ/ **hope**	/ʊ/ **book**	/u/ **too**	/aɪ/ **I**	/aʊ/ **how**
/ɔɪ/ **boy**	/ɝ/ **bird**	/ɚ/ **teacher**	/ɪr/ **ear**	/ɛr/ **air**
/ɑr/ **far**	/ɔr/ **more**	/ʊr/ **tour**	/aɪr/ **fire**	
/aʊɚ/ **hour**	/θ/ **nothing**	/ð/ **mother**	/ʃ/ **she**	
/ʒ/ **measure**	/tʃ/ **church**	/dʒ/ **jump**	/ŋ/ **long**	

USAGE work, job

Work can be anything you do to earn money, and is not always regular: *It's hard to find work in this town.* A **job** is the work someone does regularly, especially in a business: *I'm looking for a new job.*

work² * [*verb; worked, working*]
1 to do something in order to produce or achieve something: *He worked all morning to get the house clean.* | *He's **working on** a project for school.* | *You'll have to **work at** your spelling* (=try to improve it). | *They **worked hard** all day* (=worked with a lot of effort).
2 to do a particular paid job: *She **works for** a bank.* | *I **work as** a salesclerk.*
3 if a machine, substance, method, etc., works, it does what it is intended to do: *Do you know how a television works?* | *I have an idea that might work.*
4 to make a machine do something; *synonym* OPERATE: *How do you work the VCR?*
— PHRASE —
5 work your way to go somewhere or deal with things in a slow but steady way: *He worked his way to the front of the crowd.* | *She was working her way through a pile of letters.*
— PHRASAL VERB —
work out [*phrasal verb*]
6 to find the answer to a problem or question by thinking about it: **work something out** ▶ *Eventually, I worked it out.* | **work out something** ▶ *He was trying to work out the answer.*
7 to happen or continue in a satisfactory way: *I hope it works out for you.*
8 to do physical exercises: *I work out every day.*

workbook /'wɜ˞k,bʊk/ [*noun*] a book for students with questions and spaces to write the answers

worker * /'wɜ˞kɚ/ [*noun*] someone who does work or has a job: *My father is a factory worker.* | *He's a good worker.*

workman /'wɜ˞kmən/ [*noun; plural* **workmen** /'wɜ˞kmən/] a man who does physical work such as building: *The workmen had finished fixing the roof.*

workout /'wɜ˞k,aʊt/ [*noun*] a period of physical exercise that you do to make yourself healthier

worksheet /'wɜ˞k,ʃit/ [*noun*] a piece of paper with questions for students: *The teacher handed out some worksheets.*

workstation /'wɜ˞k,steɪʃən/ [*noun*] a computer used by someone in an office, or the desk where it is used

world * /wɜ˞ld/ [*noun*]
1 the whole of the earth: *She has traveled **all over the world**.* | *What's the biggest country **in the world**?*
2 a particular group of countries, organizations, or people: *the Spanish-speaking world* | *He was well-known in **the world of** education.*
— PHRASES —
3 be out of this world INFORMAL to be extremely good: *The food at the hotel was out of this world.*
4 what/where/why/how/who in the world . . . ? used to show surprise or slight anger: *What in the world are you doing in there?*

worldwide¹ /'wɜ˞ld'waɪd/ [*adjective; no comparative*] existing or happening in every part of the world: *There has been a worldwide increase in the disease.*

worldwide² [*adverb*] in every part of the world: *Pollution affects people worldwide.*

World Wide Web /'wɜ˞ld 'waɪd 'wɛb/ [*noun*]
the World Wide Web all the computer documents that are connected through the system called the Internet: *You can find all kinds of information **on the World Wide Web**.*
↪ *See also* **the Web** *at* WEB. ↪ *Compare* INTERNET.

worm * /wɜ˞m/ [*noun*] a long thin creature with no legs that lives in soil

worn¹ * /wɔrn/ [*verb*] the past participle of WEAR¹

worn² [*adjective*] weak or damaged from age or too much use: *All her rugs were old and worn.*

worn-out or **worn out** /'wɔrn 'aʊt/ [*adjective; no comparative*]
1 no longer suitable to be used because

of age or too much use: *a worn-out pair of gloves*

⇨ *See also* **wear out** *at* WEAR[1].

2 very tired, for example after doing a lot of work: *Let him sleep—he's worn out.*

worried * /ˈwɜrid/ [*adjective;* **more worried, most worried**] unhappy because you think something bad may happen or may have happened; *synonym* ANXIOUS: *I'm worried about the test tomorrow.* | *She was worried that he might have had an accident.*

worry[1] * /ˈwɜri/ [*verb;* **worries, worried, worrying**] to feel unhappy because you think something bad may happen or may have happened: *She worried about her health.* | *Don't worry—I'm sure they're safe.*

worry[2] * [*noun; plural* **worries**]
1 something that makes you worried: *My biggest worry is how to pay for college.* | *He had few worries.*
2 the feeling you have when you are worried: *Worry about his work kept him awake.*

worse[1] * /wɜrs/ [*adjective*]
1 less good; the comparative of BAD: *The weather is getting worse.* | *Her grades are much worse than mine.*
2 more sick: *The next day, he was worse.*

worse[2] * [*adverb*] less well; the comparative of BADLY: *He speaks English worse than I do!*

worse[3] [*noun*] something that is even less good than another bad thing: *The situation was already bad, but worse was to come.*

worsen /ˈwɜrsən/ [*verb;* **worsened, worsening**] to become worse or to make something worse; *opposite* IMPROVE: *The storm worsened overnight.*

worship[1] /ˈwɜrʃɪp/ [*verb;* **worshiped, worshiping**] to show respect or pray to God or a god: *The tribe worshiped many gods.*

worship[2] [*noun*] when you show respect or pray to God or a god: *The temple is a place of worship.*

worst[1] * /wɜrst/ [*adjective*] as bad as something can be; the superlative of

BAD: *That's the worst coffee I've ever tasted!*

worst[2] * [*adverb*] worse than anything else; the superlative of BADLY: *The areas worst affected by the flooding are in the north.* | *It was cold, wet, and worst of all, a long walk home.*

worst[3] * [*noun*]
1 the worst the worst thing that could happen: *You must prepare yourself for the worst.*

━━ PHRASES ━━
2 at worst used to tell someone the worst thing that could happen: *At worst, you'll have to take the test again.*
3 if worst comes to worst if the worst thing possible happens: *If worst comes to worst, I can sell my car.*

worth[1] * /wɜrθ/ [*preposition*]
1 used to say what the value of something is: *That ring is worth $500.*
2 if something is worth doing, it will be useful or enjoyable: *It's worth asking if they will reduce the price.* | *It was worth the effort.* | *All that time we spent was worth it.* | *The car is not worth repairing.* | *This book is worth reading.*
☛ When using **worth** with verbs, use only the **-ing** form of a main verb. For example, do not say "worth to be repaired" or "worth being read." Say **worth repairing** or **worth reading**.

worth[2] * [*noun*] used to mention an amount of something by saying how much it costs: *They ate five **dollars' worth of** candy.*

worthless /ˈwɜrθlɪs/ [*adjective; no comparative*] not at all valuable or useful: *They later found out the painting was worthless.* | *His advice was worthless.*

worthwhile [T] /ˈwɜrθˈwaɪl/ [*adjective;* **more worthwhile, most worthwhile**] something that is worthwhile is useful to spend time, effort, or money on: *It's worthwhile looking in several different stores.*

/i/ see	/ɪ/ big	/eɪ/ day	/ɛ/ get	/æ/ hat
/ɑ/ father, hot	/ʌ/ up	/ə/ about	/ɔ/ saw	
/oʊ/ hope	/ʊ/ book	/u/ too	/aɪ/ I	/aʊ/ how
/ɔɪ/ boy	/ɜ/ bird	/ɚ/ teacher	/ɪr/ ear	/ɛr/ air
/ɑr/ far	/ɔr/ more	/ʊr/ tour	/aɪr/ fire	
/aʊɚ/ hour	/θ/ nothing	/ð/ mother	/ʃ/ she	
/ʒ/ measure	/tʃ/ church	/dʒ/ jump	/ŋ/ long	

worthy /'wɜˑði/ [adjective; worthier, worthiest] FORMAL

═══ PHRASE ═══

be worthy of to be good enough to deserve something: *I will try to be worthy of your respect.*

would ✱ /wʊd/ [modal verb]

1 used to talk about what someone said or what you believe about the future: *He said he would be here by two o'clock.* | *He would make a great actor.*

2 used to describe a possible situation or event, or to talk about its result: *It would be nice to see her again.* | *If I had a million dollars, I would stop working.*

3 used to say what someone wants or does not want: *Would you like something to drink?* | *I would hate to disappoint my parents.*

☞ Saying **I would like** when you are asking for something is more polite than saying "I want."

4 used to say what someone did regularly in the past; synonym USED TO: *When I got home from school, I would help my mom make dinner.*

☞ Do not use **would** with the verb "be" in this meaning. For example, do not say "I would be a fast runner." Say I **used to be a fast runner.**

═══ PHRASES ═══

5 would you . . . ? used to ask someone politely to do something: *Would you tell her I called?*

6 would have used to talk about the result of something that did not actually happen: *If she had told him, he would have been angry.*

wouldn't ✱ /'wʊdənt/ the short form of "would not": *I wouldn't be surprised if they got married.*

would've ✱ /'wʊdəv/ the short form of "would have": *I would've been embarrassed if anyone had seen me!*

wound[1] ✱ /wund/ [noun] a cut or tear in someone's skin where he or she has been injured: *a bullet wound*

wound[2] ✱ /wund/ [verb; wounded, wounding] to injure someone, making a cut or tear in his or her skin: *The gunman wounded four people.*

wound[3] ✱ /waʊnd/ [verb] the past tense and past participle of WIND[2]

wounded /'wundɪd/ [adjective; no comparative] having an injury that made a cut or tear in the skin: *The wounded man was taken to the hospital.*

wove ✱ /woʊv/ [verb] the past tense of WEAVE

woven ✱ /'woʊvən/ [verb] the past participle of WEAVE

wow /waʊ/ [interjection] used when you see or hear something that is surprising or impressive: *Wow! That's amazing!*

wrap ✱ /ræp/ [verb; wraps, wrapped, wrapping]

1 to cover something completely with paper, plastic, cloth, etc.; opposite UNWRAP: *I wrapped the present in some pretty paper.* | *She wrapped the scarf around her neck.* | *He wrapped up the meat and put it in the freezer.*

═══ PHRASAL VERB ═══

wrap up [phrasal verb]

2 to put on warm clothes: *Wrap up well before you go outside.*

wrapper /'ræpɚ/ [noun] the paper, plastic, etc., around something that is sold, especially food: *a candy wrapper*

wrapping paper /'ræpɪŋ ˌpeɪpɚ/ [noun] colored paper that is used to wrap gifts

wreath /riθ/ [noun; plural wreaths /riðz/] a circle of leaves or flowers, used for decoration or to put on a grave: *a Christmas wreath*

wreck[1] /rɛk/ [verb; wrecked, wrecking] to destroy something or ruin it: *I'm worried that he'll wreck my bike.* | *The weather wrecked our plans.*

wreck[2] [noun]

1 a badly damaged ship or vehicle: *The wreck lay 260 feet below the surface.*

2 an accident in which a vehicle or plane is badly damaged: *a car wreck*

wreckage /'rɛkɪdʒ/ [noun] pieces of a vehicle, plane, ship, or building that has been destroyed: *They pulled the driver from the wreckage.*

wrench[1] /rɛntʃ/ [noun; plural wrenches] a TOOL used for fastening or undoing metal pieces

wrench[2] [*verb;* **wrenches, wrenched, wrenching**] to pull something away with a lot of force: *He wrenched the keys from her hand.*

wrestle /ˈrɛsəl/ [*verb;* **wrestled, wrestling**] to fight with someone by holding and pushing against him or her: *The boys were **wrestling with** each other on the lawn.*

wrestler /ˈrɛslɚ/ [*noun*] someone who does the sport of wrestling

wrestling /ˈrɛslɪŋ/ [*noun*] a sport in which two people hold each other and try to push each other to the ground

wriggle /ˈrɪgəl/ [*verb;* **wriggled, wriggling**] to move or twist from side to side with small movements: *Stop wriggling and let me tie your shoes.*
➪ Compare WIGGLE.

wring /rɪŋ/ [*verb;* **wrung, wringing**]
═ PHRASAL VERB ═
wring out [*phrasal verb*]
to twist a wet piece of material to remove water from it: **wring out something** ▸ *Wring out your bathing suit and hang it on the line.*

wrinkle /ˈrɪŋkəl/ [*noun*]
1 an unwanted fold in cloth: *Ironing clothes when they're damp gets rid of wrinkles.*
2 a line or fold in your skin that appears as you get older: *There were wrinkles around his eyes.*

wrinkled /ˈrɪŋkəld/ [*adjective;* **more wrinkled, most wrinkled**]
1 wrinkled cloth has unwanted folds in it: *You're not going to wear that wrinkled shirt, are you?*
2 having lines or folds in your skin: *His skin had become loose and wrinkled.*

wrist * /rɪst/ [*noun*] the part of your BODY where your hand joins your arm

wristwatch /ˈrɪstˌwætʃ/ [*noun; plural* **wristwatches**] a watch you wear around your wrist

write * /raɪt/ [*verb;* **wrote, written, writing**]
1 to put words on paper using a pen, pencil, or brush: *I wrote my name at the top of the page.* | *He can't read or write.*
2 to put words on paper in a letter and send it to someone: *I have written to*

my uncle for advice. | **write someone something** ▸ *He wrote me a long letter.*
3 to produce a book, article, piece of music, etc.: *Who wrote that play?* | *She writes for the local newspaper.*
═ PHRASAL VERBS ═
write back [*phrasal verb*]
4 to send a letter to someone who has sent you one: *He wrote back at once, accepting the invitation.*
write down [*phrasal verb*]
5 to put words on paper, for example so you do not forget information: **write down something** ▸ *He wrote down her phone number.* | **write something down** ▸ *If you have any more ideas, write them down.*
write out [*phrasal verb*]
6 to write a long list or a lot of information: **write out something** ▸ *He wrote out a list of things to do.*

writer * /ˈraɪtɚ/ [*noun*] someone who writes books, stories, etc., as a way of earning money

writing /ˈraɪtɪŋ/ [*noun*]
1 words written by someone: *There was some writing on the back of the picture.* | *I can't read her writing.*
2 the activity of writing books, stories, etc.: *You have to be good to make money from writing.*
═ PHRASE ═
3 in writing in written or printed words, and therefore official: *He wanted the offer in writing.*

written * /ˈrɪtən/ [*verb*] the past participle of WRITE

wrong[1] * /rɔŋ/ [*adjective; no comparative*]
1 not correct or right: *That's the wrong answer.* | *You're wearing the wrong kind of clothes for this job.* | *I was **wrong about** the train schedule.*
2 not acceptable, fair, or morally good; *opposite* RIGHT: *What you did was very wrong.* | *It's **wrong to** cheat.*

/i/ **see** /ɪ/ **big** /eɪ/ **day** /ɛ/ **get** /æ/ **hat**
/ɑ/ **father, hot** /ʌ/ **up** /ə/ **about** /ɔ/ **saw**
/oʊ/ **hope** /ʊ/ **book** /u/ **too** /aɪ/ **I** /aʊ/ **how**
/ɔɪ/ **boy** /ɝ/ **bird** /ɚ/ **teacher** /ɪr/ **ear** /ɛr/ **air**
/ɑr/ **far** /ɔr/ **more** /ʊr/ **tour** /aɪr/ **fire**
/aʊɚ/ **hour** /θ/ **nothing** /ð/ **mother** /ʃ/ **she**
/ʒ/ **measure** /tʃ/ **church** /dʒ/ **jump** /ŋ/ **long**

☞ Do not use **wrong** before a noun in this meaning.

━━ PHRASES ━━

3 be wrong with if something is wrong with something, it is not working or has a bad feature: *There's something wrong with the engine.* | *"I don't like this dress." "What's wrong with it?"*

☞ Do not use **wrong** before a noun in this meaning. Use it after words such as "something," "nothing," and "what."

4 what's wrong? SPOKEN used to ask someone why he or she is upset or unhappy: *"What's wrong?" "I don't understand my homework."*

wrong[2] * [*adverb*]

1 in a way that is not correct; *opposite* RIGHT: *They spelled my name wrong.*

━━ PHRASE ━━

2 go wrong to stop working or happening in the way something should: *Don't worry—nothing will go wrong.*

wrong[3] * [*noun*] actions that are not acceptable or not fair; *opposite* RIGHT: *He admitted he'd done wrong.*

wrongly /'rɔŋli/ [*adverb*] used to say that what someone did was not correct or right: *She wrongly thought that she would get the job.*

wrote * /roʊt/ [*verb*] the past tense of WRITE

wrung /rʌŋ/ [*verb*] the past tense and past participle of WRING

WWW /'dʌbəlyu'dʌbəlyu'dʌbəlyu/ [*noun*] the abbreviation of WORLD WIDE WEB

X

X * or **x** /ɛks/ [*noun; plural* Xs *or* X's, x's] the 24th letter of the English alphabet
➪ *See the usage note at* ALPHABET.

Xerox machine /'zɪrɑks məˌʃin/ [*noun*] TRADEMARK a machine that quickly makes copies of documents by taking photographs of them; *synonym* PHOTOCOPIER: *Who knows how to operate the Xerox machine?*

xl or **XL** the written abbreviation of EXTRA LARGE, especially relating to clothes sizes: *Labels are marked either s, m, l, or xl.*

Xmas /'krɪsməs/ [*noun*] used in writing as a short form of CHRISTMAS

x-ray[1] or **X-ray** /'ɛksˌreɪ/ [*noun; plural* x-rays *or* X-rays] a photograph of the inside of someone's body, taken to find out if any part of it is injured or unhealthy: *He had a chest x-ray.*

x-ray[2] or **X-ray** [*verb;* x-rays, x-rayed, x-raying *or* X-rays, X-rayed, X-raying] to take an x-ray of part of someone's body: *They x-rayed my knee.*

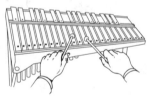

a xylophone

xylophone /'zaɪləˌfoʊn/ [*noun*] a musical instrument with wooden bars of different sizes that you hit with a small hammer: *She plays the xylophone very well.* | *a duet for xylophone and drums*

Y

Y * or **y** /waɪ/ [*noun; plural* Ys or Y's, y's] the 25th letter of the English alphabet
 ➪ *See the usage note at* ALPHABET.

yacht /yat/ [*noun*] an expensive boat used for pleasure or for racing

yam /yæm/ [*noun*] a pale orange root that is cooked and eaten as a vegetable

yank /yæŋk/ [*verb;* **yanked, yanking**] to pull something quickly and with a lot of force: *I yanked on the rope.*

Yankee /'yæŋki/ [*noun; plural* **Yankees**] someone from the northeastern states of the United States: *He's a Yankee who has never been to the south.*
 ☛ **Yankee** is often used to mean "American." However, in the U.S., only people from the Northeast are Yankees, and some people in the South use this word as an insult.

yard * /yard/ [*noun*]
 1 a unit for measuring length, equal to three feet: *The store is only 50 yards away.*
 2 an area of land around a house: *The kids were playing* **in the yard.**

yarn /yarn/ [*noun*] thick thread used for knitting or weaving

yawn[1] /yɔn/ [*verb;* **yawned, yawning**] to open your mouth and take a deep breath, when you are tired or bored: *If you can't stop yawning, take a nap.*

yawn[2] [*noun*] when you yawn: *He gave a big yawn.*

yd. [*plural* **yds.**] the written abbreviation of YARD: *The rug measures 5 yds. by 3 yds.*

yeah /yɛə/ [*adverb*] SPOKEN yes: *"Do you like school?" "Yeah, I love it."*

year * /yɪr/ [*noun*]
 1 a period of 365 or 366 days: *The building work should take about a year.* | *Many years ago, my family moved to Texas.* | *My mother died when I was* **two years old.**
 2 a period of 12 months from January 1 to December 31: *We went to Mexico* **last year** (=the year before this one). | *I started a new job* **this year** (=the year we are in now). | *We're getting married* **next year** (=the year after this one).
 3 years [*plural*] a very long time: *It'll take years to repair the flood damage.* | *I lost the book years ago.*

 ➪ *See also* **all day/night/week/ month/year** *at* ALL[1].

━━ PHRASES ━━
 4 year after year every year, for many years: *Year after year, the birds return to the same place.*
 5 a five/ten/thirty/etc.-year-old someone who is at the age of five, ten, thirty, etc.: *This is so easy a four-year-old could do it.* | *I a seven-year-old child*
 ☛ Do not use plurals with numbers in this phrase. For example, do not say "a twelve-years-old boy." Say **a twelve-year-old boy.**

yearbook /'yɪr,bʊk/ [*noun*] a book produced by a school or college every year, giving pictures and details about the students and what they did there in that year

yearly[1] * /'yɪrli/ [*adjective; no comparative*] happening, done, or produced every year; *synonym* ANNUAL: *The school puts on a yearly concert.* | *What is your yearly income?*
 ☛ Only use **yearly** before a noun.

yearly[2] [*adverb*] every year; *synonym* ANNUALLY: *Interest will be added to your account yearly.*

yeast /yist/ [*noun*] a substance used to make bread rise and to make alcoholic drinks

yell /yɛl/ [*verb;* **yelled, yelling**] to shout very loudly: *Stop yelling—I can hear you just fine!*

yellow[1] * /'yɛloʊ/ [*noun*] the color of a lemon, the sun, etc.: *Yellow doesn't look good on me.*

yellow[2] * [*adjective;* **yellower, yellowest**] of the color yellow: *The leaves on the trees had turned yellow.*

Yellow Pages /'yɛloʊ ,peɪdʒəz/ [*noun*] **the Yellow Pages** a large book with telephone numbers and advertisements for local businesses: *Fortunately, the electrician I found in the Yellow Pages was really excellent—and not too expensive.*
 ☛ Only use **the Yellow Pages** with a singular verb.

yelp /yɛlp/ [*verb;* **yelped, yelping**] if a dog or other animal yelps, it makes a short high sound: *He kicked the dog and it yelped.*

yes * /yɛs/ [*adverb*]
   1 used to give a positive answer to a question, or to agree with someone; *opposite* NO: *"Do you like my haircut?" "Yes, it looks great." | "Isn't it awful?" "Yes, it is." | "Would you like some more coffee?" "Yes please."*
   2 used to disagree with a negative statement: *"You can't say that!" "Yes I can!"*
   ↪ *See the usage note at* QUESTION¹.
   3 used to reply to someone who has said your name, to ask what he or she wants: *"Joe?" "Yes? What do you want?"*

yesterday¹ * /'yɛstərˌdeɪ/ [*adverb*] during the day before today: *We went to the beach yesterday. | I saw her **yesterday evening**.*
   ☞ Do not say "yesterday night." Say **yesterday evening** or **last night**.

yesterday² * [*noun*] the day before today: *I read about it in yesterday's paper. | No one has called me since **the day before yesterday** (=two days before today).*

yet * /yɛt/ [*adverb*]
   1 used to ask if something has already happened or to say that it has not already happened: *Have they arrived yet? | I haven't finished doing my homework yet.*
   ↪ *Compare* STILL¹.
   2 used to say that something cannot or should not be done now: *We can't leave yet—the party isn't over.*
   3 used to say that something might still happen in the future: *He may yet win.*

═ PHRASES ═

   4 yet another another, when there have been many before: *I've lost yet another umbrella.*
   5 yet again again, after happening many times before: *She's late yet again.*

yield Ⓣ /yild/ [*verb;* **yielded, yielding**] to let the cars that are already on a road you are turning onto go ahead before you enter the road: *You must **yield to** the highway traffic.*

yoga /'youɡə/ [*noun*] a kind of exercise done to gain control over your mind and body and to make you calm: ***Doing yoga** is a great way to relax.*

yogurt /'youɡərt/ [*noun*] a food made from milk that has become thick and sour, which often has fruit added: *Would you like a yogurt? | For breakfast I usually have yogurt or cereal.*

yolk /youk/ [*noun*] the soft yellow middle part of an egg: *Separate the yolks from the whites. | Next, add the beaten egg yolk to the batter.*

you * /yu/ [*pronoun*]
   1 used to mean the person or people who are being spoken to: *You look great. | Let me show you around. | I'd like to thank all of you for your help.*
   ☞ **You** can be singular or plural, and it can be the subject of a verb, or the object of a verb or preposition.
   2 used to talk about people in general: *If a bee stings you, it really hurts.*

you'd * /yud/
   1 the short form of "you had": *You'd better listen.*
   ☞ Do not use "you'd" for **you had** when **have** is the main verb. For example, do not say "You'd a phone call." Say **You had a phone call**.
   2 the short form of "you would": *You'd like the movie, I think.*

you'll * /yul/ the short form of "you will": *You'll be okay.*

young¹ * /yʌŋ/ [*adjective;* **younger, youngest**] being in the early stages of life or growth: *I loved this book when I was young. | This is still a young plant.*
   ↪ *See also* YOUTH. ↪ *Compare* OLD.

young² [*plural noun*] an animal's babies: *The mother bird collects worms for its young.*

your * /yɔr/ [*determiner*] belonging to or connected with the person or people you are talking to: *Is this your car? | Your hands are dirty.*
   ☞ Only use **your** before a noun.

you're * /yʊr/ the short form of "you are": *You're early.*
   ☞ Do not confuse **you're** and **your**. **You're** is the short form of "you are."

yours * /yɔrz/ [*pronoun*]
1 something that belongs to or is connected with the person or people you are talking to: *Is this book yours?* | *Yours must be an interesting job.*

— PHRASE ——

2 yours or **sincerely yours** used at the end of a letter, especially a formal one, before the name of the person who wrote it: *The letter was signed "Sincerely yours, Rachel White."*

yourself * /yɔr'sɛlf/ [*pronoun; plural* **yourselves** /yɔr'sɛlvz/]
1 used to say that the person or group you are talking to is affected by his, her, or its own action: *Be careful not to cut yourself.* | *You're too sick to take care of yourself.*
2 used to emphasize the word "you": *You yourselves told me it would be difficult.*
☛ Do not use **yourself** as a subject. For example, do not say "Yourself can do something." Say **You can do something yourself.**

— PHRASES ——

3 by yourself alone or without help from anyone: *I don't want to leave you by yourselves.* | *Did you make this all by yourself?*
4 to yourself not sharing something with anyone else: *You've had the car all to yourself for the whole week. It's my*

turn now. | *Please keep your opinions to yourself* (=do not say them out loud).

youth /yuθ/ [*noun; plural* **youths** /yuðz; yuθs/]
1 the period of time when you are young: *He was very handsome in his youth.*
2 [*plural*] young people: *The youth of this country are worried about the environment.* | *She belongs to the church's youth group.*
3 a young person, especially a young man: *Three youths came out of the drugstore.*
↪ *See the synonym note at* TEENAGER.

youth hostel /'yuθ ˌhɑstəl/ [*noun*] a place where young people can stay for a short time at a low cost, when they are traveling

you've * /yuv/ the short form of "you have": *You've been very helpful.*
☛ Do not use "you've" for **you have** when **have** is the main verb. For example, do not say "You've a spot on your tie." Say **You have a spot on your tie.**

yo-yo /'you you/ [*noun; plural* **yo-yos**] a round toy which goes down from your finger and up again on a piece of string

yr. the written abbreviation of YEAR or YEARS: *a 3-yr. course*

yuck /yʌk/ [*interjection*] used to show that you think something is very unpleasant: *Yuck! This food is disgusting!*

Z

Z * /zi/ or **z** [noun; plural **Zs** or **Z's, z's**] the 26th letter of the English alphabet
⊃ See the usage note at **ALPHABET**.

zebra /'zibrə/ [noun; plural **zebras** or **zebra**] an animal like a horse with black and white bands on its body

zero * /'zɪroʊ/ [number, noun; plural **zeros** or **zeroes**] the number 0: *The temperature is 15 degrees below zero.*

zigzag[1] /'zɪg,zæg/ [noun] a line that goes from side to side many times

zigzag[2] [verb; **zigzags, zigzagged, zigzagging**] to move along, going from side to side: *The skiers zigzagged down the mountain.*

zinc /zɪŋk/ [noun] a silver-white metal used to make other metals and to cover objects

zip /zɪp/ [verb; **zips, zipped, zipping**]
 1 to fasten something with a zipper; *opposite* **UNZIP**: *He zipped his bag.* | *"I'm coming" she said, zipping up her coat.*
 2 to make a large computer file smaller using a special program; *opposite*

UNZIP: *I'll zip the document and send it to you by e-mail.*

ZIP code /'zɪp ,koʊd/ [noun] *TRADEMARK* a set of numbers used in the United States that is put after an address on a piece of mail, to show what area of the country it should go to
 ⊃ See the picture at **ADDRESS**[1].

zipper /'zɪpɚ/ [noun] something used to fasten clothes, bags, etc., which has two rows of metal pieces that lock together

zodiac /'zoʊdi,æk/ [noun]
 the zodiac a system of 12 signs, based on the position of the stars and planets, which some people believe controls your character and your future: *What sign of the zodiac are you?*

zone /zoʊn/ [noun] an area of a place that is used for a particular thing: *Cars are not allowed in the bus zone.*

zoo /zu/ [noun; plural **zoos**] a place where wild animals are kept and shown to the public

zucchini /zu'kini/ [noun; plural **zucchini** or **zucchinis**] a long, round, dark green **VEGETABLE** that is white inside

SMART STUDY SECTION

CONTENTS

THE ALPHABET AND HOW IT IS PRONOUNCED

Capital	Lowercase	Pronunciation	Capital	Lowercase	Pronunciation
A	a	/eɪ/	N	n	/ɛn/
B	b	/bi/	O	o	/oʊ/
C	c	/si/	P	p	/pi/
D	d	/di/	Q	q	/kyu/
E	e	/i/	R	r	/ɑr/
F	f	/ɛf/	S	s	/ɛs/
G	g	/dʒi/	T	t	/ti/
H	h	/eɪtʃ/	U	u	/yu/
I	I	/aɪ/	V	v	/vi/
J	j	/dʒeɪ/	W	w	/ˈdʌbəl,yu/
K	k	/keɪ/	X	x	/ɛks/
L	k	/ɛl/	Y	y	/waɪ/
M	m	/ɛm/	Z	z	/zi/

REGULAR VERBS

Simple Present

I	walk	we	walk
you	walk	you	walk
he/she/it	walks	they	walk

Simple Future (will + base form)

I	will walk	we	will walk
you	will walk	you	will walk
he/she/it	will walk	they	will walk

Simple Past

I	walked	we	walked
you	walked	you	walked
he/she/it	walked	they	walked

Present Prefect (to be + present participle)

I	am walking	we	are walking
you	are walking	you	are walking
he/she/it	is	walking	they	are walking

IRREGULAR VERB CHART

Verb	Past Tense	Past Participle	Verb	Past Tense	Past Participle
arise	arose	arisen	cast	cast	cast
be	was	been	catch	caught	caught
bear	bore	borne	choose	chose	chosen
beat	beat	beaten or beat	cling	clung	clung
become	became	become	come	came	come
begin	began	begun	cost	cost	cost
bend	bent	bent	creep	crept	crept
bet	bet or betted	bet	cut	cut	cut
bid	bid	bid	deal	dealt	dealt
bind	bound	bound	dig	dug	dug
bite	bit	bitten	dive	dived or dove	dived
bleed	bled	bled	do	did	done
blow	blew	blown	draw	drew	drawn
break	broke	broken	dream	dreamed or dreamt	dreamed or dreamt
bring	brought	brought			
broadcast	broadcast	broadcast	drink	drank	drunk
build	built	built	drive	drove	driven
burst	burst	burst	eat	ate	eaten
buy	bought	bought	fall	fell	fallen

IRREGULAR VERB CHART *continued*

Verb	Past Tense	Past Participle	Verb	Past Tense	Past Participle
feed	fed	fed	lend	lent	lent
feel	felt	felt	let	let	let
fight	fought	fought	lie	lay	lain
find	found	found	light	lit	lit
flee	fled	fled	lose	lost	lost
fling	flung	flung	make	made	made
fly	flew	flown	meet	met	met
forget	forgot	forgotten	pay	paid	paid
forgive	forgave	forgiven	prove	proved	proved *or* proven
freeze	froze	frozen	put	put	put
get	got	gotten	read	read	read
give	gave	given	ride	rode	ridden
go	went	gone	ring	rang	rung
grind	ground	ground	rise	rose	risen
grow	grew	grown	run	ran	run
hang *(people)*	hanged	hanged	say	said	said
hang *(things)*	hung	hung	see	saw	seen
have	had	had	seek	sought	sought
hear	heard	heard	sell	sold	sold
hide	hid	hidden	send	sent	sent
hit	hit	hit	set	set	set
hold	held	held	sew	sewed	sewn *or* sewed
hurt	hurt	hurt	shake	shook	shaken
keep	kept	kept	shave	shaved	shaved
kneel	knelt *or* kneeled	knelt *or* kneeled	shine	shone *or* shined	shone *or* shined
know	knew	known	shoot	shot	shot
lay	laid	laid	show	showed	shown *or* showed
lead	led	led	shrink	shrank	shrunk
leave	left	left	shut	shut	shut

IRREGULAR VERB CHART *continued*

Verb	Past Tense	Past Participle	Verb	Past Tense	Past Participle
sing	sang	sung	swim	swam	swum
sink	sank *or* sunk	sunk	swing	swung	swung
sit	sat	sat	take	took	taken
sleep	slept	slept	teach	taught	taught
slide	slid	slid	tear	tore	torn
slit	slit	slit	tell	told	told
sow	sowed	sown *or* sowed	think	thought	thought
speak	spoke	spoken	throw	threw	thrown
speed	sped *or* speeded	sped *or* speeded	thrust	thrust	thrust
spend	spent	spent	tread	trod	trodden *or* trod
spill	spilled	spilled	undergo	underwent	undergone
spin	spun	spun	understand	understood	understood
spit	spit *or* spat	spit *or* spat	undertake	undertook	undertaken
split	split	split	undo	undid	undone
spoil	spoiled	spoiled	unwind	unwound	unwound
spread	spread	spread	upset	upset	upset
spring	sprang *or* sprung	sprung	wake	woke	woken
stand	stood	stood	wear	wore	worn
steal	stole	stolen	weave	wove	woven *or* wove
stick	stuck	stuck	wed	wed	wed
sting	stung	stung	wet	wet *or* wetted	wet *or* wetted
stink	stank *or* stunk	stunk	win	won	won
stride	strode	stridden	wind	wound	wound
strike	struck	struck	withdraw	withdrew	withdrawn
string	strung	strung	withhold	withheld	withheld
swear	swore	sworn	wring	wrung	wrung
sweep	swept	swept	write	wrote	written
swell	swelled	swollen *or* swelled			

ADJECTIVE WORD ORDER

In English, adjectives come before the noun they are describing. If you are using more than one adjective, you need to put them in order.

You can say: *A nice red shirt*

but you cannot say: *A red nice shirt*

Put adjectives in this order before the noun:

Deter-miner	beauty/goodness	size	age	color	origin	material	noun
A	wonderful		new			silk	skirt
The				white	German		car
My		small	old			wooden	doll
An	excellent		young		American		athlete
This	beautiful			red			balloon
A		big		yellow		cotton	dress
The	ugly		old	gray			house
Those	nice			brown	Italian		shoes

CHART OF PREFIXES AND SUFFIXES

Prefixes and suffixes are parts of words that have meaning but cannot be used alone. They are added to other basic words to make new words. Prefixes are put at the beginning, and suffixes are put at the end. Here is a list of some common prefixes and suffixes and the meanings they add to other words.

Prefix	Used With	Example
anti-	Used with nouns or adjectives to add the meaning "working against; opposed to"	antibiotic
dis-	Used with verbs or adjectives to add the meaning "opposite of; not"	dishonest, disobedient
mis-	Used with nouns, verbs, or adjectives to add the meanings "wrong; incorrectly; opposite of"	misbehave
multi-	Used with adjectives to add the meaning "many"	multicolored, multicultural
non-	Used with nouns, adjectives, or adverbs to add the meaning "not"	nonalcoholic nonsmoker,

Smart Study Section

Prefix	Used With	Example
re-	Used with nouns or verbs to add the meaning "done again"	retake, rewrite
self-	Used with nouns or adjectives to mean "done by yourself; without help from anyone"	self-control, self-service
un-	Used with adjectives to add the meaning "not, without"	unemployment, unfair

Suffix	Used With	Example
-ability	Used with adjectives that end with -able to make them nouns	reliable (adjective) → reliability (noun)
-able	Used with verbs to make adjectives that mean "able to be" or "having a particular quality"	breakable, desirable, disposable
-an	Used with nouns to tell about people who are connected to a job or an idea	electrician, Christian
-ance	Used with verbs or with adjectives that end in -ant to make nouns	fragrant (adjective) fragrance (noun); appear (noun) → appearance (noun)
-ar	Used with verbs to make nouns that tell about the person who does the job or action	beg (verb) → beggar (noun); lie (verb) → liar
-ation	Used with verbs or adjectives to make nouns	separation, creation
-en	Used with nouns or adjectives to make verbs. The suffix -en adds the meaning "to be" or "to make"	hard (adjective) → harden (verb); length (noun) → lengthen (verb)
-ence	Used with adjectives that end in -ent, or with verbs, to make nouns	disobedient (adjective) →disobedience (noun)
-er	Used with verbs to make nouns that tell about the person who does the job or action	baker, teacher
-ery	Used with verbs or nouns to make nouns that tell about the place where the action is done	bakery
-free	Used with nouns to make adjectives that are "without something"	sugar (noun) → sugar-free (adjective)
-ful	Used with nouns or verbs to make adjectives that are "full of"	beautiful, harmful

Suffix	Used With	Example
-ible	Used with verbs or nouns to make adjectives that mean "able to be"	flexible, visible
-ibility	Used with adjectives that end with -ible to make nouns	possible (adjective)→ possibility (noun)
-ic	Used with nouns to make adjectives	metal (noun) → metallic (adjective)
-ism	Used with nouns or verbs to make nouns that show the action or idea	baptism, Buddhism
-ist	Used with nouns to tell who is creating or supporting the thing or idea	Buddhist, terrorist, novelist
-ize	Used with nouns or adjectives to make verbs that mean "to make" or "to do"	computer (noun) → computerize (verb), legal (adjective) → legalize (verb)
-less	Used with nouns or verbs to make adjectives that mean "not doing" or "not having something"	careless, cordless
-like	Used with nouns to make adjectives that tell how someone is behaving or what something looks like	businesslike, lifelike
-ly	Used with adjectives to make adverbs	happy (adjective) → happily (adverb); slow (adjective) → slowly (adverb)
-ment	Used with verbs to make nouns	govern (verb) → government (noun)
-ness	Used with adjectives or verbs ending in -ing or -ed to make nouns that tell about the idea or situation	dark (adjective) → darkness (noun); deaf (adjective) → deafness (noun)
-or	Used with nouns or verbs to make nouns that tell who or what does the action	competitor, projector
-ous	Used with nouns or verbs to make adjectives meaning "full of"	glorious; nervous
-sized	Used with nouns or adjectives to tell the size of something	king-sized; life-sized medium-sized
-y	Used with nouns or verbs to make adjectives	bony, healthy, rainy

CONTRACTIONS CHARTS

Contractions are less formal than full forms. Some contractions are so informal that they are almost never written. These spoken forms have this mark *.

(s) = singular
(pl) = plural

be

I	I am = I'm
you	you are = you're
he	he is = he's
she	she is = she's
it	it is = it's
we	we are = we're
they	they are = they're
who (s)	who is = who's
who (pl)	who are
where	where's
that	that is = that's
this	this is
there	there is = there's
here	here is = here's

will

I	I will = I'll
you	you will = you'll
he	he will = he'll
she	she will = she'll
it	it will = it'll*
we	we will = we'll
they	they will = they'll
who (s)	who will = who'll
who (pl)	who will = who'll
where	where will = where'll*
that	that will = that'll*
this	this will = this'll*
there	there will = there'll*

have

I	I have = I've
you	you have = you've
he	he has = he's
she	she has = she's
it	it has = it's
we	we have = we've
they	they have = they've
who (s)	who has = who's
who (pl)	who have = who've
that	that have = that've*
there	there has = there's*
there	there have = there've*

Modal Verbs and have

could	could have = could've*
have to	have to have
might	might have = might've*
must	must have = must've*
should	should have = should've*
used to	used to have
would	would have = would've*

CONTRACTIONS CHARTS

	had		**would**
I	I had = I'd	I	I would = I'd
you	you had = you'd	you	you would = you'd
he	he had = he'd	he	he would = he'd
she	she had = she'd	she	she would = she'd
it	it had = it'd*	it	it would = it'd*
we	we had = we'd	we	we would = we'd
they	they had = they'd	they	they would = they'd
who (s)	who had = who'd*	who (s)	who would = who'd*
who (pl)	who had = who'd*	who (pl)	who would = who'd*
where	where had = where'd*	where	where would = where'd*
that	that had = that'd*	that	that would = that'd*
this	this had = this'd*	this	this would = this'd*
this	there had = there'd*	this	there would = there'd*

Negative Contractions

Infinitive	Verb	not
be	am	am not
	are	are not = aren't
	is	is not = isn't
	was	was not = wasn't
	were	were not = weren't
do	do	do not = don't
	does	does not = doesn't
	did	did not = didn't
can	can	cannot = can't
	could	could not = couldn't
have	have	have not = haven't
	has	has not = hasn't
	had	had not = hadn't
must	must	must not = mustn't
shall	shall	shall not = shan't
	should	should not = shouldn't
will	will	will not = won't
	would	would not = wouldn't

PUNCTUATION

- **Period** A period is used:
  - at the end of a sentence   *It's cold outside.*
  - after an abbreviation   *I washed the shirts, pants, socks, etc.*
  - with decimal numbers   *0.25 is equal to 25%.*
  - with money   *$25.50*

? **Question Mark** A question mark is used:
  - at the end of a question   *Do you speak English?*

! **Exclamation Point** An exclamation point is used:
  - at the end of a sentence showing strong emotion   *Leave me alone!*

, **Comma** A comma is used:
  - to separate two parts of a sentence
  When he became very cold, he walked home.
  I live in New York, but my family lives in Texas.
  - to separate things in a list
  I bought eggs, bread, spinach, and milk.

; **Semicolon** A semicolon is used:
  - to connect two parts of a sentence that could also be two complete sentences
  We crashed the car; we are lucky to be alive.

: **Colon** A colon is used:
  - to begin a list
  The punctuation marks are: the period, the question mark, the comma, the semi-colon, and the colon.
  - to separate hours from minutes in time   *1:30 A.M.   12:50 P.M.*
  - to introduce a long quotation
  Dickens' A Tale of Two Cities begins: It was the best of times, it was the worst of times.

' **Apostrophe** An apostrophe is used:
  - to show missing letters in a short form   *I'm* (=I am)   *didn't* (=did not)
  - to show ownership or possession   *the boy's hat   Susan's house*

" " **Quotation Marks** Quotation marks are used:
  - to show what someone said   *He said, "I don't understand you."*
  - for titles of short stories, poems, chapters, and songs
  The book has a poem called "Winter Love."

— **Hyphen** A hyphen is used:
- at the end of a line of text to show that a word is being divided, with part of it on the next line   *responsi-*
  bility
- to make one word out of two or more words (or parts of words), especially to make adjectives   *up-to-date   blue-green   good-looking   sweet-sour*
- to show a range of numbers   *1908-1991   2001-2*

— **Dash** A dash is used:
- to separate part of a sentence that interrupts the rest of the sentence
  She said—and I believe her—that she was telling the truth.

( ) **Parentheses** Parentheses are used:
- for extra information that is not needed for a sentence to be complete
  The books (but not the poems) were on the list of reading for the course.

[ ] **Brackets** Brackets are used
- to show explanations or missing words in a quote
  "He seemed nice at the time." [The man who sold them the car.]
- around some types of special information, such as the grammar in a dictionary   *[plural]   [noun]   [no comparative]*

STATES AND THEIR MAJOR CITIES

State and Abbreviation		Major Cities
Alabama /ˌælə'bæmə/	AL	Birmingham /'bɝˌmɪŋˌhæm/; **Mobile** /moʊ'bil/; Montgomery /mant'gʌməri/
Alaska /ə'læskə/	AK	Anchorage /'æŋkərɪdʒ/; **Juneau** /'dʒunoʊ/
Arizona /ˌærə'zoʊnə/	AZ	Phoenix /'finɪks/
Arkansas /'arkənˌsɔ/	AR	Little Rock /'lɪtəl ˌrak/
California /ˌkælə'fɔrnyə/	CA	Fresno /'freznoʊ/; **Los Angeles** /lɔs 'ændʒələs/; **San Diego** /ˌsæn di'eɪgoʊ/; **San Francisco** /ˌsæn frən'sɪskoʊ/; **San Jose** /ˌsæn hoʊ'zeɪ/; **Stockton** /'staktən/
Colorado /ˌkalə'rædoʊ/	CO	Denver /'dɛnvɚ/
Connecticut /kə'nɛtɪkət/	CT	Hartford /'hartfɚd/

Smart Study Section

State and Abbreviation		Major Cities
Delaware /'dɛlə,wɛr/	DE	Dover /'douvɚ/
Florida /'flɔrɪdə/	FL	Jacksonville /'dʒæksən,vɪl/; Miami /maɪ'æmi/; Orlando /ɔr'lændoʊ/; Tallahassee /,tælə'hæsi/; Tampa /'tæmpə/
Georgia /'dʒɔrdʒə/	GA	Atlanta /æt'læntə/
Hawaii /hə'waii/	HI	Honolulu /,hɑnə'lulu/
Idaho /'aɪdə,hoʊ/	ID	Boise /'bɔɪsi/
Illinois /,ɪlə'nɔɪ/	IL	Chicago /ʃɪ'kɑgoʊ/; Springfield /'sprɪŋ,fild/
Indiana /,ɪndi'ænə/	IN	Indianapolis /,ɪndiə'næpəlɪs/
Iowa /'aɪəwə/	IA	Des Moines /də 'mɔɪn/
Kansas /'kænzəs/	KS	Topeka /tə'pikə/; Wichita /'wɪtʃɪ,tɔ/
Kentucky /kən'tʌki/	KY	Frankfort /'fræŋkfɚt/; Louisville /'lui,vɪl/
Louisiana /lu,izi'ænə/	LA	Baton Rouge /'bætən 'ruʒ/; New Orleans /,nu 'ɔrliənz/
Maine /meɪn/	ME	Augusta /ɔ'gʌstə/; Portland /'pɔrtlənd/
Maryland /'mɛrələnd/	MD	Annapolis /ə'næpəlɪs/; Baltimore /'bɔltə,mɔr/
Massachusetts /,mæsə'tʃusɪts/	MA	Boston /'bɔstən/; Springfield /'sprɪŋ,fild/
Michigan /'mɪʃɪgən/	MI	Detroit /dɪ'trɔɪt/; Grand Rapids /'grænd 'ræpɪdz/; Lansing /'lænsɪŋ/
Minnesota /,mɪnə'soʊtə/	MN	Minneapolis /,mɪni'æpəlɪs/; St. Paul /,seɪnt 'pɔl/
Mississippi /,mɪsə'sɪpi/	MS	Jackson /'dʒæksən/
Missouri /mɪ'zʊri/	MO	Jefferson City /'dʒɛfɚ·sən 'sɪti/; Kansas City /'kænzəs 'sɪti/; St. Louis /,seɪnt 'luɪs/
Montana /mɑn'tænə/	MT	Helena /'hɛlənə/; Missoula /mɪ'zulə/
Nebraska /nə'bræskə/	NE	Lincoln /'lɪŋkən/; Omaha /'oʊmə,hɔ/
Nevada /nə'vædə/	NV	Carson City /'kɑrsən 'sɪti/; Las Vegas /lɑs 'veɪgəs/
New Hampshire /,nu 'hæmpʃɚ/	NH	Concord /'kɑnkɔrd/
New Jersey /,nu 'dʒɝ·zi/	NJ	Trenton /'trɛntən/
New Mexico /,nu 'mɛksɪ,koʊ/	NM	Albuquerque /'ælbə,kɝ·ki/; Santa Fe /'sæntə 'feɪ/

State and Abbreviation	Major Cities
New York /ˌnu 'yɔrk/	**NY** **Albany** /'ɔlbəni/; **Buffalo** /'bʌfə,loʊ/; **New York** /ˌnu 'yɔrk/; **Syracuse** /'sɪrə,kyus/
North Carolina /'nɔrθ kærə'laɪnə/	**NC** **Charlotte** /'ʃarlət/; **Greensboro** /'grinz,bɜroʊ/; **Raleigh** /'rɔli/
North Dakota /'nɔrθ də'koʊtə/	**ND** **Bismarck** /'bɪzmark/
Ohio /oʊ'haɪoʊ/	**OH** **Cincinnati** /ˌsɪnsə'næti/; **Cleveland** /'klivlənd/; **Columbus** /kə'lʌmbəs/; **Dayton** /'deɪtən/; **Toledo** /tə'lidoʊ/
Oklahoma /ˌoʊklə'hoʊmə/	**OK** **Oklahoma City** /'oʊklə'hoʊmə 'sɪti/; **Tulsa** /'tʌlsə/
Oregon /'ɔrɪgən/	**OR** **Portland** /'pɔrtlənd/; **Salem** /'seɪləm/
Pennsylvania /ˌpɛnsəl'veɪnyə/	**PA** **Allentown** /'æləntaʊn/; **Harrisburg** /'hærɪs,bɜg/ **Philadelphia** /ˌfɪlə'dɛlfiə/; **Pittsburgh** /'pɪtsbɜg/
Rhode Island /ˌroʊd 'aɪlənd/	**RI** **Providence** /'pravɪdəns/
South Carolina /'saʊθ kærə'laɪnə/	**SC** **Columbia** /kə'lʌmbiə/
South Dakota /'saʊθ də'koʊtə/	**SD** **Pierre** /pɪr/
Tennessee /ˌtɛnə'si/	**TN** **Knoxville**/'naksvɪl/; **Memphis**/'mɛmfɪs/; **Nashville** /'næʃvɪl/
Texas /'tɛksəs/	**TX** **Austin** /'ɔstən/; **Dallas** /'dæləs/; **El Paso** /ɛl 'pæsoʊ/; **Fort Worth** /ˌfɔrt 'wɜθ/; **Houston** /'hyustən/; **San Antonio** /ˌsæn æn'toʊni,oʊ/
Utah /'yutɔ/	**UT** **Salt Lake City** /'sɔlt ˌleɪk 'sɪti/
Vermont /vɚ'mant/	**VT** **Montpelier** /mant'pilyər/
Virginia /vɚ'dʒɪnyə/	**VA** **Norfolk** /'nɔrfək/; **Richmond** /'rɪtʃmənd/
Washington /'waʃɪŋtən/	**WA** **Seattle** /si'ætəl/
West Virginia /'wɛst vɚ'dʒɪnyə/	**WV** **Charleston** /'tʃarlztən/
Wisconsin /wɪs'kansən/	**WI** **Madison** /'mædəsən/; **Milwaukee** /mɪl'wɔki/
Wyoming /waɪ'oʊmɪŋ/	**WY** **Cheyenne** /ʃaɪ'ɛn/

STATES AND CAPITALS OF THE USA

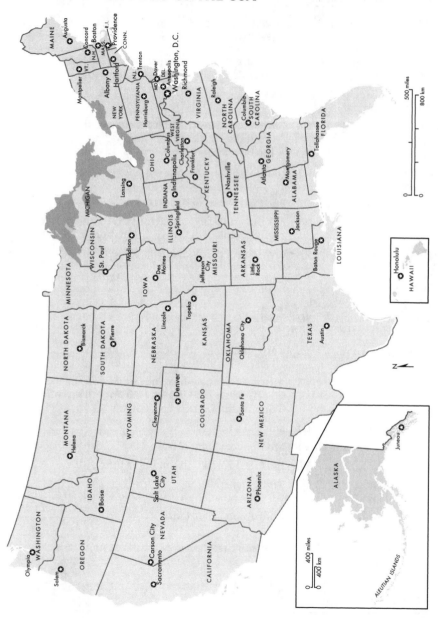

SOME COUNTRIES OF THE WORLD AND THEIR CITIZENS

Country or Area	Pronunciation	Language	Adjective
Afghanistan	/æf'gænə,stæn/	Afghan Persian; Pashtu	Afghan
Algeria	/æl'dʒɪriə/	Arabic	Algerian
Angola	/æŋ'goʊlə/	Portuguese	Angolan
Argentina	/,ɑrdʒən'tinə/	Spanish	Argentinean
Australia	/ɔ'streɪlyə/	English; local languages	Australian
Austria	/'ɔstriə/	German	Austrian
Azerbaijan	/,æzɚbaɪ'ʒɑn/	Azerbaijani	Azerbaijani
Bangladesh	/,bæŋglə'dɛʃ/	Bangala	Bangladeshi
Belarus	/,byɛlə'rus/	Byelorussian; Russian	Belarusian
Belgium	/'bɛldʒəm/	Flemish; French	Belgian
Bolivia	/bə'lɪviə/	Spanish; Quechua; Aymara	Bolivian
Brazil	/brə'zɪl/	Portuguese	Brazilian
Bulgaria	/bʌl'gɛriə/	Bulgarian	Bulgarian
Burkina Faso	/bɚ'kinə 'fɑsoʊ/	French; local languages	Burkinabe
Burundi	/bʊ'rʊndi/	French; Kirundi	Burundian
Cambodia	/kæm'boʊdiə/	Khmer	Cambodian
Cameroon	/,kæmə'run/	English; French	Cameroonian
Canada	/'kænədə/	English, French	Canadian
Chad	/tʃæd/	Arabic; French	Chadian
Chile	/'tʃɪli/	Spanish	Chilean
China	/'tʃaɪnə/	Chinese	Chinese
Colombia	/kə'lʌmbiə/	Spanish	Colombian
Democratic Republic of the Congo	/,dɛmə'krætɪk rɪ'pʌblɪk əv ðə 'kɑŋgoʊ/	French; local languages	Congolese
Republic of the Congo	/rɪ'pʌblɪk əv ðə 'kɑŋgoʊ/	French; local languages	Congolese
Costa Rica	/'kɑstə 'rikə/	Spanish	Costa Rican
Croatia	/kroʊ'eɪʃə/	Croatian	Croatian
Cuba	/'kyubə/	Spanish	Cuban
Czech Republic	/'tʃɛk rɪ'pʌblɪk/	Czech	Czech
Denmark	/'dɛnmɑrk/	Danish	Danish *Dane
Dominican Republic	/də'mɪnɪkɪn rɪ'pʌblɪk/	Spanish	Dominican

Smart Study Section

Country or Area	Pronunciation	Language	Adjective
Ecuador	/'ɛkwəˌdɔr/	Spanish	Ecuadorian
Egypt	/'idʒɪpt/	Arabic	Egyptian
El Salvador	/ɛl 'sælvəˌdɔr/	Spanish	El Salvadorian
England	/'ɪŋglənd/	English	English *English person
Ethiopia	/ˌiθi'oʊpiə/	Amharic; Tigrinya, local languages	Ethiopian
Finland	/'fɪnlənd/	Finnish	Finnish *Finn
France	/fræns/	French	French *French person
Georgia	/'dʒɔrdʒə/	Georgian	Georgian
Germany	/'dʒɝˌməni/	German	German
Ghana	/'ganə/	English	Ghanaian
Great Britain	/'greɪt 'brɪtən/	English	British *Briton; British person
Greece	/gris/	Greek	Greek
Guatemala	/ˌgwatə'malə/	Spanish	Guatemalan
Guinea	/'gɪni/	French	Guinean
Haiti	/'heɪti/	French; Haitian	Haitian
Honduras	/han'dʊrəs/	Spanish	Honduran
Hungary	/'hʌŋgəri/	Hungarian	Hungarian
India	/'ɪndiə/	Hindi; English	Indian
Indonesia	/ˌɪndə'niʒə/	Bahasa; Indonesian	Indonesian
Iran	/ɪ'ræn/	Arabic	Iranian
Iraq	/ɪ'ræk/	Arabic	Iraqi
Ireland	/'aɪrlənd/	English; Gaelic	Irish *Irish person
Israel	/'ɪzriəl/	Hebrew	Israeli
Italy	/'ɪtəli/	Italian	Italian
Ivory Coast	/'aɪvəri 'koʊst/	French	Ivorian
Japan	/dʒə'pæn/	Japanese	Japanese
Jordan	/'dʒɔrdən/	Arabic	Jordanian
Kazakhstan	/ˌkazak'stan/	Kazakh; Russian	Kazakhstani

Country or Area	Pronunciation	Language	Adjective
Kenya	/ˈkɛnyə/	English; Swahili	Kenyan
Laos	/ˈlaoʊs/	Lao; French	Laotian
Madagascar	/ˌmædəˈgæskər/	French; Malagasy	Malagasy
Malaysia	/məˈleɪʒə/	Bahasa Melayu	Malaysian
Mexico	/ˈmɛksɪkoʊ/	Spanish	Mexican
Morocco	/məˈrakoʊ/	Arabic	Moroccan
Mozambique	/ˌmoʊzæmˈbik/	Portuguese	Mozambican
Nepal	/nəˈpɔl/	Nepali	Nepalese
The Netherlands	/ðə ˈnɛðərləndz/	Dutch	Dutch *Dutch person
New Zealand	/ˌnu ˈzilənd/	English; Maori	New Zealand *New Zealander
Nicaragua	/ˌnɪkəˈragwə/	Spanish	Nicaraguan
Niger	/ˈnaɪdʒər/	French	Nigeran
Nigeria	/ˌnaɪˈdʒɪriə/	English; local languages	Nigerian
North Korea	/ˈnɔrθ kəˈriə/	Korean	North Korean
Norway	/ˈnɔrweɪ/	Norwegian	Norwegian
Pakistan	/ˈpækəˌstæn/	English; Punjabi; Sindhi	Pakistani
Panama	/ˈpænəˌma/	Spanish	Panamanian
Paraguay	/ˈpærəˌgwaɪ/	Spanish	Paraguayan
Peru	/pəˈru/	Spanish; Quechua	Peruvian
The Philippines	/ðə ˈfɪləˌpinz/	English; Tagalog	Filipino
Poland	/ˈpoʊlənd/	Polish	Polish *Pole
Portugal	/ˈpɔrtʃəgəl/	Portuguese	Portuguese
Romania	/roʊˈmeɪniə/	German; Hungarian; Romanian	Romanians
Russia	/ˈrʌʃə/	Russian	Russian
Rwanda	/ruˈandə/	English; French; Kinyarwanda	Rwandan
Saudi Arabia	/ˈsaʊdi əˈreɪbiə/	Arabic	Saudi Arabian
Scotland	/ˈskatlənd/	English; Scots	Scottish *Scot
Senegal	/ˈsɛnɪˌgɔl/	French; local languages	Senegalese

Country or Area	Pronunciation	Language	Adjective
Slovakia	/sloʊˈvakiə/	Hungarian; Slovak	Slovakian *Slovak
South Africa	/ˌsaʊθ ˈæfrɪkə/	Afrikaans; English; Ndebele; Pedi; Sotho; Swazi; Tsonga; Tswana; Venda; Xhosa; Zulu	South African
South Korea	/ˈsaʊθ kəˈriə/	Korean	South Korean
Spain	/speɪn/	Spanish	Spanish *Spaniard
Sweden	/ˈswidən/	Swedish	Swedish *Swede
Switzerland	/ˈswɪtzɚˌlənd/	French; German; Italian	Swiss
Syria	/ˈsɪriə/	Arabic; Kurdish	Syrian
Taiwan	/taɪˈwɑn/	Chinese	Taiwanese
Tajikistan	/təˈdʒɪkəˌstæn/	Taijik	Taijik
Tanzania	/ˌtænzəˈniə/	English; Kiswahili	Tanzanian
Thailand	/ˈtaɪˌlænd/	Thai	Thai
Tunisia	/tuˈniʒə/	Arabic; French	Tunisian
Turkey	/ˈtɝki/	Turkish	Turkish *Turk
Ukraine	/yuˈkreɪn/	Ukrainian	Ukrainian
The United States of America	/ðə yuˈnaɪtɪd ˈsteɪts əv əˈmɛrɪkə/	English	American
Uzbekistan	/ʊzˈbɛkəˌstan/	Uzbek	Uzbek
Venezuela	/ˌvɛnəˈzweɪlə/	Spanish	Venezuelan
Vietnam	/viˌɛtˈnam/	Vietnamese	Vietnamese
Wales	/ˈweɪlz/	English	Welsh
Yemen	/ˈyɛmən/	Arabic	Yemeni
Zambia	/ˈzæmbiə/	English	Zambian
Zimbabwe	/zɪmˈbabweɪ/	English	Zimbabwean

* Most nationality adjectives can be used as nouns to talk about a person from that country. If the noun for a citizen of a place is different from the adjective, it is shown after this mark *. You say "Danish books," but you say "a Dane."

When referring to a single citizen, many people prefer to use the adjective, not the noun. Say "A Chinese man" instead of "A Chinese." These forms are still frequently used in the plural to refer to all of the citizens of a country, for example, "The Chinese."

NUMBERS

The numbers used to count are called *cardinal* numbers.

1	one	14	fourteen	70	seventy
2	two	15	fifteen	80	eighty
3	three	16	sixteen	90	ninety
4	four	17	seventeen	100	a/one hundred
5	five	18	eighteen	101	a/one hundred and one
6	six	19	nineteen	110	a/one hundred and ten
7	seven	20	twenty	200	two hundred
8	eight	21	twenty-one	1,000	a/one thousand
9	nine	22	twenty-two	2,000	two thousand
10	ten	30	thirty	10,000	ten thousand
11	eleven	40	forty	100,000	a/one hundred thousand
12	twelve	50	fifty	1,000,000	a/one million
13	thirteen	60	sixty	1,000,000,000	a/one billion

The numbers used to put things in order are called *ordinal* numbers.

1st	first	14th	fourteenth	70th	seventieth
2nd	second	15th	fifteenth	80th	eightieth
3rd	third	16th	sixteenth	90th	ninetieth
4th	fourth	17th	seventeenth	100th	hundredth
5th	fifth	18th	eighteenth	101st	a/one hundred and first
6th	sixth	19th	nineteenth	110th	a/one hundred and tenth
7th	seventh	20th	twentieth	200th	two hundredth
8th	eighth	21st	twenty-first	1,000th	a/one thousandth
9th	ninth	22nd	twenty-second	2,000th	two thousandth
10th	tenth	30th	thirtieth	10,000th	ten thousandth
11th	eleventh	40th	fortieth	100,000th	hundred thousandth
12th	twelfth	50th	fiftieth	1,000,000th	millionth
13th	thirteenth	60th	sixtieth	1,000,000,000th	billionth

NUMBERS

What you see	What you say
	"apartment six oh three"
	"bus route six oh three"
603-5218	"My phone number is six oh three five two one eight" *or* "six zero three five two one eight"

What you write	What you say
0.063	"zero point zero six three"
603	"six hundred and three"
6,603	"six thousand, six hundred and three"
60,623	"sixty thousand, six hundred and twenty-three"
620,623	"six hundred and twenty thousand, six hundred and twenty-three"

FRACTIONS AND PERCENTAGES

	Fractions		Percentages	
●	1	a whole	100%	a/one hundred percent
◐	1/2	a/one half	50%	fifty percent
◔	1/3	a/one third	33%	thirty-three percent
◔	1/4	a/one fourth *or* a/one quarter	25%	twenty-five percent
◔	1/5	a/one fifth	20%	twenty percent

610

DATES

May 2002

M	T	W	TH	F	Sat	Sun
		1	2	3	4	5
6	7	8	9	10	11	12
13	14	15	16	17	18	19
20	21	22	23	24	25	26
27	28	29	30			

What you write	**What you say**
May 14, 2002 the 14th of May, 2002	"May fourteenth, two thousand two"
5/14/02 (in the US) 14/5/02 (in many other countries)	"the fourteenth of May, two thousand two"

Writing and saying years

1854	"eighteen fifty-four"
1906	"nineteen oh six"
2024	"twenty twenty-four"

Months of the year (and their written abbreviations)

1. January (Jan.)
2. February (Feb.)
3. March (Mar.)
4. April (Apr.)
5. May (May)
6. June (Jun.)
7. July (Jul.)
8. August (Aug.)
9. September (Sept.)
10. October (Oct.)
11. November (Nov.)
12. December (Dec.)

Days of the week (and their written abbreviations)

1. Sunday (Sun.)
2. Monday (Mon.)
3. Tuesday (Tues.)
4. Wednesday (Weds.)
5. Thursday (Thurs.)
6. Friday (Fri.)
7. Saturday (Sat.)

MATH SYMBOLS

What you write		What you say
+	$2 + 2$	two **plus** two
–	$5 - 1$	five **minus** one
×	3×4	three **times** four
÷	$12 \div 6$	twelve **divided by** six
=	$8 - 7 = 1$	eight minus seven **equals** one
.	14.35	fourteen **point** three five
%	89%	eighty-nine **percent**
$\sqrt{}$	$\sqrt{49} = 7$	**The square root of** forty-nine is seven.
x^2	$5^2 = 25$	Five **squared** is twenty-five.
x^3	$5^3 = 125$	Five **cubed** is a hundred and twenty-five.
>	$x > y$	x **is greater than** y.
<	$x < y$	y **is less than** x.
@	eggs @\$1.29/doz.	eggs **at** a dollar twenty-nine a dozen
∥	AB ∥ CD	AB **is parallel to** CD
⊥	AB ⊥ CD	AB **is perpendicular to** CD
°	$45°$	forty-five **degrees**
π	πr^2	**pi** r squared

CHARTS AND GRAPHS

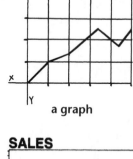

a graph

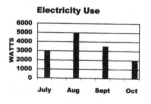

a bar graph

a chart

a pie chart

MEASUREMENTS

a ruler

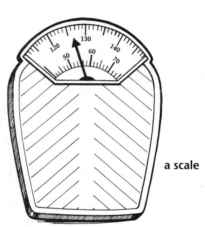

```
cm        5|         10|         15|         20|         25|         30|
inches    1|    2|    3|    4|    5|    6|    7|    8|    9|    10|    11|    12
```

1 inch (in.)

1 foot (ft.)	=	12 inches
1 yard (yd.)	=	3 feet
1 mile (mi.)	=	5280 feet

1 millimeter (mm)

1 centimeter (cm)	=	10 millimeters
1 meter (m)	=	100 centimeters
1 kilometer (km)	=	1000 meters

1 ounce

1 pound	=	16 ounces
1 ton	=	2000 pounds

1 gram

1 kilogram	= 1000 grams
1 metric ton	= 1000 kilogram

a scale

1 fluid ounce

1 pint	=	16 ounces
1 quart	=	2 pints
1 gallon	=	4 quarts

1 milliliter

1 deciliter	=	100 milliliters
1 liter	=	10 deciliters

1 pint   500 ml

8 oz

1 oz

a measuring cup

SHAPES

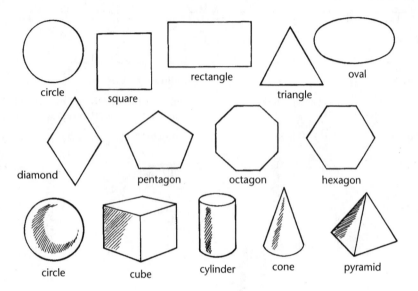

shape	adjective	pronunciation	shape	adjective	pronunciation
circle	circular	/ˈsɚkyələ˞/	octagon	octagonal	/ɑkˈtægənəl/
square	square	/skwɛr/	hexagon	hexagonal	/hɛkˈsægənəl/
rectangle	rectangular	/rɛkˈtæŋgyələ˞/	sphere	spherical	/ˈsfɪrɪkəl/
triangle	triangular	/traɪˈæŋgyələ˞/	cube	cubic	/ˈkyubɪk/
oval	oval	/ˈoʊvəl/	cylinder	cylindrical	/səˈlɪndrɪkəl/
diamond	diamond	/ˈdaɪmənd/	cone	conical	/ˈkɑnɪkəl/
pentagon	pentagonal	/pɛnˈtægənəl/	pyramid	pyramidal	/pɪrˈæmɪdəl/

TALKING ABOUT EVERYDAY THINGS

The words on pages 615-617 are all related to common subjects that you will study. Learning them can help you with speaking, and with writing essays or other assignments.

TALKING ABOUT THE WEATHER

Nouns		Adjectives		Verbs
forecast	storm	sunny	calm	the sun is shining
sunshine	lightning	bright	hot	it's raining
cloud	thunder	cloudy	warm	it's snowing
rain	rainbow	rainy	cool	it's sleeting
wind	tornado	windy	cold	
snow	hurricane	snowy	freezing	
sleet	blizzard	icy	humid	
ice	temperature	foggy	dry	
fog		stormy		

TALKING ABOUT HEALTH

(Remember to look at the BODY and SKELETON pictures too.)

Nouns		Adjectives		Verbs	
exercise	illness	healthy	tired	exercise	cough
pain	sickness	active	overweight	jog	sniff
headache	virus	strong	sore	swim	sneeze
stomachache	the flu	fit	painful	skate	break
cut	bone	in shape	itchy	climb	operate
wound	cast	out of shape	swollen	hike	recover
scratch	operation	weak	infected	play sports	get better
scar	surgery	ill	broken (bone)	ache	get well
sore throat	bandage	sick		itch	
cough				scratch	
sniff					
sneeze					

TALKING ABOUT SCHOOL

(Remember to look at the CLASSROOM picture too.)

Things and Places		People	Verbs
schedule	desk	teacher	teach
class	chalkboard	professor	assign
course	bell	principal	learn
notebook	announcement	student	study
textbook	cafeteria	librarian	write
chapter	campus	coach	memorize
page	auditorium	nurse	graduate
assignment	library	janitor	complete
essay	field	freshman	
homework	playground	sophomore	
test	gym	junior	
quiz	locker	senior	
exam	elementary school		
grade	middle school		
classroom	high school		

TALKING ABOUT WORK

Things and Places		People		Verbs
business	deal	boss	waiter/waitress	work
company	interview	employee	artist	buy
factory	profession	employer	writer	sell
office	career	worker	journalist	pay
store	skill	manager	construction	interview
bank	experience	assistant	worker	receive
hotel	contract	secretary	police officer	make a deal
restaurant	salary	salesperson	firefighter	
gallery	wage	professional	mechanic	
theater	overtime	businessperson	musician	
hospital		actor	mail carrier	
police station		doctor	hairdresser	
fire station		nurse	plumber	
salon		dentist	painter	
		lawyer	electrician	
		banker	carpenter	
		programmer	politician	

TALKING ABOUT TRANSPORTATION

(Remember to look at the CAR picture too.)

Things and Places		People	Verbs	
By air	airplane/plane	pilot	take off	fly
	airport	flight attendant	land	board
	runway	passenger	depart/leave	change planes
	gate		arrive/get in	go via somewhere
	ticket		be late	
			be on time	
By road				
automobile	highway	driver	drive	speed up
car	street	bus driver	ride	slow down
truck	intersection	cab driver	ride in	stop
van	lane	rider	ride on	cross
SUV	bus stop	cyclist	turn left	take a trip
bus	bridge		turn right	park
taxi/cab	parking place/spot		back up	honk
motorcycle	parking lot		exit	
bicycle	stoplight		get off	
traffic	traffic light		get on	
horn	crossing			
toll	fare			
By train and subway				
	train	train passenger	board	stand in line
	car	subway rider	ride	arrive/get in
	track	conductor	transfer	depart/leave
	platform	engineer	get off	
	ticket		get on	
	token			
	station			
On foot	crosswalk	pedestrian	walk	
	sidewalk		cross the street	
	block			
By boat				
	ship	sail	passenger	sail
	boat	rowboat	captain	board
	dock	oar	crew member	get on
	pier	harbor		get off
	sailboat			arrive/get in
				depart/leave

MY DICTIONARY

Use this page to add words and phrases to your dictionary. In the first column, write the word or phrase. In the second column, write the part of speech (*noun, verb*, etc.). In the third column, write your own definition. In the last column, write a sentence with the word in it, to help you remember how to use it.

Word or phrase	Part of speech	Definition	Sentence
Ms. Cartwright	name	the name of my teacher	Ms. Cartwright teaches English.

DATE DUE

BRODART, CO.   Cat. No. 23-221

Word or phrase	Part of speech	Definition	Sentence

DATE DUE

PRONUNCIATION OF AMERICAN NAMES

when more than one name is listed, the first name is the most formal.

Female names

Allison; Ally	/'æləsun/; /'æli/
Alyssa	/ə'lısə/
Anna; Anne/Ann	/'ænə/; /æn/
Brenda	/'brɛndə/
Catherine; Cathy	/'kæθərın/; /'kæθi/
Christine; Christy	/krı'stin/; /'krısti/
Cynthia; Cindy	/'sınθiə/; /'sındi/
Donna	/'danə/
Elizabeth; Beth; Liz	/ı'lızəbəθ/; /bɛθ/; /lız/
Emily; Em	/'ɛməli/; /'ɛm/
Jasmine	/'dʒæzmın/
Jennifer; Jen; Jenny	/'dʒɛnəfə-/; /'dʒɛn/; /'dʒɛni/
Jessica; Jessie	/'dʒɛsıkə/; /'dʒɛsi/
Karen	/'kærən/
Kathleen; Kate; Kathy	/kæθ'lin/; /keıt/; /'kæθi/
Kimberly; Kim	/'kımbə-li/; /kım/
Laura	/'lɔrə/
Lisa	/'lisə/
Margaret; Meg; Maggie	/'margərıt/; /mɛg/; /'mægi/
Maria	/mə'riə/
Mary	/'mɛri/
Melissa; Missy; Mel	/mə'lısə/; /'mısi/; /mɛl/
Michelle; Shelly	/mı'ʃɛl/; /'ʃɛli/
Patricia; Pat	/pə'trıʃə/; /pæt/
Rachel	/'reıtʃəl/
Rebecca; Becky	/rı'bɛkə/; /'bɛki/
Sarah	/'sɛrə/
Sharon	/'ʃærən/
Susan; Sue; Susie	/'suzən/; /su/; /'suzi/

Male names

Andrew; Andy; Drew	/'ændru/; /'ændi/; /dru/
Anthony; Tony	/'ænθəni/; /'toni/
Brian	/'braıən/
Carlos	/'karloʊs/
Charles; Charlie; Chuck	/'tʃarlz/; /'tʃarli/; /'tʃʌk/
Christopher; Chris	/'krıstəfə-/; /krıs/
Daniel; Dan	/'dænyəl/; /dæn/
David; Dave	/'deıvıd/; /deıv/
Donald; Don	/'danəld/; /dan/
Eric	/'ɛrık/
Jacob; Jake	/dʒeıkəb/; /dʒeık/
James; Jim	/dʒeımz/; /dʒım/
Jason; Jay	/'dʒeısən/; /dʒeı/
John; Johnny	/dʒan/; /'dʒani/
Jordan; Jordy	/'dʒɔrdən/; /'dʒɔrdi/
José	/hoʊ'zeı/
Joseph; Joe; Joey	/'dʒoʊzəf/; /dʒoʊ/; /'dʒoʊi/
Kenneth; Ken	/'kɛnıθ/; /kɛn/
Kevin	/'kɛvın/
Lawrence; Larry	/'lɔrıns/; /'læri/
Matthew; Matt	/'mæθyu/; /mæt/
Michael; Mike	/'maıkəl/; /maık/
Nicholas; Nick	/'nıkələs/; /nık/
Richard; Dick; Rich; Rick	/'rıtʃə-d/; /dık/; /rıtʃ/; /rık/
Robert; Bob; Rob	/'rabə-t/; /bab/; /rab/
Steven; Steve	/'stivən/; /stiv/
Thomas; Tom	/'taməs/; /tam/
Timothy; Tim	/'tıməθi/; /tım/
William; Bill; Will	/'wılyəm/; /bıl/; /wıl/